Human Resource Management

10th Edition

Gary Dessler

Florida International University

PEARSON
Prentice Hall

Upper Saddle River, New Jersey 07458

Library of Congress Cataloging-in-Publication Data
Dessler, Gary
    Human resource management / Gary Dessler.—10th ed.
       p. cm.
    Includes bibliographical references and indexes.
    ISBN 0-13-144097-7
       1. Personnel management.   I. Title.

    HF5549.D4379 2004
    658.3—dc22   2004053378

Acquisitions Editor: Jennifer Simon
Editorial Director: Jeff Shelstad
Assistant Editor: Christine V. Genneken
Editorial Assistant: Richard Gomes
Developmental Editor: Jeannine Ciliotta
Media Project Manager: Jessica Sabloff
Marketing Manager: Anke Braun
Marketing Assistant: Patrick Danzuso
Senior Managing Editor (Production): Judy Leale
Production Editor: Mary Ellen Morrell
Associate Director, Manufacturing: Vincent Scelta
Production Manager/Manufacturing Buyer: Arnold Vila
Design Manager: Maria Lange
Art Director: Steve Frim
Interior Design: Jill Little
Cover Design: Maria Lange
Cover Illustration/Photo: Burke/Triolo/Brand X Pictures/Getty Images, Inc.
Illustrator (Interior): Jade Meyers, Matrix Publishing
Permissions Coordinator: Charles Morris
Manager, Print Production: Christy Mahon
Composition/Full-Service Project Management: GGS Book Services, Atlantic Highlands
Printer/Binder: Courier/Kendallville

Credits and acknowledgments borrowed from other sources and reproduced, with permission, in this textbook appear on appropriate page within text. Photo credits appear on page 701.

Pearson Education LTD.
Pearson Education Singapore, Pte. Ltd
Pearson Education, Canada, Ltd
Pearson Education—Japan

Pearson Education Australia PTY, Limited
Pearson Education North Asia Ltd
Pearson Educación de Mexico, S.A. de C.V.
Pearson Education Malaysia, Pte. Ltd

10 9 8 7 6 5 4 3 2 1
ISBN 0-13-144097-7

Dedicated to Claudia

Brief Contents

Part 1 Introduction 2

1 The Strategic Role of Human Resource Management 2

2 Equal Opportunity and the Law 28

3 Strategic Human Resource Management and the HR Scorecard 70

Part 2 Recruitment and Placement 110

4 Job Analysis 110

5 Personnel Planning and Recruiting 150

6 Employee Testing and Selection 192

7 Interviewing Candidates 234

Part 3 Training and Development 266

8 Training and Developing Employees 266

9 Performance Management and Appraisal 308

10 Managing Careers 348

Part 4 Compensation 388

11 Establishing Strategic Pay Plans 388

12 Pay for Performance and Financial Incentives 436

13 Benefits and Services 474

Part 5 Employee Relations 514

14 Ethics, Justice, and Fair Treatment in HR Management 514

15 Labor Relations and Collective Bargaining 558

16 Employee Safety and Health 600

17 Managing Global Human Resources 654

Glossary   693

Photo Credits   701

Name and Organization Index   703

Subject Index   713

Contents

Preface xxiii
Acknowledgments xxvii

Part 1 Introduction 2

Chapter 1 The Strategic Role of Human Resource Management 2

The Manager's Human Resource Management Jobs 4
Why Is HR Management Important to All Managers? 5
Line and Staff Aspects of HRM 5
Cooperative Line and Staff HR Management: An Example 8
From Line Manager to HR Manager 9
The Changing Environment of HR Management 10
A Changing Environment 10
Measuring HR's Contribution: Strategy, Metrics, and the HR Scorecard 13
An Emphasis on Performance 14
Metrics 14
The HR Scorecard 16
The High Performance Work System 16
The New HR Manager 16
New Proficiencies 16
The Need to "Know Your Employment Law" 17
Ethics and HR 18
HR Certification 18
HR and Technology 19

■ Improving Productivity Through HRIS: The HR Portal 21
The Plan of This Book 21
The Basic Themes and Features 22
Overview 23
Part 1: Introduction 23
Part 2: Recruitment and Placement 23
Part 3: Training and Development 23
Part 4: Compensation 23
Part 5: Employee Relations 23
Summary 24
Discussion Questions 24
Individual and Group Activities 25
Experiential Exercise: Helping "The Donald" 25
Application Case: Jack Nelson's Problem 26
Continuing Case: Carter Cleaning Company 26

Chapter 2 Equal Opportunity and the Law 28

Equal Employment Opportunity 1964–1991 30
   Title VII of the 1964 Civil Rights Act 30
   Executive Orders 31
   Equal Pay Act of 1963 31
   Age Discrimination in Employment Act of 1967 31
   Vocational Rehabilitation Act of 1973 32
   Vietnam Era Veterans' Readjustment Assistance Act 32
   Pregnancy Discrimination Act of 1978 32
   Federal Agency Guidelines 32
   Sexual Harassment 32
   Early Court Decisions Regarding Equal Employment Opportunity 37
Equal Employment Opportunity 1990–91–Present 38
   The Civil Rights Act of 1991 38

■ **The New Workplace:** Enforcing the 1991 Civil Rights Act Abroad 39
   The Americans with Disabilities Act 40
   State and Local Equal Employment Opportunity Laws 44
Defense Against Discrimination Allegations 45
   Adverse Impact 46
   Bona Fide Occupational Qualification 48
   Business Necessity 49
   Other Considerations in Discriminatory Practice Defense 50

■ **Know Your Employment Law:** Discriminatory Employment Practices 50
The EEOC Enforcement Process 52
   Processing a Charge 52

■ **When You're on Your Own:** Dealing with Discrimination Issues and the EEOC 53
   Conciliation Proceedings 54
   How to Respond to Employment Discrimination Charges 54
   Mandatory Arbitration of Discrimination Claims 57
Diversity Management and Affirmative Action Programs 58
   Managing Diversity 58
   Boosting Workforce Diversity 59
   Equal Employment Opportunity Versus Affirmative Action 60

■ Improving Productivity Through HRIS: Measuring Diversity 61
   Steps in an Affirmative Action Program 61
   Reverse Discrimination 62
   Recruiting Minorities Online 63
Summary 63
Discussion Questions 64
Individual and Group Activities 64
Experiential Exercise: "Space Cadet" or Victim? 65
Application Case: A Case of Racial Discrimination? 65
Continuing Case: Carter Cleaning Company 66

Chapter 3 Strategic Human Resource Management and the HR Scorecard 70

HR's Strategic Challenges 72
   The Strategic Management Process 73
   Types of Strategic Planning 76
   Achieving Strategic Fit 77

■ **When You're on Your Own:** Using Computerized Business Planning
Software 77
　　HR and Competitive Advantage 79
HR's Strategic Roles 80

■ **The New Workplace:** Longo Builds Its Strategy on Diversity 81
　　HR's Strategy Execution Role 82
　　HR's Strategy Formulation Role 82
Creating a Strategy-Oriented HR System 83
　　The High-Performance Work System 84
　　Translating Strategy into HR Policy and Practice 84
　　HR Strategy in Action: An Example 86
The HR Scorecard Approach 87
　　Information for Creating an HR Scorecard 87
　　Using the HR Scorecard Approach 88
　　The Hotel Paris International: An Example 91

■ Improving Productivity Through HRIS: Software Systems for Managing Scorecard
Programs 96
Summary 98
Discussion Questions 98
Individual and Group Activities 99
Experiential Exercise: Developing an HR Scorecard 99
Continuing Case: The Carter Cleaning Company: The High Performance Work System 100
Appendix for Chapter 3: Establishing and Computerizing Human Resource Systems 101

 Part 2 Recruitment and Placement 110

Chapter 4 Job Analysis 110

The Nature of Job Analysis 112
　　Uses of Job Analysis Information 112
　　Steps in Job Analysis 113
Methods of Collecting Job Analysis Information 114
　　The Interview 115
　　Questionnaires 116
　　Observation 117
　　Quantitative Job Analysis Techniques 117
　　Using Multiple Sources of Information 125
Writing Job Descriptions 125
　　Job Identification 128
　　Job Summary 128
　　Relationships 128
　　Responsibilities and Duties 129

■ **Know Your Employment Law:** Writing Job Descriptions That Comply with the ADA 130
　　Standards of Performance and Working Conditions 130

■ Improving Productivity Through HRIS: Using the Internet for Writing Job Descriptions 131
Writing Job Specifications 132
　　Specifications for Trained Versus Untrained Personnel 132
　　Specifications Based on Judgment 132
　　Specifications Based on Statistical Analysis 134

■ **When You're on Your Own:** HR for Line Managers and Entrepreneurs 134
Job Analysis in a "Jobless" World 137

■ **The New Workplace:** Global Job Analysis Applications 138
    From Specialized to Enlarged Jobs 138
    Why Managers Are Dejobbing Their Companies 139
    Competency-Based Job Analysis 140

■ **The HR Scorecard:** Strategy and Results 142
    BP's Matrices 144
Summary 145
Discussion Questions 145
Individual and Group Activities 146
Experiential Exercise: The Instructor's Job Description 146
Application Case: Tropical Storm Charley 146
Continuing Case: Carter Cleaning Company 147

Chapter 5   Personnel Planning and Recruiting 150

Planning and Forecasting 152
    Forecasting Personnel Needs 153
    Forecasting the Supply of Inside Candidates 155
    Forecasting the Supply of Outside Candidates 157
Effective Recruiting 157

■ **Know Your Employment Law:** Preemployment Activities 158
    Organizing the Recruitment Function 159
    Measuring Recruiting Efforts 159
    The Recruiting Yield Pyramid 161
Internal Sources of Candidates 162
    Finding Internal Candidates 162
    Rehiring 163
    Succession Planning 163
Outside Sources of Candidates 163
    Advertising 163

■ Improving Productivity Through HRIS: Succession Planning Systems 164
    Employment Agencies 166
    Temp Agencies and Alternative Staffing 167

■ **Know Your Employment Law:** Contingent Workers 168
    Offshoring/Outsourcing White-Collar and Other Jobs 170
    Executive Recruiters 171

■ **When You're on Your Own:** Recruiting 101 172
    On Demand Recruiting Services (ODRS) 173
    College Recruiting 173
    Recruiting via the Internet 175
Recruiting a More Diverse Workforce 178
    Single Parents 178
    Older Workers 178
    Recruiting Minorities and Women 179

■ **The New Workplace:** Supervising the Graybeards 179
    Welfare to Work 180
    The Disabled 180
Developing and Using Application Forms 181
    Purpose of Application Forms 181

■ **Know Your Employment Law:** Application Forms 181
    Alternative Dispute Resolution 182

■ **Know Your Employment Law:** Mandatory Arbitration 182
    Using Application Forms to Predict Job Performance 184

■ **The HR Scorecard:** The New Recruitment Process 184
Summary 186
Discussion Questions 186
Individual and Group Activities 187
Experiential Exercise: The Nursing Shortage 187
Application Case: Finding People Who Are Passionate About What They Do 187
Continuing Case: Cater Cleaning Company 188

Chapter 6 Employee Testing and Selection 192

Why Careful Selection Is Important 194
Basic Testing Concepts 195
    Reliability 195
    Validity 195
    How to Validate a Test 197
    Equal Employment Opportunity Aspects of Testing 200
    Test Takers' Individual Rights and Test Security 201

■ **The New Workplace:** Gender Issues in Testing 201

■ **Know Your Employment Law:** The Issue of Privacy 202
    Using Tests at Work 203
    Computer-Interactive Testing 204
Types of Tests 204
    Tests of Cognitive Abilities 204
    Tests of Motor and Physical Abilities 205
    Measuring Personality and Interests 206
    Web-Based Testing 208
Work Samples and Simulations 208
    Work Sampling for Employee Selection 208
    Management Assessment Centers 209
    Video-Based Situational Testing 210
    The Miniature Job Training and Evaluation Approach 210

■ **When You're on Your Own:** Employee Testing and Selection 212
Background Investigations and Other Selection Methods 213
    Background Investigations and Reference Checks 213

■ **Know Your Employment Law:** Giving References 215
    Using Preemployment Information Services 217

■ **Improving Productivity Through HRIS:** Automated Applicant Tracking Systems
and Applicant Screening 218

■ **Know Your Employment Law:** Background Information 219
    The Polygraph and Honesty Testing 220
    Graphology 222
    Physical Examination 223
    Substance Abuse Screening 223

■ **Know Your Employment Law:** Drug Testing 223
    Complying with Immigration Law Post 9/11 224

■ **The HR Scorecard:** The New Employee Testing Program 225

Summary 227
Discussion Questions 227
Individual and Group Activities 228
Experiential Exercise: A Test for a Reservation Clerk 228
Application Case: Where's My Czar? 229
Continuing Case: Honesty Testing at Carter Cleaning Company 229

Chapter 7 Interviewing Candidates 234

Basic Features of Interviews 236
Types of Interviews 236

■ **The HR Scorecard:** The New Interviewing Program 241
Administering the Interview 243

■ Improving Productivity Through HRIS: Automated Video-Based Interview Systems 245
Are Interviews Useful? 246
What Can Undermine an Interview's Usefulness? 246
First Impressions 246
Misunderstanding the Job 247
Candidate-Order (Contrast) Error and Pressure to Hire 247
Nonverbal Behavior and Impression Management 247
Effect of Personal Characteristics: Attractiveness, Gender, Race 248
Interviewer Behavior 249
Designing and Conducting the Effective Interview 249
The Structured Situational Interview 249

■ **The New Workplace:** Applicant Disability and the Employment Interview 250
How to Conduct a More Effective Interview 252

■ **Know Your Employment Law:** Interviewing Candidates 256

■ **When You're on Your Own:** HR and the Small Business 256
Summary 259
Discussion Questions 259
Individual and Group Activities 259
Experiential Exercise: The Most Important Person You'll Ever Hire 260
Application Case: The Out-of-Control Interview 261
Continuing Case: Carter Cleaning Company 261

 ## Part 3 Training and Development 266

Chapter 8 Training and Developing Employees 266

Orienting Employees 268
The Training Process 270
The Strategic Context of Training 270
The Five-Step Training and Development Process 270
Training, Learning, and Motivation 271

■ **Know Your Employment Law:** Training and the Law 272
Analyzing Training Needs 273
Task Analysis: Assessing New Employees' Training Needs 273
Performance Analysis: Assessing Current Employees' Training Needs 273
Training Methods 275
On-the-Job Training 275
Apprenticeship Training 276

Informal Learning 277
Job Instruction Training 277
Lectures 278
Programmed Learning 279
Literacy Training Techniques 279

■ **The New Workplace 280**
Audiovisual-Based Training 280
Simulated Training 281
Computer-Based Training 281
Electronic Performance Support Systems (EPSS) 282
Distance and Internet-Based Training 283
What Is Management Development? 285

■ Improving Productivity Through HRIS: Learning Portals and Beyond 285
Managerial On-the-Job Training 286
Off-the-Job Management Training and Development Techniques 287
Managing Organizational Change and Development 290
What to Change 290

■ **When You're on Your Own:** HR for Line Managers and Entrepreneurs 291
Overcoming Resistance to Change: Lewin's Change Process 292
How to Lead the Change: A 10-Step Process 293
Using Organizational Development 294

■ **The HR Scorecard:** The New Training Program 297
Evaluating the Training Effort 299
Designing the Study 299
Training Effects to Measure 299
Summary 302
Discussion Questions 302
Individual and Group Activities 303
Experiential Exercise: Flying the Friendlier Skies 303
Application Case: Reinventing the Wheel at Apex Door Company 304
Continuing Case: Carter Cleaning Company 304

Chapter 9 Performance Management and Appraisal 308

Basic Concepts in Performance Appraisal and Performance Management 310
Comparing Performance Appraisal and Performance Management 310
Why Performance Management? 310
Defining the Employee's Goals and Work Efforts 312
An Introduction to Appraising Performance 313
Why Appraise Performance? 313
Realistic Appraisals 314
The Supervisor's Role 314
Steps in Appraising Performance 315
Graphic Rating Scale Method 315

■ **The New Workplace:** Performance Appraisals and Joint Venture Collaboration 315
Alternation Ranking Method 317
Paired Comparison Method 318
Critical Incident Method 321
Narrative Forms 322
Behaviorally Anchored Rating Scales 322
Management by Objectives (MBO) 324
Computerized and Web-Based Performance Appraisal 326

Mixing the Methods 327

Appraising Performance: Problems and Solutions 327
Potential Rating Scale Appraisal Problems 328
How to Avoid Appraisal Problems 329

■ **Know Your Employment Law:** Appraising Performance 331
Who Should Do the Appraising? 332

The Appraisal Interview 334
Types of Appraisal Interviews 335
How to Conduct the Appraisal Interview 336
Appraisals in Practice 337

Creating the Total Performance Management Process 338

■ **When You're on Your Own:** Performance Appraisal and Management 338

■ **Improving Productivity Through HRIS:** The New Performance Management System 340

■ **The HR Scorecard:** The New Performance Appraisal System 341
Summary 343
Discussion Questions 342
Individual and Group Activities 343
Experiential Exercise: Grading the Professor 344
Application Case: Appraising the Secretaries at Sweetwater U 344
Continuing Case: Carter Cleaning Company 345

Chapter 10 Managing Careers 348

The Basics of Career Management 350
Careers Today 350
Career Development 351

Roles in Career Development 352
The Employee's Role 353

■ **When You're on Your Own:** Employee Career Development 354
The Employer's Role 355
Innovative Corporate Career Development Initiatives 355

■ **Improving Productivity Through HRIS:** Integrating Career Planning into the Employer's HRIS 358

Managing Promotions and Transfers 358
Making Promotion Decisions 358
Handling Transfers 360

■ **Know Your Employment Law:** Establish Clear Guidelines for Managing Promotions 360

Enhancing Diversity Through Career Management 361
Sources of Bias and Discrimination in Promotion Decisions 361
Taking Steps to Enhance Diversity: Women's and Minorities' Prospects 363

Career Management and Employee Commitment 363
The New Psychological Contract 364
Commitment-Oriented Career Development Efforts 364

■ **The HR Scorecard:** The New Career Management System 366

Retirement 366
Summary 368
Discussion Questions 369
Experiential Exercise: Where Am I Going . . . and Why? 369
Application Case: The Mentor Relationship Turns Upside Down 370
Continuing Case: Carter Cleaning Company 370
Appendix for Chapter 10: Managing Your Career 372

➤ Part 4 Compensation 388

Chapter **11** Establishing Strategic Pay Plans 388

Determining Pay Rates 390

■ **Know Your Employment Law:** Compensation 390
Corporate Policies, Competitive Strategy, and Compensation 395
Equity and Its Impact on Pay Rates 396

■ **The New Workplace:** Globalization and Diversity: Compensating Expatriate Employees 397
Establishing Pay Rates 398
Step 1. The Salary Survey 398
Step 2. Job Evaluation 400
Step 3. Group Similar Jobs into Pay Grades 405
Step 4. Price Each Pay Grade—Wage Curves 405
Step 5. Fine-Tune Pay Rates 406

■ When You're on Your Own: Developing a Workable Pay Plan 408
Pricing Managerial and Professional Jobs 409
Compensating Managers 410
Compensating Professional Employees 411
Competency-Based Pay 412
What Is Competency-Based Pay? 412
Why Use Competency-Based Pay? 413
Competency-Based Pay in Practice 413
Competency-Based Pay: Pros, Cons, and Results 414
Other Compensation Trends 415
Broadbanding 415
Strategic Compensation 417
Comparable Worth 418

■ **The HR Scorecard:** The New Compensation Plan 419

■ Improving Productivity Through HRIS: Automating the Compensation Planning Process 421
Summary 422
Discussion Questions 422
Individual and Group Activities 422
Experiential Exercise: Ranking the College's Administrators 423
Application Case: Salary Inequities at Acme Manufacturing 423
Continuing Case: Carter Cleaning Company 424
Appendix for Chapter 11: Quantitative Job Evaluation Methods 427

Chapter **12** Pay for Performance and Financial Incentives 436

Money and Motivation: An Introduction 438
Performance and Pay 438
Individual Differences 439
Psychological Needs and Intrinsic versus Extrinsic Motivation 439
Instrumentality and Rewards: Vroom's Theory 441
Types of Incentive Plans 441

■ **Know Your Employment Law:** Incentives 442
Individual Employee Incentive and Recognition Programs 442
Piecework Plans 442
Merit Pay as an Incentive 443
Merit Pay Options 444

Incentives for Professional Employees   445
Recognition-Based Awards   445
Online Award Programs   446

■ **Improving Productivity Through HRIS:** Employee Incentive Management Systems   447
Information Technology and Incentives   447
Incentives for Salespeople   447
Salary Plan   448
Commission Plan   448
Combination Plan   448
Setting Sales Quotas   449
Strategic Sales Incentives   450
Team/Group Variable Pay Incentive Plans   450
How to Design Team Incentives   450
Pros and Cons of Team Incentives   451

■ **When You're on Your Own:** Incentives Supervisors Can Use   452
Organizationwide Variable Pay Plans   453
Profit-Sharing Plans   453
Employee Stock Ownership Plan (ESOP)   453
Scanlon and Other Gainsharing Plans   454
At-Risk Variable Pay Plans   456
Incentives for Managers and Executives   456
Short-Term Incentives: The Annual Bonus   456

■ **The HR Scorecard:** The New Incentive Plan   457
Long-Term Incentives   460

■ **The New Workplace:** Long-Term Incentives for Overseas Employees   462
Other Executive Incentives   462
Strategy and Executive Compensation   462
Designing and Executing Effective Incentive Programs   463
Why Incentive Plans Fail   464
How to Implement Effective Incentive Plans   464
Incentive Plans in Practice   465
Summary   466
Discussion Questions   466
Individual and Group Activities   467
Experiential Exercise: Motivating the Salesforce at Express Auto   467
Application Case: Inserting the Team Concept into Compensation—or Not   468
Continuing Case: Carter Cleaning Company   469

Chapter 13 Benefits and Services   474

The Benefits Picture Today   476

■ **Know Your Employment Law:** Benefits   477
Pay for Time Not Worked   479
Unemployment Insurance   479
Vacations and Holidays   480
Sick Leave   482
Parental Leave and the Family and Medical Leave Act   482
Severance Pay   484
Supplemental Unemployment Benefits   485
Insurance Benefits   485
Workers' Compensation   485
Hospitalization, Health, and Disability Insurance   486

Life Insurance 490
Benefits for Part-Time and Contingent Workers 491
Retirement Benefits 491
Social Security 491
Pension Plans 492
Pension Planning 493
Pensions and the Law 494
Pension Alternatives 494

■ Improving Productivity Through HRIS: Benefits Management Systems 495
Personal Services and Family-Friendly Benefits 496
Personal Services 496
Family-Friendly Benefits 497

■ **The New Workplace:** Domestic Partner Benefits 499
Executive Perquisites 500
Flexible Benefits Programs 500
The Cafeteria Approach 500

■ **The HR Scorecard:** The New Benefits Plan 501
Computers and Benefits Administration 504
Flexible Work Arrangements 504

■ **When You're on Your Own:** Benefits and Employee Leasing 506
Summary 507
Discussion Questions 508
Individual and Group Activities 508
Experiential Exercise: Revising the Benefits Package 508
Application Case: Striking for Benefits 509
Continuing Case: Carter Cleaning Company 509

 Part 5 Employee Relations 514

Chapter 14 Ethics, Justice, and Fair Treatment in HR Management 514

Ethics and Fair Treatment at Work 516
The Meaning of *Ethics* 517
Ethics and the Law 517
Ethics, Fair Treatment, and Justice 517

■ **The New Workplace:** Employment Contracts 519
What Shapes Ethical Behavior at Work? 519
Individual Factors 520
Organizational Factors 520
The Boss's Influence 520
Ethics Policies and Codes 522
The Organization's Culture 522
The Role of HR Management in Fostering Ethics and Fair Treatment 524
Why Treat Employees Fairly 524
HR Ethics Activities 525

■ Improving Productivity Through HRIS: Complying with Sarbanes-Oxley 529
Building Two-Way Communications 529

■ **When You're on Your Own:** Small Business Ethics 530
Employee Discipline and Privacy 531

■ **When You're on Your Own:** Disciplining an Employee 531

■ **The New Workplace:** Comparing Males and Females in a Discipline Situation 534
   Formal Disciplinary Appeals Processes 535
   Discipline without Punishment 535
   Employee Privacy 535
Managing Dismissals 537
   Grounds for Dismissal 538

■ **Know Your Employment Law:** Gross Misconduct 539
   Avoiding Wrongful Discharge Suits 540
   Personal Supervisory Liability 543
   The Termination Interview 543
   Layoffs and the Plant Closing Law 547
   Adjusting to Downsizings and Mergers 548

■ **The HR Scorecard:** The Hotel Paris's New Ethics, Justice, and Fair Treatment Process 550
Summary 553
Discussion Questions 553
Individual and Group Activities 553
Experiential Exercise: Discipline or Not? 554
Application Case: Fire My Best Salesperson? 555
Continuing Case: Carter Cleaning Company 555

Chapter 15 Labor Relations and Collective Bargaining 558

The Labor Movement 560
   A Brief History of the American Union Movement 560
   Why Do Workers Organize? 561
   What Do Unions Want? 562
   The AFL-CIO 563
Unions and the Law 563
   Period of Strong Encouragement: The Norris-LaGuardia (1932) and National Labor Relations or
      Wagner Acts (1935) 563
   Period of Modified Encouragement Coupled with Regulation: The Taft-Hartley Act (1947) 564
   Period of Detailed Regulation of Internal Union Affairs: The Landrum-Griffin Act (1959) 567

■ When You're on Your Own: New Economy Entrepreneurs and Unions 568
The Union Drive and Election 568
   Step 1. Initial Contact 568
   Step 2. Obtaining Authorization Cards 570
   Step 3. Hold a Hearing 571
   Step 4. The Campaign 571
   Step 5. The Election 572
   How to Lose an NLRB Election 573
   The Supervisor's Role 574

■ When You're on Your Own: Your Role in the Unionizing Effort 575
   Rules Regarding Literature and Solicitation 576
   Decertification Elections: Ousting the Union 576

■ **The New Workplace:** Unions Go Global 577
The Collective Bargaining Process 577
   What Is Collective Bargaining? 577
   What Is Good Faith? 578
   The Negotiating Team 579
   Bargaining Items 579
   Bargaining Stages 579
   Bargaining Hints 580

Impasses, Mediation, and Strikes 581
The Contract Agreement 584
Grievances 584
Sources of Grievances 584
The Grievance Procedure 585
Guidelines for Handling Grievances 585

■ **The HR Scorecard:** The Hotel Paris's New Labor Relations Practices 587
The Union Movement Today and Tomorrow 590
Public Employees and Unions 590
Organizing Professionals and White-Collar Employees 591

■ Improving Productivity Through HRIS: The Union Organizing Campaign 592
Employee Participation Programs and Unions 593
Summary 594
Discussion Questions 595
Individual and Group Activities 595
Experiential Exercise: The Union Organizing Campaign at Pierce U. 595
Application Case: Disciplinary Action 596
Continuing Case: Carter Cleaning Company 597

Chapter **16** Employee Safety and Health 600

Occupational Safety Law 603
OSHA Standards and Record Keeping 603
Inspections and Citations 604
Responsibilities and Rights of Employers and Employees 607

■ **When You're on Your Own:** Free On-Site Safety and Health Services for Small Businesses 610
Management Commitment and Safety 610
What Causes Accidents? 611
Unsafe Conditions and Other Work-Related Factors 611

■ **When You're on Your Own:** The Supervisor's Role in Accident Prevention 612
What Causes Unsafe Acts? (A Second Basic Cause of Accidents) 615
How to Prevent Accidents 615
Reducing Unsafe Conditions 615
Reducing Unsafe Acts by Emphasizing Safety 617
Reducing Unsafe Acts Through Selection and Placement 617
Reducing Unsafe Acts Through Training 617

■ **The New Workplace:** Safety Training for Hispanic Workers 618
Reducing Unsafe Acts Through Motivation: Posters, Incentive Programs, and Positive Reinforcement 618
Use Behavior-Based Safety 620
Use Employee Participation 620
Conduct Safety and Health Audits and Inspections 620
Safety Beyond the Plant Gate 622
Controlling Workers' Compensation Costs 622

■ **The New Workplace:** Safety at Saudi Petrol Chemical 622
Workplace Health Hazards: Problems and Remedies 623
The Basic Industrial Hygiene Program 624
Asbestos Exposure at Work 625
Infectious Diseases: The Case of SARS 625
Alcoholism and Substance Abuse 625
Stress, Burnout, and Depression 628
Computer-Related Health Problems 630

■ **Improving Productivity Through HRIS:** Internet-based Safety Improvement Solutions   631

    Aids and the Workplace   632

    Workplace Smoking   632

    Violence at Work   633

Occupational Security, Safety, and Health in a Post-9/11 World   637

    Basic Prerequisites for a Security Plan   638

    Setting Up a Basic Security Program   639

    Evacuation Plans   640

    Security for Other Sources of Property Loss   641

    Company Security and Employee Privacy   641

■ **The HR Scorecard:** The New Safety and Health Program   642

Summary   644

Discussion Questions   644

Individual and Group Activities   645

Experiential Exercise: How Safe is My University?   645

Application Case: The New Safety and Health Program   645

Continuing Case: Carter Cleaning Company   650

Chapter **17** Managing Global Human Resources   654

HR and the Internationalization of Business   656

    The HR Challenges of International Business   656

    How Intercountry Differences Affect HRM   657

Global Differences and Similarities in HR Practices   659

    Personnel Selection Procedures   659

    The Purpose of the Performance Appraisal   660

    Training and Development Practices   660

■ **When You're on Your Own:** Comparing Small Businesses, HR Practices in the United States and China   660

    The Use of Pay Incentives   661

How to Implement A Global HR System   661

    Making the Global HR System More Acceptable   661

    Developing a More Effective Global HR System   662

    Implementing the Global HR System   663

Staffing the Global Organization   664

    International Staffing: Home or Local?   664

    Offshoring   664

    Values and International Staffing Policy   665

    Why Expatriate Assignments Fail   666

    Selecting Expatriate Managers   667

■ **The New Workplace:** Sending Women Managers Abroad   669

Training and Maintaining Expatriate Employees   669

    Orienting and Training Employees on International Assignment   670

    Compensating Expatriates   671

    Appraising Expatriate Managers   673

    International Labor Relations   673

■ **Know Your Employment Law:** The Equal Employment Opportunity Responsibilities of Multinational Employers   674

    Terrorism, Safety, and Global HR   675

    Repatriation: Problems and Solutions   676

■ **Improving Productivity Through HRIS:** Taking the HRIS Global   676

    A Final Word: Auditing the HR Function   677

■ **The HR Scorecard:** Managing Global Human Resources 678
Summary 680
Discussion Questions 680
Individual and Group Activities 681
Experiential Exercise: A Taxing Problem for Expatriate Employees 681
Application Case: "Boss, I Think We Have a Problem" 681
Continuing Case: Carter Cleaning Company Going Abroad 682
Appendix for Chapter 17: HRCI Appendix 685

Glossary   693

Photo Credits   701

Name and Organization Index   703

Subject Index   713

Preface

Human Resource Management provides students in human resource management courses and practicing managers with a complete, comprehensive review of essential personnel management concepts and techniques in a highly readable and understandable form. As this new edition goes to press, I feel even more strongly than I did when I wrote the first that all managers—not just HR managers—need a strong foundation in HR/personnel management concepts and techniques to do their jobs. Because all managers do have personnel related responsibilities, I again wrote *Human Resource Management, 10th edition,* for all students of management, not just those who will someday carry the title Human Resource Manager. This edition thus continues to focus throughout on practical applications that all managers need to deal with their HR-related responsibilities. This publication is designed to provide accurate and authoritative information in regard to the subject matter covered, but it is not intended to be a source of legal or other professional advice for any purpose.

The new *When You're On Your Own* features show line managers how, for instance, to recruit and train new employees when their HR department is too busy to help, how to avoid committing management malpractice, how to more effectively address the possibility of terrorist threats, and how to deal with the trend toward outsourcing jobs to other countries.

KEY FEATURES OF THE TENTH EDITION

Integrated Strategic HR and the HR Scorecard

While this 10th edition again focuses almost entirely on essential HR management topics like job analysis, testing, compensation, and appraisal, *Strategic HR and the HR Scorecard* is now this book's integrating theme. The intensely competitive nature of business today means HR managers must be able to defend their plans and contributions in measurable terms. This textbook is the first to provide specific, actionable explanations and illustrations showing how to use devices such as the HR Scorecard (explained fully in Chapter 3) to measure HR's effectiveness in achieving the company's strategic aims.

Improving Productivity Through HRIS

HR managers increasingly rely on information technology to help support the company strategic aims. *Improving Productivity Through HRIS* features in each chapter illustrate how managers use technology to improve the productivity of HR. For example, the Chapter 6 feature explains how managers use applicant-tracking systems to compile web-based resumes, to test and prescreen applicants online, and to discover candidates hidden talents.

Know Your Employment Law

Today, virtually every HR-related decision managers make has legal implications, a fact underscored by the Human Resource Certification Institute's emphasis, in its exams, on candidates for certification having a solid knowledge of employment law. Each of this edition's chapters therefore now contains one or more new *Know Your Employment Law* features. For example, Chapter 6's explains what line managers should know about the federal and state laws governing how employers acquire and use applicants' and employees' background information. This includes, for instance, disclosure and authorization, certification, providing copies of reports, and notice of adverse action.

The New Workplace

Because globalization and diversity are central HR issues today, you will find special *The New Workplace* features devoted to these topics throughout this book. For example, the one in Chapter 4 (job analysis) explains how Mercedes-Benz uses the job analysis techniques it honed at its new Alabama factory to improve its job analysis programs at its plants around the world.

ORGANIZATION OF THE TENTH EDITION

New Chapter: Ethics, Justice and Fair Treatment in HR Management

Today's headline stories demand that ethics take a center stage in training managers. This edition therefore contains a new chapter, *Ethics, Justice and Fair Treatment in HR Management.* The chapter explains the meanings of ethics and fair treatment at work, and how HR managers can support the twin goals of improving ethical behavior and fair treatment in their companies.

New HRCI Related Exercises

The profession of HR management is becoming increasingly demanding. Responding to these new demands, thousands of HR managers have successfully passed the certification exams offered by the Human Resource Certification Institute (HRCI), thus earning the designations Professional in HR (PHR) and Senior Professional in HR (SPHR). This edition now contains, in each chapter, an *HRCI-related exercise* students can use to apply their knowledge of that chapter's material within the HRCI exam context, as well as an appendix that provides a comprehensive listing of the topics that these exams address.

Completely Updated

Adopters of previous editions will note a number of improvements in the book's end of chapter materials. In response to requests from existing and past adopters, this edition returns to using updated versions of the very successful Carter Cleaning *continuing case,* which focuses on the HR issues faced by the owners of an actual small retail service business. Each chapter's end of chapter material also contains a number of *new discussion questions and exercises*, with at least one new exercise per chapter tied to contemporary events (including one that draws on Donald Trump's "Apprentice" TV show).

Finally, I completely updated the material throughout. You'll find hundreds of *new examples and research references and topics* (including terrorism's effect on HR, and the issue of outsourcing jobs abroad), and, correspondingly, hundreds of new post-2000 *endnote citations*. Finally, with its practical, real-world orientation, *Human Resource Management* has always contained a wealth of actual HR forms, and you will find dozens of *new or updated forms* in this edition.

Summary of Selected Key Features and Changes for the Tenth Edition

New: Strategic HR and the HR Scorecard System.   Integrated throughout the book is an all-new strategic HR and HR Scorecard system, consisting of four components.

First, there is an all-new chapter (Chapter 3) devoted to strategic HR and the HR scorecard. This chapter explains the basics of strategic planning, the importance of and methods for measuring HR activities, and how to create and use an HR scorecard.

Second, each chapter (starting with Chapter 4) opens with a new strategic issues vignette. Each provides a strategic focus for the chapter, by briefly describing the strategic HR issue faced by the HR manager of the "Hotel Paris."

Third, each chapter then contains a special boxed feature entitled Strategic HR and the HR scorecard. This feature explains how the Hotel Paris's managers use the tools and techniques from that chapter to create an HR system (for instance a testing system, interviewing system, or compensation system) that contributes in a measurable way to producing the employee behaviors required to achieve the Hotel Paris's strategic goals.

Fourth, a new HR Scorecard feature within each chapter graphically illustrates and summarizes how the firm's HR activities contributed to achieving the Hotel Paris's strategic goals. The HR Scorecard is a concise measurement system. It shows the quantitative standards, or "metrics" the firm uses to measure HR activities, and to measure the employee behaviors resulting from those activities, and to measure the strategically relevant organizational outcomes of these of those employee behaviors. In so doing, it highlights, in a concise but comprehensive way, the causal links between the HR activities, and the emergent employee behaviors, and the resulting firm-wide strategic outcomes and performance.

New: When You're On Your Own Boxed Features.   Reflecting the fact that HR management is the responsibility of every manager, the tenth edition's new When You're on Your Own boxed features provide tools and techniques for line managers and entrepreneurs who have to "go it alone" when it comes to HR practices. Even in Fortune 500 companies, line managers and first-line supervisors often must supplement the broad policy assistance they receive from their HR departments with tactical, day-to-day HR skills and tools. For example, the marketing manager seeking a new assistant may want to supplement her HR department's recruiting efforts with some efforts of her own. Or, the head of business affairs may want to create a practical series of job-related challenges that can help him choose a new entry-level lawyer. The When You're on Your Own boxed features provide this sort of practical, day-to-day advice. They explain, for instance, where the line manager can turn for prepackaged training solutions, how to create valid, simple job-related tests, and how to avoid management malpractice when dealing with employment discrimination issues.

New: Know Your Employment Law Features.   Virtually every HR related decision managers make has legal implications, a factor underscored by the emphasis the HRCI's certification exams place on employment law. Each chapter therefore contains one or more new and unique Know Your Employment Law features. For example, the feature in Chapter 6 (Employee Testing and Selection) explains what the line manager needs to know about the federal and state laws governing how employers acquire and use applicants' and employees' background information, including disclosure and authorization, certification, providing copies of reports, and notice of adverse action. Chapter 11's

(Establishing Strategic Pay Plans) explain, among other things, what the manager should know about making the offer (for instance the pitfalls in quoting the offer with an annualized salary, rather than with an hourly pay rate). Chapter 5's (Personnel Planning and Recruiting) explains the legal steps the firm should take with regard to managing employment relationships with contingent workers.

TEACHING AND LEARNING RESOURCES

The following Instructor Resources are available to adopters of the Dessler textbook.

- Instructor Manual with Video Guide
- Test Item File
- Updated Videos
- Companion Website (www.prenhall.com/dessler)
- Prentice Hall Guide to the Human Resource Certification Exam
- Instructor Resource Center on CD-Rom

This Instructor's Resource Center CD-ROM is an interactive library of presentation and classroom resources. By navigating through this CD, adopters can collect materials from the text most relevant to their interests, edit to create powerful class lectures, copy them to their own computer's hard drive and/or upload them to an online course management system.

On the Instructor Resource CD, you will find the following resources:

- Instructor PowerPoints
- Instructor Manual with Video Guide
- Test Item File
- TestGen test management software

Acknowledgments

While I am of course solely responsible for the content in *Human Resource Management*, I want to thank several people for their assistance. This includes first, the faculty who reviewed this and the 9th edition: Douglas Allen, University of Denver; Jerry Bennett, Western Kentucky University; Mike Bedell, CSU-Bakersfield; Mark Butler, San Diego State; Gus Colangelo, Penn State University; Robert D. Costigan, St. John Fisher College; David Curtis, Governor's State; Beverly DeMarr, Ferris State; Pravin Kamdar, Cardinal Stritch; Gundars Kaupins, Boise State; Catherine Marsh, North Park University; Bob McCammon, College of Lake County; Harriet L. Rojas, Indiana Wesleyan University; Ed Tomlinson, Ohio State and Laura Wolfe, Louisiana State, as well as the faculty members who helped to create this edition's ancillaries: Angie Nadar; Tracy Tuten Ryan, Virginia Commonwealth University; Charlie T. Cook, University of West Alabama; and Steve Hulsey, St. Leo University.

At Prentice Hall, I am grateful for the support and dedicated assistance of many people. During the many years of my association with Prentice Hall, I have always been able to count on the continuing support and friendship of Judy Leale, Jeannine Ciliotta, and Linda Albelli and I thank them for their friendship and for all their help and support in making this book and its predecessors successful. Producing a book like this is a complicated process, and some go more smoothly than others. When the production seems to go flawlessly, as this one did, it's usually the production editor and department that should get the credit, and for that I thank Mary Ellen Morrell and Judy Leale. Once again the intelligence, editorial skills, and good humor of development editor Jeannine Ciliotta made this a far better book that it might have been. Even after 10 editions, *Human Resource Management* would likely just gather dust on someone's shelf without the dedicated efforts of all the professionals in the Prentice Hall sales force. I appreciate the efforts of senior editor Jennifer Simon for her suggestions and hard work in the development and creation of this book, of Christine Genneken for managing details associated with producing it, and of Anke Braun, Marketing Director. I want to thank Jessie Wang, Jorge Thames, and the other Pearson International professionals for their efforts in managing the internationalization of this book. At Florida International University, I appreciate the support and suggestions of my colleagues, including Ronnie Silverblatt and Herman Dorsett. To Frederick K. Easter, a great editor who saw the book's potential when I proposed its first edition, thank you for your advice, support, and encouragement.

At home, I want to acknowledge the support and patience of my wife Claudia during the many hours I spent working on editions 1-10. My son Derek, certainly the best people manager I know and a source of enormous pride, and my daughter-in-law Lisa, were always in my thoughts as I worked on these pages. My mother Laura was always a great source of support and encouragement.

Gary Dessler

After studying this chapter, you should be able to:

1. Explain what human resource management (HR) is and how it relates to the management process.

2. Give at least eight examples of how managers can use HR concepts and techniques.

3. Illustrate the HR management responsibilities of line and staff (HR) managers.

4. Provide a good example that illustrates HR's role in formulating and executing company strategy.

5. Write a short essay that addresses the topic: why metrics and measurement are crucial to today's HR managers.

6. Outline the plan of this book.

The Strategic Role of Human Resource Management

These are interesting times for human resource (HR) managers. Globalized production and sales mean more competition, and more competition means more pressure to improve—to lower costs, to make workers more productive, and to do things better and less expensively. For employers around the world, the human resource function is a key player in helping companies achieve these strategic aims. For example, more than a third of all firms now rely on computerized HR technology to more efficiently track, test, and/or select job applicants.[1] Forty-one percent of large firms (and 24% of firms overall) have human resource call centers, or intranet-enabled processes that let employees service their own HR needs (changes in benefits, for instance). At least 25% of all firms provide their employees with computer-supported and/or Web-based training. At Dell Computer, supervisors have easy access via Dell's intranet to over 30 Web applications (including automated employee appraisals), and so can do tasks by themselves that formerly required costly participation by HR department employees. At the Mercedes Benz plant in Arkansas, changes HR oversaw—such as organizing the workforce around teams—have now spread to the company's plants in Germany and South Africa.●

The main purpose of this chapter is to explain what HR managers do, and to describe more fully how today's HR function helps companies meet the challenges of globalized competition. We'll see that HR management—activities like recruiting, hiring, training, compensating, appraising, and developing employees—is part of every manager's job. And we'll see that HR is also a distinct function, with an HR manager assisting the firm's other managers in many important ways. The main topics we'll cover include the manager's human resource management jobs, crucial global and competitive trends, and how HR managers use technology and modern HR measurement systems to create the high-performance work systems employers need today.

 Explain what human resource management (HR) is and how it relates to the management process.

● THE MANAGER'S HUMAN RESOURCE MANAGEMENT JOBS

Most writers agree that all managers perform certain basic functions. These are planning, organizing, staffing, leading, and controlling. In total, they represent the **management process**. Some of the specific activities involved in each function include:

management process
The five basic functions of planning, organizing, staffing, leading, and controlling

Planning. Establishing goals and standards; developing rules and procedures; developing plans and forecasting.

Organizing. Giving each subordinate a specific task; establishing departments; delegating authority to subordinates; establishing channels of authority and communication; coordinating the work of subordinates.

Staffing. Determining what type of people should be hired; recruiting prospective employees; selecting employees; setting performance standards; compensating employees; evaluating performance; counseling employees; training and developing employees.

Leading. Getting others to get the job done; maintaining morale; motivating subordinates.

Controlling. Setting standards such as sales quotas, quality standards, or production levels; checking to see how actual performance compares with these standards; taking corrective action as needed.

We are going to focus on one of these functions in this book—the staffing, personnel management, or **human resource management (HRM)** function. Human resource management is the process of acquiring, training, appraising, and compensating employees, and attending to their labor relations, health and safety, and fairness concerns. The topics we'll discuss should therefore provide you with the concepts and techniques you need to carry out the "people" or personnel aspects of your management job. These include:

human resource management (HRM)
The policies and practices involved in carrying out the "people" or human resource aspects of a management position, including recruiting, screening, training, rewarding, and appraising.

- Conducting job analyses (determining the nature of each employee's job)
- Planning labor needs and recruiting job candidates
- Selecting job candidates
- Orienting and training new employees
- Managing wages and salaries (compensating employees)
- Providing incentives and benefits
- Appraising performance
- Communicating (interviewing, counseling, disciplining)
- Training and developing managers
- Building employee commitment

And what a manager should know about:

▌ Equal opportunity and affirmative action

▌ Employee health and safety

▌ Handling grievances and labor relations

Why Is HR Management Important to All Managers?

Why are these concepts and techniques important to all managers? Perhaps it's easier to answer this by listing some of the personnel mistakes you *don't* want to make while managing. For example, you don't want to:

▌ Hire the wrong person for the job

▌ Experience high turnover

▌ Have your people not doing their best

▌ Waste time with useless interviews

▌ Have your company taken to court because of discriminatory actions

▌ Have your company cited under federal occupational safety laws for unsafe practices

▌ Have some employees think their salaries are unfair and inequitable relative to others in the organization

▌ Allow a lack of training to undermine your department's effectiveness

▌ Commit any unfair labor practices

Carefully studying this book will help you avoid mistakes like these. And, more important, it can help ensure that you get the right results–through people. Remember, you can do everything else right as a manager—lay brilliant plans, draw clear organization charts, set up modern assembly lines, and use sophisticated accounting controls—but still fail, by hiring the wrong people or by not motivating subordinates. On the other hand, many managers—presidents, generals, governors, supervisors—have been successful even with inadequate plans, organizations, or controls. They were successful because they had the knack of hiring the right people for the right jobs and motivating, appraising, and developing them. Remember as you read this book that *getting results* is the bottom line of managing, and that, as a manager, you will have to get those results through people. As one company president summed up:

> *For many years it has been said that capital is the bottleneck for a developing industry. I don't think this any longer holds true. I think it's the work force and the company's inability to recruit and maintain a good work force that does constitute the bottleneck for production. I don't know of any major project backed by good ideas, vigor, and enthusiasm that has been stopped by a shortage of cash. I do know of industries whose growth has been partly stopped or hampered because they can't maintain an efficient and enthusiastic labor force, and I think this will hold true even more in the future.[2]*

Line and Staff Aspects of HRM

◉2 Give at least eight examples of how managers can use HR concepts and techniques.

All managers are, in a sense, HR managers, since they all get involved in activities like recruiting, interviewing, selecting, and training. Yet most firms also have a human resource department with its own top manager. How do the duties of this HR manager and his or her staff relate to "line" managers' human resource duties? Let's answer this question, starting with a short definition of line versus staff authority.

We'll see in this chapter that technology not only changes the nature of work but also creates new kinds of jobs. Katie Carmichael is a content specialist for a company called SurfControl in Scott's Valley, California. She surfs the Web every day to find sites that employers (or parents) might want to restrict, and she maintains and updates lists of those where employees at SurfControl's clients might otherwise spend unproductive time while on the job.

authority
The right to make decisions, direct others' work, and give orders.

line manager
A manager who is authorized to direct the work of subordinates and is responsible for accomplishing the organization's tasks.

staff manager
A manager who assists and advises line managers.

Line Versus Staff Authority   **Authority** is the right to make decisions, to direct the work of others, and to give orders. In management, we usually distinguish between line authority and staff authority.

Line managers are authorized to direct the work of subordinates—they're always someone's boss. In addition, line managers are directly in charge of accomplishing the organization's basic goals. (Hotel managers and the managers for production and sales are generally line managers, for example.) **Staff managers**, on the other hand, are authorized to assist and advise line managers in accomplishing these basic goals. HR managers are staff managers. They are responsible for assisting and advising line managers in areas like recruiting, hiring, and compensation.

Line Managers' HRM Responsibilities   The direct handling of people has always been an integral part of every line manager's responsibility, from president down to the lowest-level supervisor. For example, one major company outlines its line supervisors' responsibilities for effective human resource management under the following general headings:

1. Placing the right person on the right job
2. Starting new employees in the organization (orientation)
3. Training employees for jobs that are new to them
4. Improving the job performance of each person
5. Gaining creative cooperation and developing smooth working relationships
6. Interpreting the company's policies and procedures
7. Controlling labor costs
8. Developing the abilities of each person
9. Creating and maintaining department morale
10. Protecting employees' health and physical condition

In small organizations, line managers may carry out all these personnel duties unassisted. But as the organization grows, they need the assistance, specialized knowledge, and advice of a separate human resource staff. The human resource department provides this specialized assistance. In doing so, the HR manager carries out three distinct functions:

1. *A line function.* The HR manager directs the activities of the people in his or her own department and in related service areas (like the plant cafeteria). In other words, he or she exerts **line authority** within the HR department. While they generally can't wield line authority outside HR, they are likely to exert **implied authority**. This is because line managers know HR has top management's ear in areas like testing and affirmative action.

2. *A coordinative function.* HR managers also coordinate personnel activities, a duty often referred to as **functional control**. Here the HR manager and department act as the "right arm of the top executive" to ensure that line managers are implementing the firm's HR objectives, policies, and procedures (for example, adhering to its sexual harassment policies).

3. *Staff (assist and advise) functions.* Assisting and advising line managers is the heart of the HR manager's job. The HR manager assists in strategy design and execution by helping the CEO to better understand the personnel aspects of the company's strategic options. HR *assists* in hiring, training, evaluating, rewarding, counseling, promoting, and firing employees. It administers the various benefit programs (health and accident insurance, retirement, vacation, and so on). It helps line managers comply with equal employment and occupational safety laws, and plays an important role in handling grievances and labor relations. It carries out an *innovator* role, by providing "up-to-date information on current trends and new methods of solving problems"—such as today's interest in instituting systems for measuring human resource management's strategic impact. It plays an **employee advocacy** role: It helps define how management should be treating employees, makes sure employees can contest unfair practices, and represents the employees' interests within the framework of its main obligation to senior management.[3]

The size of the HR group and the number of HR specialists reflects the size of the company. For a very large company, an organization chart like the one in Figure 1-1 would be typical, containing a full complement of specialists for each HR function. At the other extreme, the HR organizational chart for a small manufacturer may contain a total of only five or six staff, and have an organization along the lines of Figure 1-2.

Examples of HR job duties include:

Recruiters. Search for qualified job applicants.

Equal employment opportunity (EEO) coordinators. Investigate and resolve EEO grievances, examine organizational practices for potential violations, and compile and submit EEO reports.

Job analysts. Collect and examine information about jobs to prepare job descriptions.

Compensation managers. Develop compensation plans and handle the employee benefits program.

Training specialists. Plan, organize, and direct training activities.

Labor relations specialists. Advise management on all aspects of union–management relations.

---

line authority
The authority exerted by an HR manager by directing the activities of the people in his or her own department and in service areas (like the plant cafeteria).

implied authority
The authority exerted by an HR manager by virtue of others' knowledge that he or she has access to top management (in areas like testing and affirmative action).

functional control
The authority exerted by an HR manager as coordinator of personnel activities.

employee advocacy
HR must take responsibility for clearly defining how management should be treating employees, make sure employees have the mechanisms required to contest unfair practices, and represent the interests of employees within the framework of its primary obligation to senior management.

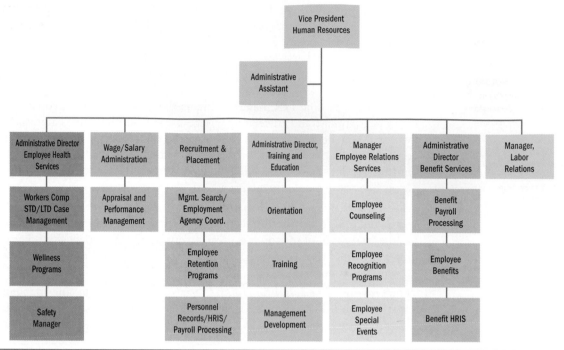

Figure 1-1
HR Department Organizational Chart (Large Company)
Source: Adapted from *BNA Bulletin to Management*, June 29, 2000.

 Illustrate the HR management responsibilities of line and staff (HR) managers.

Cooperative Line and Staff HR Management: An Example

Exactly which HR management activities are carried out by line managers and by staff managers? There's no single division of responsibilities we could apply across the board in all organizations, but we can make some generalizations.

For example, in recruiting and hiring, it's generally the line manager's responsibility to specify the qualifications employees need to fill specific positions. Then the HR staff takes over. They develop sources of qualified applicants and conduct initial screening interviews. They administer the appropriate tests. Then they refer the best applicants to the supervisor (line manager), who interviews and selects the ones he or she wants.

Some activities tend to be HR's alone. For example, 60% of firms assign responsibility for preemployment testing exclusively to HR, 75% assign college recruiting to HR, 86% assign HR insurance benefits administration, 84% assign HR exit interviews,

Figure 1-2
HR Organizational Chart (small company)

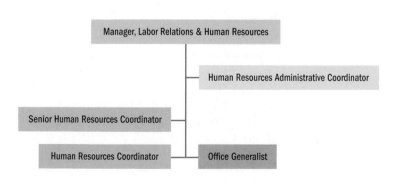

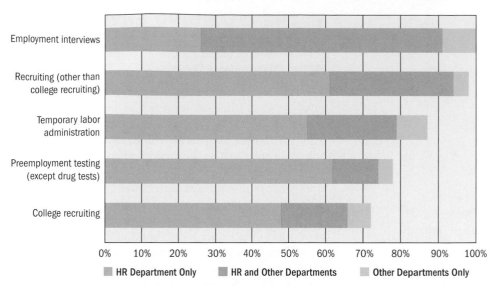

**Figure 1-3
Employment and
Recruiting—Who Handles
It? (percentage of all
employers)**
Source: HR MAGAZINE, *BNA/Society
for Human Resource Management,*
2002. Reproduced with permission
via Copyright Clearance Center.

Note: length of bars represents prevalence of activity among all surveyed employers.

and 88% assign HR personnel/HR record keeping. But employers split most activities, such as employment interviews, performance appraisal, skills training, job descriptions, and disciplinary procedures, between HR and line departments.[4]

Figure 1-3 illustrates the typical HR–line management partnership. For example, HR alone typically handles interviewing in about 25% of firms, but in about 60% of firms, HR and the other hiring departments both get involved in interviewing.

In summary, HR management is an integral part of every manager's job. Whether you're a first-line supervisor, middle manager, or president; or whether you're a production manager, sales manager, office manager, hospital administrator, county manager (or HR manager), getting results through committed people is the name of the game. And to do this, you will need a good working knowledge of the human resource management concepts and techniques in this book.

From Line Manager to HR Manager

Line managers in areas like production and sales may also make career stopovers as staff HR managers. A survey by the Center for Effective Organizations at the University of Southern California found that about one-fourth of large U.S. businesses appointed managers with no HR experience as their top HR executives. Reasons given include the fact that these people may find it easier to give the firms' HR efforts a more strategic emphasis, and the possibility that they may sometimes be better equipped to integrate the firm's HR efforts with the rest of the business.[5]

However, most top HR executives do have previous HR experience. About 80% of those in one recent survey worked their way up within HR.[6] About 37% were in employment/recruitment, and so were mostly involved in activities like recruiting and selecting employees. Thirty percent were in labor relations (union–management), and 27% worked in training and development. The other basic HR functions the top HR executives came from include compensation, benefits, EEO/affirmative action, human resource systems (HRIS), payroll, workers compensation, and safety. About 17% of these HR executives had earned the Human Resource Certification Institute's senior professional in human resources (SPHR) designation, and 13% were certified professionals in human resources (PHR).

● THE CHANGING ENVIRONMENT OF HR MANAGEMENT

HR's Changing Role

The HR department's responsibilities have gradually become broader and more strategic since the days when business people began including "personnel departments" in their organization charts. In the earliest firms, "personnel" first took over hiring and firing from supervisors, ran the payroll department, and administered benefit plans. As technology in areas like testing and interviewing began to emerge, the personnel department began to play an expanded role in employee selection, training, and promotion.[7] The emergence of union legislation in the 1930s added "protecting the firm in its interaction with unions" to the personnel department's responsibilities. Then, as new equal employment legislation created the potential for discrimination-related lawsuits and penalties, personnel's advice and oversight became even more indispensable.[8]

Today, the globalization of the world economy and several other trends are again triggering changes in how companies organize, manage, and use their personnel/HR departments. We'll look at these trends and changes next.

A Changing Environment

globalization
The tendency of firms to extend their sales, ownership, and/or manufacturing to new markets abroad.

Globalization **Globalization** refers to the tendency of firms to extend their sales, ownership, and/or manufacturing to new markets abroad. Examples are all around us. Toyota produces the Camry in Kentucky, while Dell produces and sells PCs in China. Free trade areas—agreements that reduce tariffs and barriers among trading partners—further encourage international trade. NAFTA (the North American Free Trade Area) and the EU (European Union) are examples. Doing business internationally is big business today. For example, the total value of U.S. imports rose from $799 million in 1994 to $135 *billion* in 2003; exports rose from $702 million to $88 billion in the same period.

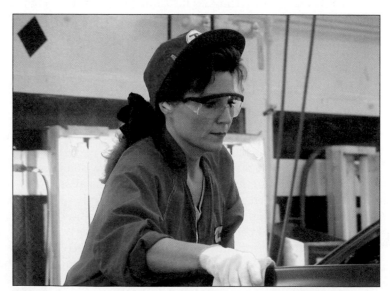

Globalization in action: This American worker is preparing a vehicle for a paint job at a Toyota facility in Georgetown, Kentucky. Toyota now manufactures its vehicles at several locations in the United States and in a number of countries around the world. Its HR operations must therefore help this huge firm integrate its global operations, for instance by providing a database of production managers who can move among facilities in different countries.

More globalization means more competition, and more competition means more pressure to be "world-class"—to lower costs, to make employees more productive, and to do things better and less expensively. As one expert puts it, "the bottom line is that the growing integration of the world economy into a single, huge marketplace is increasing the intensity of competition in a wide range of manufacturing and service industries."[9] From helping firms like Dell cut global HR communication costs, to formulating selection, training, and compensation policies for expatriate employees, managing globalization in world-class firms is a major HR challenge.

Technological Advances   Many of the improvements that make firms world-class involve technology. For example, Carrier Corporation is the world's largest manufacturer of air conditioners, and saves an estimated $100 million per year by using the Internet. In Brazil, Carrier handles all its transactions with its channel partners (its 550 dealers, retailers, and installers) over the Web. "The time required to get an order entered and confirmed by our channel partners has gone from six days to six minutes."[10] Today, HR faces the challenge of quickly applying technology to the task of improving its own operations.

Exporting Jobs   Competitive pressures and the search for greater efficiencies are also prompting more employers to export jobs abroad. For example, in 2003, Merrill Lynch said it was planning on having some of its security analysis work done in India; IBM shifted several hundred systems analysis jobs abroad; and one hospital in Boston even began a program in which radiologists abroad read digitized x-rays for the hospital's patients. Figure 1-4 summarizes the situation. It shows that between 2005 and 2015, about three million U.S. jobs, ranging from office support and computer jobs to management, sales, and even legal jobs, will likely move offshore.[11] Technology facilitates this shift, as companies like Dell find it easier to set up call centers abroad, for instance.

The Nature of Work   Technology is also changing the nature of work. Even factory jobs are more technologically demanding. For example, "knowledge-intensive high tech manufacturing in such industries as aerospace, computers, telecommunications, home electronics, pharmaceuticals, and medical instruments" are replacing factory jobs in steel, auto, rubber, and textiles.[12]

Technology is not the only trend driving this change from "brawn to brains." Today over two-thirds of the U.S. workforce is employed in producing and delivering services, not products. Between 1998 and 2008, the number of jobs in goods-producing

**Figure 1-4
Employment Exodus:
Projected Loss of Jobs and
Wages**
Source: Michael Shroeder, "States Fight Exodus of Jobs," *Wall Street Journal,* June 3, 2003, p. 84. Reproduced with permission of Dow Jones & Co. Inc. via Copyright Clearance Center.

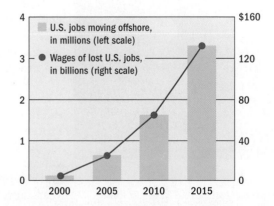

industries will stay almost unchanged, at about 25.5 million, while the number in service-producing industries will climb from 99 million to 118.8 million.[13]

Several trends account for this.[14] With global competition, more manufacturing jobs are shifting to low-wage countries, as noted. For example, Levi Strauss, one of the last major clothing manufacturers in the United States, closed the last of its American plants in 2003.

There has also been a dramatic increase in productivity that lets manufacturers produce more with fewer workers. Just-in-time manufacturing techniques link day-to-day manufacturing schedules more precisely to customer demand, thus squeezing waste out of the system and reducing inventory needs. As manufacturers integrate Internet-based customer ordering with just-in-time manufacturing systems, scheduling becomes even more precise. More manufacturers are partnering with their suppliers to create integrated supply chains. For example, when a customer orders a Dell computer, the same Internet message that informs Dell's assembly line to produce the order also signals the video screen and keyboard manufacturers to prepare for UPS to pick up their parts at a particular time. The net effect is that manufacturers have been squeezing slack and inefficiencies out of the entire production system, allowing companies to produce more products with fewer employees.

In general, the jobs that remain—and especially the manufacturing jobs—require more education and more skills. For example, the five occupations projected to grow fastest in a first decade of the 2000s depend on computers—computer engineers, computer support specialists, computer systems analysts, database administrators, and desktop publishing specialists.[15] Furthermore, automation and just-in-time manufacturing systems mean that even manufacturing jobs require more reading, mathematics, and communication skills than before.

Skilled machinist Chad Toulouse illustrates the modern blue-collar worker. After an 18-week training course, this former college student now works as a team leader in a plant where about 40 percent of the machines are automated. In older plants, machinists would manually control machines that cut chunks of metal into things like engine parts. Today, Chad and his team spend much of their time typing commands into computerized machines that create precision parts for products including water pumps. Like other modern machinists, he earns about $45,000 per year (including overtime).[16]

Also reflecting the desires to keep costs down, there has been a shift to using **nontraditional workers**. Nontraditional workers include those who hold multiple jobs, or who are "contingent" or part-time workers, or people working in alternative work arrangements (such as a mother–daughter team sharing one flight attendant job at JetBlue airlines). Today, almost 10% of American workers—13 million people—fit this nontraditional workforce category. Of these, about eight million are independent contractors who work on specific projects and move on once the projects are done.

For managers, this means a growing emphasis on knowledge workers and human capital.[17] **Human capital** refers to the knowledge, education, training, skills, and expertise of a firm's workers.[18] Today, "the center of gravity in employment is moving fast from manual and clerical workers to knowledge workers, who resist the command and control model that business took from the military 100 years ago."[19] In this environment, managers need new

nontraditional workers
Workers who hold multiple jobs or who are "contingent" or part-time workers, or people working in alternative work arrangements.

human capital
The knowledge, education, training, skills, and expertise of a firm's workers.

Today's blue-collar worker no longer does hard physical labor with dangerous machinery like this: Instead, Chad Toulouse spends most of his time as a team leader typing commands into computerized machines.

world-class HR management systems and skills to select, train, and motivate these employees and to get them to work more like committed partners.

Workforce Demographics At the same time, workforce demographics are changing. Most notably, the workforce is becoming more diverse as women, minority-group members, and older workers enter the workforce.[20] Between 1992 and 2005, workers classified as Asian and others will jump by just over 81%. Hispanics will represent 11% of the civilian labor force in 2005, up from 8% in 1992.[21] About two-thirds of all single mothers (separated, divorced, widowed, or never married) are in the labor force today, as are almost 45% of mothers with children under three years old.

The labor force also is getting older. As the baby boomers born between 1946 and 1960 prepare to leave the labor force in the next few years, employers will face what one study calls a "severe" labor shortage, and will have to "rethink attitudes toward older workers and re-examine a range of established practices, from retirement rules to employee benefits."[22] About 11% fewer Americans were born between 1966 and 1985 than were born in the 20 years after World War II, so there will be fewer people to replace the baby boomers. Furthermore, over the past 50 or so years, the proportion of women in the workforce has risen dramatically, but is now projected to stop growing. America thus can't depend on the entry of women into the labor force to counterbalance the exiting baby boomers.

With the aging of its workers, "America is facing a demographic shift as significant as the massive entry of women into the workforce that began the 1960s."[23] From the 1970s through the 1990s, many employers improved their competitive positions by instituting policies and benefits (such as more flexible work hours) that attracted more women to the workforce. Employers will now have to take similar steps to fill the openings left by retiring employees—probably by rehiring retirees.

Many firms are already instituting new policies aimed at encouraging aging employees to stay, or at attracting previously retired employees. Aerospace Corp. lets employees continue to work part-time rather than retire completely. Oracle Corp. retrains older recruits to be information technology workers. Ford offers numerous new elder care services to employees, to help current employees better cope with the demands of supporting elderly family members.

Provide a good example that illustrates HR's role in formulating and executing company strategy.

strategy
The company's long-term plan for how it will balance its internal strengths and weaknesses with its external opportunities and threats to maintain a competitive advantage.

● MEASURING HR'S CONTRIBUTION: STRATEGY, METRICS, AND THE HR SCORECARD

HR's priorities and tasks evolve over time, because they need to fit or make sense in terms of the company's strategic direction. As we'll see throughout this book, HR's central task is always to provide a set of services that make sense in terms of the company's strategy. A **strategy** is the company's plan for how it will balance its internal strengths and weaknesses with external opportunities and threats in order to maintain a competitive advantage. Ferrari therefore has different HR policies and practices than does Ford, and Wal-Mart has different HR policies and practices than does Neiman Marcus.

Trends like globalization and increased competition have placed HR front and center in most firm's strategic planning efforts. For example, we will see that HR managers today are more involved *in partnering with their top managers in both designing and implementing their companies' strategies.* Today's emphasis on gaining competitive advantage through people makes input from the department that helps to screen, train, appraise, and reward employees too important to ignore when the company is reviewing its strategic options. Today's focus on competitiveness and operational improvements also means that all managers—including HR—must be much more adept at *expressing their departmental plans and accomplishments in measurable terms.* Top management wants to see, precisely, how the HR manager's plans will make the company more valuable, for instance by boosting morale and, thereby, improving performance.

An Emphasis on Performance

A recent survey of HR professionals shows that the pressure for more performance hasn't been lost on HR managers. When asked to rate the importance of various business issues, their five top choices were competition for market share, price competition/price control, governmental regulations, need for sales growth, and need to increase productivity.[24] HR managers also know that establishing competitive, high-performance work systems under conditions of rapid change isn't easy. This helps to explain why another survey of HR executives found that their main concern is "managing change." So, today's successful HR manager must have the capacity to visualize how he or she can adapt HR systems to support the company's strategic needs, and the ability to execute the required changes. These changes may range from new incentive plans that encourage employee innovation, to centralized HR call centers to boost the HR unit's efficiency, to moving more HR activities onto the Web, and to organizing telecommuter programs.[25]

For HR, this focus on performance also requires more measurability. Management expects HR to provide measurable, benchmark-based evidence for its current efficiency and effectiveness, and for the expected efficiency and effectiveness of new or proposed HR programs. In other words, management expects solid, quantified evidence that HR is contributing in a meaningful and positive way to achieving the firm's strategic aims.

 Write a short essay that addresses the topic: why metrics and measurement are crucial to today's HR managers.

metrics
A set of quantitative performance measures HR managers use to assess their operations.

Metrics

This requirement for measurability manifests itself in several ways. First, HR managers need a set of quantitative performance measures (**metrics**) they can use to assess their operations. For example, median HR expenses as a proportion of companies' total operating costs averaged 1 to 1.1% in the early 1990s, 0.8 to 0.9% in the late 1990s, and 0.8% in 2002. There tends to be between 0.9 and one HR staff person per 100 employees. Both manufacturing and nonmanufacturing firms spend about $1,000 per employee for HR. Figures like these provide benchmark metrics managers can use as overall measures of their HR units' efficiency. Figure 1-5 provides a detailed list of HR metrics as provided by the Society for Human Resource Management (SHRM).

However, measuring HR performance requires more than current HR department performance metrics like these. Top management needs and expects more forward-looking information. For example, the CEO may ask the HR manager to defend a proposed new HR program with numbers. She may ask, for instance, "How will this new incentive compensation plan help us improve customer service, customer satisfaction, and the profitability of each of our sales?"

Furthermore, some things are easier to measure than others. "For example," says one HR executive, "we all know there are costs associated with turnover, and HR policies can definitely change our turnover rate. And we can easily compute the value [of this], because there are some very real and tangible costs associated with replacing the employees we lose."[26] On the other hand, quantifying the link between, say, the new incentive plan and customer satisfaction is more difficult, given the relative subjectivity of measuring customer satisfaction. Yet increasingly, HR managers must work with other executives to formulate such measurable links.[27]

Absence Rate	[(# days absent in month) ÷ (Ave. # of employees during mo.) × (# of workdays)] × 100	Measures absenteeism. See *BNA Job Absence Report* for benchmark and survey data. Determine if your company has an absenteeism problem. Analyze why and how to address issue. Analyze further for effectiveness of attendance policy and effectiveness of management in applying policy. See white paper entitled *Absenteeism: Analyzing Work Absences*.
Cost per Hire	(Advertising + Agency Fees + Employee Referrals + Travel cost of applicants and staff + Relocation costs + Recruiter pay and benefits) ÷ Number of Hires	Costs involved with a new hire. Use *EMA/Cost per Hire Staffing Metrics Survey* as a benchmark for your organization. Can be used as a measurement to show any substantial improvements to savings in recruitment/retention costs. Determine what your recruiting function can do to increase savings/reduce costs, etc.
Health Care Costs per Employee	Total cost of health care ÷ Total Employees	Per capita cost of employee benefits. Indicates cost of health care per employee. *Click here* for benefit data from the Bureau of Labor Statistics (BLS). See BLS's publications entitled *Employer Costs for Employee Compensation* and *Measuring Trends in the Structure and Levels of Employer Costs for Employee Compensation* for additional information on this topic.
HR expense factor	HR expense ÷ Total operating expense	HR expenses in relation to the total operating expenses of organization. In addition, determine if expenditures exceeded, met, or fell below budget. Analyze HR practices that contributed to savings, if any. See *SHRM-BNA Survey No. 66: Human Resource Activities, Budgets & Staffs, 2000–2001*.
Human Capital ROI	Revenue – (Operating Expense – [Compensation cost + Benefit cost]) ÷ (Compensation cost + Benefit cost)	Return on investment ratio for employees. Did organization get a return on its investment? Analyze causes of positive/negative ROI metric. Use analysis as opportunity to optimize investment with HR practices such as recruitment, motivation, training, and development. Evaluate if HR practices are having a causal relationship in positive changes to improving metric.
Human Capital Value Added	Revenue – (Operating Expense – ([Compensation cost + Benefit Cost]) ÷ Total Number of FTE	Value of workforce's knowledge, skill, and performance. This measurement illustrates how employees add value to organization.
Revenue Factor	Revenue ÷ Total Number of FTE	Benchmark to indicate effectiveness of company and to show employees as capital rather than as an expense. Human Capital can be viewed as an investment.
Time to fill	Total days elapsed to fill requisitions ÷ Number hired	Number of days from which job requisition was approved to new hire start date. How efficient/productive is recruiting function? This is also a process measurement. See *EMA/Cost per Hire Staffing Metrics Survey* for more information.
Training Investment Factor	Total training cost ÷ Headcount	Training cost per employee. Analyze training function further for effectiveness of training (i.e., Has productivity increased as a result of acquiring new skills and knowledge? Have accidents decreased?). If not, evaluate causes.
Turnover Costs	Cost to terminate + Cost per hire + Vacancy Cost + Learning curve loss	Factors (i.e., knowledge, skills, and abilities) and costs incurred when an employee leaves your company. *Exit interviews* are a useful tool in determining why employees are leaving your organization (see white paper *Employee Turnover Hurts Small And Large Company Profitability* for more information on this topic). Implement retention efforts. Evaluate if HR practices are having a causal relationship in positive changes to improving cost of turnover.
Turnover Rate	[# of separations during mo. ÷ Ave. # of employees during mo.] × 100	Calculate and compare metric to national average using Bureau of National Affairs *BNA Turnover Report* or www.bls.gov/jlt/home.htm. This measures the rate for which employees leave a company. Is there a trend? Has metric increased/decreased? Analyze what has caused increase/decrease to metric. Determine what organization can do to improve retention efforts. Evaluate if HR practices has a causal relationship in positive changes to improving metric (See white paper entitled *Employee Turnover: Analyzing Employee Movement Out of the Organization*).
Workers' Compensation Cost per Employee	Total WC cost for Year ÷ Average number of employees	Analyze and compare (i.e., year 1 to year 2, etc.) on a regular basis. You can also analyze Workers' Compensation further to determine trends in types of injuries, injuries by department, jobs, etc. HR practices such as safety training, *disability management*, and incentives can reduce costs. Use metric as benchmark to show causal relationship between HR practices and reduced Workers' Compensation accidents/costs.

- Compare your metrics against other organizations' metrics, survey data, etc., to evaluate your performance. Metrics can show the benefit of your HR practices and their contribution to your organization's profit.
- Benchmark data and designate time frame (plan year, fiscal year, etc.). Compare data going forward using same time frame (year 1, year 2, year 3, etc.) to show improvement/decline.

Sources: Robert Grossman, "Measuring Up," *HR Magazine*, January 2000, pp. 29–35; Peter V. Le Blanc, Paul Mulvey, and Jude T. Rich, "Improving the Return on Human Capital: New Metrics," *Compensation and Benefits Review*, January/February 2000, pp. 13–20; Thomas E. Murphy and Sourushe Zandvakili, "Data and Metrics-Driven Approach to Human Resource Practices: Using Customers, Employees, and Financial Metrics," *Human Resource Management* 39, no. 1 (Spring 2000), pp. 93–105; [*HR Planning*, Commerce Clearing House Incorporated, July 17, 1996;] SHRM/EMA 2000 Cost Pe Hire and Staffing Metrics Survey; www.shrm.org.

Figure 1-5
HR Metrics

The HR Scorecard

HR Scorecard
Measures the HR function's effectiveness and efficiency in producing employee behaviors needed to achieve the company's strategic goals.

Management ultimately judges the HR function and its initiatives based on whether they create value for the company, where "value creation" means contributing in a measurable way to achieving the company's strategic goals. HR creates value by engaging in activities that produce the employee behaviors the company needs to achieve these strategic goals. Managers often use an **HR Scorecard** to measure the HR function's effectiveness and efficiency in producing these employee behaviors and thus in achieving the company's strategic goals. The HR Scorecard is a concise measurement system. It shows the quantitative standards, or "metrics" the firm uses to measure HR activities, and to measure the employee behaviors resulting from these activities, and to measure the strategically relevant organizational outcomes of those employee behaviors. In so doing, it highlights, in a concise but comprehensive way, the causal link between the HR activities, the emergent employee behaviors, and the resulting firm-wide strategic outcomes and performance. In Chapter 3 we will discuss in detail how to devise and use an HR Scorecard, and, beginning with that chapter, we'll use an illustrative HR Scorecard to show how each chapter's material relates to supporting a company's strategic goals.

The High Performance Work System

Every company must design a set of HR policies and practices that make sense for its own strategy and situation. The employee-testing program that works for hiring engineers may not work for a retail store, for instance. And Ford Motor Corp. lost a president (Jacques Nasser) in part because he tried unsuccessfully to impose GE's famous "forced distribution" appraisal process on Ford's managers. GE's appraisal system didn't make sense for Ford.

However, research shows that the HR systems of high-performing companies do have many things in common, and that they differ in measurable ways from those of low-performing companies. Specifically, these HR systems are "high-performance work systems" (HPWS). HPWS generate more job applicants, screen candidates more effectively, provide more and better training, link pay more explicitly to performance, and provide a safer work environment, among many other things. In terms of measurable outcomes, these HPWS produce more qualified applicants per position, more employees hired based on validated selection tests, more hours of training for new employees, and a higher percentage of employees receiving regular performance appraisals. The general aim of the HPWS is to maximize the competencies and abilities of employees throughout the organization. We will look more closely at the high-performing work system in Chapter 3.

● THE NEW HR MANAGER

New Proficiencies

As you can see, being an HR manager today is a challenging task, and requires several proficiencies. One study found four categories of proficiencies: HR proficiencies, business proficiencies, leadership proficiencies, and learning proficiencies. *HR proficiencies* represent traditional knowledge and skills in areas such as employee selection, training, and compensation. *Business proficiencies* reflect the new role of HR professionals in creating profitable enterprises that serve customers effectively. Thus, today's HR managers need to be familiar with how companies operate, including strategic planning, marketing, production, and finance. They must be able to participate in a management team that formulates plans for how the company will respond to competitive pressures. Today's HR manager must be able to "speak the CFO's language" by measuring and explaining HR activities in terms managers understand, such as return on investment, payback period, and cost per unit of service.[28]

HR managers also require *leadership proficiencies*. For example, they need the ability to work with and lead management groups, and to drive the changes required, for instance, to implement new world-class employee screening and training systems. Finally, because the competitive landscape is changing so quickly and new technologies are being continually introduced, the HR manager needs *learning proficiencies*. He or she must have the ability to stay abreast of and apply all the new technologies and practices affecting the profession.

The fact that top management does understand the strategic benefits of a well-designed HR program will make the HR manager's job somewhat easier. Studies show that top management and chief financial officers recognize the critical role human resource management can play in achieving a company's strategic goals. Figure 1-6 summarizes some results. It shows they know that human capital—the employees' knowledge, skills, and experiences—can have a big effect on important organizational outcomes such as customer satisfaction and profitability.

The Need to "Know Your Employment Law"

A growing web of HR-related laws effects virtually every HR decision the HR or line manager makes. *Equal employment laws* set guidelines regarding how the company writes its recruiting ads, what questions its job interviewers ask, and how it selects candidates for training programs or evaluates its managers. *Occupational safety and health laws* mandate strict guidelines regarding safety practices at work. *Labor laws* lay out, among other things, what the supervisor can and cannot say and do when the union comes calling to organize the company's employees. As one employment lawyer sums up, "the use of such terms as probationary period, permanent employee, merit increases, white-collar . . . , annual salary in a job offer, and personality problems on the termination form now causes serious exposure to a lawsuit."[29]

Consider some examples. You discharge a worker for excessive absenteeism, but her excessive absenteeism was caused by a work-related injury. The employee sues the company, saying that you actually fired her for filing a Workers' Compensation claim.

Figure 1-6
Effects CFOs Believe Human Capital Has on Business Outcomes
Source: Steven H. Bates, "Business Partners," *HR Magazine*, September 2003, p. 49. Reproduced with permission of the Society for Human Resource Management via Copyright Clearance Center.

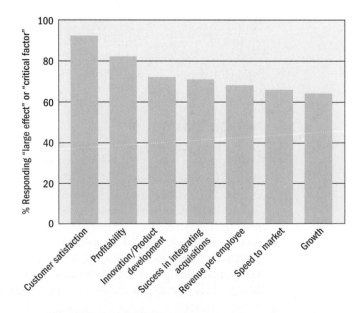

Your company may have to show in court that you did not fire the employee in retaliation for filing the claim, but for absenteeism. As another example, your company's vice president of marketing dated one of his female marketing managers for several months. He subsequently tells her that if she doesn't start dating him again, she won't get a promotion. She refuses, but he promotes her anyway. However, she still sues for sexual harassment. The law says she has a legitimate case, even though she got her promotion. The vice president created a sexually hostile environment by suggesting she may have to return the favor if he promoted her.

Because legal issues are so central to all HR activities, we will discuss equal employment law in the next chapter. Then, in each chapter, special "Know Your Employment Law" text sections will address crucial legal aspects of that chapter's topics.

Ethics and HR

Headlines regarding ethical lapses at companies ranging from Enron and MCI to Arthur Andersen and Italy's Parmalat underscore the need for ethical corporate behavior. Given that many of these firms, such as the accounting firm Arthur Andersen, were literally put out of business because of ethical lapses, it is clear that ethics needs to play a bigger role in managers' decisions.

Congress passed the Sarbanes-Oxley Act in 2003. To help ensure that managers take their ethics responsibilities seriously, Sarbanes-Oxley is intended to curb erroneous corporate financial reporting. Among other things, Sarbanes-Oxley requires CEOs and CFOs to certify their companies' periodic financial reports, prohibits personal loans to executive officers and directors, and requires CEOs and CFOs to reimburse their firms for bonuses and stock option profits if corporate financial statements subsequently require restating.[30]

HR managers need to be heavily involved in implementing ethics laws like these. For example, every employer now needs a new code of ethics for CFOs—probably promulgated by HR, which will also have to modify various company policies to include reference to Sarbanes-Oxley. The new policies must make it clear that managers may not retaliate against employees for exercising their responsibilities under the new act.

The HR manager's responsibilities for implementing Sarbanes-Oxley are just the tip of the iceberg when it comes to how HR can influence ethical practices. One survey found that six of the ten most serious ethical issues—workplace safety, security of employee records, employee theft, affirmative action, comparable work, and employee privacy rights—were HR related.[31] We will explain HR's role in promoting ethical behavior at work in each chapter, and more fully in Chapter 14.

HR Certification

As the HR manager's tasks grow more complex, human resource management is becoming more professionalized. Over 60,000 HR professionals have already passed one or both of the Society for Human Resource Management's (SHRM) HR professional certification exams. SHRM's Human Resource Certification Institute offers these exams (703-548-3440). Two levels of exams test the professional's knowledge of all aspects of HR, including management practices, staffing, HR development, compensation, labor relations, and health and safety. Those who successfully complete all requirements earn the SPHR (senior professional in HR), or PHR (professional in HR) certificate. Figure 1-7 summarizes the body of knowledge in the SHRM certification program. You will find certification-related

**Figure 1-7
2004 SHRM® Learning
System Module
Descriptions**

Module 1: Strategic Management
- The Role of Human Resources in Organizations
- The Strategic Planning Process
- Scanning the External Environment

Organizational Structure and Internal HR Partners
- Measuring Human Resource Effectiveness
- Ethical Issues Affecting Human Resources
- Human Resources and the Legislative Environment

Module 2: Workforce Planning and Employment
- Key Legislation Affecting Employee Rights
- Key Legislation Affecting Privacy and Consumer Protection
- Equal Employment Opportunity/Affirmative Action
- Gender Discrimination and Harassment in the Workplace
- Organizational Staffing Requirements
- Job Analysis and Documentation
- Recruitment
- Flexible Staffing
- Selection
- Employment Practices
- Organizational Exit
- Employee Records Management

Module 3: Human Resource Development
- Key Legislation
- Human Resource Development and the Organization
- Adult Learning and Motivation
- Assessment of HRD Needs
- HRD Program Design and Development
- HRD Program Implementation
- Evaluating HRD Effectiveness
- Career Development
- Developing Leaders
- Organizational Development Initiatives
- Performance Management

Module 4: Compensation and Benefits
- Key Legislation
- Total Compensation and the Strategic Focus of the Organization
- Pay Administration
- Compensation Systems
- Introduction to Benefit Programs
- Government-Mandated Benefits
- Voluntary Benefits
- Compensation and Benefit Programs for Employees
- Evaluating the Total Compensation System and Communicating It to Employees

Module 5: Employee and Labor Relations
- Key Legislation Affecting Employee and Labor Relations
- Employee Relations and Organizational Culture
- Employee Involvement Strategies
- Positive Employee Relations
- Work Rules
- Effective Communication of Laws, Regulations and Organizational Policies
- Discipline and Formal Complaint Resolution
- Union Organizing
- Unfair Labor Practices
- Collective Bargaining
- Strikes and Secondary Boycotts
- Public-Sector Labor Relations
- International Employee and Labor Relations

Module 6: Occupational Health, Safety, and Security
- Key Legislation
- Safety
- Health
- Security

exercises in the end-of-chapter exercises throughout this book. The test specifications for the HRCI exams are in the appendix for chapter 17 at the end of this book.

HR and Technology

Technological applications like those summarized in Table 1-1 play an increasingly important role in HR. Technology improves HR functioning in four main ways: self-service, call centers, productivity improvement, and outsourcing.[32] For example, using Dell's HR intranet, the firm's employees can *self-service* many of their HR transactions, such as updating personal information and changing benefits allocations. And, Dell's HR intranet and "data warehouse" provide its managers with desktop access to HR-related information, such as "how does turnover in my department compare to that of the other departments at Dell?" Technology also enabled Dell to create a centralized *call center*. HR specialists answer questions from all Dell's far-flung employees, reducing the need for multiple HR centers at each Dell location. The "Improving Productivity Through HRIS" box (page 21) presents another example.

More firms are installing Internet and computer-based systems for *improving HR productivity*. For example, International Paper Corp. finished installing its "Viking" HR information system in April 2001. In terms of efficiency, the goal was to achieve an

Table 1-1

**Technological
Applications for HR**

Technology	How Used by HR
Application Service Providers (ASPs) and technology outsourcing	ASPs provide software applications, for instance, for processing employment applications. The ASPs host and manage the services for the employer from their own remote computers
Web portals	Employers use these, for instance, to enable employees to sign up for and manage their own benefits packages and to update their personal information
PCs and high-speed access	Make it easier for employees to take advantage of the employers Web-assisted HR activities
Streaming desktop video	Used, for instance, to facilitate distance learning and training or to provide corporate information to employees quickly and inexpensively
The mobile Web and wireless net access	Used to facilitate employees' access to the company's Web-based HR activities
E-procurement	Used for ordering work materials more efficiently online
Internet- and network-monitoring software	Used to track employees' Internet and e-mail activities or to monitor their performance
Bluetooth	A special wireless technology used to synchronize various electronic tools like cellular phones and PCs, and thus facilitate employees' access to the employer's online HR services
Electronic signatures	Legally valid e-signatures that the employer can use to more expeditiously obtain signatures for applications and record keeping
Electronic bill presentment and payment	Used, for instance, to eliminate paper checks and to facilitate payments to employees and suppliers
Data warehouses and computerized analytical programs	Help HR managers monitor their HR systems. For example, they make it easier to assess things like cost per hire, and to compare current employees' skills with the firm's projected strategic needs

HR staff-to-employee ratio of one to 150, and a cost per employee of $800 for delivering HR services.[33] The Viking project included four components. There was a *data warehouse* which stockpiled a vast array of HR-related information on employees. It included *new technology* to upgrade the company's existing centralized HR service center (which employees can contact for answers to HR questions). The third part consisted of *new software* for managing HR activities such as payroll administration. The fourth component included an intranet-based *employee portal* that employees use to self-service certain HR-related needs (such as updating personal information).

outsourcing
Letting outside vendors provide services.

Technology also makes it easier to **outsource** HR activities to specialist service providers, by enabling service providers to have real-time, Internet-based access to the employer's HR database. Outsourcing is increasingly popular. About 84% of the HR professionals responding to one survey said their firms outsource the administration of 401(k) pension plans, 84% outsource employee assistance/counseling programs, 74% outsource retirement planning, 73% pension administration, 72%

Improving Productivity Through HRIS

The HR Portal

HR portals, usually hosted on a company's intranet, provide employees with a single access point or "gateway" to all HR information.[34] They let employees, managers, and executives interactively (and selectively) access and modify HR Information. They thereby streamline the HR process and enable HR managers to focus more on strategic issues.

Sometimes the firm's gateway HR portal supports just a few HR specialists. Anheuser-Busch used this approach when the time came for annual benefits package enrollments. HR knew there would be a large number of employee inquiries. It therefore replaced its manual inquiry process with Authoria HR, an HR portal from Authoria, Inc. (www.authoria.com). Doing so let HR digitize and aggregate through a single source (the new portal) all the former paper benefits reports, electronic spreadsheets, and benefit summaries that the firm's benefits counselors had been using. That made it much easier for specialists in Anheuser-Busch's HR call center to answer employees' questions as they came in. The aim is to eventually allow employees to research and answer their own HR questions through a browser-based interface.[35]

Wells Fargo used an HR portal when it merged with Norwest Corporation. The merger meant moving 90,000 employees to a new benefits plan, which of course triggered numerous employee inquiries. As at Anheuser-Busch, Wells Fargo armed its HR call center counselors with a specialized portal; this helped them research and answer employees' inquiries.

NCR also installed an HR portal. It is called HR eXpress, and is organized into three information areas: benefits and compensation, training and career growth, and NCR values and HR policies.[36] NCR also added a Forms Center to the site's title bar. HR eXpress gives NCR employees a shortcut to all the information they need to manage HR tasks, such as those relating to company benefits and updating their personal information. The Forms Center gives them quick access to any HR forms they need.

Putting HR services online doesn't just cut costs by letting employees research their own inquiries or by letting HR call center counselors do their jobs more easily (although it certainly does both). It also enables HR to redeploy its assets and focus on more strategic issues. As one manager put it: "We weren't looking for cost savings but to transform the work HR was doing from reactionary—dealing with paper and manual tasks—to proactive, being on the cutting edge, making people better employees."[37]

temporary staffing, and about 68% of employers outsource background checks to specialist firms.

Outline the plan of this book.

● THE PLAN OF THIS BOOK

Here we present an overview of Chapters 1–17, but do not think of these as independent, unrelated topics: Each topic interacts with and affects the others, and all should fit with the employer's strategic plan. Figure 1-8 summarizes this idea. For example, how you test and interview job candidates (Chapters 6 and 7) and train and appraise job incumbents (Chapters 8 and 9) depends on the job's specific duties and responsibilities (Chapter 4). How good a job you do selecting (Chapter 6) and training (Chapter 8) employees will affect how safely they do their jobs (Chapter 16). An employee's performance and thus his or her appraisal (Chapter 9) depends not just on the person's motivation, but on how well you identified the job's duties (Chapter 4), and screened and trained the employee (Chapters 6 and 7). Furthermore, the firm's HR strategies, and specifically the HR policies in each area—for instance, how you recruit, select, train, appraise, and compensate employees—should make sense in terms of the company's

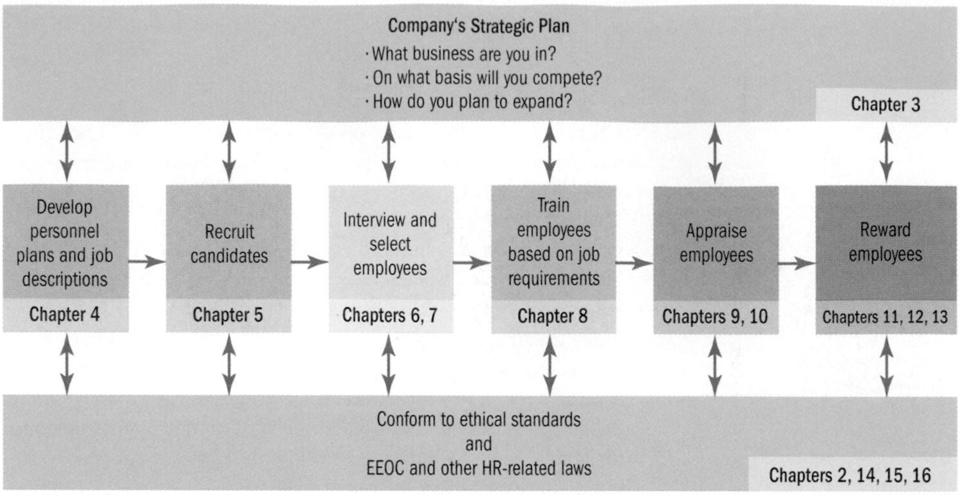
Company's Strategic Plan
· What business are you in?
· On what basis will you compete?
· How do you plan to expand?
Chapter 3
Develop personnel plans and job descriptions
Chapter 4
Recruit candidates
Chapter 5
Interview and select employees
Chapters 6, 7
Train employees based on job requirements
Chapter 8
Appraise employees
Chapters 9, 10
Reward employees
Chapters 11, 12, 13
Conform to ethical standards and EEOC and other HR-related laws
Chapters 2, 14, 15, 16

Figure 1-8
Strategy and the Basic HR Process

strategic plan. A high-end watch manufacturer like Rolex needs a different approach to hiring, training, and paying employees than does a mass producer such as Seiko. We'll look at this more closely in Chapter 3.

The Basic Themes and Features

In this book, we use several themes and features to emphasize particularly important issues, and to provide continuity from chapter to chapter. First, HR management is the *responsibility of every manager*—not just those in the HR department. Throughout this book, you'll therefore find an emphasis on practical material that you as a manager will need to perform your day-to-day management responsibilities. Even if you're a supervisor or manager in a Fortune 500 company trying to accomplish some HR-related task (like interviewing a job candidate), you may find you need more support than your HR department can provide. Even the largest employers may not always provide the sorts of day-to-day instructions and support that their line managers need. We have therefore included, in each chapter, special "When You're on Your Own" boxed features. These show you in practical terms how the manager or small business owner who is "on his or her own" can accomplish some of the chapter's key HR tasks.

Second, the intensely competitive nature of business today means HR managers must always stand ready to defend their plans and contributions in measurable terms. You'll therefore find frequent references throughout to *measuring HR's performance*. Chapter 3 explains how to use an *HR Scorecard* to measure HR's effectiveness in achieving the company's strategic aims, and each chapter after that provides an illustrated example.

Third, the HR manager must design his or her department's HR system relative to achieving the company's strategic aims. This book therefore discusses *strategic planning for HR managers* fully in Chapter 3, and uses the HR Scorecard features to illustrate how HR influences and supports the company's strategic plan.

Fourth, HR managers increasingly rely on information technology to help support the company's strategic aims. "Improving Productivity Through HRIS" features in each chapter illustrate how managers use technology to improve the productivity of HR.

Fifth, we'll see in the following chapter that virtually every HR-related decision managers make has legal implications (a fact exemplified by the emphasis SHRM certification places on the law). Each chapter therefore contains one or more relevant "Know Your Employment Law" features.

Finally, we've seen that *globalization* and *diversity* are important HR issues today, so you will find special features devoted to one or the other throughout this book.

● OVERVIEW

Following is a brief overview of the chapters.

Part 1: Introduction

Chapter 1: The Strategic Role of Human Resource Management. The manager's human resource management jobs, crucial global and competitive trends, how managers use technology and modern HR measurement systems to create high-performance work systems.

Chapter 2: Equal Opportunity and the Law. What you'll need to know about equal opportunity laws as they relate to human resource management activities such as interviewing, selecting employees, and evaluating performance.

Chapter 3: Strategic Human Resource Management and the HR Scorecard. What is strategic planning; high performance work systems; strategic HR; the HR Scorecard.

Part 2: Recruitment and Placement

Chapter 4: Job Analysis. How to analyze a job; how to determine the human resource requirements of the job, as well as its specific duties and responsibilities.

Chapter 5: Personnel Planning and Recruiting. Human resource planning and planning systems; determining what sorts of people need to be hired; recruiting them.

Chapter 6: Employee Testing and Selection. Techniques you can use to ensure that you're hiring the right people.

Chapter 7: Interviewing Candidates. How to interview candidates to help ensure that you hire the right person for the right job.

Part 3: Training and Development

Chapter 8: Training and Developing Employees. Providing the training necessary to ensure that your employees have the knowledge and skills needed to accomplish their tasks; concepts and techniques for developing more capable employees, managers, and organizations.

Chapter 9: Performance Management and Appraisal. Techniques for appraising performance and for linking performance with the organization's goals.

Chapter 10: Managing Careers. Techniques such as career planning and promotion from within that firms use to help ensure employees can achieve their potential.

Part 4: Compensation

Chapter 11: Establishing Strategic Pay Plans. How to develop equitable pay plans for your employees.

Chapter 12: Pay-for-Performance and Financial Incentives. Pay-for-performance plans such as financial incentives, merit pay, and incentives that help tie performance to pay.

Chapter 13: Benefits and Services. Providing benefits that make it clear the firm views its employees as long-term investments and is concerned with their welfare.

Part 5: Employee Relations

Chapter 14: Ethics, Justice, and Fair Treatment in HR Management. Ensuring ethical and fair treatment through discipline, grievance, and career management processes.

Chapter 15: Labor Relations and Collective Bargaining. Concepts and techniques concerning the relations between unions and management, including the union organizing campaign; negotiating and agreeing upon a collective bargaining agreement between unions and management; and managing the agreement via the grievance process.

Chapter 16: Employee Safety and Health. The causes of accidents, how to make the workplace safe, and laws governing your responsibilities for employee safety and health.

Chapter 17: Managing Global Human Resources. The growing importance of international business, and HR's role in managing the personnel side of multinational operations.

 *Review*

SUMMARY

1. All managers perform certain basic functions—planning, organizing, staffing, leading, and controlling. These represent the management process.

2. Staffing, personnel management, or human resource management includes activities like recruiting, selecting, training, compensating, appraising, and developing employees.

3. HR management is a part of every manager's responsibilities. These responsibilities include placing the right person in the right job, and then orienting, training, and compensating to improve his or her job performance.

4. The HR department carries out three main functions. The HR manager exerts line authority in his or her unit and implied authority elsewhere in the organization. He or she ensures that the organization's HR objectives and policies are coordinated and implemented. And he or she provides various staff services to line management, such as partnering with the CEO in designing the company's strategy, and assisting in the hiring, training, evaluating, rewarding, promoting, and disciplining of employees at all levels.

5. Trends such as globalization, technological advances, and deregulation mean that companies must be more competitive to thrive today. Other important trends include growing workforce diversity and changes in the nature of work, such as the movement toward a service society and a growing emphasis on human capital.

6. For the HR manager, the focus on competitiveness and productivity demands measurability. Management expects HR to provide measurable, benchmark-based evidence regarding HR's current efficiency and effectiveness, and regarding the expected efficiency and effectiveness of its new or proposed programs.

7. HR managers often use *HR Scorecards* to facilitate the measurement process. The HR Scorecard is a visual and/or computerized model that enables managers to demonstrate how HR contributes to the company's financial success. It shows the measurable, cause-and-effect links between three things: (1) HR activities (such as improving the firm's incentive plan), (2) intermediate employee results (such as improved morale), and (3) end-result company metrics (such as improved customer service and higher profits).

8. In this book, several themes and features emphasize particularly important issues, and provide continuity from chapter to chapter. For example, HR management is the *responsibility of every manager*—not just those in the HR department. HR is a *strategic partner* in the strategy development process. HR works with other top managers to formulate the company's strategy as well as to execute it.

DISCUSSION QUESTIONS

1. Explain what HR management is and how it relates to the management process.

2. Give examples of how HR management concepts and techniques can be of use to all managers.

3. Illustrate the HR management responsibilities of line and staff managers.

4. Why is it important for companies today to make their human resources into a competitive advantage? Explain how HR can contribute to doing this.

INDIVIDUAL AND GROUP ACTIVITIES

1. Working individually or in groups, develop outlines showing how trends like workforce diversity, technological innovation, globalization, and changes in the nature of work have affected the college or university you are attending now. Present in class.

2. Working individually or in groups, contact the HR manager of a local bank. Ask the HR manager how he or she is working as a strategic partner to manage human resources, given the bank's strategic goals and objectives. Back in class, discuss the responses of the different HR managers.

3. Working individually or in groups, interview an HR manager. Based on that interview, write a short presentation regarding HR's role today in building more competitive organizations.

4. Working individually or in groups, bring several business publications such as *BusinessWeek* and the *Wall Street Journal* to class. Based on their contents, compile a list entitled "What HR managers and departments do today."

5. Based on your personal experiences, list 10 examples showing how you did use (or could have used) human resource management techniques at work or school.

6. Laurie Siegel, senior vice president of human resources for Tyco International, took over her job in 2003, just after numerous charges forced the company's previous board of directors and top executives to leave the firm. Hired by new CEO Edward Breen, Siegel had to tackle numerous difficult problems starting the moment she assumed office. For example, she had to help hire a new management team. She had to do something about what the outside world viewed as a culture of questionable ethics at her company. And she had to do something about the company's top management compensation plan, which many felt contributed to the allegations by some that some former company officers had used the company as a sort of private ATM.

Siegel came to Tyco after a very impressive career. For example, she had been head of executive compensation at Allied Signal, and was a graduate of the Harvard Business School. But, as strong as her background was, she obviously had her work cut out for her when she took the senior vice president of HR position at Tyco.

Working individually or in groups, conduct an Internet search and library research to answer the following questions: What human resource management-related steps did Siegel take to help get Tyco back on the right track? Do you think she took the appropriate steps? Why or why not? What, if anything, do you suggest she do now?

EXPERIENTIAL EXERCISE

Helping "The Donald"

Purpose: The purpose of this exercise is to provide practice in identifying and applying the basic concepts of human resource management by illustrating how managers use these techniques in their day-to-day jobs.

Required Understanding: Be thoroughly familiar with the material in this chapter, and with at least several episodes of: *The Apprentice*, the TV show in which developer Donald Trump starred.

How to Set Up the Exercise/Instructions:

1. Divide the class into teams of three to four students.

2. Read this: As you may know by watching "the Donald" as he organizes his business teams for *The Apprentice*, human resource management plays an important role in what Donald Trump, and the participants on his separate teams, need to do to be successful. For example, Donald Trump needs to be able to appraise each of the participants. And, for their part, the leaders of each of his teams need to be able to staff his or her teams with the right participants, and then provide the sorts of training, incentives, and evaluations that help their companies succeed and that therefore make the participants themselves (and especially the team leaders) look like "winners" to Mr. Trump.

3. Watch several of these shows (or reruns of the shows), and then meet with your team and answer the following questions:

   a. What specific HR functions (recruiting, interviewing, and so on) can you identify Donald Trump using on this show? Make sure to give specific examples based on the show.

   b. What specific HR functions (recruiting, selecting, training, etc.) can you identify one or more of the team leaders using to help manage their teams on the show? Again, please give specific answers.

   c. Provide a specific example of how HR functions (such as recruiting, selection, interviewing, compensating, appraising, and so on) contributed to one of the participants coming across as particularly successful to Mr. Trump. Can you provide examples of how one or more of these functions contributed to a participant being told by Mr. Trump, "you're fired"?

   d. Present your team's conclusions to the class.

APPLICATION CASE

Jack Nelson's Problem

As a new member of the board of directors for a local bank, Jack Nelson was being introduced to all the employees in the home office. When he was introduced to Ruth Johnson, he was curious about her work and asked her what the machine she was using did. Johnson replied that she really did not know what the machine was called or what it did. She explained that she had only been working there for two months. She did, however, know precisely how to operate the machine. According to her supervisor, she was an excellent employee.

At one of the branch offices, the supervisor in charge spoke to Nelson confidentially, telling him that "something was wrong," but she didn't know what. For one thing, she explained, employee turnover was too high, and no sooner had one employee been put on the job than another one resigned. With customers to see and loans to be made, she continued, she had little time to work with the new employees as they came and went.

All branch supervisors hired their own employees without communication with the home office or other branches. When an opening developed, the supervisor tried to find a suitable employee to replace the worker who had quit.

After touring the 22 branches and finding similar problems in many of them, Nelson wondered what the home office should do or what action he should take. The banking firm was generally regarded as a well-run institution that had grown from 27 to 191 employees during the past eight years. The more he thought about the matter, the more puzzled Nelson became. He couldn't quite put his finger on the problem, and he didn't know whether to report his findings to the president.

Questions

1. What do you think is causing some of the problems in the bank's home office and branches?

2. Do you think setting up an HR unit in the main office would help?

3. What specific functions should an HR unit carry out? What HR functions would then be carried out by supervisors and other line managers? What role should the Internet play in the new HR organization?

Source: From Claude S. George, *Supervision in Action*, 4th ed., 1985. Adapted by permission of Prentice Hall, Inc., Upper Saddle River, NJ.

CONTINUING CASE

Carter Cleaning Company

Introduction

A main theme of this book is that HR management—activities like recruiting, selecting, training, and rewarding employees—is not just the job of a central HR group but rather a job in which every manager must engage. Perhaps nowhere is this more apparent than in the typical small service business. Here the owner/manager usually has no HR staff to rely on. However, the success of his or her enterprise (not to mention his or her family's peace of mind) often depends largely on the effectiveness through which workers are recruited, hired, trained, evaluated, and rewarded. Therefore, to help illustrate and emphasize the front-line manager's HR role, throughout this book we will use a continuing case based on an actual small business in the southeastern United States. Each chapter's segment of the case will illustrate how the case's main player—owner/manager Jennifer Carter—confronts and solves personnel problems each day at work by applying the concepts and techniques of that particular chapter. Here is background information you will need to answer questions that arise in subsequent chapters. (We also present a second, unrelated "application case" case incident in each chapter.)

Carter Cleaning Centers
Jennifer Carter graduated from State University in June 2003, and, after considering several job offers, decided to do what she really always planned to do—go into business with her father, Jack Carter.

Jack Carter opened his first laundromat in 1990 and his second in 1992. The main attraction of these coin laundry businesses for him was that they were capital- rather than labor-intensive. Thus, once the investment in machinery was made, the stores could be run with just one unskilled attendant and none of the labor problems one normally expects from being in the retail service business.

The attractiveness of operating with virtually no skilled labor notwithstanding, Jack had decided by 1996 to expand the services in each of his stores to include the dry cleaning and pressing of clothes. He embarked, in other words, on a strategy of "related diversification," by adding new services that were related to and consistent with his existing coin laundry activities. He added these in part because he wanted to better utilize the unused space in the rather large stores he currently had under lease, and partly because he was, as he put it, "tired of sending out the dry cleaning and pressing work that came in from our coin laundry clients to a dry cleaner five miles away, who then took most of what should have been our profits." To reflect the new, expanded line of services he renamed each of his two stores Carter Cleaning Centers and was sufficiently satisfied with their performance to open four more of the same type of stores over the next five years. Each store had its own on-site manager and, on average, about seven employees and annual revenues of about $500,000. It was this six-store chain of cleaning centers that Jennifer joined upon graduating from State University.

Her understanding with her father was that she would serve as a troubleshooter/consultant to the elder Carter with the aim of both learning the business and bringing to it modern management concepts and techniques for solving the business's problems and facilitating its growth.

Questions

1. Make a list of five specific HR problems you think Carter Cleaning will have to grapple with.

2. What would you do first if you were Jennifer?

KEY TERMS

management process, 4

human resource management (HRM), 4

authority, 6

line manager, 6

staff manager, 6

line authority, 7

implied authority, 7

functional control, 7

employee advocacy, 7

globalization, 10

nontraditional workers, 12

human capital, 12

strategy, 13

metrics, 14

HR Scorecard, 16

outsourcing, 20

ENDNOTES

1. See "Applicant Tracking Joins Payroll and Benefits as Top HR Apps," *Human Resource Management Reports*, Institute of Management and Administration (November 2003), p. 1.

2. Quoted in Fred. K. Foulkes, "The Expanding Role of the Personnel Function," *Harvard Business Review*, March–April, 1975, pp. 71–84. See also Michael Losey, "HR Comes of Age," *HR Magazine* 9 (1998), pp. 40–53.

3. "Employee Advocacy Remains HR Priority," *BNA Bulletin to Management*, September 26, 1996, p. 312.

4. "Human Resource Activities, Budgets and Staffs, 1999–2000," *BNA Bulletin to Management*, June 20, 2000.

5. Steve Bates, "No Experience Necessary? Many Companies Are Putting non-HR Executives in Charge of HR with Mixed Results," *HR Magazine* 46, no. 11 (November 2001), pp. 34–41.

6. "A Profile of Human Resource Executives," *BNA Bulletin to Management*, June 21, 2001, p. S5.

7. "Immigrants in the Workplace," *BNA Bulletin to Management Datagraph*, March 15, 1996, pp. 260–261. See also Tanuja Agarwala, "Human Resource Management: The Emerging Trends," *Indian Journal of Industrial Relations*, January 2002, pp. 315–331; and Shari Caudron et al., "80 People, Events and Trends that Shaped HR," *Workforce*, January 2002, pp. 26–56.

8. "Human Capital Critical to Success," *Management Review*, November 1998, p. 9.

9. Ibid., p. 9. See also "The Impact of Globalization on HR," *Workplace Visions* 5 (Society for Human Resource Management, 2000), pp. 1–8.

10. Paul Judge, "How I Saved $100 Million on the Web," *Fast Company*, February 2001, pp. 174–181.

11. Michael Schroeder, "States Fight Exodus of Jobs," *Wall Street Journal*, June 3, 2003, p. 84.

12. Roger Moncarz and Azure Reasor, "The 2000-10 Job Outlook in Brief," *Occupational Outlook Quarterly* (Spring 2002), pp. 9–44.

13. See "Future Work: Trends and Challenges for Work in the 21st Century," *Occupational Outlook Quarterly* (Summer 2000), pp. 31–37.

14. Ibid.

15. Ibid., p. 34.

16. Timothy Appel, "Better Off a Blue-Collar," *Wall Street Journal*, (July 1, 2003), p. B-1.

17. Moncarz and Reasor, "The 2000-10 Job Outlook in Brief."

18. Richard Crawford, *In the Era of Human Capital* (New York: Harper Business, 1991), p. 26.

19. Peter Drucker, "The Coming of the New Organization," *Harvard Business Review*, January–February 1998, p. 45. See also James Guthime et al., "Correlates and Consequences of High Involvement Work Practices: The Role of Competitive Strategy," *International Journal of Human Resource Management*, February 2002, pp. 183–197.

20. Gerald Ferris, Dwight Frank, and M. Carmen Galang, "Diversity in the Workplace: The Human Resources Management Challenge," *Human Resource Planning* 16, no. 1 (1993), pp. 45–51. See also "Charting the Projections: 2000–10," *Occupational Outlook Quarterly* (Winter 2001–2002), pp. 36–41.

21. "Immigrants in the Workforce."

22. See Diane Piktialis and Hal Morgan, "The Aging of the U.S. Workforce and Its Implications for Employers," *Compensation and Benefits Review*, January/February 2003, p. 57.

23. Ibid., p. 61.

24. Philip Way, "HR/IR Professionals' Educational Needs and Masters Program Curricula," *Human Resource Management Review* (2002), p. 478.

25. Christina Giannantonio and Amy Hurley, "Executive Insights into HR Practices and Education," *Human Resource Management Review* (2002), pp. 491–511.

26. Bill Leonard, "Straight Talk," *HR Magazine*, January 2002, p. 49.

27. Steve Bates, "The Metrics Maze," *HR Magazine*, December 2003, pp. 51–61; and Steve Bates, "Accounting for People," *HR Magazine*, October 2002, pp. 30–37.

28. Susan Wells, "From HR to the Top," *HR Magazine*, June 2003, p. 49.

29. Kenneth Sovereign, *Personnel Law* (Upper Saddle River, NJ: Pearson, 2001), p. 6.

30. Jonathan Seggal, "The Joy of Cooking," *HR Magazine*, November 2002, pp. 52–58.

31. Kevin Wooten, "Ethical Dilemmas in Human Resource Management," *Human Resource Management Review* 11 (2001), p. 161.

32. "The Future of HR," *Workplace Visions* 6 (Society for Human Resource Management, 2001), pp. 3–4.

33. Bill Roberts, "Process First, Technology Second," *HR Magazine*, June 2002, pp. 40–46.

34. Chris Pickering, "A Look Through the Portal," *Software Magazine* 21, no. 1 (February 2001), pp. 18–19.

35. Ibid., p. 19.

36. Jill Elswick, "How NCR Corp. Undertook an Intranet Makeover to Improve Access to HR Information," *Employee Benefit News*, January 1, 2001, item 01008001.

37. Sharon McDonnell, "More Out of ERP," *Computerworld*, October 2, 2000, p. 56.

After studying this chapter, you should be able to:

1 Cite the main features of at least five employment discrimination laws.

2 Define *adverse impact* and explain how it is proved and what its significance is.

3 Explain and illustrate two defenses you can use in the event of discriminatory practice allegations.

4 Avoid employment discrimination problems.

5 Cite specific discriminatory personnel management practices in recruitment, selection, promotion, transfer, layoffs, and benefits.

6 Define and discuss *diversity management*.

Equal Opportunity and the Law

Every time you advertise a job opening, or recruit, interview, test, or select a

candidate or appraise an employee, you have to take equal employment

laws into account. We will focus in this book on basic HR practices like

recruiting and selecting employees, and on training, appraising, and

compensating them. But as a practical matter, no manager can handle tasks

like these without eventually facing discrimination-related issues.•

The main purpose of this chapter is to provide you with the knowledge you'll need to deal effectively with equal employment opportunity questions on the job. The main topics we'll cover are equal opportunity laws from 1964 to 1991, the laws from 1991 to the present, defenses against discrimination allegations, illustrative discriminatory employment practices, the EEOC enforcement process, and diversity management and affirmative action programs.

 Cite the main features of at least five employment discrimination laws.

● EQUAL EMPLOYMENT OPPORTUNITY 1964–1991

Legislation barring discrimination against members of minority groups in the United States is certainly nothing new. For example, the Fifth Amendment to the U.S. Constitution (ratified in 1791) states, "no person shall be deprived of life, liberty, or property, without due process of the law." The Thirteenth Amendment (ratified in 1865) outlawed slavery, and courts have held it bars racial discrimination. The Fourteenth Amendment (ratified in 1868) makes it illegal for any state to "make or enforce any law which shall abridge the privileges and immunities of citizens of the United States," and the courts have generally viewed this law as barring discrimination based on sex, national origin, or race. Section 1981 of Title 42 of the U.S. Code, passed over 100 years ago as the Civil Rights Act of 1866, gives all persons the same right to make and enforce contracts and to benefit from the laws of the land.[1] Other laws as well as various court decisions made discrimination against minorities illegal by the early 1900s, at least in theory.[2]

But as a practical matter, Congress and various presidents avoided dramatic action on equal employment issues until the early 1960s. At that point, civil unrest among minorities and women prompted them to act.

Title VII of the 1964 Civil Rights Act

Title VII of the 1964 Civil Rights Act
The section of the act that says an employer cannot discriminate on the basis of race, color, religion, sex, or national origin with respect to employment.

Title VII of the 1964 Civil Rights Act was one of the first of these 1960s-era laws. Title VII (as amended by the 1972 Equal Employment Opportunity Act) states that an employer cannot discriminate based on race, color, religion, sex, or national origin. Specifically, it states that it shall be an unlawful employment practice for an employer:

(1) To fail or refuse to hire or to discharge an individual or otherwise to discriminate against any individual with respect to his/her compensation, terms, conditions, or privileges of employment, because of such individual's race, color, religion, sex, or national origin.

(2) To limit, segregate, or classify his/her employees or applicants for employment in any way that would deprive or tend to deprive any individual of employment opportunities or otherwise adversely affect his/her status as an employee, because of such individual's race, color, religion, sex, or national origin.

Who Does Title VII Cover?   Title VII bars discrimination on the part of most employers, including all public or private employers of 15 or more persons. In addition, it covers all private and public educational institutions, the federal government, and state and local governments. It bars public and private employment agencies from failing or refusing to refer for employment any individual because of race, color, religion, sex, or national origin. And it bars labor unions with 15 or more members from excluding, expelling, or classifying their membership because of race, color, religion, sex, or national origin. Joint labor–management committees established for selecting workers for apprenticeships and training similarly cannot discriminate against individuals.

Equal Employment Opportunity Commission (EEOC)
The commission, created by Title VII, is empowered to investigate job discrimination complaints and sue on behalf of complainants.

The EEOC   Title VII established the **EEOC**, which stands for **Equal Employment Opportunity Commission**. The EEOC consists of five members appointed by the president with the advice and consent of the Senate. Each member serves a five-year term. The EEOC has a staff of thousands to assist it in administering the Civil Rights law in employment settings.

The EEOC receives and investigates job discrimination complaints from aggrieved individuals. When it finds reasonable cause that the charges are justified, it attempts (through conciliation) to reach an agreement eliminating all aspects of the discrimination. If this conciliation fails, it has the power to go to court to enforce the law. Under the Equal Employment Opportunity Act of 1972, the EEOC may file discrimination charges on behalf of aggrieved individuals, or the individuals may file themselves. We'll discuss this procedure later in this chapter.

Executive Orders

affirmative action
Steps that are taken for the purpose of eliminating the present effects of past discrimination.

Office of Federal Contract Compliance Programs (OFCCP)
This office is responsible for implementing the executive orders and ensuring compliance of federal contractors.

Various U.S. presidents have issued executive orders expanding equal employment in federal agencies. For example, Executive Orders 11246 and 11375, issued by the Johnson administration (1963–1969), don't just ban discrimination; they require that contractors take **affirmative action** to ensure employment opportunity for those who may have suffered discrimination in the past. All federal contractors with contracts over $50,000 and 50 or more employees must develop and implement such programs.

These orders also established the **Office of Federal Contract Compliance Programs (OFCCP)**. It implements the orders and ensures compliance. For example, it reached a settlement with aviation contractor Triad International Management Company, which paid over $240,000 to settle claims that women and blacks were subjected to a "perversely hostile work environment," including racial slurs.[3]

Equal Pay Act of 1963

Equal Pay Act of 1963
The act requiring equal pay for equal work, regardless of sex.

The **Equal Pay Act of 1963** (amended in 1972) made it unlawful to discriminate in pay on the basis of sex when jobs involve equal work; require equivalent skills, effort, and responsibility; and are performed under similar working conditions. Differences based on a seniority system, a merit system, a system that measures earnings by quantity or quality of production, or based on any factor other than sex do not violate the act.

Age Discrimination in Employment Act of 1967

Age Discrimination in Employment Act of 1967 (ADEA)
The act prohibiting arbitrary age discrimination and specifically protecting individuals over 40 years old.

The **Age Discrimination in Employment Act of 1967 (ADEA)** made it unlawful to discriminate against employees or applicants for employment who are between 40 and 65 years of age. Subsequent amendments eliminated the age cap, effectively ending most mandatory retirement at age 65. A 1973 Supreme Court ruling held that most states and local agencies, when acting in the role of employer, must also adhere to provisions of the act that protect workers from age discrimination.

How young is young? In *O'Connor v. Consolidated Coin Caterers Corp.*, the Supreme Court held that an employee who is over 40 may sue for discrimination if he or she is replaced by a "significantly younger" employee, even if the replacement is also over 40. The Court didn't specify what "significantly younger" meant, but did seem to suggest that just three or four years would be insignificant. O'Connor had been replaced by someone 16 years younger. The ADEA is a "favored statute" among employees and lawyers, since it allows jury trials and double damages to those proving "willful" discrimination.[4]

Vocational Rehabilitation Act of 1973

The **Vocational Rehabilitation Act of 1973** requires employers with federal contracts over \$2,500 to take affirmative action in employing handicapped persons. It does not require hiring an unqualified person. It does require an employer to take steps to accommodate a handicapped worker unless doing so imposes an undue hardship on the employer. A federal district court held that compensatory damages (a payment for "future pecuniary losses, emotional pain, suffering, inconvenience, mental anguish, loss of enjoyment of life, and other nonpecuniary losses") are available under the 1973 Rehabilitation Act.[5]

Vietnam Era Veterans' Readjustment Assistance Act of 1974

The provisions of the **Vietnam Era Veterans' Readjustment Assistance Act of 1974** require that employers with government contracts of \$10,000 or more take affirmative action to employ and advance disabled veterans and qualified veterans of the Vietnam era. OFCCP administers the act.

Pregnancy Discrimination Act of 1978

Congress passed the **Pregnancy Discrimination Act (PDA)** in 1978 as an amendment to Title VII. It prohibits using pregnancy, childbirth, or related medical conditions to discriminate in hiring, promotion, suspension, or discharge, or any term or condition of employment. Also, if an employer offers its employees disability coverage, then it must treat pregnancy and childbirth like any other disability, and include it in the plan as a covered condition. The U.S. Supreme Court ruled in *California Federal Savings and Loan Association v. Guerra* that if an employer offers no disability leave to any of its employees, it can (but need not) grant pregnancy leave to a woman disabled for pregnancy, childbirth, or a related medical condition.

Federal Agency Guidelines

The federal agencies charged with ensuring compliance with these laws and executive orders issue their own guidelines. These spell out recommended procedures to follow in complying with the law.

The EEOC, Civil Service Commission, Department of Labor, and Department of Justice together have **uniform guidelines** for employers to use. They set forth "highly recommended" procedures regarding matters like employee selection, record keeping, preemployment inquiries, and affirmative action programs. As an example, they specify that employers must validate any employment selection devices (including but not limited to written tests) that screen out disproportionate numbers of women or minorities. They also explain how to validate a selection device. (We explain this procedure in Chapter 6.) The OFCCP has its own guidelines. The EEOC and other agencies also periodically issue updated guidelines clarifying and revising their positions on matters such as national origin discrimination and sexual harassment. The American Psychological Association has its own (non-legally binding) Standards for Educational and Psychological Testing.

Sexual Harassment

Harassment on the basis of sex is a violation of Title VII when such conduct has the purpose or effect of substantially interfering with a person's work performance or creating an intimidating, hostile, or offensive work environment. The EEOC's guidelines further assert that employers have an affirmative duty to maintain workplaces free of **sexual harassment** and intimidation. The Civil Rights Act of 1991 (discussed below) added teeth to this by permitting victims of intentional discrimination, including sexual harassment, to have jury trials and to collect compensatory damages for pain and suffering and punitive damages in cases in which the employer acted with "malice or reckless indifference" to the individual's rights.[6] In 1998 the U.S. Supreme Court held (in *Oncale v. Sundowner Offshore Services Inc.*) that "same-sex discrimination consisting of same-sex sexual harassment is actionable under title VII." It said that same-sex subordinates, co-workers, or superiors are liable under the theory that they create a hostile work environment for the employee.[7]

The **Federal Violence Against Women Act of 1994** provides another avenue women can use to seek relief for violent sexual harassment. It provides that a person "who commits a crime of violence motivated by gender and thus deprives another" of her rights shall be liable to the party injured.

The EEOC guidelines define sexual harassment as unwelcome sexual advances, requests for sexual favors, and other verbal or physical conduct of a sexual nature that takes place under any of the following conditions:

1. Submission to such conduct is made either explicitly or implicitly a term or condition of an individual's employment.

2. Submission to or rejection of such conduct by an individual is used as the basis for employment decisions affecting such individual.

3. Such conduct has the purpose or effect of unreasonably interfering with an individual's work performance or creating an intimidating, hostile, or offensive work environment.

Proving Sexual Harassment   There are three main ways an employee can prove sexual harassment.

1. *Quid Pro Quo.* The most direct way an employee can prove sexual harassment is to prove that rejecting a supervisor's advances adversely affected the employee's tangible benefits, such as raises or promotions. For example, in one case the employee was able to show that continued job success and advancement were dependent on her agreeing to the sexual demands of her supervisors.

2. *Hostile Environment Created by Supervisors.* It is not always necessary to show that the harassment had tangible consequences such as a demotion or termination. For example, in one case the court found that a male supervisor's sexual harassment had substantially affected a female employee's emotional and psychological ability to the point that she felt she had to quit her job. Therefore, even though no direct threats or promises were made in exchange for sexual advances, the fact that the advances interfered with the woman's performance and created an offensive work environment were enough to prove that sexual harassment had occurred. On the other hand, the courts do not interpret as sexual harassment any sexual relationships that arise during the course of employment but that do not have a substantial effect on that employment.[8] In one decision, for instance, the U.S. Supreme Court held that sexual harassment law doesn't cover ordinary "intersexual flirtation." In his ruling, Justice Antonin Scalia said courts must carefully distinguish between "simple teasing" and truly abusive behavior.[9]

3. *Hostile Environment Created by Co-Workers or Nonemployees.* Advances do not have to be made by the person's supervisor to qualify as sexual harassment: An employee's co-workers (or even the employer's customers) can cause the employer

to be held responsible for sexual harassment. In one case, the court held that a sexually provocative uniform the employer required led to lewd comments and innuendos by customers toward the employee. When she complained that she would no longer wear the uniform, she was fired. Because the employer could not show that there was a job-related necessity for requiring such a uniform and because the uniform was required only for female employees, the court ruled that the employer, in effect, was responsible for the sexually harassing behavior. EEOC guidelines also state that an employer is liable for the sexually harassing acts of its nonsupervisor employees if the employer knew or should have known of the harassing conduct.

Court Decisions   The U.S. Supreme Court used a case called *Meritor Savings Bank, FSB v. Vinson* to broadly endorse the EEOC's guidelines on sexual harassment. Two more recent U.S. Supreme Court decisions further clarified sexual harassment law.

In the first case, *Burlington Industries v. Ellerth*, the employee accused her supervisor of *quid pro quo* harassment. She said her boss propositioned and threatened her with demotion if she did not respond. The threats were not carried out, and she was in fact promoted. In the second case, *Faragher v. City of Boca Raton*, the employee accused the employer of condoning a hostile work environment. She said she quit her lifeguard job after repeated taunts from other lifeguards. The Court ruled in favor of the employees in both cases.

The Court's decisions have several important implications for employers. First, they make it clear that in a *quid pro quo* case it is *not* necessary for the employee to have suffered a tangible job action (such as being demoted) to win the case. Second, the Court spelled out an important defense against harassment suits. It said the employer must show that it took "reasonable care" to prevent and promptly correct any sexually harassing behavior and that the employee unreasonably failed to take advantage of the employer's policy.

In particular, the Court said that an employer could defend itself against sexual harassment liability by showing two things. First, it had to show "that the employer exercised reasonable care to prevent and correct promptly any sexually harassing behavior." Second, it had to demonstrate that the plaintiff "unreasonably failed to take advantage of any preventive or corrective opportunities provided by the employer." The Supreme Court specifically said that the employee's failing to use formal organizational reporting systems would satisfy the second component.

Many employers promptly took steps to ensure that they could show they did take reasonable care. For example, they promulgated strong sexual harassment policies, trained managers and employees regarding their responsibilities for complying with these policies, instituted reporting processes, investigated charges promptly, and then took corrective actions promptly, as required.[10] However, such steps, while laudable, may not be enough. Let's look at what managers and employers can do, in more detail.

What the Manager/Employer Should Do   As summarized in Figure 2-1, employers can take steps (such as issuing a strong policy statement) to minimize liability if a sexual harassment claim is filed against the organization and to prevent such claims from arising in the first place. In general, employers (1) should take steps to ensure that harassment does not take place, and (2) should take immediate corrective action, even if the offending party is a nonemployee, once it knows (or should know) of harassing conduct. A form such as the one in Figure 2-2 can facilitate this process.[11]

The manager, however, needs to keep in mind that steps like these are usually not, by themselves, enough. There are several issues to consider here. First, studies show that

Figure 2-1
HR in Practice: What
Employers Should Do to
Minimize Liability in Sexual
Harassment Claims

1. Take all complaints about harassment seriously. As one sexual harassment manual for managers and supervisors advises, when sexual conduct is observed in the workplace, the best reaction is to address the complaint or stop the conduct. If complaints are not taken seriously, or it's risky or futile to complain, then the firm's employees are likely to experience considerably higher levels of harassment.
2. Issue a strong policy statement condemning such behavior. The EEOC's standards state that an effective antiharassment policy should contain a clear explanation of the prohibited conduct; assurance of protection against retaliation for employees who make complaints or provide information related to such complaints; a clearly described complaint process that provides confidentiality and accessible avenues of complaint as well as prompt, thorough, and impartial investigations; and clear assurance that the employer will take immediate and appropriate corrective action where harassment has occurred.
3. Inform all employees about the policy prohibiting sexual harassment and of their rights under the policy.
4. Develop and implement a complaint procedure.
5. Establish a management response system that includes an immediate reaction and investigation by senior management. The likelihood of employer liability is lessened considerably when the employer's response is "adequate" and "reasonably calculated to prevent future harassment."
6. Begin management training sessions with supervisors and managers to increase their awareness of the issues. As with all training, it is advisable to make sure that the sexual harassment training programs are having the desired effect. In one study, researchers compared about 200 people who participated in a sexual harassment program with about 350 people who did not. In this study male participants in the sexual harassment program were actually *less* (not more) likely than other groups to perceive an action as sexual harassment, less willing to report sexual harassment, and more likely to blame the victim!
7. Discipline managers and employees involved in sexual harassment.
8. Keep thorough records of complaints, investigations, and actions taken.
9. Conduct exit interviews that uncover any complaints and that acknowledge by signature the reasons for leaving.
10. Re-publish the sexual harassment policy periodically.
11. Encourage upward communication through periodic written attitude surveys, hotlines, suggestion boxes, and other feedback procedures to discover employees' feelings concerning any evidence of sexual harassment and to keep management informed.

Sources: © 1991 by CCH Incorporated. All rights reserved. Reprinted with permission from *Sexual Harassment Manual for Managers and Supervisors*, published in 1991, by CCH Incorporated, a WoltersKluwer Company. Louise Fitzgerald et al., "Antecedents and Consequences of Sexual Harassment in Organizations: A Test of an Integrated Model," *Journal of Applied Psychology* 82, no. 4 (1997), pp. 577–589; "New EEOC Guidance Explains Standards of Liability for Harassment by Supervisors," *BNA Fair Employment Practices* (June 24, 1999), p. 75; "Adequate Response Bars Liability," *BNA Fair Employment Practices* (June 26, 1997), p. 74; Shereen Bingham and Lisa Scherer, "The Unexpected Effects of a Sexual Harassment Educational Program," *Journal of Applied Behavioral Science* 37, no. 2 (June 2001), pp. 125–153.

there are significant gender differences in perceptions of sexual harassment. Specifically, "women perceive a broader range of sociosexual behaviors as harassing," particularly when those behaviors involve "hostile work environment harassment, derogatory attitudes toward women, dating pressure, or physical sexual contact."[12] In other words, what is harassment to a woman may be innocent to a man.

A second reason why even apparently "reasonable" precautions may be insufficient is that employees may be reluctant to use them. This is because a sexual harassment compliance procedure may be reasonable in the legal sense, but not so reasonable to the employees who must use it. In one study, researchers surveyed about 6,000 employees in the U.S. military. Their findings made it clear that reporting incidents of harassment often triggered retaliation and could harm the victim "in terms of lower job satisfaction and greater psychological distress." Under such conditions, it's no wonder that for many of these employees, the most "reasonable" thing to do was nothing, and to avoid reporting. Managers who take preventing sexual harassment seriously therefore must ensure that the organization's culture (including management's real willingness to eradicate harassment), and not just its written rules and procedures, support employees who feel harassed.[13]

Contributing to the problem is the fact that most victims of sexual harassment don't sue or complain. Instead, they quit or try to avoid their harassers. The harassers themselves sometimes don't even realize that their abominable behavior is harassing or offending others. Sexual harassment training and policies can reduce these problems.[14]

Completion of this form is not required to formally initiate a complaint; however completing this form will assist the investigatory process. When completed please return this form to the office of the Director of Human Resources, Room 148, Joyal Administration Building. You will be contacted as soon as possible for a confidential interview to discuss the complaint.

1. Today's Date: _____

2. Your name: _____   **3.** Date of Birth: _____

4. Signature: _____

5. Status: Student-☐   Faculty-☐   Staff-☐   Manager-☐

6. Department: _____

7. Contact Information:

Home Address: _____

Office Phone: _____   Home Phone: _____

Cell or pager: _____   Email: _____

8. Person(s) against whom complaint is being made: _____

Status: Student-☐   Faculty-☐   Staff-☐   Manager-☐

9. Allegations. Include dates and locations. Use additional sheets as necessary:

_____

_____

_____

_____

_____

_____

_____

_____

10. Has anyone been notified of this incident? If so, who and when: _____

_____

11. Are there any other witnesses to the incident(s)? If so, who? _____

_____

Revised: 12/5/02

Figure 2-2
California State University, Fresno: Complaint Form for Filing a Complaint of Harassment or Discrimination
Source: California State University, Fresno.

What the Employee Can Do   An employee who believes he or she has been sexually harassed can also take several steps to address the problem. These steps are based in part on how courts define sexual harassment. For example, "hostile environment" sexual harassment generally means that the discriminatory intimidation, insults, and ridicule that permeated the workplace were sufficiently severe or pervasive to alter the conditions of employment. Courts in these cases look at several things. These include whether the discriminatory conduct is frequent or severe; whether it is physically threatening or humiliating, or a mere offensive utterance; and whether it unreasonably interferes with an employee's work performance.[15] In turn, whether an employee subjectively perceives the work environment as abusive is related to such things as whether the employee welcomed the conduct or immediately made it clear that the conduct was unwelcome, undesirable, or offensive.[16] The steps an employee can take include:

1. File a verbal contemporaneous complaint or protest with the harasser and the harasser's boss stating that the unwanted overtures should cease because the conduct is unwelcome.

2. Write a letter to the accused. This may be a polite, low-key letter that does three things: provides a detailed statement of the facts as the writer sees them; describes his or her feelings and what damage the writer thinks has been done; and states that he or she would like to request that the future relationship be on a purely professional basis. Deliver this letter in person, with a witness, if necessary.

3. If the unwelcome conduct does not cease, file verbal and written reports regarding the unwelcome conduct and unsuccessful efforts to get it to stop with the harasser's manager and/or the human resource director.

4. If the letters and appeals to the employer do not suffice, the accuser should turn to the local office of the EEOC to file the necessary claim.

5. If the harassment is of a serious nature, the employee can also consult an attorney about suing the harasser for assault and battery, intentional infliction of emotional distress, injunctive relief, and to recover compensatory and punitive damages.

Unwelcome advances in the workplace, no matter how "harmless" they may seem, constitute sexual harassment. An employee who is the victim of sexual harassment may often be reluctant to report incidents because of fear of retaliation or actual harm.

Early Court Decisions Regarding Equal Employment Opportunity

Several court decisions between 1964 and 1991 helped create the interpretive foundation for EEO laws such as Title VII.

Griggs v. Duke Power Company   *Griggs* was a landmark case, since the Supreme Court used it to define unfair discrimination. Lawyers sued the Duke Power Company on behalf of Willie Griggs, an applicant for a job as a coal handler. The company required its coal handlers to be high school graduates. Griggs claimed this requirement was illegally discriminatory because it wasn't related to success on the job and because it resulted in more blacks than whites being rejected for these jobs. Griggs won the case. The decision of the Court was unanimous, and in his written opinion, Chief Justice Burger laid out three crucial guidelines affecting equal employment legislation.

First, the Court ruled *discrimination by the employer need not be overt*. In other words, the employer does not have to be shown to have intentionally discriminated against the employee or applicant; it need only be shown that discrimination did take place. Second, the Court held that an employment practice (in this case requiring the high school degree) *must be job related* if it has an unequal impact on members of a **protected class**. (For example, if verbal ability is not required to perform the job's main functions, one should not test for it.) Third, Chief Justice Burger's opinion placed the *burden of proof on the employer* to show that the hiring practice is job related. Thus, the employer must show that the employment practice (in this case, requiring a high school degree) is necessary for satisfactory job performance if the practice discriminates against members of a protected class. In the words of Justice Burger,

protected class
Persons such as minorities and women protected by equal opportunity laws, including Title VII.

The act proscribes not only overt discrimination, but also practices that are fair in form, but discriminatory in operation. The touchstone is business necessity. If an employment practice which operates to exclude Negroes cannot be shown to be related to job performance, the practice is prohibited.[17]

Griggs established the following principles:

1. A test or other selection practice must be job related, and the burden of proof is on the employer.
2. An employer's intent not to discriminate is irrelevant.[18]
3. If a practice is "fair in form but discriminatory in operation," the courts will not uphold it.
4. *Business necessity* is the defense for any existing program that has adverse impact. The court did not define business necessity.
5. Title VII does not forbid testing. However, the test must be job related or valid, in that performance on the test must be related to performance on the job.

Albemarle Paper Company v. Moody   The *Albemarle* case is important because here the Court provided more details regarding how an employer should validate its screening tools. It helped clarify how employers could prove that the test or other screening tools are related to or predict performance on the job.[19] For example, the Court said that if an employer is to use a test to screen candidates for a job, then the nature of that job—its specific duties and responsibilities—must first be carefully analyzed and documented. Furthermore, the performance standards for employees on the job in question should be clear and unambiguous, so the employer can identify which employees are performing better than others. The Court's ruling also had the effect of establishing the EEOC (now federal) guidelines on validation as the procedures for validating employment practices.

● EQUAL EMPLOYMENT OPPORTUNITY 1990–91–PRESENT

The Civil Rights Act of 1991

Civil Rights Act of 1991 (CRA 1991)
It places burden of proof back on employers and permits compensatory and punitive damages.

Several subsequent Supreme Court rulings in the 1980s had the effect of limiting the protection of women and minority groups under equal employment laws; this prompted Congress to pass a new Civil Rights Act. President George Bush signed the **Civil Rights Act of 1991 (CRA 1991)** into law in November 1991. The effect of CRA 1991 was to roll back the clock to where it stood before the 1980s decisions, and in some respects to place even more responsibility on employers.

First, CRA 1991 addressed the issue of *burden of proof.* Today, after CRA 1991, the process of filing and responding to a discrimination charge goes something like this. The plaintiff (say, a rejected applicant) demonstrates that an employment practice (such as a test) has a disparate (or "adverse") impact on a particular group. (*Disparate impact* "means that an employer engages in an employment practice or policy that has a greater adverse impact [effect] on the members of a protected group under Title VII than on other employees, regardless of intent."[20]) Requiring a college degree for a job would have an adverse impact on some minority groups, for instance. Disparate impact claims do *not* require proof of discriminatory intent. Instead, the plaintiff must show two things. First, he or she must show that a significant disparity exists between the proportion of (say) women in the available labor pool and the proportion hired. Second, he or she must show that an apparently neutral employment practice, such as word-of-mouth advertising or a requirement that the jobholder "be able to lift 100 pounds," is causing the disparity.[21]

Then, once the plaintiff shows such disparate impact, the *employer* has the *burden of proving* that the challenged practice is job related for the position in question. For example, the employer has to show that lifting 100 pounds is actually required for the position in question, and that the business could not run efficiently without the requirement—that it is a business necessity. The New Workplace box looks at CRA 1991 in a global context.

CRA 1991 also makes it easier to sue for *money damages* in certain cases. It provides that an employee who is claiming *intentional discrimination* (which is called *disparate treatment*) can ask for (1) compensatory damages and (2) punitive damages, if it can be shown the employer engaged in discrimination "with malice or reckless indifference to the federally protected rights of an aggrieved individual."[28] This is a marked change from what prevailed until 1991. Victims of intentional discrimination who had not suffered financial loss and who sued under Title VII could not then sue for compensatory or punitive damages. All they could expect was to have their jobs reinstated (or be awarded a particular job). They were also eligible for back pay, attorneys' fees, and court costs.

Finally, CRA 1991 also states:

> *An unlawful employment practice is established when the complaining party demonstrates that race, color, religion, sex, or national origin was a motivating factor for any employment practice, even though other factors also motivated the practice.*[29]

In other words, an employer cannot avoid liability by proving it would have taken the same action—such as terminating someone—even without the discriminatory motive.[30] If there is any such motive, the practice may be unlawful. Plaintiffs in such so-called **"mixed motive"** cases recently gained an advantage from the U.S. Supreme Court

mixed motive case
A discrimination allegation case in which the employer argues that the employment action taken was motivated, not by discrimination, but by some non-discriminatory reason such as ineffective performance.

The New Workplace

Enforcing the 1991 Civil Rights Act Abroad

The 1991 Civil Rights Act marked a substantial change in the geographic applicability of equal rights legislation. Congressional legislation generally only applies within U.S. territorial borders unless specifically stated otherwise.[22] However, CRA 1991 specifically expanded coverage by amending the definition of *employee* in Title VII to mean a U.S. citizen employed in a foreign country by a U.S.-owned or -controlled company.[23] At least theoretically, U.S. citizens now working overseas for U.S. companies enjoy the same equal employment opportunity protection as those working within U.S. borders.[24]

Two factors limit the wholesale application of CRA 1991 to U.S. employees abroad, however. First, the civil rights protections are not universal or automatic because there are numerous exclusions. For example, an employer need not comply with Title VII if compliance would cause the employer to violate the law of the host country. (For instance, some foreign countries have statutes prohibiting the employment of women in management positions.)

A more vexing problem is the practical difficulty of enforcing CRA 1991 abroad. For example, the EEOC investigator's first duty in an extraterritorial case is to analyze the finances and organizational structure of the respondent, but in practice few, if any, investigators are trained for this duty and no precise standards exist for such investigations.[25] Similarly, one expert has argued that U.S. courts are "little help in overseas investigations, because few foreign nations cooperate with the intrusive enforcement of U.S. civil law."[26] It is possible, therefore, that as one expert says, "Congress' well-meaning effort to leave no American uncovered by U.S. antidiscrimination law will not have its intended effect."[27]

decision in *Desert Palace Inc. vs. Costa*. The Court decided that the plaintiff, a warehouse worker, did not have to provide evidence of explicitly discriminatory conduct (such as discriminatory employer statements), but could provide circumstantial evidence (such as lowered performance evaluations) to prove the mixed motive case.[31]

The Americans with Disabilities Act

Americans with Disabilities Act (ADA)
The act requiring employers to make reasonable accommodations for disabled employees; it prohibits discrimination against disabled persons.

The **Americans with Disabilities Act (ADA)** of 1990 prohibits employment discrimination against qualified disabled individuals.[32] Employers with 15 or more workers are prohibited from discriminating against qualified individuals with disabilities with regard to applications, hiring, discharge, compensation, advancement, training, or other terms, conditions, or privileges of employment.[33] It also says employers must make "reasonable accommodations" for physical or mental limitations unless doing so imposes an "undue hardship" on the business.

ADA does not list specific disabilities. Instead, the EEOC's guidelines say an individual is disabled when he or she has a physical or mental impairment that substantially limits one or more major life activities. Impairments include any physiological disorder or condition, cosmetic disfigurement, or anatomical loss affecting one or more of several body systems, or any mental or psychological disorder.[34] The act does specify certain conditions that are not to be regarded as disabilities, including homosexuality, bisexuality, voyeurism, compulsive gambling, pyromania, and certain disorders resulting from the current illegal use of drugs.[35]

AIDS

The EEOC's position is that the ADA prohibits discriminating against people with HIV/AIDS, and numerous state laws also protect people with AIDS from discrimination. Similarly, the Labor Department's Office of Federal Contract Compliance Programs requires treating AIDS-type diseases under the Vocational Rehabilitation Act. The bottom line for most employers is that discriminating against people with AIDS is generally unlawful.

The employer should therefore encourage its managers to persuade employees to work with HIV/AIDS-infected employees, and perhaps to discipline those who will not. But in reality, many managers are reluctant to do so. One relevant study involved obtaining questionnaires from 194 managers in various types of organizations. In many cases, the managers would not discipline the employees for refusing to work with the AIDS-infected co-workers. When the managers refused, it was usually because of a fear of AIDS, or because of the likelihood that the employee would share AIDS-related health information about the infected co-worker with the manager's other subordinates. Efforts to get employees to work with infected co-workers would therefore likely benefit from education and support.[36]

Qualified Individual

qualified individuals
Under ADA, those who can carry out the essential functions of the job.

Simply being disabled doesn't qualify someone for a job, of course. Instead, the act prohibits discrimination against **qualified individuals**—those who, with (or without) a reasonable accommodation, can carry out the *essential functions* of the job. The individual must have the requisite skills, educational background, and experience to do the job. A job function is essential when, for instance, it is the reason the position exists, or it is so highly specialized that the person is hired for his or her expertise or ability to perform that particular function.

Reasonable Accommodation

If the individual can't perform the job as currently structured, the employer must make a "reasonable accommodation" unless doing so would present an "undue hardship." Reasonable accommodation might include redesigning the job, modifying work schedules, or modifying or acquiring equipment or other devices to assist the person. Undue hardship is the rule, though: An employee with a bad back who worked as a door greeter in a Wal-Mart store asked Wal-Mart if she could sit on a stool while on duty, and the store rejected her request. She sued. The federal district court agreed with Wal-Mart that door greeters must act in an "aggressively hospitable manner," which can't be done sitting on a stool.[37] Standing was an essential job function.

Attorneys, employers, and the courts are still working through the question of what "reasonable accommodation" means. One expert noted, "three federal appeals courts have held that for it to be a reasonable accommodation, the employee must show that the costs of the accommodation do not outweigh the benefit."[38]

Many employers have successfully defended themselves. In one case, a social worker threatened to throw her co-worker out a window and to "kick her [butt]," and continued her tirade after returning from a 10-day suspension. After transfer to another job, she was diagnosed as paranoid; after telling her supervisor several times she was "ready to kill her," she was fired. She sued under ADA. The court dismissed her case because, although she had a debilitating mental illness, ADA does not require retention of employees who make threats.[39] In another case, the Court held that the employer did not discriminate against a blind bartender by requiring her to transfer to another job because she was unable to spot underage or intoxicated customers.[40] On the other hand, one U.S. circuit court held that punctuality was not an essential job function of a laboratory assistant who was habitually late. The court decided he could perform seven and a half hours of data entry even if he arrived late.[41]

Today, technological innovations make it easier for employers to accommodate disabled employees. For example, many employees with *mobility impairments* benefit from voice recognition software that allows them to input information into their computers and interactively communicate (for instance, via e-mail) without touching a keyboard. Others use alternative input devices (such as sticks held in the mouth) to strike keyboard keys. Special typing aids, including word prediction software, suggest words based on context with just one or two letters typed.

Employees with *hearing and/or speech impairments* benefit from the teletypewriter, which lets people communicate by typing and reading messages on a keyboard connected to a telephone line. Real-time translation captioning enables them to participate in lectures and meetings. Vibrating text pagers let them know when messages arrive.

Employees with *vision impairments* benefit from add-on computer devices that, among other things, allow adjustments in font size, display color, and screen magnification for specific portions of the computer screen. Voice recognition software transcription devices transcribe and speak out the written word for the employee. Special word processor software provides spoken instructions to aid the employee.[42]

Mental Impairments and the ADA

The types of disabilities alleged in ADA charges have been somewhat surprising. They haven't been common conditions associated with disability, like vision, hearing, or mobility impairments. Mental disabilities account for the greatest number of claims brought under the ADA.[43]

Under EEOC guidelines, "mental impairment" includes "any mental or psychological disorder, such as . . . emotional or mental illness." Examples include major depression, anxiety disorders, panic disorders, obsessive-compulsive disorder, and personality disorders. The

New tools for the disabled include speaking Web browsers and Braille readers that sit under a computer keyboard. James Gashel, who is blind, uses both tools in his work as director of governmental affairs for the National Federation for the Blind, an advocacy group in Baltimore, Maryland.

guidelines basically say employers should be alert to the possibility that traits normally regarded as undesirable (such as chronic lateness, hostility to co-workers, or poor judgment) may be linked to mental impairments covered by the ADA. Reasonable accommodation, says the EEOC, might then include providing room dividers, partitions, or other barriers between work spaces to accommodate individuals who have disability-related limitations.

The ADA in Practice   ADA complaints are flooding the EEOC and the courts. However, the chances of prevailing in ADA cases are against the plaintiff; employers prevailed in about 96% of federal circuit court decisions in one recent year. A main reason is that employees are failing to show that they are disabled and qualified to do the job.[44] Unlike Title VII of the Civil Rights Act, there's a heavy burden on the employee to establish that he or she is protected by the ADA. The employee has to establish that he or she has a disability that fits under the ADA's definition. Doing so is more complicated than proving that one is a particular age or race.

A U.S. Supreme Court decision typifies what plaintiffs face. An assembly-line worker sued Toyota, arguing that carpal tunnel syndrome and tendonitis prevented her from doing her job (*Toyota Motor Manufacturing of Kentucky, Inc. v. Williams*). The U.S. Supreme Court ruled that the ADA covers carpal tunnel syndrome and tendonitis only if her impairments affect not just her job performance, but her daily living activities too. The employee admitted that she could perform personal tasks and chores such as washing her face, brushing her teeth, tending her flower garden, and fixing breakfast and doing laundry. The Court said the disability must be central to the employee's daily living (not just job) to qualify under the ADA. The Court will therefore look at each case individually.[45]

Employer Obligations   The ADA imposes certain legal obligations on employers:[46]

1. An employer must not deny a job to a disabled individual if the person is qualified and able to perform the essential functions of the job. If the person is otherwise qualified but unable to perform an essential function, the employer must make a reasonable accommodation unless doing so would result in undue hardship.[47]

2. Employers are not required to lower existing performance standards or stop using tests for a job. However, those standards or tests must be job related and uniformly applied to all employees and job candidates.

3. Employers may not make preemployment inquiries about a person's disability, but they may ask questions about the person's ability to perform specific essential job functions. Table 2-1 summarizes the inquiries employers can and cannot make regarding the applicant's disabilities.

4. Similar limitations apply to medical exams for *current* employees. In one case, superiors ordered a Chicago police officer to take a blood test to determine if the level of Prozac his physician said he was taking would seriously impair his ability to do his job. At the time, the officer had not engaged in any behavior that suggested any performance problems. The court said the blood test was therefore not job related and violated the ADA's prohibition against inquiries into the nature or severity of an individual's disability.[48]

5. Employers should review job application forms, interview procedures, and job descriptions for illegal questions and statements. For example, check for questions about health, disabilities, medical histories, or previous workers' compensation claims.[49]

Table 2-1

What Inquiries Can Be Made About Disabilities?

Type	External Applicants (Pre-offer Stage)	External Applicants (Post-conditional Offer Stage)	Employees
Physical exam	No	Yes (C, D)	Yes (B, E)
Psychological exam	No	Yes (C, D)	Yes (B, E)
Health questionnaire	No	Yes (C, D)	Yes (B, E)
Workers' Compensation history	No	Yes (C, D)	Yes (B, E)
Physical agility test	Yes (A, C)	Yes (A, C)	Yes (A, C)
Drug test	Yes	Yes	Yes
Alcohol test	No	Yes (B, D)	Yes (B, E)
Specific questions (oral and written):			
About existence of a disability, its nature or severity, medical condition, physical or mental limitations	No	Yes (A, C)	Yes (B, E)
About ability to perform job-related functions (essential and nonessential)	Yes	Yes	Yes
About smoking (but not allergic to it)	Yes	Yes	Yes
About history of illegal drug use	No	Yes (B, D)	Yes (B, E)
Specific requests:			
Describe how you would perform job-related functions (essential and nonessential) with or without reasonable accommodation	Yes (D, F)	Yes (C, D)	Yes (B, E)
Provide evidence of not currently using drugs	Yes	Yes	Yes

A. If given to all similarly situated applicants/employees.

B. If job related and consistent with business necessity.

C. If only job-related criteria consistent with business necessity are used afterwards to screen out/exclude the applicant, at which point reasonable accommodation must be considered.

D. If all entering employees in same job category are subjected to it and subjected to same qualification standard.

E. But only for following purposes:

—To determine fitness for duty (still qualified or still able to perform essential functions)

—To determine reasonable accommodation

—To meet requirements imposed by federal, state, or local law (DOT, OSHA, EPA, etc.)

—To determine direct threat

F. Can be requested of a particular individual if the disability is known and may interfere with or prevent performance of a job-related function.

Source: Sue Willman, "Tips for Minimizing Abuses of the Americans with Disabilities Act," *Society for Human Resource Management Legal Report,* January–February 2003, p. 8. Copyright 2003 by Society for Human Resource Management. Reproduced with permission via Copyright Clearance Center.

6. The ADA does not require employers to have job descriptions, but it is advisable to have them. As one expert writes, "In virtually any ADA legal action, a critical question will be, what are the essential functions of the position involved? . . . in the absence of a job description that includes such function it will be difficult to convince a court that the function truly was an essential part of the job."[50]

There are several practical implications to keep in mind when dealing with ADA-related matters.[51] First, courts will tend to *define "disabilities" quite narrowly*. Employers may therefore require that the employee provide documentation of the disorder, and assess what effect that disorder has on the employee's job performance. A disability is not necessarily covered by ADA. Employers should therefore ask questions such as: Does the employee have a disability that substantially limits a major life activity? Is the employee qualified to do the job? Can the employee perform the essential functions of the job? Can any reasonable accommodation be provided without creating an undue hardship on the employer?[52] Second, it's clear from these decisions that employers "do not need to allow *misconduct or erratic performance* (including absences and tardiness), even if that behavior is linked to the disability."[53] Third, the employer does not have to *create a new job* for the disabled worker nor reassign that person to a light-duty position for an indefinite period, unless such a position exists.[54] Fourth, one expert advises, "*don't treat employees* as if they are disabled." If they can control their conditions (for instance, through medication), they usually won't be considered disabled. However, if they are treated as disabled by their employers (for instance, with respect to the jobs they're assigned), they'll normally be "regarded as" disabled and protected under the ADA.[55]

State and Local Equal Employment Opportunity Laws

In addition to the federal laws, all states and many local governments prohibit employment discrimination.

The effect of the state and local laws is usually to further restrict employers' treatment of job applicants and employees. Many state laws cover employers (like those with fewer than 15 employees) not covered by federal legislation.[56] Some extend the protection of age discrimination laws to young people, barring discrimination against not only those over 40, but those under 17; here, for instance, it would be illegal to advertise for "mature" applicants, because that might discourage some teenagers from applying.

The point is that many actions that might be legal under federal laws are illegal under state and local laws. In Arizona, for instance, the legislature amended the Arizona Civil Rights Act so that plaintiffs can bring sexual harassment claims against employers with as few as one employee. Massachusetts' Fair Employment Practice Act requires employers to adopt policies against sexual harassment, and encourages employers to conduct sexual harassment employee training. In both New York and New Jersey, genetic testing is now generally barred, as is discrimination based on genetic information.[57]

State and local equal employment opportunity agencies (often called Human Resources Commissions, Commissions on Human Relations, or Fair Employment Commissions) play a role in the equal employment compliance process. When the EEOC receives a discrimination charge, it usually defers it for a limited time to the state and local agencies that have comparable jurisdiction. If that doesn't achieve satisfactory remedies, the charges go back to the EEOC for resolution.

Table 2-2 summarizes selected equal employment opportunity laws, actions, executive orders, and agency guidelines.

Table 2-2

**Summary of
Important Equal
Employment
Opportunity Actions**

Action	What it Does
Title VII of 1964 Civil Rights Act, as amended	Bars discrimination because of race, color, religion, sex, or national origin; instituted EEOC.
Executive orders	Prohibit employment discrimination by employers with federal contracts of more than $10,000 (and their subcontractors); establish office of federal compliance; require affirmative action programs.
Federal agency guidelines	Indicate guidelines covering discrimination based on sex, national origin, and religion, as well as employee selection procedures; for example, require validation of tests.
Supreme Court decisions: *Griggs v. Duke Power Co., Albemarle v. Moody*	Rule that job requirements must be related to job success; that discrimination need not be overt to be proved; that the burden of proof is on the employer to prove the qualification is valid.
Equal Pay Act of 1963	Requires equal pay for men and women for performing similar work.
Age Discrimination in Employment Act of 1967	Prohibits discriminating against a person 40 or over in any area of employment because of age.
State and local laws	Often cover organizations too small to be covered by federal laws.
Vocational Rehabilitation Act of 1973	Requires affirmative action to employ and promote qualified handicapped persons and prohibits discrimination against handicapped persons.
Pregnancy Discrimination Act of 1978	Prohibits discrimination in employment against pregnant women, or related conditions.
Vietnam Era Veterans' Readjustment Assistance Act of 1974	Requires affirmative action in employment for veterans of the Vietnam war era.
Ward Cove v. Atonio	Made it more difficult to prove a case of unlawful discrimination against an employer.
Price Waterhouse v. Hopkins	Unlawful actions may not be discriminatory if lawful actions would have resulted in the same personnel decision.
Americans with Disabilities Act of 1990	Strengthens the need for most employers to make reasonable accommodations for disabled employees at work; prohibits discrimination.
Civil Rights Act of 1991	Reverses *Ward Cove*, *Price Waterhouse*, and other decisions; places burden of proof back on employer and permits compensatory and punitive money damages for discrimination.

Note: The actual laws (and others) can be accessed at: http://www.legal.gsa.gov/legal(#1)fcd.htm.

Define *adverse impact* and explain how it is proved and what its significance is.

● DEFENSES AGAINST DISCRIMINATION ALLEGATIONS

To understand how employers defend themselves against employment discrimination claims, we should first briefly review some basic legal theory.

Discrimination law distinguishes between disparate *treatment* and disparate *impact. Disparate treatment* means intentional discrimination. It "requires no more than a finding that women (or protected minority group members) were intentionally treated differently because of their gender" (or minority status), according to one appeals court. Disparate treatment "exists where an employer treats an individual differently because that individual is a member of a particular race, religion, gender, or ethnic group.[58]

Disparate *impact* claims do not require proof of discriminatory intent. Instead, the plaintiff must show that the apparently neutral employment practice (such as requiring a high school degree) creates an adverse impact—a significant disparity—between the proportion of (say) minorities in the available labor pool and the proportion hired. *Disparate impact* means that "an employer engages in an employment practice or policy that has a greater adverse impact (effect) on the members of a protected group under Title VII than on other employees, regardless of intent."[59] The key for the plaintiff here is thus to show that the employment practice caused an adverse impact. If it has, then the employer will probably defend itself by arguing that there is a business necessiity for the practice.

Adverse Impact

Showing **adverse impact** therefore plays a central role in discriminatory practice allegations. Under Title VII and the Civil Rights Act of 1991, a person who believes he or she was unintentionally discriminatcd against as a result of an employer's practices need only establish a *prima facie* case of discrimination. This means showing that the employer's selection procedures (like requiring a college degree for the job) did have an adverse impact on a protected minority group. Adverse impact "refers to the total employment process that results in a significantly higher percentage of a protected group in the candidate population being rejected for employment, placement, or promotion.[60]

Employers may not institute an employment practice that causes a disparate impact on a particular class of people unless they can show that the practice is job related and necessary.[61]

What does this mean? If a protected group applicant feels he or she was a victim of discrimination, the person need only show that the employer's selection process resulted in an adverse impact on his or her group. (For example, if 80% of the white applicants passed the test, but only 20% of the black applicants passed, a black applicant has a *prima facie* case proving adverse impact.) Then, once the employee has proved his or her point, the burden of proof shifts to the employer: It becomes the employer's task to prove that its test, application blank, interview, or the like is a valid predictor of performance on the job (and that it was applied fairly and equitably to both minorities and nonminorities).

How Can Someone Show Adverse Impact? It is actually not too difficult for an applicant to show that one of an employer's procedures (such as a selection test) has an adverse impact on a protected group. There are four basic approaches:

1. **Disparate rejection rates.** This means comparing the rejection rates for a minority group and another group (usually the remaining nonminority applicants). For example, ask, "Is there a disparity between the percentage of blacks among those *applying* for a particular position and the percentage of blacks among those *hired* for the position?" Or, "Do proportionately more blacks than whites fail the written examination we give to all applicants?" If the answer to either question is yes, your firm could be faced with a lawsuit.

    Federal agencies have a formula to determine disparate rejection rates: "a selection rate for any racial, ethnic or sex group which is less than four fifths or

80% of the rate for the group with the highest rate will generally be regarded as evidence of adverse impact, while a greater than four-fifths rate will generally not be regarded as evidence of adverse impact." For example, suppose 80% of male applicants are hired, but only 50% of female applicants. Since 50% is less than four-fifths of 80%, adverse impact exists as far as these federal agencies are concerned.

restricted policy
Another test for adverse impact, involving demonstration that an employer's hiring practices exclude a protected group, whether intentionally or not.

2. Restricted policy. The **restricted policy** approach means demonstrating that the employer's policy intentionally or unintentionally excluded members of a protected group. Here the problem is usually obvious—such as policies against hiring bartenders under six feet tall. Evidence of restricted policies such as these is enough to prove adverse impact and to expose an employer to litigation.

3. Population comparisons. This approach compares (1) the percentage of Hispanic (or black or other minority/protected group) and white workers in the organization with (2) the percentage of the corresponding groups in the labor market, where labor market is usually defined as the U.S. Census data for that Standard Metropolitan Statistical Area.

   For some jobs, such as laborer or secretary, it makes sense to compare the percentage of minority employees with the percentage of minorities in the surrounding community, since these employees will come from that community. However, for other jobs, such as engineer, the surrounding community may not be the relevant labor market, since recruiting may be nationwide or even global. Determining whether an employer has enough black engineers might thus involve determining the number of black engineers available nationwide rather than just in the surrounding community. Defining the relevant labor market is therefore crucial.

4. McDonnell-Douglas test. In this approach (which grew out of a case at the former McDonnell-Douglas Corporation), the applicant was qualified but the employer rejected the person and continued seeking applicants. This test is for (intentional) disparate treatment situations, rather than (unintentional) disparate impact ones (lawyers use approaches one through three for the latter).

   The U.S. Supreme Court set the following conditions for applying the McDonnell-Douglas approach: (a) that the person belongs to a protected class; (b) that he or she applied and was qualified for a job for which the employer was seeking applicants; (c) that, despite this qualification, he or she was rejected; and (d) that, after his or her rejection, the position remained open and the employer continued seeking applications from persons with the complainant's qualifications. If the plaintiff meets all these conditions, then a *prima facie* case of disparate treatment is established. At that point, the employer must articulate a legitimate nondiscriminatory reason for its action, and produce evidence but not prove that it acted on the basis of such a reason. If it meets this relatively easy standard, the plaintiff then has the burden of proving that the employer's articulated reason is merely a pretext for engaging in unlawful discrimination.

Adverse Impact: Example   Assume you turn down a member of a protected group for a job with your firm. You do this based on a test score (although it could have been interview questions, application-blank responses, or something else). Further assume that this person feels he or she was discriminated against due to being in a protected class, and decides to sue your company.

   Basically, all he or she must do is show that your HR procedure (such as the selection test) had an adverse impact on members of his or her minority group. There are four approaches that he or she can apply here: disparate rejection rates, restricted policy, population comparisons, and the McDonnell-Douglas test. Once the person shows the existence of adverse impact to the court's satisfaction, the burden of proof shifts to the employer to defend against the discrimination charges.

Note that there is nothing in the law that says that because one of your procedures has an adverse impact on a protected group, you cannot use the procedure. In fact, it could (and does) happen that some tests screen out disproportionately higher numbers of, say, blacks than whites. What the law does say is that once your applicant has made his or her case (showing adverse impact), the burden of proof shifts to you. Now you (or your company) must defend use of the procedure.

There are then basically two defenses employers use to justify an employment practice that has an adverse impact on members of a minority group: the bona fide occupational qualification (BFOQ) defense and the business necessity defense.

Bona Fide Occupational Qualification

3 Explain and illustrate two defenses you can use in the event of discriminatory practice allegations.

bona fide occupational qualification (BFOQ)
Requirement that an employee be of a certain religion, sex, or national origin where that is reasonably necessary to the organization's normal operation. Specified by the 1964 Civil Rights Act.

An employer can claim that the employment practice is a **bona fide occupational qualification (BFOQ)** for performing the job. Title VII provides that "it should not be an unlawful employment practice for an employer to hire an employee . . . on the basis of religion, sex, or national origin *in those certain instances where religion, sex, or national origin is a bona fide occupational qualification* reasonably necessary to the normal operation of that particular business or enterprise."

Courts usually interpret the BFOQ exception narrowly. It is essentially a defense to a disparate treatment case based upon direct evidence of *intentional* discrimination, and not to disparate impact (unintentional) discrimination. As a practical matter, employers use it mostly as a defense against charges of intentional discrimination based on age.

Age as a BFOQ   The Age Discrimination in Employment Act (ADEA) permits disparate treatment in those instances when age is a BFOQ. For example, age is a BFOQ when federal requirements impose a compulsory age limit, such as when the Federal Aviation Agency sets a ceiling of age 60 for pilots.[62] (In March 2001—over objections by the FAA and the two major commercial pilots unions—Congress passed new legislation allowing commercial airline pilots to fly up to age 65, if in good health—a five-year increase.[63]) Actors required for youthful or elderly roles or persons used to advertise or promote the sales of products designed for youthful or elderly consumers suggest other instances when age may be a BFOQ. However, courts set the bar high: The reason must go to the essence of the business. A court said a bus line's maximum-age hiring policy for bus drivers was a BFOQ. The court said the essence of the business was safe transportation of passengers, and given that, the employer could strive to employ the most qualified persons available.[64]

Employers using the BFOQ defense admit they based their personnel decisions on age, but seek to justify them by showing that the decisions were reasonably necessary to normal business operations (for instance, a bus line arguing its maximum-age driver requirement is necessary for safely transporting passengers). Alternatively, an employer may raise the FOA (factors other than age) defense. Here one argues that its actions were "reasonable" based on some factor other than age, such as the terminated person's poor performance.

Religion as a BFOQ   Religion may be a BFOQ in the case of religious organizations or societies that require employees to share their particular religion. For example, religion may be a BFOQ when hiring persons to teach in a denominational school. Similarly, practices, such as requiring Saturday work, that adversely affect certain religious groups are justifiable if the employer "is unable to reasonably accommodate . . . without undue hardship."[65] However, remember courts construe the BFOQ defense very narrowly.

Gender as a BFOQ   Gender may be a BFOQ for positions requiring specific physical characteristics necessarily possessed by one sex. These include positions like actor, model, and rest room attendant. However, for most jobs today, it's difficult to claim that gender is a BFOQ. For example, gender is not a BFOQ for parole and probation officers.[66] It is not a BFOQ for positions just because the positions require overtime or the lifting of heavy objects.

National Origin as a BFOQ   A person's country of national origin may be a BFOQ. For example, an employer who is running the Chinese pavilion at a fair might claim that Chinese heritage is a BFOQ for persons to deal with the public.

Business Necessity

"Business necessity" is a defense created by the courts. It requires showing that there is an overriding business purpose for the discriminatory practice and that the practice is therefore acceptable.

It's not easy to prove business necessity.[67] The Supreme Court has made it clear that business necessity does not encompass such matters as avoiding an inconvenience, annoyance, or expense to the employer. For example, an employer can't generally discharge employees whose wages have been garnished merely because garnishment (requiring the employer to divert part of the person's wages to pay his or her debts) creates an inconvenience. The Second Circuit Court of Appeals held that business necessity means an "irresistible demand," and that to be used the practice "must not only directly foster safety and efficiency" but also be essential to these goals.[68] Furthermore, "the business purpose must be sufficiently compelling to override any racial impact; and the challenged practice must effectively carry out the business purpose it is alleged to serve."[69]

However, many employers have used the business necessity defense successfully. In *Spurlock v. United Airlines*, a minority candidate sued United Airlines, stating that its requirements that pilot candidates have 500 flight hours and college degrees were unfairly discriminatory. The court agreed that the requirements did have an adverse impact on members of the person's minority group. But it held that in light of the cost of the training program and the tremendous human and economic risks involved in hiring unqualified candidates, the selection standards were a business necessity and were job related.[70]

In general, when a job requires a small amount of skill and training, the courts scrutinize closely any preemployment standards or criteria that discriminate against minorities. The employer in such instances has a heavy burden to demonstrate that the practices are job related. There is a correspondingly lighter burden when the job requires a high degree of skill, and when the economic and human risks of hiring an unqualified applicant are great.[71]

Attempts by employers to show that their selection tests or other employment practices are valid are an example of the business necessity defense. Here the employer is required to show that the test or other practice is job related—in other words, that it is a valid predictor of performance on the job. Where the employer can establish such validity, the courts have generally supported the use of the test or other employment practice as a business necessity. In this context, *validity* means the degree to which the test or other employment practice is related to or predicts performance on the job; Chapter 6 explains validation.

Other Considerations in Discriminatory Practice Defenses

There are three other points to remember about discrimination charges. First, good intentions are no excuse. As the Supreme Court held in the *Griggs* case,

> *Good intent or absence of discriminatory intent does not redeem procedures or testing mechanisms that operate as built-in headwinds for minority groups and are unrelated to measuring job capability.*

Second, do not count on hiding behind collective bargaining agreements (for instance, by claiming that the discriminatory practice is required by a union agreement). Courts have often held that equal employment opportunity laws take precedence over the rights embodied in a labor contract.[72]

Finally, remember that although a defense is often the most sensible response to charges of discrimination, it is not the only response. When confronted with the fact that one or more of your personnel practices is discriminatory, you can react by agreeing to eliminate the illegal practice and (when required) by compensating the people you discriminated against.

Avoid employment discrimination problems.

Know Your Employment Law

Discriminatory Employment Practices

Before proceeding, let's review what federal fair employment laws allow (and do not allow) you to say and do.

Federal laws like Title VII usually don't expressly ban preemployment questions about an applicant's race, color, religion, sex, or national origin. In other words, "with the exception of personnel policies calling for outright discrimination against the members of some protected group," it's not the questions but their impact.[73] For example, it is not illegal to ask a job candidate about her marital status (although at first glance such a question might seem discriminatory). You can ask such a question as long as you can show either that you do not discriminate or that you can defend the practice as a BFOQ or business necessity.

But, in practice, there are two good reasons why most employers avoid such questions. First, although federal law may not bar asking such questions, many state and local laws do. Second, the EEOC has said that it will disapprove of such practices, so just asking the questions may draw its attention.

Inquiries and practices like those on the next few pages are thus usually not illegal per se. They are "problem questions" because they tend to identify an applicant as a member of a protected group or to adversely affect members of a protected group. They become illegal if a complainant can show they are used to screen out a greater proportion of his or her protected group's applicants, and the employer can't prove the practice is required as a business necessity or BFOQ.

The EEOC approves the use of "testers"—individuals who pose as applicants to test a firm's equal employment procedures. This makes it even more important to be careful in devising selection procedures and training recruiters.[74] Let's look now at some of the potentially discriminatory HR practices you should avoid.[75]

DISCRIMINATORY RECRUITMENT PRACTICES

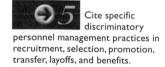

Cite specific discriminatory personnel management practices in recruitment, selection, promotion, transfer, layoffs, and benefits.

Word of Mouth You cannot rely upon word-of-mouth dissemination of information about job opportunities when your workforce is all (or substantially all) white or all members of some other class such as all female, all Hispanic, and so on. Doing so reduces the likelihood that others will become aware of the jobs and thus apply for them.

Misleading Information It is unlawful to give false or misleading information to members of any group or to fail or refuse to advise them of work opportunities and the procedures for obtaining them.

Help Wanted Ads "Help wanted—male" and "help wanted—female" advertising classifications are violations unless gender is a bona fide occupational qualification for the job. The same applies to ads that suggest you discriminate based on age. For example, you cannot advertise for a "young" man or woman.

DISCRIMINATORY SELECTION STANDARDS

Educational Requirements Courts have found educational qualifications to be illegal when (1) minority groups are less likely to possess the educational qualifications (such as a high school degree) and (2) such qualifications are also not job related. There may be jobs for which educational requirements (such as college degrees for pilot candidates) are a necessity, however.

Tests Courts deem tests unlawful if they disproportionately screen out minorities or women and are not job related. According to former Chief Justice Burger,

Nothing in the [Title VII] act precludes the use of testing or measuring procedures; obviously they are useful. What Congress has forbidden is giving these devices and mechanisms controlling force unless they are demonstrating a reasonable measure of job performance.

Preference to Relatives You cannot give preference to relatives of current employees with respect to employment opportunities if your current employees are substantially nonminority.

Height, Weight, and Physical Characteristics Requirements for physical characteristics (such as height and weight) are unlawful unless the employer can show they're job related. For example, the court held that a company's requirement that a person weigh a minimum of 150 pounds for positions on its assembly lines discriminated unfairly against women. Maximum-weight rules generally don't trigger adverse legal rulings. However, some minority groups have a higher incidence of obesity, so employers must be sure their weight rules don't adversely impact these groups. To qualify for reasonable accommodation, obese applicants must demonstrate they are 100% above their ideal weight or there is a physiological cause for their disability. In practice, employers sometimes treat overweight female applicants and employees to their disadvantage, and this is a potential problem.

Arrest Records Unless security clearance is necessary, you cannot ask an applicant whether he or she has ever been arrested or spent time in jail, or use an arrest record to disqualify a person for a position automatically. There is always a presumption of innocence until proven guilty. In addition, (1) arrest records in general are not valid for predicting job performance and (2) police have arrested a higher proportion of minorities than whites. Thus, disqualifying applicants based on arrest records automatically has an adverse impact on minorities. However, you can ask about conviction records, and then determine on a case-by-case basis whether the facts justify refusal to employ an applicant in a particular position.

Application Forms Employment applications generally shouldn't contain questions about applicants' disabilities, workers' compensation history, age, arrest record, or U.S. citizenship. Personal information required for legitimate tax or benefit reasons (such as who to contact in case of emergency) is best collected after you hire the person.[76] Note that while equal employment laws discourage employers from asking for such information, no such laws prohibit the applicants themselves from providing it. One study examined 107 résumés from Australian managerial applicants. It found that many provided information regarding marital status, ethnicity, age, and gender.[77]

Discharge Due to Garnishment A disproportionately higher number of minorities are subjected to garnishment procedures (in which creditors make a claim to a portion of the person's wages). Therefore, firing a minority member whose salary is garnished is illegal, unless you can show some overriding business necessity.

SAMPLE DISCRIMINATORY PROMOTION, TRANSFER, AND LAYOFF PRACTICES

Fair employment laws protect not just job applicants but also current employees. Any employment practices regarding pay, promotion, termination, discipline, or benefits that (1) are applied differently to different classes of persons; (2) adversely impact members of a protected group; and (3) cannot be shown to be required as a BFOQ or business necessity may be held to be illegally discriminatory. For example, the Equal Pay Act requires that equal wages be paid for substantially similar work performed by both men and women.

Personal Appearance Regulations and Title VII Employees have filed suits against employers' dress and appearance codes under Title VII, usually claiming sex discrimination but sometimes claiming racial discrimination. A sampling of what courts have ruled to be acceptable or unacceptable follows:[78]

• *Dress.* In general, employers do not violate Title VII's ban on sex bias by requiring all employees to dress conservatively. For example, a supervisor's suggestion that a female

> attorney tone down her attire was permissible when the firm consistently sought to maintain a conservative dress style and it also counseled men on dressing conservatively.
> - *Hair.* Here again, the courts usually rule in favor of the employers. For example, employer rules against facial hair do not constitute sex discrimination because they discriminate only between clean-shaven and bearded men, a type of discrimination not qualified as sex bias under Title VII. In many cases, courts also rejected arguments that grooming regulations (such as prohibitions against corn-row hair styles) are racially biased and infringe on black employees' expression of cultural identification. In one case involving American Airlines, the court decided (in favor of American) that a braided hair style is a characteristic easily changed and not worn exclusively or even predominantly by black people.
> - *Uniforms.* When it comes to discriminatory uniforms and suggestive attire, however, courts have frequently sided with the employee. For example, a bank's dress policy requiring female employees to wear prescribed uniforms consisting of five basic color-coordinated items but requiring male employees only to wear "appropriate business attire" is an example of a discriminatory policy. And requiring female employees (such as waitresses) to wear sexually suggestive attire as a condition of employment has also been ruled as violating Title VII in many cases.[79]

● THE EEOC ENFORCEMENT PROCESS

Even the most prudent employer will eventually face an employment discrimination claim, and have to deal with representatives of the EEOC. All managers should therefore have a working knowledge of the EEOC enforcement process; we describe that process in this section. Since most such claims tend to stem from the actions or inactions of first line supervisors, the following "When You're On Your Own" feature (page 53) explains some things that the supervisor and small business owner should watch out for.

Processing a Charge

Managers should have a working knowledge of the EEO enforcement process. Under CRA 1991, the discrimination claim must be filed within two years after the alleged incident took place. It must be filed in writing and under oath, by (or on behalf of) either the aggrieved person or by a member of the EEOC who has reasonable cause to believe that a violation occurred. The EEOC's common practice is to accept a charge and orally refer it to the state or local agency on behalf of the charging party. If the agency waives jurisdiction or cannot obtain a satisfactory solution, the EEOC processes it upon the expiration of the deferral period without requiring the filing of a new charge.[80]

After a charge is filed (or the state or local deferral period has ended), the EEOC has 10 days to serve notice on the employer. Figure 2-3 summarizes important questions an employer should ask after receiving a bias complaint from the EEOC. They include, for example, "To what protected group does the worker belong?" The EEOC then investigates the charge to determine whether there is reasonable cause to believe it is true; it is to make this determination within 120 days. If no reasonable cause is found, the EEOC must dismiss the charge, and must issue the charging party a Notice of Right to Sue. The person then has 90 days to file a suit on his or her own behalf.

If the EEOC does find reasonable cause for the charge, it must attempt a conciliation. If this conciliation is not satisfactory, it may bring a civil suit in a federal district court, or issue a Notice of Right to Sue to the person who filed the charge. Figure 2-4 (page 55) provides an overview of the charge-filing process.

When You're On Your Own
HR for Line Managers and Entrepreneurs

Dealing with Discrimination Issues and the EEOC

In most companies, employment discrimination issues tend to grow out of actions by individual supervisors. The supervisor makes an ill-informed or foolish comment or decision, and the employee is quick to seek redress through the EEOC or the courts. Even a "nondiscriminatory" action—like losing one's temper at a protected group employee—can trigger a discrimination claim and lawsuit. The employer may prevail, but why put the employer in the position of having to defend itself?

This has several implications for supervisors. First, in addition to the antidiscrimination training your employer may (or may not) be providing, supervisory employees should be familiar with the concepts and tools in this chapter. For example, you should understand the questions you can and cannot ask when interviewing applicants, what constitutes sexual harassment, and how equal employment opportunity law affects the full range of HR-related decisions, including those relating to appraisal, compensation, promotions, disciplinary procedures, and employee dismissals.

Second, the supervisor has to guard against committing *management malpractice*. In general, malpractice is conduct on the part of the manager that has serious consequences for the employee's personal or physical well-being, or which, as one court put it, "exceeds all bounds usually tolerated by society."[81] In such cases, the employee often alleges intentional infliction of emotional distress. The courts have sided with the plaintiff in situations where the supervisor ridiculed, threatened, humiliated, and sexually harassed an employee. In one particularly outrageous example, the employer demoted the manager to janitor and took other steps to humiliate the person. The jury subsequently awarded the former manager $3.4 million. Supervisors who commit management malpractice may be personally liable for paying a portion of the judgement.

Small business owners should understand that they certainly aren't immune from equal employment laws. Generally speaking, the EEOC enforces equal employment compliance issues against all but the very smallest of employers. For example, Title VII of the Civil Rights Act of 1964 covers employers with 15 or more employees. (Sexual harassment is one type of discrimination under Title VII). The Age Discrimination in Employment Act of 1967 covers employers with 20 or more employees. The Americans with Disabilities Act of 1990 covers employers with 15 or more employees. And, the Equal Pay Act of 1963 covers most employers with one or more employees. We've seen that these laws prohibit employment discrimination based on race, color, sex, religion, national origin, age, disability. They also prohibit retaliation for such things as opposing job discrimination, filing a charge, or participating in proceedings under these laws. (See www.EEOC.gov.) All employees, including part-time and temporary workers, are counted for purposes of determining whether an employer has a sufficient number of employees. State and local EEO laws usually cover smaller firms that come in under the EEOC's radar.

There are certain record-keeping requirements under the various EEO laws. In general, EEOC regulations require that all covered employers (including small employers) keep all personnel or employment records for one year. If the employer involuntarily terminates an employee, then the employer must keep his or her personnel records for one year from the termination date. Under the age discrimination in employment act and under the relevant fair labor standards act record-keeping requirements, employers must keep all payroll records for three years. The equal employment opportunity commission requires some employers to annually file a so-called EEO-1 report; this provides a breakdown of the employer's workforce by race and gender. Small employers are not required to file these reports, unless they employ 100 or more employees, or employ 50 or more employees and have federal contracts totaling $50,000 or more.

Figure 2-3
Questions to Ask When an Employer Receives Notice That EEOC has Filed a Bias Claim

1. Exactly what is the charge and is your company covered by the relevant statutes? (For example, Title VII and the Americans with Disabilities Act generally apply only to employees with 15 or more employees; the Age Discrimination in Employment Act applies to employers with 20 or more employees; but the Equal Pay Act applies to virtually all employers with one or more employees.) Did the employee file his or her charge on time, and was it processed in a timely manner by the EEOC?
2. What protected group does the employee belong to? Is the EEOC claiming disparate impact or disparate treatment?
3. Are there any obvious bases upon which you can challenge and/or rebut the claim? For example, would the employer have taken the action if the person did not belong to a protected group? Does the person's personnel file support the action taken by the employer? Conversely, does it suggest the possibility of unjustified discriminatory treatment?
4. If it is a sexual harassment claim, are there offensive comments, calendars, posters, screensavers, and so on, on display in the company?
5. In terms of the practicality of defending your company against this claim, who are the supervisors who actually took the allegedly discriminatory actions and how effective will they be as potential witnesses? Have you received an opinion from legal counsel regarding the chances of prevailing? Even if you do prevail, what do you estimate will be the out-of-pocket costs of taking the charge through the judicial process? Would you be better off settling the case, and what are the prospects of doing so in a way that will satisfy all parties?

Sources: Fair Employment Practices Summary of Latest Developments, January 7, 1983, p. 3, Bureau of National Affairs, Inc. (800-372-1033); Kenneth Sovereign, *Personnel Law* (Upper Saddle River, NJ: Prentice Hall, 1994), pp. 36–37; "EEOC Investigations—What an Employer Should Know," Equal Employment Opportunity Commission (http://www.eoc.gov/small/investigations.html), July 18, 2003.

Conciliation Proceedings

The EEOC has 30 days to work out a conciliation agreement between the parties before bringing suit. The EEOC conciliator meets with the employee to determine what remedy would be satisfactory and then tries to persuade the employer to accept it. If both parties accept the remedy, they sign and submit a conciliation agreement to the EEOC for approval. If the EEOC can't obtain an acceptable conciliation agreement, it may sue the employer in a federal district court. The EEOC is also experimenting with using outside mediators to settle claims in selected cities.

The EEOC seems to be getting more efficient. In fiscal year 2003, the commission obtained $385 million in awards for discrimination victims. Of this, about $116 million resulted from the EEOC's mediation program, $149 million came through litigation, and the remainder resulted from negotiations among the parties at the EEOC's administrative level, including conciliation.[82]

How to Respond to Employment Discrimination Charges

Here are some key things to keep in mind when confronted by a charge of illegal employment discrimination.

The EEOC Investigation   First, remember that EEOC investigators are not judges and aren't empowered to act as courts. They cannot make findings of discrimination on their own but they can make recommendations. If the EEOC eventually determines that an employer may be in violation of a law, its only recourse is to file a suit or issue a Notice of Right to Sue to the person who filed the charge.

Some experts advise meeting with the employee who made the complaint to clarify all the relevant issues. For example, ask: What happened? Who was involved? When did the incident take place? Did it affect the employee's ability to work? Were there any witnesses? Then prepare a written statement summarizing the complaints, facts, dates, and issues involved and request that the employee sign and date it.[83]

With respect to providing documents to the EEOC, it is often in the employer's best interests to cooperate (or to appear to be cooperative). However, remember that the

Figure 2-4
The EEOC Charge-Filing Process

Note: Parties may settle at any time.
Scource: Based on information in www.eeoc.gov/index.html.

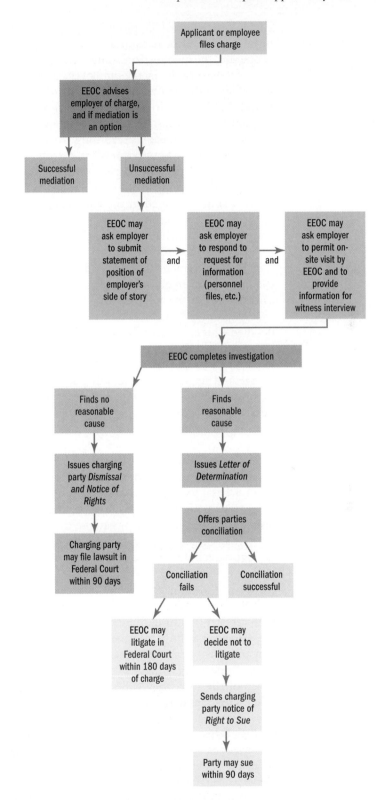

EEOC can only ask employers to submit documents and ask for the testimony of witnesses under oath. It cannot compel employers to comply. If an employer refuses to cooperate, the commission's only recourse is to obtain a court subpoena.

It may also be in the employer's best interest to give the EEOC a position statement based on its own investigation of the matter. One congressional investigation found that (at least in the EEOC's Chicago office) EEOC investigators were using the employer's position statement to write up cases because the EEOC was under pressure to resolve cases quickly. According to one management attorney, employers' position statements should contain words to the effect that "We understand that a charge of discrimination has been filed against this establishment and this statement is to inform the agency that the company has a policy against discrimination and would not discriminate in the manner charged in the complaint." Support the statement with some statistical analysis of the workforce, copies of any documents that support the employer's position, and/or an explanation of any legitimate business justification for the decision that is the subject of the complaint.[84]

If a settlement isn't reached, the EEOC will do a thorough investigation. Here there are three major principles an employer should follow. First, ensure that there is information in the EEOC's file demonstrating lack of merit of the charge. Often the best way to do that is not by answering the EEOC's questionnaire, but by providing a detailed statement describing the firm's defense in its best and most persuasive light.

Second, limit the information supplied to only those issues raised in the charge itself. For example, do not respond to an EEOC request for a breakdown of employees by age and sex if the charge only alleges sex discrimination. Releasing too much information may just invite more probing by the EEOC.[85] Third, get as much information as possible about the charging party's claim, in order to ensure that you understand the claim and its ramifications.

The Fact-Finding Conference   The EEOC says these conferences are informal meetings held early in the investigation, aimed at defining issues and determining if there is basis for negotiation. According to one expert, however, the EEOC's emphasis is on settlement. Its investigators use the conferences to find weak spots in each party's respective position that they can use as leverage to push for a settlement.

If an employer wants a settlement, the fact-finding conference can be a good place to negotiate, but there are four things to look out for. First, the only official record is the notes taken by the EEOC investigator, and the parties cannot have access to them to rectify mistakes or clarify facts. Second, the employer can bring an attorney, but the EEOC often "seems to go out of its way to tell employers that an attorney's presence is unnecessary."[86] Third, these conferences often occur soon after a charge is filed, before the employer is fully informed of the charges and facts of the case. Fourth, the parties may use witnesses' statements as admissions against the employer's interests. Therefore, before appearing, witnesses (especially supervisors) need to be aware of the legal significance of the facts they will present and of the possible claims the charging party and other witnesses may make.

EEOC Determination and Attempted Conciliation   If the fact-finding conference does not solve the matter, the EEOC's investigator will determine whether there is reason to believe ("cause") or not to believe ("no cause") that discrimination may have taken place. There are several things to keep in mind here.

First, the investigator's recommendation is often the determining factor in whether the EEOC finds cause, so it is usually best to be courteous and cooperative (within limits). Second, if there is a finding of cause, you should review the finding very carefully; make sure to point out inaccuracies in writing to the EEOC. Use this letter to again try to convince the EEOC, the charging party, and the charging party's attorney that the charge is without merit. Finally, keep in mind that even with a no-cause finding, the charging party will still get a Notice of Right to Sue letter from the EEOC, and have 90 days from receipt to bring his or her own lawsuit.

If the EEOC issues a cause finding, it has (as noted above) 30 days to work out a conciliation agreement between the parties. Some experts argue against conciliating. First, the EEOC often views conciliation not as a compromise but as complete relief to the charging party. Second, "if you have properly investigated and evaluated the case previously, there may be no real advantage in settling at this stage. It is more than likely (based on the statistics) that no suit will be filed by the EEOC."[87] Even if the EEOC or the charging party later files a suit, the employer can consider settling after receiving the complaint.

Voluntary Mediation   The EEOC refers about 10% of its charges to a voluntary mediation mechanism. It says this is "an informal process in which a neutral third party assists the opposing parties to reach a voluntary, negotiated resolution of a charge of discrimination" (www.eeoc.gov/mediate/facts). If the plaintiff agrees to mediation, the EEOC asks the employer to participate. A mediation session usually lasts up to four hours. If no agreement is reached or one of the parties rejects participation, the charge is then processed through the EEOC's usual mechanisms.[88]

The EEOC is expanding its mediation program. In the four years after the EEOC launched its mediation program in 1999, its offices had already conducted over 44,000 mediations and settled more than 30,000 charges through the program. By 2003, the EEOC had also signed more than 18 nationwide agreements and 300 local agreements for mediation with participating employers. Under this latter program, the EEOC refers all eligible discrimination charges filed against these employers to the commission's mediation unit, rather than referring it to the usual charge processing system.[89]

Faced with an offer to mediate, three responses are generally possible: Agree to mediate the charge; make a settlement offer without mediation; or prepare a "position statement" for the EEOC. If the employer does not mediate or make an offer, the position statement is required. It should include information relating to the company's business and the charging party's position; a description of any rules or policies and procedures that are applicable; and the chronology of the offense that led to the adverse action.[90]

Mandatory Arbitration of Discrimination Claims

Conciliation, mediation, and litigation are not the only options when it comes to resolving claims: Arbitration is another. The U.S. Supreme Court's decisions (in *Gilmer v. Interstate/Johnson Lane Corp.* and similar cases) make it clear that "employment discrimination plaintiffs [employees] may be compelled to arbitrate their claims under some circumstances."[91] (In *Gilmer*, the Supreme Court held that an agreement, entered into for mandatory arbitration of all employment-related disputes, can require the employee to arbitrate claims arising under the Age Discrimination in Employment Act.) Since many courts may come to view compulsory arbitration as an acceptable alternative to litigation, the following suggestions are in order:[92]

▌ Employers should immediately review all employment discrimination suits filed against them in state and federal courts to determine whether they involve an employee who is subject to some type of agreement to arbitrate. They should then decide whether to move to compel arbitration of the claim.[93]

▌ Employers "may wish to consider inserting a mandatory arbitration clause in their employment applications or employee handbooks."[94]

■ To protect such a process against appeal, the employer should institute steps to protect against arbitrator bias; allow the arbitrator to afford a claimant broad relief (including reinstatement); and allow for a reasonable amount of prehearing discovery (fact finding).

For example, after a long and expensive equal employment lawsuit, Rockwell International implemented a grievance procedure that provides for binding arbitration as the last step. Initially, Rockwell's 970 executives had to sign a mutual agreement to arbitrate employment disputes as a condition of participation in an executive stock plan. Rockwell later extended the program (called, as is traditional, an **alternative dispute resolution or ADR program**) to cover all nonunion employees at some locations. New hires at Rockwell must sign the agreement as a condition of employment, and current employees must sign it prior to promotion or transfer.[95] ADR plans are popular, although the EEOC generally opposes such plans for handling workplace bias claims.[96]

alternative dispute resolution or ADR program
Grievance procedure that provides for binding arbitration as the last step.

Define and discuss *diversity management.*

● DIVERSITY MANAGEMENT AND AFFIRMATIVE ACTION PROGRAMS

To some extent the goals of equitable and fair treatment driving equal employment legislation are being rendered moot by demographic changes and globalization. Employers, in other words, have little choice but to willingly push for more diversity. Today, as we've seen, white males no longer dominate the labor force, and women and minorities will represent the lion's share of labor force growth over the foreseeable future. Furthermore, globalization increasingly requires employers to hire minority members who have the cultural and language skills to deal with customers abroad. As a result, companies are increasingly striving for racial, ethnic, and sexual workforce balance, "not because of legal imperatives, but as a matter of enlightened economic self-interest."[97]

Although there's no unanimity about what *diversity* means, there's considerable agreement about the components of diversity. For example, in one study a majority of the respondents listed race, sex, culture, national origin, handicap, age, and religion as diversity components. In other words, these comprise the demographic building blocks that represent diversity at work and what people often think of when asked what employers mean by diversity.[98]

Managing Diversity

Managing diversity means maximizing diversity's potential advantages while minimizing the potential barriers—such as prejudices and bias—that can undermine the functioning of a diverse workforce. In practice, diversity management involves both compulsory and voluntary management actions. We've seen that there are many legally compulsory actions employers must take to minimize employment discrimination.

However, while such compulsory actions can reduce the more blatant diversity barriers, blending a diverse workforce into a close-knit and productive community also requires employers to take other steps. Based on one review of research studies, one diversity expert concluded that five sets of voluntary organizational activities are at the heart of any diversity management program. We can summarize these as follows:

■ *Provide strong leadership.* Companies with exemplary reputations in managing diversity typically have CEOs who champion the cause of diversity. Leadership means, for instance, taking a strong stand on the need for change and becoming a role model for the behaviors required for the change.

■ *Assess the situation.* The company must assess the current state of affairs with respect to diversity management. One study found that the most common tools for measuring diversity include equal employment hiring and retention metrics, employee attitude surveys, management and employee evaluations, and focus groups.[99]

■ *Provide diversity training and education.* One expert says that "the most commonly utilized starting point for . . . managing diversity is some type of employee education program."[100] Yet some argue that generalized diversity training (in terms, for instance, of getting along with others) is actually backfiring, for instance, by diminishing participants' specific attention to racial relations.[101]

■ *Change culture and management systems.* Ideally, education programs should be combined with other concrete steps aimed at changing the organization's culture and management systems—for example, change the performance appraisal procedure to emphasize that supervisors will henceforth be appraised based partly on their success in reducing intergroup conflicts.

■ *Evaluate the diversity management program.* For example, do employee attitude surveys now indicate any improvement in employees' attitudes toward diversity?

In creating diversity management programs, the employer should not ignore the obvious. For example, training immigrants in their native language can facilitate learning as well as compliance with matters such as safety rules and harassment policies, and thereby facilitate their entry into your workforce. It therefore makes sense to provide new hires with orientation sessions and employee handbooks in, for instance, Spanish.[102]

Boosting Workforce Diversity

Employers use various means to increase workforce diversity. Many companies, such as Baxter Healthcare Corporation, start by adopting strong company policies advocating the benefits of a culturally, racially, and sexually diverse workforce: "Baxter International believes that a multi-cultural employee population is essential to the company's leadership in healthcare around the world." Baxter then publicizes this philosophy throughout the company.

Next, Baxter takes concrete steps to foster diversity at work. These steps include evaluating diversity program efforts, recruiting minority members to the board of directors, and interacting with representative minority groups and networks. Diversity training is another concrete activity. It aims at sensitizing all employees about the need to value differences, build self-esteem, and generally create a more smoothly functioning and hospitable environment for the firm's diverse workforce.

As another example, minority employees' "network groups" can help companies retain managerial-level minority employees. Minority employees usually initiate network groups themselves, although management will then typically provide ongoing support (for instance, in terms of meeting space and printing expenses). The network groups' aims are to help minority employees better connect to each other and to provide mutually beneficial information, social support, and mentoring.[103] In one study, participation in network groups was associated with participants' favorable turnover intentions, feelings of social inclusion, and satisfaction with the network itself for professional and supervisory employees. Researchers found no similar positive effects for other employees, however.

Workforce diversity makes strategic sense: "as firms reach out to a broader customer base, they need employees who understand particular customer preferences and

Longo Toyota staff members at the El Monte, California, dealership. Longo's 60-person staff speaks 20 languages, and Longo has built a competitive advantage based on its employee diversity.

requirements."[104] Longo Toyota in El Monte, California, built its competitive strategy on that idea. With a 60-person salesforce that speaks more than 20 languages, Longo's staff provides a powerful competitive advantage for catering to an increasingly diverse customer base. The HR department has thereby contributed to Longo's success. While other dealerships lose half their salespeople every year, Longo retains 90% of its staff, in part by emphasizing a promotion-from-within policy that's made more than two-thirds of its minorities managers. It has also taken steps to attract more women; for instance, by adding sales management staff to spend time providing the training inexperienced salespeople usually need. In a business in which competitors can easily imitate products, showrooms, and most services, Longo has built a competitive advantage based on employee diversity.

However, while there is anecdotal evidence supporting the idea that diversity has both positive and negative effects on performance, a recent five-year study found "few positive or negative direct effects of diversity on performance."[105] How can one tell if the diversity initiatives are effective? There are some commonsense questions to ask. The employer should be able to answer the following affirmatively: Are there women and minorities reporting directly to senior managers? Do women and minorities have a fair share of the job assignments that are the traditional steppingstones to successful careers in the company? Do women and minorities have equal access to international assignments? Is the employer taking steps (including development-oriented performance appraisals and providing developmental opportunities) that ensure female and minority candidates will be in the company's career development pipeline? Are turnover rates for female and minority managers the same or lower than those for white male managers?[106] The "Improving Productivity Through HRIS" (page 61) feature shows how IT can facilitate this process.

Some employers try to boost and manage diversity through voluntary affirmative action programs. *Affirmative action* means employers make an extra effort to hire and promote those in protected groups. The aim is to voluntarily enhance employment opportunities for women and minorities (in contrast to the involuntary affirmative action programs courts have imposed on some employers since enactment of the 1964 Civil Rights Act).

Equal Employment Opportunity Versus Affirmative Action

Equal employment opportunity aims to ensure that anyone, regardless of race, color, disability, sex, religion, national origin, or age, has an equal chance for a job based on his or her qualifications. *Affirmative action* goes beyond equal employment opportunity by requiring the employer to make an extra effort to hire and promote those in a protected group. Affirmative action thus includes specific actions (in recruitment, hiring, promotions, and compensation) to eliminate the present effects of past discrimination. According to the EEOC, an affirmative action program should result in "measurable, yearly improvements in hiring, training, and promotion of minorities and females" in all parts of the organization.

While the goals are somewhat similar, note that diversity management programs differ from traditional affirmative action programs in both philosophy and method. Figure 2-5 summarizes these differences. For example, managing diversity is voluntary, while traditional affirmative action programs are often mandatory.

Improving Productivity Through HRIS

Measuring Diversity

The HR manager who wants to assess the efficiency and effectiveness of his or her company's EEOC and diversity efforts has numerous metrics from which to choose. These might include, for example, the number of EEOC claims per year; the cost of HR-related litigation; percent of minority/women promotions; and various measures for analyzing the survival and loss rate among new diverse employee groups.

Even for a company with several hundred employees, keeping track of metrics like these is expensive. The HR manager may therefore want to rely on various computerized solutions. One particular package called

"Measuring Diversity Results" provides HR managers with several diversity-related software options aimed at boosting the accuracy of the information at the manager's disposal, and reducing the costs of collecting and compiling it. Among other things, vendors' diversity management packages let the manager more easily calculate: the cost per diversity hire; a workforce profile index; the numeric impact of voluntary turnover among diverse employee groups; the effectiveness of the firm's [employment] supplier diversity initiatives; current diversity measures; and such things as direct and indirect replacement cost per hire.

Steps in an Affirmative Action Program

According to the EEOC, in an affirmative action program the employer ideally takes eight steps:

1. Issues a written equal employment policy indicating that it is an equal employment opportunity employer, as well as a statement indicating the employer's commitment to affirmative action.

2. Appoints a top official with responsibility and authority to direct and implement the program.

3. Publicizes the equal employment policy and affirmative action commitment.

4. Surveys present minority and female employment by department and job classification to determine locations where affirmative action programs are especially desirable.[107]

5. Develops goals and timetables to improve utilization of minorities, males, and females in each area where utilization has been identified.

6. Develops and implements specific programs to achieve these goals. According to the EEOC, this is the heart of the affirmative action program. Here the employer has to review its entire human resource management system (including recruitment, selection, promotion, compensation, and disciplining) to identify barriers to equal employment opportunity and to make needed changes.

Figure 2-5
Differences Between Managing Diversity and Meeting Affirmative Action Requirements

Managing Diversity	Practicing Diversity to Meet EEO/Affirmative Action Requirements
• Is voluntary	• Is often mandatory
• Focuses on productivity, efficiency, and quality	• Focuses on legal, social, moral justifications
• Includes all elements of diversity	• Includes only race, gender, and ethnicity
• Emphasizes changing systems and operations	• Emphasizes changing the mix of people
• Offers a perception of equity	• Offers a perception of preference
• Is long term and ongoing	• Is short term and limited
• Is grounded in individuality	• Is grounded in assimilation

Source: National Institutes of Health.

7. Establishes an internal audit and reporting system to monitor and evaluate progress in each aspect of the program.

8. Develops support for the affirmative action program, both inside the company (among supervisors, for instance) and outside the company in the community.[108]

When designing an affirmative action program, the **good faith effort strategy** emphasizes identifying and eliminating the obstacles to hiring and promoting women and minorities on the assumption that eliminating these obstacles will result in increased utilization of women and minorities. It may include setting goals (although strict quotas would not be advisable) and steps such as:

1. Increasing the minority or female applicant flow.

2. Demonstrating top-management support for the equal employment policy—for instance, by appointing a high-ranking EEO administrator.

3. Demonstrating equal employment commitment to the local community—for instance, by providing in-house remedial training.

4. Keeping employees informed about the specifics of the affirmative action program.

5. Broadening the work skills of incumbent employees.

6. Institutionalizing the equal employment policy to encourage supervisors' support of it—for instance, by making it part of their performance appraisals

Employers should know that voluntary affirmative action programs may conflict with the Civil Rights Act of 1991.[109] Two experts have written that "read literally, this new statutory restriction appears to bar employers from giving any consideration whatsoever to an individual's status as a racial or ethnic minority or as a woman when making an employment decision."[110] At the present time, this does not seem to be much of a problem, as long as employers emphasize the external recruitment and internal development of better-qualified minority and female employees, "while basing employment decisions on legitimate criteria."[111] However, employers have to take care that in achieving the desired goal of workforce diversity they do not inadvertently "step over the line of permissible diversity management into the realm of unlawful affirmative action (i.e., reverse discrimination)."[112] Nonbeneficiaries may react negatively when they feel such programs result in their being treated unfairly.[113] Even beneficiaries may react badly. In one study, subjects who felt they'd benefited from affirmative-action-based preferential selection gave themselves unfavorable self-evaluations.[114] Yet, in spite of this, voluntary programs are often advisable. And sometimes, the court makes them mandatory.

Reverse Discrimination

The courts have long been grappling with the use of quotas in hiring, and particularly with claims by white males of **reverse discrimination**. Many cases addressed these issues, but no consistent answer has emerged. For example, in *Bakke v. Regents of the University of California* (1978), the University of California at Davis Medical School denied admission to white student Allen Bakke, allegedly because of the school's affirmative action quota system, which required that a specific number of openings go to minority applicants. In a 5-to-4 vote, the Court struck down the policy that made race the only factor in considering applications for a certain number of class openings and thus allowed Bakke's admission.

In *Wygant v. Jackson Board of Education* (1986), the Court struck down a mechanism in a collective bargaining agreement that gave preferential treatment to minority teachers in the event of a layoff.[115] In *International Association of Firefighters v. City of Cleveland* (1986), the Court upheld a court's decree that reserved a specific number of promotions for minority firefighters and established percentage goals for minority promotions.[116] In *U.S. v. Paradise* (1987), the Court ruled that the lower courts can impose racial quotas to address the most serious cases of racial discrimination.[117] In *Johnson v. Transportation Agency, Santa Clara County* (1987), the Court held that public and private employers may voluntarily adopt hiring and promotion goals to benefit minorities and women. This ruling limited claims of reverse discrimination by white males.[118] In June 2001, the U.S. Supreme Court refused to hear Texas's challenge to a ruling that its law school affirmative action program, which gives special consideration to black and Mexican American student applicants, discriminated against whites.

Corporate affirmative action programs would not seem to be significantly affected by a U.S. Supreme Court June 2003 affirmative action decision. That decision outlawed the University of Michigan's quota-based admissions program. Since few employers now set such quotas for minority hiring, the Court's "narrow opinion" should have little effect in the workplace.[119]

Recruiting Minorities Online

Talking about hiring more minorities is one thing; actually doing it is another. In practice, many minorities are less likely to be using the Internet, for instance, and less likely to hear about good jobs from their friends. One option is to direct recruiting ads to one or more of the online minority-oriented job markets. For example, Recruiting-Online lists dozens of online diversity candidate resources (www.recruiting-online.com/course55.html). Diversity candidate Web sites with job banks include the African American Network, National Action Council of Minorities in Engineering, National Urban League, Hispanic Online, Latino Web, Society of Hispanic Engineers, Gay.com, Association for Women in Science, and Minorities Job Bank.

The National Urban League's Web site is a good example (www.nul.org/). Clicking on its Career Center tab brings you to a page with five options: Job Search; Post a Job; Resume Center; Job Agents; and Career Resources. The job agents section lets job seekers create their own job profiles. It then searches for employers' listings that may match, and sends a message to the job seeker when it finds a match.

Review

SUMMARY

1. Legislation barring discrimination is nothing new. For example, the Fifth Amendment to the U.S. Constitution (ratified in 1791) states that no person shall be deprived of life, liberty, or property without due process of law.

2. Legislation barring employment discrimination includes Title VII of the 1964 Civil Rights Act (as amended), which bars discrimination because of race, color, religion, sex, or national origin; various executive orders; federal guidelines (covering procedures for validating employee selection tools, and more); the Equal Pay Act of 1963; and the Age Discrimination in Employment Act of 1967. In addition, various court decisions (such as *Griggs v. Duke Power Company*) and state and local laws bar discrimination.

3. Title VII of the Civil Rights Act created the EEOC. It is empowered to try conciliating discrimination complaints,

but if this fails, the EEOC has the power to go to court to enforce the law.

4. The Civil Rights Act of 1991 had the effect of reversing several Supreme Court equal employment decisions. It placed the burden of proof back on employers, held that a nondiscriminatory (mixed motive) reason was insufficient to let an employer avoid liability for an action that also had a discriminatory motive, and said that Title VII applied to U.S. employees of U.S. firms overseas. It also now permits compensatory and punitive damages, as well as jury trials.

5. The Americans with Disabilities Act prohibits employment discrimination against the disabled. Specifically, qualified persons cannot be discriminated against if the firm can make reasonable accommodations without undue hardship on the business.

6. A person who feels he or she was discriminated against by a personnel procedure or decision must prove either that he or she was subjected to unlawful disparate treatment (intentional discrimination) or that the procedure in question has a disparate impact (unintentional discrimination) upon members of his or her protected class. Once a *prima facie* case of disparate treatment is established, an employer must produce evidence that its decision was based upon legitimate nondiscriminatory reasons. Once a *prima facie* case of disparate impact has been established, the employer must produce evidence that the allegedly discriminatory practice or procedure is job related and is based upon a substantial business reason.

7. There are various specific discriminatory human resource management practices that an employer should avoid in recruitment and in selection. For example, employers generally cannot advertise for "man only."

8. In practice, the EEOC often first refers a charge to a local agency. When it does proceed (and if it finds reasonable cause to believe that discrimination occurred), the EEOC has 30 days to try to work out a conciliation. Important points for the employer to remember include: (a) EEOC investigators can only make recommendations; (b) you cannot be compelled to submit documents without a court order; and (c) you may limit the information you do submit. Also, make sure to clearly document your position (as the employer).

9. An employer can use two basic defenses in the event of a discriminatory practice allegation—business necessity, and bona fide occupational qualification. An employer's "good intentions" and/or a collective bargaining agreement are not defenses. (A third defense is that the decision was made on the basis of legitimate nondiscriminatory reasons—such as poor performance—having nothing to do with the prohibited discrimination alleged.)

DISCUSSION QUESTIONS

1. Explain the main features of Title VII, Equal Pay Act, Pregnancy Discrimination Act, Americans with Disabilities Act, Civil Rights Act of 1991.

2. What important precedents were set by the *Griggs v. Duke Power Company* case? The *Albemarle v. Moody* case?

3. What is adverse impact? How can it be proved?

4. What is sexual harassment? How can an employee prove sexual harassment?

5. What are the two main defenses you can use in the event of a discriminatory practice allegation, and what exactly do they involve?

6. What is the difference between disparate treatment and disparate impact?

INDIVIDUAL AND GROUP ACTIVITIES

1. Working individually or in groups, respond to these three scenarios based on what you learned in Chapter 2. Under what conditions (if any) do you think the following constitute sexual harassment? (a) A female manager fires a male employee because he refuses her requests for sexual favors. (b) A male manager refers to female employees as "sweetie" or "baby." (c) Two male employees are overheard by a female employee exchanging sexually oriented jokes.

2. Working individually or in groups, discuss how you would set up an affirmative action program.

3. Compare and contrast the issues presented in *Bakke* with more recent court rulings on affirmative action. Working individually or in groups, discuss the current direction of affirmative action.

4. Working individually or in groups, write a paper entitled "What the manager should know about how the EEOC handles a person's discrimination charge."

5. Explain the difference between affirmative action and equal employment opportunity.

6. Assume you are the manager in a small restaurant; you are responsible for hiring employees, supervising them, and recommending them for promotion. Working individually or in groups, compile a list of potentially discriminatory management practices you should avoid.

7. The HRCI "Test Specifications" appendix at the end of this book (pages 685–689) lists the knowledge someone studying for the HRCI certification exam needs to have in each area of human resource management (such as in Strategic Management, Workforce Planning, and Human Resource

Development). In groups of four to five students, do four things: (1) review that appendix now; (2) identify the material in this chapter that relates to the required knowledge the appendix lists; (3) write four multiple choice exam questions on this material that you believe would be suit-

able for inclusion in the HRCI exam; and (4) if time permits, have someone from your team post your team's questions in front of the class, so the students in other teams can take each others' exam questions.

EXPERIENTIAL EXERCISE

"Space Cadet" or Victim?

Discrimination lawsuits are rarely simple, because the employer will often argue that the person was fired due to poor performance, rather than discrimination. So, there's often a "mixed motive" element to such situations. The facts of a case decided in December 2003, by the California State Appeals Court illustrates this (*Burk versus California Association of Realtors*, California Court of Appeals, number 161513, unpublished, 12/12/03). The facts were as follows. The California Association of Realtors maintained a hotline service to provide legal advice to real estate agents. One of the 12 lawyers who answered this hotline on behalf of the Association was a 61-year-old California attorney who worked at the Association from 1989 to 2000. Until 1996 he received mostly good reviews and salary increases. At that time, Association members began filing complaints about his advice. His supervisor told him to be more courteous and more thorough in providing advice.

Two years later, Association members were still complaining about this individual. Among other things, Association members who called in to deal with him filed complaints referring to him as "a space cadet," "incompetent," and "a total jerk." Subsequently, his supervisor contacted six Association members whom the 61-year-old lawyer had recently counseled; five of the six said they had had bad experiences. The Association fired him for mistreating Association members and providing inadequate legal advice.

The 61-year-old lawyer sued the Association, claiming that the firing was age related. To support his claim, he noted, among other things, that one colleague had told him that he was "probably getting close to retirement" and that another colleague had told him that both he and another lawyer were "getting older." The appeals court had to decide whether the Association fired the 61-year-old lawyer because of his age, or because of his performance.

Purpose: The purpose of this exercise is to provide practice in analyzing and applying knowledge of equal opportunity legislation to a real problem.

Required Understanding: Be thoroughly familiar with the material presented in this chapter. In addition, read the preceding "space cadet" case on which this experiential exercise is based.

How to Set Up the Exercise/Instructions:
1. Divide the class into groups of three to five students.
2. Each group should develop answers to the following questions:
   a. Based on what you read in this chapter, on what legal basis could the 61-year-old California attorney claim he was a victim of discrimination?
   b. On what laws and legal concepts did the employer apparently base its termination of this 61-year-old attorney?
   c. Based on what laws or legal concepts could you take the position that it is legal to fire someone for poor performance even though there may be a discriminatory aspect to the termination (which is not to say that there necessarily was such a discriminatory aspect with this case).
   d. If you were the judge called on to make a decision on this case, what would your decision be, and why?
   e. The court's decision is below, so please do not read this until you've completed the exercise.

In this case, the California State Appeals court held that "the only reasonable inference that can be drawn from the evidence is that [plaintiff] was terminated because he failed to competently perform his job of providing thorough, accurate and courteous legal advice to hotline callers." ("On Appeal, Hotheaded Hotline Lawyer Loses Age, Disability Discrimination Claims," *BNA Human Resources Report*, January 12, 2004, p. 17.)

APPLICATION CASE

A Case of Racial Discrimination?

John Peters (not his real name) was a 44-year-old cardiologist on the staff of a teaching hospital in a large city in the southeastern United States. Happily married with two teenage

children, he had served with distinction for many years at this same hospital, and in fact had done his residency there after graduating from Columbia University's medical school.

Alana Anderson (not her real name) was an attractive African American registered nurse on the staff at the same hospital with Peters. Unmarried and without children, she lived in a hospital-owned apartment on the hospital grounds and devoted almost all her time to her work at the hospital, or to taking additional coursework to further improve her already excellent nursing skills.

The hospital's chief administrator, Gary Chapman, took enormous pride in what he called the extraordinary professionalism of the doctors, nurses, and other staff members at his hospital. Although he took a number of rudimentary steps to guard against blatant violations of equal employment opportunity laws, he believed that most of the professionals on his staff were so highly trained and committed to the highest professional standards that "they would always do the right thing," as he put it.

Chapman was therefore upset to receive a phone call from Peters, informing him that Anderson had (in Peters's eyes) "developed an unwholesome personal attraction" to him and was bombarding the doctor with Valentine's Day cards, affectionate personal notes, and phone calls—often to the doctor's home. Concerned about hospital decorum and the possibility that Peters was being sexually harassed, Chapman met privately with Anderson. He explained that Peters was very uncomfortable with the personal attention she was showing to him, and asked that she please not continue to exhibit her show of affection for the doctor.

Chapman assumed that the matter was over. Several weeks later, when Anderson resigned her position at the hospital, Chapman didn't think much of it. He was therefore shocked and dismayed to receive a registered letter from a local attorney, informing him that both the hospital and Peters and Chapman personally were being sued by Anderson for racial discrimination: Her claim was that Chapman, in their private meeting, had told her, "We don't think it's right for people of different races to pursue each other romantically at this hospital." According to the lawyer, his preliminary research had unearthed several other alleged incidents at the hospital that apparently supported the idea that racial discrimination at the hospital was widespread.

Questions

1. What do you think of the way Chapman handled the accusations from Peters and his conversation with Anderson? How would you have handled them?

2. Do you think Peters had the basis for a sexual harassment claim against Anderson? Why or why not? Do you think Anderson has a legitimate case?

3. What would you do now if you were Chapman to avoid further incidents of this type?

CONTINUING CASE

Carter Cleaning Company

A Question of Discrimination

One of the first problems Jennifer faced at her father's Carter Cleaning Centers concerned the inadequacies of the firm's current HR management practices and procedures.

One problem that particularly concerned her was the lack of attention to equal employment matters. Virtually all hiring was handled independently by each store manager, and the managers themselves had received no training regarding such fundamental matters as the types of questions that should not be asked of job applicants. It was therefore not unusual—in fact, it was routine—for female applicants to be asked questions such as, "Who's going to take care of your children while you are at work?" and for minority applicants to be asked questions about arrest records and credit histories. Nonminority applicants—three store managers were white males and three were white females, by the way—were not asked these questions, as Jennifer discerned from her interviews with the managers. Based on discussions with her father, Jennifer deduced that part of the reason for the laid-back attitude toward equal employment stemmed from (1) her father's lack of sophistication regarding the legal requirements and (2) the fact that, as Jack Carter put it, "Virtually all our workers are women or minority members anyway, so no one can really come in here and accuse us of being discriminatory, can they?"

Jennifer decided to mull that question over, but before she could, she was faced with two serious equal rights problems. Two women in one of her stores privately confided to her that their manager was making unwelcome sexual advances toward them, and one claimed he had threatened to fire her unless she "socialized" with him after hours. And during a fact-finding trip to another store, an older gentleman—he was 73 years old—complained of the fact that although he had almost 50 years of experience in the business, he was being paid less than people half his age who were doing the very same job. Jennifer's review of the stores resulted in the following questions.

Questions

1. Is it true, as Jack Carter claims, that "we can't be accused of being discriminatory because we hire mostly women and minorities anyway"?

2. How should Jennifer and her company address the sexual harassment charges and problems?

3. How should she and her company address the possible problems of age discrimination?

4. Given the fact that each of its stores has only a handful of employees, is her company in fact covered by equal rights legislation?

5. And finally, aside from the specific problems, what other personnel management matters (application forms, training, and so on) have to be reviewed given the need to bring them into compliance with equal rights laws?

KEY TERMS

Title VII of the 1964 Civil Rights Act, 30

Equal Employment Opportunity Commission (EEOC), 31

affirmative action, 31

Office of Federal Contract Compliance Programs (OFCCP), 31

Equal Pay Act of 1963, 31

Age Discrimination in Employment Act of 1967 (ADEA), 31

Vocational Rehabilitation Act of 1973, 32

Vietnam Era Veterans' Readjustment Act of 1974, 32

Pregnancy Discrimination Act (PDA), 32

uniform guidelines, 32

sexual harassment, 33

Federal Violence Against Women Act of 1994, 33

protected class, 37

Civil Rights Act of 1991 (CRA 1991), 38

mixed motive case, 39

Americans with Disabilities Act (ADA), 40

qualified individuals, 40

adverse impact, 46

disparate rejection rates, 46

restricted policy, 47

bona fide occupational qualification (BFOQ), 48

alternative dispute resolution or ADR program, 58

good faith effort strategy, 62

reverse discrimination, 62

ENDNOTES

1. Commerce Clearing House, "Section 1981 Covers Racial Discrimination in Hiring and Promotion, but No Other Situation," *Human Resources Management*, June 28, 1989, p. 116.

2. Based on or quoted from *Principles of Employment Discrimination Law*, International Association of Official Human Rights Agencies, Washington, DC. See also Bruce Feldacker, *Labor Guide to Labor Law* (Upper Saddle River, NJ: Prentice Hall, 2000); and www.eeoc.gov/. Employment discrimination law is a changing field, and the appropriateness of the rules, guidelines, and conclusions in this chapter and book may also be affected by factors unique to the employer's operation. They should be reviewed by the employer's attorney before implementation.

3. "OFCCP Lists Egregious Bias Cases," *BNA Fair Employment Practices*, November 28, 1996, p. 139.

4. BNA Lawrence Kleiman and David Denton, "Downsizing: Nine Steps to ADA Compliance," *Employment Relations Today* 27, no. 3 (Fall 2000), pp. 37–45.

5. *Tanberg v. Weld County Sheriff*, SUDA Colo. No. 91-B-248, 3/18/92.

6. Larry Drake and Rachel Moskowitz, "Your Rights in the Workplace," *Occupational Outlook Quarterly* (Summer 1997), pp. 19–29.

7. Richard Wiener et al., "The Fit and Implementation of Sexual Harassment Law to Workplace Evaluations," *Journal of Applied Psychology* 87, no. 4 (2002), pp. 747–764.

8. Patricia Linenberger and Timothy Keaveny, "Sexual Harassment: The Employer's Legal Obligations," *Personnel* 58 (November/December 1981), p. 64.

9. Edward Felsenthal, "Justice's Ruling Further Defines Sexual Harassment," *Wall Street Journal*, March 5, 1998, p. B5.

10. See Mindy D. Bergman et al., "The (Un)reasonableness of Reporting: Antecedents and Consequences of Reporting Sexual

Harassment," *Journal of Applied Psychology* 87, no. 2 (2002), pp. 230–242; see also W. Kirk Turner and Christopher Thrutchley, "Employment Law and Practices Training: No Longer the Exception—It's the Rule," *Society for Human Resource Management Legal Report* (July–August 2002), pp. 1–2.

11. See the discussion in "Examining Unwelcome Conduct in a Sexual Harassment Claim," *BNA Fair Employment Practices*, October 19, 1995, p. 124. See also Molly Bowers et al., "Just Cause in the Arbitration of Sexual Harassment Cases," *Dispute Resolution Journal* 55, no. 4 (November 2000), pp. 40–55.

12. Maria Rotundo et al., "A Meta-Analysis Review of Gender Differences in Perceptions of Sexual Harassment," *Journal of Applied Psychology* 86, no. 5 (2001), pp. 914–922.

13. Bergman et al., "The (Un)reasonabless) of Reporting," p. 237.

14. Jason Janov, "Sexual Harassment and the Three Big Surprises," *HR Magazine* 46, no. 11 (November 2001), p. 123ff.

15. See the discussion in "Examining Unwelcome Conduct in a Sexual Harassment Claim," *BNA Fair Employment Practices*, October 19, 1995, p. 124.

16. Ibid., p. 124.

17. *Griggs v. Duke Power Company*, 3FEP Cases 175.

18. This is applicable only to Title VII and CRA 91; other statutes require intent.

19. James Ledvinka, *Federal Regulation of Personnel and Human Resources Management* (Boston: Kent, 1982), p. 41.

20. Bruce Feldacker, *Labor Guide to Labor Law* (Upper Saddle River, NJ: Prentice Hall, 2000), p. 513.

21. "The Eleventh Circuit Explains Disparate Impact, Disparate Treatment," *BNA Fair Employment Practices*, August 17, 2000, p. 102. See also Kenneth York, "Disparate Results in Adverse Impact Tests: The 4/5ths Rule and the Chi Square Test," *Public Personnel Management* 31, no. 2 (Summer 2002), pp. 253–262.

22. Patricia Feltes, Robert Robinson, and Ross Fink, "American Female Expatriates and the Civil Rights Act of 1991: Balancing Legal and Business Interests," *Business Horizons*, March/April 1993, pp. 82–85.

23. Ibid., p. 84.

24. Title VII does not apply to foreign operations not owned or controlled by a U.S. employer, however.

25. Based on Gregory Baxter, "Over There: Enforcing the 1991 Civil Rights Act Abroad," *Employee Relations Law Journal* 19, no. 2 (Autumn 1993), pp. 257–266.

26. Ibid., p. 265.

27. Ibid.

28. Commerce Clearing House, "House and Senate Pass Civil Rights Compromise by Wide Margin," *Ideas and Trends in Personnel*, November 13, 1991, p. 179.

29. Ibid., p. 182.

30. Mark Kobata, "The Civil Rights Act of 1991," *Personnel Journal*, March 1992, p. 48.

31. See, for example, Margaret Clark, "Direct Discrimination Evidence not Needed in Mixed Motive Case," *HR Magazine*, July 2003, pp. 25–26.

32. Elliot H. Shaller and Dean Rosen, "A Guide to the EEOC's Final Regulations on the Americans with Disabilities Act," *Employee Relations* 17, no. 3 (Winter 1991–1992), pp. 405–430. See also Brenda Sunoo, "Accommodating Workers with Disabilities," *Workforce* 80, no. 2 (February 2001), pp. 86–93.

33. "ADA: Simple Common Sense Principles," *BNA Fair Employment Practices*, June 4, 1992, p. 63.

34. Shaller and Rosen, "A Guide to the EEOC's Final Regulations," p. 408. See also James McDonald Jr., "The Rise of Psychological Issues in Employment Law," *Employee Relations Law Journal* 25, no. 3 (Winter 1999), pp. 85–97.

35. Ibid., p. 409.

36. Michael Vest et al., "Factors Influencing a Manager's Decision to Discipline Employees for Refusal to Work with an HIV/AIDS Infected Co-worker," *Employee Responsibilities and Rights* 15, no. 1 (March 2003), pp. 31–43.

37. "No Sitting for Store Greeter," *BNA Fair Employment Practices*, December 14, 1995, p. 150.

38. "Reasonable Accommodation Issues in the Workplace," *BNA Fair Employment Practices*, June 12, 1997, p. 69.

39. *Palmer v. Circuit Court of Cook County, Illinois*, c7#95-3659-6/26/97; reviewed in "No Accommodation for Violent Employee," *BNA Fair Employment Practices*, July 10, 1997, p. 79. Also see *Miller v. Illinois Department of Corrections*, CA7, 1997, 6ad cases 678; reviewed in "Courts Define Parameters of the Americans with Disabilities Act," *BNA Fair Employment Practices*, March 20, 1997, p. 34.

40. "Blind Bartender Not Qualified for Job, Court Says in Dismissing Americans with Disabilities Act Claim," *BNA Fair Employment Practices*, February 4, 1999, p. 17.

41. "Differing Views: Punctuality as Essential Job Function," *BNA Fair Employment Practices*, April 27, 2000, p. 56.

42. Sacha Cohen, "High-Tech Tools Lower Barriers for Disabled," *HR Magazine*, October 2002, pp. 60–65.

43. James McDonald Jr., "The Americans with Difficult Personalities Act," *Employee Relations Law Journal* 25, no. 4 (Spring 2000), pp. 93–107.

44. "Odds Against Getting Even Are Long in ADA Cases," *BNA Bulletin to Management*, August 20, 2000, p. 229; "Determining Employers' Responsibilities Under ADA," *BNA Fair Employment Practices*, May 16, 1996, p. 57. See also Barbara Lee, "The Implications of ADA Litigation for Employers: A Review of Federal Appellate Court Decisions," *Human Resource Management* 40, no. 1 (Spring 2001), pp. 35–50.

45. "Supreme Court Says Manual Task Limitation Needs Both Daily Living, Workplace Impact," *BNA Fair Employment Practices*, January 17, 2002, p. 8.

46. These are adapted from Wayne Barlow and Edward Hane, "A Practical Guide to the Americans with Disabilities Act," *Personnel Journal* 72 (June 1992), p. 59.

47. "Tips for Employers with Asymptomatic HIV-Positive Employees," *BNA Fair Employment Practices*, November 27, 1997, p. 141.

48. *Krocka v. Bransfield*, DC N111, #95C627, 6/24/97; reviewed in "Test for Prozac Violates ADA," *BNA Fair Employment Practices*, August 7, 1997, p. 91.

49. Elliot Shaller, "Reasonable Accommodation Under the Americans with Disabilities Act: What Does It Mean," *Employee Relations Law Journal* 16, no. 4 (Spring 1991), pp. 445–446.

50. Ibid., p. 446. See also Michael Esposito, "Are You 100 Percent ADA-Compliant?" *Management Review*, February 1993, pp. 27–29; and William R. Tracey, "Auditing ADA Compliance," *HR Magazine*, October 1994, pp. 88–90.

51. Lee, "The Implications of ADA Litigation for Employers."

52. "Determining Employers' Responsibilities Under ADA," p. 57.

53. Lee, "The Implications of ADA Litigation for Employers."

54. Ibid.

55. Timothy Bland, "The Supreme Court Focuses on the ADA," *HR Magazine*, September 1999, pp. 42–46. See also James Hall and Diane Hatch, "Supreme Court Decisions Require ADA Revision," *Workforce*, August 1999, pp. 60–66.

56. James Ledvinka and Robert Gatewood, "EEO Issues with Preemployment Inquiries," *Personnel Administrator* 22, no. 2 (February 1997), pp. 22–26.

57. "1996 State Anti-Bias Laws Focus on Harassment, Genetic Testing," *BNA Fair Employment Practices*, January 9, 1997, p. 123.

58. John Moran, *Employment Law* (Upper Saddle River, NJ: Prentice Hall, 1997), p. 166.

59. "The Eleventh Circuit Explains Disparate Impact, Disparate Treatment," p. 102.

60. John Klinefelter and James Thompkins, "Adverse Impact in Employment Selection," *Public Personnel Management*, May/June 1976, pp. 199–204.

61. Moran, *Employment Law*, p. 168.

62. *Professional Pilots Federation v. Federal Aviation Administration*, U.S. SUP CT #97-1267, cert. denied 5/18/98.

63. "Congress Legislates to Increase Commercial Pilot Age," Airline Industry Information, March 15, 2001.

64. *Usery v. Tamiami Trail Tours*, 12FEP cases 1233.

65. Ledvinka, *Federal Regulation*, p. 82. For a further discussion of religious and other types of accommodation and what they involve, see, for example, *BNA Fair Employment Practices*, January 21, 1988, pp. 9–10; *BNA Fair Employment Practices*, April 14, 1988, pp. 45–46; and James G. Frierson. "Religion in the Work Place," *Personnel Journal* 67, no. 7 (July 1988), pp. 60–67.

66. Ledvinka, *Federal Regulation*.

67. Anderson and Levin-Epstein. Primer of Equal Employment Opportunity, pp. 13–14.

68. *U.S. v. Bethlehem Steel Company*, 3FEP cases 589.

69. *Robinson v. Lorillard Corporation*, 3FEP cases 653.

70. *Spurlock v. United Airlines*, 5FEP cases 17.

71. Anderson and Levin-Epstein, Primer of Equal Employment Opportunity, p. 14.

72. This isn't ironclad, however. For example, the U.S. Supreme Court, in *Stotts*, held that a court cannot require retention of black employees hired under a court's consent decree in preference to higher-seniority white employees who were protected by a bona fide seniority system. It's unclear whether this decision also extends to personnel decisions not governed by seniority systems. *Firefighters Local 1784 v. Stotts* (BNA, April 14, 1985).

73. Ledvinka and Gatewood, "EEO Issues with Preemployment Inquiries," pp. 22–26.

74. John Wymer III and Deborah Sudbury, "Employment Discrimination 'Testers': Will Your Hiring Practices 'Pass'?" *Employee Relations Law Journal* 17, no. 4 (Spring 1992), pp. 623–633.

75. Ledvinka and Gatewood, "EEO Issues with Preemployment Inquiries," pp. 22–26.

76. Richard Connors, "Law at Work," lawatwork.com/news/applicat.html.

77. Lynn Bennington and Ruth Wein, "Aiding and Abetting Employer Discrimination: The Job Applicant's Role," *Employer Responsibilities and Rights* 14, no. 1 (March 2002), pp. 3–16.

78. This is based on *BNA Fair Employment Practices*, April 13, 1989, pp. 45–47.

79. Eric Matusewitch, "Tailor Your Dress Codes," *Personnel Journal* 68, no. 2 (February 1989), pp. 86–91; Matthew Miklaue, "Sorting Out a Claim of Bias," *Workforce* 80, no. 6 (June 2001), pp. 102–103.

80. If the charge was filed initially with a state or local agency within 180 days after the alleged unlawful practice occurred, the charge may then be filed with the EEOC within 30 days after the practice occurred or within 30 days after the person received notice that the state or local agency has ended its proceedings.

81. Kenneth Sovereign, *Personnel Law*, 4th ed. (Upper Saddle River, NJ: Prentice Hall, 1999), pp. 302–303.

82. "EEOC Reached Record of $385 Million in Benefits; Charge Filings Dropped Slightly in Fiscal 2003," *BNA Human Resources Report*, December 15, 2003, 1339.

83. "Conducting Effective Investigations of Employee Bias Complaints," *BNA Fair Employment Practices*, July 13, 1995, p. 81.

84. Based on Commerce Clearing House, *Ideas and Trends*, January 23, 1987, pp. 14–15.

85. "Tips for Employers on Dealing with EEOC Investigations," *BNA Fair Employment Practices*, October 31, 1996, p. 130.

86. Ibid., p. 219.

87. Ibid., p. 220.

88. "EEOC's New Nationwide Mediation Plan Offers Option of Informal Settlements," *BNA Fair Employment Practices*, February 18, 1999, p. 21.

89. "EEOC has 18 Nationwide, 300 Local Accords with Employers to Mediate Job Bias Claims Charges," *BNA Human Resources Report*, October 13, 2003, H-081.

90. Timothy Bland, "Sealed Without a Kiss," *HR Magazine*, October 2000, pp. 85–92.

91. Stuart Bonpey and Michael Pappas, "Is There a Better Way? Compulsory Arbitration of Employment Discrimination Claims After Gilmer," *Employee Relations Law Journal* 19, no. 3 (Winter 1993–1994), pp. 197–216.

92. These are based on ibid., pp. 210–211.

93. Ibid., p. 210.

94. Ibid.

95. David Nye, "When the Fired Fight Back," *Across-the-Board*, June 1995, pp. 31–34.

96. "EEOC Opposes Mandatory Arbitration," *BNA Fair Employment Practices*, July 24, 1997, p. 85.

97. James Coil III and Charles Rice, "Managing Work-Force Diversity in the 90s: The Impact of the Civil Rights Act of 1991," *Employee Relations Law Journal* 18, no. 4 (Spring 1993), pp. 547–565. See also Stephanie Mehta, "What Minority Employees Really Want," *Fortune*, July 10, 2000, pp. 81–188.

98. Michael Carrell and Everett Mann, "Defining Work-Force Diversity in Public Sector Organizations," *Public Personnel Management* 24, no. 1 (Spring 1995), pp. 99–111. See also Richard Koonce, "Redefining Diversity," *Training and Development Journal*, December 2001, pp. 22–33.

99. Patricia Digh, "Creating a New Balance Sheet: The Need for Better Diversity Metrics," *Mosaics* (Society for Human Resource Management, October 1999), p. 1.

100. Taylor Cox, Jr., *Cultural Diversity in Organizations: Theory, Research and Practice* (San Francisco: Berrett-Koehler, 1993), p. 236.

101. Robert Grossman, "Is Diversity Working?" *HR Magazine*, March 2000, pp. 47–50.

102. Carol Hastings, "Tapping into Your Foreign-Born, Spanish-Speaking Workforce," *Mosaics* (Society for Human Resource Management, July/August 2002), no. 3, p. 1.

103. Raymond Friedman and Books Holtom, "The Effects of Network Groups on Minority Employee Turnover Intentions," *Human Resource Management* 41, no. 4 (Winter 2002), pp. 405–421.

104. Richard Orlando, "Racial Diversity, Business Strategy, and Firm Performance: A Resource Based View," *Public Personnel Management* 24, no. 1 (Spring 1995), pp. 99–111.

105. Thomas Kochen et al., "The Effects of Diversity on Business Performance: Report of the Diversity Research Network," *Human Resource Management* 42, no. 1 (Spring 2003), pp. 3–21.

106. Bill Leonard, "Ways to Tell if a Diversity Program Is Measuring Up," *HR Magazine*, July 2002, p. 21.

107. Frank Jossi, "Reporting Race," *HR Magazine*, September 2000, pp. 87–94.

108. U.S. Equal Employment Opportunity Commission, *Affirmative Action and Equal Employment* (Washington, DC, January 1974); Antonio Handler Chayes, "Make Your Equal Opportunity Program Court Proof," *Harvard Business Review*, September 1974, pp. 81–89. See also David Kravitz and Steven Klineberg, "Reactions to Two Versions of Affirmative Action Among Whites, Blacks, and Hispanics," *Journal of Applied Psychology* 85, no. 4 (2000), pp. 597–611.

109. Coil and Rice, "Managing Work-Force Diversity in the 90s," p. 548.

110. Ibid., p. 560.

111. Ibid., pp. 562–563.

112. Ibid., p. 563.

113. Madeline Heilman, Winston McCullough, and David Gilbert, "The Other Side of Affirmative Action: Reactions of Nonbeneficiaries to Sex-Based Preferential Selection," *Journal of Applied Psychology* 81, no. 4 (1996), pp. 346–357.

114. Ibid., p. 346.

115. See Michael W. Sculnick, "The Supreme Court 1985-86 EEO Decisions: A Review," *Employment Relations Today* 13, no. 3 (Fall 1986).

116. Ibid.

117. Ibid.

118. Ann McDaniel, "A Woman's Day in Court," *Newsweek*, April 6, 1987, pp. 58–59.

119. "Lawyers, Scholars Differ on Likely Impact of Affirmative Action Rulings on Workplace," *BNA Fair Employment Practices*, July 3, 2003, pp. 79–80.

After studying this chapter, you should be able to:

1 Outline the steps in the strategic management process.

2 Explain and give examples of each type of companywide and competitive strategy.

3 Explain what a strategy-oriented HR system is and why it is important.

4 Illustrate and explain each of the seven steps in the HR Scorecard approach to creating HR systems.

Strategic Human Resource Management and the HR Scorecard

Every manager makes decisions within the context of the guidelines laid

down by his or her company's strategic plan. As we'll see in this chapter, the

company's strategic plan defines the nature of the company's business, for

instance, in terms of the markets in which it will compete and the ways in

which it will differentiate itself from its competitors. The strategic plan lays

out the broad guidelines within which the company's managers make

decisions. It thereby has a big influence on things like: "What sorts of people

should we hire?" "What kind of salesforce do we need?" "What production

methods will we use?" and "How should we build our brand image and

market our products?" In a very real sense, then, the HR manager can't

make intelligent decisions regarding how to design the company's HR

systems unless he or she understands how each of those systems helps the

company achieve its strategic goals.●

The main purpose of this chapter is to show you how to develop an HR system that supports, and makes sense in terms of, the company's strategic goals. We'll explain the strategic management process, how to develop a strategic plan, and the HR manager's role in the strategic management process. We discuss how to create a strategy-oriented HR system, and explain the step-by-step "HR Scorecard approach" to creating a strategy-oriented HR system.

● HR'S STRATEGIC CHALLENGES

strategic plan
A company's plan for how it will match its internal strengths and weaknesses with external opportunities and threats in order to maintain a competitive advantage.

The central challenge facing human resource management is always to provide a set of services that make sense in terms of the company's strategic plan. A **strategic plan** is the company's plan for how it will match its internal strengths and weaknesses with external opportunities and threats in order to maintain a competitive advantage. The basic strategic planning process involves asking, "Where are we now as a business, and where do we want to be?" The manager then formulates specific (HR and other) strategies to take the company from where it is now to where he or she wants it to be. A *strategy* is thus a course of action. The company's various strategies—its HR, sales, finance, and manufacturing strategies, for instance—need to support the company's strategic plan. Suppose the strategic plan calls for improving the quality of the company's products (such as Ford's former plan to "Make Quality Job 1"). Then one HR strategy might be to "boost employee quality consciousness through improved screening and training."

Consider another example. The essence of Dell Computer's strategic plan has always been to be what strategic planners call a "low-cost leader," by using the Internet and the phone to sell PCs directly to end users at prices competitors cannot match. The firm's HR managers have devised various HR strategies to support the firm's low-cost strategy. For example, Dell now delivers most of its HR services via the Web. A Manager Tools section on Dell's intranet contains about 30 automated Web applications (including executive search reports, hiring tools, and automated employee referrals). This allows managers to perform HR tasks that previously required costly participation by HR department personnel. The intranet also lets Dell employees administer their own 401(k) plans, check job postings, and monitor their total compensation statements. This dramatically reduces the number of HR people required to administer these activities, and thus the cost of doing so.[1]

In formulating their HR strategies, HR managers must address three basic challenges. One (as at Dell) is *the need to support corporate productivity and performance improvement efforts*. With the globalization of the world economy, competition has soared, and with it the need to continually improve organizational performance. Second is that *employees play an expanded role in employers' performance improvement efforts*. Indeed, all the elements we associate with high-performance organizations—such as technology-based production and team-based organizations—require extraordinarily high levels of employee competence and commitment. These two challenges mean that HR's attention increasingly focuses on boosting competitiveness, on managing employee performance, and, in general, on building high-performing organizations and being measured on its ability to do so.

The third challenge (stemming from the first two) is that, given its more central role in managing performance, *HR must be more involved in designing—not just executing—the company's strategic plan*. Strategy formulation was traditionally a job for the company's operating (line) managers. The president and his or her staff might decide to enter new markets, drop prod-

Bertha Renteria is a computer builder at Dell Computer Corp., in Austin, Texas. Dell managers know HR must support corporate productivity and performance improvement efforts by recruiting and hiring competent and committed employees. Hiring employees like Bertha is one of the reasons Dell has been able to meet its strategic goals and maintain its low-cost leader position.

uct lines, or embark on a five-year cost-cutting plan. Then the president would more or less entrust the personnel implications of that plan (hiring or firing new workers, hiring outplacement firms for those fired, and so on) to HR management.

Today's emphasis on gaining competitive advantage through people makes such an arrangement inadequate. In formulating its strategy, top management needs the input of the managers charged with hiring, training, and compensating the firm's employees. HR professionals therefore need to understand the basics of strategic planning.

The Strategic Management Process

Outline the steps in the strategic management process.

Strategic planning is part of the firm's strategic management process. As Figure 3-1 shows, strategic planning includes the first four strategic management tasks. It includes evaluating the firm's internal and external situation, defining the business and developing a mission, translating the mission into strategic goals, and crafting a strategy or course of action. In its simplest sense, however, strategic planning is simple: Decide what business you're in now and which ones you want to be in, formulate a strategy for getting there, and execute your plan. **Strategic management** includes the implementation phase. It is the process of identifying and executing the organization's mission, by matching the company's capabilities with the demands of its environment.

strategic management
The process of identifying and executing the organization's mission by matching its capabilities with the demands of its environment.

The strategic management process consists of several related tasks (see Figure 3-1). Let's look at the main ones.

Step 1: Define the Business and Its Mission The fundamental strategic decisions managers face are these: "Where are we now in terms of the business we're in, and what business do we want to be in, given our company's opportunities and threats, and its strengths and weaknesses?" Managers then choose strategies—courses of action such as buying competitors or expanding overseas—to get the company from where it is today to where it wants to be tomorrow.

Figure 3-1
Overview of Strategic Management Process
Source: Adapted from Fred David, *Strategic Management* (Upper Saddle River, NJ: Prentice Hall, 2001), p. 77.

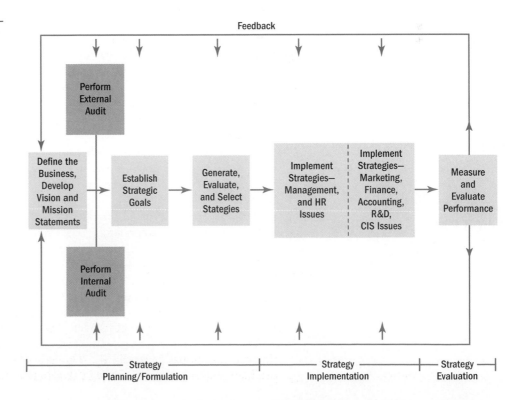

Management experts use the terms *vision* and *mission* to help define a company's current and future business. Some use the terms interchangeably. However, in general usage, vision tends to be the broader and more future-oriented of the two. The company's **vision** is a "general statement of its intended direction that evokes emotional feelings in organization members."[2] As Warren Bennis and Bert Manus say,

> *To choose a direction, a leader must first have developed a mental image of a possible and desirable future state for the organization. This image, which we call a vision, may be as vague as a dream or as precise as a goal or mission statement. The critical point is that a vision articulates a view of a realistic, credible, attractive future for the organization, a condition that is better in some important ways than what now exists.*[3]

Rupert Murdoch, chairman of News Corporation (which owns the Fox network and many newspapers and satellite TV operations), has a vision of an integrated, global satellite-based news-gathering, entertainment, and multi-media firm. WebMD CEO Jeffrey Arnold launched his business based on a vision of a Web site supplying everything a consumer might want to know about medical-related issues.[4]

The firm's **mission** is more specific and shorter term. It "serves to communicate 'who we are, what we do, and where we're headed.' "[5] Whereas visions usually lay out in very broad terms what the business should be, the mission lays out what it is supposed to be now. For example, the mission of the California Energy Commission is to "assess, and act through public/private partnerships to improve energy systems that promote a strong economy and a healthy environment." (The Commission's *vision*, by way of comparison, is "for Californians to have energy choices that are affordable, reliable, diverse, safe, and environmentally acceptable.")

Step 2: **Perform External and Internal Audits** Managers base their strategic plans on methodical analyses of their external and internal situations. The basic point of a strategic plan should be to choose a direction for the firm that makes sense, in terms of the external opportunities and threats it faces and the internal strengths and weaknesses it possesses. To facilitate this strategic external/internal audit, many managers turn to **SWOT analysis**. This involves using a SWOT chart like that in Figure 3-2 to compile and organize the process of identifying company Strengths, Weaknesses, Opportunities, and Threats.

vision
A general statement of its intended direction that evokes emotional feelings in organization members.

mission
Spells out who the company is, what it does, and where it's headed.

SWOT analysis
The use of a SWOT chart to compile and organize the process of identifying company **S**trengths, **W**eaknesses, **O**pportunities, and **T**hreats.

Figure 3-2
A SWOT Chart

| **S**trengths | **W**eaknesses |
| **O**pportunities | **T**hreats |

Step 3: Translate the Mission into Strategic Goals Saying your mission is to "assess and act through public/private partnerships to improve energy systems" is one thing; operationalizing that mission for your managers is another. The firm's managers need long-term strategic goals. For example, what exactly does that mission mean, for the next five years, in terms of how many and what specific types of partnerships to form, with whom, and when?

Business managers need specificity. WebMD's sales director needs goals regarding the number of new medical-related content providers—vitamin firms, hospitals, HMOs—it must sign up per year, as well as sales revenue targets. The business development manager needs goals regarding the number of new businesses—such as using WebMD to help manage doctors' offices online—he or she is to develop and sign. Similarly, a global financial powerhouse like Citicorp can't function solely with the broad mission "to provide integrated, comprehensive financial services worldwide." It needs specific goals, in areas including building shareholder value through growth in earnings-per-share; continuing its commitment to building customer-oriented business worldwide; maintaining superior rates of return; building a strong balance sheet; and balancing the business by customer, product, and geography.[6]

Step 4: Formulate a Strategy to Achieve the Strategic Goals The firm's strategy is a bridge connecting where the company is today with where it wants to be tomorrow. The question is, "how do we get from here to there?" A **strategy** is a course of action. It shows how the enterprise will move from the business it is in now to the business it wants to be in (as stated in its vision, mission, and strategic goals), given its opportunities and threats and its internal strengths and weaknesses.

strategy
The company's long-tem plan for how it will balance its internal strengths and weaknesses with its external opportunities and threats to maintain a competitive advantage.

Employees can't and won't implement strategies they don't buy into; therefore top companies craft strategies whose basic principles are easy to communicate. Figure 3-3 illustrates. For example, the essence of Dell's strategy has always been "be direct." Wal-Mart's strategy boils down to the familiar "low prices, every day."

A knowledge of and commitment to the strategy helps ensure that employees make decisions consistent with the company's needs. For example, the executive team's deep understanding of Nokia's strategy reportedly helps explain how the firm can make thousands of decisions each week so coherently.[7]

Step 5: Implement the Strategy Strategy implementation means translating the strategies into actions and results—by actually hiring (or firing) people, building (or closing) plants, and adding (or eliminating) products and product lines. In other words, strategy implementation involves drawing on and applying all the management functions: planning, organizing, staffing, leading, and controlling.

Step 6: Evaluate Performance Strategies don't always succeed. For example, when General Motors sold the last of its Hughes Electronics assets, it was the end of a strategy put in place about 12 years earlier. In the 1980s, GM had bought both Electronic Data Systems and Hughes Electronics, with the idea of using these

**Figure 3-3
Strategies in Brief**

Source: Arit Gadiesh and James Gilbert, "Frontline Action," *Harvard Business Review,* May 2001, p. 74.

Company	Strategic Principle
Dell	*Be direct*
eBay	*Focus on trading communities*
General Electric	*Be number one or number two in every industry in which we compete, or get out*
Southwest Airlines	*Meet customers' short-haul travel needs at fares competitive with the cost of automobile travel*
Vanguard	*Unmatchable value for the investor-owner*
Wal-Mart	*Low prices, every day*

technology firms to automate and reinvigorate automobile production and sales. GM did make a big profit when it sold the companies. However, many believe the acquisitions were actually such a distraction that they helped push GM's market share down from about 60% to 28% in the interim.[8] Similarly, Procter & Gamble announced it was selling its remaining food businesses—Jif, Crisco, and Folger's coffee—because management wants to concentrate on household and cosmetics products.[9]

strategic control
The process of assessing progress toward strategic goals and taking corrective action as needed.

Managing strategy is an ongoing process. Competitors introduce new products, technological innovations make production processes obsolete, and social trends reduce demand for some products or services while boosting demand for others. **Strategic control** keeps the company's strategy up to date. It is the process of assessing progress toward strategic goals and taking corrective action as needed. Management monitors the extent to which the firm is meeting its strategic goals, and asks why deviations exist. Management simultaneously scans the firm's strategic situation (competitors, technical advances, customer demographics, and so on) to see if it should make any adjustments. Strategic control addresses several important questions: for example, "Are all the resources of our firm contributing as planned to achieving our strategic goals?" "What is the reason for any discrepancies?" and, "Do changes in our situation suggest that we should revise our strategic plan?"

Types of Strategic Planning

② Explain and give examples of each type of companywide and competitive strategy.

Managers engage in three levels of strategic planning (see Figure 3-4). At the company-wide level, many firms consist of several businesses; for instance, PepsiCo includes Pepsi, Frito-Lay, and Pizza Hut. PepsiCo therefore needs a *corporate-level strategy*. A company's corporate-level strategy identifies the portfolio of businesses that, in total, comprise the company and the ways in which these businesses relate to each other. For example, a *diversification* corporate strategy implies that the firm will expand by adding new product lines. A *vertical integration* strategy means the firm expands by, perhaps, producing its own raw materials, or selling its products direct. *Consolidation*—reducing the company's size—and *geographic expansion*—for instance, taking the business abroad—are some other corporate strategy possibilities.

At the next level down, each of these businesses (such as Pizza Hut) needs a *business-level/competitive strategy*. A competitive strategy identifies how to build and strengthen the business's long-term competitive position in the marketplace.[10] It identifies, for instance, how Pizza Hut will compete with Papa John's or how Wal-Mart competes with Target.

competitive advantage
Any factors that allow an organization to differentiate its product or service from those of its competitors to increase market share.

Companies try to achieve competitive advantages for each business they are in. We can define **competitive advantage** as any factors that allow an organization to differentiate its product or service from those of its competitors to increase market share.

Figure 3-4
Relationships Among Strategies in Multiple-Business Firms

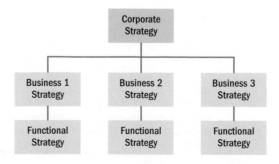

Companies use several competitive strategies to achieve competitive advantage. One, *cost leadership*, means the enterprise aims to become the low-cost leader in an industry. Wal-Mart is a typical industry cost leader: It maintains its competitive advantage through its satellite-based distribution system, and (in its early days) by keeping store location costs to a minimum by placing stores on low-cost land outside small- to medium-sized towns.

Differentiation is a second example of a competitive strategy. In a differentiation strategy, a firm seeks to be unique in its industry along dimensions that are widely valued by buyers.[11] Thus, Volvo stresses the safety of its cars, Papa John's Pizza stresses fresh ingredients, Target sells somewhat more upscale brands than Wal-Mart, and Mercedes-Benz emphasizes reliability and quality. Like Mercedes-Benz, firms can usually charge a premium price if they successfully stake a claim to being substantially different from competitors in some coveted way. Still other firms choose to compete as *focusers*. They carve out a market niche (like Ferrari), and compete by providing a product or service customers can get in no other way.

Finally, each individual business is composed of departments, such as manufacturing, sales, and HR management. *Functional strategies* identify the basic courses of action that each department will pursue in order to help the business attain its competitive goals. The firm's functional strategies should make sense in terms of its business/competitive strategy. Dell's HR strategy of putting its activities on the Web to support the parent firm's low-cost competitive strategy is one example. The "When You're on Your Own" feature illustrates a system you can use to facilitate your planning efforts.

Achieving Strategic Fit

Managers crafting strategies invariably confront a dilemma: Given a firm's opportunities and threats, and its strengths and weaknesses, should they simply "fit" capabilities to the opportunities and threats that they see, or, should they stretch well beyond their capabilities to take advantage of an opportunity? On this issue, there are two points of view.

Strategic planning expert Michael Porter emphasizes the "fit" point of view. He says that all of the firm's activities must be tailored to or fit its strategy, by ensuring that

---

When You're On Your Own
HR for Line Managers and Entrepreneurs

Using Computerized Business Planning Software

There are several business planning software packages available to assist the small business owner in writing top-notch strategic and business plans. For example, Business Plan Pro from Palo Alto software contains all the information and planning aids you need to create a business plan. It contains 30 sample plans, step-by-step instructions (with examples) for creating each part of a plan (executive summary, market analysis, and so on), financial planning spreadsheets, easy-to-use tables (for instance, for making sales forecasts), and automatic programs for creating color 3–D charts for showing things like monthly sales and yearly profits.

Business Plan Pro's planning wizard helps the manager or small business owner develop a business plan, step-by-step. The result is an integrated plan, complete with overall strategic plan, and charts, tables, and professional formatting. For example, click "start a plan," and the planning wizard presents a series of questions, including "Does your Company sell products, services or both?" "Would you like a detailed or basic business plan?" and, "Does your Company sell on credit?" Then, as you go to each succeeding part of the plan, the planning wizard shows you instructions with examples, making it easier to create your own executive summary (or other plan section, including the strategic plan). As you move into the quantitative part of your plan, such as making sales and financial forecasts, the planning wizard translates your numbers into tables and charts.

the firm's functional strategies support its corporate and competitive strategies: "It's this 'fit' that breathes life into the firm's strategy."

For example, Southwest Airlines pursues a low-cost leader strategy, and then tailors its activities to deliver low-cost, convenient service on its short-haul routes. It gets fast, 15-minute turnarounds at the gate, so it can keep its planes flying longer hours than rivals and have more departures with fewer aircraft. It also shuns frills like meals, assigned seats, and premium classes of service on which other full-service airlines build their competitive strategies.

Figure 3-5 illustrates this. The larger circles represent the activities at the heart of Southwest's low-cost activity system: limited passenger services; frequent, reliable departures; lean, highly productive ground and gate crews; high aircraft utilization; very low ticket prices; and short-haul, point-to-point routes. Various subactivities and decisions support each of these activities. For example, limited passenger service means things like no meals, no seat assignments, no baggage transfers, and limited use of travel agents. Highly productive ground crews mean high compensation, flexible union contracts, and a high level of employee stock ownership. Southwest's success reflects more than just its low-cost strategy; it's a product of a well-managed system in which each functional component fits each other component and the firm's low-cost strategy and strengths perfectly.

Strategy experts Gary Hamel and C. K. Prahalad caution against becoming too enamored with the notion of strategic fit. They agree that every company "must ultimately synchronize its resources and its responsibilities." However, they argue that being preoccupied with fit can limit growth. They argue for "stretch." They say that **leveraging** resources—supplementing what you have and doing more with what you have—can be more important than just fitting the strategic plan to current resources. For example, If modest resources were an insurmountable deterrent to future leadership, GM would not

leveraging
Supplementing what you have and doing more with what you have.

Figure 3-5
The Southwest Airlines' Activity System
Companies like Southwest tailor all their activities so that they fit and contribute to making their strategies a reality.
Source: Reprinted by permission of *Harvard Business Review.* From "What is Strategy?" by Michael E. Porter, November–December 1996. Copyright © 1996 by the President and Fellows of Harvard College, all rights reserved.

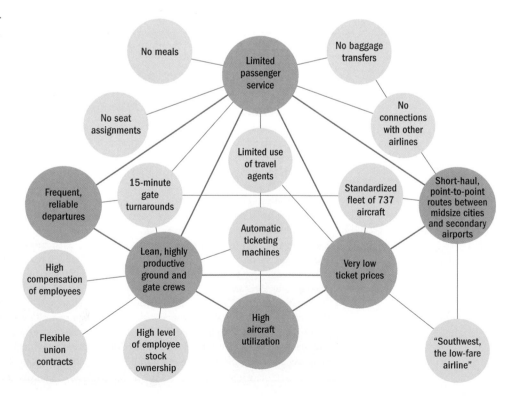

have found itself on the defensive with Honda. Wal-Mart years ago focused its relatively limited resources on building a satellite-based distribution system, thereby gaining a competitive advantage that helped it overtake Kmart.

HR and Competitive Advantage

In order to have an effective competitive strategy, the company must have one or more competitive advantages, "factors that allow an organization to differentiate its product or service."[12] Wal-Mart builds its low-cost leader strategy on the dual competitive advantages of a satellite-based inventory and distribution system, and on employment policies that help it to achieve extraordinarily low employment costs. Southwest Airlines achieves low-cost leader status through employment policies that produce a highly motivated and flexible workforce. Its workforce is its competitive advantage. Larger airlines like Delta, faced with union rules and restrictive work rules and salary structures, find it hard to compete with Southwest, whose employees eagerly rush to "turn around" an airplane in a fraction of the time it takes a Delta team. Every successful company has one or more competitive advantages around which it builds its competitive strategy.

The competitive advantage can take many forms. For a pharmaceuticals company, it may be the quality of its research team, and its patents. For a Web site like ebay, it may be a proprietary software system. Many years ago, Wal-Mart's satellite-based distribution system was so revolutionary that it was probably the firm's predominate competitive advantage. "The New Workplace" (page 81) presents another example.

Today, most companies have easy access to the same technologies, so technology itself is rarely enough to set a firm apart. It's usually the people and the management system that make the difference. For example, an operations expert from Harvard University studied manufacturing firms that installed special computer-integrated manufacturing systems to boost efficiency and flexibility. He concluded that,

> *all the data in my study point to one conclusion: operational flexibility is determined primarily by a plant's operators and the extent to which managers cultivate, measure, and communicate with them. Equipment and computer integration are secondary.*[13]

A busy Southwest ticket counter at Albany's International Airport in upstate New York. Southwest employees work hard to help the company maintain its low-cost leader position by doing more than their assigned jobs. The willingness to pitch in is a competitive advantage for Southwest, and reflects Southwest's well thought out HR strategies.

Figure 3-6
Linking Corporate and HR
Strategies
Source: © 2003, Gary Dessler, Ph.D.

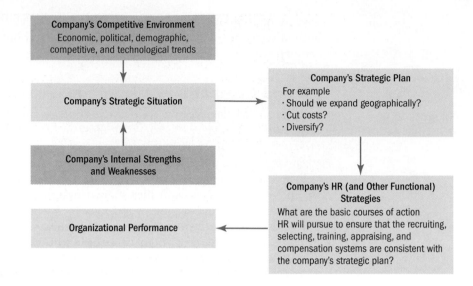

Another writer concludes:

> *In a growing number of organizations human resources are now viewed as a source of competitive advantage. . . . This is in contrast to the traditional emphasis on transferable resources such as equipment. . . . Increasingly, it is being recognized that competitive advantage can be obtained with a high quality workforce that enables organizations to compete on the basis of market responsiveness, product and service quality, differentiated products, and technological innovation.[14]*

Strategic Human Resource Management

The term *HR strategies* refers to the specific human resource management courses of action the company pursues to achieve its aims.[15] Thus, one of FedEx's strategic aims is to achieve superior levels of customer service and high profitability through a highly committed workforce. The overriding aim of its HR strategy is to build a committed workforce, preferably in a nonunion environment.[16] FedEx's specific HR strategies stem from this aim. They include: using various methods to build two-way communications; screening out potential managers whose values are not people-oriented; guaranteeing to the greatest extent possible fair treatment and employee security for all employees; and utilizing various promotion-from-within activities to give employees every opportunity to fully realize their potential. Figure 3-6 illustrates the interplay between HR strategy and the company's strategic plans and results. **Strategic human resource management** means formulating and executing HR systems—HR policies and activities—that produce the employee competencies and behaviors the company needs to achieve its strategic aims.

strategic human resource management
Formulating and executing HR systems—HR policies and activities—that produce the employee competencies and behaviors the company needs to achieve its strategic aims.

● HR'S STRATEGIC ROLES

When it comes to how involved HR managers should be in strategic planning, there is often a disconnect between what CEOs say and do. One writer says HR professionals' input is crucial: They identify problems that are critical to their companies' business strategy, and forecast potential obstacles to success.[17] When Rick Wagner

The New Workplace

Longo Builds its Strategy on Diversity

Some experts claim that diverse workforces create conflicts and rising costs. But that argument is lost on the owners of Longo Toyota in El Monte, California. Longo's HR strategy supports its strategy of catering to a highly diverse customer base by hiring and developing salespeople who speak everything from Spanish and Korean to Tagalog. And by following that HR strategy, Longo may now be one of America's top-grossing auto dealers.

With a 60-person salesforce that speaks more than 20 languages, Longo's staff provides it with a powerful competitive advantage for catering to an increasingly diverse customer base. The HR department has thereby contributed to Longo's success. While other dealerships lose half their salespeople every year, Longo retains 90% of its staff, in part by emphasizing a promotion-from-within policy that's made more than two-thirds of its managers minorities. It has also taken steps to attract more women, for instance, by adding a sales management staff to spend time providing the training inexperienced salespeople usually need. In a business in which competitors can easily imitate products, showrooms, and most services, Longo has built a competitive advantage based on employee diversity.

---

took over as CEO of General Motors, he organized a senior executive committee (the "Automotive Strategies Board"). It included GM's chief financial officer, chief information officer, and vice president of global human resources. As Wagner says, "I seek [the HR vice president's] counsel and perspective constantly. She has demonstrated a tremendous capacity to think and act strategically, which is essential to our HR function and what we want to achieve in making GM a globally competitive business."[18]

A study from the University of Michigan concluded that high-performing companies' HR professionals should be part of the firm's strategic planning executive team. These professionals identify the human issues that are vital to business strategy and help establish and execute strategy. They provide alternative insights and are involved in creating responsive and market-driven organizations. They conceptualize and execute organizational change. Another study by Mercer Consulting concluded that 39% of CEOs surveyed see HR as more of a partner than a cost center.[19] Yet another study, of 447 senior HR executives, focused on the extent to which HR had been involved in executing mergers for their companies. Figure 3-7 summarizes the findings. Mergers in which top management asked HR to apply its expertise consistently outperformed those in which HR was less involved.[20]

Yet one recent survey of 1,310 HR professionals found that, in practice, only about half said senior HR managers are involved in developing their companies' business plans.[21] A survey by the University of Southern California found that about one-fourth of large U.S. businesses appointed managers with no HR experience as top HR executives. Reasons given include the fact that they may find it easier to give the firms' HR efforts a strategic emphasis. They may also sometimes be better equipped to integrate the firm's HR efforts with the rest of the business.[22] So in practice, HR managers don't appear to be as involved in strategizing as perhaps they should be.

As HR managers do assume more strategic planning responsibilities, they will have to acquire new HR skills. This does not just mean technical skills relating to activities like selection and training. HR managers will need "an in-depth understanding of the value creating proposition of the firm." How does the company make money? What activities and processes are most critical for wealth creation as defined by customers and capital markets? Who in the firm executes these activities successfully?[23]

Figure 3-7
Percent of Mergers in
Which HR Manager Was
Involved
Source: Jeffrey Schmidt, "The Correct
Spelling of M & A Begins with HR,"
HR Magazine, June 2001, p. 105.
Reproduced with permission of Soc.
for Human Resource Mgmt. via
Copyright Clearance Center.

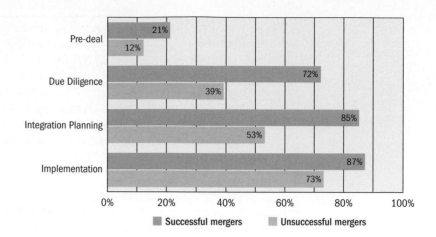

HR's Strategy Execution Role

Today's HR managers fulfill two basic strategic planning roles: *strategy execution* and *strategy formulation. Strategy execution* is traditionally the heart of the HR manager's strategic planning job. Top management formulates the company's corporate and competitive strategies. Then, it formulates broad functional strategies and policies. Like the riverbanks for a boat steaming up a waterway, the firm's functional strategies and policies set the broad limits that determine what the functional manager can and cannot do, and provide a set of signposts that the (HR or other) functional managers can use to decide the precise form the department's specific policies and activities should take. The company's HR (or other functional) strategies should thus derive directly from its company-wide and competitive strategies.

Here, the basic rule is this: The HR department's strategies, policies, and activities must make sense in terms of the company's corporate and competitive strategies, and they must support those strategies. Dell's human resource strategies—the Web-based help desk, its centralized intranet HR service bureau—help the firm better execute Dell's low-cost strategy. FedEx's HR strategies—supporting communication and employee development, for instance—help FedEx differentiate itself from its competitors by offering superior customer service.

HR management supports strategic implementation in other ways. For example, HR guides the execution of most firms' downsizing and restructuring strategies, through outplacing employees, instituting pay-for-performance plans, reducing health care costs, and retraining employees. When Wells Fargo acquired First Interstate Bancorp a few years ago, HR played a strategic role in implementing the merger—in merging two "wildly divergent" cultures and in dealing with the uncertainty and initial shock that rippled through the organizations when the merger was announced.[24]

HR's Strategy Formulation Role

While execution is important, HR increasingly plays an expanded strategic planning role today. In recent years, HR's traditional role in executing strategy has expanded to include working with top management to formulate the company's strategic plans. (HR has "a seat at the strategy planning table" is how some HR writers put this.) This expanded *strategy formulation* role reflects the reality most firms face today. Globalization means more competition, more competition means more performance, and most firms are gaining that improved performance in whole or part by boosting the competence and commitment levels of their employees. That makes HR's input crucial.

HR helps top management formulate strategy in a variety of ways. For example, formulating a company's strategic plan requires identifying, analyzing, and balancing the company's *external opportunities and threats*, on the one hand, and its *internal strengths and weaknesses*, on the other. Hopefully, the resulting strategic plans capitalize on the firm's strengths and opportunities, and minimize or neutralize its threats and weaknesses. Externally, HR management is in a unique position to supply competitive intelligence that may be useful in the strategic planning process. Details regarding competitors' incentive plans, opinion survey data from employees that elicit information about customer complaints, and information about pending legislation such as labor laws and mandatory health insurance are some examples. Furthermore:

> *From public information and legitimate recruiting and interview activities, you ought to be able to construct organization charts, staffing levels and group missions for the various organizational components of each of your major competitors. Your knowledge of how brands are sorted among sales divisions and who reports to whom can give important clues as to a competitor's strategic priorities. You may even know the track record and characteristic behavior of the executives.*[25]

As another example, HR participates in the strategy formulation process by supplying information regarding the company's internal human strengths and weaknesses. For example, IBM's decision in the 1990s to buy Lotus Software was prompted in part by the conclusion that its own human resources were insufficient to enable the firm to reposition itself as an industry leader in networking systems, or at least to do so fast enough. Some firms, thanks to HR's input, build new strategies around human resource strengths. For example, in the process of automating its factories, farm equipment manufacturer John Deere developed a workforce that was exceptionally talented and expert in factory automation. This in turn prompted the firm to establish a new-technology division to offer automation services to other companies.[26]

But, for a growing number of employers, HR is even more extensively involved in the strategy formulation process. By working closely with top management, HR is able to build a persuasive case that shows how—in specific and measurable terms—the firm's HR activities can and do contribute to creating value for the company, for instance in terms of higher profits and market value. A big part of building that case is to create a strategy-oriented HR system. We'll turn to this next.

3   Explain what a strategy-oriented HR system is and why it is important.

● CREATING A STRATEGY-ORIENTED HR SYSTEM

By way of overview, we can think of an HR process as consisting of three basic components. There are the *HR professionals* who have the strategic and other skills required to build a strategy-oriented HR system. There are the HR *policies and activities* (such as how the company recruits, selects, and trains and rewards employees) that comprise the HR system itself. And there are the *employee behaviors and competencies* that the company's strategy requires, and that hopefully emerge from the actions and policies of the firm's strategy-supporting HR system. Some HR experts refer to these three elements (the HR professionals, the HR system, and the resulting employee behaviors) as a company's basic HR architecture (see Figure 3-8).

Ideally, the HR professionals should design the HR system in such a way that it helps to produce the employee competencies and behaviors the company needs to achieve its strategic goals. It obviously does little good to design, say, training practices that produce a workforce incapable of using the company's new computerized machines.[27]

Creating a strategy-oriented HR system requires new skills on the part of HR professionals. They must have the competencies required to create HR systems that produce

Figure 3-8
The Basic Architecture of HR
Source: Adapted from Brian Becker et al., *The HR Scorecard: Linking People, Strategy, and Performance* (Boston: Harvard Business School Press, 2001), p. 12.

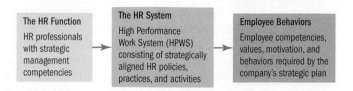

strategically relevant employee behaviors. They need to understand the strategy formulation process. They must be adept at identifying the workforce implications and requirements of the new strategy and at crafting HR policies and practices that produce those workforce requirements. They must have a sufficiently wide breadth of business knowledge to be able to understand how the company creates value, and to see how the firm's HR system can contribute to that value-creation process. The HR professional has to understand how businesses operate. Just understanding the nitty-gritty of recruiting, selecting, and training is no longer sufficient.

The High-Performance Work System

In today's competitive environment, the manager can't leave the nature of the HR system—the actual HR policies and practices—to chance. As mentioned in Chapter 1, managers usually try to create high-performance work systems (HPWS). The HPWS is a set of HR policies and practices that maximize the competencies, commitment, and abilities of the firm's employees. In practice, this means that each HPWS HR activity produces measurable superior results. For example, review Table 3-1. Note how much more extensively the high-performing companies structure their recruiting activities so as to produce qualified recruits. And, how much more extensively high-performing firms hire employees based on selection tests, and provide training to new employees. The bottom line is that management can't leave their HR systems unmanaged. Based on an ongoing research program with over 2,800 corporations, firms that use HPWS policies and practices do perform at a significantly higher level than those that do not. The evidence suggests that "high performance HR practices, [particularly] combined with new technology, produce better productivity, quality, sales, and financial performance."[28]

Table 3-1 also helps to illustrate another aspect of high-performance work systems, namely that they have a definite bias toward helping and encouraging workers to manage themselves. For example, you can see that the high-performing firms generally emphasize placing employees in self-managing, cross-functional teams. In fact, the whole thrust of the HPWS's superior recruiting, screening, training, and other HR practices is to build the sort of highly trained, empowered, self-governing, and flexible workforce that companies today need as a competitive advantage.[29]

The need for HPWS became apparent as global competition intensified in the 1990s. Companies needed a way to better utilize their human resources as they strove to improve quality, productivity, and responsiveness. In the early 1990s, the U.S. Department of Labor identified several characteristics of high-performance work organizations: multiskilled work teams; empowered front-line workers; more training; labor management cooperation; commitment to quality; and customer satisfaction.[30] HR practices like those in Table 3-1 foster these characteristics.

Translating Strategy into HR Policy and Practice

The HR manager needs a way to translate the firm's new strategy into specific, actionable HR policies and practices. The basic process, as outlined in Figure 3-9, is simple and logical. Management formulates a *strategic plan*. That strategic plan implies certain *workforce*

Table 3-1 Comparison of HR Practices in High-Performance and Low-Performance Companies*

	Low-Performance Company HR System Bottom 10% (42 firms)	High-Performance Company HR System Top 10% (43 firms)
Sample HR System HR Practices		
Number of qualified applicants per position (*Recruiting*)	8.24	36.55
Percentage hired based on a validated *selection* test	4.26	29.67
Percentage of jobs filled from within	34.90	61.46
Percentage in a *formal HR plan* including recruitment, *development*, and succession	4.79	46.72
Number of hours of *training* for new employees (less than 1 year)	35.02	116.87
Number of hours of *training* for experienced employees	13.40	72.00
Percentage of employees receiving a regular *performance appraisal*	41.31	95.17
Percentage of workforce whose *merit increase* or *incentive pay* is tied to performance	23.36	87.27
Percentage of workforce who received *performance feedback* from multiple sources (360)	3.90	51.67
Target percentile for total compensation (market rate = 50%)	43.03	58.67
Percentage of the workforce eligible for *incentive pay*	27.83	83.56
Percentage of difference in incentive pay between a low-performing and high-performing employee	3.62	6.21
Percentage of the workforce routinely working in a self-managed, *cross-functional*, or *project team*	10.64	42.28
Percentage of HR budget spent on *outsourced activities* (e.g., recruiting, benefits, payroll)	13.46	26.24
Number of employees per HR professional	253.88	139.51
Percentage of the eligible workforce covered by a union contract	30.00	8.98
Firm Performance		
Employee turnover	34.09	20.87
Sales per employee	$158,101	$617,576
Market value to book value	3.64	11.06

*Each of the variables in the "HR Outcomes" section is scaled from 1 to 6, where 1 = "not at all" and 6 = "to a very great extent."

Adapted from Becher et al., pp. 16–17.

requirements, in terms of the employee skills, attributes, and behaviors that HR must deliver to enable the business to achieve its strategic goals. (For example, must our employees dramatically improve the level of customer service?[31] Do we need more computer-literate employees to run our new machines?) Given these workforce requirements, HR management formulates *HR strategies, policies, and practices* aimed at achieving

Figure 3-9
Basic Model of How to Align HR Strategy and Actions with Business Strategy
Source: Adapted from Garrett Walker and J. Randal MacDonald, "Designing and Implementing an HR Scorecard," *Human Resources Management* 40, no. 4 (2001), p. 370.

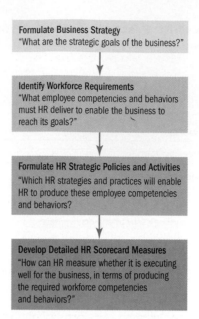

the desired workforce skills, attributes, and behaviors. (These may take the form of new selection, training, and compensation policies and practices, for instance.) Ideally, HR management then identifies "Scorecard" metrics it can use to measure the extent to which its new HR initiatives are supporting management's strategic goals.

HR Strategy in Action: An Example

An organizational change effort at the Albert Einstein Healthcare network (Einstein Medical) illustrates how companies formulate and use HR strategies to help execute their strategic plans.[32] In the early 1990s, it was apparent to Einstein's new CEO that intense competition, scientific and technological changes, the growth of managed care (HMOs and PPOs), and significant cuts in Medicare and Medicaid meant that his company needed a new strategic plan. At the time, Einstein Medical was a single acute care hospital, treating the seriously ill and infirm. His vision was to change Einstein into a comprehensive health care network providing a full range of high-quality services in various local markets.

The CEO knew that this strategic change would require numerous changes in Einstein Medical's organization and employee behaviors. Given the highly dynamic and uncertain health care environment of the 1990s, Einstein Medical would require a much more flexible, adaptable, and professional approach to delivering services. Based on that, he decided to summarize the goals of his change program in three words: "initiate," "adapt," and "deliver." To achieve Einstein Medical's strategic aims, its HR and other strategies would have to help the medical center and its employees to produce new services (initiate), capitalize on opportunities (adapt), and offer consistently high-quality services (deliver).

The CEO's next question was, "What sorts of employee competencies, skills, and behaviors would Einstein Medical need to produce these three outcomes?" Working with the HR head, the CEO chose four: Einstein employees would need to be "dedicated, accountable, generative, and resilient." They would have to be *dedicated* to Einstein's focus on initiate, adapt, and deliver. They would have to take personal *accountability* for their results. They would have to be *generative*, which means able and willing to apply new knowledge and skills in a constant search for innovative solutions. And they would have to be *resilient*, for instance, in terms of moving from job to job as the company's needs changed.

Given this, Einstein Medical's HR managers could ask, "What specific HR policies and practices would help Einstein create a dedicated, accountable, generative, and resilient workforce, and thereby help it to achieve its strategic goals?" The answer was to implement several new HR programs and practices. One was *training and communications programs* aimed at assuring that employees clearly understood the company's new vision and what it would require of all employees. *Enriching work* was another key HR initiative, and involved providing employees with more challenge and responsibility through flexible assignments and team-based work. Through new training and benefits programs, the company promoted *personal growth*, which meant helping employees take personal responsibility for their own improvement and personal development. Providing *commensurate returns* was another key HR strategy initiative; it involved tying employees' rewards to organizationwide results and providing nonmonetary rewards (such as more challenging jobs). Finally, improved selection, orientation, and dismissal procedures also helped Einstein build a more dedicated, resilient, accountable, and generative workforce.

 Illustrate and explain the steps in the HR Scorecard approach.

● THE HR SCORECARD APPROACH

Management ultimately judges the HR function based on whether it creates value for the company, where "value creation" means contributing in a measurable way to achieving the company's strategic goals. HR creates value by engaging in activities that produce the employee behaviors the company needs to achieve these strategic goals. Managers often use an **HR Scorecard** to measure the HR function's effectiveness and efficiency in producing these employee behaviors and thus in achieving the company's strategic goals. *The HR Scorecard is a concise measurement system. It shows the quantitative standards, or "metrics" the firm uses to measure HR activities, and to measure the employee behaviors resulting from these activities, and to measure the strategically relevant organizational outcomes of those employee behaviors. In so doing, it highlights, in a concise but comprehensive way, the causal link between the HR activities, and the emergent employee behaviors, and the resulting firmwide strategic outcomes and performance.*

Becker, Huselid, and Ulrich explain the need for such a measurement system this way:

> *In our view, the most potent action HR managers can take to ensure their strategic contribution is to develop a measurement system that convincingly showcases HR's impact on business performance. To design such a measurement system, HR managers must adopt a dramatically different perspective, one that focuses on how human resources can play a central role in implementing the firm's strategy. With a properly developed strategic HR architecture, managers throughout the firm can understand exactly how people create value and how to measure the value creation process.*[33]

Information for Creating an HR Scorecard

To create an HR Scorecard, the manager needs three types of information. First, he or she must know what the company's strategy is, because (as at Einstein Medical) the strategy will determine what the important employee behaviors and strategically important organizational outcomes are, and how the firm will measure organizational performance. Second, the manager must understand the causal links between the HR activities, the employee behaviors, the organizational outcomes, and the organization's performance. Figure 3-10 summarizes the basic relationships involved. Third, the manager must have **metrics** he or she can use to measure all the activities and results involved, specifically the HR activities, the emergent employee behaviors, the strategically relevant organizational outcomes, and the organizational performance.

HR scorecard
Measures the HR function's effectiveness and efficiency in producing employee behaviors needed to achieve the company's strategic goals.

metrics
Statistics used to measure the activities and results involved in a field.

**Figure 3-10
The Basic HR Scorecard
Relationships**

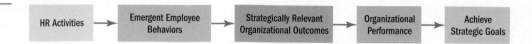

Using the HR Scorecard Approach

There are seven steps in using the HR Scorecard approach to create a strategic results oriented HR system (see Figure 3-11).[34] The seven steps are as follows:

Step 1: **Define the Business Strategy** Creating a strategy-oriented HR system starts by defining what the company's strategic plans are (such as, for Einstein Medical, expanding services and becoming a comprehensive health care network). Ideally, senior HR leaders' insights regarding the human resources in their own company and in those of the competition provide valuable planning input. Similarly, their insights regarding how HR practices and deliverables can improve the firm's performance can help top management develop a superior strategic plan. Toward the end of this stage, management translates its broad strategic plans into specific, actionable strategic goals.

Step 2: **Outline the Company's Value Chain** To achieve its strategic goals, any business must engage in certain strategically required activities. For example, Einstein Medical must devise and introduce new medical services. Microsoft must write new computer programs. Each such activity requires certain employee behaviors: Einstein Medical needs employees who have the expertise to help it devise new medical services, for instance. The point is this: any manager who wants to understand what employee behaviors are essential for his or her firm's success must first understand what the firm's required activities are.

value chain analysis
Identifying the primary activities that create value for customers and the related support activities.

For this, **value chain analysis** can be useful. The company's value chain "identifies the primary activities that create value for customers and the related support activities."[35] As Figure 3-12 illustrates, we can think of any business as consisting of a chain of crucial activities. Each activity is part of the process of designing, producing, marketing, and delivering the company's product or service. These activities might include bringing supplies and materials into the company's warehouse; bringing these materials to the shop floor and designing

**Figure 3-11
The Seven Steps in the HR
Scorecard Approach to
Formulating HR Policies,
Activities, and Strategies**
Source: Copyright © Gary Dessler, Ph.D.

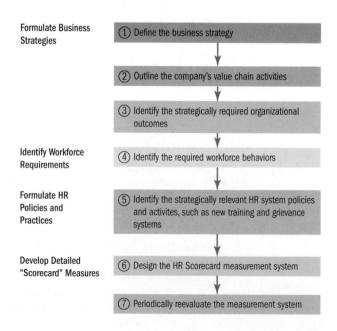

Figure 3-12
Simple Value Chain for "The Hotel Paris"
Source: Copyright © Gary Dessler, Ph.D.

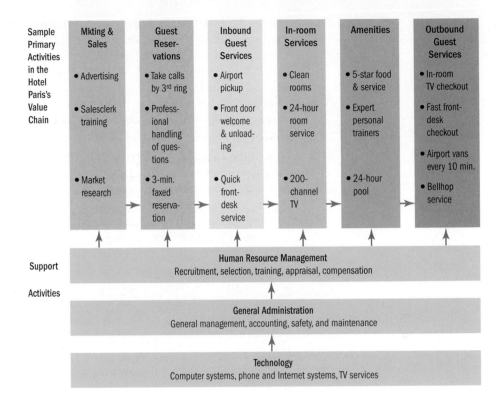

the product to customers' specifications; and the various marketing, sales, and distribution activities that attract customers and get the company's product to them. Outlining the company's value chain shows the chain of essential activities. This can help managers better understand the activities that drive performance in their company. In other words, it is a tool for identifying, isolating, visualizing, and analyzing the firm's most important activities and strategic costs.

Value chain analysis is more than just a tool for identifying the ways things are done now. It prompts questions such as: "How do our costs for this activity compare with our competitors?" "Is there some way we can gain a competitive advantage with this activity?" "Is there a more efficient way for us to deliver these services?" And, "Do we have to perform these services in-house?" Outlining and analyzing the company's value chain can also help the HR manager create an HR system that makes sense in terms of the firms' strategy. For example, it can help him or her identify the organizational outcomes the company absolutely must achieve if it is to achieve its strategic goals. (For example, at Einstein Medical, *delivering new services* was so critical to what they had to accomplish, it was obvious it had to be a core value chain activity.) This in turn can help the HR manager better understand what employee behaviors and competencies are required, and what HR policies and activities (HR system) would produce these behaviors and competencies.

Consider another example. At Dell Computer, "phone technicians competently and courteously assisting Dell customers with problems" is a crucial (or "core") value chain activity; indeed, it is a big part of what Dell has built its reputation on. The critical nature of this activity would be apparent from any outlining of Dell's value chain. Given this, Dell HR might well decide that, one way HR could add value is by improving phone technicians' performance through the use of special computerized job aids that show technicians what series of questions to ask when customers call in with problems.

Step 3: Identify the Strategically Required Organizational Outcomes Every company must produce critical, strategically relevant outcomes if it is to achieve its strategic goals. At Einstein Medical, *new services delivered* was one such required organizational outcome. At Dell, receiving *quick, competent, and courteous technical advice by phone* is one such outcome. Based on his or her understanding of how the company operates, and perhaps an analysis of the firm's value chain, the manager, in this step, now identifies and specifies the strategically relevant organizational outcomes.

Step 4: Identify the Required Workforce Competencies and Behaviors The question here is, "What employee competencies and behaviors must our employees exhibit if our company is to produce the strategically relevant organizational outcomes, and thereby achieve its strategic goals?" At Einstein Medical, employees had to take personal accountability for their results, and be willing to work proactively (be "generative") to find new and novel solutions.

Some strategic HR experts, notably Becher, Huselid, and Ulrich, refer to required workforce competencies and behaviors like these as *HR deliverables* (because the HR system's training and other activities can help to produce or "deliver" them). Competencies and behaviors such as personal accountability, working proactively, motivation, courteous behavior, and commitment produce strategically relevant organizational outcomes, and thereby drive organizational performance.

Step 5: Identify the Strategically Relevant HR System Policies and Activities Once the HR manager knows what the required employee competencies and behaviors are, he or she can turn to the task of identifying the HR activities and policies that will help to produce these employee competencies and behaviors. At Einstein Medical, *new services delivered* was one strategically relevant organizational outcome. To produce this outcome, Einstein's employees had to be willing to *work proactively to find new and novel solutions*, so this was one strategically relevant workforce competency/behavior. The question in step five is, "What HR system policies and activities will enable us to produce those workforce competencies and behaviors?" For Einstein Medical, the answer included special training programs and changing the compensation plan.

In this step, the important thing is to be specific. It is not enough to say, "We need new training programs, or disciplinary processes." Instead, the manager must now ask, "exactly what sorts of new training programs do we need, to produce the sorts of employee competencies and behaviors that we seek?" How and to what end should we change the disciplinary process? In this step, the HR manager must therefore become precise about the actual form and design of the firm's HR system. For example, all high-performing companies tend to use incentive pay. However, what precise form should the incentive plan take in this company? What specific behaviors do we want to encourage? Who will decide if the person gets the incentive pay? What percent of total pay should we base on incentives? In other words, to achieve improved organizational performance, HR management needs to *align* the HR system—the firm's HR policies and practices—with the company's specific strategic needs.

Step 6: Design the HR Scorecard Measurement System After choosing strategically required organizational outcomes, and employee competencies and behaviors, and specific HR system policies and activities, the question is, how shall we measure them all? For example, if we decide to "improve the disciplinary system," how precisely will the company measure such improvement? Perhaps in terms of number of grievances. If "higher morale" is one employee competency/behavior we want to improve, how will we measure higher morale? Perhaps with surveys that measure attitudes regarding satisfaction with supervision, and with pay.

Deciding on the proper measures or metrics requires considerable thought. For example, how exactly will we measure employee morale? What exactly constitutes a grievance? Table 3-2 presents some illustrative performance measures.

Measures like these serve two functions. First, to the extent that the manager can quantify each of these organizational outcomes, and the employee competencies, and the HR policies/activities, the measures can help the company and HR manager assess HR's performance, unambiguously and quantitatively. They make it clear whether and to what extent employee morale is up (or down), for instance. Second, they can help the HR manager to build a measurable and persuasive business case for how HR contributes to achieving the company's strategic financial goals. Hopefully, he or she will be able to show, quantitatively, how the firm's HR activities affect employee behavior, customer satisfaction, and therefore financial performance. In one recent study, 86% of HR professionals who responded said they expected measurement of the HR function to increase over the next two years, 62% said they already used metrics to assess HR performance, and 72% said they benchmark HR activities (particularly compensation and rewards, and equipment and retention, and performance appraisal) by comparing their results to other firms'.[36]

The *HR Scorecard* is crucial in this measurement process. As noted earlier, it is a visual and/or computerized model that shows the quantitative standards, or "metrics" the firm uses to measure HR activities, and to measure the employee behaviors resulting from these activities, and to measure the strategically relevant organizational outcomes of those employee behaviors. It highlights, in a concise but comprehensive way, the causal links between the HR activities, and the emergent employee behaviors, and the resulting firmwide strategic outcomes and performance. The HR Scorecard thus helps the HR manager demonstrate how HR contributes to the company's strategic and financial success. Several consulting firms provide Web-based services that make it easier to create HR Scorecards, based on metrics from best-practice, world-class firms.[37]

Step 7: Periodically Evaluate the Measurement System The HR manager cannot assume that the HR Scorecard's various measures (metrics) and links will always stay the same. Perhaps reducing grievances is not having the assumed effect on raising morale. Perhaps the company must drop some firmwide employee measures (such as front-desk customer service) and add new ones. Perhaps the measures the HR manager chose (such as number of grievances) are proving too hard to quantify. In any case, the HR manager should periodically evaluate measures and links, to make sure they are still valid.

The Hotel Paris International: An Example

Let us see how this seven-step process works by considering a fictitious company, the Hotel Paris International (Hotel Paris). Starting as a single hotel in a Paris suburb in 1990, the Hotel Paris now comprises a chain of nine hotels, with two in France, one each in London and Rome, and others in New York, Miami, Washington, Chicago, and Los Angeles. As a corporate strategy, the Hotel Paris's management and owners want to continue to expand geographically. They believe doing so will let them capitalize on their reputation for good service, by providing multicity alternatives for their satisfied guests. The problem is, their reputation for good service has been deteriorating. If they cannot improve service, it would be unwise for them to expand, since their guests might actually prefer other hotels after trying the Hotel Paris.

Sample measures for assessing employee competencies and behaviors, such as employee motivation and morale, and for assessing HR activities.
Employee attitude survey results
Employee turnover
Extent to which strategy is clearly articulated and well understood throughout the firm
Extent to which the average employee understands how his or her job contributes to the firm's success
Level of cross-cultural teamwork
Level of organizational learning
Extent to which employees are clear about their own goals
Percentage of employees making suggestions
Employee productivity
Requests for transfer to supervisor
Extent to which the employees can describe the company's core values
Employee commitment survey scores
Customer complaints/praise
Percentage of retention of high-performing key employees
Requests for transfer per employees
Percentage of employees making suggestions
Sample measures for assessing HR system activities such as testing, training, and reward policies and practices
Proportion of employees selected based on validated selection methods
Number of hours of training employees receive each year
Proportion of merit pay determined by formal performance appraisal
Percentage of workforce regularly assessed via a formal performance appraisal
Percentage of employees eligible for annual merit cash or incentive plans
Extent to which information is communicated effectively to employees
Percentage of workforce who received a performance feedback from multiple sources
Percentage of difference in incentive pay between the low-performing and high-performing employees
Percentage of the workforce routinely working in self-managed or cross-functional or project teams
Number of qualified applicants per position
Percentage of jobs filled from within

Source: Adapted from Brian Becker, Mark Huselid, and Dave Ulrich, *The HR Scorecard* (Boston: Harvard Business School Press, 2001), pp. 16–17, 63, 64, 66, 71.

A hotel's reputation for good service depends on choosing and training the right employees. Adi Dor, rooms control clerk at the New York Marriott, Brooklyn, personifies good service, hospitality, and a welcoming attitude as he greets a guest. It takes a well-thought out HR effort to create employee competencies and behaviors like these.

The Strategy   Top management, with input from the HR and other managers, and with the board of directors' approval, chooses a new competitive strategy and formulates new strategic goals. They decide: "The Hotel Paris International will use superior guest services to differentiate the Hotel Paris properties, and to thereby increase the length of stays and the return rate of guests, and thus boost revenues and profitability." All Hotel Paris managers—including the director of HR services—must now formulate strategies that support this competitive strategy.

The Value Chain   Based on discussions with other managers, the HR director, Lisa Cruz, outlines the company's value chain (see Figure 3-12, page 89). This should help her to identify those HR activities that are crucial in helping the hotel achieve its strategic goals. In a service business, the "product" is satisfied guests. Producing satisfied guests requires attending to all those activities along the Hotel Paris's value chain where the company has an opportunity to affect the guests' experiences. For the Hotel Paris, there are *inbound logistics activities* such as getting the guest from the airport and checked in. There are *operations activities* such as cleaning the guest's room. There are *outbound logistics* activities such as picking up baggage and getting the person checked out and to his or her plane. There are *marketing and sales activities* aimed at attracting guests to the hotel. There are *service activities* that provide post-stay services, such as travel awards to guests for multiple stays. And there are various *support activities*, such as purchasing, information systems, and HR.

The Strategically Required Organizational Outcomes   The Hotel Paris's basic strategy is to use superior guest services to expand geographically. Each step in the hotel's value chain provides opportunities for improving guest service. For HR director Lisa Cruz, reviewing the hotel's value chain activities makes it clear that achieving the hotel's strategic aims means achieving a number of required organizational outcomes. For examples, Lisa and her management colleagues must take steps that produce fewer customer complaints and more written compliments, more frequent guest returns and longer stays, and higher guest expenditures per visit.

The Strategically Relevant Workforce Competencies and Behaviors

The question facing Lisa, then, is this: What are the competencies and behaviors that our hotel's employees will have to exhibit, if we are to produce required organizational outcomes such as fewer customer complaints, more compliments, and more frequent guest returns? Thinking through the sorts of activities that occur at each step in the hotel's value chain helps Lisa answer that question. For example, the hotel's required employee competencies and behaviors would include, "high-quality front-desk customer service," "taking calls for reservations in a friendly manner," "greeting guests at the front door," and "processing guests' room service meals efficiently." All require motivated, high-morale employees.

The Strategically Relevant HR System Policies and Activities

The HR manager's task now is to identify and specify the HR policies and activities that will enable the hotel to produce these crucial workforce competencies and behaviors. As one example, "high-quality front-desk customer service" is one such required behavior. From this, the HR director identifies HR activities to produce such front-desk customer service efforts. For example, she decides to *institute practices to improve the disciplinary fairness and justice in the company*, with the aim of *improving employee morale*. Her assumption is that enhanced fairness will produce higher morale and that higher morale will produce improved front-desk service.

The HR Scorecard

Next, the HR director creates an HR Scorecard. This shows the cause-and-effect links among the HR activities, the workforce behaviors, and the organizational outcomes (Figure 3-13 shows the overall HR Scorecard for the Hotel Paris).

This scorecard and its linkages reflect certain assumptions on Lisa's part. For example, based on experience and discussions with the firm's other managers, she formulates the following *hypothesis* about how HR affects hotel performance: Improved grievance procedures cause improved morale, which leads to improved front-desk service, which leads to increased guest returns, which leads to improved financial performance. The HR director then chooses metrics to measure each of these factors. For example, she decides to measure "improved disciplinary procedures" in terms of how many grievances employees submit each month. She measures "improved morale" in terms of "scores on our hotel's semiannual attitude survey," and measures "high-quality front-desk customer service" in terms of "customer complaints per month."

She moves on to quantifying the cause-and-effect links among these measures. For example: "Can we show top management that there is a measurable, sequential link between improved disciplinary procedures, high morale, improved front-desk service, number of guest return visits, and hotel financial performance (revenues and profits)? If she can show such links, she has a persuasive case that shows HR's measurable contribution to the hotel's bottom-line financial performance.

In practice, the HR manager may have to rely on a largely subjective but logical argument to make the case for the cause-and-effect linkages. But ideally, she will use statistical methods such as correlation analysis to determine if links exist, and (if so) what their magnitudes are. In this way, she might find, for instance, that a 10% improvement in grievance rates is associated with an almost 20% improvement in morale. Similarly, a 20% improvement in morale is associated with a 30% reduction in customer front-desk complaints. Furthermore, a 30% reduction in complaints is associated with a 20% increase in guest return visits, and a 20% increase in return rate is associated with a 6% rise in hotel revenues. It would appear that a relatively small HR effort in reducing grievances might have a considerable effect on this hotel's bottom line!

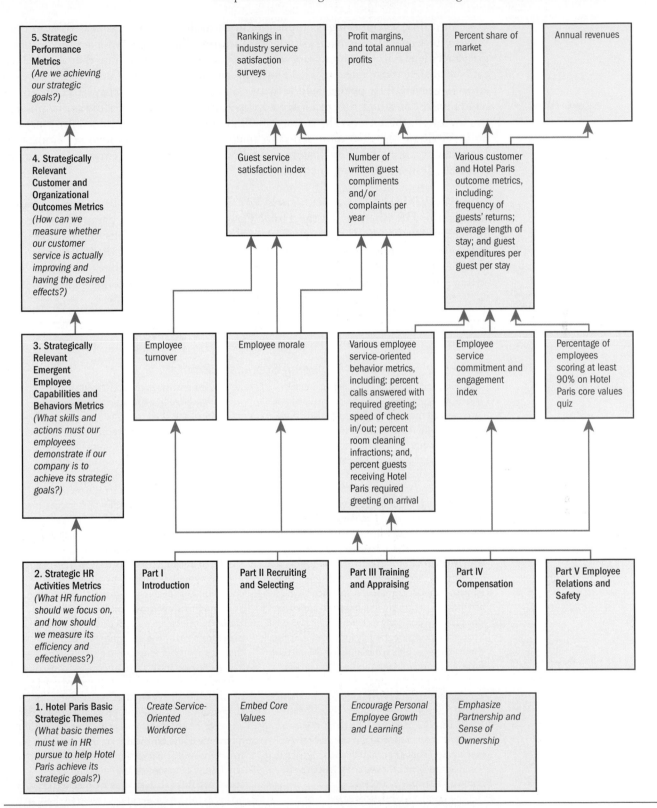

Figure 3-13
HR Scorecard for Hotel Paris International Corporation

Note: An abbreviated example showing selected HR practices and outcomes aimed at implementing the competitive strategy, "To use superior guest services to differentiate the Hotel Paris properties and thus increase the length of stays and the return rate of guests, and thus boost revenues and profitability and help the firm expand geographically.

In reality, several things complicate this measurement process. It is risky to draw cause–effect conclusions from correlation measures like these (for example do fewer grievances lead to higher morale, or vice-versa?). Furthermore, it's rare that a single factor (such as grievance rates) will have such effects alone, so we may want to measure the effects of several HR policies and activities on morale simultaneously. And (given the huge number of things that influence hotel performance) it may not always be possible to confirm all the links in the measurement chain. If not, the HR manager must rely more on logic and common sense to make her case. The following "Improving Productivity Through HRIS" feature shows how computerized systems can facilitate the scorecard design and management activities.

How We Will Use the Hotel Paris HR Scorecard   In reality, computerization enables the HR director for the Hotel Paris to create a more comprehensive HR Scorecard than the one in Figure 3-13, one that might show links among dozens of cause-and-effect metrics. For example, with computerization, the HR director need not limit herself to assessing the effects of the handful of employee behaviors (such as percentage of calls answered on time) in Figure 3-13. Instead, she could include metrics

Improving Productivity Through HRIS

Software Systems for Managing Scorecard Programs

Designing, executing, and managing an HR Scorecard containing dozens or hundreds of interrelated metrics can be challenging, and possibly futile. After all, what is the use of having all of these interrelated metrics (such as number of training hours per employee per year, employee morale, and guest satisfaction) if the company's top management can't monitor all the metrics on an ongoing basis, and take corrective action when something seems amiss? That is why many companies use special scorecard software systems to improve the productivity and effectiveness of their scorecard programs.

Most of this software, at the current time, aims to support companies' "balanced scorecard" programs. The *balanced scorecard* does for the company as a whole what the HR Scorecard does for the HR function. Specifically, the balanced scorecard is a management tool, usually a computerized model, that tracks a multitude of performance measures simultaneously and shows their interactions across the company—not just those related to HR. Thus, on a companywide basis, the firm's balanced scorecard would track all of the HR, marketing, production, and finance metrics that top management believes contribute to the company's strategic success.

The company's HR scorecard is one element of the company's overall balanced scorecard. The balanced scorecard also addresses non-HR-related activities metrics, including those in production management, marketing, and finance.

Again, managing a scorecard program can be futile unless management computerizes the scorecard itself. Several companies provide balanced scorecard software. For example, ActiveStrategy (www.activestrategy.com) provides a software system which it calls the Balanced Scorecard Dashboard Edition. It calls it the "dashboard" because top management can monitor their scorecard metrics' real-time results in a manner similar to how you might monitor your car's dashboard. Changes in speed or fuel level might suggest to you that you need to slow down, or stop for gas. Similarly, the balanced scorecard "dashboard" provides a real-time computer screen readout that top management can use to monitor their firm's metrics and to make changes as required.

ActiveStrategy's balanced scorecard software provides a basic system that management can use to create and manage its scoreboard system. For example, it provides the basis for quickly creating a scorecard, and for measuring the metrics' trends, as well as personalized user views (so employees can monitor the sections of the scorecard that relate to their own efforts). It even provides for e-mail alert notification to draw an employee's attention to the fact that his or her metrics may be trending in the wrong way.

covering the full range of HR activities, from recruitment and selection through training, appraisal, compensation, and labor relations. Her HR Scorecard model could also show the effects of all these activities on a wide range of workforce competencies and behaviors, and thus on organizational outcomes, and on the company's performance. In this way, her HR Scorecard would become a comprehensive model representing the value-adding effects of the full range of Hotel Paris HR activities.

We will use an "HR Scorecard" feature in each chapter to show how the Hotel Paris's HR director uses the concepts and techniques from that chapter to create an HR system that helps the Hotel Paris achieve its strategic goals. Table 3-3 presents some of the metrics the director could use to measure HR activities. For example, she could endeavor to improve workforce competencies and behaviors by instituting (as per Chapter 5) improved recruitment processes, and measure the latter in terms of "number of qualified applicants per position." Similarly, she may recommend to management that they change the firm's pay policies (see Chapter 11) so that the "target percentile for total compensation is in the top 25%," and show that doing so will have favorable effects on employee morale, employee customer service behavior, customer satisfaction, and the hotel chain's performance. In practice, all the HR functions we discuss in this book influence employee competencies and behaviors, and, thereby, organizational outcomes and performance.

Table 3-3

Examples of HR System Activities the Hotel Paris Can Measure as Related to Each Chapter in This Book

Chapter	Strategic Activities Metrics
2. EEOC	Number EEOC claims/year; cost of HR-related litigation; % minority/women promotions
3. Strategy	% employees who can quote company strategy/vision
4. Job Analysis	% employees with updated job descriptions
5. Recruiting	Number applicants per recruiting source; number qualified applicants/position
6. Testing	% employees hired based on validated employment test
7. Interview	% applicants receiving structured interview
8. Training	Number hours training/employee/year; number hours training new employee
9. Appraisal	Number employees getting feedback; % appraisals completed on time
10. Career Mgmt.	% employees with formal career/development plan
11. Compensation	Target percentile for total compensation (pay in top 25%)
12. Incentives	% workforce eligible for merit pay
13. Benefits	% employees 80% satisfied with benefits
14. Ethics	Number grievances/year; % employees able to quote ethics code
15. Labor Relations	% workforce in unions
16. Health and Safety	Number safety training programs/year; $ accident costs/year; hours lost time due to accidents
17. Global	% expatriates receiving predeparture screening, counseling
Overall HR Metrics	HR cost/employee; HR expense/total expenses; turnover costs

→ *Review*

SUMMARY

1. In formulating their HR strategies, HR managers must address three basic challenges: the need to support corporate productivity and performance improvement efforts; the fact that employees play an expanded role in the employer's performance improvement efforts; and the fact that HR must be more involved in designing—not just executing—the company's strategic plan.

2. There are six basic steps in the strategic management process: Define the business and its mission; perform an external and internal audit; translate the mission into strategic goals; formulate a strategy to achieve the strategic goals; implement the strategy; and evaluate performance.

3. There are three main types of strategic plans. The company's corporate-level strategy identifies the portfolio of businesses that in total comprise the company and includes diversification, vertical integration, consolidation, and geographic expansion. Each business needs a business level/competitive strategy: Differentiation and cost leadership are two examples. Finally, each individual business is composed of departments that require functional strategies. The latter identify the basic courses of action each department will pursue in order to help the business attain its strategic goals.

4. A strategy is a course of action. It shows how the enterprise will move from the business it is in now to the business it wants to be in, given its opportunities and threats and its internal strengths and weaknesses.

5. Strategic human resource management means formulating and executing HR systems that produce the employee competencies and behaviors the company requires to achieve its strategic aims.

6. The high-performance work system is designed to maximize the overall quality of human capital throughout the organization, and provides a set of benchmarks against which today's HR manager can compare the structure, content, and efficiency and effectiveness of his or her HR system.

7. The basic process of aligning HR strategies and actions with business strategy entails four steps: Formulate the business strategy; identify the workforce (employee) behaviors needed to produce the outcomes that will help the company achieve its strategic goals; formulate HR strategic policies and actions to produce these employee behaviors; and develop measures (metrics) to evaluate the HR department's performance.

8. The HR Scorecard approach to creating a strategy-oriented HR system includes seven steps: Define the business strategy; outline the company's value chain; identify the strategically required organizational outcomes; identify the required workforce competencies and behaviors; identify the strategically relevant HR system policies and activities; design the HR Scorecard measurement system; and periodically evaluate the measurement system.

9. The HR Scorecard is a concise measurement system that shows the quantitative standards the firm uses to measure HR activities, to measure the employee behaviors resulting from these activities, and to measure the strategically relevant organizational outcomes of those employee behaviors.

DISCUSSION QUESTIONS

1. What is the difference between a strategy, a vision, and a mission? Please give one example of each.

2. Define and give at least two examples of the cost leadership competitive strategy and the differentiation competitive strategy.

3. Explain how HR can be instrumental in helping a company create a competitive advantage.

4. What is a high-performance work system? Provide several specific examples of the elements in a high-performance work system.

5. Define what an HR Scorecard is, and briefly explain each of the seven steps in the HR Scorecard approach to creating a strategy-oriented HR system.

INDIVIDUAL AND GROUP ACTIVITIES

1. With three or four other students, form a strategic management group for your college or university. Your assignment is to develop the outline of a strategic plan for the college or university. This should include such things as mission and vision statements; strategic goals; and corporate, competitive, and functional strategies. In preparing your plan, make

sure to show the main strengths, weaknesses, opportunities, and threats the college faces, and which prompted you to develop your particular strategic plans.

2. Using the Internet or library resources, analyze the annual reports of five companies. Bring to class examples of how those companies say they are using their HR processes to help the company achieve its strategic goals.

3. Interview an HR manager and write a short report on the topic: "The strategic roles of the HR manager at XYZ Company."

4. Using the Internet or library resources, bring to class and discuss at least two examples of how companies are using an HR Scorecard to help create HR systems that support the company's strategic aims. Do all managers seem to mean the same thing when they refer to "HR Scorecards"? How do they differ?

5. The HRCI "Test Specifications" appendix at the end of this book (pages 685–689) lists the things someone studying for the HRCI certification exam needs to know in each area of human resource management (such as in Strategic Management, Workforce Planning, and Human Resource Development). In groups of four to five students, do four things: (1) review that appendix now; (2) identify the material in this chapter that relates to the required knowledge the appendix lists; (3) write four multiple choice exam questions on this material that you believe would be suitable for inclusion in the HRCI exam; and (4) if time permits, have someone from your team post your team's questions in front of the class, so the students in other teams can take each others' exam questions.

EXPERIENTIAL EXERCISE

Developing an HR Scorecard

Purpose: The purpose of this exercise is to give you experience in developing an HR Scorecard, by developing one for your college.

Required Understanding: You should understand the "HR Scorecard approach to creating a strategy-oriented HR system" and in particular, the seven steps in that process.

How to Set Up the Exercise/Instructions: Set up groups of three to four students for this exercise. Using whatever sources are avail-

able, including personal interviews with college administrators, each group should outline an HR Scorecard for your college by addressing each of the seven steps in the process, starting with a short definition of the business strategy for the college. Show the expected linkages among HR activities, employee behaviors, and college outcomes and performance, as well as examples of metrics you'll use to measure each.

APPLICATION CASE

Siemens Builds a Strategy-Oriented HR System

Siemens is a 150-year-old German company, but it's not the company it was even a few years ago. Until recently, Siemens focused on producing electrical products. Today the firm has diversified into software, engineering, and services, and is also global, with over 400,000 employees working in 190 countries. In other words, Siemens became a world leader by pursuing a corporate strategy that emphasized diversifying into high-tech products and services, and doing so on a global basis.

With a corporate strategy like that, global HR plays a big role at Siemens. Sophisticated engineering and services require more focus on employee selection, training, and compensation than in the average firm, and globalization requires delivering these services globally. Siemens sums up the basic themes of its HR strategy in several points. These include:

1. *A living Company is a learning Company.* The high-tech nature of Siemens's business means that employees must be able to learn on a continuing basis. Siemens uses its system

of combined classroom and hands-on apprenticeship training around the world to help facilitate this. It also offers employees extensive continuing education and management development.

2. *Global teamwork is the key to developing and using all the potential of the firm's human resources.* Because it is so important for employees throughout Siemens to feel free to work together and interact, employees have to understand the whole process, not just bits and pieces. To support this, Siemens provides extensive training and development. It also ensures that all employees feel they're part of a strong, unifying corporate identity. For example, HR uses cross-border, cross-cultural experiences as prerequisites for career advances.

3. *A climate of mutual respect is the basis of all relationships— within the Company and with society.* Siemens contends that the wealth of nationalities, cultures, languages, and outlooks

represented by its employees is one of its most valuable assets. It therefore engages in numerous HR activities aimed at building openness, transparency, and fairness, and supporting diversity.

Questions

1. Based on the information in this case, provide examples, for Siemens, of at least four strategically required organiza-tional outcomes, and four required workforce competencies and behaviors.

2. Identify at least four strategically relevant HR system policies and activities that Siemens has instituted in order to help HR contribute to achieving Siemens' strategic goals.

3. Provide a brief illustrative outline of an HR Scorecard for Siemens.

CONTINUING CASE

The Carter Cleaning Company: The High Performance Work System

As a recent graduate and person who keeps up with the business press, Jennifer is familiar with the benefits of programs such as total quality management and high-performance work systems.

Jack has actually installed a total quality program of sorts at Carter, and it has been in place for about five years. This program takes the form of employee meetings. Jack holds employee meetings periodically, but particularly when there is a serious problem in a store—such as poor-quality work or machine breakdowns. When problems like these arise, instead of trying to diagnose them himself or with Jennifer, he contacts all the employees in that store and meets with them as soon as the store closes. Hourly employees get extra pay for these meetings. The meetings have been fairly useful in helping Jack to identify and rectify several problems. For example, in one store all the fine white blouses were coming out looking dingy. It turned out that the cleaner-spotter had been ignoring the company rule that required cleaning ("boiling down") the perchloroethylene cleaning fluid before washing items like these. As a result, these fine white blouses were being washed in cleaning fluid that had residue from other, earlier washes.

Jennifer now wonders whether these employee meetings should be expanded to give the employees an even bigger role in managing the Carter stores' quality. "We can't be everywhere watching everything all the time," she said to her father. "Yes, but these people only earn about $8 per hour. Will they really want to act like mini-managers?" he replied.

Questions

1. Would you recommend that the Carters expand their quality program? If so, specifically what form should it take?

2. Assume the Carters want to institute a high-performance work system as a test program in one of their stores. Write a one-page outline summarizing what such a program would consist of.

KEY TERMS

strategic plan, 72
strategic management, 73
vision, 74
mission, 74
SWOT analysis, 74
strategy, 75

strategic control, 76
competitive advantage, 76
leveraging, 78
strategic human resource
  management, 80
HR Scorecard, 87

metrics, 87
value chain analysis, 88

ENDNOTES

1. "Human Resource Goes High-Tech: The 1999 HR Technology Conference and Exposition," *BNA Bulletin to Management*, October 14, 1999, pp. S1–S2.

2. James Higgins and Julian Vincze, *Strategic Management* (Fort Worth, TX: The Dryden Press, 1993), p. 5.

3. Warren Bennis and Bert Manus, *Leaders: The Strategies for Taking Charge* (New York: Harper & Row, 1985), quoted in Andrew Campbell and Sally Yeung, "Mission, Vision and Strategic Intent," *Long-Range Planning* 24, no. 4, p. 145. See also James M. Lucas, "Anatomy of a Vision Statement," *Management Review*, February 1998, pp. 22–26.

4. Melanie Warner, "The Young and the Loaded," *Fortune*, September 27, 1999, pp. 78–118.

5. See George Morrisey, *A Guide to Strategic Planning* (San Francisco: Jossey-Bass, 1996), p. 7.

6. Ibid., 8.

7. David Pringle, "CEO, Marking a Decade, Faces Struggling, Quickly Changing Industry," *Wall Street Journal*, January 23, 2002, p. B70.
8. Danny Hakim, "With Hughes Sale, GM Buries a Discarded Strategy," *New York Times*, October 30, 2001, p. C8.
9. Julian Barnes, "Proctor Plans to Jettison Jif and Crisco," *New York Times*, April 26, 2001, p. C1.
10. Paul Nutt, "Making Strategic Choices," *Journal of Management Studies*, January 2002, pp. 67–96.
11. Michael Porter, *Competitive Strategy* (New York: The Free Press, 1980), p. 14.
12. David Upton, "What Really Makes Factories Flexible?" *Harvard Business Review*, July–August 1995, pp. 74–86.
13. Ibid., p. 75.
14. Charles Greer, *Strategy and Human Resources*, (Upper Saddle River, NJ: Prentice Hall, 1995) p. 105.
15. Catherine Truss and Lynda Gratton, "Strategic Human Resource Management: A Conceptual Approach," *International Journal of Human Resource Management* 5, no. 3 (September 1994), p. 663.
16. Although still largely nonunionized, FedEx's pilots did vote to join the Airline Pilots Union.
17. "More on What CEOs Want from HR," *HR Focus* 80, no. 4 (April 2003), p. 5.
18. Bill Leonard, "GM Drives HR to the Next Level," *HR Magazine*, March 2002, p. 48.
19. "The New HR Agenda: 2002 Human Resource Competencies Study, Executive Summary," University of Michigan Business School (May 2003).
20. Jeffrey Schmidt, "The Correct Spelling of M&A Begins with HR," *HR Magazine*, June 2001, pp. 102–108.
21. "Strategic HR Means Translating Plans into Action," *HR Magazine* 48, no. 3 (March 2003), p. 8.
22. Steve Bates, "No Experience Necessary? Many Companies are Putting non-HR Executives in Charge of HR with Mixed Results," *HR Magazine* 46, no. 11 (November 2001), pp. 34–41.
23. "The New HR Agenda: 2002 Human Resource Competencies Study, Executive Summary," University of Michigan Business School (May 2003), 6.
24. William Henn, "What the Strategist Asks from Human Resources," *Human Resource Planning* 8, no. 4 (1985), p. 195, quoted in Greer, *Strategy and Human Resources*, pp. 117–118.
25. Samuel Greengard, "You're Next! There's No Escaping Merger Mania!" *Workforce*, April 1997, pp. 52–62.
26. Greer, op cit., p. 117
27. Brian Becker, Mark Huselid, and Dave Ulrich, *The HR Scorecard: Linking People, Strategy, and Performance* (Boston: Harvard Business School Press, 2001).
28. Alexander Colvin et al., "How High-Performance Human Resource Practices and Workforce Unionization Affect Managerial Pay," *Personnel Psychology* 54 (2001), pp. 903–934 (906).
29. Robert McNabb and Keith Whitfield, "Job Evaluation and High-Performance Work Practices: Compatible or Conflictual?" *Journal of Management Studies* 38, no. 2 (March 2001), p. 294.
30. "With High-Performance Work Organizations, Adversaries No More," *Work & Family Newsbrief*, August 2003, p. 5.
31. Garrett Walker and J. Randal MacDonald, "Designing and Implementing an HR Scorecard," *Human Resource Management* 40, no. 4 (2001), pp. 365–377.
32. Richard Shafer et al., "Crafting a Human Resource Strategy to Foster Organizational Agility: A Case Study," *Human Resource Management* 40, no. 3 (Fall 2001), pp. 197–211.
33. Quoted in Bill Macalear and Jones Shannon, "Does HR Planning Improve Business Performance?" *Industrial Management*, January/February 2003, p. 20.
34. This section is adapted in part from Becker, Huselid, and Ulrich, *The HR Scorecard: Linking People, Strategy, and Performance*.
35. Arthur Thompson, Jr. and A. J. Strickland III, *Strategic Management: Concepts and Cases* (New York: McGraw-Hill, 2001), pp. 129–131.
36. "Creating the HR Scorecard, Preliminary Findings from the Business Intelligence Report," www.business-intelligence.co.uk/hrscorecard (2001).
37. *Human Resource Department Management Report* (December 2002), p. 8; "Watson Wyatt Worldwide Creates the HR Scorecard Alliance," *InfoTrac*, downloaded September 19, 2003.

APPENDIX FOR CHAPTER 3

Establishing and Computerizing Human Resource Systems

Introduction

"The devil is in the details" someone once said, and this is certainly true with respect to designing an HR system. The HR manager may talk in broad terms about the recruiting, selection, and other HR functions he or she wants to install. But, eventually, creating the HR system requires translating the HR manager's broad preferences (for "a selection program that produces more qualified candidates," for instance) into specific, "how exactly will we do this" policies, guidelines, tools, and paperwork or computerized processes. This means actually creating the infrastructure of the HR system.

Doing so is not easy. Consider the paperwork required to breathe life into a company's HR system. Just

to start with, recruiting and hiring an employee might require a Notice of Available Position, a Help Wanted Advertising Listing, an Employment Application, an Interviewing Checklist, various verifications—of education, and immigration status, for instance—and a Telephone Reference Checklist. You'd then need an Employment Agreement, Confidentiality and Non-compete Agreements, and an Employer Indemnity Agreement. To process that new employee you might need a Hiring Authorization Form, an Employee Background Verification, a New Employee Checklist, and various forms for withholding tax and to obtain new employee data. And to keep track of the employee once on board, you'd need—just to start—an Employee Changes Form, Personnel Data Sheet, Daily and Weekly Time Records, an Hourly Employee's Weekly Time Sheet, an Overtime Permit, an Expense Report, a Vacation Request, an Absence Request, an Affirmative Action Summary, and an EEO Policy Statement and Analysis of Promotions. Then come the performance appraisal forms, a Critical Incidents Report, Notice of Probation, First (or Second) Warning Notice Form, a Disciplinary Notice, a New Employee Evaluation, a Performance Evaluation, and a Letter of Commendation, and (eventually) a Retirement Checklist, Notice of Dismissal, Reduction in Workforce Notice, Employee Check-out Record, Separation Notice, and Employment Reference Response.

In this Appendix, we'll see that the preceding list barely scratches the surface of the policies, procedures, and paperwork you'll need to run the HR system part of your business. This has several implications. First, you obviously can't wing it. Perhaps with just one or two employees you could keep track of everything in your head, or just write a separate memo for each HR action, and place it in a manilla folder for each worker. But with more than a few employees you'll need to create a human resource system comprised of standardized forms.

Very small firms can handle all or most of this sort of HR record keeping through manual paper and pencil forms and systems. But as the company grows, various parts of the HR system—payroll, or appraising, for instance—will have to be computerized if the firm is to remain competitive. (After all, you probably don't want to spend twice as much money and time on HR as do your competitors.) We'll cover manual and computerized HR systems in this Appendix.

Basic Components of Manual HR Systems

Very small employers (say, with 10 employees or less) will probably start with a manual HR system. From a practical point of view, this generally means obtaining and organizing a set of standardized personnel forms covering each important aspect of the HR—recruitment, selection, training, appraisal, compensation, safety process—as well as some means for organizing all this information for each of your employees.

The number of forms you could conceivably need even for a small firm is quite large. This is illustrated by the menu of forms shown in Table A-1, which is adapted from the Table of Contents of a compilation of HR agreements and forms.[1] A reasonable way to obtain the basic component forms of a manual HR system is to start with a compilation of forms book like that one. Another exam-

ple is James Jenks, *The Hiring, Firing (and Everything in Between) Personnel Forms Book* (Ridgefield, CT: Roundlake Publishing, 1996). The forms you want can then be adapted from these sources for your particular situation. Office supply stores (such as Office Depot and Office Max) also sell packages of personnel forms. For example, Office Depot sells packages of individual personnel forms as well as a "Human Resource Kit" containing 10 copies of each of the following: Application, Employment Interview, Reference Check, Employee Record, Performance Evaluation, Warning Notice, Exit Interview and Vacation Request, plus a Lawsuit-Prevention Guide.[2] Also available (and highly recommended) is a package of Employee Record Folders. Use the folders to maintain a file on each individual employee; on the outside of the pocket is printed a form for recording information such as name, start date, company benefits, and so on.

Several direct-mail catalog companies similarly offer a variety of HR materials. For example, HRdirect (100 Enterprise Place, Dover, DE, 19901, phone: 1-800-346-1231) offers packages of personnel forms including ones to be used for: Short- and Long-Form Employee Applications, Applicant Interviews, Mail Reference Checking, Employee Performance Reviews, Job Descriptions, Exit Interviews, Absentee Calendars and Reports, and Sexual Harassment Charge Investigation forms. Various legal-compliance forms including standardized No Weapons Policy, Harassment Policy, FMLA Notice forms, as well as posters (for instance, covering legally required postings for matters such as the Americans with Disabilities Act and Occupational Safety and Health Act) are similarly available.

G. Neil Company of Sunrise, Florida (phone: 1-800-999-9111), is another direct-mail catalog personnel materials source. In addition to a complete line of personnel forms, documents, and posters, it also offers manual paper-based systems for keeping track of matters such as attendance history, conducting job analyses, and for tracking vacation requests and safety records. A complete HR "start-up" kit is available containing 25 copies of each of the following basic components of a manual HR system: Long Form Application for Employment; Attendance History; Performance Appraisal; Payroll/Status Change Notice; Absence Report; Vacation Request & Approval; W-4 Form; I-9 Form; New Employee Data Records; Separation Notice; Interview Evaluation; Self-Appraisal; Weekly Time Sheets; Accident/Illness Report; Exit Interview; Pre-Employment Phone Reference Check; Employee Warning Notice; Performance Appraisal-Exempt Positions; and tabbed dividers, all organized in a file box.

Table A-1 **Personnel Forms**

Section 1

Recruiting and Selecting

Notice of Available Position	Employment Application Disclaimer and Acknowledgement	Request for Reference
Help Wanted Advertising Listing		Request for Transcript
Bonus for Employee Referral	Applicant Waiver	Verification of Education
Employee Referral Request	Authorization to Release Information	Verification of Employment
Prospective Employee Referral	Medical Testing Authorization	Verification of Licensure
Applicant Referral Program	Applicant Interview Schedule	Verification of Military Status
Job Bid	Rescheduled Appointment	Unsuccessful Candidate Letter
Resume Acknowledgement	Interviewing Checklist	Applicant Rejection Letter 1
Applicant Acknowledgement	Applicant Rating	Applicant Rejection Letter 2
Acknowledgement of Reference	Clerical Applicant Rating	Applicant Notification
Applicant Interview Confirmation	Applicant Interview Summary	Applicant Reply
Preliminary Employment Application	Applicant Comparison Summary	No Decision on Hiring
Veteran/Handicapped Status	Telephone Reference Checklist	Employment Confirmation
Employment Application	Medical Records Request	

Section 2

Employment Agreements

Independent Contractor's Agreement	Polygraph Examination Consent Form	General Non-Compete Agreement
Employment Agreement	Agreement to Accept Night Work	Non-Compete Agreement (Accounts)
Addendum to Employment Agreement	Expense Recovery Agreement	Non-Compete Agreement (Area)
Agreement with Sales Representative	Agreement on Inventions and Patents	Non-Disclosure of Trade Secrets
Letter Extending Sales Representative Agreement	Agreement on Proprietary Rights	Acknowledgement of Temporary Employment
Change in Terms of Sales Representative Agreement	Employees Agreement on Confidentiality Data	Employer Indemnity Agreement
Conflict of Interest Declaration	Confidentiality Agreement	Employee Indemnity Agreement
Consent for Drug/Alcohol Screen Testing	Employee's Covenants	Waiver of Liability
	Employee Secrecy Agreement	

Section 3

Processing New Employees

Rehire Form	New Personnel Checklist	Employee File
Hiring Authorization	Employee Agreement and Handbook Acknowledgement	New Employee Data
Relocation Expense Approval		Emergency Phone Numbers
Letter to New Employee 1	Job Description	Established Workday and Workweek Schedules and Policies
Letter to New Employee 2	Emergency Procedures	
Letter to New Employee 3	Summary of Employment Terms	Consent for Drug/Alcohol Screening
Letter to New Employee 4	Payroll Deduction Authorization	Receipt for Company Property
New Employee Announcement	Payroll Deduction Direct Deposit Authorization	Samples and Documents Receipt
Employee Background Verification		EEO Analysis of New Hires
New Employee Orientation Checklist	Direct Deposit Authorization	
New Employee Checklist	Withholding Tax Information	*(continued)*

Table A-1 Personnel Forms (continued)

Section 4

Personnel Management

Employment Record	Department Overtime Report	Employee Absence Report
Personnel Data Change	Department Payroll	Absence Report
Employee Information Update	Expense Report	Department Absence Report
Employee Salary Record	Mileage Reimbursement Report	Annual Attendance Record
Employment Changes	Payroll Change Notice	Employee Suggestion
Personnel Data Sheet	Pay Advice	Suggestion Plan 1
Personnel File Access Log	Payroll Summary	Suggestion Plan 2
Request to Inspect Personnel File	Vacation Request Memo	Suggestion Plan 3
Consent to Release Information	Vacation Request	Memo Regarding Drug Testing
Telephone Reference Record	Employee Health Record	Test Notice—Polygraph
Personnel Activity Report	Accident Report	Information Notice—Polygraph
Personnel Requirement Projections	Illness Report	Notice of Affirmative Action Policy
Temporary Employment Requisition	Injury Report	Affirmative Action Notice to Suppliers
Temporary Personnel Requisition	Disability Certificate	Affirmative Action Self-Identification
Employee Flextime Schedule	Physician's Report	Affirmative Action Supplier's Compliance Certificate
Weekly Work Schedule	Employee Sympathy Letter 1	
Daily Time Record	Employee Sympathy Letter 2	Affirmative Action Summary
Employee Daily Time Record	Employee Sympathy Letter 3	Equal Employment Opportunity Policy
Weekly Time Record	Employee Sympathy Letter 4	Current EEO Workforce Analysis
Hourly Employees' Weekly Time Sheet	Absence Request	EEO Analysis of Promotions
Department Overtime Request	Funeral Leave Request	Employee Transfer Request
Overtime Permit	Leave Request/Return from Leave	Off-Duty Employment Request
Overtime Authorization	Military Duty Absence	Grievance Form
Overtime Report	Late Report	

Section 5

Performance Evaluation

Employee Consultation	Disciplinary Notice	Standard Evaluation
Employee Counseling Activity Sheet	Disciplinary Warning	Temporary Employee Evaluation
Critical Incidents Report	Disciplinary Report	Employee Performance Review
Incident Report	Suspension Without Pay Notice	Performance Appraisal Interview Report
Notice of Ongoing Investigation—Polygraph	Employee Self-Evaluation	Employee Rating Response
	Performance Analysis Employee Worksheet	Performance Objectives
Notice of 30-Day Evaluation	Employee Performance Checklist	Coaching Form
Notice of Probation	New Employee Evaluation	Employee Performance Improvement Plan
Notice of Extended Probation	Managerial Evaluation	
Excessive Absenteeism Warning	Performance Evaluation	Letter of Commendation
First Warning Notice	Production Personnel Evaluation	Salary Change Request
Second Warning Notice	Sales Personnel Evaluation	

Section 6

Benefits

Accrued Benefits Statements	Resolution—Paid-Up Annuity Plan	Resolution—Tuition Benefit
Employee Benefits Analysis	Resolution—Relocation Allowance	Resolution—Scholarship Aid Program
Benefits Planning Checklist	Resolution—Performance Bonus	Resolution—Financial Counseling Plan
Employee Benefits Survey	Resolution—Low-Interest Loan	Resolution—Sabbatical Leave
Employee Benefits List	Resolution—Company Car	Resolution—Child Care Plan
Combined Resolution—Incentive Stock Option Plan	Resolution—Club Membership	Resolution—Wage Continuation Plan
Resolution—Signing Bonus	Resolution—At-Home Entertainment Allowance	Resolution—Merchandise Discount Program

Section 7

Termination/Separation

Retirement Checklist	Termination Letter for Intoxication on the Job	Employee Separation Report
Resignation		Unemployment Compensation Record
Termination Checklist	Letter Terminating Sales Representative	EEO Analysis of Terminations
Notice of Dismissal	Employee Checkout Record	Reference Report
Notice of Termination Due to Absence	General Release	Employment Reference Response
Notice of Termination Due to Work Rules Violation	Mutual Release	Refusal to Grant References
	Employee Release	Notice of Confidentiality Agreement
Reduction in Workforce Notice	Employee Exit Interview	COBRA Letter to Terminating Employee
Termination Letter for Excessive Absenteeism	Separation Notice	COBRA Employee Information Letter
Termination Letter for Lack of Work	Personnel Separation Report	COBRA Compliance

Source: Mario German, Personnel Director (Deerfield Beach, FL: EZ Legal Books, 1994), pp. vi, vii, and viii.

Automating Individual HR Tasks

As your company grows, it becomes increasingly unwieldy and uncompetitive to rely exclusively on manual HR systems. For a company with 40 or 50 employees or more, the amount of management time devoted to conducting appraisals can multiply into weeks. It is therefore at about this stage that most small- to medium-sized firms begin computerizing individual HR tasks.

Here again there are a variety of resources available. For example, at the Web site for the International Association for Human Resource Information Management, (http://www.ihrim.org), you'll find, within the Products & Services tab, a categorical buyers' guide listing software vendors. These firms provide software solutions for virtually all personnel tasks, ranging from benefits management to compensation, compliance, employee relations, outsourcing, payroll, and time and attendance systems.

Off-the-shelf software is available elsewhere, too. For example, the G. Neil Company sells off-the-shelf software packages for controlling attendance, employee record keeping, writing job descriptions, writing employee policy handbooks, and conducting computerized employee appraisals. HRdirect offers software for writing employee policy manuals, writing performance reviews, creating job descriptions, tracking attendance and hours worked for each employee, employee scheduling, writing organizational charts, managing payroll, conducting employee surveys, scheduling and tracking employee training activities, and managing OSHA compliance. A program called People Manager maintains employee records on items such as marital status, number of dependents, emergency contact and phone numbers, hire date, and job history. It also enables employers to quickly produce 30 standard reports on matters such as attendance, benefits, and ethnic information.

Establishing Human Resource Information Systems (HRIS)

Why an HRIS?   Larger companies typically integrate their separate HR systems into integrated human resource information systems (HRIS). An HRIS may be defined as interrelated components working together to collect, process, store, and disseminate information to support decision making, coordination, control, analysis, and visualization of an organization's human resource management activities.[3]

There are at least three reasons for installing such a system. First is competitiveness; an HRIS can significantly improve the efficiency of the HR operation and therefore a company's bottom line. For example, W. H. Brady Company, a Milwaukee-based manufacturer of identification products such as labels, reportedly cut several hundred thousand dollars a year from its HR budget through the use of HRIS.[4] Software producer PeopleSoft reportedly has a ratio of one HR staffer to each 110 employees, a savings of millions of dollars a year when compared with the traditional ratio of one HR staffer per 50–100 employees, and it credits that to its HRIS. The company expects the HR to employee ratio to shrink to 1:500.[5]

The HRIS can also bump the firm up to a new plateau in terms of the number and variety of HR-related reports it can produce. Citibank, for instance (now part of Citigroup), has a global database of information on all employees including their compensation, a skills inventory bank of more than 10,000 of its managers, and a compensation and benefits practices database for each of the 98 countries in which the company has employees.[6]

Finally, the HRIS can also help shift HR's attention from transactions-processing to strategic HR. As the HRIS takes over tasks such as updating employee information and electronically reviewing resumes, the types of HR staff needed and their jobs tend to change. There is less need for entry-level HR data processors, for instance, and more for analysts capable of reviewing HR activities in relation to the company's plans and engaging in activities such as management development. Let's look more closely at how these advantages come about.

HRIS in Action   How exactly can an HRIS achieve these kinds of performance improvements? At some point the employer will outgrow the separate (manual or computerized) component approach to managing HR. Some estimate that firms with fewer than 150 employees can efficiently use computerized component systems, each separately handling tasks such as attendance, and benefits and payroll management. However, beyond that point larger firms should turn to either off-the-shelf or customizable HRIS packages.[7] The advantages of moving from component systems to integrated human resource information systems arise from the following.

Improved Transaction Processing   It's been said that "the bread and butter of HRIS is still basic transaction processing."[8] One study—conducted at a pharmaceuticals a company just before it implemented an HRIS—found that 71% of HR employees' time was devoted to transactional and administrative tasks, for instance. In other words, an enormous amount of time was devoted to tasks like checking leave balances, maintaining address records, and monitoring employee benefits distributions.[9] HRIS packages are intended to be comprehensive. They therefore generally provide relatively powerful computerized processing of a wider range of the firm's HR transactions than would be possible if individual systems for each HR task had to be used.

Online Processing   Many HR information systems make it possible (or easier) to make the company's employees themselves literally part of the HRIS. For example, Merck installed employee kiosks at which employees can verify and correct their home address and work location. Estimated savings reportedly approach $640,000 for the maintenance of those data alone, and many companies report similar savings. At Provident Bank, an HR compensation system called Benelogic allows the bank's employees to enroll in all their desired benefits programs over the Internet at a secure site. One shipping company estimates it will reduce transaction processing and related paperwork from $50 down to $30 or less per employee using direct-access kiosks and integrative voice response (IVR) phone scripts.[10] Increasingly, firms like Dell are creating intranet based HR sites. These allow managers and employees to process HR related information with little or no support required from the HR group itself. But using kiosks, IVR, or (increasingly) the intranet-based systems should not only move the burden of the record keeping from HR to the employees themselves. It also should "support employees' quest for 'what if' information relating to, for example, the impact on their take-home pay of various benefits options, W-4 changes, insurance coverage, retirement planning and more."[11] Some experts refer to advanced Internet—based HR service programs like these as electronic HR or ("e-HR"). It is the "application of conventional, Web, and voice technologies to improve HR administration, transactions and process performance."

Improved Reporting Capability Because the HRIS is comprehensive with respect to the number of HR tasks it handles, the installation of such a system significantly improves HR's reporting capabilities.

For most of these systems, the number and variety of reports possible is limited only by the manager's imagination. For a start, reports might be available (company-wide and by department) for: health care cost per employee, pay and benefits as a percent of operating expense, cost per hire, report on training, volunteer turnover rates, turnover costs, time to fill jobs, and return on human capital invested (in terms of training and education fees, for instance).[12] Similarly, you might want to calculate and review: human resource cost information by business unit; personal and performance information on candidates for global assignments; demographics of the candidate pool to meet diversity reporting requirements; benefit plan funding requirements and controls; union membership information; information required for HR if a merger, acquisition, or divestiture is expected; and data on your global executive-level population for development, promotion, and transfer purposes.[13]

HR System Integration Because its software components (record keeping, payroll, appraisal, and so forth) are integrated, a true HRIS enables an employer to dramatically reengineer its entire HR function by having the information system itself take over and integrate many of the tasks formerly carried out by HR employees.

The system installed at PeopleSoft provides a good example of this:

Sophisticated workflow technology routes promotions, salary increases, transfers and other forms through the organization to the proper managers for approval. As one person signs off, it's routed to the next. If anyone forgets to process a document, a smart agent issues reminders until the task is completed. Training materials—including video—are almost entirely on line, and all payroll checks are distributed electronically.

But the company's hiring process may be the most futuristic aspect of all. Applications sent via the World Wide Web or fax are automatically deposited into a database; those submitted on paper are scanned into the computer and plugged into the same database. Once a hiring manager has selected an applicant for an interview, the system phones that person and asks him or her to select an interview time by punching buttons on a touchtone phone. At the end of the call, the client/server database notifies the interviewers of the appointment, and even offers a reminder the day of the interview. It's all handled without human interaction. And an orientation program for new hires works much the same way.[14]

HRIS Applications Because of such capabilities, even many midsize firms are installing HR information systems today. For example, Grand Casinos, Inc., installed an HRIS called the Human Resource Manager, a package from PDS, Inc., to help with the hiring of several thousand new casino employees. "This system consolidates the human resources operations of Grand Casinos' nine separate properties, and lets these operations share resumes and other applicant information."[15] State Capital Credit Union in Madison, Wisconsin, with 105 employees, installed a desktop version of an HRIS called Spectrum HR/1200. This system "tracks applicant history and status, salary and staffing changes across departments, benefits plan participation, pension plan contributions, employee training, and turnover. It maintains compliance statistics, . . . and wage and hour information."[16] State Capital's system also performs other HR tasks including internal job postings, benefits billing, payroll reconciliation, and personalized letters and labels for applicant and employee correspondence.[17] For larger installations, major IT firms including IBM provide the required HR Systems integration. For example, IBM provides software under its "On—Demand Workplace Program." Under this program IBM offers integratable HR software from several developers, including Workbrain (for instance, for labor scheduling and time and attendance), and StorePerform (for work load optimization in retail stores). Similarly, when Chiron Corp., a large pharmaceutical and biotechnology company, found it needed to integrate its existing computer-based HR system component solutions, it turned to the large information systems firm SAP. For example, SAP was able to integrate its own proprietary human resource information system with an online recruiting tool from hire.com that Chiron had been using and wanted to continue to use.

HRIS Implementation Pitfalls As most everyone knows by now, implementing a sophisticated information system is often more of a challenge than the client expects, and several potential pitfalls account for this. Cost is one problem; for example, a representative from Allstate Insurance Company reported that the costs of moving to a new HRIS had increased 10% per year for five years and that additional investment would be required to make the transition.[18] Other systems run into management resistance. At one pharmaceuticals firm, for instance, the new HRIS requires line managers to input some information (such as on performance appraisals) into the HR system, and some object to doing tasks previously performed by HR.[19] Others trigger resistance by including inconvenient or unworkable user interfaces for the employees to use; still others are installed without enough thought being given to whether or not the new HRIS will be compatible with the firm's existing HR information systems. Inadequate documentation or training can undermine the system's utility, and increase resistance to the system by exactly those employees and managers who are supposed to aid in its use.[20]

Actually installing the HRIS therefore needs to be viewed as a whole but also as a process composed of separate projects, each of which must be planned and realistically scheduled.[21] Given these sorts of hurdles a careful needs assessment obviously should be done prior to adopting an HRIS. Particularly for firms with less than 150 employees, consideration should be given to depending more on individual software packages for managing separate tasks such as attendance, benefits and payroll, and OSHA compliance.[22]

HRIS Vendors Many firms today offer HRIS packages. At the Web site for the International Association for Human Resource Information Management (mentioned above), for instance, Automatic Data Processing, Inc., Business Information Technology, Inc., Human Resource Microsystems, Lawson Software, Oracle Corporation, PeopleSoft, Inc., Restrac Web Hire, SAP America, Inc., and about 25 other firms are listed as HRIS vendors. As another example, Business Computer Systems (www.bcs-tx.com), offers a line of ABRA software products for firms ranging in size from 20 to 10,000 employees. As one example, you can point and click to find a list of employees reporting to a particular supervisor, and print over a hundred reports such as salary lists, employee profiles, and EEO reports.[23]

HR and Intranets As noted above, employers are creating internal intranets-based HR information systems. For example, LG&E Energy Corporation uses its intranet for benefits communication.[24] Employees can access the benefits homepage and (among other things) review the company's 401(k) plan investment options, get answers to frequently asked questions about the company's medical and dental plans, and report changes in family status (such as marriage) that may impact the employee's benefits.

A list of other HR-related ways in which employers use the intranet include: create an electronic employee directory; automate job postings and applicant tracking; set up training registration; provide electronic pay stubs; publish an electronic employee handbook; offer more enticing employee communications and newsletters; let employees update their personal profiles and access their accounts, such as 401(k)s; conduct open benefits enrollments; provide leave status information; conduct performance and peer reviews; manage succession planning (in part by locating employees with the right skill set to fill openings); and create discussion groups or forums.[25]

APPENDIX NOTES

1. Mario German, *Personnel Director* (Deerfield Beach, FL: E-Z Legal Books, 1994), pp. vi, vii, and viii.
2. Office Depot, Winter 2003 Catalog (Delray Beach, FL: Office Depot, 2003).
3. Adapted from Kenneth Laudon and Jane Laudon, *Management Information Systems: New Approaches to Organization and Technology* (Upper Saddle River, NJ: Prentice Hall, 1998), p. G7. See also, Michael Barrett and Randolph Kahn, "The Governance of Records Management," Directors and Boards 26, no. 3 (Spring 2002), pp. 45–48; and Anthony Hendrickson, "Human Resource Information Systems: Backbone Technology of Contemporary Human Resources," Journal of Labor Research, summer 2003, volume 24, issue three, pages 381–395
4. Samuel Greengard, "Finding Time to Be Strategic," *Personnel Journal*, October 1996, pp. 84–89.
5. Samuel Greengard, "Client/Server: HR's Helping Hand?" *Personnel Journal*, May 1996, p. 92.
6. Linda Stroh, "Integrated HR Systems Help Develop Global Leaders," *HR Magazine* 43, no. 5 (April 1998), pp. 14–18.
7. Tony Berardine, "Human Resource Information Systems Improve Management Decision-Making," *Canadian Manager*, 22, no. 5 (Winter 1997), pp. 17–18. See also, Nona Tobin, "Can Technology Ease the Pain of Salary Surveys?" *Public Personnel Management*, 31, no. 1 (Spring 2002), pp. 65–78.
8. Gerald Groe, "Information Technology and HR," *Human Resource Planning* 19, no. 1 (March 1996), pp. 56–62. See also, France Lampron, "Is an ESS Right for Your Company?" *HR Magazine* 47, no. 12 (December 2002), pp. 77–80.
9. "HR Execs Trade Notes on Human Resource Information Systems," *BNA Bulletin to Management*, December 3, 1998, p. 1. See also, Brian Walter, "But They Said Their Payroll Program Complied with the FLSA," *Public Personnel Management*, 31, no. 1 (Spring 2002), pp. 79–94.
10. Marc Miller, "Great Expectations: Is Your HRIS Meeting Them?" *HR Focus* 75, no. 4 (April 1998), pp. 1–3, see also, Vicki Gerson, "Provident Bank automates benefits administration: web-based offering from Benelogic cuts employee benefits enrollment costs," Bank Systems + Technology, September 2003, volume 40, issue 9, page 19.
11. Ibid., p. 2. See also, Ali Velshi, "Human Resources Information," The Americas Intelligence Wire, February 11, 2004.
12. Jac Fitz-enz, "Top Ten Calculations for Your HRIS," *HR Focus* 75, no. 4 (April 1998), p. 3.
13. Linda Stroh, "Integrated HR Systems," p. 16.

14. Samuel Greengard, "Client/Server: HR's Helping Hand?" *Personnel Journal*, May 1996, p. 92.

15. Stephanie Wilkinson, "Hire and Higher: Client/Server and Web-Based Systems Raise the Stakes for Solving HR Headaches," *PC Week*, July 8, 1996, pp. 45–47.

16. Mary Mink, "Software Eases HR Tasks," *Credit Union Executive* no. 6 (November–December 1996), p. 35. See also, Janet Wiscombe, "Using Technology to Cut Costs," *Workforce*, September 2001, pp. 46–51; and, "PILAT NAI expands its world-class talent management offerings with web-based strategic staffing solutions," Internet Wire, January 26, 2004

17. Ibid. See also, "Technology Trends 2002," *Workforce*, November 2001, pp. 55–58; Christina Blank and Michael G. A. R. R. Y., "Managing Smart: to improve hiring and managing of in-store employees and to reduce paperwork, retailers are turning to a host of new applications," Supermarket News, May 3, 2004, page 149; and, "How Chiron Corp. updated an old human resource information system," Human Resource Department Management Report, May 2003, page 15.

18. "HR Execs Trade Notes on Human Resource Information Systems," p. 2.

19. Ibid. p. 1.

20. Victor Haines and Andre Petit, "Conditions for Successful Human Resource Information Systems," *Human Resource Management* 36, no. 2 (Summer 1997), pp. 261–276; see also "Five critical "-tions" help you select new or replacement HRIS," Human Department Management Report, August 2003, page one.

21. James Schultz, "Avoid the DDTs of HRIS Implementation," *HR Magazine* 42, no. 5 (May 1997), pp. 37–41. See also, Bill Roberts, "The New HRIS: Good Deal or $6 Million Paperweight?" *HR Magazine* 43, no. 3, (February 1998), p. 40.

22. Tony Berardine, "Human Resource Information Systems Improve Management Decision Making," *Canadian Manager* 22, no. 4 (Winter 1997), pp. 17–19. See also, MaryAnn Hammers, "HR in a Time of Caution: Recharging Your HRMS," *Workforce*, September 2002, p. 38.

23. Jim Meade, "Below Cost Alternative to the Traditional HRIS: Best Imperative HRMS Offers Great Value," *HRMagazine* 43, no. 9 (August 1998), pp. 37–40. Note that increasing numbers of HRIS depend on so-called client/server systems. For more information see, for instance, Eric Baker, "Do You Need a Client/Server System?" *HRMagazine*, February 1997, pp. 37–43.

24. Frank Kuzmits, "Communicating Benefits: A Double Click Away," *Compensation and Benefits Review*, September/October 1998, pp. 60–64.

25. Samuel Greengard, "Increase the Value of Your Intranet," *Workforce*, March 1997, pp. 88–94; Samuel Greengard, "Achieving Greater Intranet Efficiency," *Workforce*, September 1998, pp. 71–77.

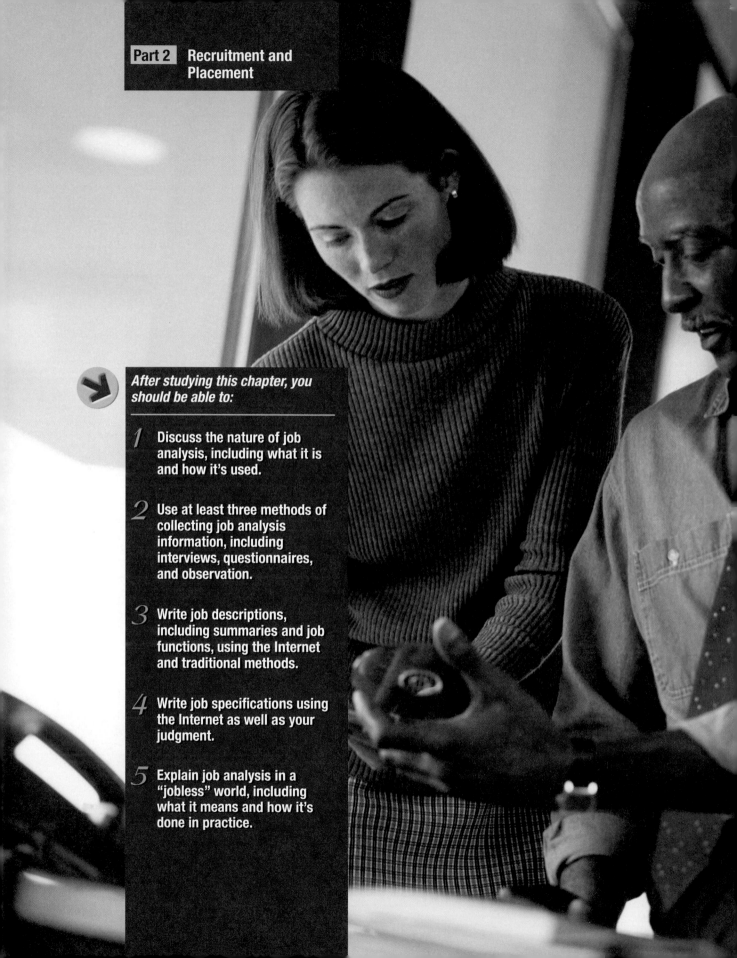

*After studying this chapter, you
should be able to:*

1 Discuss the nature of job
analysis, including what it is
and how it's used.

2 Use at least three methods of
collecting job analysis
information, including
interviews, questionnaires,
and observation.

3 Write job descriptions,
including summaries and job
functions, using the Internet
and traditional methods.

4 Write job specifications using
the Internet as well as your
judgment.

5 Explain job analysis in a
"jobless" world, including
what it means and how it's
done in practice.

Job Analysis

As an experienced HR director, the Hotel Paris's Lisa Cruz knew that

recruitment and selection processes invariably influenced employee

competencies and behavior and, through them, the company's bottom line.

Everything about the workforce—its collective skills, morale, experience, and

motivation—depended on attracting and then selecting the right employees. In

reviewing the Hotel Paris's employment systems, she was therefore concerned

to find that virtually all the company's job descriptions were out of date, and

that many jobs had no descriptions at all. She knew that without accurate job

descriptions, all her HR improvement efforts would be in vain. After all, if you

don't know a job's duties, responsibilities, and human requirements, how can

you decide who to hire or how to train them? To create HR policies and

practices that would produce employee competencies and behaviors needed

to achieve the hotel's strategic aims, Lisa's team first had to produce a set of

usable job descriptions.•

The main purpose of this chapter is to show you how to analyze a job and write job descriptions. We'll see that analyzing jobs involves determining in detail what the job entails and what kind of people the firm should hire for the job. We discuss several techniques for analyzing jobs, and how to use the Internet and more traditional methods to draft job descriptions and job specifications. Then, in the next chapter, "Personnel Planning and Recruiting," we'll turn to the methods managers use to actually find the employees they need.

 Discuss the nature of job analysis, including what it is and how it's used.

job analysis
The procedure for determining the duties and skill requirements of a job and the kind of person who should be hired for it.

job description
A list of a job's duties, responsibilities, reporting relationships, working conditions, and supervisory responsibilities—one product of a job analysis.

job specifications
A list of a job's "human requirements," that is, the requisite education, skills, personality, and so on—another product of a job analysis.

● THE NATURE OF JOB ANALYSIS

Organizations consist of positions that have to be staffed. **Job analysis** is the procedure through which you determine the duties of these positions and the characteristics of the people to hire for them.[1] Job analysis produces information used for writing **job descriptions** (a list of what the job entails) and **job specifications** (what kind of people to hire for the job).

The supervisor or HR specialist normally collects one or more of the following types of information via the job analysis:

■ *Work activities.* First, he or she collects information about the job's actual work activities, such as cleaning, selling, teaching, or painting. This list may also include how, why, and when the worker performs each activity.

■ *Human behaviors.* The specialist may also collect information about human behaviors like sensing, communicating, deciding, and writing. Included here would be information regarding job demands such as lifting weights or walking long distances.

■ *Machines, tools, equipment, and work aids.* This category includes information regarding tools used, materials processed, knowledge dealt with or applied (such as finance or law), and services rendered (such as counseling or repairing).

■ *Performance standards.* The employer may also want information about the job's performance standards (in terms of quantity or quality levels for each job duty, for instance). Management will use these standards to appraise employees.

■ *Job context.* Included here is information about such matters as physical working conditions, work schedule, and the organizational and social context—for instance, the number of people with whom the employee would normally interact. Information regarding incentives might also be included here.

■ *Human requirements.* This includes information regarding the job's human requirements, such as job-related knowledge or skills (education, training, work experience) and required personal attributes (aptitudes, physical characteristics, personality, interests).

Uses of Job Analysis Information

As summarized in Figure 4-1, job analysis information is the basis for several interrelated HR management activities.

Recruitment and Selection   Job analysis provides information about what the job entails and what human characteristics are required to perform these activities. This information, in the form of job descriptions and specifications, helps management decide what sort of people to recruit and hire.

Compensation   Job analysis information is crucial for estimating the value of each job and its appropriate compensation. Compensation (such as salary and bonus) usually depends on the job's required skill and education level, safety hazards, degree of respon-

Figure 4-1
Uses of Job Analysis
Information

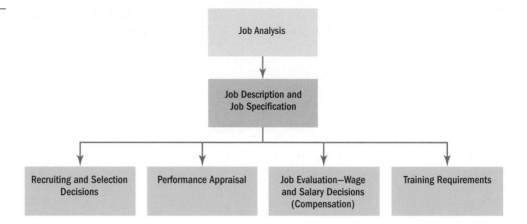

sibility, and so on—all factors you can assess through job analysis. Furthermore, many employers group jobs into classes (say, secretary III and IV). Job analysis provides the information to determine the relative worth of each job—and thus its appropriate class.

Performance Appraisal   A performance appraisal compares each employee's actual performance with his or her performance standards. Managers use job analysis to determine the job's specific activities and performance standards.

Training   The job description should show the activities and skills—and therefore the training—that the job requires.

Discovering Unassigned Duties   Job analysis can also help reveal unassigned duties. For example, your company's production manager says she's responsible for a dozen or so duties, such as production scheduling and raw material purchasing. Missing, however, is any reference to managing raw material inventories. On further study, you learn that none of the other manufacturing people are responsible for inventory management, either. You know from your review of other jobs like these that someone should be managing inventories. You've uncovered an essential unassigned duty, thanks to job analysis.

EEO Compliance   Job analysis also plays a big role in EEO compliance. U.S. Federal Agencies' Uniform Guidelines on Employee Selection stipulate that job analysis is a crucial step in validating all major personnel activities.[2] For example, employers must be able to show that their selection criteria and job performance are actually related. Doing this requires knowing what the job entails—which in turn requires a job analysis.

Steps in Job Analysis

There are six steps in doing a job analysis. Let's look at each of them.

Step 1:   Decide how you'll use the information, since this will determine the data you collect and how you collect them. Some data collection techniques—like interviewing the employee and asking what the job entails—are good for writing job descriptions and selecting employees for the job. Other techniques, like the position analysis questionnaire described later, do not provide qualitative information for job descriptions. Instead, they provide numerical ratings for each job; these can be used to compare jobs for compensation purposes.

organization chart
A chart that shows the organizationwide distribution of work, with titles of each position and interconnecting lines that show who reports to and communicates to whom.

Step 2:   Review relevant background information such as organization charts, process charts, and job descriptions.[3] **Organization charts** show the organizationwide

Figure 4-2
Process Chart for Analyzing a Job's Workflow
Source: Compensation Management: Rewarding Performance by Richard J. Henderson. Reprinted by permission of Pearson Education, Upper Saddle River, NJ.

Information Input from Plant Manager	Components Input from Suppliers

Job Under Study— Quality Control Clerk

Information Output to Plant Manager Regarding Component Quality	Product Quality Output to Plant Manager

process chart
A work flow chart that shows the flow of inputs to and outputs from a particular job.

division of work, how the job in question relates to other jobs, and where the job fits in the overall organization. The chart should show the title of each position and, by means of interconnecting lines, who reports to whom and with whom the job incumbent communicates.

A **process chart** provides a more detailed picture of the work flow. In its simplest form a process chart (like that in Figure 4-2) shows the flow of inputs to and outputs from the job you're analyzing. (In Figure 4-2 the quality control clerk is expected to review components from suppliers, check components going to the plant managers, and give information regarding component's quality to these managers.) Finally, the existing job description, if there is one, usually provides a starting point for building the revised job description.

Step 3: Select representative positions. Why? Because there may be too many similar jobs to analyze. For example, it is usually unnecessary to analyze the jobs of 200 assembly workers when a sample of 10 jobs will do.

Step 4: Actually analyze the job—by collecting data on job activities, required employee behaviors, working conditions, and human traits and abilities needed to perform the job. For this step, use one or more of the job analysis methods explained later in this chapter.

Step 5: Verify the job analysis information with the worker performing the job and with his or her immediate supervisor. This will help confirm that the information is factually correct and complete. This review can also help gain the employee's acceptance of the job analysis data and conclusions by giving that person a chance to review and modify your description of the job activities.

Step 6: Develop a job description and job specification. These are two tangible products of the job analysis. The *job description* (to repeat) is a written statement that describes the activities and responsibilities of the job, as well as its important features, such as working conditions and safety hazards. The *job specification* summarizes the personal qualities, traits, skills, and background required for getting the job done. It may be in a separate document or in the same document as the job description.

 Use at least three methods of collecting job analysis information, including interviews, questionnaires, and observation.

● METHODS OF COLLECTING JOB ANALYSIS INFORMATION

There are various ways to collect information on the duties, responsibilities, and activities of a job, and we'll discuss the most important ones in this section. In practice, you could use any one of them, or you could combine the techniques that best fit your purpose. Thus, an interview might be appropriate for creating a job description, whereas the position analysis questionnaire may be more appropriate for quantifying the worth of a job for compensation purposes.

Conducting the job analysis usually involves a joint effort by an HR specialist, the worker, and the worker's supervisor. The HR specialist (perhaps an HR manager, job analyst, or consultant) might observe and analyze the job and then develop a job description and specification. The supervisor and worker may fill out questionnaires listing the subordinate's activities. The supervisor and worker may then review and verify the job analyst's conclusions regarding the job's activities and duties.

In practice, firms usually collect job analysis data from multiple "subject matter experts" (mostly job incumbents) using questionnaires and interviews. They then average data from several employees from different departments to determine how much time a typical employee spends on each of several specific tasks. The problem is that employees who have the same job title but work in different departments may experience very different pressures. Therefore, simply adding up and averaging the amount of time that, say, HR assistants need to devote to "interviewing candidates" could end in misleading results. The point is that you must understand the job's departmental context: The way someone with a particular job title spends his or her time is not necessarily the same from department to department.

Interviews, questionnaires, observations, and diary/logs are the most popular methods for gathering job analysis data. They all provide realistic information about what job incumbents actually do. Managers use them for developing job descriptions and job specifications.

The Interview

Managers use three types of interviews to collect job analysis data—individual interviews with each employee, group interviews with groups of employees who have the same job, and supervisor interviews with one or more supervisors who know the job. They use group interviews when a large number of employees are performing similar or identical work,

The job analysis process begins when the analyst collects information from worker and supervisor about the nature of the work and the specific tasks for which the worker is responsible.

since it can be a quick and inexpensive way to gather information. As a rule, the workers' immediate supervisor attends the group session; if not, you can interview the supervisor separately to get that person's perspective on the job's duties and responsibilities.

Whichever kind of interview you use, you need to be sure the interviewee fully understands the reason for the interview, since there's a tendency for such interviews to be viewed, rightly or wrongly, as "efficiency evaluations." If so, interviewees may hesitate to describe their jobs accurately.

Pros and Cons   The interview is probably the most widely used method for identifying a job's duties and responsibilities, and its wide use reflects its advantages. It's a relatively simple and quick way to collect information, including information that might never appear on a written form. A skilled interviewer can unearth important activities that occur only occasionally, or informal contacts that wouldn't be obvious from the organization chart. The interview also provides an opportunity to explain the need for and functions of the job analysis. And the employee can vent frustrations that might otherwise go unnoticed by management.

Distortion of information is the main problem—whether due to outright falsification or honest misunderstanding.[4] Job analysis is often a prelude to changing a job's pay rate. Employees therefore may legitimately view the interview as an efficiency evaluation that may affect their pay. They may then tend to exaggerate certain responsibilities while minimizing others. Obtaining valid information can thus be a slow process, and prudent analysts get multiple inputs.

Typical Questions   Despite their drawbacks, interviews are widely used. Some typical interview questions include:

What is the job being performed?

What are the major duties of your position? What exactly do you do?

What physical locations do you work in?

What are the education, experience, skill, and [where applicable] certification and licensing requirements?

In what activities do you participate?

What are the job's responsibilities and duties?

What are the basic accountabilities or performance standards that typify your work?

What are your responsibilities? What are the environmental and working conditions involved?

What are the job's physical demands? The emotional and mental demands?

What are the health and safety conditions?

Are you exposed to any hazards or unusual working conditions?

Many interviews follow structured or checklist formats. Figure 4-3 (pages 118–119) presents one example—a job analysis questionnaire. It includes a series of detailed questions regarding matters like the general purpose of the job; supervisory responsibilities; job duties; and education, experience, and skills required. Of course, structured lists are not just for interviewers: Job analysts who collect information by personally observing the work or by using questionnaires—two methods explained below—can also use lists like these.[5] Figure 4-4 (pages 120–121) is a more unstructured questionnaire, intended for use online.

Interview Guidelines   Keep several things in mind when conducting a job analysis interview. First, the job analyst and supervisor should work together to identify the workers who know the job best—and preferably those who'll be most objective in describing their duties and responsibilities.

Second, quickly establish rapport with the interviewee. Know the person's name, speak in easily understood language, briefly review the interview's purpose, and explain how the person was chosen for the interview.

Third, follow a structured guide or checklist, one that lists questions and provides space for answers. This ensures you'll identify crucial questions ahead of time and that all interviewers (if there's more than one) cover all the required questions. (However, also make sure to give the worker some leeway in answering questions, and provide some open-ended questions like, "Was there anything we didn't cover with our questions?")

Fourth, when duties are not performed in a regular manner—for instance, when the worker doesn't perform the same job over and over again many times a day—ask the worker to list his or her duties in order of importance and frequency of occurrence. This will ensure that you don't overlook crucial but infrequently performed activities—like a nurse's occasional emergency room duties.

Finally, after completing the interview, review and verify the data. Specifically, review the information with the worker's immediate supervisor and with the interviewee.

Questionnaires

Having employees fill out questionnaires to describe their job-related duties and responsibilities is another good way to obtain job analysis information.

You have to decide how structured the questionnaire should be and what questions to include. Some questionnaires are very structured checklists. Each employee gets an inventory of perhaps hundreds of specific duties or tasks (such as "change and splice wire"). He or she is asked to indicate whether or not he or she performs each task and, if so, how much time is normally spent on each. At the other extreme, the questionnaire can be open-ended and simply ask the employee to "describe the major duties of your job." In practice, the best questionnaire often falls between these two extremes. As illustrated in Figure 4-3, a typical job analysis questionnaire might have several open-ended questions (such as "state your jobs' overall purpose") as well as structured questions (concerning, for instance, previous education required).

Whether structured or unstructured, questionnaires have both pros and cons. A questionnaire is a quick and efficient way to obtain information from a large number of employees; it's less costly than interviewing hundreds of workers, for instance. However, developing the questionnaire and testing it (perhaps by making sure the workers understand the questions) can be expensive and time-consuming.

Observation

Direct observation is especially useful when jobs consist mainly of observable physical activities—assembly-line worker and accounting clerk are examples. On the other hand, observation is usually not appropriate when the job entails a lot of mental activity (lawyer, design engineer). Nor is it useful if the employee only occasionally engages in important activities, such as a nurse who handles emergencies. And *reactivity*—the worker's changing what he or she normally does because you are watching—can also be a problem.

Managers often use direct observation and interviewing together. One approach is to observe the worker on the job during a complete work cycle. (The *cycle* is the time it takes to complete the job; it could be a minute for an assembly-line worker or an hour, a day, or longer for complex jobs.) Here you take notes of all the job activities. Then, after accumulating as much information as possible, you interview the worker. Ask the person to clarify points not understood and to explain what other activities he or she performs that you didn't observe. You can also observe and interview simultaneously, asking questions while the worker performs his or her job.

Participant Diary/Logs

diary/log
Daily listings made by workers of every activity in which they engage along with the time each activity takes.

Another approach is to ask workers to keep a **diary/log** of what they do during the day. For every activity he or she engages in, the employee records the activity (along with the time) in a log. This can produce a very complete picture of the job, especially when supplemented with subsequent interviews with the worker and the supervisor. The employee, of course, might try to exaggerate some activities and underplay others. However, the detailed, chronological nature of the log tends to mediate against this.

Some firms take a high-tech approach to diary/logs. They give employees pocket dictating machines and pagers. Then at random times during the day, they page the workers, who dictate what they are doing at that time. This approach can avoid one pitfall of the traditional diary/log method: relying on workers to remember what they did hours earlier when they complete their logs at the end of the day.

Quantitative Job Analysis Techniques

Qualitative approaches like interviews and questionnaires are not always suitable. For example, if your aim is to compare jobs for pay purposes, you may want to be able to assign quantitative values to each job. The position analysis questionnaire, the Department of Labor approach, and functional job analysis are three popular quantitative methods.

Figure 4-3
Job Analysis Questionnaire for Developing Job Descriptions

Use a questionnaire like this to interview job incumbents, or have them fill it out.
Source: www.HR.BLR.com. Reprinted with permission of the publisher © 2004 Business and Legal Reports, Inc., Old Saybrook, CT.

Job Analysis Information Sheet

Job Title_____ Date _____

Job Code_____ Dept. _____

Superior's Title _____

Hours worked _____ AM to _____ PM

Job Analyst's Name _____

1. **What is the job's overall purpose?**

_____

2. **If the incumbent supervises others,** list them by job title; if there is more than one employee with the same title, put the number in parentheses following.

_____

3. **Check those activities** that are part of the incumbent's supervisory duties.

☐ Training

☐ Performance Appraisal

☐ Inspecting work

☐ Budgeting

☐ Coaching and/or counseling

☐ Others (please specify) _____

4. **Describe the type and extent of supervision** received by the incumbent.

_____

5. **JOB DUTIES:** Describe briefly WHAT the incumbent does and, if possible, HOW he/she does it. Include duties in the following categories:

      a. daily duties (those performed on a regular basis every day or almost every day)

      _____

      b. periodic duties (those performed weekly, monthly, quarterly, or at other regular intervals)

      _____

      c. duties performed at irregular intervals

      _____

6. Is the incumbent performing duties he/she considers unnecessary? If so, describe.

_____

7. Is the incumbent performing duties not presently included in the job description? If so, describe.

_____

8. EDUCATION: Check the box that indicates the educational requirements for the job (not the educational background of the incumbent).

☐ No formal education required   ☐ Eighth grade education

☐ High school diploma (or equivalent)   ☐ 2-year college degree (or equivalent)

☐ 4-year college degree (or equivalent)   ☐ Graduate work or advanced degree
(specify:)

☐ Professional license (specify:)

Figure 4-3
(continued)

9. **EXPERIENCE:** Check the amount of experience needed to perform the job.

☐ None   ☐ Less than one month

☐ One to six months   ☐ Six months to one year

☐ One to three years   ☐ Three to five years

☐ Five to ten years   ☐ More than ten years

10. **LOCATION:** Check location of job and, if necessary or appropriate, describe briefly.

☐ Outdoor   ☐ Indoor

☐ Underground   ☐ Excavation

☐ Scaffold   ☐ Other (specify)

11. **ENVIRONMENTAL CONDITIONS:** Check any objectionable conditions found on the job and note afterward how frequently each is encountered (rarely, occasionally, constantly, etc.)

☐ Dirt   ☐ Dust

☐ Heat   ☐ Cold

☐ Noise   ☐ Fumes

☐ Odors   ☐ Wetness/humidity

☐ Vibration   ☐ Sudden temperature changes

☐ Darkness or poor lighting ☐ Other (specify)

12. **HEALTH AND SAFETY:** Check any undesirable health and safety conditions under which the incumbent must perform and note how often they are encountered.

☐ Elevated workplace   ☐ Mechanical hazards

☐ Explosives   ☐ Electrical hazards

☐ Fire hazards   ☐ Radiation

☐ Other (specify)

13. **MACHINES, TOOLS, EQUIPMENT, AND WORK AIDS:** Describe briefly what machines, tools, equipment, or work aids the incumbent works with on a regular basis:

_____

14. Have concrete work standards been established (errors allowed, time taken for a particular task, etc.)? If so, what are they?

_____

15. Are there any personal attributes (special aptitudes, physical characteristics, personality traits, etc.) required by the job?

_____

16. Are there any exceptional problems the incumbent might be expected to encounter in performing the job under normal conditions? If so, describe.

_____

17. Describe the successful completion and/or end results of the job.

_____

18. What is the seriousness of error on this job? Who or what is affected by errors the incumbent makes?

_____

19. To what job would a successful incumbent expect to be promoted?

[**Note:** this form is obviously slanted toward a manufacturing environment, but it can be adapted quite easily to fit a number of different types of jobs.]

STATE UNIVERSITY SYSTEM OF FLORIDA
FLORIDA STATE UNIVERSITY
ADMINISTRATIVE AND PROFESSIONAL
POSITION DESCRIPTION

PERSONNEL USE ONLY
Org. Chart:

DESCRIPTIVE DATA	FOR COMPLETION BY PERSONNEL UPON FINAL ACTION	Position Number:
NOTE: COMPLETE NUMBERED ITEMS PER INSTRUCTIONS	Approved Class Title:	Approved Class Code:

1. Position Number:	2. Requested Classification Action: ☐ Establish ☐ Update ☐ Change	Transaction:						Effective Date:		
3. Current Class Code:	4. Current Class Title:	UNIV 20	VP	Div.	Dept.	Sect.	S/Sect.	S/Sect.	CO
5. Vice President Division:	6. College/School:	Budget Enity	Fund Code	FTE	P/Plan 2	EEO-6	CBU	Pay Grd
7. Department:	8. Section	Signature of University Personnel Director					Date		
9. Subsection:	10. City 11. County								

RECORD INFORMATION IN AREAS PROVIDED PRIOR TO ATTACHING ADDITIONAL SHEETS

Describe functions in 12, and 13 below in terms of outcomes and results rather than method used or how a job is normally accomplished. Physical, mental and evironmental factors critical to the satisfactory performance of the job should be listed in item 17.

12.   *Essential Functions of the Job

12a   Policy-making and/or Interpretation

12b   Program Direction and Development

12c   Supervision Exercised (List titles and position numbers of positions <u>directly</u> supervised)

12d   Level of Public Contact (statement of internal and external business contact, include frequency and scope)

*NOTE: In compliance with the Americans with Disabilities Act (ADA), identify essential functions of a job required to be performed with or without reasonable accomodations. Requests to facilitate the performance of essentials functions will be given careful consideration.
**NOTE: For purposes of ADA, these functions (see 13) are marginal <u>only to</u> individuals covered under the ADA who are unable to perform these functions with or without reasonable accommodation because of a covered disability.

Figure 4-4 Example of a Questionnaire Intended for Use Online
Source: © 1999 Florida State University. (www.fsu.edu)

12e   Monetary Responsibility (amount and consequence of error)

12f   Statement of Responsibility for Confidential Data (disclosure would be prejudicial to successful operation of the SUS)

13.   **Marginal Functions of the Job

14.   Position Number and Class Title of Immediate Supervisor.

Type and extent of instructions or directions normally given to the incumbent of this position.

REQUIREMENTS
(Attach additional sheets as necessary)

15.   **Knowledge/Skills/Abilities:** In order of importance, state specific education, training, experience, knowledge, skills or abilities required for this position. Note: These requirements are in addition to the minimum qualifications stated on the official class specifications and are related to the essential functions of the position.

16.   **Required Licenses/Certifications/other specific requirements of law:** Please review statements below, check all that apply.

☐ This position requires a post-offer employment physical.
☐ This position requires a police back-ground check.
☐ This position requires fingerprinting.
☐ This position requires a child care provider security check as required under Sections 402.305 and 402.3055, Florida Statutes.

☐ This position is responsible for meeting the requirements of Section 215.422, Florida Statutes, as amended, regarding the approval and/or processing of vendors' invoices and/or distribution of warrants to vendors.

☐ This position requires licensure, certification or other special requirements described below.
☐ Other, please specifiy

17.   **Other Characteristics of the Position:** Describe other characteristics of the position such as physical, mental and environmental factors essential to the satisfactory performance of the functions of the position, or other characteristics which have not otherwise been described in the position description.

Signatures

18. I certify that I have reviewed and been provided a copy of the current position description for the position which I am assigned.

Name of Employee   Signature of Employee   Date

19. I certify that the statements above, to the best of my knowledge, accurately describes the position. I understand that intentional falsification of this documentation is in violation of State statutes and may result in disciplinary action or prosecution.

Immediate Supervisor's Name   Class Title   Position #   Signature   Date

20. **Reviewing Authority:**

(Appropriate VP, Dean, Director, Dept. Head or other Administrative Officer)   Signature   Date

Figure 4-4 (continued)

Position Analysis Questionnaire The **position analysis questionnaire (PAQ)** is a very structured job analysis questionnaire.[6] The PAQ contains 194 items, each of which (such as "written materials") represents a basic element that may or may not play an important role in the job. The job analyst decides if each item plays a role and, if so, to what extent. In Figure 4-5, for example, "written materials"

Figure 4-5
Portions of a Completed Page from the Position Analysis Questionnaire

Note: The 194 PAQ elements are grouped into six dimensions. This exhibits 11 of the "information input" questions or elements. Other PAQ pages contain questions regarding mental processes, work output, relationships with others, job context, and other job characteristics.

Information Input

1 Information Input

1.1 Sources of Job Information
Rate each of the following items in terms of the extent to which it is used by the worker as a source of information in performing his job.

	Extent of Use (U)
NA	Does not apply
1	Nominal/very infrequent
2	Occasional
3	Moderate
4	Considerable
5	Very substantial

1.1.1 Visual Sources of Job Information

1 | 4   Written materials (books, reports, office notes, articles, job instructions, signs, etc.)

2 | 2   Quantitative materials (materials which deal with quantities or amounts, such as graphs, accounts, specifications, tables of numbers, etc.)

3 | 1   Pictorial materials (pictures or picturelike materials used as *sources* of information, for example, drawings, blueprints, diagrams, maps, tracing, photographic films, x-ray films TV pictures, etc.)

4 | 1   Patterns/related devices (templates, stencils, patterns, etc., used as *sources* of information when *observed* during use; do *not* include here materials described in item 3 above)

5 | 2   Visual displays (dials, gauges, signal lights, radarscopes, speedometers, clocks, etc.)

6 | 5   Measuring devices (rulers, calipers, tire pressure gauges, scales, thickness gauges, pipettes, thermometers, protractors, etc., used to obtain visual information about physical measurements; do *not* include here devices describe in item 5 above)

7 | 4   Mechanical devices (tools, equipment, machinery, and other mechanical devices which are *sources* of information when observed during use of operation)

8 | 3   Materials in process (parts, material, objects, etc., which are *sources* of information when being modified, worked on, or otherwise processed, such as bread dough being mixed, workpiece being turned in a lathe, fabric being cut, shoe being resloed, etc.)

9 | 4   Materials *not* in process (parts, materials, objects, etc., not in the process of being changed or modified, which are *sources* of information when being inspected, handled, packaged, distributed, or selected, etc., such as items or materials in inventory, storage, or distribution channels, items being inspected, etc.)

10 | 3   Features of nature (landscapes, fields, geological samples, vegetation, cloud formations, and other features of nature which are observed or inspected to provide information)

11 | 2   Man-made features of environment (structures, buildings, dams, highways, bridges, docks, railroads, and other "man-made" or altered aspects of the indoor environment which are *observed* or *inspected* to provide job information; do not consider equipment, machines, etc., that an individual uses in his work, as covered by item 7)

received a rating of 4, indicating that written materials (like books, reports, and office notes) play a considerable role in this job. The analyst can do this online (see www.paq.com).

The advantage of the PAQ is that it provides a quantitative score or profile of any job in terms of how that job rates on five basic activities: (1) having decision-making/communication/social responsibilities, (2) performing skilled activities, (3) being physically active, (4) operating vehicles/equipment, and (5) processing information. The PAQ's real strength is thus in classifying jobs. In other words, it lets you assign a quantitative score to each job based on its decision making, skilled activity, physical activity, vehicle/equipment operation, and information-processing characteristics. You can therefore use the PAQ results to quantitatively compare jobs to one another,[7] and then assign pay levels for each job.[8]

U.S. Department of Labor (DOL) job analysis procedure
A standardized method by which different jobs can be quantitatively rated, classified, and compared based on data, people, and things scored.

Department of Labor (DOL) Procedure   The **U.S. Department of Labor (DOL) job analysis procedure** also provides a standardized method by which different jobs can be quantitatively rated, classified, and compared. The heart of this analysis is a data, people, and things rating for each job.

Here's how the procedure works. As Table 4-1 shows, a set of basic activities called *worker functions* describes what a worker can do with respect to data, people, and things. With respect to data, for instance, the basic functions include synthesizing, coordinating, and copying. With respect to people, they include mentoring, negotiating, and supervising. With respect to things, the basic functions include manipulating, tending, and handling.

Note also that each worker function gets an importance level. Thus, "coordinating" is 1, whereas "copying" is 5. If you were analyzing the job of a receptionist/clerk, for example, you might label the job 5, 6, 7, which would represent copying data, speaking—signaling people, and handling things. On the other hand, you might code a psychiatric aide in a hospital 1, 7, 5 in relation to data, people, and things. In practice, you would analyze each task that the worker performed in terms of data, people, and things.

Table 4-1

Basic Department of Labor Worker Functions

	Data	People	Things
Basic Activities	0 Synthesizing	0 Mentoring	0 Setting up
	1 Coordinating	1 Negotiating	1 Precision working
	2 Analyzing	2 Instructing	2 Operating/controlling
	3 Compiling	3 Supervising	3 Driving/operating
	4 Computing	4 Diverting	4 Manipulating
	5 Copying	5 Persuading	5 Tending
	6 Comparing	6 Speaking/signaling	6 Feeding/offbearing
		7 Serving	7 Handling
		8 Taking instructions/helping	

Note: Determine employee's job "score" on data, people, and things by observing his or her job and determining, for each of the three categories, which of the basic functions illustrates the person's job. "0" is high; "6," "8," and "7" are lows in each column.

Then the highest combination (say 4, 6, 5) would be used to identify the job, since this is the highest level that a job incumbent would be expected to attain.

As illustrated in Figure 4-6, the schedule produced from the DOL procedure contains several types of information. The job title, in this case dough mixer in a bakery, is listed first. Also listed are the industry in which this job is found and the industry's standard industrial classification code. There is a one- or two-sentence summary of the job, and the worker function ratings for data, people, and things—in this case 5, 6, 2. These numbers mean that in terms of difficulty, a dough mixer copies data, speaks/signals with people, and operates/controls with respect to things. Finally, the schedule specifies the human requirements of the job, for instance, in terms of training time required, aptitudes, temperaments. As you can see, each job ends up with a numerical score (such as 5, 6, 2). You can thus group together (and assign the same pay to) all jobs with similar scores, even for very different jobs like dough mixer and mechanic's helper.

Functional Job Analysis   **Functional job analysis** is similar to the DOL method, but differs in two ways.[9] First, functional job analysis rates the job not just on data, people, and things, but also on four more dimensions: the extent to which specific instruc-

functional job analysis
A method for classifying jobs similar to the DOL method, but additionally taking into account the extent to which instructions, reasoning, judgment, and mathematical and verbal ability are necessary for performing job tasks.

Figure 4-6
Sample Report Based on Department of Labor Job Analysis Technique

Job Analysis Schedule

1. Established Job Title _____ DOUGH MIXER _____

2. Ind. Assign _____ (bake prod.) _____

3. SIC Code(s) and Title(s) _____ 2051 Bread and other bakery products _____

4. JOB SUMMARY:

Operates mixing machine to mix ingredients for straight and sponge (yeast) doughs according to established formulas, directs other workers in fermentation of dough, and curls dough into pieces with hand cutter.

5. WORK PERFORMED RATINGS:

Worker Functions	D Data	P People	(T) Things
	5	6	2

Work Field _____ Cooking, Food Preparing _____

6. WORKER TRAITS RATING: (To be filled in by analyst)
Training time required
Aptitudes
Temperaments
Interests
Physical Demands
Environment Conditions

tions are necessary to perform the task; the extent to which reasoning and judgment are required to perform the task; the mathematical ability required to perform the task; and the verbal and language facilities required to perform the task. Second, functional job analysis also identifies performance standards and training requirements. It therefore lets you answer the question, "To do this task and meet these standards, what training does the worker require?"

You may find both the DOL and functional job analysis methods in use. However, job analysts increasingly use other methods instead, including the U.S. government's online initiatives, which we'll discuss below.

Using Multiple Sources of Information

There are obviously many ways to obtain job analysis information. You can get it from individual workers, groups, or supervisors; or from the observations of job analysts, for instance. You can use interviews, observations, or questionnaires. Some firms use just one basic approach, like having the job analyst do interviews with current job incumbents. Yet one study suggests that using just one source may not be wise.[10]

The problem is the potential inaccuracies in people's judgments. For example, in a group interview, some group members may feel forced to go along with the consensus of the group; or an employee may be careless about how he or she completes a questionnaire. What this means is that collecting job analysis data from just interviews, or just observations, may lead to inaccurate conclusions. It's better to try to avoid such inaccuracies by using several sources.[11] For example, where possible, collect job analysis data from several types of respondents—groups, individuals, observers, supervisors, and analysts; make sure the questions and surveys are clear and understandable to the respondents. And if possible, observe and question respondents early enough in the job analysis process to catch any problems while there's still time to correct the job analysis procedure you're using.

Write job descriptions, including summaries and job functions, using the Internet and traditional methods.

● WRITING JOB DESCRIPTIONS

A job description is a written statement of what the worker actually does, how he or she does it, and what the job's working conditions are. You use this information to write a job specification; this lists the knowledge, abilities, and skills required to perform the job satisfactorily.

There is no standard format for writing a job description. However, most descriptions contain sections that cover:

1. Job identification
2. Job summary
3. Responsibilities and duties
4. Authority of incumbent
5. Standards of performance
6. Working conditions
7. Job specifications

Figures 4-7 and 4-8 present two sample forms of job descriptions.

JOB TITLE: Telesales Respresentative	JOB CODE: 100001
RECOMMENDED SALARY GRADE:	EXEMPT/NON-EXEMPT STATUS: NonExempt
JOB FAMILY: Sales	EEOC: Sales Workers
DIVISION: Higher Education	REPORTS TO: District Sales Manager
DEPARTMENT: In-House Sales	LOCATION: Boston
	DATE: April 2004

SUMMARY (Write a brief summary of job)

This position is responsible for selling College textbooks, software, and multimedia products to professors, via incoming and outgoing telephone calls, and to carry out selling strategies to meet sales goals in assigned territories of smaller colleges and universities. In addition, this position will be responsible for generating a designated amount of editoria leads, and communicating to the publishing groups product feedback and market trends observed in the assigned territory.

SCOPE AND IMPACT OF JOB
Dollar responsibilities (budget and/or revenue)

This position is responsible for generating approximately $2 million in revenue, for meeting operating expense budget of approximately $4000, and a sampling budget of approximately 10,000 units.

Supervisory responsibilities (direct and indirect)

None

Other

REQUIRED KNOWLEDGE AND EXPERIENCE (Knowledge and experience necessary to do job)
Related work experience

Prior sales or publishing experience preferred. One year of company experience in a customer service or marketing function with broad knowledge of company products and services is desirable.

Formal education or equivalent
Bachelor's degree with strong acedemic performance or work equivalent experience.

Skills
Must have strong organizational and persuasive skills. Must have excellent verbal and written communications skills and must be PC proficient.

Other

Limited travel required (approx 5%)

Figure 4-7
Sample Job Description, Pearson Education
Source: Courtesy of HR Department, Pearson Education.

PRIMARY RESPONSIBILITIES (List in order of importance and list amount of time spent on task)

Driving Sales (60%)
- Achieve quantitative sales goal for assigned territory of smaller colleges and universities.
- Determine sales priorities and strategies for territory and develop a plan for implementing those strategies.
- Conduct 15–20 professor interviews per day during the academic sales year that accomplishes those priorities.
- Conduct product presentations (including texts, software, and web-site); effectively articulate author's centra vision of key titles; conduct sales interviews using the PSS model; conduct walk-through of books and technology.
- Employ telephone selling techniques and strategies.
- Sample products to appropriate faculty making strategic use of assigned sampling budgets.
- Close class test adoptions for first edition products.
- Negotiate custom publishing and special packaging agreements within company guidelines.
- Initiate and conduct in-person faculty presentations and selling trips as appropriate to maximize sales with the strategic use of travel budget. Also use internal resources to support the territory sales goals.
- Plan and execute in-territory special selling events and book-fairs
- Develop and implement in-territory promotional campaigns and targeted email campaigns.

Publishing (editorial/marketing) 25%
- Report, track, and sign editorial projects.
- Gather and communicate significant market feedback and information to publishing groups.

Territory Management 15%
- Track and report all pending and closed business in assigned database.
- Maintain records of customer sales interviews and adoption situations in assigned database.
- Manage operating budget strategically.
- Submit territory itineraries, sales plans, and sales forecasts as assigned.
- Provide superior customer service and maintain professional bookstore relations in assigned territory.

Decision-Making Responsibilities for this position:
Determine the strategic use of assigned sampling budget to most effectively generate sales revenue to exceed sales goals.
Determine the priority of customer and account contacts to achieve maximum sales potential.
Determine where in-person presentations and special selling events would be most effective to generate most sales.

Submitted By: Jim Smith, District Sales Manager	Date: April 10, 2004
Approval:	Date:
Human Resources:	Date:
Corporate Compensation:	Date:

Figure 4-7 (continued)

Figure 4-8
"Marketing Manager"
Description from Standard
Occupational Classification
Source: www.bis.gov, accessed
November 13, 2003.

20. 11-2021 Marketing Managers
Abstract: 11-2021 Marketing Managers. Determine the demand for products and services offered by a firm and Its competitors and identify potential customers. Develop pricing strategies with the goal of maximizing the firm's profits or share of the market while ensuring the firm's customers are satisfied.

Job Identification

As in Figure 4.7, the job identification section (on top) contains several types of information.[12] The *job title* specifies the name of the job, such as supervisor of data processing operations, marketing manager, or inventory control clerk. The *FLSA status* section permits quick identification of the job as exempt or nonexempt. (Under the Fair Labor Standards Act, certain positions, primarily administrative and professional, are exempt from the act's overtime and minimum wage provisions.) *Date* is the date the job description was actually written.

There may also be a space to indicate who approved the description and perhaps a space that shows the location of the job in terms of its facility/division and department/section. This section might also include the immediate supervisor's title and information regarding salary and/or pay scale. There might also be space for the grade/level of the job, if there is such a category. For example, a firm may classify programmers as programmer II, programmer III, and so on.

Job Summary

The job summary should describe the general nature of the job, and includes only its major functions or activities. Thus (in Figure 4-7), the telesales rep ". . . is responsible for selling college textbooks. . . . " For the job of materials manager, the summary might state that the "materials manager purchases economically, regulates deliveries of, stores, and distributes all material necessary on the production line." For the job of mailroom supervisor, "the mailroom supervisor receives, sorts, and delivers all incoming mail properly, and he or she handles all outgoing mail including the accurate and timely posting of such mail."[13]

Include general statements like "performs other assignments as required" with care. Such statements can give supervisors more flexibility in assigning duties. Some experts, however, state unequivocally that "one item frequently found that should never be included in a job description is a 'cop-out clause' like 'other duties, as assigned,' "[14] since this leaves open the nature of the job—and the people needed to staff it.

Relationships

There is occasionally a relationships statement (not in the example), which shows the jobholder's relationships with others inside and outside the organization. For a human resource manager, such a statement might look like this:[15]

Reports to: Vice president of employee relations.

Supervises: Human resource clerk, test administrator, labor relations director, and one secretary.

Works with: All department managers and executive management.

Outside the company: Employment agencies, executive recruiting firms, union representatives, state and federal employment offices, and various vendors.[16]

Responsibilities and Duties

This section traditionally presents a list of the job's major responsibilities and duties. As in Figure 4-7, list each of the job's major duties separately, and describe it in a few sentences. In the figure, for instance, the duties include "achieve quantitative sales goal . . . ," and "determine sales priorities. . . ." Typical duties for other jobs might include maintaining balanced and controlled inventories, making accurate postings to accounts payable, maintaining favorable purchase price variances, and repairing production-line tools and equipment.

For many years the U.S. Labor Department's *Dictionary of Occupational Titles* was the basic source that HR managers both within and outside the government turned to for standard job descriptions. However, the government has now replaced the *Dictionary* with the new **Standard Occupational Classification (SOC)** (www.bls.gov/soc/socguide.htm). The SOC classifies all workers into one of 23 major groups of jobs (see Table 4-2). These in turn contain 96 minor groups of jobs, and these in turn include 821 detailed occupations, such as the marketing manager description in Figure 4-8. The employer

Standard Occupational Classification (SOC)
Classifies all workers into one of 23 major groups of jobs which are subdivided into minor groups of jobs and detailed occupations.

Table 4-2

SOC Major Groups of Jobs

11-0000	**Management Occupations**
13-0000	**Business and Financial Operations Occupations**
15-0000	**Computer and Mathematical Occupations**
17-0000	**Architecture and Engineering Occupations**
19-0000	**Life, Physical, and Social Science Occupations**
21-0000	**Community and Social Services Occupations**
23-0000	**Legal Occupations**
25-0000	**Education, Training, and Library Occupations**
27-0000	**Arts, Design, Entertainment, Sports, and Media Occupations**
29-0000	**Healthcare Practitioners and Technical Occupations**
31-0000	**Healthcare Support Occupations**
33-0000	**Protective Service Occupations**
35-0000	**Food Preparation and Serving-Related Occupations**
37-0000	**Building and Grounds Cleaning and Maintenance Occupations**
39-0000	**Personal Care and Service Occupations**
41-0000	**Sales and Related Occupations**
43-0000	**Office and Administrative Support Occupations**
45-0000	**Farming, Fishing, and Forestry Occupations**
47-0000	**Construction and Extraction Occupations**
49-0000	**Installation, Maintenance, and Repair Occupations**
51-0000	**Production Occupations**
53-0000	**Transportation and Material Moving Occupations**
55-0000	**Military Specific Occupations**

Note: Within these major groups are 96 minor groups, 449 broad occupations, and 821 detailed occupations.

can use descriptions like these to identify the job's specific duties and responsibilities, such as "Determine the demand for products."

This section should also define the limits of the jobholder's authority, including his or her decision-making authority, direct supervision of other personnel, and budgetary limitations. For example, the jobholder might have authority to approve purchase requests up to $5,000, grant time off or leaves of absence, discipline department personnel, recommend salary increases, and interview and hire new employees.[17] You also need to comply with ADA regulations: See the "Know Your Employment Law" feature following.

Know Your Employment Law

Writing Job Descriptions That Comply with the ADA

Congress enacted the Americans with Disabilities Act (ADA) to reduce or eliminate serious problems of discrimination against disabled individuals. Under the ADA, the individual must have the requisite skills, educational background, and experience to perform the job's essential functions. A job function is essential when it is the reason the position exists or when the function is so specialized that the firm hired the person doing the job for his or her expertise or ability to perform that particular function. If the disabled individual can't perform the job as currently structured, the employer is required to make a "reasonable accommodation," unless doing so would present an "undue hardship."

As we said earlier, the ADA does not require job descriptions, but it's probably advisable to have them. Virtually all ADA legal actions will revolve around the question, "What are the essential functions of the job?" Without a job description that lists such functions, it will be hard to convince a court that the functions are essential to the job. The corollary is that you should clearly identify the essential functions: Don't just list them among the job description's other duties.

Essential job functions are the job duties that employees must be able to perform, with or without reasonable accommodation.[18] Is a function essential? Questions to ask include:

1. What three or four main activities actually constitute the job? Is each really necessary? (For example a secretary types, files, answers the phone, takes dictation.)
2. What is the relationship between each task? Is there a special sequence which the tasks must follow?
3. Do the tasks necessitate sitting, standing, crawling, walking, climbing, running, stooping, kneeling, lifting, carrying, digging, writing, operating, pushing, pulling, fingering, talking, listening, interpreting, analyzing, seeing, coordinating, etc.?
4. How many other employees are available to perform the job function? Can the performance of that job function be distributed among any other employees?
5. How much time is spent on the job performing each particular function? Are the tasks performed less frequently as important to success as those done more frequently?
6. Would removing a function fundamentally alter the job?
7. What happens if a task is not completed on time?
8. Does the position exist to perform that function?
9. Are employees in the position actually required to perform the function?[19]
10. Is there a limited number of other employees available to perform the function?
11. What is the degree of expertise or skill required to perform the function?
12. What is the actual work experience of present or past employees in the job?
13. What is the amount of time an individual actually spends performing the function?
14. What are the consequences of not requiring the performance of the function?

Standards of Performance and Working Conditions

Some job descriptions contain a standards of performance section. This lists the standards the employee is expected to achieve under each of the job description's main duties and responsibilities.

Setting standards is never an easy matter; however, most managers soon learn that just telling subordinates to "do their best" doesn't provide enough guidance. One straightforward way of setting standards is to finish the statement, "I will be completely satisfied with your work when. . . . " This sentence, if completed for each duty listed in the job description, should result in a usable set of performance standards.[20] Here are some examples:

Duty: Accurately Posting Accounts Payable

1. Post all invoices received within the same working day.
2. Route all invoices to proper department managers for approval no later than the day following receipt.
3. An average of no more than three posting errors per month.

Duty: Meeting Daily Production Schedule

1. Work group produces no less than 426 units per working day.
2. Next work station rejects no more than an average of 2% of units.
3. Weekly overtime does not exceed an average of 5%.

The job description may also list the working conditions involved on the job. These might include things like noise level, hazardous conditions, or heat. Many firms today turn to the Internet to create job descriptions, as the "Improving Productivity Through HRIS" feature illustrates.

Improving Productivity Through HRIS

Using the Internet for Writing Job Descriptions

Most employers probably still write their own job descriptions, but more are turning to the Internet. One site, www.jobdescription.com, illustrates why. The process is simple. Search by alphabetical title, keyword, category, or industry to find the desired job title. This leads you to a generic job description for that title—say, "Computers & EDP systems sales representative." You can then use the wizard to customize the generic description for this position. For example, you can add specific information about your organization, such as job title, job codes, department, and preparation date. And you can indicate whether the job has supervisory abilities, and choose from a number of possible desirable competencies and experience levels.

The U.S. Department of Labor's occupational information network, called O*NET, is another useful Web tool (you'll find it at www.doleta.gov/programs/onet). It allows users to see the most important characteristics of occupations, as well as the experience, education, and knowledge required to do each job well. Both the Standard Occupational Classification and O*NET include the specific tasks associated with many occupations. O*NET also provides skills, including basic skills such as reading and writing, process skills such as critical thinking, and transferable skills such as persuasion and negotiation. An O*NET listing also includes information on worker requirements (required knowledge, for instance), occupation requirements (based on work activities such as compiling, coding, and categorizing data), and experience requirements (including education and job training). You can also check the job's labor market characteristics (such as employment projections and earnings data).[21] The "When You're On Your Own" feature on page 134 shows you how to use O*NET.

Write job specifications using the Internet as well as your judgment.

● WRITING JOB SPECIFICATIONS

The job specification takes the job description and answers the question, "What human traits and experience are required to do this job well?" It shows what kind of person to recruit and for what qualities that person should be tested. The job specification may be a section of the job description or a separate document entirely. Often—as in Figure 4-7 on page 126—the employer presents it as part of the job description.[22]

Specifications for Trained Versus Untrained Personnel

Writing job specifications for trained employees is relatively straightforward. For example, suppose you want to fill a position for a bookkeeper (or counselor or programmer). In cases like these, your job specifications might focus mostly on traits like length of previous service, quality of relevant training, and previous job performance. Thus, it's usually not too difficult to determine the human requirements for placing already trained people on a job.

The problems are more complex when you're filling jobs with untrained people (with the intention of training them on the job). Here you must specify qualities such as physical traits, personality, interests, or sensory skills that imply some potential for performing or for being trained to do the job.

For example, suppose the job requires detailed manipulation in a circuit board assembly line. Here you might want to ensure that the person scores high on a test of finger dexterity. Your goal, in other words, is to identify those personal traits—those human requirements—that validly predict which candidates would do well on the job and which would not. Employers identify these human requirements through a subjective, judgmental approach or through statistical analysis. Let's examine both approaches.

Specifications Based on Judgment

Most job specifications come from the educated guesses of people like supervisors and human resource managers. The basic procedure here is to ask, "What does it take in terms of education, intelligence, training, and the like to do this job well?"

There are several ways to get educated guesses or judgments. You could simply create them yourself, or you could choose them from the competencies listed in Web-based job descriptions like those at www.jobdescription.com. The typical job description there lists

The job specifications for candidates, such as the customer service operator shown here, should clearly indicate which skills, like computer literacy, are job requirements.

competencies like, "Generates creative solutions" and "Manages difficult or emotional customer situations." O*NET online is another good option. Job listings there include complete listings of educational and other experience and skills required.

Use common sense when compiling a list of the job's human requirements. Certainly, job-specific human traits like those unearthed through job analysis—manual dexterity, say, or educational level—are important. However, don't ignore the fact that some work behaviors may apply to almost any job (although they might not normally surface through a job analysis).

One researcher, for example, obtained supervisor ratings and other information from 18,000 employees in 42 different hourly entry-level jobs in predominantly retail settings.[23] Regardless of the job, here are the work behaviors (with examples) that he found to be "generic"—in other words, that seem to be important to all jobs:

Job-Related Behavior	*Some Examples*
Industriousness	Keeps working even when other employees are standing around talking; takes the initiative to find another task when finished with regular work.
Thoroughness	Cleans equipment thoroughly, creating a more attractive display; notices merchandise out of place and returns it to the proper area.
Schedule flexibility	Accepts schedule changes when necessary; offers to stay late when the store is extremely busy.
Attendance	Arrives at work on time; maintains good attendance.
Off-task behavior (reverse)	Uses store phones to make personal unauthorized calls; conducts personal business during work time; lets joking friends be a distraction and interruption to work.
Unruliness (reverse)	Threatens to bully another employee; refuses to take routine orders from supervisors; does not cooperate with other employees.
Theft (reverse)	(As a cashier) Underrings the price of merchandise for a friend; cheats on reporting time worked; allows nonemployees in unauthorized areas.
Drug misuse (reverse)	Drinks alcohol or takes drugs on company property; comes to work under the influence of alcohol or drugs.

Perhaps the bigger challenge is to make sure that in doing the job analysis, you don't miss the forest for the trees. Consider a study of 50 testing engineers at a Volvo plant in Sweden. When asked what determined job competence for a testing engineer, most of the engineers focused on traditional criteria such as "to make the engine perform according to specifications." But the most effective testing engineers defined the job's main task differently: "to make sure the engine provides a customer with a good driving experience." As a result, these engineers went about their jobs testing and tuning the engines "not as engineers trying to hit a number, but as ordinary drivers—imagining themselves as seniors, students, commuters, or vacationers." This subgroup of the testing engineers worked hard to develop their knowledge of customers' driving needs, even when it meant reaching out to people outside their own group, such as designers or marketers.

The point, says the researcher, is that "if people don't recognize or value the [human] attributes that really determine success, how easy will it be for them to acquire those attributes?" Employers should therefore "shift the focus of their recruitment and training programs from flawed attribute checklists toward identifying and, if necessary, changing people's understanding of what jobs entail." In other words, in developing the job description and job specification, make sure you really understand the reason for the job and therefore the skills a person actually needs to be competent at it.[24]

Specifications Based on Statistical Analysis

Basing job specifications on statistical analysis is the more defensible approach, but it's also more difficult. The aim here is to determine statistically the relationship between (1) some predictor or human trait, such as height, intelligence, or finger dexterity; and (2) some indicator or criterion of job effectiveness, such as performance as rated by the supervisor. The procedure has five steps: (1) analyze the job and decide how to measure job performance; (2) select personal traits like finger dexterity that you believe should predict successful performance; (3) test candidates for these traits; (4) measure these candidates' subsequent job performance; and (5) statistically analyze the relationship between the human trait (finger dexterity) and job performance. Your objective is to determine whether the former predicts the latter.

This method is more defensible than the judgmental approach because equal rights legislation forbids using traits that you can't prove distinguish between high and low job performers. Hiring standards that discriminate based on sex, race, religion, national origin, or age may have to be shown to predict job performance. Ideally, this is done with a statistical validation study, as in the five-step approach above.

Many employers and managers turn to the Web for a practical approach for creating job descriptions and specifications as the "When You're on Your Own" feature illustrates.

When You're On Your Own
HR for Line Managers and Entrepreneurs

Without their own job analysts or (in many cases) HR managers, many small business owners face two hurdles when doing job analyses and job descriptions. First, they often need a more streamlined approach than those provided by questionnaires like the one shown in Figure 4-3. Second, there is always the reasonable fear that in writing their job descriptions they will overlook duties that subordinates should be assigned, or assign duties not usually associated with such positions. What they need is an encyclopedia listing all the possible positions they might encounter, including a detailed listing of the duties normally assigned to these positions.

Help is at hand: The small business owner has at least three options. The *Standard Occupational Classification*, mentioned earlier, provides detailed descriptions of thousands of jobs and their human requirements. Web sites like www.job description.com provide customizable descriptions by title and industry. And the Department of Labor's O*NET is a third alternative. We'll focus on using O*NET in this feature.

Step 1. Decide on a Plan
Start by developing at least the broad outline of a corporate plan. What do you expect your sales revenue to be next year, and in the next few years? What products do you intend to emphasize? What areas or departments in your company do you think will have to be expanded, reduced, or consolidated, given where you plan

to go with your firm over the next few years? What kinds of new positions do you think you'll need in order to accomplish your strategic plans?

Step 2. Develop an Organization Chart
Next, develop an organization chart for the firm. Show who reports to the president and to each of his or her subordinates. Complete the chart by showing who reports to each of the other managers and supervisors in the firm. Start by drawing up the organization chart as it is now. Then, depending upon how far in advance you're planning, produce a chart showing how you'd like your chart to look in the immediate future (say, in two months) and perhaps two or three other charts showing how you'd like your organization to evolve over the next two or three years.

You can use several tools here. For example, MS Word includes an organization charting function: On the insert menu, click *Object*, then *Create New*. In the *Object* type box, click *MS Organization Chart*, and then *OK*. Software packages such as OrgPublisher from TimeVision of Irving, Texas, are another option.[25]

Step 3. Use a Job Analysis/Description Questionnaire
Next, use a job analysis questionnaire to determine what the job entails. You can use one of the more comprehensive questionnaires (see Figure 4-3); however, the job description questionnaire in Figure 4-9, is a simpler and often satisfactory alternative. Fill in the required

Figure 4-9
Preliminary Job Description
Questionnaire

Source: Reprinted from
www.HR.BLR.com with the
permission of the publisher. © 2004
Business and Legal Reports, Inc.,
Old Saybrook, CT.

Instructions: Distribute copies of this questionnaire to
supervisors, managers, personnel staff members, job analysts, and
others who may be involved in writing job descriptions. Ask them
to record their answers to these questions in writing.

1. What is the job title? _____

2. Summarize the job's more important, regularly performed/duties
   in a <u>Job Summary.</u>

3. In what department is the job located? _____

4. What is the title of the supervisor or manager to whom the job holder must
   report?

5. Does the jobholder supervise other employees? If so, give their job titles
   and a brief description of their responsibilites.

Position Supervised	Responsibilites

6. What essential function duties does the jobholder perform regularly? List
   them in order of importance.

Duty	Percentage of Time Devoted to This Duty
1.	
2.	
3.	
4.	
5.	
6.	

7. Does the jobholder perform other duties periodically? Infrequently? If so,
   please list, indicating frequency.

8. What are the working conditions? List such items as noise, heat, outside
   work, and exposure to bad weather.

9. How much authority does the jobholder have in such matters as training or
   guiding other people?

10. How much education, experience, and skill are required for satisfactory job
    performance?

11. At what stage is the jobholder's work reviewed by the supervisor?

12. What machines or equipment is the jobholder responsible for operating?

13. If the jobholder makes a serious mistake or error in performing required
    duties, what would be the cost to management?

Figure 4-10
Background Data for
Examples

Example of Job Title: Customer Service Clerk

Example of Job Summary: Answers inquiries and gives directions to customers, authorizes cashing of customers' checks, records and returns lost charge cards, sorts and reviews new credit applications, works at customer service desk in department store.

Example of One Job Duty: Authorizes cashing of checks: authorizes cashing of personal or payroll checks (up to a specified amount) by customers desiring to make payment by check. Requests identification—such as driver's license—from customers and examines check to verify date, amount, signature, and endorsement. Initials check and sends customer to cashier.

information, then ask the supervisors and/or employees to list the job's duties (in the middle of the page), breaking them into daily duties, periodic duties, and duties performed at irregular intervals. You can distribute a sample of one of these duties (Figure 4-10) to supervisors and/or employees to facilitate the process.

Step 4. Obtain Lists of Job Duties from O*NET

The list of job duties you uncovered in the previous step may or may not be complete. We'll therefore use O*NET to compile a more comprehensive list. (Refer to the visual examples as you read along.) Start

A.

B.

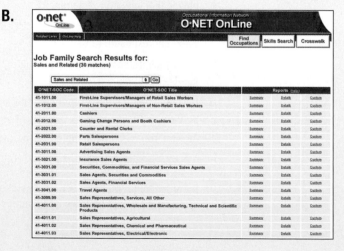

C.

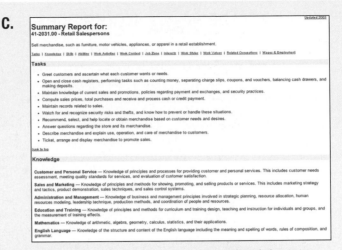

Shown in the three screen captures, O*Net easily allows the user to develop job descriptions.
Source: O*Net™ is a trademark of the U.S. Department of Labor, Employment and Training Administration. Reprinted by permission of O*Net.

by going to http://online.onetcenter.org (A.). Here, click on *Find Occupations.* Assume you want to create job descriptions for a retail salesperson. Type in *Retail Sales* for the occupational titles, and *Sales and Related* from the job families drop-down box. Click *Find Occupations* to continue, which brings you to the *Find Occupations Search Result* (B.). Clicking on *Retail Salespersons*—summary—produces the job summary and specific occupational duties for retail salespersons (C.). For a small operation, you might want to combine the duties of the retail salesperson with those of first-line supervisors/managers of retail sales workers.

Step 5. Compile the Job's Human Requirements from O*NET
Next, return to the *Snapshot for Retail Salesperson* (bottom). Here, instead of choosing occupation-specific information, choose, for example, *Worker Experiences, Occupational Requirements,* and *Worker Characteristics.* You can use this information to develop a job specification for recruiting, selecting, and training the employees.

Step 6. Complete Your Job Description
Finally, perhaps using Figure 4-9 as a guide, write an appropriate job summary for the job. Then use the information obtained in Steps 4 and 5 to create a complete listing of the tasks, duties, and human requirements of each of the jobs you will need to fill.

 Explain job analysis in a "jobless" world, including what it means and how it's done in practice.

● JOB ANALYSIS IN A "JOBLESS" WORLD

Job is generally defined as "a set of closely related activities carried out for pay," but over the past few years the concept of a job has been changing quite dramatically. As one observer put it:

> *The modern world is on the verge of another huge leap in creativity and productivity, but the job is not going to be part of tomorrow's economic reality. There still is and will always be enormous amounts of work to do, but it is not going to be contained in the familiar envelopes we call jobs. In fact, many organizations are today well along the path toward being "de-jobbed."*[26]

This "dejobbing" is a global phenomenon, as "The New Workplace" illustrates.

The New Workplace

Global Job Analysis Applications

When Mercedes-Benz opened its new factory in Alabama in the late 1990s, it gave the company an opportunity to start with a "clean sheet" for designing a car-building system for the twenty-first century. The system that evolved is similar to the "lean production systems" that Japanese manufacturers like Toyota have long been famous for. It emphasizes *just-in-time* inventory methods, so that inventories stay negligible due to the arrival "just in time" of parts for the assembly line. It emphasizes *stable production flows*, since reducing surprises (such as cars reaching the end of the line with defects that the workers must then repair) boosts quality. The new system organizes employees into *work teams*, and emphasizes the fact that all employees must dedicate themselves to *continuous improvement*.

Job analysis plays a role in this "factory of the future." Rather than having dozens or hundreds of different job descriptions, those in Mercedes-Benz's Alabama plant are relatively simplified and standardized, and there are actually relatively few different job descriptions or job titles. This makes it easier for employees to move from job to job as they work on teams, and encourages employees to look beyond their own jobs to find ways to improve the plant's operations. In just a few months' time, for instance, one team found a $.23 plastic prong that works better than the previous $2.50 prong the plant was using to keep car doors open during painting. The same team also redesigned the racks that the assembly parts move on, saving assembly workers thousands of steps per year (and thereby improving productivity and quality).

Now that this new system has proved itself in Alabama, Mercedes-Benz is extending it to plants around the world. For example, its other plants in the United States, as well as in South Africa, Brazil, and Germany, now use this new production system, including the simpler and broader job descriptions.

Source: Lindsey Chappell, "Mercedes Factories Embrace a New Order," *Automotive News*, May 28, 2001.

From Specialized to Enlarged Jobs

The term *job* as we know it today is largely an outgrowth of the industrial revolution's emphasis on efficiency. During this time, experts like Adam Smith and Frederick Taylor wrote glowingly of the positive correlation between specialized jobs and efficiency. Jobs and job descriptions, until quite recently, tended to follow their prescriptions and to be fairly detailed and specific.

By the mid-1900s other writers were reacting to what they viewed as the "dehumanizing" aspects of pigeonholing workers into highly repetitive and specialized jobs; many proposed solutions like job enlargement, job rotation, and job enrichment. **Job enlargement** means assigning workers additional same-level activities, thus increasing the number of activities they perform. Thus, the worker who previously only bolted the seat to the legs might attach the back as well. **Job rotation** means systematically moving workers from one job to another.

Psychologist Frederick Herzberg argued that the best way to motivate workers is to build opportunities for challenge and achievement into their jobs via job enrichment. **Job enrichment** means redesigning jobs in a way that increases the opportunities for the worker to experience feelings of responsibility, achievement, growth, and recognition—for instance, by letting the worker plan and control his or her own work instead of having it controlled by outsiders.

job enlargement
Assigning workers additional same-level activities, thus increasing the number of activities they perform.

job rotation
Systematically moving workers from one job to another to enhance work team performance and/or to broaden his or her experience and identify strong and weak points to prepare the person for an enhanced role with the company.

job enrichment
Redesigning jobs in a way that increases the opportunities for the worker to experience feelings of responsibility, achievement, growth, and recognition.

Why Managers Are Dejobbing Their Companies

Whether specialized, enlarged, or enriched, however, workers still generally have had specific jobs to do, and these jobs have required job descriptions. In many firms today, however, jobs are becoming more amorphous and more difficult to define. In other words, the trend is toward dejobbing.

dejobbing
Broadening the responsibilities of the company's jobs, and encouraging employees not to limit themselves to what's on their job descriptions.

   Dejobbing—broadening the responsibilities of the company's jobs, and encouraging employees not to limit themselves to what's on their job descriptions—is a result of the changes taking place in business today. Organizations need to grapple with trends like rapid product and technological change, global competition, deregulation, political instability, demographic changes, and a shift to a service economy. This has increased the need for firms to be responsive, flexible, and generally more competitive. In turn, the organizational methods managers use to accomplish this have helped weaken the meaning of *job* as a well-defined and clearly delineated set of responsibilities. Here is a sampling of organizational factors that have contributed to this weakening, and to encouraging workers not to limit themselves to narrowly defined jobs.

Flatter Organizations   Instead of traditional, pyramid-shaped organizations with seven or more management layers, flat organizations with just three or four levels are more prevalent. Most large firms have already cut their management layers from a dozen to six or fewer. Because the remaining managers have more people reporting to them, they can supervise them less, so the jobs of subordinates end up bigger in terms of both breadth and depth of responsibilities.

Work Teams   Managers increasingly organize tasks around teams and processes rather than around specialized functions. For example, at Chesebrough-Ponds USA, a subsidiary of Unilever, managers replaced a traditional pyramidal organization with multiskilled, cross-functional, and self-directed teams; the latter now run the plant's four product areas. Hourly employees make employee assignments, schedule overtime, establish production times and changeovers, and even handle cost control, requisitions, and work orders. They also are solely responsible for quality control under the plant's continuous quality improvement program.[27] In an organization like this, employees' jobs change daily; there is thus an intentional effort to avoid having employees view their jobs as a specific, narrow set of responsibilities.

boundaryless organization
Organization marked by the widespread use of teams and similar structural mechanisms that reduce and make more permeable the boundaries that typically separate departments.

The Boundaryless Organization   In a **boundaryless organization** the widespread use of teams and cross-functional task forces reduces and makes more permeable the boundaries that typically separate departments (like sales and production) and hierarchical levels.[28] Boundaryless organizations foster company responsiveness by encouraging employees to rid themselves of the "it's-not-my-job" attitudes that typically create walls between one employee's area and another's. Instead the focus is on defining the project or task at hand in terms of the overall best interests of the organization, thereby further reducing the idea of a job as a clearly defined set of duties.

reengineering
The fundamental rethinking and radical redesign of business processes to achieve dramatic improvements in critical, contemporary measures of performance, such as cost, quality, service, and speed.

Reengineering   **Reengineering** is "the fundamental rethinking and radical redesign of business processes to achieve dramatic improvements in critical contemporary measures of performance, such as cost, quality, service, and speed."[29] In their book *Reengineering the Corporation*, Michael Hammer and James Champy argue that the principles that shaped the structure and management of business for hundreds of years—like highly specialized divisions of work—should be retired. Instead, the firm should emphasize combining tasks into integrated, unspecialized processes (such as customer service) assigned to teams of employees.

At a Nissan factory in Tokyo, Japan, workers meet at a productivity session, surrounded by unfinished car frames hanging along the assembly line. Work teams like this are part of the trend toward a multiskilled, cross-functional, self-directed team organization that allows workers greater autonomy in meeting goals. In plants like these, broadly described jobs that emphasize employees' required competencies are replacing narrowly defined jobs.

competencies
Demonstrable characteristics of a person that enable performance of a job.

competency-based job analysis
Describing a job in terms of the measurable, observable, behavioral competencies an employee must exhibit to do a job well.

You can reengineer jobs in many ways. For example, you can combine several different specialized jobs into a few relatively enlarged and enriched ones.[30] Typically, in reengineered situations workers tend to become collectively responsible for overall results rather than being individually responsible for just their own tasks: "They share joint responsibility with their team members for performing the whole process, not just a small piece of it. They not only use a broader range of skills from day to day, they have to be thinking of a far greater picture."[31] Most important, "while not every member of the team will be doing exactly the same work . . . the lines between [the workers' jobs] blur," and jobs are thus very broadly defined.

Competency-Based Job Analysis

Not coincidently, many employers and job analysis experts say traditional job analysis procedures can't go on playing a central role in HR management.[32] Their basic concern is this: that in high-performance work environments in which employers need workers to seamlessly move from job to job and exercise self-control, job descriptions based on lists of job-specific duties may actually inhibit (or fail to encourage) the flexible behavior companies need. Employers are therefore shifting toward newer approaches for describing jobs, one of which, competency-based analysis, we'll focus on in this section.

What Are Competencies?   We can simply define **competencies** as demonstrable characteristics of the person that enable performance. Job competencies are always observable and measurable behaviors comprising part of a job. Unfortunately, once we get beyond that simple definition, there's some confusion over what exactly "competencies" means. Different organizations define "competencies" in somewhat different ways. Some define them more broadly, and use "competencies" synonymously with the knowledge, or skills, or abilities a person needs to do the job. Others define competencies more narrowly, in terms of measurable behaviors. Here, you would identify the job's required competencies by simply completing the phrase, "In order to perform this job competently, the employee should be able to: . . . ".

We can say that **competency-based job analysis** means describing the job in terms of the measurable, observable, behavioral competencies (knowledge, skills, and/or behaviors) that an employee doing that job must exhibit to do the job well. This contrasts with the traditional way of describing the job in terms of job duties and responsibilities.[33] Traditional job analysis focuses on "what" is accomplished—on duties and responsibilities. Competency analysis focuses more on "how" the worker meets the job's objectives or actually accomplishes the work.[34] Traditional job analysis is thus more job focused. Competency-based analysis is more worker focused—specifically, what must he or she be competent to do?

Why Use Competency Analysis?   There are three reasons to describe jobs in terms of competencies rather than duties. First, as mentioned earlier, traditional job descriptions (with their lists of specific duties) may actually backfire if a *high-performance work system* is your goal. The whole thrust of these systems is to encourage employees to work in a self-motivated way, by organizing the work around teams, by encouraging team members to rotate freely among jobs (each with its own skill set), by pushing more responsibility for things like day-to-day supervision down to the workers, and by organizing work around projects or processes in which jobs may blend or overlap. Employees here must be enthusiastic about learning and moving among jobs. Giving someone a job description with a list of specific duties may simply breed a "that's-not-my-job" attitude, by pigeonholing workers too narrowly.

Second, describing the job in terms of the skills, knowledge, and competencies the worker needs is *more strategic*. For example, Canon's strategic emphasis on miniaturization and precision manufacturing means it should encourage some employees to develop their expertise in these two strategically crucial areas.

Third, we'll see later in this book that measurable skills, knowledge, and competencies are the heart of any company's *performance management process*. As at Canon, achieving a firm's strategic goals means that employees must exhibit certain skills and competencies. **Performance management** means basing your employees' training, appraisals, and rewards on fostering and rewarding the skills and competencies he or she needs to achieve his or her goals. Describing the job in terms of skills and competencies facilitates this.

performance management
Basing your employees' training, appraisals, and rewards on fostering and rewarding the skills and competencies he or she needs to achieve his or her goals.

Examples of Competencies
In practice, managers often write paragraph-length competencies for jobs, and organize these into two or three clusters. For example, the job's required competencies might include *general competencies* (such as reading, writing, and mathematical reasoning), *leadership competencies* (such as leadership, strategic thinking, and teaching others), and *technical competencies* (which focus on the specific technical competencies required for specific types of jobs and/or occupations).

So, some technical competencies for the job of systems engineer might include the following:

- Design complex software applications, establish protocols, and create prototypes.
- Establish the necessary platform requirements to efficiently and completely coordinate data transfer.
- Prepare comprehensive and complete documentation including specifications, flow diagrams, process patrols, and budgets.[35]

Similarly, for a corporate treasurer, technical competencies might include:

- Formulate trade recommendations, by studying several computer models for currency trends, and using various quantitative techniques to determine the financial impact of certain financial trades.
- Recommend specific trades and when to make them.
- Present recommendations and persuade others to follow the recommended course of action.[36] (Note that exhibiting this competency presumes the treasurer has certain knowledge and skills that one could measure.)

Comparing Traditional versus Competency-based Job Analysis
In practice, if you pick up almost any job description today, you'll probably find that some of the job's listed duties and responsibilities are competency-based, while most are not. For example, consider the typical duties you might find in a marketing manager's job description. Which of the duties would complete the phrase, "In order to perform this job competently, the employee should be able to: . . . "?

Some familiar duties and responsibilities would not fit these requirements. For example, "works with writers and artists and overseas copywriting, design, layout, and production of promotional materials" is not particularly measurable. How could you measure the extent to which the employee "works with writers and artists" or "overseas copywriting, design, and layout"? Put another way, if you had to devise a training program for this job's incumbent, how would you determine whether you'd adequately trained the person to work with writers and artists? In fact, what sort of training would that duty and responsibility even imply? It's not clear at all. On the other hand, some of the job's typical duties and responsibilities are more easily expressed as competencies. For example, we could easily complete the phrase, "to perform this job competently, the employee should be able to" with "conduct marketing surveys on current and new-product concepts; prepare marketing activity reports; and develop and execute marketing plans and programs."

How to Write Job Competencies   Defining the job's competencies and writing them up involves a process that is similar in most respects to traditional job analysis. In other words, the manager will interview job incumbents and their supervisors, ask open-ended questions regarding job responsibilities and activities, and perhaps identify critical incidents that pinpoint success on the job. There are also off-the-shelf competencies databanks. Perhaps the largest sourcebook for standard competencies is the one created by the Department of Labor's Office of Personnel Management (see www.opm.gov).[37]

BP's Matrices

Modern, competency-based job analysis/job design techniques can help companies implement high-performance strategies. In one firm—British Petroleum's exploration division—the need for more efficient, flexible, flatter organizations and empowered employees inspired management to replace job descriptions with matrices listing skills and skill levels. Senior managers wanted to shift employees' attention from a job description/"that's-not-my-job" mentality to one that would motivate them to obtain the new skills and competencies they needed to accomplish their broader responsibilities.[38]

The solution was a skills matrix like that in Figure 4-11. They created skills matrices for various jobs held by two groups of employees, those on a management

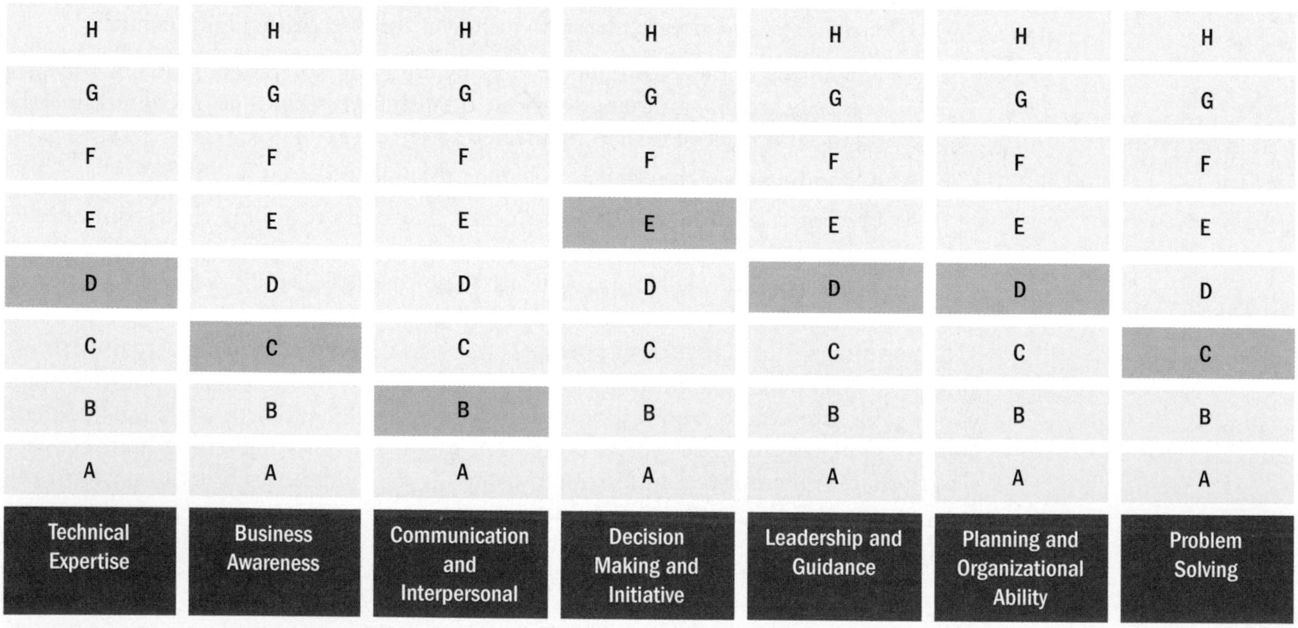

Figure 4-11
The Skills Matrix for One Job at BP

Note: The light blue boxes indicate the minimum level of skill required for the job.

track and those whose aims lay elsewhere (such as to stay in engineering). HR prepared a matrix for each job or job family (such as drilling manager). As in Figure 4-11, the matrix listed (1) the basic skills needed for that job (such as technical expertise and business awareness) and (2) the minimum level of each skill required for that job or job family. As you can see, the emphasis is no longer on specific job duties. Instead, the focus is on specifying and developing the new skills (technical expertise, business awareness, and so on) needed for the employees' broader, empowered, and relatively undefined responsibilities.

The skills matrix triggered other HR changes, and supported a performance management effort. For example, the matrices gave employees a constant reminder of what skills they must improve. The firm instituted a new skill-based pay plan that awards raises based on skills improvement. Performance appraisals now focus more on skills acquisitions. And training emphasizes developing broad skills like leadership and planning—skills applicable across a wide range of responsibilities and jobs. The HR Scorecard feature shows how Lisa Cruz applied this chapter's material.

The HR Scorecard
Strategy and Results

The Hotel Paris's competitive strategy is "To use superior guest service to differentiate the Hotel Paris properties, and to thereby increase the length of stay and return rate of guests, and thus boost revenues and profitability." HR manager Lisa Cruz must now formulate functional policies and activities that support this competitive strategy, by eliciting the required employee behaviors and competencies.

A preliminary analysis, performed jointly by Lisa and the Hotel Paris's chief financial officer, left them optimistic that HR could contribute measurably to achieving the hotel's strategic aims. Several employee competencies and behaviors including employee morale, employee commitment, and the percent of arriving guests receiving the hotel's required greeting had significant effects on customer and organizational outcomes such as guest satisfaction and frequency of guest returns. In turn, outcomes like these contributed measurably to the Hotel Paris's strategic goals, including profit margins, market share, and scores on industry satisfaction surveys. Lisa and her team now turn to creating a job analysis process that will help to produce the required employee competencies and behaviors. The accompanying HR Scorecard (Figure 4-12) outlines how the relationships involved.

Lisa Cruz knew that without accurate job descriptions, all her HR improvement efforts would be in vain since, if you don't know a job's duties, responsibilities, and human requirements, how can you decide whom to hire or how to train them?

A brief analysis, conducted with her company's CFO, reinforced that observation. They chose departments across the hotel chain that did and did not have updated job descriptions. While they understood that many other factors might be influencing the results, they believed that the statistical relationships they observed did suggest that having job descriptions had a positive influence on various employee behaviors and competencies. Perhaps having the descriptions facilitated the employee selection process, or perhaps the departments with the descriptions just had better managers. In any case, Lisa received the go-ahead to design new job descriptions for the chain.

While the resulting job descriptions included numerous traditional duties and responsibilities, most also included several competencies unique to each job. For example, job descriptions for the front-desk clerks included competencies such as "able to check a guest in or out in five minutes or less." Most service employees' descriptions included the competency, "able to exhibit patience and guest supportiveness even when busy with other activities." Lisa knew that including these competencies would make it easier for her team to devise useful employee selection, training, and evaluation processes.

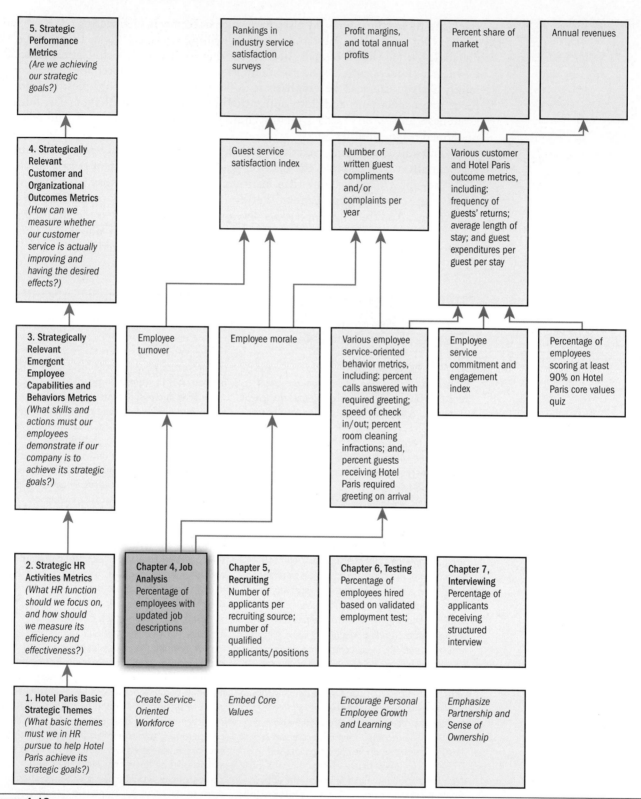

Figure 4-12
HR Scorecard for Hotel Paris International Corporation*

*Note: *(An abbreviated example showing selected HR practices and outcomes aimed at implementing the competitive strategy, "To use superior guest services to differentiate the Hotel Paris properties and thus increase the length of stays and the return rate of guests and thus boost revenues and profitability")*

Review

SUMMARY

1. Developing an organization structure results in jobs that have to be staffed. Job analysis is the procedure through which you find out (1) what the job entails and (2) what kinds of people you should hire for the job. It involves six steps: (1) determine the use of the job analysis information, (2) collect background information, (3) select the positions to be analyzed, (4) collect job analysis data, (5) review information with participants, and (6) develop a job description and job specification.

2. You can use four basic techniques to gather job analysis data: interviews, direct observation, questionnaires, and participant diary logs. These are good for developing job descriptions and specifications. The Department of Labor, functional job analysis, and PAQ approaches result in quantitative ratings of each job and are usually useful for classifying jobs for pay purposes.

3. The job description should portray the work of the position so well that the duties are clear without reference to other job descriptions. Always ask, "Will the new employee understand the job if he or she reads the job description?"

4. The job specification takes the job description and uses it to answer the question, "What human traits and experience are necessary to do this job well?" It tells what kind of person to recruit and for what qualities that person should be tested. Job specifications are usually based on the educated guesses of managers; a more accurate statistical approach to developing job specifications can also be used, however.

5. Use the Standard Occupational Classification to help you write job descriptions. Find and reproduce the descriptions that relate to the job you're describing. Then use those descriptions to "anchor" your own description and particularly to suggest duties to be included. You can also use Internet sources like jobdescription.com.

6. Firms increasingly use O*NET to create job descriptions. To use this tool, start at http://online.onetcenter.org.

7. Dejobbing is ultimately a product of the rapid changes taking place in business today. As firms try to speed decision making by taking steps such as reengineering, individual jobs are becoming broader and much less specialized. Increasingly, firms don't want employees to feel limited by a specific set of responsibilities like those listed in a job description. As a result, more employers are substituting brief job summaries, perhaps combined with summaries of the skills required for the position.

8. Competency-based analysis means describing a job in terms of measurable, observable, behavioral competencies that an employee doing the job must exhibit to do well. For example, these might include "create prototypes" and "design complex software programs."

DISCUSSION QUESTIONS

1. What items are typically included in the job description? What items are typically not shown?

2. What is job analysis? How can you make use of the information it provides?

3. We discussed several methods for collecting job analysis data—questionnaires, the position analysis questionnaire, and so on. Compare and contrast these methods, explaining what each is useful for and listing the pros and cons of each.

4. Describe the types of information typically found in a job specification.

5. Explain how you would conduct a job analysis.

6. Do you think companies can really do without detailed job descriptions? Why or why not?

7. In a company with only 25 employees, is there less need for job descriptions? Why or why not?

INDIVIDUAL AND GROUP ACTIVITIES

1. Working individually or in groups, obtain copies of job descriptions for clerical positions at the college or university where you study, or the firm where you work. What types of information do they contain? Do they give you enough information to explain what the job involves and how to do it? How would you improve on the description?

2. Working individually or in groups, use O*NET to develop a job description for your professor in this class. Based on that, use your judgment to develop a job specification. Compare your conclusions with those of other students or groups. Were there any significant differences? What do you think accounted for the differences?

3. The HRCI "Test Specifications" appendix at the end of this book (pages 685–689) lists the knowledge someone studying for the HRCI certification exam needs to have in each area of human resource management (such as in Strategic Management, Workforce Planning, and Human Resource Development). In groups of four to five students, do four things: (1) review that appendix now; (2) identify the material in this chapter that relates to the required knowledge in the appendix lists; (3) write four multiple choice exam questions on this material that you believe would be suitable for inclusion in the HRCI exam; and (4) if time permits, have someone from your team post your team's questions in front of the class, so the students in other teams can take each others' exam questions.

EXPERIENTIAL EXERCISE

The Instructor's Job Description

Purpose: The purpose of this exercise is to give you experience in developing a job description, by developing one for your instructor.

Required Understanding: You should understand the mechanics of job analysis and be thoroughly familiar with the job analysis questionnaires. (See Figures 4-3 and 4-4 and the job description questionnaire, Figure 4-10.)

How to Set Up the Exercise/Instructions: Set up groups of four to six students for this exercise. As in all exercises in this book, the groups should be separated and should not converse with each other. Half the groups in the class will develop the job description using the job analysis questionnaire (4-3), and the other half of the groups will develop it using the job description questionnaire (4-9). Each student should review his or her questionnaire (as appropriate) before joining his or her group.

1. Each group should do a job analysis of the instructor's job: half the groups will use the Figure 4-3 job analysis questionnaire for this purpose, and half will use the Figure 4-9 job description questionnaire.

2. Based on this information, each group will develop its own job description and job specification for the instructor.

3. Next, each group should choose a partner group, one that developed the job description and job specification using the alternate method. (A group that used the job analysis questionnaire should be paired with a group that used the job description questionnaire.)

4. Finally, within each of these new combined groups, compare and critique each of the two sets of job descriptions and job specifications. Did each job analysis method provide different types of information? Which seems superior? Does one seem more advantageous for some types of jobs than others?

APPLICATION CASE

Tropical Storm Charley

In August 2004, tropical storm Charley hit North Carolina and the Optima Air Filter Company. Many employees' homes were devastated, and the firm found that it had to hire almost three completely new crews, one for each of its shifts. The problem was that the "old-timers" had known their jobs so well that no one had ever bothered to draw up job descriptions for them. When about 30 new employees began taking their places, there was general confusion about what they should do and how they should do it.

The storm quickly became old news to the firm's out-of-state customers, who wanted filters, not excuses. Phil Mann, the firm's president, was at his wits' end. He had about 30 new employees, 10 old-timers, and his original factory supervisor, Maybelline. He decided to meet with Linda Lowe, a consultant from the local university's business school. She immediately had the old-timers fill out a job questionnaire that listed all their duties. Arguments ensued almost at once: Both Phil and Maybelline thought the old-timers were exaggerating to make themselves look more important, and the old-timers insisted that the lists faithfully reflected their duties. Meanwhile, the customers clamored for their filters.

Questions

1. Should Phil and Linda ignore the old-timers' protests and write up the job descriptions as they see fit? Why? Why not? How would you go about resolving the differences?

2. How would you have conducted the job analysis? What should Phil do now?

CONTINUING CASE

Carter Cleaning Company

The Job Description

Based on her review of the stores, Jennifer concluded that one of the first matters she had to attend to involved developing job descriptions for her store managers.

As Jennifer tells it, her lessons regarding job descriptions in her basic management and HR management courses were insufficient to fully convince her of the pivotal role job descriptions actually played in the smooth functioning of an enterprise. Many times during her first few weeks on the job, Jennifer found herself asking one of her store managers why he was violating what she knew to be recommended company policies and procedures. Repeatedly, the answers were either "Because I didn't know it was my job" or "Because I didn't know that was the way we were supposed to do it." Jennifer knew that a job description, along with a set of standards and procedures that specified what was to be done and how to do it, would go a long way toward alleviating this problem.

In general, the store manager is responsible for directing all store activities in such a way that quality work is produced, customer relations and sales are maximized, and profitability is maintained through effective control of labor, supply, and energy costs. In accomplishing that general aim, a specific store manager's duties and responsibilities include quality control, store appearance and cleanliness, customer relations, bookkeeping and cash management, cost control and productivity, damage control, pricing, inventory control, spotting and cleaning, machine maintenance, purchasing, employee safety, hazardous waste removal, human resource administration, and pest control.

The questions that Jennifer had to address follow.

Questions

1. What should be the format and final form of the store manager's job description?

2. Is it practical to specify standards and procedures in the body of the job description, or should these be kept separate?

3. How should Jennifer go about collecting the information required for the standards, procedures, and job description?

4. What, in your opinion, should the store manager's job description look like and contain?

KEY TERMS

job analysis, 112

job description, 112

job specifications, 112

organization chart, 113

process chart, 114

diary/log, 117

position analysis questionnaire (PAQ), 122

U.S. Department of Labor (DOL) job analysis procedure, 123

functional job analysis, 124

Standard Occupational Classification (SOC), 129

job enlargement, 138

job rotation, 138

job enrichment, 138

dejobbing, 139

boundaryless organization, 139

reengineering, 139

competencies, 140

competency-based job analysis, 140

performance management, 141

ENDNOTES

1. For a good discussion of job analysis, see James Clifford, "Job Analysis: Why Do It, and How Should It Be Done?" *Public Personnel Management* 23, no. 2 (Summer 1994), pp. 321–340.

2. James Clifford, "Manage Work Better to Better Manage Human Resources: A Comparative Study of Two Approaches to Job Analysis," *Public Personnel Management*, Spring 1996, pp. 89–102.

3. Richard Henderson, *Compensation Management: Rewarding Performance* (Upper Saddle River, NJ: Prentice Hall, 1994), pp. 139–150.

4. Wayne Cascio, *Applied Psychology in Human Resource Management* (Upper Saddle River, NJ: Prentice Hall, 1998), p. 142. See also, Michael Lundell et al., "Relationships Between Organizational Content and Job Analysis Task Ratings," *Journal of Applied Psychology* 83, no. 5 (1998), pp. 769–776.

5. See Henderson, *Compensation Management*, pp. 148–152.

6. Note that the PAQ (and other quantitative techniques) can also be used for job evaluation, which is explained in Chapter 11.

7. Again, we will see that job evaluation is the process through which jobs are compared to one another and their values determined. Although usually viewed as a job analysis technique, the PAQ is, in practice, actually as much or more of a job evaluation technique and could therefore be discussed in either this chapter or in Chapter 11. For a discussion of how to use PAQ for classifying jobs for pay purposes, see Edwin Cornelius III, Theodore Carron, and Marianne Collins, "Job Analysis Models and Job Classifications," *Personnel Psychology* 32 (Winter 1979), pp. 693–708. See also, Edwin Cornelius III, Frank Schmidt, and Theodore Carron, "Job Classification Approaches and the Implementation of Validity Generalization Results," *Personnel Psychology* 37, no. 2 (Summer 1984), pp. 247–260.

8. Jack Smith and Milton Hakel, "Comparisons Among Data Sources, Response Bias, and Reliability and Validity of a Structured Job Analysis Questionnaire," *Personnel Psychology* 32 (Winter 1979), pp. 677–692. See also, Edwin Cornelius III, Angelo DeNisi, and Allyn Blencoe, "Expert and Naive Raters Using the PAQ: Does It Matter?" *Personnel Psychology* 37, no. 3 (Autumn 1984), pp. 453–464; Robert J. Harvey et al., "Dimensionality of the Job Element Inventory: A Simplified Worker-Oriented Job Analysis Questionnaire," *Journal of Applied Psychology*, November 1988, pp. 639–646.

9. This discussion is based on Howard Olson et al., "The Use of Functional Job Analysis in Establishing Performance Standards for Heavy Equipment Operators," *Personnel Psychology* 34 (Summer 1981), pp. 351–364.

10. Frederick P. Morgeson and Michael A. Campion, "Social and Cognitive Sources of Potential Inaccuracy in Job Analysis," *Journal of Applied Psychology* 82, no. 5 (1997), pp. 627–655.

11. Ibid., p. 648.

12. Regarding this discussion, see Henderson, *Compensation Management*, pp. 175–184. See also, Louisa Wah, "The Alphabet Soup of Job Titles," *Management Review* 87, no. 6, pp. 40–43.

13. James Evered, "How to Write a Good Job Description," *Supervisory Management*, April 1981, pp. 14–19; Roger J. Plachy,

"Writing Job Descriptions That Get Results," *Personnel*, October 1987, pp. 56–58. See also, Matthew Mariani, "Replace with a Database," *Occupational Outlook Quarterly* 43, no. 1 (Spring 1999), pp. 2–9.

14. Ibid., p. 16.

15. Ibid., p. 16.

16. Ibid., p. 16.

17. Ibid., p. 17.

18. Deborah Kearney, *Reasonable Accommodations: Job Descriptions in the Age of ADA, OSHA, and Workers Comp* (New York: Van Nostrand Reinhold, 1994), p. 9. See also, Paul Starkman, "The ADA's Essential Job Function Requirements: Just How Essential Does an Essential Job Function Have to Be?" *Employee Relations Law Journal* 26, no. 4 (Spring 2001), pp. 43–102.

19. Michael Esposito, "There's More to Writing Job Descriptions Than Complying with the ADA," *Employment Relations Today*, Autumn 1992, p. 279. See also, Richard Morfopoulos and William Roth, "Job Analysis and the Americans with Disabilities Act," *Business Horizons* 39, no. 6 (November 1996), pp. 68–72; and Kristin Mitchell, George Alliger, and Richard Morfopoulos, "Toward an ADA-Appropriate Job Analysis," *Human Resource Management Review* 7, no. 1 (Spring 1997), pp. 5–16.

20. James Evered, "How to Write a Good Job Description," p. 18.

21. Matthew Mariani, "Replace with a Database: O*NET Replaces the *Dictionary of Occupational Titles*," *Occupational Outlook Quarterly* 43 (Spring 1999), pp. 2–9.

22. Based on Ernest J. McCormick and Joseph Tiffin, *Industrial Psychology* (Upper Saddle River, NJ: Prentice Hall, 1974), pp. 56–61.

23. Steven Hunt, "Generic Work Behavior: An Investigation into the Dimensions of Entry-Level, Hourly Job Performance," *Personnel Psychology* 49 (1996), pp. 51–83.

24. Jorgen Sandberg, "Understanding Competence at Work," *Harvard Business Review*, March 2001, p. 28.

25. David Shair, "Wizardry Makes Charts Relevant," *HR Magazine*, April 2000, p. 127.

26. William Bridges, "The End of the Job," *Fortune*, September 19, 1994, p. 64.

27. William H. Miller, "Chesebrough-Ponds at a Glance," *Industry Week*, October 19, 1992, pp. 14–15. For an interesting discussion of the need to move from an "it's-not-my-job" mentality from the point of view of an employee, see Kathy Shaw, "It's Not in My Job Description," *CMA Magazine*, June 1994, p. 42.

28. Larry Hirschhorn and Thomas Gilmore, "The New Boundaries of the Boundaryless Company," *Harvard Business Review*, May–June 1992, pp. 104–108. For another point of view, see George Stack Jr. and Jill Black, "The Myth of the Horizontal Organization," *Canadian Business Review*, Winter 1994, pp. 28–31.

29. Michael Hammer and James Champy, *Reengineering the Corporation* (New York: Harper Business, 1993), p. 32.

30. Ibid., p. 51.

31. Ibid., p. 68.

32. Jeffrey Shippmann et al., "The Practice of Competency Modeling," *Personnel Psychology* 53, no. 3 (2000), p. 703.

33. Ibid.

34. Ibid.

35. Adapted from Richard Mirabile, "Everything You Wanted to Know About Competency Modeling," *Training and Development* 51, no. 8 (August 1997), pp. 73–78.

36. Dennis Kravetz, "Building a Job Competency Database: What the Leaders Do," Kravetz Associates (Bartlett, Illinois, 1997).

37. www.opm.gov/.

38. Milan Moravec and Robert Tucker, "Job Descriptions for the 21st Century," *Personnel Journal*, June 1992, pp. 37–44.

After studying this chapter, you should be able to:

1 Explain the main techniques used in employment planning and forecasting.

2 List and discuss the main outside sources of candidates.

3 Effectively recruit job candidates.

4 Name and describe the main internal sources of candidates.

5 Develop a help wanted ad.

6 Explain how to recruit a more diverse workforce.

Personnel Planning and Recruiting

As a longtime HR professional, Lisa Cruz was well aware of the importance

of effective employee recruitment. If the Hotel Paris didn't get enough

applicants, it could not be selective about who to hire. And, if it could not be

selective about who to hire, it wasn't likely that the hotels would enjoy the

customer-oriented employee behaviors that the company's strategy relied

on. She was therefore disappointed to discover that the Hotel Paris was

paying virtually no attention to the job of recruiting prospective employees.

Individual hotel managers slapped together help wanted ads when they had

positions to fill, and no one in the chain had any measurable idea of how

many recruits these ads were producing or which recruiting approaches

worked the best (or worked at all). Lisa knew that it was time to step back

and get control of the Hotel Paris's recruitment function.●

Figure 5-1
Steps in Recruitment and Selection Process

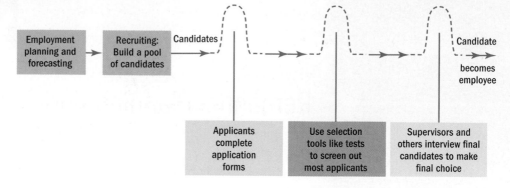

The recruitment and selection process is a series of hurdles aimed at selecting the best candidate for the job.

In the previous chapter, we discussed job analysis and the methods managers use to create job descriptions and job specifications. The purpose of this chapter is to improve your effectiveness in recruiting candidates. The topics we discuss include personnel planning and forecasting, recruiting job candidates, and developing and using application forms.

Personnel planning is the first step in the recruiting and selection process. We can conveniently view this process as a series of hurdles, as shown in Figure 5-1:

1. Decide what positions you'll have to fill through personnel planning and forecasting.

2. Build a pool of candidates for these jobs by recruiting internal or external candidates.

3. Have candidates complete application forms and perhaps undergo an initial screening interview.

4. Use selection techniques like tests, background investigations, and physical exams to identify viable candidates.

5. Decide who to make an offer to, by having the supervisor and perhaps others on the team interview the candidates.

We discuss recruitment and selection in this and the next two chapters. This chapter focuses on personnel planning and forecasting (in other words, on how to determine what positions are to be filled) and on recruiting techniques. Chapter 6 addresses selection techniques, including tests, background checks, and physical exams. Chapter 7 focuses on interviewing—by far the most widely used selection technique.

● PLANNING AND FORECASTING

employment or personnel planning
The process of deciding what positions the firm will have to fill, and how to fill them.

Employment or personnel planning is the process of deciding what positions the firm will have to fill, and how to fill them. Personnel planning covers all future positions, from maintenance clerk to CEO. However, most firms call the process of deciding how to fill the company's most important executive jobs *succession planning*.

Employment planning should be an integral part of a firm's strategic and HR planning processes. Plans to enter new businesses, build new plants, or reduce costs all influence the types of positions the firm will need to fill. Thus, when JDS Uniphase, which designs, develops, and manufactures and markets products for the fiber optics market, decided to expand its Melbourne, Florida, operations, its managers knew they'd have to expand its employment there from 140 people to almost 750. That meant they needed plans for who to hire, how to screen applicants, and when to put the plans into place. Figure 5-2 summarizes the link between strategic and personnel planning.

One big question is whether to fill projected openings from within or from outside the firm. In other words, should you plan to fill positions with current employees or by recruiting from outside? Each option produces its own set of HR plans. Current employees may require training, development, and coaching before they're ready to fill new jobs. Going outside requires a decision about what recruiting sources to use, among other things.

Like all good plans, management builds employment plans on basic assumptions about the future. Forecasting generates these assumptions. If you're planning for employment requirements, you'll usually need to forecast three things: personnel needs, the supply of inside candidates, and the supply of outside candidates. We'll start with personnel needs.

Forecasting Personnel Needs

1 Explain the main techniques used in employment planning and forecasting.

The most common personnel planning approaches involve the use of simple techniques like ratio analysis or trend analysis to estimate staffing needs based on sales projections and historical sales to personnel relationships.[1]

The usual process is to forecast revenues first, then estimate the size of the staff required to achieve this sales volume. Here, HR managers use several techniques.

trend analysis
Study of a firm's past employment needs over a period of years to predict future needs.

Trend Analysis   **Trend analysis** means studying variations in your firm's employment levels over the last few years. You might compute the number of employees in your firm at the end of each of the last five years, or perhaps the number in each subgroup (like sales, production, secretarial, and administrative) at the end of each of those years. The purpose is to identify trends that might continue into the future. Trend analysis can provide an initial estimate, but employment levels rarely depend just on the passage of time. Other factors (like changes in sales volume and productivity) also affect staffing needs.

Figure 5-2
Linking Strategy Employers to Plans

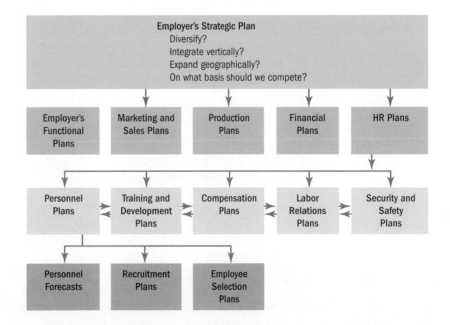

Ratio Analysis Another approach, **ratio analysis**, means making forecasts based on the ratio between (1) some causal factor (like sales volume) and (2) the number of employees required (for instance, number of salespeople). For example, suppose a salesperson traditionally generates $500,000 in sales. If the sales revenue to salespeople ratio remains the same, you would require six new salespeople next year (each of whom produces an extra $500,000) to produce a hoped-for extra $3 million in sales.

Like trend analysis, ratio analysis assumes that productivity remains about the same—for instance, that each salesperson can't be motivated to produce much more than $500,000 in sales. If sales productivity were to increase or decrease, the ratio of sales to salespeople would change. A forecast based on historical ratios would then no longer be accurate.

The Scatter Plot A **scatter plot** shows graphically how two variables—such as a measure of business activity and your firm's staffing levels—are related. If they are, then if you can forecast the level of business activity, you should also be able to estimate your personnel requirements.

For example, assume a 500-bed hospital expects to expand to 1,200 beds over the next five years. The director of nursing and the human resource director want to forecast the requirement for registered nurses. The human resource director decides to determine the relationship between size of hospital (in terms of number of beds) and number of nurses required. She calls five hospitals of various sizes and gets the following figures:

Size of Hospital (Number of Beds)	Number of Registered Nurses
200	240
300	260
400	470
500	500
600	620
700	660
800	820
900	860

Figure 5-3 shows hospital size on the horizontal axis. Number of nurses is shown on the vertical axis. If the two factors are related, then the points will tend to fall along a straight line, as they do here. If you carefully draw in a line to minimize the distances

**Figure 5-3
Determining the
Relationship Between
Hospital Size and Number
of Nurses**

Note: After fitting the line, you can project how many employees you'll need, given your projected volume.

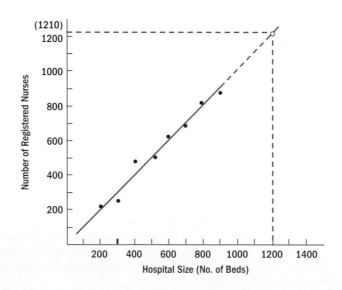

between the line and each one of the plotted points, you will be able to estimate the number of nurses needed for each hospital size. Thus, for a 1,200-bed hospital, the human resource director would assume she needs about 1,210 nurses.[2]

While simple, there are several potential drawbacks to approaches like these.[3]

1. For example, they focus exclusively (or almost exclusively) on projected sales volume and historical sales/personnel relationships, and generally assume that the firm's existing structure and activities will continue into the future.

2. They generally do not consider the impact the company's strategic initiatives may have on future staffing levels.

3. They tend to support outdated compensation plans that reward managers for managing ever-larger staffs, and will not uncover managers who continue to expand their staffs irrespective of the company's strategic needs.

4. They tend to "bake in" the nonproductive idea that increases in staffs are inevitable.

5. They tend to validate and institutionalize existing planning processes and ways of doing things, even in the face of rapid change.

Using Computers to Forecast Personnel Requirements   Employers also use computerized forecasts to estimate future personnel requirements.[4] Typical data needed include direct labor hours required to produce one unit of product (a measure of productivity), and three sales projections—minimum, maximum, and probable—for the product line in question. Based on such data, a typical program generates figures on average staff levels required to meet product demands, as well as separate **computerized forecasts** for direct labor (such as assembly workers), indirect staff (such as secretaries), and exempt staff (such as executives).

computerized forecast
Determination of future staff needs by projecting sales, volume of production, and personnel required to maintain this volume of output, using software packages.

With programs like these, employers can quickly translate projected productivity and sales levels into forecasts of personnel needs. They can then estimate the effects of various productivity and sales level assumptions on personnel requirements.[5]

Many firms use automated employee forecasting systems. In retailing, for instance, automated labor scheduling systems help retailers estimate required staffing needs based on sales forecasts and estimated store traffic.[6]

Whichever method you use, *managerial judgment* will play a big role. It's rare that any historical trend, ratio, or relationship will simply continue unchanged into the future. You will therefore have to modify the forecast based on factors—such as projected turnover or a desire to enter new markets—you believe will be important.

Forecasting the Supply of Inside Candidates

Knowing your staffing needs satisfies only half the staffing equation. Next, you have to estimate the likely supply of both inside and outside candidates. Most firms start with the inside candidates.

The main task is determining which current employees might be qualified for the projected openings. For this you need to know current employees' skills sets—their current qualifications. Sometimes it's obvious how you have to proceed. For example, when Bill Gates needed someone to lead Microsoft's new user interface project, his first question was, "Where's Kai-Fu?" His firm's voice recognition expert, Kai-Fu Lee, was in China at the time establishing a new research lab for the firm.[7] Sometimes it's not so obvious, and managers turn to **qualifications inventories**. These contain data on employees' performance records, educational background, and promotability. These help managers determine which employees are available for promotion or transfer.

qualifications inventories
Manual or computerized records listing employees' education, career and development interests, languages, special skills, and so on, to be used in selecting inside candidates for promotion.

Manual Systems and Replacement Charts   Managers use several simple manual devices to track employee qualifications. A *personnel inventory and development record form* compiles qualifications information on each employee. The information includes education, company-sponsored courses taken, career and development interests, languages, desired assignments, and skills.

Personnel replacement charts (Figure 5-4) are another option, particularly for the firm's top positions. They show the present performance and promotability for each position's potential replacement. As an alternative, you can develop a **position replacement card**. Here you create a card for each position, showing possible replacements as well as their present performance, promotion potential, and training.

Computerized Information Systems   Companies don't generally track the qualifications of hundreds or thousands of employees manually. Most firms computerize this information, using various packaged software systems.[8] (Increasingly, as we'll see, these systems are linked in with the firm's other HR systems, including its automated applicant tracking systems.)

In many of these computerized qualifications systems, the employees and the HR department enter information about employees' background, experience, and skills, often using the company intranet. When a manager needs a person for a position, he or she describes the position (for instance, in terms of education and skills). After scanning its database of possible candidates, the system produces a list of qualified candidates. Such a computerized skills inventory might include *Work experience codes; Product knowledge*, the employee's level of familiarity with the employer's product lines or services; *Industry experience*, the person's industry experiences, since for some positions work in related industries is very useful; and *Formal education*.

The Matter of Privacy   It is important to secure the data in the firm's personnel data banks. First, there is a lot of employee information in most data banks. Second, Internet/intranet access and other changes mean it's often easier for more people to

personnel replacement charts
Company records showing present performance and promotability of inside candidates for the most important positions.

position replacement card
A card prepared for each position in a company to show possible replacement candidates and their qualifications.

Figure 5-4
Management Replacement Chart Showing Development Needs of Future Divisional Vice President

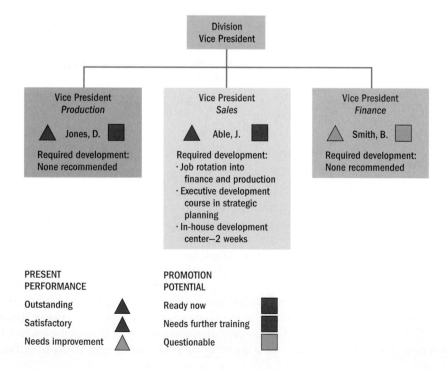

access these data.[9] Third, legislation, such as the Federal Privacy Act of 1974 and the New York Personal Privacy Act of 1985, gives some employees legal rights regarding who has access to information about their work history and job performance.

Balancing the employer's legitimate right to make this information available to those in the firm who need it with the employees' right to privacy isn't easy. One approach is to use the access matrices incorporated in many database management systems. These matrices define the rights of users (specified by name, rank, or functional identification) to various kinds of access (such as "read only" or "write only") to each database element. So the system might authorize employees in accounting to read information such as the employee's address, phone number, Social Security number, and pension status. The HR director, on the other hand, could both read and write all items.

Forecasting the Supply of Outside Candidates

If there won't be enough inside candidates to fill the anticipated openings (or you want to go outside for another reason), you need to forecast the availability of outside candidates. For example, you may want to consider general economic conditions and the expected unemployment rate. Usually, the lower the rate of unemployment, the more difficult it will be to recruit personnel.

Information like this is easy to find, both online and in hard-copy format. For example, *BusinessWeek* presents a weekly snapshot of the economy on its Outlook page, as well as a yearly forecast in December. *Fortune* magazine has a monthly forecast for the coming year. Also look for economic projections online, for example from the U.S. Congressional Budget Office (CBO), http://www.cbo.gov/showdoc.cfm?index=1824&sequence=0; the Bureau of Labor Statistics (BLS), http://www.bls.gov/news.release/ecopro.toc.htm; and from private sources such as economists at the Bank of America, http://www.bankofamerica.com/newsroom/press/press.cfm?PressID=press.20040312.02.htm.

Your plans may also require that you forecast the availability of potential job candidates in specific occupations such as nurse, computer programmer, or teacher. Recently, for instance, there has been an undersupply of nurses. The Bureau of Labor Statistics of the U.S. Department of Labor publishes annual occupational projections both online and in the *Monthly Labor Review* and in *Occupational Outlook Quarterly*. O*NET (discussed in Chapter 4) includes online projections for most occupations. The National Science Foundation regularly forecasts labor market conditions in the science and technology fields. Other federal agencies that provide occupational forecasts include the U.S. Public Health Service, the U.S. Employment Service, and the U.S. Office of Education.

List and discuss the main outside sources of candidates.

● EFFECTIVE RECRUITING

Assuming the company authorizes you to fill a position, the next step is to develop an applicant pool. It's hard to overemphasize the importance of effective recruiting. The more applicants you have, the more selective you can be in your hiring. If only two candidates apply for two openings, you may have little choice but to hire them. But if 10 or 20 applicants appear, you can use techniques like interviews and tests to screen out all but the best.

Effective recruiting is increasingly important today, for several reasons. Barring some dramatic change, there will soon be an undersupply of workers. The Bureau of Labor Statistics estimates the United States will create 22 million new jobs between 2003 and 2010, but only about 17 million new entrants will join the workforce. Several things could change this scenario. If the country continues to export white-collar jobs, then the number of new jobs added domestically will diminish. However, current estimates are for outsourcing only about three million jobs to other countries between 2003 in 2015. Therefore, the trend through 2010 seems to favor the worker.[10]

Even high unemployment, as in 2003–2004, doesn't necessarily mean that it is easy to find good candidates. For example, a survey during that period by the Department of Labor found that about half of respondents said they had "difficulty" finding qualified applicants. About 40% said it was "hard to find" good candidates.[11] Effective recruiting is thus not just important when the unemployment rate is low.

Recruiting is a more complex activity than most managers think it is. It does not just involve placing ads or calling employment agencies. For one thing, your recruitment efforts should make sense in terms of your company's strategic plans. For example, decisions to expand abroad or to fill a large number of anticipated openings imply that you've carefully thought through when and how you will do your recruiting. Second, some recruiting methods are superior to others, depending on the type of job you are recruiting for and what your resources are. Third, the success you have with your recruiting actually depends to a great extent on nonrecruitment HR issues and policies. For example, deciding to pay a 10% higher salary and better benefits than most firms in your locale should, other things being equal, help you build a bigger applicant pool faster.[12] The bottom line is that your recruiting plans (and HR plans in general) must be internally consistent, and make sense in terms of your company's strategy.

Know Your Employment Law

Preemployment Activities

As we explained in Chapter 2, numerous federal, state, and local laws and court decisions restrict what employers can and cannot do when recruiting job applicants. For example, employers can't rely on word-of-mouth dissemination of information about job opportunities when its workforce is all, or substantially all, white or all members of some other class such as all female or all Hispanic. Similarly, it is unlawful to give false or misleading information to members of any group, or to fail or to refuse to advise them of work opportunities and the procedures for obtaining them.

In practice, "the key question in all recruitment procedures is whether the method limits qualified applicants from applying."[13] So, for example, gender-specific ads that call for "busboy," or "firemen" would obviously raise red flags. Similarly, courts will often question word-of-mouth recruiting, because workers tend to nominate candidates of the same nationality, race, and religion.[14] The bottom line is that it is generally best to avoid limiting recruitment efforts to just one recruitment method; use multiple sources to reach out as widely as possible.

In choosing what to ask on the application form, some suggest thinking of the selection process as consisting of two stages. Use the first stage to determine if the applicant is qualified. Limit application form questions to identification and work history, and to those that will enable you to determine if the applicant has the knowledge or skill to perform the functions of any job vacancy. These include questions such as name, address, phone number, Social Security number, person to contact in case of emergency, previous employment, highest wages on previous jobs, and permission to contact previous employer. At this first stage, you should also determine, perhaps through testing, if the person has the knowledge and skills to do the job. If the answer is affirmative, then make a conditional job offer, but make it clear that failing to meet any of the following "second stage" conditions may result in rejection. Then, you may ask acceptable conditional job offer questions[15] such as "How long have you lived at the present address?" and "Do you have adequate means of transportation to get to work?" (see Figure 5-5).

There are two reasons to ensure that every applicant completes the application form fully, and signs a statement on it indicating that the information the person provided is true. For one thing, "The court will almost always support a discharge for falsifying information when applying for work."[16] Second, a less-than-complete job of filling in the form may reflect poor work habits. Some applicants will simply scribble "see résumé attached" on the application; this should not be acceptable.

**Figure 5-5
Sample Acceptable
Questions Once Conditional
Offer Is Made**
Source: Kenneth L. Sovereign,
Personnel Law, 4th edition © 1999.
Reprinted by permission of Pearson
Education, Inc., Upper Saddle River, NJ.

1. Do you have any responsibilities that conflict with the job vacancy?
2. How long have you lived at your present address?
3. Do you have any relatives working for this company?
4. Do you have any physical defects that would prevent you from performing certain jobs where, to your knowledge, vacancies exist?
5. Do you have adequate means of transportation to get to work?
6. Have you had any major illness (treated or untreated) in the past 10 years?
7. Have you ever been convicted of a felony or do you have a history of being a violent person? (This is a very important question to avoid a negligent hiring or retention charge.)
8. Educational background. (The information required here would depend on the job-related requirements of the position.)

Organizing the Recruitment Function

Larger firms, in particular, must decide if they will conduct all their recruiting company-wide from a central recruitment office, or decentralize recruiting to the firm's various offices. There are advantages to centralizing the recruitment function. First, centralizing makes it easier to apply the company's strategic priorities companywide. For example, General Motors North America recently switched from decentralized to centralized recruiting. Formerly, each of GM's geographical units, including its manufacturing plants, did its own recruiting. GM decided to centralize recruitment because it wanted to strengthen its employment brand. Too many potential applicants erroneously viewed GM as somewhat old-fashioned. "We wanted to break away from the old views and be portrayed more realistically" says GM's manager of talent acquisition. About 45 HR professionals in GM's "talent acquisition department" now handle recruiting for all of GM's North American plants.[17]

Recruiting centrally has other advantages. It reduces duplication (having several recruitment offices instead of one), makes it easier to spread the cost of new technologies (such as Internet-based recruitment and prescreening solutions) over more departments, builds a team of recruitment experts, and makes it easier to identify why recruitment efforts are going well (or badly). It also produces synergies. For instance, "instead of looking for one financial analyst, you can recruit for five positions from the same candidate pool."[18] On the other hand, if the firm's divisions are autonomous, or their recruitment needs are varied, it may be more sensible to decentralize the recruitment function.

Line and Staff Cooperation   The HR manager who recruits for a vacant job is seldom the one responsible for supervising its performance. He or she must therefore know exactly what the job entails, and this means speaking with the supervisor involved. For example, the recruiter might want to know about the supervisor's leadership style and about the work group—is it a tough group to get along with, for instance? He or she might also want to visit the work site, to review the job description with the supervisor to ensure that the job hasn't changed, and to obtain any additional insight into the skills and talents the new worker will need. Line and staff coordination is therefore essential.

Measuring Recruiting Effectiveness

Effectively recruit job candidates.

Even small employers may spend tens of thousands of dollars each year recruiting applicants, but few firms assess the effectiveness of their recruitment efforts. Is it more cost-effective to advertise for applicants on the Web, or in Sunday's paper? Should we use this employment agency or that one? One survey found that only about 44% of the 279 firms surveyed made formal attempts to evaluate the outcomes of their recruitment efforts.[19] This inattention flies in the face of common sense. And, it ignores evidence that organizations that engage in specific staffing practices (such as studies to determine which recruitment sources are most effective) have higher annual profits and annual profit growth.[20]

The question is what to measure and how to measure it. In terms of *what* to measure, the easy answer is, "how many applicants did we generate through each of our recruitment sources?" An Internet ad may produce more applicants than one in the Sunday paper, so at a minimum we should assess the various sources based on how many applicants they produce. This makes sense. If more applicants are generated than there are positions to fill, the firm can be more selective.[21]

The problem is that in practice more is not always better. The employer needs to attract *qualified applicants*, not just applicants. One Internet ad may produce thousands of applicants, many from so far away that there is no chance they could be viable candidates. Even with computerized prescreening and tracking software, there are still costs involved in managing applicant pools. Larger applicant pools have more applicants to correspond with and screen, raising costs and potentially extending the time required to fill vacant positions.[22] Furthermore, more applicants may not mean more selectivity. Realistically, the manager looking to hire five engineers probably won't be twice as selective with 20,000 applicants as with 10,000 applicants. At some point, the costs of processing the extra applicants outweigh the benefits of being able to be more selective. The manager must assess not just the number of applicants produced by each source, but also the applicants' quality.

One straightforward way to do this is to assess applicants from various sources, using prescreening selection devices.[23] Table 5-1 shows several selection tools managers can use to get quick assessments of whether an applicant will succeed on the job. For example, general mental ability ("IQ") tests, having applicants perform several job tasks (a "work sample" test), or testing the applicant's job knowledge, are all relatively straight-

Table 5-1

Selection Devices that Could be used to Initially Screen Applicants

Selection device	Validity for predicting job performance*
Construct	
General mental ability tests	.51
Conscientiousness tests	.31
Integrity tests	.41
Method	
Work sample tests	.54
Job knowledge tests	.48
Structured interviews	.51
Biographical data	.35
Grade point average	.23
Ratings of training and experience	.11

Note: *Higher is better.

Source: Kevin Carlson et al., "Recruitment Evaluation: The Case for Assessing the Quality of Applicants Attracted," *Personnel Psychology* 55 (2002), p. 470.

forward ways to show which applicants will succeed and which will not. You can use this information to gauge which recruiting source produces the best applicants for your situation. Having assessed the quality of each recruitment source, the employer may then want to redirect recruiting dollars from sources that produce more applicants but lower-quality ones to sources that produce fewer but better candidates.

A High-Performance Example   The methods used by one industry leader—GE Medical—illustrate how employers apply best-practices measurement techniques to the job of recruiting high-tech workers. GE Medical's competitive strategy of staying on the cutting edge of equipment design makes hiring large numbers of top-flight tech workers essential. The company hires about 500 technical workers a year to invent and make sophisticated medical devices such as CT scanners and magnetic resonance imagers. Since GE Medical must compete for talent with the likes of Microsoft, it's interesting that it has managed to cut its cost of hiring by 17%, reduced time to fill the positions by 20% to 30%, and cut in half the percentage of new hires who don't work out.[24]

GE Medical accomplished this by applying the sorts of best-practices management techniques that made its parent, General Electric Corporation, a profit powerhouse.[25] For example, GE Medical draws up a "multigenerational staffing plan" to go with each of its products' multiyear product plan. That way, management can predict two or three years ahead the sorts of specific hiring needs (such as for "absolute algorithm" experts) for which it will have to hire and train.

GE Medical has also applied some of its purchasing techniques to its dealings with recruiters. For example, it called a meeting several years ago and told 20 recruiters that it would work with only the 10 best. To measure "best," the company created measurements inspired by manufacturing techniques, such as the percentage of résumés that result in interviews and the percentage of interviews that lead to offers.

Applying a more benchmarks-oriented approach also worked with college recruiting. GE Medical's chief recruiter analyzed the division's recruiting system and found that former summer interns were twice as likely to accept a job offer as other candidates. GE Medical then tripled the size of the internship program. And to make sure they don't spend their time photocopying files, interns are given challenging group and team projects.

As another example, GE's corporatewide quality control program enabled GE Medical to discover that current employees are very effective as references for new high-tech employees. Overall, for instance, GE Medical calls for interviews just 1% of applicants whose résumés it receives, while 10% of employee referrals result not only in interviews, but in actual hires. So GE Medical took steps to double the number of employee referrals. It simplified the referral forms, eliminated bureaucratic submission procedures, and added a small reward like a Sears gift certificate for referring a qualified candidate. And it upped the ante—$2,000 if someone referred is hired, and $3,000 if he or she is a software engineer.

The Recruiting Yield Pyramid

recruiting yield pyramid
The historical arithmetic relationships between recruitment leads and invitees, invitees and interviews, interviews and offers made, and offers made and offers accepted.

Some employers use a **recruiting yield pyramid** to calculate the number of applicants they must generate to hire the required number of new employees. In Figure 5-6, the company knows it needs 50 new entry-level accountants next year. From experience, the firm also knows the ratio of offers made to actual new hires is 2 to 1; about half the people to whom it makes offers accept them. Similarly, the firm knows that the ratio of candidates interviewed to offers made is 3 to 2, while the ratio of candidates invited for

Figure 5-6
Recruiting Yield Pyramid

50	New hires
100	Offers made (2 : 1)
150	Candidates interviewed (3 : 2)
200	Candidates invited (4 : 3)
1,200	Leads generated (6 : 1)

interviews to candidates actually interviewed is about 4 to 3. Finally, the firm knows that of six leads that come in from all its recruiting efforts, only one applicant typically gets an interview—a 6-to-1 ratio. Given these ratios, the firm knows it must generate 1,200 leads to be able to invite 200 viable candidates to its offices for interviews. The firm will then get to interview about 150 of those invited, and from these it will make 100 offers. Of those 100 offers, about 50 will accept.

Name and describe the main internal sources of candidates.

● INTERNAL SOURCES OF CANDIDATES

Recruiting may bring to mind employment agencies and classified ads, but current employees are often the best source of candidates.

Filling open positions with inside candidates has many benefits. First, there's really no substitute for knowing a candidate's strengths and weaknesses. It is often therefore safer to promote employees from within, since you're likely to have a more accurate view of the person's skills. Inside candidates may also be more committed to the company. Morale may rise if employees see promotions as rewards for loyalty and competence. Inside candidates may also require less orientation and training than outsiders.

However, hiring from within can also backfire. Employees who apply for jobs and don't get them may become discontented; telling unsuccessful applicants why they were rejected and what remedial actions they might take to be more successful in the future is crucial. Many employers require managers to post job openings and interview all inside candidates. Yet the manager often knows ahead of time exactly whom he or she wants to hire. Requiring the person to interview a stream of unsuspecting inside candidates can be a waste of time for all concerned. Inbreeding is another potential drawback. When all managers come up through the ranks, they may have a tendency to maintain the status quo, when a new direction is what's required.

Finding Internal Candidates

To be effective, promotion from within requires using job posting, personnel records, and skills banks. **Job posting** means publicizing the open job to employees (often by literally posting it on bulletin boards or intranets) and listing the job's attributes, like qualifications, supervisor, work schedule, and pay rate.

Qualifications personnel inventory tools like those described earlier (such as computerized skills banks) are also important. An examination of personnel records may reveal employees who are working in jobs below their educational or skill levels. It may also reveal persons who have potential for further training or who already have the right background for the open job. Computerized records systems can help ensure that you consider qualified inside candidates for the opening.

job posting
Publicizing an open job to employees (often by literally posting it on bulletin boards) and listing its attributes, like qualifications, supervisor, working schedule, and pay rate.

Rehiring

Rehiring former employees has its pros and cons. On the plus side, former employees are known quantities (more or less), and are already familiar with the company's culture, style, and ways of doing things. On the other hand, employees who were let go may return with less-than-positive attitudes. And hiring former employees who left for greener pastures back into better positions may signal your current employees that the best way to get ahead is to leave the firm.

In any event, there are several ways to reduce the chance of adverse reactions.[26] For example, after rehired employees have been back on the job for a certain period, credit them with the years of service they had accumulated before they left. In addition, inquire (before rehiring them) about what they did during the layoff and how they feel about returning to the firm: "You don't want someone coming back who feels they've been mistreated," said one manager.[27]

Succession Planning

succession planning
The ongoing process of systematically identifying, assessing, and developing organizational leadership to enhance performance.

Forecasting the availability of inside executive candidates is particularly important in **succession planning**—the ongoing process of systematically identifying, assessing, and developing organizational leadership to enhance performance.[28]

Succession planning entails three steps: identifying and analyzing key jobs, creating and assessing candidates, and selecting those who will fill the key positions. First, based on the firm's strategic goals, top management and HR identify what the company's future key position needs will be, and formulate job descriptions and specifications for them. Thus, plans to expand abroad or to diversify the company's product line may suggest bulking up the management talent in the firm's international division, or hiring a key executive to run a new-product division. As one succession planning expert says, "A strategic business plan can only be realized when the right people are at the right place and at the right times to do the right things."[29]

After identifying future key position needs, management turns to the job of creating and assessing candidates for these jobs. "Creating" means identifying potential internal and external candidates for future key positions, and then providing them with the developmental experiences they require to be viable candidates when it's time to fill the positions. Organizations develop high-potential employees through a variety of means. Most use internal training and cross-functional experiences; they also use job rotation, external training, and global/regional assignments.[30] Finally, succession planning requires assessing these candidates and selecting those who will actually fill the key positions.[31] The HRIS feature on page 164 provides an additional perspective.

● OUTSIDE SOURCES OF CANDIDATES

Firms can't always get all the employees they need from their current staff, and sometimes they just don't want to. We'll look at the sources firms use to find outside candidates next.

➔*5* Develop a help wanted ad.

Advertising

Everyone is familiar with employment ads, and most of us have probably responded to one or more. While Web-based recruiting is replacing help wanted ads to some extent, a quick look at almost any paper or business or professional magazine will confirm that print ads are still popular. To use help wanted ads successfully, employers have to address two issues: the advertising medium and the ad's construction.

Improving Productivity Through HRIS

Succession Planning Systems

More large companies are relying on software to facilitate the succession planning process. For example, when Larry Kern became president of Dole Food Co., Inc., in 2001, the company was highly decentralized, and each of its separate operating companies handled most of their own HR activities and succession planning. Kern's strategy involved improving financial performance by reducing redundancies and centralizing certain activities, including succession planning.[32] Technology helped Dole do this. Many HRIS have optional succession planning modules. However, instead of maintaining its own expensive HR computer system and computer technicians, Dole decided to outsource these activities. It contracted with application system providers (ASPs) to handle things like payroll management. For succession management, Dole chose special software from Pilat NAI, which runs the software and keeps all the data on its own servers for a monthly fee.

The Pilat succession planning system is easy for Dole's managers to use. They get access to the program via the Web using a password. They fill out online résumés for themselves, including career interests, and note special considerations such as geographic restrictions. The managers also assess themselves on four competencies. When the manager completes his or her succession planning input, the program automatically notifies that manager's boss. The latter then assesses his or her subordinate and indicates whether the person should be promoted. The person's manager also assesses his or her overall potential. This assessment and the online résumés then go automatically to the division head and the divisional HR director. Dole's senior vice president for HR for North America then uses the information to create a career development plan for each manager, including seminars and other programs.[33]

The Media   The selection of the best medium—be it the local paper, the *Wall Street Journal*, TV, or the Internet—depends on the positions for which you're recruiting. For example, the local newspaper is usually the best source for blue-collar help, clerical employees, and lower-level administrative employees. On the other hand, if you're recruiting for workers with special skills—such as furniture finishers—you'd probably want to advertise in the Carolinas or Georgia, even if your plant is in Tennessee. The point is to target your ads where they'll reach your prospective employees.

For specialized employees, you can advertise in trade and professional journals like *American Psychologist*, *Sales Management*, *Chemical Engineering*, *Electronics News*, *Travel Trade*, and *Women's Wear Daily*. Help wanted ads in papers like the *Wall Street Journal* and *International Herald Tribune* can be good sources of middle- or senior-management personnel.

Technology is enabling companies to be more creative about how they advertise for job applicants. For example, Electronic Arts, the world's largest video game publisher, knows that "our best [job] candidates hang out online and read gaming magazines."[34] The company therefore uses its marketing programs to help solicit job applicants. For example, Electronic Arts includes information about its internship program on the back of its video game manuals. Using techniques like these, the firm now has a database of over 200,000 potential job candidates. It also uses special tracking software to identify potential applicants with specific skills, and to facilitate ongoing communications (via e-mail) with everyone in its database.

Constructing the Ad   Experienced advertisers use a four-point guide called AIDA (attention, interest, desire, action) to construct ads. You must, of course, attract attention to the ad, or readers may just miss or ignore it. Figure 5-7 shows an ad from one paper's

Figure 5-7
Help Wanted Ad:
WellCare, Inc.
Source: The *Miami Herald*, March 24, 2004, p. SF.

classified section. Why does this ad attract attention? The word "excellence" certainly helps. Employers usually advertise key positions in separate display ads.

Develop interest in the job. You can create interest by the nature of the job itself, with lines such as "outstanding opportunities for advancement." You can also use other aspects of the job, such as its location, to create interest.

Create desire by spotlighting the job's interest factors with words such as *travel* or *challenge*. Keep your target audience in mind. For example, having a graduate school nearby may appeal to engineers and professional people.

Finally, make sure the ad prompts action with a statement like "call today," or "please forward your resume."

After over 30 years of living with EEO laws, you might imagine that by now most employers are familiar with the sorts of things they can't put in ads (such as "man wanted," or "young woman preferred"). Yet the results of one study on illegal recruitment advertisement suggest that questionable or illegal ads still do slip into recruitment advertising, so this is apparently an area that continues to require caution.[35]

Employment Advertising's Effectiveness   It does pay for employers to formulate marketing campaigns aimed at making themselves more attractive to potential recruits.[36] A recent study sheds some light on how to do this. The researchers surveyed 133 students who were graduating with bachelor's or master's degrees in engineering. For these students, specific job-related advertising was significantly related to their perceptions of the company and of the job opportunities there. The results suggest that employers should try to create positive impressions of their companies through their job postings, Web sites, and other means. Building word-of-mouth reputation is also important. In their job search, these new graduate engineers relied most heavily on information about the company from other people. As the researchers conclude, "From a practical standpoint, the results indicate that expanding and capitalizing on word-of-mouth endorsements will [prove] a highly effective and economical method for increasing applicant [inquiries]."

Employment Agencies

There are three types of employment agencies: (1) public agencies operated by federal, state, or local governments; (2) agencies associated with nonprofit organizations; and (3) privately owned agencies.

Public and Nonprofit Agencies

Public and Nonprofit Agencies   Every state has a public, state-run employment service agency. The U.S. Department of Labor supports these agencies, in part through grants, and in part through other assistance such as a nationwide computerized job bank. The National Job Bank enables agency counselors in one state to advise applicants about available jobs not just in their local area, but in other areas as well.

These agencies are an important source of workers, but some employers have had mixed experiences with them. For one thing, applicants for unemployment insurance are required to register and to make themselves available for job interviews. Some of these people are not interested in getting back to work, so employers can end up with applicants who have little or no desire for immediate employment. And fairly or not, employers probably view some of these local agencies as rather lethargic in their efforts to fill area employers' jobs.

Yet these agencies' usefulness is actually on the rise. Beyond just filling jobs, for instance, counselors will visit an employer's work site, review the employer's job requirements, and even assist the employer in writing job descriptions. Most states have turned their local state employment service agencies into "one-stop" shops.[37] The 1998 Workforce Investment Act required states to give any citizen access to one-stop-shop neighborhood training/employment/educational services centers. One user says of the Queens New York One Stop Career Center in Jamaica: "I love it: I've made this place like a second home."[38] Services available to employers include recruitment services, tax credit information, training programs, and access to local and national labor market information.[39] More employers should probably be taking advantage of the 1,900 Department of Labor one-stop career centers (formerly the "unemployment offices" in many cities). One survey of 3,700 employers by the U.S. Chamber of Commerce found that less than 20% used one of the centers.

Other employment agencies are tied to nonprofit organizations. Most professional and technical societies, such as the Institute for Electrical and Electronic Engineers (IEEE), have units that help members find jobs. Many public welfare agencies try to place people who are in special categories, such as those who are physically disabled or are war veterans.

Private Agencies

Private Agencies   Private employment agencies are important sources of clerical, white-collar, and managerial personnel. They charge fees (set by state law and posted in their offices) for each applicant they place. Market conditions generally determine whether candidate or employer pays the fee. Most are fee-paid jobs, in which the employer pays the fee. Employers correctly assume that this is the best way to attract qualified currently employed applicants, who might not be so willing to pursue other jobs if they had to pay the fees.

Why turn to an agency? Reasons include:

1. Your firm doesn't have its own HR department and is not geared to doing recruiting and screening.

2. Your firm has found it difficult in the past to generate a pool of qualified applicants.

3. You must fill a particular opening quickly.

4. There is a perceived need to attract a greater number of minority or female applicants.

5. You want to reach currently employed individuals, who might feel more comfortable dealing with agencies than with competing companies.

6. You want to cut down on the time you're devoting to recruiting.[40]

Yet employment agencies also have disadvantages. For example, the employment agency's screening may let poor applicants bypass the preliminary stages of your own selection process. Unqualified applicants may go directly to the supervisors responsible for hiring, who may in turn naively hire them. Conversely, improper testing and screening at the employment agency could block potentially successful applicants from entering your applicant pool.

To help avoid such problems, experienced recruiters suggest the following:

1. Give the agency an accurate and complete job description.

2. Make sure tests, application blanks, and interviews are part of the agency's selection process.

3. Periodically review data on candidates accepted or rejected by your firm, and by the agency. Check on the effectiveness and fairness of the agency's screening process.

4. Screen the agency. Check with other managers or HR people to find out which agencies have been the most effective at filling the sorts of positions you need filled. Review the Internet and a few back issues of the Sunday classified ads to discover the agencies that handle the positions you want.

Temp Agencies and Alternative Staffing

Employers often supplement their permanent workforce by hiring contingent or temporary workers, often through temporary help employment agencies. Also known as *part-time* or *just-in-time workers*, the *contingent workforce* is big and growing. It accounts for about 20% of all new jobs created in the United States.

Today's contingent workforce isn't limited to clerical or maintenance staff. In one year, almost 100,000 people found temporary work in engineering, science, or management support occupations, for instance.[41] And growing numbers of firms use temporary workers as short-term chief financial officers, or even chief executive officers. It's estimated that 60% of the total U.S. temporary payroll is nonclerical and includes "CEOs, human resources directors, computer systems analysts, accountants, doctors, and nurses."[42]

Benefits and Costs Contingent staffing is on the rise for several reasons. Historically, of course, employers have always used "temps" to fill in for permanent employees who were out sick or on vacation. But today's desire for ever-higher productivity also contributes to temp workers' growing popularity. Productivity is measured in terms of output per hour paid for, and temps are paid only when they're working.

The benefits of contingent staffers don't come without a price. They may be more productive and less expensive to recruit and train, but contingent workers from temporary agencies generally cost employers 20% to 50% more than comparable permanent workers (per hour or per week), since the agency gets a fee. Furthermore, "people have a psychological reference point to their place of employment. Once you put them in the contingent category, you're saying they're expendable."[43]

The numbers of temporary and freelance workers are increasing all over the world. Alemi Takada is a noted Japanese freelance animator who manages her workload and does projects for companies all over the world through an Internet agency that represents about 15,000 freelancers in media and publishing.

Employers can hire temp workers either through direct hires or through temporary staff agencies. Direct hiring involves simply hiring workers and placing them on the job. The employer usually pays these people directly, as it does all its employees, but classifies them separately from regular employees.[44] The employer generally classifies these workers as casual, seasonal, or temporary employees, and often awards few if any benefits (such as pension benefits). The other approach is to retain a temp agency to supply the employees. This approach has many advantages. The agency handles all the recruiting, screening, and payroll administration for the temps, for instance. And, ideally, as we'll see, the temp employees remain employees of the temp agency alone, and simply provide their services to the client firm.

Know Your Employment Law

Contingent Workers

Whether hired directly or through agencies, temp workers can pose legal risks to the employer. The basic problem is that in many cases these "temps" are temps in name only—they are really regular employees. Microsoft Corp.—certainly a sophisticated company—had to pay a $97 million settlement several years ago to employees it had mischaracterized as "temporary." Microsoft did not pay these employees certain employee and pension benefits. A federal court held that despite their temp titles, these "temps" were actually regular Microsoft employees, eligible for the benefits.

Yet using temporary workers who come from temp agencies may actually increase the potential for problems. For example, since the employees technically work for the temp agency, not the client firm, the client's managers and supervisors may treat these people as if they have no employee rights. This sort of thinking leads the employer down a slippery slope. For example, some supervisors may assume that they can dismiss these employees arbitrarily, or ignore the federal wage and hour and employment laws. In fact, nothing could be further from the truth. Temporary workers, like all workers, have significant legal rights.

The degree to which the client firm controls the temp agency's employees' activities determines how many rights (for example, to employee benefits) these employees have. As two lawyers put it, "for purposes of most employment laws, with certain limited exceptions, employees of temporary staffing firms working in an employer's workplace will be considered to

Figure 5-8
Guidelines for Using
Temporary Employees
Source: Adapted from Bohner and Selasco, "Beware the Legal Risks of Hiring Temps," *Workforce*, October 2000, p. 53.

1. **Do not train your contingent workers.** Ask their staffing agency to handle training.
2. **Do not negotiate the pay rate of your contingent workers.** The agency should set pay.
3. **Do not coach or counsel a contingent worker on his/her job performance.** Instead, call the person's agency and request that it do so.
4. **Do not negotiate a contingent worker's vacations or personal time off.** Direct the worker to his or her agency.
5. **Do not routinely include contingent workers in your company's employee functions.**
6. **Do not allow contingent workers to utilize facilities intended for employees.**
7. **Do not let managers issue company business cards, nameplates, or employee badges to contingent workers without HR and legal approval.**
8. **Do not let managers discuss harassment or discrimination issues with contingent workers.**
9. **Do not discuss job opportunities and the contingent worker's suitability for them directly.** Instead, refer the worker to publicly available job postings.
10. **Do not terminate a contingent worker directly.** Contact the agency to do so.

be employees both of the agency and of the employer. This is the so-called 'dual employment' view espoused . . . by many courts."[45] Specifically, the more control the employer exercises over the employee's pay, work hours, and day-to-day activities, the more likely it is that the court will find that both the employer and the staffing agency have a joint employment relationship with the employee.

Under the law, it is not the label (such as "temporary worker"), or the company's policy (as in, "temporary staff will be considered as employees of the staffing agency only and not of the employer") that counts, but the facts of the case. The more control the employer and its managers and supervisors exercise over the agency's "temp" employees, the more likely it is that the court will view the temporary employees as (joint) employees of the firm. Among other things, this can conceivably mean that these employees are eligible for the same sorts of benefits (including pension benefits) as the firm's regular employees.

Employers who use employees from temporary staffing agencies therefore have to be careful how they manage the relationship with the agency, and with the temporary employees. Managers and supervisors must understand that the more control they exercise over the employee, the more likely it is that the employees will be viewed as (and in fact are) regular employees of the firm. The basic prescription is to treat the temp employees in all ways as if the temp agency is in fact his or her employer. Figure 5-8 summarizes what this involves. For instance, do not train the temp employee, or negotiate pay with him or her. Instead, let the agency do that.

In order to make temp employment relationships as fruitful as possible, anyone employing temps should understand these temp employees' main concerns. In one survey, six key concerns emerged. Temporary workers said they were:

1. Treated by employers in a dehumanizing, impersonal, and ultimately discouraging way.
2. Insecure about their employment and pessimistic about the future.
3. Worried about their lack of insurance and pension benefits.
4. Misled about their job assignments and in particular about whether temporary assignments were likely to become full-time positions.
5. "Underemployed" (particularly those trying to return to the full-time labor market).
6. In general angry toward the corporate world and its values; participants repeatedly expressed feelings of alienation and disenchantment.[46]

Finally, when working with temporary agencies, ensure that basic policies and procedures are in place, including:

Invoicing. Get a sample copy of the agency's invoice. Make sure it fits your company's needs.

Time sheets. With temps, the time sheet is not just a verification of hours worked. Once the worker's supervisor signs it, it's usually an agreement to pay the agency's fees.

Temp-to-perm policy. What is the policy if the client wants to hire one of the agency's temps as a permanent employee?

Recruitment of and benefits for temp employees. Find out how the agency plans to recruit employees and what sorts of benefits it pays.

Dress code. Specify the appropriate attire at each of your offices or plants.

Equal employment opportunity statement. Get a document from the agency stating that it is not discriminating when filling temp orders.

Job description information. Have a procedure whereby you can ensure the agency understands the job to be filled and the sort of person, in terms of skills and so forth, you want to fill it.[47]

alternative staffing
The use of nontraditional recruitment sources.

Alternative Staffing   Temporary employees are examples of **alternative staffing**—basically, the use of nontraditional recruitment sources. The use of alternative staffing sources is widespread and growing; about one of ten U.S. employees is employed in some type of alternative work arrangement. Other alternative staffing arrangements include "in-house temporary employees" (people employed directly by the company, but on an explicit short-term basis), and "contract technical employees" (highly skilled workers like engineers, who are supplied for long-term projects under contract from an outside technical services firm).

Offshoring/Outsourcing White-Collar and Other Jobs[48]

Hiring workers abroad to do the jobs of those who would otherwise work in the United States may not be the first thing managers think of when "recruitment" comes to mind. However, outsourcing jobs in this way is an increasingly important employment option. As explained in chapter one, current projections are that about three million white-collar jobs in occupations ranging from computer scientist to call-center employee to radiologist will be moving abroad in the next five or six years.

As also discussed in chapter one, the issue of sending jobs abroad is a contentious one; there are staunch advocates of both the employers' and employees' points of view. However, regardless of the pros and cons, there seems little doubt that outsourcing is an option that most HR managers will have to deal with. To take just a few recent examples, GE's Transportation division announced in 2004 that it was shifting 17 mid-level drafting jobs from Erie Pennsylvania to India. Surveys conducted in California suggest that almost 7% of employers there are or would consider offshoring IT jobs (as well as many others).

The question at hand, therefore is what sorts of specific issues should the HR manager keep in mind when formulating plans to outsource jobs abroad? Here, the experiences of other employers suggest several things to watch out for. One is the very real potential of instability or military tension in countries such as India, the Philippines and Russia. Other issues include: the likelihood of cultural misunderstandings (between your customers and the employees abroad, or between your employees here and employees there); security and privacy concerns (some U.S. customers may object to giving credit card information to strangers abroad, for instance); and the need to deal with foreign contract, liability, and legal systems issues.

Instituting programs such as these (for instance, a call-center in India) requires careful attention to various other potential obstacles as well. For example, there is the need for special training of the foreign employees (for instance, in learning to speak with American accents and idioms, and to use pseudonyms like "Jim" without discomfort). Also understand that all the expected cost savings probably won't materialize. For example, the employee abroad may earn only 10% of what someone doing comparable work in the United States would earn, but the companies supplying and managing the foreign labor will retain a portion of the savings to cover their own profits and the cost of their own infrastructure. And, of course, the HR manager's plans should include how he or she will deal with the anxiety of its U.S.-based employees and unions.

Executive Recruiters

Executive recruiters (also called headhunters) are special employment agencies retained by employers to seek out top-management talent for their clients. The percentage of your firm's positions filled by these services might be small. However, these jobs include crucial executive and technical positions. For executive positions, headhunters may be your only source of candidates. The employer always pays the fees.

There are two types of executive recruiters—contingent and retained. Members of the Association of Executive Search Consultants usually focus on executive positions paying $150,000 or more, and on "retained executive search." This means they are paid regardless of whether or not the employer eventually hires the executive through the efforts of the research firm. *Contingency-based recruiters* tend to handle junior- to middle-level management job searches in the $50,000 to $150,000 range. Whether retained or contingent, fees are beginning to drop from the usual 30% or more of the executive's first-year pay. For example, in one survey about 96% of clients paying executive search fees paid the full 30% in 2000. This dropped to 77% in 2001, and to 70% in 2002.[49]

Two trends—technology and specialization—are changing the executive search business. Most recruiting firms are establishing Internet-linked computerized databases, the aim of which, according to one senior recruiter, is "to create a long list [of potential candidates] by pushing a button."[50] Korn/Ferry launched an Internet service called Futurestep to draw more managerial applicants into its files; it also teamed up with the *Wall Street Journal*, which runs a career Web site of its own.[51]

Executive recruiters are also becoming more specialized, and the large ones are creating new businesses aimed specifically at specialized functions or industries. For example, LAI Ward Howell launched a new business specializing in financial executives, with bases in London and New York.[52]

Pros and Cons   Recruiters can be useful. They have many contacts and are especially adept at contacting qualified, currently employed candidates who aren't actively looking to change jobs. They can also keep your firm's name confidential until late into the search process. The recruiter can save top management's time by advertising for the position and screening what could turn out to be hundreds of applicants. The recruiter's fee might actually turn out to be insignificant compared with the cost of the executive time saved.

But there are pitfalls. As an employer, it is essential for you to explain completely what sort of candidate is required—and why. Some recruiters are also more salespeople than professionals. They may be more interested in persuading you to hire a candidate than in finding one who will really do the job. Recruiters also claim that what their clients say they want is often not really what the clients want. Therefore, be prepared for some in-depth dissecting of your request.

When You're On Your Own
HR for Line Managers and Entrepreneurs

Recruiting 101

There comes a time in the life of most small businesses when it dawns on the owner that his or her managers are incapable of taking the company to the next level. If the company is to expand, the entrepreneur must decide what kinds of people to hire from outside, and how to hire them. Should the owner recruit this person? Or is an outside expert required?

While most large firms don't think twice about hiring executive search firms, small-firm owners will understandably hesitate before committing to a fee that could reach $20,000 to $30,000 (with expenses) for a $60,000 to $70,000 marketing manager. As an entrepreneur, however, you should keep in mind that such thinking can be shortsighted.

Engaging in a search like this by yourself is not at all like looking for secretaries, supervisors, or data entry clerks. When you are looking to hire a key executive to help you run your firm, chances are you are not going to find your candidate by placing ads or using most of the other traditional approaches. For one thing, the person you seek is probably not reading the want ads. If he or she does happen to glance at the ads, chances are the person is happy enough not to make the effort to embark on a job search with you.

In other words, what you'll end up with is a drawer of résumés of people who are, for one reason or another, out of work, unhappy with their work, or unsuited for your job. It will then fall on you to try to find several gems in this group by devoting the time to interview and assess these applicants.

This is harder than it sounds. First, you may not even know where to begin. You won't know where to place or how to write the ads; you won't know where to search, who to contact, or how to do the sort of job that needs to be done to screen out the laggards and misfits who may appear on the surface to be viable candidates. You also won't know enough to

really do the kind of background checking that a position at this level requires. Second, this process is going to be extremely time-consuming and will divert your attention from other duties. Many business owners find that when they consider the opportunity costs (of not making sales calls, for instance), they are not saving any money at all.

If you do decide to do the job yourself, consider retaining the services of an industrial psychologist to spend four or five hours assessing the problem-solving ability, personality, interests, and energy level of the two or three candidates in which you are most interested. Although you certainly don't want the psychologist to make the decision for you, the input can provide a valuable perspective on the candidates.

Exercise special care when recruiting applicants from competing companies. Always check to see if applicants are bound by noncompete or nondisclosure agreements, for instance. And (especially when recruiting other firms' higher-level employees) you may want to check with an attorney before asking certain questions—regarding patents or potential antitrust issues, for instance.[55]

If you're a manager with an open position to fill in a *Fortune* 500 company, even you may find you have a dilemma. You may find that your local HR office will do little recruiting, other than, perhaps, placing an ad on Monster.com or other recruiting Web sites. On the other hand, your firm almost surely will not let you place your own help wanted ads. What to do? Use word of mouth to "advertise" your open position within and outside your company. Make sure everyone in your company who may conceivably know of a candidate knows that the position is open, and what it entails. And, contact your friends and colleagues in other firms to let them know you are recruiting, and to watch out for possible candidates.

Guidelines   In choosing a recruiter, guidelines include:[53]

1. Make sure the firm is capable of conducting a thorough search. Under their ethics code, a recruiter can't approach the executive talent of a former client for a vacancy with a new client for a period of two years after completing a search for the former

client. Since former clients are off limits for two years, the recruiter must search from a constantly diminishing pool.

2. Meet the individual who will actually handle your assignment. If this person hasn't the ability to seek out top candidates and sell them on your firm, it's unlikely you'll get to see the best candidates.

3. Ask how much the search firm charges. Search firm fees range from 25% to 35% of the guaranteed annual income of the position; often one-third is payable as a retainer at the outset, one-third at the end of 30 days, and one-third after 60 days. Often a fee is on a "retained" rather than on a contingency basis—it's payable whether or not the search is terminated for any reason. The out-of-pocket expenses are extra and could run to 10% to 20% of the fee itself, and sometimes more. Get the agreement in writing.[54]

On Demand Recruiting Services (ODRS)

Recently, a new type of recruiting relationship has emerged. **On demand recruiting services (ODRS)** provide short-term specialized recruiting to support specific projects without the expense of retaining traditional search firms. They are basically recruiters who get paid by the hour or project, instead of a percentage fee. For example, when the HR manager for one biotech firm had to hire several dozen people with scientific degrees and experience in pharmaceuticals, she decided an ODRS firm was her best option. She could have hired a full-time, in-house recruiter, but what would she have done with that person once the job of filling these positions was complete? A traditional recruiting firm might charge 20 to 30% of each hire's salary, a prohibitive amount for a small company. The ODRS firm charged by time, rather than per hire. It handled recruiting, analysis, and prescreening, and left the client with a short list of qualified candidates to put through the employer's own internal screening process.[56]

College Recruiting

Sending an employer's representatives to college campuses to prescreen applicants and create an applicant pool from the graduating class is an important source of management trainees, promotable candidates, and professional and technical employees. One study concluded, for instance, that new college grads filled about 38% of all externally filled jobs requiring a college degree: The percentage just for entry-level jobs requiring a college degree would probably be much higher.[57]

But on-campus recruiting is expensive and time-consuming. Schedules must be set well in advance, company brochures printed, records of interviews kept, and much time spent on campus. And recruiters themselves are sometimes ineffective, or worse. Some recruiters are unprepared, show little interest in the candidate, and act superior. Many recruiters don't screen candidates effectively. Such experiences underscore the need to train recruiters in how to interview candidates, how to explain what the company has to offer, and how to put candidates at ease.

Recruiting Goals   The campus recruiter has two primary goals. The main one is to determine whether a candidate is worthy of further consideration. Exactly which traits to look for will depend on your company's specific needs. Usual traits to assess include communication skills, education, experience, and interpersonal skills.

The other aim is to attract good candidates. A sincere and informal attitude, respect for the applicant as an individual, and prompt follow-up letters can help sell the employer to the interviewee.

Employers have to choose recruiters and schools carefully. Employers naturally look among their employees for those who can do (and, preferably, who have done) the best job of identifying top applicants and filling vacancies. Factors in selecting schools include the school's reputation and the performance of previous hires from that source.

On-Site Visits   Employers generally invite good candidates to the office or plant for an on-site visit. There are several ways to make this visit fruitful. The invitation letter should be warm and friendly but businesslike, and should give the person a choice of dates to visit the company. Someone should be assigned to meet the applicant, preferably at the airport or at his or her hotel, and to act as host. A package containing the applicant's schedule as well as other information regarding the company—such as annual reports and employee benefits—should be waiting for the applicant at the hotel.

Plan the interviews carefully and adhere to the schedule. Avoid interruptions; give the candidate the undivided attention of each person with whom he or she interviews. Luncheon should be hosted by one or more other recently hired graduates with whom the applicant may feel more at ease. Make an offer, if any, as soon as possible, preferably at the time of the visit. If this is not possible, tell the candidate when to expect a decision. If an offer is made, keep in mind that the applicant may have other offers, too. Frequent follow-ups to "find out how the decision process is going" or to "ask if there are any other questions" may help to tilt the applicant in your favor.

What sorts of things turn job candidates on or off? A study of 96 graduating students from a major Northeastern university reveals some positive and negative factors. For example, with this sample 53% mentioned "on-site visit opportunities to meet with people in positions similar to those applied for, or with higher-ranking persons" had a positive effect. Fifty-one percent mentioned "impressive hotel/dinner arrangements and having well-organized site arrangements." On the other hand, 41% were turned off by "disorganized, unprepared interviewer behavior, or uninformed, useless answers." Similarly, 40% mentioned "unimpressive cheap hotels, disorganized arrangements, or inappropriate behavior of hosts" as having negative effects.[58]

Internships   Many college students get their jobs through college internships. Internships can be win–win situations for both students and employers. For students, it may mean being able to hone business skills, learn more about potential employers, and discover their likes (and dislikes) when it comes to choosing careers. And employers, of course, can use the interns to make useful contributions while evaluating them as possible full-time employees.

Referrals and Walk-Ins

"Employee referral" campaigns are another recruiting option. The firm posts announcements of openings and requests for referrals in its intranet Web site, bulletin, and on its wallboards. Prizes or cash rewards are offered for referrals that lead to hirings. Employee referrals have been the source of almost half of all hires at AmeriCredit since the firm kicked off its "you've got friends, we want to meet them" employee referral program. Employees making a successful referral receive $1,000 awards, with the payments spread over a year. As the head of recruiting says, "Quality people know quality people. If you give employees the opportunity to make referrals, they automatically suggest high caliber people because they are stakeholders."[59]

Employee referral programs have pros and cons. Current employees can and usually will provide accurate information about the job applicants they are referring, especially since they're putting their own reputations on the line.[60] The new employees may also come with a more realistic picture of what working in the firm is like. But the success of the campaign depends a lot on employee morale.[61] And the campaign can back-fire if an employee's referral is rejected and the employee becomes dissatisfied. Using referrals exclusively may also be discriminatory if most current employees (and their referrals) are male or white.

A survey by SHRM found that of 586 employer respondents, 69% said employee referral programs are more cost-effective than other recruiting practices and 80% specifically said they are more cost-effective than employment agencies. On average, referral programs cost between $400 and $900 per hire in incentives and rewards.[62]

Referrals can also facilitate diversifying your workforce. One survey found 70% of minority/ethnic candidates do search for jobs on corporate Web sites; 67% use general job listing sites, 53% classified ads, 52% referrals, and 35% headhunter/agencies. However, only 6% listed "corporate Web site" as one of the top five ways they actually found jobs; 25% listed referrals.[63]

Particularly for hourly workers, walk-ins—direct applications made at your office—are a major source of applicants. Employers encourage walk-ins by posting HIRING signs on the property. Treat walk-ins courteously and diplomatically, for the sake of both the employer's community reputation and the applicant's self-esteem. Many employers give every walk-in a brief interview with someone in the HR office, even if it is only to get information on the applicant "in case a position should be open in the future." Good business practice also requires answering all letters of inquiry from applicants promptly and courteously. And from a practical point of view, simply posting a "Help Wanted" sign outside the door is a cost-effective way to attract good local applicants.

Recruiting via the Internet

More and more people are going online to look for jobs. One survey found that on a typical day, more than 4 million people turn to the Web looking for jobs.[64] Employers are therefore making it easy to use their Web sites to hunt for jobs: 71% of the Standard & Poor's 500 place employment information just one click away from their home pages.[65] Job seekers can submit their résumés online at 90% of the *Fortune* 500 Web sites; however, only about 25% give job seekers the option of completing online applications, although it is the method many applicants prefer, according to one expert.[66]

Some managers use the Internet to search for applicants in reverse. Rather than place their own Internet ads, they do keyword searches on sites such as HotJobs' résumé database. For example, when the HR manager for one hydraulic products company placed a Sunday ad in his local newspaper, it cost $3,000 and produced about 30 résumés, 10% of which were relevant.[67] By comparison, he found that keyword search of the HotJob database produced 52 résumés, many of which included the necessary industry experience. "I find more qualified candidates by searching for résumés than posting ads" he says.[68]

Employers list several advantages of Internet recruiting. In general, the Web is a relatively cost-effective way for firms to publicize openings. For example, Marsha Wheatley, HR director for the Washington, DC–based American Crop Protection Association, no longer runs $400 ads in the *Washington Post* when she's looking for professionals. Instead, ads on WashingtonPost.com cost only $200. And, "instead of a tiny ad that says, 'ACPA needs an accountant,' I get a whole page to describe the job, give information about the association, and include a link to our Web site."[69] Furthermore, she estimates that for half the cost of a Sunday newspaper ad, she averages nine times as many applicants' résumés via the online ad. A newspaper ad might also have a life span of perhaps 10 days, whereas the Internet ad may keep attracting applications for 30 days or more.[70] Internet recruiting can also be more timely. Responses to electronic job listings may come the day the ad is posted, whereas responses to newspaper ads can take a week just to reach an employer (although including a fax-response or e-mail address can provide quick responses, too).

Employers can also use Internet support tools such as Recruiter Toolbox to create online ads that include prescreening tests, thus further automating the recruiting process.[71] They can also supplement their own Web site ads with a variety of job search sites. Two popular recruitment Web sites are presented in Figure 5-9.

E-recruiting does have some potential legal pitfalls. For example, since more young people use the Internet, automated online application gathering and screening might mean the employer inadvertently excludes higher numbers of older applicants. Furthermore, the U.S. government's Office of Federal Contract Compliance Programs requires certain employers to track "applicant flow data." To do so, the employer needs detailed information regarding applicants, information the online screening software might not provide.[72]

Applicant Tracking   Web-based ads often produce so many applicants that most firms are installing applicant tracking systems to support their on- and offline recruiting efforts. Well-known tracking systems (such as recruitsoft.com, and Itrack-IT solutions) help employers monitor applicants.[73] They also provide several services, including requisitions management (for monitoring the firm's open jobs), applicant data collection (for scanning applicants' data into the system), and reporting (to create various recruiting-related reports such as cost per hire and hire by source).[74]

Using an E-Recruiting Applications Tracking ASP   For example, with 10,000 job openings per year, Sutter Health Corporation had to generate a lot of recruits to continue its fast-growth strategy. However, moving its job postings online not only didn't help; it actually complicated the process.[75]

Online postings did generate many more applications—300,000 a year, to be exact—but it didn't speed up the hiring process. Sutter Health had so many résumés coming in by e-mail and through its Web site that the applications ended up in a huge pile, waiting for Sutter affiliates' HR departments to get to them. If the company wanted to grow and to provide the value-added services to its affiliates it had built its reputation on, it needed a new recruiting approach.

careerbuilder.com™

CareerBuilder.com
8420 W. Bryn Mawr Avenue
Chicago, IL 60631
877-235-8978
Fax: 773-399-6313
carrie.moon@careerbuilder.com
www.careerbuilder.com
Use CareerBuilder.com's smarter search tools to target, find, and hire top-quality candidates quickly and cost-effectively. Access over 9 million candidates, expose your jobs to 2.5 million searches daily and get the exposure on 350 exceptional partner sites, including the nation's leading newspaper's Web sites. The smarter way to find better candidates.

monster®
today's the day™

Monster
5 Clock Tower Place, Ste. 500
Maynard, MA 01754
1-888-MONSTER
www.monster.com
At Monster, we're all about matching the right candidate with the right job. So we've developed hiring tools that make it fast and easy. You type in what you're looking for and we'll send the candidates who match those qualifications right to your desktop. Call 1-888-Monster for more information.

Figure 5-9
Selected Recruitment Web Sites
Source: HR Magazine, November 2003.

Sutter Health's solution was to sign on with Recruitsoft, Inc., of San Francisco. Recruitsoft is an e-recruiting applications service provider (ASP), and it now does all the work of hosting Sutter Health's job site. As an applications service provider, Recruitsoft doesn't just post Sutter Health job openings and collect its résumés; it also gives Sutter Health "an automated way to evaluate, rank and match IT and other job candidates with specific openings." For example, Recruitsoft's system automatically screens incoming résumés, compares them with Sutter's job requirements, and flags high-priority applicants. And this, says Keith Vencel, the project manager who came up with this solution, helped Sutter cut its recruiting process from weeks to days—and thereby helped ensure that Sutter's expansion strategy stays on track.

Designing Effective Internet Recruiting Programs   Designing effective Internet help wanted ads doesn't mean just recycling your newspaper ads and placing them on the Web. As one e-recruiting specialist put it, "getting recruiters out of the 'shrunken want ad mentality' is a big problem." Even for large newspaper display ads, employers are limited to brief descriptions of the job. For the more common (and brief) newspaper classified ads, they have to revert to cryptic abbreviations. It's a mistake to simply take these newspaper ads and transpose them to the Web. Figure 5-10 is an example of what happens when you do this. It is poorly written, has many needless abbreviations, and doesn't say much about why the job seeker should want that job or that employer.[76]

Now look at the effective Web ad on the bottom of Figure 5-10 from Monster.com. It uses compelling keywords such as "success driven professionals" and "independent." It provides good reasons (such as "six figure income") why you would want to work for this company. And, it starts off with an attention-grabbing opening line.

What else can you do to make your Internet recruiting more effective? There are several things to avoid. One study surveyed 256 alumni from graduate business schools. Several things about Internet job searching turned these people off. Many firms' Web-based job openings lacked relevant information (such as job descriptions). It was often

INEFFECTIVE WEB AD	EFFECTIVE WEB AD
Unix Solaris Admin/ Windows 2000 Administrator	**Work for the World's Best Boss... You!**
Exciting opportunity on ground floor project for telecom/Internet venture—local candidates only at this time. ***Might also consider subcontract if candidate has over 6 years of Solaris admin exp.*** Solaris Unix Solaris Systems Admin. MUST have Windows 2000 Admin experience. MUST have at least 3–4 years plus of System Admin experience. MUST have at least 3 solid years of Solaris exp. Looking for someone who has solid experience working with data storage and how it works in enterprise systems. (Looking for experience like RAID.) Also must have: Windows 2000 and looking for someone with specific Cisco switches and routers (5500 and 6500 Series).	Now you can be in business for yourself, have your own office, schedule your own time, and advance to management within a year. Add to that a six-figure income in the second year . . . and you have the dream career your talents deserve. We have over 140 offices nationally with over 60,000 clients. Currently, our office in Tampa seeks entrepreneurial, success-driven professionals who will welcome the independence and advantages of being a sales professional. You must have the interpersonal/communication skills and highly professional image to promote our indispensable services to the business and medical communities. We offer: · Excellent Commissions · Proven Repeat Business · Outstanding Training · No Travel, Nights or Weekends

Figure 5-10
Ineffective and Effective Web Ads
Source: Workforce, December 2001. © Crain Communication, Inc. Reprinted with permission.

difficult to format résumés and post them in the form required for the employer's recruitment site. Many subjects expressed concerns about the privacy of the information they provided. Poor graphics often made it difficult to use the Web site. And slow feedback from the employers (in terms of follow-up responses and receiving online applications to fill out) was also annoying.[77]

6   Explain how to recruit a more diverse workforce.

● RECRUITING A MORE DIVERSE WORKFORCE

Recruiting a diverse workforce isn't just socially responsible: It's a necessity, given the rapid increase in minority, older worker, and women candidates and the 70% jobless rate among disabled people. Doing so means taking special steps to recruit these people from these categories. Many employers, such as Eastman Kodak Co., include disability under their diversity initiative umbrellas. This reflects their recognition that disabled people represent a large, untapped pool of potential employees.[78]

Single Parents

About two-thirds of all single parents are in the workforce today; this group is an important source of candidates.

Attracting single parents begins with understanding the problems they face in balancing work and family life.[79] In one survey,

Many described falling into bed exhausted at midnight without even minimal time for themselves. They reported rushing through every activity and constantly feeling pressured to keep on going and do more. Vacations, which can be a time to rejuvenate, were often used for children's appointments or to handle unexpected emergencies. They often needed personal sick time or excused days off to care for sick children. As one mother noted, "I don't have enough sick days to get sick."[80]

The respondents viewed themselves as having "less support, less personal time, more stress, and greater difficulty balancing job and home life" than other working parents. However, most were hesitant to dwell on their single-parent status at work; they feared that doing so would affect their jobs and careers adversely.

Given such concerns, the first step in attracting (and keeping) single mothers is to make the workplace as user friendly for them as is practical. For example, many employers already give employees some schedule flexibility (such as one-hour windows at the beginning or end of the day). The problem is that "for some single mothers, this flexibility can help but it may not be sufficient to really make a difference in their ability to juggle work and family schedules."[81] In addition to flexibility, employers can and should train supervisors to have an increased awareness of and sensitivity to the sorts of challenges single parents face. As two researchers concluded: "Very often, the single mother's relationships with her supervisor and co-workers is a significant factor influencing whether she perceives the work environment to be supportive."[82] Ongoing support groups and other forums at which single parents can share their concerns can also help.

One important service for single working parents is day care. Companies that want to attract single mothers find it easier to do so when they offer the kinds of benefits these women need, like flexible work schedules that allow them to drop off and pick up their children at the beginning and end of the working day, or subsidized, on-site day care.

Older Workers

When it comes to hiring older workers, employers may not have much choice. Over the next few years, the fastest-growing labor force segment will be those from 45 to 64 years old. Those aged 25 to 34 will decline by almost three million, reflecting fewer births in the late 1960s and early 1970s. On the positive side, a survey by AARP and SHRM concluded that older workers tend to have lower absenteeism rates, more reliability, and better work habits than younger workers.[83] The feature, "The New Workplace," illustrates another aspect of this.

It therefore makes a lot of sense for employers to encourage older workers to stay (or to come to work at the company). How does one do this? Employers should revise policies that make it difficult for older workers to keep working (such as pension plans that penalize work after a certain age). They should offer training and workshops to eliminate age-related bias, educate managers about older workers' values, and review all HR policies (in recruiting, selection, training, appraisal, and compensation) to make sure age bias plays no role. They should also structure reward systems with older employees' needs in mind. People's occupational needs and preferences change as they grow older. One survey found that getting a raise was the main motivator for 11% of those born in the 1960s and 1970s, but just 1% for those over 65.[84] Flexibility was the main concern for 71% of baby boomers, with those who continue working preferring to do so part-time.[85] At Wrigley Company, workers over 65 can progressively shorten their work schedules; another company uses "mini shifts" to accommodate those interested in working less than full time.[86]

Recruiting Minorities and Women

Basically the same prescriptions that apply to recruiting older workers apply to recruiting minorities and women. If there is a basic guideline, it is this: to take the goal of recruiting more minorities and women seriously, and to pursue that goal energetically. In practice, this requires a three-part effort: Understand the recruitment barriers; formulate the required recruitment plans; and institute the specific day-to-day programs.[87]

Understanding the barriers that prevent minorities and women from applying is the first step. For example, to the extent that many minority applicants don't meet the educational or experience standards for the job, many companies offer remedial training

The New Workplace

Supervising the Graybeards

Recruiting and hiring older employees is one thing; supervising them—especially when they're 20 or 30 years older than their supervisors—can be a challenge.

Gregg Levin's experiences provide an example. Levin, 31, is chief executive of Perfect Curve, a company in Sudbury, Massachusetts, that makes racks for baseball caps and related products. His father—one of his employees—doesn't use a computer, but instead "takes out his legal pad and spends an hour on something that takes me 4 1/2 minutes on a computer," says Gregg. Sometimes, he says, "I feel I'm just playing. A president is in his 50s or 60s, not 31." Maintaining authority is one of the challenges in a situation like this. Gregg Levin does this in part by dressing up: "I'm always in a suit and tie," he says. "If I'm going to represent my company, I've got to do it in a mature manner."

Mary Rodas was in a similar situation when, at 24, she helped start kardz.com (which then morphed into Your Free Presentation) and then became its vice president. Kardz.com delivered inexpensive gifts matched with greeting cards. Her five subordinates at that time were much older than she was. "When people meet me, their first reaction is: 'Who's this little kid?' Or else they say, 'Can I speak to your boss?' And I point to myself and say, 'That's her.'" She says she earns respect through hard work and getting to know her workers. "I know my business, and with time people realize that I'm talking to them as an individual and an equal. I've been in this industry 11 years [she created a balloon ball at age 11 that brought in $70 million in sales for a toy company in New York], I know what I'm doing."[88]

in basic arithmetic and writing. With respect to recruiting women, anecdotal comments by women, HR managers, and diversity officers illustrate the sorts of things that can cause women to hold back from seeking or accepting jobs with particular employers. For example, among life insurers and other financial services firms, a lack of women role models make many hesitate to accept jobs as sales agents. In one retail store chain, it was similarly a lack of role models plus what the HR manager called the "rather macho culture" that stopped women from applying. Furthermore, it's also often the woman in the family who takes on much of the responsibility for the caring and schooling of the children; therefore, support services such as flexible working hours and tolerant supervisors can be especially important when women size up potential employers. At one hospital, a registered nurse summed this up by saying that even in hospitals, which traditionally have a large proportion of female employees, many managers just don't understand the different challenges that many women face in their day-to-day lives.

After recognizing what the potential impediments are, it's essential that the employer translate its good intentions into comprehensive employment plans. Preferably with the assistance of a diversity employment executive, the employer should turn to formulating comprehensive plans for attracting and retaining minorities and women, plans that may include reevaluating personnel policies, developing flexible work options, redesigning jobs, and offering flexible benefits plans.

Finally, these personnel plans must translate into specific minority and women recruitment programs. For example, since many jobseekers of Hispanic origin check with friends or relatives as a strategy for looking for jobs, encouraging your own Hispanic employees to assist, by word-of-mouth, in your recruitment efforts make sense. Other firms partner with professional organizations such as the black MBA Association, the national Society of Hispanic MBAs, and the Organization of Chinese Americans. Specialized job search web sites like those discussed elsewhere in this chapter are another auction. And, to paraphrase one successful female financial services executive, the employer who is really interested in recruiting and retaining female employees has to fully commit to supporting them, coaching them, and offering them positive reinforcement.[89]

Welfare-to-Work

The Federal Personal Responsibility and Welfare Reconciliation Act of 1996 prompted many employers to implement "welfare-to-work" programs for attracting and assimilating former welfare recipients. The act required 50% of people receiving welfare assistance to be either working or involved in a work training program by September 30, 2002.[90]

Some companies report difficulty in hiring and assimilating people previously on welfare. Applicants sometimes lack basic work skills such as reporting for work on time, working in teams, and "taking orders without losing their temper."[91] The key to a welfare-to-work program's success seems to be the employer's pretraining program, during which participants get counseling and basic skills training over several weeks.[92] For example, Marriott International hired 600 welfare recipients under its Pathways to Independence program. The heart of the program is six weeks of preemployment training focused on work and life skills and designed to rebuild self-esteem and instill positive attitudes about work.[93]

The Disabled

The EEOC estimates that nearly 70% of the disabled are jobless, but it certainly doesn't have to be that way.[94] In Germany, for instance, customers visiting Volkswagen's Wolfsburg plant are met by the receptionist, Mr. Janz. If they don't check the sign on his counter, they might assume he's ignoring them. In fact, Mr. Janz is blind, and the sign tells visitors to speak directly to him so he knows they are there.[95] Volkswagen recruited Mr. Janz because the company has a policy of integrating people with disabilities into its workforce. Similarly, thousands of employers in the United States and elsewhere have found that disabled employees provide an excellent and largely untapped source of competent, efficient labor for jobs ranging from information technology to creative advertising to receptionist.

Employers can do several things to better tap this huge potential workforce. The U.S. Department of Labor's Office of Disability Employment Policy offers several programs, including one that helps link disabled college undergraduates who are looking for summer internships with potential employers.[96] Employers also must use common sense if they want their recruiting efforts to reach the disabled. For example, employers who only post job openings online may miss potential employees who are visually impaired.[97] Beyond this, all states have local agencies (such as "Corporate Connections" in Tennessee) that provide placement services and other recruitment and training tools and information for employers seeking to hire the disabled.

● DEVELOPING AND USING APPLICATION FORMS

Purpose of Application Forms

application form
The form that provides information on education, prior work record, and skills.

Once you have a pool of applicants, the prescreening process can begin. The **application form** is usually the first step in this process (some firms first require a brief, prescreening interview).

A filled-in form provides four types of information. First, you can make judgments on substantive matters, such as whether the applicant has the education and experience to do the job. Second, you can draw conclusions about the applicant's previous progress and growth, a trait that is especially important for management candidates. Third, you can draw tentative conclusions regarding the applicant's stability based on previous work record. (Be careful not to assume that an unusual number of job changes necessarily reflects on the applicant's stability. For example, the person's last two employers may have had to lay off employees.) Fourth, you may be able to use the data in the application to predict which candidates will succeed on the job and which will not.

In practice, most organizations need several application forms. For technical and managerial personnel the form may require detailed answers to questions concerning education and training. The form for hourly factory workers might focus on the tools and equipment the applicant has used.

Know Your Employment Law

Application Forms

Employers should carefully review application forms to ensure that they comply with equal employment laws. Unfortunately, many application forms are still highly questionable. Questions to beware of include:

Education. A question on the dates of attendance and graduation from various schools—academic, vocational, or professional—is one potential violation. This question may be illegal insofar as it may reflect the applicant's age.

Arrest record. The courts have usually held that employers violate Title VII by disqualifying applicants from employment because of an arrest record. This item has an adverse impact on minorities, and employers usually can't show it's required by business necessity.

Notify in case of emergency. It is generally legal to require the name, address, and phone number of a person to notify in case of emergency. However, asking the relationship of this person to the applicant could indicate the applicant's marital status or lineage.

Membership in organizations. Many forms ask the applicant to list memberships in clubs, organizations, or societies along with offices held. Employers should add instructions not to include organizations that would reveal race, religion, physical handicaps, marital status, or ancestry.

Physical handicaps. It is usually illegal to require the listing of an applicant's physical handicaps, defects, or past illnesses unless the application blank specifically asks only for those that "may interfere with your job performance." Similarly, it is generally illegal to ask whether the applicant has ever received workers' compensation for a previous injury or illness.

Marital status. In general, the application should not ask whether an applicant is single, married, divorced, separated, or living with anyone, or the names, occupations, and ages of the applicants' spouse or children.

Housing. Asking whether an applicant *owns, rents,* or *leases* a house may also be discriminatory. It can adversely affect minority groups and is difficult to justify on grounds of business necessity.

Figure 5-11 presents one employer's approach to collecting application form information—the employment application for the FBI.

Employers need to keep several practical application form guidelines in mind. The "Employment History" section should request detailed information on each prior employer, including the name of the supervisor and his or her telephone number—all essential for following up on the reference. Also, in signing the application, the applicant should certify his or her understanding of several things: that falsified statements may be cause for dismissal; that investigation of credit and employment and driving record is authorized; that a medical examination may be required; that drug screening tests may be required; and that employment is for no definite period of time.

Alternative Dispute Resolution

While the EEOC is generally opposed to the idea, more employers are requiring applicants to sign *mandatory alternative dispute resolution* forms as part of the application process. This typically requires applicants to agree to arbitrate certain legal disputes related to their employment with or dismissal from the company (including, for instance, those relating to the Age Discrimination in Employment Act).[98]

Know Your Employment Law

Mandatory Arbitration

Different federal courts have taken different positions on the enforceability of mandatory alternative dispute resolution clauses. In 2001, the U.S. Supreme Court upheld Circuit City's use of mandatory arbitration agreements.[99] Responding to a different argument, the U.S. Court of Appeals for the Ninth Circuit called Circuit City's arbitration process "unconscionable" and unenforceable under California law.[100] The basic situation now is that mandatory arbitration agreements are enforceable in general. However, courts can strike down individual agreements based on their merits.[101]

It is therefore extremely important to create such agreements very carefully. The agreement should be a signed and dated separate agreement, not just a clause in the employment application. Use simple wording that makes it clear what the employee or potential employee is agreeing to. Provide for reconsideration and judicial appeal, for instance, if there is an error of law.[102] The employer must share in and (from a practical point of view) absorb most of the cost of the arbitration process. The arbitration process should be reasonably swift; for instance, do not require too many depositions. The mandatory arbitration should be mutual, in that the employer also agrees to arbitrate some claims it might otherwise bring against an individual. The agreement should require arbitration of all claims, not just discrimination claims. The employee, if he or she prevails, should be eligible to receive the full remedies that he or she would have had if he or she had had access to the courts. Finally, the mandatory arbitration agreement should spell out proper due process and provide for written decisions.

FEDERAL BUREAU OF INVESTIGATION

Preliminary Application for
Special Agent Position
(Please Type or Print in Black Ink)

Date: _____

FIELD OFFICE USE ONLY
Right Thumb Print
Div: _____ Program: _____

I. PERSONAL HISTORY

Name in Full (Last, First, Middle)	List College Degree(s) Already Received or Pursuing, Major, School, and Month/Year:

Marital Status: ☐ Single ☐ Engaged ☐ Married ☐ Separated ☐ Legally Separated ☐ Widowed ☐ Divorced

Birth Date (Month, Day, Year) Birth Place:	Social Security Number: (Optional)	Do you understand FBI employment requires availability for assignment anywhere in the U.S.?

Current Address

Street _____ Apt. No. _____   Home Phone _____
                                                                          Area Code   Number
City _____ State _____ Zip Code _____   Work Phone _____
                                                                          Area Code   Number

Are you: CPA ☐ Yes ☐ No   Licensed Driver ☐ Yes ☐ No   U. S. Citizen ☐ Yes ☐ No

Have you served on active duty in the U. S. Military? ☐ Yes ☐ No If yes, indicate branch of service and dates (month/year) of active duty. Include military school attendance (month/year):

How did you learn or become interested in FBI employment as a Special Agent?	Have you previously applied for FBI employment? ☐ Yes ☐ No If yes, location and date:

Do you have a foreign language background? ☐ Yes ☐ No List proficiency for each language on reverse side.

Have you ever been arrested for any crime (include major traffic violations such as Driving Under the Influence or While Intoxicated, etc.)? ☐ Yes ☐ No If so, list all such matters on a continuation sheet, even if not formally charged, or no court appearance or found not guilty, or matter settled by payment of fine or forfeiture of collateral. Include date, place, charge, disposition, details, and police agency on reverse side.

II. EMPLOYMENT HISTORY

Identify your most recent three years FULL-TIME work experience, after high school (excluding summer, part-time and temporary employment).

From Month/Year	To Month/Year	Title of Position and Description of Work	# of hrs. Per week	Name/Location of Employer

III. PERSONAL DECLARATIONS

Persons with a disability who require an accommodation to complete the application process are required to notify the FBI of their need for the accommodation.

Have you used marijuana during the last three years or more than 15 times? ☐ Yes ☐ No

Have you used any illegal drug(s) or combination of illegal drugs, other than marijuana, more than 5 times or during the last 10 years? ☐ Yes ☐ No

All Information provided by applicants concerning their drug history will be subject to verification by a preemployment polygraph examination.

Do you understand all prospective FBI employees will be required to submit to an urinalysis for drug abuse prior to employment? ☐ Yes ☐ No

Please do not write below this line.

I am aware that willfully withholding information or making false statements on this application constitutes a violation of Section 1001. Title 18, U.S. Code and if appointed, will be the basis for dismissal from the Federal Bureau of Investigation. I agree to these conditions and I hereby certify that all statements made by me on this application are true and complete, to the best of my knowledge.

_____
Signature of applicant as usually written (**Do Not Use Nickname**)

Figure 5-11
Employment Application

Using Application Forms to Predict Job Performance

Some firms use application forms to predict which candidates will be successful and which will not, in much the same way that they might use tests for screening. They do this by conducting statistical studies to find the relationship between (1) biodata responses on the application form and (2) measures of success on the job.

Here it is important to choose the biodata items (such as "does not own automobile" or "not living at home") with two things in mind. First, of course, equal employment law will obviously limit the sorts of items you'll want to use. You may also want to avoid using items that are invasive. In one study, items such as "dollar sales achieved," "received cash bonus for good job," and "grade point average in math" were perceived by subjects as not too invasive. Others such as "frequently attends religious services," "birth order," and "frequent dates as senior in high school" were more invasive. Basically, items that were seen as more verifiable, more transparent in purpose, and more impersonal were seen as less invasive.[103]

The HR Scorecard
Strategy and Results

The New Recruitment Process

The Hotel Paris's competitive strategy is, "To use superior guest service to differentiate the Hotel Paris properties, and to thereby increase the length of stay and return rate of guests, and thus boost revenues and profitability." HR manager Lisa Cruz must now formulate functional policies and activities that support this competitive strategy, by eliciting the required employee behaviors and competencies.

A preliminary analysis, performed jointly by Lisa and the Hotel Paris's chief financial officer, left them optimistic that HR could contribute measurably to achieving the hotel's strategic aims. Several employee competencies and behaviors, including employee morale, employee commitment, and the percent of arriving guests receiving the hotel's required greeting, had significant effects on customer and organizational outcomes such as guest satisfaction and frequency of guest returns. In turn, outcomes like these contributed measurably to the Hotel Paris's strategic goals, including profit margins, market share, and scores on industry satisfaction surveys. Lisa and her team now turn to creating a recruitment process that will help to produce the required employee competencies and behaviors. The accompanying HR Scorecard (Figure 5–12) outlines the relationships involved.

As they reviewed the details of the Hotel Paris's current recruitment practices, Lisa Cruz and the firm's CFO became increasingly concerned. What they found, basically, was that the recruitment function was totally unmanaged. The previous HR director had simply allowed the responsibility for recruiting to remain with each separate hotel, and the hotel managers, not being HR professionals, usually just took the path of least resistance when a job became available by placing help wanted ads in their local papers. There was no sense of direction from the Hotel Paris's headquarters regarding what sorts of applicants the company preferred, what media and alternative sources of recruits its managers should use, no online recruiting, and, of course no measurement at all of effectiveness of the recruitment process. The company totally ignored recruitment-source metrics that other firms used effectively, such as number of qualified applicants per position, percentage of jobs filled from within, the offer-to-acceptance ratio, acceptance by recruiting source, turnover by recruiting source, and selection test results by recruiting source. This despite the fact, as the CFO put it, "that high performance companies consistently score much higher than low performing firms on HR practices such as number of qualified applicants per position, and percentage of jobs filled from within."

It was safe to say that achieving the Hotel Paris's strategic aims depended largely on the quality of the people that it attracted to and then selected for employment at the firm. "What we want are employees who will put our guests first, who will use initiative to see that our guests are satisfied, and who will work tirelessly to provide our guests with services that exceed

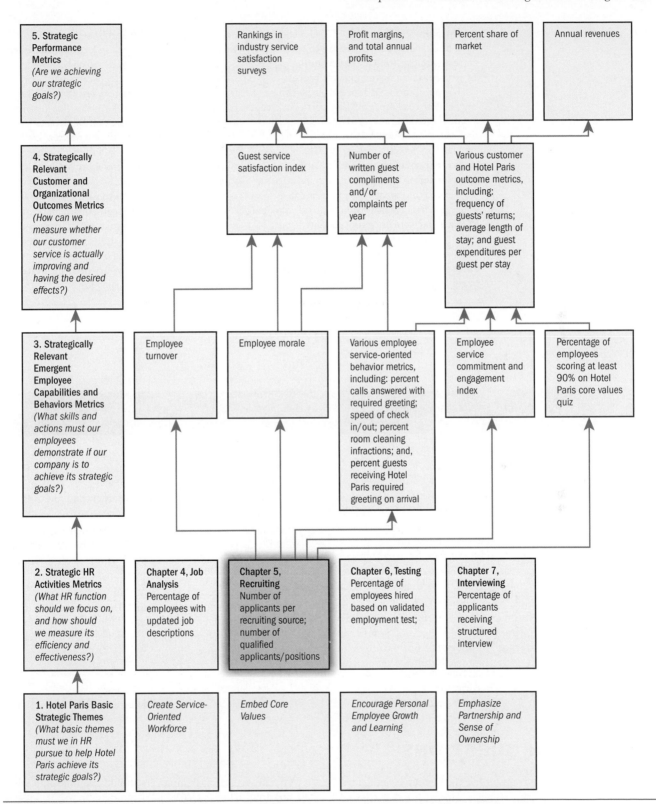

Figure 5-12
HR Scorecard for Hotel Paris International Corporation*

Note: *(An abbreviated example showing selected HR practices and outcomes aimed at implementing the competitive strategy, "To use superior guest services to differentiate the Hotel Paris properties and thus increase the length of stays and the return rate of guests and thus boost revenues and profitability") their expectations" said the CFO. Lisa and the CFO both knew this process had to start with better recruiting. The CFO gave her the green light to design a new recruitment process.

The new process had several elements. Lisa and her team had the firm's IT department create a central recruiting link for the Hotel Paris's Web site, with geographical links that each local hotel could use to publicize its openings. The HR team created a series of standard ads the managers could use for each job title. These standard ads emphasized the company's service-oriented values, and basically said (without actually saying it) that if you were not people oriented you should not apply. They also emphasized what it was like to work for the Hotel Paris, and the excellent benefits (which the HR team was about to get started on) the firm provided. It created a

new intranet-based job posting system and encouraged employees to use it to apply for open positions. For several jobs, including housekeeping crew and front-desk clerk, applicants must now first pass a short prescreening test to apply. The HR team analyzed the performance (for instance, in terms of applicants/source, and applicants hired/source) of the various local newspapers and recruiting firms the hotels had used in the past, and chose the best to be the approved recruiting sources in their local areas.

After six months with these and other recruitment function changes, the number of applicants was up on average 40%. Lisa and her team were now set to institute new screening procedures that would help them select the high-commitment, service-oriented, motivated employees they were looking for.

 *Review*

SUMMARY

1. Developing personnel plans requires three forecasts: one for personnel requirements, one for the supply of outside candidates, and one for the supply of inside candidates. To predict the need for personnel, first project the demand for the product or service. Next, project the volume of production required to meet these estimates; finally, relate personnel needs to these production estimates.

2. With personnel needs projected, the next step is to build a pool of qualified applicants. There are several sources of candidates, both internal (promotion from within) and external (advertising, employment agencies, executive

recruiters, college recruiting, the Internet, and referrals and walk-ins).

3. Remember that it is unlawful to discriminate against any individual with respect to employment because of race, color, religion, sex, national origin, or age (unless religion, sex, or origin are bona fide occupational qualifications).

4. The initial selection screening in most organizations begins with an application form. Most managers use these just to obtain background data. However, you can use application form data to make predictions about the applicant's future performance.

DISCUSSION QUESTIONS

1. What are the pros and cons of five sources of job candidates?
2. What are the four main types of information that application forms provide?
3. How, specifically, do equal employment laws apply to personnel recruiting activities?
4. What are five things employers should keep in mind when using Internet sites to find job candidates?
5. What are the five main things you would do to recruit and retain a more diverse workforce?

INDIVIDUAL AND GROUP ACTIVITIES

1. Working individually or in groups, bring to class several classified and display ads from the Sunday help wanted ads. Analyze the effectiveness of these ads using the guidelines discussed in this chapter.

2. Working individually or in groups, develop a five-year forecast of occupational market conditions for five occupations such as accountant, nurse, and engineer.

3. Working individually or in groups, visit the local office of your state employment agency. Come back to class prepared to discuss the following questions: What types of jobs seem to be available through this agency, predominantly? To what extent do you think this particular agency would be a good source of professional, technical, and/or managerial applicants? What sorts of paperwork are applicants to the state agency required to complete before their applications are processed by the agency? What other services does the office provide? What other opinions does you form about the state agency?

4. Working individually or in groups, find at least five employment ads, either on the Internet or in a local newspaper, that suggest that the company is family-friendly and should

appeal to women, minorities, older workers, and single parents. Discuss what they're doing to be family-friendly.

5. Working individually or in groups, interview a manager between the ages of 25 and 35 at a local business who manages employees age 40 or older. Ask the manager to describe three or four of his or her most challenging experiences managing older employees.

6. The HRCI "Test Specifications" appendix at the end of this book (pages 685–689) lists the knowledge someone studying for the HRCI certification exam needs to have in each area of human resource management (such as in Strategic Management, Workforce Planning, and Human Resource Development). In groups of four to five students, do four things: (1) review that appendix now; (2) identify the material in this chapter that relates to the required knowledge the appendix lists; (3) write four multiple choice exam questions on this material that you believe would be suitable for inclusion in the HRCI exam; and (4) if time permits, have someone from your team post your team's questions in front of the class, so the students in other teams can take each others' exam questions.

EXPERIENTIAL EXERCISE

The Nursing Shortage

As of March 2004, the U.S. economy was improving in many respects, but unemployment was still disappointingly high, and employers were still obviously holding back on their hiring. However, while many people were unemployed, that was not the case with nurse professionals. Virtually every hospital was aggressively recruiting nurses. Many were turning to foreign-trained nurses, for example, by recruiting nurses in the Philippines. Experts expected nurses to be in very short supply for years to come.

Purpose: The purpose of this exercise is to give you experience creating a recruitment program.

Required Understanding: You should be thoroughly familiar with the contents of this chapter, and with the nurse recruitment program of a hospital such as Lenox Hill Hospital in New York (see http://www.lenoxhillhospital.org/nursing/index.jsp, and http://www.lenoxhillhospital.org/careers/joblist.jsp).

How to Set Up the Exercise/Instructions: Set up groups of four to five students for this exercise. The groups should work separately and should not converse with each other. Each group should address the following tasks:

1. Based on information available on the hospital's Web site, create a hard-copy ad for the hospital to place in the Sunday edition of the *New York Times*. Which (geographic) editions of the *Times* would you use, and why?

2. Analyze and critique the hospital's current online nurses' ad. How would you improve on it?

3. Prepare in outline form a complete nurses' recruiting program for this hospital, including all recruiting sources your group would use.

APPLICATION CASE

Finding People Who Are Passionate About What They Do

Trilogy Software, Inc., of Austin, Texas, is a fast-growing software company, with earnings in the $100 million to $200 million range. It prides itself on its unique and unorthodox culture.

Many of its approaches to business practice are unusual, but in Trilogy's fast-changing and highly competitive environment they seem to work.

There is no dress code and employees make their own hours, often very long. They tend to socialize together (the average age is 26), both in the office's well-stocked kitchen and on company-sponsored events and trips to places like local dance clubs and retreats in Las Vegas and Hawaii. An in-house jargon has developed, and the shared history of the eight-year-old firm has taken on the status of legend. Responsibility is heavy and comes early, with a "just do it now" attitude that dispenses with long apprenticeships. New recruits are given a few weeks of intensive training, known as Trilogy University and described by participants as "more like boot camp than business school." Information is delivered as if with "a fire hose," and new employees are expected to commit their expertise and vitality to everything they do. Jeff Daniel, director of college recruiting, admits the intense and unconventional firm is not the employer for everybody. "But it's definitely an environment where people who are passionate about what they do can thrive."

The firm employs about 700 such passionate people. Trilogy's managers know the rapid growth they seek depends on having a staff of the best people they can find, quickly trained and given broad responsibility and freedom as soon as possible. Founder and CEO Joe Liemandt says, "At a software company, people are everything. You can't build the next great software company, which is what we're trying to do here, unless you're totally committed to that. Of course, the leaders at every company say, 'People are everything.' But they don't act on it."

Trilogy makes finding the right people (it calls them "great people") a companywide mission. Recruiters actively pursue the freshest, if least experienced, people in the job market, scouring college career fairs and computer science departments for talented overachievers with ambition and entrepreneurial instincts.

Top managers conduct the first rounds of interviews, letting prospects know they will be pushed to achieve but will be well rewarded. Employees take top recruits and their significant others out on the town when they fly into Austin for the standard, three-day preliminary visit. A typical day might begin with grueling interviews but end with mountain biking, Roller Blading, or laser tag. Executives have been known to fly out to meet and woo hot prospects who couldn't make the trip.

One year, Trilogy reviewed 15,000 résumés, conducted 4,000 on-campus interviews, flew 850 prospects in for interviews, and hired 262 college graduates, who account for over a third of its current employees. The cost per hire was $13,000; Jeff Daniel believes it was worth every penny.

Questions

1. Identify some of the established recruiting techniques that underlie Trilogy's unconventional approach to attracting talent.

2. What particular elements of Trilogy's culture most likely appeal to the kind of employees it seeks? How does it convey those elements to job prospects?

3. Would Trilogy be an appealing employer for you? Why or why not? If not, what would it take for you to accept a job offer from Trilogy?

4. What suggestions would you make to Trilogy for improving its recruiting processes?

Source: Chuck Salter, "Insanity, Inc.," *Fast Company*, January 1999, pp. 101–108; and www.trilogy.com/sections/careers/work, accessed 3/24/04.

CONTINUING CASE

Carter Cleaning Company

Getting Better Applicants

If you were to ask Jennifer and her father what the main problem was in running their firm, their answer would be quick and short: hiring good people. Originally begun as a string of coin-operated laundromats requiring virtually no skilled help, the chain grew to six stores, each heavily dependent on skilled managers, cleaner–spotters, and pressers. Employees generally have no more than a high school education (often less), and the market for them is very competitive. Over a typical weekend literally dozens of want ads for experienced pressers or cleaner–spotters can be found in area newspapers. All these people are usually paid around $15.00 per hour, and they change jobs frequently. Jennifer and her father are thus faced with the continuing task of recruiting and hiring qualified workers out of a pool of individuals they feel are almost nomadic in their propensity to move from area to area and job to job. Turnover in their stores (as in the stores of many of their competitors) often approaches 400%. "Don't talk to me about

human resources planning and trend analysis," says Jennifer. "We're fighting an economic war and I'm happy just to be able to round up enough live applicants to be able to keep my trenches fully manned."

In light of this problem, Jennifer's father asked her to answer the following questions:

Questions

1. First, how would you recommend we go about reducing the turnover in our stores?

2. Provide a detailed list of recommendations concerning how we should go about increasing our pool of acceptable job applicants so we are no longer faced with the need of hiring almost anyone who walks in the door. (Your recommendations regarding the latter should include completely worded online and hard-copy advertisements and recommendations regarding any other recruiting strategies you would suggest we use.)

KEY TERMS

employment or personnel planning, 152

trend analysis, 153

ratio analysis, 154

scatter plot, 154

computerized forecast, 155

qualifications inventories, 155

personnel replacement charts, 156

position replacement card, 156

recruiting yield pyramid, 161

job posting, 162

succession planning, 163

alternative staffing, 170

on demand recruiting services (ODRS), 173

application form, 181

ENDNOTES

1. Bill Macaler and Jones Shannon, "Does HR Planning Improve Business Performance?" *Industrial Management*, January/February 2003, p. 20.

2. Based on an idea in Elmer H. Burack and Robert D. Smith, *Personnel Management: A Human Resource Systems Approach* (St. Paul, MN: West, 1997), pp. 134–135. Reprinted by permission. Copyright 1997 by West Publishing Co. All rights reserved.

3. Macaler and Shannon, "Does HR Planning Improve Business Performance?" p. 16.

4. Glenn Bassett, "Elements of Manpower Forecasting and Scheduling," *Human Resource Management* 12, no. 3 (Fall 1973), pp. 35–43; Pat Sweet, "Model Future: Business Intelligence Software Is Giving Finance Directors the Time and Space to Think about the Future," *Accounting* 123 (March 1999), pp. 4–6.

5. For an example of a computerized, supply-chain-based personnel planning system, see Dan Kara, "Automating the Service Chain," *Software Magazine* 20 (June 2000), pp. 3, 42.

6. Shunyin Lam et al., "Retail Sales Force Scheduling Based on Store Traffic Forecasting," *Journal of Retailing* 74, no. 1 (Spring 1998), pp. 61–89.

7. John Markoff, "Bill Gates's Brain Cells, Dressed Down for Action," *New York Times*, March 25, 2001, pp. B1, B12.

8. For discussions of skill inventories, see, for example, John Lawrie, "Skill Inventories: Pack for the Future," *Personnel Journal*, March 1987, pp. 127–130; John Lawrie, "Skill Inventories: A Developmental Process," *Personnel Journal*, October 1987, pp. 108–110.

9. This section is based on Ibid.

10. Jennifer Schramm, "A Worker Gap Ahead," *HR Magazine*, June 2003, p. 240.

11. "Employers Still in Recruiting Bind Should Seek Government Help, Chamber Suggests," *BNA Bulletin to Management*, May 29, 2003, pp. 169–170.

12. Tom Porter, "Effective Techniques to Attract, Hire, and Retain 'Top Notch' Employees for Your Company," *San Diego Business Journal* 21, no. 13 (March 27, 2000), p. b36.

13. Kenneth Sovereign, *Personnel Law* (Upper Saddle River, NJ: Prentice Hall, 1999), pp. 47–49.

14. Ibid., p. 48.

15. Ibid., p. 50.

16. Ibid., p. 51.

17. Michelle Martinez, "Recruiting Here and There," *HR Magazine*, September 2002, p. 95.

18. Ibid.

19. Kevin Carlson et al., "Recruitment Evaluation: The Case for Assessing the Quality of Applicants Attracted," *Personnel Psychology* 55 (2002), pp. 461–490.

20. Ibid., p. 461.

21. Ibid., p. 466.

22. Ibid., p. 466.

23. Ibid.

24. Thomas Stewart, "In Search of Elusive Tech Workers," *Fortune*, February 16, 1998, pp. 171–172.

25. Ibid., p. 171.

26. "Hiring Works the Second Time Around," *BNA Bulletin to Management*, January 30, 1997, p. 40.

27. Ibid.

28. Soonhee Kim, "Linking Employee Assessments to Succession Planning," *Public Personnel Management* 32, no. 4 (Winter 2003), pp. 533–547.

29. Quoted in Susan Wells, "Who's Next," *HR Magazine*, November 2003, p. 43.

30. See "Succession Management: Identifying and Developing Leaders," *BNA* 21, no.12, (December 2003), p. 15.

31. Soonhee Kim, "Linking Employee Assessments to Succession Planning."

32. Bill Roberts, "Matching Talent with Tasks," *HR Magazine*, November 2002, pp. 91–96.

33. Ibid., p. 34.

34. Erik Krell, "Recruiting Outlook: Creative HR for 2003," *Workforce*, December 2002, pp. 40–44.

35. John Kohl, David Stephens, and Jen-Chieh Chang, "Illegal Recruitment Advertising: A Ten Year Retrospective," *Employee Responsibilities and Rights* 10, no. 3 (September 1977), pp. 213–224.

36. Christopher Collins and Cynthia Stevens, "The Relationship Between Early Recruitment Related Activities and the Application Decisions of New Labor Market Entrants: A Brand Equity Approach to Recruitment," *Journal of Applied Psychology* 87, no. 6 (2002), pp. 1121–1133.

37. Find your nearest one stop center at www.servicelocator.org/.

38. Susan Saulney, "New Jobless Centers Offer More Than a Benefit Check," *New York Times*, September 5, 2001, p. A1.

39. Lynn Doherty and E. Norman Sims, "Quick, Easy Recruitment Help: From a State?" *Workforce*, May 1998, p. 36.

40. Ibid.

41. Allison Thompson, "The Contingent Work Force," *Occupational Outlook Quarterly*, Spring 1995, p. 47.

42. Brenda Palk Sunoo, "From Santa to CEO: Temps Play All Roles," *Personnel Journal*, April 1996, pp. 34–44.

43. Shari Caudron, "Contingent Workforce Spurs HR Planning," *Personnel Journal*, (July 1994), p. 60.

44. Robert Bohner Jr. and Elizabeth Salasko, "Beware the Legal Risks of Hiring Temps," *Workforce*, October 2002, pp. 50–57.

45. Ibid.

46. Daniel Feldman, Helen Doerpinghaus, and William Turnley, "Managing Temporary Workers: A Permanent HRM Challenge," *Organizational Dynamics* 23, no. 2 (Fall 1994), p. 49.

47. This is based on or quoted from Nancy Howe, "Match Temp Services to Your Needs," *Personnel Journal*, March 1989, pp. 45–51.

48. This section is based on "Robyn Meredith, "Giant Sucking Sound," *Forbes*, September 29, 2003, volume 172, issue six, page 158; Jim McKay, "Inevitable Outsourcing, Offshoring Stirred Passions at Pittsburgh Summit," *Knight Ridder/Tribune Business News*, March 11, 2004; Peter Panepento, "General Electric Transportation to Outsource Drafting Jobs to India," *Knight Ridder/Tribune Business News*, May 5, 2004; Julie Harbin, "Recent Survey Charts Execs' Willingness to Outsource Jobs," *San Diego Business Journal*, April 5, 2004, volume 25, issue 14, pages 8–10; and Pamela Babcock, "America's Newest Export: White-Collar Jobs," HR Magazine, April 2004, volume 49, number four, pages 50–57

49. Susan Wells, "Slow Times for Executive Recruiting," *HR Magazine*, April 2003, pp. 61–67.

50. "Search and Destroy," *Economist*, June 27, 1998, p. 63.

51. Ibid.

52. Ibid.

53. John Wareham, *Secrets of a Corporate Headhunter* (New York: Playboy Press, 1981), pp. 213–225; Chip McCreary, "Get the Most Out of Search Firms," *Workforce*, August 1997, pp. S28–S30.

54. Michelle Martinez, "Working with an Outside Recruiter? Get It in Writing," *HR Magazine*, January 2001, pp. 98–105.

55. Bill Leonard, "Recruiting from the Competition," *HR Magazine*, February 2001, pp. 78–86.

56. Martha Frase-Blunt, "A Recruiting Spigot," *HR Magazine*, April 2003, pp. 71–79.

57. Sara Rynes, Marc Orlitzky, and Robert Bretz Jr., "Experienced Hiring Versus College Recruiting: Practices and Emerging Trends," *Personnel Psychology* 50 (1997), pp. 309–339.

58. Wendy Boswell et al., "Individual Job Choice Decisions and the Impact of Job Attributes and Recruitment Practices: A Longitudinal Field Study," *Human Resource Management* 42, no. 1 (Spring 2003), pp. 23–37.

59. Michelle Martinez, "The Headhunter Within," *HR Magazine*, August 2001, pp. 48–56.

60. "Employee Referrals Improve Hiring," *BNA Bulletin to Management*, March 13, 1997, p. 88.

61. Ibid., p. 13.

62. "Tell a Friend: Employee Referral Programs Earn High Marks for Low Recruiting Costs," *BNA Bulletin to Management*, June 28, 2001, p. 201.

63. Ruth Thaler Carter, "Your Recruitment Advertising," *HR Magazine*, June 2001, pp. 93–100.

64. Eric Krell, "Recruiting Outlook: Creative HR for 2003."

65. "Does Your Company's Website Click with Job Seekers?" *Workforce*, (August 2000), p. 260.

66. "Study Says Career Web Sites Could Snare More Job Seekers," *BNA Bulletin to Management*, February 1, 2001, p. 36.

67. Sarah Gale, "Internet Recruiting: Better, Cheaper, Faster," *Workforce*, December 2001, p. 76.

68. Ibid.

69. Ibid., p. 75.

70. "Internet Recruiting Holds Promise," *BNA Bulletin to Management*, July 17, 1997, p. 232.

71. "Internet Recruiting Takes Off," *BNA Bulletin to Management*, February 20, 1997, p. 64.

72. Gillian Flynn, "E-Recruiting Ushers in Legal Dangers," *Workforce*, April 2002, p. 70.

73. William Dickmeyer, "Applicant Tracking Reports Make Data Meaningful," *Workforce*, February 2001, pp. 65–67.

74. Paul Gilster, "Channel the Resume Flood with Applicant Tracking Systems," *Workforce*, January 2001, pp. 32–34; Dickmeyer, "Applicant Tracking Reports," pp. 65–67.

75. Maria Seminerio, "E-Recruiting Takes Next Step," *The Week*, April 23, 2001, pp. 49–51.

76. Sarah Gale, "Internet Recruiting: Better, Cheaper, Faster," p. 75.

77. Daniel Feldman and Brian Klass, "Internet Job Hunting: A Field Study of Appliant Experiences with Online Recruiting," *Human Resource Management* 41, no. 2 (Summer 2002), pp. 175–192.

78. "Internship Programs Helps These Recruiters Toward Qualified Students with Disabilities," *BNA Bulletin to Management* (July 17, 2003), p. 225.

79. Unless otherwise noted, this section is based on Judith Casey and Marcie Pitt-Catsouphes, "Employed Single Mothers: Balancing Job and Home Life," *Employee Assistance Quarterly* 9, no. 324 (1994), pp. 37–53.

80. Ibid., p. 42.

81. Ibid., p. 48.

82. Ibid., p. 48.

83. Phaedra Brotherton, "Tapping into an Older Workforce," *Mosaics*, March/April 2000, Society for Human Resource Management.

84. Allison Wellner, "Tapping a Silver Mine," *HR Magazine*, March 2002, p. 29.

85. Ibid.

86. For this and other examples here, see Robert Goddard, "How to Harness America's Gray Power," *Personnel Journal* (May 1987), p. 23.

87. Susan Sweetser, "Women in Financial Services—An Ideal Match," *National Underwriter Life & Health—Financial Services Edition*, January 12, 2004, volume one, issue two, pages 14–16; Charles Lauer, "Keeping the Women on Board: Hospitals Must Work Overtime to Retain the Majority of their Employees," *Modern Health Care*, October 6, 2003, volume 33, issue 40, page 21.

88. Abby Ellin, "Supervising the Graybeards," *New York Times*, January 16, 2000, p. B16.

89. "Recruitment: B&Q in Search of Female Managers," *Personnel Today*, September 2, 2003, page 4; Dina Berta, "Brinker International's Gomez Keeps Recruitment of Women, Minorities on Company's Front Burner," *Nation's Restaurant News*, November 17, 2003 volume 37 issue 46 page 16.

90. Bill Leonard, "Welfare Reform: A New Deal for HR," *HR Magazine*, March 1997, pp. 78–86; Jennifer Laabs, "Welfare Law: HR's Role in Employment," *Workforce*, January 1998, pp. 30–39.

91. "Welfare-to-Work: No Easy Chore," *BNA Bulletin to Management*, February 13, 1997, p. 56.

92. Herbert Greenberg, "A Hidden Source of Talent," *HR Magazine*, March 1997, pp. 88–91.

93. "Welfare to Work: No Easy Chore," p. 56.

94. Linda Moore, "Firms Need to Improve Recruitment, Hiring of Disabled Workers, EEO Chief Says," *Knight Ridder/Tribune Business News*, November 5, 2003, item 03309094.

95. Richard Donkin, "Making Space for a Wheelchair Workforce," *Financial Times*, November 13, 2003, p. 9.

96. "Students with Disabilities Available," *HR Briefing*, June 15, 2002, p. 5.

97. Moore, "Firms Need to Improve Recruitment."

98. Circuit City Stores, Inc., Employment Packet, January 1997.

99. *Circuit City Stores, Inc. vs. Adams*, US. No. 99–1379, 3/21/01.

100. "Court Rejects Circuit City's Arbitration Pact, Find Employer's Advantage Unconscionable," *BNA Bulletin to Management*, February 14, 2002, p. 49.

101. "Supreme Court Denies Circuit Citiy's Bid for Review of Mandatory Arbitration," *BNA Bulletin to Management*, June 6, 2002, p. 177.

102. "Supreme Court Gives the Employers Green Light to Hold Most Employees to Arbitration Pacts," *BNA Bulletin to Management*, March 29, 2001, pp. 97–98.

103. Fred Mael, Mary Connerley, and Ray Morath, "None of Your Business: Parameters of Biodata Invasiveness," *Personnel Psychology* 49 (1996), pp. 613–650.

After studying this chapter, you should be able to:

1 Explain what is meant by reliability and validity.

2 Explain how you would go about validating a test.

3 Cite and illustrate our testing guidelines.

4 Give examples of some of the ethical and legal considerations in testing.

5 List eight tests you could use for employee selection, and how you would use them.

6 Explain the key points to remember in conducting background investigations.

6

Employee Testing and Selection

As she considered what she had to do next, Lisa Cruz, the Hotel Paris's HR

director, knew that employee selection had to play a central role in her

plans. The Hotel Paris currently had an informal screening process in which

local hotel managers obtained application forms, interviewed applicants, and

checked their references. However, a pilot project using an employment test

for service people at the Chicago hotel had produced startling results. Lisa

found consistent, significant relationships between test performance and a

range of employee competencies and behaviors such as speed of check-

in/out, employee turnover, and percentage of calls answered with the

required greeting. Clearly, she was on to something. She knew that

employee capabilities and behaviors like these translated into just the sorts

of improved guest services the Hotel Paris needed to execute its strategy.

She therefore had to decide what selection procedures would be best.●

The previous chapter focused on the methods managers use to build an applicant pool. The purpose of this chapter, Employee Testing and Selection, is to show you how to use various tools and techniques to select the best candidates for the job. The main topics we'll cover include the selection process, basic testing techniques, background and reference checks, ethical and legal questions in testing, types of tests, and work samples and simulations. In the following chapter, Interviewing Candidates, we turn to the techniques you can use to improve your skills with what is probably the most widely used screening tool, the selection interview.

● WHY CAREFUL SELECTION IS IMPORTANT

With a pool of applicants, the next step is to select the best candidates for the job. This usually means whittling down the applicant pool by using the screening tools explained in this chapter: tests, assessment centers, and background and reference checks. Then the prospective supervisor can interview likely candidates and decide who to hire.

Selecting the right employees is important for three main reasons. First, your own performance always depends in part on your subordinates. Employees with the right skills and attributes will do a better job for you and the company. Employees without these skills or who are abrasive or obstructionist won't perform effectively, and your own performance and the firm's will suffer. The time to screen out undesirables is before they are in the door, not after.

negligent hiring
Hiring workers with questionable backgrounds without proper safeguards.

Second, it is important because it's costly to recruit and hire employees. Hiring and training even a clerk can cost $5,000 or more in fees and supervisory time. The total cost of hiring a manager could easily be 10 times as high once you add search fees, interviewing time, reference checking, and travel and moving expenses.

When the 3,000-room Bellagio Hotel opened in Las Vegas, it needed to hire nearly 10,000 workers in just 24 weeks. Arte Nathan, then vice president of human resources, developed a highly automated "battle plan" to get the job done. In one screening process, candidates met with staff members who checked applications and assessed their communication skills and overall demeanor. This one process eliminated about 20% of the more than 80,000 applicants.

Third, it's important because of the legal implications of incompetent hiring. For one thing (as we saw in Chapter 2), EEO laws and court decisions require nondiscriminatory selection procedures for protected groups. Furthermore, courts will find employers liable when employees with criminal records or other problems take advantage of access to customers' homes (or similar opportunities) to commit crimes. Lawyers call hiring workers with such backgrounds, without proper safeguards, **negligent hiring**.[1] In one case, *Ponticas v. K.M.S. Investments*, an apartment manager with a passkey entered a woman's apartment and assaulted her. The court found the apartment complex's owner and operator negligent in not properly checking the manager's background before hiring him.

Negligent hiring underscores the need to think through what the job's human requirements really are.[2] For example, "nonrapist" isn't likely to appear as a required knowledge, skill, or ability in a job analysis of a repair person. But it is that type of requirement that has been the focus of many negligent hiring suits.[3]

Employers protect against negligent hiring claims by:

■ Carefully scrutinizing all information supplied by the applicant on his or her employment application. For example, look for unexplained gaps in employment.

■ Getting the applicant's written authorization for reference checks, and carefully checking references.

■ Saving all records and information you obtain about the applicant.

■ Rejecting applicants who make false statements of material facts or who have conviction records for offenses directly related and important to the job in question.

■ Keeping in mind the need to balance the applicant's privacy rights with others' "need to know," especially when you discover damaging information.

■ Taking immediate disciplinary action if problems arise.[4]

Explain what is meant by reliability and validity.

● BASIC TESTING CONCEPTS

Effective selection is therefore important and depends, to a large degree, on the basic testing concepts of validity and reliability.

Reliability

reliability
The consistency of scores obtained by the same person when retested with the identical tests or with alternate forms of the same test.

Reliability is a test's first major requirement and refers to its consistency: "A reliable test is one that yields consistent scores when a person takes two alternate forms of the test or when he or she takes the same test on two or more different occasions."[5]

A test's reliability is very important; if a person scored 90 on an intelligence test on a Monday and 130 when retested on Tuesday, you probably wouldn't have much faith in the test.

There are several ways to estimate consistency or reliability. You could administer the same test to the same people at two different points in time, comparing their test scores at time two with their scores at time one; this would be a *retest estimate*. Or you could administer a test and then administer what experts believe to be an equivalent test later; this would be an *equivalent form estimate*. The Scholastic Assessment Test (SAT) is an example.

A test's *internal consistency* is another measure of its reliability. For example, suppose you have 10 items on a test of vocational interests; you believe these measure, in various ways, the person's interest in working outdoors. You administer the test and then statistically analyze the degree to which responses to these 10 items vary together. This would provide a measure of the internal reliability of the test. Psychologists refer to this as an *internal comparison estimate*. Internal consistency is one reason that you find apparently repetitive questions on some test questionnaires.

A number of things could cause a test to be unreliable. For example, the questions may do a poor job of sampling the material; test one focuses more on Chapters 1, 3, 5, and 7, while test two focuses more on Chapters 2, 4, 5, and 8. Or there might be errors due to changes in the testing conditions; for instance, the room the test is in next month may be noisy.

Validity

Reliability, while indispensable, only tells you that the test is measuring something consistently. It does not prove that you are measuring what you intend to measure. A mismanufactured 33-inch yardstick will consistently tell you that a 33-inch board is 33 inches long. Unfortunately, if what you're looking for is a board that is one full yard long, then your 33-inch yardstick, though reliable, is misleading you. What you need is a valid yardstick. Reliability is the first major requirement for a test, since if it's not measuring whatever it's measuring consistently, then you can't trust it at all. Validity is the second major requirement for a test. Validity tells you whether the test (or yardstick) is measuring what you think it's supposed to be measuring.[6]

A test is a sample of a person's behavior, but some tests are more clearly representative of the behavior being sampled than others. A typing test, for example, clearly corresponds to an on-the-job behavior. At the other extreme, there may be no apparent relationship between the items on the test and the behavior. This is the case with projective personality tests. Thus, in the Thematic Apperception Test illustrated in Figure 6-1, the

Figure 6-1
Sample Picture Card from
Thematic Apperception Test
How do you interpret this picture?
Source: Harvard University Press.
Used with permission.

psychologist asks the person to explain how he or she interprets an ambiguous picture. The psychologist uses that interpretation to draw conclusions about the person's personality and behavior. In such tests, it is more difficult to prove that the tests are measuring what they are said to measure—that they're valid.

Test validity answers the question, "Does this test measure what it's supposed to measure?"

Put another way, *validity* refers to the correctness of the inferences that we can make based on the test. For example, if Jane gets a higher score on a mechanical comprehension tests than Jim,[7] can we be sure that Jane possesses more mechanical comprehension than Jim? With respect to employee selection tests, *validity* often refers to evidence that the test is job related—in other words, that performance on the test is a valid predictor of subsequent performance on the job. A selection test must be valid since, without proof of validity, there is no logical or legally permissible reason to continue using it to screen job applicants. In employment testing, there are two main ways to demonstrate a test's validity: **criterion validity** and **content validity**.[8]

Criterion Validity Demonstrating criterion validity means demonstrating that those who do well on the test also do well on the job, and that those who do poorly on the test do poorly on the job. Thus, the test has validity to the extent that the people with higher test scores perform better on the job. In psychological measurement, a *predictor* is the measurement (in this case, the test score) that you are trying to relate to a *criterion*, like performance on the job. The term *criterion validity* reflects that terminology.

Content Validity Employers demonstrate the *content validity* of a test by showing that the test constitutes a fair sample of the content of the job. The basic procedure here is to identify job tasks and behaviors that are critical to performance, and then randomly select a sample of those tasks and behaviors to be tested. A data entry test used to hire a data entry clerk is an example. If the content you choose for the data entry test is a representative sample of what the person needs to know for the job, then the test is probably content valid.

---

test validity
The accuracy with which a test, interview, and so on measures what it purports to measure or fulfills the function it was designed to fill.

criterion validity
A type of validity based on showing that scores on the test (predictors) are related to job performance (criterion).

content validity
A test that is content valid is one that contains a fair sample of the tasks and skills actually needed for the job in question.

Demonstrating content validity sounds easier than it is in practice. Demonstrating that (1) the tasks the person performs on the test are really a comprehensive and random sample of the tasks performed on the job, and (2) the conditions under which the person takes the test resemble the work situation is not always easy. For many jobs, employers opt to demonstrate other evidence of a test's validity—such as its criterion validity.

Explain how you would go about validating a test.

How to Validate a Test

What makes a test like the Graduate Record Examination useful for college admissions directors? What makes a mechanical comprehension test useful for a manager trying to hire an engineer?

The answer to both questions is usually that people's scores on these tests predict how they perform. Thus, other things being equal, students who score high on the graduate admissions tests also do better in graduate school. Applicants who score high on the mechanical comprehension test perform better as engineers.

In order for a selection test to be useful, you should be fairly sure test scores relate in a predictable way to performance on the job. In other words, you should validate the test before using it by ensuring that scores on the test are a good predictor of some *criterion* like job performance. (In other words, you must demonstrate the test's *criterion validity*.) This validation process is usually done by an industrial psychologist. The HR department coordinates the effort. Line management's role is to describe the job and its requirements so that the human requirements of the job and its performance standards are clear to the psychologist.

The validation process consists of five steps: analyze the job, choose your tests, administer the tests, relate the test scores and the criteria, and cross-validate and revalidate.

Step 1: **Analyze the Job** The first step is to analyze the job and write job descriptions and job specifications. Here, you need to specify the human traits and skills you believe are required for adequate job performance. For example, must an applicant be verbal, a good talker? Is programming required? Must the person assemble small, detailed components? These requirements become the *predictors*. These are the human traits and skills you believe predict success on the job. In this first step, you also must define what you mean by "success on the job," since it's this success for which you want predictors. The standards of success are *criteria*. You could focus on production-related criteria (quantity, quality, and so on), personnel data (absenteeism, length of service, and so on), or judgments of worker performance (by persons like supervisors). For an assembler's job, your predictors might include manual dexterity and patience. Criteria that you would hope to predict with your test might include quantity produced per hour and number of rejects produced per hour.

Some employers make the mistake of carefully choosing predictors (such as manual dexterity) while virtually ignoring the question of which criteria best predict performance. One illustrative study involved 212 gas utility company employees. In this study, the researchers found a significant relationship between the test battery that was used as a predictor and two performance criteria—supervisor ratings of performance and objective productivity indices. However, there was virtually no relationship between the same test battery and two other criteria, namely an objective quality index or employee self-ratings.[9]

Step 2: **Choose the Tests** Next, choose tests that you think measure the attributes (predictors) important for job success. Employers usually base this choice on experience, previous research, and "best guesses." They usually don't start with just one test. Instead, they choose several tests and combine them into a *test battery*. The test battery aims to measure an array of possible predictors, such as aggressiveness, extroversion, and numerical ability.

What tests are available and where do you get them? Given the EEO and ethical issues involved, the best advice is probably to use a professional, such as a licensed industrial psychologist. However, many firms publish tests. Psychological Assessment Resources, Inc., in Odessa, Florida, is typical. It publishes and distributes many tests; some are available to virtually any purchaser, but many are available only to qualified buyers (such as those with degrees in psychology or counseling). Figure 6-2 presents several Web sites that provide information about tests or testing programs.

Some companies publish employment tests that are generally available to anyone. For example, Wonderlic Personnel Test, Inc., publishes a well-known intellectual capacity test, and also other tests, including technical skills tests, aptitude test batteries, interest inventories, and reliability inventories. G. Neil Company of Sunrise, Florida, offers employment testing materials including, for example, a clerical skills test, telemarketing ability test, service ability test, management ability test, team skills test, and sales abilities test. Again, though, don't let the widespread availability of personnel tests blind you to this important fact: You should use the tests in a manner consistent with equal employment laws, and in a manner that is ethical and protects the test taker's privacy. We'll return to this point in a moment.

Step 3: Administer the Test Next, administer the selected test(s) to employees. You have two choices here. One option is to administer the tests to employees presently on the job. You then compare their test scores with their current performance; this is *concurrent validation*. Its main advantage is that data on performance are readily available. The disadvantage is that current employees may not be representative of new applicants (who of course are really the ones for whom you are interested in developing a screening test). Current employees have already had on-the-job training and have been screened by your existing selection techniques.

Predictive validation is the second and more dependable way to validate a test. Here you administer the test to applicants before they are hired. Then hire these applicants using only existing selection techniques, not the results of the new tests you are developing. After they have been on the job for some time, measure their performance and compare it to their earlier test scores. You can then determine whether you could have used their performance on the test to predict their subsequent job performance. In the case of an assembler's job, the ideal situation would be to administer, say, the Test of Mechanical Comprehension (see page 205) to all applicants. Then ignore the test results and hire assemblers as you usually do. Perhaps six months later, measure your new assemblers' performance (quantity produced per hour, number of rejects per

---

Figure 6-2
Examples of Web Sites Offering Information on Tests or Testing Programs

- www.hr-guide.com/data/G371.htm
  Provides general information and sources for all types of employment tests.
- http://buros.unl.edu/buros/jsp/search.jsp
  Provides technical information on all types of employment and nonemployment tests.
- www.ets.org/testcoll/index.html
  Provides information on over 20,000 tests.
- www.kaplan.com/
  Information from Kaplan test preparation on how various admissions tests work.
- www.assessments.biz/default.asp?source=GW-emptest
  One of many firms offering employment tests.

hour) and compare this performance to their Mechanical Comprehension test scores (as in step 4).

Step 4: Relate Your Test Scores and Criteria The next step is to determine if there is a significant relationship between scores (the predictor) and performance (the criterion). The usual way to do this is to determine the statistical relationship between (1) scores on the test and (2) job performance through *correlation analysis*, which shows the degree of statistical relationship.

If there's a correlation between test and job performance, you can develop an **expectancy chart**. This presents the relationship between test scores and job performance graphically. To do this, split the employees into, say, five groups according to test scores, with those scoring the highest fifth on the test, the second highest fifth, and so on. Then compute the percentage of high job performers in each of these five test score groups and present the data in an expectancy chart like that in Figure 6-3. This shows the likelihood that employees who score in each of these five test score groups will be high performers. In this case, someone scoring in the top fifth of the test has a 97% chance of being rated a high performer, while one scoring in the lowest fifth has only a 29% chance of being rated a high performer.[10]

Step 5: Cross-Validate and Revalidate Before putting the test into use, you may want to check it by cross-validating, by again performing steps 3 and 4 on a new sample of employees. At a minimum, an expert should revalidate the test periodically.

The procedure you would use to demonstrate *content validity* differs from that used to demonstrate criterion validity (as described in steps 1 through 5). Content validity tends to emphasize judgment. Here, you first do a careful job analysis to identify the work behaviors required. Then combine several samples of those behaviors into a test. A typing and computer skills test for a clerk would be an example. The fact that the test is a comprehensive sample of actual, observable, on-the-job behaviors is what lends the test its content validity. Criterion validity is determined through the five-step procedure previously described. Table 6-1 summarizes important testing guidelines such as "use tests as supplements."

---

expectancy chart
A graph showing the relationship between test scores and job performance for a group of people.

Figure 6-3
Expectancy Chart

Note: This expectancy chart shows the relation between scores made on the Minnesota Paper Form Board and rated success of junior draftspersons.

Example: Those who score between 37 and 44 have a 55% chance of being rated above average and those scoring between 57 and 64 have a 97% chance.

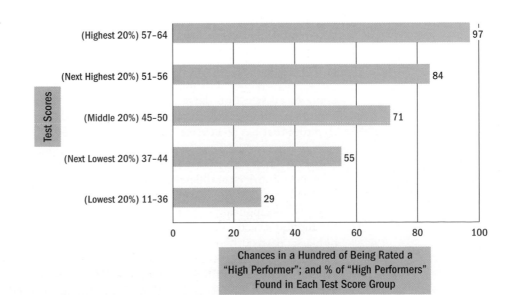

Test Scores

(Highest 20%) 57–64 — 97
(Next Highest 20%) 51–56 — 84
(Middle 20%) 45–50 — 71
(Next Lowest 20%) 37–44 — 55
(Lowest 20%) 11–36 — 29

0   20   40   60   80   100

Chances in a Hundred of Being Rated a "High Performer"; and % of "High Performers" Found in Each Test Score Group

Table 6-1

Testing Program Guidelines

1. *Use tests as supplements.* Don't make tests your only selection tool; use them to supplement other tools like interviews and background checks.

2. *Validate the tests.* It's best to validate them in your own organization. However, the fact that the same tests have proven valid in similar organizations—called validity generalization—is usually adequate.

3. *Monitor your testing/selection program.* Ask questions such as, "What proportions of minority and nonminority applicants are rejected at each stage of the hiring process?" and "Why am I using this test—what does it mean in terms of actual behavior on the job?"

4. *Keep accurate records.* Record why you rejected each applicant. A general note such as "not sufficiently well qualified" is not enough. Your reasons for rejecting the person may be subject to validation at a later date.

5. *Use a certified psychologist.* Developing, validating, and using selection standards (including tests) generally require a qualified psychologist. Most states require persons who offer psychological services to the public to be certified or licensed. A Ph.D. degree (the bachelor's degree is never sufficient) is usually one qualification. Potential consultants should provide evidence of similar work and experience in test validation, and demonstrate familiarity with federal and state equal rights laws and regulations.

6. *Manage test conditions.* Administer tests in areas that are reasonably private, quiet, well lighted, and ventilated, and make sure all applicants take the tests under the same test conditions. Once completed, keep test results confidential. Give them only to individuals with a legitimate need for the information and the ability to understand and interpret the scores (including the applicant). Train your supervisors regarding test results confidentiality.

7. *Revalidate periodically.* Employers' needs and applicants' aptitudes change over time. You should have your testing program revalidated periodically.

Cite and illustrate our testing guidelines.

Equal Employment Opportunity Aspects of Testing

As explained in Chapter 2, various federal, state, and local laws bar discrimination with respect to race, color, age, religion, sex, disability, and national origin. With respect to testing, the laws boil down to this: You must be able to prove (1) that your tests are related to success or failure on the job (validity), and (2) that your tests don't unfairly discriminate against minority or nonminority subgroups. Once the plaintiff shows that one of your selection procedures has an *adverse impact* on his or her protected class, you must demonstrate the validity and selection fairness of the allegedly discriminatory test or item. Adverse impact means there is a significant discrepancy between rates of rejection of members of the protected groups and others.

Employers can't avoid EEO laws just by avoiding tests: EEO guidelines and laws apply to all selection devices, including interviews, applications, and references. You could have to prove the validity, fairness, and job relatedness of any screening or selection tool that has an adverse impact on a protected group.[11]

Alternatives   Let's review where we are. Assume that you've used a test and that a rejected minority candidate has demonstrated adverse impact to the satisfaction of a court. How might the person have done this? One way is to show that the selection rate (for, say, the applicant's racial group) was less than four-fifths of that for the group with the highest selection rate. Thus, if 90% of white applicants passed the test but only 60% of blacks passed, then (since 60% is less than four-fifths of 90%) adverse impact exists.

The employer would then have three alternatives with respect to its testing program. One is to institute a different, valid selection procedure that does not have an adverse impact. The second is to show that the test is valid—in other words, that it is a valid predictor of performance on the job. Ideally, you would do this by conducting your own validation study. In any event, the plaintiff would then have to prove that your explanation for using the test is inadequate.

A third alternative—in this case aimed at avoiding adverse impact rather than responding to it—is to monitor the selection test to see if it has disparate (adverse) impact. If not, it's generally permissible to use the device, even if it's not valid—but why would you want to?

There are significant gender issues in the area of testing. "The New Workplace" feature illustrates this.

Give examples of some of the ethical and legal considerations in testing.

Test Takers' Individual Rights and Test Security

Test takers have rights to privacy and information under the American Psychological Association's standard for educational and psychological tests. (These guide psychologists but are not legally enforceable.) They have the right to the confidentiality of test results and the right to informed consent regarding use of these results. They have the right to expect that only people qualified to interpret the scores will have access to them, or that sufficient information will accompany the scores to ensure their appropriate interpretation. And they have the right to expect the test is fair to all. For example, no one taking it should have prior access to the questions or answers.

A complete discussion of the American Psychological Association's "Ethical Principles of Psychologists and Code of Conduct" is beyond the scope of this book, but a summary of some of its headings helps to illustrate its concerns. Main subject headings include: competence; integrity; respect for people's dignity; concern for others' welfare; social responsibility; maintaining expertise; nondiscrimination; sexual harassment; personal problems and conflicts; avoiding harm; misuse of psychologists' influence; multiple relationships; exploitation of relationships; delegation to and supervision of subordinate; competence and appropriate use of assessments and interventions; obsolete tests; maintaining confidentiality; minimizing intrusions on privacy; confidential information and databases; familiarity with the ethics code; conflicts between ethics and organizational demands; and reporting ethical violations.[12]

Research Insight   What determines perceived test fairness?[13] Following good test practices—a quiet test-taking environment, privacy, and so on—is important.[14] Another factor is the obviousness of the link between (1) the selection procedure and (2) performing the job (in other words, the selection procedure's "face validity"). In one study,

The New Workplace

Gender Issues in Testing

Employers using selection tests should know that gender issues may distort the results. TV commercials for children's toys attest to the fact that gender-role socialization is a continuing reality today: In particular, parents and others often socialize girls into traditionally female roles and boys into traditionally male roles. There is thus a "continuing over representation of women in a small number of 'pink collar' jobs such as waitress and secretary and in the traditionally female professions, including nursing, teaching, and social work,"

and a continuing underrepresentation in traditional male areas such as engineering and the sciences.[15]

Such gender-role socialization does influence men's and women's test results. For example, it can influence the occupational interests for which candidates express a preference. Males tend to score higher on aptitude tests in what some view as male fields (such as mechanical reasoning). Ironically, the interests and aptitudes tests may thus actually perpetuate the narrowing of females' career options.

259 college students from France and the United States rated the "favorability" of 10 selection procedures, and then specified what prompted them to rate some procedures as more favorable than others.[16]

The "perceived face validity of the selection procedure was the strongest correlate of favorability reactions among both samples."[17] Students' reactions were highly favorable toward interviews and work sample tests, both of which had obvious links to the job itself. They were moderately favorable toward biographical information and written ability tests. Favorability reactions were neutral toward personality and honesty tests, and negative toward graphology. In general, reactions were more favorable when the students felt the employer had the right to obtain information with a particular technique, and when the procedure was widely used in industry.

Note, then, that just because a selection technique is valid doesn't necessarily mean candidates will view it as fair. It may therefore sometimes make sense to substitute one valid test for another, if the new one comes across as more fair.[18]

Know Your Employment Law

The Issue of Privacy

Some privacy protections are embedded in U.S. law. At the federal level, the Constitution does not expressly provide for the right to privacy, but certain U.S. Supreme Court decisions do protect individuals from intrusive governmental action in a variety of contexts.[19] For example, if you are a federal employee or (in many jurisdictions) a state or local government employee, there are limits on disclosure of personnel information to individuals within or outside the agency. The Federal Privacy Act gives federal employees the right to inspect personnel files, and limits the disclosure of personnel information without the employee's consent, among other things.[20]

The common law of torts also provides some protection against disclosing information about employees to people outside the company. The best known application here involves defamation (either libel or slander). If your employer or former employer discloses information that is false and defamatory and that causes you serious injury, you may be able to sue for defamation of character.[21] In general, though, this is easier said than done. Employers providing a recommendation generally can't be sued for defamation unless the employee can show "malice"—that is, ill will, culpable recklessness, or disregard of the employee's rights. But this is usually hard to prove.[22]

Some states recognize common law as it applies to invasion of privacy. Such cases usually revolve around "public disclosure of private facts." Employees can sue employers for disclosing to a large number of people true but embarrassing private facts about the employee. (For example, your personnel file may contain private information regarding your health, test results, or job performance that you do not want disclosed outside the firm.) In invasion-of-privacy suits, truth is no defense.

One case involved a supervisor in a shouting match with an employee. The supervisor yelled out that the employee's wife had been having sexual relations with certain people. The employee and his wife sued the employer for invasion of privacy. The jury found the employer liable for invasion of the couple's privacy. It awarded damages to both of them, as well as damages for the couple's additional claim that the supervisor's conduct amounted to an intentional infliction of emotional distress.[23] Since many people sue these days, more discretion is required than some employers have shown in the past.

Guidelines to follow here include:

1. Train your supervisors regarding the importance of employee confidentiality.[24]
2. Adopt a "need to know" policy. For example, if an employee has been rehabilitated after a period of drug use and that information is not relevant to his or her functioning in the workplace, then a new supervisor may not "need to know."
3. Disclose procedures. If you know your firm can't keep information—such as test results—confidential, you may limit your liability by disclosing that fact before testing. For example, if employees who test positive on drug tests will have to use the firm's employee assistance program, explain that before giving the tests.

Using Tests at Work

Tests are widely used by employers. For example, about 41% of companies the American Management Association surveyed tested applicants for basic skills (defined as the ability to read instructions, write reports, and do arithmetic adequate to perform common workplace tasks).[25] However, some testing has actually fallen off a bit. For example, 67.6% of the respondents required employees to take job skills tests in 2001, down from 70.9% in 1999. About 29% of the respondents required some form of psychological measurement in 2001, versus 33% in 2000, and 33.4% in 1999.[26] If you want to see what such tests are like, try the short test in Figure 6-4 to see how prone you might be to on-the-job accidents.

Tests are not just for lower-level workers. For example, consultants McKinsey & Co., flew 54 MIT MBA students to Miami for two days of multiple choice business knowledge tests, case-oriented case studies, and interviews. Barclays Capital gives graduate and undergraduate job candidates aptitude tests instead of first-round interviews.[27] In general, as work demands increase (as represented by increasing skill requirements, training, and pay), employers tend to rely more on testing methods in the selection process.[28]

Employers don't use tests just to find good employees; they also use them to screen out bad ones. This can be important. By some estimates, 75% of employees have stolen from their employers at least once; 33% to 75% have engaged in behaviors such as theft, vandalism, and voluntary absenteeism; almost 25% say they've had knowledge of illicit drug use among co-workers; and 7% of a sample of employees reported being victims of physical threats.[29] Occupational fraud and abuse reportedly cost U.S. employers about $400 billion annually, or about nine dollars per day per employee or 6% of annual revenues.[30] No wonder prudent employers test their applicants.

Testing isn't just for large employers. For example, Outback Steakhouse (which now has 45,000 employees) began using preemployment tests in 1991, just two years after the company started. The testing is apparently quite successful. While annual turnover

Figure 6-4
Sample Test
Source: Courtesy of NYT Permissions.

CHECK YES OR NO	YES	NO
1. You like a lot of excitement in your life.		
2. An employee who takes it easy at work is cheating on the employer.		
3. You are a cautious person.		
4. In the past three years you have found yourself in a shouting match at school or work.		
5. You like to drive fast just for fun.		

Analysis: According to John Kamp, an industrial psychologist, applicants who answered no, yes, yes, no, no to questions 1, 2, 3, 4, and 5 are statistically likely to be absent less often, to have fewer on-the-job injuries, and, if the job involves driving, to have fewer on-the-job driving accidents. Actual scores on the test are based on answers to 130 questions.

rates for hourly employees may reach 200% in the restaurant industry, Outback's turnover ranges from 40 to 60%. Outback is looking for employees who are highly social, meticulous, sympathetic, and adaptable, and uses a test to screen out applicants who don't fit the Outback culture. This personality assessment test is part of a three-step preemployment interview process. Applicants take the test, and managers then compare the candidates' results to the profile for Outback Steakhouse employees. Those who score low on certain traits (like compassion) don't move to the next step. Those who do, move on to be interviewed by two managers. The latter focus on behavioral questions such as "What would you do if a customer asked for a side dish we don't have on the menu?"[31]

Tests come from test publishers, who provide various services to facilitate the testing process. One service is automated scoring and test interpretation. Some tests, such as the 16PF personality profile, must be professionally scored and interpreted. The 16PF is a 187-item personality profile psychologists use to measure management characteristics including creativity, independence, leadership, and self-control. Wonderlic, Inc., lets an employer administer the 16PF. The employer then faxes or mails the answer sheet to Wonderlic, which scores the candidate's profile and mails or faxes back the interpretive report in one day. Today, psychologists also easily score many psychological tests, including the MMPI personality test, online or using interpretive Windows-based software.

Computer-Interactive Testing

Computerized testing is increasingly replacing conventional paper-and-pencil and manual tests. In a large manufacturing company, researchers developed a computerized testing procedure for the selection of clerical personnel.[32] They constructed eight test components to represent actual work performed by secretarial personnel, such as maintaining and developing databases and spreadsheets, answering the telephone, filing, and handling travel arrangements. For the word processing test, applicants had three minutes (monitored by the computer) to type as much of a letter as possible; the computer recorded and corrected the manuscript. For the travel expense form completion task, applicants had to access the database file, use some of the information in it to compute quarterly expenses, and transfer this information to the travel expense form.

Some other computerized tests include numerical ability tests, reading comprehension tests, and a clerical comparing and checking test.[33] Many firms such as Kinko's (now part of FedEx) have applicants take online or offline computerized tests—sometimes by phone, using the touch-tone keypad—to quickly prescreen applicants prior to more in-depth interviews and background checks.[34]

Various other computerized selection tools are in use. For example, automated in-basket tests require job candidates to deal with a "virtual inbox" comprised of e-mails, phone calls, and documents and folders, to assess the candidates' decision-making and problem-solving skills. Candidates for architectural certification solve online architectural problems, for instance, designing building layouts to fit specified space constraints.[35]

List eight tests you could use for employee selection, and how you would use them.

● TYPES OF TESTS

We can conveniently classify tests according to whether they measure cognitive (mental) abilities, motor and physical abilities, personality and interests, or achievement.[36]

Tests of Cognitive Abilities

Cognitive tests include tests of general reasoning ability (intelligence) and tests of specific mental abilities like memory and inductive reasoning.

Intelligence Tests Intelligence (IQ) tests are tests of general intellectual abilities. They measure not a single trait but rather a range of abilities, including memory, vocabulary, verbal fluency, and numerical ability.

Originally, IQ (intelligence quotient) was literally a quotient. The procedure was to divide a child's mental age (as measured by the intelligence test) by his or her chronological age, and then multiply the results by 100. If an 8-year-old child answered questions as a 10-year-old might, his or her IQ would be 10 divided by 8, times 100, or 125.

For adults, of course, the notion of mental age divided by chronological age wouldn't make sense. Therefore, an adult's IQ score is actually a derived score. It reflects the extent to which the person is above or below the "average" adult's intelligence score.

Intelligence is often measured with individually administered tests like the Stanford-Binet Test or the Wechsler Test. Employers can administer other IQ tests such as the Wonderlic to groups of people. Other intelligence tests include the Kaufman Adolescent and Adult Intelligence Test, the Slosson Intelligence Test, the Wide Range Intelligence Test, and the Comprehensive Test of Nonverbal Intelligence.

Specific Cognitive Abilities There are also measures of specific mental abilities, such as inductive and deductive reasoning, verbal comprehension, memory, and numerical ability.

Psychologists often call such tests *aptitude tests*, since they purport to measure aptitude for the job in question. Consider the Test of Mechanical Comprehension in Figure 6-5, which tests the applicant's understanding of basic mechanical principles. It may reflect a person's aptitude for jobs—like that of machinist or engineer—that require mechanical comprehension. Other tests of mechanical aptitude include the Mechanical Reasoning Test and the SRA Test of Mechanical Aptitude. The revised Minnesota Paper Form Board Test consists of 64 two-dimensional diagrams cut into separate pieces. It provides insights into an applicant's mechanical spatial ability; you'd use it for screening applicants for jobs such as designers, draftspeople, or engineers.

Tests of Motor and Physical Abilities

You might also want to measure motor abilities, such as finger dexterity, manual dexterity, and reaction time. The Crawford Small Parts Dexterity Test is an example. It measures the speed and accuracy of simple judgment as well as the speed of finger, hand, and arm movements. Other tests here include the Stromberg Dexterity Test, the Minnesota Rate of Manipulation Test, and the Purdue Peg Board. The Roeder Manipulative Aptitude Test screens individuals for jobs where dexterity is a main requirement.

Tests of physical abilities may also be required. These include static strength (such as lifting weights), dynamic strength (like pull-ups), body coordination (as in jumping rope), and stamina.[37] Lifeguards, for example, must show they can swim a course before they're hired.

Figure 6-5
Type of Question Applicant Might Expect on a Test of Mechanical Comprehension

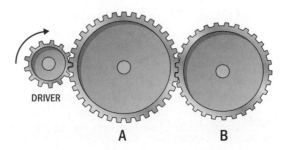

Which gear will turn the same way as the driver?

Measuring Personality and Interests

A person's cognitive and physical abilities alone seldom explain his or her job performance. Other factors, like motivation and interpersonal skills, are very important. As a consultant recently put it, most people are hired based on qualifications, but most are fired for nonperformance. And nonperformance (or performance) "is usually the result of personal characteristics, such as attitude, motivation, and especially, temperament."[38] The idea of screening out undesirables is spreading in some surprising ways. Some online dating services, like eHarmony.com, have prospective members take online personality tests, and reject those who its software judges are unmatchable.[39]

Employers use personality tests to measure and predict such intangibles. Firms including Dell, Motorola, and GE increasingly use personality tests to help screen even top-level candidates. For example, as part of its selection process for CEO candidates, Hewlett-Packard put its eventual choice, Carly Fiorina, and other finalists through a two-hour, 900-question personality test. Candidates had to indicate whether statements like "When I bump into a piece of furniture, I usually get angry" were true or false.[40]

There is no doubt that personality tests can predict job performance. For example, three researchers recently concluded: "personality constructs are indeed associated with work performance, with some traits such as conscientiousness predicting success across jobs. Other traits are correlated with specific [performance] criteria or specific occupations. For example, extraversion correlates with success in sales and management jobs, as well as with training performance."[41]

Personality tests measure basic aspects of an applicant's personality, such as introversion, stability, and motivation. Many of these tests are *projective*. The psychologist presents an ambiguous stimulus (like an ink blot or clouded picture) to the person. The psychologist then asks the person to interpret or react to it. Since the pictures are ambiguous, the person's interpretation must come from within—he or she supposedly projects into the picture his or her own emotional attitudes about life. A security-oriented person might describe the woman in Figure 6-1 (page 196) as "my mother worrying about what I'll do if I lose my job."

Other projective techniques include Make a Picture Story (MAPS), House-Tree-Person (H-T-P), and the Forer Structured Sentence Completion Test. Other examples of personality tests (more properly called personality inventories) include the Thematic Apperception Test, the Guilford-Zimmerman Temperament Survey, and the Minnesota Multiphasic Personality Inventory. The Guilford-Zimmerman survey measures personality traits like emotional stability versus moodiness and friendliness versus criticalness. The Minnesota Multiphasic Personality Inventory taps traits like hypochondria and paranoia. The Interpersonal Style Inventory is a self-report inventory composed of 300 true/false items covering scales such as sociable, sensitive, deliberate, stable, conscientious, trusting, and directive.

Wonderlic's Personal Characteristics Inventory measures five personality dimensions and links these dimensions to likely job performance. The manager administers this test, and scans or faxes it to Wonderlic, which scores it and returns the report the same day. For example, the Sales Achievement Predictor creates a report showing the individual's percentile ranked on scales such as "sales disposition" and "sales closing" and rates the test taker as highly recommended, recommended, or not recommended for sales. You'll find sample personality tests online at www.psychtests.com.

Personality tests—particularly the projective type—are the most difficult tests to evaluate and use. An expert must analyze the test taker's interpretations and reactions and infer from them his or her personality. The usefulness of such tests for selection rests on the assumption that you can find a relationship between a measurable personality trait (like introversion) and success on the job.[42]

Effectiveness   The difficulties notwithstanding, personality tests can help employers do a better job of screening. For example, researchers used the responsibility, socialization, and self-control scales of the California Psychological Inventory to successfully predict dysfunctional job behaviors among law enforcement officers.[43] At a multinational company, emotional stability, extroversion, and agreeableness predicted whether expatriates would leave their assignments early.[44] At another firm, employee testing predicted employee theft.[45]

The "Big Five"   Industrial psychologists often emphasize the "big five" personality dimensions as they apply to personnel testing: extraversion, emotional stability/neuroticism, agreeableness, conscientiousness, and openness to experience.[46]

Neuroticism represents a tendency to exhibit poor emotional adjustment and experience negative effects, such as anxiety, insecurity, and hostility. Extraversion represents a tendency to be sociable, assertive, active, and to experience positive effects, such as energy and zeal. Openness to experience is the disposition to be imaginative, nonconforming, unconventional, and autonomous. Agreeableness is the tendency to be trusting, compliant, caring, and gentle. Conscientiousness is comprised of two related facets: achievement and dependability[47]

In one study, extraversion, conscientiousness, and openness to experience were strong predictors of leadership.[48] In another "big five" study, neuroticism was negatively related to motivation, while conscientiousness was positively related to it.[49] Components of the "big five"—in particular, extraversion and openness to experience—also correlate with career interests and occupational types.[50] And, "in personality research, conscientiousness has been the most consistent and universal predictor of job performance."[51]

Researchers in one study defined career success in terms of intrinsic success (job satisfaction) and extrinsic success (income and occupational status). Conscientiousness positively predicted both intrinsic and extrinsic career success. Neuroticism negatively predicted extrinsic success. (General mental ability also positively predicted extrinsic career success.)[52]

Employers should use personality tests cautiously, particularly if the focus is on aberrant behavior. One report concluded that personality tests can help determine whether an employee's erratic behavior will pose a threat to workplace safety. However, they can also create legal problems for employers—for instance, if rejected candidates claim the results are false, or that they violate the Americans with Disabilities Act or employees' privacy.[53]

interest inventory
A personal development and selection device that compares the person's current interests with those of others now in various occupations so as to determine the preferred occupation for the individual.

Interest Inventories   **Interest inventories** compare your interests with those of people in various occupations. Thus, a person who takes the Strong-Campbell Inventory would receive a report comparing his or her interests to those of people already in occupations like accounting, engineering, management, or medical technology. These inventories have many uses. One example is career planning, since a person will likely do better in jobs that involve activities in which he or she is interested. These tests can also be useful as selection tools. Clearly, if you can select people whose interests are roughly the same as those of successful incumbents in the jobs for which you are recruiting, it is more likely that the applicants will be successful.

Achievement Tests

Achievement tests measure what a person has learned. Most of the tests you take in school are achievement tests. They measure your "job knowledge" in areas like economics, marketing, or personnel. Achievement tests are also popular at work. For example,

Person taking a Web-based employment test.

the Purdue Test for Machinists and Machine Operators tests the job knowledge of experienced machinists with questions like, "What is meant by 'tolerance'?" Other tests are available for other occupations. In addition to job knowledge, achievement tests measure the applicant's abilities; a typing test is one example.

Web-Based Testing

Firms are increasingly using the Web for testing and screening applicants. For example, in the late 1990s, the financial firm Capital One was using three paper-and-pencil tests for preemployment screening: a cognitive skills test, a math test, and a biodata job history test (which the firm used to predict job stability).[54] The process was reportedly time-consuming and inefficient: "In Tampa, we were having to process several thousand people a month just to hire 100," says a company officer. The company's new online system eliminates the paper-and-pencil process. Call center applicants working online complete the application and the upgraded math and biodata tests (which might include number of years on last job, and distance from the nearest Capital One office, for instance). They also take an online role-playing call simulation. They put on a headset, and the program plays seven different customer situations. Applicants (playing the role of operators) answer multiple choice questions online as to how they would respond. The company is in the process of expanding its online preemployment testing program to the United Kingdom and France.

● WORK SAMPLES AND SIMULATIONS

work samples
Actual job tasks used in testing applicants' performance.

Experts consider **work samples** and simulations (such as the assessment centers in this section) tests. However, they differ from most tests we've discussed, because they measure job performance directly. With video-based situational tests, for example, you present examinees with situations representative of the job for which they're applying, and evaluate their responses to these hypothetical situations.[55]

Work Sampling for Employee Selection

work sampling technique
A testing method based on measuring performance on actual basic job tasks.

The **work sampling technique** measures how a candidate actually performs some of the job's basic tasks. This has several advantages. It measures actual on-the-job tasks, so it's harder for applicants to fake answers. Work samples more clearly relate to the job you are testing for, so in terms of fairness and fair employment, you may be on safer ground. The work sample's content—the actual tasks the person must perform—is not as likely to be unfair to minorities as might a personnel test that possibly emphasized middle-class concepts and values.[56] Work sampling does not delve into the applicant's personality or psyche, so there's almost no chance of it being viewed as an invasion of privacy. Designed properly, work sampling tests also exhibit better validity than do other tests designed to predict performance.

The basic procedure is to choose several tasks crucial to performing the job and to test applicants on samples of each.[57] An observer monitors performance on each task, and indicates on a checklist how well the applicant performs. Here is an example. In developing a work sampling test for maintenance mechanics, experts first listed all possible job tasks (like "install pulleys and belts" and "install and align a motor"). Four crucial tasks were installing pulleys and belts, disassembling and installing a gearbox, installing and aligning a motor, and pressing a bushing into a sprocket.

They then broke down these four tasks into the steps required to complete them. Mechanics could perform each step in a slightly different way, of course. Since some approaches were better than others, the experts gave a different weight to different approaches.

Figure 6-6 shows one of the steps required for installing pulleys and belts—"checks key before installing." As the figure shows, possible approaches here include checking the key against (1) the shaft, (2) the pulley, or (3) neither. The right of the figure lists the weights (scores) reflecting the worth of each method. The applicant performs the task, and the observer checks off the approach used.

Management Assessment Centers

A **management assessment center** is a two- to three-day simulation in which 10 to 12 candidates perform realistic management tasks (like making presentations) under the observation of experts who appraise each candidate's leadership potential. The center itself may be a plain conference room, but it is often a special room with a one-way mirror to facilitate observation. Typical simulated exercises include:

- *The in-basket.* These exercises confront the candidate with an accumulation of reports, memos, notes of incoming phone calls, letters, and other materials collected in the actual or computerized in-basket of the simulated job he or she is about to start. The candidate must take appropriate action on each item. Trained evaluators then review the candidate's efforts.

- *Leaderless group discussion.* Trainers give a leaderless group a discussion question and tell members to arrive at a group decision. They then evaluate each group member's interpersonal skills, acceptance by the group, leadership ability, and individual influence.

- *Management games.* Participants solve realistic problems as members of simulated companies competing in a marketplace. They may have to decide, for instance, how to advertise and manufacture, and how much inventory to stock.

- *Individual presentations.* Trainers evaluate each participant's communication skills and persuasiveness by having each make an assigned oral presentation.

- *Objective tests.* A center typically includes tests of personality, mental ability, interests, and achievements.

- *The interview.* Most require an interview between at least one trainer and each participant, to assess the latter's interests, past performance, and motivation.

In practice, employers use assessment centers for selection, promotion, and development. Supervisor recommendations usually play a big role in choosing center participants. Line managers usually act as assessors and typically arrive at their ratings through a consensus process.[58]

Most experts view assessment centers as effective methods for selecting and promoting management candidates; the question is, are they worth their extra cost? They are

**Figure 6-6
Example of a Work
Sampling Question**

Checks key before installing against:	
—shaft	score 3
—pulley	score 3
—neither	score 1

Note: This is one step in installing pulleys and belts.

expensive to develop, take much longer than conventional paper and pencil tests, require managers acting as assessors, and often require psychologists. One recent study of 40 police candidates found that such centers are worth the extra cost. As the researchers concluded: "assessment center performance shows a unique and substantial contribution to the prediction of future police work success, justifying the usage of such method." In this study, peers' evaluations of candidates during the center proved especially useful.[59]

Video-Based Situational Testing

Video-based tests are also *situational tests* (which means they present examinees with situations representative of the job); other situational tests include work sampling, discussed above, and situational interviews, discussed in Chapter 7.[60] The typical video-based simulation presents the candidate with several scenarios, each followed by a multiple choice question. A scenario might depict an employee handling a situation on the job. At a critical moment, the scenario ends and the video asks the candidate to choose from among several courses of action. An example of a typical video-based scenario/judgment question, about one minute long, follows:

(*A manager is upset about the condition of the department and takes it out on one of the department's employees.*)

Manager: Well, I'm glad you're here.

Associate: Oh? Why is that?

Manager: Look at this place, that's why! I take a day off and come back to find the department in a mess. You should know better.

Associate: But I didn't work late last night.

Manager: Maybe not. But there have been plenty of times before when you've left this department in a mess.

(*The scenario stops here.*)

If you were this associate, what would you do?

a. Let the other associates responsible for the mess know that you had to take the heat.
b. Straighten up the department, and try to reason with the manager later.
c. Suggest to the manager that he talk to the other associates who made the mess.
d. Take it up with the manager's boss.[61]

While the evidence is somewhat mixed, the results suggest that video-based situational tests can be useful for selecting employees.[62]

The Miniature Job Training and Evaluation Approach

The idea here is to train candidates to perform a sample of the job's tasks, and then to evaluate their performance. The approach assumes that a person who demonstrates that he or she can learn and perform the sample of tasks will be able to learn and perform the job itself.

An example illustrates this method's usefulness. When Honda decided to build a new auto plant in Lincoln, Alabama, in 1999, it had to hire thousands of new employees in an area where few people worked in manufacturing. Working with an Alabama industrial development training agency, Honda began running help wanted ads in December 1999. The ad sought applicants for a free training program Honda was offering as a precondition for applying for jobs at the new plant. Applicants had to have at least a high school diploma or GED, employment for the past two years with no unexplainable gaps, and Alabama residency. By March 2000, 18,000 people had applied.

Honda and the Alabama agency first screened the applications by eliminating those who lacked the education or experience, and then gave preference to applicants near the plant. About 340 applicants per six-week session received special training at a new facility about 15 miles south of the plant. Since many of the applicants were already working, the training involved one-hour sessions two evenings a week. It included classroom instruction, watching videos of current Honda employees in action, and actually practicing particular jobs. Some candidates who watched the videos simply dropped out when they saw the work's pace and repetitiveness.

The training sessions serve a dual purpose. First, job candidates learn the actual skills they'll need to do the Honda jobs. Second, the training sessions provide an opportunity for special assessors from the Alabama state agency to scrutinize the trainees' work and to rate them. They then invite those who graduate to apply for jobs at the plants. Honda teams, consisting of employees from HR and departmental representatives, do the final screening. They interview the candidates, review their training records, and decide which ones to hire. New employees get a one-time drug test, but there are no other paper-and-pencil tests or credentials required. New hires get a three-day orientation. Then, assistant managers in each department coordinate their actual day-to-day training.[63]

The miniature job training approach has pros and cons. It tests applicants with actual samples of the job rather than just with paper-and-pencil tests, so it's "content relevant." It may thus be more acceptable (and fair) to disadvantaged applicants than most paper-and-pencil tests. However, it emphasizes individual instruction during training, and so is a relatively expensive screening approach.

The When You're on Your Own feature shows how a manager who's on his or her own in a large company can apply these testing concepts and tools.

Managers hired the employees at this Honda plant after seeing which of them did the best in the firm's miniature job training and evaluation program.

When You're On Your Own
HR for Line Managers and Entrepreneurs

Employee Testing and Selection

One of the ironies of being a line manager in even the largest of companies is that, when it comes to screening employees, you're often on your own. Some large firms' HR departments may work with the hiring manager to design and administer the sorts of screening tools we discussed in this chapter. But the fact is that in many of these firms, the HR departments do little more than some preliminary prescreening (for instance, administering typing tests to clerical applicants), and then follow up with background checks and drug and physical exams.

What should you do if you are, say, the marketing manager, and want to screen some of your job applicants more formally? It is possible to devise your own test battery, but caution is required here. Purchasing and then using packaged intelligence tests or psychological tests or even tests of mechanical ability could be a problem. Doing so may violate company policy, raise questions of validity, and even expose your employer to EEO liability if problems arise.

A preferred approach is to devise and use screening tools, the face validity of which is obvious. The simple work sampling test we discussed is one example. It's not unreasonable, for instance, for the marketing manager to ask an advertising applicant to spend an hour designing an ad, or to ask a marketing research applicant to spend a half hour outlining a marketing research program for a hypothetical product. Similarly, a production manager might reasonably ask an inventory control applicant to spend a few minutes using a standard inventory control model to solve an inventory problem.

However, even with relatively trouble-free tests like these, the hiring manager needs to keep the guidelines we discussed in this chapter in mind. In particular, you should protect the test taker's privacy, take steps to ensure that the person's rights are protected, and endeavor to ensure that the tests you devise are indeed a valid sample of the job.

For the small business owner, it is wise to keep in mind that while one or two hiring mistakes may not be disastrous in a big firm, they could wreak havoc in a small operation that doesn't have the resources to bounce back. A formal testing program is thus advisable.

It is also practical. Some tests are so easy to use they are particularly good for smaller firms. One is the Wonderlic Personnel Test, which measures general mental ability. It takes less than 15 minutes to administer the four-page booklet. The tester reads the instructions, and then keeps time as the candidate works through the 50 problems on the two inside sheets. The tester scores the test by totaling the number of correct answers. Comparing the person's score with the minimum scores recommended for various occupations shows whether the person achieved the minimally acceptable score for the type of job in question. The Predictive Index is another example. It measures work-related personality traits, drives, and behaviors—in particular dominance, extroversion, patience, and blame avoidance—on a two-sided sheet. A template makes scoring simple. The Predictive Index program includes 15 standard personality patterns. For example, there is the "social interest" pattern, for a person who is generally unselfish, congenial, persuasive, patient, and unassuming. This person would be good with people and a good personnel interviewer, for instance.

Computerized self-scoring testing programs are especially useful for small employers. For example, when hiring office help, many smaller employers rely on informal typing and filing tests. A better approach is to use a program like the Minnesota Clerical Assessment Battery published by Assessment Systems Corporation. It runs on a PC, and includes a typing test, proofreading test, filing test, business vocabulary test, business math test, and clerical knowledge test.

City Garage, a 200-employee chain of 25 auto service and repair shops in Dallas-Fort Worth, illustrates how one small business used a testing program to improve its operations. It had expanded rapidly since its founding in 1993, but its employee screening procedures were quite informal. The hiring process consisted of a paper-and-pencil application and one interview, immediately followed by a hire/don't hire decision. The result was high turnover, and too few managers to staff new stores.

City Garage's top managers knew they'd never be able to implement their growth strategy without a dramatic change in how they tested and hired employees. Their solution was to purchase the Personality Profile Analysis online test from Dallas-based Thomas International USA. Doing so added a third step to the application and interview process. After a quick application and background check, likely candidates take the 10-minute, 24-question PPA. City Garage staff then enter the answers into the PPA Software system, and test results are available in less than two minutes. These show whether the applicant is high or low in four personality characteristics; it also produces follow-up questions about areas that might cause problems. For example, applicants might be asked how they've handled possible weaknesses such as lack of patience in the past. If candidates answer those questions satisfactorily, they're asked back for extensive, all-day interviews, after which hiring decisions are made. The new process seems to have improved City's financial performance considerably.

Explain the key points to remember in conducting background investigations.

● BACKGROUND INVESTIGATIONS AND OTHER SELECTION METHODS

Testing is usually just part of an employer's selection process. Other tools may include background investigations and reference checks, preemployment information services, honesty testing, graphology, and substance abuse screening.

Background Investigations and Reference Checks

Most employers try to check and verify the job applicant's background information and references. In one survey of about 700 HR managers, 87% said they conduct reference checks, 69% conduct background employment checks, 61% check employee criminal records, 56% check employees' driving records, and 35% sometimes or always check credit.[64] Commonly verified data include legal eligibility for employment (in compliance with immigration laws), dates of prior employment, military service (including discharge status), education, identification (including date of birth and address to confirm identity), county criminal records (current residence, last residence), motor vehicle record, credit, licensing verification, Social Security number; and reference checks.[65]

How deeply you search depends on the position you seek to fill. For example, a credit and education check would be more important for hiring an accountant than a groundskeeper. In any case, don't limit your background checks only to new hires. It is also advisable to periodically check, say, the credit ratings of employees (like cashiers) who have easy access to company assets, and the driving records of employees who routinely use company cars.

There are two main reasons to conduct preemployment background investigations and/or reference checks—to verify factual information previously provided by the applicant, and to uncover damaging information such as criminal records and suspended drivers' licenses.[66] Lying on one's application is not unusual. For example, BellSouth's security director estimates that 15% to 20% of applicants conceal a dark secret. As he says, "It's not uncommon to find someone who applies and looks good, and then you do a little digging and you start to see all sorts of criminal history."[67]

Even relatively sophisticated companies fall prey to criminal employees, in part because they haven't conducted proper background and reference checks. In Chicago, a major pharmaceutical firm discovered it had hired gang members in mail delivery and computer repair. The crooks were stealing close to a million dollars a year in computer parts, and then using the mail department to ship them to a nearby computer store they owned.[68] Thorough background checks might have prevented the losses.

The actual background investigation/reference check can take many forms. Most employers at least try to verify an applicant's current (or former) position and salary with his or her current (or former) employer by phone (assuming doing so was cleared with the candidate). Others call the applicant's current and previous supervisors to try to discover more about the person's motivation, technical competence, and ability to work with others (although many employers have policies against providing such information). Some employers get background reports from commercial credit rating companies. The latter can provide information about credit standing, indebtedness, reputation, character, and lifestyle. Some employers ask for written references. Figure 6-7 shows a form used for phone references.

Effectiveness   The background check can be useful. It is an inexpensive and straightforward way to verify factual information about the applicant, such as current and previous job titles, current salary range, dates of employment, and educational background. There are thousands of databases and sources for finding background information, including sex offender registries, workers' compensation histories, nurses' aid registries, and sources for criminal, employment, and educational histories.[69]

However, reference checking can backfire. Laws (like the Fair Credit Reporting Act of 1970) increase the likelihood that rejected applicants will have access to the background information; they may then sue both the source of that information and the recruiting employer. In practice, it's not always easy to prove that the person deserved the bad reference. The rejected applicant has various legal remedies, including suing the source of the reference for defamation of character.[70] In one case, a court awarded a man $56,000 after he was turned down for a job because, among other things, the former employer called him a "character." This happens often enough to cause former employers to limit their comments.

It is not just the fear of legal reprisal that can undermine a reference. Many supervisors don't want to damage a former employee's chances for a job; others might prefer giving an incompetent employee good reviews if it will get rid of him or her. Even when checking references via phone, therefore, you have to be careful to ask the right questions. You must also try to judge whether the reference's answers are evasive and, if so, why.

HR managers don't seem to view reference letters as very useful. In one study, only 12% replied that reference letters were "highly valuable," 43% called them "somewhat valuable," and 30% viewed them as having "little value," or (6%) "no value." Asked whether they preferred written or telephone references, 72% favored the telephone reference, because it allows a more candid assessment and provides a more personal exchange. Not having a written record is also an appealing feature. In fact, reference letters ranked lowest—seventh out of seven—as selection tools. Ranked from top to bottom, the tools were interview, application form, academic record, oral referral, aptitude and achievement tests, psychological tests, and reference letters.[71]

Know Your Employment Law

Giving References

Federal laws that affect references include the Privacy Act of 1974, the Fair Credit Reporting Act of 1970, the Family Education Rights and Privacy Act of 1974 (and Buckley Amendment of 1974), and the Freedom of Information Act of 1966. These laws give individuals in general and students (the Buckley Amendment) the right to know the nature and substance of information in their credit files and files with government agencies, and (under the Privacy Act) to review records pertaining to them from any private business that contracts with a federal agency. It is therefore quite possible that the person you're describing may be shown your comments.

Figure 6-7
Reference Checking Form
Source: Society for Human Resource Management, © 2004. Reproduced with permission via Copyright Clearance Center.

(Verify that the applicant has provided permission before conducting reference checks)

Candidate
Name _____

Reference
Name _____

Company
Name _____

Dates of Employment:
From: _____ To: _____

Position(s)
Held _____

Salary
History _____

Reason for
Leaving _____

Explain the reason for your call and verify the above information with the supervisor (including the reason for leaving)
_____
_____
_____

1. Please describe the type of work for which the candidate was responsible.
_____
_____
_____

2. How would you describe the applicant's relationships with coworkers, subordinates (if applicable), and with superiors?
_____
_____
_____

3. Did the candidate have a positive or negative work attitude? Please elaborate
_____
_____
_____

4. How would you describe the quantity and quality of output generated by the former employee?
_____
_____
_____

5. What were his/her strengths on the job?
_____
_____
_____

6. What were his/her weaknesses on the job?
_____
_____
_____

7. What is your overall assessment of the candidate?
_____
_____
_____

8. Would you recommend him/her for this position? Why or why not?
_____
_____
_____

9. Would this individual be eligible for rehire? Why or why not?
_____
_____
_____

Other comments?
_____
_____
_____

Common law (and in particular the tort of defamation) applies to any information you supply. Communication is defamatory if it is false and tends to harm the reputation of another by lowering the person in the estimation of the community or by deterring other persons from associating or dealing with him or her. There are companies that, for a small fee, will call former employers on behalf of employees who believe they're getting bad references from the former employers. One supervisor, describing a former city employee, reportedly "used swear words, said he was incompetent and said he almost brought the city down on its knees."[72]

Another employee left his job as a supervisor of a California telecommunications company, and thought his previous employer might bad-mouth him. He hired BadReferences.com to investigate. BadReferences.com (which uses trained court reporters for its investigations) found that a supervisor at the company suggested that the employee was "a little too obsessive, . . . and not comfortable with taking risks, or making big decisions." The former employee sued his previous employer, demanding an end to defamation and $45,000 in compensation.[73]

In fact, defamation is an increasing concern. In one case, an employer fired four employees for "gross insubordination" after they disobeyed a supervisor's request to review allegedly fabricated expense account reports. The jury found that the expense reports were actually honest. The employees then argued that although their employer didn't publicize the expense account matter to others, the employer should have known that the employees would have to admit the reason for their firing when explaining and defending themselves to future employers. The court agreed and upheld jury awards to these employees totaling more than a million dollars. In another case, a manager who claimed he was wrongly accused of stealing from his former employer won $1.25 million in a slander suit.[74]

Companies fielding requests for references need policies regarding this. They should ensure that only authorized managers provide information. Other suggested guidelines for defensible references include "Don't volunteer information," "Avoid vague statements," and "Do not answer trap questions such as, 'Would you rehire this person?'" In practice, many firms have a policy of not providing any information about former employees except for their dates of employment, last salary, and position titles.[75]

Perhaps this explains why in one survey only 11% of respondents said the information they get about a candidate's violent or "bizarre" behavior is adequate. Fifty-four percent of the respondents said that they get inadequate information in this area. Of 11 types of information sought in background checks, only three were ranked by a majority of respondents as ones for which they received adequate information: dates of employment (96%), eligibility for rehire (65%), and job qualifications (56%). With regard to salary history, reasons for leaving a previous job, work habits, personality traits, human relations skills, special skills or knowledge, and employability, "fewer than half of HR managers responding to the survey said they were able to obtain adequate information."[76]

Not disclosing relevant information can be dangerous, too. In one Florida case, an employee was fired for allegedly bringing a handgun to work. After his subsequent employer fired him (for absenteeism), he returned to the second company and shot a supervisor as well as the HR director and three other people before taking his own life. The injured parties and the relatives of the murdered employees sued the original employer, who had provided the employee with a clean letter of recommendation. The letter stated his departure was not related to job performance, allegedly because that first employer didn't want to anger the employee over his firing.

Making Background Checks More Useful So what is the prospective employer to do? Is there any way to obtain better information?

Yes. First, include on the application form a statement for applicants to sign explicitly authorizing a background check, such as:

I hereby certify that the facts set forth in the above employment application are true and complete to the best of my knowledge. I understand that falsified statements or misrepresentation of information on this application or omission of any information sought may be cause for dismissal, if employed, or may lead to refusal to make an offer and/or to withdrawal of an offer. I also authorize investigation of credit, employment record, driving record, and, once a job offer is made or during employment, workers' compensation background if required.

Second, since telephone references apparently produce more candid assessments, it's probably best to rely on telephone references. Also remember that you can probably count on getting more accurate information regarding dates of employment, eligibility for rehire, and job qualifications than other background information (such as reasons for leaving a previous job).

Persistence and a sensitivity to potential red flags can also improve results. For example, if the former employer hesitates or seems to qualify his or her answer when you ask, "Would you rehire?" don't just go on to the next question. Instead, try to unearth what the applicant did to make the former employer pause.

Another suggestion is to use the references offered by the applicant as a source for other references. You might ask each of the applicant's references, "Could you please give me the name of another person who might be familiar with the applicant's performance?" In that way, you begin getting information from references who may be more objective, because they weren't referred directly by the applicant. Ask open-ended questions, such as, "How much structure does the applicant need in his/her work?" in order to get the references to talk more about the candidate.[77]

Many employers use HRIS to automate the applicant tracking and prescreening process. The following improving "Productivity Through HRIS" illustrates this process.

Improving Productivity Through HRIS

Automated Applicant Tracking Systems and Applicant Screening

Like many employers, Sutter Health, a nonprofit health care network in Sacramento, California, knew its expansion would be stifled if it couldn't fill its numerous openings. With 10,000 openings per year, Sutter's future depended on attracting huge numbers of recruits. Its first solution was to move its job opening postings online. Doing so did generate many more applications. But Sutter was hit by so many résumés—over 300,000 per year—that the applications ended up in piles, waiting for affiliates' HR departments to get to them. Project manager Keith Vencel had to devise a better solution.[78] Many firms facing challenges like these are turning to *applicant tracking systems* (ATS). Systems like these now appear to be the third-biggest example of technology use in HR (payroll management and benefits management are first and second).[79]

Today's applicant tracking systems do more than compile incoming Web-based résumés and track applicants during the hiring process. The new systems also do three things to help companies screen applicants. First, most employers also use their ATS to "knock out"

applicants who do not meet minimum, nonnegotiable job requirements, like submitting to drug tests or holding driver's licenses. Second, employers use these advanced ATS to test and screen applicants online. This includes Web-based skills testing (in accounting, for instance), cognitive skills testing (such as for mechanical comprehension), and even psychological testing. Some design their ATS to screen for intangibles. For example, Recreation Equipment, Inc., needed a system that would match applicant skills with the company's culture, and in particular, identify applicants who were naturally inclined to work in teams. The company worked with its applicant tracking system vendor to customize its system to do just that.

Third, the newer systems don't just screen out candidates, but discover "hidden talents." Thanks to the Internet, applicants often send their résumés out across a wide range of job openings, hoping a shotgun approach will help them hit a match between their résumé-based qualifications and the listed job requirements. For most employers, this is simply a screening nuisance. But for those who design their ATS to do so, the ATS can identify talents in the candidate pool that lend themselves to job matches at the company that even the applicant didn't know existed when he or she applied.

The employer thinking of adopting an ATS should seek one that meets several minimum functionality requirements.[80]

- The ATS should be easy to use, and a new user should be able to use the system in one hour or less.
- You should be able to integrate the applicant tracking system with the company's existing HRIS platform, so that, for instance, data on a newly hired candidate can flow seamlessly into the HRIS payroll system.
- The ATS should facilitate equal employment opportunity metrics reporting, and enable the employer to capture, track, and report applicant EEO data.
- The ATS should provide a strong reporting suite for employee selection performance metrics reports, including "time to fill," "cost to hire," and "applicant source statistics."
- The ATS should facilitate scheduling and tracking of candidate interviews, e-mail communications, and completed forms, including job offers.
- The ATS should provide automated screening and ranking of candidates based upon job skill profiles.

- The ATS should include an internal job posting service that supports applications from current employees and employee referral programs.
- The ATS should make it easy to cross-post jobs to commercial job boards such as monster.com.
- It should be easy to integrate the ATS job board with your company's own Web site, for instance, by linking it to your site's "careers" section.
- Since job postings normally require a preliminary signoff and approval process, the ATS should provide for requisition creation and signoff approvals.

How did Keith Vencel at Sutter Health solve his company's problem? His solution was to have Sutter sign on with a company called Recruitsoft, Inc., of San Francisco, which now handles all Sutter's applicant tracking and screening activities. Recruitsoft uses its own proprietary systems; it is an e-recruiting *applications service provider* (ASP). When applicants click on to Sutter's Web site to look for and apply for jobs, they're actually using Recruitsoft's site and software. Recruitsoft doesn't just post Sutter Health job openings and collect its résumés; it also gives Sutter Health "an automated way to evaluate, rank and match IT and other job candidates with specific openings." And this, says Keith Vencel, helped Sutter cut its recruiting process from weeks to days and thereby helped ensure that Sutter's expansion strategy stays on track.

Using Preemployment Information Services

There was a time when the only source of background information was what a candidate provided on the application form and what the employer could obtain through private investigators. Today, preemployment information services use databases to accumulate information about matters such as workers' compensation and credit histories, and conviction and driving records. For example, a south Florida firm advertises that for under $50 it will do a criminal history report, motor vehicle/driver's record report, and (after the person is hired) a workers' compensation claims report history, plus confirm identity, name, and Social Security number.

Numerous firms such as Hirecheck now provide such employment screening services (see www.hirecheck.com). In choosing a firm to use, make sure it complies with relevant laws such as the Fair Credit Reporting Act, and uses only legal data sources (more on this in a moment).[81]

There are two reasons to use caution when delving into an applicant's criminal, credit, and workers' compensation histories.[82] First (as discussed in Chapter 2), various equal employment laws discourage or prohibit the use of such information in employee screening. For example, the 1990 Americans with Disabilities Act (ADA) prohibits employers from making preemployment inquiries into the existence, nature, or severity of a disability. Therefore, asking about a candidate's previous workers' compensation claims before offering the person a job is usually unlawful. Courts might also view making employment decisions based on someone's arrest record as unfairly discriminatory. (Use of conviction information for particular jobs—for instance, where security is involved—would be less of a problem.) The EEOC says a poor credit history should not by itself preclude someone from getting a job.

Know Your Employment Law

Background Information

Second, various federal and state laws govern how employers acquire and use applicants' and employees' background information. At the federal level, the Fair Credit Reporting Act is the main directive. In addition, at least 21 states (Arizona, California, Colorado, Georgia, Kansas, Louisiana, Maine, Maryland, Massachusetts, Minnesota, Montana, New Hampshire, New Jersey, New Mexico, New York, Oklahoma, Rhode Island, Tennessee, Texas, Virginia, and Washington) impose their own requirements. Compliance essentially involves four steps, as follows:

Step 1—*Disclosure and authorization.* Before requesting consumer or investigative reports from a consumer reporting agency, the employer must disclose to the applicant or employee that a report will be requested and that copies may be provided to the employee/applicant, and the employer must obtain the employee/applicant's written authorization.

Step 2—*Certification.* The employer must certify to the reporting agency that the employer will comply with the federal and state legal requirements. (The reporting agency will generally provide the employer with a form for satisfying this requirement). The employer certifies, among other things, that the employer made the disclosures outlined above in step 1; that it obtained written consent from the employee or applicant; that the applicant or employee will have available copies of the report: that the employee or applicant was made aware that the consumer report could trigger adverse actions on the part of the employer; and that the employer hasn't violated federal or state equal employment laws.

Step 3—*Providing copies of reports.* Under federal law, the employer must provide copies of the report to the applicant or employee if adverse action (such as withdrawing an offer of employment) is contemplated. Under California law, applicants or employees must have the option of requesting a copy of the report regardless of action.

Step 4—*Notice after adverse action.* After the employer provides the employee or applicant with copies of the consumer and investigative reports and a "reasonable period" has elapsed, the employer may take an adverse action (such as withdrawing an offer, or dismissing, or not promoting the applicant or employee). If the employer anticipates taking an adverse action, the employee or applicant must receive an adverse action notice. This notice contains: the name, address, and telephone number of the consumer reporting agency; a statement that the reporting agency did not make the adverse action decision and cannot inform the consumer as to the specific reason why the employer took the adverse action; a statement of the employee/applicant's right to obtain a free copy of the report from the reporting agency; and a statement that the employee/applicant can dispute (with the consumer reporting agency) the report's accuracy or completeness. Federal law does not require the employer to provide the employee/applicant with a detailed rationale for the adverse action decision.

The employee/applicant has various remedies under the applicable laws. For example, if the employer fails to provide the required notices and/or obtain the required consents, then the employee/applicant can sue the employer in federal or state court for damages.[83]

Table 6-2 summarizes suggestions for employers regarding the collection of background information.

Table 6-2

**Collecting
Background
Information**

Some suggestions for collecting background information include the following:
1. Check all applicable state laws.
2. Review the impact of federal equal employment laws.
3. Remember the Federal Fair Credit Reporting Act.
4. Do not obtain information that you're not going to use.
5. Remember that using arrest information will be highly suspect.
6. Avoid blanket policies (such as "we hire no one with a record of workers' compensation claims").
7. Use information that is specific and job related.
8. Keep information confidential and up to date.
9. Never authorize an unreasonable investigation.
10. Make sure you always get at least two forms of identification from the applicant.
11. Always require applicants to fill out a job application.
12. Compare the application to the résumé (people tend to be more imaginative on their résumés than on their application forms, where they must certify the information).
13. Particularly for executive candidates, include background checks of such things as involvement in lawsuits, and of articles about the candidate in local or national newspapers.
14. Separate the tasks of (1) hiring and (2) doing the background check (a recruiter or supervisor anxious to hire someone may cut corners when investigating the candidate's background).

Source: Adapted from Jeffrey M. Hahn, "Pre-Employment Services: Employers Beware?" *Employee Relations Law Journal* 17, no. 1 (Summer 1991), pp. 45–69; and Shari Caudron, "Who are you really hiring?", *Workforce*, 81, no. 12 (November 2002), pp. 28–32.

The Polygraph and Honesty Testing

Some firms still use the polygraph (or lie detector) for honesty testing, even though current law severely restricts its use. The polygraph is a device that measures physiological changes like increased perspiration. The assumption is that such changes reflect changes in emotional state that accompany lying.

Complaints about offensiveness plus grave doubts about the polygraph's accuracy culminated in the Employee Polygraph Protection Act of 1988. With a few exceptions, the law prohibits employers from conducting polygraph examinations of all job applicants and most employees. (Also prohibited under this law are other mechanical or electrical devices that attempt to measure honesty or dishonesty, including psychological stress evaluators and voice stress analyzers. Federal laws don't prohibit paper-and-pencil tests and chemical testing [as for drugs].) Local, state, and federal government employers (including the FBI) can continue to use polygraph exams, but many local and state government employers are further restricted under state laws.

Other employers permitted to use polygraph tests include: industries with national defense or security contracts; certain businesses with nuclear-power-related contracts with the Department of Energy; businesses and consultants with access to highly classified information; those with counterintelligence-related contracts with the FBI or Department of Justice; and private businesses that are (1) hiring private security personnel, (2) hiring persons with access to drugs, or (3) doing ongoing investigations involving economic loss or injury to an employer's business, such as a theft.

Even in the case of ongoing investigations of theft, the law restricts employers' rights. To administer such a test during an ongoing investigation, an employer must meet four standards. First, the employer must show that it suffered an economic loss or injury. Second, it must show that the employee in question had access to the property. Third, it must have a reasonable suspicion before asking the employee to take the polygraph. Fourth, the employee must be told the details of the investigation before the test, as well as the questions to be asked on the polygraph test itself.

Paper-and-Pencil Honesty Tests   The virtual elimination of the polygraph as a screening device triggered a burgeoning market for other types of honesty testing devices. Paper-and-pencil honesty tests are psychological tests designed to predict job applicants' proneness to dishonesty and other forms of counterproductivity.[84] Most of these tests measure attitudes regarding things like tolerance of others who steal, acceptance of rationalizations for theft, and admission of theft-related activities. Tests include the Phase II profile, owned by Wackenhut Corporation of Coral Gables, Florida. London House, Inc., and Stanton Corporation publish similar tests.[85]

Technician gives a polygraph test to a woman. Test results are displayed on the computer screen facing the technician. By law, most employers cannot give these tests because of doubts about their accuracy. They are still permitted for certain government jobs that have to do with national defense, security, and intelligence.

Psychologists initially raised concerns about the proliferation of paper-and-pencil honesty tests, but recent studies support the validity of these selection tools.[86] One study focused on 111 employees hired by a major retail convenience store chain to work at store or gas station counters.[87] The firm estimated that "shrinkage" equaled 3% of sales, and internal theft was believed to account for much of this. The researchers found that scores on an honesty test successfully predicted theft in this study, as measured by termination for theft. One large-scale review of the use of such tests for measuring honesty, integrity, conscientiousness, dependability, trustworthiness, and reliability concluded that the "pattern of findings" regarding the usefulness of such tests "continues to be consistently positive."[88]

Paper-and-pencil personality testing may also help companies predict white-collar crime.[89] Subjects in one study included 329 federal prison inmates incarcerated for white-collar crime and 344 individuals from several midwestern firms employed in white-collar positions. Researchers administered three instruments, including the California Psychological Inventory (a personality inventory), the Employment Inventory (a second personality inventory), and a biodata scale. They concluded that "there are large and measurable psychological differences between white-collar offenders and nonoffenders . . ." and that it was possible to use a personality-based integrity test to differentiate between the two.[90]

What Employers Can Do   In practice, detecting dishonest candidates involves not just tests, but a comprehensive antitheft screening procedure. One expert suggests the following steps:

■ *Ask blunt questions.*[91] Ask direct questions in the face-to-face interview. For example, says this expert, there is nothing wrong with asking the applicant, "Have you ever stolen anything from an employer?" Other questions to ask include, "Have you recently held jobs other than those listed on your application?" "Have you ever been fired or asked to leave a job?" "What reasons would past supervisors give if they were asked why they let you go?" "Have past employers ever disciplined you or warned you about absences or lateness?" "Is any information on your application misrepresented or falsified?"

■ *Listen, rather than talk.* Allow the applicant to do the talking so you can learn as much about the person as possible.

■ *Do a credit check.* Include a clause in your application form that gives you the right to conduct background checks, including credit checks and motor vehicle reports.

■ *Check all employment and personal references.*

■ *Use paper-and-pencil honesty tests and psychological tests.*

■ *Test for drugs.* Devise a drug-testing program and give each applicant a copy of the policy.

■ *Establish a search-and-seizure policy and conduct searches.* Give each applicant a copy of the policy and require each to return a signed copy. The policy should state that all lockers, desks, and similar property remain the property of the company and may be inspected routinely.

The Adolf Coors Company uses a three-step honesty-screening program. First, it uses an outside lab to conduct a urinalysis test. Next, applicants take a Stanton Corporation paper-and-pencil survey on attitudes toward honesty and theft. Stanton provides a written report categorizing applicants by levels of risk. Finally, Equifax Services performs applicant references and background checks. These involve contacting previous employers and educational institutions.[92]

Honesty testing still requires some caution. Having just taken and "failed" what is fairly obviously an "honesty test," the candidate may leave the premises feeling his or her treatment was less than proper. Some "honesty" questions also pose invasion-of-privacy issues. And there are state laws to consider: For instance, Massachusetts and Rhode Island limit the use of paper-and-pencil honesty tests.

Graphology

Graphology refers to the use of handwriting analysis to determine the writer's basic personality traits. Graphology thus has some resemblance to projective personality tests, although graphology's validity is highly suspect.

In graphology, the handwriting analyst studies an applicant's handwriting and signature to discover the person's needs, desires, and psychological makeup. According to the graphologist, the writing in Figure 6-8 exemplifies "uneven pressure, poor rhythm, and uneven baselines." The variation of light and dark lines shows a "lack of control" and is "one strong indicator of the writer's inner disturbance."

Graphology's place in screening sometimes seems schizophrenic. Perhaps most importantly, studies suggest it is generally not valid, or that when graphologists do accurately size up candidates, it's because they are also privy to other background information. Yet some firms continue to use graphology—indeed, to swear by it. It tends to be bigger in Europe, where "countries like France or Germany have one central graphology institute, which serves as the certifying body."[93] Fike Corporation in Blue Springs, Missouri, a 325-employee maker of valves and other industrial products, uses profiles based on handwriting samples to design follow-up interviews. Sharon Stockham, senior HR vice president for Exchange Bank in Santa Rosa, California, says her company "lives and dies" by handwriting analysis, using it as one element for screening officer candidates.[94]

Figure 6-8
Handwriting Exhibit Used by Graphologist
Source: Kathryn Sackhein, *Handwriting Analysis and the Employee Selection Process* (New York: Quorum Books, 1990), p. 45. Reproduced with permission of Greenwood Publishing Group, Inc.

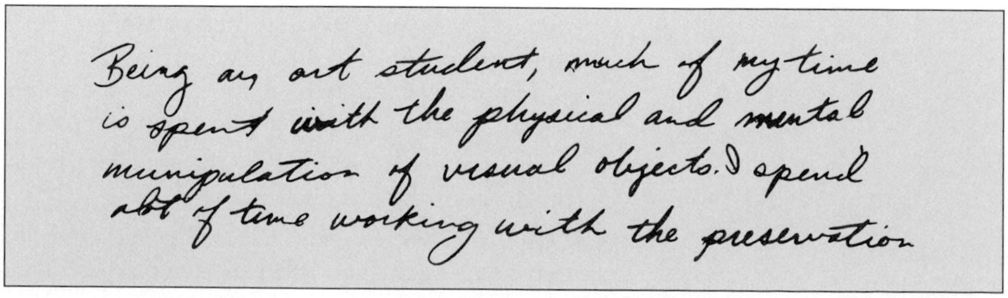

Physical Examination

Once the employer extends the person a job offer, a medical exam is often the next step in the selection process (although it may also take place after the new employee starts work).

There are several reasons for preemployment medical exams. One is to verify that the applicant meets the physical requirements of the position; another is to discover any medical limitations you should take into account in placing the applicant. The exam will also establish a record and baseline of the applicant's health for future insurance or compensation claims. By identifying health problems, the examination can also reduce absenteeism and accidents and, of course, detect communicable diseases that may be unknown to the applicant.

In the largest firms, the employer's medical department performs the exam. Smaller employers retain the services of consulting physicians. But remember that under the Americans with Disabilities Act, a person with a disability can't be rejected for the job if he or she is otherwise qualified and can perform the essential job functions with reasonable accommodation. The ADA permits a medical exam during the period between the job offer and commencement of work if such exams are standard practice for all applicants for that job category.[95]

Substance Abuse Screening

Many employers conduct drug screenings. The most common practice is to test candidates just before they're formally hired. Many also test current employees when there is reason to believe the person has been using drugs—after a work accident, or in the presence of obvious behavioral symptoms such as chronic lateness, or high absenteeism. Some firms routinely administer drug tests on a random or periodic basis, while others require drug tests when they transfer or promote employees to new positions.[96]

No drug test is foolproof. Although 96% of employers who test use urine sampling,[97] some of these tests can't distinguish between legal and illegal substances—for example, Advil and Nuprin can produce positive results for marijuana. Dr. David Feinstein, a medical review officer with Connecticut health care provider Industrial Health Care, says "anyone" can go online and purchase drug-free samples to try to beat the tests.[98] In fact, "there is a swarm of products that promise to help employees (both male and female) beat drug tests."[99]

Other employers find such tests too personal, and use hair follicle testing. The method, radio-immunoassay of hair (RIAH), requires a small sample of hair, which the lab analyzes to detect prior ingestion of illicit drugs.[100] But even here, classified ads advertise chemicals that can be added to specimens or rubbed on the scalp to fool the test.

Drug testing also raises ethical issues.[101] Unlike the roadside breathalyzer tests given to inebriated drivers, urine and blood tests for drugs indicate only whether drug residues are present; they can't measure impairment or, for that matter, habituation or addiction.[102] Without strong evidence linking blood or urine drug levels to impairment, some argue that testing is not justifiable on the grounds of boosting workplace safety.[103] Many feel the testing procedures themselves are degrading and intrusive. Others argue that use of drugs during leisure hours might have little or no relevance to the job itself.[104]

Know Your Employment Law

Drug Testing

Drug testing raises legal issues, too.[105] As one attorney writes, "It is not uncommon for employees to claim that drug tests violate their rights to privacy under common law or, in some states, a state statutory or constitutional provision."[106] Hair follicle testing is less intrusive than urinalysis but can actually produce more personal information: A three-inch hair segment will record six months of drug use.

Several federal laws affect workplace drug testing. Under the Americans with Disabilities Act, a court would probably consider a former drug user (who no longer uses illegal drugs and has successfully completed or is participating in a rehabilitation program) a qualified applicant with a disability.[107] Under the Drug Free Workplace Act of 1988, federal contractors must maintain a workplace free from illegal drugs. While this doesn't require contractors to conduct drug testing or rehabilitate affected employees, many do. Under the U.S. Department of Transportation workplace regulations, firms with over 50 eligible employees in transportation industries must conduct alcohol testing on workers with sensitive or safety-related jobs. These include mass transit workers, air traffic controllers, train crews, and school bus drivers.[108] Other laws, including the Federal Rehabilitation Act of 1973 and various state laws, protect rehabilitating drug users or those who have a physical or mental addiction.

What should an employer do when a job candidate tests positive? Most companies will not hire such candidates, and a few will immediately fire current employees who test positive. For example, 120 of the 123 companies responding to the question, "If test results are positive, what action do you take?" indicated that applicants testing positive are not hired. Current employees have more legal recourse; employers must tell them the reason for dismissal if the reason is a positive drug test.[109]

However, particularly where sensitive jobs are concerned, courts appear to side with employers. In one case, the U.S. Court of Appeals for the First Circuit (which includes Maine, Massachusetts, New Hampshire, Rhode Island, and Puerto Rico) ruled that Exxon acted properly in firing a truck driver who failed a drug test. Exxon's drug-free workplace program included random testing of employees in safety-sensitive jobs. The employee drove a tractor-trailer carrying 12,000 gallons of flammable motor fuel and tested positive for cocaine. The union representing the employee challenged the firing, an arbitrator reduced the penalty to a two-month suspension, and the appeals court reversed the arbitrator's decision. It ruled that the employer acted properly in firing the truck driver, given the circumstances.[110]

Complying with Immigration Law Post 9/11

Under the Immigration Reform and Control Act of 1986, employees hired in the United States must prove they are eligible to work in the United States. A person does not have to be a U.S. citizen to be employable. However, employers should ask a person they're about to hire whether he or she is a U.S. citizen or an alien lawfully authorized to work in the United States. To comply with this law, employers should follow these procedures:

1. Hire only citizens and aliens lawfully authorized to work in the United States.
2. Advise all new job applicants of your policy.
3. Require all new employees to complete and sign the verification form (the "I-9 form") designated by the Immigration and Naturalization Service (INS) to certify that they are eligible for employment.
4. Examine documentation presented by new employees, record information about the documents on the verification form, and sign the form.
5. Retain the form for three years or for one year past the employment of the individual, whichever is longer.
6. If requested, present the form for inspection by INS or Department of Labor officers. No reporting is required.[111]

Prospective employees can prove their eligibility for employment in two ways. One is to show a document such as a U.S. passport or alien registration card with photograph that proves both the person's identity and employment eligibility. Many prospective employees won't have either of these documents. So, the other way to verify employment eligibility is to see a document that proves the person's identity, along with a document showing the person's employment eligibility, such as a work permit.

The documents some applicants submit may be fakes. For example, a few years ago INS agents seized over two million counterfeit documents ranging from green cards and Social Security cards to driver's licenses, from nine different states.

Employers protect themselves in several ways. Systematic background checks are the most obvious. Preemployment screening should include employment verification, criminal record checks, drug screens, and reference checks. You can verify Social Security cards by calling the Social Security Administration. Employers can avoid accusations of discrimination by verifying the documents of all applicants, not just those they may think suspicious.[112]

Employers should not use the so-called I-9 Employment Eligibility Verification form to discriminate based on race or country of national origin. The requirement to verify eligibility does not provide any basis to reject an applicant just because he or she is a foreigner, or not a U.S. citizen, or an alien residing in the United States, as long as that person can prove his or her identity and employment eligibility. Employers should know that since September 11, 2001, there has been a significant rise in allegations of religious and national origin discrimination, among both employees and applicants.

Perhaps the main effect of 9/11 on immigration compliance has been the increased difficulty immigrants face in entering the United States. For example, since August 1, 2003, almost all travelers who need visas have had to have interviews at their local American consulates. However, the new Justice Department Appropriations Authorization bill, signed in 2003, authorizes the Justice Department to fight terrorism, but also actually makes it easier for foreign engineering specialists to get H-1B visas and jobs in the United States.[113]

The "HR Scorecard" feature shows how the Hotel Paris applied this chapter's ideas in creating a new testing process.

The **HR Scorecard**
Strategy and Results

The New Employee Testing Program

The Hotel Paris's competitive strategy is "To use superior guest service to differentiate the Hotel Paris properties, and to thereby increase the length of stay and return rate of guests, and thus boost revenues and profitability." HR manager Lisa Cruz must now formulate functional policies and activities that support this competitive strategy, by eliciting the required employee behaviors and competencies.

A preliminary analysis performed jointly by Lisa and the Hotel Paris's chief financial officer, left them optimistic that HR could contribute measurably to achieving the hotel's strategic aims. Several employee competencies and behaviors including employee morale, employee commitment, and the percent of arriving guests receiving the hotel's required greeting had significant effects on customer and organizational outcomes such as guest satisfaction and frequency of guest returns. In turn, outcomes like these contributed measurably to the hotel Paris's strategic goals, including profit margins, market share, and scores on industry satisfaction surveys. Lisa and her team now turn to creating a testing program that will help to produce the required employee competencies and behaviors. The accompanying HR Scorecard (Figure 6-9) outlines the relationships involved.

Lisa's team, working with an industrial psychologist, designs a test battery that they believe will produce the sorts of high-morale, patient, people-oriented employees they are

looking for. It includes a preliminary, computerized test in which applicants for the positions of front-desk clerk, door person, assistant manager, and security guard must deal with an apparently irate guest; a work sample in which front-desk clerk candidates spend 10 minutes processing an incoming "guest"; a personality test aimed at weeding out applicants who lack emotional stability; the Wonderlic test of mental ability; and the Phase II Profile for assessing candidate honesty. Their subsequent validity analysis shows that scores on the test batteries predict scores on the hotel's employee capabilities and behavior metrics. A second analysis confirmed that, as the percentage of employees hired after testing rose, so too did the hotel's employee capabilities and behaviors scores, for instance (see Figure 6-9) in terms of speed of check in/out, and percent guests receiving Hotel Paris required greeting.

Lisa and the CFO also found other measurable improvements resulting from the new testing process. For example, it took less time to fill an open position, and cost per hire diminished, so the HR department became more efficient. The new testing program thus did not only contribute to the hotel's performance by improving employee capabilities and behaviors. It also did so by directly improving profit margins and profits.

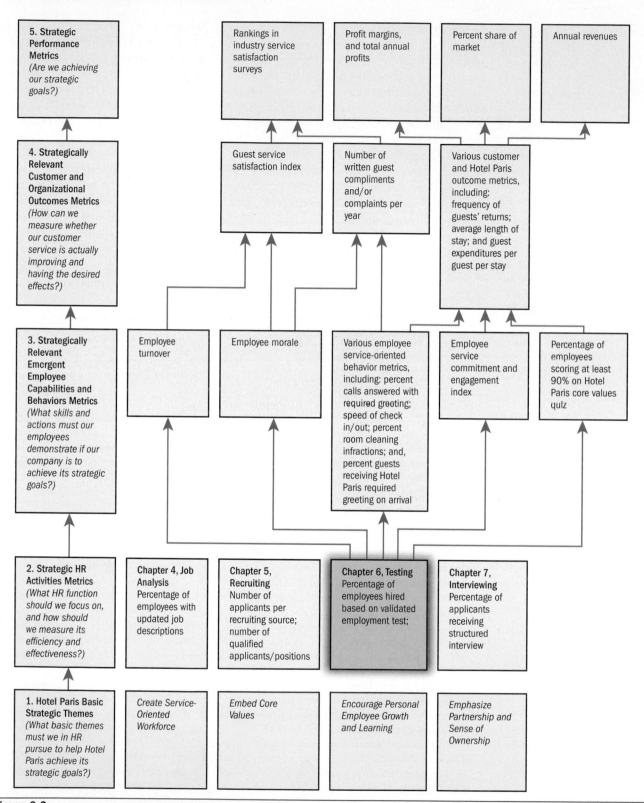

Figure 6-9
HR Scorecard for Hotel Paris International Corporation*

*Note: *(An abbreviated example showing selected HR practices and outcomes aimed at implementing the competitive strategy, "To use superior guest services to differenti-ate the Hotel Paris properties and thus increase the length of stays and the return rate of guests and thus boost revenues and profitability.")*

 *Review*

SUMMARY

1. In this chapter, we discussed techniques for screening and selecting job candidates; the first was testing.

2. As used by psychologists, the term *reliability* always means "consistency." One way to measure reliability is to administer the same (or equivalent) tests to the same people at two different points in time. Or you could focus on internal consistency, comparing the responses to roughly equivalent items on the same test.

3. Test validity answers the question, "What does this test measure?" We discussed criterion validity and content validity. Criterion validity means demonstrating that those who do well on the test do well on the job; content validity is demonstrated by showing that the test constitutes a fair sample of the content of the job.

4. There are many types of personnel tests in use, including intelligence tests, tests of physical skills, tests of achievement, aptitude tests, interest inventories, and personality tests.

5. For a selection test to be useful, scores should be predictably related to performance on the job; you must validate the test. This requires five steps: (1) analyze the job, (2) choose your tests, (3) administer the test, (4) relate test scores and criteria, and (5) cross-validate and validate the test.

6. Under equal rights legislation, an employer may have to prove that its tests are predictive of success or failure on the job. This usually requires a predictive validation study, although other means of validation are often acceptable.

7. Some basic testing guidelines include (a) use tests as supplements, (b) validate the tests for appropriate jobs, (c) analyze all current hiring and promotion standards, (d) beware of certain tests, (e) use a certified psychologist, and (f) maintain good test conditions.

8. The work sampling selection technique is based on the assumption that the best indicator of future performance is past performance. Here you use the applicant's actual performance on the same (or very similar) job to predict his or her future job performance. The steps are: (a) analyze the applicant's previous work experience, (b) have experts list component tasks for the open job, (c) select crucial tasks as work sample measures, (d) break down these tasks into steps, (e) test the applicant, and (f) relate the applicant's work sample score to his or her performance on the job.

9. Management assessment centers are another screening device and expose applicants to a series of real-life exercises. Performance is observed and assessed by experts, who then check their assessments by observing the participants when they are back at their jobs. Examples of "real-life" exercises include a simulated business game, an in-basket exercise, and group discussions.

10. Even though most people prefer not to give bad references, most companies still carry out some sort of reference check on their candidates. These can be useful in raising red flags, and questionnaires (page 214) can improve the usefulness of the responses you receive.

11. Other selection tools include the polygraph, honesty tests, and graphology. While graphology appears to have little predictive value, paper and pencil honesty tests have been used with success although they (and polygraphs) must be used with an eye toward the legal and ethical issues involved.

DISCUSSION QUESTIONS

1. What is the difference between reliability and validity? In what respects are they similar?

2. Explain how you would go about validating a test. How can this information be useful to a manager?

3. Explain why you think a certified psychologist who is specifically trained in test construction should (or should not) always be used by a small business that needs a test battery.

4. Give some examples of how to use interest inventories to improve employee selection. In doing so, suggest several examples of occupational interests that you believe might predict success in various occupations, including college professor, accountant, and computer programmer.

5. Why is it important to conduct preemployment background investigations? Outline how you would go about doing so.

6. Explain how you would get around the problem of former employers being unwilling to give bad references on their former employees.

7. How can employers protect themselves against negligent hiring claims?

INDIVIDUAL AND GROUP ACTIVITIES

1. Write a short essay discussing some of the ethical and legal considerations in testing.

2. Working individually or in groups, develop a list of specific selection techniques that you would suggest your dean use to hire the next HR professor at your school. Explain why you chose each selection technique.

3. Working individually or in groups, contact the publisher of a standardized test such as the Scholastic Assessment Test and obtain from it written information regarding the test's validity and reliability. Present a short report in class discussing what the test is supposed to measure and the degree to which you think the test does what it is supposed to do, based on the reported validity and reliability scores.

4. The HRCI "Test Specifications" appendix at the end of this book (pages 685–689) lists the knowledge someone studying for the HRCI certification exam needs to have in each area of human resource management (such as in Strategic Management, Workforce Planning, and Human Resource Development). In groups of four to five students, do four things: (1) review that appendix now; (2) identify the material in this chapter that relates to the required knowledge the appendix lists; (3) write four multiple choice exam questions on this material that you believe would be suitable for inclusion in the HRCI exam; and (4) if time permits, have someone from your team post your team's questions in front of the class, so the students in other teams can take each others' exam questions.

EXPERIENTIAL EXERCISE

A Test for a Reservation Clerk

Purpose: The purpose of this exercise is to give you practice in developing a test to measure *one specific ability* for the job of airline reservation clerk for a major airline. If time permits, you'll be able to combine your tests into a test battery.

Required Understanding: Your airline has decided to outsource its reservation jobs to Asia. You should be fully acquainted with the procedure for developing a personnel test and should read the following description of an airline reservation clerk's duties:

Customers contact our airline reservation clerks to obtain flight schedules, prices, and itineraries. The reservation clerks look up the requested information on our airline's online flight schedule systems, which are updated continuously. The reservation clerk must speak clearly, and deal courteously and expeditiously with the customer, and be able to quickly find alternative flight arrangements in order to provide the customer with the itinerary that fits his or her needs. Alternative flights and prices must be found quickly, so that the customer is not kept waiting, and so that our reservations operations group maintains its efficiency standards. It is often necessary to look under various routings, since there may be a dozen or more alternative routes between the customer's starting point and destination.

You may assume that we will hire about one-third of the applicants as airline reservation clerks. Therefore, your objective is to create a test that is useful in selecting a third of those available.

How to Set Up the Exercise/Instructions: Divide the class into teams of five or six students. The ideal candidate will obviously have to have a number of skills and abilities to perform this job well. Your job is to select a single ability and to develop a test to measure that ability. Use only the materials available in the room, please. The test should permit quantitative scoring and may be an individual or a group test.

Please go to your assigned groups and, as per our discussion of test development in this chapter, each group should make a list of the abilities relevant to success in the airline reservation clerk's job. Each group should then rate the importance of these abilities on a five-point scale. Then, develop a test to measure what you believe to be the top-ranked ability. If time permits, the groups should combine the various tests from each group into a test battery. If possible, leave time for a group of students to take the test battery.

APPLICATION CASE

Where's My Czar?

In March 2004, with the U.S. presidential campaign heating up, President Bush's White House team made what would seem to be a questionable hiring decision. It's not clear how much screening they did, or who did it, but almost as soon as the White House recommended Nebraska business executive Tony Raimondo to be the administration's assistant commerce secretary for manufacturing ("manufacturing czar"), Mr. Raimondo had to withdraw his name from consideration.

The candidate withdrew his name after blistering criticism from Democratic nominee John Kerry. Among other things, the president's manufacturing czar was supposed to develop strategies for beefing up U.S. manufacturing capacity and creating more manufacturing jobs in the United States (a crucial task, given the almost three million jobs the United States had lost in the previous three years). But, it turned out that Mr. Raimondo ran a Nebraska manufacturing business that had set up plants in China, and outsourced a portion of his company's jobs there. Senator Kerry said Mr. Raimondo therefore hardly seemed like the ideal person to champion keeping jobs in the United States.

The Bush administration said Raimondo's withdrawal was related to Nebraska political issues and not the fuss raised by Kerry. In an interview on CNBC, Commerce Secretary Don Evans said that the administration would continue to look for candidates. For a White House team known for working hard to be very corporate in the way it does things, the situation must have been somewhat embarrassing. Now, Mr. Bush has asked for your advice.

Questions

1. What should this position's job description look like?
2. What are the ideal job specifications for the person in this position?
3. How should we have gone about recruiting and screening for this position? What selection tools, specifically, would you use?
4. Where do you think we went wrong?

CONTINUING CASE

Honesty Testing at Carter Cleaning Company

Jennifer Carter, president of the Carter Cleaning Centers, and her father have what the latter describes as an easy but hard job when it comes to screening job applicants. It is easy because for two important jobs—the people who actually do the pressing and those who do the cleaning spotting—the applicants are easily screened with about 20 minutes of on-the-job testing. As with typists, as Jennifer points out, "applicants either know how to press clothes fast enough or how to use cleaning chemicals and machines, or they don't, and we find out very quickly by just trying them out on the job." On the other hand, applicant screening for the stores can also be frustratingly hard because of the nature of some of the other qualities that Jennifer would like to screen for. Two of the most critical problems facing her company are employee turnover and employee honesty. Jennifer and her father sorely need to implement practices that will reduce the rate of employee turnover. If there is a way to do this through employee testing and screening techniques, Jennifer would like to know about it because of the management time and money that are now being wasted by the never-ending need to recruit and hire new employees. Of even greater concern to Jennifer and her father is the need to institute new practices to screen out those employees who may be predisposed to steal from the company.

Employee theft is an enormous problem for the Carter Cleaning Centers, and one that is not just limited to employees who handle the cash. For example, the cleaner–spotter and/or the presser often open the store themselves, without a manager present, to get the day's work started, and it is not unusual to have one or more of these people steal supplies or "run a route." Running a route means that an employee canvasses his or her neighborhood to pick up people's clothes for cleaning and then secretly cleans and presses them in the Carter store, using the company's supplies, gas, and power. It would also not be unusual for an unsupervised person (or his or her supervisor, for that matter) to accept a one-hour rush order for cleaning or laundering, quickly clean and press the item, and return it to the customer for payment without making out a proper ticket for the item posting the sale. The money, of course, goes into the worker's pocket instead of into the cash register.

The more serious problem concerns the store manager and the counter workers who actually have to handle the cash. According to Jack Carter, "you would not believe the creativity employees use to get around the management controls we set up to cut down on employee theft." As one extreme example of this felonious creativity, Jack tells the following story: "To cut down on the amount of money my employees were stealing, I had a small sign painted and placed in front of all our cash registers. The sign said: YOUR ENTIRE ORDER FREE IF WE DON'T GIVE YOU A CASH REGISTER RECEIPT WHEN YOU PAY. CALL 552–0235. It was my intention with this sign to force all our cash-handling employees to place their receipts into the cash register where they would be recorded for my accountants. After all, if all the cash that comes in is recorded in the cash register, then we should have a much better handle on stealing in our stores, right? Well, one of our managers found a diabolical way around this. I came into the store one night and noticed that the cash register this particular manager was using just didn't look right, although the sign was dutifully placed in front of it. It turned out that every afternoon at about 5:00 P.M. when the other employees left, this character would pull his own cash register out of a box that he hid underneath our supplies. Customers coming in would notice the sign and of course the fact that he was meticulous in ringing up every sale. But unknown to them and us, for about five months the sales that came in for about an hour every day went into his

cash register, not mine. It took us that long to figure out where our cash for that store was going."

Here is what Jennifer would like you to answer:

Questions

1. What would be the advantages and disadvantages to Jennifer's company of routinely administering honesty tests to all its employees?

2. Specifically, what other screening techniques could the company use to screen out theft-prone and turnover-prone employees, and how exactly could these be used?

3. How should her company terminate employees caught stealing, and what kind of procedure should be set up for handling reference calls about these employees when they go to other companies looking for jobs?

KEY TERMS

negligent hiring, 194
reliability, 195
test validity, 196
criterion validity, 196

content validity, 196
expectancy chart, 199
interest inventory, 207
work samples, 208

work sampling technique, 208
management assessment
center, 209

ENDNOTES

1. See, for example, Ann Marie Ryan and Marja Lasek, "Negligent Hiring and Defamation: Areas of Liability Related to Pre-employment Inquiries," *Personnel Psychology* 44, no. 2 (Summer 1991), pp. 293–319.
2. Ibid.
3. Ibid.
4. Steven Mitchell Sack, "Fifteen Steps to Protecting Against the Risk of Negligent Hiring Claims," *Employment Relations Today*, August 1993, pp. 313–320.
5. Kevin Murphy and Charles Davidshofer, *Psychological Testing: Principles and Applications* (Upper Saddle River, NJ: Prentice Hall, 2001), p. 73.
6. W. Bruce Walsh and Nancy Betz, *Tests and Assessment* (Upper Saddle River, NJ: Prentice Hall, 2001).
7. Murphy and Davidshofer, *Psychological Testing*, p. 74.
8. A third, less used, way to demonstrate a test's validity is *construct validity*. A construct is an abstract trait such as happiness or intelligence. Construct validity generally addresses the question of "validity of measurement," in other words, of whether the test is really measuring, say, intelligence. To prove construct validity, an employer has to prove that the test measures the construct. Federal agency guidelines make it difficult to prove construct validity, however, and as a result few employers use this approach as part of their process for satisfying the federal guidelines. See James Ledvinka, *Federal Regulation of Personnel and Human Resource Management* (Boston: Kent, 1982), p. 113; and Murphy and Davidshofer, *Psychological Testing*, pp. 154–165.
9. Murphy and Davidshofer, *Psychological Testing*, p. 73.
10. Experts sometimes have to develop separate expectancy charts and cutting points for minorities and nonminorities if the validation studies indicate that high performers from either group (minority or nonminority) score lower (or higher) on the test.
11. Travis Gibbs and Matt Riggs, "Reducing Bias in Personnel Selection Decisions: Positive Effects of Attention to Irrelevant Information," *Psychological Reports* 74 (1994), pp. 19–26.
12. From "Ethical Principles of Psychologists and Code of Conduct," *American Psychologist* 47 (1992), pp. 1597–1611.
13. Mark Schmit and Ann Marie Ryan, "Applicant Withdrawal: The Role of Test-Taking Attitudes and Racial Differences," *Personnel Psychology* 50 (1997), pp. 855–876.
14. Robert Ployhart and Ann Marie Ryan, "Applicants' Reactions to the Fairness of Selection Procedures: The Effects of Positive Rule Violations and Time of Measurement," *Journal of Applied Psychology* 83, no. 1 (1998), pp. 3–16.
15. Walsh and Betz, *Tests and Assessment*, p. 425.
16. Dirk Steiner and Stephen Gilliland, "Fairness Reactions to Personnel Selection Techniques in France and the United States," *Journal of Applied Psychology* 81, no. 2 (1996), pp. 134–141.
17. Ibid., p. 134.
18. Russell Cropanzano and Thomas Wright, "Procedural Justice and Organizational Staffing: A Tale of Two Paradigms," *Human Resource Management Review* 13, no. 1 (Spring 2003), pp. 7–39.
19. Susan Mendelsohn and Katheryn Morrison, "The Right to Privacy at the Work Place, Part I: Employee Searches," *Personnel*, July 1988, p. 20. See also Talya Bauer et al., "Applicant Reactions to Selection: Development of the Selection Procedural Justice Scale," *Personnel Psychology* 54 (2001), pp. 387–419.

20. Mendelson and Morrison, "The Right to Privacy in the Work Place," p. 22.

21. Kenneth Sovereign, *Personnel Law*, (Upper Saddle River, NJ, Prentice Hall, 1999), pp. 204–206.

22. Ibid., p. 55.

23. *Kehr v. Consolidated Freightways of Delaware*, Docket No. 86-2126, July 15, 1987, U.S. Seventh Circuit Court of Appeals. Discussed in *Commerce Clearing House, Ideas and Trends*, October 16, 1987, p. 165.

24. For a discussion of these see *Commerce Clearing House, Ideas and Trends*, October 16, 1987, pp. 165–166.

25. http://www.amanet.org/research/pdfs/bjp_2001.pdf. Downloaded August 22, 2004.

26. Ibid.

27. Rachel Emma Silverman, "Sharpen Your Pencil," *Wall Street Journal*, December 5, 2000.

28. Steffanie Wilk and Peter Capelli, "Understanding the Determinants of the Employer Use of Selection Methods," *Personnel Psychology* 56 (2003), p. 117.

29. See Rebecca Bennett and Sandra Robinson, "Development of a Measure of Workplace Deviance," *Journal of Applied Psychology* 85, no. 3 (2000), p. 349.

30. "Employees' Dirty Deeds Caused Companies 6% of Annual Revenue, Report Says," *BNA Bulletin to Management*, August 17, 2000, p. 257.

31. Sarah Gale, "Three Companies Cut Turnover with Tests," *Workforce*, Spring 2002, pp. 66–69.

32. Neal Schmitt et al., "Computer-Based Testing Applied to Selection of Secretarial Candidates," *Personnel Psychology* 46 (1991), pp. 149–165.

33. Randall Overton et al., "The Pen-Based Computer as an Alternative Platform for Test Administration," *Personnel Psychology* 49 (1996), pp. 455–464.

34. Scott Hayes, "Kinko's Dials into Automated Applicants Screening," *Workforce*, November 1999, pp. 71–73; Gilbert Nicholson, "Automated Assessments for Better Hires," *Workforce*, December 2000, pp. 102–107.

35. Brian O'Leary et al., "Selecting the Best and Brightest," *Human Resource Management* 41, no. 3 (Fall 2002), pp. 25–34.

36. Except as noted, this is based largely on Laurence Siegel and Irving Lane, *Personnel and Organizational Psychology* (Burr Ridge, IL: McGraw-Hill, 1982), pp. 170–185. See also Cabot Jaffee, "Measurement of Human Potential," *Employment Relations Today* 17, no. 2 (Summer 2000), pp. 15–27; Maureen Patterson, "Overcoming the Hiring Crunch; Tests Deliver Informed Choices," *Employment Relations Today* 27, no. 3 (Fall 2000), pp. 77–88; Kathryn Tyler, "Put Applicants' Skills to the Test," *HR Magazine*, January 2000, p. 74; Murphy and Davidshofer, *Psychological Testing*, pp. 215–403.

37. As an example, results of meta-analyses in one study indicated that isometric strength tests were valid predictors of both supervisory ratings of physical performance, and performance on work simulations. See Barry R. Blakley, Miguel Quinones, Marnie Swerdlin Crawford, and I. Ann Jago, "The Validity of Isometric Strength Tests," *Personnel Psychology* 47 (1994), pp. 247–274.

38. William Wagner, "All Skill, No Finesse," *Workforce*, June 2000, pp. 108–116.

39. James Spencer, "Sorry, You're Nobody's Type," *Wall Street Journal*, July 30, 2003, p. D1.

40. Cora Daniels, "Does This Man Need a Shrink?" *Fortune*, February 5, 2001, pp. 205–206.

41. Murray Barrick et al., "Personality and Job Performance: Test of the Immediate Effects of Motivation Among Sales Representatives," *Journal of Applied Psychology* 87, no. 1 (2002), p. 43.

42. As per note 8, this approach calls for construct validation which, as was pointed out, is difficult to demonstrate.

43. Charles Sarchione et al., "Prediction of Dysfunctional Job Behaviors Among Law-Enforcement Officers," *Journal of Applied Psychology* 83, no. 6 (1998), pp. 904–912. See also Stephen Bates, "Personality Counts," *HR Magazine*, February 2002, pp. 28–34.

44. Paula Caligiuri, "The Big Five Personality Characteristics as Predictors of Expatriate's Desire to Terminate the Assignment and Supervisor Rated Performance," *Personnel Psychology* 53 (2000), pp. 67–68.

45. Brian Niehoff and Robert Paula, "Causes of Employee Theft and Strategies That HR Managers Can Use for Prevention," *Human Resource Management* 39, no. 1 (Spring 2000), pp. 51–64.

46. See, for example, Douglas Cellar et al., "Comparison of Factor Structures and Criterion-Related Validity Coefficients for Two Measures of Personality Based on the Five Factor Model," *Journal of Applied Psychology* 81, no. 6 (1996), pp. 694–704; and Jesus Salgado, "The Five Factor Model of Personality and Job Performance in the European Community," *Journal of Applied Psychology* 82, no. 1 (1997), pp. 30–43.

47. Timothy Judge et al., "Personality and Leadership: A Qualitative and Quantitative Review," *Journal of Applied Psychology* 87, no. 4 (2002), p. 765.

48. Ibid.

49. Timothy Judge and Remus Ilies, "Relationship of Personality to Performance Motivation: A Meta Analytic Review," *Journal of Applied Psychology* 87, no. 4 (2002), pp. 797–807.

50. Murray Barrick et al., "Meta Analysis of the Relationship between the Five Factor Model of Personality and Holland's Occupational Types," *Personnel Psychology* 56, no. 1 (Spring 2003), pp. 45–74.

51. L. A. Witt et al., "The Interactive Effects of Conscientiousness and Agreeableness on Job Performance," *Journal of Applied Psychology* 87, no. 1 (2002), pp. 164–169.

52. Timothy Judge et al., "The Big Five Personality Traits, General Mental Ability, and Career Success Across the Lifespan," *Personnel Psychology* 52 (1999), pp. 621–652.

53. See "Can Testing Prevent Violence?" *BNA Bulletin to Management*, November 28, 1996, p. 384.

54. Gilbert Nicholson, "Automated Assessments for Better Hires," *Workforce*, December 2000, pp. 102–107.

55. Jeff Weekley and Casey Jones, "Video-Based Situational Testing," *Personnel Psychology* 50 (1997), p. 25.

56. See, for example, George Burgnoli, James Campion, and Jeffrey Bisen, "Racial Bias in the Use of Work Samples for Personnel Selection," *Journal of Applied Psychology* 64, no. 2 (April 1979), pp. 119–123. See also Neal Schmitt and Amy Mills, "Traditional Tests and the Job Simulation: Minority and Majority Performance and Test Validity," *Journal of Applied Psychology* 86, no. 3 (2001), pp. 451–458.

57. Siegel and Lane, *Personnel and Organizational Psychology*, pp. 182–183.

58. Annette Spychalski, Miguel Quinones, Barbara Gaugler, and Katja Pohley, "A Survey of Assessment Center Practices in Organizations in the United States," *Personnel Psychology* 50, no. 1 (Spring 1997), pp. 71–90. See also Winfred Arthur Jr. et al., "A Meta Analysis of the Criterion Related Validity of Assessment Center Data Dimensions," *Personnel Psychology* 56 (2003), pp. 124–154.

59. Kobi Dayan et al., "Entry-Level Police Candidate Assessment Center: An Efficient Tool or a Hammer to Kill a Fly?" *Personnel Psychology* 55 (2002), pp. 827–848.

60. Weekley and Jones, "Video-Based Situational Testing," p. 26.

61. Ibid., p. 30.

62. Ibid., p. 46.

63. Robert Grossman, "Made from Scratch," *HR Magazine*, April 2002, pp. 44–53.

64. "Internet, e-mail Monitoring Common at Most Workplaces," *BNA Bulletin to Management*, February 1, 2001, p. 34.

65. Mary Mayer, "Background Checks in Focus," *HR Magazine*, January 2002, pp. 59–62; and Carroll Lachnit, "Protecting People and Profits with Background Checks," *Workforce*, February 2002, p. 52.

66. Seymour Adler, "Verifying a Job Candidate's Background: The State of Practice in a Vital Human Resources Activity," *Review of Business* 15, no. 2 (Winter 1993), p. 6.

67. Edward Robinson, "Beware—Job Seekers Have No Secrets," *Fortune*, December 29, 1997, p. 285.

68. This is based on Samuel Greengard, "Have Gangs Invaded Your Workplace?" *Personnel Journal*, February 1996, pp. 47–48.

69. Lachnit, "Protecting People and Profits with Background Checks," p. 50.

70. For additional information, see Lawrence E. Dube Jr., "Employment References and the Law," *Personnel Journal* 65, no. 2 (February 1986), pp. 87–91. See also Mickey Veich, "Uncover the Resume Ruse," *Security Management*, October 1994, pp. 75–76.

71. Thomas von der Embse and Rodney Wyse, "Those Reference Letters: How Useful Are They?" *Personnel* 62, no. 1 (January 1985), pp. 42–46.

72. "Undercover Callers Tip Off Job Seekers to Former Employers' Negative References," *BNA Bulletin to Management*, May 27, 1999, p. 161.

73. Eileen Zimmerman, "A Subtle Reference Trap for Unwary Employers," *Workforce*, April 2003, p. 22.

74. "Jury Awards Manager Accused of Theft $1.25 Million," *BNA Bulletin to Management*, March 27, 1997, p. 97.

75. James Bell, James Castagnera, and Jane Patterson Yong, "Employment References: Do You Know the Law?" *Personnel Journal* 63, no. 2 (February 1984), pp. 32–36. In order to demonstrate defamation, several elements must be present: (a) the defamatory statement must have been communicated to another party; (b) the statement must be a false statement of fact; (c) injury to reputation must have occurred; and (d) the employer must not be protected under qualified or absolute privilege. For a discussion, see Ryan and Lasek, "Negligent Hiring and Defamation," p. 307. See also James Burns Jr., "Employment References: Is There a Better Way?" *Employee Relations Law Journal* 23, no. 2 (Fall 1997), pp. 157–168.

76. "Reference Checks Hit Wall of Silence," *BNA Bulletin to Management*, July 6, 1995, p. 216.

77. "Getting Applicant Information Difficult but Still Necessary," *BNA Bulletin to Management*, February 5, 1999, p. 63. See also Robert Howie and Lawrence Shapiro, "Pre-Employment Criminal Background Checks: Why Employers Should Look Before They Leap," *Employee Relations Law Journal*, Summer 2002, pp. 63–77.

78. Gilbert Nicholson, "Automated Assessments for Better Hires," *Workforce*, December 2000, pp. 102–104.

79. Institute of Management and Administration, *Human Resource Department Report*, November 2003, 03–11, p. 1.

80. Bob Neveu, "Applicant Tracking's Top 10: Do You Know What to Look for in Applicant Tracking Systems?" *Workforce*, October 2002, p. 10.

81. Lachnit, "Protecting People and Profits with Background Checks," p. 52.

82. Jeffrey M. Hahn, "Pre-Employment Information Services: Employers Beware?" *Employee Relations Law Journal* 17, no. 1 (Summer 1991), pp. 45–69.

83. Teresa Butler Stivarius, "Background Checks: Steps to Basic Compliance in a Multistate Environment," *Society for Human Resource Management Legal Report*, March–April 2003, pp. 1–8.

84. John Jones and William Terris, "Post-Polygraph Selection Techniques," *Recruitment Today*, May–June 1989, pp. 25–31.

85. Norma Fritz, "In Focus: Honest Answers—Post Polygraph," *Personnel*, April 1989, p. 8. See also Richard White Jr., "Ask Me No Questions, Tell Me No Lies: Examining the Uses and Misuses of the Polygraph," *Public Personnel Management* 30, no. 4 (Winter 2001), pp. 483–493.

86. For a discussion of the earlier caveats see, for example, Kevin Murphy, "Detecting Infrequent Deception," *Journal of Applied Psychology* 72, no. 4 (November 1987), pp. 611–614.

87. John Bernardin and Donna Cooke, "Validity of an Honesty Test in Predicting Theft Among Convenience Store Employees," *Academy of Management Journal* 36, no. 5 (1993), pp. 1097–1108.

88. Paul Sackett and James Wanek, "New Developments in the Use of Measures of Honesty, Integrity, Conscientiousness, Dependability, Trustworthiness, and Reliability for Personnel Selection," *Personnel Psychology* 49 (1996), p. 821.

89. The following is based on Judith Collins and Frank Schmidt, "Personality, Integrity, and White Collar Crime: A Construct Validity Study," *Personnel Psychology* 46 (1993), pp. 295–311.

90. Ibid. For a description of another approach see, for example, Peter Bullard, "Pre-Employment Screening to Weed Out 'Bad Apples'," *Nursing Homes*, June 1994, pp. 29–31.

91. These are based on *Commerce Clearing House, Ideas and Trends*, December 29, 1998, pp. 222–223. See also "Divining Integrity Through Interviews," *BNA Bulletin to Management*, June 4, 1987, p. 184.

92. This example is based on *BNA Bulletin to Management*, February 26, 1987, p. 65.

93. Bill Leonard, "Reading Employees," *HR Magazine*, April 1999, pp. 67–73.

94. Ibid.

95. Mick Haus, "Pre-Employment Physicals and the ADA," *Safety and Health*, February 1992, pp. 64–65.

96. Scott MacDonald, Samantha Wells, and Richard Fry, "The Limitations of Drug Screening in the Workplace," *International Labor Review* 132, no. 1 (1993), p. 98. Not all agree that drug testing is worthwhile. See, for example, Mark Karper, Clifford Donn, and Marie Lyndaker, "Drug Testing in the Transportation Industry: The Maritime Case," *Employee Responsibilities and Rights* 71, no. 3 (September 1994), pp. 219–233.

97. Eric Rolfe Greenberg, "Workplace Testing: Who's Testing Whom?" *Personnel*, May 1989, pp. 39–45.

98. "Drug Testing: The Things People Will Do," *American Salesman* 46, no. 3 (March 2001), p. 20.

99. Diane Cadrain, "Are Your Employees' Drug Tests Accurate?" *HR Magazine*, January 2003, pp. 40–45.

100. Chris Berka and Courtney Poignand, "Hair Follicle Testing—An Alternative to Urinalysis for Drug Abuse Screening," *Employee Relations Today*, Winter 1991–1992, pp. 405–409.

101. MacDonald et al., "The Limitations of Drug Screening," pp. 102–104.

102. R. J. McCunney, "Drug Testing: Technical Complications of a Complex Social Issue," *American Journal of Industrial Medicine* 15, no. 5 (1989), pp. 589–600; discussed in MacDonald et al., "The Limitations of Drug Screening," p. 102.

103. MacDonald et al., "The Limitations of Drug Screening," p. 103.

104. For a discussion of this, see Ibid, pp. 105–106.

105. This is based on Ann M. O'Neill, "Legal Issues Presented by Hair Follicle Testing," *Employee Relations Today*, Winter 1991–1992, pp. 411–415.

106. Ibid., p. 411.

107. Ibid., p. 413.

108. Richard Lisko, "A Manager's Guide to Drug Testing," *Security Management* 38, no. 8 (August 1994), p. 92. See also Randall Kesselring and Jeffrey Pittman, "Drug Testing Laws and Employment Injuries," *Journal of Labor Research*, Spring 2002, pp. 293–301.

109. Michael A. McDaniel, "Does Pre-Employment Drug Use Predict on-the-Job Suitability?" *Personnel Psychology* 41, no. 4 (Winter 1988), pp. 717–729.

110. *Exxon Corp. v. Esso Workers Union, Inc.*, CA1#96–2241, 7/8/97; discussed in *BNA Bulletin to Management*, August 7, 1997, p. 249.

111. These are quoted from *Commerce Clearing House, Ideas and Trends*, May 1, 1987, pp. 70–71.

112. Rusell Gerbman, "License to Work," *HR Magazine*, June 2000, pp. 151–160.

113. Gillian Flynn, "Hiring of Foreign Workers in a Post-911 World," *Workforce*, July 2002, p. 78.

After studying this chapter, you should be able to:

1 List the main types of selection interviews.

2 Explain and illustrate at least six factors that affect the usefulness of interviews.

3 Explain and illustrate each guideline for being a more effective interviewer.

4 Effectively interview a job candidate.

Interviewing Candidates

One thing that concerned Lisa Cruz was the fact that the Hotel Paris's hotel

managers varied widely in their interviewing and hiring skills. Some were

quite effective, most were not. Furthermore, the company did not have a

formal employment interview-training program, nor, for that matter, did it

have standardized interview packages that hotel managers around the world

could use.

As an experienced HR professional, Lisa knew that the company's new

testing program would go only so far. She knew that at best, employment

tests accounted for perhaps 30% of employee performance. It was essential

that she and her team design a package of interviews that her hotel

managers could use to assess—on an interactive and personal basis—

candidates for various positions. It was only in that way that the hotel could

hire the sorts of employees whose competencies and behaviors would

translate into the kinds of outcomes—such as improved guest services—

that the hotel required to achieve its strategic goals.•

The previous chapter, Employee Testing and Selection, focused on important methods managers use to select employees. The purpose of the current chapter, Interviewing Candidates, is to improve your effectiveness at using what is perhaps the most important screening tool, the selection interview. The main topics we'll cover include types of interviews, the factors that can undermine an interview's usefulness, and designing and conducting an effective interview. In the following chapter, Training and Developing Employees, we'll turn to the techniques you can use to make sure the new employees you hire have the knowledge and skills they need to perform their jobs.

● BASIC FEATURES OF INTERVIEWS

An *interview* is a procedure designed to obtain information from a person through oral responses to oral inquiries; a *selection interview*, which we'll focus on in this chapter, is "a selection procedure designed to predict future job performance on the basis of applicants' oral responses to oral inquiries."[1]

Since the interview is only one of several selection tools, you could reasonably ask, "Why devote a whole chapter to this one tool?" The answer is that the interview is by far the most widely used personnel selection procedure; for instance, one study of 852 employers found that 99% used interviews for employee selection.[2] The point is that while not all companies use tests, assessment centers, or even reference checks, it would be highly unusual for a manager not to interview a prospective employee. Interviewing is thus an indispensable management tool.

As we'll see below, experts have criticized the interview for its low validity.[3] However, recent reviews have been more favorable, and an interview—at least one done properly—can be "a much better predictor of performance than previously thought and is comparable with many other selection techniques."[4]

List the main types of selection interviews.

Types of Interviews

Managers use several types of interviews in the work setting. For example, there are selection, appraisal, and exit interviews. An *appraisal interview* is a discussion, following a performance appraisal, in which supervisor and employee discuss the employee's rating and possible remedial actions. When an employee leaves a firm for any reason, HR often conducts an *exit interview*. This interview aims at eliciting information about the job or related matters that might give the employer some insight into what's right or wrong about the firm. Many techniques covered in this chapter apply equally to appraisal and exit interviews. However, we'll postpone a complete explanation of these types of interviews until Chapters 9 and 10, respectively, so we can focus here on *selection interviews*. We can classify selection interviews according to (1) how structured they are, (2) their "content"—the types of questions they contain—and (3) how the firm administers the interviews. Let's look at these.

unstructured or nondirective interview
An unstructured conversational-style interview in which the interviewer pursues points of interest as they come up in response to questions.

Structured versus Unstructured Interviews   In **unstructured or nondirective interviews**, there is generally no set format to follow, so the interview can take various directions. The lack of structure allows the interviewer to ask follow-up questions and pursue points of interest as they develop. Interviewees for the same job may or may not get the same or similar questions. A few questions might be specified in advance, but they're usually not, and there is seldom a formal guide for scoring answers. This type of interview "could even be described as little more than a general conversation."[5]

structured or directive interview
An interview following a set sequence of questions.

On the other hand, in **structured or directive interviews**, the questions and acceptable responses are specified in advance and the responses are rated for appropriateness of content.[6] McMurray's patterned interview was one early example. The interviewer followed a printed form to ask a series of questions, such as "How was the person's present job obtained?" Comments printed beneath the questions (such as "Has he/she shown self-reliance in getting his/her jobs?") then guide the interviewer in evaluating the answers.

In practice, not all structured interviews go so far as to specify acceptable answers—some are more structured than others, in other words. Figure 7-1 shows a relatively structured interview guide that stops short of specifying the answers to watch for. Indeed (as we'll explain in more detail on pages 252–253), there are different ways to structure an interview, many of which have nothing to do with using structured guides like the one in Figure 7-1.

Structured and nonstructured interviews each have pros and cons. In structured interviews, all interviewers generally ask all applicants the same questions; partly because of this, these interviews tend to be more reliable and valid. Structured interviews can also help those who may be less comfortable doing interviews to conduct better interviews. Standardizing the administration of the interview also increases consistency across candidates, enhances job relatedness, reduces overall subjectivity (and thus the potential for bias), and may "enhance the ability to withstand legal challenge."[7] On the other hand, structured interviews don't always provide enough opportunity to pursue points of interest as they develop.

Interview Content: Types of Questions We can also classify interviews based on the "content" or focus of their questions. For example, in a **situational interview**, you ask the candidate what his or her behavior would be in a given situation.[8] Thus, you might ask a supervisory candidate how he or she would respond to a subordinate coming to work late three days in a row. Interviews can be both structured and situational; here you use predetermined situational questions and answers. In such a *structured situational interview*, you might evaluate the applicant on, say, his or her choice between letting the persistently late subordinate off with a warning versus suspending the subordinate for a week.

Whereas situational interviews ask interviewees to describe how they would react to a hypothetical situation today or tomorrow, **behavioral interviews** ask interviewees to describe how they reacted to actual situations in the past.[9] For example, when Citizen's Banking Corporation in Flint, Michigan, found that 31 of the 50 people in its call center quit in one year, Cynthia Wilson, the center's head, switched to behavioral interviews. Many of those who left did so because they didn't enjoy fielding questions from occasionally irate clients. So Wilson no longer tries to predict how candidates will act based on asking them if they want to work with angry clients. Instead, she asks behavioral questions like, "Tell me about a time you were speaking with an irate person, and how you turned the situation around." Wilson says this makes it much harder to fool the interviewer, and, indeed, only four people left her center in the following year.[10] Situational questions start with phrases such as, "Suppose you were faced with the following situation . . . What would you do?" Behavioral questions might start with a phrase like, "Can you think of a time when . . . What did you do?"[11]

Behavioral or situational interviews can produce a lot of tension. "It's pretty intense," said one applicant for a consultant's job with Accenture, the consulting firm, "You can pretty much fake one or two answers, but the third time they come back to it you pretty much can't. You're pulling from real life, and you're nervous. [The interviewer] asked how I would prepare for something important. He came back to that again and again to make sure what I said was true. The whole time they are writing constantly."[12]

In a **job-related interview**, the interviewer tries to deduce what the applicant's on-the-job performance will be based on his or her answers to questions about past experiences. The questions here don't revolve around hypothetical or actual situations or scenarios. Instead, the interviewer asks job-related questions (such as, "Which courses did you like best in business school?") in order to draw conclusions about, say, the candidate's ability to handle the financial aspects of the job to be filled.

---

situational interview
A series of job-related questions that focus on how the candidate would behave in a given situation.

behavioral interviews
A series of job-related questions that focus on how the candidate reacted to actual situations in the past.

job-related interview
A series of job-related questions that focus on relevant past job-related behaviors.

Figure 7-1
Structured Interview Guide
Source: Copyright 1992. The Dartnell Corporation, Chicago, IL. Adapted with permission.

APPLICANT INTERVIEW GUIDE

To the interviewer: This Applicant Interview Guide is intended to assist in employee selection and placement. If it is used for all applicants for a position, it will help you to compare them, and it will provide more objective information than you will obtain from unstructured interviews.

Because this is a general guide, all of the items may not apply in every instance. Skip those that are not applicable and add questions appropriate to the specific position. Space for additional questions will be found at the end of the form.

Federal law prohibits discrimination in employment on the basis of sex, race, color, national origin, religion, disability, and in most instances, age. The law of most states also ban some or all of the above types of discrimination in employment as well as discrimination based on marital status or ancestry. Interviewers should take care to avoid any questions that suggest that an employment decision will be made on the basis of any such factors.

Job Interest

Name _____ Position applied for _____

What do you think the job (position) involves? _____

Why do you want the job (position)? _____

Why are you qualified for it? _____

What would your salary requirements be? _____

What do you know about our company? _____

Why do you want to work for us? _____

Current Work Status

Are you now employed? _____ Yes _____ No. If not, how long have you been unemployed? _____

Why are you unemployed? _____

If you are working, why are you applying for this position? _____

When would you be available to start work with us? _____

Work Experience

(Start with the applicant's current or last position and work back. All periods of time should be accounted for. Go back at least 12 years, depending upon the applicant's age. Military service should be treated as a job.)

Current or last
employer _____ Address _____

Dates of employment: from _____ to _____

Current or last job title _____

What are (were) your duties? _____

Have you held the same job throughout your employment with that company? _____ Yes _____ No. If not,

describe the various jobs you have had with that employer, how long you held each of them, and the main

duties of each. _____

What was your starting salary? _____ What are you earning now? _____ Comments _____

_____

Name of your last or current supervisor _____

What did you like most about that job? _____

What did you like least about it? _____

Why are you thinking of leaving? _____

  Why are you leaving right now? _____

  Interviewer's comments or observations _____

_____

(continued)

Figure 7-1
(*continued*)

What did you do before you took your last job? _____

  Where were you employed? _____

  Location _____ Job title _____

  Duties _____

  Did you hold the same job throughout your employment with that company? ____ Yes ____ No. If not, describe the jobs you held, when you held them and the duties of each. _____

  _____

  What was your starting salary? _____ What was your final salary? _____

  Name of your last supervisor _____

  May we contact that company? ____ Yes ____ No

  What did you like most about that job? _____

  What did you like least about that job? _____

  Why did you leave that job? _____

  Would you consider working there again? _____

  Interviewer: If there is any gap between the various periods of employment, the applicant should be asked about them. _____

  Interviewer's comments or observations _____

  _____

What did you do prior to the job with that company? _____

What other jobs or experience have you had? Describe them briefly and explain the general duties of each.

_____

Have you been unemployed at any time in the last five years? ____ Yes ____ No. What efforts did you make to find work? _____

What other experience or training do you have that would help qualify you for the job applied for? Explain how and where you obtained this experience or training. _____

_____

Educational Background

What education or training do you have that would help you in the job for which you have applied? _____

_____

Describe any formal education you have had. (Interviewer may substitute technical training, if relevant.) _____

_____

Off-Job Activities

What do you do in your off-hours? ___ Part-time job ___ Athletics ___ Spectator sports ___ Clubs ___ Other

Please explain. _____

Interviewer's Specific Questions

Interviewer: Add any questions to the particular job for which you are interviewing, leaving space for brief answers.

(Be careful to avoid questions which may be viewed as discriminatory.)

_____

_____

_____

Personal

Would you be willing to relocate? ____ Yes ____ No

Are you willing to travel? ____ Yes ____ No

(*continued*)

Figure 7-1
(*continued*)

What is the maximum amount of time you would consider traveling? _____
_____

Are you able to work overtime? _____

What about working on weekends? _____

Self-Assessment

What do you feel are your strong points? _____
_____

What do you feel are your weak points? _____
_____

Interviewer: Compare the applicant's responses with the information furnished on the application for employment.

Clear up any discrepancies. _____
_____

Before the applicant leaves, the interviewer should provide basic information about the organization and the job opening, if this has not already been done. The applicant should be given information on the work location, work hours, the wage or salary, type of remuneration (salary or salary plus bonus, etc.), and other factors that may affect the applicant's interest in the job.

Interviewer's Impressions

Rate each characteristic from 1 to 4, with 1 being the highest rating and 4 being the lowest.

Personal Characteristics	1	2	3	4	Comments
Personal appearance					
Poise, manner					
Speech					
Cooperation with interviewer					
Job-related Characteristics					
Experience for this job					
Knowledge of job					
Interpersonal relationships					
Effectiveness					

Overall rating for job

1	2	3	4	5
____ Superior	____ Above Average	____ Average	____ Marginal	____ Unsatisfactory
	(well qualified)	(qualified)	(barely qualified)	

Comments or remarks _____
_____
_____

Interviewer _____ Date _____

stress interview
An interview in which the applicant is made uncomfortable by a series of often rude questions. This technique helps identify hypersensitive applicants and those with low or high stress tolerance.

In a **stress interview**, the interviewer seeks to make the applicant uncomfortable with occasionally rude questions. The aim is supposedly to spot sensitive applicants and those with low or high stress tolerance. The interviewer might first probe for weaknesses in the applicant's background, such as a job that the applicant left under questionable circumstances. The interviewer then zeroes in on these weaknesses, hoping to get the candidate to lose his or her composure. Thus, a candidate for customer relations manager who obligingly mentions having had four jobs in the past two years might be told that frequent job changes reflect irresponsible and immature behavior. If the applicant then responds with a reasonable explanation of why the job changes were necessary, the interviewer might pursue another topic. On the other hand, if the formerly tranquil applicant reacts explosively with anger and disbelief, the interviewer might deduce that the person has a low tolerance for stress.

Stress interviews may help unearth hypersensitive applicants who might overreact to mild criticism with anger and abuse. However, the stress interview's invasive and ethically questionable nature demands that the interviewer be both skilled in its use and sure the job really calls for a thick skin and an ability to handle stress. This is definitely not an approach for amateur interrogators or for those without the skills to keep the interview under control.

Puzzle questions are popular today. Recruiters for technical, finance, and occasionally other types of jobs like to use them to see how candidates think under pressure. For example, an interviewer at Microsoft asked a tech service applicant this: "Mike and Todd have $21 between them. Mike has $20 more than Todd. How much money has Mike, and how much money has Todd?"[13] (You'll find the answer in paragraph 2, page 243.)

"The HR Scorecard" feature illustrates how the Hotel Paris addressed its interview program changes.

The HR Scorecard
Strategy and Results

The New Interviewing Program

The Hotel Paris's competitive strategy is "To use superior guest service to differentiate the Hotel Paris properties, and to thereby increase the length of stay and return rate of guests, and thus boost revenues and profitability." HR manager Lisa Cruz must now formulate functional policies and activities that support this competitive strategy, by eliciting the required employee behaviors and competencies.

A preliminary analysis, performed jointly by Lisa and the Hotel Paris's chief financial officer, left them optimistic that HR could contribute measurably to achieving the hotel's strategic aims. Several employee competencies and behaviors including employee morale, employee commitment, and the percent of arriving guests receiving the hotel's required greeting had significant effects on customer and organizational outcomes such as guest satisfaction and frequency of guest returns. In turn, outcomes like these contributed measurably to the Hotel Paris's strategic goals, including profit margins, market share, and scores on industry satisfaction surveys. Lisa and her team now turn to creating an interviewing program that will help to produce the required employee competencies and behaviors. The accompanying HR Scorecard (Figure 7-2) outlines the relationships involved.

Lisa receives budgetary approval to design a new employee interview system. She and her team start by reviewing the job descriptions and job specifications for the positions of front-desk clerk, assistant manager, security guard, car hop/door person, and housekeeper. Focusing on developing structured interviews for each position, the team sets about devising interview questions. For example, for the front-desk clerk and assistant manager, they formulate several *behavioral questions*, including, "Tell me about a time when you had to deal with an irate person, and what you did." And, "Tell me about a time when you had to deal with several conflicting demands at once, such as having to study for several final exams at the same time, while working. How did you handle the situation?" They also developed a number of *situational questions*, including "Suppose you have a very pushy incoming guest who insists on being checked in at once, while at the same time you're trying to process the check-out for another guest who must be at the airport in 10 minutes. How would you handle the situation?" For these and other positions, they also developed several *job knowledge* questions. For example, for security guard applicants, one question her team created was, "What are the local legal restrictions, if any, regarding using products like Mace if confronted by an unruly person on the hotel grounds?" The team combined the questions into structured interviews for each job, and turned to testing, fine-tuning, and finally using the new system.

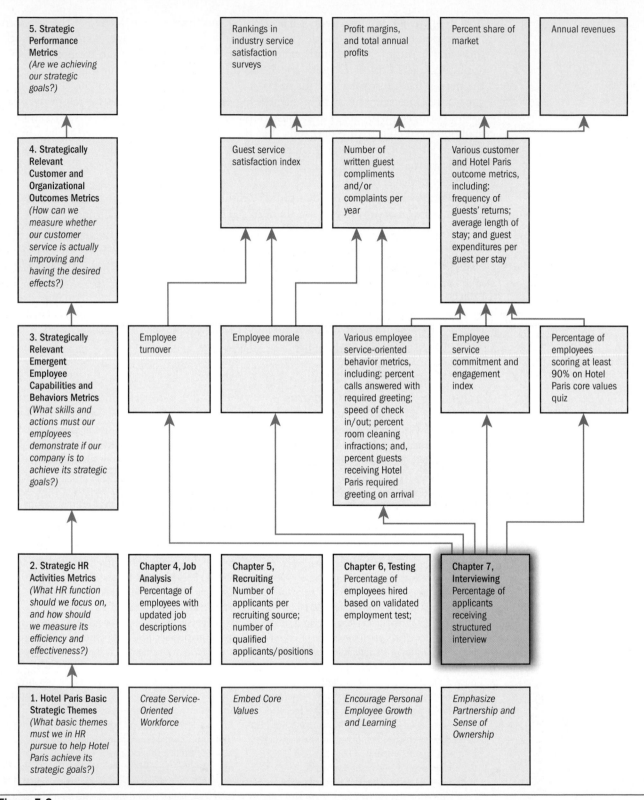

Figure 7-2
HR Scorecard for Hotel Paris International Corporation*

*Note: *(An abbreviated example showing selected HR practices and outcomes aimed at implementing the competitive strategy, "To use superior guest services to differentiate the Hotel Paris properties and thus increase the length of stays and the return rate of guests and thus boost revenues and profitability.")*

Administering the Interview

Interviews can also be administered in various ways: one on one or by a panel of interviewers; sequentially or all at once; and computerized or personally.

Personal or Individual Interviews Most interviews are individual or *one-on-one*: Two people meet alone, and one interviews the other by seeking oral responses to oral inquiries. Most interview processes are also sequential. In a *sequential or serial interview*, several persons interview the applicant, in sequence, before a decision is made. In an **unstructured sequential interview**, each interviewer may ask different questions and form an independent opinion. In a **structured sequential interview**, each interviewer rates the candidates on a standard evaluation form, using standardized questions. The hiring manager then reviews and compares the evaluations before deciding who to hire.[14] (Answer: Mike had $20.50, Todd $.50).

A **panel interview**, also known as a board interview, is defined as "an interview conducted by a team of interviewers (usually two to three), who interview the candidates simultaneously, and then combine their ratings into a final panel score." This contrasts with an *individual interview* (in which one interviewer rates one candidate), and a *serial interview* (where several interviewers assess a single candidate sequentially).[15] In a *serial* interview, candidates may cover the same ground over and over again with each interviewer. The panel format lets interviewers ask follow-up questions based on the candidate's answers, much as reporters do in press conferences. This may elicit more meaningful responses than are normally produced by a series of one-on-one interviews.

On the other hand, some candidates find panel interviews more stressful, so they may actually inhibit responses. An even more stressful variant is the **mass interview**. Here a panel interviews several candidates simultaneously. The panel poses a problem and then sits back and watches to see which candidate takes the lead in formulating an answer.

It's not clear whether, as a rule, panel interviews are more or less reliable and valid than other types of interviews, because how the employer actually conducts the panel interview has a big effect on reliability and validity. For example, structured panel interviews are more reliable and valid than unstructured ones. Panel interviews in which members use scoring sheets with descriptive scoring anchors (sample answers) are more reliable and valid than those that don't. And, training the panel interviewers may boost the interview's reliability, but probably not its validity.[16]

Some interviews are done entirely by telephone. These can actually be more accurate than face-to-face interviews for judging an applicant's conscientiousness, intelligence, and interpersonal skills. Since neither side has to worry about things like clothing and handshakes, both parties can focus on substantive answers. Or perhaps candidates—somewhat surprised by an unexpected call from the recruiter—just give more spontaneous answers.[17] In a typical study, interviewers tended to evaluate applicants more favorably in telephone versus face-to-face interviews, particularly where the interviewees were less physically attractive. However, the interviewers came to about the same conclusions regarding the interviewees whether the interview was face-to-face or by videoconference. The applicants themselves preferred the face-to-face interviews.[18]

Computerized Interviews A *computerized selection interview* is one in which a job candidate's oral and/or computerized replies are obtained in response to computerized oral, visual, or written questions and/or situations. Most computerized interviews present the applicant with a series of specific questions regarding his or her background, experience, education, skills, knowledge, and work attitudes that relate to the job for which the

unstructured sequential interview
An interview in which each interviewer forms an independent opinion after asking different questions.

structured sequential interview
An interview in which the applicant is interviewed sequentially by several persons; each rates the applicant on a standard form.

panel interview
An interview in which a group of interviewers questions the applicant.

mass interview
A panel interviews several candidates simultaneously.

Panel interviews allow each interviewer to follow up on the candidate's answers, which can give a fuller, more in-depth picture of the candidate's attitudes, qualifications, and potential.

person has applied.[19] Other, video-based computerized interviews may also confront candidates with realistic scenarios (such as irate customers) to which they must respond.

Typical computerized interviews present questions in a multiple choice format, one at a time; the applicant is expected to respond to the questions on the screen by pressing a key. For example, a sample interview question for a person applying for a job as a retail store clerk might be:

How would your supervisor rate your customer service skills?

a. Outstanding
b. Above average
c. Average
d. Below average
e. Poor[20]

Questions on a computerized interview come in rapid sequence and require the applicant to concentrate.[21] The typical computerized interview program measures the response time to each question. A delay in answering certain questions—such as "Can you be trusted?"—can flag a potential problem.

Computer-aided interviews are generally used to reject unacceptable candidates and to select those who will move on to face-to-face interviews. For example, Pic'n Pay stores, a chain of 915 self-service shoe stores headquartered in North Carolina, gives job applicants an 800 number to dial for the computerized interview, which they can take on any touch-tone phone. The interview contains 100 questions and lasts about 10 minutes. Applicants press 1 for *yes* and 0 for *no*. Every Pic'n Pay applicant then gets a follow-up live telephone interview, from one of the firm's six dedicated interviewers.

Computer-aided interviews can be advantageous. Systems like those at Pic'n Pay reduce the amount of time managers devote to interviewing what often turn out to be unacceptable candidates.[22] Applicants are reportedly more honest with computers than they would be with people, presumably because computers aren't judgmental.[23] The computer can also be sneaky; if an applicant takes longer than average to answer certain questions, he or she may be summarily screened out or at least questioned more deeply in that area by a human interviewer. Several of the interpersonal interview problems we'll discuss later in this chapter (such as making a snap judgment about the interviewee based on physical appearance) are also obviously avoided with this approach.[24] On the other hand, the mechanical nature of computer-aided interviews can leave applicants feeling that the employer is rather impersonal.

Here's how the system works at Great Western Bank. When Bonnie Dunn, 20 years old, tried out for a teller's job at Great Western Bank in Chatsworth, California, she faced a lineup of tough customers.[25] One young woman sputtered contradictory instructions about depositing a check and then blew her top when the transaction wasn't handled fast enough. Another customer had an even shorter fuse: "You people are unbelievably slow," he said.

Both tough customers appeared on a computer screen, as part of a 20-minute computerized job interview. Ms. Dunn was seated in front of a personal computer, responding via a color touch screen and a microphone. She was tested on making change and on sales skills, as well as keeping cool in tense situations.

When applicants sit down facing the computer at Great Western's bank branches, they hear it say, "Welcome to the interactive assessment aid." The computer doesn't understand what applicants say at that point, although it records their comments to be evaluated later. To begin the interview, applicants touch a label on the screen, eliciting an ominous foreword: "We'll be keeping track of how long it takes you and how many mistakes you make. Accuracy is more important than speed."

First, the computer tests the applicant on money skills, asking him or her to cash a check for $192.18, including at least three $5 bills and two dollars in quarters. Then, when an angry customer appears on the screen, the system expects candidates to grab the microphone and mollify him. Later, a bank official who listens to the recorded interviews gives applicants 5 points for maintaining a friendly tone of voice, plus up to 15 points for apologizing, promising to solve the customer's problem, and, taking a cue from the screen, suggesting that in the future he use the bank's deposit-only line.

The touchy young woman on the screen is tougher. Speaking fast, she says she wants to cash a $150 check, get $40 in cash, and put $65 in savings and the rest in checking. As an applicant struggles to sort that out, she quickly adds, "No, it has to be $50 in checking because I just wrote a check this morning." If the applicant then touches a label on the screen that says "?" the woman fumes, "How many times do I have to tell you?"

Great Western reports success with its new system. It dramatically reduced useless personal interviewing of unacceptable candidates. And, partly because the candidates see what the job's really like, those hired are reportedly 26% less likely to quit or be fired within 90 days of hiring.

"Productivity Through HRIS" illustrates how firms integrate Web-based interviews with applicant tracking.

Improving Productivity Through HRIS

Automated Video-Based Interview Systems

Many firms use the Web to assist in the employee interview process. For several years, for instance, Cisco Systems, Inc., has been equipping Cisco HR recruiters with a PC-based video camera, so they can conduct preliminary interviews via online Webcasts. The basic idea is this: The recruiter instructs the applicant to use his or her own camera-supported PC (or go to a local Kinko's or similar business). Then, at the appointed time, he or she links to Cisco via Web video for the interview. Cisco doesn't plan to eliminate face-to-face interviews. However, the Web-video interviews do reduce travel and recruiting expenses, and make things easier for candidates.

Cisco isn't alone in using the Web to streamline the interview process. For example, jobs.com conducts frequent live, interactive online career fairs. Job seekers go to the jobs.com interactive career Web site and select a city and job category. They can then participate in a live, interactive career fair event. The U.S. Army also now does online recruiting at its recruiter chat site.

Several companies integrate Web-based employment interviews with applicant tracking capabilities. The virtual interview portal from Treeba is an example (see www.TREEBA.COM/SOLUTIONS/VIPASP). The company's TreebaHire™ combines automated applicant tracking with virtual Web-based interviews. Treeba is an applications service provider. It maintains the Web-based systems on its own servers, so users are actually on the Treeba site when they click to apply for a job at the employer's own Web sites.

The TreebaHire system boosts productivity by automating the entire prescreening process. The system uses not live interviews, but previously recorded video interviews from the employer's interviewers. After the candidate successfully completes and passes the system's first-stage in-depth written screening test, the system invites the candidate, via e-mail, to participate in a virtual video interview. At this interview, the candidate responds to customized, prerecorded video interview questions and/or scenarios that the employer previously designed and recorded.

The TreebaHire system has several advantages. It eliminates the need for interviewers to schedule interview times with prospective candidates, and basically automates the entire time-consuming and expensive "prescreening" interview process. Using this system, the employer's recruiters can then, at their leisure, review the interviews and (via the Web) comment on and analyze the results with the company's other managers, and decide whom to bring in for additional screening. The system also automatically tracks each candidate's activity. It even lets the employer go back and "mine" the test and video interview databank of past and present candidates for newly created positions.

Are Interviews Useful?

While used by virtually all managers, interviews received low marks for reliability and validity in early studies. However, today (as noted previously), studies confirm that the "validity of the interview is greater than previously believed,"[26] and that the interview is "generally a much better predictor of performance than previously thought and is comparable with many other selection techniques."[27]

But there are three caveats. First, you should structure the interview.[28] The research generally suggests that structured interviews (particularly structured situational interviews) have validities about twice those of unstructured interviews.[29] Situational interviews yield a higher mean validity than do job-related (or behavioral) interviews, which in turn yield a higher mean validity than do psychological interviews.[30] However, structured interviews, regardless of content, are more valid than unstructured interviews.[31]

The second caveat is this: Be careful what sorts of traits you try to assess. A typical study illustrates why. Interviewers were able to size up the interviewee's extraversion and agreeableness. What they could *not* assess accurately were the traits that often matter most on jobs—like conscientiousness and emotional stability.[32] The implication seems to be: Do not try to focus (as many do) on hard-to-assess traits like conscientiousness. Limit yourself mostly to situational and job knowledge questions that help you assess how the candidate will actually respond to typical situations on that job. We'll explain how to do this later in the chapter. Third: Understand the factors that undermine interviews.

2 Explain and illustrate at least six factors that affect the usefulness of interviews.

● WHAT CAN UNDERMINE AN INTERVIEW'S USEFULNESS?

Hiring the right people is a crucial management job, and you can't do that job well if you don't know how to interview. Several things can undermine an interview's usefulness.

First Impressions

One of the most consistent findings is that interviewers tend to jump to conclusions—make snap judgments—about candidates during the first few minutes of the interview (or even before the interview starts, based on test scores or résumé data). One researcher estimates that in 85% of the cases, interviewers had made up their minds before the interview began, based on first impressions gleaned from candidates' application forms and personal appearance. In one study, giving interviewers candidates' test scores biased their ultimate assessment of the candidates.[33] For example, interview results related to hiring decisions only when the candidates had low passing scores on a previous selection test. For candidates with high test scores, the interview results were not related to the interviewers' decisions (assumedly because they'd already made their minds up).[34]

First impressions are thus especially damaging when the information about the candidate is negative. In another study, interviewers who previously received unfavorable reference letters about applicants gave those applicants less credit for past successes and held them more personally responsible for past failures after the interview. And their final decisions (to accept or reject applicants) were always tied to what they expected of the applicants based on the references, quite aside from the applicants' actual interview performance.[35]

In other words, interviewers seem to have a consistent negative bias. They are more influenced by unfavorable than favorable information about the candidate. Furthermore, their impressions are much more likely to change from favorable to unfavorable than from unfavorable to favorable. Indeed, a common interviewing mistake is to turn the interview into a search for negative information. In a sense, therefore, most interviews are probably loaded against the applicant. An applicant who starts well could easily end up with a low rating, because unfavorable information tends to carry more weight in the interview. An interviewee who starts out poorly will find it hard to overcome that first bad impression.[36]

One London-based psychologist who interviewed the chief executives of 80 top companies came to these conclusions about snap judgments in selection interviews: "Really, to make a good impression, you don't even get time to open your mouth . . . An interviewer's response to you will generally be preverbal—how you walk through the door, what your posture is like, whether you smile, whether you have a captivating aura, whether you have a firm, confident handshake. You've got about half a minute to make an impact and after that all you are doing is building on a good or bad first impression . . . It's a very emotional response."[37]

Misunderstanding the Job

It's also important to know what you're looking for in an ideal candidate. Interviewers who don't know precisely what the job entails and what sort of candidate is best suited for it usually make their decisions based on incorrect stereotypes of what a good applicant is. They then erroneously match interviewees with their incorrect stereotypes.

One classic study involved 30 professional interviewers.[38] Half got just a brief description of the jobs for which they were recruiting: They were told the "eight applicants here represented by their application blanks are applying for the position of secretary." The other 15 interviewers got much more explicit job information, in terms of typing speed and bilingual ability, for instance.

More job knowledge translated into better interviews. The 15 interviewers who had more job information generally agreed among themselves about each candidate's potential, while those without complete job information did not. The latter also did not discriminate as well among applicants—they tended to give them all high ratings.

Candidate-Order (Contrast) Error and Pressure to Hire

candidate-order error
An error of judgment on the part of the interviewer due to interviewing one or more very good or very bad candidates just before the interview in question.

Candidate-order (or contrast) error means that the order in which you see applicants affects how you rate them. In one study, managers had to evaluate a candidate who was "just average" after first evaluating several "unfavorable" candidates. They scored the average candidate more favorably than they might otherwise have done since, in contrast to the unfavorable candidates, the average one looked better than he actually was. This contrast effect can be huge: In some early studies, evaluators based only a small part of the applicant's rating on his or her actual potential.[39]

Pressure to hire accentuates problems like this. Researchers told one group of managers to assume they were behind in their recruiting quota. They told a second group they were ahead of their quota. Those "behind" evaluated the same recruits much more highly than did those "ahead."[40]

Nonverbal Behavior and Impression Management

The applicant's nonverbal behavior can also have a surprisingly large impact on his or her rating. In one study, 52 HR specialists watched videotaped job interviews in which the applicants' verbal content was identical, but their nonverbal behavior differed markedly. Researchers told those in one group to exhibit minimal eye contact, a low energy level, and low voice modulation. Those in a second group demonstrated the opposite behavior. Of the 26 personnel specialists who saw the high-eye-contact, high-energy-level candidate, 23 would have invited him or her for a second interview. None who saw the low-eye-contact, low-energy-level candidate would have recommended a second interview.[41] It certainly seems to pay for interviewees to "look alive."

In another study, interviewers listened to audio interviews and watched video interviews. Vocal cues (such as the interviewee's pitch, speech rates, and pauses) and visual cues (such as physical attractiveness, smile, and body orientation) correlated with the evaluator's judgments of whether or not the interviewees could be liked and trusted, and were credible.[42]

Why are the candidates' nonverbal behaviors so important? Perhaps because, accurately or not, interviewers infer the interviewee's personality from the way he or she acts in the interview. In one study, 99 graduating college seniors completed questionnaires both before and after their job interviews; the questionnaires included measures of personality, among other things.[43] They then reported their success in generating follow-up job interviews and job offers. The interviewee's personality, particularly his or her level of extraversion, had a pronounced influence on whether or not he or she received follow-up interviews and job offers. In part, this seems to be because "interviewers draw inferences about the applicant's personality based on the applicant's behavior during the interview."[44] Extraverted applicants seem particularly prone to self-promotion, and self-promotion is strongly related to the interviewer's perceptions of candidate–job fit.[45]

Of course, clever interviewees take advantage of this, by managing the impression they present. One study found some used ingratiation to persuade interviewers to like them, for instance by praising them or appearing to agree with their opinions. Others used self-promotion tactics, for instance by making complimentary comments about their own accomplishments.[46]

Yet while it's true that applicant behaviors that seem to reflect extraversion and conscientiousness probably do translate into higher ratings, it's not clear that such findings always apply in real-world settings. The problem is that much of the interviewing research uses students as raters, and hypothetical jobs, so it's not clear that we can apply the findings to the real world. For example, "In operational settings, where actual jobs are at stake, faking or socially desirable responding may be more likely to distort personality measurement and obscure relationships."[47]

Effect of Personal Characteristics: Attractiveness, Gender, Race

Interviewers also must guard against letting an applicant's attractiveness and gender distort their assessments.[48] In general, individuals ascribe more favorable traits and more successful life outcomes to attractive people.[49] In one study, subjects had to evaluate candidates for promotion based on photographs. They perceived men as being more suitable for hire and more likely to advance to a next executive level than they did equally qualified women; they preferred more attractive candidates, especially men, over less attractive ones.[50] "Even when female managers exhibited the same career-advancing behaviors as male managers, they still earned less money and were offered fewer career-progressing transfer opportunities."[51]

Race can also play a role, depending on how you conduct the interview. In one study, the interviewees appeared before three panels whose racial composition was either primarily black (75% black, 25% white), racially balanced (50% black, 50% white), or primarily white (75% white, 25% black).[52] On the primarily black panels, black and white raters judged black and white candidates similarly. In the primarily white and in the racially balanced panels, white interviewers rated white candidates higher, while black interviewers rated black candidates higher. However, in all cases, structured interviews produced less of a difference between minority and white interviewees on average than did unstructured interviews.[53] Such findings don't necessarily apply to other EEOC-protected classes. In another study of structured interviews, candidates evidencing a wide range of specific attributes and disabilities (such as child-care demands, HIV-positive status, and being wheelchair-bound) had less chance of obtaining a positive decision, even when the person performed very well in the structured interview.[54]

Recognizing that the applicant's "race, gender, hair style, teeth and even facial ticks" can influence the interview process in a discriminatory way, the European Community is considering a new directive. It would require that employers conduct recruitment interviews with screens between the applicant and the interviewers, or over a room-to-room speakerphone.[55] "The New Workplace" expands on this topic.

Interviewer Behavior

The *interviewer's* behavior also has an effect on the interviewee's performance and rating. For example, some interviewers inadvertently *telegraph* the expected answers,[65] as in: "This job calls for handling a lot of stress. You can do that, can't you?" Telegraphing isn't always so obvious. For example, subtle cues (like a smile or nod) can telegraph the desired answer.[66] Some interviewers talk so much applicants have no time to answer questions. At the other extreme, some interviewers let the applicant dominate the interview, and so don't ask all their questions.[67] Neither is a good situation. Similarly, when interviewers have favorable pre-interview impressions of the applicant, they tend to act more positively toward that person (smiling more, for instance), possibly because they want to increase the chance that the applicant will accept the job.[68]

Other interviewers play district attorney or psychologist. It's smart to be alert for inconsistencies, but uncivil to play "gotcha" by gleefully pouncing on them. Some interviewers play amateur psychologist, unprofessionally probing for hidden meanings in everything the applicants say.[69]

The demographic similarity between interviewers and applicants may also have a small effect on how interviewers rate applicants. For example, a perceived similarity in attitudes may influence how the interviewer rates the applicant's competence.[70]

● DESIGNING AND CONDUCTING THE EFFECTIVE INTERVIEW

There are two basic ways to avoid these interview problems. One is obvious: Keep them in mind and avoid them (don't play psychologist or make snap judgements, for instance). The second is not quite so obvious: Be careful how you design and structure the interview. Let's look next at structuring the interview, and at some guidelines for an effective interview.

The Structured Situational Interview

There is little doubt that the structured situational interview—a series of hypothetical, job-oriented questions with predetermined answers that interviewers ask of all applicants for the job—produces superior results.[71] Structured employment interviews using either situational questions or behavioral questions tend to yield high criteria-related validities. (This is particularly so where the raters can use descriptively anchored rating scale answer sheets to rate the interviewees' answers; these use short descriptions to illustrate good, average, or poor performance).[72] However, structured interviews with situational question formats yield the higher ratings. This may be because interviewers get more consistent (reliable) responses with situational questions (which force all

The New Workplace

Applicant Disability and the Employment Interview

In general, research findings regarding the impact of applicant disability on interview ratings are inconsistent. Some studies conclude disability has a positive impact on the applicant's ratings while others report a negative impact, or no impact.[56] However, studies do suggest that what the applicant voluntarily reveals about his on her disability does influence the hire/no-hire decision. For example, applicants who disclose a nonobvious disability tend to receive more favorable responses. Yet here again, the use of student raters means that we have to be cautious about these findings. For example, "students might give disabled applicants high ratings because, unlike real interviewers, they will not face negative feedback from supervisors who are required to exert effort to provide the hired applicant with an accommodation."[57]

A study by the Research and Evaluation Center at the National Center for Disability Services provides some insight into what disabled people who use "assistive technology" at work expect and prefer from interviewers.[58] Researchers surveyed 40 disabled people from various occupations to arrive at their conclusions. The basic finding was that, from the disabled person's point of view, interviewers tend to avoid directly addressing the disability, and therefore make their decisions without getting all the facts. What the disabled people prefer is an open discussion, one that would allow the employer to clarify his or her concerns and reach a knowledgeable conclusion. Among the questions disabled persons said they would like interviewers to ask were these:

- Is there any kind of setting or special equipment that will facilitate the interview process for you?
- Is there any specific technology that you currently use or have used in previous jobs that assists the way you work?
- Other than technology, what other kind of support did you have in previous jobs? If none, is there anything that would benefit you?
- Provide an example of how you would use technology to carry out your job duties.

- Is there any technology that you don't currently have that would be helpful in performing the duties of this position?
- In the past, did you experience any problems between your technology and the company's information systems?
- Do you foresee your technology needs changing in the near future? Why and how?
- Discuss a barrier or obstacle, if any, that you have encountered in any of your previous jobs. How was that addressed?
- Do you anticipate any transportation or scheduling issues with the work schedule expected of this position?

Remember that, under the Americans with Disabilities Act, the interviewer must limit his or her questions to whether the applicant has any physical or mental impairment that may interfere with his or her ability to perform the job's essential tasks.[59]

Employment discrimination like this is always abhorrent, but the use of employment discrimination "testers" makes nondiscriminatory interviewing even more important today. As defined by the EEOC, testers are "individuals who apply for employment which they do not intend to accept, for the sole purpose of uncovering unlawful discriminatory hiring practices."[60] Although they're not really seeking employment, testers have legal standing, with the courts[61] and with the EEOC.[62]

A case illustrates the usual approach. A private, nonprofit civil rights advocacy group sent four university students—two white, two black—to an employment agency, supposedly in pursuit of a job. The testers were given backgrounds and training to make them appear almost indistinguishable from each other in terms of qualifications: However, the white applicants and black applicants were allegedly treated differently. For example, the white tester/applicants got interviews and job offers, while the black tester/applicants got neither interviews nor offers.[63] Such unequal treatment appears to be widespread.[64]

applicants to apply the same scenario) than they do with behavioral questions (which require each applicant to find applicable experiences.)[73] In creating structured situational interviews, people familiar with the job develop situational ("What would you do if . . . ") and job knowledge questions based on the job's actual duties. They then reach consensus on what are and are not acceptable answers. The procedure is as follows.[74]

Step 1: **Job Analysis** Write a job description with a list of job duties, required knowledge, skills, abilities, and other worker qualifications.

Step 2: **Rate the Job's Main Duties** Identify the job's main duties. To do so, rate each job duty based on its importance to job success and on the time required to perform it compared to other tasks.

Step 3: **Create Interview Questions** Create interview questions that are based on actual job duties, with more questions for the important duties.

Structured situational interviews may actually contain three types of questions. *Situational questions* pose a hypothetical job situation, such as "What would you do if the machine suddenly began heating up?" *Job knowledge questions* assess knowledge essential to job performance. These often deal with technical aspects of a job (such as "What is HTML?"). *Willingness questions* gauge the applicant's willingness and motivation to meet the job's requirements—to do repetitive physical work or to travel, for instance.

The people who create the questions usually write them in terms of critical incidents. For example, for a supervisory candidate, the interviewer might ask:

> *Your spouse and two teenage children are sick in bed with colds. There are no relatives or friends available to look in on them. Your shift starts in three hours. What would you do in this situation?*

Step 4: **Create Benchmark Answers** Next, for each question, develop several descriptive answers and a five-point rating scale for each, with ideal answers for good (a 5 rating), marginal (a 3 rating), and poor (a 1 rating). Consider the preceding situational question, where the spouse and children are sick. Each member of the committee writes good, marginal, and poor answers based on things they have actually heard in an interview from people who then turned out to be good, marginal, or poor (as the case may be) on the job. After a group discussion, they reach consensus on the answers to use as benchmarks for each scenario. Three benchmark answers for the example question might be, "I'd stay home—my spouse and family come first" (1); "I'd phone my supervisor and explain my situation" (3); and "Since they only have colds, I'd come to work" (5).

Step 5: **Appoint the Interview Panel and Conduct Interviews** Companies generally conduct structured situational interviews using a panel, rather than sequentially. The panel usually consists of three to six members, preferably the same ones who wrote the questions and answers. It may also include the job's supervisor and/or incumbent, and an HR representative. The same panel interviews all candidates for the job.[75]

The panel members generally review the job description, questions, and benchmark answers before the interview. One panel member usually introduces the applicant, and asks all questions of all applicants in this and succeeding interviews (to ensure consistency). However, all panel members record and rate the applicant's answers on the rating scale sheet; they do this by indicating where the candidate's answer to each question falls relative to the ideal poor, marginal, or good answers. At the end of the interview, someone explains the follow-up procedure and answers any questions the applicant has.[76]

On the other hand, some employers seem to be quite successful without either situational or behavioral structured interviews. For example, the Container Store (which often tops the lists of best employers to work for) requires each applicant to have two to three screening interviews, each of which lasts two to three hours.[77] As one Container Store HR manager puts it, "They are often more like noninterview discussions, so that our interviews do not put people off guard. They put people at ease."

Explain and illustrate each guideline for being a more effective interviewer.

How to Conduct a More Effective Interview

You may not have the time or inclination to create structured situational interviews. However, there is still a lot you can do to make your interviews more effective. Suggestions include:

Structure Your Interview   There are several things you can do to increase the standardization of the interview or otherwise assist the interviewer to ask more consistent and job-relevant questions, without actually creating a structured situational interview.[78] They include:[79]

1. Base questions on actual job duties. This will minimize irrelevant questions. It may also reduce the likelihood of bias, because there's less opportunity to "read" things into the answer.

2. Use job knowledge, situational, or behaviorally oriented questions and objective criteria to evaluate the interviewee's responses. Questions that simply ask for opinions and attitudes, goals and aspirations, and self-descriptions and self-evaluations allow candidates to present themselves in an overly favorable manner or avoid revealing weaknesses. Structured interview questions can reduce subjectivity and therefore the chance for inaccurate conclusions, and bias.[80] Figure 7-3 illustrates some structured interview questions.

Figure 7-3
Examples of Questions That Provide Structure
Source: Michael Campion, David Palmer, and James Campion, "A Review of Structure in the Selection Interview," *Personnel Psychology* (1997), p. 668.

Situational Questions:
1. Suppose a co-worker was not following standard work procedures. The co-worker was more experienced than you and claimed the new procedure was better. Would you use the new procedure?
2. Suppose you were giving a sales presentation and a difficult technical question arose that you could not answer. What would you do?

Past Behavior Questions:
3. Based on your past work experience, what is the most significant action you have ever taken to help out a co-worker?
4. Can you provide an example of a specific instance where you developed a sales presentation that was highly effective?

Background Questions:
5. What work experiences, training, or other qualifications do you have for working in a teamwork environment?
6. What experience have you had with direct point-of-purchase sales?

Job Knowledge Questions:
7. What steps would you follow to conduct a brainstorming session with a group of employees on safety?
8. What factors should you consider when developing a television advertising campaign?

3. Train interviewers. For example, review EEO laws with prospective interviewers and train them to avoid irrelevant or potentially discriminatory questions and to avoid stereotyping minority candidates. Also train them to base their questions on job-related information.

4. Use the same questions with all candidates. When it comes to asking questions, the prescription seems to be "the more standardized, the better." Using the same questions with all candidates can also reduce bias "because of the obvious fairness of giving all the candidates the exact same opportunity."

5. Use descriptive rating scales (excellent, fair, poor) to rate answers. For each question, if possible, provide three to five possible ideal answers and a quantitative score for each. Then you can rate each candidate's answers against this scale. This ensures that all interviewers are using the same standards.

6. Use multiple interviewers or panel interviews. Doing so can reduce bias by diminishing the importance of one interviewer's idiosyncratic opinions, and by bringing in more points of view.

7. If possible, use a standardized interview form. Interviews based on structured guides like the one in Figure 7-1 usually result in the best interviews.[81] At the very least, list your questions before the interview.

8. Control the interview. Techniques here include, limiting the interviewers' follow-up questions (to ensure all interviewees get the same questions), using a larger number of questions, and prohibiting questions from candidates until after the interview.[82]

9. Take brief, unobtrusive notes during the interview. Doing so may help overcome "the recency effect" (putting too much weight on the last few minutes of the interview). It may also help avoid making a quick decision based on inadequate information early in the interview, and may also help jog your memory once the interview is complete. (Yet, the research on interview note taking is sparse. A recent study did confirm that note taking helped interviewers recall the interviewee's behavior. On the other hand, at least, in this study those who did take notes were no more accurate in sizing up interviewees than those who did not. The bottom line seems to be to take notes, but not copious ones, instead noting just the key points of what the interviewee says).[83]

Prepare for the Interview   The interview should take place in a private room where telephone calls are not accepted and you can minimize interruptions. Prior to the interview, review the candidate's application and résumé, and note any areas that are vague or that may indicate strengths or weaknesses. In one study, about 39% of the 191 respondents said interviewers were unprepared or unfocused.[84]

Remember, it's essential that you know the duties of the job, and the specific skills and traits you should be looking for. Most interviews probably fail to unearth the best candidate because the interviewer is unprepared, or overconfident, or just plain lazy. General questions like, "What are your main strengths?" or "Why did you leave your last job?" may not be totally useless. But what you really want to do is go into the interview with a set of specific questions that focus on the skills and experiences the ideal candidate for that job needs. At a minimum, review the job specifications. Go into the interview with an accurate picture of the traits of an ideal candidate, know what you're going to ask—and keep an open mind about the candidate. Remember that interviewers often make snap judgments based on first impressions. Keep a record of the answers, and review them after the interview. Make your decision then.

One key to a successful interview is often the interviewer's attitude. Greeting the person in a welcoming manner and putting him or her at ease can go a long way toward making the interview pleasant and productive for both parties.

Establish Rapport   The main reason for the interview is to find out about the applicant. To do this, you need to put the person at ease. Greet all applicants—even drop-ins—courteously and start the interview with a noncontroversial question—perhaps about the weather.

Be aware of the applicant's status. For example, if the person is unemployed, or is coming back to the workforce after many years, he or she may be exceptionally nervous, and you may want to take additional steps to put the person at ease.[85]

Ask Questions   Follow your list of questions. (Figure 7-4 presents additional sample questions.) Some do's and don'ts for actually asking questions include: Don't ask questions that can be answered yes or no; don't put words in the applicant's mouth or telegraph the desired answer; don't interrogate the applicant as if the person is a criminal, and don't be patronizing, sarcastic, or inattentive; don't monopolize the interview or let the applicant dominate the interview; do ask open-ended questions; do listen to the candidate to encourage him or her to express thoughts fully; and do draw out the applicant's opinions and feelings by repeating the person's last comment as a question (such as "You didn't like your last job?").

Does it make sense for employers to ask applicants about their extracurricular activities? In one study, researchers had 618 college students complete online surveys assessing their level of extracurricular activities. The researchers then had the students participate in an assessment center; here they evaluated the subjects in terms of four dimensions—communication, initiative, decision making, and teamwork. "The results revealed that extracurricular activities are significantly associated with each of the four interpersonal skill dimensions."[86]

Finally, when you ask for general statements of a candidate's accomplishments, ask for examples.[87] If the candidate lists specific strengths or weaknesses, follow up with "What are specific examples that demonstrate each of your strengths?"

One way to get more candid answers is to mention that you're going to conduct reference checks. Ask, "If I were to arrange for an interview with your boss, and if the boss were very candid with me, what's your best guess as to what he or she would say as your strengths, weaker points, and overall performance?"[88]

Figure 7-4
Suggested Supplementary Questions for Interviewing Applicants

Source: Reprinted from www.HR.BLR.com with permission of the publisher. © 2004 Business and Legal Reports, Inc. 141 Mill Rock Road East, Old Saybrook, CT 06475.

1. How did you choose this line of work?
2. What did you enjoy most about your last job?
3. What did you like least about your last job?
4. What has been your greatest frustration or disappointment on your present job? Why?
5. What are some of the pluses and minuses of your last job?
6. What were the circumstances surrounding your leaving your last job?
7. Did you give notice?
8. Why should we be hiring you?
9. What do you expect from this employer?
10. What are three things you will not do in your next job?
11. What would your last supervisor say your three weaknesses are?
12. What are your major strengths?
13. How can your supervisor best help you obtain your goals?
14. How did your supervisor rate your job performance?
15. In what ways would you change your last supervisor?
16. What are your career goals during the next 1–3 years? 5–10 years?
17. How will working for this company help you reach those goals?
18. What did you do the last time you received instructions with which you disagreed?
19. What are some of the things about which you and your supervisor disagreed? What did you do?
20. Which do you prefer, working alone or working with groups?
21. What motivated you to do better at your last job?
22. Do you consider your progress on that job representative of your ability? Why?
23. Do you have any questions about the duties of the job for which you have applied?
24. Can you perform the essential functions of the job for which you have applied?

Close the Interview   Leave time to answer any questions the candidate may have and, if appropriate, to advocate your firm to the candidate.

Try to end the interview on a positive note. Tell the applicant whether there is any interest and, if so, what the next step will be. Make rejections diplomatically: for instance, "Although your background is impressive, there are other candidates whose experience is closer to our requirements." If the applicant is still being considered but you can't reach a decision now, say so. If your policy is to inform candidates of their status in writing, do so within a few days of the interview.

In rejecting a candidate, one perennial question is, should you provide an explanation or not? In one study, rejected candidates who received an explanation detailing why the employer rejected them felt that the rejection process was fairer. These people were also more likely to give the employer a better recommendation, and to apply again for jobs with the firm. Unfortunately, providing detailed explanations may not be practical. As the researchers put it, "We were unsuccessful in a number of attempts to secure a site for our applied study. Of three organizations that expressed interest in our research, all eventually declined to participate in the study because they were afraid that any additional information in the rejection letters might increase legal problems. They were reluctant to give rejected applicants information that can be used to dispute the decision."[89]

Review the Interview   Once the candidate leaves, and while the interview is fresh in your mind, review your notes and fill in the structured interview guide (if you used one and if you did not fill it in during the interview).

Reviewing the interview shortly after the candidate leaves can also help minimize snap judgments and negative emphasis. Some interviewers find videotaping interviews helps them review the top candidates.[90]

Effectively
interview a job
candidate.

Know Your Employment Law

Interviewing Candidates

Various equal employment laws, including Title VII of the Civil Rights Act of 1964 and the Civil Rights Act of 1991, require that employment interviewers exercise caution in which questions they ask, lest they expose their companies to accusations of discriminatory treatment. Questions regarding an applicant's race, color, religion, sex, age, national origin, or disability trigger red flags. Again, it is generally not illegal to ask a female job candidate about marital status, or an 80-year-old applicant "how old are you?" It certainly is not advisable to do so, but the manager can ask such questions as long as he or she can show either that the employer does not discriminate or that it can defend the selection practice (in this case the interview question) as a BFOQ or business necessity. However, while inquiries like these may not be illegal, there are two good reasons to avoid them. First, although federal law may not bar asking them, many state and local laws do. Second, the EEOC has said that it disapproves of such practices as asking women their marital status or applicants their age. Such questions may thus draw the attention of the EEOC and other regulatory agencies.

If a protected group member does bring a charge of discrimination against the employer, what will sway the court to find in favor of the employer? A study of federal district court cases involving alleged employment interview discrimination provides some insights. The most important action seems to be to ensure that the interview process is structured and consistently applied. Three dimensions of interview structure, (1) having objective/job-related questions, (2) standardizing interview administration, and (3) having multiple interviewers, were related to verdicts in favor of employers.[91] Panel or series situational or behavioral structured interviews thus seem particularly defensible here.

Of course, the best approach is to avoid having job candidates file charges in the first place. Here, it is possible that "applicant perceptions of some forms of organizational justice . . . would reduce the frequency of such unfounded discrimination claims." If so, endeavor to make it clear to applicants that the interview process is fair, that the interviewer treats the interviewee with courtesy and respect, and that the interviewer is willing to explain the interview process and the nature and rationale for the questions.[92]

The following "When You're On Your Own" feature provides additional interviewing guidance for managers.

When You're On Your Own

HR for Line Managers and Entrepreneurs

HR and the Small Business

Prescriptions like "know the job," "know the skills you're looking for," and "structure the job interview" can be easier said than done, even if you're working at a *Fortune* 500 company (and, certainly if you're on your own as an entrepreneur). All the corporate resources won't do you much good if, as often happens, the company hasn't made provisions to provide employment interview training and support for its managers. There you sit with a candidate about to arrive for her job interview. What should you do?

Following this chapter's guidelines is probably the preferred approach, but perhaps you don't have the time to create, say, a structured situational interview. What follows is a streamlined procedure for crafting job-relevant questions and interviews.[93]

Preparing for the Interview

Even a busy entrepreneur or manager can quickly specify the kind of person who would be best for the job. One way to do so is to focus on four basic required factors—knowledge and experience, motivation, intellectual capacity, and personality—and to ask the following questions:

- *Knowledge and experience:* What must the candidate know to perform the job? What experience is absolutely necessary to perform the job?

- *Motivation:* What should the person like doing to enjoy this job? Is there anything the person should not dislike? Are there any essential goals or aspirations the person should have? Are there any unusual energy demands on the job?
- *Intellectual capacity:* Are there any specific intellectual aptitudes required (mathematical, mechanical, and so on)? How complex are the problems the person must solve? What must a person be able to demonstrate he or she can do intellectually? How should the person solve problems (cautiously, deductively, and so on)?
- *Personality factor:* What are the critical personality qualities needed for success on the job (ability to withstand boredom, decisiveness, stability, and so on)? How must the job incumbent handle stress, pressure, and criticism? What kind of interpersonal behavior is required in the job up the line, at peer level, down the line, and outside the firm with customers?

Specific Factors to Probe in the Interview

Next, ask a combination of situational questions, plus open-ended questions like those in Figure 7-4, to probe the candidate's suitability for the job. For example:

- *Intellectual factor.* Here, assess such things as complexity of tasks the person has performed, grades in school, test results (including scholastic aptitude tests, and so on), and how the person organizes his or her thoughts and communicates.
- *Motivation factor.* Probe such areas as: the person's likes and dislikes (for each thing done, what he or she liked or disliked about it); aspirations (including the validity of each goal in terms of the person's reasoning about why he or she chose it); and energy level, perhaps by asking what he or she does on, say, a "typical Tuesday."
- *Personality factor.* Probe by looking for self-defeating behaviors (aggressiveness, compulsive fidgeting, and so on) and by exploring the person's past interpersonal relationships. Ask questions about the person's past interactions (working in a group at school, working with fraternity

brothers or sorority sisters, leading the work team on the last job, and so on). Also, try to judge the person's behavior in the interview itself—is the candidate personable? Shy? Outgoing?
- *Knowledge and experience factor.* Probe with situational questions such as "How would you organize such a sales effort?" "How would you design that kind of Web site?"

Conducting the Interview

Have a Plan You should also devise and use a plan to guide the interview. According to interviewing expert John Drake, significant areas to cover include the candidate's:

- College experiences
- Work experiences—summer, part-time
- Work experience—full-time (one by one)
- Goals and ambitions
- Reactions to the job you are interviewing for
- Self-assessments (by the candidate of his or her strengths and weaknesses)
- Military experiences
- Present outside activities[94]

Follow Your Plan Perhaps start with an open-ended question for each topic, such as, "Could you tell me about what you did when you were in high school?" Keep in mind that you are trying to elicit information about four main traits—intelligence, motivation, personality, and knowledge and experience. You can then accumulate the information in each of these four areas as the person answers. Follow up on particular areas that you want to pursue by asking questions like, "Could you elaborate on that, please?"

Match the Candidate to the Job After following the interview plan and probing for the four factors, you should be able to draw conclusions about the person's intellectual capacity, knowledge and experience, motivation, and personality, and to summarize the candidate's general strengths and limitations. You should then compare your conclusions to both the job description and the list of behavioral specifications you developed when preparing for the interview. This should provide a rational basis for matching the candidate to the job—one based on an analysis of the traits and aptitudes the job actually requires.

You might use an interview evaluation form to compile your impressions (see Figure 7-5)

Figure 7-5
Interview Evaluation Form
Source: Reprinted from
www.HR.BLR.com with permission
of the publisher. © 2004 Business and
Legal Reports Inc. 141 Mill Rock
Road East, Old Saybrook, CT 06475.

Name of candidate:

Date interviewed:

Position:

Completed by:

Date:

Instructions: Circle one number for each criterion, then add them together for a total.

KNOWLEDGE OF SPECIFIC JOB AND JOB-RELATED TOPICS

0. No knowledge evident.
1. Less than we would prefer.
2. Meets requirements for hiring.
3. Exceeds our expectations of average candidates.
4. Thoroughly versed in job and very strong in associated areas.

EXPERIENCE

0. None for this job; no related experience either.
1. Would prefer more for this job. Adequate for job applied for.
2. More than sufficient for job.
3. Totally experienced in job.
4. Strong experience in all related areas.

COMMUNICATION

0. Could not communicate. Will be severely impaired in most jobs.
1. Some difficulties. Will detract from job performance.
2. Sufficient for adequate job performance.
3. More than sufficient for job.
4. Outstanding ability to communicate.

INTEREST IN POSITION AND ORGANIZATION

0. Showed no interest.
1. Some lack of interest.
2. Appeared genuinely interested.
3. Very interested. Seems to prefer type of work applied for.
4. Totally absorbed with job content. Conveys feeling only this job will do.

OVERALL MOTIVATION TO SUCCEED

0. None exhibited.
1. Showed little interest in advancement.
2. Average interest in advancement.
3. Highly motivated. Strong desire to advance.
4. Extremely motivated. Very strong desire to succeed and advance.

POISE AND CONFIDENCE

0. Extremely distracted and confused. Displayed uneven temper.
1. Sufficient display of confusion or loss of temper to interfere with job performance.
2. Sufficient poise and confidence to perform job.
3. No loss of poise during interview. Confidence in ability to handle pressure.
4. Displayed impressive poise under stress. Appears unusually confident and secure.

COMPREHENSION

0. Did not understand many points and concepts.
1. Missed some ideas or concepts.
2. Understood most new ideas and skills discussed.
3. Grasped all new points and concepts quickly.
4. Extremely sharp. Understood subtle points and underlying motives.

_____ **TOTAL POINTS**

ADDITIONAL REMARKS:

 *Review*

SUMMARY

1. There are several basic types of interviews—situational, nondirective, structured, sequential, panel, stress, and appraisal interviews, for instance. We can classify interviews according to content, structure, and method of administration.

2. Several factors and problems can undermine the usefulness of an interview. These are making premature decisions, letting unfavorable information predominate, not knowing the requirements of the job, being under pressure to hire, the candidate-order effect, and sending visual cues to telegraph enthusiasm.

3. The five steps in the interview are: Plan, establish rapport, question the candidate, close the interview, and review the data.

4. Guidelines for interviewers include: Use a structured guide, know the requirements of the job, focus on traits you can more accurately evaluate, let the interviewee do most of the talking, delay your decision until after the interview, and remember the EEOC requirements.

5. Increasingly, employers use computers and the Web to assist in the employee interview process. As explained in this chapter, firms now conduct at least the preliminary inter-views online, often using video-assisted scenarios. Several of the newer systems combine initial interviews with applicant tracking, to facilitate the employee selection process.

6. The steps in a structured or situational interview are: Analyze the job, evaluate the job duty information, develop interview questions with critical incidents, develop benchmark answers, appoint an interview committee, and implement.

7. A quick procedure for conducting an interview is to develop behavioral specifications; determine the basic intellectual, motivational, personality, and experience factors to probe for; use an interview plan; and then match the individual to the job.

8. As an interviewee, keep in mind that interviewers tend to make premature decisions and let unfavorable information predominate; your appearance and enthusiasm are important; you should get the interviewer to talk; it is important to prepare before walking in—get to know the job and the problems the interviewer wants solved; and you should stress your enthusiasm and motivation to work, and how your accomplishments match your interviewer's needs. (See the Appendix to this chapter, Guidelines for Interviewees.)

DISCUSSION QUESTIONS

1. Explain and illustrate the basic ways in which you can classify selection interviews.

2. Briefly describe each of the following possible types of interviews; unstructured panel interviews; structured sequential interviews; job-related structured interviews.

3. For what sorts of jobs do you think computerized interviews are most appropriate? Why?

4. Why do you think "situational interviews yield a higher mean validity than do job-related or behavioral interviews, which in turn yield a higher mean validity than do psychological interviews"?

5. Similarly, how would you explain the fact that structured interviews, regardless of content, are more valid than unstructured interviews for predicting job performance?

6. Briefly discuss and give examples of at least five common interviewing mistakes. What recommendations would you give for avoiding these interviewing mistakes?

7. Briefly discuss what an interviewer can do to improve his or her performance.

INDIVIDUAL AND GROUP ACTIVITIES

1. Prepare and give a short presentation titled, "How to Be Effective As an Employment Interviewer."

2. Use the Internet to find employers who now do preliminary selection interviews via the Web. Print out and bring examples to class. Do you think these interviews are useful? Why or why not? How would you improve them?

3. In groups, discuss and compile examples of "the worst interview I ever had." What was it about these interviews

that made them so bad? If time permits, discuss as a class.

4. In groups, prepare an interview (including a sequence of at least 20 questions) you'll use to interview candidates for the job of teaching a course in Human Resources Management. Each group should present their interview questions in class.

5. Some firms swear by unorthodox interview methods. For example, Tech Planet, of Menlo Park, California, uses weekly lunches and "wacky follow-up sessions" as substitutes for first-round job interviews. During the informal meals, candidates are expected to mingle, and they're then reviewed by the Tech Planet employees they meet at the luncheons. One Tech Planet employee asks candidates to ride a unicycle in her office to see if "they'll bond with the corporate culture or not." Toward the end of the screening process, the surviving group of interviewees has to solve brainteasers, and then openly evaluate their fellow candidates' strengths and weaknesses. What do you think of a screening process like this? Specifically, what do you think are its pros and cons? Would you recommend a procedure like this? If so, what changes, if any, would you recommend?[95]

6. In June 2003, Lockheed Martin Corp. sued the Boeing Corp. in Orlando, Florida, accusing it of using Lockheed's trade secrets to help win a multibillion-dollar government contract. Among other things, Lockheed Martin claimed that Boeing had obtained those trade secrets from a former Lockheed Martin employee who switched to Boeing.[96] But in describing methods companies use to commit corporate espionage, one writer says that hiring away the competitor's employees or hiring people to through go its dumpster are just the most obvious methods companies use to commit corporate espionage. As he says, "one of the more unusual scams—sometimes referred to as 'help wanted'—uses a person posing as a corporate headhunter who approaches an employee of the target company with a potentially lucrative job offer. During the interview, the employee is quizzed about his responsibilities, accomplishments and current projects. The goal is to extract important details without the employee realizing there is no job."[97]

Assume that you are the owner of a small high-tech company that is worried about the possibility that one or more of your employees may be approached by one of these sinister "headhunters." What would you do (in terms of employee training, or a letter from you, for instance) to try to minimize the chance that one of your employees will fall into that kind of a trap? Also, compile a list of ten questions that you think such a corporate spy might ask one of your employees.

7. The HRCI "Test Specifications" appendix at the end of this book (pages 685–689) lists the knowledge someone studying for the HRCI certification exam needs to have in each area of human resource management (such as in Strategic Management, Workforce Planning, and Human Resource Development). In groups of four to five students, do four things: (1) review that appendix now; (2) identify the material in this chapter that relates to the required knowledge the appendix lists; (3) write four multiple choice exam questions on this material that you believe would be suitable for inclusion in the HRCI exam; and (4) if time permits, have someone from your team post your team's questions in front of the class, so the students in other teams can take each others' exam questions.

EXPERIENTIAL EXERCISE

The Most Important Person You'll Ever Hire

Purpose: The purpose of this exercise is to give you practice using some of the interview techniques you learned from this chapter.

Required Understanding: You should be familiar with the information presented in this chapter, and read this: For parents, children are precious. It's therefore interesting that parents who hire "nannies" to take care of their children usually do little more than ask several interview questions and conduct what is often, at best, a perfunctory reference check. Given the often questionable validity of interviews, and the (often) relative inexperience of the father or mother doing the interviewing, it's not surprising that many of these arrangements end in disappointment. You know from this chapter that it is difficult to conduct a valid interview unless you know exactly what you're looking for and, preferably, also structure the interview. Most parents simply aren't trained to do this.

How to Set Up the Exercise/Instructions:

1. Set up groups of five or six students. Two students will be the interviewees, while the other students in the group will serve as panel interviewers. The interviewees will develop an interviewer assessment form, and the panel interviewers will develop a structured situational interview for a "Nannie."

2. Instructions for the interviewees: The interviewees should leave the room for about 20 minutes. While out of the room, the interviewees should develop an "interviewer assessment form" based on the information presented in this chapter regarding factors that can undermine the usefulness of an interview. During the panel interview, the interviewees should assess the interviewers using the interviewer assessment form. After the panel interviewers have conducted the interview, the interviewees should leave the

room to discuss their notes. Did the interviewers exhibit any of the factors that can undermine the usefulness of an interview? If so, which ones? What suggestions would you (the interviewees) make to the interviewers on how to improve the usefulness of the interview?

3. Instructions for the interviewers: While the interviewees are out of the room, the panel interviewers will have 20 minutes to develop a short structured situational interview form for a "Nannie." The panel interview team will interview two candidates for the position. During the panel interview, each interview should be taking notes on a copy of the structured situational interview form. After the panel interview, the panel interviewers should discuss their notes. What were your first impressions of each interviewee? Were your impressions similar? Which candidate would you all select for the position and why?

APPLICATION CASE

The Out-of-Control Interview

Maria Fernandez is a bright, popular, and well-informed mechanical engineer who graduated with an engineering degree from State University in June 2003. During the spring preceding her graduation, she went out on many job interviews, most of which she thought were conducted courteously and were reasonably useful in giving both her and the prospective employer a good impression of where each of them stood on matters of importance to both of them. It was, therefore, with great anticipation that she looked forward to an interview with the one firm in which she most wanted to work: Apex Environmental. She had always had a strong interest in cleaning up the environment and firmly believed that the best use of her training and skills lay in working for a firm like Apex, where she thought she could have a successful career while making the world a better place.

The interview, however, was a disaster. Maria walked into a room in which five men—the president of the company, two vice presidents, the marketing director, and another engineer—began throwing questions at her that she felt were aimed primarily at tripping her up rather than finding out what she could offer through her engineering skills. The questions ranged from unnecessarily discourteous ("Why would you take a job as a waitress in college if you're such an intelligent person?") to irrelevant and sexist ("Are you planning on settling down and starting a family anytime soon?"). Then, after the interview, she met with two of the gentlemen individually (including the president), and the discussions focused almost exclusively on her technical expertise. She thought that these later discussions went fairly well. However, given the apparent aimlessness and even mean-spiritedness of the panel interview, she was astonished when several days later she got a job offer from the firm.

The offer forced her to consider several matters. From her point of view, the job itself was perfect—she liked what she would be doing, the industry, and the firm's location. And in fact, the president had been quite courteous in subsequent discussions, as had been the other members of the management team. She was left wondering whether the panel interview had been intentionally tense to see how she'd stand up under pressure, and, if so, why they would do such a thing.

Questions

1. How would you explain the nature of the panel interview Maria had to endure? Specifically, do you think it reflected a well-thought-out interviewing strategy on the part of the firm or carelessness on the part of the firm's management? If it was carelessness, what would you do to improve the interview process at Apex Environmental?

2. Would you take the job offer if you were Maria? If you're not sure, is there any additional information that would help you make your decision, and if so, what is it?

3. The job of applications engineer for which Maria was applying requires: (a) excellent technical skills with respect to mechanical engineering; (b) a commitment to working in the area of pollution control; (c) the ability to deal well and confidently with customers who have engineering problems; (d) a willingness to travel worldwide; and (e) a very intelligent and well-balanced personality. List 10 questions you would ask when interviewing applicants for the job.

CONTINUING CASE

Carter Cleaning Company

The Better Interview

Like virtually all the other HR-related activities at Carter Cleaning Centers, the company currently has no organized approach to interviewing job candidates. Store managers, who do almost all the hiring, have a few of their own favorite questions that they ask. But in the absence of any guidance from top management, they all admit their interview performance leaves something to be desired. Similarly, Jack Carter himself is admittedly most comfortable dealing with what he calls the "nuts and bolts" machinery aspect of his business and has never felt particularly comfortable having to interview management or other job applicants. Jennifer is sure that this lack of formal interviewing practices, procedures, and training account for some of the employee turnover and theft problems. Therefore, she wants to do something to improve her company's batting average in this important area. Here are her questions:

Questions

1. In general, what can Jennifer do to improve her employee interviewing practices? Should she develop interview forms that list questions for management and nonmanagement jobs, and if so how should these look and what questions should be included? Should she initiate a computer-based interview approach, and if so why and (specifically) how?

2. Should she implement a training program for her managers, and if so, specifically what should be the content of such an interview training program? In other words, if she did decide to start training her management people to be better interviewers, what should she tell them and how should she tell it to them?

KEY TERMS

unstructured or nondirective interview, 236
structured or directive interview, 236
situational interview, 237
behavioral interviews, 237

job-related interview, 237
unstructured sequential interview, 243
structured sequential interview, 243

panel interview, 243
mass interview, 243
candidate-order error, 247

ENDNOTES

1. Michael McDaniel et al., "The Validity of Employment Interviews: A Comprehensive Review and Meta-analysis," *Journal of Applied Psychology* 79, no. 4 (1994), p. 599. See also Laura Graves and Ronald Karren, "The Employee Selection Interview: A Fresh Look at an Old Problem," *Human Resource Management* 35, no. 2 (Summer 1996), pp. 163–180.

2. L. Ulrich and D. Trumbo, "The Selection Interview Since 1949," *Psychological Bulletin* 63 (1965), pp. 100–116, quoted in Michael McDaniel et al., "The Validity of Employment Interviews," p. 599.

3. Laura Gollub Williamson et al., "Employment Interview on Trial: Linking Interview Structure with Litigation Outcomes," *Journal of Applied Psychology* 82, no. 6 (1996), p. 900.

4. Alan Huffcutt et al., "A Meta-Analytic Investigation of Cognitive Ability in Employment Interview Evaluations: Moderating Characteristics and Implications for Incremental Validity," *Journal of Applied Psychology* 81, no. 5 (1996), p. 459. See also Richard Posthuma, Frederick Morgeson, and Michael Campion, "Beyond Employment Interview Validity: A Comprehensive Narrative Review of Recent Trends over Time," *Personnel Psychology* 55 (2002), p. 18.

5. Duane Schultz and Sydney Schultz, *Psychology and Work Today* (Upper Saddle River, NJ: Prentice Hall, 1998), p. 830.

6. McDaniel et al., "The Validity of Employment Interviews," p. 602.

7. Williamson et al., "Employment Interview on Trial," p. 908.

8. Ibid., p. 601.

9. McDaniel et al., "The Validity of Employment Interviews," p. 602.

10. Bill Stoneman, "Matching Personalities with Jobs Made Easier with Behavioral Interviews," *American Banker*, November 30, 2000, p. 8a.

11. Paul Taylor and Bruce Small, "Asking Applicants What They Would Do Versus What They Did: A Meta-Analytic Comparison of Situational and Past Behavior in Employment Interview Questions," *Journal of Occupational and Organizational Psychology* 75, no. 3 (September 2002), pp. 277–295.

12. "Job Hunt as Head Trip? More Companies Use Behavioral Interviews to Screen Candidates," *Los Angeles Times*, May 20, 2001, p. W.1.

13. Martha Frase-Blunt, "Games Interviewers Play," *HR Magazine*, January 2001, pp. 104–114.

14. Kevin Murphy and Charles David Shofer, *Psychological Testing*. (Upper Saddle River, NJ: Prentice Hall, 2001) pp. 430–431.

15. Marlene Dixon et al., "The Panel Interview: A Review of Empirical Research and Guidelines for Practice," *Public Personnel Management* 31, no. 3 (Fall 2002), pp. 397–429.

16. Ibid.

17. "Phone Interviews Might Be the Most Telling, Study Finds," *BNA Bulletin to Management*, September 1998, p. 273.

18. Susan Strauss et al., "The Effects of Videoconference, Telephone, and Face-to-Face Media on Interviewer and Applicant Judgments in Employment Interviews," *Journal of Management* 27, no. 3 (2001), pp. 363–381.

19. Douglas Rodgers, "Computer-Aided Interviewing Overcomes First Impressions," *Personnel Journal*, April 1987, pp. 148–152; see also Linda Thornburg, "Computer-Assisted Interviewing Shortens Hiring Cycle," *HR Magazine*, February 1998, p. 73ff.

20. Ibid.

21. Gary Robins, "Dial-an-Interview," *Stores*, June 1994, pp. 34–35.

22. William Bulkeley, "Replaced by Technology: Job Interviews," *Wall Street Journal*, August 22, 1994, pp. B1, B7.

23. Ibid.

24. For additional information on computer-aided interviewing's benefits, see, for example, Christopher Martin and Denise Nagao, "Some Effects of Computerized Interviewing on Job Applicant Responses," *Journal of Applied Psychology* 74, no. 1 (February 1989), pp. 72–80.

25. This is quoted from or paraphrased from Bulkeley, "Replaced by Technology," pp. B1, B7.

26. Timothy Judge et al., "The Employment Interview: A Review of Recent Research and Recommendations for Future Research," *Human Resource Management* 10, no. 4 (2000), p. 392.

27. For example, structured employment interviews using either situational questions or behavioral questions tend to yield high criterion-related validities (.63 versus .47). This is particularly so where the raters can use descriptively anchored rating scale answer sheets; these use short descriptors to illustrate good, average, or poor performance. Taylor and Small, "Asking Applicants What They Would Do Versus What They Did," pp. 277–295.

28. Williamson, "Employment Interview on Trial," p. 900.

29. Ibid.

30. This validity discussion and these findings are based on McDaniel et al., "The Validity of Employment Interviews," pp. 607–610; the validities for situational, job-related, and psychological interviews were (.50), (.39), and (.29), respectively.

31. Mean validities were structured (.44) and unstructured (.33). The researchers note that in this case even the unstructured interviews were relatively structured, suggesting that "the validity of most

unstructured interviews used in practice may be lower than the validity found in this study." Ibid., p. 609.

32. Murray Barrick et al., "Accuracy of Interviewer Judgments of Job Applicant Personality Traits," *Personnel Psychology* 53 (2000), pp. 925–951.

33. McDaniel et al., "The Validity of Employment Interviews," p. 608.

34. Anthony Dalessio and Todd Silverhart, "Combining Biodata Test and Interview Information: Predicting Decisions and Performance Criteria," *Personnel Psychology* 47 (1994), p. 313.

35. S. W. Constantin, "An Investigation of Information Favorability in the Employment Interview," *Journal of Applied Psychology* 61 (1976), pp. 743–749. It should be noted that a number of the studies discussed in this chapter involve having interviewers evaluate interviews based on written transcripts (rather than face to face) and that a study suggests that this procedure may not be equivalent to having interviewers interview applicants directly. See Charles Gorman, William Grover, and Michael Doherty, "Can We Learn Anything About Interviewing Real People from 'Interviews' of Paper People? A Study of the External Validity Paradigm," *Organizational Behavior and Human Performance* 22, no. 2 (October 1978), pp. 165–192. See also John Binning et al., "Effects of Pre-interview Impressions on Questioning Strategies in Same and Opposite Sex Employment Interviews," *Journal of Applied Psychology* 73, no. 1 (February 1988), pp. 30–37; and Sebastiana Fisicaro, "A Reexamination of the Relation Between Halo Error and Accuracy," *Journal of Applied Psychology* 73, no. 2 (May 1988), pp. 239–246.

36. David Tucker and Patricia Rowe, "Relationship Between Expectancy, Causal Attribution, and Final Hiring Decisions in the Employment Interview," *Journal of Applied Psychology* 64, no. 1 (February 1979), pp. 27–34. See also Robert Dipboye, Gail Fontenelle, and Kathleen Garner, "Effect of Previewing the Application on Interview Process and Outcomes," *Journal of Applied Psychology* 69, no. 1 (February 1984), pp. 118–128.

37. Anita Chaudhuri, "Beat the Clock: Applying for Job? A New Study Shows That Interviewers Will Make Up Their Minds about You within a Minute," *The Guardian*, June 14, 2000, pp. 2–6.

38. Don Langdale and Joseph Weitz, "Estimating the Influence of Job Information on Interviewer Agreement," *Journal of Applied Psychology* 57 (1973), pp. 23–27; for a review of how to determine the human requirements of a job, see Anthony W. Simmons, "Selection Interviewing," *Employment Relations Today*, Winter 1991, pp. 305–309.

39. R. E. Carlson, "Effects of Applicant Sample on Ratings of Valid Information in an Employment Setting," *Journal of Applied Psychology* 20 (1967), pp. 259–280.

40. R. E. Carlson, "Selection Interview Decisions: The Effects of Interviewer Experience, Relative Quota Situation, and Applicant Sample on Interview Decisions," *Personnel Psychology* 20 (1967), pp. 259–280.

41. T. V. McGovern and H. E. Tinsley, "Interviewer Evaluations of Interviewees' Nonverbal Behavior," *Journal of Vocational Behavior* 13 (1978), pp. 163–171. See also Keith Rasmussen Jr., "Nonverbal Behavior, Verbal Behavior, Resume Credentials, and Selection Interview Outcomes," *Journal of Applied Psychology* 60, no. 4 (1984), pp. 551–556; Robert Gifford, Cheuk Fan Ng, and Margaret Wilkinson, "Nonverbal Cues in the Employment Interview: Links Between Applicant Qualities and Interviewer Judgments," *Journal of Applied Psychology* 70, no. 4 (1984), pp. 729–736; Scott T. Fleishmann, "The Messages of Body Language in Job Interviews," *Employee Relations* 18, no. 2 (Summer 1991), pp. 161–166.

42. Tim DeGroot and Stephen Motowidlo, "Why Visual and Vocal Interview Cues Can Affect Interviewers' Judgments and Predicted Job Performance," *Journal of Applied Psychology*, December 1999, pp. 968–984.

43. David Caldwell and Jerry Burger, "Personality Characteristics of Job Applicants and Success in Screening Interviews," *Personnel Psychology* 51 (1998), pp. 119–136.

44. Ibid., p. 130.

45. Amy Kristof-Brown et al., "Applicant Impression Management: Dispositional Influences and Consequences for Recruiter Perceptions of Fit and Similarity," *Journal of Management* 28, no. 1 (2002), pp. 27–46.

46. C. K. Stevens and A. L. Kristof, "Making the Right Impression: A Field Study of Applicant Impression Management During Interviews," *Journal of Applied Psychology* 80, pp. 587–606; Schultz and Schultz, *Psychology and Work Today*, p. 82.

47. Richard Posthuma, Frederick Morgeson, and Michael Campion, "Beyond Employment Interview Validity: A Comprehensive Narrative Review of Recent Trends Over Time," *Personnel Psychology* 55 (2002), p. 30.

48. See, for example, Madelaine Heilmann and Lewis Saruwatari, "When Beauty Is Beastly: The Effects of Appearance and Sex on Evaluation of Job Applicants for Managerial and Nonmanagerial Jobs," *Organizational Behavior and Human Performance* 23 (June 1979), pp. 360–372; and Cynthia Marlowe, Sondra Schneider, and Carnot Nelson, "Gender and Attractiveness Biases in Hiring Decisions: Are More Experienced Managers Less Biased?" *Journal of Applied Psychology* 81, no. 1 (1996), pp. 11–21.

49. Marlowe et al., "Gender and Attractiveness Biases," p. 11.

50. Ibid., p. 18.

51. Ibid., p. 11.

52. Amelia J. Prewett-Livingston et al., "Effects of Race on Interview Ratings in a Situational Panel Interview," *Journal of Applied Psychology* 81, no. 2 (1996), pp. 178–186.

53. Alan Huffcutt and Philip Roth, "Racial Group Differences in Employment Interview Evaluations," *Journal of Applied Psychology* 83, no. 2 (1998), pp. 179–189.

54. Michael Miceli et al., "Potential Discrimination in Structured Employment Interviews," *Employee Responsibilities and Rights* 13, no. 1 (March 2001), pp. 15–38.

55. "Screens Can be a Key to Unbiased Interview Process," *Personnel Today*, April 1, 2003, p. 3.

56. Posthuma, Morgeson, and Campion, "Beyond Employment Interview Validity," p. 27.

57. Ibid.

58. Andrea Rodriguez and Fran Prezant, "Better Interviews for People with Disabilities," *Workforce*, downloaded from workforce.com, November 14, 2003.

59. Pat Tammaro, "Laws to Prevent Discrimination Affect Job Interview Process and Will," *The Elected Business Journal*, June 16, 2000, p. 48.

60. This is based on John F. Wymer III and Deborah A. Sudbury, "Employment Discrimination: 'Testers'—Will Your Hiring Practices 'Pass'?" *Employee Relations Law Journal* 17, no. 4 (Spring 1992), pp. 623–633.

61. See, for example, *Lea v. Cone Mills Corp.*, 438 F2d 86 (1971).

62. Bureau of National Affairs, *Daily Labor Report*, December 5, 1990, p. D1.

63. Wymer and Sudbury, "Employment Discrimination," p. 629.

64. Ibid.

65. Arthur Pell, "Nine Interviewing Pitfalls," *Managers Magazine*, January 1994, p. 20.

66. Thomas Dougherty, Daniel Turban, and John Callender, "Confirming First Impressions in the Employment Interview: A

Field Study of Interviewer Behavior," *Journal of Applied Psychology* 79, no. 5 (1994), p. 663.

67. See Pell, "Nine Interviewing Pitfalls," p. 29; Parth Sarathi, "Making Selection Interviews Effective," *Management and Labor Studies* 18, no. 1 (1993), pp. 5–7.

68. Posthuma, Morgeson, and Campion, "Beyond Employment Interview Validity," pp. 1–87.

69. Pell, "Nine Interviewing Pitfalls," p. 30.

70. Posthuma, Morgeson, and Campion, "Beyond Employment Interview Validity," 1-87.

71. This section is based on Elliot Pursell et al., "Structured Interviewing," *Personnel Journal* 59, (November 1980), pp. 907–912; and G. Latham et al., "The Situational Interview," *Journal of Applied Psychology* 65 (1980), pp. 422–427. See also Campion, Pursell, and Brown, "Structured Interviewing," pp. 25–42; and Weekley and Gier, "Reliability and Validity of the Situational Interview," pp. 484–487.

72. .63 versus .47, op cit.; Taylor and Small, "Asking Applicants What They Would Do Versus What They Did," pp. 277–295.

73. There is some evidence that, for higher-level positions, situational question–based interviews are inferior to behavioral question–based ones, possibly because the situations are "just too simple to allow any real differentiation among candidates for higher level positions." Alan Huffcutt et al., "Comaprison of Situational and Behavioral Description Interview Questions for Higher Level Positions," *Personnel Psychology* 54, no. 3 (2001), p. 619.

74. See also Phillip Lowry, "The Structured Interview: An Alternative to the Assessment Center?" *Public Personnel Management* 23, no. 2 (Summer 1994), pp. 201–215. See also Steven Maurer, "The Potential of the Situational Interview: Existing Research and Unresolved Issues," *Human Resource Management Review* 7, no. 2 (Summer 1997), pp. 185–201.

75. Pursell et al., "Structured Interviewing," p. 910.

76. From a speech by industrial psychologist Paul Green and contained in *BNA Bulletin to Management*, June 20, 1985, pp. 2–3.

77. "Container Store Thinks Outside the Box: Award-Winning Employer Hires for Quality," *BNA Bulletin to Management*, March 1, 2001, p. 65.

78. Williamson et al., "Employment Interview on Trial," p. 901; Michael Campion, David Palmer, and James Campion, "A

Review of Structure in the Selection Interview," *Personnel Psychology* 50 (1997), pp. 655–702.

79. Unless otherwise specified, the following are based on Williamson et al., "Employment Interview on Trial," pp. 901–902.

80. Campion, Palmer, and Campion, "A Review of Structure," p. 668.

81. Carlson, "Selection Interview Decisions," pp. 259–280.

82. Campion, Palmer, and Campion, "A Review of Structure," pp. 655–702.

83. Catherine Middendorf and Therese Macan, "Note Taking in the Employment Interview: Effects on Recall and Judgment," *Journal of Applied Psychology* 87, no. 2 (2002), pp. 293–303.

84. "The Tables Have Turned," *American Management Association International*, September 1998, p. 6.

85. Edwin Walley, "Successful Interviewing Techniques," *CPA Journal*, September 1993, p. 70.

86. Robert Rubin et al., "Using Extracurricular Activity as an Indicator of Interpersonal Skill: Prudent Evaluation or Recruiting Malpractice?" *Human Resource Management* 41, no. 4 (Winter 2002), pp. 441–454.

87. Pamela Kaul, "Interviewing Is Your Business," *Association Management*, November 1992, p. 29.

88. Walley, "Successful Interviewing Techniques," p. 70.

89. Stephen Gilliland et al., "Improving Applicants' Reactions to Rejection Letters: An Application of Fairness Theory," *Personnel Psychology* 54 (2001), pp. 669–703.

90. Robin Rimmer Hurst, "Video Interviewing. Take One!" *HR Magazine*, November 1996, pp. 100–104.

91. Posthuma, Morgeson, and Campion, "Beyond Employment Interview Validity," p. 47.

92. Ibid.

93. This is based on John Drake, *Interviewing for Managers: A Complete Guide to Employment Interviewing* (New York, AMACOM, 1982).

94. Ibid.

95. Chris Maynard, "New High-Tech Recruiting Tools: Unicycles, Yahtzee and Silly Putty," *Wall Street Journal*, June 6, 2000, p. B14; see also Paul McNamara, "Extreme Interview," *Network World*, June 25, 2001, p. 65.

96. Tim Barker, "Corporate Espionage Takes Center Stage with the Boeing Revelation," *Knight Ridder/Tribune Business News*, June 15, 2003, item 03166010.

97. Ibid.

APPENDIX FOR CHAPTER 7

Guidelines for Interviewees

Before you get into a position where you have to do interviewing, you will probably have to navigate some interviews yourself. Here are some hints for excelling in your interview.

The first thing to understand is that interviews are often used to help employers determine what you are like as a person. In other words, information regarding how you get along with other people and your desire to work is often very important in the interview; your skills and technical expertise are often assessed through tests and a study of your educational and work history. Interviewers will look first for crisp, articulate answers. Specifically, whether you respond concisely, cooperate fully in answer-

ing questions, state personal opinions when relevant, and keep to the subject at hand are very important elements in influencing the interviewer's decision.

There are seven things to do to get that extra edge in the interview.

1. *Preparation is essential.* Before the interview, learn all you can about the employer, the job, and the people doing the recruiting. On the Web or at the library, look through business periodicals to find out what is happening in the employer's field. Who is the competition? How are they doing? Try to unearth the employer's problems. Be ready to explain why you

think you would be able to solve such problems, citing some of your *specific accomplishments* to make your case.

2. *Uncover the interviewer's real needs.* Spend as little time as possible answering your interviewer's first questions and as much time as possible getting him or her to describe his or her needs. Determine what the person is expecting to accomplish, and the type of person he or she feels is needed. Use open-ended questions here such as, "Could you tell me more about that?"

3. *Relate yourself to the interviewer's needs.* Once you know the type of person your interviewer is looking for and the sorts of problems he or she wants solved, you are in a good position to describe your own accomplishments *in terms of the interviewer's needs.* Start by saying something like, "One of the problem areas you've said is important to you is similar to a problem I once faced." Then state the problem, describe your solution, and reveal the results.

4. *Think before answering.* Answering a question should be a three-step process: Pause—Think—Speak. *Pause* to make sure you understand what the interviewer is driving at, *think* about how to structure your answer, and then *speak*. In your answer, try to emphasize how hiring you will help the interviewer solve his or her problem.

5. *Remember that appearance and enthusiasm are important.* Appropriate clothing, good grooming, a firm handshake, and the appearance of controlled energy are important. Remember that your *nonverbal behav-*

ior may broadcast more about you than the verbal content of what you say. Here maintaining eye contact is very important. In addition, speak with enthusiasm, nod agreement, and remember to take a moment to frame your answer (pause, think, speak) so that you sound articulate and fluent.

6. *Make a good first impression.* Remember, studies show that in most cases interviewers make up their minds about the applicant during the early minutes of the interview. A good first impression may turn to bad during the interview, but it is unlikely. Bad first impressions are almost impossible to overcome. One expert suggests paying attention to the following key interviewing considerations.
   1. Appropriate clothing
   2. Good grooming
   3. A firm handshake
   4. The appearance of controlled energy
   5. Pertinent humor and readiness to smile
   6. A genuine interest in the employer's operation and alert attention when the interviewer speaks
   7. Pride in past performance
   8. An understanding of the employer's needs and a desire to serve them
   9. The display of sound ideas
   10. Ability to take control when employers fall down on the interviewing job

7. *Ask questions.* Sample questions you can ask are presented in Figure A-1.

Figure A1
Interview Questions to Ask
Source: H. Lee Rust, *Job Search: The Complete Manual for Job Seekers* © 1991 J. Lee Rust. Published by AMACOM, division of American Management Assn. Intl., New York, NY.

1. What is the first problem that needs the attention of the person you hire?
2. What other problems need attention now?
3. What has been done about any of these to date?
4. How has this job been performed in the past?
5. Why is it now vacant?
6. Do you have a written job description for this position?
7. What are its major responsibilities?
8. What authority would I have? How would you define its scope?
9. What are the company's five-year sales and profit projections?
10. What needs to be done to reach these projections?
11. What are the company's major strengths and weaknesses?
12. What are its strengths and weaknesses in production?
13. What are its strengths and weaknesses in its products or its competitive position?
14. Whom do you identify as your major competitors?
15. What are their strengths and weaknesses?
16. How do you view the future for your industry?
17. Do you have any plans for new products or acquisitions?
18. Might this company be sold or acquired?
19. What is the company's current financial strength?
20. What can you tell me about the individual to whom I would report?
21. What can you tell me about other persons in key positions?
22. What can you tell me about the subordinates I would have?
23. How would you define your management philosophy?
24. Are employees afforded an opportunity for continuing education?
25. What are you looking for in the person who will fill this job?

After studying this chapter, you should be able to:

1. Describe the basic training process.

2. Describe and illustrate how you would go about identifying training requirements.

3. Explain how to distinguish between problems you can fix with training and those you can't.

4. Explain how to use five training techniques.

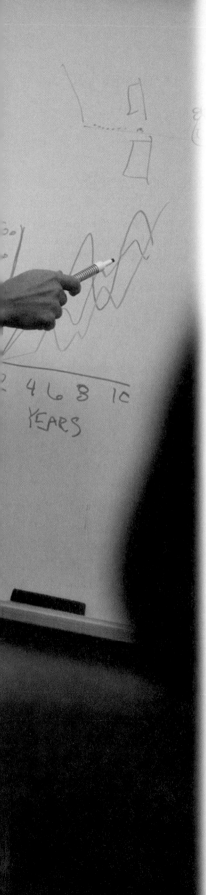

Training and Developing Employees

As she reviewed her company's training processes, Lisa had many reasons

to be concerned. For one thing, the Hotel Paris relied almost exclusively on

informal on-the-job training. New security guards attended a one-week

program offered by a law enforcement agency, but all other new hires, from

assistant manager to housekeeping crew, learned the rudiments of their jobs

from their colleagues and their supervisors, on the job. Lisa noted that the

drawbacks of this informality were evident when she compared the Hotel

Paris's performance on various training metrics with those of other hotels

and service firms. For example, in terms of number of hours training per

employee per year, number of hours training for new employees, cost per

trainee hour, and percent of payroll spent on training, the Hotel Paris was far

from the norm when benchmarked against similar firms.●

The previous chapter focused on the methods managers use to interview and select employees. Once employees are hired, the employer must train them. The purpose of this chapter is to increase your effectiveness as a trainer. The main topics we'll cover include orienting employees, the training process, training methods, training for special purposes, managerial development and training techniques, and evaluating the training effort.

● ORIENTING EMPLOYEES

Recruiting and selecting high-potential employees doesn't guarantee that they'll perform effectively. For one thing, people who don't know what to do or how to do it can't perform effectively even if they want to. Therefore your next step is to ensure that your employees know what to do and how to do it—you have to orient and train them. We will start with orientation.

employee orientation
A procedure for providing new employees with basic background information about the firm.

Employee orientation provides new employees with the basic background information required to perform their jobs satisfactorily, such as information about company rules. Programs may range from brief, informal introductions to lengthy, formal courses.

The HR specialist (or, in smaller firms, the office manager) usually performs the first part of the orientation, by explaining basic matters like working hours and vacations. That person then introduces the new employee to his or her new supervisor. The supervisor continues the orientation by explaining (see Figure 8-1) the organization of the department, and by introducing the person to his or her new colleagues, familiarizing the new employee with the workplace, and helping to reduce first-day jitters. Orientation typically includes information on employee benefits, personnel policies, the daily routine, company organization and operations, and safety measures and regulations, as well as a facilities tour.

At a minimum, new employees usually receive either printed or Internet-based *employee handbooks* covering matters like these. Under certain conditions, the courts may find that the employee handbook's contents represent legally binding employment commitments. Therefore, companies often include disclaimers to make it clear that statements of company policies, benefits, and regulations do not constitute the terms and conditions of an employment contract either expressed or implied. Also, companies generally do not insert statements such as "no employee will be fired without just cause" or statements that imply or state that employees have tenure. Indeed, it's best to emphasize that the employment relationship is strictly "at-will."

Don't underestimate the importance of orientation. Without basic information on things like rules and policies, new employees may make time-consuming or even dangerous errors. Their performance—and the firm's—will suffer. Furthermore, orientation is not just about rules. It is also about making the new person feel welcome and at home and part of the team, all potentially important if you want him or her to be productive.

Orientation programs today are moving away from routine discussions of company rules, to emphasizing the company's mission and the employee's role in that mission, and to "making the new recruit feel a productive part of a team as soon as possible."[1]

A successful orientation should accomplish four things: The new employee should feel welcome and at ease; he or she should understand the organization in a broad sense (its past, present, culture, and vision of the future), as well as key facts such as policies and procedures; the employee should be clear about what is expected in terms of work and behavior; and the person should have begun the process of becoming socialized into the firm's ways of acting and doing things.[2]

Not all new hires react to orientation in the same way.[3] Supervisors should therefore be vigilant, and follow up and encourage new employees to engage in those activities that will enable each to "learn the ropes" and quickly become productive.

NEW EMPLOYEE DEPARTMENTAL ORIENTATION CHECKLIST
(Return to Human Resources within 10 days of Hire)

NAME:	HIRE DATE:	SSN:	JOB TITLE:
DEPARTMENT:	NEO DATE:	DEPARTMENTAL ORIENTATION COMPLETED BY:	

TOPIC	DATE REVIEWED	N/A
1. HUMAN RESOURCES INFORMATION		
a. Departmental Attendance Procedures and UCSD Healthcare Work Time & Attendance Policy	a. _____	☐
b. Job Description Review	b. _____	☐
c. Annual Performance Evaluation and Peer Feedback Process	c. _____	☐
d. Probationary Period Information	d. _____	☐
e. Appearance/Dress Code Requirements	e. _____	☐
f. Annual TB Screening	f. _____	☐
g. License and/or certification Renewals	g. _____	☐
2. DEPARTMENT INFORMATION		
a. Organizational Structure-Department Core Values Orientation	a. _____	☐
b. Department/Unit Area Specific Policies & Procedures	b. _____	☐
c. Customer Service Practices	c. _____	☐
d. CQI Effort and Projects	d. _____	☐
e. Tour and Floor Plan	e. _____	☐
f. Equipment/Supplies	f. _____	☐
• Keys issued	_____	☐
• Radio Pager issued	_____	☐
• Other _____	_____	☐
g. Mail and Recharge Codes	g. _____	☐
3. SAFETY INFORMATION		
a. Departmental Safety Plan	a. _____	☐
b. Employee Safety/Injury Reporting Procedures	b. _____	☐
c. Hazard Communication	c. _____	☐
d. Infection Control/Sharps Disposal	d. _____	☐
e. Attendance at annual Safety Fair (mandatory)	e. _____	☐
4. FACILITES INFORMATION		
a. Emergency Power	a. _____	☐
b. Mechanical Systems	b. _____	☐
c. Water	c. _____	☐
d. Medical Gases	d. _____	☐
e. Patient Room	e. _____	☐
• Bed	_____	☐
• Headwall	_____	☐
• Bathroom	_____	☐
• Nurse Call System	_____	☐
5. SECURITY INFORMATION		
a. Code Triage Assignment	a. _____	☐
b. Code Blue Assignment	b. _____	☐
c. Code Red – Evacuation Procedure	c. _____	☐
d. Code 10 – Bomb Threat Procedure	d. _____	☐
e. Departmental Security Measures	e. _____	☐
f. UCSD Emergency Number 6111 or 911	f. _____	☐

This generic checklist may not constitute a complete departmental orientation or assessment. Please attach any additional unit specific orientation material for placement in the employee's HR file

I have been oriented on the items listed above_____

Figure 8-1 New Employee Departmental Orientation Checklist *Source:* UCSDHealthcare. Used with permission.

● THE TRAINING PROCESS

training
The process of teaching new employees the basic skills they need to perform their jobs.

Training refers to the methods used to give new or present employees the skills they need to perform their jobs. Training might mean showing a new Web designer the intricacies of your site, a new salesperson how to sell your firm's product, or a new supervisor how to fill out the firm's weekly payroll timesheets. Training is a hallmark of good management, and a task managers ignore at their peril. Having high-potential employees doesn't guarantee they'll succeed. Instead, they must know what you want them to do and how you want them to do it. If they don't, they'll do the jobs their way, not yours. Or they will improvise, or worse, do nothing productive at all. Good training is vital.

The Strategic Context of Training

Training used to focus mostly on teaching technical skills, such as training assemblers to solder wires or teachers to write lesson plans.[4] Today, such technical training is no longer sufficient. As one trainer puts it: "we don't just concentrate on the traditional training objectives anymore . . . We sit down with management and help them identify strategic goals and objectives and the skills and knowledge needed to achieve them. Then we work together to identify whether our staff has the skills and knowledge, and when they don't, that's when we discuss training needs."[5] In other words, the training has to make sense in terms of the company's strategic goals. A strategy to improve customer service implies the need for customer service training.

performance management
The process employers use to make sure employees are working toward organizational goals.

Training today also plays a key role in the **performance management** process. This is the integrated process employers use to make sure employees are working toward organizational goals. It means taking an integrated, goal-oriented approach to assigning, training, assessing, and rewarding employees' performance. Taking a performance management approach to training means that the training effort must make sense in terms of what the company wants each employee to contribute to achieving the company's goals.

Trends like these help explain why training is booming. Companies spent about $826 per employee for training in 2002, and offered each about 28 hours of training.[6] Training has a fairly impressive record of influencing organizational effectiveness, scoring higher than appraisal and feedback, and just below goal setting in its effect on productivity.[7]

The 9/11 attacks on the World Trade Center and the Pentagon triggered changes in both the content of employers' training programs and in how employers deliver their training. Immediately after 9/11, employers began to shift more resources to Web-based and distance learning–based training, and significantly reduced travel time for both trainers and trainees. At the same time, employers shifted more resources to diversity training (for instance, Ford Motor Company instituted several cross-cultural diversity training programs for its Muslim and non-Muslim employees), and instituted new programs on security and stress management.[8]

 Describe the basic training process.

The Five-Step Training and Development Process

Training programs consist of five steps. The first, or *needs analysis* step, identifies the specific job performance skills needed, assesses the prospective trainees skills, and develops specific, measurable knowledge and performance objectives based on any deficiencies. In the second step, *instructional design*, you decide on, compile, and produce the training program content, including workbooks, exercises, and activities; here, you'll probably use techniques like those discussed in this chapter, such as on-the-job training and computer-assisted learning. There may be a third, *validation* step, in which the bugs are worked out of the training program by presenting it to a small representative audience. The fourth step is to *implement* the program, by actually training the targeted employee group. Fifth is an *evaluation* step, in which management assesses the program's successes or failures.

Orienting and training new employees play crucial roles in socializing employees to the company's ways of doing things, and ensuring that they have the knowledge they need to perform their new jobs.

Most employers probably do not (and need not) create their own training materials, since many materials are available online and offline. For example, the professional development site thinq.com offers a wide range of Web-based courses employees can take online. And many firms, including American Media, Inc., of West Des Moines, Iowa, provide turnkey training packages. These include a training leader's guide, self-study book, and video for improving skills in areas such as customer service, documenting discipline, and appraising performance.

Training, Learning, and Motivation

Training is futile if the trainee lacks the ability or motivation to benefit from it. In terms of ability, the trainee needs (among other things) the required reading, writing, and mathematics skills, and the required educational level, intelligence, and knowledge base. Effective employee selection is obviously useful here. In addition, some employers use "miniature job training" to screen out low-potential trainees. We'll discuss this method again below, but (as first discussed in Chapter 5) it basically involves using sample tasks from the firm's training program to help decide who will and will not move on to training.[9]

The employer can take several steps to increase the trainee's motivation to learn. Providing opportunities for active practice, and letting the trainee make errors and explore alternate solutions improves motivation and learning.[10] Feedback—including periodic performance assessments and more frequent verbal critiques—is also important.[11] The employer should also make the material meaningful. For example, provide an overview of the material, and ensure that the program uses familiar examples and concepts to illustrate key points.[12] We can summarize these motivational points as follows.

Make the Learning Meaningful It is easier for trainees to understand and remember material that is *meaningful*. Therefore:

1. At the start of training, provide a bird's-eye view of the material to be presented. Knowing the overall picture facilitates learning.
2. Use a variety of familiar examples.
3. Organize the information so you can present it logically, and in meaningful units.
4. Use terms and concepts that are already familiar to trainees.
5. Use as many visual aids as possible.

Make Skills Transfer Easy Make it easy to *transfer* new skills and behaviors from the training site to the job site:

1. Maximize the similarity between the training situation and the work situation.
2. Provide adequate practice.
3. Label or identify each feature of the machine and/or step in the process.
4. Direct the trainees' attention to important aspects of the job. For example, if you're training customer service representatives in how to handle incoming calls, first explain the different types of calls they will encounter and how to recognize such calls.[13]
5. Provide "heads-up," preparatory information. For example, trainees learning to become first-line supervisors often face stressful conditions, high workload, and difficult subordinates back on the job. Studies suggest you can reduce the negative impact of such events by letting trainees know they might happen.[14]

Motivate the Learner   Here are some other ways to motivate the trainee:

1. People learn best by doing. Try to provide as much realistic practice as possible.

2. Trainees learn best when the trainers immediately reinforce correct responses, perhaps with a quick "well done."

3. Trainees learn best at their own pace. If possible, let them pace themselves.

4. Create a perceived training need in the trainees' minds.[15] In one study, pilots who had experienced pretraining, accident-related events subsequently learned more from an accident-reduction training program than did those experiencing fewer such events.[16] You could illustrate the need for the training by showing videos of simulated accidents. Similarly, "before the training, managers need to sit down and talk with the trainee about why they are enrolled in the class, what they are expected to learn and how they can use it on the job."[17]

5. The schedule is important too: The learning curve goes down late in the day, so that "full day training is not as effective as half the day or three-fourths of the day."[18]

Know Your Employment Law

Training and the Law

Managers should understand the legal implications of their training-related decisions, particularly with respect to discrimination, negligent training, and overtime pay. With respect to *discrimination*, Title VII of the Civil Rights Act of 1964 and related legislation requires that the employer avoid discriminatory actions in all aspects of its human resource management process, and that applies, of course, to selecting which employees to train. Employers face much the same consequences for discriminating against protected individuals when selecting candidates for training programs as they would in selecting candidates for jobs, or for promotion or other related decisions. Harassment training is a special case here. As explained in Chapter 2, in the late 1990s the U.S. Supreme Court ruled that courts could hold employers liable for the sexually harassing acts of their supervisors but could avoid liability by taking steps (including training) to prevent and rectify discriminatory harassment complaints. As one employment lawyer points out, "the EEOC stresses that 'if feasible, the employer should provide training to all employees to ensure they understand their [sexual harassment] rights and responsibilities.' "[19] In practical terms, this means that many lower courts, in interpreting the Supreme Court's decision, rely on the adequacy of the employer's sexual harassment training to determine whether the employer did exercise reasonable care to prevent harassment.[20]

negligent training
A situation where an employer fails to train adequately, and the employee subsequently harms a third party.

Inadequate training can also expose the employer to liability for **negligent training**. As one expert puts it, "it's clear from the case law that where an employer fails to train adequately and an employee subsequently does harm to third parties, the court will find the employer liable." Among other things, this means that the employer must confirm the applicant/employee's claims of skill and experience, provide adequate training (particularly where employees work with dangerous equipment), and evaluate the training to ensure that it is actually reducing risks.[21]

Given its frequent off-the-job nature, the question also often arises as to whether the employer has to *pay the employee* for the time the latter spends being trained. Sometimes the answer is clear. For example, if the training program is strictly voluntary, conducted outside working hours, and not directly related to the trainee's job, and the trainee does not perform any productive work, then the trainee should not expect to be compensated under the Wage and Hour laws. Similarly (as with the Honda program described in Chapter 5), employers who require job candidates to complete short training sessions as prerequisites for being considered for positions usually do not need to compensate the trainees, as long as several conditions are met. Here, for example: The training should provide no immediate benefit to the employer; the employer should not guarantee trainees they'll get jobs at the end of their training period; the employer should inform the trainees up front that they will not be paid for the time they spend training; and the training should be similar to what the trainee might expect in a vocational school, even though the employer uses its own facilities. On the other hand, if an employer tells a current employee that the company is going to terminate him or her unless the person takes the training, then the employer may have to compensate the employee for the extra time he or she spends in the company-sponsored training program.[22]

Analyzing Training Needs

Describe and illustrate how you would go about identifying training requirements.

How you analyze training needs depends on whether you're training new or current employees. The main task in analyzing *new* employees' training needs is to determine what the job entails and to break it down into subtasks, each of which you then teach to the new employee. Analyzing *current* employees' training needs can be more complex, since you have the added task of deciding whether training is the solution. For example, performance may be down because the standards aren't clear or because the person is not motivated. Some trainers use special analytical software, such as from Saba Software, Inc., to diagnose performance gaps and their causes.

Task Analysis: Assessing New Employees' Training Needs

task analysis
A detailed study of a job to identify the specific skills required.

Particularly with lower-level workers, it's common to hire inexperienced personnel and train them. Your aim here is to give these new employees the skills and knowledge they need to do the job. You use task analysis to determine the new employees' training needs.

Task analysis is a detailed study of the job to determine what specific skills—like Java (in the case of a Web developer) or interviewing (in the case of a supervisor)—the job requires. Job descriptions and job specifications are helpful here. These list the job's specific duties and skills and thus provide the basic reference point in determining the training required. You can also uncover training needs by reviewing performance standards, performing the job, and questioning current job holders and their supervisors.[23]

Some employers supplement the job description and specification with a *task analysis record form*. This consolidates information regarding required tasks and skills in a form that's especially helpful for determining training requirements. As Table 8-1 illustrates, a task analysis record form contains six types of information, such as "Skills Required."

Performance Analysis: Assessing Current Employees' Training Needs

Explain how to distinguish between problems you can fix with training and those you can't.

performance analysis
Verifying that there is a performance deficiency and determining whether that deficiency should be corrected through training or through some other means (such as transferring the employee).

For current employees, **performance analysis** is the process of verifying that there is a performance deficiency and determining if such deficiency should be corrected through training or through some other means (like transferring the employee).

There are several methods you can use to identify a current employee's training needs. These include supervisor, peer, and self performance reviews; job-related performance data (including productivity, absenteeism and tardiness, accidents, short-term sickness, grievances, waste, late deliveries, product quality, downtime, repairs, equipment utilization, and customer complaints); observation by supervisors or other specialists; interviews with the employee or his or her supervisor; tests of things like job knowledge, skills, and attendance; attitude surveys; individual employee daily diaries; and assessment centers.

The first step here is usually to compare the person's actual performance to what it should be. Examples of specific performance deficiencies include:

I expect each salesperson to make ten new contracts per week, but John averages only six.

Other plants our size average no more than two serious accidents per month; we're averaging five.

Table 8-1 **Task Analysis Record Form**

Task List	When and How Often Performed	Quantity and Quality of Performance	Conditions Under Which Performed	Skills or Knowledge Required	Where Best Learned
1. Operate paper cutter	4 times per day		Noisy pressroom: distractions		
1.1 Start motor					
1.2 Set cutting distance		± tolerance of 0.007 In.		Read gauge	On the job
1.3 Place paper on cutting table		Must be completely even to prevent uneven cut		Lift paper correctly	On the job
1.4 Push paper up to cutter				Must be even	On the job
1.5 Grasp safety release with left hand		100% of time, for safety		Essential for safety	On the job but practice first with no distractions
1.6 Grasp cutter release with right hand				Must keep both hands on releases	On the job but practice first with no distractions
1.7 Simultaneously pull safety release with left hand and cutter release with right hand					
1.8 Wait for cutter to retract		100% of time, for safety		Must keep both hands on releases	On the job but practice first with no distractions
1.9 Retract paper				Wait until cutter retracts	On the job but practice first with no distractions
1.10 Shut off		100% of time, for safety			On the job but practice first with no distractions
2. Operate printing press					
2.1 Start motor					

Note Task analysis record form showing some of the tasks and subtasks performed by a printing press operator.

Distinguishing between can't-do and won't-do problems is the heart of performance analysis. First, determine whether it is a *can't-do* problem and, if so, its specific causes. For example: The employees don't know what to do or what your standards are; there are obstacles in the system such as lack of tools or supplies; there are no job aids (such as color-coded wires that show assemblers which wire goes where), or no electronic performance support systems that provide on-screen, computerized, step-by-step instructions; you've hired people who haven't the skills to do the job; or inadequate training.

On the other hand, it might be a *won't-do* problem. Here employees could do a good job if they wanted to. Perhaps you need to change the reward system. One expert says, "perhaps the biggest trap that trainers fall into is [developing] training for problems that training just won't fix."[24]

If training is the solution, you need to set objectives. These specify what the trainee should be able to accomplish upon completing the training program—repair a copier in 30 minutes, program a simple Web site in half a day, or sell five advertising banners per day, for instance.[25]

Explain how to use five training techniques.

● TRAINING METHODS

Once you've decided to train employees and have identified their training needs and goals, you have to design the training program. You can create the content and program sequence yourself, but there is also a vast selection of online and offline content and packages from which to choose. You'll find turnkey, off-the-shelf programs on virtually any topic—from occupational safety to sexual harassment to Web design—from tens of thousands of online and offline providers. (See, for example, www.astd.org; www.trainerswarehouse.com, and www.gneil.com, among thousands of such suppliers.)

In any case, there are various methods companies use to actually deliver the training. We'll start with what is probably the most popular: on-the-job training.

On-the-Job Training

on-the-job training
Training a person to learn a job while working on it.

On-the-job training (OJT) means having a person learn a job by actually doing it. Every employee, from mailroom clerk to company president, gets on-the-job training when he or she joins a firm. In many firms, OJT is the only training available.[26]

The most familiar type of on-the-job training is the *coaching or understudy method*. Here, an experienced worker or the trainee's supervisor trains the employee. At lower levels, trainees may acquire skills by observing the supervisor. But this technique is widely used at top-management levels, too. A potential future CEO might spend a year as assistant to the current CEO, for instance. *Job rotation*, in which an employee (usually a management trainee) moves from job to job at planned intervals, is another OJT technique. Jeffrey Immelt progressed through such a process in becoming GE's new CEO. *Special assignments* similarly give lower-level executives firsthand experience in working on actual problems. The Men's Wearhouse, with 455 stores nationwide, makes extensive use of on-the-job training. It has few full-time trainers. Instead, the Men's Wearhouse has a formal process of "cascading" responsibility for training: Every manager is formally accountable for the development of his or her direct subordinates.[27]

OJT has several advantages. It is relatively inexpensive; trainees learn while producing; and there is no need for expensive off-site facilities like classrooms or programmed learning devices. The method also facilitates learning, since trainees learn by doing and get quick feedback on their performance. But there are several points to note when using OJT.

Most important, don't take the success of an on-the-job training program for granted.[28] Carefully train the trainers themselves (often the employees' supervisors), and provide the necessary training materials. Trainers should know, for instance, the principles of learning and perhaps the four-step job instruction technique that follows. Low expectations on the trainer's part may translate into poorer trainee performance (a phenomenon researchers have called "the golem effect"). Those training others should thus emphasize the high expectations they have for their trainees' success.[29]

Here are some steps to help ensure OJT success.

Step 1: Prepare the Learner

1. Put the learner at ease—relieve the tension.
2. Explain why he or she is being taught.
3. Create interest, encourage questions, find out what the learner already knows about this or other jobs.
4. Explain the whole job and relate it to some job the worker already knows.
5. Place the learner as close to the normal working position as possible.
6. Familiarize the worker with equipment, materials, tools, and trade terms.

Step 2: Present the Operation

1. Explain quantity and quality requirements.
2. Go through the job at the normal work pace.
3. Go through the job at a slow pace several times, explaining each step. Between operations, explain the difficult parts, or those in which errors are likely to be made.
4. Again go through the job at a slow pace several times; explain the key points.
5. Have the learner explain the steps as you go through the job at a slow pace.

Step 3: Do a Tryout

1. Have the learner go through the job several times, slowly, explaining each step to you. Correct mistakes and, if necessary, do some of the complicated steps the first few times.
2. Run the job at the normal pace.
3. Have the learner do the job, gradually building up skill and speed.
4. As soon as the learner demonstrates ability to do the job, let the work begin, but don't abandon him or her.

Step 4: Follow Up

1. Designate to whom the learner should go for help.
2. Gradually decrease supervision, checking work from time to time against quality and quantity standards.
3. Correct faulty work patterns before they become a habit. Show why the learned method is superior.
4. Compliment good work; encourage the worker until he or she is able to meet the quality and quantity standards.[30]

Apprenticeship Training

apprenticeship training
A structured process by which people become skilled workers through a combination of classroom instruction and on-the-job training.

More employers are implementing apprenticeship programs, an approach that began in the Middle Ages. **Apprenticeship training** is a structured process by which people become skilled workers through a combination of classroom instruction and on-the-job training. It is widely used to train individuals for many occupations.[31] It traditionally involves having the learner/apprentice study under the tutelage of a master craftsperson.[32]

Several U.S. facilities currently use this approach. For example, the Siemens Stromberg-Carlson plant in Florida has apprenticeships for adults and high school students for electronics technician jobs:

Adults work on the factory floor, receive classroom instruction at Seminole Community College, and also study at the plant's hands-on apprenticeship lab. Graduates receive Associates

Degrees in telecommunications and electronics engineering. High school students spend two afternoons per week at the apprenticeship lab.[33]

The U.S. Department of Labor's Employment and Training Administration offers apprenticeship training, along with a number of other types of training programs. Figure 8-2 lists 25 of the most popular recent apprenticeships.

Informal Learning

Employers should not underestimate the importance or value of informal training. Surveys from the American Society for Training and Development estimate that as much as 80% of what employees learn on the job they learn not through formal training programs but through informal means, including performing their jobs on a daily basis in collaboration with their colleagues.[34]

Although managers don't arrange informal learning, there's still a lot they can do to ensure that it occurs. Most of the steps are simple. For example, Siemens Power Transmission and Distribution in Raleigh, North Carolina, places tools in cafeteria areas to take advantage of the work-related discussions taking place. Even things like installing white boards and keeping them stocked with markers can facilitate informal learning.

Job Instruction Training

job instruction training (JIT)
Listing each job's basic tasks, along with key points, in order to provide step-by-step training for employees.

Many jobs consist of a logical sequence of steps and are best taught step-by-step. This step-by-step process is called **job instruction training (JIT)**. To begin, list all necessary steps in the job, each in its proper sequence. Alongside each step also list a corresponding "key point" (if any). The steps show what is to be done, and the key points show how

Figure 8-2
The 25 Most Popular Apprenticeships
Source: Olivia Crosby, "Apprenticeships," *Occupational Outlook Quarterly*, 46, no. 2 (Summer 2002), p. 5.

According to the U.S. Department of Labor apprenticeship database, the occupations listed below had the highest numbers of apprentices in 2001. These findings are approximate because the database includes only about 70% of registered apprenticeship programs—and none of the unregistered ones.

- Boilermaker
- Bricklayer (construction)
- Carpenter
- Construction craft laborer
- Cook (any industry)
- Cook (hotel and restaurant)
- Correction officer
- Electrician
- Electrician (aircraft)
- Electrician (maintenance)
- Electronics mechanic
- Firefighter
- Machinist
- Maintenance mechanic (any industry)
- Millwright
- Operating engineer
- Painter (construction)
- Pipefitter (construction)
- Plumber
- Power plant operator
- Roofer
- Sheet-metal worker
- Structural-steel worker
- Telecommunications technician
- Tool and die maker

it's to be done—and why. Here is an example of a job instruction training sheet for teaching a trainee how to operate a large, motorized paper cutter:

Steps	Key Points
1. Start motor	None
2. Set cutting distance	Carefully read scale—to prevent wrong-sized cut
3. Place paper on cutting table	Make sure paper is even—to prevent uneven cut
4. Push paper up to cutter	Make sure paper is tight—to prevent uneven cut
5. Grasp safety release with left hand	Do not release left hand—to prevent hand from being caught in cutter
6. Grasp cutter release with right hand	Do not release right hand—to prevent hand from being caught in cutter
7. Simultaneously pull cutter and safety releases	Keep both hands on corresponding releases—avoid hands being on cutting table
8. Wait for cutter to retract	Keep both hands on releases—to avoid having hands on cutting table
9. Retract paper	Make sure cutter is retracted; keep both hands away from releases
10. Shut off motor	None

Lectures

Lecturing has several advantages. It is a quick and simple way to provide knowledge to large groups of trainees, as when the salesforce needs to learn the special features of a new product. You could use written materials instead, but they may require considerably more production expense and won't encourage the give-and-take questioning that lectures do.

Here are some useful guidelines for presenting a lecture:[35]

- Give your listeners signals to help them follow your ideas. For instance, if you have a list of items, start by saying something like, "There are four reasons why the sales reports are necessary. . . . The first . . . the second . . . "

- Don't start out on the wrong foot. For instance, don't open with an irrelevant joke or story or by saying something like, "I really don't know why I was asked to speak here today."

- Keep your conclusions short. Just summarize your main point or points in one or two succinct sentences.

- Be alert to your audience. Watch body language for negative signals like fidgeting and crossed arms.

- Maintain eye contact with the trainees. At least look at each section of the audience during your presentation.

- Make sure everyone in the room can hear. Use a mike if necessary. Repeat questions that you get from trainees before you answer.

- Control your hands. Get in the habit of leaving them hanging naturally at your sides rather than letting them drift.

- Talk from notes rather than from a script. Write out clear, legible notes on large index cards or on PowerPoint slides, and use these as an outline, rather than memorizing your presentation.

- Break a long talk into a series of five-minute talks. Speakers often give a short overview introduction, and then spend the rest of a one-hour presentation going point by point through their material. Unfortunately, most people quickly lose interest in your list. Experts suggest breaking the long talk into a series of five-minute talks, each with its own introduction. Each introduction highlights what you'll discuss, why it's important to the audience, and your credibility—why they should listen to you.[36]

■ Practice. If possible, rehearse under conditions similar to those under which you will actually give your presentation.

While some view lectures as boring and ineffective training methods, studies suggest that they can in fact be quite effective.[37]

Programmed Learning

programmed learning
A systematic method for teaching job skills involving presenting questions or facts, allowing the person to respond, and giving the learner immediate feedback on the accuracy of his or her answers.

Whether the medium is a textbook, computer, or the Internet, **programmed learning** (or **programmed instruction**) is a step-by-step, self-learning method that consists of three parts:

1. Presenting questions, facts, or problems to the learner
2. Allowing the person to respond
3. Providing feedback on the accuracy of answers

Generally, programmed learning presents facts and follow-up questions. The learner can then respond, and subsequent frames provide feedback on the accuracy of his or her answers. What the next question is often depends on the accuracy of the learner's answer to the previous question.

Programmed learning's main advantage is that it reduces training time.[38] It also facilitates learning because it lets trainees learn at their own pace, provides immediate feedback, and (from the learner's point of view) reduces the risk of error. On the other hand, trainees do not learn much more from programmed learning than they would from a traditional textbook. You therefore need to weigh the cost of developing the manuals and/or software for programmed instruction against the potentially accelerated but not improved learning.

Literacy Training Techniques

Functional illiteracy—the inability to handle basic reading, writing, and arithmetic—is a serious problem at work. By one estimate, 50% of the U.S. population reads below the eighth-grade level, and about 90 million adults are functionally illiterate.[39] For example, a survey of 316 employers concluded that about 43% of all new hires required basic skill improvements, as did 37% of current employees.[40]

Employers are responding in two main ways. First, companies are testing job candidates' basic skills. Of the 1,085 companies that responded to an American Management Association (AMA) workplace testing survey, 39% indicated they conduct basic skills testing.[41] About 85% of the responding companies refuse to hire job applicants who are deficient in basic skills. About 3% test (and often reject) candidates for promotion based on their literacy scores.

The second response is to set up basic skills and literacy programs. For example, Smith and Wesson instituted a comprehensive program. A literacy audit revealed that many of the 676 factory employees fell below the required eighth-grade level. Formal classes were instituted to help employees raise their math and reading skills, and 70% of class attendees did so.[42]

Since minorities are the fastest-growing part of the U.S. workforce, language training is no longer a one-way street. In many industries (such as the gaming industry) or locales customers speak a variety of languages, and for a company to thrive, its workforce may have to be bilingual or multilingual. For example, Cash Creek Casino in Brooks, California, recently provided guest service training for its employees in English and separately in Spanish.[43]

Employees with weak reading, writing, or arithmetic skills may be reluctant to admit the problem. Supervisors therefore should watch for employees who avoid doing a particular job or using a particular tool; do not follow written directions or instructions; do not take written phone messages; take home forms to complete; or make the same mistakes repeatedly.[44] Literacy training is sometimes one aspect of diversity training programs, as "The New Workplace" feature illustrates.

The New Workplace

With an increasingly diverse workforce, more firms are implementing diversity training programs. As an HR officer for one firm put it, "We're trying to create a better sensitivity among our supervisors about the issues and challenges women and minorities face in pursuing their careers."[45] Diversity training aims to create better cross-cultural sensitivity, with the goal of fostering more harmonious working relationships among a firm's employees. According to one survey of HR directors, diversity-based programs included these elements (from most used to least used): improving interpersonal skills; understanding and valuing cultural differences; improving technical skills; socializing employees into the corporate culture; reducing stress; indoctrinating new workers into the U.S. work ethic; mentoring; improving English proficiency; improving basic math skills; and improving bilingual skills for English-speaking employees.[46] For example, Adams Mark Hotel & Resorts conducted a diversity training seminar for about 11,000 employees. It combined lectures, video, and employee role playing to emphasize sensitivity to race and religion.[47]

Most employers can probably opt for a self-contained, off-the-shelf diversity training program such as *F. A. I. R.: a practical approach to diversity and the workplace*, from VisionPoint productions. The package includes a facilitator and discussion guide, participant materials and workbook, a CD-ROM with print materials, PowerPoint slides, and two videos (the purchase price for the entire program is just under $1,000). The first video provides an overview of diversity, explains what it means to be "culturally competent," and addresses the various categories of diversity such as race, religion, ethnicity, gender, and age. The second tape presents four realistic vignettes illustrating such things as the importance of communicating, the potential pitfalls of stereotyping people, and bias in action (such as a worker whose colleagues overlook his religious faith by treating his religion's holidays with less seriousness then their own).[48]

Audiovisual-Based Training

Audiovisual-based training techniques like films, PowerPoints, videoconferencing, audiotapes, and videotapes can be very effective and are widely used.[49] The Ford Motor Company uses videos in its dealer training sessions to simulate problems and sample reactions to various customer complaints, for example.

Audiovisuals are more expensive than conventional lectures but offer some advantages. Of course, they usually tend to be more interesting. In addition, consider using them in the following situations:

1. When there is a need to illustrate how to follow a certain sequence over time, such as when teaching fax machine repair. The stop-action, instant replay, and fast- or slow-motion capabilities of audiovisuals can be useful here.

2. When there is a need to expose trainees to events not easily demonstrable in live lectures, such as a visual tour of a factory or open-heart surgery.

3. When you need organizationwide training and it is too costly to move the trainers from place to place.

Simulated Training

Simulated training (occasionally called vestibule training) is a method in which trainees learn on the actual or simulated equipment they will use on the job, but are actually trained off the job. This is a necessity when it is too costly or dangerous to train employees on the job. Putting new assembly-line workers right to work could slow production, for instance, and when safety is a concern—as with pilots—simulated training may be the only practical alternative.

Simulated training may take place in a separate room with the same equipment the trainees will use on the job. However, it often involves the use of equipment simulators. In pilot training, for instance, airlines use flight simulators for safety, learning efficiency, and cost savings, including savings on maintenance, pilot cost, fuel, and the cost of not having an aircraft in regular service.

Simulated training is increasingly computer-based. In fact, computerized and Internet-based tools have revolutionized the training process. Specific methods include computer-based training, electronic performance support systems, and learning portals.

Computer-Based Training

With computer-based training, the trainee uses computer-based and/or DVD systems to interactively increase his or her knowledge or skills.[50] For example, one employer uses computer-based training (CBT) to train interviewers to conduct correct and legally defensible interviews.[51] Trainees start with a computer screen that shows the applicant's completed employment application, as well as information about the nature of the job. The trainee then begins a simulated interview by typing in questions, which a video-taped model acting as the applicant answers, based on responses to a multitude of questions already in the computer. Some items require follow-up questions. As each question is answered, the trainee records his or her evaluation of the applicant's answer and makes a decision about the person's suitability for the position. At the end of the session, the computer tells the trainee where he or she went wrong (perhaps in asking discriminatory questions, for instance) and offers further instruction to correct these mistakes.[52] McDonald's developed about 11 different courses for its franchisees' employees, and put the programs on DVDs. The programs consist of graphics-supported lessons, and require trainees to make choices to show their understanding.[53]

CBT programs have real advantages. Interactive technologies (wherein trainees receive quick feedback) reduce learning time by an average of 50%.[54] They can also be cost-effective once designed and produced. Other advantages include instructional consistency (computers, unlike human trainers, don't have good days and bad days), mastery of learning (if the trainee doesn't learn it, he or she generally can't move on to the next step), increased retention, and increased trainee motivation (resulting from responsive feedback).

Specialist multimedia software houses like Graphic Media of Portland, Oregon, produce much of the content for CBT programs like these. They produce both custom titles and generic programs like a $999 package for teaching workplace safety.

Intelligent tutoring systems are basically supercharged programmed instruction programs. In addition to providing the trainee with guidance and directing the trainee toward the next instructional step, intelligent tutoring systems learn what questions and approaches worked and did not work and therefore adjust the suggested instructional sequence to the trainee's unique needs.

Computer-based training is increasingly interactive and realistic. For example, *interactive multimedia training* "integrates the use of text, video, graphics, photos, animation, and sound to produce a complex training environment with which the trainee interacts."[55] In training a physician, for instance, an interactive multimedia training system lets a medical student take a hypothetical patient's medical history, conduct an examination, analyze lab tests, and then (by clicking the "examine chest" button) choose a type of chest examination and even hear the sounds of the person's heart. The medical student can then interpret the sounds and draw conclusions upon which to base a diagnosis. *Virtual reality training* takes this realism a step further. Virtual reality "puts the trainee in an artificial three-dimensional environment that simulates events and situations that might be experienced on the job."[56] Sensory devices transmit how the trainee is responding to the computer, and the trainee sees and feels and hears what is going on, assisted by special goggles and auditory and sensory devices.[57]

The U.S. Armed Forces are increasingly utilizing simulation-based training programs for soldiers and officers. For example, the army developed video-game-type training programs called Full-Spectrum Command and Full-Spectrum Warrior for training troops in urban warfare. According to one description, the two games offer extremely realistic features, within a context that emphasizes real-time leadership and decision-making skills.[58]

Table 8-2 summarizes the main terminology of computer-based training.

Electronic Performance Support Systems (EPSS)

People don't remember everything they learn. The same applies to training. Dell, for example, introduces about 80 new products per year, so it's unrealistic to expect Dell's technical support people to know everything about every product. Dell's training therefore focuses on providing its employees with the skills they need every day, such as Dell's rules, culture and values, and systems and work processes. Computer-based support systems then deliver the rest of what they need to know, when they need it. For example, when a customer calls about a specific technical problem, a computerized job aid helps walk the customer rep through the solution, question by question.[59] We'll return to this in a moment.

job aid
Is a set of instructions, diagrams, or similar methods available at the job site to guide the worker.

Employers have long used job aids of one sort or another. A **job aid** is a set of instructions, diagrams, or similar methods available at the job site to guide the worker.[60] Job aids work particularly well on complex jobs that require multiple steps, or where it's dangerous to forget a step. Airline pilots use job aids (such as a checklist of things to do prior to takeoff). The General Motors Electromotive Division in Chicago gives workers job aids in the form of diagrams; these show, for example, where the locomotive wiring runs and which color wires go where.

electronic performance support systems (EPSS)
Sets of computerized tools and displays that automate training, documentation, and phone support, integrate this automation into applications, and provide support that's faster, cheaper, and more effective than traditional methods.

Electronic performance support systems (EPSS) are today's job aids. They are sets of computerized tools and displays that automate training, documentation, and phone support, integrate this automation into applications, and provide support that's faster, cheaper, and more effective than the traditional methods.[61]

When you call a Dell service representative about a problem with your new computer, he or she is probably asking questions that are prompted by an EPSS; it takes you both, step-by-step, through an analytical sequence. Without the EPSS, Dell would have to train its service reps to memorize an unrealistically large number of solutions.

Similarly, without EPSS, a new travel agent might require months of training, rather than days. At Apollo Travel Services, in Chicago, an EPSS guides travel agents' questions, and makes it harder to make mistakes. For example, when agents start to schedule an option that goes against a customer's established travel policies—such as booking managers to fly first class instead of coach—a dialogue box reminds the agent of the policy. It also asks him or her to choose from a list of appropriate reasons, if overriding the policy.[62]

Table 8-2		
Names and Descriptions of Various Computer-Based Training Techniques	**PI**	Computer-based programmed instruction (PI) programs consist of text, graphics, and perhaps multimedia enhancements that are stored in memory and connected to one another electronically. Material to be learned is grouped into chunks of closely related information. Typically, the computer-based PI program presents the trainees with the information in the chunk, and then tests them on their retention of the information. If they have not retained the material, they are cycled back to the original information, or to remedial information. If they have retained the information they move on to the next information to be learned.
	CBT	Training provided in part or in whole through the use of a computer. *Computer-based training* is the term most often used in private industry or the government for training employees using computer-assisted instruction.
	CMI	Computer-managed instruction (CMI) uses a computer to manage the administrative functions of training, such as registration, record keeping, scoring, and grading.
	ICAI	When the computer-based training system is able to provide some of the primary characteristics of a human tutor, it is often referred to as an intelligent computer-assisted instruction (ICAI) system. It is a more advanced form of PI. Expert systems are used to run the tutoring aspect of the training, monitor trainee knowledge within a programmed knowledge model, and provide adaptive tutoring based on trainee responses.
	ITS	Intelligent tutoring systems (ITS) make use of artificial intelligence to provide tutoring that is more advanced than ICAI type tutoring. ITS "learns" through trainee responses the best methods of facilitating the trainee's learning.
	Simulations	Computer simulations provide a representation of a situation and the tasks to be performed in the situation. The representation can range from identical (e.g., word processing training) to fairly abstract (e.g., conflict resolution). Trainees perform the tasks presented to them by the computer program and the computer program monitors their performance.
	Virtual Reality	Virtual reality is an advanced form of computer simulation, placing the trainee in a simulated environment that is "virtually" the same as the physical environment. This simulation is accomplished by the trainee wearing special equipment such as head gear, gloves, and so on, which control what the trainee is able to see, feel, and otherwise sense. The trainee learns by interacting with objects in the electronic environment to achieve some goal.

Source: P. Nick Blanchard and James Thacker, *Effective Training: Systems, Strategies, and Practices* (Upper Saddle River, NJ: Pearson, 2003), p. 144.

Distance and Internet-Based Training

Firms today use various forms of distance learning methods for training. Distance learning methods include traditional paper-and-pencil correspondence courses, as well as teletraining, videoconferencing, and Internet-based classes.[63]

Teletraining   With teletraining, a trainer in a central location teaches groups of employees at remote locations via television hookups. Honda America Corp., began by using satellite television technology to train engineers and now uses it for many other types of employee training. For example, its Ohio-based subsidiary purchases seminars from the National Technological University, a provider of satellite education that uses courses from various universities and specialized teaching organizations. The price per course varies, but it averages $200 to $250 per employee per seminar. "It is much more cost-effective to keep workers at home and not pay for them to travel," one of the firm's training managers says.[64]

Videoconferencing

Firms use videoconferencing to train employees who are geographically separated from each other—or from the trainer.[65] Videoconferencing allows people in one location to communicate live via a combination of audio and visual equipment with people in another city or country or with groups in several cities.[66] Keypads allow audience interactivity. For instance, in a program at Texas Instruments, the keypad system lets instructors call on remote trainees and lets the latter respond.[67]

There are several things to keep in mind before lecturing in front of the camera. For example, because the training is remote, it's particularly important to prepare a training guide ahead of time, specifically, a manual the learners can use to follow the points the trainer is making, and a script for the trainer to follow. A sampling of other hints would include: Avoid bright, flashy jewelry or heavily patterned clothing; arrive at least 20 minutes early; test all equipment you will be using; have all participants introduce themselves; avoid presenting just to the video camera and not to the in-house participants; remember that excessive physical movement will cause video image distortion with compressed telephone transmission.[68]

Training via the Internet

Internet-based learning programs are increasingly popular. Many firms simply let their employees take online courses offered by online course providers such as Click2Learn.com. Others use their proprietary internal *intranets* to facilitate computer-based training. For example, Silicon Graphics transferred many of its training materials onto its intranet. "Now employees can access the programs whenever they want. Distribution costs are zero, and if the company wants to make a change to the program, it can do so at a central location."[69]

Similarly, when the Park Avenue Bank of Valdosta, Georgia, installed its e-training program, trainees could use it 24/7 from any computer. As with most enterprisewide e-learning initiatives, the bank's training program included a learning management system that maintains a database showing employees' progress in completing courses.[70]

Delivering training online can be cost-effective. For example, Delta Airlines customer service personnel receive about 70% of their annual required FAA training via the

Videoconference at Chase Bank: Two men in one location communicate in real time with a man and a woman at another location. Videoconferencing is ideal for training employees at locations scattered all over the country or the world. Some systems include keypads that allow for interactivity.

Internet. Employees reportedly like it because it's interactive. Delta likes it because "prior to online training, employees had to travel to one of five training centers, keeping them away from their jobs for at least the day."[71]

Many employers create full-blown "learning portals" to satisfy their employees' training needs. The "Improving Productivity" feature explains how they do this.

Web-based training is popular, but, in practice, it's usually not a choice of one form of training or another. The trend is toward blended learning solutions, wherein the trainee uses several delivery methods (for instance hard-copy manuals, in class lectures, self-guided e-learning programs, and Web-based seminars or "webinars") to learn the material.[78]

Improving Productivity Through HRIS

Learning Portals and Beyond

Many firms use business portals for various purposes today. Also called Enterprise Information Portals (EIPs), they are, like Yahoo!, windows to the Internet, but also much more. Through its business portal, categories of a firm's employees—secretaries, engineers, salespeople, and so on—are able to access all the corporate applications they need to use, and "get the tools you need to analyze data inside and outside your company, and see the customized content you need, like industry news and competitive data."[72]

Companies increasingly convey their employee training through such portals. Business-to-consumer (B2C) learning portals such as thinq.com and Click2Learn.com contract with employers to deliver online training courses to the firms' employees. Some B2Cs are "vortals," or vertical industry learning portals; they target specific industries with relevant offerings. Other firms create their own learning portals for employees and customers. Called business-to-employee (B2E) portals, they let the company contract with specific training content providers, who offer their content to the firm's employees via the portal.[73]

The U.S. Post Office, with 770,000 employees, 38,000 retail offices, and revenues of nearly $66 billion per year, recently instituted such a system. It contracted with Thinq (thinq.com) to use Thinq's learning management system (LMS) to expand the Postal Service's learning activities. Thinq.'s LMS gives employees access to state-of-the-art training, and lets the Postal Service's managers monitor their organization's training progress.[74]

Learning portals put more information into everyone's hands, when they want it. Instead of limiting training opportunities to teacher-led conventional classes or to periodic training sessions, training becomes available "24/7." Employees can learn at their own pace, when they want to.[75] The portals' built-in learning management system technology doesn't just let the employee take a course. It also often grades his or her work, tracks what courses he or she has completed, and even reminds the person what courses are scheduled when. Note, however, that while e-learning is beneficial, one study, by Michigan State University researchers, found that on-site employee education programs produced better results than online training, in terms of subsequent test results.[76]

Today's learning portals tend to focus on giving employees access to a repository of training content and associated automated testing tools. Special managers' functions allow them to monitor employees' training activities. The movement is toward integrating current e-learning methods with the company's overall, enterprisewide information systems. In that way, employers can more easily combine training with the firm's already available online discussion forums and synchronous meeting tools and chat room resources.[77]

What Is Management Development?

management development
Any attempt to improve current or future management performance by imparting knowledge, changing attitudes, or increasing skills.

Management development is any attempt to improve managerial performance by imparting knowledge, changing attitudes, or increasing skills. The ultimate aim is, of course, to enhance the future performance of the company itself. The general management development process consists of (1) assessing the company's strategic needs (for instance, to fill future executive openings, or to boost competitiveness), (2) appraising the managers' current performance, and then (3) developing the managers (and future managers).

Some development programs are companywide and involve all or most new (or potential) managers. Thus, new MBAs may join Ford's management development program and rotate through various assignments and educational experiences, with the dual aims of identifying their management potential and giving them breadth of experience (in, say, production and finance). The firm may then slot superior candidates onto a "fast track," a development program that prepares them more quickly for senior-level commands.

succession planning
A process through which senior-level openings are planned for and eventually filled.

Other development programs aim to fill specific positions, such as CEO. This usually involves succession planning. **Succession planning** refers to the process through which a company plans for and fills senior-level openings. For example, GE spent several years developing, testing, and watching potential replacements for CEO Jack Welch before finally choosing Jeffrey Immelt.

The typical succession planning process involves several steps: First, *anticipate management needs* based on strategic factors like planned expansion. Next, *review your firm's management skills* inventory (data on things like education and work experience, career preferences, and performance appraisals) to assess current talent. Then, *create replacement charts* that summarize potential candidates and each person's development needs. As in an earlier example (Figure 4-4), the development needs for a future division vice president might include job rotation, executive development programs—to provide training in strategic planning—and assignment for two weeks to the employer's in-house management development center.[79] *Management development* can then begin, using methods like managerial on-the-job training, discussed below.

Managerial On-the-Job Training

On-the-job training is not just for nonmanagers. Managerial on-the-job training methods include job rotation, the coaching/understudy approach, and action learning.

job rotation
A management training technique that involves moving a trainee from department to department to broaden his or her experience and identify strong and weak points.

Job Rotation
Job rotation means moving management trainees from department to department to broaden their understanding of all parts of the business and to test their abilities. The trainee—often a recent college graduate—may spend several months in each department. The person may just be an observer in each department, but more commonly gets fully involved in its operations. The trainee thus learns the department's business by actually doing it, while discovering what jobs he or she prefers.

Coaching/Understudy Approach
Here the trainee works directly with a senior manager or with the person he or she is to replace; the latter is responsible for the trainee's coaching. Normally, the understudy relieves the executive of certain responsibilities, giving the trainee a chance to learn the job.

action learning
A training technique by which management trainees are allowed to work full-time analyzing and solving problems in other departments.

Action Learning
Action learning programs give managers and others released time to work full-time on projects, analyzing and solving problems in departments other than their own. The basics of a typical action learning program include: carefully selected teams of five to 25 members; assigning the teams real world business problems that extend beyond their usual areas of expertise; and structured learning through coaching and feedback. The employer's senior managers usually choose the projects and decide whether to accept the teams' recommendations.[80]

Pacific Gas & Electric Company (PG&E) uses an approach it calls Action-Forum Process. The idea of the Action-Forum Process is to focus on relatively narrow issues that the employees already know the most about. The program has reportedly been a success. In three years, PG&E hosted almost 80 Action-Forums and saved more than $270 million as a result of them.

The Action-Forum Process has three phases: (1) a "framework" phase of six to eight weeks—this is basically an intense planning period during which the team defines and collects data on an issue to work on; (2) the Action-Forum itself—two to three days at PG&E's learning center discussing the issue and developing action-plan recommendations; and (3) accountability sessions, when the teams meet with the leadership group at 30, 60, and 90 days to review the status of their action plans and to make any necessary changes.

RESEARCH INSIGHT   Employees often talk about the need to "shatter the glass ceiling"—the transparent but often impermeable barrier many women still face in trying to move up to top management. While it certainly makes sense to shatter the glass ceiling for equity's sake, research suggests there may be another reason to do so. With the trend toward high-involvement work teams, consensus decision making, and empowerment, the sorts of leadership styles that women already exhibit may be much more appropriate than men's.

This conclusion is based on the assumption that female managers' leadership styles are different than males', and based on research, that appears to be the case. Specifically, women scored higher than men on such traditional measures of transformational leadership as encouraging followers to question their old ways of doing things or to break with the past, providing simplified emotional appeals to increase awareness and understanding of mutually desired goals, and providing learning opportunities. On the other hand, male managers were more likely to commend followers if they complied or to discipline them if they failed.[81]

Off-the-Job Management Training and Development Techniques

There are also many off-the-job techniques for training and developing managers.

case study method
A development method in which the manager is presented with a written description of an organizational problem to diagnose and solve.

The Case Study Method   As most everyone knows, the **case study method** presents a trainee with a written description of an organizational problem. The person then analyzes the case, diagnoses the problem, and presents his or her findings and solutions in a discussion with other trainees.

Integrated case scenarios expand the case analysis concept by creating long-term, comprehensive case situations. For example, the FBI Academy created an integrated case scenario. It starts with "a concerned citizen's telephone call and ends 14 weeks later with a simulated trial. In between is the stuff of a genuine investigation, including a healthy sampling of what can go wrong in an actual criminal inquiry." To create such scenarios, scriptwriters (often employees in the firm's training group) write the scripts. The scripts include themes, background stories, detailed personnel histories, and role-playing instructions. In the case of the FBI, the scenarios are aimed at developing specific training skills, such as interviewing witnesses and analyzing crime scenes.[82]

management game
A development technique in which teams of managers compete by making computerized decisions regarding realistic but simulated situations.

Management Games   With computerized **management games**, trainees are divided into five- or six-person groups, each of which competes with the others in a simulated marketplace. Each group typically must decide, for example, (1) how much to spend on advertising, (2) how much to produce, (3) how much inventory to maintain, and (4) how many of which product to produce. Usually, the game itself compresses a two- or three-year period into days, weeks, or months. As in the real world, each company team usually can't see what decisions (such as to boost advertising) the other firms have made, although these decisions do affect their own sales.[83]

Management games can be good development tools. People learn best by being involved, and the games can be useful for gaining such involvement. They help trainees develop their problem-solving skills, as well as to focus attention on planning rather than just putting out fires. The groups also usually elect their own officers and organize themselves; they can thus develop leadership skills and foster cooperation and teamwork.

Outside Seminars Many companies and universities offer Web-based and traditional management development seminars and conferences. For example, the American Management Association provides thousands of courses in areas ranging from accounting and controls to assertiveness training, basic financial skills, information systems, project management, purchasing management, and total quality management.[84] Specialized associations, such as SHRM provide more specialized seminars for their own profession's members.

University-Related Programs Many universities provide executive education and continuing education programs in leadership, supervision, and the like. These can range from one- to four-day programs to executive development programs lasting one to four months. An increasing number of these are offered online.

The Advanced Management Program of the Graduate School of Business Administration at Harvard University is one traditional example. A class in this program consists of experienced managers from around the world. It uses cases and lectures to provide top-level management talent with the latest management skills, and with practice analyzing complex organizational problems.

Video-linked classrooms are another option. For example, a video link between the School of Business and Public Administration at California State University, Sacramento, and a Hewlett-Packard facility in Roseville, California, allows HP employees to take courses at their facility.

Role Playing The aim of **role playing** is to create a realistic situation and then have the trainees assume the parts (or roles) of specific persons in that situation.

Figure 8-3 presents a role from a classic role-playing exercise called the New Truck Dilemma. When combined with the general instructions and other roles for the exercise, role playing can trigger spirited discussions among the role player/trainees. The aim is to develop trainees' skills in areas like leadership and delegating. For example, a supervisor could experiment with both a considerate and an autocratic leadership style, whereas in the real world the person might not have the luxury of experimenting. It may also train someone to be more aware of and sensitive to others' feelings.[85]

role playing
A training technique in which trainees act out parts in a realistic management situation.

Figure 8-3
Typical Role in A Role-Playing Exercise

Source: Normal R. F. Maier and Gertrude Casselman Verser, *Psychology in Industrial Organizations,* 5th ed., p. 190. Copyright 1982 by Houghton Mifflin Company. Used by permission of the publishers.

Walt Marshall—Supervisor of Repair Crew

You are the head of a crew of telephone maintenance workers, each of whom drives a small service truck to and from the various jobs. Every so often you get a new truck to exchange for an old one, and you have the problem of deciding which of your crew members you should give the new truck. Often there are hard feelings, since each seems to feel entitled to the new truck, so you have a tough time being fair. As a matter of fact, it usually turns out that whatever you decide is considered wrong by most of the crew. You now have to face the issue again because a new truck, a Chevrolet, has just been allocated to you for assignment.

In order to handle this problem you have decided to put the decision up to the crew. You will tell them about the new truck and will put the problem in terms of what would be the fairest way to assign the truck. Do not take a position yourself, because you want to do what they think is most fair.

behavior modeling
A training technique in which trainees are first shown good management techniques in a film, are asked to play roles in a simulated situation, and are then given feedback and praise by their supervisor.

Behavior Modeling   **Behavior modeling** involves (1) showing trainees the right (or "model") way of doing something, (2) letting trainees practice that way, and then (3) giving feedback on the trainees' performance. The basic behavior modeling procedure is as follows:

1. *Modeling.* First, trainees watch films or videos that show models behaving effectively in a problem situation. The video might show a supervisor effectively disciplining a subordinate, if teaching how to discipline is the aim of the training program.
2. *Role playing.* Next, the trainees are given roles to play in a simulated situation; here they practice and rehearse the effective behaviors demonstrated by the models.
3. *Social reinforcement.* The trainer provides reinforcement in the form of praise and constructive feedback based on how the trainee performs in the role-playing situation.
4. *Transfer of training.* Finally, trainees are encouraged to apply their new skills when they are back on their jobs.

Behavioral modeling can be effective.[86] Participants in one study were 160 members of a navy construction battalion based in Gulfport, Mississippi, being trained to use new computer work stations. Three training techniques were used: conventional instruction (primarily, a lecture and slide show); computer-assisted (students received a manual at the beginning of the session, as well as the diskette-based program needed to work through exercises at their new work stations); and behavior modeling. Measures of learning and skill development were highest for behavior modeling, followed by computer-assisted training, and then conventional instruction.

Corporate Universities and In-House Development Centers   Many firms, particularly larger ones, establish **in-house development centers**. In-house development centers needn't produce all (or most) of their own training and development programs, although some do. In fact, employers are increasingly collaborating with academic institutions, training and development program providers, and Web-based educational portals to create packages of programs and materials appropriate to their employees' needs.[87]

in-house development center
A company-based method for exposing prospective managers to realistic exercises to develop improved management skills.

For many firms, learning portals are becoming their virtual corporate universities. While firms such as GE have long had their own bricks-and-mortar corporate universities, learning portals let even smaller firms have corporate universities. Bain & Company, a management consulting firm, has such a Web-based virtual university for its employees. It provides a means not only for conveniently coordinating all the company's training efforts, but also for delivering Web-based modules that cover topics from strategic management to mentoring.[88]

Executive Coaches   Many firms use executive coaches to develop their top managers' effectiveness. An *executive coach* is an outside consultant who questions the executive's boss, peers, subordinates, and (sometimes) family in order to identify the executive's strengths and weaknesses, and to counsel the executive so he or she can capitalize on those strengths and overcome the weaknesses. About two-thirds of executive coaches are reportedly female, and coaches come from a variety of backgrounds including teaching, counseling, and the mental health professions. The executive coaches' trade group, the International Coach Federation, reportedly saw its membership rise from a about 1,500 in 1999 to almost 7,000 in 2003.[89]

Executive coaching can be quite effective. Participants in one study included about 1,400 senior managers who had received "360 degree" performance feedback from bosses, peers, and subordinates. About 400 worked with an executive coach to review the feedback. Then, about a year later, these 400 managers and about 400 who did not receive coaching again received multisource feedback. It was apparent from this new feedback that managers who received executive coaching were more likely to set more effective, specific, goals for their subordinates, and to have received improved ratings from subordinates and supervisors.[90]

For the individual manager or small business owner, training and development often requires a somewhat different perspective, as we illustrate in the "When You're On Your Own" feature.

● MANAGING ORGANIZATIONAL CHANGE AND DEVELOPMENT

Helping firms manage change is a major issue for human resource managers. For example, professor Edward Lawler conducted an extensive survey of HR practices and concluded that as more employers face the need to adapt to rapid competitive change, "focusing on strategy, organizational development, and organizational change is a high payoff activity for the HR organization."[92]

What to Change

When she assumed the presidency of a troubled Avon Products Company several years ago, Andrea Jung knew she had to renew her vast organization. Sales reps were leaving, customers were demanding new, more effective products, and the firm's whole "back end" operation—its purchasing, order-taking, distribution system—lacked automation.

Faced with situations like these, managers like Andrea Jung can change one or more of five aspects of their companies—their *strategy, culture, structure, technologies,* and the *attitudes and skills* of the employees. Organizational renewal often starts with a change in the firm's strategy, mission, and vision—with *strategic change.* For example, faced with intense competition from firms like Estée Lauder, Avon under Ms. Jung more than doubled its expenditures on new-product development, with the aim of introducing a new product line that created healthier, younger looking skin. Avon also expanded its strategy to selling through select department stores, rather than just door-to-door sales reps.

Strategic changes like these invariably trigger repercussions throughout the organization. For one thing (in Avon's case), going from strictly door-to-door to adding department stores meant *cultural change,* in other words, adopting new corporate values—new notions of what employees view as right and wrong, and what they should or shouldn't do. Moving fast, embracing technology, and keeping lines of communication open were a few of the new values Avon management needed employees to adopt.

Avon's new strategy and expansion to department stores and new product lines demanded *structural change*; in other words, reorganizing the company's departmental structure, coordination, span of control, reporting relationships, tasks, and decision-making procedures; as well as *technological change,* as Ms. Jung guided Avon to automate its purchasing/distribution chain.

CEO Andrea Jung initiated a renewal program at Avon Products that demanded strategic change (doubling expenditures on new-product development) and cultural change (selling through retail outlets, not just door to door), as well as structural and technological changes to fulfill the new goals.

Of course, strategic, cultural, structural, and technological changes like these, no matter how logical, will fail without the active support of a motivated and competent workforce. Organizational renewal therefore invariably

When You're On Your Own
HR for Line Managers and Entrepreneurs

Creating Your Own Training Program

While it would certainly be ideal if supervisors in even the largest firms could tap into their companies' packaged training programs to train the new people that they hire, the fact is that many times they cannot. You often hire and are responsible for the performance of a new employee only to find that your company provides little or no specialized training for this person, beyond the new person's introductory orientation.

If so, you have several options. First, for either the individual manager or small business owner there are literally hundreds of suppliers of prepackaged training solutions. These range from self-study programs from the American Management Association (1-800-262-9699), to American Media (1-800-262-2557), Karol Media (1-800-884-0555), and Business Advantage Inc. (1-800-305-9004). Similarly, reviewing trade journals such as Occupational Hazards (www.occupational-Hazards.com) will provide you with information on numerous specialized prepackaged training program suppliers (in this case, for occupational safety and health).

Small and medium-sized companies may also want to take advantage of the new trend toward **outsourced learning**.[91] Because major consulting firms such as Accenture, and IBM Global Services can obtain increased returns to scale by providing training solutions to multiple clients, a number of employers are now productively outsourcing their companies' entire learning functions to them.

Third, you can create your own "costless" training program, using the following process.

Step 1. Set Training Objectives
First, write down your training objectives. For example, your objective might be to reduce scrap, or to get new employees up to speed within two weeks.

Step 2. Write A Detailed Job Description
A detailed job description is the heart of any training program. It should list the daily and periodic tasks of each job, along with a summary of the steps in each task.

Step 3. Develop An Abbreviated Task Analysis Record Form
For practical purposes, the individual manager or small business owner can use an abbreviated version of the Task Analysis Record Form (Table 8-1) containing just four columns. In the first, list *tasks* (including what is to be performed in terms of each of the main tasks, and the steps involved in each task). In column B, list *performance standards* (in terms of quantity, quality, accuracy, and so on). In column C, list *trainable skills* required, things the employee must know or do to perform the task. This column provides you with specific knowledge and skills (such as "Keep both hands on the wheel") that you want to stress. In the fourth column, list *aptitudes required*. These are the human aptitudes (such as mechanical comprehension, and so on) that the employee should have to be trainable for the task and for which the employee can be screened ahead of time.

Step 4. Develop A Job Instruction Sheet
Next develop a job instruction sheet for the job. As explained on page 278, a job instruction training sheet shows the steps in each task as well as key points for each.

Step 5. Prepare Training Program for the Job
At a minimum, your training package should include the job description, abbreviated Task Analysis Record Form, and job instruction sheet, all collected in a training manual. The latter should also contain a summary of the training program's objectives, the three documents mentioned earlier, and a listing of the trainable skills required for the trainee. The manual might also contain an introduction to the job, and an explanation of how the job fits with other jobs in the plant or office.

You also have to make a decision regarding which media to use in your training program. A simple but effective on-the-job training program using current employees or supervisors as trainers requires only the materials we just described. However, it could turn out that the nature of the job or the number of trainees requires producing or purchasing special audio or visual tapes or disks, a PowerPoint slide presentation, or more extensive printed materials.

outsourced learning
The outsourcing of companies' learning functions to major consulting firms.

involves bringing about *changes in the employees* themselves, and in their attitudes, skills, and behaviors.[93]

HR managers usually play a central role in organizational renewals like the one at Avon Products. Cultural change may require a reinforcement of the firm's new values with new pay plans and new performance appraisal criteria. Structural change may require performance reviews to decide who stays and who goes, as well as job analysis, personnel planning, and revised employee selection standards. Changing the employees' attitudes, skills, and behavior typically triggers a wide range of new HR efforts—recruiting and selecting new employees, instituting new training programs, and changing how the firm appraises and rewards its personnel, for instance.

One implication is that managers and HR managers need to be familiar with the techniques companies can use to bring about organizational change. At a minimum, this requires understanding three things—how to overcome resistance to change, how to lead an organizational change, and how to use a technique known as organizational development. We turn to these three topics next.

Overcoming Resistance to Change: Lewin's Change Process

Often, the trickiest part of implementing an organizational change is overcoming employees' resistance to it. The change may require the cooperation of dozens or even hundreds of managers and supervisors, many of whom might well view the change as detrimental to their well-being and peace of mind. Resistance may therefore be considerable.

Psychologist Kurt Lewin formulated the classic explanation of how to implement change in the face of resistance. To Lewin, all behavior in organizations was a product of two kinds of forces—those striving to maintain the status quo and those pushing for change. Implementing change thus meant either weakening the status quo forces or building up the forces for change. Lewin's change process consisted of these three steps:

1. *Unfreezing.* Unfreezing means reducing the forces that are striving to maintain the status quo, usually by presenting a provocative problem or event to get people to recognize the need for change and to search for new solutions.

2. *Moving.* Moving means developing new behaviors, values, and attitudes, sometimes through structural changes and sometimes through the sorts of HR-based organizational change and development techniques explained later in this chapter. The aim is to alter people's behavior.

3. *Refreezing.* Lewin assumed that organizations tend to revert to their former ways of doing things unless you reinforce the changes. How do you do this? By "refreezing" the organization into its new equilibrium. Specifically, Lewin advocated instituting new systems and procedures (such as new compensation plans and appraisal processes) to support and maintain the changes.

Writing in the *Harvard Business Review*, one organizational change expert recently provided a new and useful perspective on the change process. He says, "successful change agents I've observed employ three distinct but linked campaigns in their initiatives. A *political campaign* creates a coalition strong enough to support and guide the initiative. A *marketing campaign* taps into employees' thoughts and feelings and also effectively communicates messages about the prospective program's theme and benefits. And finally, a *military campaign* deploys executives' scarce resources of attention and time . . . " to actually carry out the change. Let us look more closely at how to actually lead the organizational change process.[94]

How to Lead the Change: A 10-Step Change Process

In practice, leading an organizational change involves a multistep process, starting with the "political" aspects of overcoming resistance and creating a guiding coalition:[95]

1. **Establish a sense of urgency.** Having become aware of the need to change, most leaders like Avon's Andrea Jung start by creating a sense of urgency. This step often takes some creativity. For example, when former Charles Schwab CEO David Pottruck kicked off his firm's new strategy, he got about 100 of the firm's senior managers together near San Francisco's Golden Gate Bridge. Each manager got a jacket that said CROSSING THE CHASM, and then together they crossed the bridge. Pottruck calls this the start of reinventing his company.

2. **Mobilize commitment through joint diagnosis of problems.** Having established a sense of urgency, the leader may then create one or more task forces to diagnose the problems facing the company. Such teams can produce a shared understanding of what they can and must improve, and thereby mobilize the commitment of those who must actually implement the change.

3. **Create a guiding coalition.** Major transformations like that at Avon are sometimes associated with just one or two highly visible leaders. But no one can really implement such changes alone. Most companies create a guiding coalition of influential people, who work together as a team to act as missionaries and implementers.

4. **Develop a shared vision.** Organizational renewal also requires a new leadership vision, "a general statement of the organization's intended direction that evokes emotional feelings in organization members." For example, when Barry Gibbons became CEO of Spec's Music some years ago, its employees, owners, and bankers—all its stakeholders—required a vision of a renewed Spec's around which they could rally. Gibbons's vision of a leaner Spec's offering a diversified blend of concerts and retail music helped provide this sense of direction.

5. **Communicate the vision.** Change expert John Kotter says, "the real power of a vision is unleashed only when most of those involved in an enterprise or activity have a common understanding of its goals and directions."[96] To do this, you have to communicate the vision. The key elements in doing so include.[97]

   - *Keep it simple.* Eliminate all jargon and wasted words. For example: "We are going to become faster than anyone else in our industry at satisfying customer needs."
   - *Use multiple forums.* Try to use every channel possible—big meetings and small, memos and newspapers, formal and informal interaction—to spread the word.
   - *Use repetition.* Ideas sink in deeply only after employees have heard them many times.
   - *Lead by example.* "Walk your talk"—make sure your behaviors and decisions are consistent with the vision you espouse.

6. **Help employees to make the change.** It's futile to communicate your vision and to have employees want to make it a reality, if they haven't the means to do so. Perhaps a lack of skills stands in the way; or policies, procedures, and the organization chart make it difficult to act; or some intransigent managers may actually discourage employees from acting. When he was CEO at the former Allied Signal, Lawrence Bossidy put every one of his 80,000 people through quality improvement training. He also created geographic "councils" (for instance, for Asia) so Allied employees in those areas could get together, share market intelligence, and compare notes.[98]

7. Generate short-term wins. Changes such as automating Avon's distribution system may take time, but the teams working on them need some intermediate reinforcement.[99] For example, one company's team set its sights on producing one successful new product about 20 months after the start of the organizational change effort.[100] They selected the product in part because they knew they could meet this goal.

8. Consolidate gains and produce more change. Such short-term wins can generate the credibility to move ahead—to change all the systems, structures, and policies that don't fit well with the company's new vision. Leaders continue to produce more change by hiring and promoting new people; by identifying selected employees to champion the continuing change; and by providing additional opportunities for short-term wins by employees.[101]

9. Anchor the new ways of doing things in the company's culture. We've seen that organizational changes usually require corresponding changes in culture and values. A "team-based, quality-oriented, adaptable organization" is not going to happen if the values employees share still emphasize selfishness, mediocrity, and bureaucratic behavior. Leaders thus take steps to role-model and communicate the company's new values.

10. Monitor progress and adjust the vision as required. Finally, the leader must monitor and assess progress. In brief, this involves comparing where the company is today with where it should be, based on measurable milestones. Ultimately, the bottom line of the leader's change efforts must be: To what extent have we achieved our strategic goals? At Avon, for instance, how many new products has the company introduced? What percentage of its sales now come from department stores? How many new door-to-door sales reps has the firm added? How efficient has our back office become?

Using Organizational Development

organizational development
A special approach to organizational change in which employees themselves formulate and implement the change that's required.

There are many ways to identify the need for an organizational change, and to implement the change itself. One of the most widely used is **organizational development (OD)**. Organizational development is a special approach to organizational change in which the employees themselves formulate the change that's required and implement it, often with the assistance of a trained consultant. Particularly in large companies, the OD process (including hiring of facilitators) is almost always handled through HR. As an approach to changing organizations, OD has several distinguishing characteristics:

1. It usually involves *action research*, which means collecting data about a group, department, or organization and then feeding the information back to the employees so they can analyze it and develop hypotheses about what the problems in the unit might be.

2. It applies behavioral science knowledge to improve the organization's effectiveness.

3. It changes the attitudes, values, and beliefs of employees so that the employees themselves can identify and implement the technical, procedural, cultural, structural, or other changes needed to improve the company's functioning.

4. It changes the organization in a particular direction—toward improved problem solving, responsiveness, quality of work, and effectiveness.

The number and variety of OD applications (also called OD interventions or techniques) have increased substantially over the years. Today, as you can see in Table 8-3, many applications are available. OD practitioners have become increasingly involved not just in changing behaviors—their original area of expertise—but also in directly altering the firm's structure, practices, strategy, and culture.

Table 8-3

Examples of OD Interventions

Interventions

Human Process

T-groups
Process consultation
Third-party intervention
Team building
Organizational confrontation meeting
Survey research

Technostructural

Formal structural change
Differentiation and integration
Cooperative union–management projects
Quality circles
Total quality management
Work design

Human Resource Management

Goal setting
Performance appraisal
Reward systems
Career planning and development
Managing workforce diversity
Employee wellness

Strategic

Integrated strategic management
Culture change
Strategic change
Self-designing organizations

There are four basic categories of OD applications: human process, technostructural, human resource management, and strategic applications. Action research—getting the employees themselves to collect the required data and to design and implement the solutions—is the basis of all four.

Human Process Applications   Human process OD techniques generally aim first at improving human relations skills. The goal is to give employees the insight and skills required to analyze their own and others' behavior more effectively, so they can then solve interpersonal and intergroup problems. These problems might include, for instance, conflict among employees, or a lack of interdepartmental communications. *Sensitivity training* is perhaps the most widely used technique in this category. Team building and survey research are others.

Sensitivity, laboratory, or t-group training (the *t* is for "training") was one of the earliest OD techniques. Its use has diminished, but you'll still find it today. Sensitivity training's basic aim is to increase the participant's insight into his or her own behavior and the behavior of others by encouraging an open expression of feelings in the trainer-guided t-group. Typically, 10 to 15 people meet, usually away from the job, with no specific agenda. Instead, the focus is on the feelings and emotions of the members in the group at the meeting. The facilitator encourages participants to portray themselves as they are in the group rather than in terms of past behaviors or future problems. The t-group's success depends on the feedback each person gets from the others, and on the participants' willingness to be candid about how they perceive each others' behavior. The process requires a climate of "psychological safety," so participants feel safe enough to reveal themselves, to expose their feelings, to drop their defenses, and to try out new ways of interacting.[102]

It's not surprising that t-group training is a controversial technique. The personal nature of such training suggests that participation should be voluntary. Some view it as unethical because you can't really consider participation "suggested" by one's superior as strictly voluntary.[103] Others argue that it can actually be a dangerous exercise if led by an inadequately prepared trainer.

OD's distinctive emphasis on action research is quite evident in *team building*, which refers to a specific process for improving team effectiveness. According to experts French and Bell, the typical team-building meeting begins with the consultant interviewing each of the group members and the leader before the meeting.[104] They are all asked what their problems are, how they think the group functions, and what obstacles are keeping the group from performing better. The consultant then categorizes the interview data into themes (such as "inadequate communications") and presents the themes to the group at the start of the meeting. The group ranks the themes in terms of importance, and the most important ones become the agenda for the meeting. The group then explores and discusses the issues, examines the underlying causes of the problems, and begins devising solutions.

Survey research, another human process OD technique, requires that employees throughout the organization fill out attitude surveys. The facilitator then uses those data as a basis for problem analysis and action planning. In general, such surveys are a convenient way to unfreeze a company's management and employees, by providing a comparative, graphic illustration of the fact that the organization does have problems to solve.[105]

Technostructural Interventions   OD practitioners are also increasingly involved in changing firms' structures, methods, and job designs using an assortment of technostructural interventions. These interventions (as well as the human resource management and strategic interventions described in the following sections) generally focus directly on improving productivity and efficiency. For example, in a *formal structural change* program, the employees collect data on the company's existing organizational structure; they then jointly redesign and implement a new one.

Human Resource Management Applications   OD practitioners increasingly use action research to enable employees to analyze and change their firm's personnel practices. Targets of change here might include the performance appraisal and reward systems, as well as installing diversity programs.

Strategic OD Applications   Strategic interventions are organizationwide OD programs aimed at achieving a fit among a firm's strategy, structure, culture, and external environment. *Integrated strategic management* is one example of how to use OD to create or change a strategy. It consists of four steps: (1) Managers and employees analyze current strategy and organizational design, (2) choose a desired strategy and organizational design, and (3) design a strategic change plan—"an action plan for moving the organization from its current strategy and organizational design to the desired future strategy and design."[106] Finally, (4) the team oversees implementing the strategic change plan, and reviewing the results to ensure that they are proceeding as planned.[107]

The "HR Scorecard" feature explains how the Hotel Paris created a Training Program to support its strategy.

The HR Scorecard
Strategy and Results

The New Training Program

The Hotel Paris's competitive strategy is "To use superior guest service to differentiate the Hotel Paris properties, and to thereby increase the length of stay and return rate of guests, and thus boost revenues and profitability." HR manager Lisa Cruz must now formulate functional policies and activities that support this competitive strategy, by eliciting the required employee behaviors and competencies.

A preliminary analysis, performed jointly by Lisa and the Hotel Paris's chief financial officer, left them optimistic that HR could contribute measurably to achieving the hotel's strategic aims. Several employee competencies and behaviors including employee morale, employee commitment, and the percent of arriving guests receiving the hotel's required greeting had significant effects on customer and organizational outcomes such as guest satisfaction and frequency of guest returns. In turn, outcomes like these contributed measurably to the Hotel Paris's strategic goals, including profit margins, market share, and scores on industry satisfaction surveys. Lisa and her team now turn to creating a training program that will help to produce the required employee competencies and behaviors. The accompanying HR Scorecard (Figure 8-4) outlines the relationships involved.

As Lisa and the CFO reviewed measures of the Hotel Paris's current training efforts, it was clear that (when compared to similar companies) some changes were in order. Most other service companies provided at least 40 hours of training per employee per year, while the Hotel Paris offered, on average, no more than five or six. Similar firms offered at least 40 hours of training per new employee, while the Hotel Paris offered, at most, 10. Even the apparently "good" metrics comparisons simply masked poor results. For example, whereas most service firms spend about 8% of their payrolls on training, the Hotel Paris spent less than 1%. The problem, of course, was that the Hotel Paris's training wasn't more efficient, it was simply nonexistent.

Given this and the commonsense links between (1) employee training and (2) employee performance, the CFO gave his go-ahead for Lisa and her team to design a comprehensive package of training programs for all Hotel Paris employees. They retained a training supplier to design a one-day training program comprised of lectures and audiovisual material for all new employees. This program covered the Hotel Paris's history, competitive strategy, and its critical employee capabilities and behaviors, including the need to be customer oriented. With a combination of lectures and video examples of correct and incorrect behaviors, the behavior-modeling part of this program aimed to cultivate in new employees the company's essential values, including, "we endeavor to do everything we can to make the guests' stay 100% pleasant."

The team developed separate training programs for each of the hotel's other individual job categories. For example, it retained a special vendor to create computer-based training programs, complete with interactive scenarios, for both the front-desk clerks and telephone operators. As with all the new training programs, they had these translated into the languages of the countries in which the Hotel Paris did business. The team chose to stay with on-the-job training for both the housekeeping and carhop/doorperson job categories, but formalized this training with special handbooks for each job category's supervisory staff. For assistant managers, the team developed a new videoconference-based training and development program. In this way, the new managers could interact with other assistant managers around the chain, even as they were learning the basics of their new jobs. Lisa and the CFO were not at all surprised to find that within a year of instituting the new training programs, scores on numerous employee capabilities and behavior metrics (including speed of check-in/out, percent of employees scoring at least 90% on Hotel Paris's values quiz, and percent room cleaning infractions) improved markedly. They knew from previous analyses that these improvements would, in turn, drive improvements in customer and organizational outcomes, and financial performance.

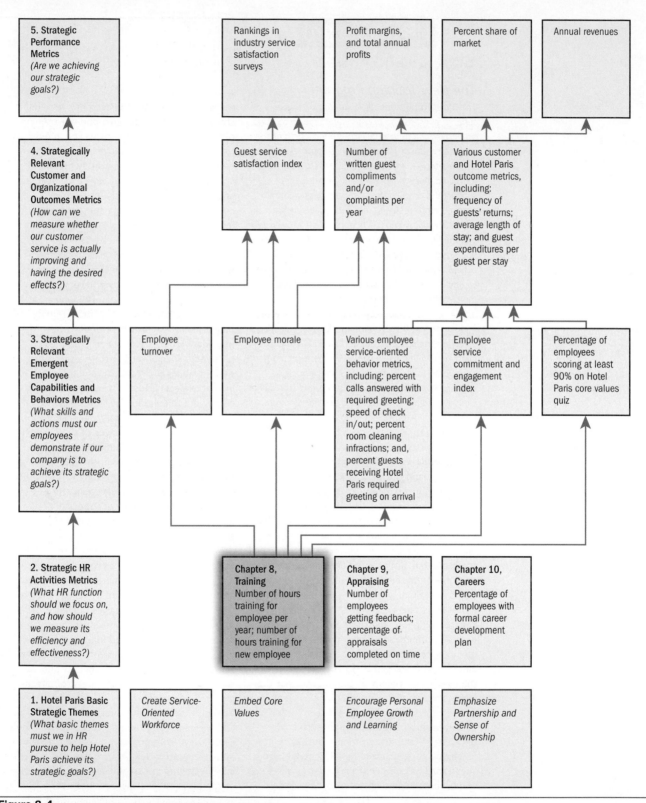

Figure 8-4
HR Scorecard for Hotel Paris International Corporation*

Note: *(An abbreviated example showing selected HR practices and outcomes aimed at implementing the competitive strategy, "To use superior guest services to differentiate the Hotel Paris properties and thus increase the length of stays and the return rate of guests, and thus boost revenues and profitability")

● EVALUATING THE TRAINING EFFORT

With today's emphasis on measuring HR management's financial impact, it is crucial that the employer make provisions to evaluate the training program. There are basically three things you can measure: participants' *reactions* to the program; what (if anything) the trainees *learned* from the program; and to what extent their on-the-job *behavior* changed as a result of the program. In one survey of about 500 U.S. organizations, 77% evaluated their training programs by eliciting reactions, 36% evaluated learning, and about 10% to 15% assessed the program's behavior and/or results.[108]

There are actually two basic issues to address when evaluating training programs. The first is the design of the evaluation study and, in particular, whether to use controlled experimentation. The second issue is: What should we measure?

Designing the Study

In evaluating the training program, the question is not just what to measure, but how to design the evaluation study. The *time series design* is one option. Here, as in Figure 8-5, you take a series of measures before and after the training program. This can provide at least an initial reading on the program's effectiveness.[109]

controlled experimentation
Formal methods for testing the effectiveness of a training program, preferably with before-and-after tests and a control group.

Controlled experimentation is a second option, and, strictly speaking, is the evaluation process of choice. A controlled experiment uses both a training group and a control group that receives no training. Data (for instance, on quantity of sales or quality of service) are obtained both before and after the group is exposed to training and before and after a corresponding work period in the control group. This makes it possible to determine the extent to which any change in performance in the training group resulted from the training rather than from some organizationwide change like a raise in pay that would have affected employees in both groups equally.[110]

In general, surveys suggest that less than half the companies responding attempted to obtain before-and-after measures from trainees; the number of organizations using control groups was negligible.[111] However, with tools such as HR Scorecards and time series studies, it is both possible and practical to estimate a training program's measurable impact. The HR manager should at least use an evaluation form like the one shown in Figure 8-6 to evaluate the training program.

Training Effects to Measure

You can measure four basic categories of training outcomes:

1. *Reaction.* Evaluate trainees' reactions to the program. Did they like the program? Did they think it worthwhile?

2. *Learning.* Test the trainees to determine whether they learned the principles, skills, and facts they were supposed to learn.

3. *Behavior.* Ask whether the trainees' on-the-job behavior changed because of the training program. For example, are employees in the store's complaint department more courteous toward disgruntled customers?

4. *Results.* Probably most important, ask: What final results were achieved in terms of the training objectives previously set? As per the HR Scorecard in Figure 8-4, did the number of customer complaints about employees drop? Did the percentage of calls answered with the required greeting rise? Reactions, learning, and behavior are important. But if the program doesn't produce measurable results, then it probably hasn't achieved its goals. If so, the problem may lie in the program. But remember that the results may be poor because the problem could not be solved by training in the first place.

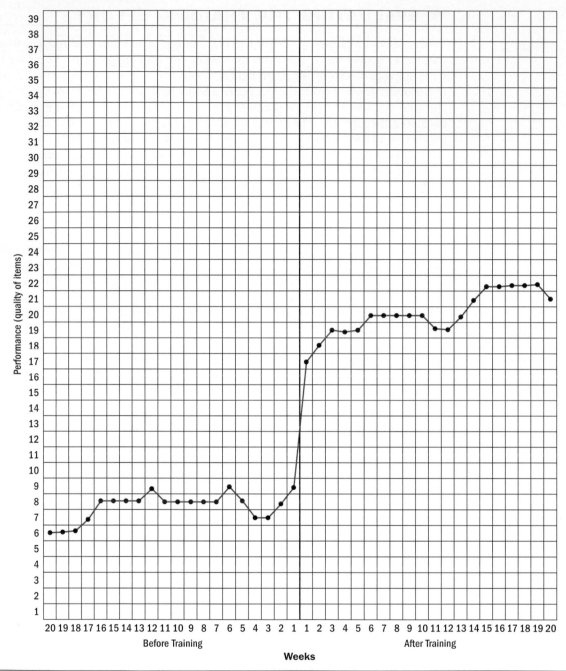

Figure 8-5
Time Series Training Evaluation Design

Evaluating any of these four is fairly straightforward. For example, Figure 8-6 presents one page from a sample evaluation questionnaire for assessing trainees' reactions. Similarly, you might assess trainees' learning by testing their new knowledge. The employer can assess the trainees' behavioral change directly or indirectly. Indirectly, for example, you might assess the effectiveness of, say, a supervisory performance appraisal training program by asking that person's subordinates questions like, "Did your supervisor take the time to provide you with examples of good and bad performance when he or she

OPM	*INSTRUCTOR HANDOUTS*	*United States Office of Personnel Management*

TRAINING EVALUATION FORM

TITLE OF COURSE: "Work and Family Issues - A Module for Supervisors and Managers"

NAME OF INSTRUCTOR:

DATE OF TRAINING
Started:_____
Ended:_____

NAME (Optional):	POSITION TITLE/GRADE:

AGENCY:	OFFICE PHONE: (Optional)	OFFICE ADDRESS: (Optional)

Rate Your Knowledge and Skill Level
(circle your rating)

Before this course Low---------------------------------------High
  1   2   3   4   5

After this course Low---------------------------------------High
  1   2   3   4   5

Overall, how would you rate this course?

__ Excellent   __Very Good __ Good

__ Fair __ Poor

EVALUATION OF COURSE
(Check appropriate box)

ITEMS OF EVALUATION How did the course sharpen your knowledge or skills in:	Excellent	Very Good	Good	Fair	Poor	Not Applicable
1. What Work and Family Programs Are	○	○	○	○	○	○
2. Who Uses Work and Family Programs	○	○	○	○	○	○
3. How to Recognize/Solve Work/Family Issues	○	○	○	○	○	○
4. Helping You Take Practical Steps on the Job	○	○	○	○	○	○

RATING OF INSTRUCTOR

	Excellent	Very Good	Good	Fair	Poor	Not Applicable
1. Presentation, organization, delivery	○	○	○	○	○	○
2. Knowledge and command of the subject	○	○	○	○	○	○
3. Use of audio-visuals or other training aids	○	○	○	○	○	○
4. Stimulation of an open exchange of ideas, participation & group interaction	○	○	○	○	○	○

STRONG POINTS OF THE COURSE

○

○

○

_____

WEAK POINTS OF THE COURSE

○

○

○

_____

ADDITIONAL DATA YOU WOULD LIKE TO HAVE COVERED IN COURSE

○

○

○

_____

ADDITIONAL COMMENTS/OR RECOMMENDATIONS

Figure 8-6
A Sample Training Evaluation Form
Source: www.opm.gov/wrkfam/.

appraised your performance most recently? Or, you can directly assess a training program's results, for instance, by measuring, say, the percentage of phone calls answered correctly.

While these four basic categories are understandable and widely used, there are several things to keep in mind. Perhaps most important, "reaction" measures (such as "How did you like the program?") generally aren't good substitutes for other training effects like learning, behavior, or results. Getting trainees' reactions—often the measurement of choice when firms evaluate training—may provide some insight into how they liked the program. However, it probably won't provide much insight into what they learned or how they'll behave once they're back on the job.[112]

Computerization is facilitating the evaluation process. For example, Bovis Land Lease in New York City offers its 625 employees numerous courses in construction and other subjects. The firm uses special learning management software to monitor which employees are taking which courses, and the extent to which employees are improving their skills.[113]

 *Review*

SUMMARY

1. The training process consists of five steps: needs analysis, instructional design, validation, implementation, and evaluation.

2. Principles of learning that are useful for training include: Make the material meaningful (by providing a bird's-eye view and familiar examples, organizing the material, splitting it into meaningful chunks, and using familiar terms and visual aids); make provision for transfer of training; and try to motivate trainees.

3. Basic training methods include on-the-job training, apprenticeship training, informal learning, job instruction training, lectures, programmed learning, audiovisual tools, simulated training, computer-based training, electronic performance support systems, and distance and Internet-based training.

4. On-the-job training is a common training technique. It might take the form of the understudy method, job rotation, or special assignments and committees. In any case, it

should have four steps: preparing the learner, presenting the operation (or nature of the job), doing performance tryouts, and following up.

5. Management development prepares employees for future jobs by imparting knowledge, changing attitudes, or increasing skills.

6. Managerial on-the-job training methods include job rotation, coaching, and action learning. Basic off-the-job techniques include case studies, management games, outside seminars, university-related programs, role playing, behavior modeling, and in-house development centers.

7. In gauging the effectiveness of a training program, there are four categories of outcomes companies can measure: reactions, learning, behavior, and results. In some cases where training seems to have failed, it may be because training was not the appropriate solution to the problem.

DISCUSSION QUESTIONS

1. "A well-thought-out orientation program is essential for all new employees, whether they have experience or not." Explain why you agree or disagree with this statement.

2. Explain how you would apply our principles of learning in developing a lecture, say, on orientation and training.

3. "John Santos" is an undergraduate business student majoring in accounting. He has just failed the first accounting course, Accounting 101, and is understandably upset. Explain how you would use performance analysis to identify what, if any, are John's training needs.

4. What are some typical on-the-job training techniques? What do you think are some of the main drawbacks of

relying on informal on-the-job training for breaking new employees into their jobs?

5. One reason for implementing global training programs is the need to avoid business losses "due to cultural insensitivity." What sort of cultural insensitivity do you think is referred to, and how might that translate into lost business? What sort of training program would you recommend to avoid such cultural insensitivity?

6. Describe the pros and cons of five management development methods.

7. Do you think job rotation is a good method to use for developing management trainees? Why or why not?

INDIVIDUAL AND GROUP ACTIVITIES

1. You're the supervisor of a group of employees whose task is to assemble disk drives that go into computers. You find that quality is not what it should be and that many of your group's devices have to be brought back and reworked; your boss says that "You'd better start doing a better job of training your workers."

    a. What are some of the "staffing" factors that could be contributing to this problem?

    b. Explain how you would go about assessing whether it is in fact a training problem.

2. Pick out some task with which you are familiar—mowing the lawn, making a salad, or studying for a test—and develop a job instruction training sheet for it.

3. Working individually or in groups, develop a short, programmed learning program on the subject "Guidelines for Giving a More Effective Lecture."

4. Working individually or in groups, use the phone or the Web to contact a provider of management development seminars. Obtain copies of its recent listings of seminar offerings. At what levels of managers are the seminar offerings aimed? What seem to be the most popular types of development programs? Why do you think that's the case?

5. Working individually or in groups, develop several specific examples to illustrate how a professor teaching human resource management could use at least four of the techniques described in this chapter in teaching his or her HR course.

6. Working individually or in groups, develop an orientation program for high school graduates entering your university as freshmen.

7. The HRCI "Test Specifications" appendix at the end of this book (pages 685–689) lists the knowledge someone studying for the HRCI certification exam needs to have in each area of human resource management (such as in Strategic Management, Workforce Planning, and Human Resource Development). In groups of four to five students, do four things: (1) review that appendix now; (2) identify the material in this chapter that relates to the required knowledge the appendix lists; (3) write four multiple choice exam questions on this material that you believe would be suitable for inclusion in the HRCI exam; and (4) if time permits, have someone from your team post your team's questions in front of the class, so the students in other teams can take each others' exam questions.

8. By mid-2003, the U.S.-led coalition in Iraq was sending hundreds of trainers to that country to train new cadres of Iraqi workers, from teachers to police officers. Perhaps no training task was more pressing than that involved in creating the country's new police force. These were the people who were to help the coalition bring security to Iraq. However, many new officers had no experience in police work. There were language barriers between trainers and trainees. And some trainees found themselves quickly under fire from insurgents when they went as trainees out into the field. Based on what you learned about training from this chapter, list the five most important things you would tell the officer in charge of training (a former U.S. big-city police chief) to keep in mind as he designs the training program.

EXPERIENTIAL EXERCISE

Flying the Friendlier Skies

Purpose: The purpose of this exercise is to give you practice in developing a training program for the job of airline reservation clerk for a major airline.

Required Understanding: You should be fully acquainted with the material in this chapter and should read the following description of an airline reservation clerk's duties:

Customers contact our airline reservation clerks to obtain flight schedules, prices, and itineraries. The reservation clerks look up the requested information on our airline's online flight schedule systems, which are updated continuously. The reservation clerk must deal courteously and expeditiously with the customer, and be able to quickly find alternative flight arrangements in order to provide the customer with the itinerary that fits his or her needs. Alternative flights and prices must be found quickly, so that the customer is not kept waiting, and so that our reservations operations group maintains its efficiency

standards. It is often necessary to look under various routings, since there may be a dozen or more alternative routes between the customer's starting point and destination.

You may assume that we just hired 30 new clerks, and that you must create a three-day training program.

How to Set Up the Exercise/Instructions: Divide the class into teams of five or six students.

Airline reservation clerks obviously need numerous skills to perform their jobs. JetBlue Airlines has asked you to quickly develop the outline of a training program for its new reservation clerks. You may want to start by listing the job's main duties, and by reviewing any work you may have done for the exercise at the end of Chapter 6. In any case, please produce the requested outline, making sure to be very specific about what you want to teach the new clerks, and what methods and aids you suggest using to train them.

APPLICATION CASE

Reinventing the Wheel at Apex Door Company

Jim Delaney, president of Apex Door, has a problem. No matter how often he tells his employees how to do their jobs, they invariably "decide to do it their way," as he puts it, and arguments ensue between Jim, the employee, and the employee's supervisor. One example is the door-design department, where the designers are expected to work with the architects to design doors that meet the specifications. While it's not "rocket science," as Jim puts it, the designers invariably make mistakes—such as designing in too much steel, a problem that can cost Apex tens of thousands of wasted dollars, once you consider the number of doors in, say, a 30-story office tower.

The order processing department is another example. Jim has a very specific and detailed way he wants the order written up, but most of the order clerks don't understand how to actually use the multipage order form. They simply improvise when it comes to a detailed question such as whether to classify the customer as "industrial" or "commercial."

The current training process is as follows. None of the jobs has a training manual per se, although several have somewhat out-of-date job descriptions. The training for new people is all on the job. Usually, the person leaving the company trains the new person during the one- or two-week overlap period, but if there's no overlap, the new person is trained as well as possible by other employees who have filled in occasionally on the job in the past. The training is basically the same throughout the company—for machinists, secretaries, assemblers, engineers, and accounting clerks, for example.

Questions

1. What do you think of Apex's training process? Could it help to explain why employees "do things their way" and if so, how?
2. What role should job descriptions play in training at Apex?
3. Explain in detail what you would do to improve the training process at Apex. Make sure to provide specific suggestions, please.

CONTINUING CASE

Carter Cleaning Company

The New Training Program

At the present time the Carter Cleaning Centers have no formal orientation or training policies or procedures, and Jennifer believes this is one reason why the standards to which she and her father would like employees to adhere are generally not followed.

The Carters would prefer that certain practices and procedures be used in dealing with the customers at the front counters. For example, all customers should be greeted with what Jack refers to as a "big hello." Garments they drop off should immediately be inspected for any damage or unusual stains so these can be brought to the customer's attention, lest the customer later return to pick up the garment and erroneously blame the store. The garments are then supposed to be immediately placed together in a nylon sack to separate them from other customers' garments. The ticket also has to be carefully written up, with the customer's name and telephone number and the date precisely and clearly noted on all copies. The counterperson is also supposed to take the opportunity to try to sell the customer additional services such as waterproofing, or simply notify the customer that "Now that people are doing their spring cleaning, we're having a special on drapery cleaning all this month." Finally, as the customer leaves, the counterperson is supposed to make a courteous comment like "Have a nice day" or "Drive safely." Each of the other jobs in the stores—pressing, cleaning and spotting, periodically maintaining the coin laundry equipment, and so forth—similarly contain cer-

tain steps, procedures, and most important, standards the Carters would prefer to see upheld.

The company has had problems, Jennifer feels, because of a lack of adequate employee training and orientation. For example, two new employees became very upset last month when they discovered that they were not paid at the end of the week, on Friday, but instead were paid (as are all Carter employees) on the following Tuesday. The Carters use the extra two days in part to give them time to obtain everyone's hours and compute their pay. The other reason they do it, according to Jack, is that "frankly, when we stay a few days behind in paying employees it helps to ensure that they at least give us a few days' notice before quitting on us. While we are certainly obligated to pay them anything they earn, we find that psychologically they seem to be less likely to just walk out on us Friday evening and not show up Monday morning if they still haven't gotten their pay from the previous week. This way they at least give us a few days' notice so we can find a replacement."

Other matters that could be covered during orientation and training, says Jennifer, include company policy regarding paid holidays, lateness and absences, health and hospitalization benefits (there are none, other than workers' compensation), and general matters like the maintenance of a clean and safe work area, personal appearance and cleanliness, time sheets, personal telephone calls and mail, company policies regarding matters like substance abuse, and eating or smoking on the job (both forbidden).

Jennifer believes that implementing orientation and training programs would help to ensure that employees know how to do their jobs the right way. And she and her father further believe that it is only when employees understand the right way to do their jobs that there is any hope their jobs will in fact be accomplished the way the Carters want them to be accomplished.

Questions

1. Specifically what should the Carters cover in their new employee orientation program and how should they convey this information?

2. In the HR management course Jennifer took, the book suggested using a job instruction sheet to identify tasks performed by an employee. "Should we use a form like this for the counterperson's job, and if so, what would the filled-in form look like?"

3. Which specific training techniques should Jennifer use to train her pressers, her cleaner–spotters, her managers, and her counterpeople, and why?

KEY TERMS

employee orientation, 268	programmed learning, 279	case study method, 287
training, 270	simulated training, 281	management game, 287
performance management, 270	job aid, 282	role playing, 288
negligent training, 272	electronic performance support	behavior modeling, 289
task analysis, 273	systems (EPSS), 282	in-house development center, 289
performance analysis, 273	management development, 285	outsourced learning, 291
on-the-job training, 275	succession planning, 286	organizational development, 294
apprenticeship training, 276	job rotation, 286	controlled experimentation, 299
job instruction training (JIT), 277	action learning, 286	

ENDNOTES

1. Charlotte Garvey, "The Whirlwind of a New Job," *HR Magazine*, June 2001, p. 111.
2. Sabrina Hicks, "Successful Orientation Programs," *Training and Development*, April 2000, p. 59. See also Howard Klein and Natasha Weaver, "The Effectiveness of an Organizational Level Orientation Program in the Socialization of New Hires," *Personnel Psychology* 53 (2000), pp. 47–66.
3. Susan Ashford and Jay Stewart Black, "Proactivity During Organizational Entry: The Role of Desire for Control," *Journal of Applied Psychology* 81, no. 2 (1996), pp. 199–214.
4. See, for example, Carolyn Wiley, "Training for the 90s: How Leading Companies Focus on Quality Improvement, Technological Change, and Customer Service," *Employee Relations Today*, Spring 1993, p. 80.
5. Christine Ellis and Sarah Gale, "A Seat at the Table," *Training*, March 2001, pp. 90–96.
6. "Companies Invested More in Training Despite Economic Setbacks, Survey Says," *BNA Bulletin to Management*, March 7, 2002, p. 73. "Employee Training Expenditures on the Rise," *American Salesman* Jan 2004 v49 i1, pp. 26–28.
7. Winfred Alfred Jr. et al., "Effectiveness of Training in Organizations: A Meta Analysis of Design and Evaluation Features," *Journal of Applied Psychology* 88, no. 2 (2003), p. 242.
8. Shari Caudron, "Training in the Post Terrorism Year," *Training and Development*, February 2002, pp. 25–30.
9. Kenneth Wexley and Gary Latham, *Developing and Training Human Resources in Organizations*, (Upper Saddle River, NJ, Prentice Hall, 2002) p. 107.
10. Ibid., p. 82.
11. Ibid., p. 87.
12. Ibid., p. 90.
13. Janice A. Cannon-Bowers et al., "Framework for Understanding Pre-Practice Conditions and Their Impact on Learning," *Personnel Psychology* 51 (1998), pp. 291–320.
14. Ibid., p. 305.
15. Kimberly A. Smith-Jentsch et al., "Can Pre-Training Experiences Explain Individual Differences in Learning?" *Journal of Applied Psychology* 81, no. 1 (1996), pp. 110–116.
16. Ibid.
17. Kathryn Tyler, "Focus on Training," *HR Magazine*, May 2000, pp. 94–102.
18. Ibid.
19. Mindy Chapman, "The Return on Investment for Training," *Compensation & Benefits Review*, January/February 2003, pp. 32–33.
20. Ibid., p.. 33.
21. Kenneth Sovereign, *Personnel Law* (Upper Saddle River, NJ: Prentice Hall, 1999), p. 204.
22. Ibid., pp. 216–217.
23. P. Nick Blanchard and James Thacker, *Effective Training: Systems, Strategies and Practices* (Upper Saddle River, NJ: Prentice Hall, 1999), pp. 138–139.
24. Tom Barron, "When Things Go Haywire," *Training and Development*, February 1999, pp. 25–27.
25. For an additional perspective, see Danny Langdon, "Objectives: Get Over Them," *Training and Development*, February 1999, pp. 54–58. See also Joan Brett and Don VandeWalle, "Goal Orientation and Goal Content As Predictors of Performance in a Training Program," *Journal of Applied Psychology* 84, no. 6 (1999), pp. 863–873.
26. Kenneth Wexley and Gary Latham, *Developing and Training Human Resources in Organizations* (Upper Saddle River, NJ: Prentice Hall, 2002), pp. 78–79.
27. Donna Goldwasser, "Me a Trainer?" *Training*, April 2001, pp. 60–66.
28. Ibid., pp. 107–112.
29. Oranit Davidson and Dov Eden, "Remedial Self-Fulfilling Prophecy: Two Field Experiments to Prevent Golem Effects Among Disadvantaged Women," *Journal of Applied Psychology* 85, no. 3 (2000), pp. 386–396.

30. Four steps in on-the-job training based on William Berliner and William McLarney, *Management Practice and Training* (Burr Ridge, IL: McGraw-Hill, 1974), pp. 442–443. See also Robert Sullivan and Donald Miklas, "On-the-Job Training That Works," *Training and Development Journal* 39, no. 5 (May 1985), pp. 118–120; Stephen B. Wehrenberg, "Supervisors as Trainees: The Long-Term Gains of OJT," *Personnel Journal* 66, no. 4 (April 1987), pp. 48–51.

31. Harley Frazis, Diane Herz, and Michael Horrigan, "Employer-Provided Training: Results from a New Survey," *Monthly Labor Review*, May 1995, p. 4.

32. "German Training Model Imported," *BNA Bulletin to Management*, December 19, 1996, p. 408.

33. Ibid.

34. Robert Weintraub and Jennifer Martineau, "The Just in Time Imperative," *Training and Development* (June 2002), p. 52.

35. Donald Michalak and Edwin G. Yager, *Making the Training Process Work* (New York: Harper & Row, 1979), pp. 108–111. See also Richard Wiegand, "Can All Your Trainees Hear You?" *Training and Development Journal* 41, no. 8 (August 1987), pp. 38–43.

36. Jacqueline Schmidt and Joseph Miller, "The Five-Minute Rule for Presentations," *Training and Development*, March 2000, pp. 16–17.

37. Arthur Winfred Jr. et al., "Effectiveness of Training in Organizations: A Meta Analysis of Design and Evaluation Features," *Journal of Applied Psychology* 88, no. 2 (2003), pp. 234–245.

38. G. N. Nash, J. P. Muczyk, and F. L. Vettori, "The Role and Practical Effectiveness of Programmed Instruction," *Personnel Psychology* 24 (1971), pp. 397–418; Duane Schultz and Sydney Ellen Shultz, *Psychology and Work Today* (Upper Saddle River, NJ: Prentice Hall, 1998), pp. 181–183.

39. Dannah Baynton, "America's $60 Billion Problem," *Training* 38, no. 5 (May 2001), p. 51.

40. "Skill Deficiencies Pose Increasing Problems," *BNA Bulletin to Management*, October 26, 1995, pp. 337–338, and "Job Applicants Lack Basic Skills," *Manufacturing News*, May 26, 2000, v7 i10, p. 12.

41. Ellen Sherman, "Back to Basics to Improve Skills," *Personnel*, July 1989, pp. 22–26, and, "Job Applicants Lack Basic Skills," op cit.

42. Baynton, "America's $60 Billion Problem," p. 51.

43. Jennifer Salopek, "Trends: Lost in Translation," *Training and Development*, December 2003, p. 15.

44. Kathryn Tyler, "Brushing Up on the Three Rs," *HR Magazine*, October 1999, p. 88.

45. See Joyce Santora, "Kinney Shoes Steps into Diversity," *Personnel Journal*, September 1991, p. 74.

46. Willie Hopkins, Karen Sterkel-Powell, and Shirley Hopkins, "Training Priorities for a Diverse Workforce," *Public Personnel Management* 23, no. 3 (Fall 1994), p. 433.

47. "Adams Mark Hotel & Resorts Launches Diversity Training Program," *Hotel and Motel Management* 216, no. 6 (April 2001), p. 15.

48. Matthew Reis, "Do-It-Yourself Diversity," *Training and Development*, March 2004, pp. 80–81.

49. Wexley and Latham, *Developing and Training*, pp. 131–133. See also Teri O. Grady and Mike Matthews, "Video . . . Through the Eyes of the Trainee," *Training* 24, no. 7 (July 1987), pp. 57–62. Erica Schroeder, "Training Takes Off, Using Multimedia," *PC Week*, August 29, 1994, pp. 33–34.

50. See, for example, Tim Falconer, "No More Pencils, No More Books!" *Canadian Banker*, March–April 1994, pp. 21–25.

51. Ralph E. Ganger, "Training: Computer-Based Training Works," *Personnel Journal* 73, no. 11 (November 1994), pp. 51–52.

52. For another example, see Mickey Williamson, "High-Tech Training," *byte*, December 1994, pp. 74–89.

53. Dina Berta, "Computer-Based Training Clicks with both Franchisees and Their Employees," *Nation's Restaurant News*, July 9, 2001, pp. 1, 18; see also Daniel Cable and Charles Parsons, "Socialization Tactics and Person–Organization Fit," *Personnel Psychology*, 54 (2001), pp. 1–23.

54. These are summarized in Rockley Miller, "New Training Looms," *Hotel and Motel Management*, April 4, 1994, pp. 26, 30.

55. P. Nick Blanchard and James Thacker, *Effective Training: Systems, Strategies, and Practices* (Upper Saddle River, NJ: Pearson, 2003), p. 247.

56. Ibid., p. 248.

57. Ibid., p. 249.

58. Paul Harris, "Simulation: The Game is On," *Training and Development*, October 2003, p. 49.

59. Tyler, "Focus on Training," p. 96. See also Allison Rosset and Erica Mohr, "Performance Support Tools: Where Learning, Work, and Results Converge," *Training and Development*, February 2004, pp. 35–37.

60. Blanchard and Thacker, *Effective Training*, p. 163.

61. Craig Marion, "What Is the EPSS Movement and What Does It Mean to Information Designers?" http://www.chesco.com/~cmarion/pcd/epssimplications.html.

62. http://www.epss.com/lb/casestud/casestud.htm.

63. Michael Blotzer, "Distance Learning," *Occupational Hazards*, March 2000, pp. 53–54.

64. "Personnel Shop Talk," *BNA Bulletin to Management*, February 12, 1998, p. 46.

65. Michael Emery and Margaret Schubert, "A Trainer's Guide to Videoconferencing," *Training*, June 1993, p. 60.

66. Ibid.

67. "Employer to Learn the Benefits of Distance Learning," *BNA Bulletin to Management*, April 25, 1996, p. 130.

68. These are based on or quoted from Emery and Schubert, "A Trainer's Guide to Videoconferencing," p. 61.

69. Larry Stevens, "The Internet: Your Newest Training Tool?" *Personnel Journal*, July 1996, pp. 27–31; see also Kenneth Brown, "Using Computers to Deliver Training: which Employees Learn and Why?" *Personnel Psychology* 54, no. 2 (Summer 2001), pp. 271–296; Jason Lewis and Dan Michaluk, "Four Steps to Building E-Learning Success," *Workforce*, May 2002, p. 42.

70. Roy Karon, "Georgia Bank Find Solutions in E-Training," *E-Learning*, May/June 2000, p. 33.

71. Ellen Zimmerman, "Better Training Is Just a Click Away," *Workforce*, January 2001, pp. 36–42.

72. David Kirkpatrick, "The Portal of the Future? Your Boss Will Run It," *Fortune*, August 2, 1999, pp. 222–227. See also Cynthia Pantazis, "Maximizing E-learning to Train the 21st Century Workforce," *Public Personnel Management*, Spring 2002, pp. 21–26.

73. Tom Barron, "A Portrait of Learning Portals," www.learningcircuits.com/may2000/barron.html.

74. "The U.S. Postal Service Turns to Thinq's LMS to Streamline Operations," *Training and Development*, December 2003, pp. 72–73.

75. Eileen Granger, "Goodbye Training, Hello Learning," *Workforce*, July 2002, pp. 35–42.

76. Brian O'Connell, "A Poor Grade for E-learning," *Workforce*, July 2002, p. 15.

77. Helen Beckett, "Blended Skills for a Better Class of E-learning," *Computer Weekly*, January 20, 2004, p. 20.

78. "The Next Generation of Corporate Learning," *Training and Development*, June 2003, p. 47.

79. For discussions of the steps in succession planning, see, for example, Kenneth Nowack, "The Secrets of Succession," *Training and*

Development, November 1994, pp. 49–55; Donald Brookes, "In Management Succession: Who Moves Up?" *Human Resources*, January–February 1995, pp. 11–13.

80. "Thrown into Deep End, Workers Surface as Leaders," *BNA Bulletin to Management*, July 11, 2002, p. 223.

81. Bernard Bass and Bruce Avolio, "Shatter the Glass Ceiling: Women May Make Better Managers," *Human Resource Management* 33, no. 4 (Winter 1994), pp. 549–560.

82. Chris Whitcomb, "Scenario-Based Training at the FBI," *Training and Development*, June 1999, pp. 42–46.

83. For a discussion of management games and also other training and development simulations, see Charlene Marner Solomon, "Simulation Training Builds Teams Through Experience," *Personnel Journal*, June 1993, pp. 100–109; Kim Slack, "Training for the Real Thing," *Training and Development*, May 1993, pp. 79–89; Bruce Lierman, "How to Develop a Training Simulation," *Training and Development*, February 1994, pp. 50–52.

84. American Management Association, Catalog of Seminars: April–December, 2003.

85. Norman Maier, Allen Solem, and Ayesha Maier, *The Role Play Technique* (San Diego, CA: University Associates, 1975), pp. 2–3. See also Alan Test, "Why I Do Not Like to Role Play," *American Salesman*, August 1994, pp. 7–20.

86. Steve Simon and Jon Werner, "Computer Training Through Behavioral Modeling, Self-Paced, and Instructional Approaches: A Field Experiment," *Journal of Applied Psychology* 81, no. 6 (1996), pp. 648–659.

87. Martha Peak, "Go Corporate U!" *Management Review* 86, no. 2 (February 1997), pp. 33–37.

88. Russell Gerbman, "Corporate Universities 101," *HR Magazine*, February 2000, pp. 101–106.

89. "Executive Coaching: Corporate Therapy," *The Economist*, November 15, 2003, p. 61.

90. James Smither et al., "Can Working with an Executive Coach Improve Multisource Feedback Ratings Over Time?" *Personnel Psychology* 56, no. 1 (Spring 2003), pp. 23–44.

91. Paul Harris, "A New Market Emerges," *Training and Development*, September 2003, pp. 30–38.

92. Edward Lawler III and Susan Mohrman, "Beyond the Vision: What Makes HR Effective?" *Human Resource Planning* 23, no. 4 (December 2000), p. 10.

93. David Upton, "What Really Makes Factories Flexible?" *Harvard Business Review*, July–August 1995, p. 75.

94. Larry Hirschhorn, "Campaigning for Change," *Harvard Business Review*, July 2002, p. 98.

95. The 10 steps are based on Michael Beer, Russell Eisenstat, and Burt Spector, "Why Change Programs Don't Produce Change," *Harvard Business Review*, November–December 1990, pp. 158–166; Thomas Cummings and Christopher Worley, *Organization Development and Change* (Minneapolis, MN: West Publishing Company, 1993); John P. Kotter, "Leading Change: Why Transformation Efforts Fail," *Harvard Business Review*, March–April 1995, pp. 59–66; and John P. Kotter, *Leading Change* (Boston: Harvard Business School Press, 1996). Change doesn't necessarily have to be painful. See, for example, Eric Abrahamson, "Change Without Pain," *Harvard Business Review*, July–August 2000, pp. 75–79, and Michael Beer and Nitin Nohria, "Cracking the Code of Change," *Harvard Business Review*, June 2000, pp. 133–141. And, some people are just more open to change than are others. As just one example, self-esteem and optimism were related to higher levels of change acceptance in one recent study: Connie Wanberg, "Predictors and Outcomes of Openness to Changes in a Reorganizing Workplace," *Journal of Applied Psychology* 85, no. 1 (2000), pp. 132–142.

96. Kotter, "Leading Change," p. 85.

97. Ibid., pp. 90–91.

98. Noel Tichy and Ram Charan, "The CEO as Coach: An Interview with Allied Signal's Lawrence A. Bossidy," *Harvard Business Review*, March–April 1995, p. 77. See also Nicholas DiFonzo and Prashant Borgia, "A Tale of Two Corporations: Managing Uncertainty During Organizational Change," *Human Resource Management* 37, nos. 3 & 4 (Winter 1998), pp. 95–304.

99. This is based on Kotter, "Leading Change," pp. 60–61.

100. This is based on Kotter, "Leading Change," pp. 60–61.

101. Beer, Eisenstat, and Spector, "Why Change Programs Don't Produce Change," p. 164.

102. Based on J. T. Campbell and M. D. Dunnette, "Effectiveness of T-Group Experiences in Managerial Training and Development," *Psychological Bulletin* 7 (1968), pp. 73–104; reprinted in W. E. Scott and L. L. Cummings, *Readings in Organizational Behavior and Human Performance* (Burr Ridge, IL: McGraw-Hill, 1973), p. 571.

103. Robert J. House, *Management Development* (Ann Arbor, MI: Bureau of Industrial Relations, University of Michigan, 1967), p. 71; Louis White and Kevin Wooten, "Ethical Dilemmas in Various Stages of Organizational Development," *Academy of Management Review* 8, no. 4 (1983), pp. 690–697.

104. Wendell French and Cecil Bell Jr., *Organization Development* (Upper Saddle River, NJ: Prentice Hall, 1995), pp. 171–193.

105. Benjamin Schneider, Steven Ashworth, A. Catherine Higgs, and Linda Carr, "Design Validity, and Use of Strategically Focused Employee Attitude Surveys," *Personnel Psychology* 49 (1996), pp. 695–705.

106. Cummings and Worley, *Organization Development and Change*, p. 501

107. For a description of how to make OD a part of organizational strategy, see Aubrey Mendelow and S. Jay Liebowitz, "Difficulties in Making OD a Part of Organizational Strategy," *Human Resource Planning* 12, no. 4 (1995), pp. 317–329.

108. Wexley and Latham, *Developing and Training Human Resources in Organizations*, p. 128.

109. Ibid., p. 153.

110. See, for example, Charlie Morrow, M. Quintin Jarrett, and Melvin Rupinski, "An Investigation of the Effect and Economic Utility of Corporate-Wide Training," *Personnel Psychology* 50 (1997), pp. 91–119.

111. R. E. Catalano and D. L. Kirkpatrick, "Evaluating Training Programs—The State of the Art," *Training and Development Journal* 22, no. 5 (May 1968), pp. 2–9. See also Basil Paquet et al., "The Bottom Line," *Training and Development Journal* 41, no. 5 (May 1987), pp. 27–33; Harold E. Fisher and Ronald Weinberg, "Make Training Accountable: Assess Its Impact," *Personnel Journal* 67, no. 1 (January 1988), pp. 73–75; Timothy Baldwin and J. Kevin Ford, "Transfer of Training: A Review and Directions of Future Research," *Personnel Psychology* 41, no. 1 (Spring 1988), pp. 63–105; Anthony Montebello and Maurine Haga, "To Justify Training, Test, Test Again," *Personnel Journal* 73, no. 1 (January 1994), pp. 83–87; John Barron et al., "How Well Do We Measure Training?" *Journal of Labor Economics* 15, no. 3 (July 1997), pp. 507–528.

112. This is based on George Alliger, Scott Tannenbaum, Winston Bennett Jr., Holly Traver, and Allison Shotland, "A Meta-Analysis of the Relations Among Training Criteria," *Personnel Psychology* 50 (1997), pp. 341–358. See also Robert Rowden, "A Practical Guide to Assessing the Value of Training in Your Company," *Employee Relations Today* 25, no. 2 (Summer 1998), pp. 65–73.

113. Todd Raphel, "What Learning Management Reports Do for You," *Workforce*, June 2001, pp. 56–58.

After studying this chapter, you should be able to:

1 Describe the appraisal process.

2 Develop, evaluate, and administer at least four performance appraisal tools.

3 Explain and illustrate the problems to avoid in appraising performance.

4 List and discuss the pros and cons of six appraisal methods.

5 Perform an effective appraisal interview.

6 Discuss the pros and cons of using different raters to appraise a person's performance.

Performance Management and Appraisal

Lisa knew that the Hotel Paris's performance appraisal system was primitive.

When the founders opened their first hotel, they went to an office-supply

store, and purchased a pad of performance appraisal forms. The hotel chain

uses these to this day. Each form is a two-sided page. Supervisors indicate

whether the employee's performance in terms of various standard traits

including quantity of work, quality of work, and dependability was excellent,

good, fair, or poor. Lisa knew that, among other flaws, this appraisal tool did

not force either the employee or the supervisor to focus the appraisal on the

extent to which the employee was helping the Hotel Paris to achieve its

strategic goals. She wanted a system that focused the employee's attention

on taking those actions that would contribute to helping the company

achieve its goals, for instance, in terms of improved customer service.●

The last three chapters addressed selecting, training, and developing employees. Once employees have been on the job for some time, you have to evaluate their performance. The purpose of this chapter is to show you how to appraise employees' performance. The main topics we cover include the performance management process, appraisal methods, appraisal performance problems and solutions, and the appraisal interview. Developing a career plan for the employee is a logical extension of the appraisal process: We'll turn to career planning in the following chapter.

● BASIC CONCEPTS IN PERFORMANCE APPRAISAL AND PERFORMANCE MANAGEMENT

performance appraisal
Evaluating an employee's current and/or past performance relative to his or her performance standards.

Virtually all companies have some formal or informal means of appraising their employees' performance. **Performance appraisal** means evaluating an employee's current and/or past performance relative to his or her performance standards. While "appraising performance" usually brings to mind specific appraisal tools such as the teaching appraisal form in Figure 9.1, the actual forms are only part of the appraisal process. Performance appraisal also always assumes that the employee understood what his or her performance standards were, and that the supervisor also provides the employee with the feedback, development, and incentives required to help the person eliminate performance deficiencies or to continue to perform above par. The aim should be to improve performance.

Comparing Performance Appraisal and Performance Management

performance management
A process that consolidates goal setting, performance appraisal, and development into a single, common system, the aim of which is to ensure that the employee's performance is supporting the company's strategic aims.

While the idea that appraisals should improve employee performance is nothing new, many managers take the integrated nature of that process—of setting goals, training employees, and then appraising and rewarding them—more seriously today than they have in the past. They call the total, integrated process **performance management**. We may define performance management as a process that consolidates goal setting, performance appraisal, and development into a single, common system, the aim of which is to ensure that the employee's performance is supporting the company's strategic aims. Performance management includes the practices through which the manager defines the employee's goals and work, develops the employee's capabilities, and evaluates and rewards the person's effort all within the framework of how the employee's performance should be contributing to achieving the company's goals.[1]

When properly designed, performance management therefore never just entails meeting with a subordinate once or twice a year to "review your performance." It means setting goals that make sense in terms of the company's strategic needs. It means daily or weekly interactions to ensure continuous improvement in the employee's capacity and performance.[2] And it involves continuously ensuring that the employee has the training and development he or she needs to perform the job. Figure 9-2 summarizes what performance management entails, in more detail.

Why Performance Management?

The increasing use by employers of performance management reflects several things. It reflects, first, the popularity of the total quality management (TQM) concepts advocated several years ago by management experts like W. Edwards Deming. Basically, Deming argued that an employee's performance is more a function of things like training, communication, tools, and supervision than of his or her own motivation.

Figure 9-1
Classroom Teaching Appraisal by Students

Source: Richard I. Miller, *Evaluating Faculty for Promotion and Tenure* (San Francisco: Jossey-Bass Publishers, 1987), pp. 164–165. Copyright © 1987, Jossey-Bass Inc., Publishers. All rights reserved. Reprinted with permission of John Wiley & Sons, Inc.

Evaluating Faculty for Promotion and Tenure
Classroom Teaching Appraisal by Students

Teacher _____ Course _____

Term _____ Academic Year _____

Thoughtful student appraisal can help improve teaching effectiveness. This questionnaire is designed for that purpose, and your assistance is appreciated. Please do not sign your name.

Use the back of this form for any further comments you might want to express.

Directions: Rate your teacher on each item, giving the highest scores for exceptional performances and the lowest scores for very poor performances. Place in the blank space before each statement the rating that most closely expresses your view.

Exceptional		Moderately Good				Very Poor	Don't Know
7	6	5	4	3	2	1	X

_____ 1. How do you rate the agreement between course objectives and lesson assignments?

_____ 2. How do you rate the planning, organization, and use of class periods?

_____ 3. Are the teaching methods and techniques employed by the teacher appropriate and effective?

_____ 4. How do you rate the competence of the instructor in the subject?

_____ 5. How do you rate the interest of the teacher in the subject?

_____ 6. Does the teacher stimulate and challenge you to think and to question?

_____ 7. Does he or she welcome differing points of view?

_____ 8. Does the teacher have a personal interest in helping you in and out of class?

_____ 9. How would you rate the fairness and effectiveness of the grading policies and procedures of the teacher?

_____ 10. Considering all the above items, what is your overall rating of this teacher?

_____ 11. How would you rate this teacher in comparison with all others you have had in the college or university?

Performance management's emphasis on the integrated nature of goal setting, appraisal, and development reflects this assumption. Second, it reflects the fact that a vast array of studies have shown that traditional performance appraisals are often not just useless but counterproductive.[3] Third, performance management as a process also explicitly recognizes that in today's globally competitive industrial environment, every employee's efforts must focus like a laser on helping the company to achieve its strategic goals. In that regard, adopting an integrated, performance management approach to guiding, developing, and appraising employees also aids the employer's continuous improvement efforts. *Continuous improvement* refers to a management philosophy that requires employers to continuously set and relentlessly meet ever-higher quality, cost, delivery, and availability goals. Continuous improvement means eradicating wastes wherever they are, including the seven wastes of overproduction, defective products, and unnecessary downtime, transportation, processing costs, motion, and inventory. Central to this philosophy is the idea that each employee must continuously improve his or her own personal performance, from one appraisal period to the next. Performance management is

Figure 9-2
The Components of an
Effective Performance
Management Process

Direction sharing means communicating the organization's higher-level goals (including its vision, mission, values, and strategy) throughout the organization and then translating these into doable departmental goals.

Role clarification means clarifying each employee's role in terms of his or her day-to-day work.

Goal setting and planning means translating organizational and departmental goals into specific goals for each employee

Goal alignment means having a process in place that allows any manager to see the link between an employee's goals and those of the department and organization

Developmental goal setting involves ensuring that each employee "thinks through, at the start of any performance period, 'what do I have to do to achieve my goals?' "

Ongoing performance monitoring includes using computer-based systems that measure and then e-mail progress and exception reports based on the person's progress toward meeting his or her performance goals.

Ongoing feedback includes both face-to-face and computer-based feedback regarding progress toward goals.

Coaching and support should be an integral part of the feedback process.

Performance assessment (appraisal) is just one element in the performance management process. The focus in performance management should be on planning and influencing how the employee's performance produces improved company results.

Rewards, recognition, and compensation all play a role in providing the consequences needed to keep the employee's goal-directed performance on track.

Workflow and process control and return on investment management means making sure that the employee's performance is linked in a meaningful way via goal setting to the company's overall measurable performance.

crucial to this process, because, as noted, it consolidates goal setting, performance appraisal, and development into a single, common system, the aim of which is to ensure that the employee's performance is supporting the company's (continuous improvement) strategic aims.[4]

Defining the Employee's Goals and Work Efforts

At the heart of performance management is the notion that the employee's effort should be goal directed.[5] There are two aspects to this. First, the manager should appraise the employee based on how that person performed with respect to achieving the specific standards by which the employee expected to be measured. Second, the employee's goals and performance standards should make sense in terms of the company's strategic goals. At the Hotel Paris, for instance, the employees' goals should reflect desirable behaviors such as speedier check ins and providing friendlier greetings.

In practice, clarifying what you expect from your employee is trickier than it may appear. For example, employers usually write job descriptions not for specific jobs, but for groups of jobs, and the descriptions rarely include specific goals. All sales managers in the firm may have the same job description, for instance. Your sales manager's job description may list duties such as "supervise salesforce" and "be responsible for all phases of marketing the divisions products." But, for strategic purposes, you may expect your sales manager to personally sell at least $600,000 worth of products per year by handling the division's two largest accounts; and to keep the salesforce happy. Unfortunately, some supervisors still tend to be lax when it comes to setting specific, strategy-oriented goals for their employees.

You have to know how to quantify your expectations. The most straightforward way to do this (for the sales manager job above, for instance) is to set measurable standards for each objective. You might measure the "personal selling" activity in terms of how many dollars of sales your manager is to generate personally; perhaps measure "keeping the salesforce happy" in terms of turnover (on the assumption that less than 10% of the salesforce will quit in any given year if morale is high). The point is that employees should always know ahead of time how and on what basis you're going to appraise them, and their goals should always stem from and support the department's and the company's broader goals.[6] Guidelines for effective goal setting include the following.

Assign Specific Goals   Employees who are given specific goals usually perform better than those who are not.

Assign Measurable Goals   Express goals in quantitative terms and include target dates or deadlines.[7] Goals set in absolute terms (such as "an average daily output of 300 units") are less confusing than goals set in relative terms (such as "improve production by 20%"). If measurable results will not be available, then "satisfactory completion"—such as "satisfactorily attended workshop" or "satisfactorily completed his or her degree"—is the next best thing. In any case, target dates or deadlines should always be set.

Assign Challenging but Doable Goals   Goals should be challenging, but not so difficult that they appear impossible or unrealistic.[8] When is a goal "too difficult" or "too hard"? One expert says:

A goal is probably too easy if it calls for little or no improvement in performance when conditions are becoming more favorable, or if the targeted level of performance is well below that of most other employees in comparable positions. A goal is probably too difficult if it calls for a large improvement in performance when conditions are worsening, or if the targeted level of performance is well above that of people in comparable positions.[9]

Encourage Participation   Throughout your management career (and often several times a day) you'll be faced with this question: Should I just tell my employees what their goals are? or, Should I let them participate with me in setting their goals? The evidence suggests that participatively set goals *do not* consistently result in higher performance than assigned goals, nor do assigned goals consistently result in higher performance than participatively set ones. *It is only when the participatively set goals are more difficult than the assigned ones that the participatively set goals produce higher performance.* Participatively set goals do tend to be set higher. It's the fact that the goal is more difficult, not that it was participatively set, that explains the higher performance.[10]

As a quick shorthand way of remembering how to set goals, many managers remember the acronym, SMART. Goals should be *specific*, and clearly state the desired results. They are *measurable*, and answer the question "how much." They are *attainable*, and not too tough or too easy. They are *relevant*, and clearly derive from what the manager and company want to achieve. And, they are *timely*, and reflect deadlines and milestones.

● AN INTRODUCTION TO APPRAISING PERFORMANCE

Why Appraise Performance?

There are several reasons to appraise subordinates' performance. First, appraisals play, or should play, an integral role in the employer's performance management process; it does little good to translate the employer's strategic goals into specific employees' goals, and then train the employees, if you don't periodically review your employees' performance. Second, the appraisal lets the boss and subordinate develop a plan for correcting any deficiencies the appraisal might have unearthed, and to reinforce the things the subordinate does correctly. Third, appraisals should serve a useful career planning purpose by providing the opportunity to review the employee's career plans in light of his or her exhibited strengths and weaknesses. And, last but not least, the appraisal almost always effects the employer's salary raise and promotional decisions.

Realistic Appraisals

In reviewing the appraisal tools we discuss below, don't miss the forest for the trees. It doesn't matter which tool you use if you're less than candid when your subordinate is underperforming. Not all managers are devotees of such candor, but some firms, like GE, are famous for hard-hearted appraisals. GE's former CEO Jack Welch has said, for instance, that there's nothing crueler than telling someone who's doing a mediocre job that he or she is doing well.[11] Someone who might have had the chance to correct bad behavior or find a more appropriate vocation may instead end up spending years in a dead-end situation, only to have to leave when a tough boss comes along.

There are many practical motivations for giving soft appraisals: the fear of having to hire and train someone new; the unpleasant reaction of the appraisee; or a company appraisal process that's not conducive to candor, for instance. Ultimately, though, it's the person doing the appraising who must decide if the potential negative effects of less-than-candid appraisals—on the appraisee's long-term peace of mind, and on the performance of the appraiser and his or her firm—outweigh the assumed benefits. They rarely do.

The Supervisor's Role

Appraising performance is both a difficult and an essential supervisory skill. The supervisor—not HR—usually does the actual appraising, and a supervisor who rates his or her employees too high or too low is doing a disservice to them, to the company, and to him- or herself. Supervisors must therefore be familiar with basic appraisal techniques, understand and avoid problems that can cripple appraisals, and know how to conduct appraisals fairly.

The HR department serves a policy-making and advisory role. Generally, the HR department provides advice and assistance regarding the appraisal tool to use, but leaves final decisions on procedures to operating division heads. In some firms, HR prepares detailed forms and procedures and insists that all departments use them. HR is also responsible for training supervisors to improve their appraisal skills. Finally, HR is responsible for monitoring the appraisal system and, particularly, for

Supervisor and worker meet to do a performance appraisal. The appraisal process includes not just evaluation, but standards-setting, and feedback to discuss the employee's progress and to make provision for any required development.

ensuring that the format and criteria being measured comply with EEO laws and aren't outdated.

Steps in Appraising Performance

Describe the appraisal process.

The performance appraisal process itself contains three steps: define the job, appraise performance, and provide feedback. *Defining the job* means making sure that you and your subordinate agree on his or her duties and job standards. *Appraising performance* means comparing your subordinate's actual performance to the standards that have been set; this usually involves some type of rating form. Third, performance appraisal usually requires one or more *feedback sessions*. Here the two of you discuss the subordinate's performance and progress, and make plans for any development required.

The manager generally conducts the appraisal itself with the aid of a predetermined and formal method like one or more of those described in this section. The two basic considerations in designing the actual appraisal tool are *what to measure* and *how to measure* it. For example, in terms of *what to measure*, we may measure the employee's performance in terms of generic dimensions such as quality, quantity, and timeliness of work. Or, we may measure performance with respect to developing one's competencies (as in the ability to use Java), or achieving one's goals. In terms of *how to measure* it, you will see that there are various methodologies, including graphic rating scales, the alternation ranking method, and "MBO." "The New Workplace" illustrates why choosing what to measure carefully is important.

Develop, evaluate, and administer at least four performance appraisal tools.

graphic rating scale
A scale that lists a number of traits and a range of performance for each. The employee is then rated by identifying the score that best describes his or her level of performance for each trait.

Graphic Rating Scale Method

The **graphic rating scale** is the simplest and still most popular technique for appraising performance. Figure 9-3 shows part of a typical rating scale. A graphic rating scale lists traits (such as quality and reliability) and a range of performance values (from unsatisfactory to outstanding) for each trait. The supervisor rates each subordinate by circling

---

The New Workplace

Performance Appraisals and Joint Venture Collaboration

Encouraging collaboration among an international joint venture's partners is an important task. For a venture in which employees from, say, the United States and Japan, or England and Spain, must work collaboratively for the venture to succeed, fostering such relationships is often the key to whether the venture succeeds. Designing the appraisal system can help in that regard.

A recent study looked at what managers can do to foster that sort of collaboration. The study involved a survey and follow-up interviews with U.S. participants in U.S.-based joint ventures between U.S. and Japanese parent companies in the auto supply industry. The study focused on the variables that influenced the U.S. employees' collaborative attitudes.

The researchers found that, among other things, the venture's appraisal system contributed to collaboration at the operational level in these joint ventures. Specifically, they concluded that to encourage collaboration, employee performance appraisal systems "should include measures of initiative and success in developing productive working relationships with counterparts." Appraising these employees in part based on information-sharing with counterparts, as well as participation in sponsored events and informal get-togethers are two examples. Managers are fond of saying, "you get what you measure." That certainly appears to apply to encouraging global joint ventures' employees to be collaborative.[12]

Performance Appraisal

Employee Name _____ Title _____

Department _____ Employee Payroll Number _____

Reason for Review: ☐ Annual ☐ Promotion ☐ Unsatisfactory Performance

☐ Merit ☐ End Probation Period ☐ Other _____

Date employee began present position ____ / ____ / ____

Date of last appraisal ____ / ____ / ____ Scheduled appraisal date ____ / ____ / ____

Instructions: Carefully evaluate employee's work performance in relation to current job requirements. Check rating box to indicate the employee's performance. Indicate N/A if not applicable. Assign points for each rating within the scale and indicate in the corresponding points box. Points will be totaled and averaged for an overall performance score.

RATING IDENTIFICATION

O—Outstanding—Performance is exceptional in all areas and is recognizable as being far superior to others.

V—Very Good—Results clearly exceed most position requirements. Performance is of high quality and is achieved on a consistent basis.

G—Good—Competent and dependable level of performance. Meets performance standards of the job.

I—Improvement Needed—Performance is deficient in certain areas. Improvement is necessary.

U—Unsatisfactory—Results are generally unacceptable and require immediate improvement. No merit increase should be granted to individuals with this rating.

N—Not Rated—Not applicable or too soon to rate.

GENERAL FACTORS	RATING SCALE		SUPPORTIVE DETAILS OR COMMENTS
1. Quality—The accuracy, thoroughness, and acceptability of work performed.	O ☐ 100–90 V ☐ 90–80 G ☐ 80–70 I ☐ 70–60 U ☐ below 60	Points	_____
2. Productivity—The quantity and efficiency of work produced in a specified period of time.	O ☐ 100–90 V ☐ 90–80 G ☐ 80–70 I ☐ 70–60 U ☐ below 60	Points	_____
3. Job Knowledge—The practical/technical skills and information used on the job.	O ☐ 100–90 V ☐ 90–80 G ☐ 80–70 I ☐ 70–60 U ☐ below 60	Points	_____
4. Reliability—The extent to which an employee can be relied upon regarding task completion and follow-up.	O ☐ 100–90 V ☐ 90–80 G ☐ 80–70 I ☐ 70–60 U ☐ below 60	Points	_____
5. Availability—The extent to which an employee is punctual, observes prescribed work break/meal periods, and the overall attendance record.	O ☐ 100–90 V ☐ 90–80 G ☐ 80–70 I ☐ 70–60 U ☐ below 60	Points	_____
6. Independence—The extent of work performed with little or no supervision.	O ☐ 100–90 V ☐ 90–80 G ☐ 80–70 I ☐ 70–60 U ☐ below 60	Points	_____

Figure 9-3
One Page of a Two-Page Graphic Rating Scale with Space for Comments

or checking the score that best describes his or her performance for each trait. The assigned values for the traits are then totaled.

What to Measure? As noted earlier, the employer must decide exactly what performance to measure. Here, there are many options. As in Figure 9-3, the employer may opt for *generic dimensions* such as quality and quantity. Another option is to appraise performance on the *job's actual duties*. For example, Figure 9-4 shows part of an appraisal form for an administrative secretary. The form assesses the job's five main sets of duties, one of which is "maintaining records." Here you would assess how well the employee did in exercising his or her specific job duties. *Competency-based appraisals* are another option. Here, the idea is to focus on the extent to which the employee exhibits the competencies that the employer values for this job. In any case, the employer will want to appraise the employee based on the extent to which he or she is meeting his or her standards in each of these areas.

It is not unusual at all to design a tool that measures several things. Thus, Figure 9-5 (I, II, III) explicitly measures both competencies and objectives. With respect to competencies, the employee is expected to develop and exhibit competencies such as "identifies and analyzes problems," and "maintains harmonious and effective work relationships with co-workers and constituents." The employee and supervisor would fill in the "objectives" section at the start of the year, and then set new ones as part of the appraisal.

Alternation Ranking Method

alternation ranking method
Ranking employees from best to worst on a particular trait, choosing highest, then lowest, until all are ranked.

Ranking employees from best to worst on a trait or traits is another option. Since it is usually easier to distinguish between the worst and best employees, an **alternation ranking method** is most popular. First, list all subordinates to be rated, and then cross out the names of any not known well enough to rank. Then, on a form like that in Figure 9-6 (page 321) indicate the employee who is the highest on the characteristic being measured and also the one who is the lowest. Then choose the next highest and the next lowest, alternating between highest and lowest until all employees have been ranked.

Name ______________________
Rating period from ____________ to ____________
Rater name ______________________
Rater title ______________________
Department ______________________

Rating Scale Key
1 Fails to meet job requirements
2 Meets most job requirements
3 Fully meets all job requirements
4 Exceeds all job requirements

Part II: Rating Scales for Task Areas

Position: Administrative Secretary Duties and Responsibilities	
Duty: Maintaining Departmental Personnel Records PCT. (30%)	RATING: 1 ☐ 2 ☐ 3 ☐ 4 ☐
Using spreadsheets and other computerized forms: Ensure all recorded personnel information is up to date and accurate, including name, address, and contact information; maintain accurate records of all personal leave taken annually, as well as vacation schedules; maintain accurate records of all employees' benefits.	Comments

Figure 9-4
Portion of an Administrative Secretary's Sample Performance Appraisal Form

SECTION I   **Success and Effectiveness in Meeting Specific Job Responsibilities/Objectives and Performance Standards in Support of Departmental Goals**

Primary Performance Expectations: Responsibilities/Objectives and Standards	Mid-Year Progress Notes	End of Period Rating of Success and Effectiveness Comment and Place X on Scale to Rate
		Not Strong Strong Very
Objective 1:		⊢—┼—┼—┼—┤
Objective 2:		⊢—┼—┼—┼—┤
Objective 3:		⊢—┼—┼—┼—┤
Objective 4:		⊢—┼—┼—┼—┤
Objective 5:		⊢—┼—┼—┼—┤

Objectives for new rating period reviewed and agreed to:		Mid-Year Review:	
Evaluator Date	Employee Date	Evaluator Date	Employee Date

Figure 9-5
Performance Management Outline
Source: www.cwru.edu.

Paired Comparison Method

The **paired comparison method** helps make the ranking method more precise. For every trait (quantity of work, quality of work, and so on), you pair and compare every subordinate with every other subordinate.

Suppose you have five employees to rate. In the paired comparison method, you make a chart, as in Figure 9-7 (page 321), of all possible pairs of employees for each trait. Then, for each trait, indicate (with a + or −) who is the better employee of the pair. Next, add up the number of +s for each employee. In Figure 9-7, Maria ranked highest (has the most + marks) for quality of work, whereas Art was ranked highest for creativity.

Forced Distribution Method   The **forced distribution method** is similar to grading on a curve. With this method, you place predetermined percentages of ratees into performance categories. For example, you may decide to distribute employees as follows:

15% high performers   20% low-average performers

20% high-average performers   15% low performers

30% average performers

SECTION II

Success in Measuring Required Performance Competencies

	Mid-Year Progress Notes	End of Period Rating of Success and Effectiveness Comment and Place X on Scale to Rate		
		Not Strong	Strong	Very
Job Knowledge/Competency: Demonstrates the knowledge and skills necessary to perform the job effectively. Understands the expectations of the job and remains current regarding new developments in areas of responsibility. Performs responsibilities in accordance with job procedures and policies. Acts as a resource person upon whom others rely for assistance.		├──┼──┼──┼──┤		
Quality/Quantity of Work: Completes assignments in a thorough, accurate, and timely manner that achieves expected outcomes. Exhibits concern for the goals and needs of the department and others that depend on services or work products. Handles multiple responsibilities in an effective manner. Uses work time productively.		├──┼──┼──┼──┤		
Planning/Organization: Establishes clear objectives and organizes duties for self based on the goals of the department, division, or management center. Identifies resources required to meet goals and objectives. Seeks guidance when goals or priorities are unclear.		├──┼──┼──┼──┤		
Initiative/Commitment: Demonstrates personal responsibility when performing duties. Offers assistance to support the goals and objectives of the department and division. Performs with minimal supervision. Meets work schedule/attendance expectations for the position.		├──┼──┼──┼──┤		
Problem Solving/Creativity: Identifies and analyzes problems. Formulates alternative solutions. Takes or recommends appropriate actions. Follows up to ensure problems are resolved.		├──┼──┼──┼──┤		
Teamwork and Cooperation: Maintains harmonious and effective work relationships with co-workers and constituents. Adapts to changing priorities and demands. Shares information and resources with others to promote positive and collaborative work relationships.		├──┼──┼──┼──┤		
Interpersonal Skills: Deals positively and effectively with co-workers and constituents. Demonstrates respect for all individuals.		├──┼──┼──┼──┤		
Communication (Oral and Written): Effectively conveys information and ideas both orally and in writing. Listens carefully and seeks clarification to ensure understanding.		├──┼──┼──┼──┤		

Competencies Reviewed and Discussed:	Mid-Year Review	
Evaluator	Date	Employee Date

Figure 9-5 (continued)

(The proportions in each category need not be symmetrical; GE uses top 20%, middle 70%, and bottom 10% for managers.)

As for students at school, forced distribution means two things for employees: Not everyone can get an A; and one's performance is always rated relative to one's peers. One practical, if low-tech, way to do this is to write each employee's name on a separate index card. Then, for each trait (quality of work, creativity, and so on), place the employee's card in the appropriate performance category.

More firms are adopting this practice. Sun Microsystems force-ranks all of its 43,000 employees. Sun managers appraise employees in groups of about 30, and those in the bottom 10% of each group get 90 days to improve. If they're still in the bottom 10% in 90 days, they get a chance to resign and take severance pay. Some decide to stay, but "If it doesn't work out," the firm fires them without severance.[13]

SECTION III   **End of Period Summary Performance Rating**

Based on a review of Section I, Success and Effectiveness in Position Responsibilities/Accomplishing Objectives and Standards, and Section II, Performance Competencies, provide a summary performance rating:

Comments: _____

_____

_____

_____

_____

_____

■ Performance consistently and significantly above standards in virtually all areas; far exceeds normal expectations.

■ Performance well above standards in many important aspects; usually exceeds normal expectations.

■ Performance meets standards in all important aspects; good contributor.

■ Performance slightly below standards in some important aspects, but meets standards in others; performance generally acceptable but improvement needed to fully achieve functional performance level.

■ Performance below standards in a number of critical aspects; substantial improvement needed.

_____   _____
Evaluator Signature   Date

I have read this appraisal and it had been discussed with me. I understand that signing this appraisal does not necessarily mean I agree with all of the information in it or that I forfeit my right for review.

_____   _____
Employee Signature   Date

Figure 9-5 (continued)

As most students know, forced distribution grading systems are more unforgiving than most other means of appraising performance. With a forced distribution system, you're either in the top 5% or 10% (and thus get that "A"), or you're not. And, if you're in the bottom 5% or 10%, you get an "F," no questions asked. Your professor hasn't the wiggle room to give everyone As, Bs, and Cs. Some students have to fail. Given this, employers need to be doubly careful to protect their appraisal plans from managerial abuse. Office politics and managerial bias can taint ratings. To protect against bias claims, employers should take several steps.[14] Appoint a review committee to review any employee's low ranking. Train raters to be objective; and consider using multiple raters in conjunction with the forced distribution approach.

In any case, the problem, even with forced ranking, is that choosing performance extremes is usually not the problem: "It is not difficult to identify the good performer and the bad performer and to make decisions accordingly. The challenge is for processes to differentiate meaningfully between the other 80%.[15] Enhancing their performance is the primary challenge."

What becomes of those in the bottom 10%? Some firms transfer them. However, dismissal is more likely, reflecting the fact that top employees often outperform average ones (let alone low ones) by as much as 100%.[16]

Figure 9-6
Alternation Ranking Scale

ALTERNATION RANKING SCALE

For the Trait: _____

For the trait you are measuring, list all the employees you want to rank. Put the highest-ranking employee's name on line 1. Put the lowest-ranking employee's name on line 20. Then list the next highest ranking on line 2, the next lowest ranking on line 19, and so on. Continue until all names are on the scale.

Highest-ranking employee

1. _____   11. _____

2. _____   12. _____

3. _____   13. _____

4. _____   14. _____

5. _____   15. _____

6. _____   16. _____

7. _____   17. _____

8. _____   18. _____

9. _____   19. _____

10. _____   20. _____

Lowest-ranking employee

Critical Incident Method

critical incident method
Keeping a record of uncommonly good or undesirable examples of an employee's work-related behavior and reviewing it with the employee at predetermined times.

With the **critical incident method,** the supervisor keeps a log of positive and negative examples (critical incidents) of a subordinate's work-related behavior. Every six months or so, supervisor and subordinate meet to discuss the latter's performance, using the incidents as examples.

Figure 9-7
Ranking Employees by the Paired Comparison Method

Note: + means "better than." − means "worse than." For each chart, add up the number of +'s in each column to get the highest-ranked employee.

FOR THE TRAIT "QUALITY OF WORK"

Employee Rated:

As Compared to:	A Art	B Maria	C Chuck	D Diane	E José
A Art		+	+	−	−
B Maria	−		−	−	−
C Chuck	−	+		+	−
D Diane	+	+	−		+
E José	+	+	+	−	

Maria Ranks Highest Here

FOR THE TRAIT "CREATIVITY"

Employee Rated:

As Compared to:	A Art	B Maria	C Chuck	D Diane	E José
A Art		−	−	−	−
B Maria	+		−	+	+
C Chuck	+	+		−	+
D Diane	+	−	+		−
E José	+	−	−	+	

Art Ranks Highest Here

This method has several advantages. It provides actual examples of good and poor performance the supervisor can use to explain the person's rating. It ensures that the manager or supervisor thinks about the subordinate's appraisal all during the year. The rating does not just reflect the employee's most recent performance. The list hopefully provides examples of what specifically the subordinate can do to eliminate any deficiencies. However, without some numerical rating, this method is not too useful for comparing employees or making salary decisions.

It's useful to accumulate incidents that are tied to the employee's goals. In Table 9-1, one of the assistant plant manager's continuing duties was to supervise procurement and to minimize inventory costs. The critical incident log shows that the assistant plant manager let inventory storage costs rise 15%; this provides a specific example of what performance must be improved in the future.

Narrative Forms

The final written appraisal is often in narrative form. For example, Figure 9-8 presents a performance improvement plan worksheet. The person's supervisor is responsible for providing his or her assessment of the employee's past performance and required areas of improvement. This aids the employee in understanding where his or her performance was good or bad, and how to improve that performance.

Behaviorally Anchored Rating Scales

behaviorally anchored rating scale (BARS)
An appraisal method that aims at combining the benefits of narrative critical incidents and quantified ratings by anchoring a quantified scale with specific narrative examples of good and poor performance.

A **behaviorally anchored rating scale (BARS)** combines the benefits of narratives, critical incidents, and quantified (graphic rating type) scales by anchoring a rating scale with specific behavioral examples of good or poor performance. Its proponents say it provides better, more equitable appraisals than do the other tools we discussed.[17]

Developing a BARS typically requires five steps:

1. *Generate critical incidents.* Ask persons who know the job (jobholders and/or supervisors) to describe specific illustrations (critical incidents) of effective and ineffective performance.

Table 9-1

Examples of Critical Incidents for an Assistant Plant Manager

Continuing Duties	Targets	Critical Incidents
Schedule production for plant	90% utilization of personnel and machinery in plant; orders delivered on time	Instituted new production scheduling system; decreased late orders by 10% last month; increased machine utilization in plant by 20% last month
Supervise procurement of raw materials and inventory control	Minimize inventory costs while keeping adequate supplies on hand	Let inventory storage costs rise 15% last month; overordered parts "A" and "B" by 20%; underordered part "C" by 30%
Supervise machinery maintenance	No shutdowns due to faulty machinery	Instituted new preventative maintenance system for plant; prevented a machine breakdown by discovering faulty part

Figure 9-8
Appraisal-Coaching
Worksheet
Source: Reprinted from www.HR.
BLR.com with permission of the
publisher, © 2004 *Business and Legal
Reports,* Inc. 141 Mill Rock Road East,
Old Saybrook, CT.

Appraisal-Coaching Worksheet

Instructions: This form is to be filled out by supervisor and employee prior to each performance review period.

Employee: _____   Position: _____

Supervisor: _____   Department: _____

Date: _____ Period of Work under Consideration: From _____ to _____

1. What areas of the employee's work performance are meeting job performance standards?

2. In what areas is improvement needed during the next six to twelve months?

3. What factors or events that are beyond the employee's control may affect (positively or negatively) his/her ability to accomplish planned results during the next six to twelve months?

4. What specific strengths has the employee demonstrated on this job that should be more fully used during the next six to twelve months?

5. List two or three areas (if applicable) in which the employee needs to improve his/her performance during the next six to twelve months (gaps in knowledge or experience, skill development needs, behavior modifications that affect job performance, etc.)

6. Based on your consideration of items 1–5 above, summarize your mutual objectives:

A. What supervisor will do:

B. What employee will do:

C. Date for next progress check or to reevaluate objectives:

D. Data/evidence that will be used to observe and/or measure progress.

_____
Signature-Employee   Signature-Supervisor

_____
Date

---

2. *Develop performance dimensions.* Have these people cluster the incidents into a smaller set of (5 or 10) performance dimensions, and define each dimension, such as "salesmanship skills."

3. *Reallocate incidents.* Another group of people who also know the job then reallocate the original critical incidents. They get the cluster definitions and the critical incidents, and must reassign each incident to the cluster they think it fits best. Retain a critical incident if some percentage (usually 50% to 80%) of this second group assigns it to the same cluster as did the first group.

4. *Scale the incidents.* This second group then rates the behavior described by the incident as to how effectively or ineffectively it represents performance on the dimension (7- to 9-point scales are typical).

5. *Develop a final instrument.* Choose about six or seven of the incidents as the dimension's behavioral anchors.[18]

RESEARCH INSIGHT   Three researchers developed a BARS for grocery checkout clerks.[19] They collected critical incidents, and then clustered these into eight performance dimensions:

Knowledge and Judgment

Conscientiousness

Skill in Human Relations

Skill in Operation of Register

Skill in Bagging

Organizational Ability of Check-stand Work

Skill in Monetary Transactions

Observational Ability

They then developed behaviorally anchored rating scales (similar to the one in Figure 9-9) for each of these dimensions. Each contained a scale (ranging from 1 to 9) for rating performance from "extremely poor" to "extremely good." Then a specific critical incident (such as "by knowing the price of items, this checker would be expected to look for mismarked and unmarked items") helped anchor or specify what was meant by "extremely good" (9) performance. Similarly, they used several other critical incident anchors along the performance scale from (8) down to (1).

Advantages   While more time-consuming than other appraisal tools, BARS seems to have some advantages.

1. *A more accurate gauge.* People who know and do the job and its requirements better than anyone develop the BARS. This should produce a good gauge of job performance.

2. *Clearer standards.* The critical incidents along the scale make clear what to look for in terms of superior performance, average performance, and so forth.

3. *Feedback.* The critical incidents make it easier to explain the ratings to appraisees.

4. *Independent dimensions.* Systematically clustering the critical incidents into five or six performance dimensions (such as "salesmanship skills") should help to make the performance dimensions more independent of one another. For example, a rater should be less likely to rate an employee high on all dimensions simply because he or she was rated high in "salesmanship skills."

5. *Consistency.* [20]BARS-based evaluations also seem to be relatively consistent and reliable, in that different raters' appraisals of the same person tend to be similar.

management by objectives (MBO)
Involves setting specific measurable goals with each employee and then periodically reviewing the progress made.

Management by Objectives (MBO)

Stripped to its basics, **management by objectives (MBO)** requires the manager to set specific measurable goals with each employee and then periodically discuss the latter's progress toward these goals. You could engage in a modest and informal MBO program

Figure 9-9
Example of a Behaviorally Anchored Rating Scale for the Dimension Salesmanship Skill
Source: Walter C. Borman, "Behavior Based Rating Scales," in Ronald A. Berk (ed.), *Performance Assessment: Methods and Applications* (Baltimore, MD: Johns Hopkins University Press, 1986), p. 103.

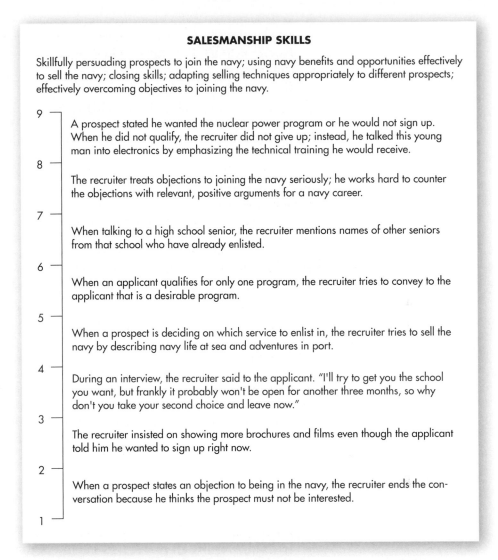

SALESMANSHIP SKILLS

Skillfully persuading prospects to join the navy; using navy benefits and opportunities effectively to sell the navy; closing skills; adapting selling techniques appropriately to different prospects; effectively overcoming objectives to joining the navy.

9 — A prospect stated he wanted the nuclear power program or he would not sign up. When he did not qualify, the recruiter did not give up; instead, he talked this young man into electronics by emphasizing the technical training he would receive.

8 — The recruiter treats objections to joining the navy seriously; he works hard to counter the objections with relevant, positive arguments for a navy career.

7 — When talking to a high school senior, the recruiter mentions names of other seniors from that school who have already enlisted.

6 — When an applicant qualifies for only one program, the recruiter tries to convey to the applicant that is a desirable program.

5 — When a prospect is deciding on which service to enlist in, the recruiter tries to sell the navy by describing navy life at sea and adventures in port.

4 — During an interview, the recruiter said to the applicant. "I'll try to get you the school you want, but frankly it probably won't be open for another three months, so why don't you take your second choice and leave now."

3 — The recruiter insisted on showing more brochures and films even though the applicant told him he wanted to sign up right now.

2 — When a prospect states an objection to being in the navy, the recruiter ends the conversation because he thinks the prospect must not be interested.

1

with subordinates by jointly setting goals and periodically providing feedback. However, the term *MBO* generally refers to a comprehensive and formal organizationwide goal-setting and appraisal program consisting of six steps:

1. *Set the organization's goals.* Establish, based on the firm's strategic plan, an organizationwide plan for next year and set specific company goals.
2. *Set departmental goals.* Next, department heads take these company goals (like "boost 2004 profits by 20%") and, with their superiors, jointly set goals for their departments.
3. *Discuss departmental goals.* Department heads discuss the department's goals with all subordinates, often at a departmentwide meeting. They ask employees to set their own preliminary individual goals; in other words, how can each employee contribute to the department's goals?
4. *Define expected results* (set individual goals). Department heads and their subordinates set short-term individual performance targets.

5. *Performance reviews.* Department heads compare each employee's actual and targeted performance.
6. *Provide feedback.* Department heads and employees discuss and evaluate the latters' progress.

There are three problems in using MBO. Setting unclear, unmeasurable objectives is the main one. An objective such as "will do a better job of training" is useless. On the other hand, "will have four subordinates promoted during the year" is a measurable objective.

Second, MBO is time-consuming. Setting objectives, measuring progress, and giving feedback can take several hours per employee per year, over and above the time you already spend doing each person's appraisal.

Third, setting objectives with the subordinate sometimes turns into a tug-of-war, with you pushing for higher quotas and the subordinate pushing for lower ones. Knowing the job and the person's ability is important. To motivate performance, the objectives must be fair and attainable. The more you know about the job and the person's ability, the more confident you can be about the standards you set.

Computerized and Web-Based Performance Appraisal

Several relatively inexpensive performance appraisal software programs are on the market. These generally enable managers to keep notes on subordinates during the year, and then to electronically rate employees on a series of performance traits. The programs then generate written text to support each part of the appraisal.

Employee Appraiser (developed by the Austin-Hayne Corporation, San Mateo, California) presents a menu of more than a dozen evaluation dimensions, including dependability, initiative, communication, decision making, leadership, judgment, and planning and productivity. Within each dimension are various performance factors, again presented in menu form. For example, under "communication" are separate factors for writing, verbal communication, receptivity to feedback and criticism, listening skills, ability to focus on the desired results, keeping others informed, and openness. When the user clicks on a performance factor, the person sees a relatively sophisticated version of a graphic rating scale. Instead of a scale with numbers, however, Employee Appraiser uses behaviorally anchored examples. For example, for verbal communication, there are six choices, ranging from "presents ideas clearly" to "lacks structure." After the manager picks the phrase that most accurately describes the worker, Employee Appraiser generates sample text for the employee's appraisal.

PerformanceReview.com, from KnowledgePoint of Petaluma, California, lets managers evaluate employees online based on their competencies, goals, and development plans. Managers can choose from standard competencies such as "communications," or create their own.[21]

The Web site improvenow.com lets employees fill out a 60-question assessment online with or without their supervisor's approval, and then gives the supervisor the team's feedback with an overall score.[22] Evaluators rated two appraisal packages outstanding: PeopleSoft HR management, and SAP r/3 hr.[23] About a third of employers use online performance management tools to facilitate the process for at least some employees.[24]

electronic performance monitoring (EPM)
Having supervisors electronically monitor the amount of computerized data an employee is processing per day, and thereby his or her performance.

Electronic performance monitoring (EPM) is in some respects the ultimate in computerized appraising. EPM means having supervisors electronically monitor the

amount of computerized data an employee is processing per day, and thereby his or her performance.[25] As two researchers note, "organizations now use computer networks, sophisticated telephone systems, and both wireless audio and video links to monitor and record the work activities of employees." It's estimated that as many as 26 million U.S. workers have their performance monitored electronically. This fact has already triggered congressional legislation aimed at requiring that employees receive precise notification of when they will be monitored.

How do employees react to EPM? Studies suggest two things. First, "participants [employees] with the ability to delay or prevent electronic performance monitoring indicated higher feelings of personal control and demonstrated superior task performance." In other words, let employees have some control over how and when they're monitored.[26] If you can't, then the findings suggest this: Don't let them know when you're actually monitoring them. Participants who knew exactly when the monitoring was taking place actually expressed lower feelings of personal control than did those who did not know when the monitoring was on.

Mixing the Methods

Most firms combine several appraisal tools. Figure 9-3 presents one example. Basically, this is a graphic rating scale, with descriptive phrases included to define each trait. However, it also has a section for comments below each trait. This lets the rater provide several critical incidents. The quantifiable rating facilitates comparing employees, and is useful for salary, transfer, and promotion decisions. The critical incidents provide specific examples for developmental discussions.

● APPRAISING PERFORMANCE: PROBLEMS AND SOLUTIONS

Few of the things managers do are fraught with more peril than appraising subordinates' performance. Employees in general tend to be overly optimistic about what their ratings will be. You and they know their raises, career progress, and peace of mind may well hinge on how you rate them. This alone makes it difficult to rate performance; but of even greater concern, are the numerous technical problems that can cast doubt on how fair the whole process is. Let's turn to some of these more technical appraisal problems and how to solve them, and to several other pertinent appraisal issues.

Potential Rating Scale Appraisal Problems

Most employers still depend on graphic-type rating scales to appraise performance, but these scales are especially susceptible to several problems: unclear standards, halo effect, central tendency, leniency or strictness, and bias.

unclear standards
An appraisal that is too open to interpretation.

Unclear Standards   Table 9-2 illustrates the **unclear standards** problem. This graphic rating scale seems objective, but would probably result in unfair appraisals because the traits and degrees of merit are ambiguous. For example, different supervisors would probably define "good" performance, "fair" performance, and so on differently. The same is true of traits such as "quality of work" or "creativity."

There are several ways to fix this problem. The best way is to develop and include descriptive phrases that define each trait, as in Figure 9-3. There the form specified what was meant by "outstanding," "superior," and "good" quality of work. This specificity results in appraisals that are more consistent and more easily explained.

halo effect
In performance appraisal, the problem that occurs when a supervisor's rating of a subordinate on one trait biases the rating of that person on other traits.

Halo Effect   Experts define **halo effect** as "the influence of a rater's general impression on ratings of specific ratee qualities."[27] For example, supervisors often rate unfriendly employees lower on all traits, rather than just for the trait "gets along well with others." Being aware of this problem is a major step toward avoiding it. Supervisory training can also alleviate the problem, as can using a BARS.

central tendency
A tendency to rate all employees the same way, such as rating them all average.

Central Tendency   Some supervisors stick to the middle when filling in rating scales. For example, if the rating scale ranges from 1 to 7, they tend to avoid the highs (6 and 7) and lows (1 and 2) and rate most of their people between 3 and 5. If you use a graphic rating scale, this **central tendency** could mean that you rate all employees "average." That may distort the evaluations, making them less useful for promotion, salary, or counseling purposes. Ranking employees instead of using graphic rating scales can reduce this problem, since ranking means you can't rate them all average.

strictness/leniency
The problem that occurs when a supervisor has a tendency to rate all subordinates either high or low.

Leniency or Strictness   Other supervisors tend to rate all their subordinates consistently high (or low), just as some instructors are notoriously high or low graders. This **strictness/leniency** problem is especially severe with graphic rating scales, particularly when firms don't insist that their supervisors avoid giving all their employees high (or

Table 9-2

A Graphic Rating Scale with Unclear Standards

	Excellent	Good	Fair	Poor
Quality of work				
Quantity of work				
Creativity				
Integrity				

Note: For example, what exactly is meant by "good," "quantity of work," and so forth?

low) ratings. On the other hand, ranking forces supervisors to distinguish between high and low performers.

Therefore, if a graphic rating scale must be used, it may be a good idea to impose a distribution—that, say, about 10% of the people should be rated "excellent," 20% "good," and so forth. In other words, try to get a spread (unless, of course, you're sure all your people really do fall into just one or two categories).

The appraisal you do may be less objective than you think. One study focused on how personality influenced the evaluations students gave their peers. Raters who scored higher on "conscientiousness" tended to give their peers lower ratings—they were more strict, in other words; those scoring higher on "agreeableness" gave higher ratings—they were more lenient.[28]

It's not just the appraiser's tendencies but the purpose of the appraisal that causes strictness/leniency. Two researchers reviewed 22 studies of performance appraisal leniency. They concluded that "performance appraisal ratings obtained for administrative purposes [such as pay raises or promotions] were nearly one-third of a standard deviation larger than those obtained for research or employee development purposes."[29]

Bias Appraisees' personal characteristics (such as age, race, and sex) can affect their ratings, often quite apart from each ratee's actual performance. Managers should not underestimate this problem. Appraisals frequently say more about the appraiser than about the appraised.[30] Studies suggest that "rater idiosyncratic biases account for the largest percentage of the observed variances in performance ratings."[31]

bias
The tendency to allow individual differences such as age, race, and sex to affect the appraisal ratings employees receive.

RESEARCH INSIGHT One study illustrates how bias can influence the way one person appraises another. In this study, researchers sought to determine the extent to which pregnancy is a source of bias in performance appraisals.[32] The subjects were 220 undergraduate students between the ages of 17 and 43 attending a midwestern university.

Two videotapes of a female "employee" were prepared. Each video showed three five-minute scenarios in which this "employee" interacted with another woman. For example, she acted as a customer representative to deal with an irate customer, tried to sell a computer system to a potential customer, and dealt with a problem subordinate. In each case, the performance level of the "employee" was designed to be average or slightly above average. The "employee" was the same in both videotapes, and the videotapes were identical—except for one difference. Researchers shot the first videotape in the "employee's" ninth month of pregnancy, the second about five months later. The aim of the study was to investigate whether the "employee's" pregnancy influenced the performance appraisal ratings she received in the various situations.

Several groups of student raters watched either the "pregnant" or "not pregnant" tape. They rated the "employee" on a 5-point graphic rating scale for individual characteristics such as "ability to do the job," "dependability," and "physical mannerisms."

The results suggest that pregnant women may face more workplace discrimination than do women in general. Despite seeing otherwise identical behavior by the same woman, the student raters "with a remarkably high degree of consistency" assigned lower performance ratings to a pregnant woman as opposed to a nonpregnant one.[33]

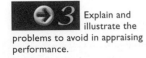
Explain and illustrate the problems to avoid in appraising performance.

How to Avoid Appraisal Problems

It's probably safe to say that problems like these can make an appraisal worse than no appraisal at all. Would an employee not be better off with no appraisal than with a seemingly objective but actually biased one? Problems like these aren't inevitable, though, and you can minimize them.

First, learn and understand the potential problems, and the solutions (like clarifying standards) for each. Understanding the problem can help you avoid it.

Second, use the right appraisal tool. Each tool has its own pros and cons. For example, the ranking method avoids central tendency but can cause bad feelings when employees' performances are in fact all "high"; and the ranking and forced distribution methods both provide relative—not absolute—ratings. Table 9-3 summarizes each tool's pros and cons.

Third, train supervisors to reduce rating errors such as halo, leniency, and central tendency. In one training program, raters watched a videotape of people at work, and then rated the workers. The trainers then placed the supervisors' ratings of these workers on a flip chart, and explained and illustrated the various errors (such as leniency and halo). Packaged training programs are available. For example, Harvard Business School Publishing offers *Assessing Performance,* for about $150. It lists the steps and things to consider in preparing for and conducting the appraisal interview.[34]

Training isn't always the solution, however. In practice, several factors—including the extent to which employees' pay is tied to performance ratings, union pressure, employee turnover, time constraints, and the need to justify ratings—may be more important than training. This means that improving appraisal accuracy calls not just for training, but also for reducing the effect of outside factors such as union pressure and time constraints.

A *fourth* solution—diary keeping—is worth the effort.[35] One study involved 112 first-line supervisors from a large electronics firm. Some attended a special training program on diary keeping. The program explained the role of critical incidents, and how the supervisors could compile these incidents into a diary or incident file to use later as a reference for a subordinate's appraisal. Then came a practice session, followed by a feedback and group discussion session aimed at reinforcing the importance of recording both positive and negative incidents.

The conclusion of this and similar studies is that you can reduce the adverse effects of appraisal problems by having raters compile positive and negative critical incidents as

4 List and discuss the pros and cons of six appraisal methods.

Table 9-3

Important Advantages and Disadvantages of Appraisal Tools

Tool	Advantages	Disadvantages
Graphic rating scale	Simple to use; provides a quantitative rating for each employee.	Standards may be unclear; halo effect, central tendency, leniency, bias can also be problems.
BARS	Provides behavioral "anchors." BARS is very accurate.	Difficult to develop.
Alternation ranking	Simple to use (but not as simple as graphic rating scales). Avoids central tendency and other problems of rating scales.	Can cause disagreements among employees and may be unfair if all employees *are,* in fact, excellent.
Forced distribution method	End up with a predetermined number or % of people in each group.	Employees' Appraisal results depend on your choice of cutoff points.
Critical incident method	Helps specify what is "right" and "wrong" about the employee's performance; forces supervisor to evaluate subordinates on an ongoing basis.	Difficult to rate or rank employees relative to one another.
MBO	Tied to jointly agreed-upon performance objectives.	Time-consuming.

they occur during the appraisal period. Maintaining such records instead of relying on memories is definitely the preferred approach.[36]

Diary keeping is preferred but not foolproof. In one study, raters were required to keep a diary, but the diary keeping actually undermined the performance appraisal's objectiveness.[37] What could account for such apparently bizarre findings? One possibility is that managers may develop positive or negative feelings toward ratees. The managers may then seek out and record incidents that are consistent with how they feel about the ratees. In any case, it's apparent that even diary keeping is no guarantee of objectivity, and that as a rater you must always keep the cognitive nature of the appraisal process in mind. Raters bring to the task a bundle of biases, inclinations, and decision-making shortcuts (such as stereotyping people based on age), so that, potentially at least, the appraisal is bound to be a product (or victim, some might argue) of the rater's biases and inclinations.

The manager should also keep in mind the intensely interpersonal nature of the appraisal process. As one writer puts it, "performance ratings amplify the quality of the personal relationship between boss and employee." Good relationships tend to create good experiences, bad relationships bad ones."[38] Knowing the employment law that applies to appraisals is also important, a point to which we now turn.

Know Your Employment Law

Appraising Performance

Appraisals affect promotions, raises, and dismissals. Since passage of Title VII in 1964, courts have therefore addressed the link between appraisals and personnel actions. They have often found that the inadequacies of an employer's appraisal system lay at the root of illegal discriminatory actions, particularly in cases concerning layoffs, promotions, discharges, merit pay, or combinations of these.[39]

An illustrative case involved layoff decisions. The court held that the firm had violated Title VII when it laid off several Hispanic-surnamed employees on the basis of poor performance ratings. The court concluded that the practice was illegal because:

1. The firm based the appraisals on subjective supervisory observations.
2. It didn't administer and score the appraisals in a standardized fashion.
3. Two of the three supervisory evaluators did not have daily contact with the employees they appraised.

Personal bias, unreasonably rating everyone high (or low), and relying just on recent events are some other reasons courts gave for deciding that firms' appraisal processes and subsequent personnel actions were unfair.[40] Furthermore, *legal* doesn't always mean *ethical*, but ethics should be the bedrock of an appraisal. Most managers (and college students) understand that appraisers or professors can "stick to the rules" and do lawful performance reviews but still fail to provide honest assessments. As one commentator puts it:

The overall objective of high-ethics performance reviews should be to provide an honest assessment of performance and to mutually develop a plan to improve the individual's effectiveness. That requires that we tell people where they stand and that we be straight with them.[41]

Here are some guidelines for developing a legally defensible appraisal process.[42]

1. Make sure you know what you mean by "successful performance." Conduct a job analysis to establish the criteria and standards.
2. Incorporate these criteria and standards into a rating instrument (BARS, graphic rating scale, and so on).
3. Communicate performance standards to employees and to those rating them, in writing.
4. When using graphic rating scales, avoid abstract trait names (such as "loyalty" or "honesty"), unless you can define them in terms of observable behaviors.
5. Use subjective supervisory ratings (essays, for instance) as only one component of the overall appraisal process.

6. Train supervisors to use the rating instrument properly. Give instructions on how to apply performance appraisal standards ("outstanding," and so on) when making judgments. (In 6 of 10 cases decided against the employer, the plaintiffs were able to show that supervisors applied subjective standards unevenly to minority and majority employees.) At least provide raters with written instructions for using the rating scale.
7. Allow appraisers substantial daily contact with the employees they're evaluating.
8. Base your appraisals on separate ratings for each of the job's performance dimensions. Using a single overall rating of performance is not acceptable to the courts, which often characterize such systems as vague.[43] Courts generally require combining separate ratings for each performance dimension with some formal weighting system to yield a summary score.
9. Whenever possible, have more than one appraiser conduct the appraisal, and conduct all such appraisals independently. This can help to cancel out individual errors and biases.
10. One appraiser should never have absolute authority to determine a personnel action.
11. Employees should have the opportunity to review and make comments, written or verbal, about their appraisals before they become final, and should have a formal appeals process through which to appeal their ratings.
12. Document all information and reasons bearing on any personnel decision: "Without exception, courts condemn informal performance evaluation practices that eschew documentation."[44]
13. Where appropriate, provide corrective guidance to assist poor performers in improving their performance.

If your case gets to court, which of these guidelines will most influence the judge's decision? A review of almost 300 U.S. court decisions is informative. Actions reflecting fairness and due process were most important. In particular, performing a job analysis, providing raters with written instructions, permitting employee review of results, and obtaining agreement among raters were the four practices that seemed to have the most consistent impact in most of the judicial decisions. The courts placed little emphasis on whether or not the employers formally validated their performance appraisal tools or processes.[45]

Who Should Do the Appraising?

Traditionally, the person's direct supervisor appraises his or her performance. However, other options are certainly available and are increasingly used. We'll look at the main ones.

The Immediate Supervisor   Supervisors' ratings are the heart of most appraisals. This makes sense: The supervisor should be—and usually is—in the best position to observe and evaluate the subordinate's performance, and is responsible for that person's performance.

Peer Appraisals   With more firms using self-managing teams, peer or team appraisals—the appraisal of an employee by his or her peers—are becoming more popular. For example, an employee chooses an appraisal chairperson each year. That person then selects one supervisor and three other peers to evaluate the employee's work.

Peer appraisals can predict future management success. In one study of military officers, peer ratings were quite accurate in predicting which officers would be promoted and which would not.[46] Peer ratings have other benefits. One study involved placing undergraduates into self-managing work groups. The researchers found that peer appraisals had "an immediate positive impact on [improving] perception of open communication, task motivation, social loafing, group viability, cohesion, and satisfaction."[47] However, *logrolling*—when several peers collude to rate each other highly—can be a problem.

Rating Committees   Many employers use rating committees. These committees usually contain the employee's immediate supervisor and three or four other supervisors.

Performance appraisals are most typically done by immediate supervisors, who can coach and monitor employees on a continuous basis.

Using multiple raters makes sense. While there may be a discrepancy among ratings by individual supervisors, the composite ratings tend to be more reliable, fair, and valid. Such ratings have higher inter-rater reliability or consistency than do ratings obtained from several peers.[48] Several raters can also help cancel out problems like bias and halo effects. Furthermore, when there are differences in ratings, they usually stem from the fact that raters at different levels observe different facets of an employee's performance, and the appraisal ought to reflect these differences. Even when a committee is not used, it is customary to have the manager immediately above the one who makes the appraisal review it.

Self-Ratings   Should employees appraise themselves? The basic problem, of course, is that employees usually rate themselves higher than they are rated by supervisors or peers. In one study, it was found that when asked to rate their own job performances, 40% of the employees in jobs of all types placed themselves in the top 10% ("one of the best"), while virtually all remaining employees rated themselves either in the top 25% ("well above average"), or at least in the top 50% ("above average").[49] Usually no more than 1% or 2% will place themselves in a below-average category, and then almost invariably in the top below-average category. One study concludes that individuals do not necessarily always have such positive illusions about their own performances, although in rating the performance of their group, group members did consistently give the group unrealistically high performance ratings.[50] Supervisors requesting self-appraisals to accompany their own should therefore know that doing so may accentuate differences and rigidify positions, rather than aid the process. Furthermore, even if you don't ask for a self-appraisal, your employee will almost certainly enter the performance review with his or her own self-appraisal in mind, and this will usually be higher than your rating. Therefore, come prepared for a dialogue, with specific critical incidents to make your point.

Appraisal by Subordinates   More firms today let subordinates anonymously rate their supervisor's performance, a process some call *upward feedback*.[51] The process helps top managers diagnose management styles, identify potential "people" problems, and take corrective action with individual managers as required. Subordinate ratings are especially valuable when used for developmental rather than evaluative purposes.[52] Managers who receive feedback from subordinates who identify themselves view the upward appraisal process more positively than do managers who receive anonymous feedback. However, subordinates (not surprisingly) are more comfortable giving anonymous responses, and those who have to identify themselves tend to provide inflated ratings.[53] Sample upward feedback items include: I can tell my manager what I think; my manager tells me what is expected; and my manager listens to my concerns.

RESEARCH INSIGHT   How effective is upward feedback in improving supervisors' behavior? Very, to judge from the evidence. One study involved 92 managers who were rated by one or more subordinates in each of four administrations of an upward feedback survey over two years.[54] The subordinates rated themselves and their managers on 33 behavioral statements. The feedback managers received included results from previous administrations of the survey, so they could track their performance over time.

The results were impressive. According to the researchers, "managers whose initial level of performance (defined as the average rating from subordinates) was 'low' improved between administrations one and two, and sustained this improvement two years later."[55] The results also suggest that it's not necessarily the specific feedback that caused the performance improvement (since low-performing managers seemed to improve over time even if they didn't receive any feedback). Instead, learning what the critical supervisory behaviors were (as a result of themselves filling out the appraisal surveys), plus knowing their subordinates would be appraising them, may have been enough to cause the improved behavior.

360-Degree Feedback   Many firms have expanded the idea of upward and peer feedback into "360-degree feedback." Ratings are collected "all around" an employee, from supervisors, subordinates, peers, and internal or external customers.[56] According to one study, 29% of the responding employers use 360-degree feedback (also called "multisource assessment"), and another 11% had plans to implement it.[57] The feedback is generally used for development rather than for pay increases.

Most 360-degree feedback systems contain several common features. Appropriate parties—peers, supervisors, subordinates, and customers, for instance—complete surveys on an individual. The surveys take many forms but often include items such as "returns phone calls promptly," "listens well," or "[my manager] keeps me informed." Computerized and Web-based systems then compile this feedback into individualized reports that HR presents to the ratees. The ratees are often the only ones who get these completed reports. They then meet with their own supervisors and sometimes with their subordinates and share the information they feel is pertinent for developing a self-improvement plan.

Some doubt the practicality of 360-degree feedback. Employees usually do these reviews anonymously, so those with an ax to grind can misuse the system. A "Dilbert" cartoon strip, announcing that evaluations by co-workers will help decide raises, has one character asking, "If my co-workers got small raises, won't there be more available in the budget for me?"[58] Yet one study found significant correlations between 360-degree ratings (by peers and managers) and conventional performance ratings.[59]

Thus, 360-degree appraisal systems are the subject of considerable debate. One study, by the HR consulting firm Watson Wyatt, found that companies using 360-degree-type feedback have lower market value (in terms of stock price). For example, those using peer review have a market value about 5% lower than similar companies that don't use peer reviews, and those that allow subordinates to evaluate their managers are valued almost 6% lower than similar firms that don't. These findings don't necessarily suggest a cause-and-effect relationship between nontraditional appraisal methods and market value, but they are a red flag. The findings suggest that any firm implementing 360-degree feedback should carefully assess the potential costs of the program, focus any feedback very clearly on concrete goals, carefully train the people that are giving and receiving the feedback, and not rely solely on 360-degree feedback for performance appraisal.[60] And, particularly with so many appraisers involved, the company should make doubly sure that the feedback the person receives is productive, unbiased, and development-oriented.[61]

Today, the use of the procedure is diminishing. After much initial fanfare, some firms, like GE, backed off from 360-degree appraisals. Some found the paperwork overwhelming; others found that some employees colluded with peers to give each other high ratings. But others still argue that progressive executives, at least, welcome 360-degree feedback, since "by laying themselves open to praise and criticism from all directions and inviting others to do the same, they guide their organizations to new capacities for continuous improvement."[62]

● THE APPRAISAL INTERVIEW

appraisal interview
An interview in which the supervisor and subordinate review the appraisal and make plans to remedy deficiencies and reinforce strengths.

An appraisal typically culminates in an **appraisal interview**. Here, supervisor and subordinate review the appraisal and make plans to remedy deficiencies and reinforce strengths. Interviews like these are potentially uncomfortable, since few people like to receive—or give—negative feedback. Adequate preparation and effective implementation are therefore essential.

Types of Appraisal Interviews

There are four basic types of appraisal interviews, each with its own objectives:

Satisfactory—Promotable is the easiest of the four appraisal interviews: The person's performance is satisfactory and there is a promotion ahead. Your objective is to discuss the person's career plans and to develop a specific action plan for the educational and professional development the person needs to move to the next job.

Satisfactory—Not promotable is for employees whose performance is satisfactory but for whom promotion is not possible. Perhaps there is no more room in the company. Some employees are also happy where they are and don't want a promotion. Your objective here is to maintain satisfactory performance. This is not easy. The best option is usually to find incentives that are important to the person and enough to maintain satisfactory performance. These might include extra time off, a small bonus, additional authority to handle a slightly enlarged job, and reinforcement, perhaps in the form of an occasional "well done!"

When the person's performance is *unsatisfactory but correctable*, the interview objective is to lay out an action plan (see Figure 9-10) for correcting the unsatisfactory performance.

Figure 9-10
Performance Contract
Source: David Antonion, "Improving the Performance Management Process Before Discontinuing Performance Appraisals," *Compensation and Benefits Review* May–June 1994, p. 33, 34.

PERFORMANCE CONTRACT

Within the next year, I understand that our organization's objectives are _____ _____ and that the goals of our department are _____ . I also understand that our work unit goals are _____ .

My key internal customers are _____ and their work needs and expectations are _____ .

To make my contribution toward attaining the goals stated above, I understand that I am expected to do the following:

My individual performance goals are _____ .

My goals for improving work methods (process) are _____ .

My goals for improving specific interpersonal work behaviors when I interact with the following _____ are _____ .

I believe these goals are acceptable and attainable. I also understand that I will be evaluated by multiple appraisal sources (supervisor, peers, internal, and, if appropriate, external customers).

Compensation for my work performance will be based on whether my performance was (1) outstanding, (2) fully competent, or (3) unsatisfactory. I understand that the following forms of compensation will be considered: (1) merit award for my individual performance goal attainment, (2) enhancement and utilization of my skills, (3) my work unit's or team's performance (gainsharing), and (4) our organization's performance (profit sharing).

_____   _____
Your signature   Supervisor's signature

If the employee is *unsatisfactory* and the situation is *uncorrectable*, you can usually skip the interview. You either tolerate the person's poor performance for now, or dismiss the person.

Perform an effective appraisal interview.

How to Conduct the Appraisal Interview

First, prepare for the interview. Assemble the data. Study the person's job description, compare performance to the standards, and review the employee's previous appraisals. Next, prepare the employee. Give the employee at least a week's notice to review his or her work, read over the job description, analyze problems, and gather questions and comments. Finally, choose the time and place. Find a mutually agreeable time for the interview and allow enough time for the entire interview. Interviews with lower-level personnel like clerical workers and maintenance staff should take no more than an hour. Interviews with management employees often takes two or three hours. Be sure the interview is done in a private place where you won't be interrupted by phone calls or visitors.

There are four things to keep in mind in actually conducting the interview:

1. *Talk in terms of objective work data.* Use examples such as absences, tardiness, quality records, inspection reports, scrap or waste, orders processed, productivity records, material used or consumed, timeliness of tasks or projects, control or reduction of costs, numbers of errors, costs compared to budgets, customers' comments, product returns, order processing time, inventory level and accuracy, accident reports, and so on.

2. *Don't get personal.* Don't say, "You're too slow in producing those reports." Instead, try to compare the person's performance to a standard. ("These reports should normally be done within 10 days.") Similarly, don't compare the person's performance to that of other people. ("He's quicker than you are.")

3. *Encourage the person to talk.* Stop and listen to what the person is saying; ask open-ended questions such as, "What do you think we can do to improve the situation?" Use a command such as "Go on," or "Tell me more." Restate the person's last point as a question, such as, "You don't think you can get the job done?"

4. *Don't tiptoe around.* Don't get personal, but do make sure the person leaves knowing specifically what he or she is doing right and doing wrong. Give specific examples; make sure the person understands; and get agreement before he or she leaves on how things will be improved, and by when. Develop an action plan showing steps and expected results.

How to Handle a Defensive Subordinate   Defenses are an important and familiar aspect of our lives. When a supervisor tells someone his or her performance is poor, the first reaction is often denial. By denying the fault, the person avoids having to question his or her own competence. Others react to criticism with anger and aggression. This helps them let off steam and postpones confronting the immediate problem until they are able to cope with it. Still others react to criticism by retreating into a shell.

In any event, understanding and dealing with defensiveness is an important appraisal skill. In his book *Effective Psychology for Managers*, psychologist Mortimer Feinberg suggests the following:

1. Recognize that defensive behavior is normal.

2. Never attack a person's defenses. Don't try to "explain someone to themselves" by saying things like, "You know the real reason you're using that excuse is that you

can't bear to be blamed for anything." Instead, try to concentrate on the act itself ("sales are down") rather than on the person ("you're not selling enough").

3. Postpone action. Sometimes it is best to do nothing at all. People frequently react to sudden threats by instinctively hiding behind their "masks." But given sufficient time, a more rational reaction takes over.

4. Recognize your own limitations. Don't expect to be able to solve every problem that comes up, especially the human ones. More important, remember that a supervisor should not try to be a psychologist. Offering your people understanding is one thing; trying to deal with psychological problems is another matter entirely.

How to Criticize a Subordinate   When criticism is required, do it in a manner that lets the person maintain his or her dignity and sense of worth. Criticize in private, and do it constructively. Provide examples of critical incidents and specific suggestions of what could be done and why. Avoid once-a-year "critical broadsides" by giving feedback on a daily basis, so that the formal review contains no surprises. Never say the person is "always" wrong (since no one is ever "always" wrong or right). Finally, criticism should be objective and free of any personal biases on your part.

How to Ensure the Interview Leads to Improved Performance   Whether subordinates express satisfaction with their appraisal interview depends on factors such as (1) not feeling threatened during the interview; (2) having an opportunity to present their ideas and feelings and to influence the course of the interview; and (3) having a helpful and constructive supervisor conduct the interview.

But, of course, you don't just want subordinates to be satisfied with their appraisal interviews. Your main aim is to get them to improve their subsequent performance. Here, clearing up job-related problems with the employee and setting measurable performance targets and a schedule for achieving them—an action plan—are essential.

However, providing the necessary development and support for the change is crucial. Many managers bring to the appraisal an erroneous (though unstated) assumption: that simply revealing the gap between where the employee should be and is will trigger improved performance. But in most human endeavors, that's not enough. For example, if getting someone to lose weight merely required a scale, there'd be little need for the thousands of diet programs on the market. Similarly, identifying the gap is just the first step in improving an employee's performance. Doing so often requires providing the tools and support the person needs to move ahead.[63]

How to Handle a Formal Written Warning   There will be times when an employee's performance is so poor that a formal written warning is required. Such written warnings serve two purposes: (1) They may serve to shake your employee out of his or her bad habits, and (2) they can help you defend your rating, both to your own boss and (if needed) to the courts. Written warnings should identify the standards by which the employee is judged, make it clear that the employee was aware of the standard, specify any deficiencies relative to the standard, and show the employee had an opportunity to correct his or her performance.

6 Discuss the pros and cons of using different raters to appraise a person's performance.

Appraisals in Practice

Surveys shed light on how and why companies appraise employees.[64] In one survey, about 89% of 250 SHRM members reported that performance appraisal was required for all their employees. Many reported using more than one appraisal format. About 32% said they used MBO, 24% used the graphic rating scale, 10% used "other," and, about 34%

used a narrative essay format; here raters take an open-ended approach to describing their employees' behaviors. None of those responding used behaviorally anchored rating scales. Eighty percent conduct annual evaluations; most of the rest do semiannual appraisals, and 92% require a review and feedback session as part of the appraisal process. A second survey found that of 100 large organizations, 52% use appraisals for promotions, 60% do *not* link appraisals to pay raises, and 68% say they don't even link the appraisals to determining other rewards, such as bonuses. About half used appraislas for succession planning.

● CREATING THE TOTAL PERFORMANCE MANAGEMENT PROCESS

We have seen that for many employers, the traditional "performance appraisal" is just part of the firm's overall performance management process. In a sense, performance management starts at the end and works back. Top management says, "What is our strategy and what are our goals?" Each manager in the chain of command then asks, "What does this mean for the goals we set for our employees, and for how we train, appraise, promote, and reward them?" The performance appraisal is just one link in that process.

Perhaps the best way to illustrate how to create a total performance management process is to look at how several companies—a small firm (NCCI), a large firm (TRW), and the Hotel Paris—actually did so. We will begin with a smaller organization, as illustrated next in the accompanying "When You're On Your Own" feature.

When You're On Your Own
HR for Line Managers and Entrepreneurs

Performance Management and Appraisal

At the Boca Raton, Florida–based National Council on Compensation Insurance (NCCI), management integrated performance management with the firm's HR Scorecard system.[65] Strategically, NCCI wanted to improve its own performance (in terms of customer satisfaction) by focusing its service representatives' attention on their specific roles in improving customer service. As part of its new performance management system, NCCI therefore had each employee and supervisor devise goals for the employee to achieve over the following 12 months, with a follow-up meeting after six months to assess progress and take remedial action.

NCCI's performance management process specifically recognizes how each employee's efforts link with the company's performance. It does this through an MBO type process. Senior management and the company's board establish company-wide planning objectives. Then the various departments set goals consistent with that plan, and memorialize these on a special HR Scorecard that shows how these goals link up to NCCI's strategic goals.

For example, NCCI's corporate goals include improving the firm's performance by providing its clients with more service, and selling them more software products. As part of NCCI's performance management process, each individual customer service consultant identifies what he or she could do to help achieve these aims. Then, each month, employees "get a report showing how much time they've spent with customers, how many problems they solved, and how many new products they sold. We roll these stats up through the division to the corporate level, so that they can see how both they and the company are progressing toward the goals. A person can look at that and see how his or her small piece is part of the big picture."[66] In this way, NCCI encourages each employee to continuously improve his or her performance in a way that helps the firm achieve its goals.

What does the individual manager in a large firm do if the employer simply has no such system? Certainly, there is generally no reason why the manager cannot legitimately adopt the employer's standard appraisal process to include some aspects of the performance management process. For example, discuss the company's goals with the employee, and then set some goals for the coming year that make sense in terms of them. Provide feedback continuously, rather than once a year. Make sure the employee has the training he or she needs.

Performance management notwithstanding, the individual supervisor will often find him- or herself uncomfortable at the prospect of what may well turn out to be a tense appraisal interview. Here, there is usually no substitute for fairness and candor, particularly in those tough situations where candor is required. Beyond that, it may be useful to review the checklist on Figure 9-11 just before the appraisal.

Implementing a performance management system like NCCI's in a larger company usually requires considerable technological support. The "Improving Productivity Through HRIS" feature illustrates how TRW, Inc., instituted such a system.

What steps did Lisa Cruz and her team take to formulate a new performance management process? We end this chapter with a summary of how in "The HR Scorecard."

Figure 9-11
Checklist During the Appraisal Interview
Source: Reprinted from www.HR.BLR.com with permission of the publisher, © 2004 *Business and Legal Reports, Inc.* 141 Mill Rock Road East, Old Saybrook, CT.

CHECKLIST DURING THE APPRAISAL INTERVIEW

Yes No

- Did you discuss each goal or objective established for this employee? ☐ ☐
- Are you and the employee clear on the areas of agreement? disagreement? ☐ ☐
- Did you and the employee cover all positive skills, traits, accomplishments, areas of growth, etc.? Did you reinforce the employee's accomplishments? ☐ ☐
- Did you give the employee a sense of what you thought of his or her potential or ability? ☐ ☐
- Are you both clear on areas where improvement is required? expected? demanded? desired? ☐ ☐
- What training or development recommendations did you agree on? ☐ ☐
- Did you indicate consequenses for noncompliance, if appropriate? ☐ ☐
- Did you set good objectives for the next appraisal period? ☐ ☐
  - Objective? ☐ ☐
  - Specific? ☐ ☐
  - Measurable? ☐ ☐
- Standard to be used for evaluation? ☐ ☐
  - Time frame? ☐ ☐
- Did you set a time for the next evaluation? ☐ ☐
- Did you confirm what your part would be? Did the employee confirm his or her part? ☐ ☐
- Did you thank the employee for his or her efforts? ☐ ☐

Improving Productivity Through HRIS

TRW's New Performance Management System

With over 100,000 employees in 36 countries on five continents, administering employee appraisals and managing performance is obviously a complicated process in a company like TRW.[67] In 2001, the firm was deeply in debt, and the company's heavy investment in the automotive business was a drain on its profits. TRW's top management knew it had to take steps to make the firm more competitive and performance driven. At the time, TRW had a traditional, paper-based employee appraisal system, and most of the firm's far-flung departments even used their own appraisal systems. As they reviewed what had to be done next, top management decided that a companywide performance management system was a top priority.

Top management identified a special team and charged it with creating a "one company, one system" performance management system. The team consisted of several information technology experts, and key HR representatives from each of the business units. Because team members were scattered around the world, the team and its team meetings were entirely Web-based, and virtual. Their aim was to quickly develop a performance management system that was both consistent and comprehensive. It had to be *consistent* in that employees in all of TRW's far-flung organization could use the same system. It had to be *comprehensive* in that it consolidated the various components of performance management into a single common system. For TRW, these components included goal setting, performance appraisal, professional development, and succession planning.

The team created an online system, one in which most TRW employees and supervisors worldwide could input and review their data electronically. (The team subsequently created an equivalent paper-based system, for use by certain employees abroad, who did not have easy access to the Web.) The Web-based performance management system consisted of the information in Figure 9-12.

To facilitate filling in the online form's pages, the team created a wizard that leads the user from step to step. The system also includes embedded prompts, and pull-down menus. For example, in the "demonstrated strengths" area, the pull-down menus allow the user to select specific competencies such as "financial acumen."

In practice, either the employee or the manager can trigger the performance management process by completing the appraisal and sending it to the other, although it's usually the employee that begins the process. Once the employee finishes the online form, a system-generated e-mail notifies the manager that the form is ready for review. Then the two fine-tune the appraisal by meeting in person, and by interacting online.

The new performance management system has produced benefits well beyond systematizing the performance appraisal and performance management process. The new system focuses everyone's attention on goal-oriented performance, for instance in terms of required employee "TRW Behaviors." It identifies development needs that are both organizationally relevant and of interest to the employee. It gives managers instantaneous access to employee performance-related data (for example, by clicking a "managing employees" function on the online system, a manager can see an onscreen

Figure 9-12
Information Required for TRW's Web-Based Performance Management System

Page one biographical data	Overall performance—manager's overall rating and comments
Identification information	
Education	**Page four development summary**
Experience summary	Demonstrated strengths
Pages 2–3 performance summary	Improvement opportunities
Accomplishments against previous year goals	Performance goals for the upcoming year
TRW behaviors	Professional development activities for the
TRW initiatives	upcoming year
Legal and ethical conduct/diversity and cultural	Future potential/positions (employee perspective)
sensitivity	Future potential/positions (manager perspective)
Previous year's professional development activities	Electronic sign-off from both employee and
Employee comments	manager

Source: D. Bradford Neary, "Creating a Company-Wide, Online, Performance Management System: A Case Study at TRW, Inc.," *Human Resource Management* 41, no 4 (Winter 2002), p. 495.

overview of the assessment status of each of his or her direct reports). It gives all managers access to an employee database so that, for instance, a search for a mechanical engineer with Chinese language skills takes just a few minutes.

And, the system lets the manager quickly review the development needs of all his or her employees. The result is an integrated, goal-oriented employee development and appraisal "Performance Management Process."

The HR Scorecard
Strategy and Results

The New Performance Management System

The Hotel Paris's competitive strategy is "To use superior guest service to differentiate the Hotel Paris properties, and to thereby increase the length of stay and return rate of guests, and thus boost revenues and profitability." HR manager Lisa Cruz must now formulate functional policies and activities that support this competitive strategy, by eliciting the required employee behaviors and competencies.

A preliminary analysis, performed jointly by Lisa and the Hotel Paris's chief financial officer, left them optimistic that HR could contribute measurably to achieving the hotel's strategic aims. Several employee competencies and behaviors including employee morale, employee commitment, and the percent of arriving guests receiving the hotel's required greeting had significant effects on customer and organizational outcomes such as guest satisfaction and frequency of guest returns. In turn, outcomes like these contributed measurably to the Hotel Paris's strategic goals, including profit margins, market share, and scores on industry satisfaction surveys. Lisa and her team now turn to creating an appraisal process that will help to produce the required employee competencies and behaviors. The accompanying HR Scorecard (Figure 9-13) outlines the relationships involved.

Both Lisa Cruz and the firm's CFO were concerned by the current disconnect between (1) what the current appraisal process was focusing on and (2) what the company wanted to accomplish in terms of its strategic goals. They wanted the firm's new performance management system to help breathe life into the firm's HR Scorecard, by focusing employees' behavior specifically on the performances that would help the Hotel Paris achieve its strategic goals.

Lisa and her team created a performance management system that focused on both competencies and objectives. In designing the new system, their starting point was the job descriptions they had created for the hotel's employees. These descriptions each included

required competencies. Consequently, using a form similar to Figure 9-5, the front-desk clerks' appraisals now focus on competencies such as "able to check a guest in or out in five minutes or less." Most service employees' appraisals include the competency, "able to exhibit patience and guest support of this even when busy with other activities." There were other required competencies. For example, the Hotel Paris wanted all service employees to show initiative in helping guests, to be customer oriented, and to be team players (in terms of sharing information and best practices). Each of these competencies derives from the Hotel's aim of becoming more service-oriented. Each employee now also receives one or more strategically relevant objectives for the coming year. (One, for a housecleaning crewmember, said, "Martha will have no more than three room cleaning infractions in the coming year," for instance.)

Thus, each employee's appraisal made sense in the context of the sort of customer oriented hotel the Hotel Paris sought to become. In addition to the goals and competencies-based appraisals, other Hotel Paris performance management system forms laid out the development efforts that the employee would undertake in the coming year. Instructions also reminded the supervisors that, in addition to the annual and semiannual appraisals, they should continuously interact with and update their employees. The result was a comprehensive performance management system: The supervisor appraised the employee based on goals and competencies that were driven by the company's strategic needs. And, the actual appraisal resulted in new goals for the coming year, as well as in specific development plans that made sense in terms of the company's and the employees' needs and preferences.

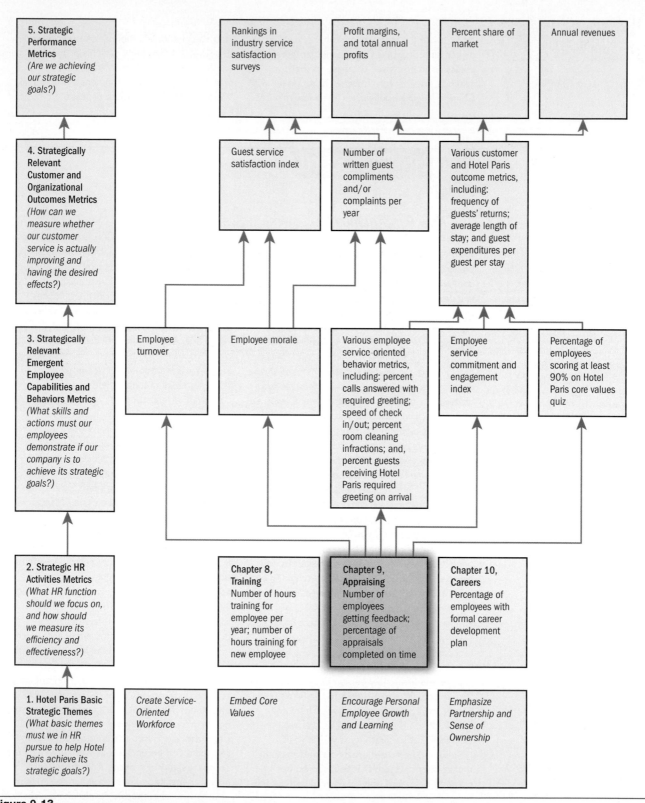

Figure 9-13
HR Scorecard for Hotel Paris International Corporation*

Note: *(An abbreviated example showing selected HR practices and outcomes aimed at implementing the competitive strategy, "To use superior guest services to differentiate the Hotel Paris properties and thus increase the length of stays and the return rate of guests, and thus boost revenues and profitability")

 *Review*

SUMMARY

1. Most companies have some formal or informal means of appraising their employees' performance. *Performance appraisal* means evaluating an employee's current and/or past performance relative to his or her performance standards.

2. We defined *performance management* as a process that consolidates goal setting, performance appraisal, and development into a single, common system, the aim of which is to ensure that the employee's performance is supporting the company's strategic aims.

3. Performance management includes practices through which the manager defines the employee's goals and work, develops the employee's capabilities, and evaluates and rewards the person's effort.

4. The employer must decide exactly what sort of performance to measure. The employer may opt for *generic dimensions* such as quality and quantity, or appraise performance on the *job's actual duties*. With *competency-based appraisals* the idea is to focus on the extent to which the employee exhibits the competencies that the employer values for this job. The employer may also want to appraise the employee based on the extent to which he or she is achieving his or her *objectives*.

5. Performance appraisal tools include the graphic rating scale, alternation ranking method, forced distribution method, BARS, MBO, critical incident method, and computer and Web-based methods.

6. Appraisal problems to beware of include unclear standards, halo effect, central tendency, leniency or strictness problems, and bias.

7. Most subordinates probably want a specific explanation or examples regarding why they were appraised high or low, and for this, compiling a record of positive and negative critical incidents can be useful.

8. There are three types of appraisal interviews: unsatisfactory but correctable performance; satisfactory but not promotable; and satisfactory—promotable.

9. To bring about constructive change in a subordinate's behavior, get the person to talk in the interview. Use open-ended questions, state questions in terms of a problem, use a command question, use questions to try to understand the feelings underlying what the person is saying, and restate the person's last point as a question. On the other hand, don't do all the talking, don't use restrictive questions, don't be judgmental, don't give free advice, and don't get involved with name calling, ridicule, or sarcasm.

DISCUSSION QUESTIONS

1. What is the purpose of a performance appraisal?

2. Discuss the pros and cons of four performance appraisal tools.

3. Explain how you would use the alternation ranking method, the paired comparison method, and the forced distribution method.

4. Explain in your own words how you would go about developing a behaviorally anchored rating scale.

5. Explain the problems to be avoided in appraising performance.

6. Discuss the pros and cons of using different potential raters to appraise a person's performance.

7. Compare and contrast performance management and performance appraisal.

8. Answer the question, "How would you get the interviewee to talk during an appraisal interview?"

INDIVIDUAL AND GROUP ACTIVITIES

1. Working individually or in groups, develop a graphic rating scale for the following jobs: secretary, professor, directory assistance operator.

2. Working individually or in groups, describe the advantages and disadvantages of using the forced distribution appraisal method for college professors.

3. Working individually or in groups, develop, over the period of a week, a set of critical incidents covering the classroom performance of one of your instructors.

4. The HRCI "Test Specifications" appendix at the end of this book (pages 685–689) lists the knowledge someone studying for the HRCI certification exam needs to have in each area of human resource management (such as in Strategic Management, Workforce Planning, and Human Resource Development). In groups of four to five students, do four things: (1) review that appendix now; (2) identify the material in this chapter that relates to the required knowledge the appendix lists; (3) write four

multiple choice exam questions on this material that you believe would be suitable for inclusion in the HRCI exam; and (4) if time permits, have someone from your team post your team's questions in front of the class, so the students in other teams can take each others' exam questions.

5. Every week, like clockwork, during the 2004 TV season, Donald Trump told another "apprentice," "You're fired."

Review recent (or archived) episodes of Donald Trump's *Apprentice* show and answer this: What performance appraisal system did Mr. Trump use, and do you think it resulted in valid appraisals? What techniques discussed in this chapter did he seem to apply? How would you suggest he change his appraisal system to make it more effective?

EXPERIENTIAL EXERCISE

Grading the Professor

Purpose: The purpose of this exercise is to give you practice in developing and using a performance appraisal form.

Required Understanding: You are going to develop a performance appraisal form for an instructor and should therefore be thoroughly familiar with the discussion of performance appraisals in this chapter.

How to Set Up the Exercise/Instructions: Divide the class into groups of four or five students.

Instructions
1. First, based on what you now know about performance appraisal, do you think Figure 9-1 is an effective scale for appraising instructors? Why? Why not?

2. Next, your group should develop its own tool for appraising the performance of an instructor. Decide which of the appraisal tools (graphic rating scales, alternation ranking, and so on) you are going to use, and then design the instrument itself.

3. Next, have a spokesperson from each group put his or her group's appraisal tool on the board. How similar are the tools? Do they all measure about the same factors? Which factor appears most often? Which do you think is the most effective tool on the board?

4. The class should select the top 10 factors from all of the appraisal tools presented to create what the class perceives to be the most effective tool for appraising the performance of the instructor.

APPLICATION CASE

Appraising the Secretaries at Sweetwater U

Rob Winchester, newly appointed vice president for administrative affairs at Sweetwater State University, faced a tough problem shortly after his university career began. Three weeks after he came on board in September, Sweetwater's president, Rob's boss, told Rob that one of his first tasks was to improve the appraisal system used to evaluate secretarial and clerical performance at Sweetwater U. Apparently, the main difficulty was that the performance appraisal was traditionally tied directly to salary increases given at the end of the year. So most administrators were less than accurate when they used the graphic rating forms that were the basis of the clerical staff evaluation. In fact, what usually happened was that each administrator simply rated his or her clerk or secretary as "excellent." This cleared the way for all support staff to receive a maximum pay increase every year.

But the current university budget simply did not include enough money to fund another "maximum" annual increase for every staffer. Furthermore, Sweetwater's president felt that the custom of providing invalid feedback to each secretary on his or her year's performance was not productive, so he had asked the new vice president to revise the system. In October, Rob sent a memo to all administrators telling them that in the future no more

than half the secretaries reporting to any particular administrator could be appraised as "excellent." This move, in effect, forced each supervisor to begin ranking his or her secretaries for quality of performance. The vice president's memo met widespread resistance immediately—from administrators, who were afraid that many of their secretaries would begin leaving for more lucrative jobs in private industry; and from secretaries, who felt that the new system was unfair and reduced each secretary's chance of receiving a maximum salary increase. A handful of secretaries had begun quietly picketing outside the president's home on the university campus. The picketing, caustic remarks by disgruntled administrators, and rumors of an impending slowdown by the secretaries (there were about 250 on campus) made Rob Winchester wonder whether he had made the right decision by setting up forced ranking. He knew, however, that there were a few performance appraisal experts in the School of Business, so he decided to set up an appointment with them to discuss the matter.

He met with them the next morning. He explained the situation as he had found it: The present appraisal system had been set up when the university first opened 10 years earlier, and the appraisal form had been developed primarily by a committee of secretaries. Under that system, Sweetwater's administrators filled out forms similar to the one shown in Table 9-2. This once-a-year appraisal (in March) had run into problems almost immediately, since it was apparent from the start that administrators varied widely in their interpretations of job standards, as well as in how conscientiously they filled out the forms and supervised their secretaries. Moreover, at the end of the first year it became obvious to everyone that each secretary's salary increase was tied directly to the March appraisal. For example, those rated "excellent" received the maximum increases, those rated "good" received smaller increases, and those given neither rating received only the standard across-the-board cost-of-living increase. Since universities in general—and Sweetwater in particular—have paid secretaries somewhat lower salaries than those prevailing in private industry, some secretaries left in a huff that first year. From that time on, most administrators simply rated all secretaries excellent in order to reduce staff turnover, thus ensuring each a maximum increase. In the process, they also avoided the hard feelings aroused by the significant performance differences otherwise highlighted by administrators.

Two Sweetwater experts agreed to consider the problem, and in two weeks they came back to the vice president with the following recommendations. First, the form used to rate the secretaries was grossly insufficient. It was unclear what "excellent" or "quality of work" meant, for example. They recommended instead a form like that in Figure 9-3. In addition, they recommended that the vice president rescind his earlier memo and no longer attempt to force university administrators to arbitrarily rate at least half their secretaries as something less than excellent. The two consultants pointed out that this was, in fact, an unfair procedure since it was quite possible that any particular administrator might have staffers who were all or virtually all excellent— or conceivably, although less likely, all below standard. The experts said that the way to get all the administrators to take the appraisal process more seriously was to stop tying it to salary increases. In other words, they recommended that every administrator fill out a form like that in Figure 9-3 for each secretary at least once a year and then use this form as the basis of a counseling session. Salary increases would have to be made on some basis other than the performance appraisal, so that administrators would no longer hesitate to fill out the rating forms honestly.

Rob thanked the two experts and went back to his office to ponder their recommendations. Some of the recommendations (such as substituting the new rating form for the old) seemed to make sense. Nevertheless, he still had serious doubts as to the efficacy of any graphic rating form, particularly if he were to decide in favor of his original forced ranking approach. The experts' second recommendation—to stop tying the appraisals to automatic salary increases—made sense but raised at least one very practical problem: If salary increases were not to be based on performance appraisals, on what were they to be based? He began wondering whether the experts' recommendations weren't simply based on ivory tower theorizing.

Questions

1. Do you think that the experts' recommendations will be sufficient to get most of the administrators to fill out the rating forms properly? Why? Why not? What additional actions (if any) do you think will be necessary?
2. Do you think that Vice President Winchester would be better off dropping graphic rating forms, substituting instead one of the other techniques we discussed in this chapter, such as a ranking method? Why?
3. What performance appraisal system would you develop for the secretaries if you were Rob Winchester? Defend your answer.

CONTINUING CASE

Carter Cleaning Company

The Performance Appraisal

After spending several weeks on the job, Jennifer was surprised to discover that her father had not formally evaluated any employee's performance for all the years that he had owned the business. Jack's position was that he had "a hundred higher-priority things to attend to," such as boosting sales and lowering costs, and, in any case, many employees didn't stick around long enough to be appraisable anyway. Furthermore, contended Jack, manual workers such as those doing the pressing and the cleaning did periodically get positive feedback in terms of praise from Jack for a job well done, or criticism, also from Jack, if things did not look right during one of his swings through the stores. Similarly, Jack was never shy about telling his managers about store problems so that they, too, got some feedback on where they stood.

This informal feedback notwithstanding, Jennifer believes that a more formal appraisal approach is required. She believes that there are criteria such as quality, quantity, attendance, and punctuality that should be evaluated periodically even if a worker is paid on piece rate. Furthermore, she feels quite strongly that the managers need to have a list of quality standards for matters such as store cleanliness, efficiency, safety, and adherence to budget on which they know they are to be formally evaluated.

Questions

1. Is Jennifer right about the need to evaluate the workers formally? The managers? Why or why not?
2. Develop a performance appraisal method for the workers and managers in each store.

KEY TERMS

performance appraisal, 310

performance management, 310

graphic rating scale, 315

alternation ranking method, 317

paired comparison method, 318

forced distribution method, 318

critical incident method, 321

behaviorally anchored rating scale (BARS), 322

management by objectives (MBO), 324

electronic performance monitoring (EPM), 326

unclear standards, 328

halo effect, 328

central tendency, 328

strictness/leniency, 328

bias, 329

appraisal interview, 334

ENDNOTES

1. Peter Glendinning, "Performance Management: Pariah or Messiah," *Public Personnel Management* 31, no. 2 (Summer 2002), pp. 161–178.

2. Clinton Wingrove, "Developing an Effective Blend of Process and Technology in the New Era of Performance Management," *Compensation and Benefits Review*, January/February 2003, p. 27.

3. Mushin Lee and Byoungho Son, "The Effects of Appraisal Review Content on Employees' Reactions and Performance," *International Journal of Human Resource Management* 1 (February 1998), p. 283; David Antonioni, "Improve the Management Process Before Discontinuing Performance Appraisals," *Compensation and Benefits Review*, May–June 1994, p. 29. See also Jonathan Siegel, "86 Your Appraisal Process?" *HR Magazine*, October 2000, pp. 199–206; Steve Bates, "Performance Appraisals: Some Improvement Needed," *HR Magazine* April 2003, p. 12.

4. Clinton Wingrove, "Developing an Effective Blend of Process and Technology" p. 27; See also, "IBM was named a recipient of Intel Corporation's prestigious 2003 supplier continuous improvement award," Purchasing, May 6, 2004, v133, i8, p. 26.

5. Vesa Vuutari and Marja Tahbanainen, "The Antecedents of Performance Management Among Finnish Expatriates," *Journal of Human Resource Management* 13, no. 1 (February 2002), pp. 53–75.

6. See, for example, Doug Cederblom and Dan Pemerl, "From Performance Appraisal to Performance Management: One Agency's Experience," *Personnel Management* 31, no. 2 (Summer 2002), pp. 131–140.

7. Gary Yukl, *Skills for Managers and Leaders* (Englewood Cliffs, NJ: Prentice Hall, 1991), pp. 132–33; see also Gary Latham, "Cognitive and Motivational Effects of Participation: A Mediator Study," *Journal of Organizational Behavior*, January 1994, 49–64.

8. Yukl, *Skills for Managers and Leaders*, p. 133. See also Miriam Erez, Daniel Gopher, and Nira Arzi, "Effects of Goal Difficulty, Self-Set Goals, and Monetary Rewards on Dual Task Performance," *Organizational Behavior and Human Decision Processes*, December 1990, pp. 247–269; and Thomas Lee, "Explaining the Assigned Goal-Incentive Interaction: The Role of Self-Efficacy and Personal Goals," *Journal of Management*, July–August 1997, 541–550.

9. Yukl, *Skills for Manager and Leaders*, p. 133.

10. See, for example, Robert Renn, "Further Examination of the Measurement of Properties of Leifer & McGannon's 1998 Goal Acceptance and Goal Commitment Scales," *Journal of Occupational and Organizational Psychology*, March 1999, pp. 107–114.

11. John (Jack) Welch, broadcast interview at Fairfield University, C-Span (May 5, 2001).

12. Kurt H. Loess and Ugur Yavas, "Human Resource Collaboration Issues in International Joint Ventures: A Study of U.S.-Japanese Auto Supply IJVs," *Management International Review* 43, no. 13 (July 2003), p. 311.

13. Del Jones, "More Firms Cut Workers Ranked at Bottom to Make Way for Talent," *USA Today*, May 30, 2001, p. B01.

14. "Straight Talk About Grading Employees on a Curve," *BNA Bulletin to Management*, November 1, 2001, p. 351.

15. Clinton Wingrove, "Developing an Effective Blend of Process and Technology", p. 26.

16. Steve Bates, "Forced Ranking," *HR Magazine*, June 2003, pp. 63-68.

17. See, for example, Timothy Keaveny and Anthony McGann, "A Comparison of Behavioral Expectation Scales and Graphic Rating Scales," *Journal of Applied Psychology*, 60 (1975), pp. 695–703. See also John Ivancevich, "A Longitudinal Study of Behavioral Expectation Scales: Attitudes and Performance," *Journal of Applied Psychology* 30, no. 3 (Autumn 1986), pp. 619–628.

18. Based on Donald Schwab, Herbert Heneman III, and Thomas DeCotiis, "Behaviorally Anchored Scales: A Review of the Literature," *Personnel Psychology*, 28 (1975), pp. 549–562. For a discussion, see also Uco Wiersma and Gary Latham, "The Practicality of Behavioral Observation Scales, Behavioral Expectation Scales, and Trait Scales," *Personnel Psychology* 30, no. 3 (Autumn 1986), pp. 619–689.

19. Lawrence Fogli, Charles Hullin, and Milton Blood, "Development of First Level Behavioral Job Criteria," *Journal of Applied Psychology* 55 (1971), pp. 3–8. See also Terry Dickenson and Peter Fellinger, "A Comparison of the Behaviorally Anchored Rating and Fixed Standard Scale Formats," *Journal of Applied Psychology*, April 1980, pp. 147–154; and Joseph Maiorca, "How to Construct Behaviorally Anchored Rating Scales (BARS) for Employee Evaluations," *Supervision*, August 1997, pp. 15–19.

20. Kevin R. Murphy and Joseph Constans, "Behavioral Anchors as a Source of Bias in Rating," *Journal of Applied Psychology* 72, no. 4 (November 1987), pp. 573–577; Aharon Tziner, "A Comparison of Three Methods of Performance Appraisal with Regard to Goal Properties, Goal Perception, and Ratee Satisfaction," *Group and Organization Management* 25, no. 2 (June 2000), pp. 175–191.

21. Gary Meyer, "Performance Reviews Made Easy, Paperless," *HR Magazine*, October 2000, pp. 181–184.

22. Ann Harrington, "Workers of the World, Rate Your Boss?" *Fortune* 2000, pp. 340–342.

23. "Appraisal Puts 15 Leading HRIS's to the Test," *BNA Bulletin to Management*, October 26, 2000, p. 340.

24. "Software Simplifies Performance Reviews, But Is It Affecting Employee Development," *BNA Bulletin to Management*, March 27, 2003, p. 97.

25. Jeffrey Stanton and Janet Barnes-Farrell, "Effects of Electronic Performance Monitoring on Personal Control, Task Satisfaction, and Task Performance," *Journal of Applied Psychology* 81, no. 6 (1996), p. 738.

26. Ibid.

27. Andrew Solomonson and Charles Lance, "Examination of the Relationship Between True Halo and Halo Effect in Performance Ratings," *Journal of Applied Psychology* 82, no. 5 (1997), pp. 665–674.

28. Ted Turnasella, "Dagwood Bumstead, Will You Ever Get That Raise?" *Compensation and Benefits Review*, September–October 1995, pp. 25–27. See also Solomonson and Lance, "Examination of the Relationship Between True Halo and Halo Effect," pp. 665–674.

29. I. M. Jawahar and Charles Williams, "Where All the Children Are Above Average: The Performance Appraisal Purpose Effect," *Personnel Psychology* 50 (1997), p. 921.

30. Clinton Wingrove, "Developing an Effective Blend of Process and Technology," pp. 25–30.

31. Gary Gregures et al., "A Field Study of the Effects of Rating Purpose on the Quality of Multisource Ratings," *Personnel Psychology* 56 (2003), pp. 1–21.

32. Jane Halpert, Midge Wilson, and Julia Hickman, "Pregnancy as a Source of Bias in Performance Appraisals," *Journal of Organizational Behavior* 14 (1993), pp. 649–663.

33. Ibid., p. 655.

34. "Assessing Performance," *Training and Development* 55, no. 5 (May 2001), p. 133.

35. Angelo DeNisi and Lawrence Peters, "Organization of Information in Memory and the Performance Appraisal Process: Evidence from the Field," *Journal of Applied Psychology* 81, no. 6 (1996), pp. 717–737.

36. Juan Sanchez and Philip DeLaTorre, "A Second Look at the Relationship Between Rating and Behavioral Accuracy in Performance Appraisal," *Journal of Applied Psychology* 81, no. 1 (1996), p. 7.

37. Arup Varna et al., "Interpersonal Affect and Performance Appraisal: A Field Study," *Personnel Psychology* 49 (1996), pp. 341–360.

38. Annette Simmons, "When Performance Reviews Fail," *Training and Development* 57, no. 9 (September 2003), pp. 47–53.

39. David Martin et al., "The Legal Ramifications of Performance Appraisal: The Growing Significance," *Public Personnel Management* 29, no. 3 (Fall 2000), pp. 381–383.

40. This is based on Kenneth L. Sovereign, *Personnel Law* (Upper Saddle River, NJ: Prentice Hall, 1994), pp. 113–114. See also "Avoiding HR Lawsuits," *Credit Union Executive*, November–December 1999, p. 6.

41. Larry Axline, "Ethical Considerations of Performance Appraisals," *Management Review*, March 1994, p. 62.

42. Wayne Cascio and H. John Bernardin, "Implications of Performance Appraisal Litigation for Personnel Decisions," *Personnel Psychology*, Summer 1981, pp. 211–212; Gerald Barrett and Mary Kernan, "Performance Appraisal and Terminations: A Review of Court Decisions since *Brito v. Zia* with Implications for Personnel Practices," *Personnel Psychology* 40, no. 3 (Autumn 1987), pp. 489–504.

43. James Austin, Peter Villanova, and Hugh Hindman, "Legal Requirements and Technical Guidelines Involved in Implementing Performance Appraisal Systems," in Gerald Ferris and M. Ronald Buckley (eds.), *Human Resources Management*, 3rd ed. (Upper Saddle River, NJ: Prentice Hall, 1996), pp. 271–288.

44. Ibid., p. 282.

45. Jon Werner and Mark Bolino, "Explaining U.S. Courts of Appeals' Decisions Involving Performance Appraisal: Accuracy, Fairness, and Validation," *Personnel Psychology* 50 (1997), pp. 1–24.

46. R. G. Downey, F. F. Medland, and L. G. Yates, "Evaluation of a Peer Rating System for Predicting Subsequent Promotion of Senior Military Officers," *Journal of Applied Psychology* 61 (April 1976); see also Julie Barclay and Lynn Harland, "Peer Performance Appraisals: The Impact of Rater Competence, Rater Location, and Rating Correctability on Fairness Perceptions," *Group and Organization Management* 20, no. 1 (March 1995), pp. 39–60.

47. Vanessa Druskat and Steven Wolf, "Effects and Timing of Developmental Peer Appraisals in Self-Managing Workgroups," *Journal of Applied Psychology* 84, no. 1 (1999), pp. 58–74.

48. Chockalingam Viswesvaran, Denize Ones, and Frank Schmidt, "Comparative Analysis of the Reliability of Job Performance Ratings," *Journal of Applied Psychology* 81, no. 5 (1996), pp. 557–574.

49. George Thornton III, "Psychometric Properties of Self-Appraisal of Job Performance," *Personnel Psychology* 33 (Summer 1980), p. 265. See also Cathy Anderson, Jack Warner, and Cassie Spencer, "Inflation Bias in Self-Assessment Evaluations: Implications for Valid Employee Selection," *Journal of Applied Psychology* 69, no. 4 (November 1984), pp. 574–580; and Shaul Fox and Vossi Dinur, "Validity of Self-Assessment: A Field Evaluation," *Personnel Psychology* 41, no. 3 (Autumn 1988), pp. 581–592.

50. Forest Jourden and Chip Heath, "The Evaluation Gap in Performance Perceptions: Illusory Perceptions of Groups and Individuals," *Journal of Applied Psychology* 81, no. 4 (August 1996), pp. 369–379.

51. Manuel London and Arthur Wohlers, "Agreement Between Subordinates and Self-Ratings in Upward Feedback," *Personnel Psychology* 44, no. 2 (Summer 1991), pp. 375–391.

52. Ibid., p. 376.

53. David Antonioni, "The Effects of Feedback Accountability on Upward Appraisal Ratings," *Personnel Psychology* 47, no. 2 (Summer 1994), pp. 349–355.

54. Richard Reilly, James Smither, and Nicholas Vasilopoulos, "A Longitudinal Study of Upward Feedback," *Personnel Psychology* 49 (1996), pp. 599–612.

55. Ibid., p. 599.

56. Kenneth Nowack, "360-Degree Feedback: The Whole Story," *Training and Development*, January 1993, p. 69.

57. "360-Degree Feedback on the Rise, Survey Finds," *BNA Bulletin to Management*, January 23, 1997, p. 31. See also Christopher Mabey, "Closing the Circle: Participant Views of a 360-Degree Feedback Program," *Human Resource Management Journal* 11, no. 1 (2001), pp. 41–53.

58. Carol Hymowitz, "Do 360-Degree Job Reviews by Colleagues Promote Honesty or Insults?" B-1.

59. Terry Beehr et al., "Evaluation of 360-Degree Feedback Ratings: Relationships with Each Other and with Performance and Selection Predictors," *Journal of Organizational Behavior* 22, no. 7 (November 2001), pp. 775–778.

60. Bruce Pfau and Ira Kay, "Does a 360-degree Feedback Negatively Affect the Company Performance?" *HR Magazine*, June 2002, pp. 55-59.

61. Scott Wimer, "The Dark Side of 360-Degree Feedback," *Training and Development*, September 2002, pp. 37–42.

62. Maury Pieperl, "Getting 360-Degree Job Feedback Right," *Harvard Business Review*, January 2001, p. 147.

63. Annette Simmons, "When Performance Reviews Fail," *Training and Development* 57, no. 9 (September 2003), pp. 47–53.

64. Brian Smith et al., "Current Trends in Performance Appraisal: An Examination of Managerial Practice," *SAM Advanced Management Journal* 61, no. 3 (Summer 1996), p. 16; "Companies appraise to improve development," *Personnel Today*, Feb. 25, 2003, p. 51.

65. Patrick Kiger, "How Performance Management Reversed NCCI's Fortunes," *Workforce*, May 2002, pp. 48-52.

66. Andrew Frank, "Technology Can Improve—Not Just Measure—Performance," *HR Briefing*, February 15, 2003, pp. 5–6.

67. D. Bradford Neary, "Creating a Company-Wide, Online, Performance Management System: A Case at TRW, Inc.," *Human Resource Management* 41, no. 4, (Winter 2002), pp. 491–498.

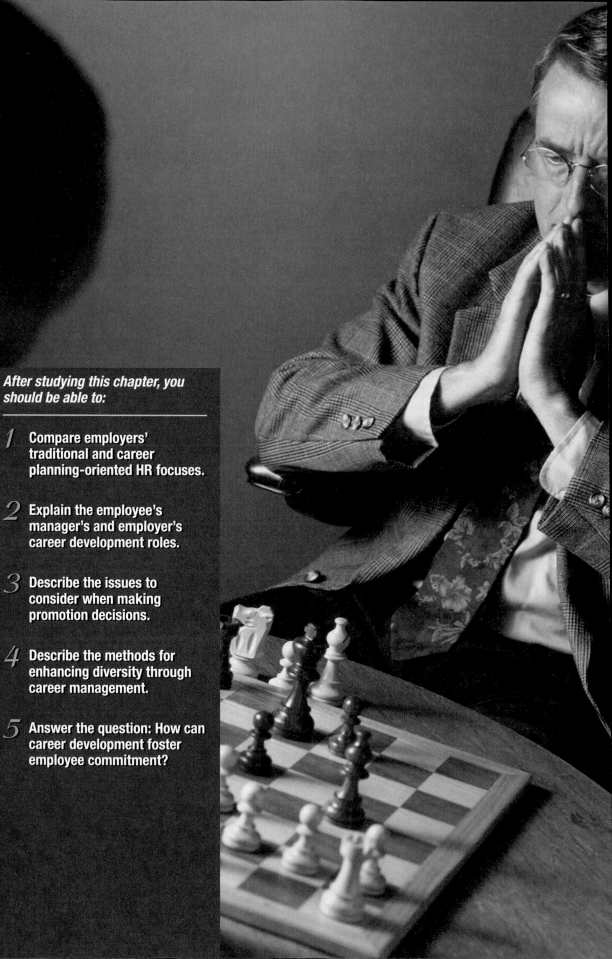

After studying this chapter, you
should be able to:

1 Compare employers'
traditional and career
planning-oriented HR focuses.

2 Explain the employee's
manager's and employer's
career development roles.

3 Describe the issues to
consider when making
promotion decisions.

4 Describe the methods for
enhancing diversity through
career management.

5 Answer the question: How can
career development foster
employee commitment?

Managing Careers

Lisa Cruz knew that as a hospitality business, the Hotel Paris was uniquely dependent upon having committed, high-morale employees. In a factory or small retail shop, the employer might be able to rely on direct supervision to make sure that the employees were doing their jobs. But in a hotel, just about every employee is "on the front line." There is usually no one there to supervise the limousine driver when he or she picks up a guest at the airport, or when the valet takes the guest's car, or the front-desk clerk signs the guest in, or the housekeeping clerk needs to handle a guest's special request. If the hotel wanted satisfied guests, they had to have committed employees who did their jobs as if they owned the company, even when the supervisor was nowhere in sight. But for the employees to be committed, Lisa knew the Hotel Paris had to make it clear that the company was also committed to its employees.

From her experience, she knew that one way to do this was to help her employees have successful and satisfying careers, and she was therefore concerned to find that the Hotel Paris had no career management process at all. Supervisors weren't trained to discuss employees' developmental needs or promotional options during the performance appraisal interviews. Promotional processes were informal. And the firm made no attempt to provide any career development services that might help its employees to develop a better understanding of what their career options were, or should be. Lisa was sure that committed employees were key to improving the experiences of its guests, and that she couldn't boost employee commitment without doing a better job of attending to her employees' career needs.•

Chapter 9 focused on appraising employees' performance. Once you've appraised their performance, it's often necessary to address career-related issues and to communicate these issues to the subordinates. The main purpose of this chapter is to help you be more effective at managing your employees' careers. We discuss the employees', managers', and employers' roles in career development, and the procedures for managing promotions and transfers. We also discuss the important topic of enhancing diversity through career management, and, finally, the career management steps an employer can take to foster employee commitment. The appendix to this chapter provides specific tools and techniques for making career choices and finding the right job. This chapter completes Part 3, which addressed training, appraisal, and development. Once you've trained and appraised employees, you need to turn to the question of how to pay them, the topic we cover in the next three chapters.

career
The occupational positions a person has had over many years.

We may define **career** as the "occupational positions a person has had over many years." Many people look back on their careers with satisfaction, knowing that what they might have achieved they did achieve, and that their career goals were satisfied. Others are less fortunate and feel that, at least in their careers, their lives and their potential went unfulfilled.

● THE BASICS OF CAREER MANAGEMENT

Employers have a significant impact on employees' careers, through their effects on the HR process. Recruiting, selecting, placing, training, appraising, rewarding, promoting, and separating the employee all affect the person's career, and therefore career satisfaction and success. Some firms institute relatively formal *career management* processes, while other firms do relatively little. We can define **career management** as a process for enabling employees to better understand and develop their career skills and interests, and to use these skills and interests most effectively both within the company and after they leave the firm. **Career development** is the lifelong series of activities (such as workshops) that contribute to a person's career exploration, establishment, success, and fulfillment. **Career planning** is the deliberate process through which someone becomes aware of personal skills, interests, knowledge, motivations, and other characteristics; acquires information about opportunities and choices; identifies career-related goals; and establishes action plans to attain specific goals.

career management
The process for enabling employees to better understand and develop their career skills and interests, and to use these skills and interests more effectively.

career development
The lifelong series of activities that contribute to a person's career exploration, establishment, success, and fulfillment.

career planning
The deliberate process through which someone becomes aware of personal skills, interests, knowledge, motivations, and other characteristics; and establishes action plans to attain specific goals.

Careers Today

Careers today are not what they were several years ago. "Careers were traditionally viewed as an upward, linear progression in one or two firms or as stable employment within a profession."[1] Today, someone's career is more likely to be "driven by the person, not the organization [and] reinvented by the person from time to time, as the person and the environment change."[2] Some even suggest that tomorrow's career won't be so much a gradual mountain climb as a series of short hills or learning stages, as the person switches from job to job and from firm to firm. (Thus, the sales rep, laid off by a publishing firm that's just merged, may reinvent her career for the next few years as a security analyst specializing in media companies, or as an account executive at a brokerage firm.)

What does this mean for HR? For one thing, the psychological contract between employers and workers has changed. Yesterday, employees traded loyalty for job security.[3] Today, "employees exchange performance for the sort of training and learning and development that will allow them to remain marketable."[4] This in turn means that the aims of HR activities like selection and training are now somewhat broader. In addition to serving the company's needs, these activities must now be designed to serve employees' long-run interests. In particular, they must encourage the employee to grow and realize his or

Table 10-1

Traditional Versus Career Development Focus

HR Activity	Traditional Focus	Career Development Focus
Human resource planning	Analyzes jobs, skills, tasks—present and future. Projects needs. Uses statistical data.	Adds information about individual interests, preferences, and the like to data.
Training and development	Provides opportunities for learning skills, information, and attitudes related to job.	Provides career path information. Adds individual growth orientation.
Performance appraisal	Rating and/or rewards.	Adds development plans and individual goal setting.
Recruiting and placement	Matching organization's needs with qualified individuals.	Matches individual and jobs based on a number of variables including employees' career interests.
Compensation and benefits	Rewards for time, productivity, talent, and so on.	Adds non-job-related activities to be rewarded, such as United Way leadership positions.

Source: Adapted from Fred L. Otte and Peggy G. Hutcheson, *Helping Employees Manage Careers* (Upper Saddle River, NJ: Prentice Hall, 1992), p. 10.

career planning and development
The deliberate process through which a person becomes aware of personal career-related attributes and the lifelong series of steps that contribute to his or her career fulfillment.

 Compare employers' traditional and career planning-oriented HR focuses

her full potential. Table 10-1 summarizes how activities such as training and appraisal can be used to provide more of such a **career planning and development** focus.

John Madigan, vice president of HR for the Hartford Insurance Company's 3,500-member IT group, discovered how important development activities can be. He conducted a survey. Of the employees who left the organization, "Ninety percent of people who left voluntarily talked about [the lack of] career and professional development and the level of support their managers gave them in this area," he says.[5]

Career Development

Career development programs tend to have a new focus today. Corporate career development programs used to focus on the employee's future with that particular firm—in other words, on managing the person's career with the firm. Figure 10-1 illustrates this approach.[6] Today, the reality for most people is that they'll have to change employers (and perhaps careers) several times during their work lives. The emphasis now is thus on facilitating self-analysis, development, and management.[7]

Providing employees with the career planning tools they need benefits all concerned. It gives the employee the perspective he or she needs to understand his or her career options, and what he or she can do to pursue the most attractive ones. And, to the extent that the person develops the skills he or she needs for a career move, it makes the person more mobile and more likely to achieve career success.

For the employer, the career development partnership serves several functions. As two experts put it, "employers provide the tools, environment, and skill development opportunities for employees, and then employees are better equipped to serve the company and build it to its potential."[8] Career development may also cultivate employee commitment. Often, one of the best things an employer can do to maintain employee commitment is to emphasize how the company will partner with the employee in continuously developing his or her skills and knowledge: "The most attractive proposition an employer can make today is that in five years the employee will have more knowledge and be more employable than now. That should be the acid test for any career development program."[9]

**Figure 10-1
Employee Career
Development Plan**
Source: Reprinted from www.HR.
BLR.com with permission of the
publisher, © 2004 *Business and Legal
Reports Inc.*, 141 Mill Rock Road East,
Old Saybrook, CT.

Employee Career Development Plan

Employee: _____   **Position:** _____

Manager: _____   **Department:** _____

Date of Appraisal: _____

1. What is the next logical step up for this employee, and when do you think he/she will be ready for it?

Probable Next Job:	When Ready:			
	Now	6 Months	1 Year	2 Years
1.	☐	☐	☐	☐
2.	☐	☐	☐	☐
3.	☐	☐	☐	☐

2. What is the highest probable promotion within five years?

3. What does this employee need to prepare for promotion?

- Knowledge: _____
  _____

  Action Plan: _____
  _____

- Still Training: _____
  _____

  Action Plan: _____
  _____

- Management Training: _____
  _____

  Action Plan: _____
  _____

Career development programs needn't be complicated. Employees report that receiving performance feedback, having individual development plans, and having access to non-technical skills training would probably reduce the likelihood they'd leave their firms. Yet, only about a fourth of the respondents in one survey had individual development plans.[10]

Explain the employee's manager's and employer's career development roles

● ROLES IN CAREER DEVELOPMENT

The employee, the manager, and the employer all play roles in planning, guiding, and developing the employee's career (see Table 10-2). However, the employee must always accept full responsibility for his or her own career development and career success. This is one task that no employee should ever leave to a manager or employer. For the individual employee, the career planning process means matching individual strengths and weaknesses with occupational opportunities and threats. The person wants to pursue

Table 10-2

Roles in Career Development

Individual
• Accept responsibility for your own career.
• Assess your interests, skills, and values.
• Seek out career information and resources.
• Establish goals and career plans.
• Utilize development opportunities.
• Talk with your manager about your career.
• Follow through on realistic career plans.
Manager
• Provide timely performance feedback.
• Provide developmental assignments and support.
• Participate in career development discussions.
• Support employee development plans.
Organization
• Communicate mission, policies, and procedures.
• Provide training and development opportunities.
• Provide career information and career programs.
• Offer a variety of career options.

Source: Fred L. Otte and Peggy G. Hutcheson, *Helping Employees Manage Careers* (Upper Saddle River, NJ: Prentice Hall, 1992), p. 56.

occupations, jobs, and a career that capitalize on his or her interests, aptitudes, values, and skills. He or she wants to choose occupations, jobs, and a career that make sense in terms of projected future demand for various types of occupations.

Of course, career planning only gets one so far. During 2000–2003, many people who had previously worked hard to train as computer systems analysts were devastated to find that the dot-com collapse had dramatically reduced the need for systems analysts. However, uncertainties like these only underscore the need for keeping one's finger on the pulse of the job market, so as to be better positioned to move when a career change is required.

Many people make the mistake of changing occupations (or of remaining unhappily in their present jobs) when they could be happier without making a big career change. For some people, a little fine-tuning will often suffice. The employee, if dissatisfied at work, has to figure out where the problem lies. Some people may like their occupations and the employers for whom they work, but not how their specific jobs are structured. Others may find their employers' ways of doing things are the problem. In any case, it's not always the occupation that's the problem. Why decide to switch from being a lawyer to a teacher, when it's not the profession but that law firm's 80-hour weeks that's the problem?

The Employee's Role

Making decisions like these is the employee's responsibility. For example, an employee can do several things short of changing occupations. Ask yourself what you're looking for in a job, and to what extent your current position is fulfilling your needs. Get rid of energy-draining, low-impact responsibilities. Enhance your networks, for instance, by joining a cross-functional team at work, discussing your career goals with role models, conducting informational interviews with people whose jobs interest you, and becoming a board member for a nonprofit organization so you can interact with new people. If you are satisfied with your occupation and where you work, but not with your job as it is currently organized, reconfigure your job. For example, consider alternative work arrangements such as part-time work, flexible hours, or telecommuting; delegate or eliminate the job functions you least prefer; and seek out a "stretch assignment" that will let you work on something that you find challenging.[11]

Studies also suggest that having a mentor—a senior person who can be a sounding board for your career questions and concerns, and provide career-related guidance and assistance—can significantly enhance career satisfaction and success.[12] Here, again, the employer can play an important role, for instance, by encouraging and rewarding senior managers to serve as mentors. But again, it is ultimately the employee's responsibility to find a mentor and to maintain a productive relationship. Suggestions for doing so include:

- Choose an appropriate potential mentor. The mentor should be able to remain objective to offer good career advice, so someone who doesn't have direct supervisory responsibility over you may be best. Many people seek out someone who is one or two levels above their current boss, or possibly even someone in another company.

- Don't be surprised if you're turned down. Not everyone is willing to undertake this time-consuming professional commitment, so do not be surprised if your first one or two choices turn you down.

- Make it easier for a potential mentor to agree to your request by making it clear ahead of time what you expect in terms of time and advice.

- Have an agenda. Bring an agenda to your first mentoring meeting that lays out key issues and topics for discussion.

- Respect the mentor's time. Be selective about the work-related issues that you bring to the table—this person isn't there to be your personal management consultant. Furthermore, the mentoring relationship generally should not involve personal problems or issues.[13]

In this chapter, we'll focus primarily on the manager's and the employer's role in the employee's career development process. The "When You're on Your Own" feature illustrates the manager's role in the employee's career development. The appendix to this

When You're On Your Own
HR for Line Managers and Entrepreneurs

Employee Career Development

Whether or not the employer has a career development program, the individual manager can easily do several things to support his or her subordinates' career development needs. For example, when the subordinate first begins his or her job, you can discuss the importance of developing a career plan, as well as ways in which you can help the employee achieve career goals. The manager can schedule regular performance appraisals and, at these reviews, focus on the extent to which the employee's current skills and performance are consistent with the person's career goals. The manager can provide the employee with an informal career development plan like that in Figure 10-1. And, the manager can provide mentoring assistance, and keep subordinates informed about how they can utilize the firm's current career-related benefits.[14]

chapter, "Managing Your Career" (see page 372) explains the career planning process from the employee's point of view. Let's look now at the employer's role.

The Employer's Role

A survey illustrates the range of career management practices employers can engage in. The researchers surveyed 524 organizations in the United Kingdom to determine how often they used 17 career management practices. "Posting job openings" was the most popular practice. The other top career practices, in descending order, were: formal education; career-oriented performance appraisals; counseling by managers; lateral, developmental moves; counseling by HR; retirement preparation; and succession planning.[15] Sun Microsystems has a relatively formal and well-thought-out program. It maintains a career development center staffed by certified counselors to help employees fill development gaps and choose career opportunities at Sun. The firm believes its program helps explain why its average employee tenure of four years is more than twice that estimated at other Silicon Valley firms.[16]

> The employer's career development responsibilities depend somewhat on how long the employee has been with the firm. Before hiring, *realistic job previews* can help prospective employees more accurately gauge whether the job is indeed for them, and particularly whether a job's demands are a good fit with a candidate's skills and interests. Especially for recent college graduates, the first job can be crucial for building confidence and a more realistic picture of what he or she can and cannot do: Providing *challenging first jobs* (rather than relegating new employees to "jobs where they can't do any harm"), and having an experienced mentor who can help the person learn the ropes, are important. Some refer to this as preventing **reality shock**, a phenomenon that occurs when a new employee's high expectations and enthusiasm confront the reality of a boring, unchallenging job.

> After the person has been on the job for a while, an employer can take steps to contribute in a positive way to the employee's career. *Career-oriented appraisals*—in which the manager is trained not just to appraise the employee but also to match the person's strengths and weaknesses with a feasible career path and required development work—is one important step. Similarly, providing periodic, planned **job rotation** can help the person develop a more realistic picture of what he or she is (and is not) good at, and thus the sort of future career moves that might be best.

> Firms can also provide **mentoring** opportunities. Mentoring may be formal or informal. Informally, mid- and senior-level managers may voluntarily help less experienced employees—for instance, by giving them career advice and helping them navigate political pitfalls. Other informal means—such as increasing the opportunities for networking and interactions among diverse employees—can also be effective.[17] Firms may also have formal mentoring programs. For instance, the employer may pair protégés with potential mentors. Many provide instructional manuals to help mentor and protégé better understand their respective responsibilities.

Innovative Corporate Career Development Initiatives

Employers' corporate career development initiatives may also include innovative programs like those listed below.

1. *Provide each employee with an individual budget.* He or she can use this budget for learning about career options and personal development.[18]

reality shock
Results of a period that may occur at the initial career entry when the new employee's high job expectations confront the reality of a boring, unchallenging job.

job rotation
Moving an employee through a preplanned series of positions in order to prepare the person for an enhanced role with the company.

mentoring
Formal or informal programs in which mid- and senior-level managers help less experienced employees—for instance, by giving them career advice and helping them navigate political pitfalls.

Mentoring can be formal or informal, but usually consists of mid- or senior-level managers helping less experienced colleagues with career advice and tips on how to avoid political problems and move up the ladder.

2. *Offer on-site or online career centers.* These might include an on or off-line library of career development materials, career workshops, workshops on related topics (such as time management), and also provide individual career coaches for career guidance. For example, Dow Chemical instituted a "People Success System" to facilitate employees' career planning and development. The system includes a list of competencies for every job in the company. Employees can review the competencies required for their own jobs (or for others they might be interested in), and identify their own developmental needs. They can then use the People Success System database to find training and development options.[19] The employer may also organize an online career center using tools like those we describe in the chapter appendix.

3. *Encourage role reversal.* Have employees temporarily work in different positions in order to develop a better appreciation of their occupational strengths and weaknesses.

4. *Establish a "corporate campus."* Make career and development courses and programs available, perhaps through partnerships with local colleges or consultants.

5. *Help organize "career success teams."* These are small groups of employees from the same or different departments who meet periodically to network and support one another in achieving their career goals.

6. *Provide career coaches.* For example, Allmerica Financial Corp., hired 20 career development coaches to assist its 850-person information technology staff. This coaching program was part of a broader organizational change program, to centralize information technology and create small information technology teams. The coaches help individual IT employees identify their development needs, and obtain the training, professional development, and networking opportunities that they need to satisfy those needs.[20]

   Career coaches usually focus on career counseling and development advice. For example, they might work one-on-one with individual employees to help them use career assessment tools and identify their training and development options.[21] However, a new breed of coach is emerging. Used mostly for companies' highest-level managers, the coaches often double as therapists. These "executive coaches" provide assessment and advice that often digs quite deeply into the executive's personality, and into how the person's personal life may be influencing his or her career.

   Career coaches should help employees create clear one- to five-year plans showing where their careers with the firm may lead. Then, base developmental plans on the skills employees will need to succeed at the firm.[22]

7. *Provide Career Planning Workshops.* A career planning workshop is "a planned learning event in which participants are expected to be actively involved, completing career planning exercises and inventories and participating in career skills practice sessions."[23] A typical workshop includes three main activities: self-assessment, an environmental assessment, and goal-setting and action-planning segment. See Figure 10-2 for a typical agenda.

8. *Computerized on- and offline programs are available for improving the organizational career planning process.* For example, WorkforceVision from Criterion, Inc., in Irving, Texas, helps the company analyze an employee's training needs. Clicking on the employee's name launches his or her work history, competencies, career path, and other information. For each competency (such as leadership and customer focus), a bar chart graphically shows "gap analysis" highlighting the person's strengths and weaknesses. The firm can then organize developmental activities around the person's needs.[24]

9. *First USA Bank has what it calls the Opportunity Knocks program.* Its purpose is to help employees crystallize their career goals and achieve them within the company.

In addition to career development training and follow-up support, First USA Bank has also outfitted special career development facilities at its work sites that employees can use on company time. These contain materials such as career assessment and planning tools.[25]

Before the program—Two weeks prior to the workshop participants receive a letter confirming their participation in the program and package of work to be completed before coming to the workshop. The exercises in this package include skills inventory, values identification, life accomplishments inventory, and a reading describing career direction options.

Day 1

8:30–10:00 **Introduction and Overview of Career Planning**

Welcome and Introduction to Program

Welcome by general manager
Overview of agenda and outcomes
Participant introductions (statements of expectations for the program)

Overview of Career Development

Company's philosophy
Why career planning is needed
What career planning is and is not
Career planning model

10:00–Noon **Self-Assessment: Part 1**

Individual Self-Assessment: Values

Values card sort exercise
Reconciling with values pre-work
Introduce career planning summary work sheet

Individual Self-Assessment: Skills

Motivated skills exercise
Examining life accomplishments (synthesize with pre-work)
Identifying accomplishment themes
Preferred work skills (from pre-work inventory)
Fill in career planning summary work sheet

1:00–3:00 **Self-Assessment: Part 2**

Individual Self-Assessment: Career Anchors

Career anchoring pattern exercise
Small group discussions
Fill in career planning summary work sheet

Individual Self-Assessment: Preferences

What success means to me
Skills, knowledge, personal qualities
Fill in career planning summary work sheet

Individual Self-Assessment: Career Path Pattern

Synthesize with direction options from pre-work
Fill in career planning summary work sheet

3:30–4:30 **Environmental Assessment**

Information About the Company
Goals, growth areas, expectations, turnover, competition for jobs, skills for the future
Fill in career planning summary work sheet
Personal career profile
Reality test, how you see self at this point by sharing

Day 2

8:30–10:00 **Goal Setting**

Warm-Up Exercise
Review of where we've been and where we're going
Setting goals—where do I want to be?
Creating an ideal future
Future skills and accomplishments
Desired lifestyle
Life and career goals

10:15–1:30 **Environmental Assessment: Part 2**

Career resources in the company
Introduce support services and hand out information
Marketing yourself—what it takes to achieve your goals here
Describe resource people who will be with the group for lunch and brainstorm questions/issues to be discussed
Lunch with resource people
Review lunch discussions

1:30–4:30 **Developing Career Action Plans**

Making career decisions
Identifying long-range alternatives
Identifying short-range alternatives
Improving career decisions
Decision styles and ways to enhance them
Creating your career plan
Reconciling your goals with options
Next career steps
Development action plan
Contingency planning
Making It Happen—Making Commitments to Next Steps
Summary and Adjourn

Figure 10-2
Sample Agenda—Two-Day Career Planning Workshop
Source: Fred L. Otte and Peggy Hutcheson, *Helping Employees Manage Careers* (Upper Saddle River, NJ: Prentice Hall, 1992), pp. 22–23.

Improving Productivity Through HRIS

Integrating Career Planning into the Employer's HRIS

Realistically, it doesn't make much sense to compartmentalize activities like career planning, succession planning, performance appraisal, and training and development. Ideally, the employee's career planning and development needs should certainly reflect the strengths and weaknesses that the performance appraisal brings to light. And, of course, eliminating those deficiencies should ideally (and automatically) involve the employee tapping into the firm's training and development offerings. Similarly, it would be ideal if the same integrated information system gave management a bird's-eye view of their employees' career interests, progress, and appraisal results, so as to expedite the firm's succession planning process.

That is why more employers are moving toward integrating their career planning and development systems with their firms' performance appraisal, succession planning, and training and development information systems. Thus, rather than just offering employees a stand-alone career planning and development product, they get access to the firm's companywide HRIS, which, among other things, integrates all these functions.

For example, Alyeska, the company that manages the trans-Alaska pipeline, has a user-friendly portal that lets employees "see their full training history, development plans and upcoming deadlines, register for courses, or do career planning—usually without having to ask for help."[26] At the same time, "managers can get a quick picture of the training needs for a particular group, or see all the employees who have a specific qualification."[27]

One information system that lets employers integrate appraisal, career development, training, and succession planning systems is Kenexa CareerTracker. CareerTracker "helps organizations optimize workforce productivity by providing an easily accessible platform for ongoing employee performance management, succession planning, and career development."[28]

For both the employer and employee, it often makes more sense to merge the firm's career development and training and appraisal systems together as an integrated online package. The "Improving Productivity Through HRIS" feature illustrates this.

promotions
Advancements to positions of increased responsibility.

transfers
Reassignments to similar positions in other parts of the firm.

● MANAGING PROMOTIONS AND TRANSFERS

Promotions and transfers are integral parts of most people's careers. **Promotions** traditionally refer to advancements to positions of increased responsibility; **transfers** are reassignments to similar positions in other parts of the firm.

Making Promotion Decisions

Describe the issues to consider when making promotion decisions

Most working people look forward to promotions, which usually mean more pay, responsibility, and (often) job satisfaction. For employers, promotions can provide opportunities to reward exceptional performance, and to fill open positions with tested and loyal employees. Yet the promotion process isn't always a positive experience for either employee or employer. Unfairness, arbitrariness, or secrecy can diminish the effectiveness of the process for all concerned. Several decisions, therefore, loom large in any firm's promotion process.

Decision 1: Is Seniority or Competence the Rule?   Probably the most important decision is whether to base promotion on seniority or competence, or some combination of the two.

Today's focus on competitiveness favors competence, as does the fact that promotion based on competence is the superior motivator. However, a company's ability to use competence as the criterion depends on several things, most notably whether or not union agreements or civil service requirements govern promotions. Union agreements sometimes contain clauses that emphasize seniority, such as: "In the advancement of employees to higher paid jobs when ability, merit, and capacity are equal, employees with the highest seniority will be given preference."[29] And civil service regulations that stress seniority rather than competence often govern promotions in many public-sector organizations.

Decision 2: How Should We Measure Competence?   If the firm opts for competence, how should it define and measure competence? Defining and measuring past performance is relatively straightforward: Define the job, set standards, and use one or more appraisal tools to record performance. But promotions require something more: You also need a valid procedure for predicting a candidate's future performance.

Most employers use prior performance as a guide, and assume that (based on his or her prior performance) the person will do well on the new job. This is the simplest procedure. Others use tests or assessment centers to evaluate promotable employees and to identify those with executive potential.

An increasing number of employers take a more comprehensive approach. For example (particularly given the public safety issues involved), police departments have traditionally taken a relatively systematic approach when evaluating candidates for promotion to command positions. Traditional promotional reviews include a written knowledge test, an assessment center, credit for seniority, and a score based on recent performance appraisal ratings. Other departments are adding a personnel records review. This includes evaluation of job-related dimensions such as supervisory-related education and experience, ratings from multiple sources, and systematic evaluation of behavioral evidence.[30]

Decision 3: Is the Process Formal or Informal?   Many firms have informal promotion processes. They may or may not post open positions, and key managers may use their own "unpublished" criteria to make decisions. Here employees may (reasonably) conclude that factors like "who you know" are more important than performance, and that working hard to get ahead—at least in this firm—is futile.

Many employers establish formal, published promotion policies and procedures. These have several components. Employees get a *formal promotion policy* describing the criteria by which the firm awards promotions. A *job-posting policy* states the firm will post open positions and their requirements, and circulate these to all employees. As explained in Chapter 5, many employers also maintain *employee qualification briefs*, and use replacement charts and computerized employee information systems.

Decision 4: Vertical, Horizontal, or Other?   Promotions aren't necessarily as simple as they may appear. For example, how do you motivate employees with the prospect of promotion when your firm is downsizing? And how do you provide promotional opportunities for those, like engineers, who may have little or no interest in administrative roles?

Several options are available. Some firms, such as the exploration division of British Petroleum, create two parallel career paths, one for managers, and another for "individual contributors" such as high-performing engineers. At BP, individual contributors can move up to nonsupervisory but senior positions, such as "senior engineer." These jobs have most of the financial rewards attached to management-track positions at that level.

Another option is to move the person horizontally. For instance, move a production employee to HR so as to develop his or her skills and to test and challenge his or her aptitudes. And in a sense, "promotions" are possible even when leaving the person in the same job. For example, you can usually enrich the job, and provide training to enhance the opportunity for assuming more responsibility.

Sophie Brouchard with her husband and sons on moving day. When Bouchard, a top sales rep for executive recruiting firm TMP Worldwide, Inc., was offered a transfer from Montreal to London, her major concern was her husband. Stephane Licari would have to leave his own promising sales career behind. Bouchard mentioned the problem to her boss, who immediately set up an interview for Licari with the head of European sales, and he was offered a job in London as well.

Handling Transfers

A *transfer* is a move from one job to another, usually with no change in salary or grade. Employees seek transfers for many reasons, including personal enrichment, more interesting jobs, greater convenience—better hours, location of work, and so on—or to jobs offering greater advancement possibilities. Employers may transfer a worker to vacate a position where he or she is no longer needed, to fill one where he or she is needed, or more generally to find a better fit for the employee within the firm. Many firms today boost productivity by consolidating positions. Transfers are a way to give employees who might have nowhere else to go a chance for another assignment and, perhaps, some personal growth.

Many firms have had policies of routinely transferring employees from locale to locale, either to expose them to a wider range of jobs or to fill open positions with trained employees. Such easy-transfer policies have now fallen into disfavor. This is partly because of the cost of relocating employees (paying moving expenses, and buying back the employee's current home, for instance) and partly because firms assumed that frequent transfers had a damaging effect on transferees' family life.

One study suggests that the latter argument, at least, is without merit.[31] The main finding was that there were few differences between mobile and stable families. Few families in the mobile group believed moving is easy. However, they were as satisfied with all aspects of their lives (except social relationships—making friends at work, for instance) as were stable families.

Know Your Employment Law

Establish Clear Guidelines for Managing Promotions

In general, the employer's promotion processes must comply with all the same anti-discrimination laws as do procedures for recruiting and selecting employees or any other HR actions. For example, Title VII of the 1964 Civil Rights Act states, "it shall be an unlawful employment practice for an employer to fail or refuse to hire or to discharge an individual or otherwise to discriminate against any individual with respect to his/her compensation, terms, conditions, or privileges of employment, because of such individual's race, color, religion, sex, or national origin." Similarly, the Age Discrimination in Employment Act of 1967 made it unlawful to discriminate against older employees or applicants for employment in any manner, including promotion.

Beyond such general caveats, there are several specific things to keep in mind regarding the employment law aspects of promotional decisions. One concerns potential problems caused by claims of *retaliation*. Most federal and state employment laws contain anti-retaliation provisions. As long as the employee (or former employee) was acting in good faith when he or she filed the EEOC (or other protected) claim against the employer, the person may claim retaliation if he or she subsequently suffers an adverse employment action.[32] More than 27% of all EEOC charges filed recently were retaliation charges. In such charges, the employee basically claims that (1) the employee tried to blow the whistle on the company for doing something illegal, or filed an EEOC charges or workers' compensation claim, or safety complaint, or lawsuit against the company; (2) the employer then fired, demoted, failed to promote, or cut the pay of that employee; and (3) the HR action was caused by the employee's legally protected activity.

Because withholding promotions is one of the more drastic actions an employer can take with respect to current employees, the manager should establish safeguards to make sure that the promotion decision does not prompt such a claim of retaliation, as it often does. For example, the Fifth U.S. Circuit Court of Appeals allowed her claim of retaliation to proceed when a female employee provided evidence that she was turned down for promotion because a supervisor she had previously accused of sexual harassment made comments that persuaded her current supervisor not to promote her.[33] The evidence confirmed that in a meeting at which supervisors reviewed the person's performance, the former supervisor (and object of the sexual harassment accusation) made comments regarding the employee's "ability to work effectively with others."

One way for the employer to defend itself against such claims is to make sure that its promotion procedures are clear and objective. For example, the Eighth U.S. Circuit Court of Appeals recently held that a company's failure to set objective guidelines and procedures for promoting current employees may suggest employment discrimination.[34] (In this case, the court found that the organization, a community college, did not consistently use the same procedures for hiring and promotions at different times, did not clarify when and under what conditions vacant positions were announced, or whether or not there were application deadlines.) In another case, the employer turned down the 61-year-old applicant for a promotion because of his interview performance; the person who interviewed him said he did not "get a real feeling of confidence" from the candidate.[35] In this case, "the court made it clear that while subjective reasons can justify adverse employment decisions, an employer must articulate any clear and reasonably specific factual bases upon which it based its decision." In other words, you should be able to provide objective evidence supporting your subjective assessment for promotion.

Describe the methods for enhancing diversity through career management

● ENHANCING DIVERSITY THROUGH CAREER MANAGEMENT

Sources of Bias and Discrimination in Promotion Decisions

Women and people of color tend to experience relatively less career progress in organizations, and bias and more subtle barriers are often the cause. Yet this is not necessarily the result of decision makers' racist sentiments.[36] Instead, secondary factors—such as having few people of color employed in the hiring department—may be the cause. Sometimes, the bias may be unintentional and uninformed. In one study, the people of color applying for promotions actually had more work experience, and were therefore ironically seen as plateaued.[37] In any case, the bottom line seems to be that whether it's bias or some other reason, questionable hurdles like these do exist, and need to be found and eliminated.

Similarly, women still don't make it to the top of the career ladder in numbers proportionate to their numbers in U.S. industry. Women constitute 40% of the workforce, but hold less than 2% of top-management positions. Blatant or subtle discrimination, including the belief that "women belong at home and are not committed to careers," inhibits many managers from taking women as seriously as men. The "old-boy network" of informal friendships forged over lunch, at social events, or at club meetings is usually not open to women, although it's often here that promotional decisions are made. A lack of women mentors makes it harder for women to find the role models and supporters they need to help guide their careers. Unlike many men, women must also make the "career versus family" decision, since the responsibilities of raising the children and managing the household still fall disproportionately on women:

> *Balancing work and family life can be a challenge. For example, Brenda Barnes gave up her job as head of PepsiCo's North American beverage business in order to spend more time with her family. Linda Noonan, an auditor with Deloitte & Touche, left to join a smaller accounting firm after trying to balance a 70-hour workweek with her responsibilities as a new mother. Her situation also illustrates what employers can do to resolve such work–family conflicts. When Deloitte instituted a new flexible work schedule, Noonan went back to work there. She signed an agreement to work 80% of the hours normally expected of her position. She also arranged to work more hours from January to March (when the workload is heaviest), and to take more time off the rest of the year to spend with her two daughters.[38]*

Women and men also face different challenges as they advance through their careers. Women report greater barriers (such as being excluded from informal networks) than do men, and greater difficulty getting developmental assignments and geographic mobility opportunities. Women had to be more proactive to get such assignments. Because developmental experiences like these are so important, "organizations that are interested in helping female managers advance should focus on breaking down the barriers that interfere with women's access to developmental experiences."[39]

In these matters, minority women may be particularly at risk. By 2006, the number of African American, Asian American, and Hispanic women in the U.S. workforce will grow by 35%, 78%, and 25%, respectively. Yet women of color hold only a small percentage of professional and managerial private-sector positions. Minority and nonminority women differ somewhat in their views of what makes a successful career. The minority women in one survey said the main factors contributing to career advancement included access to high-visibility assignments (51%), performing above expectations (49%), communicating well (47%), and having influential mentors or sponsors (44%). In a separate study, white female executives chose consistently exceeding performance expectations (77%) as most important, followed by developing a style with which men are comfortable (61%), seeking difficult or high-visibility assignments (50%), and having an influential mentor (37%). The minority women reported that the main barriers to advancement included not having an influential mentor (47%), lack of informal networking with influential colleagues (40%), lack of company role models for members of the same racial or ethnic group (29%), and a lack of high-visibility assignments (28%).[40]

Adding to the problem is the fact that some corporate career development programs may actually be inconsistent with the needs of minority and nonminority women. For example, many programs assume that the workplace plays a central role in people's lives, but family needs may well play the major role in many women's (and men's) lives. Similarly, such programs may assume that career paths are orderly, sequential, and continuous; yet the need to stop working for a time to attend to family needs may well punctuate the career paths of many people of color and women (and perhaps men).[41] And, in any case, a study of male and female corporate expatriates concluded that three organizational career development activities—fast-track programs, individual career counseling, and career planning workshops—were less available to women than to men.[42] Many refer to this combination of subtle and not-so-subtle barriers to womens' career progress as the *glass ceiling*.

Taking Steps to Enhance Diversity: Women's and Minorities' Prospects

Employers can take steps to enhance women's and minorities' promotional and career prospects. Perhaps the most important thing is to focus on *taking the career interests of women and minority employees seriously*. In other words, accept that there are problems, and work on eliminating the barriers. Other advisable steps include the following.

Eliminate Institutional Barriers   Many practices (such as required late-night meetings) may seem gender neutral but in fact disproportionately affect women and minorities. Employers need to identify such practices and make their practices more accommodating.

Improve Networking and Mentoring   To improve female employees' networking opportunities, Marriott International instituted a series of leadership conferences for women. Speakers offered practical tips for career advancement, and shared their experiences. More important, the conferences provided numerous informal opportunities— over lunch, for instance—for the Marriott women to meet and forge business relationships. Accountants Deloitte & Touche instituted a formal mentoring program: "We want to involve most of our senior partners and say to them, 'we want you to spend 200 hours over the next year [mentoring] a manager—and we're going to be checking in with you to see how it's going.' "[43]

Eliminate the Glass Ceiling   Eliminating glass ceiling barriers requires more than an order from the CEO, because the problem is usually systemic. As one expert puts it, "the roots of gender discrimination are built into a platform of work practices, cultural norms and images that appear unbiased . . . People don't even notice them, let alone question them. But they create a subtle pattern of disadvantage that blocks all women." Complicating things is the fact that when they come up against these obstacles, women may attribute them not to structural ("glass ceiling") barriers, but to their own personal inadequacies. For example, numerous after-hours meetings may be the norm in a fast-driving company. For women with family responsibilities, not being able to attend could cripple their advancement prospects. Rescheduling late meetings will therefore (as noted above) make a difference for women with child-care responsibilities.

Institute Flexible Schedules and Career Tracks   Inflexible promotional ladders (such as "you must work eight years of 70-hour weeks to apply for partner) can put women—who often have more responsibility for child-raising chores—at a disadvantage. In many large accounting firms, for instance, "more men successfully logged the dozen or so years normally needed to apply for a position as partner. But fewer women stuck around, so fewer applied for or earned these prized positions."[44] One solution, as at Deloitte & Touche, is to institute career tracks (including reduced hours, and more flexible year-round work schedules) that enable women to periodically reduce their time at work, but still remain on a partnership track.

5   Answer the question: How can career development foster employee commitment?

● CAREER MANAGEMENT AND EMPLOYEE COMMITMENT

The globalization of the world economy has been a boon in many ways. For products and services ranging from cars to computers to air travel, it has powered lower prices, better quality, and higher productivity and living standards.

But these advances haven't come without a price. At least in the short run, the same cost-efficiencies, belt-tightening, and productivity improvements that globalization produced have also triggered numerous and ongoing workforce dislocations. The desire for

Breaking the glass ceiling: Jenny Ming, president of Gap Inc.'s Old Navy chain since April 1999, and a *BusinessWeek* top manager that year, is one of the few women in upper-level executive positions in major corporations.

efficiencies drove firms to downsize, and to "do more with less." It prompted thousands of mergers, large and small, many of which—as when NCNB bought BankAmerica—aimed specifically to "eliminate redundancies"; in other words, to close duplicate branches and back office operations. And with every buyout, merger, and downsizing, more employees found themselves out of work. Partly as a reaction to these changes, and to the bubble economy of the late 1990s, and to the recession of 2000–2003, the U.S. economy lost over three million jobs in the early 2000s, or about 2% of the country's jobs.

The New Psychological Contract

As mentioned earlier in this chapter, changes like these understandably prompt many employees to ask why they should be loyal to their employers. "Why," they might ask, "should I be loyal to you if you're just going to dump me when you decide to cut costs again?" To paraphrase the author of the book *Pack Your Own Parachute*, the smart employee today thus tends to think of him or herself as a free agent, there to do a good job but also to prepare for the next career move, to another firm. Yesterday's employee–employer "psychological contract" may have been something like, " do your best and be loyal to us, and we'll take care of your career." Today, it is "do your best for us and be loyal to us for as long as you're here, and we'll provide you with the developmental opportunities you'll need to move on and have a successful career." In such situations, employers must think through what they're going to do to maintain employee commitment, and thereby minimize voluntary departures, and maximize employee effort.

Commitment-Oriented Career Development Efforts

The employer's career planning and development process can and should play a central role in this process. As we've seen, it is through this process that the employer supports the employee's efforts to test and develop viable career goals, and to develop the skills and experiences that accomplishing those goals requires. Managed effectively, the employer's career development process should send the signal that the employee cares about the employee's career success, and thus deserves the employee's commitment. Career development programs and career-oriented appraisals can facilitate this.

Career Development Programs For example, we've seen that most large (and many smaller) employers provide career planning and development services. Consider the program at Saturn Corporation's Spring Hill, Tennessee, plant. A career workshop uses vocational guidance tools (including a computerized skills assessment program and other career gap analysis tools) to help employees identify career-related skills and the development needs they possess. This workshop, according to one employee, "helps you assess yourself, and takes four to six hours. You use it for developing your own career potential. The career disk identifies your weaknesses and strengths: you assess yourself, and then your team assesses you."[45] Tuition reimbursement and other development aids are also available to help employees develop the skills they need to get ahead.

Programs like these can help foster employee commitment. Here is how one Saturn employee put it:

> *I'm an assembler now, and was a team leader for two-and-a-half years. My goal is to move into our people-systems [HR] unit. I know things are tight now, but I know that the philosophy here is that the firm will look out for me—they want people to be all they can be. I know here I'll go as far as I can go; that's one reason I'm so committed to Saturn.[46]*

Career-Oriented Appraisals Similarly, as mentioned earlier, few situations at work provide a better opportunity for discussing career-related issues then does the annual or semi-annual appraisal. Performance appraisals should not only be about telling someone how he or she has done. They also provide the ideal occasion to link the employee's performance, career interests, and developmental needs into a coherent career plan. A form like the one in Figure 10-3 can facilitate this process, by helping the

HR Management Checklists

A. Employee's Major Strengths

    1. _____

    2. _____

    3. _____

B. Areas for Improvement/Development

    1. _____

    2. _____

    3. _____

C. Development Plans: Areas for Development

    1. _____

    2. _____

    3. _____

    4. _____

Development Strategy:

_____

_____

_____

D. Employee's Comments on This Review: _____

_____

_____

_____

E. Reviewer's Comments: _____

_____

_____

_____

Growth potential in present position and future growth potential for increased responsibilities: _____

_____

_____

Employer's Signature: _____ Date: _____

Reviewer's Signature: _____ Date: _____

Reviewer's Manager's Signature: _____ Date: _____

Figure 10-3
Sample Performance Review Development Plan

Source: Reprinted from www.HR.BLR.com with permission of the publisher, © 2004 *Business and Legal Reports, Inc.*, 141 Mill Rock Road East, Old Saybrook, CT.

The HR Scorecard
Strategy and Results

The New Career Management System

The Hotel Paris's competitive strategy is "To use superior guest service to differentiate the Hotel Paris properties, and to thereby increase the length of stay and return rate of guests, and thus boost revenues and profitability." HR manager Lisa Cruz must now formulate functional policies and activities that support this competitive strategy, by eliciting the required employee behaviors and competencies.

A preliminary analysis, performed jointly by Lisa and the Hotel Paris's chief financial officer, left them optimistic that HR could contribute measurably to achieving the hotel's strategic aims. Several employee competencies and behaviors including employee morale, employee commitment, and the percent of arriving guests receiving the hotel's required greeting had significant effects on customer and organizational outcomes such as guest satisfaction and frequency of guest returns. In turn, outcomes like these contributed measurably to the Hotel Paris's strategic goals, including profit margins, market share, and scores on industry satisfaction surveys. Lisa and her team now turn to creating a career management process that will help to produce the required employee competencies and behaviors. The accompanying HR Scorecard (Figure 10-4) outlines the relationships involved.

For Lisa Cruz and the CFO, their preliminary research left little doubt about the advisability of instituting a new career management system at the Hotel Paris. Based on their pilot project, employees in those Hotel Paris hotels who had been working under the new career management system were more committed, received more complementary letters from guests, and received higher performance appraisal ratings than did employees who did not have career plans. The CFO therefore gave the go-ahead to design and institute a new Hotel Paris career management program.

Lisa and her team knew that they already had most of the building blocks in place, thanks to the new performance management system they had instituted just a few weeks earlier (as noted in the previous chapter). For example, the new performance management system already required that the supervisor appraise the employee based on goals and competencies that were driven by the company's strategic needs; and the appraisal itself produced new goals for the coming year and specific development plans for the employee. Of course, these development plans had to make sense in terms of the company's and the employee's needs and preferences.

In addition to the new performance management system, Lisa and her team created an online "Hotel Paris Career Center." With links to a choice of career assessment tools such as the self-directed search, www.self-directed-search.com, and wizard-based templates for developing one's own career plan, the site went far toward providing the Hotel Paris's employees with the career assistance that they required. Also on the site, a new "International job openings" link made it easier for Hotel Paris employees to identify positions for which they might be qualified. The results exceeded Lisa and the CFO's expectations. Virtually every employee produced a career plan within the first six months. The appraisal interviews often turned into animated, career-oriented development sessions, and soon the various measures of employee commitment and guest service were trending up.

---

manager and employee to translate the latter's performance-based experiences for the year into tangible development plans and goals.

"The HR Scorecard" illustrates how the Hotel Paris put these career development ideas into practice.

● RETIREMENT

retirement
The point at which one gives up one's work, usually between the ages of 60 and 65.

Retirement for many employees is a mixed blessing. The employee may be free of the daily requirements of his or her job, but at the same time be slightly adrift because of not having a job. About 30% of the employers in one survey therefore reported having for-

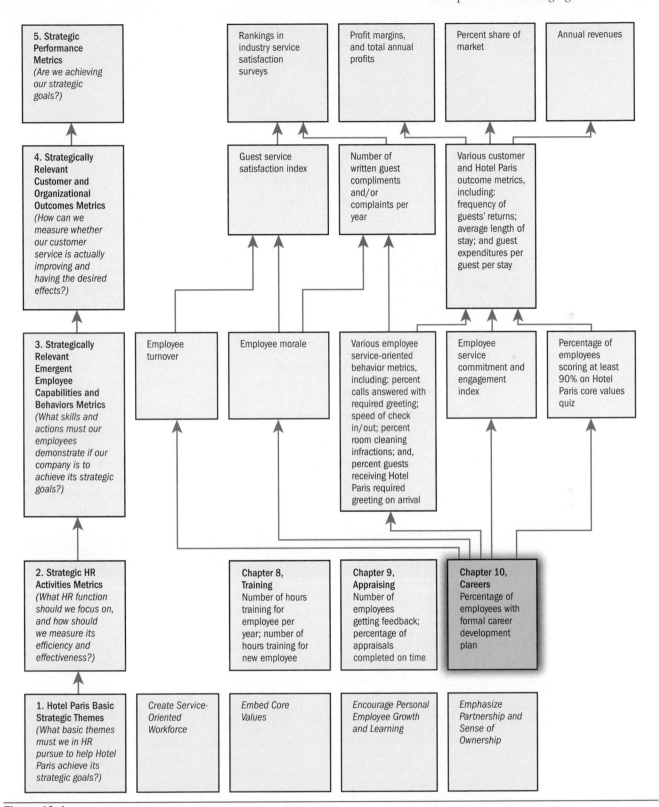

Figure 10-4
HR Scorecard for Hotel Paris International Corporation*

Note: *(An abbreviated example showing selected HR practices and outcomes aimed at implementing the competitive strategy, "To use superior guest services to differentiate the Hotel Paris properties and thus increase the length of stays and the return rate of guests, and thus boost revenues and profitability")

preretirement counseling
Counseling provided to employees who are about to retire, which covers matters such as benefits advice, second careers, and so on.

mal **preretirement counseling** aimed at easing the passage of their employees into retirement. The most common preretirement practices were:

Explanation of Social Security benefits (reported by 97% of those with preretirement education programs)

Leisure time counseling (86%)

Financial and investment counseling (84%)

Health counseling (82%)

Psychological counseling (35%)

Counseling for second careers outside the company (31%)

Counseling for second careers inside the company (4%)

There's no reason to wait until a person is ready to retire to provide retirement planning assistance. For example, American Express introduced an online asset allocation tool for use by its employer-clients' retirement plan participants. The Web-based tool, called Retirement Guidance Planner, lets an employer's retirement plan participants calculate and keep track of progress toward retirement income goals and more easily allocate assets among different investments online.[47] Many firms, including Vanguard, and Fidelity, offer similar online programs.

Another important trend is granting part-time employment to employees as an alternative to outright retirement. Several surveys of blue- and white-collar employees showed that about half of all employees over age 55 would like to continue working part-time after they retire.[48] And with many employers predicting an imminent employee shortage, such programs help employers, too.

Retirement procedures must comply with the law. For example, current and former agents of New York Life Insurance Company filed a suit alleging that the company defrauded about 10,000 agents of their retirement and health insurance benefits. Among other things, the suit claims that agents were systematically forced out as they got close to the 20 years of service that would qualify them for full retirement benefits. New York Life says most of the terminations were for other reasons, such as compliance problems or the agents' own decisions to move on.[49]

 *Review*

SUMMARY

1. We may define *career* as the occupational positions a person has had over many years. *Career planning* is the deliberate process through which someone becomes aware of personal skills, interests, knowledge, motivations, and other characteristics; acquires information about opportunities and choices; identifies career-related goals; and establishes action plans to attain specific goals.

2. Corporate career development programs used to focus on the employee's future with that particular firm. Today, the emphasis is more on self-analysis, development, and career management to enable the individual to develop the career plans and skills he or she will need to move on to the next step in his or her career, quite probably with another employer.

3. Employers play an important role in the career management process. Among other things, the employer may provide on-

site or online career centers, implement formal mentoring programs, and provide career coaches and/or mentors.

4. Studies suggest that having a mentor can be an important element in furthering an employee's career. Guidelines here include: Choose an appropriate potential mentor, don't be surprised if you're turned down, have an agenda, and respect the mentors time.

5. In making promotion decisions, the employer must decide between seniority and competence, a formal or informal system, and ways to measure competence.

6. Enhancing diversity through career management requires some special preparations on the part of the employer. Guarding against intentional or unintentional bias and discrimination in promotion decisions is one issue. For example, blatant or subtle discrimination often explains the rela-

tively low success rate in women moving to the top rungs of organizational career ladders.

7. Career management-related steps to enhance diversity include: Eliminate institutional barriers, improve networking and mentoring, eliminate the glass ceiling barriers, and institute flexible schedules.

8. The employer's career planning and development process can and should play a central role in helping employees crystallize their career goals and thereby increase their commitment to the employer. Career development programs and career-oriented appraisals are two important components in this process.

DISCUSSION QUESTIONS

1. What is the employee's role in the career development process? The manager's role? The employer's role?

2. Describe the specific corporate career development initiatives that an employer can take.

3. What are four specific steps employees can take to support diverse employees' career progress?

4. Give several examples of career development activities that employers can use to foster employee commitment.

INDIVIDUAL AND GROUP ACTIVITIES

1. Write a one-page essay stating, "where I would like to be career-wise 10 years from today."

2. Explain the career-related factors to keep in mind when making the employee's first assignments.

3. In groups of four or five students, meet with several administrators and faculty members in your college or university, and, based on this, write a two-page paper on the topic, "The faculty promotion process at our college." What do you think of the process? Could you make any suggestions for improving it?

4. In groups of four or five students, at your place of work or at your college, interview the HR manager with the aim of writing a two-page paper addressing the topic, "Steps we are taking in this organization to enhance diversity through career management."

5. Develop a résumé for yourself, using the guidelines presented in this chapter's appendix.

6. Working individually or in groups, choose three occupations (such as management consultant, HR manager, or salesperson) and use some of the sources described in the appendix to this chapter to make an assessment of the future demand for this occupation in the next 10 years or so. Does this seem like a good occupation to pursue? Why or why not?

7. The HRCI "Test Specifications" appendix at the end of this book (pages 685–689) lists the knowledge someone studying for the HRCI certification exam needs to have in each area of human resource management (such as in Strategic Management, Workforce Planning, and Human

Resource Development). In groups of four to five students, do four things: (1) review that appendix now; (2) identify the material in this chapter that relates to the required knowledge the appendix lists; (3) write four multiple choice exam questions on this material that you believe would be suitable for inclusion in the HRCI exam; and (4) if time permits, have someone from your team post your team's questions in front of the class, so the students in other teams can take each others' exam questions.

8. A 2003 survey of recent college graduates in the United Kingdom found that although many hadn't found their first jobs, most were already planning "career breaks" and to keep up their hobbies and interests outside work. As one report of the findings put it, "the next generation of workers is determined not to wind up on the hamster wheel of long hours with no play."[50] Part of the problem seems to be that many already see their friends "putting in more than 48 hours a week" at work. Career experts reviewing the results concluded that many of these recent college grads "are not looking for high pay, high-profile jobs anymore."[51] Instead, they seem to be looking to "compartmentalize" their lives; to keep the number of hours they spend at work down, so they can maintain their hobbies and outside interests. So, do you think these findings are as popular in the United States as they appear to be in the United Kingdom? If so, if you were mentoring one of these people at work, what three specific bits of career advice would you give him or her?

EXPERIENTIAL EXERCISE

Where am I going . . . and why?

Purpose: The purpose of this exercise is to provide you with experience in analyzing your career preferences.

Required Understanding: Students should be thoroughly familiar with the "managing your career" appendix to this chapter.

How to Set Up the Exercise/Instructions: Using at least three of the methods described in this chapter's appendix (identify your occupational orientation, identify your career directions, and so forth), analyze your career-related inclinations (you can take the self-directed search for about eight dollars at www.self-directed-search.com). Based on this analysis, answer the following questions (you may, if you wish, do this analysis in teams of three or four students)

1. What does your research suggest to you about what would be your preferable occupational options?
2. Based on research sources like those we listed in the appendix to this chapter, what are the prospects for these occupations?

3. Given these prospects and your own occupational inclinations, outline a brief, one-page career plan for yourself including current occupational inclinations, career goals, and an action plan listing four or five development steps you will need to take in order to get from where you are now career-wise to where you want to be, based on your career goals.

APPLICATION CASE

The Mentor Relationship Turns Upside Down

"I wish I could talk this problem over with Walter," Carol Lee thought. Walter Lemaire had been her mentor for several years at Larchmont Consulting, yet now he was her problem.

Carol thought back to the beginning of her association with Larchmont and with Walter. She had joined the firm as a writer and editor; her job during those early years had been to revise and polish the consultants' business reports. The work brought her into frequent contact with Walter, who was a senior vice president at the time. Carol enjoyed discussing the consultants' work with him, and when she decided to try to join the consulting team, she asked for his help. Walter became her mentor as well as her boss and guided her through her successful transition to consultant and eventually partner.

At each promotion to various supervisory jobs along the way to partner, Carol cemented her relationship with her new subordinates by acknowledging the inevitable initial awkwardness and by meeting with each person individually to forge a new working relationship. Her career prospered, and when Walter moved on to run a start-up software publishing venture for Larchmont, Carol was promoted to take his place. However, his new venture faltered, and the partners decided someone else would have to step in. Despite the fact that Carol was much younger than Walter and once had worked for him, she was given the assignment of rescuing the start-up operation.

Carol's discomfort over the assignment only grew as she began to review the history of the new venture. Her rescue mission was going to entail undoing much of what Walter had done, reversing his decisions about everything from product design to marketing and pricing. Carol was so reluctant to second-guess her old mentor and boss that she found herself all but unable to discuss any of her proposed solutions with him directly. She doubted that any of her past experience had prepared her to assume the role of Walter's boss, and in these difficult circumstances her need to turn the operation around would be, she felt, like "pouring salt on his wounds."

Questions

1. What is Carol's role in Walter's career development now? Should Larchmont have any such role? Why or why not?
2. What advice would you offer Carol for approaching Walter?
3. If Carol has to dismiss Walter, how specifically would you suggest she proceed?
4. Assume Carol has heard a rumor that Walter has considered resigning. What should she do about it?

Note: The incident in this case is based on an event at an unidentified firm described in Jennifer Frey, "Pride and Your Promotion," *Working Woman*, October 1996.

CONTINUING CASE

Carter Cleaning Company

The Career Planning Program

Career planning has always been a pretty low-priority item for Carter Cleaning, since "just getting workers to come to work and then keeping them honest is enough of a problem," as Jack likes to say. Yet Jennifer thought it might not be a bad idea to give some thought to what a career planning program might involve for Carter. A lot of their employees had been with them for years in dead-end jobs, and she frankly felt a little badly for them: "Perhaps we could help them gain a better perspective on what they want to do," she thought. And she definitely believed that the store management group needed better career direction if Carter Cleaning was to develop and grow.

Questions

1. What would be the advantages to Carter Cleaning of setting up such a career planning program?
2. Who should participate in the program? All employees? Selected employees?
3. Outline and describe the career development program you would propose for the cleaners, pressers, and counterpeople and managers at the Carter Cleaning Centers.

KEY TERMS

career, 350

career management, 350

career development, 350

career planning, 350

career planning and
   development, 351

reality shock, 355

job rotation, 355

mentoring, 355

promotions, 358

transfers, 358

retirement, 366

preretirement counseling, 368

career cycle, 372

growth stage, 372

exploration stage, 372

establishment stage, 372

trial substage, 372

stabilization substage, 373

midcareer crisis substage, 373

maintenance stage, 373

decline stage, 373

career anchors, 375

ENDNOTES

1. Sherry Sullivan, William Carden, and David Martin, "Careers in the Next Millennium: Directions for Future Research," *Human Resource Management Review* 8, no. 2 (1998), p. 165.

2. Douglas Hall, "Protean Careers of the 21st Century," *Academy of Management Executive* 10, no. 4 (1996), p. 8.

3. Kenneth Brousseau, Michael Driver, Kristina Eneroth, and Rikerd Larsson, "Career Pandemonium: Realigning Organizations and Individuals," *Academy of Management Executive* 10, no. 4 (1996), pp. 52–66; Brent Allred, Charles Snow, and Raymond Miles, "Characteristics of Managerial Careers in the 21st Century," *Academy of Management Executive* 10, no. 4 (1996), pp. 17–27.

4. Sullivan, Carden, and Martin, "Careers in the Next Millennium," p. 165; see also Richard Koonce, "Plan on a Career That Bobs and Weaves," *Training and Development Journal* 52, no. 4 (April 1998), pp. 14–16.

5. Carla Joinson, "Career Management and Commitment," *HR Magazine*, May 2001, pp. 60–64.

6. Jim Bright, "Career Development: Empowering Your Staff to Excellence," *Journal of Banking and Financial Services* 17, no. 3 (July 2003), p. 12.

7. Jan Selmer, "Usage of Corporate Career Development Activities by Expatriate Managers and the Extent of Their International Adjustment," *International Journal of Commerce and Management* 10, no. 1 (Spring 2000), p. 1.

8. Barbara Greene and Liana Knudsen, "Competitive Employers Make Career Development Programs a Priority," *San Antonio Business Journal* 15, no. 26 (July 20, 2001), p. 27.

9. Bright, "Career Development: Empowering Your Staff to Excellence," p. 12.

10. Carla Joinson, "Employee, Sculpt Thyself with a Little Help," *HR Magazine*, May 2001, pp. 61–64.

11. Deb Koen, "Revitalize Your Career," *Training and Development*, January 2003, pp. 59–60.

12. Michael Doody, "A Mentor Is a Key to Career Success," *Health-Care Financial Management* 57, no. 2 (February 2003), pp. 92–94.

13. "Preparing Future Leaders in Health-Care," Leaders, c/o Witt/Kieffer, 2015 Spring Road, Suite 510, Oak Brook, IL 60523.

14. Bill Hayes, "Helping Workers with Career Goals Boosts Retention Efforts," *Boston Business Journal* 21, no. 11 (April 20, 2001), p. 38.

15. Yehuda Baruch and Maury Pieperl, "Career Management Practices: An Empirical Survey and Implications," *Human Resource Management* 39, no. 4 (Winter 2000), pp. 347–366.

16. "Career Guidance Steers Workers Away from Early Exits," *BNA Bulletin to Management*, September 7, 2000, p. 287.

17. Belle Rose Ragins, "Diversified Mentoring Relationships in Organizations: A Power Perspective," *Academy of Management Review* 22, no. 2 (1997), p. 513.

18. Greene and Knudsen, "Competitive Employers Make Career Development Programs a Priority," p. 27.

19. Jim Warner and Jackie Keagy, "Creating a Virtual Career Development Center," *HR Focus* 74, no. 10 (October 1997), pp. 11–13.

20. Julekha Dash, "Coaching to Aid IT Careers, Retention," *Computerworld*, March 20, 2000, p. 52.

21. P. Sandlin, "Coaching Takes to the Couch: CEO's Increasing Use of Coaches," *Chief Executive*, December 2002, pp. 42–46.

22. David Foote, "Wanna Keep Your Staff Happy? Think Career," *Computerworld*, October 9, 2000, p. 38.

23. Fred Otte and Peggy Hutcheson, *Helping Employees Manage Careers* (Upper Saddle River, NJ: Prentice Hall, 1992), p. 143.

24. Jim Meade, "Boost Careers and Succession Planning," *HR Magazine*, October 2000, pp. 175–178.

25. Patrick Kiger, "First USA Bank, Promotions and Job Satisfaction," *Workforce*, March 2001, pp. 54–56.

26. Tim Harvey, "Enterprise Training System Is Trans Alaska Pipeline's Latest Safety Innovation," *Pipeline and Gas Journal* 229, no. 12 (December 2002), pp. 28–32.

27. Ibid.

28. "Kenexa Announces a Latest Version of Kenexa Career Tracker," *Internet Wire*, March 22, 2004, p. NA.

29. See, for example, Daniel Quinn Mills, *Labor–Management Relations* (New York: McGraw-Hill, 1986), pp. 387–396.

30. George Thornton III and David Morris, "The Application of Assessment Center Technology to the Evaluation of Personnel Records," *Public Personnel Management* 30, no. 1 (Spring 2001), p. 55.

31. See, for example, Richard Chanick, "Career Growth for Baby Boomers," *Personnel Journal* 71, no. 1 (January 1992), pp. 40–46.

32. Robin Shay, "Don't Get Caught in the Legal Wringer When Dealing with Difficult to Manage Employees," www.SHRM.org.

33. *Gee v. Pincipi*, 5th Cir., number 01-50159, April 18, 2002, "Alleged Harasser's Comments Tainted Promotion Decision," www.SHRM.org, downloaded March 2, 2004.

34. Maria Danaher, "Unclean Promotion Procedures Smack of Discrimination," www.shrm.org, downloaded March 2, 2004.

35. Elaine Herskowitz, "The Perils of Subjective Hiring and Promotion Criteria," www.shrm.org.

36. See, for example, Gary Powell and D. Anthony Butterfield, "Effect of Race on Promotions to Top Management in a Federal Department," *Academy of Management Journal* 40, no. 1 (1997), pp. 112–128.

37. Ibid., p. 124.

38. In Susan Wells, "Smoothing the Way," *HR Magazine*, June 2001, pp. 52–58.

39. Karen Lyness and Donna Thompson, "Climbing the Corporate Ladder: Do Female and Male Executives Follow the Same Route?" *Journal of Applied Psychology* 85, no. 1 (2000), pp. 86–101.

40. "Minority Women Surveyed on Career Growth Factors," *Community Banker*, 9, no. 3 (March 2000), p. 44.

41. In Ellen Cook et al., "Career Development of Women of Color and White Women: Assumptions, Conceptualization, and Interventions from an Ecological Perspective," *Career Development Quarterly* 50, no. 4 (June 2002), pp. 291–306.

42. Jan Selmer and Alicia Leung, "Are Corporate Career Development Activities Less Available to Female than to Male Expatriates?" *Journal of Business Ethics*, March 2003, pp. 125–137.

43. Wells, "Smoothing the Way," p. 55.

44. Kathleen Melymuka, "Glass Ceilings & Clear Solutions," *Computerworld*, May 29, 2000, p. 56.

45. Personal interview, March 1992.

46. Personal interview, March 1992.

47. "American Express Adds Tools to Retirement Section," *Financial Net News* 6, no. 17 (April 30, 2001), p. 3.

48. "Preretirement Education Programs," *Personnel* 59 (May–June 1982), p. 47. For a discussion of why it is important for retiring employees to promote aspects of their lives aside from their careers, see Daniel Halloran, "The Retirement Identity Crisis—and How to Beat It," *Personnel Journal* 64 (May 1984), pp. 38–40. See also, "Pay Policies," *BNA Bulletin to Management*, March 29, 1990, no. 10 (March 5, 2001), pp. 49–50.

49. "Agents Sue New York Life Over Retirement Benefits," *National Underwriter Life and Health Financial Services Edition* 105, no. 10 (March 5, 2001), pp. 49–50.

50. "New Trend in Career Hunt," *Europe Intelligence Wire*, February 10, 2004, p. NA.

51. Ibid.

APPENDIX FOR CHAPTER 10

Managing Your Career

Managing your career has never been as important as it is today.[1] The individual must be responsible for creating and managing his or her own career. And, in today's job marketplace, employee ability replaces job security.[2]

The first step in planning a career for yourself or someone else is to learn as much as possible about your interests, aptitudes, and skills.

MAKING CAREER CHOICES

Identify Your Career Stage

Each person's career goes through stages, and the stage you are in will influence your knowledge of and preference for various occupations. The main stages of this **career cycle** follows.

Growth Stage   The **growth stage** lasts roughly from birth to age 14 and is a period during which the person develops a self-concept by identifying with and interacting with other people such as family, friends, and teachers. Toward the beginning of this period, role playing is important, and children experiment with different ways of acting; this helps them to form impressions of how other people react to different behaviors and contributes to their developing a unique self-concept or identity. Toward the end of this stage, the adolescent (who by this time has developed preliminary ideas about what his or her interests and abilities are) begins to think realistically about alternative occupations.

Exploration Stage   The **exploration stage** is the period (roughly from ages 15 to 24) during which a person seriously explores various occupational alternatives.

The person attempts to match these alternatives with what he or she has learned about them and about his or her own interests and abilities from school, leisure activities, and work. Tentative broad occupational choices are usually made during the beginning of this period. Then toward the end of this period, a seemingly appropriate choice is made and the person tries out for a beginning job.

Probably the most important task the person has in this and the preceding stage is that of developing a realistic understanding of his or her abilities and talents. Similarly, the person must make sound educational decisions based on reliable sources of information about occupational alternatives.

Establishment Stage   The **establishment stage** spans roughly ages 24 to 44 and is the heart of most people's work lives. During this period, it is hoped a suitable occupation is found and the person engages in those activities that help him or her earn a permanent place in it. Often, and particularly in the professions, the person locks onto a chosen occupation early. But in most cases, this is a period during which the person is continually testing his or her capabilities and ambitions against those of the initial occupational choice.

The establishment stage is itself comprised of three substages. The **trial substage** lasts from about ages 25 to 30. During this period, the person determines whether or not the chosen field is suitable; if it is not, several changes might be attempted. (Jane Smith might have her heart set on a career in retailing, for example, but after several months of constant travel as a newly hired assistant buyer for a department store, she might decide that a less travel-oriented career such as one in market research is more in tune with her needs.) Roughly between the ages of 30 and 40, the person goes through a **stabilization substage**. Here firm occupational goals are set and the person does more explicit career planning to determine the sequence of promotions, job changes, and/or any educational activities that seem necessary for accomplishing these goals.

Finally, somewhere between the mid-thirties and mid-forties, the person may enter the **midcareer crisis substage**. During this period, people often make a major reassessment of their progress relative to original ambitions and goals. They may find that they are not going to realize their dreams (such as being company president) or that having been accomplished, their dreams are not all they were purported to be. Also during this period, people have to decide how important work and career are to be in their lives. It is often during this midcareer substage that some people face, for the first time, the difficult choices between what they really want, what really can be accomplished, and how much must be sacrificed to achieve it.

Maintenance Stage   Between the ages of 45 and 65, many people simply slide from the stabilization substage into the **maintenance stage**. During this latter period, the person has typically created a place in the world of work and most efforts are now directed at maintaining that place.

Decline Stage   As retirement age approaches, there is often a deceleration period in the **decline stage**. Here many people face the prospect of having to accept reduced levels of power and responsibility and learn to accept and develop new roles as mentor and confidante for those who are younger. There is then the more or less inevitable retirement, after which the person hopefully finds alternative uses for the time and effort formerly expended on his or her occupation.

Identify Your Occupational Orientation

Career-counseling expert John Holland says that personality (including values, motives, and needs) is one career choice determinant. For example, a person with a strong social orientation might be attracted to careers that entail interpersonal rather than intellectual or physical activities and to occupations such as social work. Based on research with his Vocational Preference Test (VPT), Holland found six basic personality types or orientations (see www.self-directed-search.com).[3]

1. *Realistic orientation.* These people are attracted to occupations that involve physical activities requiring skill, strength, and coordination. Examples include forestry, farming, and agriculture.

2. *Investigative orientation.* Investigative people are attracted to careers that involve cognitive activities (thinking, organizing, understanding) rather than affective activities (feeling, acting, or interpersonal and emotional tasks). Examples include biologist, chemist, and college professor.

3. *Social orientation.* These people are attracted to careers that involve interpersonal rather than intellectual or physical activities. Examples include clinical psychology, foreign service, and social work.

4. *Conventional orientation.* A conventional orientation favors careers that involve structured, rule-regulated activities, as well as careers in which it is expected that the employee subordinate his or her personal needs to those of the organization. Examples include accountants and bankers.

5. *Enterprising orientation.* Verbal activities aimed at influencing others characterize enterprising personalities. Examples include managers, lawyers, and public relations executives.

6. *Artistic orientation.* People here are attracted to careers that involve self-expression, artistic creation, expression of emotions, and individualistic activities. Examples include artists, advertising executives, and musicians.

Most people have more than one occupational orientation (they might be social, realistic, and investigative, for example), and Holland believes that the more similar or compatible these orientations are, the less internal conflict or indecision a person will face in making a career choice. To help illustrate this, Holland suggests placing each orientation in one corner of a hexagon, as in Figure 10A-1. As you can see, the model has six corners, each of which represents one personal orientation (for example, enterprising). According to Holland's research, the closer two orientations are in this figure, the more compatible they are. If your number-one and number-two orientations fall side by side, you will have an easier time choosing a career. However, if your orientations turn out to be opposite (such as realistic and social), you may experience more indecision in making a career choice because your interests are driving you toward very different types of careers. In Table 10A-1, we have summarized some of the occupations found to be the best match for each of these six orientations. You can, for about $8.00 take Holland's SDS online (see www.self-directed-search.com).

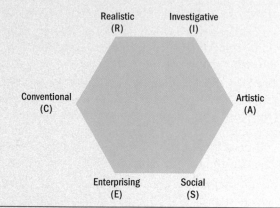

Figure 10-A1
Choosing an Occupational Orientation

The SDS has an excellent reputation, but the career seeker needs to be somewhat wary of some of the other online career assessment sites. One study of 24 no-cost online career assessment Web sites concluded that they were easy to use, but suffered from a lack of validation, limited confidentiality controls, and limited information on test interpretation. However, a number of online career assessment instruments such as the career key (www.careerkey.org/english) do reportedly provide validated and useful information.[4]

Identify Your Career Directions

MBA students at the Harvard Business School sometimes take a quiz to help them identify career directions and make career choices in which they'll be happy.[5] To take a short-form version of this quiz, you'll need three types of information. First (see Figure 10A-2), this approach assumes that all executive work is based on one or more of eight core activities such as "quantitative analysis" and "managing people." Begin by reading each of those activities.

Next (see Figure 10A-3), quickly go through each of the second figure's pairs of statements and indicate which one is more interesting to you. Then add the letters for your total score on each core function and record that score in the second figure.

Then, use Figure 10A-4 to see what kind of successful businesspeople share your career direction's interests. For example, if you scored high in Figure 10A-3 on "Enterprise Control" and "Managing People," then CEOs, Presidents, Division Managers, and General Managers are the sorts of people whose career interests are most similar to yours.

Identify Your Skills

Successful performance also depends on ability. You may have a conventional orientation, but whether you have *the skills* to be an accountant, banker, or credit manager will largely determine which occupation you ultimately choose. Therefore, you have to identify your skills.

An Exercise   One useful exercise for identifying occupational skills is to take a blank piece of paper and head it "The School or Occupational Tasks I Was Best At." Then write a short essay that describes the tasks. Make sure to go into as much detail as you can about your duties and responsibilities and what it was about each task that you found enjoyable. (In writing your essay, by the way, notice that it's not necessarily the most enjoyable *job* you've had, but the most enjoyable *task* you've had to perform; you may have had jobs that you really didn't like except for one of the specific duties or tasks in the job, which you really enjoyed.) Next, on other sheets of paper, do the same thing for two other tasks you have had. Now go through your three essays and underline the skills that you mentioned the most often. For example, did you enjoy putting together and coordinating the school play when you worked in the principal's office one year? Did you especially enjoy the hours you spent in

Table 10-A1 Example of Some Occupations that May Typify Each Occupational Theme

Realistic	Investigative	Artistic	Social	Enterprising	Conventional
				A Wide Range of Managerial Occupations, including:	
Engineers	Physicians	Advertising Executives	Auto Sales Dealers	Military Officers	Accountants
Carpenters	Psychologists	Public Relations Executives	School Administrators	Chamber of Commerce Executives	Bankers
	Research and Development Managers			Investment Managers	Credit Managers
				Lawyers	

Figure 10-A2
Finding the Job You Should Want (Part 1)
Source: James Waldroop and Timothy Butler, "Finding the Job You *Should* Want," *Fortune,* March 2, 1998, p. 211.

the library doing research for your boss when you worked one summer as an office clerk?[6]

Aptitudes and Special Talents
For career planning purposes, a person's aptitudes are usually measured with a test battery such as the general aptitude test battery (GATB), which most state one stop career centers make available. This instrument measures various aptitudes including intelligence and mathematical ability. You can also use specialized tests, such as for mechanical comprehension. However, even Holland's Self Directed Search will provide some insights into your aptitudes.[7]

Identify Your Career Anchors

Edgar Schein says that career planning is a continuing process of discovery—one in which a person slowly develops a clearer occupational self-concept in terms of what his or her talents, abilities, motives, needs, attitudes, and values are. Schein also says that as you learn more about yourself, it becomes apparent that you have a dominant **career anchor**, *a concern or value that you will not give up if a [career] choice has to be made.*

Career anchors, as their name implies, are the pivots around which a person's career swings; a person becomes conscious of them as a result of learning, through experience, about his or her talents and abilities, motives and needs, and attitudes and values. Based on his research at the Massachusetts Institute of Technology, Schein believes that career anchors are difficult to predict because they are evolutionary and a product of a process of discovery. Some people may never find out what their career anchors are until they have to make a major choice—such as whether to take the promotion to the headquarters staff or strike out on their own by starting a business. It is at this point that all the person's past work experiences, interests, aptitudes, and orientations converge into a meaningful pattern that helps show what (career anchor) is the most important factor in driving the person's career choices.

Based on his study of MIT graduates, Schein identified five career anchors.[8]

Technical/Functional Competence
People who had a strong technical/functional career anchor tended to avoid decisions that would drive them toward general management. Instead, they made decisions that would enable them to remain and grow in their chosen technical or functional fields.

Part 2: *Reread the brief description of the eight sets of activities on the previous page, then quickly go through each of the following pairs and indicate which one is more interesting to you by placing the bold letter for that choice in the box to the left. Don't leave any out and don't record any ties. Mark your first intuitive response.*

1. Creative **P**roduction or **I**nfluence Through Language and Ideas
2. **M**anaging People or Creative **P**roductions
3. **E**nterprise Control or **A**pplication of Technology
4. **T**heory Development or Creative **P**roduction
5. **M**anaging People or **C**ounseling and Mentoring
6. **Q**uantitative Analysis or **T**heory Development
7. **I**nfluence Through Language and Ideas or **E**nterprise Control
8. **Q**uantitative Analysis or **E**nterprise Control
9. **A**pplication of Technology or **I**nfluence Through Language and Ideas
10. **I**nfluence Through Language and Ideas or **Q**uantitative Analysis
11. **T**heory Development or **C**ounseling and Mentoring
12. **A**pplication of Technology or Creative **P**roduction
13. **A**pplication of Technology or **M**anaging People
14. **T**heory Development or **I**nfluence Through Language and Ideas
15. Creative **P**roduction or **C**ounseling and Mentoring
16. **C**ounseling and Mentoring or **Q**uantitative Analysis
17. **T**heory Development or **E**nterprise Control
18. **E**nterprise Control or Creative **P**roduction

19. **M**anaging People or **T**heory Development
20. **A**pplication of Technology or **T**heory Development
21. **E**nterprise Control or **C**ounseling and Mentoring
22. Creative **P**roduction or **Q**uantitative Analysis
23. **C**ounseling and Mentoring or **I**nfluence Through Language and Ideas
24. **Q**uantitative Analysis or **M**anaging People
25. **E**nterprise Control or **M**anaging People
26. **A**pplication of Technology or **C**ounseling and Mentoring
27. **M**anaging People or **I**nfluence Through Language and Ideas
28. **A**pplication of Technology or **Q**uantitative Analysis

Add the bold letters for your total score on each core function and record that score below:

- **Application of Technology**
- **Counseling and Mentoring**
- **Quantitative Analysis**
- **Managing People**
- **Theory Development and Conceptual Thinking**
- **Enterprise Control**
- **Creative Production**
- **Influence Through Language and Ideas**

Based on the scores above, identify your most significant interests. Most people will find one to three clear leaders. What does it all mean? Turn the page to find out.

Figure 10-A3
Finding the Job You Should Want (Part 2)
Source: James Waldroop and Timothy Butler, "Finding the Job You *Should* Want," *Fortune*, March 2, 1998, p. 212.

Part 3: *Now that you know which combinations you prefer, see what kind of successful business people share your interests.*

ENTERPRISE CONTROL and MANAGING PEOPLE: CEOs, presidents, division managers, and general managers who enjoy both strategy and the operations aspects of the position—the CEO who enjoys playing the COO role as well.

ENTERPRISE CONTROL and QUANTITATIVE ANALYSIS: Investment bankers, other financial professionals, who enjoy deal making, partners in Big Six firms, top-level executives in commercial and investment banks, investment managers.

APPLICATION OF TECHNOLOGY and QUANTITATIVE ANALYSIS: Individual contributors who have a strong interest in engineering analysis (systems analysis, tech consultants, process consultants); production and operations managers.

CREATIVE PRODUCTION and INFLUENCE THROUGH LANGUAGE AND IDEAS: Advertising executives, brand managers, corporate trainers, salespeople, public relations specialists; people in the fashion, entertainment, and media industries.

COUNSELING AND MENTORING and MANAGING PEOPLE: Human resources managers, managers who enjoy coaching and developing the people reporting to them, managers in nonprofit organizations with an altruistic mission.

ENTERPRISE CONTROL and INFLUENCE THROUGH LANGUAGE AND IDEAS: Executives (CEOs, presidents, general managers) whose leadership style relies on persuasion and consensus building; marketing managers, salespeople.

APPLICATION OF TECHNOLOGY and ENTERPRISE CONTROL: Managers and senior executives in high technology, telecommunications, biotech, information systems (internally or consulting), and other engineering-related fields.

THEORY DEVELOPMENT and QUANTITATIVE ANALYSIS: Economic-model builders quantitative analysis, "knowledge base" consultants, market forecasters, business professors.

CREATIVE PRODUCTION and ENTERPRISE CONTROL: Solo entrepreneurs, senior executives in industries where the product or service is of a creative nature (fashion, entertainment, advertising, media).

CREATIVE PRODUCTION: Entrepreneurs who partner with a professional manager, short-term project managers, new-product developers, advertising "creatives"; individual contributors in fashion, entertainment, and media.

Figure 10-A4
Finding the Job You Should Want (Part 3)
Source: James Waldroop and Timothy Butler, "Finding the Job You *Should* Want," *Fortune*, March 2, 1998, p. 214.

Managerial Competence   Other people show a strong motivation to become managers and their career experience enabled them to believe they had the skills and values required. A management position of high responsibility is their ultimate goal. When pressed to explain why they believed they had the skills necessary to gain such positions, many in Schein's research sample answered that they were qualified for these jobs because of what they saw as their competencies in a combination of three areas: (1) analytical competence (ability to identify, analyze, and solve problems under conditions of incomplete information and uncertainty); (2) interpersonal competence (ability to influence, supervise, lead, manipulate, and control people at all levels); and (3) emotional competence (the capacity to be stimulated by emotional and interpersonal crises rather than exhausted or debilitated by them, and the capacity to bear high levels of responsibility without becoming paralyzed).

Creativity   Some of the graduates had gone on to become successful entrepreneurs. To Schein these people seemed to have a need "to build or create something that was entirely their own product—a product or process that bears their name, a company of their own, or a personal fortune that reflects their accomplishments." For example, one graduate had become a successful purchaser, restorer, and renter of townhouses in a large city; another had built a successful consulting firm.

Autonomy and Independence Some seemed driven by the need to be on their own, free of the dependence that can arise when a person elects to work in a large organization where promotions, transfers, and salary decisions make them subordinate to others. Many of these graduates also had a strong technical/functional orientation. Instead of pursuing this orientation in an organization, they had decided to become consultants, working either alone or as part of a relatively small firm. Others had become professors of business, freelance writers, and proprietors of a small retail business.

Security A few of the graduates were mostly concerned with long-run career stability and job security. They seemed willing to do what was required to maintain job security, a decent income, and a stable future in the form of a good retirement program and benefits. For those interested in *geographic security*, maintaining a stable, secure career in familiar surroundings was generally more important than pursuing superior career choices, if choosing the latter meant injecting instability or insecurity into their lives by forcing them to pull up roots and move to another city. For others, security meant *organizational security*. They might today opt for government jobs, where tenure still tends to be a way of life. They were much more willing to let their employers decide what their careers should be.

Assessing Career Anchors To help you identify career anchors, take a few sheets of blank paper and write out your answers to the following questions:[9]

1. What was your major area of concentration (if any) in high school? Why did you choose that area? How did you feel about it?

2. What is (or was) your major area of concentration in college? Why did you choose that area? How did you feel about it?

3. What was your first job after school? (Include military if relevant.) What were you looking for in your first job?

4. What were your ambitions or long-range goals when you started your career? Have they changed? When? Why?

5. What was your first major change of job or company? What were you looking for in your next job?

6. What was your next major change of job, company, or career? Why did you initiate or accept it? What were you looking for? (Do this for each of your major changes of job, company, or career.)

7. As you look back over your career, identify some times you have especially enjoyed. What was it about those times that you enjoyed?

8. As you look back, identify some times you have not especially enjoyed. What was it about those times you did not enjoy?

9. Have you ever refused a job move or promotion? Why?

10. Now review all your answers carefully, as well as the descriptions for the five career anchors (managerial competence, technical/functional, security, creativity, autonomy). Based on your answers to the questions, rate, for yourself, each of the anchors from 1 to 5; 1 equals low importance, 5 equals high importance.

Managerial competence _____

Technical/functional competence _____

Security _____

Creativity _____

Autonomy _____

What Do You Want to Do?

We have explained occupational orientations, skills, and career anchors and the role these play in choosing a career. But there is at least one more exercise that can prove enlightening. On a sheet of paper, answer the question: "If you could have any kind of job, what would it be?" Invent your own job if need be, and don't worry about what you can do—just what you want to do.[10]

Identify High-Potential Occupations

Learning about yourself is only half the job of choosing an occupation. You also have to identify those occupations that are right (given your occupational orientations, skills, career anchors, and occupational preferences) as well as those that will be in high demand in the years to come.

Not surprisingly, the most efficient way to learn about and compare and contrast occupations is through the Internet. The U.S. Department of Labor's online (www.bls.gov/oco/) *Occupational Outlook Handbook 2004–2005* (updated each year) provides detailed descriptions and information on hundreds of occupations (see Figure 10A-5). The New York State Department of Labor

Figure 10-A5
Occupational Outlook
Handbook Online

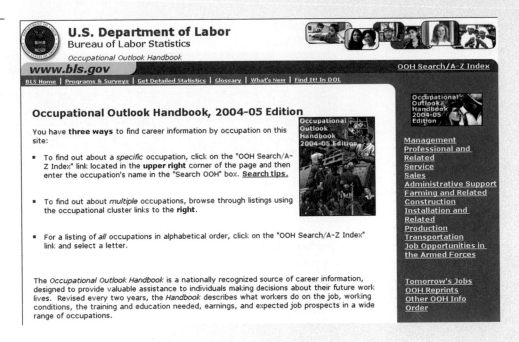

(http://nycareerzone.org) similarly provides excellent information on careers categorized in clusters, such as Arts and Humanities, Business and Information Systems, and Engineering and Technology. Both these sites include information regarding demand for and employment prospects for the occupations they cover. Figure 10A-6 lists other sites to turn to both for occupational information and for information on where to turn to when searching for a job—the subject to which we ourselves now turn.

The U.S. government's One-Stop Career Centers are another excellent source. In them, job seekers can now apply for unemployment benefits, register with the state job service, talk to career counselors, use computers to write résumés and access the Internet, take tests, and use career libraries, which offer books and videos on various employment topics. In some centers job hunters can even make use of free telephones, fax machines, and photocopiers to facilitate job searches.

FINDING THE RIGHT JOB

You have identified your occupational orientation, skills, and career anchors and have picked out the occupation you want and made plans for a career. If necessary, you have embarked on the required education and training. Your next step is to find a job that you want in the company and locale in which you want to work.

Job Search Techniques

Do Your Own Local Research   Perhaps the most direct way of unearthing the job you want, where you want it, is to pick out the geographic area in which you want to work, and find out all you can about the companies in that area that appeal to you, and the people you have to contact in those companies to get the job you want. Sometimes this research is decidedly low-tech. For example, the reference librarian in one Fairfax County, Virginia, library suggested the following sources for patrons seeking information about local businesses:

Industrial Directory of Virginia
Industrial Directory of Fairfax County
Principal Employers of the Washington Metro Area
The Business Review of Washington

Other general reference materials you can use includes *Who's Who in Commerce and Industry*, *Who's Who in America*, *Who's Who in the East*, and *Poor's Register*. Using these guides, you can find the person in each organization who is ultimately responsible for hiring people in the position you seek.

But the Internet is generally a better bet, especially if you're in one city and your ideal job would be in another. Most of the large online job search sites such as monster.com (and those in Figure 10A-6, have local-area

Figure 10-A6
Occupational and Job
Search Sources Online

Source: Printed with permission from Mapping Your Future, a public service Web site providing career, college, financial aid, and financial literacy information and services to students, families, and schools (http://mapping-your-future.org).

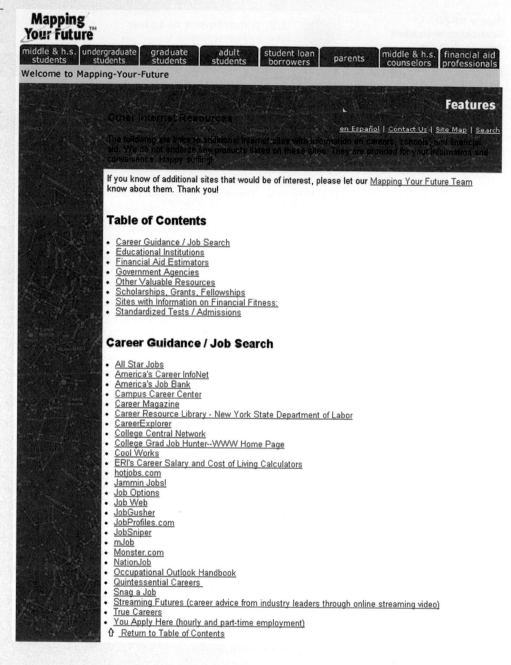

search capabilities, for instance. Use the *Wall Street Journal's* career Web site (http://www.careerjournal.com/) to search for jobs by occupation and location (see Figure 10A-7). The U.S. government's America's JobBank (http://www.ajb.dni.us/) (see Figure 10A-8) is another excellent online job search resource. And, most big-city newspapers have their own (or links to) online local job listings.

In addition to the giant general-purpose career Web sites (like Monster), most large companies, indus-

tries, and crafts have their own specialized sites.[11] For example, the Air Conditioning Contractors in America (www.acca.org/careers/) and Financial Executives International (www.fei.org) make it easy for industry employers and prospective employees to match their needs.

When job hunting, you can post your résumé on the Web. But while many people do so, Web-based résumés can cause problems. "Once I put my résumé on the Internet, I couldn't do anything to control it," said

Figure 10-A7
CareerJournal.com

Source: Wall Street Journal by Career
Journal.com © 2004. Reproduced
with permission of Dow Jones & Co.
Inc. via Copyright Clearance Center.

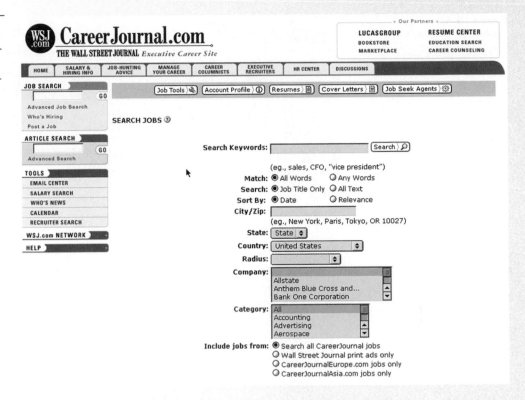

one technical consultant after his boss had stumbled across the fact that several months before he had been job hunting. If you do post your résumé on the Web, experts suggest taking precautions. At a minimum, date your résumé (in case it lands on your boss's desk two years from now); insert a disclaimer forbidding unauthorized transmission by headhunters; check ahead of time to see who has access to the database on which you're posting your résumé; and try to cloak your identity by listing your capabilities but not your name or employer—just an anonymous e-mail account to receive inquiries.[12]

Personal Contacts   Generally, the most popular way to seek job interviews is to rely on personal contacts such as friends and relatives.[13] So, let as many responsible people as possible know that you are in the market for a job and specifically what kind of job you want. (Beware, though, if you are currently employed and don't want your job search getting back to your current boss. If that is the case, better just pick out two or three very close friends and tell them it is absolutely essential that they be discreet in seeking a job for you.)

No matter how close your friends or relatives are to you, by the way, you don't want to impose too much on them. It is usually best to ask them for the name of someone they think you should talk to in the kind of firm in which you'd like to work, and then do the digging yourself.

Answering Advertisements   Most experts agree that answering ads is a low-probability way to get a job, and it becomes increasingly less likely that you will get a job this way as the level of jobs increases. Answering ads, in other words, is fine for jobs that pay under $30,000 per year, but it's highly unlikely that as you move up in management you are going to get your job by simply answering classified ads. Nevertheless, good sources of classified ads for professionals and managers include the *New York Times*, the *Wall Street Journal*, and specialized journals in your field that list job openings. All these sources also post the positions online, of course.

In responding to ads, be sure to create the right impression with the materials you submit; check the typing, style, grammar, neatness, and so forth, and check your résumé to make sure it is geared to the job for which you are applying. In your cover letter, be sure to have a paragraph or so in which you specifically address why your background and accomplishments are appropriate to the job being advertised; you must respond clearly to the company's identified needs.[14]

Figure 10-A8
America's JobBank

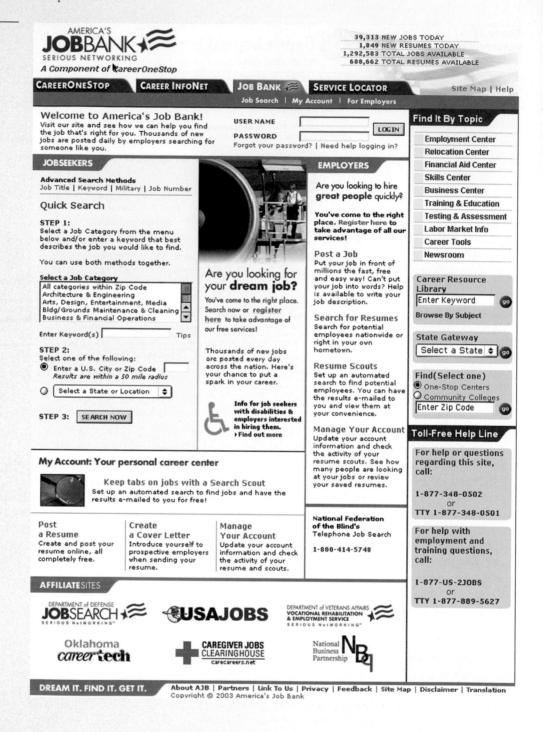

Be very careful in replying to blind ads, however (those with just a post office box). Some executive search firms and companies will run ads even when no position exists just to gauge the market, and there is always the chance that you can be trapped into responding to your own firm.

Employment Agencies Agencies are especially good at placing people in jobs paying up to about $40,000, but they can be useful for higher-paying jobs as well. Their fees for professional and management jobs are usually paid by the employer. Assuming you know the job you want, review a few back issues of your paper's Sunday classified ads to identify the agencies that consistently handle the positions you want. Approach three or four initially, preferably in response to specific ads, and avoid signing any contract that gives an agency the exclusive right to place you.

Executive Recruiters Executive recruiters are retained by employers to seek out top talent for their clients, and their fees are always paid by the employer. They do not do career counseling, but if you know the job you want, it pays to contact a few. Send your résumé and a cover letter summarizing your objective in precise terms, including job title and the size of company you want, work-related accomplishments, current salary, and salary requirements. Firms are usually listed in the Yellow Pages under "Executive Search Consultants." However, beware, because some firms today call themselves executive search or career consultants but do no searches: They just charge a (often hefty) fee to help you manage your search. Remember that with a search firm you never pay a fee.

What sorts of things will the headhunter look for? Ten important items include:[15] You have demonstrated the ability to get results; you come well recommended by your peers and competitors; you understand who the search consultant works for and what he is trying to do; you are likeable and presentable, and your ego is in check; you can think strategically and understand how to institute change in an organized direction; you have achieved the results you have because of the way you treat others, not in spite of it; you can sell yourself concisely; you have at least some of the key specific experiences that the job entails; you are honest, fair, and a good source and even take the time when somebody calls you as a source to give them other sources that you believe are high potential; and you know who you are and what you want.[16]

Career Counselors Career counselors will not help you find a job per se; rather, they specialize in aptitude testing and career counseling. They are listed under "Career Counseling" or "Vocational Guidance." Their services usually cost $300 or so and include psychological testing and interviews with an experienced career counselor. Check the firm's services, prices, and history as well as the credentials of the person you will be dealing with.

Executive Marketing Consultants Executive marketing consultants manage your job-hunting campaign. They generally are not recruiters and do not have jobs to fill. Depending on the services you choose, your cost will range from $400 to $5,000 or more. The process may involve months of weekly meetings. Services include résumé and letter writing, interview skill building, and developing a full job-hunting campaign. Before approaching a consultant, though, you should definitely do in-depth self-appraisal (as explained in this chapter) and read books like Richard Bolles's *The Quick Job Hunting Map* and *What Color Is Your Parachute?*

Then check out three or four of these firms (they are listed in the Yellow Pages under "Executive Search Consultants") by visiting each and asking: What exactly is your program? How much does each service cost? Are there any extra costs, such as charges for printing and mailing résumés? What does the contract say? After what point will you get no rebate if you're unhappy with the services? Then review your notes, check the Better Business Bureau, and decide which of these firms (if any) is for you.

Employers' Web Sites With more and more companies listing job openings on their Web sites any serious job hunter should be using this valuable source. Doing so requires some special résumé preparations, as we'll see next.

Writing Your Résumé

Your résumé is probably your most important selling document, one that can determine whether you get offered a job interview. Here are some résumé pointers, as offered by employment counselor Richard Payne and other experts.[17] An example of a good résumé is presented in Figure 10A-9.

Introductory Information Start your résumé with your name, home and e-mail address, and telephone number. Using your office phone number can indicate either that (1) your employer knows you are leaving or (2) you don't care whether he or she finds out. You're usually better off using your home or cell phone number.

Job Objective State your job objective next. This should summarize in one sentence the specific position you want, where you want to do it (type and size of company), and a special reason an employer might have for wanting you to fill the job. For example, "Production manager in a medium-size manufacturing company in a situation in which strong production scheduling and control experience would be valuable." Always try to put down the most senior title you know you can expect to

CONRAD D. STAPLETON
77 Pleasantapple Way
Coltsville, NY 10176
747-1012 conrad@Pearson.com

CONFIDENTIAL

JOB OBJECTIVE	*Senior Production Manager* in a situation requiring extensive advertising and promotion experience.
PRESENT POSITION	VALUE-PLUS DIVISION, INTERCONTINENTAL CORPORATION
2000–Present	*Product Manager,* NEW PRODUCTS, LAUDRYON SOAP and CARBOLENE CLEANER, reporting to Group Product Manager.

Recommended and obtained test market authorization, then managed all phases of development of THREE test brands, scheduled for introduction during Fall/Winter 1993. Combined first year national volume projects to $20 million, with advertising budget of $6 million. Concurrently developing several new products for 1994 test marketing.

Also responsible for two established brands: LAUNDRYON SOAP, a $7 million brand, and CARBOLENE CLEANER, a $4 million regional brand. Currently work with three advertising agencies on test and established brands.

1997–2000   *Product Manager,* WEEKENDER PAINTS, a $6 million brand.

Developed and implemented a repositioning of this brand (including new copy and new package graphics) to counter a 10-year sales downtrend averaging 10% a year. Repositioning increased test market volume 16%, and national volume 8% the following year.

Later initiated development of new, more competitive copy than advertising used during repositioning. Test area sales increased 35%. National airing is scheduled for Fall 1991.

Developed plastic packaging that increased test market volume 10%.

Also developed and implemented profit improvement projects which increased net profit 33%.

1996   *Product Manager,* SHINEZY CAR WASH, a $4 million brand.

Initiated and test marketed an improved aerosol formula and a liquid refill. Both were subsequently expanded nationally and increased brand volume 26%.

RICHARDS-DONALDS COMPANY

1995–1996   *Assistant Product Manager,* reporting to Product Manager.

Concurrent responsibility on PAR and SHIPSHAPE detergents. Developed locally tailored annual promotion plans. These resulted in 30% sales increase on PAR and stabilization of SHIPSHAPE volume.

1994–1995   *Product Merchandising Assistant*

Developed and implemented SUNSHINE SUDS annual promotion plan.

1993–1994   Academic Leave of Absence to obtain MBA. See EDUCATION.

1991–1993   *Account Manager,* Field Sales.

Account Manager for Shopper's Pal, the most difficult chain in Metropolitan West Chester. Achieved sales increase of 10% and distribution of all Lever products, introduced while I was on territory. Based on this performance was awarded Food'N Things Co-operatives, the second most difficult account, and achieved similar results.

1990–1991   READING SCHOOL, University of Maryland

MBA in Marketing Management. Average grade 3.5 out of 4.0. Thesis: "The Distribution of Pet Supplies through Supermarkets," graded 4.0 out of 4.0. Courses included quantitative methods, finance, accounting, and international business.

1986–1990   ELTON COLLEGE, Kansas City, Missouri

BA in Liberal Arts. Was one of 33, out of freshman class of 110, who completed four years of this academically rigorous program. These required each year. Judge in Student Court during senior year.

Figure 10-A9
Example of a Good Résumé
Source: Adapted from Richard Payne, *How to Get a Better Job Quicker* (New York: Signet, 1988), pp. 80–81.

secure, keeping in mind the specific job for which you are applying.

Job Scope   Indicate the scope of your responsibility in each of your previous jobs, starting with your most recent position. For each of your previous jobs, write a paragraph that shows job title, whom you reported to directly and indirectly, who reported to you, how many people reported to you, the operational and human resource budgets you controlled, and what your job entailed (in one sentence).

Your Accomplishments   Next (and this is very important), indicate your "worth" in each of the positions you held. This is the heart of your résumé. It shows for each of your previous jobs: (1) the concrete action you took and why you took it and (2) the specific result of your action—the "payoff." For example, "As production supervisor, I introduced a new process to replace costly hand soldering of component parts. The new process reduced assembly time per unit from 30 to 10 minutes and reduced labor costs by over 60%." Use several of these worth statements for each job.

Length   Keep your résumé to two pages or less, and list education, military service (if any), and personal background (hobbies, interests, associations) on the last page.

Personal Data   Do not put personal data regarding age, marital status, or dependents on top of page one. If you must include it, do so at the end of the résumé, where it will be read after the employer has already formed an opinion of you.

Finally, two last points. First, do not produce a slipshod résumé: Avoid overcrowded pages, difficult-to-read copies, typographical errors, and other problems of this sort. Second, do not use a make-do résumé—one from 10 years ago. Produce a new résumé for each job you are applying for, gearing your job objective and worth statements to the job you want.

Make Your Résumé Scannable   For many job applications it's important to write a scannable résumé, in other words, one that is electronically readable by a computer system. Many medium- and larger-sized firms that do extensive recruiting and hiring—especially online and with the aid of applicant tracking systems—now use software to quickly and automatically review large numbers of résumés, screening out those that don't seem to match (often based on the absence of certain key words that the employer is looking for).

There are several guidelines to keep in mind for writing scannable résumés.[18] These can be summarized as follows:

Use type no smaller than 10 points and no larger than 14 points.

Do not use italicized type, and do not underline words.

Use type styles that work well for résumés and can be scanned as well as read, such as Helvetica, Futura, Optima, Times Roman, New Century Schoolbook, Courier, Univers, and Bookman.

When submitting hard copies, submit only high-resolution documents. Documents produced on a laser printer work best. Many photocopies and faxes are not clean enough for scanning.

Make sure to present your qualifications using powerful key words appropriate to the job or jobs for which you are applying. For example, trainers might use key words and phrases such as: computer-based training, interactive video, and group facilitator.

Handling the Interview

You have done all your homework and now the big day is almost here; you have an interview next week with the person who is responsible for hiring for the job you want. What must you do to excel in the interview? Here are some suggestions.

Prepare, Prepare, Prepare   First, remember that preparation is essential. Before the interview, learn all you can about the employer, the job, and the people doing the recruiting. Search the Internet (or your library) to find out what is happening in the employer's field. Who is the competition? How are they doing?

Uncover the Interviewer's Needs   Spend as little time as possible answering your interviewer's first questions and as much time as possible getting the person to describe his or her needs—what the person is looking to get accomplished and the type of person needed. Use open-ended questions, such as "Could you tell me more about that?"

Relate Yourself to the Person's Needs   Once you understand the type of person your interviewer is looking for and the sorts of problems he or she wants solved, you are in a good position to describe your own accomplishments in terms of the interviewer's needs. Start by saying something like, "One of the problem areas you've indicated is important to you is similar to a problem I once faced." Then state the problem, describe your solution, and reveal the results.

Think Before Answering   Answering a question should be a three-step process: pause, think, speak. Pause to make sure you understand what the interviewer is driving at, think about how to structure your answer, and then speak. In your answer, try to emphasize how hiring you will help the interviewer solve his or her problem.

Make a Good Appearance and Show Enthusiasm   Appropriate clothing, good grooming, a firm handshake, and the appearance of controlled energy are important. Remember that studies of interviews show that in almost 80% of the cases, interviewers make up their minds about the applicant during the first few moments of the interview. A good first impression may turn bad during the interview, but it is unlikely. Bad first impressions are almost impossible to overcome.

APPENDIX GLOSSARY

career cycle   The various stages a person's career goes through.

growth stage   The period from birth to age 14 during which a person develops a self-concept by identifying with and interacting with other people.

exploration stage   The period (roughly from ages 15 to 24) during which a person seriously explores various occupational alternatives.

establishment stage   Spans roughly ages 24 to 44 and is the heart of most people's work lives.

trial substage   Period that lasts from about ages 25 to 30 during which the person determines whether or not the chosen field is suitable; if not, changes may be attempted.

stabilization substage   Firm occupational goals are set and the person does more explicit career planning.

midcareer crisis substage   Period during which people often make major reassessments of their progress relative to original ambitions and goals.

maintenance stage   Period between ages 45 and 65 when many people slide from the stabilization substage into an established position and focus on maintaining that place.

decline stage   Period where many people face having to accept reduced levels of power and responsibility, and must learn to develop new roles as mentors or confidantes for younger people.

career anchors   Pivots around which a person's career swings; require self-awareness of talents and abilities, motives and needs, and attitudes and values.

APPENDIX ENDNOTES

1. Rebecca Sohn, "Career Management in a Jobless Economy," Westchester County Business Journal, April 5, 2004, v 43, i14, p. 4.
2. Ibid.
3. John Holland, *Making Vocational Choices: A Theory of Careers* (Upper Saddle River, NJ: Prentice Hall, 1973).
4. Edward Levinson et al., "A Critical Evaluation of the Web-Based Version of the Career Key," *Career Development Quarterly* 50, no. 1 (September 1, 2002), pp. 26–36.
5. This is based on James Waldroop and Timothy Butler, "Finding the Job You *Should* Want," *Fortune*, March 2, 1998, pp. 211–214.
6. Richard Bolles, *What Color Is Your Parachute?* (Berkeley, CA: Ten Speed Press, 2003), pp. 5–6.
7. Ibid., p. 5.
8. Edgar Schein, *Career Dynamics*, (Reading, MA; Addison Wesley, 1978) pp. 128–129; and Edgar Schein, "Career Anchors Revisited: Implications for Career Development in the 21st Century," *Academy of Management Executive* 10, no. 4 (1996), pp. 80–88.
9. Ibid., pp. 257–262.
10. This example is based on Richard Bolles, *The Three Boxes of Life* (Berkely, CA: Ten Speed Press, 1976). See also Richard Bolles, *What Color Is Your Parachute?*
11. "Resume Banks Launched," *Financial Executives* 17, no. 6 (September 2001), p. 72; James Siegel, "The ACCA Launches Online Career Center," *A/C, Heating & Refrigeration News*, June 16, 2003, p. 5.
12. "Read This Before You Put a Resume Online," *Fortune*, May 24, 1999, pp. 290–291.

13. See, for example, Deborah Wright Brown and Alison Konrad, "Job Seeking in a Turbulent Environment: Social Networks and the Importance of Cross-Industry Ties to An Industry Change," *Human Relations*, August 2001, v 54, i8, p. 1018. See also John Wareham, "How to Make a Headhunter Call You," *Across-the-Board* 32, no. 1 (January 1995), pp. 49–50.

14. See, for example, "Job Search Tips The America's Intelligence Wire," May 17, 2004, and "What to Do When Your Job Search Stalls," Business Week online, March 16, 2004.

15. John Rau, "And the Winner Is . . . ," *Across-the-Board* 54, no. 10 (November/December 1997), pp. 38–42.

16. Based on Ibid., pp. 32–42.

17. Richard Payne, "How to Get a Better Job Quicker," (New York, Mentor, 1987) pp. 54–87. See also Larry Salters, "Resume Writing for the 1990s," *Business and Economics Review* 40, no. 3 (April 1994), pp. 11–18.

18. Erica Gordon Sorohan, "Electrifying a Job Search," *Training and Development*, October 1994, pp. 7–9; "Electronic Resumes Help Searchers Get in Job Hunt," Knight Ridder/Tribune Business News, April 6, 2004, ITEM 04097013.

After studying this chapter, you should be able to:

1 List the basic factors in determining pay rates.

2 Explain in detail how to establish pay rates.

3 Explain how to price managerial and professional jobs.

4 Discuss competency-based pay and other current trends in compensation.

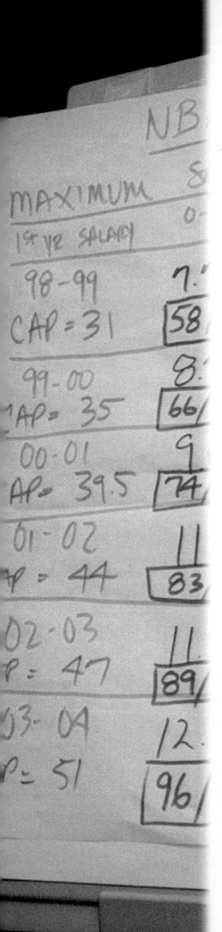

Establishing Strategic Pay Plans

Like several other HR systems at the Hotel Paris, the compensation program

was unplanned and unsophisticated. The company has a narrow target

range for what it will pay employees in each job category (front-desk clerk,

security guard, and so forth). Each hotel manager decides where to start a

new employee within that narrow pay range. The company has given little

thought to tying general pay levels or individual employees' pay to the

company's strategic goals. For example, the firm's policy is simply to pay its

employees a "competitive salary," by which it means about average for what

other hotels in the city are paying for similar jobs. Lisa knows that pay

policies like these may actually run counter to what the company wants to

achieve strategically, in terms of creating an extraordinarily service-oriented

workforce. How can you hire and retain a top workforce, and channel their

behaviors toward high-quality guest services, if you don't somehow link

performance and pay? She and her team therefore turn to the task of

assessing and redesigning the company's compensation plan.●

Once employees have done their jobs and been appraised, they expect to be paid. The main purpose of this chapter is to show you how to establish a pay plan. We explain "job evaluation" techniques—techniques for finding the relative worth of a job—, and how to conduct online and offline salary surveys. We also show you how to price the jobs in your firm by developing pay grades and ranges. In the next chapter, we'll focus specifically on pay-for-performance and incentive plans.

 **List the basic factors in determining pay rates.**

employee compensation
All forms of pay or rewards going to employees and arising from their employment.

direct financial payments
Pay in the form of wages, salaries, incentives, commissions, and bonuses.

indirect payments
Pay in the form of financial benefits such as insurance.

● DETERMINING PAY RATES

Employee compensation refers to all forms of pay or rewards going to employees and arising from their employment. It has two main components, **direct financial payments** (wages, salaries, incentives, commissions, and bonuses), and **indirect payments** (financial benefits like employer-paid insurance and vacations).

In turn, there are basically two ways to make direct financial payments to employees: you can base them on increments of time or on performance. Time-based pay is still the foundation of most employers' pay plans. Blue-collar workers get hourly or daily wages, for instance, and others, like managers or Web designers, tend to be salaried and paid by the week, month, or year. The second direct payment option is to pay for performance. Piecework is an example. It ties compensation to the amount of production (or number of "pieces") the worker turns out. For instance, you divide a worker's target hourly wage by the standard number of units he or she is to produce in one hour. Then for each unit he or she produces, the person earns the calculated rate per piece. Or, for each unit he or she produces over the standard hourly number of units, the person might earn a piece rate as an incentive. Sales commissions are another example of performance-based (in this case, sales-based) compensation. Of course, employers often create pay plans in which employees receive some combination of time-based pay plus incentives. In this chapter, we explain how to formulate plans for paying employees a time-based wage or salary; subsequent chapters cover performance-based financial incentives and bonuses, and employee benefits.

Several basic factors influence the design of any pay plan: legal, union, company policy, and equity. We'll start with legal factors.

Davis-Bacon Act (1931)
A law that sets wage rates for laborers employed by contractors working for the federal government.

Walsh-Healey Public Contract Act (1936)
A law that requires minimum wage and working conditions for employees working on any government contract amounting to more than $10,000.

Title VII of the 1964 Civil Rights Act
This act makes it unlawful for employers to discriminate against any individual with respect to hiring, compensation, terms, conditions, or privileges of employment because of race, color, religion, sex, or national origin.

Know Your Employment Law

Compensation
The area of compensation management is heavily regulated, and it is easy for managers to inadvertently violate one or more of these laws and thereby cause their firms to incur substantial penalties.

OVERVIEW OF COMPENSATION LAWS
Various laws specify things like minimum wages, overtime rates, and benefits.[1] For example, the 1931 **Davis-Bacon Act** allows the secretary of labor to set wage rates for laborers and mechanics employed by contractors working for the federal government. Amendments provide for paid employee benefits. The 1936 **Walsh-Healey Public Contract Act** sets basic labor standards for employees working on any government contract that amounts to more than $10,000. It contains minimum wage, maximum hour, and safety and health provisions, and requires time-and-a-half pay for work over 40 hours a week. **Title VII of the 1964 Civil Rights Act** makes it unlawful for employers to discriminate against any individual with respect to hiring, compensation, terms, conditions, or privileges of employment because of race, color, religion, sex,

or national origin. Other significant compensation-related laws include the 1938 Fair Labor Standards Act, the 1963 Equal Pay Act, and the 1974 Employer Retirement Income Security Act.

1938 FAIR LABOR STANDARDS ACT

Fair Labor Standards Act (1938)
This act provides for minimum wages, maximum hours, overtime pay, and child labor protection. The law has been amended many times and covers most employees.

The Fair Labor Standards Act, originally passed in 1938 and since amended many times, contains minimum wage, maximum hours, overtime pay, equal pay, record-keeping, and child labor provisions that are familiar to most working people. It covers the majority of U.S. workers—virtually all those engaged in the production and/or sale of goods for interstate and foreign commerce. In addition, agricultural workers and those employed by certain larger retail and service companies are included. State fair labor standards laws cover most employers not covered by the FLSA.

One familiar provision governs *overtime pay*. It says employers must pay overtime at a rate of at least one and a half times normal pay for any hours worked over 40 in a workweek. Thus, if a worker covered by the act works 44 hours in one week, he or she must be paid for four of those hours at a rate equal to one and a half times the hourly or weekly base rate the person would have earned for 40 hours. For example, if the person earns $8 an hour (or $320 for a 40-hour week), he or she would be paid at the rate of $12 per hour (8 times 1.5) for each of the four overtime hours worked, or a total of $48 extra. If the employee instead receives time off for the overtime hours, the employer must also compute the number of hours granted off at the one-and-a-half-times rate. So the person would get six hours off for the four hours of overtime, in lieu of overtime pay.

The act also sets a *minimum wage*, which sets a floor for employees covered by the act (and usually bumps up wages for practically all workers when Congress raises the minimum). The minimum wage in 2004 was $5.15 for the majority of those covered by the act. *Child labor provisions* prohibit employing minors between 16 and 18 years old in hazardous occupations, and carefully restrict employment of those under 16. Several states have their own minimum wage laws. For example, the minimum wage in California as of June 2004, was $6.75. About 80 localities, including Boston and Chicago, require businesses that have contracts with the city to pay employees wages ranging from $6 to $12 an hour.[2]

Specific categories of employees are exempt from the act or certain provisions of the act, and particularly from the act's overtime provisions—they are "exempt employees." A person's exemption depends on his or her responsibilities, duties, and salary. Bona fide executive, administrative (like office managers), and professional employees (like architects) are generally exempt from the minimum wage and overtime requirements of the act.[3] Figure 11-1 provides examples of those who are and are not exempt.

If an employee is exempt from the FLSA's minimum wage provisions, then he or she is also exempt from its overtime pay provisions. However, certain employees are always exempt from overtime pay provisions. They include, among others: agricultural employees; live-in household employees; taxicab drivers; and employees of motion picture theaters.

Violating provisions of this act can be costly. For example, several years ago a federal judge ordered the owners of a Colorado beef processing plant to pay nearly $2 million in back wages to 5,071 employees. The firm violated the Fair Labor Standards Act by not paying those employees one and a half times their regular pay rate for hours worked in excess of 40 per week, and for not keeping required records.[4]

Equal Pay Act (1963)
An amendment to the Fair Labor Standards Act designed to require equal pay for women doing the same work as men.

In August 2004, the U.S. Department of Labor issued new rules regarding who is exempt. In general, under these new rules, most employees earning less than $455 per week are non-exempt and earn overtime.[5]

1963 Equal Pay Act The **Equal Pay Act**, an amendment to the Fair Labor Standards Act, states that employees of one sex may not be paid wages at a rate lower than that paid to employees of the opposite sex for doing roughly equivalent work. Specifically, if the work requires equal skills, effort, and responsibility and involves similar working conditions, employees of both sexes must receive equal pay, unless the differences in pay stem from a seniority system, a merit system, the quantity or quality of production, or "any factor other than sex."

Employee Retirement Income Security Act (ERISA)
The law that provides government protection of pensions for all employees with company pension plans. It also regulates vesting rights (employees who leave before retirement may claim compensation from the pension plan).

1974 Employee Retirement Income Security Act (ERISA) The **Employee Retirement Income Security Act** This act provided for the creation of government-run, employer-financed corporations to protect employees against the failure of their employers' pension plans. In

Figure 11-1
Who Is Exempt? Who Is Not Exempt?

Exempt, Nonexempt Examples

Exempt Professionals
Attorneys
Physicians
Dentists
Pharmacists
Optometrists
Architects
Engineers
Teachers
Certified public accountants
Scientists
Computer systems analysts

Nonexempt
Paralegals
Nonlicensed accountants
Accounting clerks
Newspaper writers

Exempt Executives
Corporate officers
Supervisors

Superintendents
General managers
Individual who is in sole charge of an "independent establishment" or branch

Nonexempt
Working foreman/forewoman
Working supervisor
Lead worker
Management trainees

Exempt Administrators
Executive assistant to the president
Personnel directors
Accountants
Purchasing agents

Nonexempt
Secretaries
Clerical employees
Inspectors
Statisticians

Note: These lists are general in nature, and exceptions exist. Any questionable allocation of exemption status should be reviewed by labor legal counsel.
Source: Jeffrey Friedman, "The Fair Labor Standards Act Today: A Primer," Compensation, January/February 2002, p. 53. Reprinted with permission of Sage Publications, Inc.

addition, it sets regulations regarding vesting rights (*vesting* refers to the equity or ownership the employees build up in their pension plans should their employment be terminated before retirement). ERISA also regulates *portability rights* (the transfer of an employee's vested rights from one organization to another) and contains fiduciary standards to prevent dishonesty in pension plan funding.

Other Legislation Affecting Compensation
Various other laws influence compensation decisions. For example, the Age Discrimination in Employment Act prohibits age discrimination against employees who are 40 years of age and older in all aspects of employment, including compensation.[6] The Americans with Disabilities Act prohibits discrimination against qualified persons with disabilities in all aspects of employment, including compensation. The Family and Medical Leave Act aims to entitle eligible employees, both men and women, to take up to 12 weeks of unpaid, job-protected leave for the birth of a child or for the care of a child, spouse, or parent. And various executive orders require employers that are federal government contractors or subcontractors to not discriminate, and to take affirmative action in certain employment areas, including compensation.

Each of the 50 states has its own workers' compensation laws, which cover over 85 million workers. Among other things, these aim to provide prompt, sure, and reasonable income to victims of work-related accidents. The Social Security Act of

Two executives discuss a print layout; one happens to be in a wheelchair. Federal law mandates that the wheelchair-bound employee not suffer discrimination in compensation.

1935 (as amended) aims to protect workers from destitution in the event of termination of employment beyond their control. Employers and employees contribute equally to the benefits it provides. This act also provides for unemployment compensation—jobless benefits—for workers unemployed through no fault of their own for up to 26 weeks. (We'll discuss Social Security payments—payments to those who are disabled or retired, for instance—in Chapter 13.) The federal wage garnishment law limits the amount of an employee's earnings that employers can withhold (garnish) per week, and protects the worker from discharge due to garnishment. Some special applications of the law to compensation follow.

COMPENSATION LAW IN PRACTICE: MAKING THE OFFER

The manager needs to exercise care in how he or she words the letter of offer. Some employers quote an annual salary, perhaps because even a modest hourly pay rate may look impressive when annualized ("$20,000 per year" may sound better than "$10 per hour," for instance). The problem with making offers in terms of annual salaries is that in some jurisdictions doing so can create an implied (one-year) contract between employer and new employee. Not many courts have taken that position, but as one labor lawyer points out, "The problem in the use of annual salary is that it creates exposure to a lawsuit win or lose."[7] It's therefore usually best to describe prospective pay in terms of hourly pay rate or monthly salary.

COMPENSATION LAW IN PRACTICE: THE WORKDAY

Employers also need to be vigilant about employees who arrive early or leave late, lest the extra time spent on the employer's property obligate the employer to compensate the employee for that time. For example, a diligent employee may get dropped off at work early and spend, say, 20 minutes before his or her day actually starts doing work-related chores such as compiling a list of clients to call that day. While there is no hard and fast rule, some courts follow the rule that employees who arrive 15 or more minutes early are presumed to be working unless the employer can prove otherwise.[8] If using time clocks, employers should always instruct employees not to clock in more than 5–10 minutes early (or out 5–10 minutes late).

COMPENSATION LAW IN PRACTICE: THE INDEPENDENT CONTRACTOR

Whether or not the business relationship is one of employee–employer or independent contractor is a continuing issue for employers, with even major firms allegedly misclassifying some employees. Microsoft paid almost $97 million to settle one such suit, for instance.[9]

For employers, there are several advantages to claiming that someone doing work for them is an independent contractor. Among other things, the FLSA's requirements do not apply, and the employer does not have to pay unemployment compensation payroll taxes, Social Security taxes, or city, state, and federal income taxes or compulsory workers' compensation for that worker. If the person is truly an independent contractor, the relationship can also be advantageous to him or her. For example, it gives the worker more flexibility regarding things like when and where he or she works, and often gives the person more options, for instance, in terms of deducting business expenses.

The problem is that many so-called independent contractor relationships are not really independent contractor relationships. The U.S. Department of Labor says there is no single rule or test for determining whether an individual is an independent contractor or an employee. Instead, it is the total activity or situation at which the courts will look. The major consideration is this: The more the employer controls what the worker does, the more likely it is that the courts will find the worker is actually an employee. Figure 11-2 lists some factors the courts will consider in deciding whether the relationship is employee–employer or independent contractor.

Penalties for the employer who misclassifies an employee as an independent contractor can be severe. For example, the employer can be retroactively liable for the IRS taxes that it did not withhold (plus penalties), as well as for overtime pay, unemployment compensation taxes, and back Social Security taxes plus interest.

Figure 11-2
Independent Contractor

Source: Reprinted from www.HR. BLR.com with permission of the publisher, © 2004 *Business and Legal Reports Inc.*, 141 Mill Rock Road East, Old Saybrook, CT.

Independent Contractor

Managers are to use the following checklist to classify individuals as independent contractors. If more than 3 questions are answered "yes", the manager will confer with human resources regarding the classification. (EE = Employees, IC = Independent Contractors)

Factors which show control:

	Yes/EE	No/IC	N/A
1. Worker must comply with instructions.	☐	☐	☐
2. Worker is trained by person hired.	☐	☐	☐
3. Worker's services are integrated in business.	☐	☐	☐
4. Worker must personally render services.	☐	☐	☐
5. Worker cannot hire or fire assistants.	☐	☐	☐
6. Work relationship is continuous or indefinite.	☐	☐	☐
7. Work hours are present.	☐	☐	☐
8. Worker must devote full time to this business.	☐	☐	☐
9. Work is done on the employer's premises.	☐	☐	☐
10. Worker cannot control order or sequence.	☐	☐	☐
11. Worker submits oral or written reports.	☐	☐	☐
12. Worker is paid at specific intervals.	☐	☐	☐
13. Worker's business expenses are reimbursed.	☐	☐	☐
14. Worker is provided with tools or materials.	☐	☐	☐
15. Worker has no significant investment.	☐	☐	☐
16. Worker has no opportunity for profit/loss.	☐	☐	☐
17. Worker is not engaged by many different firms.	☐	☐	☐
18. Worker does not offer services to public.	☐	☐	☐
19. Worker may be discharged by employer.	☐	☐	☐
20. Worker can terminate without liability.	☐	☐	☐

Union Influences on Compensation Decisions

Unions and labor relations laws also influence pay plan design. The National Labor Relations Act of 1935 (or Wagner Act) and associated legislation and court decisions legitimized the labor movement. It gave unions legal protection and granted employees the right to organize, to bargain collectively, and to engage in concerted activities for the purpose of collective bargaining or other mutual aid or protection. Historically, the wage rate has been the main issue in collective bargaining. However, unions also negotiate other pay-related issues, including time off with pay, income security (for those in industries with periodic layoffs), cost-of-living adjustments, and benefits like health care.

The 1935 Act created the National Labor Relations Board (NLRB) to oversee employer practices and ensure that employees receive their rights. Its rulings underscore the need to involve union officials in developing the compensation package. For example, employers must give the union a written explanation of the employer's "wage curves"—the graph that relates job to pay rate. The union is also entitled to know the salary of each employee it is representing.[10]

Corporate Policies, Competitive Strategy, and Compensation

The compensation plan should further the firm's strategic aims—management should produce an *aligned reward strategy*. In other words, management should ask, "How can I construct a total portfolio of reward programs that all link to both short- and longer-term business success, drive shareholder value, encourage the behaviors that we need, and deliver true value to our employees?"[11] The employer's basic task is always to create a bundle of rewards—a total reward package—specifically aimed at eliciting the employee behaviors the firm needs to support and achieve its competitive strategy. Table 11-1 summarizes this cause-and-effect HR Scorecard-type process.

Exactly how the firm will use its pay plan to further its strategic aims will manifest itself in the firm's pay policies. The HR or compensation manager will write the policies in conjunction with top management, in a manner such that the policies are consistent with the firm's strategic aims. For example, will the firm be a leader or a follower regarding pay?[12] A top hospital like Johns Hopkins might have a policy of starting nurses at a wage of 20% above the prevailing market wage, as might the Hotel Paris.

Yet, paying higher salaries is no guarantee that the employer will be able to hire more qualified employees, since other factors may influence the quality of the people it hires. For example, in a study of public schools, the researcher found that for nonunion school districts there was a statistically significant relationship between teacher salaries and that school district's probability of hiring well-qualified teachers. The researcher did not find a pay–teacher quality relationship in unionized school districts.[13]

Whether to emphasize seniority or performance is another compensation policy issue. For example, U.S. federal employees get raises based on longevity. The government groups jobs into grades based on things like skill and education, and there are 15

Table 11-1 **Developing an Aligned Reward Strategy**	Questions to Ask:
	1. What are our company's key success factors? What must our company do, to be successful in fulfilling its mission or achieving its desired competitive position?
	2. What are the employee behaviors or actions necessary to successfully implement this competitive strategy?
	3. What compensation programs should we use to reinforce those behaviors? What should be the purpose of each program in reinforcing each desired behavior?
	4. What measurable requirements should each compensation program meet to be deemed successful in fulfilling its purpose?
	5. How well do our current compensation programs match these requirements?
	Source: Adapted from Jack Dolmat-Connell, "Developing a Reward Strategy that Delivers Shareholder and Employee Value," *Compensation and Benefits Review*, March–April 1999, p. 51.

salary steps within each grade. It takes 18 years for an employee to progress from step one to step nine. Seniority-based pay may be advantageous to the extent that employees perceive seniority as an objective standard. One disadvantage, though, is that top performers may get the same raises as poor ones.

Other policies usually cover the pay cycle, as well as how to award salary increases and promotions, overtime pay, probationary pay, and leaves for military service, jury duty, and holidays. For example, pay cycle policies vary from weekly to monthly. In one survey, 24% of respondents issued weekly paychecks, 48% paid biweekly, 22% paid twice a month, and 5% paid monthly.[14]

salary compression
A salary inequity problem, generally caused by inflation, resulting in longer-term employees in a position earning less than workers entering the firm today.

Salary Compression   How to handle salary compression is another policy issue. **Salary compression**, which means longer-term employees' salaries are lower than those of workers entering the firm today, is a creature of inflation. Prices (and starting salaries) go up faster than the company's salaries, and firms need a policy to handle it. Writing one is tricky. On the one hand, you don't want to treat current employees unfairly or to have them leave with their knowledge and expertise. However, mediocre performance or lack of assertiveness, not salary compression, may explain some low salaries. One policy is to install a more aggressive merit pay program. Others authorize supervisors to recommend "equity" adjustments for selected employees who are both highly valued and victims of pay compression.

Geography   Geography also plays a policy role. Cost-of-living differences between cities can be considerable. For example, a family of four might live in Miami for just over $39,000 per year, while the same family's annual expenditures in Chicago or Los Angeles would be over $56,000.

Employers handle cost-of-living differentials in several ways. One is to give the transferred person a nonrecurring payment, usually in a lump sum or perhaps spread over one to three years. Others pay a differential for ongoing costs in addition to a one-time allocation. For example, one employer pays a differential of $6,000 per year to people earning $35,000 to $45,000 whom it transfers from Atlanta to Minneapolis. Others simply raise the employee's base salary. Compensating expatriate employees is still another policy problem, as "The New Workplace" feature illustrates.

Equity and Its Impact on Pay Rates

In studies conducted at Emory University, researchers investigated how Capuchin monkeys reacted to inequitable pay. They trained monkeys to trade pebbles for food. Some monkeys got grapes in return for pebbles, others got cucumber slices. Those receiving the sweeter grapes willingly traded in their pebbles. But if a monkey receiving a cucumber slice saw one of its neighbors get a grape, it slammed down the pebble or refused to eat the cucumber.[15] The moral, it would seem, is that even lower primates may be genetically programmed to be treated fairly when it comes to being paid.

Higher up the primate line, *the equity theory of motivation* postulates that people have a need for, and therefore value and seek, fairness at work. People are strongly motivated to maintain a balance between what they perceive as their inputs or contributions, and their rewards. Equity theory states that if a person perceives an inequity, a tension or drive will develop in the person's mind, and the person will be motivated to reduce or eliminate the tension and perceived inequity. Research tends to support equity theory, particularly as it applies to people who are underpaid.[16]

With respect to compensation, managers should address four forms of equity: *external*, *internal*, *individual*, and *procedural*.[17] *External equity* refers to how a job's pay rate in one company compares to the job's pay rate in other companies. *Internal equity* refers to how fair the job's pay rate is, when compared to other jobs within the same

The New Workplace

Globalization and Diversity: Compensating Expatriate Employees

The question of cost-of-living differentials has particular significance to multinational firms. The annual cost of keeping a U.S. expatriate in France might average $193,000, while in neighboring Germany the cost is closer to $246,000.[18]

How should multinationals compensate expatriate employees—those it sends overseas? Two basic international compensation policies are popular: home-based and host-based plans.[19]

With a *home-based salary plan*, an international transferee's base salary reflects his or her home country's salary. The employer then adds allowances for cost-of-living differences—housing and schooling costs, for instance. This is a reasonable approach for short-term assignments, and avoids the problem of having to change the employee's base salary every time he or she moves.

In the *host-based plan*, the firm ties the international transferee's base salary to the host country's salary structure. In other words, the manager from New York who is sent to France would have his or her base salary changed to the prevailing base salary for that position in France, rather than keep the New York base salary. The firm usually tacks on cost-of-living, housing, schooling, and other allowances here as well.

A survey of multinational enterprises suggests most set expatriates' salaries according to their home-country base pay.[20] (Thus, a French manager assigned to Kiev by a U.S. multinational will generally have a base salary that reflects the salary structure in the manager's home country, in this case France.) In addition, the person typically gets allowances including cost-of-living, relocation, housing, education, and hardship allowances (the latter for countries with a relatively hard quality of life, such as China). The employer also usually pays any extra tax burdens resulting from taxes the manager is liable for over and above those he or she would have to pay in the home country. In time, globalization of business may lead to more global standardizing of pay rates for most occupations around the world.[21]

company (for instance, is the sales manager's pay fair, when compared to what the production manager is earning?). *Individual equity* refers to the fairness of an individual's pay as compared with what his or her co-workers are earning for the same or very similar jobs within the company, based on each individual's performance. *Procedural equity* refers to the "perceived fairness of the processes and procedures used to make decisions regarding the allocation of pay."[22]

Managers use various methods to address each of these equity issues. For example, they use salary surveys to monitor and maintain external equity. They use job analysis and job evaluation (discussed below) to maintain internal equity. They use performance appraisal and various types of incentive pay to maintain individual equity. And they use communications, grievance mechanisms, and employees' participation in developing the company's pay plan to help ensure that employees view the pay process as transparent and fair. Some firms administer surveys to monitor employees' attitudes regarding the pay plan. Questions typically include, "How satisfied are you with your pay?" "What criteria were used for your recent pay increase?" and "What factors do you believe are used when your pay is determined?"[23]

Even large, sophisticated companies aren't immune to pay inequities. With morale down due to widespread concerns about racial discrimination suits, layoffs, and possibly inequitable salaries, Coca-Cola Co. undertook a salary review of companies ranging from PepsiCo to Procter & Gamble and Yahoo. Management then announced raises ranging from about $1,000 to as much as $15,000 for most of its employees. When inequities do arise, conflict can ensue. To head off discussions of internal or individual equity, some firms maintain strict secrecy over pay matters, with mixed results. But for external equity, online pay forum sites like vault.com, combined with easy access to salary data on sites like Salary.com, make it easy for employees to discover that they could earn more elsewhere.

The process of establishing pay rates while ensuring external, internal, and (to some extent) procedural equity consists of five steps:

1. Conduct a salary survey of what other employers are paying for comparable jobs (to help ensure external equity).
2. Determine the worth of each job in your organization through job evaluation (to ensure internal equity).
3. Group similar jobs into pay grades.
4. Price each pay grade by using wave curves.
5. Fine-tune pay rates.

The next section focuses on each of these steps.

 Explain in detail how to establish pay rates.

● ESTABLISHING PAY RATES

Step 1. The Salary Survey

salary survey
A survey aimed at determining prevailing wage rates. A good salary survey provides specific wage rates for specific jobs. Formal written questionnaire surveys are the most comprehensive, but telephone surveys and newspaper ads are also sources of information.

benchmark job
A job that is used to anchor the employer's pay scale and around which other jobs are arranged in order of relative worth.

It's difficult to set pay rates if you don't know what others are paying, so salary surveys play a big role in pricing jobs. Virtually every employer conducts at least an informal telephone, newspaper, or Internet **salary survey**.[24]

Employers use these surveys in three ways. First, they use survey data to price **benchmark jobs**. They then use these as the anchors around which they slot their other jobs, based on each job's relative worth to the firm. (Job evaluation, explained next, helps determine the relative worth of each job.) Second, employers typically price 20% or more of their positions directly in the marketplace (rather than relative to the firm's benchmark jobs), based on a formal or informal survey of what comparable firms are paying for comparable jobs. (A dot-com firm might do this for jobs like Web programmer, whose salaries fluctuate widely and often.) Third, surveys also collect data on benefits like insurance, sick leave, and vacations to provide a basis for decisions regarding employee benefits.

Salary surveys can be formal or informal.[25] Informal telephone or Internet surveys are good for checking on a relatively small number of easily identified and quickly recognized jobs, such as when a bank's HR director wants to confirm the salary at which to advertise a newly open cashier's job. Such informal techniques are also good for checking discrepancies, such as when the HR director wants to find out if some area banks are really paying tellers on some sort of incentive plan. Perhaps 20% of large employers use their own formal questionnaire surveys to collect compensation information from other employers. Most of these ask about things like number of employees, overtime policies, starting salaries, and paid vacations.

Commercial, Professional, and Government Salary Surveys Many employers use surveys published by consulting firms, professional associations, or government agencies. For example, the U.S. Department of Labor's Bureau of Labor Statistics (BLS) conducts three annual surveys: (1) area wage surveys; (2) industry wage surveys; and (3) professional, administrative, technical, and clerical (PATC) surveys.

About 200 annual area wage surveys provide data for a variety of clerical and manual occupations ranging from secretary to messenger to office clerk. Area wage surveys also provide data on weekly work schedules, paid holidays and vacation practices, health insurance and pension plans, as well as on shift operations and differentials. Industry wage surveys provide similar data, but by industry. They provide national pay data for workers in selected jobs for industries like building, trucking, and printing. PATC surveys collect pay data on 80 occupations, including accounting, legal services, personnel management, engineering, chemistry, buying, clerical supervisory, drafting, and clerical. They provide information about earnings as well as production bonuses, commissions, and cost-of-living increases. The BLS recently organized its various pay surveys into a new national compensation survey, and began publishing this information on the Web. The Internet site is http://stats.bls.gov.

Private consulting and/or executive recruiting companies like Hay Associates, Heidrick and Struggles, and Hewitt Associates publish data covering compensation for top and middle management and members of boards of directors. Professional organizations like the Society for Human Resource Management and the Financial Executives Institute publish surveys of compensation practices among members of their associations.

Watson Wyatt Data Services of Rochelle Park, New Jersey, publishes several compensation surveys. Its top management compensation surveys cover dozens of top positions, including chief executive officer, top real estate executive, top financial executive, top sales executive, and top claims executive, all categorized by function and industry. Watson Wyatt also offers middle management compensation surveys, supervisory management compensation surveys, sales and marketing personnel surveys, professional and scientific personnel surveys, and surveys of technician trades, skilled trades, and office personnel, among others. The surveys generally cost about $500 to $700 each, but can be worth the expense if they help avoid the dual hazards of (1) paying too much or (2) suffering turnover because of uncompetitive pay.

Using the Internet to Do Compensation Surveys   Finding salary data is not as mysterious as it used to be, thanks to the Internet. A rapidly expanding array of Internet-based options makes it easy for anyone to access published compensation survey information. Table 11-2 shows some popular salary survey Web sites.

To get a real-time picture of what employers in your area are paying for, say, accounting clerks, it's useful to access the online Internet sites of one or two of your local newspapers. In this case, the *South Florida Sun-Sentinel* has a site called careerbuilder. It lists career opportunities—in other words, just about all the jobs listed in the newspaper by category and, in many instances, wage rates (http://www.sun-sentinel.com/classified/jobs). From this listing, you'll find jobs listed for "Accounts receivable clerks—$10.00 per hour," "Accounting clerk—$25k," "Accounting clerk—credit clerk, to $22k," and "Accounts payable clerk, $22–26k," among many others. Switching to the *Miami Herald*'s online Web site (www.miami.com/mld/miamiherald/classifieds/employment) classifieds, you similarly find a list of several dozen related job listings. For example, there is a "Payroll clerk, Doral area, $25k," an "Accounting clerk—City of Hialeah starting at $594 biweekly," and "Accounting assistant—Miami Lakes area, to $29k." More Web sites for compensation purposes are available from consulting firms; others are listed in this textbook's Web site page for this chapter, and in Table 11-2.

The Internet provides numerous fee-based sources of international salary data. For example, William M. Mercer, Inc., an international consulting firm (http://www.mercer.com), publishes an annual global compensation planning report summarizing compensation trends for more than 40 countries plus representative pay data for four common benchmark jobs.[26]

In most cases, salary survey data are used to price benchmark jobs, around which other jobs are then slotted based on the job's relative worth. Determining the relative worth of a job is the purpose of job evaluation, which we'll address next.

Table 11-2 Some Pay Data Web Sites

Sponsor	Internet Address	What It Provides	Downside
Salary.com	Salary.com	Salary by job and zip code, plus job and description, for hundreds of jobs	Adapts national averages by applying local cost-of-living differences
Wageweb	www.wageweb.com	Average salaries for more than 150 clerical, professional, and managerial jobs	Charges $100 for breakdowns by industry, location, etc. location, etc.
Exec-U-Net	www.execunet.com	Salary, bonus, and options for about 650 management posts	Charges an initial $125 for job details
Futurestep*	www.futurestep.com	Pay analyses for people eligible for managerial posts paying about $50,000 to $200,000 a year	Participants automatically subject to queries from Korn/Ferry recruiters
U.S. Office of Personnel Management	www.opm.gov/oca/ 04tables/index.asp	Salaries and wages for U.S. government jobs	Limited to U.S. government jobs
Job Smart	http://jobsmart.org/tools/ salary/sal-prof.cfm	Profession-specific salary surveys	Necessary to review numerous salary surveys for each profession

*An alliance between recruiters Korn/Ferry International and the *Wall Street Journal*.

Source: Adapted from Joann S. Lublin, "Web Transforms Art of Negotiating Raises," *Wall Street Journal*, Sept. 22, 1998, p. B1, and Susan Marks, "Can the Internet Help You Hit the Salary Mark?" *Workforce*, 80 no. 1 (Jan. 2001), pp. 86–93.

Step 2. Job Evaluation

job evaluation
A systematic comparison done in order to determine the worth of one job relative to another.

Job evaluation is aimed at determining a job's relative worth. It is a formal and systematic comparison of jobs to determine the worth of one job relative to another and eventually results in a wage or salary hierarchy. The basic principle is this: Jobs that require greater qualifications, more responsibilities, and more complex job duties should be paid more highly than jobs with lesser requirements.[27] The basic procedure is to compare the jobs in relation to one another—for example, in terms of required effort, responsibility, and skills. Suppose you know (based on your salary survey) how to price key benchmark jobs, and then use job evaluation to determine the relative worth of all the other jobs in your firm relative to these key jobs. You are then well on your way to being able to price all the jobs in your organization equitably.

Compensable Factors You can use two basic approaches to compare several jobs. First, you can take an intuitive approach. You might decide that one job is more important than another and not dig any deeper into why. As an alternative, you could compare the jobs by focusing on certain basic factors the jobs have in common. Compensation management specialists call these **compensable factors**. They are the factors that establish how the jobs compare to one another, and that determine the pay for each job.

compensable factor
A fundamental, compensable element of a job, such as skills, effort, responsibility, and working conditions.

Some employers develop their own compensable factors. However, most use factors popularized by packaged job evaluation systems or by federal legislation. For example, the Equal Pay Act focuses on four compensable factors—skills, effort, responsibility, and working conditions. The method popularized by the Hay consulting firm focuses on three factors: know-how, problem solving, and accountability. In 2004, Wal-Mart instituted a new wage structure based on knowledge, problem solving skills and accountability requirements.

Identifying compensable factors plays a central role in job evaluation. You usually compare each job with all comparable jobs using the same compensable factors. However, the compensable factors you use depend on the job and the job evaluation method. For example, you might choose to include "decision making" for a manager's job, though it might be inappropriate for a cleaner's job.[28]

Preparing for the Job Evaluation   Job evaluation is mostly a judgmental process, one demanding close cooperation among supervisors, HR specialists, and employees and union representatives. The main steps include identifying the need for the program, getting cooperation, and then choosing an evaluation committee. The committee then performs the actual evaluation.

Identifying the need for job evaluation should not be difficult. For example, dissatisfaction reflected in high turnover, work stoppages, or arguments may result from paying employees different rates for similar jobs. Managers may express uneasiness with an informal way of assigning pay rates to jobs, accurately sensing that a more systematic assignment would be more equitable.

Next (since employees may fear that a systematic evaluation of their jobs may actually reduce their pay rates), getting employees to cooperate in the evaluation is a second important step. You can tell employees that as a result of the impending job evaluation program, pay rate decisions will no longer be made just by management whim; that job evaluation will provide a mechanism for considering the complaints they have been expressing; and that no present employee's rate will be adversely affected as a result of the job evaluation.

Next, choose a job evaluation committee. There are two reasons for doing so. First, the committee should include several people who are familiar with the jobs in question, each of whom may have a different perspective regarding the nature of the jobs. Second, if the committee is composed at least partly of employees, the committee approach can help ensure greater employee acceptance of the job evaluation results.

So the composition of the committee is important. The group usually consists of about five members, most of whom are employees. Management has the right to serve on such committees, but employees may view this with suspicion. However, an HR specialist can usually be justified on the grounds that he or she has a more impartial outlook than line managers and can provide expert assistance. One option is to have this person

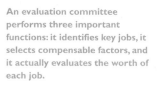

An evaluation committee performs three important functions: it identifies key jobs, it selects compensable factors, and it actually evaluates the worth of each job.

serve in a nonvoting capacity. Union representation is possible. In most cases, though, the union's position is that it is accepting the results of the job evaluation only as an initial decision and is reserving the right to appeal actual job pricing decisions through grievance or bargaining channels.[29] Once appointed, each committee member should receive a manual explaining the job evaluation process, and instructions that explain how to conduct the job evaluation.

The evaluation committee performs three main functions. First, it usually identifies 10 or 15 key benchmark jobs. These will be the first jobs to be evaluated and will serve as the anchors or benchmarks against which the relative importance or value of all other jobs can be compared. Next, the committee may select compensable factors (although the HR department will usually choose these as part of the process of determining the specific job evaluation technique the firm will use). Finally, the committee performs its most important function—actually evaluating the worth of each job. For this, the committee will probably use one of the following methods: ranking, job classification, point method, or factor comparison.

Job Evaluation Methods: Ranking   The simplest job evaluation method ranks each job relative to all other jobs, usually based on some overall factor like "job difficulty." There are several steps in the job **ranking method**.

ranking method
The simplest method of job evaluation that involves ranking each job relative to all other jobs, usually based on overall difficulty.

1. *Obtain job information.* Job analysis is the first step: Job descriptions for each job are prepared, and the information they contain about the job's duties is usually the basis for ranking jobs. (Sometimes job specifications are also prepared. However, the ranking method usually ranks jobs according to the whole job, rather than a number of compensable factors. Therefore, job specifications—which list the job's demands in terms of problem solving, decision making, and skills, for instance—are not as necessary with this method as they are for other job evaluation methods.)

2. *Select and group jobs.* It is often not practical to make a single ranking for all jobs in an organization. The usual procedure is to rank jobs by department or in clusters (such as factory workers or clerical workers). This eliminates the need for direct comparison of, say, factory jobs and clerical jobs.

3. *Select compensable factors.* In the ranking method, it is common to use just one factor (such as job difficulty) and to rank jobs based on the whole job. Regardless of the number of factors you choose, it's advisable to explain the definition of the factor(s) to the evaluators carefully so that they evaluate the jobs consistently.

4. *Rank jobs.* For example, give each rater a set of index cards, each of which contains a brief description of a job. Then they rank these cards from lowest to highest. Some managers use an "alternation ranking method" for making the procedure more accurate. Here you take the cards, first choosing the highest and the lowest, then the next highest and next lowest, and so forth until you've ranked all the cards. Table 11-3 illustrates a job ranking. Jobs in this small health facility are ranked from orderly up to office manager. The corresponding pay scales are on the right. After ranking, it is possible to slot additional jobs between those already ranked and to assign an appropriate wage rate.

5. *Combine ratings.* Usually, several raters rank the jobs independently. Then the rating committee (or the employer) can simply average the rankings.

This is the simplest job evaluation method, as well as the easiest to explain. And it usually takes less time than other methods.

Table 11-3

Job Ranking by Olympia Health Care

Ranking Order	Annual Pay Scale
I. Office manager	$43,000
2. Chief nurse	42,500
3. Bookkeeper	34,000
4. Nurse	32,500
5. Cook	31,000
6. Nurse's aide	28,500
7. Orderly	25,500

Some of its drawbacks derive more from how it's used than from the method itself. For example, there's a tendency to rely too heavily on "guesstimates." Similarly, ranking provides no yardstick for quantifying the value of one job relative to another. For example, job number 4 may in fact be five times "more valuable" than job number 5, but with the ranking system all you know is that one job ranks higher than the other. Ranking is usually more appropriate for small organizations that can't afford the time or expense of developing a more elaborate system.

Job Evaluation Methods: Job Classification **Job classification** (or **job grading**) is a simple, widely used method in which raters categorize jobs into groups; all the jobs in each group are of roughly the same value for pay purposes. The groups are called **classes** if they contain similar jobs, or **grades** if they contain jobs that are similar in difficulty but otherwise different. Thus, in the federal government's pay grade system, a "press secretary" and a "fire chief" might both be graded "GS-10" (GS stands for "General Schedule"). On the other hand, in its job class system, the state of Florida might classify all "secretary IIs" in one class, all "maintenance engineers" in another, and so forth.

There are several ways to actually categorize jobs. One is to write class or grade descriptions (similar to job descriptions) and place jobs into classes or grades based on how well they fit these descriptions. Another is to draw up a set of compensable factor-based rules for each class (for instance, how much independent judgment, skill, physical effort, and so on, does the class of jobs require?). Then categorize the jobs according to these rules.

Probably the most popular procedure is to choose compensable factors and then develop class or grade descriptions for each class or grade in terms of amount or level of the compensable factor(s) in those jobs. The federal classification system in the United States, for example, employs the following compensable factors: (1) difficulty and variety of work, (2) supervision received and exercised, (3) judgment exercised, (4) originality required, (5) nature and purpose of interpersonal work relationships, (6) responsibility, (7) experience, and (8) knowledge required. Based on these compensable factors, raters write a **grade definition** like that in Figure 11-3. This one shows one grade description (GS-7) for the federal government's pay grade system. Then the evaluation committee reviews all job descriptions and slots each job into its appropriate grade, by comparing each job description to the rules in each grade description. For instance, the federal government system classifies the positions automotive mechanic, welder, electrician, and machinist in grade GS-10.

The classification method has several advantages. The main one is that most employers usually end up grouping jobs into classes anyway, regardless of the evaluation

job classification (or grading) method
A method for categorizing jobs into groups.

classes
Grouping jobs based on a set of rules for each group or class, such as amount of independent judgment, skill, physical effort, and so forth, required. Classes usually contain similar jobs.

grades
A job classification system like the class system, although grades often contain dissimilar jobs, such as secretaries, mechanics, and firefighters. Grade descriptions are written based on compensable factors listed in classification systems.

grade definition
Written descriptions of the level of, say, responsibility and knowledge required by each grade. Similar jobs can then be combined into grades or classes.

Figure 11-3
Example of A Grade Level Definition
This is a summary chart of the key grade level criteria for the GS-7 level of clerical and assistance work. Do not use this chart alone for classification purposes; additional grade level criteria are in the Web-based chart.
Source: http://www.opm.gov/fedclass. gscler.pdf. August 29, 2001.

GRADE	NATURE OF ASSIGNMENT	LEVEL OF RESPONSIBILITY
GS-7	Performs specialized duties in a defined functional or program area involving a wide variety of problems or situations; develops information, identifies interrelationships, and takes actions consistent with objectives of the function or program served.	Work is assigned in terms of objectives, priorities, and deadlines; the employee works independently in resolving most conflicts; completed work is evaluated for conformance to policy; guidelines, such as regulations, precedent cases, and policy statements require considerable interpretation and adaptation.

method they use. They do this to avoid having to work with and price an unmanageable number of jobs. Of course the job classification automatically groups the employer's jobs into classes. The disadvantages are that it is difficult to write the class or grade descriptions, and considerable judgment is required to apply them. Yet many employers (including the U.S. government) use this method with success.

point method
The job evaluation method in which a number of compensable factors are identified and then the degree to which each of these factors is present on the job is determined.

Job Evaluation Methods: Point Method   The **point method** is a more quantitative technique. It involves identifying (1) several compensable factors, each having several degrees, as well as (2) the degree to which each of these factors is present in the job. Assume there are five degrees of "responsibility" a job could contain. Further assume you assign a different number of points to each degree of each factor. Once the evaluation committee determines the degree to which each compensable factor (like "responsibility" and "effort") is present in the job, it can calculate a total point value for the job by adding up the corresponding points for each factor. The result is a quantitative point rating for each job. The point method is apparently the most widely used job evaluation method; the appendix to this chapter explains it in detail.

factor comparison method
A widely used method of ranking jobs according to a variety of skill and difficulty factors, then adding up these rankings to arrive at an overall numerical rating for each given job.

Job Evaluation Methods: Factor Comparison   The **factor comparison method** is actually a refinement of the ranking method. With the ranking method, you generally look at each job as an entity and rank the jobs on some overall factor like job difficulty. With the factor comparison method, you rank each job several times—once for each of several compensable factors. For example, you might first rank jobs in terms of the compensable factor "skill." Then rank them according to their "mental requirements," and so forth. Then combine the rankings for each job into an overall numerical rating for the job. This too is a widely used method, also found in more detail in the appendix to this chapter.

Computerized Job Evaluations   Using quantitative job evaluation methods such as the point or factor comparison plans can be time-consuming. Accumulating the information about "how much" of each compensable factor the job contains traditionally involves a tedious process in which evaluation committees debate the level of each compensable factor in a job. They then write down their consensus judgments and manually compute each job's point values.

CAJE—computer-aided job evaluation—can streamline this process. Computer-aided job evaluation, says one expert, can simplify job analysis, help keep job descriptions up to date, increase evaluation objectivity, reduce the time spent in committee meetings, and ease the burden of system maintenance. CAJE includes electronic data entry, computerized checking of compensable factor questionnaire responses, and automated output of job evaluations and of a variety of compensation reports.[30]

Most of these computerized systems have two main components. There is, first, a structured questionnaire. This contains items such as "enter total number of employees who report functionally to this position." Second, all CAJE systems use statistical models. These allow the computer program to price jobs more or less automatically, by assigning points or factor comparison rankings to things like number of employees reporting to the positions, prices of benchmark jobs, current pay, and current pay grade midpoints.

Step 3. Group Similar Jobs into Pay Grades

pay grade
A pay grade is comprised of jobs of approximately equal difficulty.

Once it has used job evaluation to determine the relative worth of each job, the committee can turn to the task of assigning pay rates to each job; however, it will usually want to first group jobs into **pay grades**. It could, of course, just assign pay rates to each individual job.[31] But for a large employer, such a plan would be difficult to administer, since there might be different pay rates for hundreds or even thousands of jobs. And even in smaller organizations, there's a tendency to try to simplify wage and salary structures as much as possible. Therefore, the committee will probably group similar jobs (in terms of their ranking or number of points, for instance) into grades for pay purposes. Instead of having to deal with hundreds of pay rates, it might only have to focus on, say, 10 or 12.

A pay grade is comprised of jobs of approximately equal difficulty or importance as established by job evaluation. If the committee used the point method, then the pay grade consists of jobs falling within a range of points. With the ranking method, the grade consists of all jobs that fall within two or three ranks. The classification method automatically categorizes jobs into classes or grades. (With the factor comparison method, the grade consists of a specified range of pay rates, as the appendix to this chapter explains.) Ten to 16 grades per "job cluster" (a *cluster* is a logical grouping, such as factory jobs, clerical jobs, and so on) are now common. However, as we'll explain shortly, there's a trend toward reducing the number of pay grades within each cluster, so that each grade includes more jobs.

Step 4. Price Each Pay Grade—Wage Curves

wage curve
Shows the relationship between the value of the job and the average wage paid for this job.

The next step is to assign pay rates to your pay grades. (Of course, if you chose not to slot jobs into pay grades, you would have to assign individual pay rates to each individual job.) You'll typically use a **wage curve** to help assign pay rates to each pay grade (or to each job).

The wage curve shows the pay rates currently paid for jobs in each pay grade, relative to the points or rankings assigned to each job or grade by the job evaluation. Figure 11-4 presents an example. Note that it shows pay rates on the vertical axis, and pay grades (in terms of points) along the horizontal axis. The purpose of the wage curve is to show the relationships between (1) the value of the job as determined by one of the job evaluation methods and (2) the current average pay rates for your grades.

The pay rates on the wage curve are traditionally those now paid by the employer. However, if there is reason to believe the current pay rates are out of step with the market rates for these jobs, choose benchmark jobs within each pay grade, and price them via a compensation survey. These new market-based pay rates then replace the current rates on the wage curve. Then slot in your other jobs (and their pay rates) around the benchmark jobs.[32]

There are several steps in pricing jobs with a wage curve. First, find the average pay for each pay grade, since each of the pay grades consists of several jobs. Next, plot the pay rates for each pay grade as was done in Figure 11-4. Then fit a line, called a *wage line*, through the points just plotted. You can do this freehand or by using a statistical method. Finally, price the jobs. For this, wages along the wage line are the target wages or salary rates for the jobs in each pay grade. If the current rates being paid for any of your jobs or grades fall well above or below the wage line, raises or a pay freeze for that job may be in order. Your next step, then, is to fine-tune your pay rates.

Figure 11-4
Plotting a Wage Curve

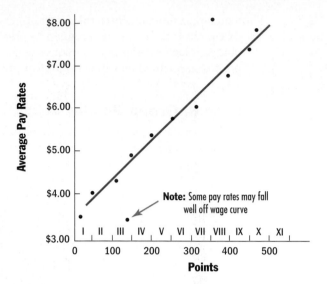

Step 5. Fine-Tune Pay Rates

Fine-tuning involves developing pay ranges and correcting out-of-line rates.

pay ranges
A series of steps or levels within a pay grade, usually based upon years of service.

Developing Pay Ranges   Most employers do not pay just one rate for all jobs in a particular pay grade. For example, GE Medical won't want to pay all its accounting clerks, from beginners to long tenure, at the same rate. Instead, employers develop vertical pay (or "rate") ranges for each horizontal pay grade. These **pay ranges** may appear as vertical boxes within each grade, showing minimum, maximum, and midpoint pay rates for that grade, as in Figure 11-5. (Specialists call this graph a *wage structure*. It graphically depicts the range of pay rates—in this case, per hour—paid for each pay grade.) Or you may depict the pay range on the vertical axis as steps or levels, with specific corresponding pay rates for each step within each grade. Table 11-4 shows the pay rates and steps for some federal government grades. As of the time of this pay schedule, for instance, employees in positions classified in grade GS-10 could be paid annual salaries between $39,969 and $51,964, depending on the level or step at which they were hired into the grade, the amount of time they were in the grade, and their merit increases (if any).

There are several reasons for employers to use pay ranges for each pay grade. First, it lets the employer take a more flexible stance in the labor market. For example, it makes it easier to attract experienced, higher-paid employees into a pay grade at the top of the range, since the starting salary for the pay grade's lowest step may be too low to attract them. Pay ranges also let companies provide for performance differences between employees within the same grade or between those with different seniorities. As in Figure 11-5, most employers structure their pay ranges to overlap a bit, so an employee in one grade who has more experience or seniority may earn more than an entry-level position in the next higher pay grade.

The wage line or curve usually anchors each pay range. The firm might then arbitrarily decide on a maximum and minimum rate for each grade, such as 15% above and below the wage line. As an alternative, some employers allow the pay range for each grade to become wider (covering more pay rates) for the higher pay ranges, reflecting the greater demands and performance variability inherent in more complex jobs.

Correcting Out-of-Line Rates   The wage rate for a particular job may fall well off the wage line or well outside the rate range for its grade, as shown in Figure 11-4. This means that the average pay for that job is currently too high or too low, relative to

Figure 11-5
Wage Structure

Note: This shows overlapping wage classes and maximum–minimum wage ranges.

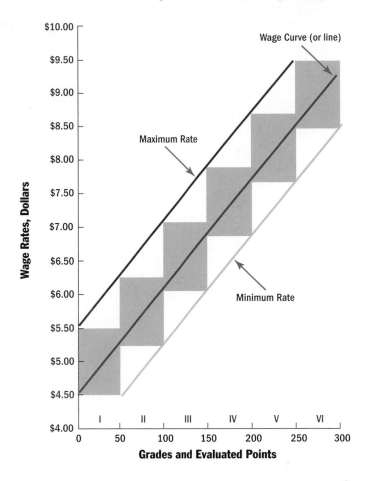

other jobs in the firm. You should raise the wages of underpaid employees to the minimum of the rate range for their pay grade.

Points falling above are a different story. These are "red circle," "flagged," or "overrates," and there are several ways to cope with this problem. One is to freeze the rate paid to employees until general salary increases bring the other jobs into line. A second option is to transfer or promote some or all of the employees involved to jobs for which you can legitimately pay them their current pay rates. The third option is to freeze the rate for six months, during which time you try to transfer or promote the overpaid employees. If you cannot, then cut the rate you pay these employees to the maximum in the pay range for their pay grade.

Table 11-4 **Federal Government Pay Schedule: Grades GS-8–GS-10, New York, Northern New Jersey, Long Island, January 2000**

	Annual Rates for Steps (in dollars)									
Grade	**1**	**2**	**3**	**4**	**5**	**6**	**7**	**8**	**9**	**10**
GS-8	32,859	33,954	35,049	36,145	37,140	38,335	39,430	40,525	41,620	42,715
GS-9	36,295	37,504	38,714	39,923	41,133	42,342	43,551	44,761	45,970	47,180
GS-10	39,969	41,302	42,635	43,967	45,300	46,633	47,966	42,298	50,631	51,964

Source: **info@fedamerica.com**.

When You're On Your Own
HR for Line Managers and Entrepreneurs

Developing a Workable Pay Plan

Developing a pay plan is as important in a small firm as a large one. Paying wage rates that are too high may be unnecessarily expensive, and paying less may guarantee inferior help and high turnover. And internally inequitable wage rates will reduce morale and cause endless badgering by employees demanding raises "the same as Joe down the hall." The president who wants to concentrate on major issues like sales would thus do well to institute a rational pay plan promptly.

First, conduct a wage survey. Four sources can be especially useful. The Sunday classified newspaper ads should yield useful information on wages offered for jobs similar to those you are trying to price. Second, local Job Service "One Stop" offices can provide a wealth of information, as they compile extensive information on pay ranges and averages for many of the jobs listed on O*NET. Third, local employment agencies, always anxious to establish ties that could grow into business relationships, should be able to provide good data. Fourth, the Internet and Web sites like Salary.com can yield a wealth of information on area pay rates.

Smaller firms are making use of the Internet in other ways. StockHouse Media Corp., is an international provider of online financial content and community development products with 210 employees from the United States to Canada, Japan, and Singapore. Shawnee Love, the firm's global HR director, makes extensive use of the Web for determining salaries for all the firm's personnel. For example, she uses e-mail to request salary data from professional groups like the Society for Human Resource Management, and surfs the Internet to monitor rates and trends by periodically checking job boards, company Web sites, and industry associations. "We source information that is both industry related as well as functionally related and of varying geographies, such as state, provincial, countrywide versus marketing, sales, HR, tech, etc.," she says.[33]

If you employ more than 20 employees or so, conduct at least a rudimentary job evaluation. You will need job descriptions, since these will be the source of data regarding the nature and worth of each job. Checking a Web site like JobDescription.com can be useful here.

You may find it easier to split employees into three clusters—managerial/professional, office/clerical, and plant personnel. For each of the three groups, choose compensable factors and then rank or assign points to each job based on the job evaluation. For each job or class of jobs (such as assemblers), you will want to create a pay range. In general, you should choose as the midpoint of that range the target salary required by your job evaluation, and then produce a range of about 30% around this average, broken into a total of five steps. (Thus, assemblers might earn from $6.00 to $9.60 per hour, in five steps.)

As noted earlier in this chapter, compensation policies are important, too. For example, you need a policy on when and how to compute raises. Many small business owners make the mistake of appraising employees on their anniversary date, a year after they are hired. The problem here is that the raise for one employee then becomes the standard for the next, as employees have time to compare notes. This produces a never-ending cycle of appraisals and posturing for ever-higher raises.

The better alternative is to have a policy of once-a-year raises following a standard one-week appraisal period, preferably about four weeks before you produce the budget for next year. In this way, the administrative headache of conducting these appraisals and awarding raises is dealt with during a one-week (or two-week) period, and the raises are known before the budget is compiled. Other required compensation policies include amount of holiday and vacation pay (as explained in Chapter 13), overtime pay policy, method of pay (weekly, biweekly, monthly), garnishments, and time card or sign-in sheet procedures. (For sources of sample policies, see the HR systems discussion on p. 101.) The small business owner can then use the checklist in Figure 11-6 to judge the new plan's completeness.

Figure 11-6
Compensation
Administration Checklist

A good compensation administration program is comprehensive and flexible and ensures optimum performance from employees at all levels. The following checklist may be used to evaluate a company's program. The more questions answered "yes," the more thorough has been the planning for compensation administration.
Source: Reprinted from www.HR.BLR.com with permission of the publisher, © 2004 Business and Legal Reports Inc., 141 Mill Rock Road East, Old Saybrook, CT.

	Yes	No
• Is your plan for salary administration in writing?	☐	☐
• Do you have stated goals for your plan, such as:		
—Compliance with applicable law?	☐	☐
—Consistently rewarding performance?	☐	☐
—Attracting quality employees?	☐	☐
—Reducing turnover?	☐	☐
• Does your plan include the following topics?	☐	☐
—Annual wage and hour surveys?	☐	☐
—Explanations for salary schedules?	☐	☐
—Evaluations of job classifications?	☐	☐
—Premium, bonus, vacation pay?	☐	☐
—Paid medical leave, long-term disability?	☐	☐
—Temporary positions, part-time positions?	☐	☐
• Is there a written analysis for each job in your company?	☐	☐
• Does each analysis include a listing of the following job requirements?	☐	☐
—Knowledge/skills/experience/personal characteristics?	☐	☐
• Do you periodically review and update each job description?	☐	☐
• Have you set salary ranges for each job category?	☐	☐
• Do you provide regular, written performance evaluations for employees?	☐	☐
• Are the evaluations used to decide promotions and pay increases?	☐	☐
• Do you communicate your job evaluation plan to your employees through:	☐	☐
—Orientation/supervisors?	☐	☐
—Bulletin boards/handbooks?	☐	☐
• Have you developed a written system of merit increases?	☐	☐
• Do you have stated goals for the system, such as:	☐	☐
—Increase productivity/quality?	☐	☐
—Reduce errors/cost?	☐	☐
• Do you respond to suggestions from employees about your compensation plan?	☐	☐

3 Explain how to price managerial and professional jobs.

PRICING MANAGERIAL AND PROFESSIONAL JOBS

Developing compensation plans for managers or professionals is similar in many respects to developing plans for any employee. The basic aim is the same: to attract and keep good employees. And job evaluation—classifying jobs, ranking them, or assigning points to them, for instance—is as applicable to managerial and professional jobs as to production and clerical ones.

There are some big differences, though. For one thing, job evaluation provides only a partial answer to the question of how to pay managers and professionals. These jobs tend to stress harder-to-quantify factors like judgment and problem solving more than do production and clerical jobs. There is also more emphasis on paying managers and professionals based on results—based on their performance or on what they can do—rather than on the basis of static job demands like working conditions. Developing compensation plans for managers and professionals therefore tends to be relatively complex. Job evaluation, while still important, usually plays a secondary role to nonsalary issues like bonuses, incentives, and benefits.

Compensating Managers

Compensation for a company's top executives usually consists of four main elements: base pay, short-term incentives, long-term incentives, and executive benefits and perks.[34] *Base pay* includes the person's fixed salary as well as, often, guaranteed bonuses such as "10% of pay at the end of the fourth fiscal quarter, regardless of whether or not the company makes a profit." *Short-term incentives* are usually cash or stock bonuses for achieving short-term goals, such as year-to-year increases in sales revenue. *Long-term incentives* aim to encourage the executive to take actions that drive up the value of the company's stock, and include things like stock options; these generally give the executive the right to purchase stock at a specific price for a specific period. Finally, *executive benefits and perks* might include supplemental executive retirement pension plans, supplemental life insurance, and health insurance without a deductible or coinsurance. With so many complicated elements, employers must be alert to the tax and securities law implications of their executive compensation decisions.[35]

What Really Determines Executive Pay?   Salary is the cornerstone of executive compensation; it's the element on which employers layer benefits, incentives, and perquisites—all normally bestowed in proportion to base pay. Executive compensation emphasizes performance incentives more than do other employees' pay plans, since organizational results are likely to reflect executives' contributions more directly than those of lower-echelon employees. Incentives equal 31% or more of a typical executive's base pay in many countries, including the United States, United Kingdom, France, and Germany.[36] We'll discuss short- and long-term incentives in Chapter 13.

The traditional wisdom is that company size significantly affects top managers' salaries. Yet studies show that the usual standards, like company size and company performance, explain only about 30% of the variation in CEO pay. Instead, each firm seems to take a unique approach: "In reality, CEO pay is set by the board taking into account a variety of factors such as the business strategy, corporate trends, and most importantly where they want to be in a short and long term."[37] Another study concluded that CEOs' pay depends on the complexity and unpredictability of the decisions they make.[38] In this study, complexity was a function of such things as the number of businesses controlled by the CEO's firm, the number of corporate officers in each firm, and the level of R&D and capital investment activity.[39] Regardless of performance, firms paid CEOs based on the complexity of the jobs they filled.

In any event, shareholder activism has tightened the restrictions on what top executives are paid.[40] For example, the Securities and Exchange Commission now has rules regarding executive compensation communications. The company must disclose the chief executive officer's pay, as well as other officers' pay if their compensation (salary and bonus) exceeds $100,000. One result is that boards of directors must act responsibly in reviewing and setting executive pay. That, says one expert, includes determining the key performance requirements of the executive's job; assessing the appropriateness of the firm's current compensation practices; conducting a pay-for-performance survey; and testing shareholder acceptance of the board's pay proposals.[41] The government also changed the federal tax code in the early 1990s to make CEO pay above $1 million a year nondeductible as a corporate business expense if the pay was not related to performance.[42]

Increasingly, shareholders are rebelling at what they see as excessive executive pay, particularly when their companies are less than successful. For example, shareholders in the pharmaceutical firm GlaxoSmithKline voted to reject the board's recommendation to pay its chief executive $35 million if he lost his job and to enhance the pension plans of both him and his wife.[43]

The bottom line is that boards are reducing the relative importance of base salary while boosting the emphasis on performance-based pay.[44] The big issue here is identifying the appropriate performance standards and then determining how to link these to pay. Typical short-term measures of shareholder value include revenue growth and operating profit margin. Long-term shareholder value measures include rate of return above some predetermined base, and what is known as economic value added. (We'll discuss these in Chapter 12.)

Performance-based pay can focus a manager's attention. When heavy truck production tumbled, CEO Joseph Magliochetti saw sales of his auto parts maker Dana Corp. drop by 6%, and profits by 44%. At the end of the year, he still got his $850,000 salary. But his board of directors eliminated his bonus and stock grant, which the year before had earned him $1.8 million. The board said he had failed to beat the profit goals it had set for him.[45]

Managerial Job Evaluation   Despite questions about the rationality of executive pay, job evaluation is still important in pricing executive and managerial jobs in most large firms. The basic approach is to classify all executive and management positions into a series of grades, to which a series of salary ranges is attached.

As with nonmanagerial jobs, one alternative is to rank the executive and management positions in relation to each other, grouping those of equal value. However, firms also use the job classification and point evaluation methods, with compensable factors like position scope, complexity, difficulty, and creative demands. Job analysis, salary surveys, and the fine-tuning of salary levels around wage curves also play central roles.

Compensating Professional Employees

Compensating nonsupervisory professional employees like engineers and scientists presents unique problems.[46] Analytical jobs like these emphasize creativity and problem solving, compensable factors not easily compared or measured. Furthermore, how do you measure performance? The professional's economic impact on the firm often relates only indirectly to his or her actual efforts. For example, the success of an engineer's invention depends on many factors, like how well the firm markets it.

Employers can use job evaluation for professional jobs. Compensable factors here tend to focus on problem solving, creativity, job scope, and technical knowledge and expertise. Firms use the point method and factor comparison methods, although job classification seems most popular. (Here, recall that you slot jobs into grades based on grade descriptions.) Yet in practice, firms rarely use traditional job evaluation methods for professional jobs, since it is so difficult to quantify factors such as creativity that make a difference in professional work.

Most employers use a market-pricing approach. They price professional jobs in the marketplace as best they can, to establish the values for benchmark jobs. Then they slot these benchmark jobs and their other professional jobs into a salary structure. Each professional discipline (like engineering or R&D) usually ends up having four to six grade levels, each with a broad salary range. This helps employers remain competitive when bidding for professionals whose skills and attainments vary widely, and who literally have global employment possibilities.[47]

Discuss competency-based pay and other current trends in compensation.

● COMPETENCY-BASED PAY

Introduction

We've seen that employers traditionally base a job's pay on the relative worth of the job. The compensation team compares jobs—actually, compares each job's set of duties—using compensable factors such as effort and responsibility. This allows them (1) to compare jobs to one another (as in, "based on its duties, this job seems to require about twice the effort of that one"), and (2) to assign internally equitable pay rates for each job. Thus, the pay rate for the job principally depends on the job itself, not on who is doing it.

For reasons which we'll explain shortly, an increasing number of compensation experts and employers are moving away from assigning pay rates to jobs based on the jobs' numerically rated, intrinsic duties. Instead, they advocate basing the job's pay rate on the level of "competencies" the job demands of those who fill it.[48] "Title and tenure have been replaced with performance and competencies," is how one expert puts it.[49] Compensation specialists call this second approach *competency-based pay*.

What Is Competency-based Pay?

competency-based pay
Where the company pays for the employee's range, depth, and types of skills and knowledge, rather than for the job title he or she holds.

In a nutshell, **competency-based pay** is where the company pays for the employee's range, depth, and types of skills and knowledge, rather than for the job title he or she holds.[50] Experts variously call it competence-, knowledge-, or skill-based pay. With competency-based pay, an employee in a class I job who could (but may not have to at the moment) do class II work gets paid as a class II worker, not a class I. We can simply define **competencies** as "demonstrable characteristics of the person, including knowledge, skills, and behaviors, that enable performance."[51]

competencies
Demonstrable characteristics of a person, including knowledge, skills, and behaviors, that enable performance.

Unfortunately (as we explained in chapter 4), there's some confusion over what exactly "competencies" means. Different organizations define "competencies" in somewhat different ways. Some, like the U.S. Office of Personnel Management, take a broader approach. They use "competencies" synonymously with the knowledge, or skills, or abilities required to do the job. Another approach is to express competencies more narrowly, in terms of measurable behaviors.[52] Here, you would identify the job's required competencies by completing the phrase, "In order to perform this job competently, the employee should be able to . . . ".[53]

Whether narrowly or broadly defined, several things distinguish the competency-based pay approach. Employees build job competencies through *experience* on the same or similar jobs. And, competency-based pay ties the person's pay to his or her competencies—pay is more *person oriented*. Employees here get paid based on what they can do—even if, at the moment, they don't have to do it. Traditional job evaluation–based pay plans tie the worker's pay to the worth of the job based on the job's duties—pay here is more *job oriented*. Employees are paid mostly based on what their current jobs demand.

In practice, competency-based pay usually comes down to using one or both of two basic types of pay programs: *pay for knowledge* or *skill-based pay*.[54] Pay-for-knowledge pay plans reward employees for learning organizationally relevant knowledge—for instance, you might pay a new waiter more once he or she memorizes the menu. With skill-based pay, the employee earns more after developing organizationally relevant skills—Microsoft pays programmers more as they master the skill of writing new programs.

Why Use Competency-Based Pay?

Why pay employees based on the skill, knowledge, or competency level they achieve, rather than based on the duties of the jobs they're assigned to? For example, why pay an Accounting Clerk II who has achieved a certain mastery of accounting techniques the same (or more than) someone who is an Accounting Clerk IV? There are several good reasons for doing so.

First, traditional pay plans may actually backfire if a *high-performance work system* is your goal. The whole thrust of these systems is to encourage employees to work in a self-motivated way, by organizing the work around teams, by encouraging team members to rotate freely among jobs (each with its own skill set), by pushing more responsibility for things like day-to-day supervision down to the workers, and by organizing work around projects or processes where jobs may blend or overlap. In such systems, you obviously want employees to be enthusiastic about learning and moving among other jobs. Pigeonholing workers by classifying them too narrowly into jobs based on the job's points may actually discourage such enthusiasm and flexibility.

There is evidence that analytical types of job evaluation (such as the point or factor comparison methods) do conflict with the high-performance work approach.[55] In one study, the researchers found that "workplaces in which the high-performance approach has been most fully implemented are less likely to have the more formal, analytical type of job evaluation. Furthermore, those [workplaces] with both analytical job evaluation and the high-performance work system are less likely to have high above average financial performance than those with either of these on a single basis."[56] The less quantitative, more subjective job evaluation methods such as classifying, grading, or ranking jobs didn't seem to be a problem.

Second, paying for skills, knowledge, and competencies is *more strategic*. For example, Canon's strategic emphasis on miniaturization and precision manufacturing means it should reward some employees based on the skills and knowledge they develop in these two strategically crucial areas, not just based on the jobs to which they're assigned.

Third, measurable skills, knowledge, and competencies are the heart of any company's *performance management process*. As at Canon, achieving the firm's strategic goals means that employees must apply certain skills and competencies. In performance management terms, its employees' goals, training, appraisals, and rewards must therefore focus in an integrated way on nurturing these skills and competencies. At Canon, this might mean, for some employees, setting goals for and training, appraising, and paying them based on their miniaturization and precision manufacturing competencies.

Competency-Based Pay in Practice

In practice, skill/competency/knowledge–based pay programs generally contain four main components: (1) a system that defines specific skills, and a process for tying the person's pay to his or her skill; (2) a training system that lets employees seek and acquire skills; (3) a formal competency testing system; and (4) a work design that lets employees move among jobs to permit work assignment flexibility.[57]

For example, a General Mills manufacturing facility implemented one such plan.[58] This facility paid workers based on attained skill levels. Management created four clusters (or "blocks") of jobs, corresponding to the four production areas: mixing, filling, packaging, and materials. Within each block, workers could attain three levels of skill.

Level 1 indicates limited ability, such as knowledge of basic facts and ability to perform simple tasks without direction.[59] Level 2 means the employee attained partial proficiency and could, for instance, apply technical principles on the job. Attaining Level 3 means the employee is fully competent in the area and could, for example, analyze and solve production problems. Each production block had a different average wage rate. There were, therefore, 12 pay levels (four blocks with three pay levels each) in the plant.

General Mills set the wages for the 12 skill levels (four blocks with three levels each) in part by making the pay for the lowest of the three pay levels in each block equal to the average entry-level pay rate for similar jobs in the community. A new employee could start in any block, but always at Level 1. If after several weeks he or she was certified at the next higher skill level, General Mills raised his or her salary. Employees freely rotated from block to block, as long as they could achieve Level 2 performance within their current block. The plan appeared to boost flexibility.

Competency-Based Pay: Pros, Cons, and Results

Competency-based pay has its detractors. Many companies report implementation problems when instituting competency-based pay.[60] Some pay experts point out that competency-based pay "ignores the cost implications of paying for knowledge, skills and behaviors even if they are not used."[61] There may also be simpler ways to encourage learning. For example, one aerospace firm has a quasi-skill-based pay program. It has all exempt employees negotiate "learning contracts" with their supervisors. The employees then get raises for meeting learning (skills-improvement) objectives.[62]

Whether skill-based pay improves productivity is an open question. When used in conjunction with team-building and worker involvement and empowerment programs, it does appear to lead to higher quality as well as lower absenteeism rates and fewer accidents.[63] A study of one such skill-based pay program concluded that it had probably resulted in about 58% greater productivity, 16% lower labor cost per part, and an 82% reduction in scrap, versus a comparison facility.[64] However, the findings in another firm, which are not conclusive, suggest that productivity was higher at its non-skill-based-pay facility.[65]

One thing to keep in mind is that if the skill-based pay program doesn't motivate employees to learn new skills, it will fail. Does it motivate the employee to seek and apply new skills? Here, the expectancy theory of motivation can be of some use. It sug-

To be successful, skill-based pay programs have to motivate employees like these workers at an Ameristeel fabrication plant to learn and apply new skills.

gests that the program's success will depend on the value to the employee of the improved pay associated with the new skills, the degree to which the employee sees skills improvement as actually leading to better pay, and the person's training, self-efficacy, and ability to successfully use the new skill.[66]

● OTHER COMPENSATION TRENDS

The movement toward competency-based pay is one important compensation trend. This section looks at two others: broadbanding, strategic compensation and comparable worth.

Broadbanding

Most firms end up with pay plans that slot jobs into classes or grades, each with its own vertical pay rate range. For example, the U.S. government's pay plan consists of 18 main grades (GS-1 to GS-18), each with its own pay range. For an employee whose job falls in one of these grades, the pay range for that grade dictates his or her minimum and maximum salary.

The question is, "How wide should the salary grades be, in terms of the number of job evaluation points they include?" (For example, might the U.S. government want to collapse its 18 salary grades into six or seven broader bands?) There is a downside to having narrow grades. For instance, if you want someone whose job is in grade 2 to fill in for a time in a job that happens to be in grade 1, it's difficult to reassign that person without lowering his or her salary. Similarly, if you want the person to learn about a job that happens to be in grade 3, the employee might object to the reassignment without a corresponding raise to grade 3 pay. Traditional grade pay plans thus breed inflexibility.

That is why some firms are broadbanding their pay plans. **Broadbanding** means collapsing salary grades and ranges into just a few wide levels or bands, each of which contains a relatively wide range of jobs and salary levels. Figure 11-7 illustrates this. In this case the company's previous six pay grades are consolidated into two broad bands.

A company may create broadbands for all its jobs, or for specific groups such as managers or professionals. The pay rate range of each broadband is relatively large, since it ranges from the minimum pay of the lowest grade the firm merged into the broadband up to the maximum pay of the highest merged grade. Thus, for example, instead of having 10 salary grades, each of which contains a salary range of $15,000, the firm might collapse the 10 grades into three broadbands, each with a set of jobs such that the difference between the lowest- and highest-paid jobs might be $40,000 or more. For the jobs that fall in this broadband, there is therefore a much wider range of pay rates. You can move employees from job to job within the broadband more easily, without worrying about the employees moving outside the relatively narrow rate range associated with a traditional narrow pay grade. Broadbanding therefore breeds flexibility.

Companies broadband for several reasons, most often to support strategic performance improvement initiatives. Broadbanding's basic advantage is that it injects greater flexibility into employee assignments.[67] It is especially sensible where firms flatten their hierarchies and organize into self-managing teams. The new, broad salary bands can include both supervisors and subordinates and also facilitate moving employees slightly up or down along the pay scale, without bumping the person into a new salary range. For example, "the employee who needs to spend time in a lower-level job to develop a certain skill set can receive higher-than-usual pay for the work, a circumstance considered impossible under traditional pay systems."[68] One expert argues that traditional quantitative evaluation plans actually reward unadaptability.[69] He argues that jobs narrowly defined by compensable factors such as "know-how" are unlikely to encourage job incumbents to be flexible. Instead, the tendency may be for workers to take a "that's not my job" attitude and to concentrate on their specific tasks.

broadbanding
Consolidating salary grades and ranges into just a few wide levels or "bands," each of which contains a relatively wide range of jobs and salary levels.

Figure 11-7
Broadbanded Structure and
How It Relates to Traditional
Pay Grades and Ranges

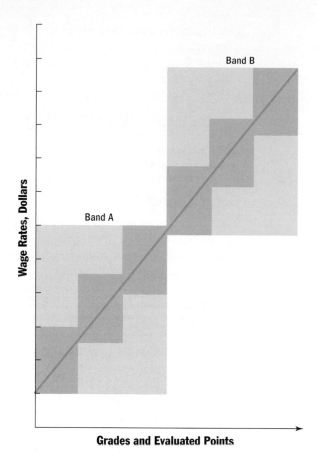

However, broadbanding can be unsettling, particularly for new employees. For example, Home Depot has used broadbanding for over 10 years, and "when employees want to learn something new, they play to the level [on that project] that they're capable of," says the firm's head of information systems. That is motivating once you get used to it. However, it can make a new employee feel adrift: "There's a sense of a permanence in the set of job responsibilities often attached to job titles," he says. That sense of permanence isn't nearly as clear when employees can (and are expected to) move frequently from project to project and job to job.[70]

A survey of 783 employers found that about 15% were using broadbanding.[71] One British company does so to support its strategy of cutting costs and flattening and downsizing the organization. The flattening meant fewer jobs, each of which had broader responsibilities, and broadbanding made it easier to get employees to assume their new, broader roles.[72] Dow Jones & Company implemented broadbanding for its 1,000 IT professionals several years ago.

Even with trends like competence/skill-based pay and broadbanding, 60% to 70% of U.S. firms use point and factor comparison plans. Job evaluation's relative ease of use and familiarity are probably the main reasons. And neither skill-based pay nor broadbanding eliminates the need for evaluating the worth of one job relative to others.[73]

Broadbanding involves several steps. First, you need to decide on the number of bands and how many points they will include, and assign each band a salary range. The bands usually have wide salary ranges and overlap substantially. A band may consist of a number of jobs, each with a market wage rate. More often, bands contain several skill levels. Workers must increase their skills and knowledge to get raises.

Strategic Compensation

As most everyone knows by now, IBM is a classic example of an organizational renewal. It dominated its industry through the early 1980s. But by the 1990s, it was failing to exploit new technologies and losing touch with its customers.[74] Its board hired Louis Gerstner. His first strategic aim was to transform IBM from a sluggish giant to a lean winner.

Accomplishing this meant doing more than downsizing and reorganizing the firm; Gerstner had to transform IBM's culture—the shared values, attitudes, and behavior patterns that guided employees' behavior. He sought to emphasize winning, execution, speed, and decisiveness. He knew he had to use the compensation plan to support IBM's strategic aims.[75]

IBM's existing compensation pay plan did the opposite. Everyone in this huge company was in a job whose relative worth was based on a decades-old, point-factor-based job evaluation. What were some of the implications? For one thing, maintaining the point system for over 100,000 employees required "a massive and cumbersome" attention to point-factor-manual-based evaluations. This structure also cultivated a preoccupation with internal equity rather than with market-driven, competitive rates of pay. Gerstner knew he had to change the pay plan to drive the new culture he sought to create.

To change this situation, Gerstner's team made four major changes in what became the firm's new strategic compensation plan:

1. *The marketplace rules.* The company switched from its previous single salary structure (for nonsales employees) to different salary structures and merit budgets for different job families. This enabled IBM to take different compensation actions for different job families (for instance, for accountants, engineers, programmers, and so on). In particular, this enabled IBM to concentrate on paying employees in different job families in a more market-oriented way. The new approach sent the strong cultural signal that "a market-driven company must watch the market closely and act accordingly."[76]

2. *Fewer jobs, evaluated differently, in broadbands.* Second, IBM scrapped its point-factor job evaluation system and its traditional salary grades. The new system has no points at all. The old system contained 10 different compensable factors; the new one slots jobs into 10 bands based on just three (skills, leadership requirements, and scope/impact).

   In the United States, the number of separate job titles dropped from over 5,000 to fewer than 1,200[77] and 24 salary grades dropped to 10 broadbands. This communicated a new organizational model: IBM was to be a flatter organization that could "deliver goods and services to market faster."[78]

3. *Managers manage.* The previous compensation plan based raises on a complex comparison that linked performance appraisal scores to salary increases measured in tenths of a percent. The new system is streamlined. Managers get a budget and some coaching, the essence of which is: "Either differentiate the pay you give to stars versus acceptable performers or the stars won't be around too long."[79] The new approach lets managers rank employees on a variety of factors (such as critical skills, and results). The managers decide which factors are used and what weights they're given.

4. *Big stakes for stakeholders.* As IBM was floundering in the early 1990s, every nonexecutive employee's cash compensation (outside the sales division) consisted of base salary (plus overtime, shift premiums, and some other adjustments). Pay for performance was a foreign concept. Within a year or two after Gerstner arrived, most IBM employees around the world "had 10% or more of their total cash compensation tied to performance."[80] In the new system, there are only three performance appraisal ratings. "A top-rated employee receives two-and-one-half times the award of an employee with the lowest ranking. (Awards are calibrated as percentages of pensionable earnings.)[81]

The changes at IBM illustrate the nuts and bolts of *strategic compensation*, which means using the compensation plan to support the company's strategic aims. IBM's new pay plan refocused its employees' attention on the values of winning, execution, and speed, and on being better, faster, and more competitive. The "HR Scorecard" feature shows how the Hotel Paris applied principles like these in creating its own strategy-oriented compensation plan.

Comparable Worth

comparable worth
The concept by which women who are usually paid less than men can claim that men in comparable rather than in strictly equal jobs are paid more.

Comparable worth refers to the requirement to pay men and women equal wages for jobs that are of *comparable* (rather than strictly *equal*) value to the employer. In its broadest sense, comparable worth may mean comparing quite dissimilar jobs, such as nurses to truck mechanics or secretaries to technicians.[82] The problem "comparable worth" seeks to address is this: women often have jobs that are quite dissimilar to those of men. Should you pay women who are performing jobs *equal* to men's or just *comparable* to men's the same as men? If it's only for equal jobs, then the tendency may be to limit pay comparisons to other lower paid jobs in which women predominate. This is the basic issue in comparable worth.

For years, "equal" was the standard in the United States, though "comparable" was and is used in Canada and many European countries.[83] As a result of court rulings, some experts[84] believe that comparable worth may become more important in the United States.[85] This issue is not going away. For example, representative Eleanor Holmes Norton (D-DC) has advocated a new "fair pay act" under which employers would have to provide equal pay for different but "comparable" jobs.[86]

County of Washington v. Gunther (1981) was a pivotal case for comparable worth. It involved Washington County, Oregon, prison matrons who claimed sex discrimination. The county had evaluated comparable but nonequal men's jobs as having 5% more "job content" (based on a point evaluation system) than the women's jobs, but paid the men 35% more.[87] After seesawing through the courts to the U.S. Supreme Court, Washington County finally agreed to pay 35,000 employees in female-dominated jobs almost $500 million in pay raises over seven years to settle the suit.

Comparable worth has implications for job evaluation procedures. Virtually every comparable worth case that reached a court involved the use of the point method of job evaluation. (Here, you'll recall, each job is evaluated in terms of several factors like effort, skill, and responsibility, and then assigned points based on the degree of each factor present in the job.) Point plans therefore facilitate comparability ratings among different jobs.

So, can firms still use point-type plans? Perhaps the wisest approach is for employers to price their jobs as they see fit (with or without point plans), but to ensure that women have equal access to all jobs. In other words, eliminate the wage discrimination issue by eliminating sex-segregated jobs.

All this notwithstanding, the fact is that women in the United States still earn only about 77% as much as men. However, generation X women—those aged 25 to 34—earned about 82% of what men in the same age group earned in 2000, up from 70% in 1979. They also increased their presence in executive, administrative, and managerial occupations from about 9% in 1983 to 16% in 2000.[88]

What accounts for such differences? One specialist cites four factors: women's starting salaries are traditionally lower, because employers traditionally view them as having less leverage; salary increases for women in professional jobs do not reflect their above-average performance, whereas men with equal performance receive bigger raises; in white-collar jobs, men tend to change jobs more frequently, which enables them to be promoted to higher-level jobs over women with more seniority; and in blue-collar jobs, women tend to be placed in departments with lower-paying jobs.[89] Employers can and should establish procedures to eliminate such inequitable practices.

The HR Scorecard
Strategy and Results

The New Compensation Plan

The Hotel Paris's competitive strategy is "To use superior guest service to differentiate the Hotel Paris properties, and to thereby increase the length of stay and return rate of guests, and thus boost revenues and profitability." HR manager Lisa Cruz must now formulate functional policies and activities that support this competitive strategy, by eliciting the required employee behaviors and competencies.

A preliminary analysis, performed jointly by Lisa and the Hotel Paris's chief financial officer, left them optimistic that HR could contribute measurably to achieving the hotel's strategic aims. Several employee competencies and behaviors including employee morale, employee commitment, and the percent of arriving guests receiving the hotel's required greeting had significant effects on customer and organizational outcomes such as guest satisfaction and frequency of guest returns. In turn, outcomes like these contributed measurably to the Hotel Paris's strategic goals, including profit margins, market share, and scores on industry satisfaction surveys. Lisa and her team now turn to creating a compensation plan that will help to produce the required employee competencies and behaviors. The accompanying HR Scorecard (Figure 11-8) outlines the relationships involved.

Even the most casual review by Lisa Cruz and the CFO made it clear that the company's compensation plan wasn't designed to support the firm's new strategic goals. For one thing, they knew that they should pay somewhat more, on average, than did their competitors if they expected employees to consistently exceed expectations when it came to serving guests. Yet their review of a variety of metrics (including the Hotel Paris's salary/competitive salary ratios, the total compensation expense per employee, and the target percentile for total compensation) suggested that in virtually all job categories the Hotel Paris paid no more than average, and, occasionally, paid somewhat less.

The current compensation policies had also bred what one hotel manager called an "I don't care" attitude on the part of most employees. What she meant was that most Hotel Paris employees quickly learned that regardless of what their performance was, they always ended up getting paid about the same as employees who performed better and worse than they did. So, the firm's compensation plan actually created a disconnect between pay and

performance: It was not channeling employees' behaviors toward those required to achieve the company's goals. In some ways, it was doing the opposite.

Lisa and the CFO knew they had to institute a new, strategic compensation plan. They wanted a plan that improved employee morale, contributed to employee commitment, reduced employee turnover, and rewarded (and thus encouraged) the sorts of service-oriented behaviors that boosted guest satisfaction. After meeting with the company's CEO and the Board, the CFO gave Lisa the go-ahead to redesign the company's compensation plan, with the overall aim of creating a new plan that would support the company's strategic aims.

Lisa and her team (which included a consulting compensation expert) set numerous new measurable compensation policies for the Hotel Paris, and these new policies formed the heart of the new compensation plan. A new job evaluation study provided a more rational and fair basis upon which the company could assign pay rates. A formal compensation survey by the consultant established, for the first time at the Hotel Paris, a clear picture of what competitive hotels and similar businesses were paying in each geographic area, and enabled the Hotel Paris team to more accurately set targets for what each position at the hotel should be paying. Rather than just paying at the industry average, or slightly below, the new policy called for the Hotel Paris to move all its salaries into the 75th percentile over the next three years.

As they instituted the new compensation policies, Lisa and the CFO were pleased to learn from feedback from the various hotel managers that the latter were already noting several positive changes. The number of applicants for each position had increased by over 50% on average, turnover dropped by 80%, and surveys of morale and commitment were producing higher results. Lisa and her team now began to consider how to inject more of a "pay for performance" element into the company's compensation plan, perhaps by instituting new bonuses and incentives. We will see what she did in the following chapter.

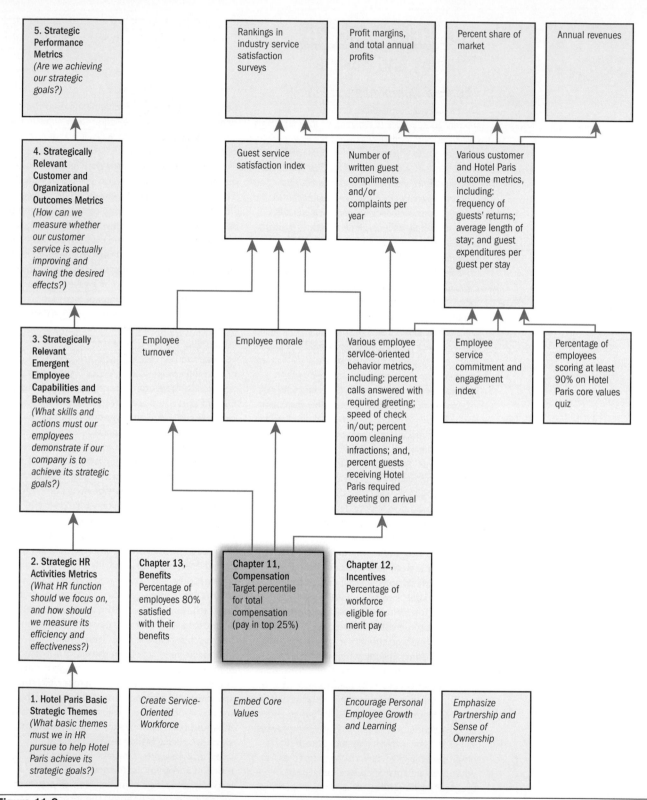

Figure 11-8
HR Scorecard for Hotel Paris International Corporation*

Note: *(An abbreviated example showing selected HR practices and outcomes aimed at implementing the competitive strategy, "To use superior guest services to differentiate the Hotel Paris properties and thus increase the length of stays and the return rate of guests and thus boost revenues and profitability")

For many employees, integrating their compensation programs with their HRIS is one of the more pressing current compensation trends. "Improving Productivity Through HRIS" shows how companies can do this.

Improving Productivity Through HRIS

Automating the Compensation Planning Process

All companies, whether large or small, must engage in *compensation planning*. Compensation planning is the process of ensuring that managers allocate salary increases equitably across the organization while staying within budget guidelines.[90] Usually, the company identifies set times during the year (called "focal reviews") when all the firm's managers review employees' performance, and match these with budgetary constraints and formulate pay raise recommendations for the coming year.

As employers like IBM have moved toward linking their compensation plans more closely with strategic considerations, the job of developing salary raise recommendations has become increasingly complex. It's no longer just a case of the manager allocating raises across the board, or allocating raises based just on performance appraisals. Instead, (as at IBM) numerous issues (including strategic concerns, geographic considerations, the effects of paying employees based on competencies rather than job duties, and the need to take into consideration a variety of elements including bonus payments and stock option grants) make allocating equitable raises while staying within budget quite a challenge.

Making raise decisions has always been cumbersome, even when there were fewer complexities involved. In the 1980s and early 1990s, employers used spreadsheets to administer these compensation planning periods. The firm's HR department would create individual spreadsheets for each manager, and the managers would use these to record their salary increase recommendations for all their subordinates. HR (and its compensation unit) would then have to assemble the spreadsheets by unit, department, division, and, finally, companywide. This was obviously a very labor-intensive and costly process.

In the late 1990s, firms began moving toward mainframe or client-server-based applications for facilitating this compensation planning process. This usually required developing custom-designed compensation planning software for each customer. It also tended to lack the flexibility most companies desired, for instance, to add new compensation components, such as when a company moves to competency-based pay.

Today, companies are moving toward intranet-based compensation planning programs. Using an intranet-based compensation planning application has many advantages. It lets the company control and distribute its application centrally, so that it can quickly update its compensation programs, without having to modify the software on individual managers' computers. Automating the system can also produce huge cost savings for even medium-sized businesses. For example, one company estimated that it cost them about $35 to complete a single manual compensation transaction (such as combining the raise budgets for two departments), but about $16 if it automated this process. Using a centralized application saves money in other ways. For example, employers often assign pay raise budgets to all their managers, only to find that (once the various department budgets all come together) the accumulated excess raises amount to millions of dollars. This generally doesn't happen with an automated system.

In acquiring a system like this for your company, there are several criteria to keep in mind. First, *look for the most intuitive, easiest to use application*. Second, make sure the application includes *decision-support tools* such as pop-up windows with guideline alerts, calculators, and additional supporting information to make it easy for managers to make intelligent compensation allocation decisions. Third, the application should be *flexible*, so that, for instance, the employer can easily add different pay raise components (merit pay, yearly bonuses, and so on) for various departments. Fourth, the application should be *robust*, in that it can easily handle all of the business rules and actual calculations that the system aims to support. Fifth, the compensation planning application has to be *compatible with a variety of HRIS* (such as payroll systems) so that the employer has no problem integrating systems from several vendors without costly code customization.

 *Review*

SUMMARY

1. There are two bases on which to pay employee compensation—increments of time and volume of production. The former includes hourly or daily wages and salaries. Basing pay on volume of production ties compensation directly to the amount of product (or number of "pieces") the worker generates.

2. Establishing pay rates involves five steps: Conduct salary surveys, evaluate jobs, develop pay grades, use wage curves, and fine-tune pay rates.

3. Job evaluation determines the relative worth of a job. It compares jobs to one another based on their content, which is usually defined in terms of compensable factors like skills, effort, responsibility, and working conditions.

4. The five-step ranking method of job evaluation is simple to use, but there is a tendency to rely too heavily on estimates. The classification (or grading) method is a second qualitative approach that categorizes jobs based on a class description or classification rules for each class.

5. Quantitative methods include the point method, which requires identifying a number of compensable factors and then determining the degree to which each of these factors is present in the job. The factor comparison method entails deciding which jobs have more of certain compensable factors than others.

6. Most managers group similar jobs into wage or pay grades for pay purposes. These are comprised of jobs of approximately equal difficulty or importance as determined by job evaluation.

7. Developing a compensation plan for executive, managerial, and professional personnel is complicated by the fact that factors like performance and creativity must take precedence over static factors like working conditions. Market rates, performance, and incentives and benefits thus play a much greater role than does job evaluation for these employees.

8. Competence-, knowledge-, or skill-based pay means paying for the employee's range, depth, and types of skills and knowledge, rather than for the job title he or she holds. We defined *competencies* as "demonstrable characteristics of the person, including knowledge, skills, and behaviors, that enable performance."

9. We listed three reasons for considering a competency-based pay plan. First, traditional pay plans may actually backfire if a *high-performance work system* is your goal. Second, paying for skills, knowledge, and competencies is *more strategic*. Third, measurable skills, knowledge, and competencies are the heart of any company's *performance management process*.

10. Other trends in compensation include broadbanding, strategic compensation, and adjustments for comparable worth.

DISCUSSION QUESTIONS

1. What is the difference between exempt and nonexempt jobs?

2. Should the job evaluation depend on an appraisal of the jobholder's performance? Why? Why not?

3. What is the relationship between compensable factors and job specifications?

4. Compare and contrast the following methods of job evaluation: ranking, classification, factor comparison, and point method.

5. What are the pros and cons of broadbanding, and would you recommend your current employer (or some other firm you're familiar with) use it? Why or why not?

6. It was recently reported in the news that the average pay for most university presidents ranged around $250,000 per year, but that a few earned much more. For example, the new president of Vanderblit received $852,000 in 2003. Discuss why you would (or would not) pay university presidents as much or more than many corporate CEO's.

7. Do small companies need to develop a pay plan? Why or why not?

INDIVIDUAL AND GROUP ACTIVITIES

1. Working individually or in groups, conduct salary surveys for the following positions: entry-level accountant and entry-level chemical engineer. What sources did you use, and what conclusions did you reach? If you were the HR

manager for a local engineering firm, what would you recommend that you pay for each job?

2. Working individually or in groups, develop compensation policies for the teller position at a local bank. Assume that

there are four tellers: two were hired in May and the other two were hired in December. The compensation policies should address the following: appraisals, raises, holidays, vacation pay, overtime pay, method of pay, garnishments, and time cards.

3. Working individually or in groups, access relevant online Web sites to determine what equitable pay ranges are for these jobs: chemical engineer, marketing manager, and HR manager, all with a bachelor's degree and five years of experience in the following cities: New York, New York; San Francisco, California; Houston, Texas; Denver, Colorado; Miami, Florida; Atlanta, Georgia; Chicago, Illinois; Birmingham, Alabama; Detroit, Michigan; and Washington, D.C. For each position in each city, what are the pay ranges and the average pay? Does geographical location impact the salaries of the different positions? If so, how?

4. The HRCI "Test Specifications" appendix at the end of this book (pages 685–689) lists the knowledge someone studying for the HRCI certification exam needs to have in each area of human resource management (such as in Strategic Management, Workforce Planning, and Human Resource Development). In groups of four to five students, do four things: (1) review that appendix now; (2) identify the material in this chapter that relates to the required knowledge the appendix lists; (3) write four multiple choice exam questions on this material that you believe would be suitable for inclusion in the HRCI exam; and (4) if time permits, have someone from your team post your team's questions in front of the class, so the students in other teams can take each others' exam questions.

5. Some of America's CEOs came under fire in 2004 because their pay seemed to some to be excessive, given their firms' performances. To choose just two of very many: Citigroup CEO Sandy Weill got a $29 million cash bonus, and Sprint's CEO Gary Forsee got $14 million. However, big institutional investors are no longer sitting back and not complaining. For example, TV's *Nightly Business Line* says that pension manager TIAA-CREF is talking to 50 companies about executive pay. What do you think it was about the period 2000–2004 that got so many big investors to rebel against "excessive" executive pay? Do you think they were right to make a fuss? Why?

EXPERIENTIAL EXERCISE

Ranking the College's Administrators

Purpose: The purpose of this exercise is to give you experience in performing a job evaluation using the ranking method.

Required Understanding: You should be thoroughly familiar with the ranking method of job evaluation and obtain job descriptions for your college's dean, department chairperson, director of admissions, library director, registrar, and your professor.

How to Set Up the Exercise/Instructions: Divide the class into groups of four or five students. The groups will perform a job

evaluation of the positions of dean, department chairperson, and professor using the ranking method.

1. Perform a job evaluation by ranking the jobs. You may use one or more compensable factors.

2. If time permits, a spokesperson from each group can put his or her group's rankings on the board. Did the groups end up with about the same results? How did they differ? Why do you think they differed?

APPLICATION CASE

Salary Inequities at Acme Manufacturing

Joe Black was trying to figure out what to do about a problem salary situation he had in his plant. Black recently took over as president of Acme Manufacturing. The founder and former president, Bill George, had been president for 35 years. The company was family owned and located in a small eastern Arkansas town. It had approximately 250 employees and was the largest employer in the community. Black was a member of the family that owned Acme, but he had never worked for the company prior to becoming president. He had an MBA and a law degree, plus five years of management experience with a large manufacturing organization, where he was senior vice president for human resources before making his move to Acme.

A short time after joining Acme, Black started to notice that there was considerable inequity in the pay structure for salaried employees. A discussion with the human resources director led him to believe that salaried employees' pay was very much a matter of individual bargaining with the past president. Hourly paid factory employees were not part of the problem because they were unionized and their wages were set by collective bargaining. An examination of the salaried payroll showed that there were 25 employees, ranging in pay from that of the president to that of the receptionist. A closer examination showed that 14 of the salaried employees were female. Three of these were front-line factory supervisors and one was the human resources director. The other 10 were nonmanagement.

This examination also showed that the human resources director appeared to be underpaid, and that the three female supervisors were paid somewhat less than any of the male supervisors. However, there were no similar supervisory jobs in which there were both male and female job incumbents. When asked, the HR director said she thought the female supervisors may have been paid at a lower rate mainly because they were women, and perhaps George, the former president, did not think that women needed as much money because they had working husbands. However, she added she personally thought that they were paid less because they supervised less-skilled employees than did the male supervisors. Black was not sure that this was true.

The company from which Black had moved had a good job evaluation system. Although he was thoroughly familiar with and capable in this compensation tool, Black did not have time to make a job evaluation study at Acme. Therefore, he decided to hire a compensation consultant from a nearby university to help him. Together, they decided that all 25 salaried jobs should be in the same job evaluation cluster; that a modified ranking method of job evaluation should be used; and that the job descriptions recently completed by the HR director were current, accurate, and usable in the study.

The job evaluation showed that the HR director and the three female supervisors were being underpaid relative to comparable male salaried employees.

Black was not sure what to do. He knew that if the underpaid female supervisors took the case to the local EEOC office, the company could be found guilty of sex discrimination and then have to pay considerable back wages. He was afraid that if he gave these women an immediate salary increase large enough to bring them up to where they should be, the male supervisors would be upset and the female supervisors might comprehend the total situation and want back pay. The HR director told Black that the female supervisors had never complained about pay differences.

The HR director agreed to take a sizable salary increase with no back pay, so this part of the problem was solved. Black believed he had four choices relative to the female supervisors:

1. To do nothing.
2. To gradually increase the female supervisors' salaries.
3. To increase their salaries immediately.
4. To call the three supervisors into his office, discuss the situation with them, and jointly decide what to do.

Questions

1. What would you do if you were Black?
2. How do you think the company got into a situation like this in the first place?
3. Why would you suggest Black pursue the alternative you suggested?

Source: This case was prepared by Professor James C. Hodgetts of the Fogelman College of Business and Economics of the University of Memphis. All names are disguised. Used by permission.

CONTINUING CASE

Carter Cleaning Company

The New Pay Plan

Carter Cleaning Centers does not have a formal wage structure nor does it have rate ranges or use compensable factors. Wage rates are based mostly on those prevailing in the surrounding community and are tempered with an attempt on the part of Jack Carter to maintain some semblance of equity between what workers with different responsibilities in the stores are paid.

Needless to say, Carter does not make any formal surveys when determining what his company should pay. He peruses the want ads almost every day and conducts informal surveys among his friends in the local chapter of the laundry and cleaners trade association. While Jack has taken a "seat-of-the-pants" approach to paying employees, his salary schedule has been guided by several basic pay policies. While many of his colleagues adhere to a policy of paying absolutely minimum rates, Jack has always followed a policy of paying his employees about 10% above what he feels are the prevailing rates, a policy that he believes reduces turnover while fostering employee loyalty. Of somewhat more concern to Jennifer is her father's informal policy of paying men about 20% more than women for the same job. Her father's explanation is, "They're stronger and can work harder for longer hours, and besides they all have families to support."

Questions

1. Is the company at the point where it should be setting up a formal salary structure based on a complete job evaluation? Why?
2. Is Jack Carter's policy of paying 10% more than the prevailing rates a sound one, and how could that be determined?
3. Similarly, is Carter's male–female differential wise and if not, why not?
4. Specifically, what would you suggest Jennifer do now with respect to her company's pay plan?

KEY TERMS

employee compensation, 390

direct financial payments, 390

indirect financial payments, 390

Davis-Bacon Act (1931), 390

Walsh-Healey Public Contract Act
(1936), 390

Title VII of the 1964 Civil Rights
Act, 390

Fair Labor Standards Act
(1938), 391

Equal Pay Act (1963), 391

Employee Retirement Income
Security Act (ERISA), 391

salary compression, 396

salary survey, 398

benchmark job, 398

job evaluation, 400

compensable factor, 400

ranking method, 402

job classification (or grading)
method, 403

classes, 403

grades, 403

grade definition, 403

point method, 404

factor comparison method, 404

pay grade, 405

wage curve, 405

pay ranges, 406

competency-based pay, 412

competencies, 412

broadbanding, 415

comparable worth, 418

ENDNOTES

1. Richard Henderson, *Compensation Management* (Reston, VA: Reston, 1980); Joseph Martocchio, *Strategic Compensation*, (Upper Saddle River, NJ: Prentice Hall, 2004), pp. 44–60.

2. "The Evolution of Compensation," *Workplace Visions*, The Society for Human Resource Management, 2002, p. 2, www.dol.gov/esa/minwage/america.htm, accessed June 3, 2004.

3. For a description of exemption requirements see Jeffrey Friedman, "The Fair Labor Standards Act Today: A Primer," *Compensation*, (January/February 2002) pp. 51–54.

4. www.dol.gov/_sec/media/speeches/541_Side_By_Side.htm, and "FLSA Exemptions Flow Chart," www.shrm.org.

5. "Employer Ordered to Pay $2 Million in Overtime," *BNA Bulletin to Management*, September 26, 1996, pp. 308–309. See also "Restaurant Managers Awarded $2.9 Million in Overtime Wages for Nonmanagement Work," *BNA Bulletin to Management*, August 30, 2001, p. 275.

6. Robert Nobile, "How Discrimination Laws Affect Compensation," *Compensation and Benefits Review*, July/August 1996, pp. 38–42.

7. Kenneth Sovereign, *Personnel Law* (Upper Saddle River, NJ: Prentice Hall, 1999), p. 165.

8. Ibid., p. 215.

9. "Microsoft Agrees to Pay $96.9 Million to Settle Contingent Workers' Lawsuits," *BNA Bulletin to Management*, December 14, 2000, p. 395.

10. Henderson, *Compensation Management*, pp. 101–127; see also Barry Hirsch and Edward Schumacher, "Unions, Wages, and Skills," *Journal of Human Resources* 33, no. 1 (Winter 1998), p. 115.

11. Jack Dolmat-Connell, "Developing a Reward Strategy That Delivers Shareholder and Employee Value," *Compensation and Benefits Review* March/April 1999, pp. 46–53.

12. Note that the assumption that low wage rates make a firm more competitive may be a "dangerous myth." It's the firm's overall relative labor costs that determine how competitive it will be, and such costs are driven not just by pay rates but by productivity. As one expert points out, "managers should remember that the issue is not just what you pay people, but also what they produce." Jeffrey Pfeffer, "Six Dangerous Myths About Pay," *Harvard Business Review*, May/June 1998, pp. 109–119.

13. David Figlio, "Better Qualified Teachers?" *Industrial and Labor Relations Review* 55, no. 4 (July 2002), pp. 686–700.

14. Carla Joinson, "Pay Attention to Pay Cycles," *HR Magazine*, November 1998, pp. 71–78.

15. Nicholas Wade, "Play Fair: Your Life May Depend on It," *New York Times*, September 12, 2003, p. 12.

16. Robert Bretz and Stephen Thomas, "Perceived Inequity, Motivation, and Final Offer Arbitration in Major League Baseball," *Journal of Applied Psychology*, June 1992, pp. 280–289.

17. David Terpstra and Andre Honoree, "The Relative Importance of External, Internal, Individual, and Procedural Equity to Pay Satisfaction," *Compensation and Benefits Review*, November/December 2003, pp. 67–74.

18. Jack Anderson, "Compensating Your Overseas Executives, Part II: Europe in 1992," *Compensation and Benefits Review*, July/August 1990, p. 28.

19. This is based on ibid., pp. 29–31. See also Maureen Minehan, "The New 'Face' of Global Competition," *Global Workforce Magazine* 45, no. 12 (December 2000), pp. 4–5.

20. Richard Hodgetts and Fred Luthans, "U.S. Multinationals' Expatriates' Compensation Strategies," *Compensation and Benefits Review*, January/February 1993, pp. 57–62.

21. George Milkovich and Matt Bloom, "Rethinking International Compensation," *Compensation and Benefits Review* 30, no. 2 (January/February 1998), pp. 15–24.

22. Ibid., p. 68.

23. Vicki Kaman and Jodie Barr, "Employee Attitude Surveys for Strategic Compensation Management," *Compensation and Benefits Review*, January/February 1991, pp. 52–65.

24. Henderson, *Compensation Management*, pp. 260–269.

25. For more information on these surveys, see the company's brochure, "Domestic Survey References," Watson Wyatt Data Services, 218 Route 17 North, Rochelle Park, NJ 07662, 1998.

26. "International Sources of Salary Data," *Compensation and Benefits Review*, May/June 1998, p. 23.

27. Martocchio, *Strategic Compensation*, p. 138. See also Nona Tobin, "Can Technology Ease the Pain of Salary Surveys?" *Public Personnel Management* 31, no. 1 (Spring 2002), pp. 65–78.

28. You may have noticed that job analysis as discussed in Chapter 4 can be a useful source of information on compensable factors, as well as on job descriptions and job specifications. For example, a quantitative job analysis technique like the position analysis questionnaire generates quantitative information on the degree to which the following five basic factors are present in each job: having decision-making/communication/social responsibilities, performing skilled activities, being physically active, operating vehicles or equipment, and processing information. As a result, a job analysis technique like the PAQ is actually as (or some say, more) appropriate as a job evaluation technique (than for job analysis) in that jobs can be quantitatively compared to one another on those five dimensions and their relative worth thus ascertained. Another point worth noting is that you may find that a single set of compensable factors is not adequate for describing all your jobs. This is another reason why many managers therefore divide their jobs into job clusters. For example, you might have a separate job cluster for factory workers, for clerical workers, and for managerial personnel. You would then probably have a somewhat different set of compensable factors for each job cluster.

29. Michael Carrell and Christina Heavrin, Labor Relations and Collective Bargaining (Upper Saddle River, NJ: Prentice Hall, 2004) pp. 300–303.

30. Sondra O'Neal, "CAJE: Computer-Aided Job Evaluation for the 1990's," *Compensation and Benefits Review*, November/December 1990, pp. 14–19.

31. If you used the job classification method, then of course the jobs are already classified.

32. In other words, on the graph, plot the benchmark jobs' points (as determined by job evaluation) and their corresponding market pay rates (as determined by the salary survey). Then slot in the other jobs based on their evaluations, to determine what their target pay rates should be.

33. Susan Marks, "Can the Internet Help You Hit the Salary Mark?" *Workforce*, January 2001, pp. 86–93.

34. Mark Meltzer and Howard Goldsmith, "Executive Compensation for Growth Companies," *Compensation and Benefits Review*, November/December 1997, pp. 41–50.

35. Douglas Tormey, "Executive Compensation: Creating 'Legal' Checklist," *Compensation and Benefits Review*, July/August 1996, pp. 12–36. See also Bruce Ellig, "Executive Pay: A Primer," *Compensation and Benefits Review*, January/February 2003, pp. 44–50.

36. "Executive Pay," *Wall Street Journal*, April 11, 1996, pp. R16, R170, and Fay Hansen, "Current Trends in Compensation and Benefits," *Compensation and Benefits Review*, v. 36, no. 2 (March/April 2004), pp. 7–8.

37. James Reda, "Executive Pay Today and Tomorrow," *Corporate Board* 22, no. 126 (January 2001), p. 18.

38. Andrew Henderson and James Frederickson, "Information-Processing Demands as a Determinant of CEO Compensation," *Academy of Management Journal* 39, no. 2 (1996), pp. 576–606.

39. Ibid., pp. 585–586.

40. William White, "Managing the Board Review of Executive Pay," *Compensation and Benefits Review*, November/December 1992, pp. 35–41.

41. Ibid., pp. 38–40; see also H. Anthony Hampson, "Tying CEO Pay to Performance: Compensation Committees Must Do Better," *Business Quarterly* 55, no. 4 (Spring 1991), pp. 18–22.

42. Geoffrey Colvin, "It's a Banner Year for CEO Pay," *Fortune*, April 26, 1999, p. 422.

43. "Revolting Shareholders," *The Economist*, May 24, 2003, p. 13.

44. William White and Raymond Fife, "New Challengers for Executive Compensation in the 1990's," *Compensation and Benefits Review*, January/February 1993, pp. 27–35. See also W.G. Jurgensen, "Crafting an Executive Stock Purchase Program," *Directors and Boards* 24, no. 1 (Fall 1999), pp. 39–41; Allison Wellner, "Golden Handcuffs," *HR Magazine*, October 2000, pp. 129–136.

45. Louis Lavelle, "While the CEO Gravy Train May Be Slowing Down, It Hasn't Jumped the Rails," *BusinessWeek*, April 16, 2001, pp. 76–80.

46. See for example Martocchio, *Strategic Compensation*.

47. See also Bernisha Bridges, "The Role of Rewards in Motivating Scientific and Technical Personnel: Experience in England AFB," *National Productivity Review*, Summer 1993, pp. 337–348.

48. See, for example, Robert Henneman and Peter LeBlanc, "Development of and Approach for Valuing Knowledge Work," *Compensation and Benefits Review*, July/August 2002, p. 47.

49. Kevin Foote, "Competencies in the Real World: Performance Management for the Rationally Healthy Organization," *Compensation and Benefits Review*, July/August 2001, p. 25.

50. Gerald Ledford Jr., "Paying for the Skills, Knowledge and Competencies of Knowledge Workers," *Compensation and Benefits Review*, July/August 1995, p. 56; see also Richard Sperling and Larry Hicks, "Trends in Compensation and Benefits Strategies," *Employment Relations Today* 25, no. 2 (Summer 1998), pp. 85–99.

51. Ledford, "Three Case Studies on Skill-Based Pay," *Compensation and Benefits Review*, (March/April 1991), p. 12. See also Kathryn Cofsky, "Critical Keys to Competency-Based Pay," *Compensation and Benefits Review*, November/December 1993, pp. 46–52; Brian Murray and Barry Gerhart, "Skill-Based Pay and Skills Seeking," *Human Resource Management Review* 10, no. 3 (2000), pp. 271–287.

52. Foote, "Competencies in the Real World," p. 29.

53. Duncan Brown, "Using Competencies and Rewards to Enhance Business Performance and Customer Service at The Standard Life Assurance Company," *Compensation and Benefits Review*, July/August 2001, pp. 17, 19.

54. Joseph Martocchio, *Strategic Compensation*, p. 168.

55. Robert McNabb and Keith Whitfield, "Job Evaluation and High-Performance Work Practices: Compatible or Conflictual?" *Journal of Management Studies* 38, no. 2 (March 2001), pp. 294–311.

56. Ibid., p. 293.

57. Gerald Ledford, "Three Case Studies on Skill-Based Pay," p. 12. See also Cofsky, "Critical Keys to Competency-Based Pay," pp. 46–52; Murray and Gerhart, "Skill-Based Pay and Skills Seeking," pp. 271–287.

58. Gerald Ledford Jr., and Gary Bergal, "Skill-Based Pay Case Number 1: General Mills," *Compensation and Benefits Review*, March/April 1991, pp. 24–38; see also Gerald Barrett, "Comparison of Skill-Based Pay with Traditional Job Evaluation Techniques," *Human Resource Management Review* 1, no. 2 (Summer 1991), pp. 97–105; Barbara Dewey, "Changing to Skill-Based Pay: Disarming the Transition Land Mines," *Compensation and Benefits Review*, January/February 1994, pp. 38–43.

59. This is based on Ledford and Bergal, "Skill-Based Pay Case Number 1," pp. 28–29.

60. Brown, "Using Competencies and Rewards," p. 14.

61. Robert Henneman and Peter LeBlanc, "Work Evaluation Addresses the Shortcomings of Both Job Evaluation and Market Pricing," *Compensation and Benefits Review*, January/February 2003, p. 8.

62. Ledford, "Paying for the Skills, Knowledge, and Competencies of Knowledge Workers," p. 55.

63. Kevin Parent and Carline Weber, "Case Study: Does Paying for Knoweldge Pay Off? " *Compensation and Benefits Review*, September/October 1994, pp. 44–50; and Edward Lawler III, Gerald Ledford Jr., and Lei Chang, "Who Uses Skill-Based Pay, and Why?" *Compensation and Benefits Review*, November/December 1996, pp. 20–26.

64. Brian Murray and Barry Gerhard, "An Empirical Analysis of a Skill-Based Pay Program and Plan Performance and Outcomes," *Academy of Management Journal* 41, no. 1 (1998), pp. 68–78.

65. Parent and Weber, "Case Study." For a good discussion of the conditions under which competency-based pay is more effective, see Edward Lawler III, "Competencies: A Poor Foundation for the New Pay," *Compensation and Benefits Review*, November/December 1996, pp. 20–26.

66. Bryan Murray and Barry Gerhard, "Skill Based Pay and Skill Seeking," *Human Resource Management Review* 1, no. 3 (Fall 2000), pp. 271–287.

67. David Hofrichter, "Broadbanding: A 'Second Generation' Approach," *Compensation and Benefits Review*, September/October 1993, pp. 53–58. See also "The Future of Salary Management," *Compensation and Benefits Review*, July/August 2001, pp. 7–12.

68. Ibid., p. 55.

69. For example, see Sondra Emerson, "Job Evaluation: A Barrier to Excellence?" *Compensation and Benefits Review*, January/February 1991, pp. 39–52; Nan Weiner, "Job Evaluation Systems: A Critique," *Human Resource Management Review* 1, no. 2 (Summer 1991), pp. 119–132; and Brian Klass, "Compensation in the Jobless Organization," *Human Resource Management Review* 12, no. 1 (Spring 2002), pp. 43–62.

70. Dawne Shand, "Broadbanding the IT Worker," *Computerworld* 34, no. 41 (October 9, 2000).

71. "Broadbanding Pay Structures Does Not Receive Flat-Out Support from Employers, Survey Finds," *BNA Bulletin to Management*, January 13, 2000, p. 11.

72. Duncan Brown, "Broadbanding: A Case Study of Company Practices in the United Kingdom," *Compensation and Benefits Review*, November/December 1996, p. 43.

73. Emerson, "Job Evaluation," p. 39.

74. Andrew Richter, "Paying the People in Black at Big Blue," *Compensation and Benefits Review*, May/June 1998, p. 51. See also McNabb and Whitfield, "Job Evaluation and High-Performance Work Practices," pp. 293–313.

75. Ibid., pp. 53–54.

76. Ibid., p. 54.

77. Ibid.

78. Ibid.

79. See ibid., p. 55.

80. Ibid., p. 56.

81. Ibid., p. 56.

82. Helen Remick, "The Comparable Worth Controversy," *Public Personnel Management Journal*, Winter 1981, p. 38; U.S. Department of Labor, *Perspectives on Working Women: A Data Book*, October 1980.

83. Remick, "The Comparable Worth Controversy," p. 377.

84. Ibid.

85. Martocchio, *Strategic Compensation*, p. 191.

86. "Comparable Worth Wages: Lawmakers Rethink Equal Pay," *Foodservice Director* 14, no. 6 (June 15, 2001), p. 18.

87. *County of Washington v. Gunther*, U.S. Supreme Court no. 80-426, June 8, 1981.

88. "Generation X Women Earn More Than Predecessors," *BNA Bulletin to Management*, June 6, 2002, p. 181.

89. "Women Still Earned Less Than Men, BLS Data Show," *BNA Bulletin to Management*, June 8, 2000, p. 72. However, there is some indication that there is less gender-based pay gap among full-time workers ages 21 to 35 living alone. Kent Hoover, "Study Finds No Pay Gap for Young, Single Workers," *Tampa Bay Business Journal* 20, no. 19 (May 12, 2000), p. 10.

90. Al Wright, "Tools for Automating Complex Compensation Programs," *Compensation and Benefits Review*, November/December 2003, pp. 53–61.

APPENDIX FOR CHAPTER 11

QUANTITATIVE JOB EVALUATION METHODS

The Factor Comparison Job Evaluation Method

The factor comparison technique is a *quantitative* job evaluation method. It has many variations and appears to be the most accurate, the most complex, and one of the most widely used job evaluation methods.

It is actually a refinement of the ranking method and entails deciding which jobs have more of certain compensable factors. With the ranking method you generally look at each job as an entity and rank the jobs. With the factor comparison method you rank each job several times—*once for each compensable factor you choose*. For example, jobs might be ranked first in terms of the factor "skill." Then they are ranked according to their "mental requirements." Next they are ranked according to their "responsibility," and so forth. Then these rankings are combined for each job into an overall numerical rating for the job. Here are the required steps.

Step 1. Obtain Job Information This method requires a careful, complete job analysis. First, job descriptions are written. Then job specifications are developed, preferably in terms of the compensable factors the job evaluation committee has decided to use. For the factor comparison method, these compensable factors are usually (1) mental requirements, (2) physical requirements, (3) skill requirements, (4) responsibility, and (5) working conditions. Typical definitions of each of these five factors are presented in Figure 11-A1.

Step 2. Select Key Benchmark Jobs Next, 15 to 25 key jobs are selected by the job evaluation commit-

tee. These jobs will have to be representative benchmark jobs, acceptable reference points that represent the full range of jobs to be evaluated.

Step 3. Rank Key Jobs By Factor Here evaluators are asked to rank the key jobs on each of the five factors (mental requirements, physical requirements,

**Figure 11-A1
Sample Definitions of Five Factors Typically Used in Factor Comparison Method**
Source: Jay L. Otis and Richard H. Leukart, *Job Evaluation: A Basis for Sound Wage Administration*, p. 181. © 1954, revised 1983. Reprinted by permission of Prentice Hall, Upper Saddle River, NJ.

1. Mental Requirements
Either the possession of and/or the active application of the following:
A. (inherent) Mental traits, such as intelligence, memory, reasoning, facility in verbal expression, ability to get along with people, and imagination.
B. (acquired) General education, such as grammar and arithmetic; or general information as to sports, world events, etc.
C. (acquired) Specialized knowledge such as chemistry, engineering, accounting, advertising, etc.

2. Skill
A. (acquired) Facility in muscular coordination, as in operating machines, repetitive movements, careful coordinations, dexterity, assembling, sorting, etc.
B. (acquired) Specific job knowledge necessary to the muscular coordination only; acquired by performance of the work and not to be confused with general education or specialized knowledge. It is very largely training in the interpretation of sensory impressions.
Examples
1. In operating an adding machine, the knowledge of *which* key to depress for a subtotal would be skill.
2. In automobile repair, the ability to determine the significance of a certain knock in the motor would be skill.
3. In hand-firing a boiler, the ability to determine from the appearance of the firebed how coal should be shoveled over the surface would be skill.

3. Physical Requirements
A. Physical effort, such as sitting, standing, walking, climbing, pulling, lifting, etc.; both the amount exercised and the degree of the continuity should be taken into account.
B. Physical status, such as age, height, weight, sex, strength, and eyesight.

4. Responsibilities
A. For raw materials, processed materials, tools, equipment, and property.
B. For money or negotiable securities.
C. For profits or loss, savings or methods' improvement.
D. For public contact.
E. For records.
F. For supervision.
1. Primarily the complexity of supervision *given* to subordinates; the number of subordinates is a secondary feature. Planning, direction, coordination, instruction, control, and approval characterize this kind of supervision.
2. Also, the degree of supervision *received*. If Jobs A and B gave no supervision to subordinates, but A received much closer immediate supervision than B, then B would be entitled to a higher rating than A in the supervision factor.
To summarize the four degrees of supervision:
Highest degree—gives much—gets little
High degree—gives much—gets much
Low degree—gives none—gets little
Lowest degree—gives none—gets much

5. Working Conditions
A. Environmental influences such as atmosphere, ventilation, illumination, noise, congestion, fellow workers, etc.
B. Hazards—from the work or its surroundings.
C. Hours.

Table 11-A1 **Ranking Key Jobs by Factors**[1]

	Mental Requirements	Physical Requirements	Skill Requirements	Responsibility	Working Conditions
Welder	1	4	1	1	2
Crane operator	3	1	3	4	4
Punch press operator	2	3	2	2	3
Security guard	4	2	4	3	1

[1] 1 is high, 4 is low.

skill requirements, responsibility, and working conditions). This ranking procedure is based on job descriptions and job specifications. Each committee member usually makes this ranking individually, and then a meeting is held to develop a consensus on each job. The result of this process is a table, as in Table 11A-1. This shows how each key job ranks on each of the five compensable factors.

Step 4. Distribute Wage Rates By Factors
This is where the factor comparison method gets a bit more complicated. In this step the committee members have to divide up the present wage now being paid for each key job, distributing it among the five compensable factors. They do this in accordance with their judgments about the importance to the job of each factor. For example, if the present wage for the job of laborer in

Mexico is $4.26, our evaluators might distribute this wage as follows:

Mental requirements	$0.36
Physical requirements	$2.20
Skill requirements	$0.42
Responsibility	$0.28
Working conditions	$1.00
Total	$4.26

You make such a distribution for all key jobs.

Step 5. Rank Key Jobs According To Wages Assigned To Each Factor
Here you again rank each job, factor by factor, but the ranking is based on the wages assigned to each factor. As shown in Table 11A-2,

Table 11-A2 **Ranking Key Jobs by Wage Rates**[1]

	Hourly Wage	Mental Requirements	Physical Requirements	Skill Requirements	Responsibility	Working Conditions
Welder	$9.80	4.00(1)	0.40(4)	3.00(1)	2.00(1)	0.40(2)
Crane operator	5.60	1.40(3)	2.00(1)	1.80(3)	0.20(4)	0.20(4)
Punch press operator	6.00	1.60(2)	1.30(3)	2.00(2)	0.80(2)	0.30(3)
Security guard	4.00	1.20(4)	1.40(2)	0.40(4)	0.40(3)	0.60(1)

[1] 1 is high, 4 is low.

Table 11-A3 Comparison of Factor and Wage Rankings

	Mental Requirements		Physical Requirements		Skill Requirements		Responsibility		Working Conditions	
	A^1	$\$^2$	A^1	$\$^2$	A^1	$\$^2$	A^1	$\$^2$	A^1	$\$^2$
Welder	1	1	4	4	1	1	1	1	2	2
Crane operator	3	3	1	1	3	3	4	4	4	4
Punch press operator	2	2	3	3	2	2	2	2	3	3
Security guard	4	4	2	2	4	4	3	3	1	1

[1]Amount of each factor based on step 3.
[2]Ratings based on distribution of wages to each factor from step 5.

for example, for the "mental requirements" factor, the welder job ranks first, whereas the security guard job ranks last.

Each member of the committee first makes this distribution working independently. Then the committee meets and arrives at a consensus concerning the money to be assigned to each factor for each key job.

Step 6. Compare the Two Sets of Rankings to Screen Out Unusable Key Jobs

You now have two sets of rankings for each key job. One was your original ranking (from step 3). This shows how each job ranks on each of the five compensable factors. The second ranking reflects for each job the wages assigned to each factor. You can now draw up a table like the one in Table 11A-3.

For each factor, this shows both rankings for each key job. On the left is the ranking from step 3. On the right is the ranking based on wages paid. For each factor, the ranking based on the amount of the factor (from step 3) should be about the same as the ranking based on the wages assigned to the job (step 5). (In this case they are.) If there's much of a discrepancy, it suggests that the key job might be unusable, and from this point on, it is no longer used as a key job. (Many managers don't bother to screen out unusable key jobs. To simplify things, they skip over our steps 5 and 6, going instead from step 4 to step 7; this is an acceptable alternative.)

Step 7. Construct the Job-Comparison Scale

Once you've identified the usable, true key jobs, the next step is to set up the job-comparison scale (Table 11A-4).

(Note that there's a separate column for each of the five comparable factors.) To develop it, you'll need the assigned wage tables from steps 4 and 5.

For each of the factors for all key jobs, you write the job next to the appropriate wage rate. Thus, in the assigned wage rate table (Table 11A-2), the welder job has $4.00 assigned to the factor "mental requirements." Therefore, on the job-comparison scale (Table 11A-4) write "welder" in the "mental requirements" factor column, next to the "$4.00" row. Do the same for all factors for all key jobs.

Step 8. Use the Job-Comparison Scale

Now all the other jobs to be evaluated can be slotted, factor by factor, into the job-comparison scale. For example, suppose you have a job of plater that you want to slot in. You decide where the "mental requirements" of the plater job would fit as compared with the "mental requirements" of all the other jobs listed. It might, for example, fit between punch press operator and inspector. Similarly, you would ask where the "physical requirements" of the plater's job fit as compared with the other jobs listed. Here you might find that it fits just below crane operator. You would do the same for each of the remaining three factors.

An Example Let us work through an example to clarify the factor-comparison method. We'll just use four key jobs to simplify the presentation—you'd usually start with 15 to 25 key jobs.

Table 11-A4 **Job (Factor)-Comparison Scale**

	Mental Requirements	Physical Requirements	Skill Requirements	Responsibility	Working Conditions
.20				Crane Operator	Crane Operator
.30					Punch Press Operator
.40		Welder	Sec. Guard	Sec. Guard	Welder
.50					
.60					Sec. Guard
.70					
.80				Punch Press Operator	
.90					
1.00				(Plater)	
1.10					
1.20	Sec. Guard				
1.30		Punch Press Operator			
1.40	Crane Operator	Sec. Guard	(Inspector)	(Plater)	
1.50		(Inspector)			(Inspector)
1.60	Punch Press Operator				
1.70	(Plater)				
1.80			Crane Operator	(Inspector)	
1.90					
2.00		Crane Operator	Punch Press Operator	Welder	
2.20		(Plater)			
2.40	(Inspector)				(Plater)
2.60					
2.80					
3.00			Welder		
3.20					
3.40					
3.60					
3.80					
4.00	Welder				
4.20					
4.40					
4.60					
4.80					

Step 1: First, we do a job analysis.

Step 2: Here we select our four key jobs: welder, crane operator, punch press operator, and security guard.

Step 3: Based on the job descriptions and specifications, here we rank key jobs by factor, as in Table 11A-1.

Step 4: Here we distribute wage rates by factor, as in Table 11A-2.

Step 5: Then we rank our key jobs according to wage rates assigned to each key factor. These rankings are shown in parentheses in Table 11A-2.

Step 6: Next compare your two sets of rankings (see Table 11A-3). In each left-hand column (marked A) is the job's ranking from step 3 based on the amount of the compensable factor. In each right-hand column (marked $) is the job's ranking from step 5 based on the wage assigned to that factor. In this case, there are no differences between any of the pairs of A (amount) and $ (wage) rankings, so all our key jobs are usable. If there had been any differences (for example, between the A and $ rankings for the welder job's "mental requirements" factor), we would have dropped that job as a key job.

Step 7: Now we construct our job-comparison scale as in Table 11A-4. For this, we use the wage distributions from step 4. For example, let us say that in steps 4 and 5 we assigned $4.00 to the "mental requirements" factor of the welder's job. Therefore, we now write "welder" on the $4.00 row under the "mental requirements" column as in Table 11A-4.

Step 8: Now all our other jobs can be slotted, factor by factor, into our job-comparison scale. We do not distribute wages to each of the factors for our other jobs to do this. We just decide where, factor by factor, each of our other jobs should be slotted. We've done this for two other jobs in the factor comparison scale: They're shown in parentheses. Now we also know what the wages for these two jobs should be, and we can also do the same for all our jobs.

A Variation   There are several variations to this basic factor-comparison method. One converts the dollar values on the factor comparison chart (Table 11A-4) to points. (You can do this by multiplying each of the dollar values by 100, for example.) The main advantage in making this change is that your system would no longer be "locked in" to your present wage rates. Instead, each of your jobs would be compared with one another, factor by factor, in terms of a more constant point system.

Pros and Cons   We've presented the factor-comparison method at some length because it is (in one form or another) a very widely used job evaluation method. Its wide use derives from several advantages: First, it is an accurate, systematic, quantifiable method for which detailed, step-by-step instructions are available. Second, jobs are compared to other jobs to determine a relative value. Thus, in the job-comparison scale you not only see that a welder requires more mental ability than a plater; you also can determine about *how much* more mental ability is required—apparently about twice as much ($4.00 versus $1.70). (This type of calibration is not possible with the ranking or classification methods.) Third, this is also a fairly easy job evaluation system to explain to employees.

Complexity is probably the most serious disadvantage of the factor-comparison method. Although it is fairly easy to explain the factor-comparison scale and its rationale to employees, it is difficult to show them how to build one. In addition, the use of the five factors is an outgrowth of the technique developed by its originators. However, using the same five factors for all organizations and for all jobs in an organization may not always be appropriate.

The Point Method of Job Evaluation

The point method is widely used. It requires identifying several compensable factors (like skills and responsibility), each with several degrees, and also the degree to which each of these factors is present in the job. A different number of points is usually assigned for each degree of each factor. So once you determine the degree to which each factor is present in the job, you need only add up the corresponding number of points for each factor and arrive at an overall point value for the job.[1] Here are the steps:

Step 1. Determine Clusters of Jobs to be Evaluated   Because jobs vary widely by department, you usually will not use one point-rating plan for all jobs in the organization. Therefore, the first step is usually to cluster jobs, for example, into shop jobs, clerical jobs, sales jobs, and so forth. Then the committee will generally develop a point plan for one group or cluster at a time.

Step 2. Collect Job Information   This means performing a job analysis and writing job descriptions and job specifications.

Step 3. Select Compensable Factors

Here select compensable factors, like problem solving, physical requirements, or skills. Each cluster of jobs may require its own compensable factors.

Step 4. Define Compensable Factors

Next, carefully define each compensable factor. This is done to ensure that the evaluation committee members will each apply the factors with consistency. Figure 11A-2 (top) shows one such definition. The definitions are often drawn up or obtained by the human resource specialist.

Step 5. Define Factor Degrees

Next define each of several degrees for each factor so that raters may judge the amount or degree of a factor existing in a job. Thus, for the factor "complexity" you might choose to have six degrees, ranging from "seldom confronts new problems" through "uses independent judgement." (Definitions for each degree are shown in Figure 11A-2.) The number of degrees usually does not exceed five or six, and the actual number depends mostly on judgment. Thus, if all employees either work in a quiet, air-conditioned office or in a noisy, hot factory, then two degrees would probably suffice for the factor "working conditions." You need not have the same number of degrees for each factor, and you should limit degrees to the number necessary to distinguish among jobs.

Step 6. Determine Relative Values of Factors

The next step is to decide how much weight (or how many total points) to assign to each factor. This is important because for each cluster of jobs some factors are bound to be more important than others. Thus, for executives the "mental requirements" factor would carry far more weight than would "physical requirements." The opposite might be true of factory jobs.

The process of determining the relative values or weights that should be assigned to each of the factors is generally done by the evaluation committee. The committee members carefully study factor and degree definitions and then determine the relative value of the factors for the cluster of jobs under consideration. Here is one method for doing this:

First, assign a value of 100% to the highest-ranking factor. Then assign a value to the next highest factor as a

---

**Figure 11-A2
Example of One Factor (Complexity/Problem Solving) in a Point Factor System**

Source: Richard W. Beatty and James R. Beatty, "Job Evaluation," in Ronald A. Berk (ed.), *Performance Assessment: Methods and Applications* (Baltimore, MD: Johns Hopkins University Press, 1986), p. 322.

The mental capacity required to perform the given job as expressed in resourcefulness in dealing with unfamiliar problems, interpretation of data, initiation of new ideas, complex data analysis, creative or developmental work.

Level	Point Value	Description of Characteristics and Measures
0	0	Seldom confronts problems not covered by job routine or organizational policy; analysis of data is negligible. *Benchmark:* Telephone operator/receptionist.
1	40	Follows clearly prescribed standard practice and demonstrates straightforward application of readily understood rules and procedures. Analyzes noncomplicated data by established routine. *Benchmark:* Statistical clerk, billing clerk.
2	80	Frequently confronts problems not covered by job routine. Independent judgment exercised in making minor decisions where alternatives are limited and standard policies established. Analysis of standardized data for information of or use by others. *Benchmark:* Social worker, executive secretary.
3	120	Exercises independent judgment in making decisions involving nonroutine problems with general guidance only from higher supervision. Analyzes and evaluates data pertaining to nonroutine problems for solution in conjunction with others. *Benchmark:* Nurse, accountant, team leader.
4	160	Uses independent judgment in making decisions that are subject to review in the final stages only. Analyzes and solves nonroutine problems involving evaluation of a wide variety of data as a regular part of job duties. Makes decisions involving procedures. *Benchmark:* Associate director, business manager, park services director.
5	200	Uses independent judgment in making decisions that are not subject to review. Regularly exercises developmental or creative abilities in policy development. *Benchmark:* Executive director.

Table 11-A5 Evaluation Points Assigned to Factors and Degrees

	First-Degree Points	Second-Degree Points	Third-Degree Points	Fourth-Degree Points	Fifth-Degree Points
Decision making	41	82	123	164	204
Problem solving	35	70	105	140	174
Knowledge	24	48	72	96	123

percentage of its importance to the first factor, and so forth. For example,

Decision making	100%
Problem solving	85%
Knowledge	60%

Next, sum up the total percentage (in this case 100% + 85% + 60% = 245%). Then convert this 245% to a 100% system as follows:

Decision making:	100 ÷ 245 = 40.82 = 40.8%
Problem solving:	85 ÷ 245 = 34.69 = 34.7%
Knowledge:	60 ÷ 245 = 24.49 = 24.5%
Totals	100.0%

Step 7. Assign Point Values to Factors and Degrees   In step 6, total weights were developed for each factor in percentage terms. Now assign points to each factor as in Table 11A-5. For example, suppose it is decided to use a total number of 500 points in the point plan. Because the factor "decision making" had a weight of 40.8%, it would be assigned a total of 40.8% x 500 = 204 points.

Thus, it was decided to assign 204 points to the decision-making factor. This automatically means that the highest degree for the decision-making factor would also carry 204 points. Then assign points to the other degrees for this factor, usually in equal amounts from the lowest to the highest degree. For example, divide 204 by the number of degrees (say, 5); this equals 40.8. Then the lowest degree here would carry about 41 points. The second degree would carry 41 plus 41, or 82 points. The third degree would carry 123 points. The fourth degree would carry 164 points. Finally, the fifth and highest degree would carry 204 points. Do this for each factor (as in Table 11A-5).

Step 8. Write the Job Evaluation Manual
Developing a point plan like this usually culminates in a *point manual* or *job evaluation manual*. This simply consolidates the factor and degree definitions and point values into one convenient manual.

Step 9. Rate the Jobs   Once the manual is complete, the actual evaluations can begin. Raters (usually the committee) use the manual to evaluate jobs. Each job based on its job description and job specification is evaluated factor by factor to determine the number of points that should be assigned to it. First, committee members determine the degree (first degree, second degree, and so on) to which each factor is present in the job. Then they note the corresponding points (see Table 11A-5) that were previously assigned to each of these degrees (in step 7). Finally, they add up the points for all factors, arriving at a total point value for the job. Raters generally start with rating key jobs and obtain consensus on these. Then they rate the rest of the jobs in the cluster.

"Packaged" Point Plans   Developing a point plan of one's own can obviously be a time-consuming process. For this reason a number of groups (such as the National Electrical Manufacturer's Association and the National Trade Association) have developed standardized point plans. These have been used or adapted by thousands of organizations. They contain ready-made factor and degree definitions and point assessments for a wide range of jobs and can often be used with little or no modification.

Pros and Cons   Point systems have their advantages, as their wide use suggests. This is a quantitative technique that is easily explained to and used by employees. On the other hand, it can be difficult to develop a point plan, and this is one reason many organizations have opted for ready-made plans. In fact, the availability of a number of ready-made plans probably accounts in part for the wide use of point plans in job evaluation.

APPENDIX NOTES

1. For a discussion, see, for example, Roger Plachy, "The Point Factor Job Evaluation System: A Step-by-Step Guide, Part I," *Compensation and Benefits Review*, July/August 1987, pp. 12–27; Roger Plachy, "The Case for Effective Point-Factor Job Evaluation, Viewpoint I," *Compensation and Benefits Review*, March/April 1987, pp. 45–48; Roger Plachy, "The Point-Factor Job Evaluation System: A Step-by-Step Guide, Part II," *Compensation and Benefits Review*, September/October 1987, pp. 9–24; and Alfred Candrilli and Ronald Armagast, "The Case for Effective Point-Factor Job Evaluation, Viewpoint II," *Compensation and Benefits Review*, March/April 1987, pp. 49–54. See also Robert J. Sahl, "How to Install a Point-Factor Job Evaluation System," *Personnel*, 66, no. 3 (March 1989), pp. 38–42.

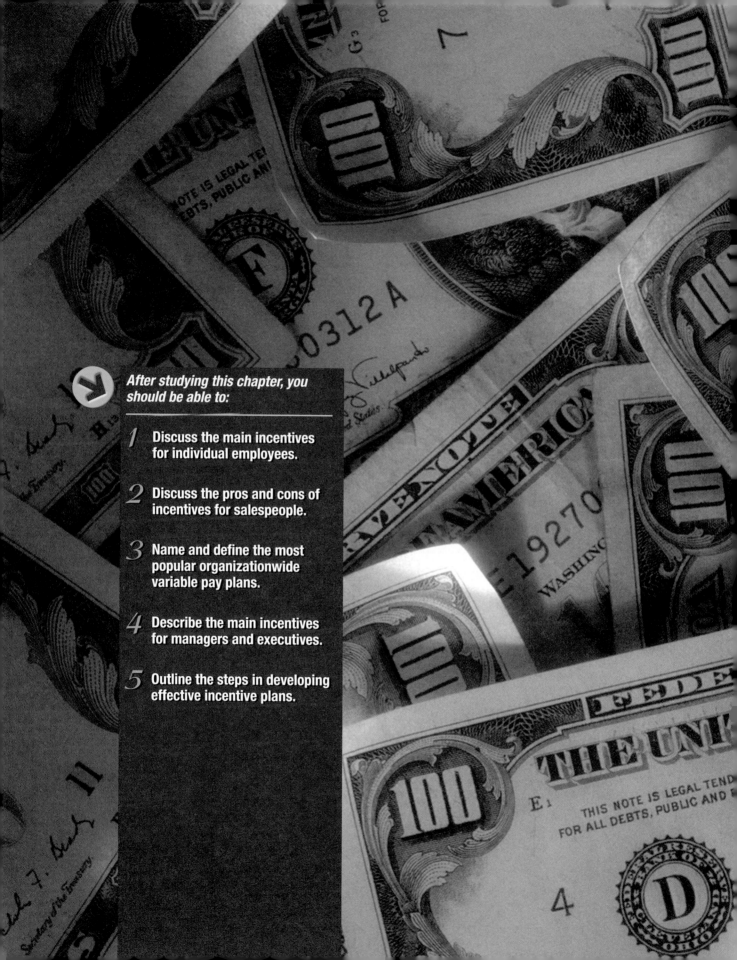

After studying this chapter, you should be able to:

1 Discuss the main incentives for individual employees.

2 Discuss the pros and cons of incentives for salespeople.

3 Name and define the most popular organizationwide variable pay plans.

4 Describe the main incentives for managers and executives.

5 Outline the steps in developing effective incentive plans.

Pay for Performance and Financial Incentives

One of Lisa Cruz's biggest pay-related concerns is that the Hotel Paris compensation plan does not link pay to performance in any effective way. Because salaries were historically barely competitive, supervisors tended to award merit raises across the board. So, employees who performed well got only about the same raises as did those who performed poorly. Similarly, there was no bonus or incentive plan of any kind aimed at linking employee performance to strategically relevant employee capabilities and behaviors such as greeting guests in a friendly manner or providing expeditious check-ins and check-outs. The bottom line for Lisa and the CFO was that the company's financial rewards system—potentially, the single biggest tool they had for channeling employee performance toward accomplishing the Hotel Paris's goals—was totally inadequate. She and her team thus turned to the job of deciding what sort of incentive-based reward systems to install.•

Chapter 11 focused on developing pay plans and on non-performance-based compensation elements such as salaries and wages. The main purpose of this chapter is to explain how to use performance-based incentives to motivate employees. We'll discuss incentives for individual employees, incentives for managers and executives, incentives for salespeople, incentives for professionals, and organizationwide variable pay plans. We'll explain why incentive plans fail, and provide a checklist for creating an effective plan. In the next chapter, Benefits and Services, we'll turn to financial and nonfinancial benefits and services, such as pay for time not worked and insurance benefits, which are the final part of the compensation package.

● MONEY AND MOTIVATION: AN INTRODUCTION

There is nothing new about using incentives to motivate workers. Frederick Taylor popularized the use of financial incentives—financial rewards paid to workers whose production exceeds some predetermined standard—in the late 1800s. As a supervisory employee of the Midvale Steel Company, Taylor had become concerned with what he called "systematic soldiering"—the tendency of employees to work at the slowest pace possible and to produce at the minimum acceptable level. What especially intrigued him was the fact that some of these workers had the energy to run home and work on their homes, even after a 12-hour day. Taylor knew that if he could find some way to harness this energy during the workday, his firm could achieve huge productivity gains. His answer, in part, was to institute employee incentive programs.

Performance and Pay

Maximizing shareholder value under conditions of enormous competition and turbulence is a necessity today, and this has produced a resurgence of interest in financial incentive/pay-for-performance plans. Studies show why: because incentives can work. One study involved 34 stores of a large retailer, 15 of which installed a new sales incentive plan. The researchers found that installing the plan "enables a store to capture more customers from its competitors [especially] when there is more intense competition."[1] The new plan was most effective in the stores facing the greatest competition. Another study focused on 20 *Fortune* 500 companies.[2] The researchers concluded, "our data showed that organizations in which turbulence was greater shifted the financial risk to their managers by paying proportionally higher levels of variable pay."[3] (Turbulence included reductions in force, sale of assets, acquisition by another company, mergers, joint ventures, and attempted takeovers.)

The problem is that other surveys suggest that most incentive plans are less than effective. For example, Mercer Human Resource Consulting found that just 28% of the 2,600 U.S. workers it surveyed said they were personally motivated by their companies' incentive plans. Only 29% said their firms rewarded their performance when they did a good job. "Employees don't see a strong connection between pay and performance, and their performance is not particularly influenced by the company's incentive plan," is how one Mercer pay expert summed up the findings.[4]

What accounts for the fact that about 70% of these employees felt that their firms' pay-for-performance plans were ineffective? In many cases, those devising the pay for performance plan simply don't understand the motivational underpinnings and effects of the plan. Not everyone reacts to a reward in the same way, and not all rewards are suited to all situations. Compensation experts therefore argue that managers should understand the motivational bases of pay-for-performance plans.[5] We'll review some of this basic information next.

For our purposes, there are three sets of psychological insights that the manager will find useful in devising his or her incentive plan. These are the concepts of *individual differences*, and the twin motivational theories relating to *psychological needs*, and *employee expectancies*.

Individual Differences

law of individual differences
The fact that people differ in personality, abilities, values, and needs.

The manager devising an incentive plan should remember, first, that different people react to different incentives in different ways. Psychologists explain this was what they call the **law of individual differences**. This means that people differ in personality, abilities, values, and needs, and these differences manifest themselves in different desires and in different reactions.

Personality is one of the many individual differences that affect how people react to incentives. For example, one recent study focused on high "positive affective" (PA) individuals, and low PA individuals. High PAs are energetic, active and alert, while low PAs are more lethargic, listless, and apathetic.[6] In this study, low PAs responded much more favorably to merit raises than did high PAs, perhaps because the raise gave the (relatively unhappy) low PAs relatively more to be happy about.[7] The moral: know your employees and fine-tune the incentives you offer to their needs.

A survey of how employees react to non-cash incentive recognition rewards (such as gift certificates) further illustrates this common sense prescription. Employees have different needs, and therefore consistently prefer to choose the rewards they receive. Figure 12-1 summarizes employee preferences for non-cash incentives based on one recent survey.

Psychological Needs and Intrinsic versus Extrinsic Motivation

Abraham Maslow   Psychologist Abraham Maslow argued that people have a hierarchy of five increasingly higher-level needs, which he called physiological, security, social, self-esteem, and self-actualization. (Self-actualization refers to the need people have to be what they are capable of becoming.)[8] Most writers envision Maslow's hierarchy as a stepladder. Basically, they assume that for a need to motivate behavior, the next

**Figure 12-1
Employee Preferences for Noncash Incentives**
Source: Darryl Hutson, "Shopping for Incentives," *Compensation and Benefits Review,* March/April 2002, p. 76. Reprinted with permission of Sage Publications, Inc.

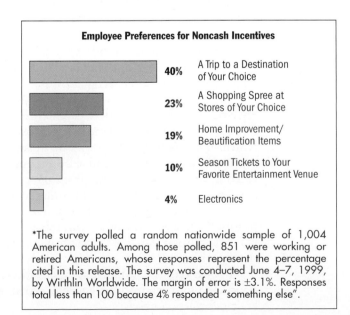

Employee Preferences for Noncash Incentives

40%	A Trip to a Destination of Your Choice
23%	A Shopping Spree at Stores of Your Choice
19%	Home Improvement/ Beautification Items
10%	Season Tickets to Your Favorite Entertainment Venue
4%	Electronics

*The survey polled a random nationwide sample of 1,004 American adults. Among those polled, 851 were working or retired Americans, whose responses represent the percentage cited in this release. The survey was conducted June 4–7, 1999, by Wirthlin Worldwide. The margin of error is ±3.1%. Responses total less than 100 because 4% responded "something else".

lower level needs must first be satisfied.[9] For example, the theory would suggest that someone who is desperately hungry or cold would be relatively uninterested in an offer of a more interesting, enriched job; the person just wants to eat. The corollary: if you want to motivate someone with recognition and a challenging job, make sure the person's lower level needs are satisfied.

There is actually little research evidence to support this idea, but it remains highly popular, in part, no doubt, due to its intuitive attractiveness.[10] Maslow, later in his career, suggested it might be more useful to think of his five needs as comprising a two-step not a five-step hierarchy.[11] The bottom rung contains needs best satisfied by things like extrinsically supplied job security and food and shelter. The second, upper rung contains needs for achievement and self-actualization, needs best satisfied by intrinsic rewards like the sense of achievement one derives from doing a challenging job and doing it well.

Frederick Herzberg   Frederick Herzberg's famous hygiene—motivator theory of motivation similarly divides Maslow's hierarchy into lower level (physiological, safety, social) and higher-level (achievement, self-actualization) needs. He says the best way to motivate someone is to organize the job so that doing it provides the feedback and challenge that helps satisfy the person's higher-level needs. These needs are relatively insatiable, says Herzberg, and so recognition and challenging work provides a sort of built-in motivation generator.

Herzberg calls the two factors at the heart of his theory *hygienes* and *motivators*. He says the factors (hygienes) that satisfy lower-level needs are different from those (motivators) that satisfy or partially satisfy higher-level needs. If *hygiene* factors (factors outside the job itself, such as working conditions, salary, and incentive pay) are inadequate, employees become dissatisfied. However, adding more of these hygienes (like incentives) to the job (supplying what Herzberg calls extrinsic motivation) is an inferior way to try to motivate someone, because lower-level needs are quickly satisfied. Soon the person simply says, in effect, "What have you done for me lately? I want another raise."

Instead of relying on hygienes, says Herzberg, the employer interested in creating a self-motivated workforce should emphasize "job content" or *motivator* factors. Managers do this by enriching workers' jobs so that the jobs are more challenging, and by providing feedback and recognition. Here, it's the sense of enjoyment and achievement that provides the motivation, not some extrinsic element like pay or supervision. The motivation, in a sense, come from within the person, and just doing the job provides the motivation. Among other things, Herzberg's theory makes the point that relying exclusively on financial incentives is risky, and that the employer should not ignore the benefits of providing the recognition and challenging work that most people desire.

Edward Deci   The work of psychologist Edward Deci underscores another potential downside to relying too heavily on extrinsic rewards: They may backfire. He says, "Intrinsically motivated behaviors are those behaviors that are motivated by the underlying need for competence and self-determination." Deci found that extrinsic rewards could at times actually detract from the person's intrinsic motivation.[12] For example, a Samaritan who risks danger by rushing to an accident victim's aid might be insulted if the victim said, "thanks, here's some money for your trouble." The point may be stated thusly: Be cautious in devising incentive pay for highly motivated employees, lest you inadvertently demean and detract from the desire they have to do the job out of a sense of responsibility.[11]

Since extrinsic and intrinsic motivation stems from different needs, it follows that it's unwise to try to institute a single "one size fits all" financial incentive plan, without also considering how the firm will address the employees' intrinsic needs. As three compensation experts put it, "an organization . . . needs a rewards strategy for the specific behaviors driven by extrinsic motivation and a recognition strategy for those behaviors driven by intrinsic motivation.[13] For the manager, the question is not "What motivates employees?" Instead, he or she should ask, how is *this particular* behavior motivated? Which motivational subsystem (extrinsic or intrinsic) is at work?" Some behaviors are best motivated by job challenge and recognition, others by financial rewards.

Instrumentality and Rewards: Vroom's Theory

expectancy
A person's expectation that his or her effort will lead to performance.

instrumentality
The perceived relationships between successful performance and obtaining the reward.

valence
The perceived value a person attaches to the reward.

Another important motivational fact is that, in general, people won't pursue rewards they find unattractive, or engage in tasks on which the odds of success are very low. Psychologist Victor Vroom's motivation theory echoes these commonsense observations. He says a person's motivation to exert some level of effort is a function of three things: the person's **expectancy** (in terms of probability) that his or her effort will lead to performance;[14] **instrumentality**, or the perceived connection (if any) between successful performance and actually obtaining the rewards; and **valence**, which represents the perceived value the person attaches to the reward.[15] In Vroom's theory, motivation is thus a product of three things: Motivation = $(E \times I \times V)$, where, of course, E represents expectancy, I instrumentality, and V valence. If E or I or V is zero or inconsequential, there will be no motivation.

Vroom's theory has three implications for how managers design pay-for-performance plans. First (looking first at just "E"), if employees don't expect that effort will produce performance, no motivation will occur. So, managers must ensure that their employees have the skills to do the job, and believe they can do the job. That is why training, job descriptions, and confidence building and support are important. Second, (with respect to "I"), Vroom's theory also suggests that employees must see the instrumentality of their efforts—they must believe that successful performance will in fact lead to getting the reward. Managers can accomplish this in many ways—by creating easy to understand incentive plans, and by communicating success stories, so that employees see they will be rewarded for doing well. Last but not least, (with respect to "V"), the reward itself must be of value to the employee. Here (as explained above), the manager should take individual employee preferences into account, and endeavor to use extrinsic and intrinsic rewards that make sense in terms of the specific behaviors you want to encourage. Toward the end of this chapter, we'll summarize what we know about how to implement effective incentive plans.

Types of Incentive Plans

variable pay
Any plan that ties pay to productivity or profitability, usually as one-time lump payments.

Managers often use two terms synonymously with incentive plans. *Variable pay* is a team or group incentive plan that ties pay to some measure of the firm's (or the facility's) overall profitability;[16,17] profit-sharing plans (discussed below) are one example.[18] However, confusing as it may be, some experts do include individual incentive plans within the category of variable pay.[19] Traditionally, all incentive plans are *pay-for-performance* plans. They pay all employees based on the employees' performance. To structure our discussion, we will organize the remainder of this chapter around individual employee incentive and recognition programs, sales compensation programs, team/group-based variable pay programs, organizationwide incentive programs, executive incentive compensation programs, and executing effective incentive programs. We first take a brief look at how employment law affects one's choice of financial incentives.

Know Your Employment Law

Incentives

Several federal laws apply to employer incentive plans. For one thing, the employer must comply with the overtime provisions of the Fair Labor Standards Act when designing and administering its incentive plans. If the incentive is in the form of a prize or cash award, the employee generally must include the value of that award when calculating the worker's overtime pay.[20]

Specifically, overtime rates are paid to nonexempt employees based on their previous week's earnings, and unless you structure the incentive bonuses properly, the bonus itself becomes part of the week's wages. It must then be included in base pay when computing any overtime that week.[21]

Certain bonuses are excludable from overtime pay calculations. For example, Christmas and gift bonuses that are not based on hours worked, or are so substantial that employees don't consider them a part of their wages, do not have to be included in overtime pay calculations. Similarly, purely discretionary bonuses in which the employer retains discretion over how much if anything to pay are excludable.

The problem is that many other types of incentive pay must be included. Under the FLSA, bonuses to be included in overtime pay computations include those promised to newly hired employees, those provided in union contracts or other agreements, and those announced to induce employees to work more productively, steadily, rapidly, or efficiently or to induce them to remain with the company. Such bonuses would include individual and group production bonuses, bonuses for quality and accuracy of work, efficiency bonuses, attendance bonuses, length-of-service bonuses, and sales commissions.[22]

Consider the following example: Alison works 45 hours in a particular week at a straight time rate of $6 an hour. In that week she also earns a production bonus of $18. Her new regular rate for that week becomes 45 × $6 = $270 + $18 = $288, and $288 divided by 45 = $6.40 per hour. Her new hourly rate is therefore $6.40 per hour for that week. Additional half-time pay ($3.20 per hour) is due her for the 5 hours overtime she worked as part of her 45 hours. Her total weekly pay for that week is, therefore, $288 + (5 × 3.20) = $304.

The Sarbanes-Oxley act of 2002, affects how employers formulate their executive incentive programs. Congress passed Sarbanes-Oxley to inject a higher level of responsibility into executives' and board members' decisions. It makes them personally liable for violating their fiduciary responsibilities to their shareholders. The act also requires that CEOs and CFOs of public companies repay any bonuses, incentives, or equity-based compensation received from the company during the 12-month period following the issuance of a financial statement that the company must restate due to material noncompliance with a financial reporting requirement as a result of misconduct.[23]

Discuss the main incentives for individual employees.

INDIVIDUAL EMPLOYEE INCENTIVE AND RECOGNITION PROGRAMS

Several incentive plans are particularly suited for use with individual employees.

Piecework Plans

piecework
A system of pay based on the number of items processed by each individual worker in a unit of time, such as items per hour or items per day.

Piecework is the oldest individual incentive plan and is still the most widely used. Here you pay the worker a sum (called a *piece rate*) for each unit he or she produces. Thus, if Tom the Web surfer gets $.40 for each e-mail sales lead he finds for the firm, he would make $40 for bringing in 100 a day and $80 for 200.

In a perfect world, developing a workable piece rate plan requires industrial engineering (that's how Frederick Taylor got his start). The crucial issue is the production standard, and industrial engineers usually set this—for instance, in terms of a standard number of e-mail leads per hour or a standard number of minutes per e-mail lead. In

Tom's case, a job evaluation indicated that his Web surfing job was worth $8 an hour. The industrial engineer determined that 20 good leads per hour was the standard production rate. Therefore, the piece rate (for each lead) was $8 divided by 20, or $.40 per sales lead. (Of course, we need to ensure that Tom makes at least the minimum wage, so we'd probably pay him $5.15 per hour—the minimum wage—whether or not he brought in 13 leads, and then pay him $.40 per lead for each over 13.)

straight piecework
An incentive plan in which a person is paid a sum for each item he or she makes or sells, with a strict proportionality between results and rewards.

Piecework generally implies **straight piecework**, which entails a strict proportionality between results and rewards regardless of output. However, some piecework plans allow for sharing productivity gains between employer and worker, such that the worker receives extra income for some above-normal production.[24] So if Tom starts bringing in 30 leads per hour instead of the "standard" 20, his piece rate for leads above 25 might bump to $.45 each.

Piecework plans have pros and cons. They are understandable, appear equitable in principle, and can be powerful incentives, since rewards are proportionate to performance. However, workers on piecework may resist attempts to revise production standards, even if the change is justified. Indeed, these plans may promote rigidity: Employees concentrate on output and are less willing to concern themselves with meeting quality standards or switching from job to job (since doing so could reduce their productivity).[25] Attempts to introduce new technology or processes may trigger resistance, for much the same reason. Options in such an event include team-based incentives and gainsharing programs, both discussed below.

standard hour plan
A plan by which a worker is paid a basic hourly rate but is paid an extra percentage of his or her rate for production exceeding the standard per hour or per day. Similar to piecework payment but based on a percent premium.

The **standard hour plan** is like the piece rate plan, with one difference. Instead of getting a rate per piece, the worker gets a premium equal to the percent by which his or her performance exceeds the standard. So if Tom's standard is 160 leads per day (and thus $64 per day), and he brings in 200 leads, he'd get an extra 25%, or $80 for the day. Some firms find that expressing the incentive in percentages reduces the workers' tendency to link their production standard to pay (thus making the standard easier to change). It also eliminates the need to recompute piece rates whenever hourly wage rates are changed.[26]

In some industries, the term *piecework* has a poor reputation, (and not just because managers have a history of changing the production standards). For example, some garment manufacturers had operators assemble items (like shirts) in their homes, and paid them for each piece they completed. Unfortunately, the hourly pay for this work didn't always fulfill the minimum wage requirements of the Wage and Hour Act. The problem continues today, in a more modern form. For example, an electronics firm had a woman who assembled cables for the firm during the day take home parts to assemble at night. Working with her sister, the two reportedly assembled cables in their downtown San Jose, California, apartment, allegedly averaging only $2 to $2.50 an hour for the piecework—less than half the minimum wage.[27]

While still widely used, even industries that traditionally stressed piecework incentive plans, such as textiles, are reportedly moving to other plans. "People did work harder under these programs, but they posed problems. For one thing, they created quality problems," says one expert. Firms also tend to be more interested in incentive plans "that focus on profitability and profitability-related accomplishments," rather than just production volume, says another expert. More firms are therefore moving to the team incentive plans, gainsharing plans, and organizationwide incentive pay programs we'll discuss later in this chapter.[28]

Merit Pay as an Incentive

merit pay (merit raise)
Any salary increase awarded to an employee based on his or her individual performance.

Merit pay or a **merit raise** is any salary increase the firm awards to an individual employee based on his or her individual performance. It is different from a bonus in that it usually becomes part of the employee's base salary, whereas a bonus is a one-time payment. Although the term *merit pay* can apply to the incentive raises given to any employee—exempt or nonexempt, office or factory, management or nonmanagement—the term is more often used for white-collar employees and particularly professional, office, and clerical employees.

Merit pay is the subject of much debate. Advocates argue that only pay or other rewards tied directly to performance can motivate improved performance. They contend that the effect of awarding pay raises across the board (without regard to individual merit) may actually detract from performance, by showing employees they'll be rewarded regardless of how they perform.

Detractors present good reasons why merit pay can backfire. One is the dubious nature of many firms' appraisal processes. Since the appraisals are unfair, so too will be the merit pay you base them on.[29] Similarly, supervisors often tend to minimize differences in employee performance when computing merit raises. They give most employees about the same raise, either because of a reluctance to alienate some employees or because of a desire to give everyone a raise that will at least help them stay even with the cost of living. A third problem is that almost every employee thinks he or she is an above-average performer, so getting a below-average merit increase can be demoralizing.[30]

One study focused on the relationship between performance ratings and merit pay raises for 218 workers in a nuclear waste facility. The researchers found a "very modest relationship between merit pay increase and performance rating."[31] Yet, while problems like these can undermine a merit pay plan, there seems little doubt that merit pay can improve performance. But you must be sure to conduct the appraisals and allocations fairly and effectively.

Merit Pay Options

Two adaptations of merit pay plans are popular. One awards merit raises in a lump sum once a year and does *not* make the raises part of the employee's salary (making them, in effect, short-term bonuses for lower-level workers). The other ties merit awards to both individual and organizational performance. Traditional merit increases are cumulative, but most *lump-sum merit raises* are not. This produces two potential benefits. First, the rise in payroll expenses can be significantly slowed. (Traditionally, someone with a salary of $30,000 per year might get a 5% increase. This moves the employee to a new base salary of $31,500. If the employee gets another 5% increase next year, then the new merit increase of 5% is tacked on not just to the $30,000 base salary, but to the extra $1,500 the employee received last year.) Lump-sum merit increases can also be more dramatic motivators than traditional merit pay raises. For example, a 5% lump-sum merit payment to our $30,000 employee is $1,500 cash, as opposed to a traditional weekly merit payout of $29 for 52 weeks.

Tying lump-sum merit pay to both individual and organizational performance is another option. Table 12-1 presents a sample matrix for doing so. In this example, you might measure the company's performance by, say, rate on return, or sales divided by payroll costs. Company performance and the employee's performance (using his or her performance appraisal) receive equal weight in computing the merit pay. Here an outstanding performer would receive 70% of his or her maximum lump-sum award even if the organization's performance were marginal. However, employees with marginal or unacceptable performance would get no lump-sum awards even in years in which the firm's performance was outstanding. The bonus plan at Discovery Communications is an example. Executive assistants can receive bonuses of up to 10% of their salaries. The boss's evaluation of the assistant's individual performance accounts for 80% of the potential bonus; 10% is based on how the division does, and 10% on how the company as a whole does.[32]

Table 12-1 **Lump-Sum Award Determination Matrix (an example)**

The Employee's Performance rating (Weight = .50)	The Company's Performance (Weight = 0.50)				
	Outstanding	**Excellent**	**Good**	**Marginal**	**Unacceptable**
Outstanding	1.00	0.90	0.80	0.70	0.00
Excellent	0.90	0.80	0.70	0.60	0.00
Good	0.80	0.70	0.60	0.50	0.00
Marginal	—	—	—	—	—
Unacceptable	—	—	—	—	—

To determine the dollar value of each employee's incentive award: (1) multiply the employee's annual, straight-time wage or salary as of June 30 times his or her maximum incentive award and (2) multiply the resultant product by the appropriate percentage figure from this table. For example, if an employee had an annual salary of $20,000 on June 30 and a maximum incentive award of 7% and if her performance and the organization's performance were both "excellent," the employee's award would be $1,120: ($20,000 × 0.07 × 0.80 = $1,120).

Incentives for Professional Employees

Professional employees are those whose work involves the application of learned knowledge to the solution of the employer's problems. They include lawyers, doctors, economists, and engineers.

Making incentive pay decisions for professional employees can be challenging. For one thing, firms usually pay professionals well anyway. For another, they're already driven—by the desire to produce high-caliber work and receive recognition from colleagues. In some cases, (as experts like Deci would argue) offering financial rewards to people like these may actually diminish their intrinsic motivation—not add to it.[33]

However, that's not to say that professionals don't want financial incentives, particularly those in high-demand jobs like software and systems developers for information technology (IT) firms. A survey of 300 IT departments found that 77% were paying bonuses and incentives, including stock options and profit sharing, to IT professionals.[34] Many are also offering benefits that are highly attractive to professionals, including better vacations, more flexible work hours,[35] equipment for home offices,[36] and improved pension plans.[37] Texas Instruments began offering stock option grants to about a third of its engineers when it discovered it was losing about 15% of them to the competition.[38] Several firms, including IBM and Motorola, award bonuses to employees whose work wins patents for the firms.[39]

Recognition-Based Awards

Studies show that recognition has a positive impact on performance, either alone or in conjunction with financial rewards. For example, in one study, combining financial rewards with nonfinancial ones (like recognition), produced a 30% performance improvement in service firms, almost twice the effect of using each reward alone.[40] The Minnesota Department of Natural Resources conducted one study of recognition. Respondents said they "highly valued" day-to-day recognition from supervisors, peers, and team members. More than two-thirds said it was important to believe that others appreciated their work.[41]

Employers are therefore increasingly using performance-based recognition programs today.[42] According to one survey, 78% of CEOs and 58% of HR vice presidents

Many firms, like Spartech
Corporation, hold annual awards
and recognitions meetings to
recognize and thank selected
employees for their contributions
to the firm.

Many firms, like Spartech Corporation, hold annual awards and recognitions meetings to recognize and thank selected employees for their contributions to the firm.

said their firms were using performance recognition programs.[43] Dallas-based Texas Instruments, for instance, offers bonuses as well as nonfinancial recognition, including personalized plaques, parties, movie tickets, golf lessons, and team shirts and jackets. The number of individual Texas Instruments employees recognized in this way jumped by 400% in one recent year, from 21,970 to 84,260.[44] At Metro Motors in Montclair, California, the name of the employee of the month goes up on the electronic billboard over the dealership.[45] Managers at American Skandia, which provides insurance and financial planning products and services, regularly evaluate their customer service reps based on specific standards. Those who exceed those standards receive a plaque, a $500 check, their photo and story on the firm's internal Web site, and a dinner for them and their teams.[46]

Online Award Programs

If there's a downside to recognition programs, it's that they're expensive to administer. For example, many firms run anniversary awards programs to recognize employees on significant dates like their fifth year with the company. The HR department usually has to choose the merchandise, create the rewards catalog, print and mail the catalog, and monitor everyone's anniversary dates and make sure the employee actually gets his or her award. This can be very time-consuming.

Many firms—including Nortel Networks, Nextel Communications, Levi Strauss & Co., Barnes & Noble, Citibank, and Wal-Mart—now partner with online incentive firms to improve and expedite the whole process. Management consultant Hewitt Associates uses www.bravanta.com to help its managers more easily recognize exceptional employee service with special awards. After just eight days, the number of award requests online exceeded those from both its offline programs, in part because the whole system makes recognizing employees and letting them choose the awards so much easier: "the gifts are good and easy to order from the desktop . . . and we value the ability to update gift choices easily, so the program doesn't become stagnant," says Hewitt's program's administrator.[47] Internet incentive/recognition sites include bravanta.com, premierchoiceaward.com, givenanything.com, incentivecity.com, netcentives.com, salesdriver.com, and kudoz.com.

Improving Productivity Through HRIS

Employee Incentive Management Systems

With over 1,000 sales representatives, First Tennessee Bank was having problems managing its sales incentive programs.[48] Bank employees had to laboriously enter by hand sales information for each of the 1,000 sales reps onto Excel spreadsheets. The process, said one officer, "was more labor-intensive than it needed to be" and "had begun to spiral out of control." Citizens Financial Group in Providence, Rhode Island, had a similar problem. It used 96 full-time employees spending 75,000 hours a year to enter data for the firm's 7,000 salespeople and 15 sales programs. And, that does not include the thousands of hours that the salespeople themselves have to spend tracking their own sales and rechecking the other employees' work.

For a large business with thousands of sales reps, employee incentive management (EIM) systems can cost between $1 million and $10 million to install. But when you consider that it costs an average of $1,500 a year per employee to manage a manual system, an EIM system can pay for itself in the first year or two. More firms are therefore improving the productivity of their incentive systems by installing EIM software systems. According to the Gartner Inc., consulting group, the market for EIM systems will grow from about $200,000 in 2003, to $3 billion by 2006.

There are many reasons to use sites like these to manage your awards program. The sites can offer a much broader range of products than most employers could catalog and offer themselves. And perhaps most important, the whole process is expedited—it's much easier to bestow and deliver the awards. That in turn lets companies like Nortel reinforce superior performance at once, when it will have the biggest impact.[49] Texas instruments maintains an online "TI mall" that helps its 102 divisional managers provide merchandise and individual travel awards to employees who do a good job.[50] At Intuit, an extended weekend for two including airfare, hotel, and spending money is the most popular Web-based recognition award.[51]

Information Technology and Incentives

Incentives are becoming increasingly complicated. For one thing, more and more employees now receive incentives. Furthermore, the range of behaviors for which employees can earn incentives extends from better cost to cutting cost to answering more calls per hour.[52] Tracking performance of dozens or hundreds of measures like these and then computing individual employees' incentives is obviously very time-consuming. A number of firms such as Incentives Systems Inc., provide sophisticated automated support for calculating, monitoring, and awarding and generally maintaining such pay plans.

Compensation experts refer to this software as enterprise incentive management (EIM). As one says, "EIM software automates the planning, calculation, modeling and management of incentive compensation plans, enabling companies to align their employees with corporate strategy and goals."[53] The "Improving Productivity Through HRIS" feature illustrates its use.

Discuss the pros and cons of incentives for salespeople.

● INCENTIVES FOR SALESPEOPLE

Sales compensation plans typically rely heavily on incentives in the form of sales commissions. However, some salespeople get straight salaries, and most receive a combination of salary and commissions.

Salary Plan

Some firms pay salespeople fixed salaries (perhaps with occasional incentives in the form of bonuses, sales contest prizes, and the like).[54] Straight salaries make particular sense when the main job involves prospecting (finding new clients), or when it mostly involves account servicing, such as developing and executing product training programs for a customer's salesforce or participating in national and local trade shows. You'll often find jobs like these in industries that sell technical products. This is one reason why the aerospace and transportation equipment industries emphasize sales salary plans.

The straight salary approach has pros and cons. Straight salary makes it simple to switch territories or to reassign salespeople, and it can foster loyalty among the sales staff. Commissions tend to shift the salesperson's emphasis to making the sale rather than to prospecting and cultivating long-term customers. The main disadvantage, of course, is that pay isn't proportionate to results.[55] This can constrict sales and demotivate potentially high-performing salespeople.

Commission Plan

Commission plans pay salespeople for results, and only for results. Under these plans salespeople have the greatest incentive, and there's a tendency to attract high-performing salespeople who see that effort clearly leads to rewards. Sales costs are proportionate to sales rather than fixed, and the company's fixed sales costs are low. It's a plan that's easy to understand and compute.

However, it is not without drawbacks. Salespeople tend to focus on making the sale and on high-volume items, and may neglect nonselling duties like servicing small accounts, cultivating dedicated customers, and pushing hard-to-sell items. Wide variations in income may occur; this can lead to a feeling that the plan is inequitable. In addition, pay is often excessive in boom times and low in recessions. Also keep in mind that sales performance—like any performance—is a product of not just motivation, but of ability too. If the person hasn't the sales skills, then commissions won't produce sales.

Research evidence provides further insights into the pros and cons of sales commissions. One study addressed whether commission plans influenced salesperson turnover. One potential drawback of commission-only plans is that working without a financial safety net may induce salespeople to leave. When pay is 100% at risk, as one sales representative put it,

> *If I go on vacation, I lose money. If I'm sick, I lose money. If I'm not willing to drop everything on a moment's notice to close with a customer, I lose money. I can't see how anyone could stay in this job for long. It's like a trapeze act and I'm working without a net.*[56]

In this study, paying salespersons under maximally contingent reward conditions—in other words, where commissions accounted for 100% of pay—was the situation with by far the highest turnover. Turnover was much lower when salespersons were paid a combination of a base pay plus commissions.[57] These findings suggested that 100% commissions can drive higher sales by focusing strong-willed salespeople on maximizing sales. However, it can also undermine the desire of less-strong-willed salespeople to stay. Thus, the effects of a commission plan depend on the salesperson's skills and personality.

Combination Plan

Most companies pay salespeople a combination of salary and commissions, usually with a sizable salary component. Early studies suggested that the most popular salary/commission split was 80% base salary and 20% incentives, with 70/30 and 60/40 splits being the second and third most frequently reported arrangements.[58] These splits have not appeared to change dramatically over the years. For example, one compensation expert used a 70% base salary/30% incentive mix as a target; this cushioned the downside risk for the salesperson, while limiting the risk that the upside rewards would get out of hand from the firm's point of view.[59]

Combination plans have pros and cons. They give salespeople a floor to their earnings, let the company specify what services the salary component is for (such as servicing current accounts), and still provide an incentive for superior performance. However, the salary component isn't tied to performance, so the employer is obviously trading away some incentive value. Combination plans also tend to become complicated, and misunderstandings can result.

This might not be a problem with a simple salary-plus-commission plan, but most plans are not so simple. For example, in a "commission-plus-drawing-account" plan, a salesperson is paid on commissions but can draw on future earnings to get through low sales periods. Similarly, in the "commission-plus-bonus" plan, the firm pays its salespeople mostly based on commissions. However, they also get a small bonus for directed activities like selling slow-moving items.

An example can help illustrate the complexities of the typical combination plan. In one company, the following three-step formula is applied:

Step 1: Sales volume up to $18,000 a month. Base salary plus 7% of gross profits plus 0.5% of gross sales.

Step 2: Sales volume from $18,000 to $25,000 a month. Base salary plus 9% of gross profits plus 0.5% of gross sales.

Step 3: Over $25,000 a month. Base salary plus 10% of gross profits plus 0.5% of gross sales.

In all cases, base salary is paid every two weeks, while the earned percentage of gross profits and gross sales is paid monthly.[60]

The salesforce also may get various special awards. Oakite Company, for instance, uses several recognition awards to boost sales. A President's Cup is awarded to the top division manager, and there is a VIP Club for the top 105 of the salesforce in total dollar sales. Oakite publicizes the VIP Club within the firm, and belonging carries a lot of prestige. Other firms such as Airwick Industries award televisions and Lenox china as special sales awards.

When Metiom, Inc., a New York–based e-commerce infrastructure firm, needed a sales incentive program, it set up one called the "inner circle." After meeting specific sales quotas, the firm's 30 top salespeople and their significant others got a trip to Paradise Island in the Bahamas. The program not only motivated the company's salesforce, but had the added benefit of encouraging family support for the salesperson's success.[61]

As noted above, employers increasingly use the Web to support their sales incentive programs. For example, SalesDriver, in Maynard, Massachusetts, runs Web-based sales-performance-based incentive programs. Firms like these specialize in setting up online sales incentive programs; sales managers just have to make some choices. SalesDriver can help a company launch a campaign template in a day or less. Using the template, the sales manager can select from a catalog of 1,500 reward items, and award these to sales and marketing reps for meeting quotas for things like lead generation and total sales.[62]

Setting Sales Quotas

There are several things to consider when choosing sales quotas. One is whether to lock them in for a period of time. Experts traditionally suggested "locking in" sales quotas and incentive plans, on the assumption that frequent changes undermine motivation and morale. But in today's fast-changing business scene, such inflexibility is usually not advisable. One expert says, "Now that product life cycles are often in the six-month to even six-week range, the traditional approaches to most sales plans cannot accommodate the pace. The sales organization and its emphasis must become more flexible than it has been." Firms therefore tend to review their sales compensation plans and quotas more often.[63]

There are other things to consider. Questions to ask include: Have we communicated quotas to the salesforce within one month of the start of the period? Does the salesforce know exactly how its quotas are set? Do you combine bottom-up information (like account forecasts) with top-down requirements (like the company business plan)? Do 60% to 70% of the salesforce generally hit their quota? Do high performers hit their targets consistently? Do low performers show improvement over time? Are quotas stable through the performance period? Are returns and debookings reasonably low? Has your firm generally avoided compensation-related lawsuits?[64] Is 10% of the salesforce achieving higher performance than previously? And, is 5% to 10% of the salesforce achieving below quota performance and receiving coaching?[65]

It may seem obvious, but also make sure the commission rates let the company pay its bills. There is a tendency to set commission rates informally, without considering how much each sale must contribute to covering expenses. Each salesperson's effort should contribute to covering his or her share of fixed costs and variable costs, and to the company's profit. Fixed costs include the person's salary and benefits, as well as his or her share of office space, utilities, and salaries for support staff and management. Variable costs include telephone charges and travel expenses. In computing the sales commission rates, ensure that what's left over from the sale (after commissions) contributes to profits, too.[66]

An Example: Auto Dealers   Commission rates vary by industry, but a look at how auto dealers set their salespersons' commission rates provides some interesting insights into how to set rates to achieve specific aims. Compensation for car salespeople ranges from a high of 100% commission to a small base salary with commission accounting for most of total compensation. Commission is generally based on the net profit on the car when it's delivered to the buyer. This promotes precisely the sorts of behaviors the car dealer wants to encourage. For example, it encourages the salesperson to hold firm on the retail price, and to push "after-sale products" like floor mats, side moldings, undercoating, car alarms, and trunk-mounted CDs. Car dealers also use short-term incentives. For helping sell slow-moving vehicles, the salesperson may be offered a "spiff"—a car dealer term for an extra incentive bonus over commission.[67]

Strategic Sales Incentives

Employers increasingly link sales commissions to strategic non-volume-based measures. Procter & Gamble measures and rewards its salespeople (which it calls "customer consultants") commissions based on their success in helping customers lower their inventories.[68] At Siebel systems, about 40% of each salesperson's incentive is based on factors like customers' reported satisfaction with service. The firm's vice president of technical services says, "I think our people are better sales reps because of it. There's a lot of value to using this metric as opposed to using only traditional quotas.[69]

● TEAM/GROUP VARIABLE PAY INCENTIVE PLANS

How to Design Team Incentives

Firms increasingly use teams to manage much of their work. In such cases, they need incentive plans that both encourage teamwork and focus team members' attention on performance.

team or group incentive plan
A plan in which a production standard is set for a specific work group, and its members are paid incentives if the group exceeds the production standard.

Team or group incentive plans pay incentives to the team based on the team's performance.[70] One way to do this is to set work standards for each team member and then calculate each member's output. Members are then paid based on one of three formulas: (1) All members receive the pay earned by the highest producer, (2) all members receive the pay earned by the lowest producer, or (3) all members receive pay equal to the average pay earned by the group. A second approach is to set an engineered production standard based on the output of the group as a whole: All members then receive the same pay, based on the piece rate for the group's job. This group incentive can use the piece rate or standard hour plan, but the latter is more prevalent.

A third option is to tie rewards to goals based on some overall standard of group performance, such as "total labor hours per final product." Doing so avoids the need for a precisely engineered piecework standard.[71] One company established such an incentive plan for its teams. If the firm reached 100% of its goal, the employees would share in about 5% of the improvement (in labor costs saved). The firm divided the 5% pool by the number of employees to compute the value of a "share." Each work team then received two goals, and if the team achieved both goals, each employee earned one share in addition to his or her base pay. If the teams achieved one goal, they each got half a share. The results of this plan—in terms of changing employee attitudes and focusing teams on strategic goals—were reportedly "extraordinary."[72]

Pros and Cons of Team Incentives

Team incentives often make a lot of sense. Much work today is organized around teams—project teams publish books, assembly teams assemble cars, and new-product teams launch new products. Performance here reflects not just individual but team effort, so team incentives make sense. Team-based plans reinforce team planning and problem solving, and help ensure collaboration.[73] In Japan, one rule is, never reward only one individual. Instead, Japanese companies reward the group—to reduce jealousy, to make group members indebted to one another, and to encourage a sense of cooperation. Team incentives also facilitate training, since each member has an interest in getting new members trained as fast as possible.

Toyota inspectors examine a finished car coming off the assembly line in Miyazaki, Japan. Japanese companies reward the group to encourage cooperation. Toyota is known for its team- and work-group-based systems, which are used successfully in U.S. plants as well.

The main disadvantage is that a worker's pay may not be proportionate to his or her own efforts, which may demotivate hard workers. Workers who share in the team's pay but don't put their hearts into the effort can be a problem. Solutions include having team members commit in writing to putting the goals of the team before their own, and basing part of each worker's pay on individual (not just team) performance.[74]

The "When You're On Your Own" feature illustrates some incentives the supervisor can easily use.

When You're On Your Own
HR for Line Managers and Entrepreneurs

Incentives Supervisors Can Use

The individual line manager probably would not want to rely exclusively on the employer's incentive plans for motivating his or her subordinates. First, the firm's plans may not be very complete. And, even if they are, there are simply too many opportunities to motivate your employees on a day-to-day basis to let those opportunities pass. The manager or small business owner might therefore want to keep the following motivation-related suggestions in mind.

First, your simplest and best option for motivating employees is usually just to ensure that the employee has a doable *goal* and that he or she agrees with that. It makes little sense to try to motivate employees in other ways (such as with financial incentives) if they don't know their goals or don't agree with them. The research evidence on this point is quite clear. Psychologist Edwin Locke and his colleagues have consistently found that specific, challenging goals lead to higher task performance than specific, unchallenging goals, or vague goals or no goals. From this research it seems apparent that the most straightforward way to motivate your employee may simply be to make sure that he or she has (and understands) an acceptable, challenging goal, and has the ability to achieve it. You should set SMART goals— make them Specific, Measurable, Attainable, Relevant, and Timely.

Second, keep in mind that *recognizing an employee's contribution* is a simple and powerful motivation tool. Studies show that recognition has a positive impact on performance, either alone or in combination with financial rewards. For example, in one study, combining financial rewards with nonfinancial ones (as noted) produced a 30% performance improvement in service firms, almost twice the effect of using each reward alone. When the Minnesota Department of Natural Resources conducted a study of recognition, respondents said they highly valued day-to-day recognition from supervisors, peers, and team members. More than two-thirds said it was important to believe that others appreciated their work.[75]

Third, there are a multitude of *positive reinforcement rewards* you can use on a day-to-day basis, independent of your company's incentive plans. A short list would include:

- Challenging work assignments
- Freedom to choose own work activity
- Having fun built into work
- More of preferred task
- Role as boss's stand-in when he or she is away
- Role in presentations to top management
- Job rotation
- Encouragement of learning and continuous improvement
- Being provided with ample encouragement
- Being allowed to set own goals
- Compliments
- Expression of appreciation in front of others
- Note of thanks
- Employee-of-the-month award
- Special commendation
- Bigger desk
- Bigger office or cubicle

Name and define the most popular organizationwide variable pay plans.

● ORGANIZATIONWIDE VARIABLE PAY PLANS

Many employers have incentive plans in which most employees can participate. These variable pay plans include profit sharing, employee stock ownership (ESOP), and Scanlon/gainsharing plans.

Profit-Sharing Plans

profit-sharing plan
A plan whereby employees share in the company's profits.

Profit-sharing plans (in which all or most employees receive a share of the firm's annual profits) are popular today.[76] Ford Motor Co. introduced a profit-sharing plan for salaried employees,[77] and General Motors increased its profit-sharing payout when profits improved.[78]

Yet research on such plans' effectiveness is sketchy. One study concludes that there is "ample" evidence that profit- sharing plans boost productivity, but that their effect on profits is insignificant, once you factor in the costs of the plans' payouts.[79]

There are several types of profit-sharing plans. In *cash plans*, the most popular, the firm simply distributes a percentage of profits (usually 15% to 20%) as profit shares to employees at regular intervals. The *Lincoln incentive system*, first instituted at the Lincoln Electric Company of Ohio, is a more complex plan. In one version, employees work on a guaranteed piecework basis, and the firm distributes total annual profits (less taxes, 6% dividends to stockholders, and a reserve for investment) each year among employees based on their merit rating.[80] The Lincoln plan also includes a suggestion system that pays individual workers rewards for savings resulting from their suggestions. The plan has been quite successful.

There are also *deferred profit-sharing plans*: The firm places a predetermined portion of profits in each employee's account under a trustee's supervision. There is a tax advantage here, since income taxes on the distributions are deferred, often until the employee retires and the money is taxed at a lower rate.

Employee Stock Ownership Plan (ESOP)

employee stock ownership plan (ESOP)
A corporation contributes shares of its own stock to a trust in which additional contributions are made annually. The trust distributes the stock to employees on retirement or separation from service.

Employee stock ownership plans are companywide plans in which a corporation contributes shares of its own stock—or cash to be used to purchase such stock—to a trust established to purchase shares of the firm's stock for employees. The firm generally makes these contributions annually in proportion to total employee compensation, with a limit of 15% of compensation. The trust holds the stock in individual employee accounts, and distributes it to employees upon retirement (or other separation from service), assuming the person has worked long enough to earn ownership of the stock. (Stock options, as discussed elsewhere in this chapter, go directly to the employees individually to use as they see fit, rather than into a retirement trust. One study compared performance of 229 "new economy" firms offering broad-based stock options to that of their non-stock-option counterparts. Those offering the stock options had higher shareholder returns than did those not offering the options.[81])

ESOPs have several advantages. The company gets a tax deduction equal to the fair market value of the shares that are transferred to the trustee, and can also claim an income tax deduction for dividends paid on ESOP-owned stock.[82] Employees aren't taxed until they receive a distribution from the trust, usually at retirement when their tax rate is lower. The Employee Retirement Income Security Act (ERISA) allows a firm to borrow against employee stock held in trust and then repay the loan in pretax rather than after-tax dollars, another tax incentive for using such plans.[83]

ESOPs can also help the shareholders of closely held corporations (in which, for instance, a family owns virtually all the shares) to diversify their assets by placing some of their own shares of the company's stock into the ESOP trust and purchasing other marketable securities for themselves in their place.[84]

Research suggests that ESOPs do encourage employees to develop a sense of ownership in and commitment to the firm. They do so in part because the ESOPs provide increased financial incentives, create a new sense of ownership, and help to build teamwork.[85] The following example illustrates how one company "shares the wealth" through a combination of companywide cash bonuses and stock ownership plans.

The annual employee bonus at Thermacore, Inc., is one way the firm lets employees share in the wealth generated by operations during the year. All employees of Thermacore and its parent corporation, DTX, are eligible. The unique aspect of the program is that all employees receive the same amount of bonus regardless of total compensation, seniority, or position in the company.

The bonus pool is based on pretax income minus a minimum, threshold guarantee to the stockholders. The guarantee is typically 15% of the firm's equity at the beginning of the year. The amount of income to place in the bonus pool is determined by multiplying company income (less the 15%-of-equity guarantee) by an employee bonus pool percentage determined by the board of directors and senior management. Regular employees then receive a full share, and part-time employees receive a share based on the percentage of time worked. In one typical year, the bonus pool rate was 12%, and the full bonus share was more than $1,300 per employee.

Thermacore also has a stock ownership plan for all employees. Each year, the stockholders and the board of directors approve a dollar value of stock to offer to employees. For example, the board may decide to make available $100,000 of company stock. No one employee may subscribe for more than $10,000 worth of stock. Thermacore is a private company, so the stock trades only within the company. The firm sells shares to the employees at a discount. The company has the right of first refusal should the employee wish to leave the company or sell stock. Employees can pay for the stock in cash at the closing of the subscription period or by payroll deduction.[86]

Scanlon and Other Gainsharing Plans

Few would argue with the fact that the most powerful way of ensuring employee commitment is to synchronize the organization's goals with those of its employees—to ensure that the two sets of goals overlap, and that by pursuing his or her goals, the worker pursues the employer's goals as well. Experts have proposed many techniques for attaining this idyllic state, but few are used as widely or successfully as the **Scanlon plan**, an incentive plan developed in 1937 by Joseph Scanlon, a United Steel Workers Union official.[87] It is still popular today.

Scanlon plan
An incentive plan developed in 1937 by Joseph Scanlon and designed to encourage cooperation, involvement, and sharing of benefits.

The Scanlon plan is remarkably progressive, considering that it is now about 70 years old. As currently implemented, Scanlon plans have the following basic features.[88] The first is Scanlon's *philosophy of cooperation*. This philosophy assumes that managers and workers must rid themselves of the "us" and "them" attitudes that normally inhibit employees from developing a sense of ownership in the company.

A second feature of the plan is what its practitioners call *identity*. This means that to focus employee involvement, the company must clearly articulate its mission or purpose, and employees must understand how the business operates in terms of customers, prices, and costs. *Competence* is a third basic feature. The program today, say three experts, "explicitly recognizes that a Scanlon plan demands a high level of competence from employees at all levels."[89]

The fourth feature of the plan is the *involvement system*. Employees present improvement suggestions to the appropriate departmental-level committees, which transmit the valuable ones to the executive-level committee. The latter then decides whether to implement the suggestion.

The fifth element of the plan is the *sharing of benefits formula*. If a suggestion is implemented and successful, all employees usually share in 75% of the savings. For example, assume that the normal monthly ratio of payroll costs to sales is 50%. (Thus, if sales are $600,000, payroll costs should be $300,000.) Assume the firm implements suggestions that result in payroll costs of $250,000 in a month when sales were $550,000 and payroll costs should have been $275,000 (50% of sales). The savings attributable to these suggestions is $25,000 ($275,000 minus $250,000). Workers would typically share in 75% of this ($18,750), while $6,250 would go to the firm. In practice, the firm sets aside a portion, usually one-quarter of the $18,750, for the months in which labor costs exceed the standard.

Gainsharing Plans   The Scanlon plan is one early version of what we call today a **gainsharing plan**. Gainsharing is an incentive plan that engages many or all employees in a common effort to achieve a company's productivity objectives, with any resulting cost-savings gains shared among employees and the company.[90] In addition to the Scanlon plan, other types of gainsharing plans include the Rucker and Improshare plans.

gainsharing plan
An incentive plan that engages employees in a common effort to achieve productivity objectives and share the gains.

The basic difference among these plans is the formula used to determine employee bonuses. For example, the Scanlon formula divides payroll expenses by total sales. The Rucker formula uses sales value minus materials and supplies, all divided into payroll expenses. Most firms use custom-designed versions of these plans.

Implementing a Gainsharing Plan   In general there are eight basic steps in implementing a gainsharing plan:[91]

1. Establish general plan objectives. These might include boosting productivity or lowering costs.
2. Choose specific performance measures. For example, use productivity measures such as labor hours per unit produced, or financial measures like return on net assets to measure employee performance.
3. Decide on a funding formula. What portion of gains will employees receive? In one study, employees received, by formula, an average of 46.7% of incremental gains; the remainder stayed with the company.[92]
4. Decide on a method for dividing and distributing the employees' share of the gains. Standard methods include equal percentage of pay or equal shares; however, some plans also modify awards based on individual performance.
5. Choose the form of payment. This is usually cash, but occasionally is common stock.
6. Decide how often to pay bonuses. Firms tend to compute financial performance measures for this purpose annually, and labor productivity measures quarterly or monthly.
7. Develop the involvement system. The most commonly used systems include steering committees, update meetings, suggestion systems, coordinators, problem-solving teams, department committees, training programs, newsletters, inside auditors, and outside auditors.
8. Implement the plan.

As an example, assume a supplier wants to boost quality. Doing so would translate into fewer customer returns, less scrap and rework, and therefore higher profits.[93] Historically, $1 million in output results in $200,000 (2%) scrap, returns, and rework. The company tells its employees that if next month's production results in only 1% scrap, returns, and rework, the 1% saved would be a gain, to be split 50/50 with the workforce, less a small amount for reserve for months in which scrap exceeds 2%. The firm posts awards monthly but allocates them quarterly.[94]

At-Risk Variable Pay Plans

at-risk variable pay plans
Plans that put some portion of the employee's weekly pay at risk, subject to the firm's meeting its financial goals.

At-risk variable pay plans are essentially plans that put some portion of the employee's weekly pay at risk. If employees meet or exceed their goals, they earn incentives. If they fail to meet their goals, they forgo some of the pay they would normally have earned.

At one DuPont division, the employee's at-risk pay is a maximum of 6%. This means each employee's base pay will be 94% of his or her counterpart's salary in other (non-at-risk) DuPont divisions.[95] Employees can then match or exceed their counterparts' pay if their department reaches certain predetermined financial goals. Saturn initially designed its at-risk component to be about 20%, but then cut it back to 5%.

"The HR Scorecard" feature illustrates how the Hotel Paris applied these ideas.

 Describe the main incentives for managers and executives.

● INCENTIVES FOR MANAGERS AND EXECUTIVES

Managers play a central role in influencing divisional and corporate profitability, and most firms therefore put considerable thought into how to reward them. Most managers get short-term bonuses and long-term incentives in addition to salary.[96] For firms offering short-term incentive plans, virtually all—96%—provide those incentives in cash. For those offering long-term incentive plans, about 48% offer stock options, which are intended to motivate and reward management for long-term corporate growth, prosperity, and shareholder value. For mature companies, executives' base salary, short-term incentives, long-term incentives, and benefits might be 60%, 15%, 15%, and 10%, respectively. For growth companies, the corresponding figures might be 40%, 45%, 25%, and 10%.[97] About 69% of companies in one survey had short-term incentives, although nearly a third of those said they didn't consider them effective in boosting employee performance.[98]

Short-Term Incentives: The Annual Bonus

annual bonus
Plans that are designed to motivate short-term performance of managers and are tied to company profitability.

Most firms have **annual bonus** plans aimed at motivating the short-term performance of managers and executives. Short-term bonuses can easily result in plus or minus adjustments of 25% or more to total pay. There are three basic issues to consider when awarding short-term incentives: eligibility, fund size, and individual awards.

Eligibility   Most firms opt for broad eligibility—they include both top- and lower-level managers—and mainly decide who's eligible in one of two ways. Based on one survey, about 25% of companies decide eligibility based on job level or job title. About 54% decide eligibility based on a combination of factors, including job level/title, base salary level, and discretionary considerations (such as identifying key jobs that have a measurable impact on profitability). Base salary level alone is the sole determinant in less than 3% of the companies polled.[99]

The size of the bonus is usually greater for top-level executives. Thus, an executive earning $150,000 in salary may be able to earn another 80% of his or her salary as a bonus, while a manager in the same firm earning $80,000 can earn only another 30%. Similarly, a supervisor might be able to earn up to 15% of his or her base salary in bonuses. Average bonuses range from a low of 10% to a high of 80% or more. A typical company might establish a plan whereby executives could earn 45% of base salary, managers 25%, and supervisory personnel 12%.

Fund Size   The firm must also decide the total amount of bonus money to make available—fund size. Some use a *nondeductible formula*. They use a straight percentage (usually of the company's net income) to create the short-term incentive fund. Others

The HR Scorecard
Strategy and Results

The New Incentive Plan

The Hotel Paris's competitive strategy is "To use superior guest service to differentiate the Hotel Paris properties, and to thereby increase the length of stay and return rate of guests, and thus boost revenues and profitability." HR manager Lisa Cruz must now formulate functional policies and activities that support this competitive strategy, by eliciting the required employee behaviors and competencies.

A preliminary analysis, performed jointly by Lisa and the Hotel Paris's chief financial officer, left them optimistic that HR could contribute measurably to achieving the hotel's strategic aims. Several employee competencies and behaviors including employee morale, employee commitment, and the percent of arriving guests receiving the hotel's required greeting had significant effects on customer and organizational outcomes such as guest satisfaction and frequency of guest returns. In turn, outcomes like these contributed measurably to the Hotel Paris's strategic goals, including profit margins, market share, and scores on industry satisfaction surveys. Lisa and her team now turn to creating an incentive program that will help to produce the required employee competencies and behaviors. The accompanying HR Scorecard (Figure 12-2) outlines the relationships involved.

Based on their analysis, Lisa Cruz and the CFO concluded that by any metric, their company's incentive plan was totally inadequate. The percentage of the workforce whose merit increase or incentive pay is tied to performance is effectively zero, because managers awarded merit pay across the board. No more than 5% of the workforce (just the managers) was eligible for incentive pay. And, the percentage of difference in incentive pay between a low-performing and a high-performing employee was less than 2%. Lisa knew from industry studies that in top firms, over 80% of the workforce had merit pay or incentive pay tied to performance. She also knew that in high-performing firms, there was at least a 5% or 6% difference in incentive pay between a low-performing and a high-performing employee. The CFO authorized Lisa to design a new strategy-oriented incentive plan for the Hotel Paris's employees. Their overall aim was to incentivize the pay plans of just about all the company's employees.

Lisa and the company's CFO laid out three measurable criteria that the new incentive plan had to meet. First, at least 90% (and preferably all) of the Hotel Paris's employees must be eligible for a merit increase or incentive pay that is tied to performance. Second, there must be at least a 10% difference in incentive pay between a low-performing and high-performing employee. Third, the new incentive plan had to include specific bonuses and evaluative mechanisms that linked employee behaviors in each job category with strategically relevant employee capabilities and behaviors. For example, front-desk clerks were to be rewarded in part based on the friendliness and speed of their check-ins and check-outs, and the housecleaning crew was to be evaluated and rewarded in part based on the percentage of room cleaning infractions.

With these criteria in mind, Lisa and her team turned to designing the new merit and incentive pay plan. They created a larger merit pay pool, and instructed supervisors that employees scoring in the lower 10% of performance were to receive no merit pay, while the difference in merit pay between the top category and medium category employees was to be 10%. They contracted with an online employee recognition firm and instituted a new "Hotel Paris instantaneous thank you award program." Under this program, any guest or any supervisor could recommend any hotel employee for an instantaneous recognition award; if approved by the department manager, the employee could choose the recognition award by going to the company's Web site. The incentive structure for all the company's managers, including hotel managers, assistant managers, and departmental managers, now ties at least 10% of each manager's annual pay to the degree to which his or her hotel achieves its strategic aims. The plan measures this in terms of ratings on the guest satisfaction index, average length of guest stay, and frequency of guest returns. Ratings on all these metrics soon began to rise.

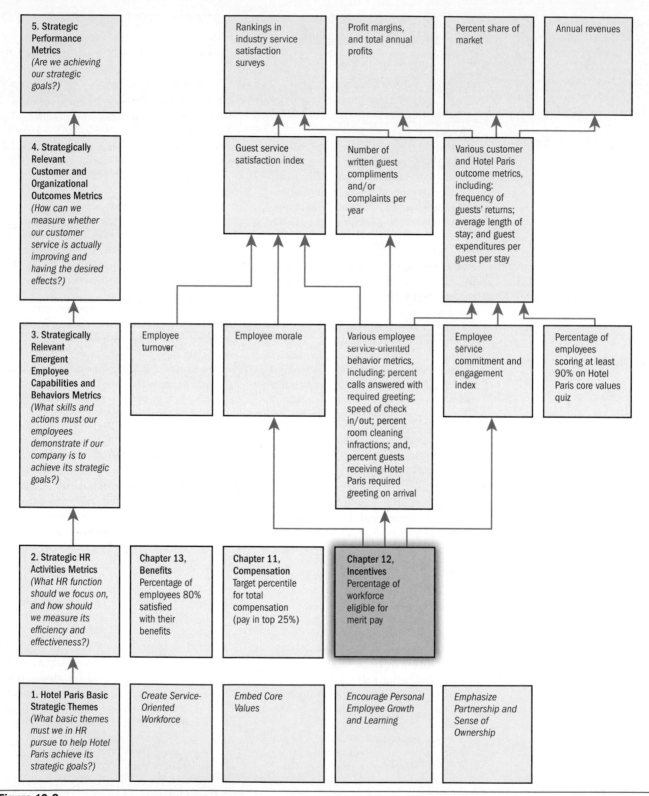

Figure 12-2
HR Scorecard for Hotel Paris International Corporation*

*Note: *(An abbreviated example showing selected HR practices and outcomes aimed at implementing the competitive strategy, "To use superior guest services to differentiate the Hotel Paris properties and thus increase the length of stays and the return rate of guests and thus boost revenues and profitability")*

The boss hands an employee her bonus check, with smiles all around. Annual bonuses can add significantly to total pay and are used to motivate short-term performance.

use a *deductible formula*, on the assumption that the fund should start to accumulate only after the firm has met a specified level of earnings. Some firms don't use a formula at all, but make that decision on a totally discretionary basis.[100]

There are no hard-and-fast rules about the proportion of profits to pay out. One alternative is to reserve a minimal amount of the profits, say, 10%, for safeguarding stockholders' investments, and then to establish a fund for bonuses equal to, say, 20% of the corporate operating profit before taxes in excess of this base amount. Thus, if the operating profits were $200,000, then the management bonus fund might be 20% of $180,000 or $36,000. Other illustrative formulas used for determining the executive bonus fund are as follows:

1. Ten percent of net income after deducting 5% of average capital invested in business.
2. Twelve and one-half percent of the amount by which net income exceeds 6% of stockholders' equity.
3. Twelve percent of net earnings after deducting 6% of net capital.[101]

Individual Awards   The third task is deciding the actual individual awards. Typically, a target bonus (as well as maximum amount, perhaps double the target bonus) is set for each eligible position, and the actual award reflects the person's performance. The firm computes performance ratings for each manager, computes preliminary total bonus estimates, and compares the total amount of money required with the bonus fund available. If necessary, it then adjusts the individual bonus estimates.

One question is whether managers will receive bonuses based on individual performance, corporate performance, or both. The basic rule should be: Outstanding managers should receive at least their target bonuses, and marginal ones should receive at best below-average awards. Firms usually tie top-level executive bonuses to overall corporate results (or divisional results if the executive heads a major division). But as one moves farther down the chain of command, corporate profits become a less accurate gauge of a manager's contribution. For, say, supervisors or the heads of functional departments, it often makes more sense to tie the bonus to individual performance.

Many firms tie short-term bonuses to both organizational and individual performance. Perhaps the simplest way is the split-award method, which breaks the bonus into two parts. Here the manager actually gets two separate bonuses, one based on his or her individual effort and one based on the organization's overall performance. Thus, a manager might be eligible for an individual performance bonus of up to $10,000, but receive only $2,000 at the end of the year, based on his or her individual performance evaluation. But the person might also receive a second bonus of $3,000, based on the firm's profits for the year. Give the money you save from the poor performers to the outstanding ones.

One drawback to this approach is that it may give marginal performers too much—for instance, someone could get a company-based bonus, even if his or her own performance is mediocre. One way to get around this is to use the multiplier method. In other words, make the bonus a product of both individual and corporate performance. As Table 12-2 illustrates, multiply the target bonus by 1.00 or .80 or zero (if the firm's performance is excellent, and the person's performance is excellent, good, fair, or poor). A manager whose own performance is poor does not even receive the company-based bonus.

Table 12-2

Multiplier Approach to Determining Annual Bonus

		Company Performance (based on sales targets, weight .50)			
		Excellent	**Good**	**Fair**	**Poor**
Individual Performance	Excellent	1.00	.90	.80	.70
(based on appraisal. weight .50)	Good	.80	.70	.60	.50
	Fair	0.00	0.00	0.00	0.00
	Poor	0.00	0.00	0.00	0.00

Note: To determine the dollar amount of a manager's award, multiply the maximum possible (target) bonus by the appropriate factor in the matrix.

Long-Term Incentives

Employers use long-term incentives to inject a long-term perspective into their executives' decisions. With only short-term criteria to shoot for, a manager could boost profitability by reducing plant maintenance, for instance; this tactic might catch up with the company two or three years later. Long-term incentives also encourage executives to stay with the company by letting them accumulate capital (usually options to buy company stock) that can only be cashed in after a certain number of years—"golden handcuffs."

Firms don't just use stock options as long-term incentives. Other popular long-term incentives (discussed below) include cash, stock, stock appreciation rights, and phantom stock. The popularity of these plans changes over time due to economic and market conditions and trends, internal company financial pressures, changing attitudes toward long-term incentives, changes in tax law, and other factors.

stock option
The right to purchase a stated number of shares of a company stock at today's price at some time in the future.

Stock Options   A **stock option** is the right to purchase a specific number of shares of company stock at a specific price during a specific period of time; the executive thus hopes to profit by exercising his or her option to buy the shares in the future but at today's price. The assumption is that the price of the stock will go up. Unfortunately, this depends partly on considerations outside the manager's control, such as general economic and market conditions. When the market for Internet stocks plummeted in 2000, many managers saw their options go "underwater." Many of these firms then had to scramble to sweeten their managers' incentive plans. *Nonqualified stock options* are the most popular. They are options to purchase stock at a stated price, usually the fair market value at the time of the grant.[102]

The chronic problem with stock options is that firms have traditionally used them to reward managers for even lackluster performance. There is therefore a trend toward using new types of options, tied more explicitly to specific goals. For example, with *indexed options*, the option's exercise price fluctuates with the performance of, say, a market index. Then, if the company's stock does no better than the index, the manager's options are worthless. With *premium priced options*, the exercise price is higher than the stock's closing price on the date of the grant, so the executive can't profit from the options until the stock has made significant gains.[103]

In the past few years, firms have begun deemphasizing stock option plans, for several reasons. With the numerous corporate scandals in the early 2000s, many believe enormous stock options provided too much incentive for questionable managerial decisions. Furthermore, until recently, most companies did not treat the stock options they awarded as an expense, which has the potential of distorting financial performance. (For example, while the stock options were very much a part of each manager's compensation, the cost of those stock options didn't show up as an expense on the companies' financial statements.) With more companies today trying to emphasize accuracy and transparency in financial statements, more are expensing stock options. Having to show the stock options as an immediate expense reduces, to some degree, the attractiveness to the companies of awarding the options. As one compensation consultant puts it, "The fact that this is now 'costing' them something will mean that they will have to do more of the cost/benefit analysis to see which [compensation plan] design will give them the best return for their dollar."[104]

Other Stock Option Plans   Different employees tend to have different stock option plans. Plans for key employees (such as top executives) typically provide for a very significant upside in the value of stock the employee can receive. On the other hand, more companies today are implementing broad-based stock option plans in which the potential appreciation is relatively modest, but in which all or most employees can participate. Why do this? As two compensation experts put it, "Companies are asking more from employees than ever before. They have cut out layers of management, downsized, outsourced, empowered employees.[105] "By giving stock options to non-executives, companies make good the promise of letting employees share in the company's success."[106]

The *key employee program* may go to a handful of top executives and provides significant economic incentives to motivate these people and to keep them on board. On the other hand, a nonkey program like one in place at IBM offers a broad list of employees a highly competitive total compensation package to emphasize that the company intends to share its success with its employees.[107]

Too many stock options can be too much of a good thing. "Executives with increasingly large stock option holdings have an added incentive to undertake riskier business strategies." Their options provide an incentive to go for spectacular results, but since they have not actually bought the stock yet, they don't risk their own money. The solution is to draft the option plan so it forces recipients to convert their options to stock more quickly.[108]

Other Plans   There are several other stock-related, long-term incentive plans. *Stock appreciation rights* permit the recipient to exercise the stock option (by buying the stock) or to take any appreciation in the stock price in cash, stock, or some combination of these. A *performance achievement plan* awards shares of stock for the achievement of predetermined financial targets, such as profit or growth in earnings per share. With *restricted stock plans*, the firm usually awards shares without cost to the executive: The employee can sell the stock (for which he or she paid nothing), but is restricted from doing so for, say, five years. Under *phantom stock plans*, executives receive not shares but "units" that are similar to shares of company stock. Then at some future time, they receive value (usually in cash) equal to the appreciation of the "phantom" stock they own.

Performance Plans   Traditional executive incentives (like stock options) often don't build in any real risk for the executive, so the executives' and the shareholders' interests could diverge.[109] Often, for instance, managers can exercise options with little or no cash outlay, and then quickly sell their stock.[110]

The solution is to design the plan so that executives don't prosper unless the company does. Performance plans are one means for doing so. They are "plans whose payment or value is contingent on financial performance measured against objectives set at the start of a multi-year period.[111] They are essentially bonuses, but the measurement period is longer than a year. For example, the plan may award zero to 300 "performance units" worth $2,000 per unit, depending on the company's earnings-per-share growth over several years. Thus, at the end of the period, the executive might be eligible to

The New Workplace

Long-term Incentives for Overseas Executives

Developing long-term incentives for a firm's overseas operations presents some tricky problems, particularly with regard to taxation. For example, extending a U.S. stock option plan to local nationals in a firm's overseas operations could subject them to immediate local taxation on the stocks, even though the shares could not be sold because of requirements built into the company's plan.[112]

The problem extends to U.S. executives stationed overseas. For example, it's not unusual for an executive to be taxed $40,000 on $140,000 of stock option income if he or she is based in the United States. However, if that person receives the same stock option income while stationed overseas, he or she may be subject to both the $40,000 U.S. tax and a foreign income tax (depending on the country) of perhaps $94,000. Therefore, ignoring the overseas country's tax burden has the effect of virtually eliminating the incentive value of the stock from the executive's point of view, or dramatically boosting the cost of the stock to the company (assuming the company pays the foreign income tax). In any case, firms cannot assume that they can simply export their executives' incentive programs. Instead, they must consider various factors, including tax treatment, the regulatory environment, and foreign exchange controls.[113]

receive, say, a $300,000 cash grant, in proportion to his or her success in meeting his or her financial goals. "The New Workplace" illustrates some global aspects of the executive pay issue.

Other Executive Incentives

golden parachutes
Payments companies make in connection with a change in ownership or control of a company.

Companies also provide various incentives to persuade executives to remain with the firm. For example, **golden parachutes** are payments companies make in connection with a change in ownership or control of a company. For example, a company's golden parachute clause might state that, should there be a change in ownership of the firm, the executive would receive a one-time payment of $2 million. Under recently issued IRS regulations, companies cannot deduct "excess" golden parachute payments made to executives, and the executive must pay a 20% excise tax on the golden parachute payments.[114] Other firms, perhaps more dubiously, guarantee large loans to directors and officers, for instance, to buy company stock. Thus, directors and officers of Conseco Inc., owed the company more than $500 million for such loans when shares of the company stock dropped precipitously.[115]

Strategy and Executive Compensation

Few HR practices can have as profound or obvious an impact on strategic success as the company's long-term incentives. Whether expanding through joint ventures abroad, consolidating operations, or following some other strategy, few firms can fully implement strategies in just one or two years. As a result, the long-term signals you send your managers and executives regarding what you will (or won't) reward can have a big effect on whether your strategy succeeds. A strategy to boost sales by expanding abroad might suggest linking long-term rewards to increased sales abroad. A cost-reduction strategy might require linking them to improved profit margins.

Employers designing long-term incentives thus ignore their firm's strategy at their peril. Compensation experts suggest first defining the strategic context for the executive compensation plan, and then creating the compensation package itself in what is basically an HR Scorecard-type process:

1. Define the strategic context for the executive compensation program, including the internal and external issues that face the company, and the firm's business objectives. For example, ask: What are our organization's long-term goals, and how can the compensation structure support them? What defines the organization's work culture—its basic values regarding what people should and should not do—and how will the compensation program mold that culture? What competitive challenges do we face?[116]

2. Based on your strategic aims, shape each component of the executive compensation package (base salary, short-term incentives, long-term incentives, and benefits and perquisites), and then group the components into a balanced plan that makes sense in terms of motivating executive behavior to achieve these aims. Each component should help to focus the manager's attention on the behaviors required to achieve the company's strategic goals.

3. Create a stock option plan that gives the executive compensation package the special character it needs to meet the unique needs of the executives and the company and its strategy.

4. Check the executive compensation plan for compliance with all legal and regulatory requirements and for tax effectiveness.

5. Install a process for reviewing and evaluating the executive compensation plan whenever a major business change occurs.

Preferably, translate goals and aims into measurable terms. First, try to identify the main financial factors that drive the company's business.[117] One expert says, "In many companies, a careful analysis of historical financials shows that well over 90% of economic value change is driven by a few simple items that can be separated out."[118] For example, you may find that about 10 or 15 financial items—pricing, discounts, raw material costs, and net sales, for instance—are the controllable factors that drive the improvements in the value of the company and the value of the shareholders' investment.[119] Then, link executives' incentives to these items, to motivate the required behaviors.

One popular strategy today is to improve supply chain efficiencies. For example, Dell Computer encourages its customers to monitor their order status online, since doing so reduces the need for Dell employees to answer order status questions. Airlines encourage fliers to book their travel online, since this means less need for reservations clerks—and fewer commissions to travel agents.

The problem is, companies often spend millions on technology for supply chain efficiencies, only to find they fail because employees resist the changes. Many firms are therefore using incentives to support these change programs.[120] For example, one incentive program at Sun Microsystems focuses on customer satisfaction metrics. Employees receive incentives based on achieving supply-chain-related improvements in activities like ontime delivery and customer returns. K*Tec electronics established a similar incentive system. Each of the firm's program management teams has a dedicated customer. K*Tec teams are rewarded based on how well they manage supply-chain-related activities such as inventory turnover and capital invested. The programs are mostly for mid- to upper-level managers.

● DESIGNING AND EXECUTING EFFECTIVE INCENTIVE PROGRAMS

5 Outline the steps in developing effective incentive plans.

As we saw at the start of this chapter, roughly 70% of employees feel that their firms' incentive plans are ineffective. We turn here to why such plans fail, and how to improve their effectiveness.[121]

Why Incentive Plans Fail

Experts have proposed many explanations for why incentive plans fail. We can summarize their reasoning with the following points:

■ *Performance pay can't replace good management.* Performance pay is supposed to motivate workers, but lack of motivation is not always the culprit. Ambiguous instructions, lack of clear goals, inadequate employee selection and training, unavailability of tools, and a hostile workforce (or management) are some other factors that impede performance.

■ *You get what you pay for.* An incentive plan that rewards a group based on how many pieces they produce may lead to rushed production and lower quality. A plantwide incentive for reducing accidents may simply reduce the number of reported accidents.

■ *"Pay is not a motivator."* [122] Recall that psychologist Frederick Herzberg says employers should provide adequate financial rewards, and then build other, more effective motivators (like opportunities for achievement and psychological success) into jobs. More challenging jobs and employee regulations often make more sense than do financial incentive plans.

■ *Rewards punish.* Many view punishment and reward as two sides of the same coin. They say "Do this and you'll get that" is not very different from "Do this or you won't get that." [123]

■ *Rewards rupture relationships.* Incentive plans have the potential for encouraging individuals (or individual groups) to pursue financial rewards for themselves.

■ *Rewards can have unintended consequences.* One expert says: "Tell people that their income will depend on their productivity or performance rating, and they will focus on the numbers. Sometimes they will manipulate the schedule for completing tasks or even engage in patently unethical and illegal behavior." [124]

■ *Rewards may undermine responsiveness.* When employees' main focus is on achieving some specific goal like cutting costs, any changes or distractions make achieving that goal harder for the employees. Incentive plans can therefore mediate against change and responsiveness.

■ *Rewards undermine intrinsic motivation.* Edward Deci said that contingent financial rewards (incentives) may actually undermine the intrinsic motivation that often results in optimal performance. [125] The argument is that financial incentives undermine the feeling that the person is doing a good job voluntarily.

How to Implement Effective Incentive Plans

What can you do to make your incentive plan more effective? Some guidelines follow:

1. *Ask: Is effort clearly instrumental in obtaining the reward?* Sometimes incentive pay doesn't make sense. For example: when employees are unable to control quantity or output (such as on machine-paced assembly lines). In general, it makes more sense to use an incentive plan when there is a clear relationship between employee effort and quantity or quality of output, the job is standardized, the work flow is regular, delays are few or consistent, and quality is less important than quantity—or, if quality is important, employees can easily measure and control it. [126]

2. *Link the incentive with your strategy.* Decide how the incentive plan will contribute to implementing the firm's strategy and objectives. The key thing is that, "in the best of all possible worlds, each item on your awards menu earns its keep by delivering on its promise, whether to inspire higher performance, reduce costs or any of a range of results that fit your business and its strategic plan."[127]

3. *Make sure effort and rewards are directly related.* The incentive plan should reward employees in direct proportion to increased productivity or quality. Employees must also perceive that they can actually do the tasks required. The standard has to be attainable, and you have to provide the necessary tools, equipment, and training.[128]

4. *Make the plan easy for employees to understand.* Employees should be able to calculate their rewards for various levels of effort.

5. *Set effective standards.* Make standards high but reasonable—there should be about a 60% to 70% chance of success. And the goal should be specific—this is much more effective than telling someone to "do your best."

6. *View the standard as a contract with your employees.* Once the plan is working, use caution before decreasing the size of the incentive. Rate cuts have long been the nemesis of incentive plans.

7. *Get employees' support for the plan.* Restrictions by members of the work group can undermine the plan.

8. *Use good measurement systems.* In the case of merit pay, for instance, the process used to appraise performance must be clear and fair if the plan is to be of any use.[129]

9. *Emphasize long-term as well as short-term success.* [130] For example, just paying assembly workers for quantity produced may be shortsighted: Longer-term improvements like those deriving from work-improvement suggestions are often equally important in increasing the firm's value.

10. *Adopt a comprehensive, commitment-oriented approach.* From the employees' point of view, incentive plans don't exist in isolation. For example, trying to motivate employees with a new incentive plan when they don't have the skills to do the job, or are demoralized by unfair supervisors, a boring job, or a lack of respect, might well fail. Therefore, it's best to install the program within a framework of HR-related practices that promote employee commitment by making the company a place in which employees want to work and do feel like partners.

HR activities that contribute to building commitment include: clarifying and communicating the goals and mission of the organization; guaranteeing organizational justice—for instance, by having a comprehensive grievance procedure and extensive two-way communications; creating a sense of community by emphasizing teamwork and encouraging employees to interact; supporting employee development, perhaps by emphasizing promotion from within, developmental activities, and career-enhancing activities; and generally committing to being supportive of your employees.[131]

Incentive Plans in Practice

In practice, most companies have several incentive plans, including individual performance awards, team awards, and gainsharing plans. Based on one sample of 1,244 companies, about 41% have individual performance awards, 25% had team awards, and 19% have gainsharing plans.

For example, Nucor Corp., is the largest steel producer in the United States, and also has the highest productivity, highest wages, and lowest labor cost per ton in the

American steel industry.[132] Employees earn bonuses of 100% or more of base salary, and all Nucor employees participate in one of four performance-based incentive plans. With the production incentive plan, operating and maintenance employees and supervisors get weekly bonuses based on their work groups' productivity. The department manager incentive plan pays department managers annual incentive bonuses based mostly on the ratio of net income to dollars of assets employed for their division. With the professional and clerical bonus plan, employees who are not in one of the two previous plans get bonuses based on their divisions' net income return on assets. Finally, under the senior officers incentive plan, Nucor senior managers (whose base salaries are lower than those of executives in comparable firms) get bonuses based on Nucor's annual overall percentage of net income to stockholders equity.[133]

 *Review*

SUMMARY

1. The scientific use of financial incentives can be traced back to Frederick Taylor. Although such incentives subsequently became somewhat less popular, most writers today agree that they can be quite effective.

2. Different people react to different incentives in different ways. Psychologists explain this with what they call the law of individual differences, the fact that people differ in personality, abilities, values, and needs.

3. Psychologists distinguish between intrinsic and extrinsic motivation. Abraham Maslow argued that people have a hierarchy of five increasingly higher-level needs which he called physiological, security, social, self-esteem, and self-actualization. Similarly, Frederick Herzberg's hygiene-motivator motivation theory divides Maslow's hierarchy into lower-level and higher-level needs. Victor Vroom says a person's motivation to exert some level of effort is a function of three things: the person's expectancy that his or her effort will lead to performance, instrumentality, and valence.

4. Piecework, where a worker is paid a piece rate for each unit he or she produces, is the oldest type of incentive plan. With a straight piecework plan, workers are paid on the basis of the number of units produced. With a guaranteed piecework plan, each worker receives his or her base rate (such as the minimum wage) regardless of how many units he or she produces.

5. Other useful incentive plans include the standard hour plan and group incentive plans. The former rewards workers by a percent premium that equals the percent by which their performance is above standard. Group incentive plans are useful where the workers' jobs are highly interrelated.

6. Most sales personnel are paid on some type of salary plus commission (incentive) basis. Management employees are often paid according to a bonus formula that ties the bonus to, for example, increased sales. Stock options are one of the most popular executive incentive plans.

7. Profit sharing and the Scanlon plan are examples of organizationwide incentive plans. Gainsharing and merit plans are two other popular plans. The problem with such plans is that the link between a person's efforts and rewards is sometimes unclear. On the other hand, such plans may contribute to developing a sense of commitment among employees.

8. Incentive plans work best when units of output are easily measured, when employees can control output, when the effort—reward relationship is clear, when work delays are under employees' control, when quality is not paramount, and when the organization must know precise labor costs anyway (to stay competitive).

DISCUSSION QUESTIONS

1. Compare and contrast six types of incentive plans.

2. Explain five reasons why incentive plans fail.

3. Describe the nature of some important management incentives.

4. When and why would you pay a salesperson a combined salary and commission?

5. What is merit pay? Do you think it's a good idea to award employees merit raises? Why or why not?

6. In this chapter, we listed a number of reasons experts give for not instituting a pay-for-performance plan (such as "rewards punish"). Do you think these points (or any of them) are valid? Why or why not?

7. What is a Scanlon plan? Based on what you've read in this chapter, what features of an effective incentive program does the Scanlon plan include?

8. Give four examples of when you would suggest using team or group incentive programs rather than individual incentive programs.

INDIVIDUAL AND GROUP ACTIVITIES

1. Working individually or in groups, develop an incentive plan for the following positions: chemical engineer, plant manager, used-car salesperson. What factors did you have to consider in reaching your conclusions?

2. A state university system in the Southeast instituted a "Teacher Incentive Program" (TIP) for its faculty. Basically, faculty committees within each university's colleges were told to award $5,000 raises (not bonuses) to about 40% of their faculty members based on how good a job they did teaching undergraduates, and how many they taught per year. What are the potential advantages and pitfalls of such an incentive program? How well do you think it was accepted by the faculty? Do you think it had the desired effect?

3. The HRCI "Test Specifications" appendix at the end of this book (pages 685–689) lists the knowledge someone studying for the HRCI certification exam needs to have in each area of human resource management (such as in Strategic Management, Workforce Planning, and Human Resource Development). In groups of four to five students, do four things: (1) review that appendix now; (2) identify the material in this chapter that relates to the required knowledge the appendix lists; (3) write four multiple choice exam questions on this material that you believe would be suitable for inclusion in the HRCI exam; and (4) if time permits, have someone from your team post your team's questions in front of the class, so the students in other teams can take each others' exam questions.

4. In March 2004, the pension plan of the Utility Workers Union of America proposed changing the corporate bylaws of Dominion Resources, Inc., so that in the future, management had to get shareholder approval of executive pay exceeding $1 million, as well as detailed information about the firm's executive incentive plans. Many unions—most of which have pension funds with huge investments in U.S. companies—are taking similar steps. They point out that, usually, under Internal Revenue Service regulations, corporations can't deduct more than $1 million in pay for any of a company's top five paid executives. Under the new rules the unions are pushing, boards of directors will no longer be able to approve executive pay above $1 million; instead, shareholders would have to vote on it. In terms of effectively running a company, what do you think are the pros and cons of the unions' recommendations? Would you vote for or against the unions' recommendation? Why or why not?

EXPERIENTIAL EXERCISE

Motivating the Salesforce at Express Auto

Purpose: The purpose of this exercise is to give you practice developing an incentive plan.

Required Understanding: Be thoroughly familiar with this chapter, and read the following:

    Express Auto, an automobile megadealership with over 600 employees that represents 22 brands, has just received a very discouraging set of survey results. Customer satisfaction scores have fallen for the ninth straight quarter. Customer complaints include:

- It was hard to get prompt feedback from mechanics by phone.
- Salespeople often did not return phone calls.
- The finance people seemed "pushy."
- New cars were often not properly cleaned or had minor items that needed immediate repair or adjustment.

- Cars often had to be returned to have repair work redone.

    Table 12-3 describes Express Auto's current compensation system.

How to Set Up the Exercise/Instructions: Divide the class into groups of four–five students. Assign one or more groups to analyzing each of the five teams in column one. Each student group should analyze the compensation package for its Express Auto team. Each group should address these questions:

1. In what ways might your team's compensation plan contribute to the customer service problems?

2. What recommendations would you make to improve the compensation system in a way that would likely improve customer satisfaction?

Table 12-3

Express Auto Compensation System

Express Auto Team	Responsibility of Team	Current Compensation Method
1. Sales force	Persuade buyer to purchase a car.	Very small salary (minimum wage) with commissions. Commission rate increases with every 20 cars sold per month.
2. Finance office	Help close the sale; persuade customer to use company finance plan.	Salary, plus bonus for each $10,000 financed with the company.
3. Detailing	Inspect cars delivered from factory, clean, and make minor adjustments	Piecework paid on the number of cars detailed per day.
4. Mechanics	Provide factory warranty service, maintenance, and repair.	Small hourly wage, plus bonus based on (1) number of cars completed per day and (2) finishing each car faster than the standard estimated time to repair.
5. Receptionists/phone service personnel	Primary liaison between customer and salesforce, finance, and mechanics.	Minimum wage.

APPLICATION CASE

Inserting the Team Concept into Compensation—or Not

One of the first things Sandy Caldwell wanted to do in his new position at Hathaway Manufacturing was improve productivity through teamwork at every level of the firm. As the new human resource manager for the suburban plant, Sandy set out to change the culture to accommodate the team-based approach he had become so enthusiastic about in his most recent position.

Sandy started by installing the concept of team management at the highest level, to oversee the operations of the entire plant. The new management team consisted of manufacturing, distribution, planning, technical, and human resource plant managers. Together they developed a new vision for the 500-employee facility, which they expressed in the simple phrase "Excellence Together." They drafted a new mission statement for the firm that focused on becoming customer driven and team based, and that called upon employees to raise their level of commitment and begin acting as "owners" of the firm.

The next step was to convey the team message to employees throughout the company. The communication process went surprisingly well, and Sandy was happy to see his idea of a "workforce of owners" begin to take shape. Teams trained together, developed production plans together, and embraced the technique of 360-degree feedback, in which an employee's performance evaluation is obtained from supervisors, subordinates, peers, and internal or external customers. Performance and morale improved, and productivity began to tick upward. The company even sponsored occasional celebrations to reward team achievements, and the team structure seemed firmly in place.

Sandy decided to change one more thing. Hathaway's long-standing policy had been to give all employees the same annual pay increase. But Sandy felt that in the new team environment, outstanding performance should be the criterion for pay raises. After consulting with CEO Regina Cioffi, Sandy sent a memo to all employees announcing the change to team-based pay for performance.

The reaction was immediate and 100% negative. None of the employees was happy with the change, and among their complaints, two stood out. First, because the 360-degree feedback system made everyone responsible in part for someone else's performance evaluation, no one was comfortable with the idea that pay raises might also somehow be linked to peer input. Second, there was a widespread perception that the way the change was decided upon, and the way it was announced, put the firm's commitment to team effort in doubt. Simply put, employees felt left out of the decision process.

Sandy and Regina arranged a meeting for early the next morning. Sitting in her office over their coffee, they began a painful debate. Should the new policy be rescinded as quickly as it was adopted, or should it be allowed to stand?

Questions

1. Does the pay-for-performance plan seem like a good idea? Why or why not?

2. What advice would you give Regina and Sandy as they consider their decision?

3. What mistakes did they make in adopting and communicating the new salary plan? How might Sandy have approached this major compensation change a little differently?

4. Assuming the new pay plan were eventually accepted, how would you address the fact that in the new performance evaluation system, employees' input affects their peers' pay levels?

Note: The incident in this case is based on an actual event at Frito-Lay's Kirkwood, New York, plant, as reported in C. James Novak, "Proceed with Caution When Paying Teams," *HR Magazine*, April 1997, p. 73.

CONTINUING CASE

Carter Cleaning Company

The Incentive Plan

The question of whether to pay Carter Cleaning Center employees an hourly wage or an incentive of some kind has always intrigued Jack Carter.

His basic policy has been to pay employees an hourly wage, except that his managers do receive an end-of-year bonus depending, as Jack puts it, "on whether their stores do well or not that year."

He is, however, considering using an incentive plan in one store. Jack knows that a presser should press about 25 "tops" (jackets, dresses, blouses) per hour. Most of his pressers do not attain this ideal standard, though. In one instance, a presser named Walt was paid $8 per hour, and Jack noticed that regardless of the amount of work he had to do, Walt always ended up going home at about 3:00 P.M., so he earned about $300 at the end of the week. If it was a holiday week, for instance, and there were a lot of clothes to press, he might average 22 to 23 tops per hour (someone else did pants) and so he'd earn perhaps $300 and still finish up each day in time to leave by 3:00 P.M. so he could pick up his children at school. But when things were very slow in the store, his productivity would drop to perhaps 12 to 15 pieces an hour, so that at the end of the week he'd end up earning perhaps $280, and in fact not go home much earlier than he did when it was busy.

Jack spoke with Walt several times, and while Walt always promised to try to do better, it gradually became apparent to Jack that Walt was simply going to earn his $300 per week no matter what. While Walt never told him so directly, it dawned on Jack that Walt had a family to support and was not about to earn less than his "target" wage regardless of how busy or slow the store was. The problem was that the longer Walt kept pressing each day, the longer the steam boilers and compressors had to be kept on to power his machines, and the fuel charges alone ran close to $6 per hour. Jack clearly needed some way short of firing Walt to solve the problem, since the fuel bills were eating up his profits.

His solution was to tell Walt that instead of an hourly $8 wage he would henceforth pay him $0.33 per item pressed. That way, said Jack to himself, if Walt presses 25 items per hour at $0.33 he will in effect get a small raise. He'll get more items pressed per hour and will therefore be able to shut the machines down earlier.

On the whole, the experiment worked well. Walt generally presses 25 to 35 pieces per hour now. He gets to leave earlier, and with the small increase in pay he generally earns his target wage. Two problems have arisen, though. The quality of Walt's work has dipped a bit, plus, his manager has to spend a minute or two each hour counting the number of pieces Walt pressed that hour. Otherwise Jack is fairly pleased with the results of his incentive plan and he's wondering whether to extend it to other employees and other stores.

Questions

1. Should this plan in its present form be extended to pressers in the other stores?

2. Should other employees (cleaner-spotters, counter people) be put on a similar plan? Why? Why not? If so, how, exactly?

3. Is there another incentive plan you think would work better for the pressers?

4. A store manager's job is to keep total wages to no more than 30% of sales and to maintain the fuel bill and the supply bill at about 9% of sales each. Managers can also directly affect sales by ensuring courteous customer service and by ensuring that the work is done properly. What suggestions would you make to Jennifer and her father for an incentive plan for store managers?

KEY TERMS

law of individual differences, 439
expectancy, 441
instrumentality, 441
valence, 441
variable pay, 441
piecework, 442
straight piecework, 443

standard hour plan, 443
merit pay (merit raise), 443
team or group incentive plan, 451
profit-sharing plan, 453
employee stock ownership plan
(ESOP), 453
Scanlon plan, 454

gainsharing plan, 455
at-risk variable pay plans, 456
annual bonus, 456
stock option, 460
golden parachutes, 462

ENDNOTES

1. Rajiv Banker, Seok-Young Lee, Gordon Potter, and Dhinu Srinivasan, "Contextual Analysis of Performance Impacts of Outcome-Based Incentive Competition," *Academy of Management Journal* 39, no. 4 (1996), pp. 940–941.
2. Linda Stroh, Jeanne Brett, Joseph Baumann, and Anne Reilly, "Agency Theory and Variable Pay Compensation Strategies," *Academy of Management Journal* 39, no. 3 (1996), pp. 751–767.
3. Ibid., p. 762. See also Richard Allen and Marilyn Helms, "Reward Practices and Organizational Performance," *Compensation and Benefits Review*, July/August 2001, pp. 74–80.
4. "Few Employees See the Pay for Performance Connection," *Compensation and Benefits Review*, June 2003, vol. 17, issue 2, "Most Workers Not Motivated by Cash," *Incentive Today*, July–August, 2004 p. 19, and "Pay-for Performance Plans' Impact Uncertain: Study," *Modern Healthcare*, May 24, 2004, p. 34.
5. James Shaw et al., "Reactions to Merit Pay Increases: A Longitudinal Test of a Signal Sensitivity Perspective," *Journal of Applied Psychology* 88, no. 3 (2003), pp. 538–544.
6. Ibid.
7. Ted Turnasella, "Pay and Personality," *Compensation and Benefits Review*, March/April 2002, pp. 45–59.
8. Ernest R. Hilgard, *Introduction to Psychology* (New York: Harcourt Brace and World, 1962), pp. 124–125.
9. See, for instance, R. Kanfer, "Motivation Theory," in M. D. Dunnette and L. M. Hough (eds.), *Handbook of Industrial and Organizational Psychology* (Palo Alto, CA: Consulting Psychologists Press, 1990). See also Robert Heresy, "A Practitioner's View of Motivation," *Journal of Managerial Psychology*, May 1993, pp. 110–115; and Kenneth Kovatch, "Employee Motivation: Addressing a Crucial Factor in Your Organization's Performance," *Employee Relations Today*, Summer 1995, pp. 93–107.
10. See Douglas M. McGregor, "The Human Side of Enterprise," in Michael Matteson and John M. Ivanovich (eds.), *Management Classics* (Santa Monica, CA: Goodyear, 1977), pp. 43–49. See also Weart Woolridge, "Time to Stand Maslow's Hierarchy on Its Head?" *People Management* 21, (December 1995), p. 17.
11. See, for example, Clay Alderfer, "Theories Reflecting My Personal Experiences and Life Development," *Journal of Applied Behavioral Science*, November 1989, pp. 351–366.
12. See, for example, Edward Deci, *Intrinsic Motivation* (New York: Plenum, 1975).
13. Frederick Hansen et al., "Rewards and Recognition in Employee Motivation," *Compensation and Benefits Review*, September/October 2002, p. 67.
14. Kanfer, "Motivation Theory," p. 113.
15. For a discussion, see John P. Campbell and Robert Prichard, "Motivation Theory in Industrial and Organizational Psychology," in Marvin Dunnette (ed.), *Industrial and Organizational Psychology* (Chicago: Rand McNally, 1976), pp. 74–75; and Kanfer, "Motivation Theory," pp. 115–116.
16. "Designing a Variable Pay Plan," *BNA Bulletin to Management*, June 20, 1996, p. 200.
17. Ibid., p. 200.
18. "Employers Use Pay to Lever Performance," *BNA Bulletin to Management*, August 21, 1997, p. 272.
19. See, for example, Kenan Abosch, "Variable Pay: Do We Have the Basics in Place?" *Compensation and Benefits Review*, July/August 1998, pp. 2–22.
20. See, for example, Diane Cadrain, "Cash Versus Non-cash Rewards," *HR Magazine*, April 2003, pp. 81–87.
21. This is based on William E. Buhl, "Keeping Incentives Simple for Nonexempt Employees," *Compensation and Benefits Review*, March/April 1989, pp. 14–19.
22. Ibid., pp. 15–16.
23. "Impact of Sarbanes-Oxley on Executive Compensation," downloaded December 11, 2003, from www.thelenreid.com, Thelen, Reid, and Priest L. L. P.
24. Richard Henderson, *Compensation Management* (Upper Saddle River, NJ: Prentice Hall, 2000), p. 463; Philip Lewis, "Managing Performance-Related Pay Based on Evidence from the Financial Services Sector," *Human Resource Management Journal* 8, no. 2 (1998), pp. 66–77.
25. For a discussion of these, see Thomas Wilson, "Is It Time to Eliminate the Piece Rate Incentive System?" *Compensation and Benefits Review*, March/April 1992, pp. 43–49.
26. Measured day work is a third type of individual incentive plan for production workers. See, for example, Mitchell Fein, "Let's Return to MDW for Incentives," *Industrial Engineering*, January 1979, pp. 34–37.
27. Oanh Ha, "California Workers Named in Articles Not Asked to Help in Piecework Probe," *Knight Ridder/Tribune News*, March 23, 2000, item 0008408e.
28. William Atkinson, "Incentive Pay Programs that Work in Textile," *Textile World* 151, no. 2 (February 2001), pp. 55–57.
29. Donald Campbell et al., "Merit Pay, Performance Appraisal, and Individual Motivation: An Analysis and Alternative," *Human Resource Management* 37, no. 2 (Summer 1998), pp. 131–146.
30. Dan Gilbert and Glenn Bassett, "Merit Pay Increases Are a Mistake," *Compensation and Benefits Review*, March/April 1994, pp. 20–25.

31. The average uncorrected cross-sectional correlation was 17. Michael Harris et al., "A Longitudinal Examination of a Merit Pay System: Relationships Among Performance Ratings, Merit Increases, and Total Pay Increases," *Journal of Applied Psychology* 83, no. 5 (1998), pp. 825–831.

32. Jonathan Glater, "Varying the Recipe Helps TV Operations Solve Morale Problem," *New York Times*, March 7, 2001, p. C1.

33. Edward Deci and Richard Ryan, *Intrinsic Motivation and Self-Determination in Human Behavior* (New York: Plenum Press, 1985).

34. Esther Shein, "Team Spirit: IT is Getting Creative with Compensation to Foster Collaboration," *PC Week*, May 11, 1998, pp. 69–72. See also, Fay Hansen, "Short-Term Incentive Programs Are Most Effective in Driving IT Performance," *Compensation and Benefits Review*, November/December 2003, pp. 11–12.

35. Rose-Robin Pedone, "Engineering the Job Market," *LI Business News*, July 7, 1998, p. 1B.

36. Julia King, "Name Your Price, As Talent Plays Hardball with Software Firms," *Computerworld*, September 16, 1996, p. 32.

37. Richard Arnold, "Catching a Star," *CA Magazine*, October 1998, pp. 107–112.

38. Ann Harrington, "Saying 'We Love You' With Stock Options," *Fortune*, October 11, 1999, p. 316.

39. Betty Sosin, "A Patent on the Back," *HR Magazine*, March 2000, pp. 107–112.

40. Scott Hays, "Pros and Cons of Pay for Performance," *Workforce*, February 1999, pp. 69–74, and "Incentives: Is Employee Recognition Key to Corporate Goals?" *Occupational Hazards*, November 2003, vol. 65, issue iii, p. 23.

41. Bob Nelson, *1001 Ways to Reward Employees* (New York: Workmen Publishing, 1994), p. 5.

42. "Round-the-Clock Recognition: Any Time Is a Good Time to Give Workers Their Due," *BNA Bulletin To Management*, February 13, 2003, p. 49.

43. Leslie Yerkes, "Motivating Workers in Tough Times," *Incentives* 75, no. 10, (October 2001), p. 120.

44. Libby Estell, "I See London, I See France . . . ," *Incentives*, August 2001, pp. 58–62.

45. Sarah Baley, "Getting Technical: The Incentive Business Gets Wired Slowly," *Meetings and Conventions*, October 1997, p. 13.

46. Ibid. See also, Chris Taylor, "On-the-Spot Incentives," *HR Magazine*, May 2004, pp. 80–85.

47. Paul Glister, "Online Incentives Sizzle—and You Shine," *Workforce*, January 2001, p. 46. See also Andrea Poe, "On-line Recognition," *HR Magazine*, June 2002, pp. 95–103.

48. Jeremy Wuittner, "Plenty of Incentives to Use E.I.M. Software Systems," *American Banker* 168, no. 129 (July 8, 2003), p. 680.

49. Mark Stiffler, "Incentive Compensation and the Web," *Compensation and Benefits Review*, January/February 2001, pp. 15–19.

50. "Striking a Chord: Texas Instruments Uses All the Right Tools to Recognize Top Performers," *Incentives* 177, no. 3 (March 2003), p. 34.

51. Karen Gines, "Unify and Simplify," *Incentives* 176, no. 9 (September 2002), p. 8.

52. William Bulkeley, "Incentives Systems Fine-Tune Pay/Bonus Plans," *Wall Street Journal*, August 16, 2001, p. B4.

53. Nina McIntyre, "EIM Technology to Successfully Motivate Employees," *Compensation and Benefits Review*, July/August 2001, pp. 57–60.

54. Straight salary by itself is not, of course, an incentive compensation plan as we use the term in this chapter.

55. Sonjun Luo, "Does Your Sales Incentive Plan Pay for Performance?" *Compensation and Benefits Review*, January/ February 2003, pp. 18–24.

56. David Harrison, Meghan Virick, and Sonja William, "Working Without a Net: Time, Performance, and Turnover Under Maximally Contingent Rewards," *Journal of Applied Psychology* 81, no. 4 (1996), p. 332.

57. Ibid., pp. 331–345.

58. John Steinbrink, "How to Pay Your Salesforce," *Harvard Business Review*, 57 (July-August 1978), p. 115.

59. Bill O'Connell, "Dead Solid Perfect: Achieving Sales Compensation Alignment," *Compensation and Benefits Review*, March/April 1996, pp. 46–47.

60. In the salary bonus plan, salespeople are paid a basic salary and are then paid a bonus for carrying out specific activities.

61. Jeanie Casisom, "Jumpstart Motivation," *Incentives* 175, no. 5 (May 2001), p. 77.

62. Kathleen Cholewka, "Tech Tools," *Sales and Marketing Management* 152, no. 7 (July 2001), p. 24.

63. Bill Weeks, "Setting Sales Force Compensation in the Internet Age," *Compensation and Benefits Review*, March/April 2000, pp. 25–34, and David Fiedler, "Should You Adjust Your Sales Compensation?" *HR Magazine*, February 2003, pp. 78–80.

64. S. Scott Sands, "Ineffective Quotas: The Hidden Threat to Sales Compensation Plans," *Compensation and Benefits Review*, March/April 2000, pp. 35–42.

65. Peter Gundy, "Sales Compensation Programs: Built to Last," *Compensation and Benefits Review*, September/October 2002, pp. 21–28.

66. David Cocks and Dennis Gould, " 'Sales Compensation' A New Technology—The Enabled Strategy," *Compensation and Benefits Review*, January/February 2001, pp. 27–31.

67. Peter Glendinning, "Kicking the Tires of Automotive Sales Compensation," *Compensation and Benefits Review*, September/ October 2000, pp. 47–53, and Michele Marchetti, "Why Sales Contests Don't Work," *Sales and Marketing Management*, January 2004, vol. 156, p. 19.

68. Eileen Zimmerman, "Quota Busters," *Sales and Marketing Management* 153, no. 1 (January 2001), pp. 58–63.

69. Ibid.

70. Henderson, *Compensation Management*, pp. 367–368. See also Shari Caudron, "Tie Individual Pay to Team Success," *Personnel Journal* 73, no. 10 (October 1994), pp. 40–46.

71. Other suggestions are as follows: equal payments to all members on the team; differential payments to team members based on their contributions to the team's performance; and differential payments determined by a ratio of each group member's base pay to the total base pay of the group. See Kathryn Bartol and Laura Hagmann, "Team Based Pay Plans: A Key to Effective Team Work," *Compensation and Benefits Review*, November–December 1992, pp. 24–29. See also, Charlotte Garvey, "Steer Teams with the Right Pay," *HR Magazine*, May 2002, pp. 70–71.

72. Richard Seaman, "The Case Study: Rejuvenating an Organization with Team Pay," *Compensation and Benefits Review*, September/ October 1997, pp. 25–30.

73. James Nickel and Sandra O'Neal, "Small Group Incentives: Gainsharing in the Microcosm," *Compensation and Benefits Review*, March/April 1990, p. 24. See also Jane Pickard, "How Incentives Can Drive Teamworking," *Personnel Management*, September 1993, pp. 26–32; and Caudron, "Tie Individual Pay to Team Success," pp. 40–46.

74. Robert Heneman and Courtney Von Hippel, "Balancing Group and Individual Rewards: Rewarding Individual Contributions to the Team," *Compensation and Benefits Review*, July/August 1995, pp. 63–68.

75. Nelson, *1001 Ways to Reward Employees*, p. 19.

76. "American Airlines' Profit Sharing Tops $250 Million," *Knight-Ridder/Tribune Business News*, February 27, 1998, p. 227.

77. "Ford Motor Co. Profit-Sharing Plan," *Wall Street Journal*, October 13, 1998, p. B5.

78. "Sharing the Wealth—GM," *Ward's Auto World*, March 1998, p. 7.

79. Seongsu Kim, "Does Profit Sharing Increase Firms' Profits?" *Journal of Labor Research* (Spring 1998), pp. 351–371. See also Jacqueline Coyle-Shapiro et al., "Using Profit-Sharing to Enhance Employee Attitudes: A Longitudinal Examination of the Effects on Trust and Commitment," *Human Resource Management* 41, no. 4 (Winter 2002), pp. 423–449.

80. David Belcher, *Compensation Administration* (Upper Saddle River, NJ: Prentice Hall, 1977), p. 351.

81. James Sesil et al., "Broad-based Employee Stock Options in U.S. New Economy Firms," *British Journal of Industrial Relations* 40, no. 2 (June 2002), pp. 273–294.

82. See James Brockardt and Robert Reilly, "Employee Stock Ownership Plans After the 1989 Tax Law: Valuation Issues," *Compensation and Benefits Review*, September/October 1990, pp. 29–36.

83. For a discussion of the effects of employee stock ownership on employee attitudes, see John Gamble, "ESOPs: Financial Performance and Federal Tax Incentives," *Journal of Labor Research* 19, no. 3 (Summer 1998), pp. 529–542.

84. Steven Etkind, "ESOPs Create Liquidity for Share Holders and Help Diversify Their Assets," *Estate Planning* 24, no. 4 (May 1998), pp. 158–165.

85. William Smith, Harold Lazarus, and Harold Murray Kalkstein, "Employee Stock Ownership Plans: Motivation and Moral Issues," *Compensation and Benefits Review*, September/October 1990, pp. 37–46.

86. Best Manufacturing Practices Center of Excellence, copyright 1998.

87. Brian Moore and Timothy Ross, *The Scanlon Way to Improved Productivity: A Practical Guide* (New York: Wiley, 1978), p. 2.

88. These are based in part on Steven Markham, K. Dow Scott, and Walter Cox Jr., "The Evolutionary Development of a Scanlon Plan," *Compensation and Benefits Review*, March/April 1992, pp. 50–56.

89. Markham et al., "The Evolutionary Development of a Scanlon Plan," p. 51.

90. Barry W. Thomas and Madeline Hess Olson, "Gainsharing: The Design Guarantees Success," *Personnel Journal*, May 1998, pp. 73–79. See also "Aligning Compensation with Quality," *Bulletin to Management*, BNA Policy and Practice Series, April 1, 1993, p. 97.

91. Paul Rossler and C. Patrick Koelling, "The Effect of Gainsharing on Business Performance at a Paper Mill," *National Productivity Review* (Summer 1993), pp. 365–382.

92. O'Dell and McAdams, *People, Performance and Pay*, p. 42.

93. This is paraphrased from Woodruff Imbermann, "Boosting Plant Performance with Gainsharing," *Business Horizons*, November–December 1992, p. 77.

94. For other examples, see Timothy Ross and Larry Hatcher, "Gainsharing Drives Quality Improvement," *Personnel Journal*, November 1992, p. 77.

95. Robert McNutt, "Sharing Across the Board: DuPont's Achievement Sharing Program," *Compensation and Benefits Review*, July/August 1990, pp. 17–24.

96. Mark Meltzer and Howard Goldsmith, "Executive Compensation for Growth Companies," *Compensation and Benefits Review*, November/December 1997, pp. 41–50, and Barbara Kiviat, "Everyone into the Bonus Pool," *Time*, December 15, 2003, vol. 162, issue 24, p. A5.

97. Ibid. See also, Eric Krell, "Getting a Grip on Executive Pay," *Workforce*, February 2003, pp. 30–32.

98. "Short-Term Incentives Considered Ineffective, Survey Reveals," *Society for Human Resource Management*, January 2000, p. 5.

99. Meltzer and Goldsmith, "Executive Compensation for Growth Companies," pp. 44–45. See also Robert E. Wood et al., "Bonuses, Goals, and Instrumentality Effects," *Journal of Applied Psychology* 84, no. 5 (1999), pp. 703–720.

100. Ibid., pp. 188. Meltzer and Goldsmith, "Executive Compensation for Growth Companies," p. 44. Fay Hansen, "Salary and Wage Trends," *Compensation and Benefits Review*, March/April 2004, pp. 9–10.

101. Bruce Ellig, *Executive Compensation: A Total Pay Perspective*, (New York: McGraw-Hill, 1962), p. 189. See also, Joseph Martocchio, *Strategic Compensation* (Upper Saddle River, NJ: Prentice Hall, 2004), pp. 412–414.

102. Meltzer and Goldsmith, "Executive Compensation," pp. 47–48.

103. Louis Lavelle, "How to Hold the Options Express," *BusinessWeek*, September 9, 2002.

104. Elaine Denby, "Weighing Your Options," *HR Magazine*, November 2002, pp. 44–49.

105. Jeff Staiman and Cary Thompson, "Designing and Implementing a Broad-Based Stock Option Plan," *Compensation and Benefits Review*, July/August 1998, p. 23.

106. Ibid., p. 23. See also Don Delves, "Stock Options: Overused and Underwater," *Workforce*, January 2003, pp. 50–54.

107. Ibid., p. 25.

108. "Study Finds That Directly Owning Stock Shares Leads to Better Results," *Compensation and Benefits Review*, March/April 2001, p. 7.

109. Ira Kay, "Beyond Stock Options: Emerging Practices in Executive Incentive Programs," *Compensation and Benefits Review*, November/December 1991, p. 19. Fay Hansen, "Executive Compensation," *Compensation and Benefits Review*, September/October 2003, pp. 9–10.

110. For a discussion, see ibid., pp. 18–29.

111. Jeffrey Kanter and Mathew Ward, "Long-Term Incentives for Management, Part 4: Performance Plans," *Compensation and Benefits Review*, January/February 1990, p. 36; Meltzer and Goldsmith, "Executive Compensation for Growth Companies," pp. 46–47. With the new plan at IBM, executives only benefit if the stock rises at least 10%. See "Stock Option Update," *HR Focus*, April 2004, p. 7.

112. Robert Klein, "Compensating Your Overseas Executives, Part 3: Exporting U.S. Stock Option Plans to Expatriates," *Compensation and Benefits Review*, January/February 1991, pp. 27–38.

113. For a discussion, see ibid.

114. "Final Regs Issued for Golden Parachute Payments," *Executive Tax and Management Report* 66, no. 17 (September 2003), p. 1.

115. "Conseco Not Alone on Executive Perks," *Knight-Ridder/Tribune Business News*, August 28, 2003, item 03240015.

116. This section is based on Meltzer and Goldsmith, "Executive Compensation for Growth Companies," pp. 41–50. See also James Nelson, "Linking Compensation to Business Strategy," *Journal of Business Strategy* 19, no. 2 (March/April 1998), pp. 25–28.

117. Richard Semler, "Developing Management Incentives That Drive Results," *Compensation and Benefits Review*, July/August 1998, pp. 41–48.

118. Ibid., p. 44.

119. Ibid., p. 47.

120. Jennifer Schott, "Compensation Ties Incentives to Change," *ebusiness*, March 12, 2001, p. 4.

121. Peter Kurlander, "Building Incentive Compensation Management Systems: What Can Go Wrong?" *Compensation and Benefits Review*, July/August 2001, pp. 52–56.

122. The following five points are based on Alfie Kohn, "Why Incentive Plans Cannot Work," *Harvard Business Review*, September/October 1993, pp. 54–63.

123. Ibid., p. 58.

124. Ibid., p. 62.

125. Ibid.; see also Bruce Tulgan, "Real Pay for Performance," *Journal of Business Strategy* 22, no. 3 (May/June 2001), pp. 19–22.

126. Reed Taussig, "Managing Cash Based Incentives," *Compensation and Benefits Review*, March/April 2002, pp. 65–68. See also Nigel Nicholson, "How to Motivate Your Problem People," *Harvard Business Review*, January 2003, pp. 57–65.

127. "Frameworks for a More ROI Minded Rewards Plan," *Pay for Performance Report*, (February 2003), p. 1, and Alan Robinson and Dean Schroeder, "Rewards That Really Work," *Security Management*, July 2004, pp. 30–34.

128. See, for example, James Gutherie and Edward Cunningham, "Pay for Performance: The Quaker Oats Alternative," *Compensation and Benefits Review*, March/April 1992, pp. 18–23.

129. Alfie Kohn, "Challenging Behaviorist Dogma: Myths About Money and Motivation," *Compensation and Benefits Review*, March/April 1998, pp. 27–32.

130. Ibid., pp. 30–31.

131. Gary Dessler, "How to Earn Your Employees' Commitment," *Academy of Management Executive* 13, no. 2 (1999), pp. 58–67; Steven Gross and Jeffrey Bacher, "The New Variable Pay Programs: How Some Succeed, Why Some Don't," *Compensation and Benefits Review*, January/February 1993, pp. 55–56. See also Nina Gupta and Jason Shaw, "Financial Incentives Are Effective!" *Compensation and Benefits Review*, March/April 1998, pp. 28–32.

132. Janet Wiscombe, "Can Pay for Performance Really Work?" *Workforce*, August 2001, p. 30.

133. Susan Marks, "Incentives That Really Reward and Motivate," *Workforce*, June 2001, pp. 108–114.

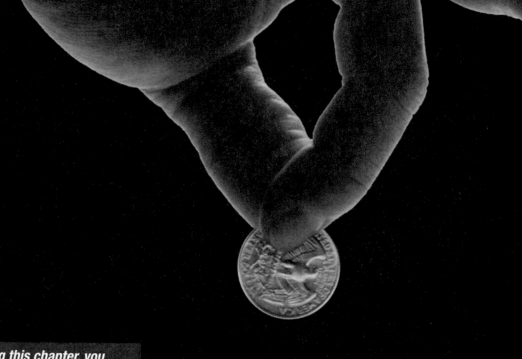

After studying this chapter, you should be able to:

1. Name and define each of the main pay for time not worked benefits.

2. Describe each of the main insurance benefits.

3. Discuss the main retirement benefits.

4. Outline the main employees' services benefits.

5. Explain the main flexible benefit programs.

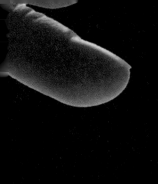

Benefits and Services

While the Hotel Paris's benefits (in terms of things like holidays and health care) were comparable to other hotels', Lisa Cruz knew they weren't good enough to support the high-quality service behaviors her company sought. Indeed, the fact that they were roughly comparable to those of similar firms didn't seem to impress the Hotel Paris's employees, at least 60% of whom consistently said they were deeply dissatisfied with the benefits they were getting. Lisa's concern (with which the CFO concurred) was that dissatisfaction with benefits contributed to morale and commitment being below what they should be, and thus to inhibiting the Hotel Paris from achieving its strategic aims. Lisa therefore turned to the task of assessing and redesigning the company's benefits plans.●

The previous chapter explained how to use financial incentives to motivate employees. The main purpose of this chapter is to improve your ability to weigh the pros and cons of various employee benefit plans. We discuss four main types of plans: supplemental pay benefits (such as sick leave and vacation pay); insurance benefits (such as workers' compensation); retirement benefits (such as pensions); and employee services (such as child-care facilities). We'll see that employees' preferences for various benefit plans differ, and that it's therefore useful to individualize benefits packages.

This chapter completes our discussion of employee compensation and benefits. The next chapter, Ethics, Justice, and Fair Treatment in HR Management, starts a new part of this book, and focuses on another important HR task, employee relations.

● THE BENEFITS PICTURE TODAY

benefits
Indirect financial and nonfinancial payments employees receive for continuing their employment with the company.

"What are your benefits?" is the first question many applicants ask. **Benefits**—indirect financial and nonfinancial payments employees receive for continuing their employment with the company—are an important part of just about every employee's compensation.[1] They include things like health and life insurance, pensions, time off with pay, and child-care facilities.

Most full-time employees in the United States receive benefits. Virtually all employers—99%—offer some health insurance coverage.[2] However, the percentage of Americans covered by job-based health insurance fell from 63.6% in 2000 to 61.3% in 2002.[3]

Benefits are a major expense for most employers. Employee benefits account for about one-third of wages and salaries (or about 28% of total payrolls), with legally required benefits, followed by health insurance, the most expensive single benefit cost.[4] As Figure 13-1 summarizes, annual health care costs have increased steadily for the past few years. Consultants Towers Perrin estimate that the 2004 cost of medical coverage alone was about $314 per month for employee-only coverage, $627 per month for employee plus one dependent coverage, and $888 per month for family coverage.[5] Figure 13-2 summarizes the breakdown of benefits as a percentage of wages and salaries as of June 2003. As you can see, legally required payments for things like unemployment compensation represent the biggest benefits expense.

Figure 13-1
Annual Health Care Cost Increases—National Averages
Source: Eric Parmenter, "Controlling Health-Care Costs," *Compensation and Benefits Review*, September/October 2002, p. 44. Reprinted by permission of Sage Publications, Inc.

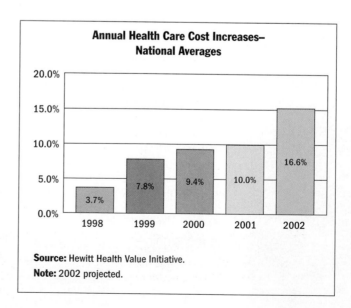

Annual Health Care Cost Increases–National Averages

- 1998: 3.7%
- 1999: 7.8%
- 2000: 9.4%
- 2001: 10.0%
- 2002: 16.6%

Source: Hewitt Health Value Initiative.
Note: 2002 projected.

Figure 13-2
Private-Sector Employer
Compensation Costs, June
2003
Source: "Total Employer Costs Rose
to 22.61 in Second Quarter," *BNA*
Bulletin to Management, September 11,
2003, p. 293.

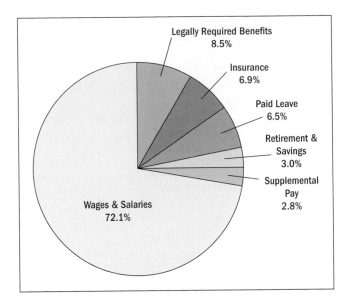

Employees do seem to understand the value of health benefits. One study concluded that employees whose firms provided such benefits accepted wages about 20% lower than what they would have received working at firms without such benefits.[6] But another survey, of 10,000 employees, found that only 43% were satisfied with the overall performance of their health plans, and less than half trust their employers to design health plans that provide the coverage they need.[7]

In developing benefits plans, employers must address numerous policy issues. These include: what benefits to offer; who receives coverage; whether to include retirees in the plan; whether to deny benefits to employees during initial "probationary" periods; how to finance benefits; the degree of employee choice in determining benefits; cost-containment procedures; and how to communicate benefits options to employees.[8] Many of these decisions involve federal law.

Know Your Employment Law

Benefits

Some benefits are required by federal (or most state) law, while others are discretionary (see Table 13-1). However, while not required under federal law, these "discretionary" benefits are regulated—often extensively—by federal law.

While "equal employment law" may jump to mind when managers think of work-related regulations, *employee benefits* are probably as much or more regulated. A surprisingly wide range of federal law applies here, and in most instances (such as setting up pension plans), it is basically impossible to proceed without expert help. For example, the Employee Retirement Income Security Act of 1975 (ERISA) covers pension plans, and requires employers to have written plan documents that establish terms (such as eligibility and participation).[9] The Economic Growth and Tax Relief Conciliation Act of 2001 contains provisions governing retirement plans. In 2002, President Bush signed into law the Job Creation and Worker Assistance Act (the "economic stimulus law"). This provides guidelines regarding what rates of return employers should use in computing their pension plan values. The Newborn Mother's Protection Act of 1996 prohibits an employer's health plan from using incentives to encourage employees to leave the hospital after childbirth after less than the legislatively determined minimum stay. The Mental Health Parity Act of 1996 limits health plans' ability to set annual or lifetime maximums on mental and nervous

Table 13-1

Benefits Required by Federal or Most State Law	Benefits Discretionary on Part of Employer*
Social Security	Disability, Health, and Life Insurance
Unemployment Insurance	Pensions
Workers' Compensation	Paid Time Off for Vacations, Holidays, Sick Leave, Personal Leave, Jury Duty, etc.
Leaves under Family Medical Leave Act	Employee Assistance and Counseling Programs
	"Family Friendly" benefits for Child Care, Elder Care, Flexible Work Schedules, etc.
	Executive Perquisites

While not required under federal law, all these benefits are regulated in some way by federal law, as explained in this chapter.

disorders benefits. Several organizations, including CALPERS, California's pension management authority, were found by courts to have violated the Age Discrimination in Employment Act by discriminating against older employees in the way they calculated retirement benefits.[10]

Employers who provide health care services (such as in-house counseling or medical facilities) also have to follow the privacy rules of the Health Insurance Portability and Accountability Act of 1996 (HIPAA). These rules set minimum requirements for protecting individuals' health care data accessibility and confidentiality.[11]

Of course, employers also must adhere to the laws of the states in which they do business. For example, California recently passed legislation requiring most state contractors to provide domestic partner benefits for employees who are in same-sex relationships.[12]

On a more day-to-day basis, many of the manager's benefits-related legal questions will involve employee leaves. Different types of employee leaves involve different levels of employer legal liability. Personal leave, vacation leave, and paid sick leave are generally matters of company policy, rather than statutory law.[13] Most employers grant personal leave in renewable increments for things like non-health-related personal crises. The main legal obligation here is to ensure that the company awards and extends personal leaves in a nondiscriminatory manner. If the employee fails to return once the unpaid personal leave expires, then the manager should invoke the company's job abandonment or attendance discipline policies.[14]

No federal law requires private-sector employers to grant paid vacation leave or paid holidays. One question that may arise is whether the employer has the right to cancel an employee's scheduled vacation, for instance, due to an unanticipated rush of orders. Here it's important that the employer formulate its vacation policy so it is clear that the employer reserves the right to require vacation cancellation and rescheduling if production so demands.[15] If the employee works during what would otherwise be his or her vacation period, the employee should then be paid both his or her regular pay and vacation pay for the period ("pay in lieu of vacation"), assuming the employer does not simply reschedule the vacation.

While federal law does not require vacation benefits, the employer must still formulate vacation policy with care. As another example, the employer generally must pay the employee for his or her earned but unused vacation when the employee terminates. However, the employer defines "earned." For example, if the employer's vacation policy requires that a new employee pass his or her first employment anniversary before becoming entitled to a vacation, the employee gets no vacation pay if he or she leaves for any reason during that first year. Similarly, if the vacation policy simply says that an employee receives, say, a two-week vacation after two years with the company, he or she may not be eligible for any pro rata vacation if he or she leaves before the end of two years. Many employers write a vacation policy that says vacation pay accrues, say, on a biweekly basis. By doing so they obligate themselves to pay employees pro rata vacation pay when they leave the firm.

Under the Family and Medical Leave Act (FMLA), the Americans with Disabilities Act (ADA), or state workers' compensation laws, certain leaves are statutorily required. For example, under the FMLA the employer must grant an employee 12 weeks of leave in a 12-month period for the birth or care of a newborn child; placement of a child for adoption or foster care; to care for a spouse, child, or parent with a serious health condition; or to care for the employee's own serious health condition. Under the Americans with Disabilities Act, a qualified employee with a disability may be eligible for a leave if such a leave is necessary to reasonably accommodate the employee. And, as we will see later in this chapter, under various state workers' compensation laws, employees may be eligible for medical expense reimbursement and disability income and leave in connection with work-related injuries.

Employers have recently expressed some dissatisfaction with the FMLA. A survey of 416 HR professionals found that about half said they approved leaves they believed were not legitimate, but felt they had to grant because of vague interpretations of the law.[16] Therefore, the employer who wants to avoid granting FMLA leaves that are not really required by law needs to understand some FMLA details. For example, to be eligible for leave under the FMLA, the employee must have worked for the employer for at least a total of 12 months and have worked (not just been paid) for 1,250 or more hours in the past 12 consecutive months.[17] The employee must also be assigned to a job site that employs 50 or more employees within a 75-mile radius. If either does not apply, no leave is required.

Here again, the employer needs to be careful how it formulates its policies. For example, if it uses a calendar or fiscal year for its 12-month FMLA period, then an employee could conceivably take his or her two 12-week leaves back-to-back. To avoid this, write the policy so that the clock starts again on the date the employee returns from his or her last leave. Similarly, keep in mind that under the FMLA the employee must give the employer 30 days' advance notice if the need is foreseeable, and (again) must have worked at least 1,250 hours in the past 12 months—not just been paid for those hours—as he or she might have been if on paid leave. We discuss the FMLA further on page 482.

There are many benefits and various ways to classify them. We will classify them as (1) pay for time not worked, (2) insurance benefits, (3) retirement benefits, and (4) services. We start our discussion with pay for time not worked.

● PAY FOR TIME NOT WORKED

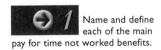

1 Name and define each of the main pay for time not worked benefits.

supplemental pay benefits
Benefits for time not worked such as unemployment insurance, vacation and holiday pay, and sick pay.

Pay for time not worked—also called **supplemental pay benefits**—is one of an employer's most costly benefits, because of the large amount of time off that many employees receive. Common time-off-with-pay periods include holidays, vacations, jury duty, funeral leave, military duty, personal days, sick leave, sabbatical leave, maternity leave, and unemployment insurance payments for laid-off or terminated employees.

Unemployment Insurance

unemployment insurance
Provides benefits if a person is unable to work through some fault other than his or her own.

All states have **unemployment insurance** or compensation laws. These provide for benefits if a person is unable to work through no fault of his or her own. The benefits derive from a tax on employers that can range from 0.1% to 5% of taxable payroll in most states. An employer's unemployment tax rate reflects its rate of personnel terminations. States have their own unemployment laws, but they all follow federal guidelines.

Firms aren't required to let everyone they dismiss receive unemployment benefits—only those released through no fault of their own. Thus, strictly speaking, a worker

The jury takes the oath before the full courtroom (judge, clerk of the court, defendant, lawyers, and onlookers). Jury duty is one of a number of supplemental pay benefits, or pay for time not worked, that are very costly for employers because of the amount of time an employee may be off the job.

fired for chronic lateness can't legitimately claim benefits. But many managers take a lackadaisical attitude toward protecting their employers against unwarranted claims. Employers therefore spend thousands of dollars per year on unemployment taxes that would not be necessary if they protected themselves.

Following the checklist in Table 13-2 can help protect the employer. Determine whether you could answer "yes" to questions such as, "Do you have a rule that three days' absence without calling is reason for automatic discharge?" Doing so should enable you to better demonstrate that a dismissal was a result of the person's inadequate performance rather than lack of work or some other cause beyond his or her control.

Vacations and Holidays

The number of paid employee vacation days varies considerably from employer to employer. In the United States, the average is about 10 days per year. However, even for the same employer, long-term employees traditionally get more vacation days. Thus, a typical U.S. company policy might call for:

1. One week after 6 months to 1 year of service;
2. Two weeks after 1 to 5 years of service;
3. Three weeks after 5 to 10 years of service;
4. Four weeks after 15 to 25 years of service; and
5. Five weeks after 25 years of service.[18]

The number of paid holidays also varies considerably from employer to employer, from a minimum of about 5 days to 13 or more. The most common paid holidays include New Year's Day, Memorial Day, Independence Day, Labor Day, Thanksgiving Day, and Christmas Day. Other common holidays include Martin Luther King Jr. Day, Good Friday, Presidents' Day, Veterans' Day, the Friday after Thanksgiving, the day before Christmas Day, and the day before New Year's Day.[19]

Firms have to address several holiday- and vacation-related policy issues. They must decide, of course, how many days off employees will get, and what (if any) the

Table 13-2

An Unemployment Insurance Cost-Control To-Do Checklist

Cause—Do You:

1. Keep documented history of lateness, absence, and warning notices

2. Warn chronically late employees before discharging them

3. Have policy that three days' absence without calling in is reason for automatic discharge

4. Request doctor's note on return to work after absence

5. Make written approval for personal leave mandatory

6. Stipulate date for return to work from leave

7. Obtain a signed resignation statement

8. Mail job abandonment letter if employee fails to return on time

9. Require new employees to stipulate in writing their availability to work overtime, night shifts, etc.

10. Set probationary periods to evaluate new employees

11. Conduct follow-up interviews one to two months after hire

12. Document all instances of poor performance, recording when and how employees did not meet job requirements

13. Require supervisors to document the steps taken to remedy the situation

14. Require supervisors to document employee's refusal of advice and direction

15. Make sure all policies and rules of conduct are understood by all employees

16. Require all employees to sign a statement acknowledging acceptance of firm's policies and rules

17. File the protest against a former employee's unemployment claim on time (usually within 10 days)

18. Use proper terminology on claim form and attach documented evidence regarding separation

19. Attend hearings and appeal unwarranted claims

20. Check every claim against the individual's personnel file

21. Routinely conduct exit interviews to produce information for protesting unemployment claims

22. Hold periodic workshops with supervisors to review procedures and support effort to reduce turnover costs

23. Identify turnover problems as they occur by

a) location

b) department

c) classification of employee

paid holidays will be. Other policy decisions include: Will employees get their regular base pay while on vacation, or vacation pay based on average earnings (which may include overtime)? Will employees get paid for accrued vacation time if they leave before taking their vacations? Will we pay employees for a holiday if they don't come to work the day before and the day after the holiday? And, should we pay some premium—such as time and a half—when employees must work on holidays? Wage surveys and Web sites like hrtools.com provide sample policies for inclusion in the firm's employee manual.

Sick Leave

Sick leave provides pay to employees when they're out of work due to illness. Most sick leave policies grant full pay for a specified number of sick days—usually up to about 12 per year. The sick days usually accumulate at the rate of, say, one day per month of service.

Sick leave pay causes difficulty for many employers. The problem is that while many employees use their sick days only when they are legitimately sick, others use sick leave as extensions to vacations, whether they are sick or not. In one survey, for instance, personal illnesses accounted for only about 45% of unscheduled sick leave absences. Family issues (27%), personal needs (13%), a mentality of "entitlement" (9%), and stress (6%) were other reasons cited.[20] While the figure varies considerably by size of firm, unscheduled absenteeism for all employers averages about 1.6% of all scheduled work hours. Thus, a company with 10 employees and a 40-hour workweek might expect to have employees calling in with unscheduled absences at the rate of about .016 × 400 or 6.4 hours per week.[21] One survey found that the average cost of absenteeism per employee per year was $789 in 2002, with personal illness accounting for about a third of the absences.[22]

Employers have tried several tactics to reduce the problem. Some repurchase unused sick leave at the end of the year by paying their employees a daily equivalent sum for each sick leave day not used. The drawback is that the policy can encourage legitimately sick employees to come to work despite their illness. Others have experimented with holding monthly lotteries in which only employees with perfect monthly attendance are eligible for a cash prize. Marriott has a program called BeneTrade through which employees can trade the value of some sick days for other benefits. Others aggressively investigate all absences, for instance, by calling the absent employees at their homes when they are out sick.

Many companies use pooled paid leave plans. These plans lump together sick leave, vacation, and holidays into a single leave pool. Their use grew from 21% of firms surveyed about five years ago to 66% recently.[23] For example, one hospital previously granted new employees 25 days off per year (10 vacation days, three personal days, and 12 sick days). Employees used, on average, five of those 12 sick days (as well as all vacations and personal days).[24] The new pooled paid leave plan allowed new employees to accrue 18 days to use as they saw fit. ("Catastrophic leaves"—defined as short-term illnesses causing absences for more than five consecutive workdays, as well as special absences like jury duty and bereavement leave—were handled with separate accounts.) The new plan reportedly resulted in a saving of almost $400,000 over three years in lower overtime, and $350,000 in reduced temporary help.

Parental Leave and the Family and Medical Leave Act

Parental leave is an important benefit. About half of workers are women, and about 80% will become pregnant during their work lives. Furthermore, many women and men are heads of single-parent households. Partly as a response, former president Clinton signed the Family and Medical Leave Act of 1993 (FMLA). Among its provisions (as noted earlier) the law stipulates that:

1. Private employers of 50 or more employees must provide eligible employees up to 12 weeks of unpaid leave for their own serious illness, the birth or adoption of a child, or the care of a seriously ill child, spouse, or parent.

2. Employers may require employees to take any unused paid sick leave or annual leave as part of the 12-week leave provided in the law.

3. Employees taking leave are entitled to receive health benefits while they are on unpaid leave, under the same terms and conditions as when they were on the job.

4. Employers must guarantee employees the right to return to their previous or equivalent position with no loss of benefits at the end of the leave; however, the law provides a limited exception from this provision to certain highly paid employees.

Seven states (California, Illinois, Louisiana, Massachusetts, Minnesota, North Carolina, and Vermont) and the District of Columbia have expanded upon the Family Medical and Leave Act by instituting "small necessities leave" laws. These provide leave for things like visiting physicians and attending school activities.[25]

This request and the U.S. Department of Labor Certification of Health Care Provider form should be sent to Human Resources Salary Administration, Box 7210, NCSU, Raleigh, NC 27695 CALS-Cooperative Extension Personnel should forward their forms to CALS Personnel Office, Box 7602, NCSU, Raleigh, NC 27695

Employee Name _____ PeopleSoft ID# _____

Telephone _____ (work) _____ (home)

Department _____

Supervisor Name _____ Telephone _____

Leave Coordinator Name _____ Telephone _____

Leave to Begin _____ / / _____ Return to Work _____ / / _____

While on Family Illness Leave I plan to use: (check all that apply)

☐ **Leave Without Pay (LWOP)**   ☐ **Sick Leave**   ☐ **Comp Time**
☐ **Annual Leave**   ☐ **Bonus Leave**

I have applied for participation in the Shared Leave Program   ☐ Yes   ☐ No

I understand that if I am taking this leave as LWOP, I will need to pay for my health benefits should I want them to continue while I am on Family Illness Leave. I also understand that I must provide written notice of my intention to return to work prior to the end of my leave and return to duty within or at the end of the time granted, or notify the department immediately when there is a decision not to return. Failure to report at the expiration of a leave, unless an extension has been requested and approved, may be considered as a resignation.

Employee Signature _____ **Date** _____

Supervisor Signature _____ **Date** _____

Human Resources Signature _____ **Date** _____

Figure 13-3
North Carolina State University Family Illness Leave Request

Some employers have found complying with the FMLA somewhat onerous. "We have found that basically any illness is now covered by the law," said one benefits director. Another contends that her company can no longer "impose any discipline—even the downgrading of attendance ratings—for absences due to any cause covered by the law."[26] Employees also seem to be surprisingly aware of their rights under the act, with over half the complaints filed with the Department of Labor's Wage and Hour Division in some recent years stemming from the act.[27] And courts have found supervisors (not just employers) liable under the act for improperly preventing workers from exercising their FMLA rights.[28]

Family and Medical Leave Act leaves are usually unpaid (see Figure 13-3), but they're not costless to the employer. One study concluded that the costs associated with recruiting new temporary replacement workers, training them, and compensating for their lower productivity could represent a significant expense over and above what employers would normally pay full-time employees.[29] (Find out more about the FMLA at www.dol.gov/elaws.)

As noted earlier, employers therefore need clear procedures for leaves of absence (including those awarded under the Family and Medical Leave Act). In general, no employee should be given a leave until it's clear what the leave is for. If the leave is for medical or family reasons, the employer should obtain medical certification from the attending physician or medical practitioner. A standard form should also place on record the employee's expected return date, and the fact that without an authorized extension, the firm may terminate his or her employment. One employment lawyer says employers should "kind of bend over backward" when deciding if an employee is eligible for leave based on an FMLA situation, and not be too abrupt in turning the person down.[30] However, employers can require independent medical assessments before approving paid FMLA disability leaves.[31]

Severance Pay

severance pay
A one-time payment some employers provide when terminating an employee.

Many employers provide **severance pay**—a one-time payment when terminating an employee. Severance pay makes sense on several grounds. It is a humanitarian gesture, and good public relations. In addition, most managers expect employees to give them at least one or two weeks' notice if they plan to quit; it therefore seems appropriate to provide at least one or two weeks' severance pay if an employee is being dismissed. Avoiding litigation from disgruntled former employees is another reason for severance pay. And the Worker Adjustment and Retraining Notification ("plant closing") Act requires covered employers to give employees 60 days' written notice (but not severance pay) of plant closures or mass layoffs. Finally, severance pay plans help reassure employees who stay on after the employer downsizes its workforce that they'll receive some financial help if the employer lets them go, too.

For whatever reason, severance pay is common. In one survey of 3,000 HR managers, 82% of responding organizations (ranging from 66% for very small firms to over 90% for larger firms) reported having a severance policy.[32] Just about all full time employees of "old economy" U.S. companies (such as steel and autos) and about half their part time workers are eligible for severance pay. The reason for the dismissal affects whether the employee gets severance pay. For example, about 95% of employees dismissed due to downsizings got severance pay, while only about a third of employers offered severance in cases of termination for poor performance. About half the employees receiving severance pay get lump-sum amounts; the other half receive salary continuation for a time. The average maximum severance is 39 weeks for executives and about 30 weeks for other downsized employees.[33] Severance pay at the rate of one week of severance pay for each year of service is the policy at about half the firms responding to another survey.[34]

Supplemental Unemployment Benefits

supplemental unemployment benefits
Provide for a "guaranteed annual income" in certain industries where employers must shut down to change machinery or due to reduced work. These benefits are paid by the company and supplement unemployment benefits.

In some industries, such as automaking, shutdowns to reduce inventories or change machinery are common, and laid-off or furloughed employees must depend on unemployment insurance. Some companies pay **supplemental unemployment benefits**. As the name implies, these supplement the employee's unemployment compensation, and help the person maintain his or her standard of living for the time he or she is out of work. They provide benefits over and above state employment compensation for three contingencies: layoffs, reduced workweeks, and relocations.

Describe each of the main insurance benefits.

● INSURANCE BENEFITS

Most employers also provide a number of required or voluntary insurance benefits, such as workers' compensation and health insurance.

Workers' Compensation

workers' compensation
Provides income and medical benefits to work-related accident victims or their dependents regardless of fault.

Workers' compensation laws aim to provide sure, prompt income and medical benefits to work-related accident victims or their dependents, regardless of fault. Every state has its own workers' compensation law and administrative commission, and some run their own insurance programs. However, most require employers to carry workers' compensation insurance with private, state-approved insurance companies. Neither the state nor the federal government contributes any funds for workers' compensation.

How Benefits Are Determined   Workers' compensation benefits can be monetary or medical. In the event of a worker's death or disablement, the person's dependents are paid a cash benefit based on prior earnings—usually one-half to two-thirds the worker's average weekly wage, per week of employment. In most states, there is a set time limit—such as 500 weeks—for which benefits can be paid. If the injury causes a specific loss (such as an arm), the employee may receive additional benefits based on a statutory list of losses, even though he or she may return to work. In addition to these cash benefits, employers must furnish medical, surgical, and hospital services as required for the employee.

For workers' compensation to cover an injury or work-related illness, one must only prove that it arose while the worker was on the job. It does not matter that he or she may have been at fault; if the person was on the job when the injury occurred, he or she is entitled to workers' compensation. For example, suppose you instruct all employees to wear safety goggles when at their machines. One worker does not and experiences an injury while on the job. The company must still provide workers' compensation benefits.

The employment provisions of the Americans with Disabilities Act (ADA) influence employers' workers' compensation procedures. For one thing, ADA provisions generally prohibit employers from inquiring about an applicant's workers' compensation history, a practice that was widespread before passage of the act. Furthermore, the ADA makes it more important that injured employees get back to work quickly or be accommodated if their injury leads to a disability. Failing to let an employee who is on workers' compensation because of an injury return to work, or failing to accommodate him or her, could lead to lawsuits under ADA.[35]

Controlling Workers' Compensation Costs   Minimizing the number of workers' compensation claims (and therefore accidents and lost hours) is an important goal for all employers. While the employer's insurance company usually pays the claims, the costs of the premiums depend on the number and dollar amount of claims. Workers' compensation benefits costs are rising: They recently grew by 3.5% overall while wages grew by just 2.4%.[36]

While many workers' compensation claims are legitimate, some are not. Supervisors should be aware of typical red flags for fraudulent claims, including: vague accident details; minor accidents resulting in major injuries; lack of witnesses; injuries occurring late Friday or very early Monday; and late reporting.[37]

In practice, there are several ways to reduce such claims. You can screen out accident-prone workers. You can reduce accident-causing conditions in your facilities. And you can reduce the accidents and health problems that trigger these claims—for instance, by instituting effective safety and health programs and complying with government safety standards.

It's also important to get injured employees back on the job as fast as possible, since workers' compensation costs accumulate as long as the person is out of work. Many firms have rehabilitation programs that include physical therapy (including exercise equipment); career counseling to guide injured employees into new, less strenuous jobs; and nursing assistance to help reintegrate recipients back into your workforce.[38] Employers can also affect their premiums by selecting insurers based on their level of service and flexibility in negotiating rates.[39]

Case management is an increasingly popular cost-control option. It is "the treatment of injured workers on a case-by-case basis by an assigned manager, usually a registered nurse, who coordinates with the physician and health plan to determine which care settings are the most effective for quality care and cost.[40] Respondents in one survey found that safety/injury protection and case management were the most common workers' compensation cost-containment measures. Other effective techniques included monitoring health care providers for compliance with their fee schedules, and auditing medical bills.[41]

Hospitalization, Health, and Disability Insurance

Health and hospitalization insurance looms large in many people's choice of employer, because such insurance is so expensive. Most employers therefore offer their employees some type of hospitalization, medical, and disability insurance. Along with life insurance, these benefits form the cornerstone of most benefits programs. Table 13-3 illustrates the prevalance of health-related benefits.

Hospitalization, health, and disability insurance helps protect against hospitalization costs and the loss of income arising from off-the-job accidents or illness. Many employers purchase the insurance from life insurance companies, casualty insurance companies, or Blue Cross (for hospital expenses) and Blue Shield (for physician expenses) organizations. Others contract with health maintenance organizations or preferred provider organizations.

Most health insurance plans provide at least basic hospitalization and surgical and medical insurance for all eligible employees at group rates. Insurance is generally available to all employees—including new nonprobationary ones—regardless of health or physical condition. Most basic plans pay for hospital room and board, surgery charges, and medical expenses (such as doctors' visits to the hospital). Some also provide major medical coverage to meet the high medical expenses resulting from long-term or serious illnesses. Employers' health and hospitalization plans must comply with the Americans with Disabilities Act.[42] For example, the plan shouldn't make distinctions based on disability unless those distinctions are justified by recognized differences based on actuarial data or historic costs.[43]

Most employers also sponsor insurance plans that help cover health-related expenses like eye care and dental services. In most employer-sponsored dental plans, employees pay a specific amount of deductible dental expenses before the plan kicks in with benefits. In most cases, the premiums are paid entirely by the employers.

Table 13-3

Percent of Employers Offering Health Benefits

	Number Responding	Yes
Prescription drug program coverage	580	98%
Life insurance	582	97%
Dental insurance	581	96%
PPO (preferred provider organization)	578	87%
Mental health insurance	578	76%
Vision insurance	580	71%
Employee assistance program	579	67%
Vaccinations on-site (example: flu shots)	581	60%
Chiropractic insurance	576	59%
Wellness program, resources, and information	578	57%
CPR training/first aid	581	55%
HMO (health maintenance organization)	576	54%

Source: Adapted from SHRM/SHRM Foundation 2003 Benefits Survey.

Other plans pay for diagnostic visits to the doctor's office, vision care, hearing aids, and prescription drugs. *Accidental death and dismemberment* coverage provides a lump-sum benefit in addition to life insurance benefits when death is accidental. It also provides benefits in case of accidental loss of limbs or sight. Employers must provide the same health care benefits to employees over the age of 65 that they do to younger workers, even though the older workers are eligible for federally funded Medicare health insurance. *Disability insurance* provides income protection for loss of salary due to illness or accident. Payments usually start when normal sick leave payments end, and may continue until age 65 or beyond. The benefits usually range from 50% to 75% of the employee's base pay if he or she is disabled.

Many employers offer membership in a **health maintenance organization (HMO)** as a hospital/medical option. The HMO itself is a medical organization consisting of specialists (surgeons, psychiatrists, and so on) operating out of a community-based health care center. It provides routine medical services to employees who pay a nominal fee. The HMO also receives a fixed annual fee per employee from the employer (or employer and employee), regardless of whether it provides that person service.

Preferred provider organizations (PPOs) are a cross between HMOs and the traditional doctor–patient arrangement: They are "groups of health care providers that contract with employers, insurance companies, or third-party payers to provide medical care services at a reduced fee."[44] Unlike HMOs (whose relatively limited lists of health care providers are often located in one health care center), PPOs let employees select providers (like doctors) from a relatively wide list, and see them in their offices. The providers agree to provide discounts and submit to certain utilization controls, such as on the number of diagnostic tests they can order.[45]

New Trends in Health Care Cost Control Employers are taking steps to try to rein in spiraling health care costs.[46] Many are using *cost-containment specialists*—companies that specialize in helping employers reduce their health care costs. For example,

health maintenance organization (HMO)
A prepaid health care system that generally provides routine round-the-clock medical services as well as preventive medicine in a clinic-type arrangement for employees, who pay a nominal fee in addition to the fixed annual fee the employer pays.

preferred provider organizations (PPOs)
Groups of health care providers that contract with employers, insurance companies, or third-party payers to provide medical care services at a reduced fee.

health care containment companies can use their network of contacts with PPOs to help employers obtain the best PPO coverage for their needs.

Getting employees more *involved and empowered* in the health care program is another cost-containment trend. To manage health care costs, it's crucial that employees have a stake in the process. As one cost control expert puts it, "the biggest criticism of managed care . . . is that the health care consumer has little financial stake in treatment decisions. Today's typical patients consume as much health care as they wish, and someone else pays for it."[47] The solution, in part, is to make sure employees know the costs of the medical decisions they're making, and to involve them more in plan administration. For example, employers use their HR intranets to provide employees with access to basic health care coverage and benefits information, promote in-network services to employees, and encourage employees to reevaluate their health care market options frequently. *Online selection software* allows employees to choose the most appropriate of the employer's health care offerings based on estimates from employees concerning matters like doctor visits, prescriptions, and use of specialists. Other big savings come from *automating health care plan administration*, for instance, by making online enrollment mandatory.[48]

Other employers are moving toward *defined contribution health care plans*. These are similar to 401(k) retirement programs, but focus on health care costs. The employer commits to making a specific dollar amount contribution toward each employee's health care coverage. Under defined contribution health plans, each employee has a medical allotment that he or she can use for copayments or discretionary medical costs, rather than a specified health care benefits package with open-ended costs. Yet other firms are moving toward offering plans with *high deductibles*—more than $1,000—for individual coverage.[49]

Outsourcing is another option. For example,[50] 84% of firms in one survey said they were outsourcing employee assistance and counseling, and 53% were outsourcing health care benefits administration.

Many firms are cutting their health care costs by reducing or *eliminating retiree health care coverage*. One study found that about 13% of surveyed employers had reduced subsidized health benefits for their future retirees in the previous two years.[51] (About 17,000 unionized blue-collar employees at GE recently staged a two-day strike protesting increased premiums for the firm's 25,000 early retirees.)[52]

Small firms are increasingly joining *benefits purchasing alliances*. The assumption here is that by banding together to purchase health care benefits, these employers will obtain better choice, purchasing power, human resource management efficiencies, and cost savings than they would if they pursue these benefits alone.[53] Figure 13-4 summarizes other cost-saving strategies.

Mental Health Benefits   Mental illnesses account for a large portion of the disabilities in the United States, Canada, and Western Europe. The World Health Organization estimates that in the United States, for instance, more than 34 million people between the ages of 18 and 64 suffer from mental illness.[54] Mental illnesses represent about 24% of all reported disabilities, considerably more than disabling injuries, respiratory diseases, cardiovascular diseases, and cancer combined.

Mental health treatment costs are rising because of widespread drug and alcohol problems, an increase in the number of states that require employers to offer a minimum package of mental health benefits, and the fact that other health care claims are higher for employees with high mental health claims. The Mental Health Parity Act of 1996 sets minimum mental health care benefits at the national level.[55]

Some employers are slowing the rise in mental health benefits by monitoring the benefit's process. One New York financial services firm, faced with a big jump in mental health costs in one year, rejected the idea of placing across-the-board limits on coverage.

**Figure 13-4
Other Cost-Saving
Strategies**
Source: Shari Caudron, "Health Care
Costs: HR's Crisis Has Real
Solutions," *Workforce*, February 2002,
p. 30. © Crain Communications, Inc.

1. **Wellness programs:** Corporate wellness efforts have been around for a long time but they've recently entered the Internet age. For example, companies such as 3Com, Chevron, and General Mills utilize an online health management program developed by WellMed to give employees immediate access to personalized health information. Giving employees access to health resources via home or work is another way that companies are encouraging employees to take responsibility for their own health management.
2. **Disease management:** Employers that contract with disease-management programs such as those offered by Milwaukee-based Innovative Resource Group are able to identify and manage the care of employees with chronic conditions such as asthma or diabetes. This helps to avoid the high costs associated with lost productivity and unmanaged medical conditions.
3. **Absence management:** Many companies are realizing that the cost of health insurance is only one piece of the puzzle. Such things as lost productivity and worker absences contribute to the hidden costs of health care. For this reason, more employers are starting to recognize that absences have to be managed holistically so that when employees are absent, their return to work is managed more aggressively.
4. **On-site primary care:** Cleveland-based Whole Health Management, which provides on-site medical and fitness centers, recently started offering clients such as American Airlines on-site primary-care services. Geared to self-insured employers with at least 2,000 workers at a site, on-site primary care enables employees to obtain such things as physical exams and preventive health care screenings without leaving the work site. According to Whole Health's calculations, employers receive a $5 return for every $1 spent.
5. **Eliminating cost-inefficient plans:** Companies are taking a closer look at health plans they currently offer and, by reviewing quality and financial factors, are beginning to eliminate those that aren't cost-effective.
6. **Moving toward PPO:** According to Hewitt Associates, employers are continuing to transition from point-of-service plans to preferred provider organizations. PPOs offer lower administrative fees, competitive discounts, and greater freedom for employees, and can be relatively cost-neutral to organizations.

Instead, it redesigned the mental health portion of its health plan. The plan now includes a utilization review to certify treatment, increased outpatient benefits, and a network of cost-efficient providers.[56]

The Pregnancy Discrimination Act   As explained earlier, this act requires employers to treat women affected by pregnancy, childbirth, or related medical conditions the same as any employees not able to work, with respect to all benefits, including sick leave and disability benefits, and health and medical insurance. Thus, it is illegal for most employers to discriminate against women by providing benefits of lower amount or duration for pregnancy, childbirth, or related medical conditions. For example, if an employer provides up to 26 weeks of temporary disability income to employees for all illnesses, it must provide up to 26 weeks for pregnancy and childbirth, too.

COBRA Requirements   The ominously titled COBRA—Comprehensive Omnibus Budget Reconciliation Act—requires most private employers to continue to make health benefits available to terminated or retired employees and their families for a period of time, generally 18 months. The former employee must pay for the coverage, as well as a small fee for administrative costs.

Employers who fail to follow COBRA's regulations do so at their peril. For one thing, you don't want terminated or retired employees to become injured and then claim you never told them their insurance coverage could have been continued. Therefore, when a new employee first becomes eligible for your company's insurance plan, that person must receive (and acknowledge receiving) an explanation of his or her COBRA rights. Similarly, all employees separated from the company for any reason should sign a form acknowledging that they received and understand the information about their COBRA rights. Figure 13-5 provides a COBRA checklist.

Long-Term Care   Today, the oldest baby boomers are in their 60s, and long-term care insurance—care to support people in their old age—is a key employee benefit.[57] The Health Insurance Portability and Accountability Act, enacted in 1996, lets

Figure 13-5
COBRA Record-keeping
Compliance Checklist
Source: Reprinted from www.HR.
BLR.com with permission of the
publisher, © 2004 *Business and Legal
Reports, Inc.*, 141 Mill Rock Road East,
Old Saybrook, CT.

Detailed record keeping is crucial for COBRA compliance. The following checklist is designed to ensure that the proper records are maintained for problem-free COBRA compliance.

	Yes	No
• Do you maintain records so that is easily determined who is covered by your group health care plan?	☐	☐
• Do you record terminations of covered employees as soon as terminations occur?	☐	☐
• Do you track reduction of hours of employees covered by group health care plans?	☐	☐
• Do you track deaths of employees covered by group health care plans?	☐	☐
• Do you track leaves of absence of employees covered by group health care plans?	☐	☐
• Do you track Medicare eligibility of employees covered by group health care plans?	☐	☐
• Do you track the disability status of employees covered by group health care plans?	☐	☐
• Do you track retirees covered by group health care plans?	☐	☐
• Do you maintain current addresses of employees?	☐	☐
• Do you maintain current addresses of individuals receiving COBRA benefits?	☐	☐
• Do you require employees to provide a written acknowledgement that they have received notice of their COBRA rights?	☐	☐
• Do you have a system to determine who has paid COBRA premiums on time?	☐	☐
• Do you have a system to determine who has obtained other group health coverage so that they are no longer eligible for COBRA under your plan?	☐	☐
• Do you maintain a telephone log of calls received about COBRA?	☐	☐
• Do you maintain a record of changes in your plan?	☐	☐
• Do you maintain a record of how premiums are calculated?	☐	☐
• Do you maintain a log of those employees who are denied COBRA coverage?	☐	☐
• Do you maintain a log of why employees are denied COBRA coverage?	☐	☐

employers and employees deduct the cost of long-term care insurance premiums from their annual income taxes, making this particular benefit even more attractive.[58] Employers can provide insurance benefits for several types of long-term care, such as adult day care, assisted living, and custodial care.

Life Insurance

group life insurance
Provides lower rates for the employer or employee and includes all employees, including new employees, regardless of health or physical condition.

In addition to hospitalization and medical benefits, most employers provide **group life insurance** plans. As with health insurance, employees can obtain lower rates in a group plan. And group plans usually accept all employees—including new nonprobationary ones—regardless of health or physical condition.

In many cases, the employer pays 100% of the base premium, which usually provides life insurance equal to about two years' salary. The employee then pays for any additional coverage. In some cases, the cost of the base premium is split 50/50 or 80/20 between employer and employee. In general, there are three key personnel policies to address: the benefits-paid schedule (the amount of life insurance benefits is usually tied to the employee's annual earnings), supplemental benefits (continued life insurance coverage after retirement, and so on); and financing (the amount and percent that the employee contributes).

Benefits for Part-Time and Contingent Workers

The Bureau of Labor Statistics, which defines part-time work as less than 35 hours a week, says 13.6% of the nation's workforce—about 19 million people—work part-time. An aging workforce, more phased retirement programs, a desire to better balance work and family life issues, and more women in the workforce help explain this phenomenon. In any case, a study found that 80% of the firms surveyed provide holiday, sick leave, and vacation benefits, and over 70% offer some form of health care benefits to part-time workers.[59]

A related issue concerns misclassifying as "independent contractors" or "consultants" contingent workers whose ongoing relationships with the employer actually make them employees. As explained in Chapter 5, the Internal Revenue Service and other entities apply various tests to assess the degree to which the employer actually controls the worker's actions and work schedule. As three attorneys put it, "Short-term, just in time workers provided by staffing agencies are not an issue. However the employer's policy for workers who are still on the job after 1,000 to 1,500 hours should require that they be provided with benefits, either through the staffing agency or by outsourcing their administration to an administrative employer who can provide benefits."[60]

Discuss the main retirement benefits.

● RETIREMENT BENEFITS

The first contingent of baby boomers turns 65 in the year 2011, and many reportedly won't wait that long to retire. Most still retire before age 65, although more are opting to not retire or to "un-retire."[61] Employers are therefore being more aggressive about enhancing their retirement plans.[62] The major retirement benefits are the federal Social Security program and employer pension/retirement plans, like the 401(k).

Social Security

Social Security
Federal program that provides three types of benefits: retirement income at the age of 62 and thereafter; survivor's or death benefits payable to the employee's dependents regardless of age at time of death; and disability benefits payable to disabled employees and their dependents. These benefits are payable only if the employee is insured under the Social Security Act.

Most people assume that **Social Security** provides income only when they are over 62, but it actually provides three types of benefits. The familiar *retirement benefits* provide an income if you retire at age 62 or thereafter and are insured under the Social Security Act. Second are *survivor's* or *death benefits*. These provide monthly payments to your dependents regardless of your age at death, again assuming you are insured under the Social Security Act. Finally, there are *disability payments*. These provide monthly payments to employees who become totally disabled (and their dependents) if they work and meet certain requirements. The Social Security system also administers the Medicare program, which provides a wide range of health services to people 65 or over. "Full retirement age" traditionally was 65—the usual age for retirement. However, full retirement age for Social Security is rising: It is 67 for those born in 1960 or later.

A tax on the employee's wages, shared equally by employees and employers, funds Social Security (technically, it is called "Federal Old Age and Survivor's Insurance"). As of 2004, the maximum amount of earnings subject to Social Security tax was $87,900.[63] Employer and employee each paid 7.65%.

Pension Plans

pension plans
Plans that provide a fixed sum when employees reach a predetermined retirement age or when they can no longer work due to disability.

Pensions provide income to individuals in their retirement, and just over half of full-time workers participate in some type of **pension plan** at work. However, the actual rate of participation depends on several things. For example, older workers tend to have a higher participation rate, and employees of larger firms have participation rates as much as three times as high as those in small firms.

We can classify pension plans in three basic ways: *contributory versus noncontributory* plans; *qualified versus nonqualified* plans; and *defined contribution versus defined benefit* plans.[64] The employee contributes to the contributory pension plan, while the employer makes all contributions to the noncontributory pension plan. Employers derive certain tax benefits from contributing to qualified pension plans, such as tax deductions for contributions; nonqualified pension plans get less favorable tax treatment for employees and employers.

defined benefit pension plan
A plan that contains a formula for determining retirement benefits.

With **defined benefit plans**, the employee knows ahead of time the pension benefits he or she will receive. The defined pension benefit itself is usually set by a formula that ties the person's retirement pension to an amount equal to a percentage of the person's preretirement pay (for instance, to an average of his or her last five years of employment), multiplied by the number of years he or she worked for the company.

defined contribution pension plan
A plan in which the employer's contribution to employees' retirement savings funds is specified.

Defined contribution plans specify what contribution the employee and employer will make to the employee's retirement or savings fund. Here, in other words, the contribution is defined, not the pension. With a defined benefit plan, the employee knows what his or her retirement benefits will be upon retirement. With a defined contribution plan, the person's pension will depend on the amounts contributed to the fund and on the retirement fund's investment earnings. Defined contribution plans are increasingly popular among employers today, because of their relative ease of administration, favorable tax treatment, and other factors.

401(k) plan
A defined contribution plan based on section 401(k) of the Internal Revenue Code.

Economic Growth and Tax Relief Reconciliation Act (2001) (EGTRRA)
An act that improves the attractiveness of retirement benefits like 401(k) plans by boosting individual employees' elective deferred limits to $15,000, effective in 2006.

401(k) Plans   Plans based on section 401(k) of the Internal Revenue Code, called **401(k) plans**, are popular defined contribution plans. Here an employee authorizes the employer to deduct a certain amount of money from his or her paycheck before taxes and to invest it in the 401(k) plan. This results in a pretax reduction in pay, so the employee pays no tax on those set-aside dollars until after he or she retires (or removes the money from the 401(k) plan). The employee decides how much the employer will deduct and deposit in the 401(k) plan; the person can deduct up to the legal maximum (the IRS sets an annual dollar limit—$13,000 in 2004). The employer arranges, usually with an investment company such as Fidelity Investments, to actually manage the 401(k) plan and to make various investment options available to the company's 401(k) plan. The options typically include mutual stock funds and bond funds. The **Economic Growth and Tax Relief Reconciliation Act of 2001 (EGTRRA)** improves the attractiveness of retirement benefits like 401(k) plans, by boosting individual employees' elective deferral limits to $14,000 in 2005 and to $15,000 in 2006.[65]

"We never could afford this," says Carmela Owens of Kosola & Associates, speaking of the firm's new 401K plan, whose adoption she spearheaded. "Now I'm actually going to have a retirement, and my kids will have money if something happens to me."

Employers should choose their 401(k) providers with the utmost care, not only because of the employer's responsibility to its employees but also because changing 401(k) providers can be a "grueling venture."[66] About 50 million American workers, or about 40% of the U.S. workforce, have 401(k) plans.[67]

In addition to reliability, employers want a 401(k) plan provider that makes it easy for employer and employee to participate in the plan. For example, Ford Motor Company helps employees manage their accounts by offering Fidelity Investment's Internet-based retirement portfolio planning tool to its 145,000 401(k) plan participants.[68] Firms such as Vanguard, Fidelity and others can establish online, fully Web-based 401(k) plans even for small firms with 10 to 50 employees. Employees get various online tools—such as an "asset allocation planner."

Other Types of Defined Contribution Plans   There are several types of defined contribution plans.[69] In a **savings and thrift plan** (of which a 401(k) is one example), employees contribute a portion of their earnings to a fund; the employer usually matches this contribution in whole or in part. The employer's contributions can be considerable, particularly where competition for employees is intense. For example, Harleysville Group, Inc., matches up to 100% of an employee's contribution up to 6% of his or her salary, in an effort to attract and retain information technology (IT) workers. However, Radio Shack Corporation in Fort Worth, Texas, probably sets a record: It matches 401(k) contributions at 159%.[70]

In **deferred profit-sharing plans**, employers typically contribute a portion of their profits to the pension fund, regardless of the level of employee contribution. An **employee stock ownership plan (ESOP)** is a qualified, tax-deductible stock bonus plan in which employers contribute stock to a trust for eventual use by employees. Overall, about 91% of employers offer 401(k) salary reduction plans; 67% also offer defined benefit pension plans alongside their 401(k)s, and 18% offer other deferred profit-sharing savings plans.[71]

Pension Planning

Pension planning is complicated, partly because of the many federal laws governing pensions. For example, companies (and employees) usually want to ensure their pension contributions are "qualified," or tax deductible, so they must follow the pertinent income tax codes. The **Employee Retirement Income Security Act (ERISA)** of 1974 restricts what companies can, cannot, and must do in regard to pension plans (more on this in a moment). In unionized companies, the employer must let the union participate in pension plan administration.

In developing pension plans to meet their unique needs, employers have to consider several key policy issues:[72]

■ *Membership requirements.* For example, what is the minimum age or minimum service at which employees become eligible for a pension?

■ *Benefit formula.* This usually ties the (defined) pension to the employee's final earnings, or an average of his or her last three or four years' earnings.

■ *Plan funding.* How will you fund the plan? Will it be contributory or noncontributory?

■ *Vesting.* **Vested funds** are the money employer and employee have placed in the latter's pension fund that cannot be forfeited for any reason. The employees' contributions are always theirs, of course. However, until the passage of ERISA, the employer's contribution in many pension plans didn't vest until the employee retired. So you could have worked for a company for 30 years and been left with no pension if the company went out of business one year before you were to retire. That generally can't happen today, although, as we'll see, that's no guarantee that some employees won't get lower pensions than they expected if their plans fail.

---

savings and thrift plan
Plan in which employees contribute a portion of their earnings to a fund; the employer usually matches this contribution in whole or in part.

deferred profit-sharing plan
A plan in which a certain amount of profits is credited to each employee's account, payable at retirement, termination, or death.

employee stock ownership plan (ESOP)
A qualified, tax-deductible stock bonus plan in which employers contribute stock to a trust for eventual use by employees.

Employee Retirement Income Security Act (ERISA)
Signed into law by President Ford in 1974 to require that pension rights be vested and protected by a government agency, the PBGC.

vested funds
Money placed in a pension fund that cannot be forfeited for any reason.

Pensions and the Law

Passage of ERISA was a pivotal step in protecting the pensions of workers and stimulating the growth of pension plans. Today, under ERISA, participants in pension plans must have a nonforfeitable right to 100% of their accrued benefits after five years of service; as an alternative, the employer may choose to phase in vesting over a period of three to seven years. Under the Tax Reform Act of 1986, an employer can require that an employee complete a period of no more than two years' service to the company before becoming eligible to participate in the plan. However, if you require more than one year of service before eligibility, the plan must grant employees full and immediate vesting rights at the end of that period.

ERISA established the **Pension Benefits Guarantee Corporation (PBGC)** to oversee and insure pensions should a plan terminate without sufficient funds to meet its vested obligations. However, the PBGC guarantees only defined benefit plans, not defined contribution plans. Furthermore, it will only pay an individual a pension of up to about $27,000 per year.[73]

Pension Benefits Guarantee Corporation (PBGC)
Established under ERISA to ensure that pensions meet vesting obligations; also insures pensions should a plan terminate without sufficient funds to meet its vested obligations.

Pension Alternatives

Many firms, faced with the need to reduce their workforces, are offering early retirement windows and other voluntary separation arrangements.

Early Retirement Windows   Some plans take the form of **early retirement window** arrangements in which specific employees (often age 50-plus) are eligible to participate. The "window" means that for a limited time, the company opens up the opportunity for employees to retire earlier than usual. The financial incentive is generally a combination of improved or liberalized pension benefits plus a cash payment.

early retirement window
A type of offering by which employees are encouraged to retire early, the incentive being liberal pension benefits plus perhaps a cash payment.

Employers should use programs like these cautiously. Age discrimination is the fastest-growing type of discrimination claim, and unless structured properly, early retirement programs can be challenged as de facto methods for forcing the discharge of older employees against their will. While it is generally legal to use incentives to encourage individuals to choose early retirement, the employee's decision must be voluntary. In fact, in several cases individuals who were eligible for and elected early retirement later challenged their early retirement by claiming their decisions weren't voluntary. In one case (*Paolillo v. Dresser Industries, Inc.*), the employer told employees on October 12 that they were eligible to retire under a "totally voluntary" early retirement program, and must inform the company of their decision by October 18. However, employees didn't get the details of the program until October 15. The employees subsequently sued, claiming coercion. The U.S. Court of Appeals for the Second Circuit (New York) agreed with them, arguing that an employee's decision to retire must be voluntary and made without undue strain.[74]

Employers must therefore exercise caution in encouraging employees to take early retirement. The waiver of future claims they sign should meet EEOC guidelines. In particular, it must be knowing and voluntary, not provide for the release of prospective rights or claims, and not be an exchange for benefits to which the employee was already entitled. It should give the employee ample opportunity to think over the agreement and to seek advice from legal counsel. The Older Workers' Benefit Protection Act (OWBPA), signed into law in 1990, imposes specific limitations on waivers that purport to release a terminating employee's potential claims against his or her employer based on age discrimination.[75]

Portability   Today's needs for flexible staffing and the realities of ongoing corporate restructurings are also prompting employers to make their pension plans more *portable*. Employers often do this by switching from defined benefit to defined contribution plans, since the former are more appropriate for employees who plan to stay with the firm until retirement. Another approach is to allow workers who leave the firm before retirement to receive initial benefits at a younger age.[76]

Cash Balance Pension Plans   These are defined benefit plans for federal tax purposes, but they work differently. In a typical defined benefit plan, the employer multiplies the employee's average pay over the last few years of his or her employment by a predetermined multiple, based on years with the firm, and the result represents the person's annual retirement income. This approach tends to favor older employees (whose income is often higher and who have been with the firm for a number of years). Younger employees who may not be planning to stay with the firm their entire careers may prefer **cash balance plans**. Under these plans, the employer contributes a percentage of employees' current pay to the employees' pension plans every year, and employees earn interest on this amount. Cash balance plans therefore provide the portability of defined contribution plans with the employer funding of defined benefit plans.[77] Federal courts recently ruled against both IBM Corp. and Xerox Corp., saying that their cash balance plans violated ERISA—they allegedly discriminated against older, longer tenure employees—so these plans are under something of a cloud.[78]

The "Improving Productivity Through HRIS" feature illustrates how employers use HRIS to more efficiently manage their benefits programs.

cash balance plans
Defined benefit plans under which the employer contributes a percentage of employees' current pay to employees' pension plans every year, and employees earn interest on this amount.

Improving Productivity Through HRIS

Benefits Management Systems

With health care and drug costs rising 12% to 15% per year, HR managers are struggling to find ways to make their benefits dollars go further. As we explained earlier in this chapter, they are therefore implementing various health care cost-control strategies, including boosting copays and, in some cases, reducing benefits.

One of the main ways HR managers are increasing the productivity of their benefits dollars is by increasing the utilization of technology. One recent survey, by the Institute of Management and Administration, found that about 57% of the 192 HR and benefits managers who responded said they will focus on getting more out of existing benefits technology and automation, while 30% of benefits managers said they would be investing in new benefits technology soon.[79]

Benefits administration can be an enormously labor-intensive and time-consuming activity for an HR department. Left unautomated, it can require the employer to devote hundreds or thousands of HR professionals' hours to transactions such as answering employees' questions about comparative benefits, and updating employees' benefits information. Tasks like these clearly demand intranet-based self-service benefits management applications.

For example, when the organization that assists Pennsylvania school districts with their insurance needs decided to assist the school boards with automating their benefits administration, they interviewed four solution providers. They chose a company called BeneLogic.[80] The solution, called the Employee Benefit Electronic Service Tool, "lets users manage all aspects of benefits administration, including enrollment, plan descriptions, eligibility, and premium reconciliation, via Microsoft Internet Explorer and Netscape Navigator."[81]

BeneLogic's benefits management system provides the school boards with numerous advantages. BeneLogic hosts and maintains the Web support application on its own servers, and creates customized, Web-based applications for each school district. The system facilitates Web-based employee benefit enrollment, provides centralized call center support for benefit-related questions, and even handles benefits-related payroll, HRIS, and similar functions by partnering with companies like ADP (which manages many of the school boards' payroll functions), and PeopleSoft (which provides and services many of the school boards' human resource information systems). Each school board employee accesses the BeneLogic site via a link on his or her own board's Web site.

Outline the main employees' services benefits.

● PERSONAL SERVICES AND FAMILY-FRIENDLY BENEFITS

While time off, insurance, and retirement benefits account for the lion's share of benefits costs, most employers also provide various services, including personal services (such as legal and personal counseling), job-related "family-friendly" services (such as child-care facilities), educational subsidies, and executive perquisites (such as company cars and planes for its executives).

Personal Services

Many companies provide the sorts of personal services that most employees need at one time or another. These include credit unions, legal services, counseling, and social and recreational opportunities.

Credit Unions   Credit unions are usually separate businesses established with the employer's assistance to help employees with borrowing and saving needs. Employees usually become members by purchasing a share of the credit union's stock for $5 or $10. Members can then deposit savings that accrue interest at a rate determined by the credit union's board of directors. Perhaps more important to most employees, loan eligibility and the loan's rate of interest are usually more favorable than those of banks and finance companies. Many credit unions are large, multibranch operations. For example, Arrowhead Credit Union has 100,000 members and 17 branches, with ATMs, checking, and a full range of banking services.[82]

employee assistance program
A formal employer program for providing employees with counseling and/or treatment programs for problems such as alcoholism, gambling, or stress.

Employee Assistance Programs (EAPs)   **Employee assistance programs (EAPs)** provide counseling and advisory services, which might include, for instance, personal legal and financial services, child and elder care referrals, adoption assistance, mental health counseling, and life event planning.[83] EAPs are increasingly popular, with more than 60% of larger firms offering such programs. The trend is toward offering one-stop-shopping EAP benefits from large, off-site providers. One study found that personal mental health was the most common problem addressed by employee assistance programs, followed by family problems.[84]

For the company, programs like these produce advantages, not just costs. For example, sick family members and health problems such as depression account for many of the sick leave days employees take. These absences can be reduced with employee assistance programs that provide advice on issues like elder care referrals and disease management.[85]

Key steps for launching a successful EAP program include:

■ *Develop a policy statement.* Define the program's purpose, employee eligibility, the roles and responsibilities of various personnel in the organization, and procedures for using the plan.

■ *Ensure professional staffing.* Consider the professional and state licensing requirements.

■ *Maintain confidential record-keeping systems.* Everyone involved with the EAP, including supervisors, secretaries, and support staff, must understand the importance of confidentiality. Also ensure files are locked, access is limited and monitored, and identifying information is minimized.

■ *Be aware of legal issues.* For example, in most states counselors must disclose suspicions of child abuse to an appropriate state agency. Get legal advice on establishing the EAP, carefully screen the credentials of the EAP staff, and obtain professional liability insurance for the EAP.[86]

Family-Friendly Benefits

Several trends are changing the landscape of benefits administration: There are more households in which both adults work; more one-parent households; more women in the workforce; more workers over 55. And there's the "time bind"—people working harder and longer, without the time to do all they'd like to do.

The pressures of balancing work and family life have led many employers to bolster what they call their family-friendly benefits. While there is no single list of what does or does not constitute a "family-friendly benefit," they generally include child care, elder care, fitness facilities, and flexible work schedules that enable employees to better meet the demands of their family and work lives. As two experts put it:

On-site child care, fitness and medical facilities, flexible work scheduling, telecommuting, occasional sabbaticals, loan programs for home computers, stock options, concierge services, even insurance for the family pet are all part of the compensation package in the new workplace.[87]

Ninety percent of responding employees in one survey said such work/life benefits were "important" or "very important" to them; important benefits included on-site day care, flexible work schedules, referral services for child care and elder care, long-term care insurance, and family leave.[88]

Many more employers have therefore added these kinds of benefits. A survey by the Society for Human Resource Management (SHRM) found that about 29% of employers provided at least some type of child-care assistance in 2003, up from 23% in 1999.[89] The SHRM survey also found that, of the firms responding, 55% offer flextime, 31% offer compressed workweeks, and 34% permit some telecommuting.[90]

First Tennessee Bank in Memphis calls its family-friendly benefits program Family Matters. Its main emphasis is on flexibility: For example, the bank's previous policy forced employees to take vacations in two-week blocks and required dismissal for any employee who missed more than eight days per year. With Family Matters, employees can now follow flextime schedules, scale back to working as few as 20 hours a week and still keep benefits, and schedule more hours of work early in the month to take time off late in the month if that's what they need to do.[91]

Family-friendly firms routinely turn up on "best companies to work for" lists. For example, BMC (56th on *Fortune*'s list of the 100 best companies to work for) includes a kitchen on each floor with free fruit, popcorn, soda, and TV. Forty-six of *Fortune*'s 100 best companies offer take-home meals; 26 have concierge services to help with time-consuming details like buying birthday presents.[92] More firms offer job sharing as a benefit.[93]

Software giant **SAS Institute, Inc.,** offers generous employee benefits. The North Carolina firm keeps turnover at 4% in an industry where 20% is typical, in large part by offering family-friendly benefits like paid maternity leave, day care on site, lunchtime piano concerts, massages, and yoga classes like this one.

Effect on Performance   But do these family-friendly programs improve productivity? There is not a lot of evidence. Many firms that implement these plans do so as part of broader commitment-building programs. These typically also include emphasizing employee development, promotion from within, and open communications.[94] Implemented in this manner, studies suggest work/life benefits may in fact contribute to employees' willingness to "go the extra mile" for their employers.[95]

On the other hand, benefits like these don't come cheap. For example, the CEO of one firm that provides concierge services to employees estimates that for a large company, concierge services cost $100,000 per year. Aetna found it saved $400,000 by making employees at its Blue Bell, Pennsylvania, office buy their own coffee and tea. Excite@home saved $165,000 by eliminating free sodas.[96] We'll look at some specific family-friendly benefits.

Subsidized Child Care   Most employees still make private provisions to take care of their children; relatives accounted for 48% of all child-care providers in one study.[97] Organized day care centers of all types accounted for another 30% of child-care arrangements, and nonrelatives accounted for most of the remaining arrangements.

How do employers help? Many employers (about 18% in 2003) simply investigate the day care facilities in their communities and recommend certain ones to interested employees. But more employers are setting up company-sponsored day care facilities, both to attract employees and to reduce absenteeism. Often (as at the Wang Laboratories day care facility in Lowell, Massachusetts), the center is a private, tax-exempt venture run separately from but subsidized by the firm. Employees pay about $30 a week for a child's care. Successful day care facilities are usually close to the workplace (often in the same building), and the employer covers at least half of the operating costs.[98]

By establishing subsidized day care centers, employers can gain via improved recruiting results, lower absenteeism, improved morale, favorable publicity, and lower turnover. But to ensure that the program is worthwhile and cost-effective, good planning is required. This often starts with a questionnaire to employees to answer questions like, "What would you be willing to pay for care for one child in a child-care center near work?" and "Have you missed work during the past six months because you needed to find new care arrangements?"

Elder Care   Elder care benefits are important for much the same reasons as are child-care benefits: The responsibility for caring for an aging relative can affect the employee's performance at work.[99] One study found that 64% took sick days or vacation time, 33% decreased work hours, 22% took leaves of absence, 20% changed their job status from full- to part-time, 16% quit their jobs, and 13% retired early. The problem will grow more acute as the segment of the population over age 65 grows from about 35 million today to 82 million in 2050.

How are firms responding? Citing the "human toll on caregivers," more employers are providing elder care services. For example, the United Auto Workers and Ford Motor Company provide elder care referral service for Ford's salaried employees. They provide a detailed assessment of the elderly relative's needs, and recommendations on the care that would be best.[100] The national council on the aging has a useful Web site to help elders and caregivers find benefit programs: www.benefitscheckup.org.

Other Job-Related Benefits   Some employers provide subsidized *employee transportation*. In one such program, Seattle First National Bank negotiated contracts with a transit system to provide free year-round transportation to more than 3,000 of the bank's employees. *Food services* are provided in some form by many employers; they let employees purchase meals, snacks, or coffee, usually at relatively low prices. Most food operations are nonprofit, and, in fact, some firms provide food services below cost.

Educational subsidies such as tuition refunds have long been popular benefits for employees seeking to continue or complete their educations. Payments range from all tuition and expenses to some percentage of expenses to a flat fee of several hundred dollars per year. Many employers provide in-house college programs, where faculty teach on the employer's premises. Other in-house educational programs include remedial work in basic literacy and training for improved supervisory skills.

As far as tuition reimbursement programs are concerned, one survey found that about 72% of the 579 companies surveyed pay for college courses related to an employee's present job. Most companies also reimburse non-job-related courses (such as a Web designer taking an accounting class) that pertain to the company business. Some employers pay for self-improvement classes, such as foreign language study, even though they are unrelated to company business or the employee's job.[101] DaimlerChrysler, Ford, and General Motors provide $1,000 annually to dependents of current or retired UAW members for tuition.[102]

September 11   With respect to employee benefits, the September 11 terrorist attacks (1) prompted many firms to expand their trauma counseling services, and also (2) made most insurance-related benefits much more expensive to obtain. Many firms, particularly in New York City, quickly instituted or expanded their employee assistance programs immediately after the World Trade Center attacks. For example, Merrill Lynch instituted various counseling services to help employees cope with the stress of the tragedy. In terms of costs, workers' compensation insurance skyrocketed after 9/11, when claims reached almost $3 billion. "Today, for companies with large concentrations of employees—in other words, firms with more than 1,500 workers—a 75% increase [in workers' compensation premium costs] is considered a good deal."[103] The general effect of 9/11 on insurance benefits has been to prompt insurers to analyze their potential liabilities by geographic area much more carefully, and to take steps to reduce their risks should a calamity affect numerous employers in one area.[104]

"The New Workplace" describes another personal/family benefit.

The New Workplace

Domestic Partner Benefits

A recent survey by the Society for Human Resource Management found that of 578 companies responding, about 23% offer same-sex domestic partner benefits, 31% offer opposite-sex partner benefits, and about 2% plan to do one or both.[105] Among large companies, for instance, Northrop Grumman Corp., extends domestic partner benefits to the 9,500 salaried workers at its Newport News shipyard.[106]

When employers provide *domestic partner benefits* to employees, it generally means that employees' same-sex or opposite-sex domestic partners are eligible to receive the same benefits (health care, life insurance, and so forth) as do the husband, wife, or legal dependent of one of the firm's employees.

Under Internal Revenue Service guidelines, "dependents" include the taxpayer's son or daughter or a descendant of either, stepson or stepdaughter, brother, sister, stepbrother, or stepsister, father, mother or ancestor of either, stepfather stepmother, niece or nephew, aunt or uncle, or in-law for whom the taxpayer pays more than half the support.[107] With the recent passage of the Defense of Marriage Act, Congress provided that employers may not treat same-sex domestic partners the same as employees' spouses for purposes of federal law, so there is considerable doubt as to whether the benefits extended to domestic partners will be federal tax free, as they generally are for the relatives enumerated above.

Executive Perquisites

When you reach the pinnacle of the organizational pyramid—or at least get close to the top—you will find, waiting for you, the Executive Perk. Perquisites (perks, for short) usually only go to a few top executives. Perks can range from substantial to almost insignificant.

Many popular perks fall between these extremes. These include management loans (which typically enable senior officers to exercise their stock options); salary guarantees (also known as golden parachutes), to protect executives if their firms become targets of acquisitions or mergers; financial counseling (to handle top executives' investment programs); and relocation benefits, often including subsidized mortgages, purchase of the executive's current house, and payment for the actual move.[108] A selection of other executive perks includes time off with pay (including sabbaticals and severance pay), outplacement assistance, company cars, chauffeured limousines, security systems, company planes and yachts, executive dining rooms, physical fitness programs, legal services, tax assistance, liberal expense accounts, club memberships, season tickets, credit cards, and children's education. As you can see, employers have many ways of making their hardworking executives' lives as pleasant as possible!

"The HR Scorecard" illustrates the new benefits program at the Hotel Paris.

● FLEXIBLE BENEFITS PROGRAMS

When given the opportunity to choose, employees prefer flexibility in their benefits plans. In a survey of working couples, for instance, 83% took advantage of flexible hours, 69% took advantage of the sorts of flexible-style benefits options packages we'll discuss next; and 75% said that flexible-style benefits plans are the sorts of plans they would like to see their companies offer. About 70% of employers in one survey chose flexible health care options.[109]

The online job listing service jobtrak.com asked college students and recent graduates, "Which benefit do you desire most?" More than 3,000 responded. Thirty-five percent sought flexible hours; 19% stock options; 13% more vacation time; 12% a better health plan; and 9% wanted a signing bonus. Most of the preferred benefits had to do with lifestyle issues rather than financial ones.[110] Given findings like these and the enormous cost of benefits, it is prudent to survey employees' benefits preferences and needs, perhaps using a form like that in Figure 13-7 (page 503).

The Cafeteria Approach

*flexible benefits plan/
cafeteria benefits plan*
Individualized plans allowed by employers to accommodate employee preferences for benefits.

Because employees do have different preferences for benefits, employers often let employees individualize their benefits plans. The "cafeteria" approach is one way to do this. (The terms **flexible benefits plan** and **cafeteria benefits plan** are generally used synonymously.) A cafeteria plan is one in which the employer gives each employee a benefits fund budget, and lets the person spend it on the benefits he or she prefers, subject to two constraints. First, the employer must carefully limit total cost for each benefits package. Second, each benefits plan must include certain required items—for example, Social Security, workers' compensation, and unemployment insurance. Employees can often make midyear changes to their plans if, for instance, their dependent care costs rise and they want to divert more contributions to this expense.[111]

The HR Scorecard
Strategy and Results

The New Benefits Plan

The Hotel Paris's competitive strategy is "To use superior guest service to differentiate the Hotel Paris properties, and to thereby increase the length of stay and return rate of guests, and thus boost revenues and profitability." HR manager Lisa Cruz must now formulate functional policies and activities that support this competitive strategy, by eliciting the required employee behaviors and competencies.

A preliminary analysis, performed jointly by Lisa and the Hotel Paris's chief financial officer, left them optimistic that HR could contribute measurably to achieving the hotel's strategic aims. Several employee competencies and behaviors including employee morale, employee commitment, and the percent of arriving guests receiving the hotel's required greeting had significant effects on customer and organizational outcomes such as guest satisfaction and frequency of guest returns. In turn, outcomes like these contributed measurably to the Hotel Paris's strategic goals, including profit margins, market share, and scores on industry satisfaction surveys. Lisa and her team now turn to creating a benefits program that will help to produce the required employee competencies and behaviors. The accompanying HR Scorecard (Figure 13-6) outlines the relationships involved.

As they reviewed the numbers relating to their benefits plan, Lisa Cruz and the CFO became increasingly concerned. They computed several benefits-related metrics for their firm, including *benefits costs as a percentage of payroll, sick days per full-time equivalent employee per year, benefits cost/competitor's benefits cost ratio,* and *workers' compensation experience ratings.* The results, as the CFO put it, offered a "good news–bad news" situation. On the good side, the ratios were generally similar to those of most competing hotels. The bad news was that the measures were strikingly below what they were when compared with the results for high-performing service-oriented businesses. The CFO authorized Lisa to design and propose a new benefits plan.

Lisa knew there were several things she wanted to accomplish with this plan. She wanted a plan that contributed to improved employee morale and commitment. And, she wanted the plan to include elements that made it easier for her employees to do their jobs—so that, as she put it, "they could come to work and give their full attention to giving our guests great service, without worrying about child care and other major family-oriented distractions."

The new plan that she and her team designed therefore had the following components. Its centerpiece was a proposal for dramatically improved family-friendly benefits. Because so many of each hotel's employees were single parents, and because each hotel had to run 24 hours a day, Lisa's team proposed, and the Board approved, setting aside a room in each hotel for an on-site child-care facility and for hiring a trained professional attendant. They considered instituting a flexible work schedule program, but for most of the jobs this was impractical, because each front-line employee simply had to be there at his or her appointed hour. However, they were able to propose and institute a new job-sharing program so that, for instance, two people could share one housekeeping or front-desk clerk job, as long as the job was covered.

One of the metrics Lisa and her team specifically wanted to address was the relatively high absence rate at the Hotel Paris. Because so many of these jobs are front-line jobs—car hops, limousine drivers, and front-desk clerks, for instance—it's impossible to do without someone in the position if there is absence. As a result, poor attendance had a particularly serious effect on metrics like overtime pay and temporary help costs. Here, at the urging of her compensation consultant, Lisa decided to opt for a system similar to Marriott's "BENETRADE." With this benefit program, employees can trade the value of some sick days for other benefits. As Lisa put it, "I'd rather see our employees using their sick day pay for things like additional health care benefits, if it means they'll think twice before taking a sick day to run a personal errand."

After just less than a year, Lisa and the CFO believe the new program is having the desired effects. Their studies suggest that the improved benefits are directly contributing to improved employee morale and commitment, sick days have diminished by 40%, and employee turnover is down 60%. Furthermore, when the hotels advertise for their open positions, their job interview surveys suggest that over 60% of the applicants cite "family-friendly benefits" as one of the top reasons for applying to work at the Hotel Paris.

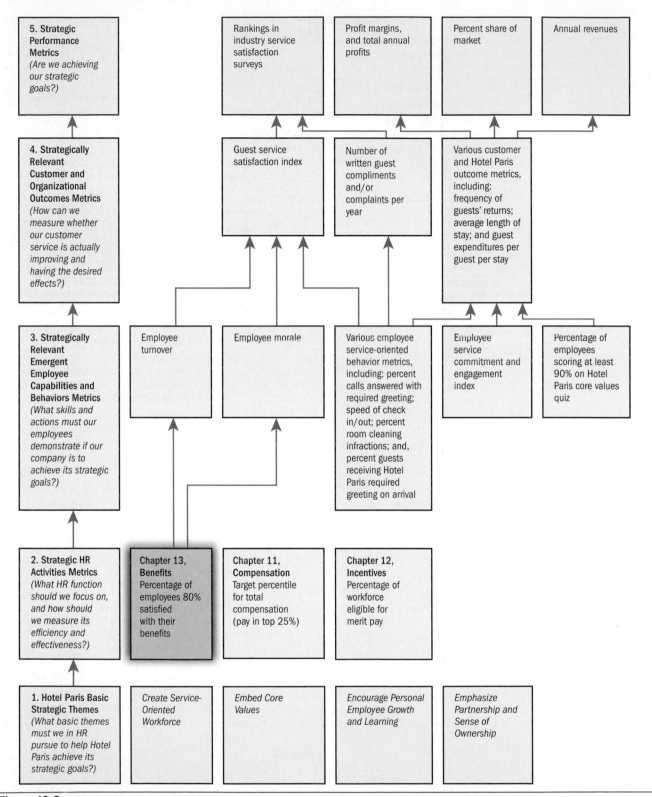

Figure 13-6
HR Scorecard for Hotel Paris International Corporation*

Note: *(An abbreviated example showing selected HR practices and outcomes aimed at implementing the competitive strategy, "To use superior guest services to differentiate the Hotel Paris properties and thus increase the length of stays and the return rate of guests and thus boost revenues and profitability")*

Indicate the level of Importance of the following benefits to you and your family:

	Low Importance	High Importance
Single health coverage	_____	_____
Family health coverage	_____	_____
Preventive health care	_____	_____
Flexibility in choice of physician	_____	_____
Prescription coverage	_____	_____
Vision coverage	_____	_____
Dependent care assistance	_____	_____
Educational assistance	_____	_____
Paid maternity leave	_____	_____
Disability insurance	_____	_____

Indicate any two benefits listed below that you feel can be enhanced by the company, and include a comment suggesting how:

Health care coverage	_____
Prescription coverage	_____
Vision coverage	_____
Dependent care assistance	_____
Educational assistance	_____
Maternity leave	_____
Disability insurance	_____

If the company could spend additional money on benefits, rank in order of importance (1 = *most important*; 7 = *least important*) which of the following benefits you suggest should be funded:

_____ Health care coverage

_____ Prescription coverage

_____ Vision coverage

_____ Dependent care assistance

_____ Educational assistance

_____ Maternity leave

Figure 13-7
Sample Survey of Employee Needs

Source: Michelle Buckley, "Checkup for Health Benefit Offerings," *Compensation and Benefits Review*, September/October 2000, p. 43. Reprinted by permission of Sage Publications, Inc.

Cafeteria plans come in several varieties. To give employees more flexibility in what benefits they use, about 70% of employers offer *flexible spending accounts* for medical and other expenses. This option lets employees pay for certain benefits expenses with pretax dollars. During the open enrollment period, the employee may choose how much salary reduction dollars the employer will deposit in this account. To encourage employees to use this option without laying out cash, some firms are offering *debit cards* that employees can use at their medical provider or pharmacy.[112] *Core plus option plans* establish a core set of benefits (such as medical insurance), which are usually mandatory for all employees. Beyond the core, employees can then choose from various benefits options.[113]

The "Life Plan" at Pitney Bowes provides an example.[114] Pitney Bowes attaches a "price" to every benefit offered and allows employees to "shop" for the benefits they need each year. Each employee gets a certain number of "flex dollars" to spend each year on the benefits he or she prefers. Employees can buy whatever benefits they want up to the limit of their available flex dollars; they can even supplement that amount with their personal funds if they so choose.

The flex dollars themselves are awarded based on an employee's salary, length of service, age, and number of dependents covered by benefits.[115] In establishing the program, Pitney Bowes included numerous traditional benefits such as medical, dental, short-term disability insurance, pension plans, and vacations. In addition, however, it expanded its choices to include things like group legal services, a loan broker to help employees shop for the best college financing, and unlimited personal financial planning (for a special fee of $175 per year).[116]

Computers and Benefits Administration

Whether it is flexible benefits or some other plan, computers play an important role in benefits administration. PC-based systems let employees interactively update and manipulate their benefits packages, as do various Web sites like www.401k.com. Inter- and intranet systems enable employees to get medical information about hospitals and doctors and to do interactive financial planning and investment modeling.[117] Firms also use computerized systems to let employees update their benefits plans, and to inform employees about their benefits and to answer routine questions that might otherwise go unasked or take up a human resource manager's time. Such questions include: "In which option of the medical plan am I enrolled?" "Who are my designated beneficiaries for the life insurance plan?" "If I retire in two years, what will be my monthly retirement income?" and "What is the current balance in my company savings plan?"

Systems like these are not just for *Fortune* 500 companies. Administering the benefits for even a company with 25 or 30 employees can be a chore. For example, consider the paperwork involved when an employee asks, "Can I take my vacation next week?" Answering may require digging through time cards, spreadsheets, and HR folders, and then considering whether the request falls under the Family and Medical Leave Act or COBRA. Even smaller firms thus often use software like HROffice, from Ascentis Software Corporation. HROffice includes over 100 built-in reports on matters ranging from attendance and benefits to performance reviews and bonuses.[118] They may also use employee leasing, as the "When You're On Your Own" feature illustrates.

Flexible Work Arrangements

➔5 Explain the main flexible benefit programs.

Flextime   **Flextime** is a plan whereby employees' workdays are built around a core of mid-day hours, such as 11:00 A.M. to 2:00 P.M. Workers determine their own starting and stopping hours. For example, they may opt to work from 7:00 A.M. to 3:00 P.M. or from 11:00 A.M. to 7:00 P.M. The number of employees in formal flextime programs—from 4% of operators to 17% of executive employees—doesn't tell the whole story. Many more employees, about 46%, actually take advantage of informal flexible work schedules.[119]

In practice, most employers give employees only limited freedom regarding the hours they work. Most hold fairly close to the traditional 9:00 A.M. to 5:00 P.M. workday. For example, in about half the firms, employees can't start work later than 9:00 A.M., and employees in about 40% of the firms must be in by 10:00 A.M. Therefore, the effect of flextime for most employees is to give them about one hour of leeway before 9:00 A.M. or after 5:00 P.M. SHRM found that in 2003, about half of all firms offered flexible hours options.

Compressed Workweeks

Many employees, like airline pilots, do not work conventional five-day, 40-hour workweeks. It would hardly do, for instance, for the pilot on a 12-hour flight to have to clock out midway across the Atlantic. Similarly, hospitals may want doctors and nurses to provide continuing care to a patient, or manufacturers may want to reduce the productivity lost whenever workers change shifts.

Nonconventional ("compressed") workweeks come in many flavors. Some firms have four-day workweeks, with four 10-hour days. Others have employees work two days on, two days off, three days on, then two days off, two days on, and so forth. Some workers—in hospitals, for instance—work three 12-hour shifts, and then are off for the next four days. About half of 500 employers in one recent survey said they now use 12-hour shifts for many of their employees.[120]

Effectiveness of Flextime and Compressed Workweek Programs

How effective are flextime and compressed workweek programs? One review suggests the following. Flexible work schedules do have positive effects on employee productivity, job satisfaction, satisfaction with work schedule, and employee absenteeism; the positive effect on absenteeism was much greater than on productivity. Compressed workweeks positively affected job satisfaction and satisfaction with work schedule; absenteeism did not increase, and productivity was not positively affected. Highly flexible programs were actually less effective than less flexible ones.[121]

Some experts argue that longer, 12-hour shifts may increase fatigue, and therefore accidents. However, one report suggests 12-hour shifts can actually be safer, in some respects. For example, the "general workplace confusion" that often occurs during shift changes is reduced with 12-hour shifts, since there are fewer shift changes. To further reduce potential detrimental side effects, a Texas DuPont plant provides portable treadmills and exercise bikes that shift workers can use to get their "blood pumping." A south Texas power plant installed a special "light box" that mimics daytime sun by providing intense, full-spectrum light.[122]

job sharing
Allows two or more people to share a single full-time job.

work sharing
Refers to a temporary reduction in work hours by a group of employees during economic downturns as a way to prevent layoffs.

telecommuting
Where employees work at home, usually with computers, and use phones and the Internet to transmit letters, data, and completed work to the home office.

Other Flexible Work Arrangements

Employers are taking other steps to accommodate employees' scheduling needs. **Job sharing** allows two or more people to share a single full-time job. For example, two people may share a 40-hour-per-week job, with one working mornings and the other working afternoons. About 22% of the firms questioned in one survey indicated that they allow job sharing.[123] These include Gannett newspapers and PepsiCo, which has offered it for more than 20 years.[124] **Work sharing** refers to a temporary reduction in work hours by a group of employees during economic downturns as a way to prevent layoffs. Thus, 400 employees may all agree to work (and get paid for) only 35 hours per week, to avoid a lay-off of 30 workers.

Telecommuting is another option. Here employees work at home, usually with computers, and use phones and the Internet to transmit letters, data, and completed work to the home office. For example, Best Western Hotels i... residents of the Arizona Center for Women, a minimum-security ...mmuting office staff, and Dell has call centers in India.

Daniel Briddle, owner of Mesa, Arizona–based PC ...nology Services, proves that you don't have to be a hermit to teleco... about 80% of his work time interacting continuously with custom... office and spends the rest of the time doing on-site tech support f... ...osting service.

Like most telecommuters today, Briddle's business d... rely on his being able to communicate in real time via the Inte... digital assistants. For one thing, he carries a text-based pager, an... account configured to forward messages straight to the device. He... e number where clients can leave him both voice and fax messa... a message on this number, the service e-mails him a message ... he goes online to hear the message over the Internet or listen by phone. "It works perfectly for me. Plus, my clients see that I have a toll-free number." He also carries a personal digital assistant (a Palm), into which he inserts a lot of the technical information about each client's system. That makes it even easier for him to respond quickly when a client has a problem.[125]

Many businesses—particularly smaller ones—don't have the resources or employee base to support the cost of many of the benefits we discussed in this chapter. The "When You're on Your Own" feature describes one solution.

When You're On Your Own
HR for Line Managers and Entrepreneurs

Benefits and Employee Leasing

The 40 employees at First Weigh Manufacturing in Sanford, Florida, may not work for a giant company, but they get employee benefits and HR services as if they do. That's because Tom Strasse, First Weigh's owner, signed up with ADP Total Source, a professional employee organization that now handles all First Weigh's HR processes. "I didn't have the time or the personnel to deal with the human resources, safety and OSHA regulations," Strasse says. "We were always looking for new insurance."[126]

Strasse's experience is typical of small businesses that turn to *employee leasing*. Employee leasing firms (generally called professional employer organizations, or staff leasing firms) arrange to have all the employer's employees transferred to the employee leasing firm's payroll. The leasing firm becomes the employees' legal employer, and usually handles all employee-related activities such as recruiting, hiring (with client

firms' supervisors' approvals), and paying taxes (Social Security payments, unemployment insurance, and so on).

However, benefits management is often the big attraction. Getting health and other insurance can be a big problem for smaller firms. Even group rates for life or health insurance can be quite high when only 20 or 30 employees are involved. First Weigh Manufacturing's health insurance carrier dropped the firm after its first two years, and Strasse had to go scrambling to find a new carrier—which he did, with premiums that were 30% higher.

That's where the leasing firm comes in. Remember that the leasing firm is the legal employer of your employees. The employees therefore are absorbed into a much larger insurable group, along with other employers' former employees. As a result, a small business owner may be able to get insurance for its people that it couldn't otherwise afford. An added benefit: The Alexandria, Virginia–based National Association of Professional Employer Organizations (which represents employee leasing firms) estimates that the average cost of regulations, paperwork, and tax compliance for smaller firms is about $5,000 per employee per year.[127] With expenses like that, it's understandable that many small business owners figure what they save on not managing their own HR activities pretty much pays for the employee leasing firm's fees. Now, for instance, when Strasse has a question about HR legal issues or safety concerns, he can just call his representative at the employee leasing firm.

Employee leasing may sound too good to be true, and it often is. Many employers aren't comfortable letting a third party become the legal employer of their employees (who literally have to be terminated by the employer and rehired by the leasing firm). However, there are other, more concrete risks to consider. Several years ago, for instance, the employee leasing industry tarnished itself when one or two firms manipulated the pension benefits offered to higher-paid employees.[128] The arrangement can also raise liability concerns. For example, in the typical employee leasing arrangement, the professional employer organization and the client employer agree to share the various responsibilities, a concept known as co-employment. So, for instance, in states where courts have not universally upheld workers' compensation as the sole remedy for injuries at work (there are some such states), it's very important to specify whether the client company or the leasing firm is insuring the workers' compensation exposure.[129]

Review

SUMMARY

1. Financial incentives are usually paid to specific employees whose work is above standard. Employee benefits, on the other hand, are available to all employees based on their membership in the organization.

2. There are four basic types of benefits plans: pay supplements, insurance, retirement benefits, and services.

3. Supplemental pay benefits provide pay for time not worked. They include unemployment insurance, vacation and holiday pay, severance pay, and supplemental unemployment benefits.

4. Insurance benefits include workers' compensation, group hospitalization, accident and disability insurance, and group life insurance.

5. Employee benefits are highly regulated by federal and state laws. Benefits required by federal or most state law include Social Security, unemployment insurance, workers' compensation, and leaves under the Family Medical Leave Act. Discretionary (non–legally required) benefits include disability, health and life insurance, pensions, and paid time off for vacations and holidays.

6. Employers are trying to rein in spiraling health care costs, and taking several specific steps to do this. These include using cost-containment specialists, getting employees more involved and empowered in the health care program, moving toward defined contribution health care plans, and outsourcing benefits such as employee assistance and counseling.

7. Retirement benefits include Social Security and pension plans. Social Security does not cover just retirement benefits but survivor's and disability benefits as well. Pension plans include defined benefit plans, defined contribution plans, deferred profit sharing, and savings plans. One of the critical issues in pension planning is vesting. ERISA basically ensures that pension rights become vested and protected after a reasonable amount of time.

8. Most employers also provide benefits in the form of employee services. These include food services, recreational opportunities, legal advice, credit unions, and counseling.

9. The employee's age, marital status, and sex clearly influence choice of benefits. This suggests the need for individualizing the organization's benefits plans.

10. Flexible benefits plans, also called the cafeteria approach, allow the employee to put together his or her own benefits plan, subject to total cost limits and the inclusion of certain nonoptional items. Many firms have installed cafeteria plans; they require considerable planning and computer assistance.

DISCUSSION QUESTIONS

1. You are applying for a job as a manager and are at the point of negotiating salary and benefits. What questions would you ask your prospective employer concerning benefits? Describe the benefits package you would try to negotiate for yourself.

2. What is unemployment insurance? Is an organization required to pay unemployment benefits to all dismissed employees? Explain how you would go about minimizing your organization's unemployment insurance tax.

3. Explain how ERISA protects employees' pension rights.

4. What is "portability"? Why do you think it is (or isn't) important to a recent college graduate?

5. What are the provisions of the FMLA?

INDIVIDUAL AND GROUP ACTIVITIES

1. Working individually or in groups, research the unemployment insurance rate and laws of your state. Write a summary detailing your state's unemployment laws. Assuming Company X has a 30% rate of annual personnel terminations, calculate Company X's unemployment tax rate in your state.

2. Assume you run a small business. Working individually or in groups, visit the Web site www.dol.gov/elaws. (See the Small Business Retirement Savings Advisor.) Write a two-page summary explaining: (1) the various retirement savings programs available to small business employers, and (2) which retirement savings program you would choose for your small business and why.

3. You are the HR consultant to a small business with about 40 employees. At the present time the firm offers only five days of vacation, five paid holidays, and legally mandated benefits such as unemployment insurance payments. Develop a list of other benefits you believe it should offer, along with your reasons for suggesting them.

4. The HRCI "Test Specifications" appendix at the end of this book (pages 685–689) lists the knowledge someone studying for the HRCI certification exam needs to have in each area of human resource management (such as in Strategic Management, Workforce Planning, and Human Resource Development). In groups of four to five students, do four things: (1) review that appendix now; (2) identify the material in this chapter that relates to the required knowledge the appendix lists; (3) write four multiple choice exam questions on this material that you believe would be suitable for inclusion in the HRCI exam; and (4) if time permits, have someone from your team post your team's questions in front of the class, so the students in other teams can take each others' exam questions.

EXPERIENTIAL EXERCISE

Revising the Benefits Package

Purpose: The purpose of this exercise is to provide practice in developing a benefits package for a small business.

Required Understanding: Be very familiar with the material presented in this chapter. In addition, review Chapter 11 to reacquaint yourself with sources of compensation survey information, and come to class prepared to share with your group the benefits package for the small business in which you work or in which someone with whom you're familiar works.

How to Set Up the Exercise/Instructions: Divide the class into groups of four or five students. Your assignment is as follows: Maria Cortes runs a small personnel recruiting office in Miami and has decided to start offering an expanded benefits package to her 25 employees. At the current time, the only benefits are seven paid holidays per year and five sick days per year. In her company, there are two other managers, as well as 17 full-time recruiters and five secretarial staff members. In the time allotted, your group should create a benefits package in keeping with the size and requirements of this firm.

APPLICATION CASE

Striking for Benefits

By February 2004, the strike by Southern California grocery workers against the state's major supermarket chains was almost five months old. Because so many workers were striking (70,000), and because of the issues involved, unions and employers across the country were closely following the negotiations. Indeed, grocery union contracts were set to expire in several cities later in 2004, and many believed the California settlement—assuming one was reached—would set a pattern.

The main issue was employee benefits, and specifically how much (if any) of the employees' health care costs the employees should pay themselves. Based on their existing contract, Southern California grocery workers had unusually good health benefits. For example, they paid nothing toward their health insurance premiums, and paid only $10 copayments for doctor visits. However, supporting these excellent health benefits cost the big Southern California grocery chains over $4.00 per hour per worker.

The big grocery chains were not proposing cutting health care insurance benefits for their existing employees. Instead, they proposed putting any new employees hired after the new contract went into effect into a separate insurance pool, and contributing $1.35 per hour for their health insurance coverage. That meant new employees' health insurance would cost each new employee perhaps $10 per week. And, if that $10 per week wasn't enough to cover the cost of health care, then the employees would have to pay more, or do without some of their benefits.

It was a difficult situation for all the parties involved. For the grocery chain employers, skyrocketing health care costs were undermining their competitiveness; and the current employees feared any step down the slippery slope that might eventually mean cutting their own health benefits. The unions didn't welcome a situation in which they'd end up representing two classes of employees, one (the existing employees) who had excellent health insurance benefits, and another (newly hired employees) whose benefits were relatively meager, and who might therefore be unhappy from the moment they took their jobs and joined the union.

Questions

1. Assume you are mediating this dispute. Discuss five creative solutions you would suggest for how the grocers could reduce the health insurance benefits and the cost of their total benefits package without making any employees pay more.

2. From the grocery chains' point of view, what is the downside of having two classes of employees, one of which has superior health insurance benefits? How would you suggest they handle the problem?

3. Similarly, from the point of view of the union, what are the downsides of having to represent two classes of employees, and how would you suggest handling the situation?

Source: Based on "Settlement Nears for Southern California Grocery Strike," *Knight-Ridder/Tribune Business News*, February 26, 2004, item 04057052.

CONTINUING CASE

Carter Cleaning Company

The New Benefit Plan

Carter Cleaning Centers has traditionally provided only legislatively required benefits for its employees. These include participation in the state's unemployment compensation program, Social Security, and workers' compensation (which is provided through the same insurance carrier that insures the stores for such hazards as theft and fire). The principals of the firm— Jack, Jennifer, and their families—have individual, family-supplied health and life insurance.

At the present time, Jennifer can see several potential problems with the company's policies regarding benefits and services. One is turnover. She wants to do a study to determine whether similar companies' experiences with providing health and life insurance benefits suggest they enable these firms to

reduce employee turnover and perhaps pay lower wages. Jennifer is also concerned with the fact that her company has no formal policy regarding vacations or paid days off or sick leave. Informally, at least, it is understood that employees get one week's vacation after one year's work, but in the past the policy regarding paid vacations for days such as New Year's Day and Thanksgiving Day has been very inconsistent. Sometimes employees who had been on the job only two or three weeks were paid fully for one of these holidays, while at other times employees who had been with the firm for six months or more had been paid for only half a day. Jennifer knows that this policy must be made more consistent.

She also wonders whether it would be advisable to establish some type of day care center for the employees' children. She knows that many of the employees' children either have no place to go during the day (they are preschoolers) or have no place to go after school, and she wonders whether a benefit such as day care would be in the best interests of the company.

Questions

1. Draw up a policy statement regarding vacations, sick leave, and paid days off for Carter Cleaning Centers.

2. What would you tell Jennifer are the advantages and disadvantages to Carter Cleaning Centers of providing its employees with health, hospitalization, and life insurance programs?

3. Would you advise establishing some type of day care center for the Carter cleaning employees? Why or why not?

KEY TERMS

benefits, 476	Social Security, 491	Employee Retirement Income Security Act (ERISA) , 493
supplemental pay benefits, 479	pension plans, 492	vested funds, 493
unemployment insurance, 479	defined benefit pension plan, 492	Pension Benefits Guarantee Corporation (PBGC), 494
sick leave, 482	defined contribution pension plan, 492	early retirement window, 494
severance pay, 484	401(k) plan, 492	cash balance plans, 495
supplemental unemployment benefits, 485	Economic Growth and Tax Relief Reconciliation Act (2001) (EGTRRA), 492	employee assistance program, 496
workers' compensation, 485	savings and thrift plan, 493	flexible benefits plan/cafeteria benefits plan, 500
health maintenance organization (HMO) , 487	deferred profit-sharing plan, 493	job sharing, 505
preferred provider organizations (PPOs) , 487	employee stock ownership plan (ESOP) , 493	work sharing, 505
group life insurance, 490		telecommuting, 505

ENDNOTES

1. Based on Frederick Hills, Thomas Bergmann, and Vida Scarpello, *Compensation Decision Making* (Fort Worth, TX: The Dryden Press, 1994), p. 424. See also L. Kate Beatty, "Pay and Benefits Break Away from Tradition," *HR Magazine*, November 1994, pp. 63–68, and Fay Hansen, "The Cutting Edge of Benefit Cost Control," *Workforce*, March 2003, pp. 36–42.

2. "Survey Finds 99 Percent of Employers Providing Health-Care Benefits," *Compensation and Benefits Review*, September/October 2002, p. 11.

3. "Decline in Job Based Health Coverage Links to Growth of U.S. Uninsured," *BNA Human Resources Report*, December 8, 2003, p. 30.

4. Eric Parmenter, "Controlling Health-Care Costs," *Compensation and Benefits Review*, September/October 2002, p. 44.

5. "Employers Face Fifth Successive Year of Major Health Cost Increases, Survey Finds," *BNA Human Resources Report*, October 6, 2003, p. 1050.

6. Craig Olson, "Will Workers Accept Lower Wages in Exchange for Health Benefits?" *Journal of Labor Economics* 20, no. 2 (April 2002), pp. S91–S114.

7. "Survey Finds 57 Percent of Employees Satisfied with Health Plans," *Compensation and Benefits Review*, March/April 2002, p. 11.

8. Joseph Martocchio, *Strategic Compensation* (Upper Saddle River, NJ: Prentice Hall, 2001), p. 262.

9. This is based on Eric Parmenter, "Employee Benefit Compliance Checklist," *Compensation and Benefits Review*, May/June 2002, pp. 29–38.

10. John Vater Jr., "Traps for the Unwary in Administration of Employee Health Benefits," *Compensation and Benefits Review*, May/June 2002, pp. 40–46.

11. Larri Short and Eileen Kahanar, "Unlocking the Secrets of the New Privacy Rules," *Occupational Hazards*, September 2002, pp. 51–54.

12. "California Domestic Partner Benefits Mandate Carries Likely Impact Beyond State's Borders," *BNA Bulletin to Management*, November 6, 2003, p. 353.

13. Based on Dennis Grant, "Managing Employee Leaves: A Legal Primer," *Compensation and Benefits Review*, July/August 2003, pp. 36–46.

14. Ibid., pp. 36–37.

15. Ibid., p. 37.

16. "Ten Years After It Was Signed into Law, FMLA Needs Makeover, Advocates Contend," *BNA Bulletin to Management*, February 20, 2003, p. 58.

17. Based on Dennis Grant, "Managing Employee Leaves: A Legal Primer," p. 41.

18. K. Matthes, "In Pursuit of Leisure: Employees Want More Time Off," *HR Focus* 7 (1992).

19. Richard Henderson, *Compensation Management* (Upper Saddle River, NJ: Prentice Hall, 1994), p. 555.

20. Ibid., p. 116. See also, "Spurious Sick-Notes Spiral Upwards," *The Safety and Health Practitioner*, June 2004, vol. 22, issue 6, p. 3.

21. "BNA's Quarterly Report on Job Absence and Turnover, Third Quarter 1997," *BNA Bulletin to Management*, December 11, 1997, pp. 1–4.

22. "Unscheduled Employee Absences Cost Companies More Than Ever," *Compensation and Benefits Review*, March/April 2003, p. 19.

23. "SHRM Benefits Survey Finds Growth in Employer Use of Paid Leave Pools," *BNA Bulletin to Management*, March 21, 2002, p. 89.

24. This is based on M. Michael Markowich and Steve Eckberg, "Get Control of the Absentee-Minded," *Personnel Journal*, March 1996, pp. 115–120.

25. "Review of State Law Reveals Six Trends Expected to Put Employers on the Hook," *BNA Bulletin to Management*, March 28, 2002, p. 97.

26. "Employers Complain About Leave Law and Absences," *BNA Bulletin to Management*, June 19, 1997, p. 193.

27. "Military Duty, Family Leave Laws Produce Complaints," *BNA Bulletin to Management*, June 13, 1996, p. 186.

28. "Individual Liability Under FMLA," *BNA Fair Employment Practices*, November 30, 1995, p. 139.

29. Dawn Gunch, "The Family Leave Act: A Financial Burden?" *Personnel Journal*, September 1993, p. 49.

30. Gillian Flynn, "Employers Need an FMLA Brush-Up," *Workforce*, April 1997, pp. 101–104. See also "Worker Who Was Employee for Less than One Year Can Pursue FMLA Claim, Federal Court Determines," *BNA Fair Employment Practices*, April 26, 2001, p. 51.

31. "Workers Who Come and Go Under FMLA Complicate Attendance Policies, Lawyer Says," *BNA Bulletin to Management*, March 16, 2000, p. 81.

32. "Severance Practices," *BNA Bulletin to Management*, January 11, 1996, pp. 12, 13, and Neil Grossman, "Shrinking the Workforce in an Economic Slowdown," *Compensation and Benefits Review*, Spring 2002, pp. 12–23.

33. Ibid, and, "Severance/Retention Practices: 2002; Pension Benefits, October 2002, p. 11.

34. "Severance Pay Common for Workers Who Lose Jobs," *BNA Bulletin to Management*, August 31, 1995, p. 273.

35. "Workers' Compensation and ADA," *BNA Bulletin to Management*, August 6, 1992, p. 248.

36. "Workers' Compensation Costs are Rising Faster Than Wages," *BNA Bulletin to Management*, July 31, 2003, p. 244.

37. "Workers' Comp Claims Rise with Layoffs, But Employers Can Identify, Prevent Fraud," *BNA Bulletin to Management*, October 4, 2001, p. 313.

38. See, for example, Betty Bialk, "Cutting Workers' Compensation Costs," *Personnel Journal*, July 1987, pp. 95–97.

39. Steve Lattanzio, "What Can Employer Do to Influence the Cost of Its Workers' Compensation Program?" *Compensation and Benefits Review*, 1997, pp. 20–30.

40. "Using Case Management in Workers' Compensation," *BNA Bulletin to Management*, June 6, 1996, p. 181.

41. "Firms Cite Own Efforts as Key to Controlling Costs," *BNA Bulletin to Management*, March 21, 1996, p. 89. See also "Workers' Compensation Outlook: Cost Control Persists," *BNA Bulletin to Management*, January 30, 1997, pp. 33–44, and Annmarie Lipold, "The Soaring Costs of Workers' Comp," *Workforce*, February 2003, p. 42ff.

42. Richard Gisonny and Michael Langan, "EEOC Provides Guidance on Application of ADA on Health Plans," *Benefits Law Journal* 6, no. 3 (Autumn 1993), pp. 461–467.

43. Johnathan Mook, "The ADA and Employee Benefits: A Regulatory and Litigation Update," *Benefits Law Journal* 7, no. 4 (Winter 1994–95), pp. 407–429.

44. Hills, Bergmann, and Scarpello, *Compensation Decision Making*, p. 137.

45. George Milkovich and Jerry Newman, *Compensation* (Burr Ridge, IL: McGraw-Hill, 1993), p. 445.

46. Except as noted, this section is based on Sean Smith, "New Trends in Health-Care Cost Control," *Compensation and Benefits Review*, January 18, 2002, p. 121.

47. Ibid., p. 40.

48. "As Workers Feel the Effect of Cost Hikes, Employers Turn to Health Remedies," *BNA Bulletin to Management*, April 18, 2002, p. 121.

49. "High Deductible Plans Might Catch On," *BNA Human Resources Report*, September 15, 2003, p. 967.

50. "HR Outsourcing: Managing Costs and Maximizing Provider Relations," *BNA, Inc.* 21, no. 11 (Washington, DC: November 2003), p. 10.

51. "One in Five Big Firms May Drop Coverage for Future Retirees, Health Survey Finds," *BNA Bulletin to Management*, December 12, 2002, p. 393.

52. Dale Busse, "Health Care," *HR Magazine*, April 2003, pp. 49–51.

53. Robert Christadore, "Benefits Purchasing Alliances: Creating Stability in an Unstable World," *Compensation and Benefits Review*, September/October 2001, pp. 49–53.

54. "Mental Health Trends," *Workplace Editions, No. 2*, Society for Human Resource Management, Alexandria, VA.

55. Ronald Bachman, "Time for Another Look," *HR Magazine*, March 1997, pp. 93–96.

56. Ibid., pp. 35–36.

57. James Weil, "Baby Boomer Needs Will Spur Growth of Long-Term Care Plans," *Compensation and Benefits Review*, March/April 1996, p. 49.

58. Carolyn Hirschman, "Will Employers Take the Lead in Long-Term Care?" *HR Magazine*, March 1997, pp. 59–66.

59. Bill Leonard, "Recipes for Part-Time Benefits," *HR Magazine*, April 2000, pp. 56–62.

60. Bob Lanza et al., "Legal Status of Contingent Workers," *Compensation and Benefits Review*, July/August 2003, pp. 47–60.

61. Brenda Pol Sunoo, "Millions May Retire," *Workforce*, December 1997, p. 48. See also "Many Older Workers Choose to 'Un-Retire' or Not Retire at All," *Knight Ridder/Tribune Business News*, September 28, 2003, item 03271012, "Older Workers: Recent Trends in Employment and Retirement, Patrick Purcell, *Journal of Deferred Compensation*, Spring 2003, vol. 8, issue 3, pp. 30–54, and "For Many Seniors, a Job Beats Retirement," *Knight Ridder/Tribune Business News*, February 9. 2003, item 3040001.

62. Ibid.

63. "Social Security Wage Base Up $900; Benefits Adjusted 2.1 Percent for 2004," *BNA Human Resources Report*, October 27, 2003, p. 1133.

64. Martocchio, *Strategic Compensation*, pp. 245–248, and Lin Grensing-Pophal, "A Pension Formula that Pays Off," *HR Magazine*, February 2003, pp. 58–62.

65. Ronald Grossman, "Reshaping the Retirement Benefit Bucket, EGTRRA Style," *Society for Human Resource Management Legal Report*, September/October 2001, p. 1.

66. Lindsay Wyatt, "401(k) Conversion: It's as Easy as Riding a Bike," *Workforce*, April 1997, p. 66. See also Carolyn Hirschman, "Growing Pains. Employers and Employees Alike Have Lots to Learn About 401(k) Plans," *HR Magazine*, June 2002, pp. 30–38.

67. "401(k) Is Now a Mainstay for Retirement Benefits," *HR Magazine*, April 2000, p. 31.

68. Arlene Jacobius, "Ford Offers Fidelity Planning Tool to Its Participants: The 401(k) Feature Includes Customized Model Portfolios," *Pension and Investments*, May 3, 1999, p. 36.

69. Wyatt, "401(k) Conversion," p. 20.

70. Matt Hamblin, "Benefits and Then Some: When It Comes to Basic Job Perks, IT Pros Want Them All—Plus a Fat Paycheck," *Computerworld*, July 19, 2000.

71. Victor Infante, "Retirement Plan Trends," *Workforce*, November 2000, pp. 69–76.

72. For an explanation of how to minimize employee benefits litigation related to pension and health benefits claims, see Thomas Piskorski, "Minimizing Employee Benefits Litigation Through Effective Claims Administration Procedures," *Employee Relations Law Journal* 20, no. 3 (Winter 1994–1995), pp. 421–431.

73. For a discussion, see Milton Zall, "Understanding the Risks to Pension Benefits," *Personnel Journal*, January 1992, pp. 62–69.

74. *Paolillo v. Dresser Industries*, 821F.2d81 (2d cir., 1987).

75. Arthur Silbergeld, "Release Agreements Must Comply with the Older Workers' Benefit Protection Act," *Employment Relations Today*, Winter 1992–1993, pp. 457–460.

76. Kathleen Murray, "How HR Is Making Pensions Portable," *Personnel Journal*, July 1993, pp. 36–46.

77. Harold Burlingame and Michael Culotta, "Cash Balance Pension Plan Facilitate Restructuring the Workforce at AT&T," *Compensation and Benefits Review*, November/December 1998, pp. 25–31; Eric Lekus, "When Are Cash Balance Pension Plans the Right Choice?" *BNA Bulletin to Management*, January 28, 1999, p. 7.

78. "Cash Balance Plans: IBM, Xerox Found in Violation of Pension Law," *BNA Bulletin to Management*, August 7, 2003, p. 249. See also Susan Bernstein, "Cash Balance Plans: Cloud of Uncertainty Continues," *Compensation and Benefits Review*, May/June 2003, pp. 51–60; and Elayne Demby, "Cash Balance Makes a Comeback," *Workforce*, May 2003, pp. 39–43.

79. "Benefits Cost Control Solutions to Consider Now," *HR Focus* 80, no. 11 (November 2003), p. 1.

80. Johanna Rodgers, "Web Based Apps Simplify Employee Benefits," *Insurance and Technology* 28, no. 11 (November 2003), p. 21.

81. Ibid.

82. Tina Carlson, "Arrowhead C.U. to Open Branch on used Car Lot," *Credit Union Journal*, January 22, 2001, p. 6.

83. Joseph O'Connell, "Using Employee Assistance Programs to Avoid Crises," *Long Island Business News*, April 19, 2002, p. 10.

84. See Scott MacDonald et al., "Absenteeism and Other Workplace Indicators of Employee Assistance Program and Matched Controls," *Employee Assistance Quarterly* 15, no. 3 (2000), pp. 51–58.

85. "Making Up for Lost Time: How Employers Can Curb Excessive Unscheduled Absences," *BNA Human Resources Report*, October 20, 2003, p. 1097.

86. See Harry Turk, "Questions and Answers: Avoiding Liability for EAP Services," *Employment Relations Today*, Spring 1992, pp. 111–114.

87. Maureen Hannay and Melissa Northam, "Low-Cost Strategies for Employee Retention," *Compensation and Benefits Review*, July/August 2000, pp. 65–72.

88. "Work/Life Perks Often Avoided by Workers, Poll Finds," *BNA Bulletin to Management*, March 19, 1998, p. 81.

89. Mary Burke, Euren Esen, and Jessica Cullison, *2003 Benefits Survey*, SHRM/SHRM Foundation 1800 Duke Street, Alexandria VA, 2003, pp. 8–9.

90. Ibid.

91. Gillian Flynn, "Making a Business Case for Balance," *Workforce*, March 1997, pp. 68–74.

92. Jerry Useem, "Welcome to the New Company Town," *Fortune*, January 10, 2000, pp. 62–70.

93. Patricia Nakache, "One VP, Two Brains," *Fortune*, December 20, 1999, pp. 327–328.

94. P. Osterman, "Work/Family Programs and the Employment Relationship," *Administrative Science Quarterly* 40 (1995), pp. 681–700.

95. Susan Lambert, "Added Benefits: The Link Between Work Life Benefits and Organizational Citizenship Behavior," *Academy of Management Journal* 43, no. 5 (2000), pp. 801–815.

96. Mathew Boyle, "How to Cut Perks Without Killing Morale," *Fortune*, February 19, 2001, pp. 241–244.

97. "Child Care Options," *BNA Bulletin to Management*, July 4, 1996, p. 212. See also, "Child Care Report Boasts Its Benefit to California Economy," *Knight Ridder/Tribune Business News*, January 9, 2003, item 03009011.

98. This is based on ibid., pp. 212–214. See also, Todd Raphael, "Business Can Make Child Care Work," *Workforce*, December 2001, vol. 80, issue 12, p. 88.

99. Kelli Earhart, R. Dennis Middlemist, and Willi Hopkins, "Elder Care: An Emerging Assistance Issue," *Employee Assistance Quarterly* 8, no. 3 (1993), pp. 1–10. See also, "Finding a Balance Between Conflicting Responsibilities: Work and Caring for Aging Parents," *Monday Business Briefing*, July 7, 2004, and "Employers Feel Impact of Eldercare: Some Expanded Benefits for Workers," *Knight Ridder/Tribune Business News*, June 13, 2004, item 04165011.

100. Rudy Yandrick, "Elder Care Grows Up," *HR Magazine*, November 2001, pp. 72–77.

101. SHRM, 2003 Benefits Survey, op cit, p. 30.

102. "Chrysler Benefits to Cover Tuition, Dependent Care," *BNA Bulletin to Management*, October 2, 1997, p. 313.

103. Russa Banham, "Working It Out: Rates in the Workers' Compensation Market Have Increased More Than Any Other Line of Insurance Since September 11," *Reactions* 22, no. 9 (September 2002), pp. 80–84.

104. David Pilla et al., "One Year Later," *Benefits Review*, September 2002, p. 103.

105. SHRM/SHRM Foundation, 2003 Benefits Survey, p. 2.

106. Carolyn Shapiro, "More Companies Cover Benefits for Employee's Domestic Partners," *Knight-Ridder/Tribune Business News*, July 20, 2003.

107. "What You Need to Know to Provide Domestic Partner Benefits," *HR Focus* 80, no. 3 (August 2003), p. 3.

108. Martocchio, *Strategic Compensation*, pp. 308–309.

109. "Couples Want Flexible Leave, Benefits," *BNA Bulletin to Management*, February 19, 1998, p. 53, SHRM, 2003 Benefits Survey, op cit, p. 14.

110. "Money Isn't Everything," *Journal of Business Strategy* 21, no. 2 (March 2000), p. 4.

111. Carolyn Hirshman, "Kinder, Simpler Cafeteria Rules," *HR Magazine*, January 2001, pp. 74–79.

112. "Debit Cards for Health-Care Expenses Received Increased Employer Attention," *BNA Bulletin to Management*, September 25, 2003, p. 305.

113. Martocchio, *Strategic Compensation*, p. 263.

114. David Hom, "How Pitney Bowes Broadens Benefit Choices with Value-Added Services," *Compensation and Benefits Review*, March/April 1996, pp. 60–66.

115. Ibid., p. 60

116. Ibid., p. 62.

117. "Technology Revolutionizes Administration," *BNA Bulletin to Management*, November 9, 1995; "Benefits Merge onto Information Superhighway," *BNA Bulletin to Management*, February 29, 1996, p. 66; Miriam Scott, "Incentive Benefits Systems Save Time and Dollars for Employers, Employees," *Employee Benefits Plan Review*, February 1995, pp. 16–18. See also Neil Schelberg et al., "Paperless Benefit Plan Administration," *Compensation and Benefits Review*, July/August 2000, pp. 58–64.

118. Jim Meade, "Affordable HRIS Strong on Benefits," *HR Magazine*, April 2000, pp. 132–135.

119. "Slightly More Workers Are Skirting 9–5 Tradition," *BNA Bulletin to Management*, June 20, 2002, p. 197.

120. "Improving Well-Being and Morale 24 Hours a Day," *BNA Bulletin to Management*, August 19, 1999.

121. Boris Baltes et al., "Flexible and Compressed Workweek Schedules: A Meta-Analysis of Their Effects on Work-Related Criteria," *Journal of Applied Psychology* 84, no. 4 (1999), pp. 496–513.

122. "Improving Well-Being and Morale 24 Hours a Day."

123. "2003 Benefits Survey," SHRM, op cit, p. 2.

124. Judith Letterman, "Two People, One Job," *New York Times*, January 14, 2001, p. 8.

125. William Van Winkle, "Your Away-from-Home Office," *Home Office Computing* 19, no. 1 (January 2001), p. 54.

126. Jane Applegate, "Employee Leasing Can Be a Savior For Small Firms," *Business Courier Serving Cincinnati-Northern Kentucky*, January 28, 2000, p. 23.

127. Harriet Tramer, "Employee Leasing Agreement Can Ease Personnel Concerns," *Cranes Cleveland Business*, July 24, 2000, p. 24.

128. Applegate, "Employee Leasing Can Be Savior for Small Firms," p. 23.

129. Diana Reitz, "Employee Leasing Breeds Liability Questions," *National Underwriter Property and Casualty Risk and Benefits Management* 104, no. 18 (May 2000), p. 12.

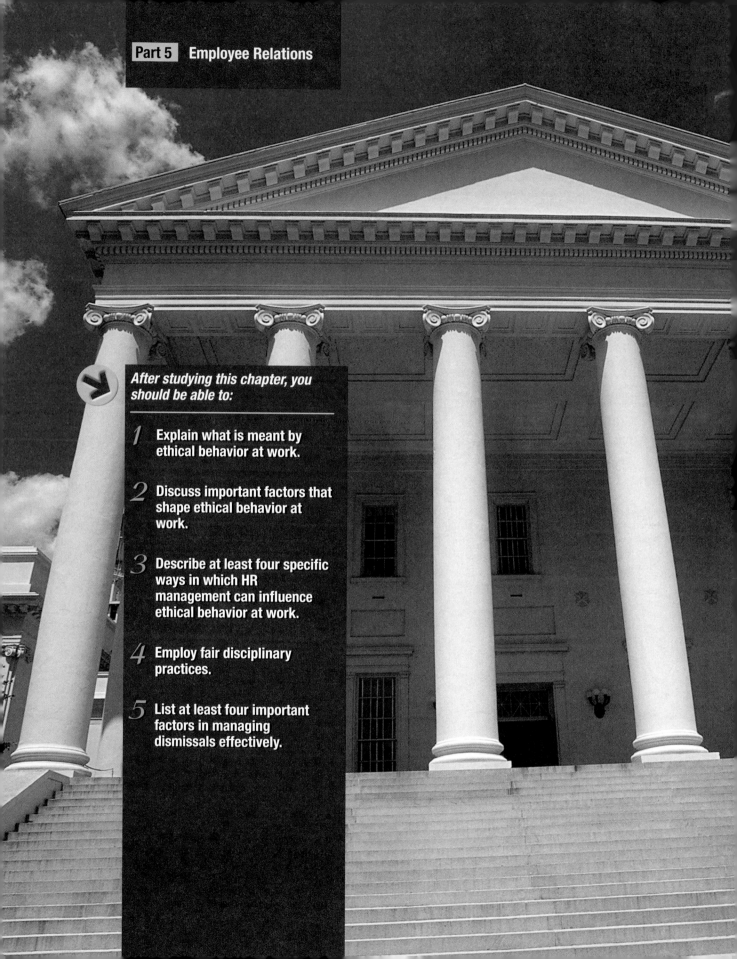

After studying this chapter, you should be able to:

1 Explain what is meant by ethical behavior at work.

2 Discuss important factors that shape ethical behavior at work.

3 Describe at least four specific ways in which HR management can influence ethical behavior at work.

4 Employ fair disciplinary practices.

5 List at least four important factors in managing dismissals effectively.

Ethics, Justice, and Fair Treatment in HR Management

As the head of HR for the Hotel Paris, Lisa Cruz was especially concerned about her company maintaining the highest ethical standards. Her concerns were twofold. First, from a practical point of view, there are, in a hotel chain, literally thousands of opportunities on any given day for guests to have bad experiences, ethically speaking. For example, in any single hotel each day there are at least a dozen people (including housekeepers, front-desk clerks, security guards, and so on) with easy access to guests' rooms, and to their personal belongings. Guests—many younger, and many unwary—are continually walking the halls unprotected. So, in a service company like this, there is simply no margin for ethical errors.

But she was concerned about ethics for a second reason. She'd been around long enough to know that employees do not like being treated unfairly, and that unfairness in any form could manifest itself in low morale and commitment, and in diminished performance. Indeed, perhaps her employees' low morale and commitment—as measured by her firm's attitude surveys—stemmed, in part, from what they perceived as unjust treatment by the hotel's managers. Lisa therefore turned to the task of assessing and redesigning the Hotel Paris's ethics, justice, and fair treatment practices. •

515

This chapter starts a new part of the book, Part 5, Employee Relations. Part 4 focused on employee compensation, including salaries, incentives, and benefits. Now, in Part 5 we turn to issues relating to employee justice, safety, and union relations. The current chapter focuses on ethics, justice, and fair treatment in HR, matters that lie at the heart of excellent relations with employees. Topics we'll cover here include ethics and fair treatment at work, the factors that shape ethical behavior at work, HR's role in fostering improved workplace ethics, employee discipline and privacy, and managing dismissals.

Explain what is meant by ethical behavior at work.

● ETHICS AND FAIR TREATMENT AT WORK

You face ethical choices every day. Is it wrong to use company e-mail for personal reasons? Is a $50 gift to a boss unacceptable? Compare your answers to those of Americans by answering the quiz in Figure 14-1.

In organizations, the manager's HR-related activities are a frequent source of ethical questions. As the executive director of the Ethics Officer Association put it, HR activities such as disciplinary fairness, sexual harassment, and equity in performance reviews often trigger ethics-related issues.[1] One survey of 747 HR professionals found that 54% had observed misconduct ranging from violations of Title VII, to violations of

---

Office Technology

1. Is it wrong to use company e-mail for personal reasons?
   ❑ Yes ❑ No

2. Is it wrong to use office equipment to help your children or spouse do schoolwork?
   ❑ Yes ❑ No

3. Is it wrong to play computer games on office equipment during the workday?
   ❑ Yes ❑ No

4. Is it wrong to use office equipment to do internet shopping?
   ❑ Yes ❑ No

5. Is it unethical to blame an error you made on a technological glitch?
   ❑ Yes ❑ No

6. Is it unethical to visit pornographic Web sites using office equipment?
   ❑ Yes ❑ No

Gifts and Entertainment

7. What's the value at which a gift from a supplier or client becomes troubling?
   ❑ $25 ❑ $50 ❑ $100

8. Is a $50 gift to a boss unacceptable?
   ❑ Yes ❑ No

9. Is a $50 gift *from* the boss unacceptable?
   ❑ Yes ❑ No

10. Of gifts from suppliers: Is it OK to take a $200 pair of football tickets?
    ❑ Yes ❑ No

11. Is it OK to take a $120 pair of theater tickets?
    ❑ Yes ❑ No

12. Is it OK to take a $100 holiday food basket?
    ❑ Yes ❑ No

13. Is it OK to take a $25 gift certificate?
    ❑ Yes ❑ No

14. Can you accept a $75 prize won at a raffle at a supplier's conference?
    ❑ Yes ❑ No

Truth and Lies

15. Due to on-the-job pressure, have you ever abused or lied about sick days?
    ❑ Yes ❑ No

16. Due to on-the-job pressure, have you ever taken credit for someone else's work or idea?
    ❑ Yes ❑ No

Figure 14-1
The *Wall Street Journal* Workplace-Ethics Quiz

The spread of technology into the workplace has raised a variety of new ethical questions, and many old ones still linger. Compare your answers with those of other Americans surveyed, on pages 554–555.

Source: Wall Street Journal, October 21, 1999, pp. B1–B4; © 1999 by Dow Jones & Co. Inc. Reproduced with permission via Copyright Clearance Center.

the Occupational Safety and Health Act, to employees using drugs or alcohol or falsifying work records.[2] Another found that six of the 10 most serious ethical issues—workplace safety, security of employee records, employee theft, affirmative action, comparable work, and employee privacy rights—were HR related.[3]

Of course, HR activities need not just be a potential hotbed of ethical problems. Instead, HR activities can drive positive ethical change, and can play a central role in the company's ethics efforts. We'll focus on how in this and the following sections. Let's look first at what *ethics* means.

The Meaning of *Ethics*

ethics
The principles of conduct governing an individual or a group; specifically, the standards you use to decide what your conduct should be.

Ethics refers to "the principles of conduct governing an individual or a group,"[4] and specifically to the standards you use to decide what your conduct should be. Ethical decisions are always characterized by two things. First, they always involve *normative judgments.*[5] A normative judgment implies that something is good or bad, right or wrong, better or worse. "You are wearing a skirt and blouse" is a nonnormative statement; "That's a great outfit!" is a normative one.

Ethical decisions also involve *morality,* which is society's accepted standards of behavior. Moral standards differ from other standards in several ways. They address behaviors of serious consequence to society's well-being, such as murder, lying, and slander. They cannot be established or changed by decisions of authoritative bodies like legislatures, and they should override self-interest. Many people believe that moral judgments are never situational. They argue that something that is morally right (or wrong) in one situation is right (or wrong) in another. Moral judgments tend to trigger strong emotions. Violating moral standards may make individuals feel ashamed or remorseful.[6]

It would simplify things if it was always clear which decisions were ethical and which were not. Unfortunately, it is not. If the decision makes the person feel ashamed or remorseful, or involves a matter of serious consequence such as murder, then chances are it's probably unethical. On the other hand, in some countries, bribery may be so ingrained that their citizens don't view it as wrong. True, "Everyone is doing it" is no excuse. However, the fact that a society doesn't view bribery as wrong may suggest that the person offering a bribe there may not be doing something wrong, at least in terms of his or her frame of reference.

Ethics and the Law

Furthermore, the law is not the best guide about what is ethical, because something may be legal but not right, and something may be right but not legal. You can make a decision that involves ethics (such as firing an employee) based on what is legal. However, that doesn't mean the decision will be ethical. Firing a 38-year-old employee with 20 years' tenure without notice or cause may be unethical, but it is still legal, for instance. Patrick Gnazzo, vice president for business practices at United Technologies Corp. (and a former trial lawyer), put it this way: "Don't lie, don't cheat, don't steal. We were all raised with essentially the same values. Ethics means making decisions that represent what you stand for, not just what the laws are."[7] Sometimes behavior is illegal and unethical. For example, one huge meat producer and processor recently had to respond to a federal indictment charging it with smuggling illegal immigrants from Mexico to cut factory costs.[8]

Ethics, Fair Treatment, and Justice

Managing human resources often requires making decisions in which fairness plays a big role. You hire one candidate and reject another, promote one and demote another, pay one more and one less, and settle one's grievances while rejecting another's. How employees react to these decisions depends, to a large extent, on whether they think the decisions and the processes that led up to them were fair.

Fairness is an integral part of what most people think of as "justice." A company that is just is, among other things, equitable, fair, impartial, and unbiased in the ways it does things. With respect to employee relations, experts generally define *organizational justice* in terms of its three components—distributive justice, procedural justice, and interpersonal or interactive justice. **Distributive justice** refers to the fairness and justice of the decision's result (for instance, did I get an equitable pay raise?). **Procedural justice** refers to the fairness of the process (for instance, is the process my company uses to allocate merit raises fair?). **Interactional** or **interpersonal justice** refers to "the manner in which managers conduct their interpersonal dealings with employees," and in particular to the degree to which they treat employees with dignity as opposed to abuse or disrespect (for instance, "does my supervisor treat me with respect?")[9]

Companies where fairness and justice prevail also tend to be ethical companies. One study focused on how employees reacted to fair treatment. It concluded that "to the extent that survey respondents believed that employees were treated fairly . . . [they] reported less unethical behavior in their organizations. They also reported that employees and their organizations were more aware of ethical issues [and] more likely to ask for ethical advice.[10] Similarly, "[H]iring, performance evaluation, discipline, and terminations can be ethical issues because they all involve honesty, fairness, and the dignity of the individual.[11] In practice, fair treatment reflects concrete actions such as "employees are trusted," "employees are treated with respect," and "employees are treated fairly" (see Figure 14-2).[12] Most employees associate fairness with ethical behavior.[13]

Workplace unfairness can be blatant. Some supervisors are "workplace bullies," yelling at or ridiculing subordinates, humiliating them, and sometimes even making threats. The employer should, of course, always prohibit such behavior, and many firms do have antiharassment policies. For example, at the Oregon Department of

Margin glossary

distributive justice
The fairness and justice of a decision's result.

procedural justice
The fairness of the process.

interactional (interpersonal) justice
The manner in which managers conduct their interpersonal dealings with employees.

Figure 14-2
Perceptions of Fair Interpersonal Treatment Scale

Sources: Michelle A. Donovan et al., "The Perceptions of Their Interpersonal Treatment Scale: Development and Validation of a Measure of Interpersonal Treatment in the Workplace," *Journal of Applied Psychology*, 83, no. 5 (1998), p. 692. Copyright © 1997 by Michelle A. Donovan, Fritz Drasgow, and Liberty J. Munson at the University of Illinois at Urbana-Champaign. All rights reserved.

What is your organization like most of the time? Circle YES if the item describes your organization, NO if it does not describe your organization, and ? if you cannot decide.

IN THIS ORGANIZATION:

1. Employees are praised for good work	Yes	?	No
2. Supervisors yell at employees (R)	Yes	?	No
3. Supervisors play favorites (R)	Yes	?	No
4. Employees are trusted	Yes	?	No
5. Employees' complaints are dealt with effectively	Yes	?	No
6. Employees are treated like children (R)	Yes	?	No
7. Employees are treated with respect	Yes	?	No
8. Employees' questions and problems are responded to quickly	Yes	?	No
9. Employees are lied to (R)	Yes	?	No
10. Employees' suggestions are ignored (R)	Yes	?	No
11. Supervisors swear at employees (R)	Yes	?	No
12. Employees' hard work is appreciated	Yes	?	No
13. Supervisors threaten to fire or lay off employees (R)	Yes	?	No
14. Employees are treated fairly	Yes	?	No
15. Co-workers help each other out	Yes	?	No
16. Co-workers argue with each other (R)	Yes	?	No
17. Co-workers put each other down (R)	Yes	?	No
18. Co-workers treat each other with respect	Yes	?	No

Note:: R = the item is reverse scored.

The New Workplace

Employment Contracts

Businesses expanding abroad soon discover that hiring employees in Europe requires much more stringent communication than does hiring people in the United States. For example, the European Union (EU) has a directive that requires employers to provide employees with very explicit contracts of employment, usually within two months of their starting work.

How employers must comply with this law varies by country. For example, in the United Kingdom the employee must be given a written contract specifying, among other things, name of employer, grievance procedure, job title, rate of pay, disciplinary rules, pension plan, hours of work, vacation and sick leave policies, pay periods, and date when employment began. In Germany, the contracts need not be in writing, although they customarily are, given the amount of detail they must cover, including minimum notice prior to layoff, wages,

vacations, maternity/paternity rights, equal pay, invention rights, noncompetition clause, and sickness pay. The contract need not be in writing in Italy, but again, it usually is. Items covered include start date, probationary period, working hours, job description, place of work, basic salary, and a noncompetition clause. In France, the contract must be in writing, and specify information such as the identity of the parties, place of work, type of job or job descriptions, notice period, dates of payment, and work hours.

Although employment contract requirements differ from one European country to another, one thing can be said with certainty. When it comes to outlining the nature of the employment relationship, employers can't take fair treatment lightly, but instead must be very explicit about what the nature of the employer–employee relationship is to be.

Transportation, "It is the policy of the department that all employees, customers, contractors and visitors to the work site are entitled to a positive, respectful and productive work environment, free from behavior, actions, [and] language constituting workplace harassment."[14] Not surprisingly, employees of abusive supervisors are more likely to quit their jobs, and to report lower job and life satisfaction and higher stress if they remain in those jobs.[15]

Some of the things that motivate managers to be fair may (or may not) be surprising. For one thing, the old saying, "the squeaky wheel gets the grease" seems to be true. One study investigated the extent to which assertiveness on the subordinate's part influenced the fairness with which the person's supervisor treated him or her.[16] Did supervisors treat pushier employees more fairly? Yes, they did: "Individuals who communicated assertively were more likely to be treated fairly by the decision maker." Studies also suggest that large organizations have to work particularly hard to set up procedures that make the workplace seem fair to employees.[17]

Fair treatment tends to be more formalized in Europe. "The New Workplace" illustrates this.

● WHAT SHAPES ETHICAL BEHAVIOR AT WORK?

→ 2 Discuss important factors that shape ethical behavior at work.

Whether or not a person acts ethically at work is usually not a result of any one thing. For example, it's not just the employee's *ethical tendencies*, since even "ethical" employees can have their actions influenced by *organizational* factors. So, the manager's first task is to understand what shapes ethical behavior, and then to take concrete steps to ensure that employees make ethical choices. Let's look first at the factors that shape ethical behavior. Then, in the following section, we turn to the steps the HR manager can take to help ensure ethical behavior.

Individual Factors

Because people bring to their jobs their own ideas of what is morally right and wrong, the individual must shoulder much of the credit (or blame) for the ethical choices he or she makes. One survey of CEOs of manufacturing firms explored their intention to engage (or to not engage) in two questionable business practices: soliciting a competitor's technological secrets and making payments to foreign government officials to secure business. The researchers concluded that personal predispositions more strongly affected decisions than did environmental pressures or organizational characteristics.[18]

In any case, honesty testing (discussed in Chapter 6) shows that some people are more inclined toward making the wrong ethical choice. How would you rate your own ethics? Figure 14-3 presents a short self-assessment survey to help you answer that question.

Organizational Factors

In March 2004, Michael Sullivan, WorldCom's former CFO, pleaded guilty to helping the firm's former chairman, Bernard Ebbers, mask WorldCom's deteriorating financial situation. Among other things, the government accused him of instructing underlings to fraudulently book accounting entries, and of filing false statements with the SEC. Why, as a star CFO and someone trained to protect the interests of his shareholders, would the CFO do such a thing? "I took these actions, knowing they were wrong, in a misguided attempt to preserve the company to allow it to withstand what I believed were temporary financial difficulties."[19]

The scary thing about unethical behavior at work is that it's usually not driven by personal interests. Table 14-1 summarizes the results of one survey of the principal causes of ethical lapses, as reported by six levels of employees and managers. As you can see, being under the gun to meet scheduling pressures was the number-one factor in causing ethical lapses. For most of these employees, "meeting overly aggressive financial or business objectives," and "helping the company survive" were the two other top causes. "Advancing my own career or financial interests" ranked toward the bottom of the list. Thus (at least in this case) most ethical lapses occurred because employees felt pressured to do what they thought was best to help their companies. Several years ago, three former CUC International executives pleaded guilty to federal charges. Authorities then called it "the largest and longest" accounting fraud in history. The former executives said they had done it to keep the price of the company stock high.[20]

Having rules on the books forbidding this sort of thing does not, by itself, seem to work. For example, in 2002, New York's attorney general filed charges against Merrill Lynch, alleging that several of its analysts had issued optimistic rating on stocks, while privately expressing concerns about those same stocks. The allegation was that they did so (in violation of company rules) to aid and support Merrill Lynch's investment banking relationships with these companies.

The Boss's Influence

The boss sets the tone, and by his or her actions sends signals about what is right or wrong. According to one report, for instance, "the level of misconduct at work dropped dramatically when employees said their supervisors exhibited ethical behavior." Only 25% of employees who agreed that their supervisors "set a good example of ethical business behavior" said they had observed misconduct in the last year, compared with 72% of those who did not feel that their supervisors set good ethical examples.[21]

A study by the American Society of Chartered Life Underwriters found that 56% of all workers felt some pressure to act unethically or illegally, and that the problem

Figure 14-3
How Do My Ethics Rate?

Source: Adapted from A. Reichel and Y. Neumann, *Journal of Instructional Psychology,* March 1988, pp. 25–53. With permission of the authors.

Instrument

Indicate your level of agreement with these 15 statements using the following scale:

1 = Strongly disagree
2 = Disagree
3 = Neither agree nor disagree
4 = Agree
5 = Strongly agree

1. The only moral of business is making money.	1	2	3	4	5
2. A person who is doing well in business does not have to worry about moral problems.	1	2	3	4	5
3. Act according to the law, and you can't go wrong morally.	1	2	3	4	5
4. Ethics in business is basically an adjustment between expectations and the ways people behave.	1	2	3	4	5
5. Business decisions involve a realistic economic attitude and not a moral philosophy.	1	2	3	4	5
6. "Business ethics" is a concept for public relations only.	1	2	3	4	5
7. Competitiveness and profitability are important values.	1	2	3	4	5
8. Conditions of a free economy will best serve the needs of society. Limiting competition can only hurt society and actually violates basic natural laws.	1	2	3	4	5
9. As a consumer, when making an auto insurance claim, I try to get as much as possible regardless of the extent of the damage.	1	2	3	4	5
10. While shopping at the supermarket, it is appropriate to switch price tags on packages.	1	2	3	4	5
11. As an employee, I can take home office supplies; it doesn't hurt anyone.	1	2	3	4	5
12. I view sick days as vacation days that I deserve.	1	2	3	4	5
13. Employees' wages should be determined according to the laws of supply and demand.	1	2	3	4	5
14. The business world has its own rules.	1	2	3	4	5
15. A good businessperson is a successful businessperson.	1	2	3	4	5

ANALYSIS AND INTERPRETATION

Rather than specify "right" answers, this instrument works best when you compare your answer to those of others. With that in mind, here are mean responses from a group of 243 management students. How did your responses compare?

1. 3.09	6. 2.88	11. 1.58
2. 1.88	7. 3.62	12. 2.31
3. 2.54	8. 3.79	13. 3.36
4. 3.41	9. 3.44	14. 3.79
5. 3.88	10. 1.33	15. 3.38

seems to be getting worse.[22] Here are examples of how supervisors knowingly (or unknowingly) lead subordinates astray:

■ Tell staffers to do whatever is necessary to achieve results.

■ Overload top performers to ensure that work gets done.

■ Look the other way when wrongdoing occurs.

■ Take credit for others' work or shift blame.[23]

Table 14-1

Principal Causes of Ethical Compromises

	Senior Mgmt.	Middle Mgmt.	Front-Line Supv.	Prof. Non-Mgmt.	Admin. Salaried	Hourly
Meeting schedule pressure	1	1	1	1	1	1
Meeting overly aggressive financial or business objectives	3	2	2	2	2	2
Helping the company survive	2	3	4	4	3	4
Advancing the career interests of my boss	5	4	3	3	4	5
Feeling peer pressure	7	7	5	6	5	3
Resisting competitive threats	4	5	6	5	6	7
Saving jobs	9	6	7	7	7	6
Advancing my own career or financial interests	8	9	9	8	9	8
Other	6	8	8	9	8	9

Note: 1 is high, 9 is low.

Sources: O. C. Ferrell and John Fraedrich, *Business Ethics*, 3rd ed. (New York: Houghton Mifflin, 1997), p. 28; adapted from Rebecca Goodell, *Ethics in American Business: Policies, Programs, and Perceptions* (1994), p. 54. Permission provided courtesy of the Ethics Resource Center, 1120 6th Street NW, Washington, DC: 20005.

Ethics Policies and Codes

An ethics policy and code is one signal that the firm is serious about ethics. Sometimes ethics codes work, and sometimes they don't. Enron was a huge energy company that collapsed due to falsified accounting. Enron's ethical principles were widely available on the company's Web site. They state, among other things, that "as a partner in the communities in which we operate, Enron believes it has a responsibility to conduct itself according to certain basic principles." Those include, "respect, integrity, communication and excellence."[24]

Some firms urge employees to apply a quick "ethics test" to evaluate whether what they're about to do fits the company's code of conduct. For example, the Raytheon Company asks employees who are faced with ethical dilemmas to ask:

Is the action legal?

Is it right?

Who will be affected?

Does it fit Raytheon's values?

How will it "feel" afterwards?

How will it look in the newspaper?

Will it reflect poorly on the company?[25]

The Organization's Culture

It is clear that ethics codes alone cannot prevent unethical behavior. About three-fourths of U.S. firms have formal ethics codes, and most offer ethics training. (About 95% of the largest *Fortune* 50 firms provide such training.) Yet about four of every 10 employees in

Finance executive Mary Ann Adams of Southwest Airlines leans from the cockpit of a Southwest airliner: Southwest's culture of "let's have fun" permeates all levels of the organization.

the United States say they have witnessed serious legal or ethical problems where they work. In one survey over 50% of all workers in the financial services and insurance industries said they felt under pressure to act illegally or unethically. Just under half reported participating in such activities.[26] What accounts for this disconnect between what the ethics codes say and how these employees feel?

One factor is that it's usually not just one or two things that create the environment in which unethical behavior can flourish. Several things—the individual, the boss, the ethics code, and the degree of competition, for instance—interact. Another is that when it comes to ethical behavior, it's not what you say that's important; it's what you do. Parents can talk about being ethical, but if their children see them always cutting ethical corners—bringing home "free" office supplies from where they work, for instance—the children may assume that being unethical is really okay.

The same is true at work. Southwest Airlines nurtures a "let's have fun" organizational culture all its own. New employees are sometimes the butt of practical jokes, cabin attendants have been known to sing from the overhead racks, and the firm's CEO, after one company masquerade party, walked out to the mechanics on the tarmac still wearing his night's costume, a long lacy dress and high heels. JetBlue Airlines cultivates its own unique culture. The firm's CEO, David Neeleman, wants to make sure that all employees get the message that "we're all in this company together." You'll therefore often find him or one of the firm's other officers helping out at the gate, or handing luggage up into the plane, or assisting the cabin attendants while in flight. By the signals they send, and the examples they set, both CEOs set the tone—nurture the cultures—of their companies. The manager sets values and creates a culture through what he or she says and does. Employees take their signals from that behavior and from that culture, and this influences how they themselves behave.

organizational culture
The characteristic values, traditions, and behaviors a company's employees share.

What Is Organizational Culture?   **Organizational culture** is the characteristic values, traditions, and behaviors a company's employees share. A *value* is a basic belief about what is right or wrong, or about what you should or shouldn't do. ("Honesty is the best policy" would be a value.) Values are important because they guide and channel

David Neeleman, JetBlue Airways, CEO, opens the Nasdaq with a group of cheering company employees.

behavior. Managing people and shaping their behavior therefore depends on shaping the values they use as behavioral guides. The firm's culture should therefore send clean signals about what is and isn't acceptable behavior.

To an outside observer, a company's culture reveals itself in several ways. You can see it in employees' *patterns of behavior*, such as ceremonial events and written and spoken commands. For example, managers and employees may engage in behaviors such as hiding information, politicking, or expressing honest concern when a colleague requires assistance. You can also see it in the *physical manifestations* of a company's behavior, such as written rules, office layout, organizational structure, and dress codes. In turn, these cultural symbols and behaviors tend to reflect the firm's shared *values*, such as "the customer is always right" or "don't be bureaucratic." If management and employees really believe "honesty is the best policy," the written rules they follow and the things they do should reflect this value.

The Manager's Role   When it comes to creating a corporate culture, effective managers like JetBlue's David Neeleman do not leave it to chance. Managers have to think through ways to send the right signals to their employees. Here is how they can do it:

- *Clarify Expectations.* First, they make clear their expectations with respect to the values they want subordinates to follow. One way to do this is to publish a corporate ethics code. For example, the Johnson & Johnson credo says, "We believe our first responsibility is to the doctors, nurses and patients, to mothers and fathers and all others who use our products and services."

- *Use Signs and Symbols. Symbolism*—what the manager actually does and thus the signals he or she sends—ultimately does the most to create and sustain the company's culture. Southwest Airlines sets the tone by what it does from the day a person is hired. New employees "are welcomed with balloons, games, toys, and gifts. New hires, even pilots, learn company songs or cheers during orientation."[27] Managers need to "walk the talk."

- *Provide Physical Support.* The physical manifestations of the manager's values—the firm's incentive plan, appraisal system, and disciplinary procedures, for instance—send strong signals regarding what employees should and should not do. Does the firm reward ethical behavior or penalize it?

- *Use Stories.* Stories can illustrate important company values. IBM has such stories, like the one about how IBM salespeople drove all night through storms to get parts to customers.

- *Organize Rites and Ceremonies.* At JCPenney, new management employees are inducted into the "Penney Partnership." Each inductee receives an HCSC lapel pin. The letters stand for JCPenney's core values of honor, confidence, service, and cooperation.

3   Describe at least four specific ways in which HR management can influence ethical behavior at work.

● THE ROLE OF HR MANAGEMENT IN FOSTERING ETHICS AND FAIR TREATMENT

Why Treat Employees Fairly?

For most people the question, *Why treat employees fairly?* is a rhetorical one, since most learn, at an early age, some version of the golden rule. Management guru Peter Drucker put it this way, "They're not employees, they're people," when he warned managers, in a *Harvard Business Review* article, to treat their employees with dignity and respect.

But there are also some practical reasons for taking care that you treat the firm's employees with the fairness and justice that all employees deserve. An increasingly litigious workforce is one reason. The manager wants to be sure disciplinary and discharge procedures will survive the scrutiny of arbitrators and the courts, and they will not if the procedures are blatantly unfair. Furthermore, perceptions of fairness relate to enhanced employee commitment; to enhanced satisfaction with the organization, with jobs, and with leaders; and to organizational citizenship behaviors (in general, the steps employees take to support their employers' interests).[28] Applicants who believed they were treated unfairly expressed more desire to appeal the outcome (and, one would assume, to file suit). Applicants who view the firm's testing programs as fair not only react more favorably to the selection procedure, but view the company and the job as more attractive. Employees who view the firm's drug testing program as unfair report lower job satisfaction and less commitment to the company.[29]

A recent study provides a vivid illustration. College instructors completed surveys regarding the extent to which they saw their colleges as treating them with procedural and distributive justice. The procedural justice questions included, for example, "In general, the department/college's procedures allow for requests for clarification for additional information about a decision." The distributive justice questions included, "I am fairly rewarded considering the responsibilities I have." These instructors also completed organizational commitment questionnaires. These included questions such as, "I am proud to tell others that I am part of this department/college." Their students then completed surveys. These contained items such as "The instructor put a lot of effort into planning the content of this course," "The instructor was sympathetic to my needs," and "The instructor treated me fairly."

The results were telling. Instructors who perceived high distributive and procedural justice reported higher organizational commitment. Furthermore, their students reported higher levels of instructor effort, pro-social behaviors, and fairness, as well as more positive reactions to their instructors. "Overall," as the researcher says, "the results imply that fair treatment of employees has important organizational consequences."[30]

HR Ethics Activities

There's no single cause of unethical behavior at work, so it is not surprising that there's no "silver bullet" to prevent it. Creating a culture that encourages employees to do the right thing is a key step, though it's not so simple to do. Employers must take several steps to ensure ethical behavior by their employees, and many of these actions are clearly within the realm of HR. Let's consider some specific examples.

Staffing and Selection   One writer says, "The simplest way to tune up an organization, ethically speaking, is to hire more ethical people."[31] Indeed, screening out undesirables can actually start before the applicant even applies, if the HR department creates recruitment materials containing explicit references to the company's emphasis on integrity and ethics. The U.S. Datatrust site in Figure 14-4 is an example. Employers can then use tools such as honesty tests and meticulous background checks (discussed in Chapter 6) to screen out those who may not fit.[32]

The selection process also sends signals about what the company's values and culture really are, in terms of ethical and fair treatment. For example, "If prospective employees perceive that the hiring process does not treat people fairly, they may assume that ethical behavior is not important in the company, and that 'official' pronouncements about the importance of ethics can be discounted."[33]

The manager can do several things to ensure that others view the firm's assessment methods as fair. For example, the employee will tend to view the *formal procedure* (such

Figure 14-4
U.S.DataTrust

Source: Reprinted with permission of
U.S. Data Trust Corporation.

as the selection interview) as fair to the extent that it tests job-related criteria, provides an opportunity to demonstrate competence, provides a way of redressing an error, and is used consistently with all applicants (or employees). The person's *interpersonal treatment* should reflect such things as the propriety of the questions, the politeness and respect of the person doing the assessing, and the degree to which there was an opportunity for two-way communication. Finally, candidates appreciate employers' *providing explanations*. Evidence suggests that individuals see a system as fair to the extent that the employer provides useful knowledge both about the employee's or candidate's own performance and about the employer's assessment procedures.[34]

Applicants or employees thus tend to view some selection tools as fairer than others. For example, to the extent that work sample tests (discussed in Chapter 6) are clearly job-related, give applicants an opportunity to perform, and provide specific feedback, applicants tend to view them as fair. Effective interviews that provide for two-way communication, let the applicant display skills, offer feedback, and have high face validity (in terms of measuring what they're purported to measure), are also viewed as fair. On the other hand, subjects in several studies actually preferred honesty tests or urinalysis to personality assessment tests, probably because of the lack of obvious job relevance of personality assessment.

Training   Ethics training typically plays a big role in helping employers nurture a culture of ethics and fair play. Such training usually includes showing employees how to recognize ethical dilemmas, how to use ethical frameworks (such as codes of conduct) to resolve problems, and how to use HR functions (such as interviews and disciplinary practices) in ethical ways. Training like this needn't be complicated. For example,

Lockheed Martin provides its training session employees with short, "what-if" scenarios that highlight how to identify and deal with conflict of interest situations. The problem is that an emphasis on the mechanics of compliance may not be enough. Instead, the training should also emphasize the moral underpinnings of the ethical choice and the company's deep commitment to integrity and ethics. The participation of top managers underscores that commitment.[35]

Consider an example. Perhaps not surprisingly, findings regarding sexual harassment training programs indicate that trainees who don't view sexual harassment as an ethical/moral matter may be more inclined to engage in such behavior than those who do. The problem is that many sexual harassment training sessions focus, not on ethics, but on the desire to avoid legal liability. The result of such training is an emphasis on what is legal rather than on what is right.[36] Such ethics training may simply be futile, if it ignores changing the mind-sets of those trainees who don't view harassment as unethical.[37]

Ethics training is often Internet-based. For example, Lockheed Martin Corp. uses its intranet to let its 160,000 employees take ethics and legal compliance training online. Lockheed's ethics software also keeps track of how well the company and its employees are doing in terms of maintaining high ethical standards. The program helped top management see that in one recent year, 4.8% of the company's ethics allegations involved conflicts of interest, and that it takes about 30 days to complete an ethics violation internal investigation.[38]

Figure 14-5 summarizes the tools and techniques employers use as part of their ethics training programs. As you can see, new-hire orientation, annual refresher training, and distributing the companies' policies and handbooks are all quite important.

Performance Appraisal   The firm's performance appraisal processes provide another opportunity to emphasize its commitment to ethics and fairness. First, the appraisal can make it clear that the company not only professes to adhere to high ethical standards, but also actually measures (and then rewards) employees who follow those standards.

Second, how the supervisors do the appraisals is important. Studies confirm that, in practice, some managers ignore accuracy and honesty in performance appraisals and instead use the process for political purposes (such as encouraging employees with whom they don't get along to leave the firm).[39] To send the signal that fairness and ethics are paramount, standards should be clear, employees should understand the basis upon which they're going to be appraised, and the appraisals themselves should be performed objectively and fairly.

Reward and Disciplinary Systems   To the extent that behavior is a function of its consequences, it is the company's (and HR's) responsibility to ensure that the firm rewards ethical behavior and penalizes unethical behavior. In fact, research suggests that "employees expect the organization to dole out relatively harsh punishment for unethical conduct."[40] If the company does not deal swiftly with unethical behavior, it's often the ethical employees (not the unethical ones) who feel punished.

Workplace Aggression and Violence   We will see in Chapter 16 that workplace aggression and violence are increasingly serious problems, as well as problems that often stem from real or perceived inequities. Employees who see themselves as unfairly underpaid may take negative actions ranging from employee theft to destruction of company property. Many HR actions, including layoffs, being passed over for promotion, terminations, and discipline can prompt perceptions of unfair treatment that translate into dysfunctional behavior. (One employee, believing his dismissal was inhumane, retaliated by causing almost $20 million in damage to his employer's computer systems.)

Figure 14-5
The Role of Training in Ethics

Source: Susan Wells, "Turn Employees into Saints," *HR Magazine*, December 1999, p. 52. © 1999 by Soc. for Human Resource Management. Reproduced with permission via Copyright Clearance Center.

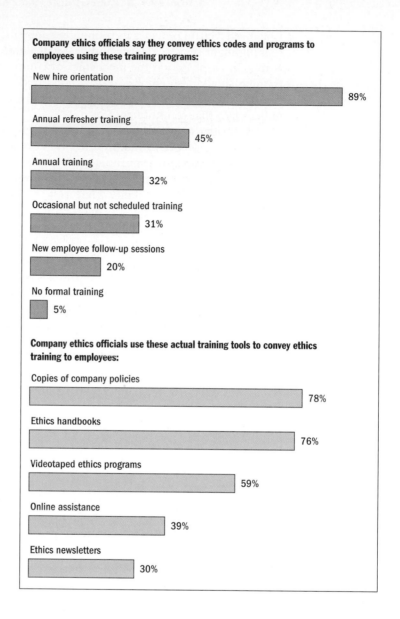

Company ethics officials say they convey ethics codes and programs to employees using these training programs:

New hire orientation — 89%
Annual refresher training — 45%
Annual training — 32%
Occasional but not scheduled training — 31%
New employee follow-up sessions — 20%
No formal training — 5%

Company ethics officials use these actual training tools to convey ethics training to employees:

Copies of company policies — 78%
Ethics handbooks — 76%
Videotaped ethics programs — 59%
Online assistance — 39%
Ethics newsletters — 30%

Other HR Ethics Activities   In the post-Sarbanes-Oxley era, HR supports the employer's ethics programs in other ways. For example, usually either HR or the firm's legal department heads up its ethical compliance efforts. One study of *Fortune* 500 companies concluded than an HR officer was responsible for the program in 28% of responding firms. Another 28% gave the firm's legal officers responsibility, and 16% established separate ethics or compliance departments. The rest of the firms spread the responsibility among auditing departments, or positions such as public affairs and corporate communications.[41]

Employers' ethics committees will often include HR professionals. These committees ensure that senior company leaders engage in discussions about ethical issues. Every two years Lockheed Martin surveys its employees regarding their adherence to the Lockheed ethics code. It then institutes new ethics training programs based on the feedback it receives. Johnson & Johnson uses its famous "credo" (its set of core ethical principles) as part of its management development programs.[42]

Many employers use information systems to help manage their ethics programs. The "Improving Productivity Through HRIS" feature illustrates this.

Improving Productivity Through **HRIS**

Complying with Sarbanes-Oxley

Particularly in very large companies, designing and managing ethics programs isn't easy or cheap. As we've seen, doing so requires the almost continuous attention of the company's top managers, as well as a considerable investment in setting up and monitoring ethics codes, and training employees.

Passage of the Sarbanes-Oxley Act of 2002 made ethics compliance even more expensive. Among other things, the act requires that the CEO and the CFO of publicly traded companies personally attest to the accuracy of their companies' financial statements, and also to the fact that its internal controls are adequate.[43] As one lawyer put it, "Sarbanes-Oxley has added a wide range of new issues to the traditional compliance function."[44]

With their personal credibility on the line, the new law has focused top management's attention on ensuring that all the firm's employees take ethics very seriously. This means big, publicly traded firms are becoming much more serious about providing ethics-related education and training, and about

making sure they can prove that their employees actually got trained.

The problem is, training and following up programs like this can be very expensive. Larger firms need a cost-effective way of making such training available. That's why when DTE Energy, with 14,000 employees, needed an ethics training system, it turned to a Web-based program from Integrity Interactive Corp. of Waltham, Massachusetts. Now, all the company's employees have easy access to a standardized ethics training program through their PCs, and DTE can easily track who has taken the training and who has not. The employees can take the training when they want to, and the company can monitor their progress. As one officer at Integrity Interactive puts it,

It would have been easy in the 1990s for companies to say, "we have 30,000 employees and 40% turnover. There's no way to train all these people in our code of conduct and ethical compliance . . . The Internet has taken that excuse away. It is now physically possible to reach anyone, anywhere on the globe—and what's more, to prove that you're doing it."[45]

Building Two-Way Communications

The opportunity for two-way communication plays an important role in our perceptions of how fairly we're being treated. Studies support this commonsense observation. One study concluded that three actions contributed to perceived fairness in business settings: *engagement* (involving individuals in the decisions that affect them by asking for their input and allowing them to refute the merits of others' ideas and assumptions); *explanation* (ensuring that everyone involved and affected understands why final decisions are made and the thinking that underlies the decisions); and *expectation clarity* (making sure everyone knows up front by what standards they will be judged and the penalties for failure).[46] A U.S. Supreme Court decision (*Reeves v. Sanderson Plumbing Products*) suggests that poor employee relations—for instance, untruthful or incomplete communications with or about employees—may overwhelm otherwise good defenses to discrimination claims when the claims reach the courts.[47]

For this reason, many employers facilitate two-way communication. For example, at many firms including Toyota Motor Manufacturing in Lexington, Kentucky, a *hotline* gives employees an anonymous method of bringing questions or problems to management's attention. The plant hotline is available 24 hours a day. Employees can pick up any phone, dial the hotline extension (the number is posted on the plant bulletin boards), and deliver their message to the recorder. The HR manager reviews and answers all messages. As a related matter, nationwide 1-800 hotlines often play a central role in employers' ethics efforts, by making it easier for employees to report unethical behavior. Other firms administer periodic *opinion surveys*. For example, the FedEx Survey Feedback Action (SFA) program includes an anonymous survey that lets employees express their feelings—about the company and their managers, and to some extent about service, pay, and benefits. Each manager then has an opportunity to discuss the department results with subordinates, and create an action plan for improving work group commitment. Sample questions include:

I can tell my manager what I think.

My manager tells me what is expected.

My manager listens to my concerns.

My manager keeps me informed.

Ethics programs are not just important for large companies. The "When You're On Your Own" feature illustrates this.

When You're On Your Own
HR for Line Managers and Entrepreneurs

Small Business Ethics

When people think of unethical corporate behavior, big companies like Enron, WorldCom, and Arthur Andersen come to mind, because they've been in the headlines. Yet studies suggest that small and midsize enterprises are prone to the same unethical corporate behavior as big firms. For example, one study of 20 small to midsize firms found that bribery, corrupt dealings, payoffs to local gangsters, and a general tone of dishonesty were all "business as usual" at many of these firms.[48] Sometimes, these firms were clever about their corrupt dealings. When doing business abroad, one U.S. business tried to keep its hands clean by forming a "strategic alliance" with a local firm. The latter then did the dirty work, for example, handling the local bribes, while the U.S. firm's managers looked the other way.

There are several reasons why smaller firms have to be particularly alert to the possibility of unethical behavior. For one thing, small firms may tend to be lax, on the assumption that "we're one big family" and so are all operating from the same set of ethical rules. Smaller firms also don't have the resources for things like ethics hotlines, extensive ethics code–building, and ethics training that big firms have. This helps to explain why, while virtually every major company has an ethics code, ethics guidelines, and provides ethics training, only about 58% of small to midsize firms have ethics guidelines, and only 41% offer ethics training.[49]

The irony is that ethical lapses that might be trivial to big firms could be devastating to small ones. For example, having an unethical accountant in a billion-dollar firm embezzle $10 million would be a nuisance, but not deadly. But if the European sales manager of a $10 million firm walks off with $1 million cash, it could be the end.

There are several steps a small business owner can take to establish a workable, simple ethics program. First, *size up your company's current ethics-related activities* as they stand now. Even a self-audit based on guidelines like those in this chapter (the availability of an ethics code, ethics training, internal controls to monitor ethical behavior, and so on) can be worthwhile. Second, *create a code of conduct*, and make it clear to all employees that you take it seriously. Third, *train your people*. Training needn't be complicated. For example, one expert suggests having your managers develop scenarios illustrating which behaviors are ethical and which are not, and then meeting periodically for training sessions to discuss these. Fourth, make it easier to *solicit feedback* from your employees, so that they can more easily provide you with suspicions of unethical behavior. And, last, but not least, *walk the talk*. Particularly in a small business, the owner or CEO is so visible that employees will take their ethical signals from him or her.

Employ fair
disciplinary
practices.

● EMPLOYEE DISCIPLINE AND PRIVACY

The purpose of *discipline* is to encourage employees to behave sensibly at work (where *sensible* is defined as adhering to rules and regulations). In an organization, rules and regulations serve about the same purpose that laws do in society; discipline is called for when one of these rules or regulations is violated.[50] A fair and just discipline process is based on three pillars: clear rules and regulations, a system of progressive penalties, and an appeals process.

First, rules and regulations address issues such as theft, destruction of company property, drinking on the job, and insubordination. Examples include:

▍ *Poor performance is not acceptable.* Each employee is expected to perform his or her work properly and efficiently and to meet established standards of quality.

▍ *Alcohol and drugs do not mix with work.* The use of either during working hours and reporting for work under the influence of either are both strictly prohibited.

▍ *The vending of anything in the plant without authorization is not allowed; nor is gambling in any form permitted.*

Rules inform employees ahead of time what is and is not acceptable behavior. Upon hiring, tell employees, preferably in writing, what is not permitted. The employee orientation handbook usually contains the rules and regulations.

A system of progressive penalties is a second pillar of effective discipline. Penalties may range from oral warnings to written warnings to suspension from the job to discharge. The severity of the penalty is usually a function of the type of offense and the number of times the offense has occurred. For example, most companies issue warnings for the first unexcused lateness (see form in Figure 14-6). For a fourth offense, discharge is the usual disciplinary action. Finally, an appeals process including the right to grieve the decision helps to ensure that supervisors mete out discipline fairly and equitably (see Figure 14-7).

The "When You're On Your Own" feature provides additional guidance for the front-line supervisor.

When You're On Your Own
HR for Line Managers and Entrepreneurs

Disciplining an Employee

Even if you're a manager in a *Fortune* 500 company, you may find yourself without company guidelines when you're thinking of disciplining or discharging an employee for violating company rules. In such a situation, fair discipline guidelines would include:

• Make sure the evidence supports the charge of employee wrongdoing.
• Ensure that the employee's due process rights are protected.
• Warn the employee of the disciplinary consequences.
• The rule that was allegedly violated should be "reasonably related" to the efficient and safe operation of the particular work environment.

• Fairly and adequately investigate the matter before administering discipline.
• The investigation should produce substantial evidence of misconduct.
• Rules, orders, or penalties should be applied evenhandedly.
• The penalty should be reasonably related to the misconduct and to the employee's past work history.
• Maintain the employee's right to counsel.
• Don't rob a subordinate of his or her dignity.
• Remember that the burden of proof is on you.
• Get the facts. Don't base a decision on hearsay or on your general impression.
• Don't act while angry.

Figure 14-6
Disciplinary Action Form I
Source: Reprinted from www.HR.
BLR.com with permission of the
publisher, © 2004 *Business and Legal
Reports, Inc.*, 141 Mill Rock Road East,
Old Saybrook CT.

Disciplinary Action Form

Date: _____

Name: _____

Dept.: _____

Disciplinary Action:

❑ Verbal*   ❑ Written   ❑ Written & Suspension   ❑ Discharge

To the employee:

Your performance has been found unsatisfactory for the reasons set
forth below. Your failure to improve or avoid a recurrence will be
cause for further disciplinary action.

Details: _____

_____

_____

_____

_____

_____

A copy of this warning was personally delivered to the above
employee by:

Supervisor _____

Date _____

I have received and read this warning notice. I have been informed
that a copy of this notice will be placed in my personnel file.

Employee _____

Date _____

*Completion of this form shall serve as documentation only and
should not be filed in the employee's personnel file.

When disciplinary decisions reach arbitration, clarity and fairness loom large in arbitrators' decisions. One study surveyed 45 published arbitration awards in which tardiness had triggered discipline and/or discharge. When arbitrators overturned employers' decisions, it was usually because the employer had failed to clarify what it meant by "tardy," or because there was a lack of clarity regarding how often an employee may be late over a given period, or because of an inappropriately severe penalty.[51] An overly severe disciplinary procedure can backfire in other ways. For example, an unfair disciplinary procedure (such as one with harsh supervisory behaviors) can trigger retaliatory employee mischief, and thus actually encourage misbehavior.[52] There are also gender issues in discipline, as "The New Workplace" illustrates.

NC STATE UNIVERSITY
EMPLOYEE GRIEVANCE FORM

To file a formal grievance, an employee is required to complete and submit this form to the Division of Human Resources in accordance with the guidlines of the University's regulation regarding Grievance - SPA Grievance and Appeal. All sections must be completed. (Attach additional sheets if necessary.)

A.   EMPLOYEE INFORMATION

Name _____

Position Title _____   Department _____

Campus Address _____   Work Telephone _____

Home Address _____   Home Telephone _____

Date of Incident _____   Supervisor _____

B.   Grievance Type: (please check one)

- ❑ a violation or misapplication of university policies
- ❑ a violation or misapplication of rules pertaining to employment in the respective department
- ❑ inaccurate or misleading information in a personnel file
- ❑ a violation or misapplication of applicable laws or regulations, including anti-discrimination laws
- ❑ a suspension without pay, demotion, or dismissal
- ❑ unlawful workplace harassment

C.   State the specific reason(s) for grievance:

_____

_____

_____

_____

_____

_____

D.   State the specific resolution being requested:

_____

_____

_____

_____

_____

_____

_____

_____   _____
Employee Signature   Date

Figure 14-7
Employee Grievance Form
Source: NC State University. Used with permission.

The New Workplace

Comparing Males and Females in a Discipline Situation

Watching a movie like *King Arthur* may lead you to the conclusion that chivalry in general and a protective attitude toward women in particular is a well-established value in many societies, but that may not be the case. Not only is chivalry not necessarily a prevailing value, but there is even a competing hypothesis in the research literature. What several researchers call "The Evil Woman Thesis" certainly doesn't argue that women are evil. Instead it "argues that women who commit offenses violate stereotypic assumptions about the proper behavior of women. These women will be penalized for their inappropriate sex role behavior in addition to their other offenses."

In other words, the unfortunately titled "Evil Woman Thesis" argues that when a woman doesn't act the way other men and women think she should act, they tend to overreact and treat her more harshly than they might if the alleged misdeed was done by a man.

While such a thesis might seem ridiculous on its face, the results of at least one careful study seem to indicate that it may in fact have considerable validity. In this study, 360 graduate and undergraduate university business school students in a southern city (split about 50–50 between men and women) were asked to review a labor arbitration case. The case involved two employees, one male and one female, with similar work records and tenure with their employers. Both were discharged for violation of company rules related to alcohol and drugs. The case portrays one worker's behavior as a more serious breach of company rules: The more culpable worker (a male in half the study and a female in the other half) had brought the intoxicant to the work setting.

The male and female decision-maker students were asked to express their agreement with two alternative approaches to arbitrating the dispute that arose when the culpable employee was discharged. The researchers assumed that only the male decision-maker students might come down more harshly on the culpable employee when that employee was a woman, and they were therefore surprised at their results.

In their study, they found evidence of a bias against the culpable woman employee by both the male and female students making the decisions about how to discipline the worker. In other words, the culpable female workers in the labor case clearly received harsher treatment from both the men and women student decision makers. As the researchers conclude, "note that women, as decision makers, appear to be as willing as men to impose harsher discipline on women than upon men." In most respects, including the willingness to fire the culpable worker, it was the woman worker who could expect the harsher treatment, not the man.

In this study, it was student decision makers who were asked to come to some conclusions regarding discipline based on what they read in the case, so there is no way to conclude based solely on this study that the findings would necessarily apply in real-world settings or under different conditions. However, the results of this study certainly provide food for thought regarding the fact that women just might be treated more harshly than men in a discipline situation.

A related question is, Do male and female supervisors differ in how they discipline subordinates? A second study shed some light on this. The researchers interviewed 163 workers. The workers held a range of jobs and their bosses had disciplined them in various ways, from firings to just reminding them to do better. About 40% of the workers changed their behavior after scoldings, whether the boss was a man or woman. However, the male bosses were much more severe than the women. For example, the men were three times as likely to suspend or sack a subordinate, and only half as likely to just give an oral scolding. That harshness seemed to have a predictable effect: For example, 82% of female subordinates who were disciplined by males felt responsible for their bad behavior, while only 48% of those with female bosses felt responsible.

Sources: This is based on Sandra Hartman et al., "Males and Females in a Discipline Situation: Exploratory Research on Completing Hypotheses," *Journal of Managerial Issues* 6, no. 1 (Spring 1994), pp. 57, 64–68; "A Woman's Place," *The Economist* 356, no. 8184 (August 19, 2000), p. 56.

Formal Disciplinary Appeals Processes

Grievance-type disciplinary appeal procedures aren't limited to unionized firms. Consider FedEx's *guaranteed fair treatment* multistep program. In *step 1, management review*, the complainant submits a written complaint to a member of management (manager, senior manager, or managing director) within seven calendar days of the occurrence of the eligible issue. If not satisfied with that decision, then in *step 2, officer complaint*, the complainant submits a written appeal to the vice president or senior vice president of the division within seven calendar days of the step 1 decision. Finally, in *step 3, executive appeals review*, the complainant may submit a written complaint within seven calendar days of the step 2 decision to the employee relations department. This department then investigates and prepares a case file for the executive review appeals board. The appeals board—the CEO, the COO, the chief personnel officer, and three senior vice presidents—then reviews all relevant information and makes a decision to uphold, overturn, or initiate a board of review, or to take other appropriate action.

Discipline without Punishment

Traditional discipline has two potential flaws. First, no one likes being punished (although fairness guidelines like those previously mentioned can take the edge off this). A second shortcoming is that forcing rules on employees may gain short-term compliance, but not cooperation when you are not around to enforce the rules.

nonpunitive discipline
Discipline without punishment, usually involving a system of oral warnings and paid "decision-making leaves" in lieu of more traditional punishment.

Discipline without punishment (or **nonpunitive discipline**) aims to avoid these disciplinary problems. It does this by gaining employees' acceptance of the rules and by reducing the punitive nature of the discipline itself. Here is how it works:

1. *Issue an oral reminder.* As a supervisor, your goal is to get the employee to agree to solve the disciplinary problem.

2. *Should another incident arise within six weeks, issue a formal written reminder, a copy of which is placed in the employee's personnel file.* In addition, hold a second private discussion with the employee, again without any threats.

3. *Give a paid, one-day "decision-making leave."* If another incident occurs in the next six weeks or so, the employee is told to take a one-day leave with pay to stay home and consider whether the job is right for him or her and whether he or she wants to abide by the company's rules. When the employee returns to work, he or she meets with you and gives you a decision regarding whether or not he or she will follow the rules.

4. *If no further incidents occur in the next year or so, the one-day paid suspension is purged from the person's file.* If the behavior is repeated, the next step is dismissal (see later discussion).[53]

The process would not apply to exceptional circumstances. Criminal behavior or in-plant fighting might be grounds for immediate dismissal, for instance. And if several incidents occurred at very close intervals, the supervisor might skip step 2—the written warning.

Employee Privacy

The four main types of employee privacy violations upheld by courts are intrusion (locker room and bathroom surveillance), publication of private matters, disclosure of medical records, and appropriation of an employee's name or likeness for commercial purposes.[54] Background checks, monitoring off-duty conduct and lifestyle, drug testing, workplace searches, and monitoring of workplace activities trigger most privacy violations.[55]

Companies have focused more resources on employee monitoring since September 11, 2001. For example, one survey, by the Society of Human Resource Management, found that about two-thirds of companies monitor e-mail activity, three-quarters monitor employee Internet use, and about 40% monitor phone calls.[56] Employers say they do so mostly to improve productivity and protect themselves from computer viruses, leaks of confidential information, and harassment suits.[57] Employees who use company computers to do things like swap and download music files can also ensnare employers in illegal activities—another reason for employers to make clear what employees can and cannot use their company computers for.[58]

New software can secretly record everything anyone does online on a particular computer. Other software lets you find out everything your spouse, children, and employees do online with e-mail. "This program works so well it's scary," says someone who has used it.[59] When Turner Broadcasting System Inc., noticed that employees at its CNN London business bureau were piling up overtime claims, they installed new software to monitor every Web page every worker used. As the firm's network security specialist puts it, "If we see people were surfing the Web all day, then they don't have to be paid for that overtime."[60] Pillsbury fired a regional manager after intercepting a supposedly private e-mail message making threatening comments about supervisors.

There are two main restrictions on workplace monitoring: the **Electronic Communications Privacy Act (ECPA)**, and common-law protections against invasion of privacy. Congress intended the ECPA to help restrict interception and monitoring of oral and wire communications, but the law has two exceptions. The "business purpose exception" permits employers to monitor communications if they can show a legitimate business reason for doing so. The second, "consent exception" allows employers to monitor communications if they have their employees' consent to do so.[61]

Electronic eavesdropping is legal—at least to a point. For example, federal law and most state laws allow employers to monitor employees' phone calls in the ordinary course of business, but they must stop listening once it becomes clear that a conversation is personal rather than business related. You can also intercept e-mail service to protect the property rights of the e-mail provider. However, to be safe, employers often issue e-mail and online service usage policies. These warn employees that those systems are meant to be used for business purposes only. Employers also have employees sign e-mail and telephone monitoring acknowledgment statements like that in Figure 14-8.

One reason for explicit, signed policy statements is the possibility that employers may be held liable for illegal acts their employees commit by via e-mail. For example, messages sent by supervisors that contain sexual innuendo, or ones defaming an employee, can ensnare employers that haven't taken steps to prohibit e-mail system misuse.

Electronic Communications Privacy Act (ECPA)
Intended in part to restrict interception and monitoring of oral and wire communications, but with two exceptions: employers who can show a legitimate business reason for doing so, and employers who have employees' consent to do so.

Figure 14-8
Sample Telephone Monitoring Acknowledgement Statement
Source: Reprinted with permission from *Bulletin to Management* (BNA Policy and practice Series) 48, no. 14, Part II, (April 3, 1997), p. 7. Copyright 1997 by The Bureau of National Affairs, Inc.

I understand that my telephone and e-mail communications will be monitored periodically by my supervisor and other [company] management staff. I understand that the purpose of this monitoring is to improve:

- The quality of customer service provided to policyholders and prospective customers
- My product knowledge and presentation skills

Signature   Date

Print Name   Department

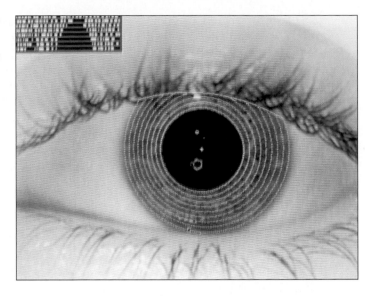

Computer screen image of the iris of an eye being scanned as part of a computer recognition program. White concentric circles cover the iris while mapping landmarks and deviations in the surface. Each person's iris is as individual as a fingerprint.

Videotaping in the workplace seems to call for more legal caution. In one case, the U.S. Court of Appeals for the First Circuit ruled that an employer's continuous video surveillance of employees in an office setting did not constitute an unconstitutional invasion of privacy.[62] But a Boston employer had to pay over $200,000 to five workers it secretly videotaped in an employee locker room, after they sued in state court.[63]

Increasingly security-conscious firms are implementing new forms of employee monitoring devices. Biometrics—using physical traits such as fingerprints or iris scans for identification—is one example. With the most typical types of fingerprint technology, the user passes his or her fingertip over an optical reader, or presses it directly onto a computer chip. Iris scanning is more limited, but tends to be the most accurate authorization device. Some organizations like the Federal Aviation Authority use it to control employees' access to its network information systems.[64]

 List at least four important factors in managing dismissals effectively.

● MANAGING DISMISSALS

dismissal
Involuntary termination of an employee's employment with the firm.

Dismissal is the most drastic disciplinary step the manager can take. Because of this, special care is required to ensure that sufficient cause exists for it. Furthermore, dismissal should occur only after all reasonable steps to rehabilitate or salvage the employee have failed. However, there are undoubtedly times when dismissal is required, perhaps at once.

Of course, the best way to "handle" a dismissal is to avoid it in the first place. Many dismissals start with bad hiring decisions. Using sound selection practices including assessment tests, reference and background checks, drug testing, and clearly defined job descriptions can reduce the need for many dismissals.[65]

For more than 100 years, the prevailing rule in the United States was that without a contract, either the employer or the employee can *terminate at will* the employment relationship. In other words, the employee can resign for any reason, at will, and the employer can similarly dismiss an employee for any reason, at will. Today, however, dismissed employees are increasingly taking their cases to court, and many employers have found they no longer have a blanket right to fire. Instead, federal EEO and other laws and various state laws and court rulings increasingly limit management's right to dismiss employees. For example, firing a "whistle-blower" might trigger "public policy" exceptions to firing at will; or a statement in an employee handbook may imply a contractual agreement to keep an employee on.

Three main statutory and common law protections against wrongful discharge have eroded the at-will doctrine—the public policy exception, the implied contract exception, and the covenant of good faith exception. Under the *public policy exception*, courts have held the discharge to be wrongful when it was against an explicit, well-established public policy (for instance, the employer fired the employee for refusing to break the law). Under the *implied contract exception*, courts have held that, even in the absence of an express written instrument to that effect, an implied contract existed based on representations in an employee handbook. The *covenant of good faith exception* suggests that employers should not fire employees without good cause. However, only 11 U.S. states recognize it, and most courts reject it. (Under this third exception a longtime employee might argue, for instance, that the employer fired the person without cause, to avoid having to pay retirement benefits.)[66]

Grounds for Dismissal

There are four bases for dismissal:

■ unsatisfactory performance
■ misconduct
■ lack of qualifications for the job
■ changed requirements of (or elimination of) the job.

unsatisfactory performance
Persistent failure to perform assigned duties or to meet prescribed standards on the job.

misconduct
Deliberate and willful violation of the employer's rules.

Unsatisfactory performance may be defined as persistent failure to perform assigned duties or to meet prescribed standards on the job.[67] Specific reasons include excessive absenteeism, tardiness, a persistent failure to meet normal job requirements, or an adverse attitude toward the company, supervisor, or fellow employees. **Misconduct** is deliberate and willful violation of the employer's rules and may include stealing, rowdy behavior, and insubordination. *Lack of qualifications* for the job is an employee's inability to do the assigned work although he or she is diligent. Because in this case the employee may be trying to do the job, it is reasonable for the employer to do what's possible to salvage him or her—perhaps by assigning the employee to another job, or retraining the person. *Changed requirements of the job* is an employee's inability to do the work assigned, after the nature of the job has changed. Similarly, an employer may have to dismiss an employee when his or her job is eliminated. Again, the employee may be industrious, so it is reasonable to retrain or transfer this person, if possible.

insubordination
Willful disregard or disobedience of the boss's authority or legitimate orders; criticizing the boss in public.

Insubordination, a form of misconduct, is sometimes grounds for dismissal. Stealing, chronic tardiness, and poor-quality work are concrete grounds for dismissal, but insubordination is sometimes harder to translate into words. It may be useful to remember that some acts are or should be deemed insubordinate whenever and wherever they occur. These include, for instance:

1. Direct disregard of the boss's authority. At sea, this is mutiny.
2. Flat-out disobedience of, or refusal to obey, the boss's orders—particularly in front of others.
3. Deliberate defiance of clearly stated company policies, rules, regulations, and procedures.
4. Public criticism of the boss. Contradicting or arguing with him or her is also negative and inappropriate.
5. Blatant disregard of reasonable instructions.
6. Contemptuous display of disrespect; making insolent comments, for example; and, more important, portraying these feelings while on the job.

7. Disregard for the chain of command, shown by going around the immediate supervisor or manager with a complaint, suggestion, or political maneuver. Although the employee may be right, that may not be enough to save him or her from charges of insubordination.

8. Participation in (or leadership of) an effort to undermine and remove the boss from power.[68]

Know Your Employment Law

Gross Misconduct

There are instances in which the employee's conduct is so outrageous that it qualifies as "gross misconduct." The employer may not wish to be as flexible in allowing employees like this to return to work, as might be the case when the infraction is relatively minor. Furthermore, the employer is not obligated under the law to provide the usual ongoing COBRA benefits for employees dismissed for gross misconduct.

It is not clear what Congress meant by "gross misconduct" when it wrote the COBRA law, and given this ambiguity, courts will tend to decide in favor of the employee. However, the following Gross Misconduct Checklist provides an idea of what such behavior involves.[69]

Policy on Gross Misconduct

The following factors extracted from court decisions on gross or willful misconduct by employees in other contexts will aid the employer in writing its policy on gross misconduct for COBRA, and in determining whether the cause of a termination was "gross misconduct." (The more "Yes" answers, the more likely the cause was gross misconduct.)

- Was anyone physically harmed? If so, how badly?
- Has the employee violated the same rule several times before?
- Did the employee realize the seriousness of his or her actions?
- Will the employee be denied unemployment benefits based on the conduct?
- Did the conduct seriously harm the business of the employer?
- Was work severely disrupted?
- Were other employees significantly affected?
- Was the employer exposed to bad publicity that would greatly harm its business?
- Was the employer's reputation severely damaged?
- Will the employer lose significant business or otherwise suffer economic harm because of the misconduct?
- Will the employer be heavily fined because of the misconduct?
- Could the employer lose its business license because of the employee's misconduct?
- Has the harm to the employer already occurred?
- Will the employee lose any license needed to work for the employer (e.g., driver's license)?
- Was there criminal activity involved?
- Was it a felony?
- Does it relate to harm to a person?
- Was fraud involved?
- Was any safety statute violated?
- Was any civil statute violated?
- Was the conduct purposeful?
- Was the conduct on duty?
- Is the policy violated well-known to employees?
- Does the conduct justify immediate termination?
- Has the employer immediately fired other employees who did something similar?
- Did the employee have an opportunity to explain the conduct prior to the determination that it was gross misconduct?

"Yes" answers to the following questions suggest the employer needs to exercise caution before denying COBRA continuation coverage for gross misconduct.

- Does the employee have a reasonable explanation for the conduct?
- Was there any provocation leading to the employee's conduct?
- Is this the first time the employee violated any company policy?
- Is the harm to the employer merely a potential?
- Is only a misdemeanor as opposed to a felony involved?
- Does any criminal activity relate to property as opposed to harm to a person?
- Was the conduct off duty?
- Has the employer only reprimanded other employees who did something similar?

Dismissals are never pleasant, but there are several things you can do to ensure that the person views the dismissal as fair. One study found that "individuals who reported that they were given full explanations of why and how termination decisions were made were more likely to (1) perceive their layoff as fair, (2) endorse the terminating organization, and (3) indicate that they did not wish to take the past employer to court."[70] Instituting a formal multistep procedure (including warning) and a neutral appeal process also fosters fairness.

Who actually does the dismissing is important. One study focused on an R&D facility.[71] Survivors whose managers informed them of an impending layoff viewed the entire dismissal procedure as much fairer than did those told by, say, HR. (The quality of the pre-layoff relationship between the employee and the manager did affect whether or not the employee preferred to get the news from the manager.) Based on this study, at least, one has to question the wisdom of centralizing responsibility for matters like these in the HR department, particularly where the relationship between employees and supervising manager has been good. Amazon.com took what some feel was a less diplomatic approach to dismissing some employees in the Seattle area. The firm had an in-person meeting to announce the downsizing, but telecommuter employees who were unable to attend got the news by e-mail, once the meeting was underway.

High-Performance Insight   Security measures are important whenever dismissals take place. Common sense has always dictated using a checklist to ensure that dismissed employees returned all keys and company property, and (often) accompanying them out of their offices and out of the building. Widespread Internet access makes security measures even more important today. For example, it's necessary to disable passwords and accounts of former employees, to plug holes that could allow an ex-employee to exploit someone else's user account to gain illegal access, and to have formal rules for return of company laptops and handhelds. "Measures range from simply disabling access and changing passwords to reconfiguring the network and changing IP addresses, remote access procedures and telephone numbers," says one chief technology officer. When a Verizon employee is terminated, it's that person's immediate supervisor who must ensure that all access privileges are cut off and all accounts deleted; the company's security group then checks to make sure all processes have been followed.[72]

Avoiding Wrongful Discharge Suits

wrongful discharge
An employee dismissal that does not comply with the law or does not comply with the contractual arrangement stated or implied by the firm via its employment application forms, employee manuals, or other promises.

Wrongful discharge occurs when an employee's dismissal does not comply with the law or with the contractual arrangement stated or implied by the firm via its employment application forms, employee manuals, or other promises. (In a *constructive discharge* claim, the plaintiff argues that he or she quit, but had no choice because the employer made the situation so intolerable at work.)[73] The time to protect against such suits is before the suits are filed.

Figure 14-9
Typical Severance Pay

Source: www.shrm.org, downloaded
March 6, 2004.

- *Nonexempt employee*—one week of pay for each year with a minimum of four weeks and maximum of two months.
- *Exempt employee to $90,000*—two weeks for each year with a minimum of two months and a maximum of six months.
- *Exempt employee over $90,000 to director or VP level*—two to three weeks for each year with a minimum of three months and maximum of nine months.
- *Director or VP to company officer*—three weeks for each year with a minimum of four months and maximum of a year.
- *Officer*—usually covered by an employment contract or Change of Control provisions and can be all the way from one year of pay to three or four years, with other perks that may be continued.

Avoiding wrongful discharge suits requires a two-pronged approach. First, set up employment policies and dispute resolution procedures (such as those outlined in this chapter) that make employees feel they are treated fairly. People who are fired and who walk away with the feeling that they've been embarrassed, stripped of their dignity, or treated unfairly financially (for instance, in terms of severance pay) are more likely to seek retribution in the courts. To some extent, employers can use severance pay to blunt a dismissal's sting. Figure 14-9 summarizes typical severance policies in manufacturing and service industries. There is no way to make a termination pleasant, but an employer's first line of defense is to handle the dismissal with fairness and justice.

Second, do the preparatory work—starting with the employment application—that will help avoid such suits. Pay particular attention to the employee handbook. It should include an acknowledgment form like that in Figure 14-10 which makes clear that the material in the handbook does not constitute a contract. Steps to take include the following:

- Have applicants sign the employment application and make sure it contains a clearly worded statement that employment is for no fixed term and that the employer can terminate at any time. In addition, the statement should inform the job candidate that "nothing on this application can be changed."
- Review your employee manual to look for and delete statements that could prejudice your defense in a wrongful discharge case. For example, delete any reference to the fact that "employees can be terminated only for just cause" (unless you really mean that).
- Have clear written rules listing infractions that may require discipline and discharge, and then make sure to follow the rules.
- If a rule is broken, get the worker's side of the story in front of witnesses, and preferably get it signed. Then make sure to check out the story, getting both sides of the issue.
- Be sure to appraise employees at least annually. If an employee shows evidence of incompetence, give that person a warning and provide an opportunity to improve. All evaluations should be in writing and signed by the employee.
- Keep careful confidential records of all actions such as employee appraisals, warnings or notices, memos outlining how improvement should be accomplished, and so on.
- A final 10-step checklist to reduce exposure to wrongful discharge litigation would include: (1) Is employee covered by any type of written agreement, including a collective bargaining agreement? (2) Have written or oral

representations been made to form a contract? (3) Is a defamation claim likely? (4) Is there a possible discrimination allegation? (5) Is there any workers' compensation involvement? (6) Have reasonable rules and regulations been communicated and enforced? (7) Has employee been given an opportunity to explain any rule violations or to correct poor performance? (8) Have all monies been paid within 24 hours after separation? (9) Has employee been advised of his or her rights under COBRA? (10) Has employee been advised of what the employer will tell a prospective employer in response to a reference inquiry?[74]

Telling the employee the reason for the dismissal is important. While some managers try to avoid hurting the person's feelings or triggering an argument, not being frank and honest can backfire. A U.S. Supreme Court decision suggests that in certain cases an employee who simply shows that the employer's stated reason for discharging him or her is a lie could have the right to take the case to a jury.[75]

Figure 14-10
TJP Inc. Employee
Handbook Acknowledgment
Form

TJP INC. EMPLOYEE HANDBOOK ACKNOWLEDGMENT FORM

This employee handbook has been given to _____

on (date) _____

by _____ (title) _____

Employee's effective starting date _____

Employee's pay period _____

Employee's hours and workweek are _____

Welcome to TJP Inc. Below are a list of your benefits with their effective date:

Benefit	**Effective Date**
Hospitalization _____	_____
Life insurance _____	_____
Retirement _____	_____
Vacation _____	_____
Sick leave _____	_____
Holidays _____	_____
Personal days _____	_____
Bereavement _____	_____
Worker's compensation _____	_____
Social Security _____	_____
Your first performance appraisal will be on _____	_____

I understand that my employee handbook is for informational purposes only and that I am to read and refer to the employee handbook for information on employment work rules and company policies. TJP Inc. may modify, revoke, suspend or terminate any and all policies, rules, procedures and benefits at any time without prior notice to company employees. This handbook and its statements do not create a contract between TJP Inc. and its employees. This handbook and its statements do not affect in any way the employment-at-will relationship between TJP Inc. and its employees.

(Employee's signature) _____

(Date) _____

If humanitarianism and wrongful discharge suits aren't enough to encourage you to be fair, consider this. One study found that managers run double their usual risk of suffering a heart attack during the week after they fire an employee.[76] During one five-year period, physicians interviewed 791 working people who had just undergone heart attacks to find out what might have triggered them. The researchers concluded that the stress associated with firing someone doubled the usual risk of a heart attack for the person doing the firing, during the week following the dismissal.

Personal Supervisory Liability

Courts sometimes hold managers personally liable for their supervisory actions, particularly with respect to actions covered by the Fair Labor Standards Act and the Family and Medical Leave Act.[77] The Fair Labor Standards Act defines *employer* to include "any person acting directly or indirectly in the interest of an employer in relation to any employee . . . ," and this can mean the individual supervisor.

There are several ways to avoid creating situations in which personal liability becomes an issue. Managers should be fully familiar with applicable federal, state, and local *statutes* and know how to uphold their requirements. *Follow company policies and procedures*, since an employee may initiate a claim against an individual supervisor whom he or she alleges did not follow company policies and procedures. The essence of many charges is that the plaintiff was treated differently than others, so *consistent application* of the rule or regulation is important. Administer the discipline in a manner that does not add to the *emotional hardship* on the employee (as would dismissing them in the middle of the workday when they have to publicly collect their belongings and leave the office). Most employees will try to present their side of the story, and allowing them to do so can provide the employee some measure of satisfaction. *Do not act in anger*, since doing so personalizes the situation and undermines any appearance of objectivity. Finally, *utilize the HR department* for advice regarding how to handle difficult disciplinary matters.

The Termination Interview

termination interview
The interview in which an employee is informed of the fact that he or she has been dismissed.

Dismissing an employee is one of the most difficult tasks you can face at work. The dismissed employee, even if warned many times in the past, may still react with disbelief or even violence. Guidelines for the **termination interview** itself are as follows:[78]

1. *Plan the interview carefully.* According to experts at Hay Associates, this includes:
   - Make sure the employee keeps the appointment time.
   - Never inform an employee over the phone.
   - Allow 10 minutes as sufficient time for the interview.
   - Use a neutral site, never your own office.
   - Have employee agreements, the human resource file, and a release announcement (internal and external) prepared in advance.
   - Be available at a time after the interview in case questions or problems arise.
   - Have phone numbers ready for medical or security emergencies.

2. *Get to the point.* Do not beat around the bush by talking about the weather or making other small talk. *As soon as the employee enters*, give the person a moment to get comfortable and then inform him or her of your decision.

3. *Describe the situation.* Briefly, in three or four sentences, explain why the person is being let go. For instance, "Production in your area is down 6%. We have talked about these problems several times in the past three months, and the solutions are not being followed through. We have to make a change." Remember to describe the situation rather than attack the employee personally by saying things like, "Your production is just not up to par." Also emphasize that the decision is final and irrevocable.

4. *Listen.* Continue the interview until the person appears to be talking freely and reasonably calmly about the reasons for his or her termination and the support package (including severance pay).

5. *Review all elements of the severance package.* Describe severance payments, benefits, access to office support people, and the way references will be handled. However, under no conditions should any promises or benefits beyond those already in the support package be implied.

6. *Identify the next step.* The terminated employee may be disoriented and unsure what to do next. Explain where the employee should go next, upon leaving the interview.

Outplacement Counseling

outplacement counseling
A systematic process by which a terminated person is trained and counseled in the techniques of self-appraisal and securing a new position.

Outplacement counseling is a systematic process by which someone you've terminated is trained and counseled in the techniques of conducting a self-appraisal and securing a new job appropriate to his or her needs and talents. As the term is generally used, outplacement does not imply that the employer takes responsibility for placing the person in a new job. Instead, it is a counseling service whose purpose is to provide the person with advice, instructions, and a sounding board to help formulate career goals and successfully execute a job search. Outplacement counseling is part of the terminated employee's support or severance package and is often done by specialized outside firms.

Outplacement firms do more than counsel displaced employees; they also help the employer devise its dismissal plan. For about two months before announcing its downsizing plan, MacLean, Virginia–based Getroncis worked with an outplacement firm to develop a plan regarding how to break the news, deal with dismissed employees' emotional reactions, and institute the appropriate severance pay and equal opportunity employment plans.[79]

Exit Interview

exit interviews
Interviews with employees who are leaving the firm, conducted for the purpose of obtaining information about the job or related matters, to give the employer insight about the company.

Many employers conduct **exit interviews** with employees who are leaving the firm. The HR department usually does this. They aim to elicit information about the job or related matters that might give the employer a better insight into what is right—or wrong—about the company. The assumption, of course, is that because the employee is leaving, he or she will be candid.

Exit interview questions to ask include: How were you recruited? Why did you join the company? Was the job presented correctly and honestly? Were your expectations met? What was the workplace environment like? What was your supervisor's management style like? What did you like most/least about the company? Were there any special problem areas? Why did you decide to leave, and how was the departure handled?[80] Figure 14-11 presents a form used for this purpose.

Based on one survey, the quality of information you can expect from exit interviews is questionable. The researchers found that at the time of separation, 38% of those leaving blamed salary and benefits, and only 4% blamed supervision. Followed up 18 months later, however, 24% blamed supervision and only 12% blamed salary and benefits. Getting to the real problem during the exit interview may thus require some heavy digging.[81] Yet these interviews can be useful. When Blue Cross of Northeastern Pennsylvania laid off employees, many said, in exit interviews, "This is not a stable place to work." The firm took steps to correct that misperception for those who stayed with Blue Cross.

We are interested in identifying opportunities to improve the work environment at NC State. Please respond to each of the following questions with honesty and candor. Monthly, questionnaires are forwarded to the appropriate Dean's or Vice Chancellor's office to determine factors that contribute to turnover. Your feedback is greatly appreciated.

Name (optional) _____   **Date** _____

1. Department _____

2. College/Division _____

3. Current Rank/Title _____

 □ Full-time □ Part-time   □ EPA □ SPA

4. Date of Separation ___ / ___ / ___   **5. NCSU Length of Service** ___ Years ___ Months

6. Gender   □ Female   □ Male

7. Race   □ White   □ Black   □ Asian/Pacific Islander   □ Hispanic   □ American Indian/Alaskan Native
  □ Other _____

8. EPA Classification, if applicable: □ Administrator   □ EPA Professional
  □ Tenured/Tenure Track Faculty   □ Non-Tenure Track Faculty

9. Which factors attracted you to NC State: (circle all that apply)

A. Interesting position   C. Academic environment
B. Opportunities for training, advancement, career growth   D. Pay
Other _____

10. What did you enjoy most about your job at NC State: (circle all that apply)

A. Pay   E. Benefits   I. Opportunities for advancement
B. Communications   F. Meaningful work   J. Recognition of work
C. Co-workers   G. Quality of supervision   K. Work environment
D. Convenient location H. Training/educational opportunities L. Parking
Other _____

11. What did you enjoy least about your job at NC State: (circle all that apply)

A. Pay   E. Benefits   I. Opportunities for advancement
B. Communications   F. Meaingful work   J. Recognition of work
C. Co-workers   G. Quality of supervision   K. Work environment
D. Convenient location H. Training/educational opportunities L. Parking
Other _____

12. Primary reasons for leaving NC State: (circle all that apply)

A. Change in career   G. Family or personal needs   M. Retirement
B. Health issues   H. Moving from area   N. Pay dissatisfaction
C. Lack of recognition for work   I. Work environment   O. Quality of supervision
D. Lack of advancement opportunites J. To further education   P. Workload or work hours
E. Laid off (RIF)   K. Discontinuation of funding   Q. Anticipated/Denial of tenure
F. Non-renewal of contract or position L. Benefits dissatisfaction
Other _____

Figure 14-11
Exit Interview Questionnaire
Source: NC State University. Used with permission.

13. **Which <u>one factor</u> was most important in your decision to leave? Please select only one.**

_____

14. **Would you recommend employment in your department or at NC State to a friend or colleague?**
☐ Yes ☐ No   **Please explain.** _____

_____

15. **What mosted helped you achieve your goals at NC State?**

_____

_____

16. **What was least helpful to you?**

_____

_____

17. **What constructive suggestions do you have for improving employment at NC State?**

_____

_____

_____

18. **Future Employer**
   A. Private employment (e.g., business, industry)   C. Government – ☐ Local ☐ State ☐ Federal
   B. Self-employment   D. Other University/College _____

                                    Which college/University? _____

   Other _____

19. **What makes your future employer/position more attractive than your current position?**

_____

_____

20. **Have you completed an Asset Tracking Form verifying the return of all assigned university assets?**
☐ Yes ☐ No   Comments _____

21. **Any further comments you would like to add...**

_____

_____

_____

_____

Please complete the attached supplement specific to your classification.
If SPA or EPA professional, please bring or mail this completed to Human Resources, Administrative Services Center,
NCSU Box 7210, Raleigh, NC 27695-7210. Call (919) 515-6575 with questions.
If EPA faculty, please bring or mail this completed form to the Office for Equal Opportunity, Holladay Hall, NCSU Box
7530, Raleigh, NC 27695-7530. Call (919) 513-1234 with questions.

Thank you for your employment at NC State University and for completing this survey.

Figure 14-11 (continued)

Layoffs and the Plant Closing Law

Nondisciplinary separations are a fact of corporate life. For the employer, reduced sales or profits may required *layoffs* or *downsizing*. Employees may terminate their employment to retire or to seek better jobs.

Ironically, today's emphasis on "human capital" notwithstanding, layoffs and downsizings rose in the early 2000s. For example, annual layoffs reached a 10-year high of over 1.5 million in 2001. This prompted experts to suggest considering alternatives to reducing employee head counts. Suggestions include finding volunteers who are interested in reducing hours or part-time work; using attrition; opting for voluntary early retirement packages; and networking with local employers concerning temporary or permanent redeployments.[82] As the economy improved, employment rose after 2003.

The Plant Closing Law   Until 1989, there were no federal laws requiring notification of employees when an employer decided to close a facility. However, in that year the Worker Adjustment and Retraining Notification Act (popularly known as the *plant closing law*) became law. It requires employers of 100 or more employees to give 60 days' notice before closing a facility or starting a layoff of 50 people or more. The law does not prevent the employer from closing down, nor does it require saving jobs. It simply gives employees time to seek other work or retraining by giving them advance notice of the shutdown.

Employers are responsible for giving notice to employees who will (or who reasonably may be expected to) experience a covered "employment loss." *Covered employment losses* include *terminations* (other than discharges for cause; voluntary departures, or retirement); *layoffs* exceeding six months, and reductions of more than 50% in employee's work hours during each month of any six-month period. Generally, the firm needn't notify workers it reassigns or transfers to certain employer-sponsored programs or who get an opportunity to transfer or relocate to another company location within a reasonable commuting distance. While there are exceptions to the law, the penalty for failing to give notice is fairly severe: one day's pay and benefits to each employee for each day's notice that should have been given, up to 60 days.

The law is not entirely clear about how to notify employees. However, if you write a letter to individual employees, a paragraph that might suit the purpose would be as follows:

> *Please consider this letter to be your official notice, as required by the federal plant closing law, that your current position with the company will end 60 days from today because of a [layoff or closing] that is now projected to take place on [date]. After that day your employment with the company will be terminated, and you will no longer be carried on our payroll records or be covered by any company benefit programs. Any questions concerning the plant closing law or this notice will be answered in the HR office.*[83]

A layoff, in which workers are sent home for a time, is a situation in which three conditions are present: (1) there is no work available for these employees, (2) management expects the no-work situation to be temporary and probably short term, and (3) management intends to recall the employees when work is again available. A layoff is therefore not a termination, which is a permanent severing of the employment relationship. After the World Trade Center attack, most U.S. airlines laid off ("furloughed") about 20% of their employees, but expected eventually to (and did) bring them back. Some employers, however, use the term *layoff* as a euphemism for discharge or termination.

Bumping/Layoff Procedures   Employers who encounter frequent business slowdowns and layoffs may have procedures that let employees use their seniority to remain on the job. Most such **bumping/layoff procedures** have these features in common:

1. Seniority is usually the ultimate determinant of who will work.
2. Seniority can give way to merit or ability, but usually only when no senior employee is qualified for a particular job.
3. Seniority is usually based on the date the employee joined the organization, not the date he or she took a particular job.
4. Because seniority is usually companywide, an employee in one job can usually bump or displace an employee in another job, provided the more senior person can do the job without further training. When the New York Stock Exchange recently eliminated all "reporter" jobs on the exchange, many of these people applied for and "bumped" lower seniority employees, for instance, from "messenger" jobs.

Alternatives to Layoffs   Given the investments they have in recruiting, screening, and training employees, many employers are hesitant to lay off people at the first sign of business decline.

There are several alternatives. With the *voluntary reduction in pay plan*, all employees agree to reductions in pay to keep everyone working. Other employers arrange for all or most employees to concentrate their vacations during slow periods. They don't have to hire temporary help for vacationing employees during peak periods, and staffing automatically declines when business declines. For example, Sun (as well as many Silicon Valley employers) had all employees stay home for a week when the economy slowed in mid-2001. Other employees agree to take *voluntary time off*, which again has the effect of reducing the employer's payroll and avoiding layoffs.

Many firms, including IBM, reduce layoffs with a *rings of defense approach*. They hire temporary employees, often as independent contractors, with the understanding their work is temporary. When layoffs come, they are the first to leave. Some seek volunteers as an alternative to dismissing large numbers of employees. Procter & Gamble offered buyout packages to about 20,000 nonmanufacturing U.S. employees, in its quest to find enough volunteers to avoid dismissing 5,600 people.[84]

Adjusting to Downsizings and Mergers

Firm's often use **downsizing**—reducing, usually dramatically, the number of people the firm employs—to better their financial position. Yet many firms discover operating earnings don't rise after major cuts. Low morale among those remaining may be part of the problem.

From a practical point of view, firms can take steps to reduce the remaining employees' uncertainty and to boost their morale.[85] A postdownsizing program at Duracell, Inc. (now part of Dow), illustrates what you can do. The program had postdownsizing-announcement activities, including a full staff meeting at the facility; immediate follow-up in which remaining employees were split into groups with senior managers to express their concerns and have their questions answered; and long-term support, for instance, by encouraging supervisors to meet with employees frequently and informally to encourage an open-door atmosphere. Other companies, such as the Diners Club subsidiary of

Citigroup, used attitude surveys to help management monitor how postdownsizing efforts are progressing.

Regardless of why you're downsizing, think through the process, both to avoid unnecessary consequences and to ensure the process is fair. Here are some guidelines for implementing a reduction in force.[86]

- *Identify objectives and constraints.* For example, decide how many positions to eliminate at which locations, and what criteria to use to pinpoint the employees to whom you'll offer voluntary exit incentives.
- *Form a downsizing team.* This management team should prepare a communication strategy for explaining the downsizing; establish hiring and promotion levels; produce a downsizing schedule; and supervise the displaced employees' benefit programs.
- *Address legal issues.* You'll want to ensure that others won't view the downsizing as a subterfuge to lay off protected classes of employees. Therefore, review factors such as age, race, and gender before finalizing and communicating any dismissals.
- *Plan postimplementation actions.* Activities such as surveys and explanatory meetings can help maintain morale. Similarly, some suggest a hiring freeze of at least six months after the layoffs have taken effect.
- *Address security concerns.* As with any large layoffs, it may be wise to have security personnel in place in case there's a problem from one or two employees, and to follow the *dismissal checklist discussed earlier in this chapter.*

Downsizings needn't necessarily suggest the horror stories the press occasionally characterizes them as. *Information sharing* (in terms of providing advanced notice regarding the layoff), and *interpersonal sensitivity* (in terms of the manager's demeanor during layoffs) can both help cushion the otherwise negative effects.[87]

One lawyer contends that when employees seek out lawyers after layoffs it's often because they're unhappy with how the layoff was achieved. The people who will actually be announcing the downsizing and dealing with the employees need to be able to explain factually what is happening and what the employees' rights are, and must limit their comments to what is true.[88]

In terms of dismissal, *mergers and acquisitions* are usually one-sided: One company essentially acquires the other, and it is often the employees of the latter who find themselves looking for new jobs. In such a situation, the remaining employees in the acquired firm may be hypersensitive to mistreatment of their colleagues. It thus behooves the manager to treat those whom you let go fairly. Seeing your former colleagues fired is bad enough for morale. Seeing them fired under conditions that smack of unfairness poisons the relationship. As a rule, therefore:

- Avoid the appearance of power and domination.
- Avoid win–lose behavior.
- Remain businesslike and professional in all dealings.
- Maintain as positive a feeling about the acquired company as possible.
- Remember that the degree to which your organization treats the acquired group with care and dignity will affect the confidence, productivity, and commitment of those who remain.[89]

For example, Jack Brown, chairman of Slater Brothers, knew it was crucial to maintain good relations with the employees of the 33 Albertson's and 10 Lucky Stores his company acquired. Slater first created a transition team headed by a top executive, who, among other things, offered jobs to all employees of the 43 stores. His firm also devoted a great deal of time and effort to communicating with the new employees. As he says, "I took a month and talked to all of them . . . All people got to stay at the same store with the same pay, the same benefits, and the same seniority."[90]

"The HR Scorecard" shows how the Hotel Paris applied these ideas.

The HR Scorecard
Strategy and Results

The Hotel Paris's New Ethics, Justice, and Fair Treatment Process

The Hotel Paris's competitive strategy is "To use superior guest service to differentiate the Hotel Paris properties, and to thereby increase the length of stay and return rate of guests, and thus boost revenues and profitability." HR manager Lisa Cruz must now formulate functional policies and activities that support this competitive strategy, by eliciting the required employee behaviors and competencies.

A preliminary analysis, performed jointly by Lisa and the Hotel Paris's chief financial officer, left them optimistic that HR could contribute measurably to achieving the hotel's strategic aims. Several employee competencies and behaviors including employee morale, employee commitment, and the percent of arriving guests receiving the hotel's required greeting had significant effects on customer and organizational outcomes such as guest satisfaction and frequency of guest returns. In turn, outcomes like these contributed measurably to the Hotel Paris's strategic goals, including profit margins, market share, and scores on industry satisfaction surveys. Lisa and her team now turn to creating a fair treatment process that will help to produce the required employee competencies and behaviors. The accompanying HR Scorecard (Figure 14-12) outlines the relationships involved.

When she sat down with the CFO to discuss her proposal for the Hotel Paris's fairness, justice, and ethics system, Lisa came armed with some research, and it certainly caught the CFO's attention. The study could not have been more germane. In 2003, the *Journal of Applied Psychology* published a study that showed how improving the level of interpersonal and procedural justice in a service company can lead to improved employee attitudes and performance and thus to improved hotel performance. And the study was done in a hotel chain.

In this study, the researchers collected employee survey data from a hotel chain's 111 different hotel properties in the United States and Canada. The employee services department of this hotel chain obtained completed surveys from 8,832 of the hotel's employees. The researchers also obtained data on employee turnover as well as on the employees' commitment, employees' intentions to remain with the organization, and guest satisfaction.

The following figures help summarize what the researchers found: note the links. Clearly, having fair and just procedures in place effected employee morale and behavior, and thus company performance. Note Figure A on the top. It shows that in this hotel chain, procedural justice and interpersonal justice were related to increased levels of employees' satisfaction with supervision. Procedural justice and satisfaction with supervision were both related to improved employee commitment. And employee commitment was related to intention to remain with the hotel, and therefore to reducing employee turnover. Figure B on the bottom shows a related sequence. This one shows that procedural and interpersonal justice led to improved employee satisfaction with supervision and commitment, and thus, to improved employee discretionary service behaviors, and ultimately to higher guest service satisfaction.

For Lisa and the CFO, these results provided a concrete and measurable rationale for moving ahead with improving the Hotel Paris's fairness, justice, and ethics practices. The results supported, in a measurably defensible way, the idea that spending the money required to improve procedural and interpersonal justice would likely improve employee attitudes and behaviors (employee commitment, discretionary service behavior, and employee turnover), and, thereby, improve guest satisfaction and company performance. The results even suggested by

Employee Morale and Behavior Improves When Justice Prevails

Source: Tony Simons and Quinetta Roberson, "Why Managers Should Care about Fairness. The Effects of Aggregate Justice Perceptions on Organizational Outcomes," *Journal of Applied Psychology* 88, no. 3 (2003), p. 432.

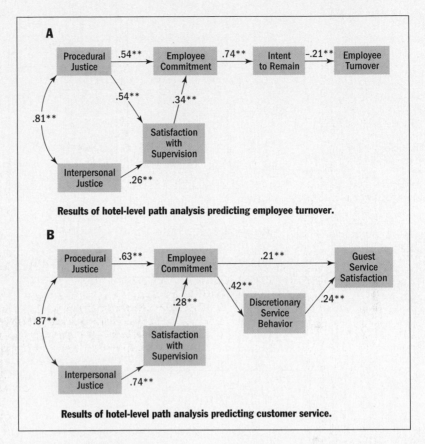

Results of hotel-level path analysis predicting employee turnover.

Results of hotel-level path analysis predicting customer service.

"how much" improving morale and justice might boost guest satisfaction.

Lisa and her HR team took a number of steps to institute new ethics, justice, and fair treatment practices at the Hotel Paris. Working with the company's general counsel, they produced and presented to the CEO a new Hotel Paris code of ethics, as well as a more complete set of ethical guidelines. These now appear on the Hotel Paris's careers Web site link, and are part of each new employee's orientation packet. They contracted with a vendor to provide a customized, Web-based ethics training program, and made it clear that the first employees to participate in it were the company's top executives.

Lisa and her team then proceeded methodically through the company's entire HR process, starting with recruitment and selection. For example, the new selection process now includes an honesty test. New guidelines ensure an open and fair performance appraisal process, including required signatures from the appraising supervisor's own boss. The team completely revamped the hotel's

disciplinary process. They instituted a new appeals process that included appeals to each hotel's manager, and then to Lisa Cruz, and finally to a top management executive appeals committee. They instituted a new discipline without punishment system. They instituted new guidelines outlining grounds for dismissal. The new procedure requires that someone from HR approve any dismissal before it is final, and be present when any employee who's been with the firm for more than a year is dismissed.

After six months of operating under the new system, several changes are already evident. Surveys the team took before the new program commenced, and now, indicate a significant upward movement in the employees' perceptions of "consistent and equitable treatment of all employees." Grievances are down by 80%, 95% of employees are able to quote the ethics code, employee morale and commitment are up, and, in general, employee service type behaviors (such as greeting guests in a friendly manner) have increased too. Lisa and the CFO are pleased with the new system, and are optimistic it will also help to improve customer service satisfaction.

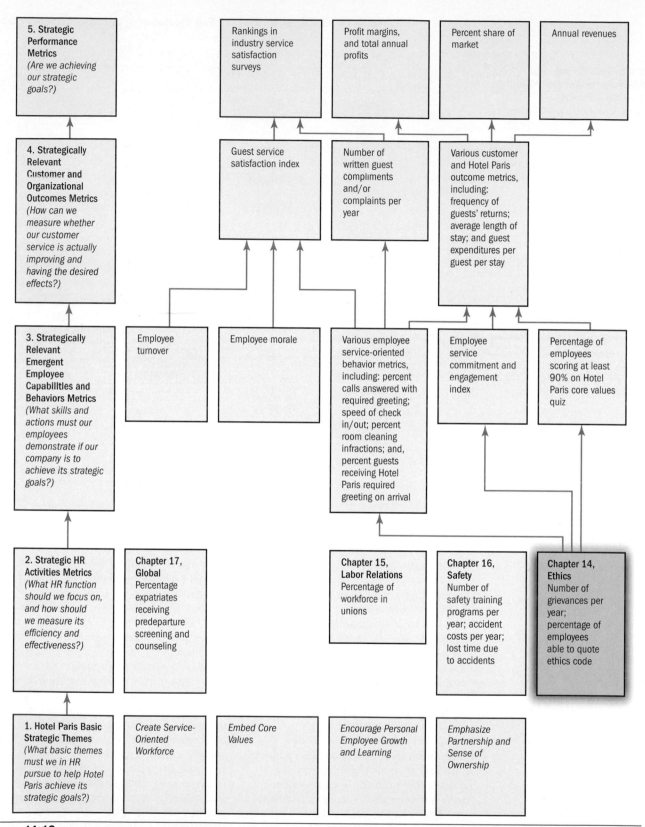

Figure 14-12

HR Scorecard for Hotel Paris International Corporation*

Note: *(An abbreviated example showing selected HR practices and outcomes aimed at implementing the competitive strategy,"To use superior guest services to differentiate the Hotel Paris properties and thus increase the length of stays and the return rate of guests and thus boost revenues and profitability")

 *Review*

SUMMARY

1. Ethics refers to the principles of conduct governing an individual or a group, and specifically to the standards you use to decide what your conduct should be.

2. Ethical decisions are always characterized by two things. First, they always involve normative judgments. Second, ethical decisions also always involve morality, which is society's accepted standards of behavior.

3. Numerous factors shape ethical behavior at work. These include individual factors, organizational factors, the boss's influence, ethics policies and codes, and the organization's culture.

4. HR management can influence ethics and fair treatment at work in numerous ways. Some examples: A fair and open selection process can emphasize the company's stress on integrity and ethics, the company can have special ethics training programs, employees' adherence to high ethical standards can be measured during performance appraisals, and ethical (or unethical) work-related behavior can be rewarded or punished.

5. A fair and just discipline process is based on three prerequisites: rules and regulations, a system of progressive penalties, and an appeals process. Following discipline guidelines is important.

6. The basic aim of discipline without punishment is to gain an employee's acceptance of the rules by reducing the punitive nature of the discipline itself.

7. Managing dismissals is an important part of any supervisor's job. Among the reasons for dismissal are unsatisfactory performance, misconduct, lack of qualifications, changed job requirements, and insubordination. In dismissing one or more employees, however, remember that termination at will as a policy has been weakened by exceptions in many states. Furthermore, great care should be taken to avoid wrongful discharge suits.

8. Dismissing an employee is always difficult, and the termination interview should be handled properly. Plan the interview carefully (for instance, early in the week), get to the point, describe the situation and then listen until the person has expressed his or her feelings. Then discuss the severance package and identify the next step.

9. Nondisciplinary separations such as layoffs and retirement occur all the time. The plant closing law (the Worker Adjustment and Retraining Notification Act) outlines requirements to be followed with regard to official notice before operations with 50 or more people are to be closed down.

DISCUSSION QUESTIONS

1. Explain how you would ensure fairness in disciplining, discussing particularly the prerequisites to disciplining, disciplining guidelines, and the discipline without punishment approach.

2. Why is it important in our highly litigious society to manage dismissals properly?

3. What techniques would you use as alternatives to traditional discipline? What do such alternatives have to do with "organizational justice"? Why do you think alternatives like these are important, given industry's need today for highly committed employees?

INDIVIDUAL AND GROUP EXERCISES

1. Working individually or in groups, interview managers or administrators at your employer or college in order to determine the extent to which the employer or college endeavors to build two-way communication, and the specific types of programs used. Do the managers think they are effective? What do the employees (or faculty members) think of the programs in use at the employer or college?

2. Working individually or in groups, obtain copies of the student handbook for your college and determine to what extent there is a formal process through which students can air grievances. Based on your contacts with other students, has it been an effective grievance process? Why or why not?

3. Working individually or in groups, determine the nature of the academic discipline process in your college. Do you

think it is effective? Based on what you read in this chapter, would you recommend any modifications?

4. The HRCI "Test Specifications" appendix at the end of this book (pages 685–689) lists the knowledge someone studying for the HRCI certification exam needs to have in each area of human resource management (such as in Strategic Management, Workforce Planning, and Human Resource Development). In groups of four to five students, do four things: (1) review that appendix now; (2) identify the material in this chapter that relates to the required knowledge the appendix lists; (3) write four multiple choice exam questions on this material that you believe would be suitable for inclusion in the HRCI exam; and (4) if time permits, have someone from your team post your team's

questions in front of the class, so the students in other teams can take each others' exam questions.

5. In a recent research study at Ohio State University, a professor found that even honest people, left to their own devices, will steal from their employers.[91] In this study, the researchers gave financial services workers the opportunity to steal a small amount of money after participating in an after-work project for which the pay was inadequate. Would the employees steal to make up for the underpayment? In most cases, yes. Employees who scored low on an honesty test stole whether or not their office had an ethics program that said stealing from the company was illegal. Employees who scored high on the honesty test also stole, but only if their office did not have such an employee ethics program—the "honest" people didn't steal if there was an ethics policy.

In groups of four or five students, answer these questions: Do you think findings like these are generalizable? In other words, would they apply across the board to employees in other types of companies and situations? If your answer is yes, what do you think this implies about the need for and wisdom of having an ethics program?

EXPERIENTIAL EXERCISE

Discipline or Not?

Purpose: The purpose of this exercise is to provide you with some experience in analyzing and handling an actual disciplinary action.

Required Understanding: Students should be thoroughly familiar with the following case, titled "Botched Batch." **Do not read the "award" or "discussion" sections until after the groups have completed their deliberations.**

How to Set Up the Exercise/Instructions: Divide the class into groups of four or five students. Each group should take the arbitrator's point of view and assume that they are to analyze the case and make the arbitrator's decision. Review the case again at this point, but please do not read the award and discussion.

Each group should answer the following questions:

1. Based on what you read in this chapter, including all relevant guidelines, what would your decision be if you were the arbitrator? Why?
2. Do you think that after their experience in this arbitration the parties will be more or less inclined to settle grievances by themselves without resorting to arbitration?

Botched Batch

Facts: A computer department employee made an entry error that botched an entire run of computer reports. Efforts to rectify the situation produced a second set of improperly run reports. As a result of the series of errors, the employer incurred extra costs of $2,400, plus a weekend of overtime work by other computer department staffers. Management suspended the employee for three days for negligence, and also revoked a promotion for which the employee had previously been approved.

Protesting the discipline, the employee stressed that she had attempted to correct her error in the early stages of the run by notifying the manager of computer operations of her mistake. Maintaining that the resulting string of errors could have been avoided if the manager had followed up on her report and stopped the initial run, the employee argued that she had been treated unfairly because the manager had not been disciplined even though he compounded the problem, whereas she was severely punished. Moreover, citing her "impeccable" work record and management's acknowledgment that she had always been a "model employee," the employee insisted that the denial of her previously approved promotion was "unconscionable."

(*Please do **not** read beyond this point until after you have answered the two questions.*)

Award: The arbitrator upholds the three-day suspension, but decides that the promotion should be restored.

Discussion: "There is no question," the arbitrator notes, that the employee's negligent act "set in motion the train of events that resulted in running two complete sets of reports reflecting improper information." Stressing that the employer incurred substantial cost because of the error, the arbitrator cites "unchallenged" testimony that management had commonly issued three-day suspensions for similar infractions in the past. Thus, the arbitrator decides, the employer acted with just cause in meting out an "evenhanded" punishment for the negligence.

Turning to the denial of the already approved promotion, the arbitrator says that this action should be viewed "in the same light as a demotion for disciplinary reasons." In such cases, the arbitrator notes, management's decision normally is based on a pattern of unsatisfactory behavior, an employee's inability to perform, or similar grounds. Observing that management had never before reversed a promotion as part of a disciplinary action, the arbitrator says that by tacking on the denial of the promotion in this case, the employer substantially varied its disciplinary policy from its past practice. Because this action on management's part was not "evenhanded," the arbitrator rules, the promotion should be restored.[91]

Ethics Quiz Answers

Quiz is on Page 516—Figure 14-1.

1. 34% said personal e-mail on company computers is wrong.
2. 37% said using office equipment for schoolwork is wrong.
3. 49% said playing computer games at work is wrong.
4. 54% said Internet shopping at work is wrong.
5. 61% said it's unethical to blame your error on technology.
6. 87% said it's unethical to visit pornographic sites at work.
7. 33% said $25 is the amount at which a gift from a supplier or client becomes troubling, while 33% said $50, and 33% said $100.

8. 35% said a $50 gift to the boss is unacceptable.
9. 12% said a $50 gift *from* the boss is unacceptable.
10. 70% said it's unacceptable to take the $200 football tickets.
11. 70% said it's unacceptable to take the $120 theater tickets.
12. 35% said it's unacceptable to take the $100 food basket.

13. 45% said it's unacceptable to take the $25 gift certificate.
14. 40% said it's unacceptable to take the $75 raffle prize.
15. 11% reported they lie about sick days.
16. 4% reported they take credit for the work or ideas of others.

APPLICATION CASE

Fire My Best Salesperson?

Greg Johns, sales director for International Widget Industries (IWI) had a problem. He was just told that his top salesperson, Bob Pollock, was stealing from the company. Pollock had been inflating expense reports and exaggerating his sales (by double booking sales orders). He therefore got higher expense reimbursements and commissions than he deserved. The accounting department had proof that Pollock was stealing. IWI's CEO has told Johns to either rectify the situation or lose his own job. Johns is in a quandary about what to do. He doesn't want to lose his best salesperson, and he thinks perhaps there might be extenuating circumstances—such as family pressures—that explain Pollock's behavior. The question is, what should Johns do now?[92]

Questions

Assume you are Johns. Specifically,
1. What should you do now?
2. Why should you do it?
3. How would you do it?

Please answer that three-part question before moving on to see what actually happened, by reading the following:

In this case, there's no question of what to do. The company must terminate this salesperson. According to the people who are actually involved in this situation, no company can tolerate stealing on the part of its employees. If you cannot trust the salesperson, his presence with your company will have a corrosive effect on all that he deals with, including customers and co-workers.

The consensus is to confront him. First, confirm that the information is accurate. Show him the evidence, get his response, and assuming the accusations are true, have the person surrender all his company account information and leads in return for a quiet termination.

Now, knowing what IWI actually did, what do you think of their response? What, if anything, would you have done differently?

CONTINUING CASE

Carter Cleaning Company

Guaranteeing Fair Treatment

Being in the laundry and cleaning business, the Carters have always felt strongly about not allowing employees to smoke, eat, or drink in their stores. Jennifer was therefore surprised to walk into a store and find two employees eating lunch at the front counter. There was a large pizza in its box, and the two of them were sipping colas and eating slices of pizza and submarine sandwiches off paper plates. Not only did it look messy, but there were also grease and soda spills on the counter and the store smelled from onions and pepperoni, even with the four-foot-wide exhaust fan pulling air out through the roof. In addition to being a turnoff to customers, the mess on the counter increased the possibility that a customer's order might actually become soiled in the store.

While this was a serious matter, neither Jennifer nor her father felt that what the counter people were doing was grounds for immediate dismissal, partly because the store manager had apparently condoned their actions. The problem was, they didn't know what to do. It seemed to them that the matter called for more than just a warning but less than dismissal.

Questions

1. What would you do if you were Jennifer, and why?
2. Should a disciplinary system be established at Carter's Cleaning Centers?
3. If so, what should it cover, and how would you suggest it deal with a situation such as the one with the errant counter people?
4. How would you deal with the store manager?

KEY TERMS

ethics, 517
distributive justice, 518
procedural justice, 518
interactional (interpersonal) justice, 518
organizational culture, 523
nonpunitive discipline, 535
Electronic Communications Privacy Act (ECPA), 536

dismissal, 537

unsatisfactory performance, 538

misconduct, 538

insubordination, 538

wrongful discharge, 540

termination interview, 543

outplacement counseling, 544

exit interviews, 544

bumping/layoff procedures, 548

downsizing, 548

ENDNOTES

1. "What Role Should HR Play in Corporate Ethics?" *HR Focus* 81, no. 1 (January 2004), p. 3.

2. Paul Schumann, "A Moral Principles Framework for Human Resource Management Ethics," *Human Resource Management Review* 11 (2004), p. 94.

3. Kevin Wooten, "Ethical Dilemmas in Human Resource Management: An Application of a Multidimensional Framework, A Unifying Taxonomy, and Applicable Codes," *Human Resource Management Review* 11 (2001), p. 161.

4. Manuel Velasquez, *Business Ethics: Concepts and Cases* (Upper Saddle Rive, NJ: Prentice Hall, 1992), p. 9. See also Kate Walter, "Ethics Hot Lines Tap into More Than Wrongdoing," *HR Magazine*, September 1995, pp. 79–85; and Skip Kaltenheuser, "Bribery Is Being Outlawed Virtually Worldwide," *Business Ethics*, May 1998, p. 11.

5. The following discussion, except as noted, is based on Manuel Velasquez, *Business Ethics*, pp. 9–12.

6. For further discussion of ethics and morality, see Tom Beauchamp and Norman Bowie, *Ethical Theory and Business* (Upper Saddle River, NJ: Prentice Hall, 2001), pp. 1–19.

7. Richard Osborne, "A Matter of Ethics," *Industry Week*, September 4, 2000, pp. 41–42.

8. Carroll Lachnit, "Recruiting Trouble for Tyson," *Workforce, HR Trends and Tools for Business Results* 81, no. 2 (February 2002), p. 22.

9. Daniel Skarlicki and Robert Folger, "Fairness and Human Resources Management," *Human Resource Management Review* 13, no. 1 (2003), p. 1.

10. Gary Weaver and Linda Trevino, "The Role of Human Resources in Ethics/Compliance Management: A Fairness Perspective," *Human Resource Management Review* 11 (2001), p. 115.

11. Linda Trevino and Katherine Nelson, *Managing Business Ethics* (New York: John Wiley & Sons, 1999), p. 134.

12. Michelle Donovan et al., "The Perceptions of Their Interpersonal Treatment Scale: Development and Validation of a Measure of Interpersonal Treatment in the Workplace," *Journal of Applied Psychology* 83, no. 5 (1998), pp. 683–692.

13. Weaver and Trevino, "The Role of Human Resources," pp. 113–134.

14. Rudy Yandrick, "Lurking in the Shadows," *HR Magazine*, October 1999, pp. 61–68.

15. Bennett Tepper, "Consequences of Abusive Supervision," *Academy of Management Journal* 43, no. 2 (2000), pp. 178–190.

16. M. Audrey Korsgaard, Loriann Roberson, and R. Douglas Rymph, "What Motivates Fairness? The Role of Subordinate Assertive Behavior on Managers' Interactional Fairness," *Journal of Applied Psychology* 83, no. 5 (1998), pp. 731–744.

17. Marshall Schminke et al., "The Effect of Organizational Structure on Perceptions of Procedural Fairness," *Journal of Applied Psychology* 85, no. 2 (2000), pp. 294–304.

18. Sara Morris et al., "A Test of Environmental, Situational, and Personal Influences on the Ethical Intentions of CEOs," *Business and Society*, August 1995, pp. 119–247.

19. "Former CEO Joins WorldCom's Indicted," *Miami Herald*, March 3, 2004, p. 4C.

20. Floyd Norris and Diana Henriques, "Three Admit Guilt in Falsifying CUC's Books," *New York Times*, June 15, 2000, p. C1.

21. "Ethics Policies are Big with Employers, but Workers See Small Impact on the Workplace," *BNA Bulletin to Management*, June 29, 2000, p. 201.

22. Discussed in Samuel Greengard, "Cheating and Stealing," *Workforce*, October 1997, pp. 45–53.

23. From Guy Brumback, "Managing Above the Bottom Line of Ethics," *Supervisory Management*, December 1993, p. 12.

24. James Kunen, "Enron Division (and Values) Thing," *New York Times*, January 19, 2002, p. A19.

25. Dayton Fandray, "The Ethical Company," *Workforce*, December 2000, pp. 74–77.

26. S. Greengard, "50 Percent of Your Employees are Lying, Cheating, and Stealing," *Workforce*, October 1997, pp. 44–53.

27. "Promoting Workplace Fun Draws Serious Attention," *BNA Bulletin to Management*, August 8, 1999, p. 215.

28. Weaver and Trevino, "The Role of Human Resources," p. 117.

29. Russell Cropanzano and Thomas Wright, "Procedural Justice and Organizational Staffing: A Tale of Two Paradigms," *Human Resource Management Review* 13, no. 1 (2003), pp. 7–40.

30. Suzanne Masterson, "A Trickle-Down Model of Organizational Justice: Relating Employees' and Customers' Perceptions of and Reactions to Fairness," *Journal of Applied Psychology* 86, no. 4 (2001), pp. 594–601.

31. J. Krohe Jr., "The Big Business of Business Ethics," *Across the Board* 34 (May 1997), pp. 23–29; Deborah Wells and Marshall Schminke, "Ethical Development and Human Resources Training: An Integrator Framework," *Human Resource Management Review* 11 (2001), pp. 135–158.

32. Editorial: "Ethical Issues in the Management of Human Resources," *Human Resource Management Review* 11 (2001), p. 6.

33. Weaver and Trevino, "The Role of Human Resources," p. 123.

34. Cropanzano and Wright, "Procedural Justice and Organizational Staffing," pp. 7–40.

35. Weaver and Trevino, "The Role of Human Resources," p. 123.

36. Wells and Schminke, "Ethical Development and Human Resources Training," pp. 135–158.

37. Michael J. McCarthy, "How One Firm Tracks Ethics Electronically," *Wall Street Journal*, October 21, 1999, pp. B1, B4.

38. M. Ronald Buckley et al., "Ethical Issues in Human Resources Systems," *Human Resource Management Review* 11, nos. 1, 2 (2001), pp. 11, 29.

39. Weaver and Trevino, "The Role of Human Resources," pp. 113–134.

40. Weaver and Trevino, "The Role of Human Resources," p. 114.

41. "Corporations' Drive to Embrace Ethics Gives HR Leaders Chance to Take Reins," *BNA Bulletin to Management*, November 7, 2002, p. 353.

42. Max Rexroad and Joyce Ostrosky, "Sarbanes-Oxley: What It Means to the Marketplace," *Journal of Accountancy* 197, no. 2 (February 2004), pp. 43–48.

43. Michael Burr, "Corporate Governance: Embracing Sarbanes-Oxley," *Public Utilities Fortnightly*, October 15, 2003, pp. 20–22.

44. Ibid.
45. W. Chan Kim and Rene Mauborgne, "Fair Process: Managing in the Knowledge Economy," *Harvard Business Review*, July/August 1997, pp. 65–75.
46. William Kandel, "After Reeves: Proving Pretext, Imprecision or Imperfection?" *Employee Relations Law Journal* 26, no. 3 (Winter 2000), pp. 5–29.
47. "Ethics: It Isn't Just the Big Guys," *The American Intelligence Wire*, July 28, 2003, p. 10.
48. Ibid.
49. Lester Bittel, *What Every Supervisor Should Know* (New York: McGraw-Hill, 1974), p. 308; Paul Falcone, "The Fundamentals of Progressive Discipline," *HR Magazine*, February 1997, pp. 90–92.
50. Donald Petersen, "The Arbitration of Tardiness Cases," *Journal of Collective Negotiations in the Public Sector* 29, no. 2 (2000), pp. 167–174.
51. Dick Grote, "Discipline without Punishment," *Across the Board* 38, no. 5 (September 2001), pp. 52–57.
52. David Campbell et al., "Discipline Without Punishment—At Last," *Harvard Business Review*, July/August 1995, pp. 162–178.
53. Milton Zall, "Employee Privacy," *Journal of Property Management* 66, no. 3 (May 2001), p. 16.
54. Morris Attaway, "Privacy in the Workplace on the Web," *Internal Auditor* 58, no. 1 (February 2001), p. 30.
55. Declam Leonard and Angela France, "Workplace Monitoring: Balancing Business Interests with Employee Privacy Rights," *Society for Human Resource Management Legal Report*, May–June 2003, pp. 3–6.
56. Eileen Zimmerman, "HR Must Know When Employee Surveillance Crosses the Line," *Workforce*, February 2002, pp. 38–44.
57. "Workers Sharing Music, Movies at Work Violates Copyrights, Employer Finds," *BNA Bulletin to Management*, June 19, 2003, p. 193.
58. Cynthia Kemper, "Big Brother," *Communication World* 18, no. 1 (December 2000/January 2001), pp. 8–12.
59. Michael McCarthy, "Now the Boss Knows Where You're Clicking," *Wall Street Journal*, October 21, 1999, p. B1.
60. Leonard and France, "Workplace Monitoring," p. 4.
61. *Vega-Rodriguez v. Puerto Rico Telephone Company*, CA1,#962061, 4/8/97, discussed in "Video Surveillance Withstands Privacy Challenge," *BNA Bulletin to Management*, April 17, 1997, p. 121.
62. "Secret Videotaping Leads to $200,000 Settlement," *BNA Bulletin to Management*, January 22, 1998, p. 17.
63. Bill Roberts, "Are You Ready for Biometrics?" *HR Magazine*, March 2003, pp. 95–96.
64. Andrea Poe, "Make Foresight 20/20," *HR Magazine*, February 2000, pp. 74–80.
65. Charles Muhl, "The Employment at Will Doctrine: Three Major Exceptions," *Monthly Labor Review* 124, no. 1 (January 2001), pp. 3–11.
66. Joseph Famularo, *Handbook of Modern Personnel Administration* (New York: McGraw-Hill, 1982), pp. 65.3–65.5.
67. Ibid., pp. 65.4–65.5.
68. Kenneth Sovereign, *Personnel Law* (Upper Saddle River, NJ: Prentice Hall, 1999), p. 148.
69. Ibid; and Connie Wanderg et al., "Perceived Fairness of Layoffs Among Individuals Who Have Been Laid Off: A Longitudinal Study," *Personnel Psychology* 2 (1999), pp. 59–84.
70. Dana Mansour-Cole and Susanne Scott, "Hearing It Through the Grapevine: The Influence of Source, Leader-Relations, and Legitimacy on Survivors' Fairness Perceptions," *Personnel Psychology* 51 (1998), pp. 25–54.
71. Jaikumar Vijayan, "Downsizings Leave Firms Vulnerable to Digital Attacks," *Computerworld* 25 (2001), pp. 6–7.
72. Paul Falcon, "Give Employees the (Gentle) Hook," *HR Magazine*, April 2001, pp. 121–128.
73. Based on James Coil III and Charles Rice, "Three Steps to Creating Effective Employee Releases," *Employment Relations Today*, Spring 1994, pp. 91–94. See also Jeffrey Conner, "Disarming Terminated Employees," *HR Magazine*, January 2000, pp. 113–116; and Richard Bayer, "Termination with Dignity," *Business Horizons* 43, no. 5 (September 2000), pp. 4–10.
74. Gillian Flynn, "Grounds for Dismissal," *Workforce*, August 2000, pp. 86–90.
75. "One More Heart Risk: Firing Employees," *Miami Herald*, March 20, 1998, pp. C1, C7.
76. Edward Isler et al., "Personal Liability and Employee Discipline," *Society for Human Resource Management Legal Report*, September–October 2000, pp. 1–4.
77. Based on Coil and Rice, "Three Steps to Creating Effective Employee Releases," pp. 91–94.
78. Kemba Dunham, "The Kinder Gentler Way to Lay Off Employees—More Human Approach Helps," *Wall Street Journal*, March 13, 2001, p. B-1.
79. Paul Brada, "Before You Go . . . ," *HR Magazine*, December 1998, pp. 89–102.
80. Joseph Zarandona and Michael Camuso, "A Study of Exit Interviews: Does the Last Word Count," *Personnel* 62, no. 3 (March 1981), pp. 47–48. For another point of view, see "Firms Can Profit from Data Obtained from Exit Interviews," *Knight-Ridder/Tribune Business News*, February 13, 2001, Item 0104 4446.
81. Marlene Piturro, "Alternatives to Downsizing," *Management Review*, October 1999, pp. 37–42; "How Safe Is Your Job?" *Money*, December 1, 2001, p. 130.
82. Commerce Clearing House, *Ideas and Trends*, August 9, 1988, p. 133. See also Nancy Ryan, "Complying with the Worker Adjustment and Retraining Notification Act (WARNACT)," *Employee Relations Law Journal* 18, no. 1 (Summer 1993), pp. 169–176.
83. Emily Nelson, "The Job Cut Buyouts Favored by P&G Pose Problems," *Wall Street Journal*, June 12, 2001, p. B01.
84. See, for example, "Cushioning the Blow of Layoffs," *BNA Bulletin to Management*, July 3, 1997, p. 216; and "Levi Strauss Cushions Blow of Plant Closings," *BNA Bulletin to Management*, November 20, 1997, p. 370.
85. These are suggested by attorney Ethan Lipsig and discussed in "The Lowdown on Downsizing," *BNA Bulletin to Management*, January 9, 1997, p. 16.
86. Stephen Gilliland and Donald Schepers, "Why We Do the Things We Do: A Discussion and Analysis of Determinants of Just Treatment in Layoff Implementation Decisions," *Human Resource Management Review* 13, no. 1 (2003), pp. 59–84.
87. "Communication Can Reduce Problems, Litigation After Layoffs, Attorneys Say," *BNA Bulletin to Management*, April 24, 2003, p. 129.
88. See Robert Ford and Pamela Perrew, "After the Layoff: Closing the Barn Door Before All the Horses Are Gone," *Business Horizons*, July–August 1993, pp. 34–40.
89. Steve Weinstein, "The People Side of Mergers," *Progressive Grocer* 80, no. 1 (January 2001), pp. 29–31.
90. Based on "Theft is Unethical," *HE Solutions* 34 (October 2002), p. 66.
91. Bureau of National Affairs, *Bulletin to Management*, Sept. 13, 1985, p. 3.
92. Based on "What Would You Do?" *Sales & Marketing Management* 155 (January 2003), pp. 52–54.

After studying this chapter, you should be able to:

1. Give a brief history of the American labor movement.

2. Discuss the main features of at least three major pieces of labor legislation.

3. Present examples of what to expect during the union drive and election.

4. Describe five ways to lose an NLRB election.

5. Illustrate with examples bargaining that is not in good faith.

6. Develop a grievance procedure.

Labor Relations and Collective Bargaining

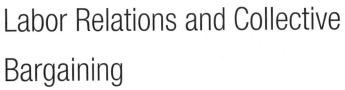

Lisa Cruz's parents were both union members, and she had no strong philosophical objections to unions, per se. However, as the head of HR for the Hotel Paris, she did feel very strongly that her employer should do everything legally possible to remain union-free. She knew that this is what the hotel chain's owners and top executives wanted. Furthermore, the evidence seemed to support their position. At least one study that she'd seen concluded that firms with 30% or more of their eligible workers in unions were in the bottom 10% in terms of performance, while those with 8% to 9% of eligible workers in unions scored in the top 10%.[1] The problem was that the Hotel Paris really had no specific policies and procedures in place to help its managers and supervisors deal with union activities. With all the laws regarding what employers and their managers could and could not do to respond to a union's efforts, Lisa knew her company was "a problem waiting to happen." She turned her attention to deciding what steps she and her team should take with regard to labor relations and collective bargaining.●

The previous chapter focused on employee ethics and justice—always important when dealing with unions. The main purpose of this chapter is to provide you with information you'll need to deal effectively with unions and grievances. After briefly discussing the history of the American labor movement, we describe some basic labor legislation, including the subject of unfair labor practices. We explain labor negotiations, including the union actions you can expect during the union campaign and election. And we explain what you can expect during the actual bargaining sessions, and how to handle grievances, an activity often called "contract administration." In the next chapter, Employee Safety and Health, we'll turn to the techniques managers use to provide employees with a safe and healthy workplace.

● THE LABOR MOVEMENT

Today, just over 16 million U.S. workers belong to unions—around 13.2% of the total number of men and women working in this country.[2] Many are still traditional blue-collar workers, but unions increasingly appeal to while-collar workers, too. For instance, workers including doctors, psychologists, graduate teaching assistants, and even fashion models are forming or joining unions.[3] Federal, state, and local governments employ about seven million union members, who account for almost 40% of total government employees. And in some industries— including transportation and public utilities, where over 26% of employees are union members—it's still hard to get a job without joining a union.[4] Union membership in other countries is declining, but is still very high: 37% of employed workers in Canada, 43% in Mexico, 44% in Brazil, 44% in Italy, and 24% in Japan.[5] Why are unions important? How did they get that way? Why do workers join them? How do employers and unions hammer out agreements? These are questions we'll address in this chapter.

Give a brief history of the American labor movement.

A Brief History of the American Union Movement

To understand what unions are and what they want, it is useful to understand "where they've been." The history of the union movement in the United States has been one of alternate expansion and contraction. As early as 1790, skilled craftsmen (shoemakers, tailors, printers, and so on) organized themselves into trade unions. They posted their minimum wage demands and had "tramping committees" go from shop to shop to ensure that no member accepted a lesser wage. Union membership grew until a major depression around 1837 resulted in a membership decline. Membership then began increasing as the United States entered its industrial revolution. In 1869, a group of tailors met and formed the Knights of Labor. The Knights were interested in political reform. By 1885, they had 100,000 members, which (as a result of winning a major strike against a railroad) exploded to 700,000 the following year. Partly because of their focus on social reform, and partly due to a series of unsuccessful strikes, the Knights' membership dwindled rapidly thereafter, and the group dissolved in 1893.

In 1886, Samuel Gompers formed the American Federation of Labor. It consisted mostly of skilled workers and, unlike the Knights, focused on practical, bread-and-butter gains for its members. The Knights of Labor had engaged in a class struggle to alter the form of society, and thereby get a bigger chunk of benefits for its members. Gompers aimed to reach the same goal by raising day-to-day wages and improving working conditions. The AFL grew rapidly until after World War I, at which point its membership exceeded 5.5 million people.

The 1920s was a period of stagnation and decline for the U.S. union movement. This was a result of several events, including a postwar depression, manufacturers'

Making fenders at an early Ford factory in Ypsilanti, Michigan. In addition to heavy physical labor, workers faced health hazards—poor lighting, dust, and dangerous machinery.

renewed resistance to unions, Samuel Gompers's death, and the apparent prosperity of the 1920s. By late 1929, due to the Great Depression, millions of workers (including many union members) had lost their jobs, and by 1933 union membership was down to under three million workers.

Membership began to rise again in the mid-1930s. As part of his New Deal programs, President Franklin Delano Roosevelt passed the National Industrial Recovery Act, which made it easier for labor to organize. Other federal laws as well as prosperity and World War II also contributed to the rapid increase in members, which topped out at about 21 million workers in the 1970s. Union membership has consistently fallen since then, due to factors such as the shift from manufacturing to service jobs, and new legislation (such as occupational safety laws) that provide the sorts of protections that workers could once only obtain from their unions. Indeed, hundreds of local, state, and federal laws and regulations now address the sorts of concerns that helped drive the early union movement.[6]

Why Do Workers Organize?

Experts have spent much time and money trying to discover why workers unionize, and they've proposed many theories. Yet there is no simple answer to the question, partly because each worker probably joins for his or her own reasons.

It does seem clear that workers don't unionize just to get more pay or better working conditions, though these are very important. In fact, weekly earnings of union members are much higher than those of nonunion workers: about $50 a week more in service jobs, $60 in manufacturing, $130 in government, and as much as $300 a week more in construction jobs, for instance.[7] Union workers receive significantly more holidays, sick leave, unpaid leave, insurance plan benefits, long-term disability benefits, and various other benefits than do nonunion workers.[8] On the other hand, the main issue is not always pay. As an example, the UAW recently restarted efforts to organize workers at Nissan motors' Smyrna, Tennessee, auto plant. The issue here isn't pay, since Nissan plant employees earn about the same per hour as UAW workers at other plants. Of greater concern, "are increasing workloads, mounting injuries and what union officials described as inadequate retirement benefits at the Smyrna plant."[9]

Thus, the urge to unionize often seems to boil down to the belief on the part of workers that it is only through unity that they can get their fair share of the pie and also protect themselves from management whims. (For example, several years ago angry FedEx pilots for a time rejected a proposed agreement backed by their own union leaders, in part, said one pilot, because "there was a trust relationship that has deteriorated."[10]) In practice, therefore, low morale, fear of job loss, and arbitrary management actions help foster unionization. And in some respects, these factors have not changed in years. Here is how one writer describes the motivation behind the early unionization of automobile workers:

> *In the years to come, economic issues would make the headlines when union and management met in negotiations. But in the early years the rate of pay was not the major complaint of the autoworkers. . . . Specifically, the principal grievances of the autoworkers were the speed-up of production and the lack of any kind of job security. As production tapered off, the order in which workers were laid off was determined largely by the whim of foremen and other supervisors. . . . The worker had no way of knowing when he would be laid off, and had no assurance when, or whether, he would be recalled. . . . Generally, what the workers revolted against was the lack of human dignity and individuality, and a working relationship that was massively impersonal, cold, and nonhuman. They wanted to be treated like human beings—not like faceless clockcard numbers.[11]*

What Do Unions Want?

We can generalize by saying that unions have two sets of aims, one for *union security* and one for *improved wages, hours, working conditions*, and *benefits* for their members.

Union Security   First and probably foremost, unions seek security for themselves. They fight hard for the right to represent a firm's workers and to be the exclusive bargaining agent for all employees in the unit. (As such, they negotiate contracts for all employees, including those not members of the union.) Five types of union security are possible:

1. **Closed shop.** The company can hire only union members. Congress outlawed this in 1947, but it still exists in some industries (such as printing).
2. **Union shop.** The company can hire nonunion people, but they must join the union after a prescribed period of time and pay dues. (If not, they can be fired.)
3. **Agency shop.** Employees who do not belong to the union still must pay union dues on the assumption that the union's efforts benefit all the workers.
4. **Open shop.** It is up to the workers whether or not they join the union—those who do not, do not pay dues.
5. Maintenance of membership arrangement. Employees do not have to belong to the union. However, union members employed by the firm must maintain membership in the union for the contract period.

Not all states give unions the right to require union membership as a condition of employment. **Right to work** "is a term used to describe state statutory or constitutional provisions banning the requirement of union membership as a condition of employment."[12] Section 14(b) of the Taft-Hartley Act (discussed below) permits states to forbid the negotiation of compulsory union membership provisions, not just for firms engaged in intrastate commerce, but those in interstate commerce, too. Right to work laws don't outlaw unions. They do outlaw (within those states) any of the forms of union security. This understandably inhibits union formation in those states. Twenty-one "right to work states," from Florida to Mississippi to Wyoming, ban all forms of union security.

---

closed shop
A form of union security in which the company can hire only union members. This was outlawed in 1947 but still exists in some industries (such as printing).

union shop
A form of union security in which the company can hire nonunion people, but they must join the union after a prescribed period of time and pay dues. (If they do not, they can be fired.)

agency shop
A form of union security in which employees who do not belong to the union must still pay union dues on the assumption that union efforts benefit all workers.

open shop
Perhaps the least attractive type of union security from the union's point of view, the workers decide whether or not to join the union; and those who join must pay dues.

right to work
A term used to describe state statutory or constitutional provisions banning the requirement of union membership as a condition of employment.

Improved Wages, Hours, and Benefits for Members   Once their security is assured, unions fight to improve wages, hours, and working conditions. The typical labor agreement also gives the union a role in other HR activities, including recruiting, selecting, compensating, promoting, training, and discharging employees.

The AFL-CIO

The American Federation of Labor and Congress of Industrial Organizations (AFL-CIO) is a voluntary federation of about 100 national and international labor unions in the United States. The separate AFL and CIO merged in 1955, with the AFL's George Meany as its first president. For many people in the United States, the AFL-CIO is synonymous with the word *union*. Most, but not all, unionized workers belong to unions affiliated with the AFL-CIO.

There are three layers in the structure of the AFL-CIO (and other U.S. unions). First, there is the local union. This is the union the worker joins, and to which he or she pays dues. The local union also usually signs the collective bargaining agreement determining the wages and working conditions. The local is in turn a single chapter in the national union. For example, if you were a teacher in Detroit, you would belong to the local union there, which is one of hundreds of local chapters of the American Federation of Teachers. The third layer in the structure is the national federation, in this case, the AFL-CIO. This federation is composed of about 100 national and international unions, which in turn are comprised of over 60,000 local unions.

Most people tend to think of the AFL-CIO as the most important part of the labor movement, but it is not. The AFL-CIO itself really has little power, except what its constituent unions let it exercise. Thus, the president of the teachers' union wields more power in that capacity than in her capacity as a vice president of the AFL-CIO. Yet as a practical matter, the AFL-CIO does act as a spokesperson for labor, and its president, John Sweeney, has political clout far in excess of a figurehead president.

● UNIONS AND THE LAW

Until about 1930, there were no special labor laws. Employers were not required to engage in collective bargaining with employees and were virtually unrestrained in their behavior toward unions; the use of spies, blacklists, and firing of union agitators were widespread. "Yellow dog" contracts, whereby management could require nonunion membership as a condition for employment, were widely enforced. Most union weapons—even strikes—were illegal.

This one-sided situation lasted until the Great Depression (around 1930). Since then, in response to changing public attitudes, values, and economic conditions, labor law has gone through three clear periods: from "strong encouragement" of unions, to "modified encouragement coupled with regulation," and finally to "detailed regulation of internal union affairs."[13]

 Discuss the main features of at least three major pieces of labor legislation.

Norris-LaGuardia Act (1932)
This law marked the beginning of the era of strong encouragement of unions and guaranteed to each employee the right to bargain collectively "free from interference, restraint, or coercion."

Period of Strong Encouragement: The Norris-LaGuardia (1932) and National Labor Relations or Wagner Acts (1935)

The **Norris-LaGuardia Act of 1932** set the stage for a new era in which union activity was encouraged. It guaranteed to each employee the right to bargain collectively "free from interference, restraint, or coercion." It declared yellow dog contracts unenforceable. And it limited the courts' abilities to issue injunctions (stop orders) for activities such as peaceful picketing and payment of strike benefits.

Yet this act did little to restrain employers from fighting labor organizations by whatever means they could find. So in 1935, Congress passed the **National Labor Relations (or Wagner) Act** to add teeth to Norris-LaGuardia. It did this by (1) banning certain unfair labor practices; (2) providing for secret-ballot elections and majority rule for determining whether a firm's employees would unionize; and (3) creating the **National Labor Relations Board (NLRB)** to enforce these two provisions.

As part of its duties, the NLRB periodically issues interpretive rulings. For example, the NLRB ruled that temporary employees could join the unions of permanent employees in the companies where their temporary employment agencies assign them to work.[14]

Unfair Employer Labor Practices   The Wagner Act deemed "statutory wrongs" (but not crimes) five unfair labor practices used by employers:

1. It is unfair for employers to "interface with, restrain, or coerce employees" in exercising their legally sanctioned right of self-organization.
2. It is unfair for company representatives to dominate or interfere with either the formation or the administration of labor unions. Among other specific management actions found to be unfair under these first two practices (1 and 2) are bribing employees, using company spy systems, moving a business to avoid unionization, and black-listing union sympathizers.
3. Employers are prohibited from discriminating in any way against employees for their legal union activities.
4. Employers are forbidden to discharge or discriminate against employees simply because the latter file unfair practice charges against the company.
5. Finally, it is an unfair labor practice for employers to refuse to bargain collectively with their employees' duly chosen representatives.

Unions file an unfair labor practice charge (see Figure 15-1) with the National Labor Relations Board. The board then investigates the charge and decides if it should take action. Possible actions include dismissal of the complaint, request for an injunction against the employer, or an order that the employer cease and desist.

Such complaints are not unusual. When Knight Ridder consolidated the separate online operations of several of its papers into the new KnightRidder.com, it triggered a labor dispute. Citing possible unfair labor practices, the unions asked the NLRB to investigate whether KnightRidder.com violated labor law by not negotiating the transfer of workers with the union.[15]

From 1935 to 1947   Union membership increased quickly after passage of the Wagner Act in 1935. Other factors such as an improving economy and aggressive union leadership contributed to this rise. But by the mid-1940s, after the end of World War II, the tide had begun to turn. Largely because of a series of massive postwar strikes, public policy began to shift against what many viewed as union excesses. The stage was set for passage of the Taft-Hartley Act.

Period of Modified Encouragement Coupled with Regulation: The Taft-Hartley Act (1947)

The **Taft-Hartley (or Labor Management Relations) Act of 1947** reflected the public's less enthusiastic attitude toward unions. It amended the National Labor Relations (Wagner) Act by limiting unions in four ways: (1) prohibiting unfair union labor

Figure 15-1
NLRB Form 501: Filing an
Unfair Labor Practice

FORM NLRB 501
(2 81)

FORM EXEMPT UNDER
44 U.S.C. 3512

UNITED STATES OF AMERICA
NATIONAL LABOR RELATIONS BOARD
CHARGE AGAINST EMPLOYER

INSTRUCTIONS: File an original and 4 copies of this charge with NLRB Regional Director for the region in which the alleged unfair labor practice occurred or is occurring.	DO NOT WRITE IN THIS SPACE	
	CASE NO.	DATE FILE

1. EMPLOYER AGAINST WHOM CHARGE IS BROUGHT

a. NAME OF EMPLOYER	b. NUMBER OF WORKERS EMPLOYED	
c. ADDRESS OF ESTABLISHMENT (*street and number, city, State, and ZIP code*)	d. EMPLOYER REPRESEN-TATIVE TO CONTACT	e. PHONE NO.
f. TYPE OF ESTABLISHMENT (*factory, mine, wholesaler, etc.*)	g. IDENTIFY PRINCIPAL PRODUCT OR SERVICE	

h. THE ABOVE-NAMED EMPLOYER HAS ENGAGED IN AND IS ENGAGING IN UNFAIR LABOR PRACTICES WITHIN THE MEANING OF SECTION 8(a), SUBSECTIONS (1) AND _____ OF THE NATIONAL
(*list subsections*)
LABOR RELATIONS ACT, AND THESE UNFAIR LABOR PRACTICES ARE UNFAIR LABOR PRACTICES AFFECTING COMMERCE WITHIN THE MEANING OF THE ACT.

2. BASIS OF THE CHARGE (*be specific as to facts, names, addresses, plants involved, dates, places, etc.*)

BY THE ABOVE AND OTHER ACTS, THE ABOVE-NAMED EMPLOYER HAS INTERFERED WITH, RESTRAINED, AND COERCED EMPLOYEES IN THE EXERCISE OF THE RIGHTS GUARANTEED IN SECTION 7 OF THE ACT.

3. FULL NAME OF PARTY FILING CHARGE (*if labor organization, give full name, including local name and number*)

4a. ADDRESS (*street and number, city, State, and ZIP code*)	4b. TELEPHONE NO.

5. FULL NAME OF NATIONAL OR INTERNATIONAL LABOR ORGANIZATION OF WHICH IT IS AN AFFILIATE OR CONSTITUENT UNIT (*to be filled in when charge is filed by a labor organization*)

6. DECLARATION

I declare that I have read the above charge and that the statements therein are true to the best of my knowledge and belief.

By _____
(signature of respresentative or person filing charge)   (title, if any)

Address _____
(telephone number)   (date)

WILLFULLY FALSE STATEMENTS ON THIS CHARGE CAN BE PUNISHED BY FINE AND IMPRISONMENT
(*U.S. CODE, TITLE 18, SECTION 1001*)

practices, (2) enumerating the rights of employees as union members, (3) enumerating the rights of employers, and (4) allowing the president of the United States to temporarily bar national emergency strikes.

Unfair Union Labor Practices   The Taft-Hartley Act enumerated several labor practices that unions were prohibited from engaging in:

1. First, it banned unions from restraining or coercing employees from exercising their guaranteed bargaining rights. Some specific union actions the courts have held illegal under this provision include stating to an anti-union employee that he or she will lose his or her job once the union gains recognition, and issuing patently false statements during union organizing campaigns.

2. It is also an unfair labor practice for a union to cause an employer to discriminate in any way against an employee in order to encourage or discourage his or her membership in a union. In other words, the union cannot try to force an employer to fire a worker because he or she doesn't attend union meetings, opposes union policies, or refuses to join a union. There is one exception: Where a closed or union shop prevails (and union membership is therefore a prerequisite to employment), the union may demand discharge for a worker who fails to pay his or her initiation fees and dues.

3. It is an unfair labor practice for a union to refuse to bargain in good faith with the employer about wages, hours, and other employment conditions. Certain strikes and boycotts are also unfair practices.

4. It is an unfair labor practice for a union to engage in "featherbedding" (requiring an employer to pay an employee for services not performed).

Rights of Employees   The Taft-Hartley Act also protected the rights of employees against their unions. For example, many people felt that compulsory unionism violated the basic right of freedom of association. Legitimized by Taft-Hartley, new right-to-work laws sprang up in 19 states (mainly in the South and Southwest). These outlawed labor contracts that made union membership a condition for keeping one's job. In New York, for example, many printing firms have union shops. You can't work as a press operator unless you belong to a printers' union. In Florida, such union shops—except those covered by the Railway Labor Act—are illegal, and printing shops typically employ both union and nonunion press operators. Even today, union membership varies widely by state, from a high of 26.8% in New York to a low of 3.7% in South Carolina (other representative membership densities are California, 16.5%; Florida, 7.4%; Texas, 6.5%; Michigan, 23.9%; and Ohio, 19.4%).[16] This employee rights provision also allowed an employee to present grievances directly to the employer (without going through the union). And it required the employee's authorization before the union could have dues subtracted from his or her paycheck.

In general, the National Labor Relations Act does not restrain unions from unfair labor practices to the extent that it does employers. Unions may not restrain or coerce employees. However "violent or otherwise threatening behavior or clearly coercive or intimidating union activities are necessary before the NLRB will find an unfair labor practice."[17] Examples here would include physical assaults or threats of violence, economic reprisals, and mass picketing that restrains the lawful entry or leaving of a work site. In one typical case, *Pattern Makers vs. National Labor Relations Board*, the U.S. Supreme Court found the union guilty of an unfair labor practice when it tried to fine some members for resigning from the union and returning to work during a strike.[18]

Rights of Employers   The Taft-Hartley Act also explicitly gave employers certain rights. First, it gave them full freedom to express their views concerning union organization. For example, you as a manager can tell your employees that in your opinion unions are worthless, dangerous to the economy, and immoral. You can even, generally speaking, hint that unionization and subsequent high-wage demands might result in the permanent closing of the plant (but not its relocation). Employers can set forth the union's record concerning violence and corruption, if appropriate. In fact, the only major restraint is that employers must avoid threats, promises, coercion, and direct interference with workers who are trying to reach a decision. There can be no threat of reprisal or force or promise of benefit.[19]

Furthermore, the employer (1) cannot meet with employees on company time within 24 hours of an election or (2) suggest to employees that they vote against the union while they are at home or in the employer's office, although he or she can do so while in their work area or where they normally gather.

national emergency strikes
Strikes that might "imperil the national health and safety."

National Emergency Strikes   The Taft-Hartley Act also allows the U.S. president to intervene in **national emergency strikes**. These are strikes (for example, on the part of railroad workers) that might "imperil the national health and safety." The president may appoint a board of inquiry and, based on its report, apply for an injunction restraining the strike for 60 days. If the parties don't reach a settlement during that time, the president can have the injunction extended for another 20 days. During this last period, employees take a secret ballot to ascertain their willingness to accept the employer's last offer.

Period of Detailed Regulation of Internal Union Affairs: The Landrum-Griffin Act (1959)

Landrum-Griffin Act (1959)
The law aimed at protecting union members from possible wrongdoing on the part of their unions.

In the 1950s, Senate investigations revealed unsavory practices on the part of some unions, and the result was the **Landrum-Griffin Act** (officially, the **Labor Management Reporting and Disclosure Act) of 1959**. An overriding aim of this act was to protect union members from possible wrongdoing on the part of their unions. Like Taft-Hartley, it also amended the National Labor Relations (Wagner) Act.

First, the law contains a bill of rights for union members. Among other things, it provides for certain rights in the nomination of candidates for union office. It also affirms a member's right to sue his or her union and ensures that no member can be fined or suspended without due process, which includes a list of specific charges, time to prepare a defense, and a fair hearing.

This act also laid out rules regarding union elections. For example, national and international unions must elect officers at least once every five years, using some type of secret-ballot mechanism. And it regulates the kind of person who can serve as a union officer. For example, persons convicted of felonies (bribery, murder, and so on) are barred from holding union officer positions for a period of five years after conviction.

Senate investigators also discovered flagrant examples of employer wrongdoing. Employers and their "labor relations consultants" had bribed union agents and officers, for example. That had been a federal crime starting with the passage of the Taft-Hartley Act. But Landrum-Griffin greatly expanded the list of unlawful employer actions. For example, companies can no longer pay their own employees to entice them not to join the union. The act also requires reports from unions and employers covering such practices as the use of labor relations consultants.

Union laws like these aren't just issues for big companies like FedEx and GE. They're increasingly an issue for high-tech entrepreneurs too, as the following "When You're On Your Own" illustrates.

When You're On Your Own
HR for Line Managers and Entrepreneurs

New Economy Entrepreneurs and Unions

High-tech "new economy" entrepreneurs are getting an unexpected lesson in labor relations. For most of their relatively short corporate lives, they have assumed that new economy jobs like Web designer were immune from union efforts. But with several e-commerce firms (including Amazon.com) facing union organizing efforts, they've had to change those assumptions.

There are many reasons why these firms are not as immune to unions as their entrepreneur founders thought they'd be. For one thing, many employees at new economy online retailers such as Amazon.com are doing very "old economy" tasks like loading and unloading trucks and packing shipments. Even many of the Web designers, programmers, and other high-tech employees—who traditionally see themselves playing big roles in their dot-com companies—got increasingly frustrated as stock options lost most of their value in 2000–2001 and dot-coms went out of business or shrank drastically.

When it comes to attracting unions, many of these entrepreneurs have been their own worst enemies. Focusing on sales and meeting customer demand, many paid little attention to writing personnel policies, developing effective performance appraisal systems, or staying in touch with employees' concerns. As one labor attorney puts it, "they have been lax about overtime, pay scales, and just having an employee handbook with policies and procedures clearly defined. . . . The high-tech industry has always been so confident that none of their own would ever want the union that they've been amazingly ignorant of basic labor law." Even the entrepreneurs' love affairs with their intranets may work against them. For example, many store all personal information regarding employees in computer files that are easily accessed by employees who want to start union organizing campaigns.

What is an entrepreneur to do? Revise (or enact) written personnel policies and practices, so union organizers have less reason to view your firm as a loosely run and vulnerable target. Improve the security of employee records files. And (since unionization attempts in dot-coms tend to focus on support services such as call centers, distribution, and help desks)—one labor lawyer says—"don't lose touch with the people taking the calls. And don't think it is just about compensation. It is also the work environment. An hourly call center employee who punches a clock day after day while watching the engineers come and go as they please may get ideas."[20]

● THE UNION DRIVE AND ELECTION

Present examples of what to expect during the union drive and election.

It is through the union drive and election that a union tries to be recognized to represent employees. This process has five basic steps.

Step 1. Initial Contact

During the initial contact stage, the union determines the employees' interest in organizing, and establishes an organizing committee.

The initiative for the first contact between the employees and the union may come from the employees, from a union already representing other employees of the firm, or from a union representing workers elsewhere. In any case, there is an initial contact between a union representative and a few employees.

Once an employer becomes a target, a union official usually assigns a representative to assess employee interest. The representative visits the firm to determine whether enough employees are interested to make a union campaign worthwhile. He or she also identifies employees who would make good leaders in the organizing campaign and calls them together to create an organizing committee. The objective here is to educate the committee about the benefits of forming a union and the law and procedures involved in forming a local union.

The union must follow certain rules when it starts contacting employees. The law allows organizers to solicit employees for membership as long as the effort doesn't endanger the performance or safety of the employees. Therefore, much of the contact takes place off the job, for example, at home or at eating places near work. Organizers can also safely contact employees on company grounds during off hours (such as lunch or break time). Yet, in practice, there will be much informal organizing going on at the workplace as employees debate the merits of organizing. In any case, this initial contact stage may be deceptively quiet. Sometimes the first inkling management has of the campaign is the distribution or posting of handbills soliciting union membership.

Technology, in the form of e-mail, is affecting the organizing process. However, preventing union employees from sending pro-union e-mail messages on company e-mail is easier said than done. Prohibiting only union e-mail may violate NLRB decisions, for instance. And instituting a rule barring workers from using e-mail for all non-work-related topics may also be futile if the company actually does little to stop e-mail other than pro-union messages.

Labor Relations Consultants   Both management and unions now use outside advisers, and these labor relations consultants are increasingly influencing the unionization process. The consultants may be law firms, researchers, psychologists, labor relations specialists, or public relations firms. In any case, their role is to provide advice and related services not just when a vote is expected (although this is when most of them are used), but at other times, too. For the employer, the consultant's services may range from ensuring that the firm properly fills out routine forms to managing the whole union campaign. Unions may use public relations firms to improve their image, or specialists to manage corporate campaigns aimed at pressuring shareholders and creditors to get management to agree to the union's demands.

The widespread use of such consultants—only some of whom are actually lawyers—has raised the question of whether some have advised their clients to engage in activities that are illegal or questionable under labor laws. One tactic, for instance, is to delay the union vote with lengthy hearings at the NLRB. The longer the delay in the vote, they argue, the more time the employer has to drill anti-union propaganda into the employees. During these delays, employers can also try to eliminate employees who are not anti-union, and pack the bargaining unit with pro-management employees. Others accuse consultants of advising employers to lie to the NLRB, for example, by backdating memos in order to convince the board that the wage increase being offered was decided months before the union campaign ever began.[21]

Union Salting   Unions are not without creative ways to win elections. **Union salting** is an organizing tactic by which full-time undercover union organizers are hired by unwitting employers. A U.S. Supreme Court decision held the tactic to be legal.[22] The U.S. Supreme Court has also ruled that union salts are "employees" under the National Labor Relations Act, and the NLRB will require that employers pay salts if they fire them for trying to organize the workplace.[23] For employers, the solution is to make sure you know who you're hiring.[24]

However, employers must proceed with care. Recently, for instance, the National Labor Relations Board concluded that an employer did commit an unfair labor practice by refusing to consider hiring nine members of Plumbers and Pipe Fitters, Local 520. Not hiring the people simply because as members of the local union they might be pro-union or union salts would be discriminatory. On the other hand, if the

union salting
A union organizing tactic by which workers who are in fact employed full-time by a union as undercover organizers are hired by unwitting employers.

employer could show that it would not hire the applicants regardless of their union affiliation—perhaps because they didn't have the qualifications for the position, or others were more qualified—then the refusal to hire them is defensible.[25] The NLRB said its local office had to review each case to determine if the employer's decisions were nondiscriminatory.

Step 2. Obtaining Authorization Cards

For the union to petition the NLRB for the right to hold an election, it must show that a sizable number of employees may be interested in organizing. The next step is thus for union organizers to try to get the employees to sign **authorization cards**. Among other things, these usually authorize the union to seek a representation election and state that the employee has applied to join the union. Thirty percent of the eligible employees in an appropriate bargaining unit must sign before the union can petition the NLRB for an election.

authorization cards
In order to petition for a union election, the union must show that at least 30% of employees may be interested in being unionized. Employees indicate this interest by signing authorization cards.

During this stage, both union and management use various forms of propaganda. The union claims it can improve working conditions, raise wages, increase benefits, and generally get the workers better deals. Management can attack the union on ethical and moral grounds and cite the cost of union membership. Management can also explain its track record, express facts and opinions, and explain the law applicable to organizing campaigns. However, neither side can threaten, bribe, or coerce employees. And an employer may not make promises of benefits to employees or make unilateral changes in terms and conditions of employment that were not planned to be implemented prior to the onset of union organizing activity.

Management can take several steps with respect to the authorization cards themselves. For example, the NLRB ruled an employer may lawfully inform employees of their right to revoke their authorization cards, even when employees have not solicited such information. The employer can also distribute pamphlets that explain just how employees can revoke their cards. However, management can go no further than explaining to employees the procedure for card revocation and furnishing resignation language. The law prohibits any material assistance such as postage or stationery. The employer also cannot check to determine which employees have actually signed or revoked their authorization cards.

What else can you do to educate employees who have not yet decided whether to sign their cards? It is an unfair labor practice to tell employees they can't sign a card. What you can do is prepare supervisors so they can explain what the card actually authorizes the union to do. For example, the typical authorization card actually does three things. It lets the union seek a representation election (it can be used as evidence that 30% of your employees have an interest in organizing). It designates the union as a bargaining representative in all employment matters. And it states that the employee has applied for membership in the union and will be subject to union rules and bylaws. The latter is especially important. The union, for instance, may force the employee to picket and fine any member who does not comply with union instructions. Explaining the serious legal and practical implications of signing the card can thus be an effective management weapon.

One thing management should *not* do is look through signed authorization cards if confronted with them by union representatives. The NLRB could construe that as an unfair labor practice, as spying on those who signed. It could also later form the basis of a charge alleging discrimination due to union activity, if the firm subsequently disciplines someone who signed a card.

During this stage, unions can picket the company, subject to three constraints: (1) The union must file a petition for an election within 30 days after the start of picketing;

(2) the firm cannot already be lawfully recognizing another union; and (3) there cannot have been a valid NLRB election during the past 12 months. Unions today use the Internet to distribute and collect authorization cards.

Step 3. Hold a Hearing

Once the union collects the authorization cards, one of three things can occur. If the employer chooses not to contest *union recognition* at all, then the parties need no hearing, and a special "consent election" is held. If the employer chooses not to contest the union's *right to an election*, and/or the scope of the bargaining unit, and/or which employees are eligible to vote in the election, no hearing is needed and the parties can stipulate an election. If an employer *does* wish to contest the union's right, it can insist on a hearing to determine those issues. An employer's decision about whether to insist on a hearing is a strategic one based on the facts of each case and whether it feels it needs additional time to try to persuade a majority of its employees not to elect a union to represent them.

Most companies do contest the union's right to represent their employees, claiming that a significant number of them don't really want the union. It is at this point that the National Labor Relations Board gets involved. The union usually contacts the NLRB, which requests a hearing. The regional director of the NLRB then sends a hearing officer to investigate. The examiner sends both management and union a notice of representation hearing (NLRB Form 852; see Figure 15-2) that states the time and place of the hearing.

The hearing addresses several issues. First, does the record indicate there is enough evidence to hold an election? (For example, did 30% or more of the employees in an appropriate bargaining unit sign the authorization cards?) Second, the examiner must decide what the bargaining unit will be. The latter is a crucial matter for the union, for employees, and for the employer. The **bargaining unit** is the group of employees that the union will be authorized to represent and bargain for collectively. If the entire organization is the bargaining unit, the union will represent all nonsupervisory, nonmanagerial, and nonconfidential employees, even though the union may be oriented mostly toward blue-collar workers. (Professional and nonprofessional employees can be included in the same bargaining unit only if the professionals agree to it.) If your firm disagrees with the examiner's decision regarding the bargaining unit, it can challenge the decision. This will require a separate step and NLRB ruling.

The NLRB hearing addresses other questions. These include: "Does the employer qualify for coverage by the NLRB?" "Is the union a labor organization within the meaning of the National Labor Relations Act?" and, "Do any existing collective bargaining agreements or prior elections bar the union from holding a representation election?"

If the results of the hearing are favorable for the union, the NLRB will order holding an election. It will issue a Notice of Election (NLRB Form 707) to that effect, for the employer to post.

bargaining unit
The group of employees the union will be authorized to represent.

Step 4. The Campaign

During the campaign that precedes the election, union and employer appeal to employees for their votes. The union emphasizes that it will prevent unfairness, set up grievance and seniority systems, and improve unsatisfactory wages. Union strength, they'll say, will give employees a voice in determining wages and working conditions. Management will stress that improvements like the union promises don't require unionization, and that wages are equal to or better than they would be with a union. Management will also emphasize the financial cost of union dues; the fact that the union is an "outsider"; and that if the union wins, a strike may follow. It can even attack the union on ethical and moral grounds, while insisting that employees will not be as well off and may lose freedom. But neither side can threaten, bribe, or coerce employees.

Figure 15-2
NLRB Form 852: Notice of Representation Hearing

FORM NLRB-852
(6-61)

UNITED STATES OF AMERICA
BEFORE THE NATIONAL LABOR RELATIONS BOARD

Case No.

NOTICE OF REPRESENTATION HEARING

The Petitioner, above named, having heretofore filed a Petition pursuant to Section 9 (c) of the National Labor Relations Act, as amended, 29 U.S.C. Sec 151 et seq., copy of which Petition is hereto attached, and it appearing that a question affecting commerce has arisen concerning the representation of employees described by such Petition.

YOU ARE HEREBY NOTIFIED that, pursuant to Section 3(b) and 9(c) of the Act, on the day of   , 20   , at

a hearing will be conducted before a hearing officer of the National Labor Relations Board upon the question of representation affecting commerce which has arisen, at which time and place the parties will have the right to appear in person or otherwise, and give testimony.

Signed at   on the   day of   , 20

Regional Director, Region
National Labor Relations Board

Step 5. The Election

The election is held within 30 to 60 days after the NLRB issues its Decision and Direction of Election. The election is by secret ballot; the NLRB provides the ballots (see Figure 15-3), voting booth, and ballot box, and counts the votes and certifies the results.

The union becomes the employees' representative if it wins the election, and winning means getting a majority of the votes *cast*, not a majority of the total workers in the bargaining unit. (Also keep in mind that if an employer commits an unfair labor practice, the NLRB may reverse a "no union" election. As representatives of their employer, supervisors must therefore be careful not to commit unfair practices.) Several things influence whether the union wins the certification election. Unions have a higher probability of success in geographic areas with a higher percentage of union workers, in part because union employees enjoy higher wages and benefits. High unemployment seems to lead to poorer results for the

Figure 15-3
Sample NLRB Ballot

UNITED STATES OF AMERICA

National Labor Relations Board

OFFICIAL SECRET BALLOT

FOR CERTAIN EMPLOYEES OF

_____

Do you wish to be represented for purposes of collective bargaining by —

_____

MARK AN "S" IN THE SQUARE OF YOUR CHOICE

YES

NO

DO NOT SIGN THIS BALLOT. Fold and drop in ballot box.
If you spoil this ballot return it to the Board Agent for a new one.

union, perhaps because employees fear that unionization efforts might result in reduced job security or employer retaliation. Unions usually carefully pick the size of their bargaining unit (all clerical employees in the company, only those at one facility, and so on), because it's clear that the larger the bargaining unit, the smaller the probability of union victory. The more workers vote, the less likely a union victory, probably because more workers who are not strong supporters vote. The union is important, too: The Teamsters union is less likely to win a representation election than other unions, for instance.[26]

How to Lose an NLRB Election

The unions won 55.9% of elections in 2002, up slightly from 54.1% in 2001.[27] According to expert Mathew Goodfellow, there is no sure way employers can win elections. However, there are five sure ways to lose one.[28]

Describe five ways to lose an NLRB election.

Reason 1. Asleep at the Switch   In one study, in 68% of the companies that lost to the union, executives were caught unaware. In these companies, turnover and absenteeism had increased, productivity was erratic, and safety was poor. Grievance procedures were rare. When the first reports of authorization cards began trickling back to top managers, they usually responded with a barrage of letters describing how the company was "one big family" and calling for a "team effort." As Goodfellow observes,

Yet the best strategy is to not be caught asleep in the first place: Overall, prudence dictates that management spend time and effort even when the atmosphere is calm testing the temperature of employee sentiments and finding ways to remove irritants. Doing that cuts down on the possibility that an election will ever take place.[29]

Reason 2. Appointing a Committee   Of the losing companies, 36% formed a committee to manage the campaign. According to the expert, there are three problems in doing so: (1) Promptness is essential in an election situation, and committees are notorious for moving slowly. (2) Most committee members are NLRB neophytes. Their views therefore are mostly reflections of wishful thinking rather than experience. (3) A committee's decision is usually a compromise decision. The result is often close to the most conservative opinion—but not necessarily the most knowledgeable or most effective one. This expert suggests giving full responsibility to a single, decisive executive. A human resource director and a consultant or adviser with broad experience in labor relations should in turn assist this person.

Reason 3. Concentrating on Money and Benefits

In 54% of the elections studied, the company lost because top management concentrated on the wrong issues: money and benefits. As this expert puts it:

> *Employees may want more money, but quite often if they feel the company treats them fairly, decently, and honestly, they are satisfied with reasonable, competitive rates and benefits. It is only when they feel ignored, uncared for, and disregarded that money becomes a major issue to express their dissatisfaction.*[30]

Reason 4. Industry Blind Spots

The researcher found that in some industries, employees felt more ignored and disregarded than in others. In highly automated industries (such as paper manufacturing and automobiles), there was some tendency for executives to ignore hourly employees, although this is changing today as firms implement more quality improvement programs. Here (as in reason 3), the solution is to pay more attention to employees' needs and attitudes.

Reason 5. Delegating Too Much to Divisions

For companies with plants scattered around the country, organizing several of the plants gives the union a wedge to tempt other plants' workers. Unionizing one or more plants tends to lead to unionizing others. Part of the solution is to keep the first four reasons above in mind, and thus diminish the union's ability to organize those first few plants. Also, don't abdicate all personnel and industrial relations decisions to plant managers.[31] Dealing effectively with unions—monitoring employees' attitudes, reacting properly when the union appears, and so on—generally requires centralized guidance from the main office and its HR staff.

The Supervisor's Role

Supervisors are an employer's first line of defense when it comes to the unionizing effort. They are often in the best position to sense evolving employee attitude problems, for instance, and to discover the first signs of union activity. Unfortunately, there's another side to that coin: They can also inadvertently take actions that hurt their employer's union-related efforts.

Supervisors therefore need special training. Specifically, they must be knowledgeable about what they can and can't do to legally hamper organizing activities. Unfair labor practices could (1) cause the NLRB to hold a new election after your company has won a previous election, or (2) cause your company to forfeit the second election and go directly to contract negotiation.

In one case, a plant superintendent reacted to a union's initial organizing attempt by prohibiting distribution of union literature in the plant's lunchroom. Since solicitation of off-duty workers in nonwork areas is generally legal, the company subsequently allowed the union to post union literature on the company's bulletin board and to distribute union literature in nonworking areas inside the plant. However, the NLRB still ruled that the initial act of prohibiting distribution of the literature was an unfair labor practice, one not "made right" by the company's subsequent efforts. The NLRB used the superintendent's action as one reason for invalidating an election that the company had won. The "When You're On Your Own" feature provides guidelines for the front-line manager.

Your Role in the Unionizing Effort

One company helps its supervisors remember what they may and may not do with respect to unionization with the acronyms TIPS and FORE.[32] For example, the manager should remember TIPS for what he or she *may not* do:

T—Threaten. Do not threaten or imply the company will take adverse action of any kind for supporting the unions.[33] Do not threaten to terminate employees because of their union activities, and don't threaten to close the facility if the union wins the election.

I—Interrogate. Don't interrogate or ask employees their position concerning unions, or how they are going to vote in an election.

P—Promise. Don't promise employees a pay increase, special favors, better benefits, or promotions.

S—Don't spy at any union activities or attend a union meeting, even if invited.

And to remember what the supervisor *may do* to discourage unionization, remember FORE:

F—Facts. Do tell employees that by signing the authorization card the union may become their legal representative in matters regarding wages and hours, and do tell them that by signing a union authorization card it does not mean they must vote for the union.

O—Opinion. You may tell employees that management doesn't believe in third-party representation, and that management believes in having an open-door policy to air grievances.

R—Rules. Provide factually correct advice such as telling employees that the law permits the company to permanently replace them if there's a strike, and that the union can't make the company agree to anything it does not want to during negotiations.

E—Experience. The supervisor may share personal experiences he or she may have had with a union.[34]

Figure 15-4 summarizes some other things to avoid.

**Figure 15-4
Union Avoidance:
What Not to Do**

Source: From the BLR Newsletter "Best Practices in HR." Copyright © 2004, *Business & Legal Reports, Inc.*, 141 Mill Rock Road East, Old Saybrook, CT. Reprinted with permission of the publisher.

Human resources professionals must be very careful to do the following during union activities at their companies:

- Watch what you say. Angry feelings of the moment may get you in trouble.

- Never threaten workers with what you will do or what will happen if a union comes in. Do not say, for example, that the business will close or move, that wages will go down or overtime will be eliminated, that there will be layoffs, etc.

- Don't tell union sympathizers that they will suffer in any way for their support. Don't terminate or discipline workers for engaging in union activities.

- Don't interrogate workers about union sympathizers or organizers.

- Don't ask workers to remove union screensavers or campaign buttons if you allow these things for other organizations.

- Don't treat pro-union or anti-union workers any differently.

- Don't transfer workers on the basis of union affiliation or sympathies.

- Don't ask workers how they are going to vote or how others may vote.

- Don't ask employees about union meetings or any matters related to unions. You can listen, but don't ask for any details.

- Don't promise workers benefits, promotions, or anything else if they vote against the union.

- Avoid becoming involved—in any way—in the details of the union's election or campaign, and don't participate in any petition movement against the union.

- Don't give financial aid or any support to any unions.

Any one of these practices may result in a finding of "unfair labor practices," which may in turn result in recognition of a union without an election, as well as fines for your company.

Rules Regarding Literature and Solicitation

There are steps you can take to legally restrict union organizing activity.[35]

1. Employers can always bar nonemployees from soliciting employees during their work time—that is, when the employee is on duty and not on a break. Thus, if the company cafeteria is open to whomever is on the premises, union organizers can solicit off-duty employees who are in the cafeteria, but not the cafeteria workers (such as cooks) who are not on a break.

2. Employers can usually stop employees from soliciting other employees for any purpose if one or both employees are on paid-duty time and not on a break.

3. Most employers (not including retail stores, shopping centers, and certain other employers) can bar nonemployees from the building's interiors and work areas as a right of private property owners. They can also sometimes bar nonemployees from exterior private areas—such as parking lots—if there is a business reason (such as safety) and the reason is not just to interfere with union organizers.

    Whether or not employers must give union representatives permission to organize on employer-owned property at shopping malls is a matter of legal debate. The U.S. Supreme Court ruled in *Lechmere, Inc. v. National Labor Relations Board* that employers may bar nonemployees from their property if the nonemployees have reasonable alternative means of communicating their message to the intended audience. However, if the employer lets other organizations like the Salvation Army set up at their workplaces, the NLRB may view discriminating against the union organizers as an unfair labor practice.[36]

4. Employers can deny on- or off-duty employees access to interior or exterior areas only if they can show the rule is required for reasons of production, safety, or discipline.

Such restrictions are valid only if the employer doesn't discriminate against the union. For example, if the employer lets employees collect money for wedding, shower, and baby gifts, to sell Avon products or Tupperware, or to engage in other solicitation during their working time, it may not be able to lawfully prohibit them from union soliciting during work time. To do so would discriminate based on union activity, which is an unfair labor practice. Here are two examples of specific rules aimed at limiting union organizing (or other) activity:

Solicitation of employees on company property during working time interferes with the efficient operation of our business. Nonemployees are not permitted to solicit employees on company property for any purpose. Except in break areas where both employees are on break or off the clock, no employee may solicit another employee during working time for any purpose.

Distribution of literature on company property not only creates a litter problem but also distracts us from our work. Nonemployees are not allowed to distribute literature on company property. Except in the performance of his or her job, an employee may not distribute literature unless both the distributor and the recipient are off the clock or on authorized break in a break area or off company premises. Special exceptions to these rules may be made by the company for especially worthwhile causes such as United Way, but written permission must first be obtained and the solicitation will be permitted only during break periods.[37]

Decertification Elections: Ousting the Union

Winning an election and signing an agreement do not necessarily mean that the union is in the company to stay. The same law that grants employees the right to unionize also gives them a way to legally terminate their union's right to represent them. The process

The New Workplace

Unions Go Global

Any company that thinks it can avoid unionization by sending manufacturing and jobs abroad is sorely mistaken.[41] Today, as we've seen, most businesses are "going global," and regional trade treaties like the North American Free Trade Agreement (NAFTA) are further boosting the business done by firms abroad. This fact is not lost on unions, some of which are already expanding their influence abroad.

For example, U.S. unions are helping Mexican unions to organize, especially in U.S.-owned factories. Thus, the United Electrical Workers is subsidizing organizers at Mexican plants of the General Electric Company. And when the Campbell Soup Company threatened to move some operations to Mexico, the Farm Labor Organizing Committee, a midwestern union, discouraged the move by helping its Mexican counterpart win a stronger contract, one that would have cost Campbell Soup higher wages if it made the move.

Reebok's experience provides another example of how unions reach across national boundaries. It has been working with the AFL-CIO to make the unions representing its overseas factories' employees more effective in protecting its workers' human rights.[42] Safety and work conditions are thus improving.

U.S. unions gain several things by forming alliances with unions abroad. By helping workers in other countries unionize, they help raise the wages and living standards of local workers. That may in turn discourage corporate flight from the United States in search of low wages. Unions also help their own positions in the United States with the added leverage they get from having unions abroad that can help them fight their corporate campaigns—campaigns aimed at swaying the views of the employer's owners, directors and banks.

---

decertification
Legal process for employees to terminate a union's right to represent them.

is **decertification**. There are around 450 to 500 decertification elections each year, of which unions usually win around 30%.[38] That's actually a more favorable rate for management than the rate for the original, representation elections.

Decertification campaigns don't differ much from certification campaigns.[39] The union organizes membership meetings and house-to-house visits, mails literature into the homes, and uses phone calls, NLRB appeals, and (sometimes) threats and harassment to win the election.[40] For its part, management uses meetings—including one-on-one meetings, small-group meetings, and meetings with entire units—as well as legal or expert assistance, letters, improved working conditions, and subtle or not-so-subtle threats to try to influence the votes.

"The New Workplace" illustrates some global aspects of union–management relations.

● THE COLLECTIVE BARGAINING PROCESS

What Is Collective Bargaining?

When and if the union becomes your employees' representative, a day is set for management and labor to meet and negotiate a labor agreement. This agreement will contain specific provisions covering wages, hours, and working conditions.

collective bargaining
The process through which representatives of management and the union meet to negotiate a labor agreement.

What exactly is **collective bargaining**? According to the National Labor Relations Act:

> *For the purpose of [this act,] to bargain collectively is the performance of the mutual obligation of the employer and the representative of the employees to meet at reasonable times and confer in good faith with respect to wages, hours, and terms and conditions of*

employment, or the negotiation of an agreement, or any question arising thereunder, and the execution of a written contract incorporating any agreement reached if requested by either party, but such obligation does not compel either party to agree to a proposal or require the making of a concession.

In plain language, this means that both management and labor are required by law to negotiate wage, hours, and terms and conditions of employment "in good faith." In a moment, we will see that the specific terms that are negotiable (since "wages, hours, and conditions of employment" are too broad to be useful in practice) have been clarified by a series of court decisions.

What Is Good Faith?

5 Illustrate with examples bargaining that is not in good faith.

good faith bargaining
Both parties are making every reasonable effort to arrive at agreement; proposals are being matched with counterproposals.

Good faith bargaining is the cornerstone of effective labor–management relations. It means that both parties communicate and negotiate, that they match proposals with counterproposals, and that both make every reasonable effort to arrive at an agreement. It does not mean that one party compels another to agree to a proposal. Nor does it require that either party make any specific concessions (although as a practical matter, some may be necessary).

When is bargaining not in good faith? As interpreted by the NLRB and the courts, a violation of the requirement for good faith bargaining may include the following:

1. *Surface bargaining.* Going through the motions of bargaining without any real intention of completing a formal agreement.
2. *Inadequate concessions.* Unwillingness to compromise, even though no one is required to make a concession.
3. *Inadequate proposals and demands.* The NLRB considers the advancement of proposals to be a positive factor in determining overall good faith.
4. *Dilatory tactics.* The law requires that the parties meet and "confer at reasonable times and intervals." Obviously, refusal to meet with the union does not satisfy the positive duty imposed on the employer.
5. *Imposing conditions.* Attempts to impose conditions that are so onerous or unreasonable as to indicate bad faith.
6. *Making unilateral changes in conditions.* This is a strong indication that the employer is not bargaining with the required intent of reaching an agreement.
7. *Bypassing the representative.* The duty of management to bargain in good faith involves, at a minimum, recognition that the union representative is the one with whom the employer must deal in conducting negotiations.
8. *Committing unfair labor practices during negotiations.* Such practices may reflect poorly upon the good faith of the guilty party.
9. *Withholding information.* An employer must supply the union with information, upon request, to enable it to understand and intelligently discuss the issues raised in bargaining.
10. *Ignoring bargaining items.* Refusal to bargain on a mandatory item (one must bargain over these) or insistence on a permissive item (one may bargain over these).[43]

Of course, requiring good faith bargaining doesn't mean that negotiations can't grind to a halt. For example, Northwest Airlines wouldn't let its negotiators meet with mechanics' union representatives because, Northwest said, the union didn't respond to company proposals the last three times they met.[44] Claiming that Bryant College negotiators were not sufficiently responsive with respect to wages and benefits, the Service Employees International Union, Local 134, filed an unfair labor practice claiming Bryant failed to negotiate in good faith.[45]

The Negotiating Team

Both union and management send a negotiating team to the bargaining table, and both teams usually go into the bargaining sessions having "done their homework." Union representatives will have sounded out union members on their desires and conferred with representatives of related unions.

Management uses several techniques to prepare for bargaining. First, it prepares the data on which to build its bargaining position.[46] It compiles data on pay and benefits that include comparisons with local pay rates and to rates paid for similar jobs within the industry. Data on the distribution of the workforce (in terms of age, sex, and seniority, for instance) are also important, because these factors determine what the company will actually pay out in benefits. Internal economic data regarding cost of benefits, overall earnings levels, and the amount and cost of overtime are important as well.

Management will also "cost" the current labor contract and determine the increased cost—total, per employee, and per hour—of the union's demands. It will use information from grievances and feedback from supervisors to determine what the union's demands might be, and prepare counteroffers and arguments.[47] Other popular tactics are attitude surveys to test employee reactions to various sections of the contract that management may feel require change, and informal conferences with local union leaders to discuss the operational effectiveness of the contract and to send up trial balloons on management ideas for change.

Bargaining Items

Labor law sets out categories of items that are subject to bargaining: These are mandatory, voluntary, and illegal items.

voluntary bargaining items
Items in collective bargaining over which bargaining is neither illegal nor mandatory—neither party can be compelled against its wishes to negotiate over those items.

Voluntary (or permissible) bargaining items are neither mandatory nor illegal; they become a part of negotiations only through the joint agreement of both management and union. Neither party can compel the other to negotiate over voluntary items. You cannot hold up signing a contract because the other party refuses to bargain on a voluntary item.

illegal bargaining items
Items in collective bargaining that are forbidden by law; for example, a clause agreeing to hire "union members exclusively" would be illegal in a right-to-work state.

Illegal bargaining items are forbidden by law. A clause agreeing to hire union members exclusively would be illegal in a right-to-work state, for example.

mandatory bargaining items
Items in collective bargaining that a party must bargain over if they are introduced by the other party—for example, pay.

Table 15-1 presents some of the 70 or so **mandatory bargaining items**, over which bargaining is mandatory under the law. They include wages, hours, rest periods, layoffs, transfers, benefits, and severance pay. Others, such as drug testing, are added as the law evolves.

Bargaining Stages

The actual bargaining typically goes through several stages.[48] First, each side presents its demands. At this stage, both parties are usually quite far apart on some issues. Second, there is a reduction of demands. At this stage, each side trades off some of its demands to gain others. Third come the subcommittee studies; the parties form joint subcommittees to try to work out reasonable alternatives. Fourth, the parties reach an informal settlement, and each group goes back to its sponsor. Union representatives check informally with their superiors and the union members; management representatives check with top management. Finally, once everything is in order, the parties fine-tune and sign a formal agreement.

Table 15-1

Bargaining Items

Mandatory	Permissible	Illegal
Rates of pay	Indemnity bonds	Closed shop
Wages	Management rights as to union affairs	Separation of employees based on race
Hours of employment		
Overtime pay	Pension benefits of retired employees	Discriminatory treatment
Shift differentials	Scope of the bargaining unit	
Holidays		
Vacations	Including supervisors in the contract	
Severance pay		
Pensions	Additional parties to the contract such as the international union	
Insurance benefits		
Profit-sharing plans	Use of union label	
Christmas bonuses	Settlement of unfair labor changes	
Company housing, meals, and discounts	Prices in cafeteria	
Employee security	Continuance of past contract	
Job performance		
Union security	Membership of bargaining team	
Management–union relationship	Employment of strike breaker	
Drug testing of employees		

Source: Michael R. Carrell and Christina Heavrin, *Labor Relations and Collective Bargaining: Cases, Practices, and Law* (Upper Saddle River, NJ: Prentice Hall, 2001), p. 177.

Bargaining Hints

Expert Reed Richardson has the following advice for bargainers:

1. Be sure to set clear objectives for every bargaining item, and be sure you understand the reason for each.
2. Do not hurry.
3. When in doubt, caucus with your associates.
4. Be well prepared with firm data supporting your position.
5. Always strive to keep some flexibility in your position.
6. Don't concern yourself just with what the other party says and does; find out why.
7. Respect the importance of face saving for the other party.
8. Be alert to the real intentions of the other party—not only for goals, but also for priorities.

9. Be a good listener.

10. Build a reputation for being fair but firm.

11. Learn to control your emotions and use them as a tool.

12. As you make each bargaining move, be sure you know its relationship to all other moves.

13. Measure each move against your objectives.

14. Pay close attention to the wording of every clause negotiated; they are often a source of grievances.

15. Remember that collective bargaining is a compromise process. There is no such thing as having all the pie.

16. Try to understand people and their personalities.

17. Consider the impact of present negotiations on those in future years.[49]

Impasses, Mediation, and Strikes

impasse
Collective bargaining situation that occurs when the parties are not able to move further toward settlement, usually because one party is demanding more than the other will offer.

In collective bargaining, an **impasse** occurs when the parties are not able to move further toward settlement. An impasse usually occurs because one party is demanding more than the other will offer. Sometimes an impasse can be resolved through a third party—a disinterested person such as a mediator or arbitrator. If the impasse is not resolved in this way, the union may call a work stoppage, or strike, to put pressure on management.

mediation
Intervention in which a neutral third party tries to assist the principals in reaching agreement.

Third-Party Involvement   Negotiators use three types of third-party interventions to overcome an impasse: mediation, fact finding, and arbitration. With **mediation**, a neutral third party tries to assist the principals in reaching agreement. The mediator usually holds meetings with each party to determine where each stands regarding its position, and then uses this information to find common ground for further bargaining. The mediator is always a go-between, and does not have the authority to dictate terms or make concessions. He or she communicates assessments of the likelihood of a strike, the possible settlement packages available, and the like.

fact finder
A neutral party who studies the issues in a dispute and makes a public recommendation for a reasonable settlement.

In certain situations, as in a national emergency dispute, a fact finder may be appointed. A **fact finder** is a neutral party who studies the issues in a dispute and makes a public recommendation for a reasonable settlement.[50] Presidential emergency fact-finding boards have successfully resolved impasses in certain critical transportation disputes.

arbitration
The most definitive type of third-party intervention, in which the arbitrator usually has the power to determine and dictate the settlement terms.

Arbitration is the most definitive type of third-party intervention, because the arbitrator often has the power to determine and dictate the settlement terms. Unlike mediation and fact finding, arbitration can guarantee a solution to an impasse. With *binding arbitration*, both parties are committed to accepting the arbitrator's award. With *nonbinding arbitration*, they are not. Arbitration may also be voluntary or compulsory (in other words, imposed by a government agency). In the United States, voluntary binding arbitration is the most prevalent.

There are two main topics of arbitration. *Interest arbitration* always centers on working out a labor agreement; the parties use it when such agreements do not yet exist or when one or both parties are seeking to change the agreement. *Rights arbitration* really means "contract interpretation arbitration." It usually involves interpreting existing contract terms, for instance, when an employee questions the employer's right to have taken some disciplinary action.[51]

strike
A withdrawal of labor.

economic strike
A strike that results from a failure to agree on the terms of a contract that involve wages, benefits, and other conditions of employment.

unfair labor practice strike
A strike aimed at protesting illegal conduct by the employer.

wildcat strike
An unauthorized strike occurring during the term of a contract.

sympathy strike
A strike that takes place when one union strikes in support of the strike of another.

picketing
Having employees carry signs announcing their concerns near the employer's place of business.

Strikes   A **strike** is a withdrawal of labor, and there are four main types of strikes. An **economic strike** results from a failure to agree on the terms of a contract. Unions call **unfair labor practice strikes** to protest illegal conduct by the employer. A **wildcat strike** is an unauthorized strike occurring during the term of a contract. A **sympathy strike** occurs when one union strikes in support of the strike of another union.[52] For example, in sympathy with employees of the *Detroit News*, *Detroit Free Press*, and *USA Today*, the United Auto Workers enforced a nearly six-year boycott that prevented the papers from being sold at Detroit-area auto plants, cutting sales by about 20,000 to 30,000 copies a day.[53]

The number of major work stoppages (those involving 1,000 workers or more) held fairly steady (between 20 and 40) during the 1990s, reaching a record low of 19 in 2002. These numbers are down dramatically from the 1960s and 1970s, when the number of work stoppages peaked at about 400 per year, between 1965 and 1975.

Picketing, or having employees carry signs announcing their concerns near the employer's place of business, is one of the first activities to occur during a strike. Its purpose is to inform the public about the existence of the labor dispute and often to encourage others to refrain from doing business with the struck employer.

Employers can make several responses when they become the object of a strike. One is to shut down the affected area and halt operations until the strike is over. A second is to contract out work in order to blunt the effects of the strike. A third response is to continue operations, perhaps using supervisors and other nonstriking workers to fill in for the striking workers. A fourth alternative is hiring replacements for the strikers.

Diminished union leverage plus competitive pressures now prompt more employers to *replace* (or at least consider replacing) *strikers* with permanent replacement workers. One study of HR managers found that of those responding, 18% "would not consider striker replacements" in the event of a strike, while 31% called it "not very likely," 23% "somewhat likely" and 21% "very likely."[54]

Employers generally can replace strikers. In one very important labor relations case known as *Mackay*, the U.S. Supreme Court ruled that while the National Labor Relations Act does prohibit employers from interfering with employees' right to strike, employers still have the right to continue their operations and, therefore, to replace strikers. Subsequent decisions by the National Labor Relations Board put some limitations on *Mackay*. For example, employers cannot permanently replace strikers who are protesting unfair labor practices, cannot grant replacement workers pay raises not offered to strikers, and must rehire strikers who apply for reinstatement unconditionally.

When a strike is imminent, plans must be made to deal with it. For example, as negotiations between the Hibbing Taconite Steel Plant in Minnesota and the United Steelworkers of America headed toward a deadline, the firm began preparations that included bringing in security workers and trailers to house them.

Two experts say that following these guidelines can minimize confusion:

- Pay all striking employees what you owe them on the first day of the strike.
- Secure the facility. Management should control access to the property. The company should consider hiring guards to protect replacements coming to and from work and to watch and control the picketers, if necessary.

Janitors march through the streets of Long Beach, California, during a strike. Placards and t-shirts display their demands in English and Spanish, and the march through the streets brings the strike to public attention.

▮ Notify all customers, and prepare a standard official response to all queries.

▮ Contact all suppliers and other persons who will have to cross the picket line. Establish alternative methods of obtaining supplies.

▮ Make arrangements for overnight stays in the facility and for delivered meals in case the occasion warrants such action.

▮ Notify the local unemployment office of your need for replacement workers.

▮ Photograph the facility before, during, and after picketing. If necessary, install videotape equipment and devices to monitor picket line misconduct.

▮ Record all facts concerning strikers' demeanor and activities and such incidents as violence, threats, mass pickets, property damage, or problems. Record the police response to requests for assistance.

▮ Gather the following evidence: number of pickets and their names; time, date, and location of picketing; wording on every sign carried by pickets; and descriptions of picket cars and license numbers.[55]

Other Alternatives   Management and labor each have other weapons they can use to try to break an impasse and achieve their aims. The union, for example, may resort to a corporate campaign. A **corporate campaign** is an organized effort by the union that exerts pressure on the employer by pressuring the company's other unions, shareholders, corporate directors, customers, creditors, and government agencies, often directly. Thus, the union might surprise individual members of the board of directors by picketing their homes, and organizing a **boycott** of the company's banks.[56]

The Web is another potent union tool. For example, when the Hotel Employees and Restaurant Employees Union, Local 2, wanted to turn up the heat on the San Francisco Marriott, it launched a new Web site. The site explains the union's eight-month boycott and provides a helpful list of union-backed hotels where prospective guests can stay. It also lists organizations that decided to stay elsewhere in response to the boycott.[57]

Inside games are another union tactic, one often used in conjunction with corporate campaigns. **Inside games** are union efforts to convince employees to impede or to disrupt production—for example, by slowing the work pace, refusing to work overtime, filing mass charges with government agencies, refusing to do work without receiving detailed instructions from supervisors, and engaging in other disruptive activities such as sick-outs.[58] Inside games are basically strikes—albeit "strikes" in which the employees are being supported by the company, which continues to pay them. In one inside game at Caterpillar's Aurora, Illinois, plant, United Auto Workers' grievances in the final stage before arbitration rose from 22 to 336. The effect was to clog the grievance procedure and tie up workers and management in unproductive endeavors on company time.[59]

For their part, employers can try to break an impasse with lockouts. A **lockout** is a refusal by the employer to provide opportunities to work. It (sometimes literally) locks out employees and prohibits them from doing their jobs (and getting paid). The NLRB generally doesn't view lockouts as an unfair labor practice. For example, if your product is a perishable one (such as vegetables), then a lockout may be a legitimate tactic to neutralize or decrease union power. The NLRB views lockouts as an unfair labor practice only when the employer acts for a prohibited purpose. It is not a prohibited purpose to try to bring about a settlement on terms favorable to the employer. Lockouts are not widely used today; employers are usually reluctant to cease operations when employees are willing to continue working (even though there may be an impasse at the bargaining table).

---

corporate campaign
An organized effort by the union that exerts pressure on the corporation by pressuring the company's other unions, shareholders, directors, customers, creditors, and government agencies, often directly.

boycott
The combined refusal by employees and other interested parties to buy or use the employer's products.

inside games
Union efforts to convince employees to impede or to disrupt production—for example, by slowing the work pace.

lockout
A refusal by the employer to provide opportunities to work.

Both employers and unions can seek an injunction from the courts if they believe the other side is taking actions that could cause irreparable harm to the other party. An **injunction** is a court order compelling a party or parties either to resume or to desist from a certain action.[60]

injunction
A court order compelling a party or parties either to resume or to desist from a certain action.

The Contract Agreement

The actual contract agreement may be a 20- or 30-page document; or it may be even longer. It may contain just general declarations of policy, or detailed rules and procedures. The tendency today is toward the longer, more detailed contract. This is largely a result of the increased number of items the agreements have been covering.

The main sections of a typical contract cover subjects such as these:

(1) management rights, (2) union security and automatic payroll dues deduction, (3) grievance procedures, (4) arbitration of grievances, (5) disciplinary procedures, (6) compensation rates, (7) hours of work and overtime, (8) benefits: vacations, holidays, insurance, pensions, (9) health and safety provisions, (10) employee security seniority provisions, and (11) contract expiration date.

Develop a grievance procedure.

● GRIEVANCES

Hammering out a labor agreement is not the last step in collective bargaining. No labor contract can cover all contingencies and answer all questions. For example, suppose the contract says you can only discharge an employee for "just cause." You subsequently discharge someone for speaking back to you in harsh terms. Was it within your rights to discharge this person? Was speaking back to you harshly "just cause"?

grievance
Any factor involving wages, hours, or conditions of employment that is used as a complaint against the employer.

The labor contract's **grievance** procedure usually handles problems like these. This procedure provides an orderly system whereby both employer and union determine whether some action violated the contract.[61] It is the vehicle for administering the contract on a day-to-day basis. The grievance process allows both parties to interpret and give meaning to various clauses, and transforms the contract into a "living organism." Remember, though, that this day-to-day collective bargaining involves interpretation only; it usually doesn't involve negotiating new terms or altering existing ones.

Sources of Grievances

From a practical point of view, it is probably easier to list those items that *don't* precipitate grievances than to list the ones that do. Employees may use just about any factor involving wages, hours, or conditions of employment as the basis of a grievance.

However, certain grievances are more serious, since they're usually more difficult to settle. Discipline cases and seniority problems including promotions, transfers, and layoffs would top this list. Others would include grievances growing out of job evaluations and work assignments, overtime, vacations, incentive plans, and holidays.[62] Here are four examples of grievances:

- *Absenteeism.* An employer fired an employee for excessive absences. The employee filed a grievance stating that there had been no previous warnings or discipline related to excessive absences.

- ▪ *Insubordination.* An employee on two occasions refused to obey a supervisor's order to meet with him, unless a union representative was present at the meeting. As a result, the employee was discharged and subsequently filed a grievance protesting the discharge.
- ▪ *Overtime.* The employer discontinued Sunday overtime work after a department was split. Employees affected filed a grievance protesting loss of the overtime work.
- ▪ *Plant rules.* The plant had a posted rule barring employees from eating or drinking during unscheduled breaks. The employees filed a grievance claiming the rule was arbitrary.[63]

A grievance is often a symptom of an underlying problem. Sometimes, bad relationships between supervisors and subordinates are to blame: This is often the cause of grievances over "fair treatment," for instance. Organizational factors such as automated jobs or ambiguous job descriptions that frustrate or aggravate employees also cause grievances. Union activism is another cause; the union may solicit grievances from workers to underscore ineffective supervision. Problem employees are yet another underlying cause of grievances. These are individuals, who, by their nature, are negative, dissatisfied, and prone to complaints. Discipline and dismissal, explained in Chapter 14, are also both major sources of grievances.

The Grievance Procedure

Most collective bargaining contracts contain a very specific grievance procedure. It lists the various steps in the procedure, time limits associated with each step, and specific rules such as "all charges of contract violation must be reduced to writing." Virtually every labor agreement signed today contains a grievance procedure clause. (Nonunionized employers need such procedures, too, as explained in Chapter 14.)

Union grievance procedures differ from firm to firm. Some contain simple, two-step procedures. Here the grievant, union representative, and company representative meet to discuss the grievance. If they don't find a satisfactory solution, the grievance is brought before an independent, third-party arbitrator, who hears the case, writes it up, and makes a decision. Figure 15-5 shows a Grievance Record Form.

At the other extreme, the grievance procedure may contain six or more steps. The first step might be for the grievant and shop steward to meet informally with the grievant's supervisor to try to find a solution. If they don't find one, the employee files a formal grievance, and there's a meeting with the employee, shop steward, and the supervisor's boss. The next steps involve the grievant and union representatives meeting with higher-level managers. Finally, if top management and the union can't reach agreement, the grievance may go to arbitration.

Sometimes the grievance process gets out of hand. For example, in the first half of 2001, members of American Postal Workers Union, Local 482, filed 1,800 grievances at the Postal Service's Roanoke mail processing facility (the usual rate is about 800 grievances per year). The employees apparently were responding to job changes, including transfers triggered by the Postal Service's efforts to further automate its processes.[64]

Guidelines for Handling Grievances

The best way to handle a grievance is to develop a work environment in which grievances don't occur in the first place. Hone your ability to recognize, diagnose, and correct the causes of potential employee dissatisfaction (such as unfair appraisals, inequitable wages, or poor communications) before they become grievances.

Figure 15-5
A Standard Grievance
Record Form
Source: Michael Carrell and Christina Heavrin, *Labor Relations and Collective Bargaining* (Upper Saddle River, NJ: Prentice Hall, 2001), p. 415.

GRIEVANCE NUMBER *97-003*   DATE FILED *4/23/03*   UNION *Local 1233*

NAME OF GRIEVANT(S) *Davis, Henry*   CLOCK # *0379*

DATE CAUSE OF GRIEVANCE OCCURRED *4/20/03*

CONTRACTUAL PROVISIONS CITED *Articles III, VII, and others*

STATEMENT OF THE GRIEVANCE

    On April 20, Foreman George Moore asked Henry Davis to go temporarily to the Rolling Mill for the rest of the turn. Davis said he preferred not to, and that he was more senior to others who were available. The foreman never ordered Davis to take the temporary assignment. He only requested that Davis do so.

    Davis was improperly charged with insubordination and suspended for three days. The foreman did not have just cause for the discipline.

RELIEF SOUGHT:

    Reinstatement with full back pay and seniority.

GRIEVANT'S SIGNATURE   *Henry Davis*   DATE *4/22/03*

STEWARD'S SIGNATURE   *Jim Bob Smith*   DATE *4/23/03*

STEP 1

DISPOSITION:

    Foreman Moore gave Davis clear instructions to report temporarily to the Rolling Mill for the remainder of the shift. Davis refused to do so and was warned that it could result in discipline. When he again refused the foreman's directive, he was disciplined.

    The discipline was for just cause. The grievance is rejected.

SIGNATURE OF
EMPLOYER REPRESENTATIVE   *Paul Roberts*   DATE *4/26/03*

_____ Grievance Withdrawn or ✓ Referred to Step 2

SIGNATURE OF
UNION REPRESENTATIVE   *Jim Bob Smith*   DATE *4/28/03*

The manager is on the firing line and must steer a course between treating employees fairly and maintaining management's rights and prerogatives. One expert has developed a list of do's and don'ts as useful guides in handling grievances.[65] Some critical ones include:

Do:

1. Investigate and handle each case as though it may eventually result in arbitration.
2. Talk with the employee about his or her grievance; give the person a full hearing.
3. Require the union to identify specific contractual provisions allegedly violated.
4. Comply with the contractual time limits for handling the grievance.
5. Visit the work area of the grievance.
6. Determine whether there were any witnesses.
7. Examine the grievant's personnel record.
8. Fully examine prior grievance records.
9. Treat the union representative as your equal.
10. Hold your grievance discussions privately.
11. Fully inform your own supervisor of grievance matters.

Don't:

12. Discuss the case with the union steward alone—the grievant should be there.

13. Make arrangements with individual employees that are inconsistent with the labor agreement.

14. Hold back the remedy if the company is wrong.

15. Admit to the binding effect of a past practice.

16. Relinquish to the union your rights as a manager.

17. Settle grievances based on what is "fair." Instead, stick to the labor agreement.

18. Bargain over items not covered by the contract.

19. Treat as subject to arbitration claims demanding the discipline or discharge of managers.

20. Give long written grievance answers.

21. Trade a grievance settlement for a grievance withdrawal.

22. Deny grievances because "your hands have been tied by management."

23. Agree to informal amendments in the contract.

"The HR Scorecard" illustrates how the Hotel Paris applied these union–management concepts.

The **HR Scorecard**
Strategy and Results

The Hotel Paris's New Labor Relations Practices

The Hotel Paris's competitive strategy is "To use superior guest service to differentiate the Hotel Paris properties, and to thereby increase the length of stay and return rate of guests, and thus boost revenues and profitability." HR manager Lisa Cruz must now formulate functional policies and activities that support this competitive strategy, by eliciting the required employee behaviors and competencies.

A preliminary analysis, performed jointly by Lisa and the Hotel Paris's chief financial officer, left them optimistic that HR could contribute measurably to achieving the hotel's strategic aims. Several employee competencies and behaviors including employee morale, employee commitment, and the percent of arriving guests receiving the hotel's required greeting had significant effects on customer and organizational outcomes such as guest satisfaction and frequency of guest returns. In turn, outcomes like these contributed measurably to the Hotel Paris's strategic goals, including profit margins, market share, and scores on industry satisfaction surveys. Lisa and her team now turn to creating a labor relations process that will help to

produce the required employee competencies and behaviors. The accompanying HR Scorecard (Figure 15-6) outlines the relationships involved.

Lisa and the CFO knew that unionization was a reality for the Hotel Paris. About 5% of the hotel chain's U.S. employees were already unionized, and unions in this area were quite active. For example, as they were surfing the Internet to better gauge the situation, Lisa and the CFO came across the accompanying Web site from the Hotel Employees Restaurant Union, local 26. It describes their success in negotiating a contract and their accomplishments at several local hotels including ones managed by the Westin and Hilton chains. The CFO and Lisa agreed that it was important that she and her team develop and institute a new set of policies and practices that would enable the Hotel Paris to deal more effectively with unions.

They set about that task with the aid of a labor-management attorney. Together, the team developed a 20-page "What You Need

Boston Hotel Employees and Restaurant Employees Union

Local 26

Harvard Contract 2001	Master Hotel Contract 2001	Westin Contract 2000	Logan Airport Hilton 1999

 Return Home

 About Local 26

 Union Officers

 Contact Info

Links & Resources

 Member Services

 Business Agents

 Organize Now!

 Research Department

Campaigns

Master Hotel Contract 2001

STRENGTH, UNITY AND ACTION

Our strength comes from Local 26 members who participate in the fight–whether you were a member of the Negotiating Committee, joined the Contract Committee, signed up to be a picket captain, volunteered to distribute food, served as a marshal at the Strike Authorization vote and rally, went on delegations to management or came to rallies and meetings - our victory was the result of your hard work and determination. Our union is strong because of our members. You made it clear to everyone who was watching this Fall that Local 26 is a strong union. Take pride in our new contract, because we earned it together.

Below: Local 26 Members at the Strike Authorization Vote and Rally

to Know When the Union Calls" manual for Hotel Paris managers and supervisors. This manual contained three sets of information. First, it provided a succinct outline of *labor relations law*, particularly as it relates to the company's managers. Second, it laid a *detailed set of guidelines* regarding what supervisors could and could not do with respect to union organizing activities. Third, it identified all line supervisors as the company's "front-*line eyes and ears*" with respect to union organizing activity. Here, the manual provided examples of activities that might suggest that a union was trying to organize the hotel's employees, and whom the supervisor should notify.

Lisa and her team also decided to take a more proactive approach to ensuring that their company was sufficiently responsive to its employees' concerns. Here, they assumed that the best way to "win" a union campaign was to reduce the chances that the employees wanted a union. Lisa and her team believed that many of the steps they'd taken earlier should help. For example, improving salaries and wages, providing financial incentives, and instituting the new ethics, justice, and fairness programs already seemed to be having a measurable effect on employee morale. One year after the hotel's new labor relations efforts went into effect, the percentage of eligible employees in unions was down to 3%.

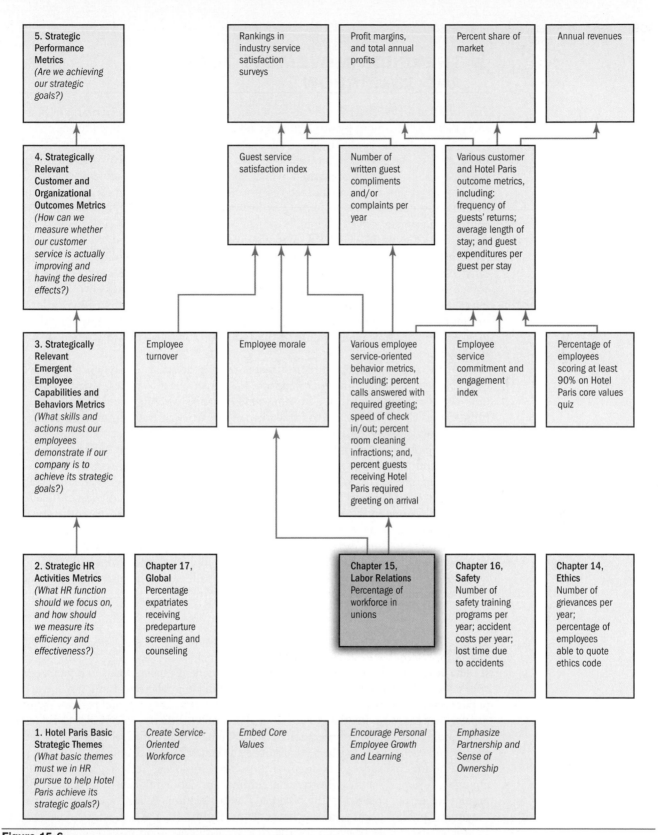

Figure 15-6

HR Scorecard for Hotel Paris International Corporation*

*Note: *(An abbreviated example showing selected HR practices and outcomes aimed at implementing the competitive strategy, "To use superior guest services to differentiate the Hotel Paris properties and thus increase the length of stays and the return rate of guests and thus boost revenues and profitability")*

● THE UNION MOVEMENT TODAY AND TOMORROW

The 1980s and 1990s were hard times for unions. About 35% of the nonfarm U.S. work-force belonged to unions by the 1960s. By 2002, that figure had dropped to about 13.2%.

Several things contributed to this decline. Laws like OSHA and Title VII of the Civil Rights Act reduced the need for the traditional protective role unions play. Increased global competition and new technologies like the Internet and Just-In-Time inventory systems forced manufacturers to reduce inefficiencies and cut costs—often by reducing payrolls by automating or by sending jobs abroad. New foreign-owned southern auto plants from Toyota, Nissan, BMW, and DaimlerChrysler largely stayed union free. The number of U.S. manufacturing jobs has declined, while service jobs have increased. The shift from manufacturing to services is exemplified by "new econ-omy" high-tech firms like Amazon and Cisco, whose white-collar workers have largely stayed union free. Some union leaders also believe that the new attempts at labor–management cooperation such as employee participation teams undermine unions' traditional prerogatives, by giving employees more say over how they do their jobs. The union movement's share of the U.S. workforce has thus dwindled, as noted, to about 13.2% today.

Yet that 13.2% figure underestimates the impact that unions have on the U.S. economy. For one thing (as noted above), union membership varies widely by state, so unions are still quite influential in some states (such as Michigan and New York). And, fully 35% of the nation's blue-collar workers—in particular those in manufacturing and construction jobs—belong to unions.

The problem is that only about 15% of U.S. workers are now employed in manufactur-ing and construction, a figure that's down from about 25% 20 years ago. So, unions' traditional membership sources are shrinking. As two experts put it, "[The union movement's] inability to recruit white-collar workers on any significant scale has been primarily responsible for its slipping from representing 35% of the labor force in 1959, and 20% of U.S. workers in 1983, to its current position of representing only 13.5%" [several years ago].[66]

Yet there are some bright spots for labor unions. For example, about 40% of all col-lege faculty members, 45,000 physicians, 50,000 engineers, and almost 100,000 nurses belong to unions (as do most major league baseball, football, basketball, and hockey players). Furthermore, about 40% of all federal, state, and local government employees belong to unions, a point to which we now turn.

Public Employees and Unions

If there is a notable bright spot for the union movement, it's their success in organizing fed-eral, state, and municipal workers. With at least 7 million public-sector union members, the public sector represents at least 44% of total U.S. union membership, and perhaps the union movement's biggest potential growth area. Three public unions—the National Education Association, the American Federation of State, County and Municipal Employees, and the American Federation of Teachers—are among the largest nine U.S. unions.

The unions' success in organizing public employees reflects, in part, years of changes in public sector collective bargaining and labor relations legislation. Public employees are not covered by the National Labor Relations Act. However, other laws do extend to public employees much the same rights. In 1871, Congress passed the Pendleton Act. This provided for the first Civil Service Commission, which, among other things, protected federal employees from certain arbitrary dismissals, and admin-istered competitive examinations to determine who would get federal jobs.

Public-sector union membership increased dramatically starting in 1960, due to several presidential executive orders, and new legislation. In 1962, President John F. Kennedy signed executive order 10988. This recognized federal employees' rights to join or refrain from joining labor organizations and granted recognition to those organizations. In 1978, Congress passed the Civil Service Reform Act of 1978. Title VII of this act (known as the Federal Labor Relations Act) is similar to the National Labor Relations Act. It gave the new Federal Labor Relations Authority new authority to oversee federal public-sector labor relations. Among other things, this Title VII prohibits the government from restraining or coercing employees in the exercise of their organizational rights, or from encouraging or discouraging union membership. Similarly, labor organizations may not interfere with the employees' rights to unionize or to refrain from organizing.[67]

Organizing Professionals and White-Collar Employees

Unions are also making inroads into traditionally hard-to-organize worker segments like professionals and white-collar workers, as even these employees see their job security and perquisites under attack. Recent reports of IBM sending systems analysts' jobs abroad, of Merrill Lynch having more security analysis done abroad by foreign nationals, and of hospitals having digitized X-rays read and interpreted by doctors abroad illustrate the concerns many professionals have. As noted above, thousands of teachers, doctors, nurses, and professionals have already joined unions, and employers' continuing attempts to squeeze ever more productivity out of these workers may well prompt more to consider doing so. Boeing Corp., provides one example. Several years ago the firm began focusing more on cost cutting and financial results and (from its engineers' point of view) less on engineering excellence. Engineers' morale reportedly dropped, and Boeing was caught by surprise when its engineers joined the Seattle Professional Engineering Employees Association.[68] Today, white-collar workers and professionals (many in the public sector) now represent close to half of all union members.[69]

The "Improving Productivity Through HRIS" feature shows how todays' unions are using information technology to boost their effectiveness.

A striking doctor speaks to other striking doctors outside the Woodhull Medical and Mental Center in Brooklyn, New York, after an unprecedented walkout. They belong to a doctors' union, and the issues were pay and the quality of patient care.

Improving Productivity Through HRIS

The Union Organizing Campaign

Employers are not the only ones benefiting from improved productivity through HRIS. As one expert recently asked, "If faster and more powerful ways of communicating enable companies to compete in a quickly changing and challenging environment, shouldn't they also make unions stronger and more efficient as organizations and workplace representatives?"[70]

In fact, employers need to know that the Internet is revolutionizing union activity, much as it revolutionized how firms do business. E-mail and the Internet mean unions can mass e-mail announcements to collective bargaining unit members, and use mass e-mail to reach supporters and government officials for their corporate campaigns.

Union-based Web sites are becoming integral parts of many such unionization campaigns; Alliance@IBM provides one example. Managed by the Communications Workers of America, Alliance@IBM seeks to encourage IBM employees to join the Communications Workers of America. It does so by providing information on a range of issues, such as why IBM employees need a union, questions and concerns about unions, and how employees can join the union and get involved. For example, one page addresses the issue "Why We Need Alliance@IBM."

Source: Marcos Camacho, A law corporation, 29700 Woodford Tehachapird, Keene, CA 93531.

Another page provides background information and instructions for Alliance organizers at IBM. It contains downloadable, online flyers for distribution; articles on topics like "Renewing a Union in the New Economy" and "Working Hard, Earning Less: The Story of Job Growth in America." The site even includes a downloadable authorization card.

The Web site for the United Farmworkers (www.ufw.org) provides another example. Particularly with union membership down, unions need more efficient ways to interact with their members, potential members, and contributors. The accompanying UFW Web site illustrates this. For example, it provides an efficient way for the union to organize its Gallo campaign, and to sign up new contributors for its other efforts.

Employee Participation Programs and Unions

Employers and unions are also grappling with the question of how to deal with employee participation programs. A UPS program is typical. Under this program, hourly employees in self-directed teams establish priorities on how to do their jobs. UPS argues that employee involvement and teamwork can produce higher productivity. The Teamsters union (which represents the company's drivers and other hourly workers) is suspicious that the program is merely a tactic for subverting the union's influence on its members.[71]

To understand the problem, it's useful to know that one goal of the National Labor Relations (or Wagner) Act was to outlaw "sham unions." Two years before passage of the NLRA, the National Recovery Act (1933) tried to give employees the right to organize and to bargain collectively. This triggered an increase in unions that were actually company-supported organizations aimed at keeping legitimate unions out. This helped lead to passage of the National Labor Relations Act.

The problem is that, because of how the courts often interpret the NLRA, courts might view participative programs like UPS's as sham unions. After all, the NLRA defines a labor organization as

Any organization of any kind, or any agency or employee representation committee or plan, in which employees participate and which exists for the purpose, in whole or in part, of dealing with employers concerning grievances, labor disputes, wages, rates of pay, hours of employment, or conditions of work.[72]

Whether a court views an employer's participation program as impermissible revolves around two main criteria. One is dominance. For example, if the employer formulates the idea for the committees, creates them, controls the development of their constitution or governing rules, or maintains control over the committees' functions, they could be viewed as unfairly dominated by the employer.[73] Second is the program's actual role. If the committees focus just on issues such as quality and productivity improvement, courts are more likely to view them as outside the scope of the National Labor Relations Act. Being involved in union-type matters such as wages, working conditions, and hours of work may be more questionable. For example, the NLRB recently ruled that one company had let its worker committees essentially supervise themselves (within certain parameters), and that because the plant manager rarely overruled the committees, "it cannot be doubted that each committee exercises as a group authority that in the traditional plant setting would be considered to be supervisory." The court hearing this case therefore found that because each of the 87 committees had final decision-making authority and because the committees limited their activities to job-related matters such as deciding how to do their jobs, the committee structure did not violate labor law.[74]

For now, employers can take these steps to avoid having their employee participation programs viewed as sham unions:[75]

■ Involve employees in the formation of these programs to the greatest extent practical.

■ Continually emphasize to employees that the committees exist for the exclusive purpose of addressing issues such as quality and productivity. They are not intended as vehicles for dealing with management on mandatory bargaining-type items such as pay and working conditions.

■ Don't try to establish such committees at the same time union organizing activities are beginning in your facility.

■ Fill the committees with volunteers rather than elected employee representatives, and rotate membership to ensure broad employee participation.

■ Minimize your participation in the committees' day-to-day activities, to avoid unlawful interference or, worse, the perception of domination.

 *Review*

SUMMARY

1. Union membership has been alternately growing and shrinking since as early as 1790. A major milestone was the creation in 1886 of the American Federation of Labor (AFL) by Samuel Gompers. Today, the AFL-CIO is a national federation of about 100 national and international unions. Most recently the trend in unionization has been toward organizing white-collar workers, particularly since the proportion of blue-collar workers has been declining.

2. In addition to improved wages and working conditions, unions seek security when organizing. We discussed five possible arrangements, including the closed shop, the union shop, the agency shop, the open shop, and maintenance of membership.

3. The Norris-LaGuardia Act and the Wagner Act marked a shift in labor law from repression to strong encouragement of union activity. They did this by banning certain types of unfair labor practices, by providing for secret-ballot elections, and by creating the National Labor Relations Board.

4. The Taft-Hartley Act reflected the period of modified encouragement coupled with regulation. It enumerated the rights of employees with respect to their unions, enumerated the rights of employers, and allowed the U.S. president to temporarily bar national emergency strikes. Among other things, it also enumerated certain unfair union labor practices. And employers were explicitly given the right to express their views concerning union organization.

5. The Landrum-Griffin Act reflected the period of detailed regulation of internal union affairs. It grew out of discoveries of wrongdoing on the part of both management and union leadership and contained a bill of rights for union members.

6. There are five steps in a union drive and election: the initial contact, obtaining authorization cards, holding a hearing with the NLRB, the campaign, and the election itself. The union need only win a majority of the votes cast, not a majority of the workers in the bargaining unit eligible to vote.

7. There are five surefire ways to lose an NLRB election: Be caught sleeping at the switch, form a committee, emphasize money and benefits, have an industry blind spot, and delegate too much to divisions.

8. Bargaining collectively in good faith is the next step if and when the union wins the election. Good faith means that both parties communicate and negotiate, and that proposals are matched with counterproposals. Bargaining items are categorized as mandatory, voluntary, or illegal.

9. An impasse occurs when the parties aren't able to move further toward settlement. Third-party involvement—namely, arbitration, fact finding, or mediation—is one alternative. Sometimes, though, a strike occurs. Boycotts and lockouts are two other anti-impasse weapons sometimes used by labor and management.

10. Grievance handling has been called day-to-day collective bargaining. It involves the continuing interpretation of the collective bargaining agreement but usually not its renegotiation.

11. Most agreements contain a carefully worded grievance procedure ranging from two to six or more steps. The steps usually involve union-management meetings at each step up the chain of command until (if agreement isn't reached) the grievance goes to arbitration. Grievance handling is as important in nonunion organizations as in those that are unionized.

12. Several things contributed to the union movement's declining membership. These include laws, like OSHA and Title VII, global competition and new technologies, declining numbers of U.S. manufacturing jobs, and possibly, the new attempts at labor–management cooperation such as employee participation teams.

13. There are some bright spots for labor unions. For example, many professional employees belong to unions, as do about 40% of all federal, state, and local government employees. The unions' success in organizing public employees reflects, in part, years of changes in public-sector collective bargaining and labor relations legislation. In 1962, President John F. Kennedy signed executive order 10988. This recognized federal employees' rights to join or refrain from joining labor organizations and granted recognition to those organizations. And, in 1978, Congress passed the Civil Service Reform Act.

DISCUSSION QUESTIONS

1. Why do employees join unions? What are the advantages and disadvantages of being a union member?
2. Discuss five sure ways to lose an NLRB election.
3. Describe important tactics you would expect the union to use during the union drive and election.
4. Briefly illustrate how labor law has gone through a cycle of repression and encouragement.
5. Explain in detail each step in a union drive and election.
6. What is meant by good faith bargaining? Using examples, explain when bargaining is not in good faith.
7. Define impasse, mediation, and strike, and explain the techniques that are used to overcome an impasse.

INDIVIDUAL AND GROUP ACTIVITIES

1. You are the manager of a small manufacturing plant. The union contract covering most of your employees is about to expire. Working individually or in groups, discuss how to prepare for union contract negotiations.
2. Working individually or in groups, use Internet resources to find situations where company management and the union reached an impasse at some point during their negotiation process, but eventually resolved the impasse. Describe the issues on both sides that led to the impasse. How did they move past the impasse? What were the final outcomes?
3. The HRCI "Test Specifications" appendix at the end of this book (pages 685–689) lists the knowledge someone studying for the HRCI certification exam needs to have in each area of human resource management (such as in Strategic Management, Workforce Planning, and Human Resource Development). In groups of four to five students, do four things: (1) review that appendix now; (2) identify the material in this chapter that relates to the required knowledge the appendix lists; (3) write four multiple choice exam questions on this material that you believe would be suitable for inclusion in the HRCI exam; and (4) if time permits, have someone from your team post your team's questions in front of the class, so the students in other teams can take each others' exam questions.
4. In October 2003, 8,000 Amtrak workers agreed not to disrupt service by walking out, at least not until a court hearing was held. Amtrak had asked the courts for a temporary restraining order, and the Transport Workers Union of America was actually pleased to postpone its walkout. The workers were apparently not upset at Amtrak, but at Congress, for failing to provide enough funding for Amtrak. What if anything can an employer do when employees threaten to go on strike, not because of what the employer did, but what a third party—in this case, Congress—has done or not done? What laws would prevent the union from going on strike in this case?

EXPERIENTIAL EXERCISE

The Union-Organizing Campaign at Pierce U.

Purpose: The purpose of this exercise is to give you practice in dealing with some of the elements of a union organizing campaign.

Required Understanding: You should be familiar with the material covered in this chapter, as well as the following incident, "An Organizing Question on Campus."

INCIDENT: An Organizing Question on Campus: Art Tipton is human resource director of Pierce University, a private university located in a large urban city. Ruth Zimmer, a supervisor in the maintenance and housekeeping services division of the university, has just come into Art's office to discuss her situation. Zimmer's division is responsible for maintaining and cleaning physical facilities of the university. Zimmer is one of the department supervisors who supervises employees who maintain and clean on-campus dormitories.

In the next several minutes, Zimmer proceeds to express her concerns about a union organizing campaign that has begun among her employees. According to Zimmer, a representative of the Service Workers Union has met with several of her employees, urging them to sign union authorization cards. She has observed several of her employees "cornering" other employees to talk to them about joining the union and to urge them to sign union authorization (or representation) cards. Zimmer even observed this during working hours as employees were going about their normal duties in the dormitories. Zimmer reports that a number of her employees have come to her asking for her opinions about the union. They told her that several other supervisors in the department had told their employees not to sign any union authorization cards and not to talk about the union at any time while they were on campus. Zimmer also reports that one of her fellow supervisors told his employees that anyone who was caught talking about the union or signing a union authorization card would be disciplined and perhaps dismissed.

Zimmer says that her employees are very dissatisfied with their wages and with the conditions that they have endured from students, supervisors, and other staff people. She says that several employees told her that they had signed union cards because they believed that the only way university administration would pay attention to their concerns was if the employees had a union to represent them. Zimmer says that she made a list of employees whom she felt had joined or were interested in the union, and she could share these with Tipton if he wanted to deal with them personally. Zimmer closed her presentation with the comment that she and other department supervisors need to know what they should do in order to stomp out the threat of unionization in their department.

How to Set Up the Exercise/Instructions: Divide the class into groups of four or five students. Assume that you are labor relations consultants retained by the university to identify the problems and issues involved and to advise Art Tipton on the university's rights and what to do next. Each group will spend about 45 minutes discussing the issues. Then, outline those issues, as well as an action plan for Tipton. What should he do next?

If time permits, a spokesperson from each group should list on the board the issues involved and the group's recommendations. What should Art do?

APPLICATION CASE

Disciplinary Action

The employee, a union shop steward, was on her regularly scheduled day off at home. She was called by her supervisor and told to talk to three union members and instruct them to attend a work function called a "Quest for Quality Interaction Committee" meeting. The Quest for Quality program was a high priority with the employer for improving patient care at the hospital facility and was part of a corporate program. The union had objected to the implementation of the Quest for Quality program and had taken the position that employees could attend the program if their jobs were threatened, but they should do so under protest and then file a grievance afterward.

On the day in question, the union shop steward, in a conference call with the three employees, said she would not order them to attend the Quest for Quality meeting, although her supervisor had asked her to. The supervisor who had called the union shop steward had herself refused to order the employees to attend the meeting, but relied on the union shop steward to issue the order to the employees. When the shop steward failed to order the employees to attend the meeting, the employer suspended her for two weeks. She grieved the two-week suspension.

The union position was that the company had no authority to discipline the union shop steward on her day off for failure to give what it termed a "management direction to perform the specific job function of attending a mandatory corporate meeting." The union pointed out that it was unfair that the employer refused to order the employees directly to attend the meeting but then expected the union shop steward to do so. The union argued that while it is not unusual to call a union shop steward for assistance in problem solving, the company had no right to demand that he or she replace supervisors or management in giving orders and then discipline the union official for refusing to do so.

The company position was that the opposition of the union to the Quest for Quality meetings put the employees in a position of being unable to attend the meetings without direction from the union shop steward; that the union shop steward was given a job assignment of directing the employees to attend the meeting; and that failure to follow that job assignment was insubordination and just cause for her suspension.

Nonetheless, the union contended that the arbitrator must examine the nature of the order when deciding whether the insubordination was grounds for discipline. As to the nature of the order in this case, the employer had to demonstrate that the order was directly related to the job classification and work assignment of the employee disciplined. The refusal to obey such an order must be shown to pose a real challenge to supervisory authority. The employee did not dispute the fact that she failed to follow the orders given to her by her supervisor, but pointed out that she was not on duty at the time and that the task being given to her was not because of her job with the company but because of her status as a union shop steward.

Questions

1. As the arbitrator, do you think the employer had just cause to discipline the employee? Why or why not?

2. If the union's opposition to the Quest for Quality program encouraged the employees not to participate, why shouldn't the union be held responsible for directing the employees to attend?

Source: Adapted from Cheltenham Nursing Rehabilitation Center 89 LA 361 (1987); discussion in Michael Carrell and Christina Heavrin, *Labor Relations and Collective Bargaining* (Upper Saddle River, NJ: Prentice Hall, 1995), pp. 100–101.

CONTINUING CASE

Carter Cleaning Company

The Grievance

On visiting one of Carter Cleaning Company's stores, Jennifer was surprised to be taken aside by a long-term Carter employee, who met her as she was parking her car. "Murray (the store manager) told me I was suspended for two days without pay because I came in late last Thursday," said George. "I'm really upset, but around here the store manager's word seems to be law, and it sometimes seems like the only way anyone can file a grievance is by meeting you or your father like this in the parking lot." Jennifer was very disturbed by this revelation and promised the employee she would look into it and discuss the situation with her father. In the car heading back to headquarters she began mulling over what Carter Cleaning Company's alternatives might be.

Questions

1. Do you think it is important for Carter Cleaning Company to have a formal grievance process? Why or why not?

2. Based on what you know about the Carter Cleaning Company, outline the steps in what you think would be the ideal grievance process for this company.

3. In addition to the grievance process, can you think of anything else that Carter Cleaning Company might do to make sure that grievances and gripes like this one get expressed and also get heard by top management?

KEY TERMS

closed shop, 562	union salting, 569	strike, 582
union shop, 562	authorization cards, 570	economic strike, 582
agency shop, 562	bargaining unit, 571	unfair labor practice strike, 582
open shop, 562	decertification, 577	wildcat strike, 582
right to work, 562	collective bargaining, 577	sympathy strike, 582
Norris-LaGuardia Act (1932) , 563	good faith bargaining, 578	picketing, 582
National Labor Relations (or Wagner) Act, 564	voluntary bargaining items, 579	corporate campaign, 583
	illegal bargaining items, 579	boycott, 583
National Labor Relations Board (NLRB), 564	mandatory bargaining items, 579	inside games, 583
	impasse, 581	lockout, 583
Taft-Hartley Act (1947), 564	mediation, 581	injunction, 584
national emergency strikes, 567	fact finder, 581	grievance, 584
Landrum-Griffin Act (1959), 567	arbitration, 581	

ENDNOTES

1. Brian Becker et al., *The HR Scorecard* (Boston: Harvard Business School Press, 2001), p. 16.
2. "Union Membership Dipped Slightly in 2002, BLS Reports," *BNA Bulletin to Management*, March 13, 2003, p. 85.
3. Stephen Greenhouse, "Labor, Revitalized with New Recruiting, Has Regained Power and Prestige," *New York Times*, October 9, 1999, p. A10. One high-profile effort to unionize professionals sputtered. See Michael Romano, "Backpedaling: AMA Rethinks Unionizing Efforts, Cites Recent Ruling," *Modern Health Care*, June 11, 2001.
4. "Union Ranks in U.S. Workforce Lessen in 2000", *BNA Bulletin to Management*, March 1, 2001, p. 69.
5. "Union Membership Around the World," *BNA Bulletin to Management*, November 13, 1997, pp. 364–365.
6. James Bennett and Jason Taylor, "Labor Unions: Victims of Their Political Success?" *Journal of Labor Research* 22, no. 2 (Spring 2001), pp. 261–273.

7. "Union Membership and Earnings," *BNA Bulletin to Management*, February 13, 1997, pp. 52–53; "Union Membership Fell Again in 1997," *BNA Bulletin to Management*, February 26, 1998, p. 60.
8. William Wiatrowski, "Employee Benefits for Union and Nonunion Workers," *Monthly Labor Review*, February 1994, p. 35.
9. Jeffrey Ball, "United Auto Workers Asks for a Vote on Unionization at Nissan Factory," *Wall Street Journal*, August 15, 2001, p. A4; see also Jerry Fuller Jr. and Kim Hester, "A Closer Look at the Relationship Between Justice Perceptions and Union Participation," *Journal of Applied Psychology* 86, no. 6 (2001), pp. 1096–1105.
10. Nicole Harris, "Flying into a Rage?" *BusinessWeek*, April 27, 1998, p. 119.
11. Warner Pflug, *The UAW in Pictures* (Detroit: Wayne State University Press, 1971), pp. 11–12.
12. Benjamin Taylor and Fred Witney, *Labor Relations Law* (Upper Saddle River, NJ: Prentice Hall, 1992), pp. 170–171.

13. The following material is based on Arthur Sloane and Fred Witney, *Labor Relations* (Upper Saddle River, NJ: Prentice Hall, 2001), pp. 46–124.

14. Karen Robinson, "Temp Workers Gain Union Access," *HR News, Society for Human Resource Management* 19, no. 10 (October 2000), p. 1.

15. Elizabeth Bennett, "Online Staffers in Dispute with Papers," *Philadelphia Business Journal*, January 12, 2001, p. 6.

16. "Union Membership by State and Industry," *BNA Bulletin to Management*, May 29, 1997, pp. 172–173; "Regional Trends: Union Membership by State and Multiple Jobholding by State," *Monthly Labor Review* 123, no. 9 (September 2000), pp. 40–41.

17. Michael Carrell and Christina Heavrin, *Labor Relations and Collective Bargaining* (Upper Saddle River, NJ: Pearson, 2004), p. 180.

18. Ibid., p. 179.

19. Sloane and Witney, *Labor Relations*, p. 121.

20. Ben Foster, "Tech Firms a New Target for Union Organizers," *Baltimore Business Journal*, February 16, 2001, p. 14; Mark Leon, "A Union of Their Own," *InfoWorld*, March 12, 2001, pp. 41–42; Loretta Prencipe, "E-mail and the Internet Are Changing the Labor/Management Powerplay," *InfoWorld*, March 12, 2001, p. 46; Scott Tillett, "Dot-com Workers Take New Path to Unions," *Internet Week*, January 15, 2001, p. 9.

21. *Labor Relations Consultants: Issues, Trends, Controversies* (Rockville, MD: Bureau of National Affairs, 1985), p. 72.

22. For a discussion, see Cory Fine, "Beware the Trojan Horse," *Workforce*, May 1998, pp. 45–51.

23. "Spurned Union Salts Entitled to Back Pay, D.C. Court Says, Affirming Labor Board," *BNA Bulletin to Management*, June 21, 2001, p. 193.

24. Cory Fine, "Beware the Trojan Horse," p. 46.

25. Diane Hatch and James Hall, "Salting Cases Clarified by NLRB," *Workforce*, August 2000, p. 92.

26. Edwin Arnold et al., "Determinants of Certification Election Outcomes in the Service Sector," *Labor Studies Journal* 25, no. 3 (Fall 2000), p. 51.

27. "Number of Elections, Union Wins Increased in 2002," *BNA Bulletin to Management*, June 19, 2003, p. 197.

28. This section is based on Matthew Goodfellow, "How to Lose an NLRB Election," *Personnel Administrator* 23 (September 1976), pp. 40–44. See also Gillian Flynn, "When the Unions Come Calling," *Workforce*, November 2000, pp. 82–87.

29. Ibid.

30. Ibid.

31. Harry Katz, "The Decentralization of Collective Bargaining: A Literature Review and Comparative Analysis," *Industrial and Labor Relations Review* 47, no. 1 (October 1993), p. 11.

32. Carrell and Heavrin, *Labor Relations and Collective Bargaining*.

33. Ibid., p. 166.

34. Ibid., pp. 167–168.

35. Jonathon Segal, "Unshackle Your Supervisors to Stay Union Free," *HR Magazine*, June 1998, pp. 62–65.

36. "Union Access to Employer's Customers Restricted," *BNA Bulletin to Management*, February 15, 1996, p. 49; "Workplace Access for Unions Hinges on Legal Issues," *BNA Bulletin to Management*, April 11, 1996, p. 113.

37. Ibid., pp. 4–65. The appropriateness of these sample rules may be affected by factors unique to an employer's operation, and they should therefore be reviewed by the employer's attorney before implementation.

38. "Union Decertifications Up in First Half of 1998," *BNA Bulletin to Management*, December 24, 1998, p. 406. See also, Clyde Scott and Edwin Arnold, "Deauthorization and Decertification Elections: An Analysis and Comparison of Results," *Working USA*, Winter 2003, vol. 7, issue 3, pp. 6–20.

39. Carrell and Heavrin, *Labor Relations and Collective Bargaining*, pp. 120–121.

40. See for example David Meyer and Trevor Bain, "Union Decertification Election Outcomes: Bargaining Unit Characteristics and Union Resources," *Journal of Labor Research* 15, no. 2 (Spring 1994), pp. 117–136.

41. This is based on David Moberg, "Like Business, Unions Must Go Global," *New York Times*, December 19, 1993, p. 13.

42. Doug Cahn, "Reebok Takes the Sweat Out of Sweatshops," *Business Ethics* 14, no. 1 (January 2000), p. 9.

43. Carrell and Heavrin, *Labor Relations and Collective Bargaining*, pp. 176–177.

44. "No Talks Until Mechanics Union Softens Demand, Northwest Airlines Says," *Knight-Ridder/Tribune Business News*, March 28, 2001, Item 01087165.

45. "Bryant Union Says College is Bargaining in Good Faith," *Providence Business News*, March 12, 2001, p. 19.

46. John Fossum, *Labor Relations* Dallas: BPI, 1982, pp. 246–250.

47. Boulwareism is the name given to a strategy, now generally held in disfavor, by which the company, based on an exhaustive study of what it thought its employees wanted, made but one offer at the bargaining table and then refused to bargain any further unless convinced by the union on the basis of new facts that its original position was wrong. The NLRB subsequently found that the practice of offering the same settlement to all units, insisting that certain parts of the package could not differ among agreements, and communicating to the employees about how negotiations were going amounted to an illegal pattern. Fossum, *Labor Relations*, p. 267. See also William Cooke, Aneil Mishra, Gretchen Spreitzer, and Mary Tschirhart, "The Determinants of NLRB Decision-Making Revisited," *Industrial and Labor Relations Review* 48, no. 2 (January 1995), pp. 237–257.

48. See for example, Arthur Sloane and Fred Witney, *Labor Relations* (Upper Saddle River, NJ, Prentice Hall, 2004) pp. 177–218.

49. Reed Richardson, *Collective Bargaining*, by objectives (Englewood Cliffs, NJ: Prentice Hall, 1977) p. 150.

50. Fossum, *Labor Relations*, p. 312. See also Thomas Watkins, "Assessing Arbitrator Competence," *Arbitration Journal* 47, no. 2 (June 1992), pp. 43–48.

51. Carrell and Heavrin, *Labor Relations and Collective Bargaining*, p. 501.

52. Fossum, *Labor Relations*, p. 317.

53. Mark Fitzgerald, "UAW Lifts Boycott," *Editor and Publisher*, February 26, 2001, p. 9.

54. "Striker Replacements," *BNA Bulletin to Management*, February 6, 2003, p. S7.

55. Stephen Cabot and Gerald Cuerton, "Labor Disputes and Strikes: Be Prepared," *Personnel Journal* 60 (February 1981), pp. 121–126. See also Brenda Sunoo, "Managing Strikes, Minimizing Loss," *Personnel Journal* 74, no. 1 (January 1995), pp. 50ff.

56. For a discussion, see Herbert Northrup, "Union Corporate Campaigns and Inside Games as a Strike Form," *Employee Relations Law Journal* 19, no. 4 (Spring 1994), pp. 507–549.

57. Jessica Materna, "Union Launches Web Site to Air Grievances Against San Francisco Marriott" *San Francisco Business Times*, May 4, 2001, p. 15.

58. Northrup, "Union Corporate Campaigns and Inside Games," p. 513.

59. Ibid., p. 518.

60. Clifford Koen Jr., Sondra Hartmen, and Dinah Payne, "The NLRB Wields a Rejuvenated Weapon," *Personnel Journal*, December 1996, pp. 85–87.

61. Sloane and Witney, *Labor Relations*, 10th ed., pp. 221–227.

62. Carrell and Heavrin, *Labor Relations and Collective Bargaining*, pp. 417–418.

63. Richardson, *Collective Bargaining*.

64. Duncan Adams, "Worker Grievances Consume Roanoke, VA Mail Distribution Center," *Knight-Ridder/Tribune Business News*, March 27, 2001, Item 01086009.

65. See Newport, Supervisory Management, p. 273, for an excellent checklist. See also Mark Lurie, "The Eight Essential Steps in Grievance Processing," *Dispute Resolution Journal* 54, no. 4 (November 1999), pp. 61–65.

66. Sloane and Witney, *Labor Relations*, 11th ed., p. 2.

67. Carrell and Heavrin, *Labor Relations and Collective Bargaining*, pp. 34–36.

68. Woodrow Timberman, "Why Engineers Strike: The Boeing Story," *Business Horizons* 44, no. 6 (November 2001), pp. 35–39.

69. "White Collar Workers Flocking to Unions," The Labor Research Organizations, http://www.laborresearch.org/story2.php/323.

70. Gary Chaison, "Information Technology: The Threat to Unions," *Journal of Labor Research* 23, no. 2 (Spring 2002), pp. 249–260.

71. "Union Fights Team Program at UPS," *BNA Bulletin to Management*, March 14, 1996, p. 88.

72. Jenero and Lyons, "Employee Participation Programs," p. 539.

73. See ibid., p. 551; Mary Pivec and Howard Robbins, "Employee Involvement Remains Controversial," *HR Magazine*, November 1996, pp. 145–150; Darren McCabe, "Total Quality Management: Anti-Union Trojan Horse or Management Albatross," *Work Employment and Society* 13, no. 4 (December 1999), pp. 665–691.

74. "Employer's System of Worker Empowerment Does not Fall Prey to Labor Act, NLRB Rules," *BNA Bulletin to Management*, August 2, 2001, p. 241.

75. These are based on ibid., pp. 564–565.

You Have a Right to a Sa
and Healthful Workplac
IT'S THE LA

- You have the right to notify your employer or OSHA about workplace hazards. You may ask OSHA to keep your name confidential.

- You have the right to request an OSHA inspection if you believe that there are unsafe and unhealthful conditions in your workplace. You or your representative may participat nspection.

  file a complaint with OSHA within 30 days of nation by your employer for making safety and heal nts or for exercising your rights under the *OSH Act.*

  e a right to see OSHA citations issued to your er. Your employer must post the citations at or nea e of the alleged violation.

  nployer must correct workplace hazards by the date d on the citation and must certify that these hazard en reduced or eliminated.

  e the right to copies of your medical records or of your exposure to toxic and harmful substances tions.

  nployer must post this notice in your workplace.

After studying this chapter, you should be able to:

1 Explain the basic facts about OSHA.

2 Explain the supervisor's role in safety.

3 Minimize unsafe acts by employees.

4 Explain how to deal with important occupational health problems.

Employee Safety and Health

While "hazardous conditions" might not be the first thing that comes to mind

when you think of hotels, Lisa Cruz knew that hazards and safety were in

fact serious issues for the Hotel Paris. Indeed, everywhere you look—from

the valets leaving car doors open on the driveways to slippery areas around

the pools, to tens of thousands of pounds of ammonia, chlorine, and other

caustic chemicals that the hotels use each year for cleaning and laundry,

hotels provide a fertile environment for accidents. Obviously, hazardous

conditions are bad for the Hotel Paris. They are inhumane for the workers.

High accident rates probably reduce employee morale and thus service. And

accidents raise the company's costs and reduce its profitability, for instance

in terms of workers' compensation claims and absences. Lisa knew that she

had to clean up her firm's occupational safety and health systems. ●

The previous chapter explored union–management relations, and the issues unions typically focus on when negotiating agreements. Employee safety is usually one of these. The main purpose of this chapter is to provide you with the basic knowledge you'll need to deal more effectively with employee safety and health problems at work. Today, every manager needs a working knowledge of OSHA—the Occupational Safety and Health Act—and so we discuss it at some length. Specifically, we review its purpose, standards, and inspection procedures, as well as the rights and responsibilities of employees and employers under OSHA. We also stress the importance of the supervisor and of top management commitment to organizationwide safety. We'll see that there are three basic causes of accidents: chance occurrences, unsafe conditions, and unsafe acts—and several techniques for preventing accidents. We'll also discuss several important employee health problems, such as substance abuse and workplace violence, and what to do about them.

Why Safety Is Important   Safety and accident prevention concern managers for several reasons, one of which is the staggering number of work-related accidents. For example, over 5,500 U.S. workers died annually in the early 2000s in workplace incidents, and there were over 4.7 million nonfatal injuries and illnesses resulting from accidents at work—roughly 5.1 cases per 100 full-time workers in the United States per year. Many safety experts believe such figures actually underestimate the true numbers. Many injuries and accidents, the theory goes, just go unreported.

And injuries aren't just a problem in traditionally "unsafe" industries like mining and construction. For example, every year over 15,000 reportable injuries or illnesses occur among semiconductor workers, another 15,000 among circuit board assemblers, and another 15,000 among manufacturers of computers and computer peripherals.[1] In fact, an increasingly technology-based economy is triggering new health concerns. Even new computers contribute to "sick building syndrome"—symptoms like headaches and sniffles, which some experts blame on poor ventilation and dust and fumes from on-site irritants.[2] Two engineers found that new computers emit chemical fumes (which, however, diminish after the computer runs constantly for a week[3]). And "safe" office work is actually susceptible to many other health and safety problems, including "repetitive trauma injuries related to computer use, respiratory illnesses stemming from indoor air quality, and high levels of stress, which are associated with a variety of factors, including task design."[4]

But even facts like these don't tell the whole story. They don't reflect the human suffering incurred by the injured workers and their families or the economic costs incurred by employers, nor do they reflect the legal implications. When a boiler explosion at Ford's Rouge Power Plant killed six workers and injured 14, Ford was slapped with a $1.5 million fine, and also agreed to spend almost $6 million instituting various safety measures. The state of Michigan concluded that Ford hadn't followed safety procedures, and that gas had leaked into the furnace because employees hadn't closed valves properly.[5] One senator recently said he was planning to introduce legislation making it a federal crime punishable by up to 10 years' imprisonment to cause a worker's death through willfully violating OSHA regulations.[6]

Yet, even with all of this attention on health and safety, there apparently still are many employers who may take safety less seriously then they should. For example, the *New York Times* recently described, in a story entitled "A Family's Profits, Wrung from Blood and Sweat," a cast-iron business that "has been cited for more than 400 safety violations since 1995, four times more than its six major competitors combined," and an environment in which managers allegedly marked for dismissal employees who protested unsafe conditions.[7]

1 Explain the basic facts about OSHA.

● OCCUPATIONAL SAFETY LAW

Occupational Safety and Health Act
The law passed by Congress in 1970 "to assure so far as possible every working man and woman in the nation safe and healthful working conditions and to preserve our human resources."

Congress passed the **Occupational Safety and Health Act** in 1970 "to assure so far as possible every working man and woman in the nation safe and healthful working conditions and to preserve our human resources."[8] The only employers it doesn't cover are self-employed persons, farms in which only immediate members of the employer's family work, and some workplaces already protected by other federal agencies or under other statutes. The act covers federal agencies, though its provisions usually don't apply to state and local governments in their role as employers.

Occupational Safety and Health Administration (OSHA)
The agency created within the Department of Labor to set safety and health standards for almost all workers in the United States.

The act created the **Occupational Safety and Health Administration (OSHA)** within the Department of Labor. OSHA's basic purpose is to administer the act and to set and enforce the safety and health standards that apply to almost all workers in the United States. The Department of Labor enforces the standards, and OSHA has inspectors working out of branch offices around the country to ensure compliance.

OSHA Standards and Record Keeping

OSHA operates under the "general" standard clause that each employer:

> *shall furnish to each of his [or her] employees employment and a place of employment which are free from recognized hazards that are causing or are likely to cause death or serious physical harm to his [or her] employees.*

To carry out this basic mission, OSHA is responsible for promulgating legally enforceable standards. These are contained in five volumes covering general industry standards, maritime standards, construction standards, other regulations and procedures, and a field operations manual.

The standards are very complete and seem to cover just about every conceivable hazard in great detail. (Figure 16-1 presents a small part of the standard governing handrails for scaffolds.) And OSHA regulations don't just list specific chemical or structural-type standards. For example, OSHA's standard on respiratory protection also includes requirements for program administration; work-site-specific procedures; requirements regarding the selection, use, cleaning, maintenance, and repair of respirators; employee training; respirator fit tests; and medical evaluations of the employees who use the respirators.[9]

occupational illness
Any abnormal condition or disorder caused by exposure to environmental factors associated with employment.

Under OSHA, employers with 11 or more employees must maintain records of, and report, occupational injuries and occupational illnesses. An **occupational illness** is any abnormal condition or disorder caused by exposure to environmental factors associated with employment. This includes acute and chronic illnesses caused by inhalation, absorption, ingestion, or direct contact with toxic substances or harmful agents.

As summarized in Figure 16-2, employers must report all occupational illnesses.[10] They must also report most occupational injuries, specifically those that result in medical treatment (other than first aid), loss of consciousness, restriction of work (one or more lost workdays), restriction of motion, or transfer to another job.[11] If an on-the-job

Figure 16-1
OSHA Standards Examples

Guardrails not less than 2″ × 4″ or the equivalent and not less than 36″ or more than 42″ high, with a midrail, when required, of a 1″ × 4″ lumber or equivalent, and toeboards, shall be installed at all open sides on all scaffolds more than 10 feet above the ground or floor. Toeboards shall be a minimum of 4″ in height. Wire mesh shall be installed in accordance with paragraph [a] (17) of this section.

Source: General Industry Standards and Interpretations, U.S. Department of Labor, OSHA (Volume 1: Revised 1989, Section 1910.28(b) (15)), p. 67.

Figure 16-2
What Accidents Must Be
Reported Under the
Occupational Safety and
Health Act (OSHA)?

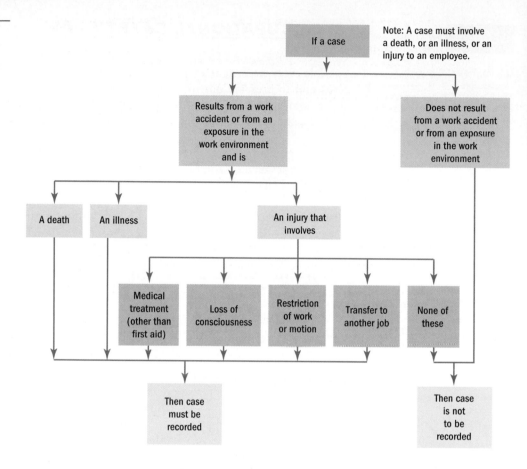

accident results in the death of an employee or in the hospitalization of five or more employees, all employers, regardless of size, must report the accident in detail to the nearest OSHA office. OSHA's latest record-keeping rules streamline the job of reporting occupational injuries or illnesses.[12] The rules continue to presume that an injury or illness that resulted from an event in or exposure to the work environment is work related. However, it allows the employer to conclude that the event was not job related (and needn't be reported) if the facts so warrant—such as if a worker breaks an ankle after catching his foot on his car's seat belt when parked on the company lot.

Yet, OSHA's record-keeping requirements are still broader than you might think, because its definition of occupational injuries and illnesses is so broad.[13] Examples of recordable conditions include: food poisoning suffered by an employee after eating in the employer's cafeteria, colds compounded by drafty work areas, and ankle sprains that occur during voluntary participation in a company softball game at a picnic the employee was required to attend. OSHA pursues record-keeping violations during investigations, so it behooves employers to record injuries or illnesses incurred at work carefully. Figure 16-3 shows the OSHA form used to report occupational injuries or illness.

Inspections and Citations

OSHA enforces its standards through inspections and (if necessary) citations. OSHA may not conduct warrantless inspections without an employer's consent. However, it may inspect after acquiring an authorized search warrant or its equivalent.[14]

Occupational Safety and Health Administration
Supplementary Record of
Occupational Injuries and Illnesses

U.S. Department of Labor

This form is required by Public Law 91-596 and must be kept in the establishment for 5 years.
Failure to maintain can result in the issuance of citations and assessment of penalties.

Case or File No.

Form Approved
O.M.B. No. 1218-0176

See OMB Disclosure
Statement on reverse.

Employer
1. Name

2. Mail address (No. and street, city or town, State, and zip code)

3. Location, if different from mail address

Injured or Ill Employee
4 Name (First, middle, and last)

Social Security No.

5. Home address (No. and street, city or town, State, and zip code)

6. Age

7. Sex (Check one)   Male ☐   Female ☐

8. Occupation (Enter regular job title, not the specific activity he was performing at the time of injury.)

9. Department (Enter name of department or division in which the injured person is regularly employed, even though he may have been temporarily working in another department at the time of injury.)

The Accident or Exposure to Occupational Illness
If accident or exposure occurred on employer's premises, give address of plant or establishment in which it occurred. Do not indicated department or division within the plant or establishment. If accident occurred outside employer's premises at an identifiable address, give that address. If it occurred on a public highway or at any other place which cannot be identified by number and street, please provide place references locating the place of injury as accurately as possible.

10. Place of accident or exposure (No. and street, city or town, State, and zip code)

11. Was place of accident or exposure on employer's premises?   Yes ☐   No ☐

12. What was the employee doing when injured? (Be specific. If he was using tools or equipment or handling material, name them and tell what he was doing with them.)

13. How did the accident occur? (Describe fully the events which resulted in the injury or occupational illness. Tell what happened and how it happened. Name any objects or substances involved and tell how they were involved. Give full details on all factors which led or contributed to the accident. Use separate sheet for additional space.)

Occupational Injury or Occupational Illness
14. Describe the injury or illness in detail and indicate the part of body affected. (E.g., amputation of right index finger at second joint; fracture of ribs; lead poisoning; dermatitis of left hand, etc.)

15. Name the object or substance which directly injured the employee. (For example, the machine or thing he struck against or which struck him; the vapor or poison he inhaled or swallowed; the chemical or radiation which irriatated his skin; or in cases of strains, hernias, etc., the thing he was lifting, pulling, etc.)

16. Date of injury or initial diagnosis of occupational illness

17. Did employee die? (Check one)   Yes ☐   No ☐

Other
18. Name and address of physician

19. If hospitalized, name and address of hospital

Date of report | Prepared by | Official position

OSHA No. 101 (Feb. 1981)

(See Next Page/Reverse)

Figure 16-3
Form Used to Record Occupational Injuries and Illnesses
Source: U.S. Department of Labor.

Inspection Priorities   Imminent danger situations get top priority. Here, it's likely there is a danger that can immediately cause death or serious physical harm. Second priority is catastrophes, fatalities, and accidents that have already occurred. (Employers must report such situations to OSHA within 48 hours.) Third priority is valid employee complaints of alleged violation standards. Next in priority are periodic, special-emphasis inspections aimed at high-hazard industries, occupations, or substances. Random inspections and reinspections generally have last priority. (Most inspections result from employee complaints.)

Under its priority system, OSHA conducts an inspection within 24 hours when a complaint indicates an immediate danger, and within three working days when a serious hazard exists. For a "nonserious" complaint filed in writing by a worker or a union, OSHA will respond within 20 working days. OSHA handles other nonserious complaints by writing to the employer and requesting corrective action.

The Inspection Itself   The inspection itself begins when the OSHA officer arrives at the workplace.[15] He or she displays official credentials and asks to meet an employer representative. (Always insist on seeing the officer's credentials, which include photograph and serial number.) The officer explains the visit's purpose, the scope of the inspection, and the standards that apply. An authorized employee representative accompanies the officer during the inspection. The inspector can also stop and question workers (in private, if necessary) about safety and health conditions. The act protects each employee from discrimination for exercising his or her disclosure rights. OSHA rules require employee involvement in OSHA's on-site consultations, and that employees be informed of the inspections' results.[16]

OSHA inspectors look for violations of all types, but some potential problem areas—such as scaffolding and fall protection—seem to grab more of their attention. The five most frequent OSHA inspection violation areas are scaffolding, fall protection, hazard communication, lockout/tagout (electrical repairs), and respiratory problems.

Finally, after checking the premises and employer's records, the inspector holds a closing conference with the employer's representative. Here the inspector discusses apparent violations for which OSHA may issue or recommend a **citation** and penalty. At this point, the employer can produce records to show compliance efforts. Figure 16-4 lists the hazards that accounted for the greatest number of citations in one recent year. Inadequate or unsafe scaffolding was the most frequently cited hazard.

citation
Summons informing employers and employees of the regulations and standards that have been violated in the workplace.

Penalties   OSHA can also impose penalties. These generally range from $5,000 up to $70,000 for willful or repeat serious violations, although in practice the penalties can be far higher—$1.5 million at the Ford Rouge plant, for instance. The parties settle many

Figure 16-4
Most Frequently Cited OSHA Standards: The Top 10 for 2002
Source: James Nash, "Enforcement: Scaffolding Is Still No. 1," *Occupational Hazards*, Penton Media, Inc. January 2003, p. 14.

Standard	Subject	No. of Citations
1926.451	Scaffolding, General Requirements	8,423
1910.120	Hazard Communication	6,951
1926.501	Fall Protection	5,461
1910.134	Respiratory Protection	4,250
1910.147	Lockout/Tagout	3,973
1910.305	Electrical, Wiring Methods	3,202
1910.212	Machines, General Requirements	2,878
1910.178	Powered Industrial Trucks	2,574
1910.303	Electrical Systems Design	2,291
1910.219	Mechanical Power-Transmission Apparatus	2,088

Note: Data shown reflect Federal OSHA citations issued during the period October 2001 through September 2002.

OSHA cases before litigation, in "pre-citation settlements." Here, OSHA issues the citation and agreed-on penalties simultaneously, after negotiations with the employer.[17] There is also a maximum of $7,000 a day in penalties for failure to correct a violation.

In general, OSHA calculates penalties based on the gravity of the violation and usually takes into consideration factors like the size of the business, the firm's compliance history, and the employer's good faith.[18] In practice, OSHA must have a final order from the independent Occupational Safety and Health Review Commission (OSHRC) to enforce a penalty.[19] An employer who files a notice of contest can drag out an appeal for years. Many employers do appeal their citations, at least to the OSHA district office.

Inspection Guidelines   What should managers do when OSHA inspectors unexpectedly show up? Suggestions include:

Initial Contact

Refer the inspector to your OSHA coordinator.

Check the inspector's credentials.

Ask the inspector why he or she is inspecting your workplace: Complaint? Regular scheduled visit? Fatality or accident follow-up? Imminent danger?

If the inspection stems from a complaint, you are entitled to know whether the person is a current employee, though not the person's name.

Notify your counsel, who should review all requests for documents and information, as well as documents and information you provide.

Opening Conference

Establish the focus and scope of the planned inspection.

Discuss the procedures for protecting trade secret areas.

Show the inspector you have safety programs in place. He or she may not go to the work floor if paperwork is complete and up to date.

Walk-Around Inspection

Accompany the inspector and take detailed notes.

If the inspector takes a photo or video, you should, too.

Ask for duplicates of all physical samples and copies of all test results.

Be helpful and cooperative, but don't volunteer information.

To the extent possible, immediately correct any violation the inspector identifies.[20]

Responsibilities and Rights of Employers and Employees

Both employers and employees have responsibilities and rights under the Occupational Safety Health Act. Employers, for example, are responsible for meeting their duty to provide "a workplace free from recognized hazards," for being familiar with mandatory OSHA standards, and for examining workplace conditions to make sure they conform to applicable standards. Employers have the right to seek advice and off-site consultation from OSHA, request and receive proper identification of the OSHA compliance officer before inspection, and to be advised by the compliance officer of the reason for an inspection.

Employees also have rights and responsibilities, but OSHA can't cite them for violations of their responsibilities. They are responsible, for example, for complying with all applicable OSHA standards, for following all employer safety and health rules and regulations, and for reporting hazardous conditions to the supervisor. Employees have a right to demand safety and health on the job without fear of punishment. The act prohibits

FedEx follows OSHA noise guidelines by frequently monitoring noise levels, testing employees' hearing annually, conducting hearing protection programs, and providing earplugs and earmuffs. These FedEx employees drag air freight containers through the fuselage of a FedEx plane wearing protective headgear.

employers from punishing or discriminating against workers who complain to OSHA about job safety and health hazards. (See the accompanying OSHA safety poster, in Figure 16-5.)

Dealing with Employee Resistance   While employees have a responsibility to comply with OSHA standards, they often resist, and in most such cases the employer remains liable for any penalties. The refusal of some workers to wear hard hats as mandated by the OSHA requirements typifies this problem. Employers have attempted to defend themselves against penalties for such noncompliance by citing worker intransigence and their own fear of wildcat strikes and walkouts. In most cases, courts have held employers liable for safety violations at the workplace regardless of the fact that the violations were due to employee resistance.

Yet it is possible for employers to reduce their liability, since "courts have recognized that it is impossible to totally eliminate all hazardous conduct by employees."[21] In the event of a problem, the courts may take into consideration facts such as whether the employer's safety procedures were adequate; whether the training really gave employees the understanding, knowledge, and skills required to perform their duties safely; and whether the employer really required employees to follow the procedures.

There are several other ways to address the liability problem.[22] First, an employer can bargain with its union for the right to discharge or discipline any employee who disobeys an OSHA standard. As a second alternative, a formal employer-employee arbitration process could provide a relatively quick method for resolving an OSHA-related dispute. Other employers have turned to positive reinforcement and training for gaining employee compliance; more on this shortly. However, the only surefire way to eliminate liability is to ensure that no safety violations occur.

The magazine *Occupational Hazards* conducted a survey of 12 health and safety experts, and asked them to identify the "10 best ways" to get into trouble with OSHA. The experts ranged from former OSHA compliance officers and lawyers to consultants and safety managers. Here's what they said (starting with the best way to incur OSHA's wrath):[23]

1. Ignore or retaliate against employees who raise safety issues.
2. Antagonize or lie to OSHA during an inspection.
3. Keep inaccurate OSHA logs and have disorganized safety files.
4. Do not correct hazards OSHA has cited you for and ignore commonly cited hazards.

Figure 16-5
OSHA Safety Poster

You Have a Right to a Safe and Healthful Workplace.
IT'S THE LAW!

- You have the right to notify your employer or OSHA about workplace hazards. You may ask OSHA to keep your name confidential.
- You have the right to request an OSHA inspection if you believe that there are unsafe and unhealthful conditions in your workplace. You or your representative may participate in the inspection.
- You can file a complaint with OSHA within 30 days of discrimination by your employer for making safety and health complaints or for exercising your rights under the *OSH Act.*
- You have a right to see OSHA citations issued to your employer. Your employer must post the citations at or near the place of the alleged violation.
- Your employer must correct workplace hazards by the date indicated on the citation and must certify that these hazards have been reduced or eliminated.
- You have the right to copies of your medical records or records of your exposure to toxic and harmful substances or conditions.
- Your employer must post this notice in your workplace.

The *Occupational Safety and Health Act of 1970 (OSH Act),* P.L. 91-596, assures safe and healthful working conditions for working men and women throughout the Nation. The Occupational Safety and Health Administration, in the U.S. Department of Labor, has the primary responsibility for administering the *OSH Act.* The rights listed here may vary depending on the particular circumstances. To file a complaint, report an emergency, or seek OSHA advice, assistance, or products, call 1-800-321-OSHA or your nearest OSHA office: • Atlanta (404) 562-2300 • Boston (617) 565-9860 • Chicago (312) 353-2220 • Dallas (214) 767-4731 • Denver (303) 844-1600 • Kansas City (816) 426-5861 • New York (212) 337-2378 • Philadelphia (215) 861-4900 • San Francisco (415) 975-4310 • Seattle (206) 553-5930. Teletypewriter (TTY) number is 1-877-889-5627. To file a complaint online or obtain more information on OSHA federal and state programs, visit OSHA's website at www.osha.gov. If your workplace is in a state operating under an OSHA-approved plan, your employer must post the required state equivalent of this poster.

1-800-321-OSHA
www.osha.gov

U.S. Department of Labor • Occupational Safety and Health Administration • OSHA 3165

5. Fail to control the flow of information during and after an inspection. (The employer should not hand over to the OSHA inspector any information he or she does not ask for, and should also keep tabs on everything the employer has given to the inspector.)

6. Do not conduct a safety audit, or identify a serious hazard and do nothing about it.

7. Do not use appropriate engineering controls.

8. Do not take a systemic approach toward safety. (As one expert put it, "an OSHA officer can see right away if [your company] does not place a priority on safety."

9. Do not enforce safety rules.

10. Ignore industrial hygiene issues. (It's easier to focus on day-to-day physical safety because these problems tend to be more apparent then hygiene issues such as airborne contaminants. You often cannot see exposure problems such as these, although their effects on employees may be severe.)

When You're On Your Own
HR for Line Managers and Entrepreneurs

Free On-Site Safety and Health Services for Small Businesses

Small businesses have some unique challenges when it comes to managing safety. Without HR or safety departments, they often don't know where to turn for advice on promoting employee safety. And, many have the (inaccurate) notion that small firms like theirs aren't covered by the occupational safety and health act.[24] Small businesses are indeed almost always covered by the act, and one option for them is to turn to OSHA for free advice and consultation.

OSHA provides free on-site safety and health services for small businesses. This service uses safety experts from state governments, and provides consultations, usually at the employer's workplace. According to OSHA, this safety and health consultation program is completely separate from the OSHA inspection effort, and no citations are issued or penalties proposed.

The employer triggers the process by requesting a voluntary consultation. There is then an opening conference with a safety expert, a walk-through, and a closing conference at which the employer and safety expert discuss the latter's observations. The consultant then sends you a detailed report explaining the findings. The employer's only obligation is to commit to correcting serious job safety and health hazards in a timely manner.

For example, when Jan Anderson, president of her own steel installation company in Colorado, realized her workers' compensation costs were higher than her payroll, she knew she had to do something. Anderson joined with similar Colorado firms for help. At the group's request, OSHA helped draft new safety systems, created educational materials, and provided inspections that were more cooperative than adversarial. As a result, says Anderson, "Our workers' compensation costs have decreased significantly, we have had no accidents, and there is an awareness that we take safety seriously."[25]

To the chagrin of some employers, OSHA is using technology to report its inspection results. For example, OSHA's Web site (www.osha.gov) gives you easy access to your company's (or your competitors') OSHA enforcement history. The "When You're On Your Own" feature shows how OSHA can help smaller businesses comply with safety rules and laws.

● MANAGEMENT COMMITMENT AND SAFETY

On the next few pages, we'll see that reducing accidents often boils down to reducing accident-causing conditions and accident-causing acts—but do not miss the forest for the trees. Telling supervisors to watch for spills and telling employees to work safely is futile if everyone in the firm believes management isn't serious about safety. Safety starts with and depends on top management commitment.

Historically, for instance, DuPont's accident rate has been much lower than that of the chemical industry as a whole. This good safety record is partly due to an organizational commitment to safety, which is evident in the following description:

One of the best examples I know of in setting the highest possible priority for safety takes place at a DuPont Plant in Germany. Each morning at the DuPont Polyester and Nylon Plant the director and his assistants meet at 8:45 to review the past 24 hours. The first matter they discuss is not production, but safety. Only after they have examined reports of accidents and near misses and satisfied themselves that corrective action has been taken do they move on to look at output, quality, and cost matters.[26]

All employees should see convincing evidence of top management's commitment. This requires top management's being personally involved in safety activities; giving safety matters high priority in meetings and production scheduling; giving the company safety officer high rank and status; and including safety training in new workers' training. Ideally, "safety is an integral part of the system, woven into each management competency and a part of everyone's day-to-day responsibilities."[27] In addition:

- Institutionalize management's commitment with a safety policy, and publicize it. This should emphasize that the firm will do everything practical to eliminate or reduce accidents and injuries.
- Analyze the number of accidents and safety incidents and then set specific achievable safety goals. Georgia-Pacific reduced its workers' compensation costs with a policy that forces managers to halve accidents or forfeit 30% of their bonuses.

Committing to safety is not just a case of humanitarianism (although that is important).[28] Safety programs also pay for themselves. One safety program at a Missouri ABB Business Services plant resulted in total OSHA cases reduced 80% in one year; OSHA lost-time rate reduced 86% in one year; and $560,000 contributed to profit. One study of two organizations concluded that their safety activities paid for themselves by a ratio of 10 to 1, just in direct savings of workers' compensation expenses over a period of four years.[29]

● WHAT CAUSES ACCIDENTS?

There are three basic causes of workplace accidents: chance occurrences, unsafe conditions, and unsafe acts on the part of employees. Chance occurrences (such as walking past a plate-glass window just as someone hits a ball through it) are more or less beyond management's control. We will therefore focus on unsafe conditions and unsafe acts.

Unsafe Conditions and Other Work-Related Factors

unsafe conditions
The mechanical and physical conditions that cause accidents.

Unsafe conditions are one main cause of accidents. They include such things as:

Improperly guarded equipment

Defective equipment

Hazardous procedures in, on, or around machines or equipment

Unsafe storage—congestion, overloading

Improper illumination—glare, insufficient light

Improper ventilation—insufficient air change, impure air source[30]

The basic remedy here is to identify and eliminate the unsafe conditions. OSHA standards address these mechanical and physical accident-causing conditions. HR and the firm's top managers should play a central role in and accept responsibility for identifying unsafe conditions. However, as the employer's front-line managers, supervisors play a crucial role in this process too, as the "When You're On Your Own" feature explains.

While accidents can happen anywhere, there are some special danger zones. About one-third of industrial accidents occur around forklift trucks, wheelbarrows, and other handling and lifting areas. The most serious accidents usually occur near metal and woodworking machines and saws, or around transmission machinery like gears, pulleys, and flywheels. Falls on stairs, ladders, walkways, and scaffolds are the third

Explain the supervisor's role in safety.

When You're On Your Own
HR for Line Managers and Entrepreneurs

The Supervisor's Role in Accident Prevention

After inspecting a work site in which workers were installing sewer pipes in a four-foot trench, the OSHA inspector cited the employer for violating the OSHA rule requiring employers to have a "stairway, ladder, ramp or other safe means of egress" in trench excavations that are four or more feet in depth.[31] In the event the trench caved in, workers needed a quick way out.

As in most such cases, the employer and its top management had the primary responsibility for the safety breakdown, but the local supervisor was responsible for the day-to-day inspections. The OSHA rule for which the company was cited requires that a competent person make daily inspections of trenches like this to make sure that its walls aren't shifting and its ladders are functioning properly. Here, the supervisor did not properly do his daily inspection.

Whether you're the manager in the IT department of a *Fortune* 500 company or

you're managing an excavation or dry cleaning store, daily safety inspections should always be part of your routine. As one safety recommendation recently put it, "a daily walk-through of your workplace—whether you are working in outdoor construction, indoor manufacturing, or any place that poses safety challenges—is an essential part of your work."[32]

Exactly what you should look for during your daily safety inspection depends on the sort of workplace for which you're responsible, of course. For example, construction sites and dry cleaning stores have hazards all their own. However, in general you can use a checklist of unsafe conditions such as the one in Figure 16-6 to spot problems. We present another, more extensive checklist in Figure 16-12 at the end of this chapter. And you may use a checklist such as Figure 16-7 for training a new employee in his or her safety duties.

most common cause of industrial accidents. Hand tools (like chisels and screwdrivers) and electrical equipment (extension cords, electric droplights, and so on) are other major causes of accidents.[33] In addition to unsafe conditions, three other work-related factors contribute to accidents: the job itself, the work schedule, and the psychological climate of the workplace.

Certain jobs are inherently more dangerous. For example, the job of crane operator results in about three times more accident-related hospital visits than does the job of supervisor.

Work schedules and fatigue also affect accident rates. Accident rates usually don't increase too noticeably during the first five or six hours of the workday. But after that, the accident rate increases faster than the increase in the number of hours worked. This is due partly to fatigue and partly to the fact that accidents occur more often during night shifts.

Unfortunately, some of the most important working-condition-related causes of accidents are not as obvious, because they involve workplace psychology. For example, one researcher reviewed the official hearings regarding fatal accidents suffered by off-shore oil workers in the British sector of the North Sea.[34] A strong pressure within the organization to complete the work as quickly as possible, employees who are under a great deal of stress, and a poor safety climate—for instance, supervisors who never mention safety—were a few of the psychological conditions leading to accidents. Similarly, accidents occur more frequently in plants with a high seasonal layoff rate and where there is hostility among employees, many garnished wages, and blighted living conditions.

I.   GENERAL HOUSEKEEPING

Adequate and wide aisles—no materials protruding into aisles

Parts and tools stored safely after use—not left in hazardous positions that could cause them to fall

Even and solid flooring—no defective floors or ramps that could cause falling or tripping accidents

Waste cans and sand pails—safely located and properly used

Material piled in safe manner—not too high or too close to sprinkler heads

Floors—clean and dry

Firefighting equipment—unobstructed

Work benches orderly

Stockcarts and skids safely located, not left in aisles or passageways

Aisles kept clear and properly marked; no air lines or electric cords across aisles

II.   MATERIAL HANDLING EQUIPMENT AND CONVEYANCES

On all conveyances, electric or hand, check to see that the following items are all in sound working conditions:

Brakes—properly adjusted

Not too much play in steering wheel

Warning device—in place and working

Wheels—securely in place; properly inflated

Fuel and oil—enough and right kind

No loose parts

Cables, hooks, or chains—not worn or otherwise defective

Suspended chains or hooks conspicuous

Safely loaded

Properly stored

III.   LADDERS, SCAFFOLD, BENCHES, STAIRWAYS, ETC.

The following items of major interest to be checked:

Safety feet on straight ladders

Guardrails or handrails

Treads, not slippery

No cracked, or rickety

Properly stored

Extension ladder ropes in good condition

Toeboards

IV.   POWER TOOLS (STATIONARY)

Point of operation guarded

Guards in proper adjustment

Gears, belts, shafting, counterweights guarded

Foot pedals guarded

Brushes provided for cleaning machines

Adequate lighting

Properly grounded

Tool or material rests properly adjusted

Adequate work space around machines

Control switch easily accessible

Safety glasses worn

Gloves worn by persons handling rough or sharp materials

No gloves or loose clothing worn by persons operating machines

V.   HAND TOOLS AND MISCELLANEOUS

In good condition—not cracked, worn, or otherwise defective

Properly stored

Correct for job

Goggles, respirators, and other personal protective equipment worn where necessary

VI.   WELDING

Arc shielded

Fire hazards controlled

Operator using suitable protective equipment

Adequate ventilation

Cylinder secured

Valves closed when not in use

VII.   SPRAY PAINTING

Explosion-proof electrical equipment

Proper storage of paints and thinners in approved metal cabinets

Fire extinguishers adequate and suitable; readily accessible

Minimum storage in work area

VIII.   FIRE EXTINGUISHERS

Properly serviced and tagged

Readily accessible

Adequate and suitable for operations involved

Figure 16-6
Checklist of Mechanical or Physical Accident-Causing Conditions
Source: Courtesy of the American Insurance Association. From "A Safety Committee Man's Guide," p. I–64.

Supervisors: Please review each relevant item with your new employee to ensure a safe and healthful workplace. Check off items as information is explained to the employee or note "NA" for not applicable. Environmental Health and Safety requires that this form be completed and signed before the employee is allowed to start work.

Employee _____ Date Begin _____

Dept _____ Job Title _____

Supervisor _____ Box # _____

Safety

_____ 1. Review hazardous elements specific to job (chemicals; discuss routes of entry and effects of overexposure, extreme heat; machinery; etc.)

_____ 2. Review hazardous elements specific to job (chemicals; discuss routes of entry and effects of overexposure, extreme heat; machinery; etc.)

_____ 3. Review administrative control in effect (limited exposure time, rotating jobs, distance from operation, etc.)

_____ 4. Review applicable safe work procedures (proper lifting techiques, two-man jobs, etc.)

_____ 5. Distribute and review use of personal protective equipment required (explain why equipment is needed)

_____ 6. Review Health and Safety manual

_____ 7. Review wtitten Hazard Communication program and MSDS for chemicals specific to the operation

_____ 8. Review Lockout/Tagout program

_____ 9. Review Safe Operating Procedures (SOPs) for equipment employee will be expected to use

Safety

_____ 1. Review evacuation procedure in case of fire or disaster (walk employee through primary and secondary emergency exit routes for his/her work area)

_____ 2. Identify all fire extinguishers, type of fire to be used on, and review fire extinguisher operation

_____ 3. Identify all fire alarm pull boxes

Health

_____ 1. Identify first-aid stations and services/equipment available

_____ 2. Inform employee of person(s) to contact in case of emergency

_____ 3. Identify emergency response personnel

_____ 4. Review employee right-to-access exposure and medical records

Accident Reporting

_____ 1. Review accident/incident reporting procedure (encourage employee to bring to your attention any unsafe conditions or unsafe work practices)

_____ 2. Review rights and internal assistance available with regard to workers' compensation

_____   _____   _____
Supervisor's Signature   Supervisor Print Name   Date

_____   _____
Employee's Signature   Date

Figure 16-7
Safety Checklist

RESEARCH INSIGHT   A related study involved a survey of about 16,000 employees in Australia. The study focused on the relationships among (1) "high-quality jobs," (2) employee satisfaction, and (3) occupational injuries. The researchers defined high-quality jobs as those that involved extensive training, variety, and autonomy.[35] They measured high-quality jobs with questions such as "the employer provided job training last year." They measured job satisfaction with items such as "I am satisfied with management treatment." They measured occupational injuries by, for instance, having respondents indicate whether they had experienced an injury in the past year.

   The researchers found that "the results of this study show clearly that high-quality work has direct and indirect (via job satisfaction) effects on occupational injuries." Providing employees with high-quality work (in terms of increased opportunities for autonomy, increased involvement, and more training) seems to improve safety-conscious behavior directly by promoting employee learning, heightening problem solving, and enabling preventive action. High-quality work also improves safety indirectly: It enhances job satisfaction, and it is clear from this study and others that higher job satisfaction is associated with employee safety.[36]

What Causes Unsafe Acts? (A Second Basic Cause of Accidents)

Unsafe acts can undo even the best attempts to minimize unsafe conditions, but there are no easy answers to the question of what causes people to act recklessly. For years psychologists assumed that some employees were simply more accident prone than others, and that accident-prone people generally caused more accidents. However, studies have failed to consistently support this assumption.[37]

   Therefore, while some believe that most accident-prone people are impulsive, most experts today doubt that accident proneness is universal—that some people will have more accidents no matter what the situation. Instead, the consensus is that the person who is accident prone on one job may not be so on a different job. They say that accident proneness is situational.

   Various human traits do relate to accident proneness in specific situations. For example, accident-prone drivers performed worse on a test of motor skills than did drivers with fewer accidents, and older adults with impaired vision were at a higher risk for falls and motor vehicle crashes. People who were more fatalistic, negative, and cynical were more likely to exhibit violent behavior on the job.[38] We'll turn to how employers reduce unsafe acts and conditions next.

● HOW TO PREVENT ACCIDENTS

In practice, accident prevention boils down to two basic activities: (1) reducing unsafe conditions and (2) reducing unsafe acts. In most large facilities, the chief safety officer has responsibility for these activities. The chief safety officer often has the title Environmental Health and Safety Officer. Virtually all these people—98%—have responsibility for safety. According to one survey, 78.2% also have responsibility for occupational health, 69.3% for industrial hygiene, 60% for fire protection, 56.8% for environmental issues, and 52.2% for workers' compensation.[39]

Reducing Unsafe Conditions

Reducing unsafe conditions is always an employer's first line of defense. Safety engineers should design jobs so as to remove or reduce physical hazards. In addition, supervisors and managers play a role in reducing unsafe conditions. A checklist like the one in Figure 16-6 or the self-inspection checklist in Figure 16-12 can help identify and remove potential hazards.

Employers increasingly use computerized tools to design safer equipment. For example, Designsafe (from Designsafe Engineering, Ann Arbor, Michigan) facilitates hazard analysis, risk assessment, and the identification of safety control options. Designsafe helps the safety designer identify the task's main processes and sub-processes, and the worker behaviors associated with them. It then helps the designer choose the most appropriate safety control device for keeping the worker safe, from a list of devices such as adjustable enclosures, presence-sensing devices, and personal protective equipment.[40]

Sometimes the solution for eliminating an unsafe condition is obvious, and sometimes it's more subtle. For example, slips and falls at work are often the result of debris or a slippery floor.[41] Relatively obvious remedies for problems like these include slip-reducing floor coatings, floor mats, better lighting, and a system to quickly block off spills. But perhaps less obviously, special safety gear can also reduce the problems associated with otherwise unsafe conditions. For example, slip-resistant footwear with grooved soles can reduce slips and falls. Cut-resistant gloves reduce the hazards of working with sharp objects. Figure 16-8 illustrates what's available.

Getting employees to wear personal protective equipment can be a famously difficult chore. Including the employees in planning the program, reinforcing appropriate behaviors, and addressing comfort issues can smooth the way for more widespread use of protective equipment.[42] Wearability is important. In addition to providing reliable barrier protection and durability, protective clothing should fit properly; be easy to care for, maintain, and repair; be flexible and lightweight; provide comfort and reduce heat stress; have rugged construction; be relatively easy to put on and take off; and be easy to clean, dispose of, and recycle.[43]

Again, reducing unsafe conditions—by designing the job properly and having managers watch for hazards—should always be the first choice. Then come administrative controls, such as job rotation to reduce long-term exposure to the hazard. Only then should you turn to personal protective equipment.[44]

Reducing unsafe acts—through screening, training, or incentive programs, for example—is the second basic way to reduce accidents. Let's look at how to do this.

**Figure 16-8
Cut-Resistant Gloves
Web Ad**
Source: Courtesy of Occupational Hazards, Penton Media, Inc.

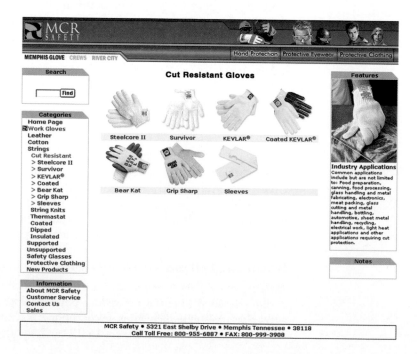

Minimize unsafe acts by employees.

Reducing Unsafe Acts by Emphasizing Safety

As mentioned above, it is the supervisor's responsibility to set the tone so subordinates want to work safely. This involves more than talking up safety, ensuring that workers wipe up spills, or enforcing safety rules, although such things are important. It's also necessary to show by both word and deed that safety is crucial. For example, supervisors should:

Praise employees when they choose safe behaviors;

Listen when employees offer safety suggestions, concerns, or complaints;

Be a good example, for instance, by following every safety rule and procedure;

Visit plant areas regularly;

Maintain open safety communications—for instance, by telling employees as much as possible about safety activities such as testing alarms and changing safety equipment or procedures;

Link managers' bonuses to safety improvements.[45]

Creating the right safety climate isn't just academic. One study assessed safety climate in terms of items such as "my supervisor says a good word whenever he sees the job done according to the safety rules." The study found that (1) employees did develop consistent perceptions concerning supervisory safety practices, and (2) these safety climate perceptions predicted safety records in the months following the survey.[46]

Reducing Unsafe Acts Through Selection and Placement

Screening is another way to reduce unsafe acts. Here, the manager's aim is to isolate the trait (such as visual skill) that might predict accidents on the job in question, then screen candidates for this trait. As noted above, tests have distinguished between those who do and do not have more car accidents, falls, and violent outbursts. Studies suggest that a test like the Employee Reliability Inventory (ERI) can help employers reduce unsafe acts at work. The ERI purportedly measures reliability dimensions such as emotional maturity, conscientiousness, safe job performance, and courteous job performance.[47] While the findings of one study were not definitive, using the ERI in the selection process did seem to be associated with reductions in work-related accidents.[48]

Also, ask a few safety-related questions during the selection interview—for instance, "What would you do if you saw another employee working in an unsafe way?" and "What would you do if your supervisor gave you a task, but didn't provide any training on how to perform it safely?"[49]

The Americans with Disabilities Act has particular relevance for safety-related screening. For example, under the ADA it is unlawful to inquire (prior to hiring) about an applicant's workers' compensation injuries and claims. You also cannot ask applicants whether they have a disability, or require them to take tests that tend to screen out those with disabilities. However, you can usually ask whether an applicant has the ability to perform a job. You can even ask, "Do you know of any reason why you would not be able to perform the various functions of the job you are seeking?"[50]

Reducing Unsafe Acts Through Training

Safety training is another way to reduce unsafe acts, especially for new employees. You should instruct them in safe practices and procedures, warn them of potential hazards, and work on developing a safety-conscious attitude. OSHA has published two useful booklets, "Training Requirements Under OSHA" and "Teaching Safety and Health in the Workplace."

The New Workplace

Safety Training for Hispanic Workers

Bilingual safety training is important. With increasing numbers of Hispanic workers in the United States, sometimes in hazardous jobs, experts are expressing concern about the level of safety training they're receiving. For example, while total fatalities in construction only rose about 1% from 1997 to 2002, the number of Hispanic fatalities in construction rose by almost 50%, because so many more Hispanics are working in construction jobs.[51]

Faced with statistics like these, many construction companies are offering specialized training programs for Hispanic workers. One example is a 40-hour training course provided for construction workers at the Dallas-Fort Worth airport expansion project. The construction firms here credit at least part of the safety improvements at the airport site to the new training program. For example, the project's safety record (in terms of incidence of injuries and illnesses per 100 full-time workers) is far better than national averages. The project's workers' compensation claims are about 20% lower than those in Texas in general.

Based on this program's apparent success, there are several useful conclusions one can draw about what a program like this should look like. First, the program should *speak the workers' language*. OSHA requirements already demand this, of course: It would hardly be useful to provide safety training in English to someone with modest English comprehension, and believe that you've accomplished your training aims. What they learned at Dallas-Fort Worth, however, is that teaching the program in Spanish was only part of "speaking the workers' language." They also recruit instructors who are from the ethnic groups they are training, and try to use instructors who worked in construction. The program also provides some *multilingual cross-training* for specific phrases. For example, the course teaches non-Hispanic trainees to say "peligro" [danger] or "cuidado" (be careful) if you see someone with his or her back to dangerous equipment.[52]

There are some other suggestions we can draw from the airport program. The program should address *cultural differences*. For example, they found that some workers, such as those from Panama, usually want to be greeted first, instead of just told, "you are doing something wrong." Another conclusion: *Don't skimp on training*. Because of the added cultural and multilingual aspects, experts contend that a 24-hour course is the absolute minimum. The 40-hour course at Dallas-Fort Worth airport cost about $500 tuition per student (not counting the worker's wages).

You can't just provide training and assume it will be successful. OSHA standards require demonstrated proficiency in numerous areas. For example, OSHA's respiratory protection standard requires that each employee be able to demonstrate how to inspect, put on, remove, use, and check respirator seals.[53] "The New Workplace" provides an additional perspective.

Reducing Unsafe Acts Through Motivation: Posters, Incentive Programs, and Positive Reinforcement

Employers also use various tools to motivate workers to work more safely. *Safety posters* are one. In one study, their use apparently increased safe behavior by more than 20%. However, posters are no substitute for a comprehensive safety program. Employers should combine them with other techniques (like screening and training) to reduce unsafe conditions and acts, and also change the posters often.

Incentive programs have also been successful at reducing workplace injuries. For example, UPS has given its drivers safety awards for years.[54] Clariant Corporation annually evaluates managers and employees on meeting goals in four key areas, including safety performance; bonuses (up to 8% of gross pay) then depend on their safety records.[55]

One way to motivate and encourage safety in a factory is to tell employees how much management values it: This safety poster on an exterior factory wall tells employees how well they are doing.

Some contend that safety incentive programs are misguided. OSHA has argued, for instance, that they don't cut down on actual injuries or illnesses, but only on injury and illness *reporting*. One option is to emphasize "nontraditional" incentives—for instance, giving employees recognition awards for attending safety meetings, for identifying hazards, or for demonstrating their safety and health proficiency.[56]

Positive Reinforcement Programs   Others use *positive reinforcement programs* to improve safety at work. Researchers introduced one program in a wholesale bakery.[57] An analysis of the safety-related conditions existing in the plant before the study suggested a number of areas that needed improvement. For example, new hires received no formal safety training, and managers rarely mentioned safety on a day-to-day basis.

The new safety program included positive reinforcement and training. The firm set and communicated a reasonable goal (in terms of observed incidents performed safely). A training phase was next. Employees received safety information during a 30-minute training session by viewing pairs of slides depicting scenes that the researchers staged in the plant. One slide, for example, showed the supervisor climbing over a conveyor; the parallel slide showed the supervisor walking around the conveyor. After viewing an unsafe act, employees had to describe what was wrong ("what's unsafe here?"). Then, after airing the problem, the researchers demonstrated the same incident again but performed in a safe manner, and explicitly stated the safe-conduct rule ("go around, not over or under, conveyors").

At the conclusion of the training phase, supervisors showed employees a graph with their pretraining safety record (in terms of observed incidents performed safely) plotted. They were encouraged to consider increasing their performance to the new safety goal for the following reasons: for their own protection, to decrease costs for the company, and to help the plant get out of last place in the safety ranking of the parent company. Then the researchers posted the graph and a list of safety rules in a conspicuous place in the work area.

The graph helped provide positive reinforcement. Whenever observers walked through the plant collecting safety data, they posted on the graph the percentage of incidents they had seen performed safely by the group as a whole, thus providing the workers with feedback. Workers could compare their current safety performance with both their previous performance and their assigned goal. In addition, supervisors praised workers when they performed selected incidents safely. Safety in the plant subsequently improved markedly.

Use Behavior-Based Safety

Behavior-based safety means identifying the worker behaviors that contribute to accidents and then training workers to avoid these behaviors. For example, Tenneco Corporation (which manufactures automobile exhaust systems and Monroe brand suspensions) implemented a behavior-based safety program at its 70 manufacturing sites in 20 countries. The firm selected internal consultants from among its quality managers, training managers, engineers, and production workers. After training, the internal consultants identified five critical behaviors for Tenneco's first safety program, such as: *Eyes on task: Does the employee watch his or her hands while performing a task?* The consultants made observations, collected data regarding the behaviors, and then instituted on-site training programs to get employees to perform these activities properly.[58]

Use Employee Participation

There are at least two reasons to get the employees involved in designing the safety program. First, those actually doing the jobs are often management's best source of ideas about what the potential problems are and how to solve them. Second, it is generally easier to get employees to accept and enthusiastically follow the safety program when they've had a hand in designing it.

For example, when the International Truck and Engine Corp. began designing its new plant in Springfield, Ohio, management opted to involve employees in designing a safer and more efficient facility.[59] This modern plant was to use new types of robot equipment with which the firm had little experience. Management therefore decided that it would be best to involve employee and plant safety representatives as well as the usual product engineering and facilities engineering managers in designing the plant.

Employee participation took several forms. Management appointed joint labor–management safety teams for each department. Several years before the equipment was to arrive, project engineers began speaking with safety team representatives to start designing safeguard systems for the robot equipment. The company sent one safety team, including the union safety chairman, to Japan to watch the robot machines in action, and to develop a checklist of items that the safety teams needed to address. Then, back in Ohio, members of this team worked with employee safety representatives to identify possible hazards and to develop new devices such as color-coded locks to better protect the employees. Once they are committed to the idea of safety, a checklist as in Figure 16-9 can provide employees with a useful reminder of what to watch out for.

Conduct Safety and Health Audits and Inspections

Again, however, programs for reducing unsafe acts are no substitute for eliminating hazards. Routinely inspect all premises for possible safety and health problems, using checklists as aids. Investigate all accidents and "near misses." Have a system in place for letting employees notify managers about hazards.[60] Use employee safety committees to do the inspecting. Committee activities include evaluating safety adequacy, monitoring safety audit findings, and suggesting strategies for improving health and safety performance.[61]

The manager can expedite the safety audit process considerably by using a personal digital assistant such as a PalmPilot. For example, one Microsoft Windows application for designing and completing safety audit questionnaires is called Process and Performance Measurement (PPM). To use this application, the manager or

Figure 16-9
Employee Safety Responsibilities Checklist
Source: Reprinted from www.HR.BLR.com with permission of the publisher, © 2004 *Business and Legal Reports, Inc.*, 141 Mill Rock Road East, Old Saybrook, CT.

> **Employee Safety Responsibilities Checklist**
> ❑ Know what constitutes a safety hazard.
> ❑ Be constantly on the lookout for safety hazards.
> ❑ Correct or report safety hazards immediately.
> ❑ Know and use safe work procedures.
> ❑ Avoid unsafe acts.
> ❑ Keep the wotk area clean and uncluttered.
> ❑ Report accidents, injuries, illnesses, exposures to hazardous substances, and near misses immediately.
> ❑ Report acts and conditions that don't seem right even if you aren't sure if they're hazards.
> ❑ Cooperate with internal inspections and job hazard analyses.
> ❑ Follow company safety rules.
> ❑ Look for ways to make the job safer.
> ❑ Participate actively in safety training.
> ❑ Treat safety as one of your most important job responsibilities.

safety official gives the safety audit a name, enters the audit questions, and lists possible answers. For example, typical questions for a fire extinguisher audit might include, "Are fire extinguishers clearly identified and accessible?" and "Are only approved fire extinguishers used in the workplace?"[62] The supervisor or employee then uses the PalmPilot to record the audit and to automatically transmit it to the firm's safety office.

Table 16-1 summarizes actions for reducing unsafe conditions and acts.

Table 16-1

Reducing Unsafe Conditions and Acts: A Summary

Reduce Unsafe Conditions
Identify and eliminate unsafe conditions.
Use administrative means, such as job rotation.
Use personal protective equipment.
Reduce Unsafe Acts
Emphasize top management commitment.
Emphasize safety.
Establish a safety policy.
Reduce unsafe acts through selection.
Provide safety training.
Use posters and other propaganda.
Use positive reinforcement.
Use behavior-based safety programs.
Encourage worker participation.
Conduct safety and health inspections regularly.

Safety Beyond the Plant Gate

Off-work safety programs are important, too. Experts estimate, for instance, that U.S. businesses pay about $400 per employee yearly to cover the health care costs resulting from off-the-job injuries to employees and their families.[63] In 2000, OSHA tried to extend its health and safety guidelines to workers who work at home, but the resulting complaints forced it to rescind the policy.[64]

A volunteer employee safety team at Rohm & Haas's Deerpark, Texas, facility organized several programs to reduce off-the-job injuries. One month the safety team conducted a seat belt check: "If employees had their seat belts on when they drove up to the plant, they received a scratch-off lottery ticket and information on seat belt safety."[65]

Safety management is a high priority for companies around the world, as "The New Workplace" illustrates.

Controlling Workers' Compensation Costs

In the event an accident does occur, the employee may turn to the employer's workers' compensation insurance to cover his or her expenses and losses. In turn, the employer's workers' compensation premiums reflect the number and size of its claims. There is, therefore, both a humanitarian and financial impetus for reducing claims.

Before the Accident The time to start "controlling" workers' compensation claims is before the accident happens, not after. This involves taking all the safety steps described above. The approach doesn't have to be complicated. For example, LKL Associates, Inc., of Orem, Utah, cut its workers' compensation premiums in half by communicating written safety and substance abuse policies to workers and then strictly enforcing those policies.[66]

The New Workplace

Safety at Saudi Petrol Chemical

The industrial safety and security manager for the Saudi Petrol Chemical Co., in Jubail City, Saudi Arabia, says that his company's excellent safety record is a result of the fact that "our employees are champions of safety."[67] Employees are involved in every part of the safety process. They serve on safety committees, develop and lead daily and monthly safety meetings, and conduct job safety analyses, for instance.

Safety begins with the company's top management. Senior management representatives serve on the company's Management Health and Safety Committee. This committee meets monthly to review incident reports, establish health and safety goals, review safety statistics, and endorse and sponsor safety programs.

The firm cultivates its "safety first" culture from the day a new employee arrives at work.

For example, new employees are encouraged to participate in the safety process during orientation. Then (about six weeks later) they attend a one-day orientation where company officials explain and emphasize the importance of the company's health, safety, and environmental policies and programs. Employees also participate in monthly departmental training sessions to discuss departmental safety issues and safety suggestions. They work with their departmental committees to conduct monthly safety audits, to review and document departmental job safety, and to submit safety suggestions (about 60 suggestions are submitted per month). Employees are required to report every safety incident and near miss, and more than 600 reports are submitted each year.

After the Accident   The injury can be traumatic for the employee, and how the employer handles it is important. The employee will have questions, such as where to go for medical help and whether he or she gets paid for time off. It's also usually at this point that the employee decides whether to retain a workers' compensation attorney to plead his or her case. Here it is important for the employer to be proactive. Provide first aid, and make sure the worker gets quick medical attention; make it clear that you are interested in the injured worker and his or her fears and questions; document the accident; file required accident reports; and encourage a speedy return to work.[68]

It doesn't help that half the employees who return after workers' comp face indifference, criticism, or dismissal.[69] Perhaps the most important thing an employer can do is develop an aggressive return-to-work program, including making light-duty work available. The best solution, for both employer and employee, is for the worker to become a productive member of the company again instead of a victim living on benefits.[70]

Analyzing Claims   Claims-tracking software is crucial for helping employers understand what's driving their workers' compensation claims. For example, a health services agency in Bangor, Maine, purchased CompWatch, a workers' compensation claims management and tracking program, from Benefit Software, Inc. CompWatch enables an employer to track and analyze each of its workers' compensation claims. The agency entered all its previous claims, including near-miss incidents, and used CompWatch to analyze trends. For example, CompWatch could divide automobile accidents into those in which its driver was at fault, and those in which another person caused the accident (or the responsibility could not be determined). The agency discovered some of the auto accidents were apparently due to its drivers' need for training, so the agency introduced a driver safety program. Doing so reduced accidents. In one department, this apparently led to a 42% reduction in auto accidents from one year to the next.[71]

Explain how to deal with important occupational health problems.

● WORKPLACE HEALTH HAZARDS: PROBLEMS AND REMEDIES

Most workplace health hazards aren't obvious ones like unguarded equipment or slippery floors. Many are unseen hazards (like mold) that the company inadvertently produces as part of its production processes. Other problems, like drug abuse, the employees may create for themselves. In either case, these health hazards are often as much or more dangerous to workers' health and safety than are obvious hazards like slippery floors. The manager must therefore address them. Typical workplace exposure hazards may include:

1. Chemicals and other hazardous materials.
2. Excessive noise and vibrations.
3. Temperature extremes.
4. Biohazards including those that are normally occurring (such as mold) and man-made (such as anthrax).
5. Ergonomic hazards (such as poorly designed equipment that forces workers to do their jobs while contorted in unnatural positions).
6. And, the more familiar safety-related hazards such as slippery floors and blocked passageways.[72]

As an example, Table 16-2 lists some OSHA substance-specific health standards. Hazardous substances like these require air sampling and other preventive and

Table 16-2

OSHA Substance-Specific Health Standards

Substance	Permissable Exposure Limits
Asbestos	.1001
Vinyl chloride	.1017
Inorganic arsenic	.1018
Lead	.1025
Cadmium	.1027
Benzene	.1028
Coke oven emissions	.1029
Cotton dust	.1043
1,2-Dibromo-3-chloropropane	.1044
Acrylonitrile	.1045
Ethylene oxide	.1047
Formaldehyde	.1048
4,4′-Methylene-dianaline	.1050
Methylene chloride	.1051

Source: John F. Rekus, "If You Thought Air Sampling Was Too Difficult to Handle, This Guide Can Help You Tackle Routine Sampling with Confidence, Part I," *Occupational Hazards,* May 2003, p. 43.

precautionary measures. They are also more widespread than most managers realize. For example, cadmium pigments provide color to many paints and coatings, and ethyl alcohol is often used as a solvent in industrial processes. Altogether, OSHA standards lists permissible exposure limits for about 600 chemicals.

The Basic Industrial Hygiene Program

Recognizing and developing precautions for hazards like these has become especially important since the 9/11 incidents and the anthrax mail scares of 2001–2002. Managing exposure hazards like these comes under the category of *industrial hygiene*, and involves a process of recognition, evaluation, and control. First, the facility's health and safety officers (possibly working with teams of supervisors and employees) must *recognize* possible exposure hazards. Doing so typically involves conducting plant/facility walk-around surveys, employee interviews, records reviews, and reviews of government and nongovernmental standards regarding various occupational exposure hazards.

Having identified a possible hazard, the *evaluation* phase involves determining how severe the hazard is. This usually requires measuring the exposure, comparing the measured exposure to some benchmark (as in Table 16-2), and determining whether the risk is within tolerances.[73]

Finally, the hazard *control* phase involves taking steps to eliminate or reduce the hazard so that it no longer ranks as dangerous. In this regard, familiar personal protective equipment such as face masks or shoe guards are generally the *last* recommended option for dealing with such problems, not the first. Before relying on these, the employer must install engineering controls (such as process enclosures or ventilation), and administrative controls (including training and improved housekeeping); this is mandatory under OSHA.

Asbestos Exposure at Work

Exposure to asbestos is a major potential source of occupational respiratory disease. This worker wears protective clothing and a respirator to remove asbestos from ceiling panels in a classroom.

There are four major sources of occupational respiratory diseases: asbestos, silica, lead, and carbon dioxide. Of these, asbestos has become a major concern, in part because of publicity surrounding asbestos in buildings such as schools constructed before the mid-1970s. Major efforts are still under way to rid these buildings of the substance.

OSHA standards require several actions with respect to asbestos. Companies must monitor the air whenever an employer expects the level of asbestos to rise to one-half the allowable limit. (You would therefore have to monitor if you expected asbestos levels of 0.1 fiber per cubic centimeter.) Engineering controls—walls, special filters, and so forth—are required to maintain an asbestos level that complies with OSHA standards. Only then can employers use respirators if additional efforts are still required to achieve compliance.

Infectious Diseases: The Case of SARS

With many employees traveling to and from international destinations, monitoring and controlling infectious diseases like Ebola and SARS has become an important safety issue. In 2003 there were 400 potential SARS candidates and 70 confirmed cases in the United States, and, in 2004, SARS reappeared in China. This, therefore, does not seem to be a problem that is about to go away. The Centers for Disease Control (CDC) says workers who traveled to areas with known SARS outbreaks in the last 10 days or who had close contact with people with suspected SARS, may be at risk for developing the disease.[74] Obviously, employers must make provisions for ensuring that a returning employee does not inadvertently infect one or more colleagues.

Employers can take a number of steps to prevent the entry or spread of infectious diseases like SARS into their workplaces. These include:

1. Closely monitor CDC travel alerts. The CDC issues travel advisories (which recommend deferring nonessential travel) and travel alerts (which simply inform travelers of health concerns and provides precautions). You can access this information at www.cdc.gov.

2. Provide daily medical screenings for employees returning from SARS-infected areas.

3. Deny access to your facility for 10 days to employees or visitors returning from affected areas, particularly those who have had contact with suspected infected individuals.

4. Tell employees to stay home if they have a fever or respiratory system symptoms.

5. Clean work areas and surfaces regularly.

6. Stagger breaks. Offer several lunch periods to reduce overcrowding.

7. Emphasize to employees the importance of frequent handwashing, and make sanitizers containing alcohol easily available throughout the workplace.

Alcoholism and Substance Abuse

Alcoholism and substance abuse are serious and widespread problems at work. While the percentage of full-time U.S. workers engaging in illegal drug use has reportedly dropped in the last 15 years or so, about 15% of workers still report having used illicit drugs in the past year. Studies suggest that 70% of illicit drug users aged 18 to 49 work full-time, and that drug-using employees are over three and a half times more likely to be involved in workplace accidents.[75]

Some experts estimate that as many as 50% of all "problem employees" in industry are actually alcoholics. One estimate places the cost of a substance abuser's damage to a company at $7,000 per abuser per year.[76]

The effects of alcoholism on the worker and the work are severe.[77] Both the quality and quantity of the work decline, and a form of "on-the-job absenteeism" occurs as efficiency declines. The alcoholic's on-the-job accidents usually don't increase significantly, apparently because he or she becomes much more cautious (but effectiveness suffers). However, the off-the-job accident rate is higher than for nonalcoholics. Morale of other workers drops as they have to shoulder the work of their alcoholic peer.

Recognizing the alcoholic on the job is another problem. Early symptoms such as tardiness can be similar to those of other problems and thus hard to classify. The supervisor is not a psychiatrist, and without specialized training, identifying—and dealing with—the alcoholic is difficult.

Table 16.3 presents a chart showing observable behavior patterns that indicate alcohol-related problems. As you can see, alcohol-related problems range from tardiness in the earliest stages of alcohol abuse to prolonged, unpredictable absences in its later stages.

Dealing with Substance Abuse   As explained earlier in this book, most firms test applicants and (often) current employees for drugs. Such testing is generally effective. Preemployment drug testing discourages those on drugs from applying for work or coming to work for employers who do testing. One study found that over 30% of regular drug users employed full-time said they were less likely to work for a company that conducted preemployment screening.[78] Some applicants or employees may try to evade the test, for instance, by purchasing "clean" specimens to use. Several states, including New Jersey, North Carolina, Virginia, Oregon, South Carolina, Pennsylvania, Louisiana, Texas, and Nebraska have passed laws making drug-test fraud a crime.[79]

The big question is what to do when a current employee tests positive for alcohol or drugs. Disciplining, discharge, in-house counseling, and referral to an outside agency are the four traditional prescriptions. In practice, each employer tends to develop its own approach to dealing with substance abuse problems. One HR director says: "We present the employee with the option of a mandatory professional assessment (which may result in rehab and/or counseling depending on the results of the assessment). If the employee refuses the professional assessment, employment is terminated."[80] Another describes her company's policy this way:

> *Some employers have zero tolerance and terminate immediately. Some employers don't have a choice (pharmaceutical labs, for example). Others are lenient. Our policy is a three-strikes-and-you're-out process. The first step is a warning notification and permission given to us to test the employee at any time we want—for a period of five years. The second step is a mandatory substance abuse rehabilitation program at the employee's own expense . . . the third step is immediate termination for cause.[81]*

Other steps involve training of supervisors or company policy. Training supervisors to identify alcoholics or drug abusers and the problems they create is advisable. Employers should also establish and communicate a company policy. This policy should state management's position on alcohol and drug abuse and on the use and possession of illegal drugs on company premises. It should also list the methods (such as urinalysis) used to determine the causes of poor performance; state the company's views on rehabilitation, including workplace counseling; and specify

Table 16-3 **Observable Behavior Patterns Indicating Possible Alcohol-Related Problems**

Stage	Absenteeism	General Behavior	Job Performance
I Early	Tardiness Quits early Absence from work situations ("I drink to relieve tension")	Complaints from fellow employees for not doing his or her share Overreaction Complaints of not "feeling well" Makes untrue statements	Misses deadlines Commits errors (frequently) Lower job efficiency Criticism from the boss

II
Middle
	Frequent days off for vague or implausible
	  reasons
	
	("I feel guilty about sneaking drinks"; "I have
	  tremors")
		Marked changes
		Undependable statements
		Avoids fellow employees
		Borrows money from fellow employees
		Exaggerates work accomplishments
		Frequent hospitalization
		Minor injuries on the job
		  (repeatedly)
			General deterioration
			Cannot concentrate
			Occasional lapses of memory
			Warning from boss

III Late	Frequent days off; several days at a time	Aggressive and belligerent behavior Domestic problems interfere with work	Far below expectation Punitive disciplinary action

Middle	Does not return from lunch
	("I don't feel like eating"; "I don't want to
	  talk about it"; "I like to drink alone")
		Financial difficulties (garnishments, and
		  so on)
		More frequent hospitalization
		Resignation: Does not want to discuss
		  problems
		Problems with the laws in the
		  community	

IV Approaching Terminal Stage	Prolonged unpredictable absences ("My job interferes with my drinking")	Drinking on the job (probably) Completely undependable Repeated hospitalization Serious financial problems Serious family problems: divorce	Uneven Generally incompetent Faces termination or hospitalization

Note: Based on content analysis of files of recovering alcoholics in five organizations. From *Managing and Employing the Handicapped: The Untapped Potential*, by Gopal C. Patl and John I. Adkins Jr., with Clenn Morrison (Lake Forest, IL: Brace-Park, Human Resource Press, 1981).

Source: Gopal C. Patl and John I. Adkins Jr., "The Employer's Role in Alcoholism Assistance," *Personnel Journal* 62, no. 7 (July 1983), p. 570.

penalties for policy violations. Additional steps employers take include conducting workplace inspections (searching employees for illegal substances) and using undercover agents.

Supervisors are in a tricky position: They should be the company's first line of defense in combating workplace drug abuse, but should avoid becoming detectives or medical diagnosticians. Guidelines supervisors should follow include these:

■ If an employee appears to be under the influence of drugs or alcohol, ask how the employee feels and look for signs of impairment such as slurred speech. Send an employee judged unfit for duty home. (See Table 16-3.)

▌ Make a written record of your observations and follow up each incident. In addition, inform workers of the number of warnings the company will tolerate before requiring termination.

▌ Refer troubled employees to the company's employee assistance program.

Workplace Substance Abuse and the Law   The federal Drug-Free Workplace Act requires employers with federal government contracts or grants to ensure a drug-free workplace by taking (and certifying that they have taken) a number of steps. For example, to be eligible for contract awards or grants, employers must agree to:

▌ Publish a policy prohibiting the unlawful manufacture, distribution, dispensing, possession, or use of controlled substances in the workplace.

▌ Establish a drug-free awareness program that informs employees about the dangers of workplace drug abuse.

▌ Inform employees that they are required, as a condition of employment, not only to abide by the employer's policy but also to report any criminal convictions for drug-related activities in the workplace.[82]

The U.S. Department of Transportation also has its own rules regarding drug testing in the transportation industry.[83] These rules require random breath alcohol tests as well as preemployment, postaccident, reasonable suspicion, and return-to-duty testing for workers in safety-sensitive jobs in transportation industries including aviation, interstate motor carrier, railroad, pipeline, and commercial marine.

Legal Risks   Dealing with alcoholism and drugs at work does entail legal risks. Employees have sued for invasion of privacy, wrongful discharge, defamation, and illegal searches. Therefore, before implementing any drug control program, ask:

▌ How will you inform workers about your substance abuse policy? Use employee handbooks, bulletin board postings, pay inserts, and the like to publicize your substance abuse plans.

▌ What testing, such as urinalysis, will be required of prospective and current employees? Explain the conditions under which testing may occur and the procedures for handling employees who refuse to be tested.

▌ What accommodations would you make for employees who voluntarily seek treatment? Substance abuse is a physical handicap under federal and some state laws. You may be required to make reasonable accommodations for employees who enter alcohol or drug treatment programs.

Stress, Burnout, and Depression

Problems such as alcoholism and drug abuse sometimes result from stress, especially job stress. Here, job-related factors such as overwork, relocation, and problems with customers eventually put the person under so much stress that a pathological reaction such as drug abuse or depression occurs.

A variety of external factors can lead to job stress. These include work schedule, pace of work, job security, route to and from work, and the number and nature of customers or clients. Even noise, including people talking and telephones ringing, contributes to stress: 54% of office workers in one recent survey said such noise often bothered them.[84]

However, no two people react to the job in the same way, because personal factors also influence stress. For example, Type A personalities—people who are workaholics and who feel driven to always be on time and meet deadlines—normally place themselves under greater stress than do others. Similarly, your tolerance for ambiguity, patience, self-esteem, health and exercise, and work and sleep patterns can also affect how you react to stress. Add to job stress the stress caused by nonjob problems like divorce and, as you might imagine, many workers are problems waiting to happen.

Job stress has serious consequences for both employer and employee. The human consequences include anxiety, depression, anger, and various physical consequences, such as cardiovascular disease, headaches, and accidents. For the organization, consequences include reductions in the quantity and quality of performance, increased absenteeism and turnover, and increased grievances and health care costs.[85] A study of 46,000 employees concluded that stress and depression may cause employees to seek medical care for vague physical and psychological problems and can in fact lead to more serious health conditions. High-stress workers' health care costs were 46% higher than those of their less-stressed co-workers.[86]

Reducing Job Stress   There are a number of ways to alleviate dysfunctional stress. These range from commonsense remedies (such as getting more sleep and eating better) to more exotic remedies like biofeedback and meditation. Finding a more suitable job, getting counseling, and planning and organizing each day's activities are other sensible responses. In his book *Stress and the Manager*, Dr. Karl Albrecht suggests the following ways for a person to reduce job stress:

- Build rewarding, pleasant, cooperative relationships with colleagues and employees.
- Don't bite off more than you can chew.
- Build an especially effective and supportive relationship with your boss.
- Negotiate with your boss for realistic deadlines on important projects.
- Learn as much as you can about upcoming events and get as much lead time as you can to prepare for them.
- Find time every day for detachment and relaxation.
- Take a walk around the office to keep your body refreshed and alert.
- Find ways to reduce unnecessary noise.
- Reduce the amount of trivia in your job; delegate routine work whenever possible.
- Limit interruptions.
- Don't put off dealing with distasteful problems.
- Make a constructive "worry list" that includes solutions for each problem.[87]

The employer and its HR specialists and supervisors can also play a role in identifying and reducing job stress. Supportive supervisors and fair treatment are two obvious steps. Based on a survey of 1,299 employers by one insurance company, other steps include:

- Reduce personal conflicts on the job.
- Have open communication between management and employees.
- Support employees' efforts, for instance, by regularly asking how they are doing.
- Ensure effective job–person fit, since a mistake can trigger stress.[88]
- Give employees more control over their jobs.[89]
- Provide employee assistance programs including professional counseling.[90]

burnout
The total depletion of physical and mental resources caused by excessive striving to reach an unrealistic work-related goal.

Burnout   **Burnout** is a phenomenon closely associated with job stress. Experts define burnout as the total depletion of physical and mental resources caused by excessive striving to reach an unrealistic work-related goal. Burnout doesn't just spontaneously appear. Instead, it builds gradually, manifesting itself in symptoms such as irritability, discouragement, entrapment, and resentment.[91]

What can a burnout candidate do? Here are some suggestions:

■ *Break your patterns.* First, survey how you spend your time. Are you doing a variety of things or the same one repeatedly? The more well rounded your life is, the better protected you are against burnout.

■ *Get away from it all periodically.* Schedule occasional periods of introspection during which you can get away from your usual routine, perhaps alone, to seek a perspective on where you are and where you are going.

■ *Reassess your goals in terms of their intrinsic worth.* Are the goals you've set for yourself attainable? Are they really worth the sacrifices you'll have to make?

■ *Think about your work.* Could you do as good a job without being so intense or by also pursuing outside interests?

RESEARCH INSIGHT   If you're thinking of taking a vacation to eliminate your burnout, you might as well save your money, according to one study.[92] In this study, 76 clerks in an administrative department in the headquarters of an electronics firm in central Israel completed questionnaires measuring job stress and burnout twice before a vacation, once during the vacation, and twice after the vacation.

The clerks' burnout certainly did decline during the vacation. The problem was the burnout quickly returned to pre-vacation levels by the time of the second post-vacation survey. At least for these 76 clerks, burnout moved partway back toward its pre-vacation level by three days after the vacation, and all the way by three weeks after they returned to work.[93]

The good news, of course, is that burnout can apparently be reduced by removing the stressors that caused it in the first place. The bad news is that (without other changes) the burnout will quickly return once the vacation is over. One implication, as these researchers point out, is that mini vacations during the workday—"such as time off for physical exercise, meditation, power naps, and reflective thinking"—might help reduce stress and burnout.[94]

Employee depression is a serious problem at work. Experts estimate that depression results in more than 200 million lost workdays in the United States annually, and may cost U.S. businesses as much as $24 billion per year just in absenteeism and lost productivity.[95] Depressed people also tend to have worse safety records.[96]

Employers therefore need to take steps to train supervisors to identify warning signs of depression, and to counsel and encourage those who may need such services to take advantage of the firm's employee assistance program. Typical warning signs of depression (if they last for more than two weeks) include: persistent sad, anxious, or "empty" moods, sleeping too little, reduced appetite, loss of interest in activities once enjoyed, restlessness or irritability, and difficulty concentrating.[97]

Managing workplace health hazards can be a costly process. "Improving Productivity Through HRIS" shows how information systems can help improve the efficiency of this process.

Computer-Related Health Problems

The fact that many workers spend hours each day working with computers is creating health problems at work. Short-term eye problems like burning, itching, and tearing as well as eyestrain and eye soreness are common complaints among video display users.

Improving Productivity Through HRIS

Internet-based Safety Improvement Solutions

In today's business environment, companies need to obtain efficiencies wherever they can, and Internet-based systems can help them manage their safety programs much more efficiently. For example, consider the matter of **material safety data sheets (MSDS)**. Any employees handling hazardous chemicals must be familiar with those chemicals' MSDS. These sheets, from OSHA, describe the precautions employees are to take when dealing with the chemicals, and what to do if problems arise. In a dry cleaning store, for instance, the cleaner–spotter is supposed to be knowledgeable about the MSDS for chemicals like hydrafluorous acid (used for stain removal) and perchloroethylene (used for cleaning).

Particularly for large firms, managing the MSDS can cost millions of dollars annually. The employer needs to distribute the appropriate MSDS to each employee, ensure that the employees study and learn their contents, and continually update the data sheets based on new information from OSHA. Many firms (particularly pharmaceuticals manufacturers and chemical companies) are therefore putting their MSDS programs online. The Web-based systems provide a platform upon which the employer can mount all its relevant MSDS, make these available to the employees who need them, monitor and test employees on the sheets' use, and update the MSDS as required. Systems like these provide an inexpensive way to boost the productivity and effectiveness of one essential aspect of an employer's safety and health program.

A good MSDS information system should offer several basic features.[98]

- *Customization and ease of access.* The system you choose should provide for indexing and retrieval of the key information your employees need, and allow the employer to customize the system for its own unique needs.
- *Platform.* Preferably use software which an applications service provider makes available on its own Web platform, so that the employer can easily change its own software and hardware without having to modify or maintain the MSDS system.

- *Revision management.* The MSDS' applications service provider company should provide comprehensive updates and revision management, including contacting chemical manufacturers on a regular basis.
- *Conversion of hard copy to electronic.* In general, software vendors that simply scan the hard-copy data sheets and related information cannot provide the same level of legibility as suppliers that can convert hard copy to traditional text files.
- *Searchability.* The system should allow the employer and its employees to search by chemical or generic names, as well as conduct searches for words or phrases anywhere in the body of the text.
- *The depth and diversity of specialized services.* The service provider must have the capability to provide service to all the employer's national and international sites. Ideally, the vendor should also have the ability to adapt its software to the company's own enterprisewide software. For example, it should be able to link its MSDS system with the employer's existing online training systems, as well as its maintenance, inventory, and purchasing systems.

Employers also turn to the Web to support their safety training programs. For example, puresafety.com (www.puresafety.com) enables firms to create their own training Web sites, complete with a "message from the safety director." Once an employer arranges to install the puresafety Web site, it can populate the site with courses from companies that supply health and safety courses via puresafety.com. The courses themselves are available in various formats, including digital versions of videotape training, and PowerPoint presentations. Puresafety.com also develops or modifies existing courses for employers.

Sites like puresafety.com make it easy for an employer to quickly organize and launch a health and safety program for its employees, and to efficiently deliver individual courses to employees, when and where they want them.[99]

material safety data sheets (MSDS)
Sheets that describe the precautions required by OSHA that employees are to take when dealing with hazardous chemicals, and what to do if problems arise.

Backaches and neckaches are other frequent complaints. These often occur because employees try to compensate for problems like glare by maneuvering into awkward body positions. There may also be a tendency for computer users to suffer from cumulative motion disorders, such as carpal tunnel syndrome, caused by repetitive use of the hands and arms at uncomfortable angles.[100] However, a recent study reported in the journal *Neurology* concluded that heavy computer work does not increase the risk of carpal tunnel syndrome.[101]

NIOSH has provided general recommendations regarding the use of video displays. These include:

1. Give employees rest breaks. The institute recommends a 15-minute rest break after two hours of continuous work for operators under moderate workloads.

2. Design maximum flexibility into the work station so it can be adapted to the individual operator. For example, use adjustable chairs with midback supports.

3. Reduce glare with devices such as shades over windows, and recessed or indirect lighting.

4. Give workers a complete preplacement vision exam to ensure properly corrected vision for reduced visual strain.

5. Place the keyboard in front of the employee, tilted away with the rear portion lower than the front.

6. Place the computer mouse and mouse pad as close to the user as possible, and ensure there are no obstructions on the desk that impede mouse movement.[102]

7. Allow the user to position his or her wrists at the same level as the elbow.

8. Put the monitor at or just below eye level, at a distance of 18 to 30 inches from the eyes.

9. Let the wrists rest lightly on a pad for support.

10. Put the feet flat on the floor, or on a footrest.[103]

AIDS and the Workplace

Some of employers' most important AIDS-related questions concern their legal responsibilities in dealing with AIDS sufferers.[104] The employer cannot single out an employee for AIDS testing, because doing so would subject the person to discriminatory treatment under the ADA. Similarly, while you can probably require a physical exam that includes an AIDS test as a condition of employment, refusing to hire the person because of positive test results could put you at risk of an ADA discrimination suit. Mandatory leave cannot be required of a person with AIDS unless work performance has deteriorated. And, preemployment inquiries about AIDS or other illnesses or disabilities would not be advisable, given the prohibitions of the Americans with Disabilities Act.

All employees (including managers) should be familiar with their obligations under the Americans with Disabilities Act and the Family and Medical Leave Act. For example, make sure supervisors know to provide reasonable accommodations such as refrigerator access for storage of medicines, and periodic daily medical breaks.

Workplace Smoking

Smoking is a serious health and cost problem for both employees and employers. For employers, these costs derive from higher health and fire insurance, as well as increased absenteeism and reduced productivity (which occurs when, for instance, a smoker takes a 10-minute break to finish a cigarette behind the store). In general, "smoking employees are less healthy than nonsmokers, are absent more, make more and more expensive claims for health and disability benefits, and endanger co-workers who breathe smoky air."[105]

Nonsmoking employees who are concerned with inhaling secondhand smoke are suing their employers. The California Environmental Protection Agency estimates that each year in the United States, secondhand smoke causes 3,000 deaths due to lung cancer and 35,000 to 62,000 illnesses due to heart problems (not all work related).[106]

What You Can and Cannot Do   Can the employer institute a smoking ban? The answer depends on several things, including the state in which you are located, whether or not your firm is unionized, and the details of the situation. For example, instituting a smoking ban in a unionized facility which formerly allowed employees to smoke means altering conditions of work. It is therefore subject to collective bargaining.[107] Many states and municipalities now ban indoor smoking in public areas. In general, the best advice seems to be to proceed one step at a time, starting with restrictions that are not too confining.

In general, you can deny a job to a smoker as long as you don't use smoking as a surrogate for some other kind of discrimination. A "no-smokers-hired" policy does not, according to one expert, violate the Americans with Disabilities Act (since smoking is not considered a disability), and in general "employers' adoption of a no-smokers-hired policy is not illegal under federal law."[108] The problem arises, as noted above, when you try to implement smoking restrictions for current employees in a facility.

Violence at Work

Violence against employees has become an enormous problem at work. Homicide is the second biggest cause of fatal workplace injuries, and surveys by the National Institute of Occupational Safety and Health (NIOSH) found that nonfatal workplace assaults resulted in more than 876,000 lost workdays and about $16 billion in lost wages in one recent year.

While robbery was the primary motive for homicide at work, a co-worker or personal associate committed roughly one of seven workplace homicides.[109] And these numbers are just the tip of the iceberg. For example, 29 U.S. Postal Service supervisors and colleagues were slain by disgruntled postal workers in one 10-year period, but there were also 350 assaults by postal workers in one year alone.[110]

While men have more fatal occupational injuries than do women, the proportion of women who are victims of assault is much higher. The Gender-Motivated Violence Act, part of the comprehensive Violence Against Women Act passed by Congress in 1994, imposes significant liabilities on employers whose women employees become violence victims.[111]

Fatal workplace violence against women has three main sources. Over two-thirds of all women (many working in retail establishments) murdered at work were victims of random criminal violence carried out by an assailant unknown to the victim, as might occur during a robbery. Co-workers, family members, or previous friends or acquaintances carried out the remaining homicides. Specifically, in a survey of nearly 600 full-time men and women workers nationwide, clients, patients, and other strangers accounted for 68% of all violent attacks.[112] Co-workers accounted for about 20% of the attacks, and an employer or boss about 7%.

With respect to bosses, one report refers to bullying as the "silent epidemic" of the workplace, "where abusive behavior, threats, and intimidation often go unreported."[113] And, workplace violence doesn't just affect people. It can also manifest itself in sabotaging the firm's property, software, or information databases.[114]

Violence is more associated with some jobs than others. In one study, researchers constructed a "risk for violence scale." In its final form, this listed 22 job characteristics that the researchers found correlated with violence on the job. Jobs with a high likelihood for violence include those jobs that involve physical care of others, decisions that influence other people's lives, involve handling guns, exercise security functions, exercise physical control over others, interact with frustrated individuals, and handle weapons other than guns, for instance.[115]

Employers need to eliminate workplace violence on humanitarian grounds, but there are also legal reasons for doing so. For example, the employee-victim may sue the employer, on the theory that the employer negligently hired or retained someone the employer should have known could be violent.[116]

Employers can take several steps to reduce workplace violence. Let's look at them.

Heightened Security Measures   Heightened security measures are an employer's first line of defense against workplace violence, whether that violence comes from co-workers, customers, or outsiders. NIOSH suggests these sensible precautions for reducing the risk of workplace violence:[117] Improve external lighting; use drop safes to minimize cash on hand and post signs noting that only a limited amount of cash is on hand; install silent alarms and surveillance cameras; increase the number of staff on duty; provide staff training in conflict resolution and nonviolent response; and close establishments during high-risk hours late at night and early in the morning.[118] Employers can also issue a weapons policy that states, for instance, that employees cannot bring firearms and other dangerous or deadly weapons onto the facility.

Because about half of workplace homicides occur in the retail industry, OSHA issued voluntary recommendations aimed at reducing homicides and injuries in such establishments. Particularly for late-night or early-morning retail workers, the suggestions include: Install mirrors and improved lighting; provide silent and personal alarms; reduce store hours during high-risk periods; install drop safes and signs that indicate little cash is kept on hand; erect bullet-resistance enclosures; and increase staffing during high-risk hours.[119]

Improved Employee Screening   Screening out potentially explosive employees and applicants is the employer's next line of defense. At a minimum, this means a rigorous preemployment investigation. Obtain a detailed employment application and solicit an applicant's employment history, educational background, and references. A personal interview, personnel testing, and a review and verification of all information provided should also be included. Sample interview questions to ask might include, for instance, "What frustrates you?" and "Who was your worst supervisor and why?"[120]

That testing can screen out those prone to workplace aggression is clear. In one study researchers measured the relationship among personal characteristics such as "trait anger" (for instance, how participants feel about having a fiery temper when they do not receive recognition for doing good work) and "attitude toward revenge" (which of course measures a person's attitude toward revenge). The researchers concluded that measurable individual differences variables like trait anger "account for more than 60% of the variance in our measure of the incidence of workplace aggression."[121]

Certain background circumstances indicate the need for a more in-depth background investigation of the applicant. Red flags include:[122]

An unexplained gap in employment.

Incomplete or false information on the résumé or application.

A negative, unfavorable, or false reference.

Prior insubordinate or violent behavior on the job.

A criminal history involving harassing or violent behavior.

A prior termination for cause with a suspicious (or no) explanation.

A history of depression or significant psychiatric problems.

A history of drug or alcohol abuse.

Strong indications of instability in the individual's work or personal life as indicated, for example, by frequent job changes or geographic moves.

Lost licenses or accreditations.[123]

Workplace Violence Training   Employers should supplement enhanced security and screening with workplace training. Several firms offer video training programs that explain what workplace violence is, identify its causes and signs, and offer tips on how to prevent it and what to do when it occurs. Firms should also train supervisors to identify the clues that typically precede violent incidents. These include:[124]

■ *Verbal threats.* Individuals often talk about what they may do. An employee might say, "Bad things are going to happen to so-and-so," or "That propane tank in the back could blow up easily."

■ *Physical actions.* Troubled employees may try to intimidate others, gain access to places where they do not belong, or flash a concealed weapon in the workplace to test reactions.

■ *Frustration.* Most cases do not involve a panicked individual; a more likely scenario would involve an employee who has a frustrated sense of entitlement to a promotion, for example.

■ *Obsession.* An employee may hold a grudge against a co-worker or supervisor, and some cases stem from romantic interest.[125]

Organizational Justice   A related step is to create a workplace culture emphasizing mutual respect, justice, and civility. Of course, this is easier said than done. In general, management should emphasize by word and deed that it believes deeply in and demands civility.[126] Instituting safeguards to ensure that managers treat employees fairly can reduce violent behavior at work. As three researchers recently noted, "from the emerging empirical evidence, it appears that even though revenge can be motivated by non-justice concerns, such as organizational politics, it typically occurs in response to a perceived injustice."[127]

Consider one study. The researchers asked respondents to reply to the following item: "Think back over your time as an employee in your current organization when you've been offended by another person. Please write a description of the offense below." The researchers also asked the respondents how they reacted to the injustice.

The findings provide insight into the mechanisms of revenge. First (not surprisingly), they found that the employees were more willing to exact revenge against less powerful offenders.[128] Second, high-status victims were less likely to try to get revenge against low-status employees, possibly because of societal norms that people in positions of power should not take retaliatory action. Third, it was clear that blame was positively related to revenge; an employee who blamed another for some injustice or personal affront was more likely to try to seek revenge, and less likely to seek reconciliation. The implication is that instituting policies and training that reduce the potential for unjust actions will likely reduce the chances that employees will express frustration with violence or revenge.

Enhanced Attention to Employee Retention/Dismissal   Particularly given the potential liability of retaining employees who subsequently commit violent acts, employers also need effective procedures for deciding which employees should be retained. Circumstances to watch out for in deciding whether or not to retain employees include:

An act of violence on or off the job.

Erratic behavior evidencing a loss of awareness of actions.

Overly defensive, obsessive, or paranoid tendencies.

Overly confrontational or antisocial behavior.

Sexually aggressive behavior.

Isolationist or loner tendencies.

Insubordinate behavior with a suggestion of violence.

Tendency to overreact to criticism.

Exaggerated interest in war, guns, violence, catastrophes.

The commission of a serious breach of security.

Possession of weapons, guns, knives at the workplace.

Violation of privacy rights of others such as searching desks or stalking.

Chronic complaining and frequent, unreasonable grievances.

A retribution-oriented or get-even attitude.[129]

Dismissing Violent Employees   The manager should use caution when firing or disciplining potentially violent employees. Analyze and anticipate, based on the person's history, what kind of aggressive behavior to expect. Have a security guard or a violence expert present when the dismissal takes place. Clear away furniture and things the person might throw. Don't wear loose clothing that the person might grab. Don't make it sound as if you're accusing the employee; instead say that according to company policy, you're required to take action. Maintain the person's dignity and try to emphasize something good about the employee. Providing job counseling for terminated employees may also help get the employee over the traumatic postdismissal adjustment.[130]

Consider the case of an executive suspected of sabotaging his former employer's computer system, causing up to $20 million in damage. What made this man, who'd been earning $186,000 a year, do such a thing? A note he wrote anonymously to the president provides some insight: "I have been loyal to the Company in good and bad times for over thirty years. . . . What is most upsetting is the manner in which you chose to end our employment. I was expecting a member of top management to come down from his ivory tower to face us directly with a layoff announcement, rather than sending the kitchen supervisor with guards to escort us off the premises like criminals. . . . We will not wait for God to punish you—we will take measures into our own hands."[131]

The employer should also consider obtaining restraining orders against those who have exhibited a tendency to act violently in the workplace. The HR manager should thus understand where to obtain restraining orders, what they do, and the process for obtaining them.[132]

Dealing with Angry Employees   What do you do when confronted by an angry, potentially explosive employee? Here are some suggestions:[133]

Make eye contact.

Stop what you are doing and give your full attention.

Speak in a calm voice and create a relaxed environment.

Be open and honest.

Let the person have his or her say.

Ask for specific examples of what the person is upset about.

Be careful to define the problem.

Ask open-ended questions and explore all sides of the issue.

Listen: As one expert says, "Often, angry people simply want to be listened to. They need a supportive, empathic ear from someone they can trust."[134]

Legal Constraints on Reducing Workplace Violence   As sensible as it is to try to screen out potentially violent employees, doing so incurs the risk of liability and lawsuits. Most states have policies that encourage the employment and rehabilitation of ex-offenders, and some states therefore limit the use of criminal records in hiring decisions.[135] For example, except in certain limited instances, Article 23-A of the New York Corrections Law makes it unlawful to discriminate against job applicants based on their prior criminal convictions. Similarly, courts have interpreted Title VII of the Civil Rights Act of 1964 as restricting employers from making employment decisions based on arrest records, since doing so may unfairly discriminate against some minority groups.

Aside from federal law, most states prohibit discrimination under any circumstances based on arrest records, and on prior convictions unless a direct relationship exists between the prior conviction and the job, or the employment of the individual presents an unreasonable risk to people or property.[136] And developing a "violent employee" profile could end up merely describing a mental impairment and thus violate the Americans with Disabilities Act.[137] Eliminating workplace violence while safely navigating the legal shoals is, therefore, a risky business.

● OCCUPATIONAL SECURITY, SAFETY, AND HEALTH IN A POST-9/11 WORLD

The 9/11 World Trade Center and Pentagon attacks accounted for about one-third of the 8,600 workplace fatalities in 2001, and prompted employers to start focusing more attention on security. One post-9/11 survey found that 52% of employers had instituted new security arrangements since the attacks.[138] Figure 16-10 illustrates immediate steps employers took to upgrade safety and security immediately following the 9/11 terrorist attacks. For example, about 46% of the surveyed employers issued gloves, masks, or other personnel protective equipment to at least specific employees (such as mail room workers). Forty-three percent instituted new, more stringent, building entry procedures. Forty-six percent implemented new emergency/disaster recovery plans.

Another survey (sponsored by Hartford Financial Services Group) found that employers instituted much stricter facility screening requirements. For example, the number of unauthorized visitors entering facilities dropped from 32% to 13% in the two years following the 9/11 attacks, and the number of firms instituting identification requirements or hiring security personnel rose by 15% between December 2001 and July 2002. Many firms are also instituting special handling procedures for suspicious mail packages, and holding regular emergency evacuation drills. Some are even setting aside special "safe room" shelters, complete with food and water supplies to last several days in the event of a chemical, radioactive, or biological attack.

Figure 16-10
Safety, Security, and Emergency Planning Initiatives Following Terrorist Incidents
Source: Adapted from "After Sept. 11th, Safety and Security Moved to the Fore," *BNA Bulletin to Management,* January 17, 2002, p. 52.

Initiatives	Percent of Employers
	(146)
Safety and Security	
Personal protective equipment	46%
New/more stringent building entry procedures	43
Restricted access to some areas	19
Closed entrances/areas	17
New/additional security personnel	12
Extended work hours for security personnel	10
New security devices (e.g., metal detectors)	10
New/more stringent applicant screening	7
Physical barriers to building entry	5
Emergency Planning and Disaster Recovery	
Review emergency/disaster recovery plan(s)	46
Revise emergency/disaster recovery plan(s)	32
New/revised evacuation drills	23
Form committee or task force to address emergency planning/disaster recovery	15
Develop emergency/disaster recovery plan(s)	14
Develop/revise procedures for data backup	14
Develop/revise procedures for tracking employee whereabouts	10

The attacks caused most employers to reprioritize their security concerns. Before 9/11, the top workplace security concerns were as follows:[139]

1. Workplace violence
2. Internet/intranet security
3. Employee selection and screening
4. Fraud and white-collar crime
5. Business interruption and disaster recovery
6. General employee theft
7. Hardware/software theft
8. Workplace drug and alcohol use
9. Unethical business conduct
10. Property crime, such as external theft and vandalism

After the attacks, *physical security* quickly joined the top 10 list.

Basic Prerequisites for a Security Plan

As one recent corporate security summary put it, "workplace security involves more than keeping track of who comes in a window, installing an alarm system, or employing guards for an after-hours watch. Organizations that are truly security conscious plan and implement policies and programs that involve employees in protecting against identified risks and threats."[140]

Ideally, a comprehensive corporate security program should start with the following prerequisites:

1. Company philosophy and policy on crime—In particular, make sure employees understand that no crime is acceptable and that the employer has a zero tolerance policy with respect to workers who commit crimes.
2. Investigations of job applicants—Make sure to conduct a full background check as part of your selection process for every position.
3. Security awareness training—Make it clear, during training and orientation programs, that the employer takes a tough approach to workplace crime.
4. Crisis management—Establish and communicate the procedures employees should follow in the event of a terrorist threat, bomb threat, fire, or other emergency.

Setting Up a Basic Security Program

In simplest terms, instituting a basic security program[141] requires four steps: analyzing the current level of risk, and then installing mechanical, natural, and organizational security systems.

Security programs often start with an analysis of the facility's *current level of risk*. The employer, preferably with the aid of security experts, should assess the company's exposure. Here, it is logical to start with the obvious. For example, what is the neighborhood like? Does your facility (such as the office building you're in) house other businesses or individuals (such as federal law enforcement agencies) that might bring unsafe activities to your doorstep? Is your facility close to major highways or railroad tracks (where, for instance, toxic fumes from the trains could present a problem)?

As part of its initial current threat assessment, the employer should also review at least these six areas:

1. *Access to the reception area*, including number of access points, and need for a "panic button" for contacting emergency personnel;
2. *Interior security*, including possible need for key cards, secure restrooms, and better identification and existence of exits;
3. *Authorities' involvement*, in particular security plans that include emergency procedures developed with local law enforcement authorities;
4. *Mail handling*, including how employees screen and open mail and where it enters the building;
5. *Evacuation*, including a full review of evacuation procedures and training; and,
6. *Backup systems* that allow the company to capture computer information at alternative locations if disaster strikes.

Having assessed the potential current level of risk, the employer then turns its attention to assessing and improving three basic sources of facility security: mechanical security, natural security, and organizational security.[142]

natural security
Taking advantage of the facility's natural or architectural features in order to minimize security problems.

Natural security means taking advantage of the facility's natural or architectural features in order to minimize security problems. For example, do stacks of boxes in front of your windows prevent police officers from observing what's happening in your facility at night? Are there unlit spots in your parking lot? And, does having too many entrances mean it is difficult to control facility access?

Organizational security requires making sure security staff have clearly defined duties and know what to do in case of an emergency. It also means doing proper background checks. Here a uniformed guard checks surveillance monitors in a factory office.

mechanical security
The utilization of security systems such as locks, intrusion alarms, access control systems, and surveillance systems.

Mechanical security is the utilization of security systems such as locks, intrusion alarms, access control systems and surveillance systems in a cost-effective manner that will reduce the need for continuous human surveillance.[143] Here, technological advances are making it easier for employers to institute new security arrangements. Many mail rooms now use special scanners to check the safety of incoming mail. And for access security, biometric scanners that read thumb or palm prints or retina or vocal patterns make it easier to enforce plant security. However, critics say these also may undermine employee privacy, for instance, by identifying where the employee is at any point in time.[144]

organizational security
Using good management to improve security.

Finally, **organizational security** means using good management to improve security. For example, it means properly training and motivating security staff and lobby attendants. As another example, it means making sure that security staff have written orders that clearly define their duties, especially in situations such as fire, elevator entrapment, hazardous materials spills, medical emergencies, hostile intrusions, hostage situations, bomb or terrorist attacks, suspicious packages, civil disturbances, and workplace violence.[145] Organizational security also means instituting other sensible human resource management–related steps. For example, are you properly investigating the backgrounds of new hires? Are you requiring the same types of background checks for the contractors who supply security and other personnel to your facility? And, do you provide new employees with security orientations?

Evacuation Plans

The 9/11 terrorist attacks also prompted more employers to formulate comprehensive evacuation plans. Of course, attacks are only one reason for triggering employee evacuation. Others include fires, explosions, chemical releases, power outages, and severe weather.[146]

Evacuation plans should contain several elements. These include *early detection of a problem, methods for communicating the emergency externally,* and *communications plans for initiating an evacuation and for providing information to those the employer wants to evacuate.* Regarding the latter, a simple alarm often does not suffice. Ideally, an initial alarm should come first. The employer should then follow the initial alarm with an announcement providing specific information about the emergency, and letting employees know what action they should take next.[147]

Security for Other Sources of Property Loss

The attacks also prompted employers to focus more on traditional sources of property loss, including fraud, theft, sabotage, and vandalism. Protecting property (including intellectual property) often begins with a *security audit* involving steps like the following:

1. Identify all major assets, including intellectual property;
2. Trace the work processes that control each asset;
3. Identify where opportunities for crime exist, and identify areas where protective measures are needed;
4. Test security controls periodically to ensure sufficient protection.

Tracing the work processes is especially important. For example, much of today's corporate communications flow through computer systems. The employer must therefore review work processes, including authorization procedures and access activities, in order to understand the extent of the threat to the computer and other systems and where these threats may arise.

Data security should be a major concern for all employers. A study by the American Society for Industrial Security concluded that American firms lost almost $60 billion in proprietary information or intellectual property in the one year from July 1, 2002 to June 30, 2003. Much of these losses involved research and development, and finance departments. Furthermore, while computer hackers may seem the most logical culprits here, current and former employees, on-site contractors, and domestic competitors were actually the biggest thieves.[148]

Company Security and Employee Privacy

Security programs like these have been accompanied by a significant rise in the monitoring of employee communications and workplace activities, and this has prompted many to ask, Are employee privacy rights being violated?

Employers must consider employee privacy when using monitoring to investigate possible employee security breaches. For example, the Federal Wire Act (technically, the Federal Electronic Communications Privacy Act) prohibits someone from intercepting oral, wire, or electronic communication. However, this act does permit employees to consent to the monitoring of business communications. Ideally, employers should get employees' express consent for such monitoring, for instance, when employees sign for receipt of company policy forms during orientation. However, the employer may also use monitoring if it is clear from its policies that employees should have known that such monitoring might take place. But, even getting express permission doesn't give employers carte blanche to monitor employee communications. Several state courts have held that monitoring phone conversations (even on company phones) invades employees' privacy once it becomes apparent that the conversation is personal.

The employer can take several steps to make it easier to investigate employees for potential security breaches. These include:[149]

1. Distribute a policy that says the company reserves the right to inspect and search employees as well as their personal property, electronic media, and files; and emphasizes that company-provided conveniences such as lockers and desks remain the property of the company and are subject to its control and search;

2. Train investigators to focus on the facts and avoid making accusations;

3. Make sure your investigators know that employees can request that an employee representative be present during the interview;

4. Make sure all investigations and searches are evenhanded and nondiscriminatory.

"The HR Scorecard" shows how the Hotel Paris applied many of this chapter's health and safety concepts.

The HR Scorecard
Strategy and Results

The New Safety and Health Program

The Hotel Paris's competitive strategy is "To use superior guest service to differentiate the Hotel Paris properties, and to thereby increase the length of stay and return rate of guests, and thus boost revenues and profitability." HR manager Lisa Cruz must now formulate functional policies and activities that support this competitive strategy, by eliciting the required employee behaviors and competencies.

A preliminary analysis, performed jointly by Lisa and the Hotel Paris's chief financial officer, left them optimistic that HR could contribute measurably to achieving the hotel's strategic aims. Several employee competencies and behaviors including employee morale, employee commitment, and the percent of arriving guests receiving the hotel's required greeting had significant effects on customer and organizational outcomes such as guest satisfaction and frequency of guest returns. In turn, outcomes like these contributed measurably to the Hotel Paris's strategic goals, including profit margins, market share, and scores on industry satisfaction surveys. Lisa and her team now turn to creating a safety and health program that will help to produce the required employee competencies and behaviors. The accompanying HR Scorecard (Figure 16-11) outlines the relationships involved.

Lisa and the CFO reviewed their company's safety records, and what they found disturbed them deeply. In terms of every safety-related metric they could find, including accident costs per year, lost time due to accidents, workers' compensation per employee, and number of safety training programs per year, the Hotel Paris compared unfavorably with most other hotel chains and service firms. "Why, just in terms of extra workers' compensation costs, the Hotel Paris must be spending $500,000 a year more than we should be," said the CFO. And that

didn't include lost time due to accidents, or the likely negative effect accidents had on employee morale, or the cost of litigation (as when, for instance, one guest accidentally burned himself with chlorine that a pool attendant had left unprotected). The CFO authorized Lisa to develop a new safety and health program.

Lisa and her team began by hiring a safety and health consultant, someone who had been an inspector and then manager with OSHA. Based on their analysis, the team then took numerous steps, including the following. First, specially trained teams consisting of someone from Lisa's HR group, the local hotel's assistant manager, and three local hotel employees went through each local hotel "with a fine tooth comb," as Lisa put it. They used an extensive checklist to identify and eliminate unsafe conditions.

Lisa's team took other steps. They convinced the Hotel Paris's board of directors and chairman and CEO to issue a joint statement emphasizing the importance of safety, and the CEO, during a one-month period, visited each hotel to meet with all employees and emphasize safety. The Hotel Paris also contracted with a safety training company. This firm created special online safety programs for the company's managers, and developed five-day training seminars for the hotels' staffs.

The new programs seem to be effective. Lisa and the CFO were pleased to find, after about a year, that accident costs per year, lost time due to accidents, and workers' compensation expenses were all down at least 40%. And anecdotal evidence from supervisors suggested that employees feel better about the company's commitment to them, and were providing better service as a result.

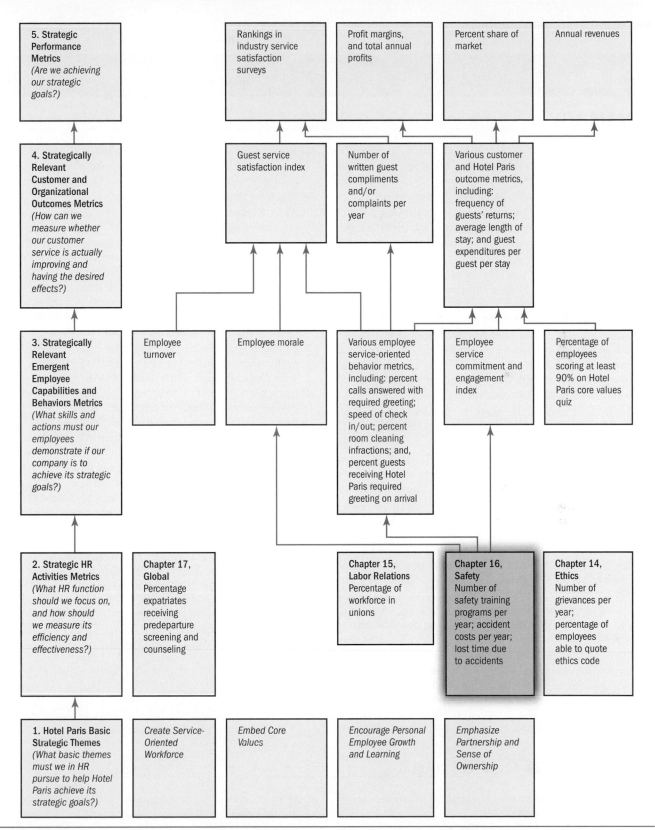

Figure 16-11
HR Scorecard for Hotel Paris International Corporation*

Note: *(An abbreviated example showing selected HRP practices and outcomes aimed at implementing the competitive strategy, "To use superior guest services to differentiate the Hotel Paris properties and thus increase the length of stays and the return rate of guests and thus boost revenues and profitability")

➡ *Review*

SUMMARY

1. The area of safety and accident prevention is of concern to managers at least partly because of the staggering number of deaths and accidents occurring at work. There are also legal and economic reasons for safety programs.

2. The purpose of OSHA is to ensure every working person a safe and healthful workplace. OSHA standards are very complete and detailed and are enforced through a system of workplace inspections.

3. Supervisors play a key role in monitoring workers for safety. Workers in turn have a responsibility to act safely. A commitment to safety on the part of top management is an important aspect of any safety program.

4. There are three basic causes of accidents: chance occurrences, unsafe conditions, and unsafe acts on the part of employees. In addition, three other work-related factors (the job itself, the work schedule, and the psychological climate) also contribute to accidents.

5. Most experts doubt that there are accident-prone people who have accidents regardless of the job. Instead, the consensus seems to be that the person who is accident prone in one job may not be on a different job.

6. There are several approaches to preventing accidents. One is to reduce unsafe conditions. The other approach is to reduce unsafe acts—for example, through an emphasis on safety, selection and placement, training, and positive reinforcement.

7. Alcoholism, drug addiction, stress, and emotional illness are four important and growing health problems among employees. Alcoholism is a particularly serious problem and one that can drastically lower the effectiveness of your organization. Disciplining, discharge, in-house counseling, and referrals to an outside agency are techniques used to deal with these problems.

8. Stress and burnout are other potential health problems at work. Asbestos, video display health problems, AIDS, and workplace smoking are other employee health problems discussed in this chapter.

9. Violence against employees is an enormous problem at work. Steps that can reduce workplace violence include improved security arrangements, better employee screening, and violence-reduction training.

10. Most workplace health hazards aren't obvious ones like unguarded equipment or slippery floors. Many are unseen hazards. Typical workplace exposure hazards may include chemicals and other hazardous materials, excessive noise and vibrations, temperature extremes, biohazards, ergonomic hazards, and safety-related hazards such as slippery floors. Managing exposure hazards like these comes under the category of *industrial hygiene*, and involves a process of recognition, evaluation, and control.

11. With many employees traveling to and from international destinations, monitoring and controlling infectious diseases like Ebola and SARS has become an important safety issue. Steps include: Closely monitor CDC travel alerts; provide daily medical screenings; deny access to your facility for 10 days to employees or visitors from affected areas; and tell employees to stay home if they have a fever or respiratory system symptoms.

12. The 9/11 World Trade Center and Pentagon attacks caused most employers to reprioritize their security concerns. After 9/11, physical security quickly joined the top 10 list. Ideally, a comprehensive corporate security program should include: a company philosophy and policy, investigations of job applicants, security awareness training, and crisis management. Instituting a basic security program involves four steps: analyzing the current level of risk, and then installing mechanical, natural, and organizational security systems. Evacuation plans are important. They should include early detection of a problem, methods for communicating the emergency externally, and communications plans for initiating an evacuation.

DISCUSSION QUESTIONS

1. Explain how to reduce the occurrence of unsafe acts on the part of your employees.
2. Discuss the basic facts about OSHA—its purpose, standards, inspections, and rights and responsibilities.
3. Explain the supervisor's role in safety.
4. Explain what causes unsafe acts.
5. Describe at least five techniques for reducing accidents.
6. Analyze the legal issues concerning AIDS.
7. Explain how you would reduce stress at work.
8. Describe the steps employers can take to reduce workplace violence.

INDIVIDUAL AND GROUP ACTIVITIES

1. Working individually or in groups, answer the question, "Is there such a thing as an accident prone person?" Develop your answer using examples of actual people you know who seemed to be accident prone on some endeavor.

2. Working individually or in groups, compile a list of the factors at work or in school that create dysfunctional stress for you. What methods do you use for dealing with the stress?

3. The HRCI "Test Specifications" appendix at the end of this book (pages 685–689) lists the knowledge someone studying for the HRCI certification exam needs to have in each area of human resource management (such as in Strategic Management, Workforce Planning, and Human Resource Development). In groups of four to five students, do four things: (1) review that appendix now; (2) identify the material in this chapter that relates to the required knowledge the appendix lists; (3) write four multiple choice exam questions on this material that you believe would be suitable for inclusion in the HRCI exam; and (4) if time permits, have someone from your team post your team's questions in front of the class, so the students in other teams can take each others' exam questions.

4. The March 2004 issue of the journal *Occupational Hazards* presented some information about what happens when

OSHA refers criminal complaints about willful violations of OSHA standards to the U.S. Department of Justice (DOJ). Between 1982 and 2002, OSHA referred 119 fatal cases allegedly involving willful violations of OSHA to DOJ for criminal prosecution. The DOJ declined to pursue 57% of them, and some were dropped for other reasons. Of the remaining 51 cases, the DOJ settled 63% with pretrial settlements involving no prison time. So, counting acquittals, of the 119 cases OSHA referred to the DOJ, only nine resulted in prison time for at least one of the defendants. "The Department of Justice is a disgrace," charged the founder of an organization for family members of workers killed on the job. One possible explanation for this low conviction rate is that the crime in cases like these is generally a misdemeanor, not a felony, and the DOJ generally tries to focus its attention on felony cases. Given this information, what implications do you think this has for how employers and their managers should manage their safety programs, and why do you take that position?

5. In February 2004 a 315-foot-tall, 2-million-pound erection crane collapsed on a construction site in East Toledo, Ohio, killing four ironworkers. Do you think catastrophic failures like this are avoidable? If so, what steps would you suggest the general contractor take to avoid a disaster like this?

EXPERIENTIAL EXERCISE

How Safe Is My University?

Purpose: The purpose of this exercise is to give you practice in identifying unsafe conditions.

Required Understanding: You should be familiar with material covered in this chapter, particularly that on unsafe conditions and that in Figures 16-6 and Figure 16-12.

How to Set Up the Exercise/Instructions: Divide the class into groups of four.

Assume that each group is a safety committee retained by your college or university's safety engineer to identify and

report on any possible unsafe conditions in and around the school building. Each group will spend about 45 minutes in and around the building you are now in for the purpose of identifying and listing possible unsafe conditions. (Make use of the checklists in Figures 16-6 and 16-12.)

Return to the class in about 45 minutes. A spokesperson for each group should list on the board the unsafe conditions you think you have identified. How many were there? Do you think these also violate OSHA standards? How would you go about checking?

APPLICATION CASE

The New Safety and Health Program

At first glance, a dot-com company is one of the last places you'd expect to find potential safety and health hazards—or so the owners of LearnInMotion.com thought. There's no danger of moving machinery, no high-pressure lines, no cutting or heavy lifting, and certainly no forklift trucks. However, there are safety and health problems.

In terms of accident-causing conditions, for instance, the one thing dot-com companies have lots of is cables and wires. There are cables connecting the computers to each other and

to the servers, and in many cases separate cables running from some computers to separate printers. There are 10 telephones in this particular office, all on 15-foot phone lines that always seem to be snaking around chairs and tables. There is, in fact, an astonishing amount of cable considering this is an office with less than 10 employees. When the installation specialists wired the office (for electricity, high-speed DSL, phone lines, burglar alarms, and computers), they estimated they used well over five miles of cables of one sort or another.

GENERAL

		OK	ACTION NEEDED

1. Is the required OSHA workplace poster displayed in your place of business as required where all employees are likely to see it? ☐ ☐
2. Are you aware of the requirement to report all workplace fatalities and any serious accidents (where 5 or more are hospitalized) to a federal or state OSHA office within 48 hours? ☐ ☐
3. Are workplace injury and illness records being kept as required by OSHA? ☐ ☐
4. Are you aware that the OSHA annual summary of workplace injuries and illnesses must be posted by February 1 and must remain posted until March 1? ☐ ☐
5. Are you aware that employers with 10 or fewer employees are exempt from the OSHA record-keeping requirements, unless they are part of an official BLS or state survey and have received specific instructions to keep records? ☐ ☐
6. Have you demonstrated an active interest in safety and health matters by defining a policy for your business and communicating it to all employees? ☐ ☐
7. Do you have a safety committee or group that allows participation of employees in safety and health activities? ☐ ☐
8. Does the safety committee or group meet regularly and report, in writing, its activities? ☐ ☐
9. Do you provide safety and health training for all employees requiring such training, and is it documented? ☐ ☐
10. Is one person clearly in charge of safety and health activities? ☐ ☐
11. Do all employees know what to do in emergencies? ☐ ☐
12. Are emergency telephone numbers posted? ☐ ☐
13. Do you have a procedure for handling employee complaints regarding safety and health? ☐ ☐

WORKPLACE
ELECTRICAL WIRING, FIXTURES AND CONTROLS

OK   ACTION NEEDED

1. Are your workplace electricians familiar with the requirements of the National Electrical Code (NEC)? ☐ ☐
2. Do you specify compliance with the NEC for all contract electrical work? ☐ ☐
3. If you have electrical installations in hazardous dust or vapor areas, do they meet the NEC for hazardous locations? ☐ ☐
4. Are all electrical cords strung so they do not hang on pipes, nails, hooks, etc.? ☐ ☐
5. Is all conduit, BX cable, etc., properly attached to all supports and tightly connected to junction and outlet boxes? ☐ ☐
6. Is there no evidence of fraying on any electrical cords? ☐ ☐
7. Are rubber cords kept free of grease, oil, and chemicals? ☐ ☐
8. Are metallic cable and conduit systems properly grounded? ☐ ☐
9. Are portable electric tools and appliances grounded or double insulated? ☐ ☐

Develop Your Own Checklist.

10. Are all ground connections clean and tight? ☐ ☐
11. Are fuses and circuit breakers the right type and size for the load on each circuit? ☐ ☐
12. Are all fuses free of "jumping" with pennies or metal strips? ☐ ☐

These Are Only Sample Questions.

13. Do switches show evidence of overheating? ☐ ☐
14. Are switches mounted in clean, tightly closed metal boxes? ☐ ☐
15. Are all electrical switches marked to show their purpose? ☐ ☐
16. Are motors clean and kept free of excessive grease and oil? ☐ ☐
17. Are motors properly maintained and provided with adequate overcurrent protection? ☐ ☐
18. Are bearings in good condition? ☐ ☐
19. Are portable lights equipped with proper guards? ☐ ☐
20. Are all lamps kept free of combustible material? ☐ ☐
21. Is your electrical system checked periodically by someone competent in the NEC? ☐ ☐

Figure 16-12
Self-Inspection Safety and Health Checklist

EXITS AND ACCESS

	OK	ACTION NEEDED

1. Are all exits visible and unobstructed? ☐ ☐
2. Are all exits marked with a readily visible sign that is properly illuminated? ☐ ☐
3. Are there sufficient exits to ensure prompt escape in case of emergency? ☐ ☐
4. Are areas with limited occupancy posted and is access/egress controlled by persons specifically authorized to be in those areas? ☐ ☐
5. Do you take special precautions to protect employees during construction and repair operations? ☐ ☐

Develop Your Own Checklist.

These Are Only Sample Questions.

FIRE PROTECTION

	OK	ACTION NEEDED

1. Are portable fire extinguishers provided in adequate number and type? ☐ ☐
2. Are fire extinguishers inspected monthly for general condition and operability and noted on the inspection tag? ☐ ☐
3. Are fire extinguishers recharged regularly and properly noted on the inspection tag? ☐ ☐
4. Are fire extinguishers mounted in readily accessible locations? ☐ ☐
5. If you have interior standpipes and valves, are these inspected regularly? ☐ ☐
6. If you have a fire alarm system, is it tested at least annually? ☐ ☐
7. Are plant employees periodically instructed in the use of extinguishers and fire protection procedures? ☐ ☐
8. If you have outside private fire hydrants, were they flushed within the last year and placed on a regular maintenance schedule? ☐ ☐
9. Are fire doors and shutters in good operating condition? ☐ ☐
   Are they unobstructed and protected against obstruction? ☐ ☐
10. Are fusible links in place? ☐ ☐
11. Is your local fire department well acquainted with your plant, location, and specific hazards? ☐ ☐
12. Automatic Sprinklers:
    Are water control valves, air and water pressures checked weekly? ☐ ☐
    Are control valves locked open? ☐ ☐
    Is maintenance of the system assigned to responsible persons or a sprinkler contractor? ☐ ☐
    Are sprinkler heads protected by metal guards where exposed to mechanical damage? ☐ ☐
    Is proper minimum clearance maintained around sprinkler heads? ☐ ☐

HOUSEKEEPING AND GENERAL WORK ENVIRONMENT

	OK	ACTION NEEDED

1. Is smoking permitted in designated "safe areas" only? ☐ ☐
2. Are NO SMOKING signs prominently posted in areas containing combustibles and flammables? ☐ ☐
3. Are covered metal waste cans used for oily and paint-soaked waste? ☐ ☐
   Are they emptied at least daily? ☐ ☐
4. Are paint spray booths, dip tanks, etc., and their exhaust ducts cleaned regularly? ☐ ☐
5. Are stand mats, platforms, or similar protection provided to protect employees from wet floors in wet processes? ☐ ☐
6. Are waste receptacles provided, and are they emptied regularly? ☐ ☐
7. Do your toilet facilities meet the requirements of applicable sanitary codes? ☐ ☐
8. Are washing facilities provided? ☐ ☐
9. Are all areas of your business adequately illuminated? ☐ ☐
10. Are floor load capacities posted in second floors, lofts, storage areas, etc.? ☐ ☐
11. Are floor openings provided with toe boards and railings on a floor hole cover? ☐ ☐
12. Are stairways in good condition with standard railings provided for every flight having four or more risers? ☐ ☐

Figure 16-12 (continued)

13. Are portable wood ladders and metal ladders adequate for their purpose, in good condition and provided with secure footing? □ OK □ ACTION NEEDED

14. If you have fixed ladders, are they adequate, and are they in good condition and equipped with side rails or cages or special safety climbing devices, if required? □ □

15. For Loading Docks:

Are dockplates kept in serviceable condition and secured to prevent slipping? □ □

Do you have means to prevent car or truck movement when dockplates are in place? □ □

MACHINES AND EQUIPMENT

OK ACTION NEEDED

1. Are all machines or operations that expose operators or other employees to rotating parts, pinch points, flying chips, particles, or sparks adequately guarded? □ □

2. Are mechanical power transmission belts and pinch points guarded? □ □

3. Is exposed power shafting less than 7 feet from the floor guarded? □ □

4. Are hand tools and other equipment regularly inspected for safe condition? □ □

5. Is compressed air used for cleaning reduced to less than 30 psi? □ □

6. Are power saws and similar equipment provided with safety guards? □ □

7. Are grinding wheel tool rests set to within $1/8$ inch or less of the wheel? □ □

8. Is there any system for inspecting small hand tools for burred ends, cracked handles, etc.? □ □

9. Are compressed gas cylinders examined regularly for obvious signs of defects, deep rusting, or leakage? □ □

10. Is care used in handling and storing cylinders and valves to prevent damage? □ □

11. Are all air receivers periodically examined, including the safety valves? □ □

12. Are safety valves tested regularly and frequently? □ □

13. Is there sufficient clearance from stoves, furnaces, etc., for stock, woodwork, or other combustible materials? □ □

14. Is there clearance of at least 4 feet in front of heating equipment involving open flames, such as gas radiant heaters, and fronts of firing doors of stoves, furnaces, etc.? □ □

15. Are all oil and gas fired devices equipped with flame failure controls that will prevent flow of fuel if pilots or main burners are not working? □ □

16. Is there at least a 2-inch clearance between chimney brickwork and all woodwork or other combustible materials? □ □

17. For Welding or Flame Cutting Operations:

Are only authorized, trained personnel permitted to use such equipment? □ □

Have operators been given a copy of operating instructions and asked to follow them? □ □

Are welding gas cylinders stored so they are not subjected to damage? □ □

Are valve protection caps in place on all cylinders not connected for use? □ □

Are all combustible materials near the operator covered with protective shields or otherwise protected? □ □

Is a fire extinguisher provided at the welding site? □ □

Do operators have the proper protective clothing and equipment? □ □

Develop Your Own Checklist.

These Are Only Sample Questions.

MATERIALS

OK ACTION NEEDED

1. Are approved safety cans or other acceptable containers used for handling and dispensing flammable liquids? □ □

2. Are all flammable liquids that are kept inside buildings stored in proper storage containers or cabinets? □ □

3. Do you meet OSHA standards for all spray painting or dip tank operations using combustible liquids? □ □

4. Are oxidizing chemicals stored in areas separate from all organic material except shipping bags? □ □

5. Do you have an enforced NO SMOKING rule in areas for storage and use of hazardous materials? □ □

6. Are NO SMOKING signs posted where needed? □ □

Figure 16-12 (continued)

	OK	ACTION NEEDED
7. Is ventilation equipment provided for removal of air contaminants from operations such as production grinding, buffing, spray painting and/or vapor degreasing, and is it operating properly?	☐	☐
8. Are protective measures in effect for operations involved with X-rays or other radiation?	☐	☐
9. For Lift Truck Operations:		
Are only trained personnel allowed to operate forklift trucks?	☐	☐
Is overhead protection provided on high lift rider trucks?	☐	☐
10. For Toxic Materials:		
Are all materials used in your plant checked for toxic qualities?	☐	☐
Have appropriate control procedures such as ventilation systems, enclosed operations, safe handling practices, proper personal protective equipment (e.g., respirators, glasses or goggles, gloves, etc.) been instituted for toxic materials?	☐	☐

EMPLOYEE PROTECTION

	OK	ACTION NEEDED
1. Is there a hospital, clinic, or infirmary for medical care near your business?	☐	☐
2. If medical and first-aid facilities are not nearby, do you have one or more employees trained in first aid?	☐	☐
3. Are your first-aid supplies adequate for the type of potential injuries in your workplace?	☐	☐
4. Are there quick water flush facilities available where employees are exposed to corrosive materials?	☐	☐
5. Are hard hats provided and worn where any danger of falling objects exists?	☐	☐
6. Are protective goggles or glasses provided and worn where there is any danger of flying particles or splashing of corrosive materials?	☐	☐
7. Are protective gloves, aprons, shields, or other means provided for protection from sharp, hot, or corrosive materials?	☐	☐
8. Are approved respirators provided for regular or emergency use where needed?	☐	☐
9. Is all protective equipment maintained in a sanitary condition and readily available for use?	☐	☐
10. Where special equipment is needed for electrical workers, is it available?	☐	☐
11. When lunches are eaten on the premises, are they eaten in areas where there is no exposure to toxic materials, and not in toilet facility areas?	☐	☐
12. Is protection against the effect of occupational noise exposure provided when the sound levels exceed those shown in Table G-16 of the OSHA noise standard?	☐	☐

Develop Your Own Checklist.

These Are Only Sample Questions.

Figure 16-12 (continued)

Most of these are hidden in the walls or ceilings, but many of them snake their way from desk to desk, and under and over doorways. Several employees have tried to reduce the nuisance of having to trip over wires whenever they get up by putting their plastic chair pads over the wires closest to them. However, that still leaves many wires unprotected. In other cases, they brought in their own packing tape, and tried to tape down the wires in those spaces where they're particularly troublesome, such as across doorways.

The cables and wires are only one of the more obvious potential accident-causing conditions. The firm's programmer, before he left the firm, had tried to repair the main server while the unit was still electrically alive. To this day, they're not sure exactly where he stuck the screwdriver, but the result was that

he was "blown across the room," as one manager put it. He was all right, but it was still a scare. And while they haven't received any claims yet, every employee spends hours at his or her computer, so carpal tunnel syndrome is a risk, as are a variety of other problems such as eye strain and strained backs.

One recent accident particularly scared the owners. The firm uses independent contractors to deliver the firm's book- and DVD–based courses in New York and two other cities. A delivery person was riding his bike east at the intersection of Second Avenue and East 64th Street in New York when he was struck by a car going south on Second Avenue. Luckily he was not hurt, but the bike's front wheel was wrecked, and the close call got the firm's two owners, Mel and Jennifer, thinking about their lack of a safety program.

It's not just the physical conditions that concern the company's two owners. They also have some concerns about potential health problems such as job stress and burnout. While the business may be (relatively) safe with respect to physical conditions, it is also relatively stressful in terms of the demands it makes in hours and deadlines. It is not at all unusual for employees to get to work by 7:30 or 8 o'clock in the morning and to work through until 11 or 12 o'clock at night, at least five and sometimes six or seven days per week. Just getting the company's new on-line calendar fine-tuned and operational required 70-hour workweeks for three weeks from five of LearnInMotion.com's employees.

The bottom line is that both Jennifer and Mel feel quite strongly that they need to do something about implementing a health and safety plan. Now, they want you, their management consultants, to help them actually do it. Here's what they want you to do for them.

Questions and Assignments

1. Based upon your knowledge of health and safety matters and your actual observations of operations that are similar to theirs, make a list of the potential hazardous conditions employees and others face at LearnInMotion.com. What should they do to reduce the potential severity of the top five hazards?

2. Would it be advisable for them to set up a procedure for screening out stress-prone or accident-prone individuals? Why or why not? If so, how should they screen them?

3. Write a short position paper on the subject, "What should we do to get all our employees to behave more safely at work?"

4. Based on what you know and on what other dot-coms are doing, write a short position paper on the subject, "What can we do to reduce the potential problems of stress and burnout in our company?"

CONTINUING CASE

Carter Cleaning Company

The New Safety Program

Employees' safety and health are very important matters in the laundry and cleaning business. Each facility is a small production plant in which machines, powered by high-pressure steam and compressed air, work at high temperatures washing, cleaning, and pressing garments, often under very hot, slippery conditions. Chemical vapors are continually produced, and caustic chemicals are used in the cleaning process. High-temperature stills are almost continually "cooking down" cleaning solvents in order to remove impurities so that the solvents can be reused. If a mistake is made in this process—like injecting too much steam into the still—a boilover occurs, in which boiling chemical solvent erupts out of the still and over the floor, and on anyone who happens to be standing in its way.

As a result of these hazards and the fact that chemically hazardous waste is continually produced in these stores, several government agencies (including OSHA and the EPA) have instituted strict guidelines regarding the management of these plants. For example, posters have to be placed in each store notifying employees of their right to be told what hazardous chemicals they are dealing with and what the proper method for handling each chemical is. Special waste-management firms must be used to pick up and properly dispose of the hazardous waste.

A chronic problem the Carters (and most other laundry owners) have is the unwillingness on the part of the cleaning–spotting workers to wear safety goggles. Not all the chemicals they use require safety goggles, but some—like the hydrofluorous acid used to remove rust stains from garments—are very dangerous. The latter is kept in special plastic containers, since it dissolves glass. The problem is that wearing safety goggles can be troublesome. They are somewhat uncomfortable, and they also become smudged easily and thus cut down on visibility. As a result, Jack has always found it almost impossible to get these employees to wear their goggles.

Questions

1. How should the firm go about identifying hazardous conditions that should be rectified? Use checklists such as Figures 16-6 and 12-12 to list at least 10 possible dry cleaning store hazardous conditions.

2. Would it be advisable for the firm to set up a procedure for screening out accident-prone individuals? How should they do so?

3. How would you suggest the Carters get all employees to behave more safely at work? Also how would you advise them to get those who should be wearing goggles to do so?

KEY TERMS

Occupational Safety and Health Act, 603

Occupational Safety and Health Administration (OSHA), 603

occupational illness, 603

citation, 606

unsafe conditions, 611

behavior-based safety, 620

burnout, 630

material safety data sheets (MSDS), 631

natural security, 639

mechanical security, 640

organizational security, 640

ENDNOTES

1. Greg Hom, "Protecting Eyes from High-Tech Hazards," *Occupational Hazards*, March 1999, pp. 53–55; "Workplace Injuries by Industry, 2002," *Safety Compliance Letter*, February 2004, issue 2438, p. 12; Leigh Strope, "Deaths at Work Rise Slightly to 5,559 in 2003, with Most Occurring in Construction, Transportation," AP News, September 22, 2004, 11:45 p.m. GMT, downloaded September 23, 2004.

2. "Blame New Computers for Sick Buildings," *USA Today* 129, no. 2672 (May 2001), p. 8.

3. Michael Pinto, "Why Are Indoor Air Quality Problems So Prevalent Today?" *Occupational Hazards*, January 2001, pp. 37–39.

4. Sandy Moretz, "Safe Havens?" *Occupational Hazards*, November 2000, pp. 45–46.

5. Todd Nighswonger, "Rouge Settlement Sparks Safety Initiative at Ford," *Occupational Hazards*, October 1999, pp. 101–102. Karen Gaspers, "It's Painful for the Bottom Line, Too," *Safety and Health*, October 2003, vol. 168, issue 14, p. 323.

6. James Nash, "OSHA Targets Recalcitrant Employers," *Occupational Hazards*, May 2003, p. 12. See also, "Judge Sentences Man to Prison For Scaffolding Deaths," *Occupational Hazards*, February 2004, p. 14.

7. David Barstow and Lowell Bergman, "A Family's Profits, Wrung from Blood and Sweat," *New York Times*, January 9, 2003, p. 81.

8. Much of this is based on "All about OSHA" (revised), U.S. Department of Labor, Occupational Safety and Health Administration (Washington, DC).

9. "Safety Rule on Respiratory Protection Issues," *BNA Bulletin to Management*, January 8, 1998, p. 1. See also, "Staying on Top of OSHA Terms Helps Measure Safety," *Safety and Health*, July 2004, vol. 170, issue 1, p. 44.

10. "OSHA Hazard Communication Standard Enforcement," *BNA Bulletin to Management*, February 23, 1989, p. 13. See also William Kincaid, "OSHA vs. Excellence in Safety Management," *Occupational Hazards*, December 2002, pp. 34–36.

11. "What Every Employer Needs to Know About OSHA Record Keeping," U.S. Department of Labor, Bureau of Labor Statistics (Washington, DC), report 412–3, p. 3.

12. Arthur Sapper and Robert Gombar, "Nagging Problems Under OSHA's new Record-keeping Rules," *Occupational Hazards*, March 2002, p. 58.

13. Brian Jackson and Jeffrey Myers, "Just When You Thought You Were Safe: OSHA Record-Keeping Violations," *Management Review*, May 1994, pp. 62–63.

14. "Supreme Court Says OSHA Inspectors Need Warrants," *Engineering News Record*, June 1, 1978, pp. 9–10; W. Scott Railton, "OSHA Gets Tough on Business," *Management Review* 80, no. 12 (December 1991), pp. 28–29. Steve Hollingsworth, "How to Survive an OSHA Inspection," *Occupational Hazards*, March 2004, pp. 31–33.

15. This section is based on "All About OSHA," pp. 23–25. See also Robert Sand, "OSHA Access to Privileged Materials: Criminal Prosecutions; Damages for Fear of Cancer," *Employee Relations Law Journal* 19, no. 1 (Summer 1993), pp. 151–157; "OSHA Final Rule Expands Employees' Role in Consultations, Protects Employer Records," *BNA Bulletin to Management*, November 2, 2000, p. 345.

16. Diane Hatch and James Hall, "A Flurry of New Federal Regulations," *Workforce*, February 2001, p. 98.

17. "Settling Safety Violations Has Benefits," *BNA Bulletin to Management*, July 31, 1997, p. 248.

18. "Enforcement Activity Increased in 1997," *BNA Bulletin to Management*, January 29, 1998, p. 28.

19. Ibid., p. 28.

20. Robert Grossman, "Handling Inspections: Tips from Insiders," *HR Magazine*, October 1999, pp. 41–50.

21. Charles Chadd, "Managing OSHA Compliance: The Human Resources Issues," *Employee Relations Law Journal* 20, no. 1 (Summer 1994), p. 106.

22. These are based on Roger Jacobs, "Employee Resistance to OSHA Standards: Toward a More Reasonable Approach," *Labor Law Journal*, April 1979, pp. 227–230. See also, "Half of All Working Americans Feel Immune to Workplace Injuries, Nationally Workplace Deaths Up by 6% in 2001," *Internet Wire*, June 13, 2003, p. 100816442584.

23. These are based on James Nash, "The Top Ten Ways to Get into Trouble with OSHA," *Occupational Hazards*, December 2003, pp. 27–30.

24. Sean Smith, "OSHA Resources Can Help Small Businesses with Hazards," *Westchester County Business Journal*, August 4, 2003, p. 4.

25. Lisa Finnegan, "Industry Partners with OSHA," *Occupational Hazards*, February 1999, pp. 43–45.

26. Willie Hammer, *Occupational Safety Management and Engineering* (Englewood Cliffs, NJ: Prentice Hall, 1985) pp. 62–63. See also, "DuPont's 'STOP' Helps Prevent Workplace Injuries and Incidents," *Asia Africa Intelligence Wire*, May 17, 2004.

27. F. David Pierce, "Safety in the Emerging Leadership Paradigm," *Occupational Hazards*, June 2000, pp. 63–66.

28. "Safety Program Results at ABB Business Services Missouri Plant," *Occupational Hazards*, July 2000, p. 23.

29. Donald Hantula et al., "The Value of Workplace Safety: A Time Based Utility Analysis Model," *Journal of Organizational Behavior Management* 21, no. 2 (2001), pp. 79–98.

30. "A Safety Committee Man's Guide," Aetna Life and Casualty Insurance Company, Catalog 87684. See also Dan Petersen, "The Barriers to Safety Excellence," *Occupational Hazards*, December 2000, pp. 37–39.

31. "Did This Supervisor Do Enough to Protect Trench Workers?" *Safety Compliance Letter*, October 2003, p. 9.

32. Ibid.

33. "A Safety Committee Man's Guide," pp. 17–21.

34. For a discussion of this, see David Hofmann and Adam Stetzer, "A Cross-Level Investigation of Factors Influencing Unsafe Behaviors and Accidents," *Personnel Psychology* 49 (1996), pp. 307–308.

35. Julian Barling et al., "High-Quality Work, Job Satisfaction, and Occupational Injuries," *Journal of Applied Psychology* 88, no. 2 (2003), pp. 276–283.

36. Ibid., p. 280.

37. Duane Schultz and Sydney Schultz, *Psychology and Work Today* (Upper Saddle River, NJ: Prentice Hall, 1998), p. 351.

38. Cynthia Owsley et al., "Visual Processing Impairment and Risk of Motor Vehicle Crash Among Older Adults," *Journal of the American Medical Association*, April 8, 1998, pp. 1083–1089; Hosam Kamel et al., "The Activities of Daily Vision Scale: A Useful Tool to Assess for Risk in Older Adults with Vision Impairment," *Journal of the American Geriatrics Society* 48, no. 11 (November 2000), pp. 1474–1478; Hiroshi Matsuoka, "Development of a Short Test for Accident Proneness," *Perceptual and Motor Skills* 85, no. 3 (December 1997), pp. 903–907; Janice Marra, "Profiling Employees and Assessing the Potential for Violence," *Public Management* 82, no. 2 (February 2000), pp. 25–26.

39. Todd Nighswonger, "Threat of Terror Impacts Workplace Safety," *Occupational Hazards*, July 2002, pp. 24–26.

40. Michael Blotzer, "Safety by Design," *Occupational Hazards*, May 1999, pp. 39–40.

41. Susannah Figura, "Don't Slip Up on Safety," *Occupational Hazards*, November 1996, pp. 29–31. See also Russ Wood, "Defining the Boundaries of Safety," *Occupational Hazards*, January 2001, pp. 41–43.

42. Tom Andrews, "Getting Employees Comfortable with PPE," *Occupational Hazards*, January 2000, pp. 35–38.

43. James Zeigler, "Protective Clothing: Exploring the Wearability Issue," *Occupational Hazards*, September 2000, pp. 81–82.

44. "The Complete Guide to Personal Protective Equipment," *Occupational Hazards*, January 1999, pp. 49–60.

45. William Kincaid, "10 Habits of Effective Safety Managers," *Occupational Hazards*, November 1996, pp. 41–43.

46. Dov Zohar, "A Group Level Model of Safety Climate: Testing the Effect of a Group Climate on Microaccidents in Manufacturing Jobs," *Journal of Applied Psychology* 85, no. 4 (2000), pp. 587–596. See also Judith Erickson, "Corporate Culture: The Key to Safety Performance," *Occupational Hazards*, April 2000, p. 45.

47. Gerald Borofsky, Michelle Bielema, and James Hoffman, "Accidents, Turnover, and Use of a Pre-employment Screening Interview," *Psychological Reports*, 1993, pp. 1067–1076.

48. Ibid., p. 1072.

49. Dan Hartshorn, "The Safety Interview," *Occupational Hazards*, October 1999, pp. 107–111.

50. *Workers' Compensation Manual for Managers and Supervisors*, pp. 22–23.

51. James Nash, "Construction Safety: Best Practices in Training Hispanic Workers," *Occupational Hazards*, February 2004, pp. 35–38.

52. Ibid., p. 37.

53. John Rekus, "Is Your Safety Training Program Effective?" *Occupational Hazards*, August 1999, pp. 37–39.

54. Jennifer Laabs, "Cashing in on Safety," *Workforce*, August 1997, p. 57.

55. Gregg LaBar, "Awards and Incentives in Action," *Occupational Hazards*, January 1997, pp. 91–92.

56. James Nash, "Rewarding the Safety Process," *Occupational Hazards*, March 2000, pp. 29–34.

57. Judi Komaki, Kenneth Barwick, and Lawrence Scott, "A Behavioral Approach to Occupational Safety: Pinpointing and Reinforcing Safe Performance in a Food Manufacturing Plant," *Journal of Applied Psychology* 63 (August 1978), pp. 434–445. See also Anat Arkin, "Incentives to Work Safely," *Personnel Management* 26, no. 9 (September 1994), pp. 48–52; Peter Making and Valerie Sutherland, "Reducing Accidents Using a Behavioral Approach," *Leadership and Organizational Development Journal* 15, no. 5 (1994), pp. 5–10. Sandy Smith, "Why Cash Isn't King," *Occupational Hazards*, March 2004, pp. 37–38.

58. Stan Hudson and Tim Gordon, "Tenneco's Drive to Become Injury Free," *Occupational Hazards*, May 2000, pp. 85–87. See also William Atkinson, "Behavior-Based Safety," *Management Review* 89, no. 2 (February 2000), pp. 41–45.

59. Kim McDaniel, "Employee Participation: A Vehicle for Safety by Designing," *Occupational Hazards*, May 2002, pp. 71–76.

60. Linda Johnson, "Preventing Injuries: The Big Payoff," *Personnel Journal*, April 1994, pp. 61–64; David Webb, "The Bathtub Effect: Why Safety Programs Fail," *Management Review*, February 1994, pp. 51–54.

61. Lisa Cullen, "Safety Committees: A Smart Business Decision," *Occupational Hazards*, May 1999, pp. 99–104.

62. Michael Blotzer, "PDA Software Offers Auditing Advances," *Occupational Hazards*, December 2001, p. 11.

63. Virginia Sutcliffe, "Employee Safety: Beyond the Plant Gate," *Occupational Hazards*, December 1998, pp. 41–42.

64. "OSHA Backs Off on Home Rules," *Occupational Hazards*, February 2000, p. 8.

65. Sutcliffe, "Employee Safety," p. 42.

66. "Strict Policies Mean Big Cuts in Premiums," *Occupational Hazards*, May 2000, p. 51.

67. S. L. Smith, "Sadaf Drives for Safety Excellence," *Occupational Hazards*, November 1998, p. 41. For further discussion, see also Kathy Seabrook, "10 Strategies for Global Safety Management," *Occupational Hazards*, June 1999, pp. 41–43.

68. See, for example, *Workers' Compensation Manual for Managers and Supervisors*, pp. 36–39.

69. "Study: No Warm Welcome After Comp Leave," *Occupational Hazards*, February 2001, p. 57.

70. Ibid., p. 51.

71. Donna Clendenning, "Taking a Bite Out of Workers' Comp Costs," *Occupational Hazards*, September 2000, pp. 85–86.

72. This is based on Paul Puncochar, "The Science and Art to Identifying Workplace Hazards," *Occupational Hazards*, September 2003, pp. 50–54.

73. Ibid, p. 52.

74. Sandy Smith, "SARS: What Employers Need to Know," *Occupational Hazards*, July 2003, pp. 33–35.

75. Todd Nighswonger, "Just Say Yes to Preventing Substance Abuse," *Occupational Hazards*, April 2000, pp. 39–41.

76. "Facing Facts About Workplace Substance Abuse," *Rough Notes* 144, no. 5 (May 2001), pp. 114–118.

77. See, for example, Kathryn Tyler, "Happiness from a Bottle?" *HR Magazine*, May 2002, pp. 30–37.

78. William Corinth, "Pre-Employment Drug Testing," *Occupational Hazards*, July 2002, p. 56.

79. Diane Cadrain, "Are Your Employees' Drug Tests Accurate?" *HR Magazine*, January 2003, pp. 41–45.

80. Brenda Sunoo, "Positive Drug Test Results: Terminate or Rehabilitate?" *Personnel Journal*, December 1996, p. 94.

81. Ibid., p. 94.

82. This is quoted from "Drug-Free Workplace: New Federal Requirements," *BNA Bulletin to Management*, February 9, 1989, pp. 1–4. Note that the Drug-Free Workplace Act does not mandate or mention testing employees for illegal drug use.

83. "Alcohol Misuse Prevention Programs: Department of Transportation Final Rules," *BNA Bulletin to Management*, March 24, 1994, pp. 1–8.

84. Eric Sundstrom et al., "Office Noise, Satisfaction, and Performance," *Environment and Behavior* 26, no. 2 (March 1994), pp. 195–222.

85. Michael Manning, Conrad Jackson, and Marceline Fusilier, "Occupational Stress, Social Support, and the Costs of Health Care," *Academy of Management Journal* 39, no. 3 (1996), pp. 738–750.

86. "Stress, Depression Cost Employers," *Occupational Hazards*, December 1998, p. 24. See also Charlene Solomon, "Stressed to the Limit," *Workforce*, September 1999, pp. 48–54.

87. Karl Albrecht, *Stress and the Manager* (Englewood Cliffs, NJ: Spectrum, 1979). For a discussion of the related symptoms of depression, see James Krohe Jr., "An Epidemic of Depression?" *Across-the-Board*, September 1994, pp. 23–27, and Todd Nighswonger, "Stress Management," *Occupational Hazards*, September 1999, p. 100.

88. "Solutions to Workplace Stress," *BNA Bulletin to Management*, February 11, 1993, p. 48. See also Christopher Bachler, "Workers Take Leave of Job Stress," *Personnel Journal*, January 1995, p. 38.

89. Pascale Carayon, "Stressful Jobs and Non-Stressful Jobs: A Cluster Analysis of Office Jobs," *Ergonomics* 37, no. 2 (1994), pp. 311–323.

90. "Managing Stress in the Workplace," *BNA Bulletin to Management*, January 18, 1996, p. 24.

91. Madan Mohan Tripathy, "Burnout Stress Syndrome in Managers," *Management and Labor Studies* 27, no. 2 (April 2002), pp. 89–111.

92. Mina Westman and Dov Eden, "Effects of a Respite from Work on Burnout: Vacation Relief and Fade-Out," *Journal of Applied Psychology* 82, no. 4 (1997), pp. 516–527.

93. Ibid., p. 516.

94. Ibid., p. 526.

95. Todd Nighswonger, "Depression: The Unseen Safety Risk," *Occupational Hazards*, April 2002, pp. 38–42.

96. Ibid., p. 40.

97. Ibid.

98. Marco Wysong, "A Prescription for Managing Chemicals: Use These Strategies for Successful Electronic MSDS," *Industrial Safety and Hygiene News* 37, no. 1 (January 2003), p. 42.

99. Michael Blotzer, "PDA Software Offers Auditing Advances," p. 11.

100. "Carpal Tunnel Claims Up, But Cost Per Claim Down," *BNA Bulletin to Management*, July 25, 1996, p. 233.

101. "Risk of Carpal Tunnel Syndrome Not Linked to Heavy Computer Work, Study Says," *BNA Bulletin to Management*, June 28, 2001, p. 203.

102. These are based on "Inexpensive Ergonomic Innovations," *BNA Bulletin to Management*, February 1, 1996, p. 40.

103. Sondra Lotz Fisher, "Are Your Employees Working Ergosmart?" *Personnel Journal*, December 1996, pp. 91–92.

104. Maureen Mineham, "New AIDS Survival Rates Mean Patients Returning to Work," *HR Magazine*, October 1997, p. 208.

105. Daniel Warner, "We Do Not Hire Smokers: May Employers Discriminate Against Smokers?" *Employee Responsibilities and Rights Journal* 7, no. 2 (1994), p. 129.

106. Ronald Davis, "Exposure to Environmental Tobacco Smoke: Identifying and Protecting Those at Risk," *Journal of the American Medical Association*, December 9, 1998, pp. 147–148; see also Al Karr, "Lighting Up," *Safety and Health* 162, no. 3 (September 2000), pp. 62–66.

107. Kenneth Sovereign, *Personnel Law* (Upper Saddle River, NJ: Prentice Hall, 1999), pp. 76–79.

108. Warner, "We Do Not Hire Smokers," p. 138.

109. Gus Toscano and Janaice Windau, "The Changing Character of Fatal Work Injuries," *Monthly Labor Review*, October 1994, p. 17. See also Robert Grossman, "Bulletproof Practices," *HR Magazine*, November 2002, pp. 34–42.

110. Based on Louis DiLorenzo and Darren Carroll, "The Growing Menace: Violence in the Workplace," *New York State Bar Journal*, January 1995, p. 24.

111. Kenneth Diamond, "The Gender-Motivated Violence Act: What Employers Should Know," *Employee Relations Law Journal* 25, no. 4 (Spring 2000), pp. 29–41.

112. "Workplace Violence: Sources and Solutions," *BNA Bulletin to Management*, November 4, 1993, p. 345. See also Danny Fogelman, "Minimizing the Risk of Violence in the Workplace," *Employee Relations Today* 27, no. 1 (Spring 2000), pp. 83–99.

113. "Bullies Trigger 'Silent Epidemic' at Work, but Legal Cures Remain Hard to Come By," *BNA Bulletin to Management*, February 24, 2000, p. 57.

114. Jennifer Laabs, "Employee Sabotage," *Workforce*, July 1999, pp. 33–42.

115. Manon Mireille LeBlanc and E. Kevin Kelloway, "Predictors and Outcomes of Workplace Violence and Aggression," *Journal of Applied Psychology* 87, no. 3 (2002), pp. 444–453.

116. Alfred Feliu, "Workplace Violence and the Duty of Care: The Scope of an Employer's Obligation to Protect Against the Violent Employee," *Employee Relations Law Journal* 20, no. 3 (Winter 1994–95), pp. 381–406.

117. "Workplace Violence: Sources and Solutions," *BNA Bulletin to Management*, November 4, 1993, p. 345.

118. Ibid.

119. "OSHA Addresses Top Homicide Risk," *BNA Bulletin to Management*, May 14, 1998, p. 148.

120. Dawn Anfuso, "Workplace Violence," *Personnel Journal*, October 1994, pp. 66–77.

121. Scott Douglas and Mark Martinko, "Exploring the Role of Individual Differences in the Prediction of Workplace Aggression," *Journal of Applied Psychology* 86, no. 4 (2001), p. 554.

122. Feliu, "Workplace Violence and the Duty of Care," p. 395.

123. Quoted from ibid., p. 395.

124. "Preventing Workplace Violence," *BNA Bulletin to Management*, June 10, 1993, p. 177. See also Jenny McCune, "Companies Grapple with Workplace Violence," *Management Review* 83, no. 3 (March 1994), pp. 52–57.

125. Quoted or paraphrased from Younger, "Violence Against Women in the Workplace," p. 177, and based on recommendations from Chris Hatcher.

126. Shari Caudron, "Target: HR," *Workforce*, August 1998, p. 48.

127. Karl Acquino et al., "How Employees Respond to Personal Offense: The Effect of the Blame Attribution, Victim Status, and Offender Status on Revenge and Reconciliation in the Workplace," *Journal of Applied Psychology* 86, no. 1 (2001), pp. 52–59.

128. Ibid. p. 57.

129. Feliu, "Workplace Violence," pp. 401–402.

130. Shari Caudron, "Target HR," *Workforce*, August 1998, pp. 44–52.

131. Eve Tahmincioglu, "Vigilance in the Face of Layoff Rage," *New York Times*, August 1, 2001, pp. C1, C6.

132. Diane Cadrain, "And Stay Out! Using Restraining Orders Can Be an Effective and Proactive Way of Preventing Workplace Violence," *HR Magazine*, August 2002, pp. 83–86.

133. Donna Rosato, "New Industry Helps Managers Fight Violence," *USA Today*, August 8, 1995, p. 1.

134. Helen Frank Bensimon, "What to Do About Anger in the Workplace," *Training and Development* 51, no. 9 (September 1997), pp. 28–32.

135. DiLorenzo and Carroll, "The Growing Menace," p. 25.

136. Quoted from Feliu, "Workplace Violence," p. 393.

137. DiLorenzo and Carroll, "The Growing Menace," p. 27.

138. This is based on "New Challenges for Health and Safety in the Workplace," Society for Human Resource Management, *Workplace Vision*, no. 3 (2003), pp. 2–4. See also, "Protecting Chemical Plants From Terrorists: Opposing Views," *Occupational Hazards*, February 2004, pp. 18–20.

139. "Focus on Corporate Security," *BNA HR Executive Series*, Fall 2001.

140. Ibid., p. 4.

141. Unless otherwise noted, following based on Richard Maurer, "Keeping Your Security Program Active," *Occupational Hazards*, March 2003, pp. 49–52.

142. Ibid., p. 50.

143. Ibid., p. 50.

144. Della Roberts, "Are Your Ready for Biometrics?" *HR Magazine*, March 2003, pp. 95–99.

145. Maurer, "Keeping Your Security Program Alive," p. 52.

146. Craig Schroll, "Are Your Employees Ready to Leave the Building? Evacuation Planning: A Matter of Life-and-Death," *Occupational Hazards*, June 2002, pp. 49–51.

147. Ibid., p. 52.

148. "Firms see Former Workers, Contractors Biggest Source of Data Theft," *BNA Bulletin to Management*, October 24, 2002, p. 339.

149. Louis Obdyke, "Investigating Security Breaches, Workplace Theft, and Employee Fraud," *Society for Human Resource Management Legal Report*, January–February 2003, pp. 1–2.

After studying this chapter, you should be able to:

1 List the HR challenges of International Business.

2 Illustrate how intercountry differences affect HRM.

3 Discuss the global differences and similiarities in HR practices.

4 Explain five ways to improve international assignments through selection.

5 Discuss how to train and maintain international employees.

Managing Global Human Resources

With hotels in 11 cities in Europe and the United States, Lisa knew that the

company had to do a better job of managing its global human resources. For

example, there was no formal means of identifying or training management

employees for duties abroad (either for those going to the United States or to

Europe). As another example, recently, after spending upwards of $200,000

on sending a U.S. manager and her family abroad, they had to return her

abruptly when the family complained bitterly of missing their friends back

home. Lisa knew this was no way to run a multinational business. She

turned her attention to developing the HR practices her company required to

do business more effectively internationally.●

To this point in the book, we've discussed the basic concepts and techniques of HR management, including job analysis, recruitment, selection, training, appraisal, compensation, and labor relations and safety. The purpose of the current (and final) chapter is to make you more effective at managing the international aspects of your HR duties. The topics we'll focus on include the internationalization of business, intercountry differences affecting HR, improving international assignments through selection, and training and maintaining international employees.[1]

● HR AND THE INTERNATIONALIZATION OF BUSINESS

U.S.-based companies are increasingly doing business abroad. Huge firms like Procter & Gamble, IBM, and Citicorp have long had extensive overseas operations, of course. But with the expansion of the European union into Eastern Europe, and the rapid development of demand in Asia and other parts of the world, even small firms are finding that success depends on their ability to market and manage overseas.

This presents firms with some interesting management challenges. Market, product, and production plans must be coordinated on a worldwide basis, for instance, and organization structures capable of balancing centralized home-office control with adequate local autonomy must be created. And, of course, the firm must extend its HR policies and systems to service its staffing needs abroad: For example, "Should we staff the local offices with local or U.S. managers?" "How should we appraise and pay our local employees?" "How should we deal with the unions in our offices abroad?"

List the HR challenges of International Business.

The HR Challenges of International Business

When researchers asked senior international HR managers in eight large companies, "What are the key global pressures affecting human resource management practices in your firm currently and for the projected future?" the three that emerged were:[2]

■ *Deployment:* Easily getting the right skills to where we need them, regardless of geographic location.

■ *Knowledge and innovation dissemination.* Spreading state-of-the-art knowledge and practices throughout the organization regardless of where they originate.

■ *Identifying and developing talent on a global basis.* Identifying who can function effectively in a global organization and developing his or her abilities.[3]

Dealing with global staffing pressures like these is quite complex. For example, it involves addressing, on a global basis, activities including candidate selection, assignment terms and documentation, relocation processing and vendor management, immigration processing, cultural and language orientation and training, compensation administration and payroll processing, tax administration, career planning and development, and handling of spouse and dependent matters.[4]

At firms like Ford Motor Company, having a global HR perspective "requires understanding different cultures, what motivates people from different societies, and how that's reflected in the structure of international assignments."[5] In China, for instance, special insurance should cover emergency evacuations for serious health problems; telephone communication can be a "severe handicap" in Russia; and medical facilities in Russia may not meet international standards.[6] So the challenge of conducting

HR activities abroad comes not just from the vast distances involved (though this is important), but also from the cultural, political, legal, and economic differences among countries and their peoples. Let's look at this.

Illustrate how intercountry differences affect HRM.

How Intercountry Differences Affect HRM

Companies operating only within the borders of the United States generally have the luxury of dealing with a relatively limited set of economic, cultural, and legal variables. The United States is a capitalist, competitive society. And while the U.S. workforce reflects a multitude of cultural and ethnic backgrounds, shared values (such as an appreciation for democracy) help to blur potentially sharp cultural differences. Although the different states and municipalities certainly have their own laws affecting HR, a basic federal framework helps produce a fairly predictable set of legal guidelines regarding matters such as employment discrimination, labor relations, and safety and health.

A company operating multiple units abroad isn't blessed with such homogeneity. For example, minimum legally mandated holidays range from none in the United Kingdom to five weeks per year in Luxembourg. And while Italy has no formal requirements for employee representatives on boards of directors, they're required in Denmark for companies with more than 30 employees. The point is that the need to adapt personnel policies and procedures to the differences among countries complicates HR management in multinational companies. For example, consider the following intercountry differences.

Cultural Factors   Countries differ widely in their *cultures*—in other words, in the basic values their citizens adhere to, and in the ways these values manifest themselves in the nation's arts, social programs, politics, and ways of doing things.

Cultural differences from country to country necessitate corresponding differences in management practices among a company's subsidiaries. For example, in a study of about 330 managers from Hong Kong, the People's Republic of China, and the United States, the U.S. managers tended to be most concerned with getting the job done. Chinese managers were most concerned with maintaining a harmonious environment, and Hong Kong managers fell between these extremes.[7] A classic study by Professor Geert Hofstede identified other international cultural differences. For example, Hofstede says societies differ in *power distance*—in other words, the extent to which the less powerful members of institutions accept and expect an unequal distribution of power.[8] He concluded that acceptance of such inequality was higher in some countries (such as Mexico) than in others (such as Sweden).

Studies show how such cultural differences can influence HR policies.[9] For example, compared to U.S. employees, "Mexican workers expect managers to keep their distance rather than to be close, and to be formal rather than informal." In Mexico, individualism is not valued as highly as it is in the United States. As a result, some workers tend to expect to receive a wider range of services and benefits (such as food baskets and medical attention for themselves and their families) from their employers.[10]

In fact, the list of cultural differences is endless. In Germany, you should never arrive even a few minutes late and should always address senior people formally, with their titles.[11] Such cultural differences are a two-way street, and employees from abroad need orientation to avoid the culture shock of coming to work in the United States.[12] For example, in the Intel booklet "Things You Need to Know About Working in the U.S.A.," topics covered include sexual harassment, recognition of gay and lesbian rights, and Intel's expectations about behavior.[13]

Economic Systems   Differences in economic systems also translate into differences in HR practices. For one thing, some countries are more wedded to the ideals of free enterprise than are others. For instance, France—though a capitalist society—

Economic, cultural, and legal differences make managing global enterprises tricky. In Germany, for instance, workers like those in this Audi auto factory never arrive even a few minutes late and always address senior people formally. Their hourly pay is higher than that of similar workers in the United States, they work fewer hours per year, and they get 18 vacation days per year after six months of service.

imposed tight restrictions on employers' rights to discharge workers, and limited the number of hours an employee could legally work each week.

Differences in labor costs are also substantial. Hourly compensation costs in U.S. dollars for production workers range from $2.38 in Mexico to $5.41 in Taiwan, $17.47 in the United Kingdom, $21.33 in the United States, and $25.08 in Germany, for instance.[14]

There are other labor costs to consider. For example, there are wide gaps in hours worked. Portuguese workers average about 1,980 hours of work annually, while German workers average 1,648 hours. Several European countries, including the United Kingdom and Germany, require substantial severance pay to departing employees, usually equal to at least two years' service in the United Kingdom and one year's in Germany.[15] Compared to the usual two or three weeks of U.S. vacation, workers in France can expect two and a half days of paid holiday per full month of service per year, Italians usually get between four and six weeks off per year, and Germans get 18 vacation days per year after six months of service.[16]

Legal and Industrial Relations Factors   Legal as well as industrial relations (the relationships among the worker, the union, and the employer) factors also vary from country to country. For example, the U.S. practice of employment at will does not exist in Europe, where firing and laying off workers is usually time-consuming and expensive. And in many European countries, *work councils* replace the informal or union-based worker–management mediations typical in U.S. firms. Works councils are formal, employee-elected groups of worker representatives that meet monthly with managers to discuss topics ranging from no-smoking policies to layoffs.[17]

codetermination
Employees have the legal right to a voice in setting company policies.

Codetermination is the rule in Germany and several other countries. **Codetermination** means employees have the legal right to a voice in setting company policies. Workers elect their own representatives to the supervisory board of the employer, and there is a vice president for labor at the top management level.[18] In the United States, HR policies on most matters such as wages and benefits are set by the employer, or by the employer in negotiations with its labor unions. The codetermination laws, including the Works Constitution Act, largely determine the nature of HR policies in many German firms.

The European Union   In the 1990s, the separate countries of the former European Community (EC) were unified into a common market for goods, services, capital, and even labor called the European Union (EU). Tariffs for goods moving across borders from one EU country to another generally disappeared, and employees (with some exceptions) now find it easy to move freely between jobs in the EU countries. The introduction of a single currency—the euro—has further blurred many of these differences. The euro replaced the local currencies of most member countries in early 2002.

In addition to participative processes (like codetermination) found in some EU countries, European Union law currently requires multinationals to consult workers about certain corporate actions such as mass layoffs. However, a new EU directive will greatly expand this requirement. By 2008, more companies—including all those with 50 or more employees in the EU—must "inform and consult" employees about employee-related actions, even if the firms don't operate outside their own countries' borders. And the consultation will then be "ongoing" rather than just for major, strategic decisions.[19]

However, intra-EU differences remain. Many countries have minimum wages while others don't, and workweek hours permitted vary from no maximum in the United Kingdom to 48 per week in Greece and Italy. Other differences exist in minimum number of annual holidays, and minimum advance notice of termination. Employment contracts are another big difference. For most U.S. positions, written correspondence is normally limited to a short letter listing the date, job title, and initial compensation for the new hire.[20] In most European countries, employers are usually required to provide a detailed statement of the job. The European Union, for instance, has a directive requiring employers to provide such a statement (including details of terms and conditions of work) within two months of the employee's starting work.[21]

Even within the EU, however, these requirements vary. In England, a detailed written statement is required, including rate of pay, date employment began, hours of work, vacation entitlement, place of work, disciplinary rules, and grievance procedure. While Germany doesn't require a written contract, it's still customary to have one specifying most particulars about the job and conditions of work. In Italy, as in Germany, written agreements aren't legally required. However, "even more so than in Germany, prudence dictates providing written particulars in the complex, and at times confusing, legal structure in Italy."[22]

The EU's increasing internal coordination will gradually reduce these differences.[23] However, cultural differences will remain, and will translate into differences in management practices. Such differences "may strain relations between headquarters and subsidiary personnel or make a manager less effective when working abroad than at home."[24] Firms therefore risk operational problems abroad unless they take special steps to select, train, and compensate their international employees and assignees.

Discuss the global differences and similarities in HR practices.

GLOBAL DIFFERENCES AND SIMILARITIES IN HR PRACTICES

Since countries differ in cultures, legal/political systems, and economies, it should not be surprising that HR practices tend to differ from country to country, too. One study in particular helps to illustrate this. Beginning in the early 1990s, human resource management scholars from 13 countries or regions used the *Best International Human Resource Management Practices Survey* to assess human resource management practices around the world.[25] The results provide a snapshot of the differences and similarities of HR practices in a wide range of countries. We'll look at some of these next.

Personnel Selection Procedures

Employers around the world tend to use similar criteria and methods for selecting employees. As in the United States, employers around the world usually rank "personal interviews," "the person's ability to perform the technical requirements of the job," and "proven work experiences in a similar job" at or near the top of the criteria or methods they use. The top rankings were the same or similar in the United States, Australia, and Latin America, for instance. Cultural differences did have some impact across countries, however. In Mexico, "having the right connections" was a top consideration in being hired. "Employee tests" were one of the three top selection practices in the People's Republic of China, Indonesia, and Korea, but not in the United States. And, "the person's ability to get along well with others already working here" was one of the three personnel selection criteria in Japan and Taiwan, but not in other countries.

The Purpose of the Performance Appraisal

There tends to be more variation in how employers in different countries use the results of performance appraisals.[26] For example, employers in Taiwan, the United States, and Canada rank "to determine pay" as one of the top three reasons for appraising performance, while that purpose is of relatively little import in Korea and Mexico. Employers in the United States, Taiwan, and Australia emphasize using the appraisal to "document the employee's performance," while in Mexico and the People's Republic of China this purpose is far down the list. "To recognize subordinate" was a main purpose for appraisals in Japan and Mexico, but nowhere else.

Training and Development Practices

When it comes to the purposes of training and development programs, there are usually more similarities than differences across countries.[27] In particular, employers just about everywhere rank "to improve technical abilities" as the main purpose for providing employees with training.

While the main reason for providing training tends to be the same regardless of country, the amount of training firms provide does vary substantially from country to country.[28] For example, training expenditures per employee range from a low of $241 per employee in Asia (outside Japan) to $359 in Japan and $724 in the United States. Similarly, the total hours of training per eligible employees per year ranges from 26 total training hours in Asia up to just over 49 total hours of training per year in Europe.

When You're On Your Own
HR for Line Managers and Entrepreneurs

Comparing Small Businesses, HR Practices in the United States and China

Cross-country differences like these tend to manifest themselves in small businesses, too. For example, one study compared compensation practices in 248 small U.S. companies with those in 148 small Chinese companies. (The researchers defined "small companies" as those with 500 or fewer employees.)[29] First, in terms of *job analysis*, jobs in small Chinese companies tend to be more narrowly defined and set in stone than those in small U.S. businesses. Work in small Chinese firms appears to be more structured than in comparably sized U.S. firms. The small Chinese firms have more up-to-date job descriptions, their employees deviate from their assigned job duties less frequently, their job descriptions tend to cover all the job's duties, and in general the Chinese job descriptions shape the job's duties, rather than the employee.

Similarly, the researchers found significant differences in *performance appraisal practices* between U.S. and Chinese firms. In Chinese firms, compared to the U.S., performance appraisals more often focus on the bottom line; appraisal feedback is evaluative rather than developmental; the appraisal focuses on objective, quantifiable results; and the main objective is to improve performance (rather than to develop the employee). Perhaps surprisingly, therefore, performance appraisals in small Chinese companies tend to be more hard-nosed than are those in the United States.

These differences extend to the firms' *actual pay practices*. Again (perhaps surprisingly given China's communist roots), there's significantly more emphasis on incentive pay than guaranteed salaries in China's small businesses. Employees in the Chinese firms are more likely to receive bonuses based on the company's profits, to receive bonuses based on companywide gainsharing plans, to get stock or stock options as incentives, and to be paid based mostly on an incentive plan rather than on a guaranteed income plan. On the other hand, there tends to be less variation among Chinese employees in pay, and more emphasis than in U.S. firms on seniority.

On the other hand, employers around the world are quite consistent in their use of training delivery methods. Classroom training represents the lion's share of training time in all countries and regions (although in the six or so years since this study, the use of technological "learning technologies" has undoubtedly risen).

The Use of Pay Incentives

Findings regarding the use of financial incentives were somewhat counterintuitive. Given the emphasis on pay for performance in the United States, and the People's Republic of China's communist roots, one might have expected U.S. managers to stress incentives more heavily than their Chinese colleagues. However, that was not the case. Based on this survey, in terms of their use, incentives play an only "moderate" role in U.S. pay packages. In the People's Republic of China, Japan, and Taiwan incentives play a relatively important role.[30]

Owners of small businesses are not immune to global differences like these. The "When You're On Your Own" feature illustrates this.

● HOW TO IMPLEMENT A GLOBAL HR SYSTEM

Given cross-cultural differences like these in HR practices around the world, one could reasonably ask, "Is it realistic for a company to try to institute a standardized HR system in all or most of its facilities around the world?" A recent study suggests that the answer is "yes." It shows that the employer may have to defer to local managers on some specific issues. However, in general, the fact that there are currently global differences in HR practices doesn't mean that these differences are necessary or even advisable. The important thing is knowing how to create and implement the global HR system.

In this study, the researchers interviewed HR personnel from six global companies—Agilent, Dow, IBM, Motorola, Procter & Gamble, and Shell Oil Co.—as well as international HR consultants.[31] Their overall conclusion was that employers who successfully implement global HR systems apply various international HR best practices in doing so. This enables them to create global HR systems that are globally *acceptable*, that they can *develop* more effectively, and that their HR staffs can then *implement* more effectively. Let's look at each.

Making the Global HR System More Acceptable

First, employers engage in three best practices so that the global HR systems they eventually develop will be acceptable to their local managers around the world.

1. *Remember that global systems are more accepted in truly global organizations.* These companies and all their managers think of themselves as global in scope and perspective, and all or most functions and business units operate on a truly global basis. They are not simply aggregates of numerous more or less independent local entities. For example, truly global organizations require their managers to work on global teams, and identify and recruit and place the employees they hire globally. As one Shell manager put it, "If you're truly global, then you are hiring here [the United States] people who are going to immediately go and work in the Hague, and vice versa."[32] This makes it easier for managers everywhere to accept the global imperative for having a more standardized HR system.

2. *Investigate pressures to differentiate and determine their legitimacy.* HR managers seeking to standardize selection, training, appraisal, compensation, or other HR practices worldwide will always meet resistance from local managers who insist, "you can't do that here, because we are different culturally and in other ways." Based on their research, these investigators found that these "differences" are usually not persuasive. For example, when Dow wanted to implement an online employee recruitment and selection tool in a particular region abroad, the hiring managers there told Dow that there was no way their managers would use it. After investigating the supposed cultural roadblocks and then implementing the new system, "what we found is that the number of applicants went through the roof when we went online, and the quality of the applicants also increased."[33]

However, the operative word here is "investigate"—it does not mean ramming through a change without ascertaining whether there may in fact be some reason for using a more locally appropriate system. Carefully assess whether the local culture or other differences might in fact undermine the new system. Be knowledgeable about local legal issues, and be willing to differentiate where necessary. Then, market-test the new HR tool.

3. *Try to work within the context of a strong corporate culture.* A strong corporate culture helps override geographical differences. Companies that create a strong corporate culture find it easier to obtain agreement among far-flung employees when it comes time to implement standardized practices worldwide. For example, Procter & Gamble has a strong corporate culture. Because of how P&G recruits, selects, trains, and rewards them, its managers have a strong sense of shared values. For instance, Procter & Gamble emphasizes orderly growth, and its culture therefore encourages a relatively high degree of conformity among managers. New recruits quickly learn to think in terms of "we" instead of "I." They learn to value thoroughness, consistency, self-discipline and a methodical approach. Because all P&G managers worldwide tend to share these values, they are in a sense more similar to each other than they are geographically different. Having such global unanimity makes it easier to develop and implement standardized HR practices worldwide.

Developing a More Effective Global HR System

Similarly, researchers found that these companies engaged in several best practices in developing effective worldwide HR systems.

1. *Form global HR networks.* The firm's HR managers around the world should feel that they're not merely local HR managers, but are part of a greater whole, namely, the firm's global HR network. These six firms did this in various ways. For instance, they formed global HR development teams, and involved them in developing the new HR systems. In fact, these researchers found that in developing global HR systems, the most critical factor for success is "creating an infrastructure of partners around the world that you use for support, for buy-in, for organization of local activities, and to help you better understand their own systems and their own challenges."[34] Treat the local HR managers as equal partners, not just implementers.

2. *Remember that it's more important to standardize ends and competencies than specific methods.* For example, (with regard to screening applicants) the researchers conclude that "while companies may strive to standardize tools globally, the critical point is [actually] to standardize what is assessed but to be flexible in how it is assessed."[35] Thus, IBM uses a more or less standardized recruitment and selection process worldwide, but "details such as who conducts the interview (hiring manager vs. recruiter) or whether the prescreen is by phone or in person, differ by country."[36]

Implementing the Global HR System

Finally, in actually implementing the global HR systems, several best practices can help ensure a more effective implementation.

1. *Remember, "You can't communicate enough."* For example, "there's a need for constant contact with the decision makers in each country, as well as the people who will be implementing and using the system."[37]
2. *Dedicate adequate resources for the global HR effort.* For example, do not expect local HR offices to suddenly start implementing the new job analysis procedures unless the head office provides adequate resources for these additional activities. Table 17-1 summarizes these best practices for instituting global HR systems.

Table 17-1

Summary of Best Global HR Practices

Do . . .	Don't . . .
• Work within existing local systems—integrate global tools into local systems	• Try to do everything the same way everywhere
• Create a strong corporate culture	• Yield to every claim that "we're different"—make them prove it
• Create a global network for system development—global input is critical	• Force a global system on local people
• Treat local people as equal partners in system development	• Use local people just for implementation
• Assess common elements across geographies	• Use the same tools globally, unless you can show that they really work and are culturally appropriate
• Focus on what to measure and allow flexibility in how to measure	• Ignore cultural differences
• Allow for local additions beyond core elements	• Let technology drive your system design—you can't assume every location has the same level of technology investment and access
• Differentiate when necessary	• Assume that "if we build it they will come"—you need to market your tools or system and put change management strategies in place
• Train local people to make good decisions about which tools to use and how to do so	
• Communicate, communicate, communicate!	
• Dedicate resources for global HR efforts	
• Know, or have access to someone who knows, the legal requirements in each country	

Source: Ann Marie Ryan et al., "Designing and Implementing Global Staffing Systems: Part 2—Best Practices," *Human Resource Management* 42, no. 1 (Spring 2003), p. 93.

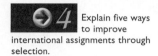

Explain five ways to improve international assignments through selection.

● STAFFING THE GLOBAL ORGANIZATION

Staffing the employer's global organization is the heart of international HR. The process involves identifying and selecting the people who will fill your positions abroad, and then placing them in those positions.

International Staffing: Home or Local?

expatriates (expats)
Noncitizens of the countries in which they are working.

home-country nationals
Citizens of the country in which the multinational company has its headquarters.

third-country nationals
Citizens of a country other than the parent or the host country.

Multinational companies (MNCs) employ several types of international managers. *Locals* are citizens of the countries where they are working. **Expatriates ("expats")** are noncitizens of the countries in which they are working.[38] **Home-country nationals** are citizens of the country in which the multinational company has its headquarters. **Third-country nationals** are citizens of a country other than the parent or the host country—for example, a British executive working in the Tokyo branch of a U.S. multinational bank.[39] Expatriates still represent a minority of multinationals' managers. Thus, "most managerial positions are filled by locals rather than expatriates in both headquarters or foreign subsidiary operations."[40]

There are several reasons to rely on local managers to fill your foreign subsidiary's management ranks. Many people don't want to work in a foreign country, and the cost of using expatriates is usually far greater than the cost of using local workers.[41] Locals may view the multinational as a "better citizen" if it uses local management talent, and some governments even press for the "nativization" of local management.[42] There may also be a fear that expatriates, knowing they're posted to the foreign subsidiary for only a few years, may overemphasize short-term projects rather than more necessary long-term tasks.[43]

Yet there are also reasons for using expatriates—either home-country or third-county nationals—for staffing subsidiaries. The major reason is usually technical competence: In other words, employers often can't find local candidates with the required technical qualifications. Multinationals also view a successful stint abroad as a required step in developing top managers. (For instance, after a term abroad, the head of General Electric's Asia-Pacific region was transferred back to a top executive position as vice chairman at GE.) Control is another important reason to use expatriates. The assumption is that home-office managers are already steeped in the firm's policies and culture, and thus more likely to implement headquarters' instructions and ways of doing things.

Offshoring

offshoring
Having local employees abroad do jobs that the firm's domestic employees previously did in-house.

Offshoring—having local employees abroad do jobs that the firm's domestic employees previously did in-house—is growing by leaps and bounds. Forrester Research projects that about 588,000 U.S. jobs will move offshore between 2000 and 2005, and that that total will grow to about one and a half million jobs by 2010, two and a half million jobs by 2013, and over three million jobs by 2015.[44] Put another way, a report from the McKinsey Global Institute says that the total value of offshoring (also called outsourcing) will grow from about $33 billion in 2002, to over $100 billion in 2008.

Offshoring jobs is very controversial. In the 1980s and 1990s, it was mostly manufacturing jobs that employers shipped overseas. Between 2000 and 2015, the U.S. Labor Department and Forrester Research estimate that about 288,000 management jobs will go offshore, 472,000 computer jobs, 184,000 architecture jobs, almost 75,000 legal jobs, and about 1.7 million office jobs. Offshoring's opponents naturally worry that this jobs drain will mean millions fewer white-collar jobs for American workers. Proponents contend that employers must offshore jobs to remain globally competitive, and that the money employers thereby save boosts research and development and, eventually, create even more domestic jobs for U.S. workers.

IBM staffer leaves the offices of IBM Argentina. HR plays a big role in offshoring: recruiting and hiring the best people; providing information on local wage rates, working conditions, and productivity; making sure there is a supervisory and management structure in place; and seeing that required screening and training is done.

The pros and cons notwithstanding, there's no doubt that offshoring is a matter that HR managers are going to have to deal with. For one thing, offshoring tends to be a uniquely HR-dependent activity. Typically, when firms go abroad, they do so to develop new markets or to open up new manufacturing facilities to serve local markets. In such cases, marketing, sales, and production executives tend to play the pivotal role in where the firm locates its new facilities. Offshoring, on the other hand, mostly involves HR. Employers look to their HR directors to help identify high-quality, low-cost talent abroad and to provide the necessary background data on things like wage rates, working conditions, and productivity.

One thing the HR manager needs to watch out for when offshoring is missing the forest for the trees. Finding a city abroad that provides a wealth of low-paid, high-quality technically competent workers is only part of the task of making offshoring succeed. Among other things, the HR manager also needs to make sure that there is an effective *supervisory and management structure* in place to manage these workers, and that all the employees receive the *screening* and *training* that they require. Furthermore, particularly given the vast distances involved, the HR manager also needs to ensure that the compensation policies and working conditions are satisfactory. Offshoring, after all, is a fast-growing industry, and these local employees are just the sorts of mobile talent who can easily move to new employers.

Values and International Staffing Policy

What determines whether firms use locals or expats? Hopefully, purely rational reasons like cost and competency will prevail. However, the firms' top executives' values will also undoubtedly play a role. Experts sometimes classify top executives' values as ethnocentric, polycentric, or geocentric, and these values translate into corresponding corporate behaviors and policies. In an ethnocentrically run corporation, "the prevailing attitude is that home country attitudes, management style, knowledge, evaluation criteria, and managers are superior to anything the host country might have to offer."[45] In the polycentric corporation, "there is a conscious belief that only host country managers can ever really understand the culture and behavior of the host country market; therefore, the foreign subsidiary should be managed by local people."[46] Geocentric executives believe they must scour the firm's whole management staff on a global basis, on the assumption that the best manager for a specific position anywhere may be in any of the countries in which the firm operates.

These values translate into three broad international staffing policies. With an **ethnocentric** staffing policy, the firm fills key management jobs with parent-country nationals.[47] At Royal Dutch Shell, for instance, most financial officers around the world are Dutch nationals. Reasons given for ethnocentric staffing policies include lack of qualified host-country senior management talent, a desire to maintain a unified corporate culture and tighter control, and the desire to transfer the parent firm's core competencies (for instance, a specialized manufacturing skill) to a foreign subsidiary more expeditiously.[48]

A **polycentric**-oriented firm would staff its foreign subsidiaries with host-country nationals, and its home office with parent-country nationals. This may reduce the local cultural misunderstandings that might occur if it used expatriate managers. It will also almost undoubtedly be less expensive. One expert estimates that an expatriate executive can cost a firm up to three times as much as a domestic executive because of relocation expenses and other expenses such as schooling for children, annual home leave, and the need to pay income taxes in two countries.[49]

A **geocentric** staffing policy "seeks the best people for key jobs throughout the organization, regardless of nationality"—similar to what Ford Motor Company does.[50] This may let the global firm use its human resources more efficiently by transferring the best person to the open job, wherever he or she may be. It can also help build a stronger and more consistent culture and set of values among the entire global management team.

ethnocentric
The notion that home-country attitudes, management style, knowledge, evaluation criteria, and managers are superior to anything the host country has to offer.

polycentric
A conscious belief that only the host-country managers can ever really understand the culture and behavior of the host-country market.

geocentric
The belief that the firm's whole management staff must be scoured on a global basis, on the assumption that the best manager of a specific position anywhere may be in any of the countries in which the firm operates.

Why Expatriate Assignments Fail

Because international assignments are the heart of international HR, it's disconcerting to see how often such assignments fail. The exact number of failures is hard to quantify, in part because "failure" means different things to different people. An early return rate is perhaps the most obvious indicator. However, some expatriates may fail less conspicuously, quietly running up the hidden costs of reduced productivity and poisoned customer and staff relations.[51] However, there is some evidence that the rate of early departures, at least, is declining, from about 8% in the 1990s to 3.2% in 2002. This appears to be because more employers are taking steps to reduce expats' problems abroad, for example, by selecting expats more carefully, helping spouses to get jobs abroad, and providing more ongoing support to the expat and his or her family.[52]

Discovering why such assignments fail is an important research task, and experts have made considerable progress. *Personality* is one factor. For example, in a study of 143 expatriate employees, extroverted, agreeable, and emotionally stable individuals were less likely to want to leave early.[53] Furthermore, the person's *intentions* are important. For example, people who want expatriate careers try harder to adjust to such a life.[54] Nonwork factors like *family pressures* usually loom large in expatriate failures. In one study, U.S. managers listed, in descending order of importance for leaving early: inability of spouse to adjust, managers' inability to adjust, other family problems, managers' personal or emotional immaturity, and inability to cope with larger overseas responsibility.[55] Managers of European firms emphasized only the inability of the manager's spouse to adjust as an explanation for the expatriate's failed assignment. Other studies similarly emphasize dissatisfied spouses' effects on the international assignment.[56]

These findings underscore a truism regarding international assignee selection: It's usually not incompetence, but family and personal problems that undermine the international assignee. As one expert puts it:

The selection process is fundamentally flawed. . . . Expatriate assignments rarely fail because the person cannot accommodate to the technical demands of the job. The expatriate selections are made by line managers based on technical competence. They fail because of family and personal issues and lack of cultural skills that haven't been part of the process.[57]

Given the role of family problems in expat failures, it's important that the employer understand just how unhappy and cut off the expat manager's spouse can feel in a foreign environment. One relevant study involved analyzing questionnaire data from 221 international assignee couples working in 37 countries.[58] Perhaps the most poignant finding concerned the degree to which many spouses often felt cut off and adrift; consider this quote:

It's difficult to make close friends. So many expats have their guard up, not wanting to become too close. Too many have been hurt, too many times already, becoming emotionally dependent on a friend only to have the inevitable happen—one or the other gets transferred. It's also difficult to watch your children get hurt when their best friend gets transferred. Although I have many acquaintances, I have nowhere near the close friends I had in the states. My spouse therefore has become my rock.[59]

One study identified three things that helped make it easier for the spouse to adjust. Language fluency was one. Since spouses will obviously feel even more cut off from their new surroundings if they can't make themselves understood, the employer should provide the spouse—not just the employee—with *language training*. The couple's family situation is important too. For example, having *preschool-age children* (rather than school-age children or no children) seemed to make it easier for the spouse to adjust. "This suggests that younger children, perhaps because of their increased dependency, help spouses retain that part of their social identities: as parents, their responsibilities for these children remain the same."[60] It also clearly helps that there be a *strong bond of closeness* and mutual sharing between spouse and expat partner, to provide the continuing emotional and social support many spouses find lacking abroad.

There are other useful steps the employer can take. Providing realistic previews of what to expect, careful screening, improved orientation, and improved benefits packages are some obvious solutions. A less obvious solution is to institute procedures that ensure your firm treats its employees fairly—treating them with respect, providing an appeal process, and so on. In one study of international assignees, nonwork problems were "significantly less pronounced when the organization's procedures were judged to be more fair."[61]

One way to reduce assignment problems is simply to shorten the length of the assignment, something employers are doing. A recent survey reports that 23% of the employers' overseas assignments lasted over three years, down from 32% in 1996.[62]

Selecting Expatriate Managers

The processes firms use to select managers for their domestic and foreign operations obviously have many similarities. For either assignment, the candidate should have the technical knowledge and skills to do the job, and the intelligence and people skills to be a successful manager.[63]

However, we've seen that foreign assignments are different. There is the need to cope with colleagues whose culture may be drastically different from one's own, and the stress that being alone in a foreign land can put on the single manager. And if spouse and children will share the assignment, there are the complexities and pressures that the family will have to confront, from learning a new language to finding new friends and attending new schools.

Selecting managers for these assignments therefore sometimes means testing them for traits that predict success in adapting to new environments. One study asked 338 international assignees from various countries and organizations to specify which traits were important for the success of managers on foreign assignment. The researchers identified five factors that contribute to success in such assignments: job knowledge and motivation, relational skills, flexibility/adaptability, extracultural openness, and family situation (spouse's positive opinion, willingness of spouse to live abroad, and so on). Figure 17-1 shows some of the specific items that make up each of the five factors. The five factors were not equally important in the foreign assignees' success, according to the assignees. "Family situation was generally found to be the most important factor, a finding consistent with other research on international assignments and transfers."[64]

Adaptability Screening   With flexibility and adaptability often appearing high in studies like these, **adaptability screening** is sometimes part of the expatriate screening process. Often conducted by a psychologist or psychiatrist, adaptability screening aims to assess the assignee's (and spouse's) probable success in handling the foreign transfer, and to alert them to issues (such as the impact on children) the move may involve.[65] Here, experience is often the best predictor of future success. Companies like Colgate-Palmolive therefore look for overseas candidates whose work and nonwork experience, education, and language skills already demonstrate a commitment to and facility for living and working with different cultures.[66] Even several successful summers spent traveling overseas or participating in foreign student programs might provide some basis to believe that the potential transferee can adjust when he or she arrives overseas.

Many firms also use paper-and-pencil tests such as the Overseas Assignment Inventory. This test reportedly identifies the characteristics and attitudes international assignment candidates should have. Realistic previews about the problems to expect in the new job (such as mandatory private schooling for the children) as well as about the cultural benefits, problems, and idiosyncrasies of the country are another important part of the screening process. The rule, say some experts, should always be to "spell it all out" ahead of time, as many multinationals do for their international transferees.[67]

adaptability screening
A process that aims to assess the assignee's (and spouse's) probable success in handling a foreign transfer.

Figure 17-1
Five Factors Important in International Assignee Success, and Their Components
Source: Adapted from Arthur Winfred Jr., and Winston Bennett Jr., "The International Assignee: The Relative Importance of Factors Perceived to Contribute to Success," *Personnel Psychology* 18 (1995), pp. 106–107.

I. Job Knowledge and Motivation
Managerial ability
Organizational ability
Imagination
Creativity
Administrative skills
Alertness
Responsibility
Industriousness
Initiative and energy
High motivation
Frankness
Belief in mission and job
Perseverance

II. Relational Skills
Respect
Courtesy and fact

Display of respect
Kindness
Empathy
Non-judgmentalness
Integrity
Confidence

III. Flexibility/Adaptability
Resourcefulness
Ability to deal with stress
Flexibility
Emotional stability
Willingness to change
Tolerance for ambiguity
Adaptability
Independence
Dependability
Political sensitivity
Positive self-image

IV. Extracultural Openness
Variety of outside interests
Interest in foreign cultures
Openness
Knowledge of local language[s]
Outgoingness and extroversion
Overseas experience

V. Family Situation
Adaptability of spouse and family
Spouse's positive opinion
Willingness of spouse to live abroad
Stable marriage

The New Workplace

Sending Women Managers Abroad

Women are underrepresented as managerial expatriates. For example, while women represent about 50% of the middle management talent in U.S. companies, they represent only 14% of expat managers sent abroad. What accounts for this? Line managers make most of these assignments, and many of these managers suffer from misperceptions that inhibit them from recommending women to work abroad. Consider the results of one survey, by the International Personnel Association.[68] Many managers assume that women don't want to work abroad, or are reluctant to move their families abroad, or can't get their spouses to move because the husband is the main breadwinner. In fact, this survey found, women do want international assignments, they are not less inclined than male managers to move their families abroad, and their male spouses are not necessarily the families' main breadwinners.

What other perceptions (or misperceptions) inhibit managers from recommending women to work abroad? Safety is often an issue. Employers tend to assume that women posted abroad are more likely to become crime victims. However, most of the surveyed women expats said that safety was no more an issue with women than it was with men. As one said,

"it doesn't matter if you're a man or woman. If it's a dangerous city, it's dangerous for whomever."[69]

Fear of cultural prejudices against women is another common issue. Here, there's no doubt that in some cultures women have to follow different rules than do their male counterparts, for instance, in terms of their attire. But even here, as one expat said, "even in the more harsh cultures, once they recognize that the women can do the job, once your competence has been demonstrated, it becomes less of a problem."[70]

There are several proactive steps the employer can take to short-circuit misperceptions like these, and to identify more women to assign abroad. For example, formalize a process for identifying employees who are willing to take assignments abroad. (At Gillette, for instance, supervisors use the performance review interview to identify the subordinate's career interests, including the possibility of assigning the person abroad.) Train managers to understand how employees really feel about going abroad, and what the real safety and cultural issues are. Let successful female expats help recruit prospective female expats, and discuss with them the pros and cons of assignments abroad. Provide the expat's spouse with employment assistance.[71]

Unfortunately, theory doesn't always translate into practice. The importance of adaptability screening notwithstanding, 70% of respondents in one survey listed "skills or competencies" as the most important selection criteria when choosing candidates for international assignments. They ranked "job performance" second. The ability to adapt to new cultural conditions—as measured by items like "prior international living experience or assignment," and "familiarity with assignment country"—were rarely ranked as most important or second most important.[72] One study found that selection for positions abroad is so informal that the researchers called it "the coffee machine system": Two colleagues meet at the office coffee machine, strike up a conversation about the possibility of a position abroad, and based on that and little more a selection decision is made.[73] Perhaps this helps explain the high failure rate of foreign assignees. "The New Workplace" provides a perspective on how such informality can affect women managers.

 Discuss how to train and maintain international employees.

● TRAINING AND MAINTAINING EXPATRIATE EMPLOYEES

Careful screening is just the first step in ensuring the foreign assignee's success. The employee may then require special training, and the firm will also need special international HR policies for compensating the firm's overseas employees and for maintaining healthy labor relations.

Orienting and Training Employees on International Assignment

When it comes to providing the orientation and training required for success overseas, the practices of most U.S. firms reflect more form than substance. One consultant says that despite many companies' claims, there is generally little or no systematic selection and training for assignments overseas. In one survey, a sample of company executives agreed that international business required that employees be firmly grounded in the economics and practices of foreign countries. However, few of their companies actually provide such training to their employees. A survey of U.S. companies that assign employees abroad found that only 42% have a "formal program for briefing employees regarding conditions in the host country."[74]

What sort of special training do overseas candidates need? One firm specializing in such programs prescribes a four-step approach.[75] Level 1 training focuses on the impact of cultural differences, and on raising trainees' awareness of such differences and their impact on business outcomes. Level 2 aims at getting participants to understand how attitudes (both negative and positive) are formed and how they influence behavior. (For example, unfavorable stereotypes may subconsciously influence how a new manager responds to and treats his or her new foreign subordinates.) Level 3 training provides factual knowledge about the target country, while Level 4 provides skill building in areas like language and adjustment and adaptation skills.

Beyond these special training needs, managers abroad continue to need traditional training and development. At IBM, for instance, such development includes rotating assignments that permit overseas managers to grow professionally. IBM and other firms also have management development centers around the world where executives can hone their skills. And classroom programs (such as those at the London Business School, or at INSEAD in France) provide overseas executives the sorts of educational opportunities (to acquire MBAs, for instance) that similar stateside programs do for their U.S.-based colleagues.

In addition to developing these managers' skills, international management development activities can also have more subtle effects on the managers and their firms. For example, rotating assignments can help managers form bonds with colleagues around the world, and these contacts can help the managers make cross-border decisions more expe-

Classroom programs like those at the London Business School or at INSEAD in France, where these executives attend a lecture, offer overseas executives educational opportunities comparable to those available to their U.S.-based colleagues.

ditiously. Activities such as periodic seminars (in which the firm brings together managers from its global subsidiaries and steeps them for a week or two in the firm's values, strategy, and policies) are also useful. They can help provide consistency of purpose and thereby improve control, by building a unifying set of values, standards, and corporate culture.

Trends in Expatriate Training   There are several trends in expatriate training and development. First, rather than providing only predeparture cross-cultural training, more firms are providing continuing, in-country cross-cultural training during the early stages of an overseas assignment. Second, employers are using returning managers as resources to cultivate the "global mind-sets" of their home-office staff. For example, automotive equipment producer Bosch holds regular seminars in which newly arrived returnees pass on their knowledge and experience to relocating managers and their families.

There's also increased use of software and the Internet for cross-cultural training. For example, *Bridging Cultures* is a self-training multimedia package for people who will be traveling and/or living overseas. It uses short video clips to introduce case study intercultural problems, and then guides users to selecting the strategy to best handle the situation. Cross-cultural training firms' Web sites include: www.bennettinc.com/indexie.htm; www.livingabroad.com; www.worldwise-inc.com; and www.globaldynamics.com.[76]

Compensating Expatriates

The whole area of international compensation presents some tricky problems. On the one hand, there is logic in maintaining companywide pay scales and policies so that, for instance, divisional marketing directors throughout the world are paid within the same narrow range. This reduces the risk of perceived inequities, and dramatically simplifies the job of keeping track of disparate, country-by-country wage rates.

Yet not adapting pay scales to local markets can produce more problems than it solves. The fact is, it can be enormously more expensive to live in some countries (like Japan) than others (like Greece); if these cost-of-living differences aren't considered, it may be almost impossible to get managers to take "high-cost" assignments. However, the answer is usually not just to pay, say, marketing directors more in one country than in another. For one thing, you could get resistance when you tell a marketing director in Tokyo who's earning $4,000 per week to move to your division in Spain, where his or her pay for the same job will drop by half (cost of living notwithstanding). One way to handle the problem is to pay a similar base salary companywide, and then add on various allowances according to individual market conditions.[77]

Determining equitable wage rates in many countries is no simple matter. There is a wealth of "packaged" compensation survey data available in the United States, but such data are not so easy to come by overseas. As a result, one of the greatest difficulties in managing multinational compensation is establishing consistent compensation measures between countries.

Some multinational companies conduct their own local annual compensation surveys. For example, Kraft conducts an annual study of total compensation in Belgium, Germany, Italy, Spain, and the United Kingdom. It focuses on the total compensation paid to each of 10 senior management positions held by local nationals in these firms. The survey covers all forms of compensation including cash, short- and long-term incentives, retirement plans, medical benefits, and perquisites.[78] This information becomes the basis for annual salary increases and proposed changes in the benefits package.

The Balance Sheet Approach   The most common approach to formulating expatriate pay is to equalize purchasing power across countries, a technique known as the balance sheet approach.[79] More than 85% of North American companies reportedly use this approach.

The basic idea is that each expatriate should enjoy the same standard of living he or she would have had at home. With the balance sheet approach, four main home-country groups of expenses—income taxes, housing, goods and services, and discretionary expenses (child support, car payments, and the like)—are the focus of attention. The employer estimates what each of these four expenses is in the expatriate's home country, and what each will be in the host country. The employer then pays any differences—such as additional income taxes or housing expenses.

In practice, this usually boils down to building the expatriate's total compensation around five or six separate components. For example, base salary will normally be in the same range as the manager's home-country salary. In addition, however, there might be an overseas or foreign service premium. The executive receives this as a percentage of his or her base salary, in part to compensate for the cultural and physical adjustments he or she will have to make.[80] There may also be several allowances, including a housing allowance and an education allowance for the expatriate's children. Income taxes represent another area of concern. A U.S. manager posted abroad must often pay not just U.S. taxes but also income taxes in the host country.

Table 17-2 illustrates the balance sheet approach. In this case, the manager's annual earnings are $80,000, and she faces a U.S. income tax rate of 28%, and a Belgium income tax rate of 70%. The other costs are based on the index of living costs abroad published in the "U.S. Department of State Indexes of Living Costs Abroad, Quarters Allowances, and Hardship Differentials," available at http://www.state.gov.

Incentives   While the situation is changing, performance-based incentives still tend to be less prevalent abroad. In Europe, firms traditionally emphasize a guaranteed annual salary and companywide bonus.[81] European compensation directors do want to see more performance-based pay. However, they first have to overcome several problems—including the public relations aspects of such a move (such as selling the idea of more emphasis on performance-based pay). U.S. firms that offer overseas managers long-term incentives use overall corporate performance criteria (like worldwide profits) when awarding incentive pay—although, ironically, a manager's local performance may have little or no effect on how the company as a whole performs.

What U.S. companies do offer are various incentives to get expatriates to accept and stay on international assignment. **Foreign service premiums** are financial payments over and above regular base pay, and typically range between 10% and 30% of base pay. Note, though, that since managers tend to get these premiums in small increments with their base pay, it's easy to misconstrue these as regular "pay raises," and then to become disillusioned when the premium stops upon the expatriates' return. **Hardship allowances**

foreign service premiums
Financial payments over and above regular base pay, typically ranging between 10% and 30% of base pay.

hardship allowances
Compensate expatriates for exceptionally hard living and working conditions at certain locations.

Table 17-2

The Balance Sheet Approach (Assumes Base Salary of $80,000)

Annual Expense	Chicago, U.S.	Brussels, Belgium (U.S.$ equivalent)	Allowance
Housing & utilities	$35,000	$67,600	$32,600
Goods & services	6,000	9,500	3,500
Taxes	22,400	56,000	33,600
Discretionary income	10,000	10,000	0
Total	$73,400	$143,100	$69,700

Source: Joseph Martocchio, *Strategic Compensation: A Human Resource Management Approach*, 2nd edition (Upper Saddle River, NJ: Prentice Hall, 2001), Table 12-15, p. 294.

mobility premiums
Typically, lump-sum payments to reward employees for moving from one assignment to another.

compensate expatriates for exceptionally hard living and working conditions at certain foreign locations. Employers also usually pay these incrementally (with each paycheck), so it's important to make it clear that this is not a permanent raise. **Mobility premiums** are typically lump-sum payments to reward employees for moving from one assignment to another.

Yet, in general, executive compensation systems around the world are becoming more similar: "The structures have common broadband base salary ranges, flexible annual incentive targets/maximums and internationally established share option guideline awards."[82] And, as in the United States, more multinational employers are granting more stock options to a broader group of their employees overseas, a step that requires even more attention to complying with local tax laws.[83]

Appraising Expatriate Managers

Several things complicate the task of appraising an expatriate's performance. For one thing, the question of who actually appraises the expatriate is crucial. Obviously, local management must have some input, but cultural differences here may distort the appraisals. Thus, host-country bosses might evaluate a U.S. expatriate manager in India somewhat negatively if they find his or her use of participative decision making culturally inappropriate. On the other hand, home-office managers may be so out of touch that they can't provide valid appraisals, since they're not fully aware of the situation the manager faces locally. Similarly, the procedure may be to measure the expatriate by objective criteria such as profits and market share, but local events (such as political instability) may affect the manager's performance while remaining "invisible" to home-office staff.

Suggestions for improving the expatriate appraisal process include:

1. Stipulate the assignment's difficulty level, and adapt the performance criteria to the situation.
2. Weigh the evaluation more toward the on-site manager's appraisal than toward the home-site manager's.
3. If the home-office manager does the actual written appraisal, have him or her use a former expatriate from the same overseas location for advice.

International Labor Relations

Firms opening subsidiaries abroad will find substantial differences in labor relations practices among the world's countries and regions. This is important; remember that while union membership as a percentage of wage and salary earners is dropping in the United States, it is still relatively high in most industrialized countries compared with the United States.

The following synopsis illustrates some of these labor relations differences by focusing on Europe. However, similarly significant differences would exist as we move, say, to South and Central America, and to Asia.[84]

■ *Centralization.* In general, collective bargaining in Western Europe is likely to be industrywide or regionally oriented, whereas in the United States it generally occurs at the enterprise or plant level.

■ *Union structure.* European collective bargaining is more centralized, and local unions tend to have less autonomy and decision-making power than in the United States.

■ *Employer organization.* Due to the prevalence of industrywide bargaining in Europe, employer associations (rather than individual employers) tend to perform the employer's collective bargaining role.

■ *Union recognition.* Union recognition for collective bargaining purposes in Western Europe is much less formal than in the United States. For example, in Europe there is no legal mechanism requiring an employer to recognize a particular union; even if a union claims to represent 80% of an employer's workers, another union can try to organize and bargain for the other 20%.

■ *Union security.* Union security in the form of formal, closed-shop agreements is largely absent in continental Western Europe.

■ *Content and scope of bargaining.* U.S. labor–management agreements tend to focus on wages, hours, and working conditions. European agreements tend to be brief and to specify minimum wages and employment conditions, with individual employers free to institute more generous terms. This is because industrywide bargaining makes it difficult to write detailed contracts applicable to individual enterprises. And in Europe, the government is heavily involved in setting terms of employment (such as vacations and working conditions).

■ *Grievance handling.* In Western Europe, grievances occur much less often than in the United States; when raised, legislated machinery outside the union's formal control usually handles them.

■ *Strikes.* With some exceptions, strikes generally occur less frequently in Europe. This is probably due to industrywide bargaining, which generally elicits less management resistance than in the United States, where union demands "cut deeper into the individual enterprise's revenues."[85]

■ *Worker participation.* Worker participation has a long history in Western Europe, where it tends to go far beyond matters such as pay and working conditions. The aim is to create a system by which workers can participate directly in the management of the enterprise. Works councils and codetermination are two examples.[86]

Know Your Employment Law

The Equal Employment Opportunity Responsibilities of Multinational Employers

U.S. employers doing business abroad, or foreign firms doing business in the United States or its territories,[87] have wide-ranging responsibilities to their employees under American equal employment opportunity laws, including Title VII, the ADEA, and the ADA. For example, *foreign multinational employers* that operate in the United States or its territories (American Samoa, Guam, the Commonwealth of the Northern Mariana Islands, Puerto Rico, and the U.S. Virgin Islands) must abide by EEO laws to the same extent as U.S. employers, unless the employer is covered by a treaty or other binding international agreement that limits the full applicability of U.S. antidiscrimination laws. Similarly, *U.S. employers*—those that are incorporated or based in the United States or are controlled by U.S. companies—that employ U.S. citizens outside the United States or its territories are subject to Title VII, the ADEA, and the ADA with respect to those employees. U.S. EEO laws do not apply to *non-U.S. citizens* working for U.S. (or foreign) firms *outside* the United States or its territories.

If equal employment opportunity laws conflict with the laws of the country in which the U.S. employer is operating, the laws of the local country generally take precedence. In particular, U.S. employers are not required to comply with requirements of Title VII, the ADEA, or the ADA if adherence to that law would violate the law of the country where the workplace is located. For example, an employer would have a "Foreign Laws Defense" for a mandatory retirement policy if the law in the country in which the company is located requires mandatory requirement. However, a U.S. employer may not transfer an employee to another country in order to disadvantage the employee because of his or her race, color, sex, religion, national origin, age, or disability. For example, an employer may not transfer an older worker to a country with a mandatory retirement age for the purpose of forcing the worker's retirement.

Terrorism, Safety, and Global HR

The increased threat of terrorism is affecting HR activities both domestically and abroad. Domestically, for instance, anecdotal evidence suggests that the new federal anti-terrorism laws and procedures are affecting employers' ability to import and export workers.[88] For example, since the September 11 terrorist attacks, getting working papers for foreign workers now takes weeks or months instead of days. This is because in most cases, the prospective employee must have an interview at his or her local U.S. Embassy, and scheduling these is a relatively time-consuming process.

Employers are also facing more resistance from prospective expats. More are reluctant to accept foreign postings and take their families abroad, and those that do are demanding more compensation.[89] And for their employees and facilities abroad, employers have had to institute more comprehensive safety plans, including, for instance, evacuation plans to get employees to safety, if that becomes necessary. Even before the September 11 attacks, the threats facing expat employees were on the rise. For example, the number of overseas kidnappings more than doubled from 830 to 1,728 during the mid- to late 1990s.[90] Developments like these had already prompted employers to take steps to better protect their expat employees.

Taking Protective Measures   Employers are doing so in a variety of ways. In the movie *Proof of Life*, Russell Crowe heads up a "crisis team" sent in to negotiate the release of and then rescue a kidnapped employee, and in this case, fiction reflects real life. Many employers do retain such crisis team services. They then call on these crisis management teams, for instance, when they receive notice that criminal elements have kidnapped or detained one of their expats, or threatened the person with harm unless a ransom is paid. As one insurance executive puts it, "when you have a specialist, there's a better chance to get the person back. You want a specialist in there because you don't want the employee coming home in a body bag."[91]

Kidnapping and Ransom (K&R) Insurance   Hiring crisis teams and paying ransoms can be prohibitively expensive for all but the largest firms, so most employers with many employees abroad buy kidnapping and ransom (K&R) insurance. Any one or more of several events may trigger payments under such policies. The obvious ones are kidnapping (for instance, the employee is a hostage until the employer pays a ransom), extortion (threatening bodily harm), and detention (holding an employee without any ransom demand). Other triggering events include threats to property or products unless the employer makes a payment.

The insurance itself typically covers several costs associated with kidnappings, abductions, or extortion attempts. These costs might include, for instance, hiring a crisis team, the actual cost of the ransom payment to the kidnappers or extortionists, ensuring the ransom money in case it's lost in transit, legal expenses, and employee death or dismemberment.[92]

Keeping business travelers out of crime's way is a specialty all its own, but suggestions here include:[93]

■ Provide expatriates with general training about traveling, living abroad, and the place they're going to, so they're more oriented when they get there.

■ Tell them not to draw attention to the fact that they're Americans—by wearing flag emblems or t-shirts with American names, or by using American cars, for instance.

■ Have travelers arrive at airports as close to departure time as possible and wait in areas away from the main flow of traffic where they're not as easily observed.

■ Equip the expatriate's car and home with adequate security systems.

■ Tell employees to vary their departure and arrival times and take different routes to and from work.

■ Keep employees current on crime and other problems by regularly checking, for example, the State Department's travel advisory service and consular information sheets (http://travel.state.gov/travel_warnings.html). These provide up-to-date information on possible threats in almost every country of the world.

■ Advise employees to remain confident at all times: Body language can attract perpetrators, and those who look like victims often become victimized.[94]

As another matter, firms like Coca-Cola and Exxon increasingly acknowledge that the AIDS epidemic can have devastating effects on the citizens of many of the countries in which they do business—and on their local employees. Thus, Exxon is providing HIV prevention education for employees, and Chevron donated $250,000 in medical supplies for state-of-the-art blood testing.[95]

The following "Improving Productivity Through HRIS" shows how global firms can use their HRIS to integrate the HR efforts globally.

Repatriation: Problems and Solutions

One of the most confounding and worrisome facts about sending employees abroad is that 40% to 60% of them will probably quit within three years of returning home. One study suggests that a three-year assignment abroad for one employee with a base salary of about $100,000 costs the employer $1 million, once extra living costs, transportation,

Improving Productivity Through HRIS

Taking the HRIS Global

As a company grows, relying on manual HR systems to manage activities like worldwide safety, benefits administration, payroll, and succession planning becomes unwieldy. As we've seen, more firms are therefore automating and integrating their HR systems into human resource information systems (HRIS).[96]

For global firms, it makes particular sense to expand the firm's human resource information systems abroad. For example, electrical components manufacturer Thomas & Betts once needed 83 faxes to get a head count of its 26,000 employees in 24 countries; it can now do so with the push of a button, thanks to its global HRIS system.[97] Most global HRIS uses are more sophisticated. Without a database of a firm's worldwide management talent, for instance, selecting employees for assignments abroad and keeping track of each unit's compensation plans, benefits, and personnel practices and policies can be overwhelming. However, any HRIS is no better than the accuracy of its data (information on salaries, employee skills, and appraisals, for instance), and "such a database needs to be constantly reviewed and updated."[98]

Integrating and updating a firm's HR systems, particularly in a global firm, makes using an Internet-based HRIS especially beneficial. For example, when Buildnet, Inc., decided to integrate its separate HR systems, it chose a Web-based software package called MyHRIS, from NuView, Inc. (www.nuviewinc. com). This is an Internet-based system that includes human resource and benefits administration, applicant tracking and résumé scanning, training administration, and succession planning and development.[99] With MyHRIS, managers at any of the firm's locations around the world can access and update more than 200 built-in reports such as "termination summary" or "open positions."[100] And the firm's home-office managers can monitor global HR activities on a real-time basis.

and family benefits are included.[101] Given the investment the employer makes in training and sending these often high-potential people abroad, it obviously makes sense to do everything possible to make sure that they stay with the firm. For this, formal repatriation programs can be quite useful. For instance, one study found that about 5% of returning employees resigned if their firms had formal repatriation programs, while about 22% of those left if their firms had no such programs.[102]

The heart and guiding principle for any repatriation program is this: Make sure that the expatriate and his or her family don't feel that the company has left them adrift. For example, AT&T has an effective three-part repatriation program, one that actually starts before the employee leaves for the assignment abroad.[103] First, AT&T *matches the expat and his or her family with a psychologist* trained in repatriation issues. The psychologist meets with the family before they go abroad. The psychologist discusses the challenges they will face abroad, assesses with them how well he or she think they will adapt to their new culture, and stays in touch with them throughout their assignment. (Other firms, like Dow, also provide written repatriation agreements. These guarantee in writing that the company won't keep the expat abroad for more than some period, such as three years, and that on return he or she will receive a mutually acceptable job.)

Second, AT&T makes sure that *the employee always feels that he or she is still "in the loop"* with what's happening back at the home office. For example, AT&T assigns the expat a mentor, and brings the expat back to the home office periodically for meetings and to socialize with his or her colleagues.

Third, once it's time for the expat employee and his or her family to return home, AT&T *provides formal repatriation services.* About six months before the overseas assignment ends, the psychologist and an HR representative meet with the expat and the family, to start preparing them for the return. For example, they help plan the employee's next career move, help the person update his or her résumé, and begin putting the person in contact with supervisors back home. They work with the person's family on the logistics of the move back home. Then, about a month after returning home, the expat and family attend a "welcome home" seminar, where they discuss matters like the stress of repatriation.[104]

"The HR Scorecard" shows how the Hotel Paris used concepts like those in this chapter to create a strategy-oriented global HR effort.

A Final Word: Auditing the HR Function

A manager would be lax not to periodically follow up to see how effective his or her HR policies and procedures have been. With its focus on translating specific HR activities into measurable organizational outcomes, the HR Scorecard is the method of choice here. However, the HR manager can use other approaches. One is to tap the opinions of HR and line managers regarding the HR function's effectiveness. The process involves five steps: (1) HR and line managers answer the question, "What should HR's functions be?" (2) Participants then rate each of these functions to answer the question, "How important are each of these functions?" (3) Next, they answer the question, "How well are each of the functions performed?" (4) Next, compare (2) and (3) to focus on "What needs improvement?" (5) Then, top management needs to answer the question, "Overall, how effectively does the HR function allocate its resources? In other words, are there steps that we can take—such as creating a centralized HR call center, or putting more HR activities on the Web—that can improve how our firm uses its HR resources, given the results of questions 1–4?"

Sometimes an HR audit requires more of an expert opinion. An HR review like the one above can help pinpoint concerns and suggestions from the firm's managers about things they'd like to see HR change. However, there is often no substitute for having outside HR experts methodically audit each step in the firm's HR process. The usual procedure is to evaluate each of the firm's HR activities, including job descriptions, recruitment and selection

The HR Scorecard
Strategy and Results

Managing Global Human Resources

The Hotel Paris's competitive strategy is, "To use superior guest service to differentiate the Hotel Paris properties, and to thereby increase the length of stay and return rate of guests, and thus boost revenues and profitability." HR manager Lisa Cruz must now formulate functional policies and activities that support this competitive strategy, by eliciting the required employee behaviors and competencies.

A preliminary analysis, performed jointly by Lisa and the Hotel Paris's chief financial officer, left them optimistic that HR could contribute measurably to achieving the hotel's strategic aims. Several employee competencies and behaviors including employee morale, employee commitment, and the percent of arriving guests receiving the hotel's required greeting had significant effects on customer and organizational outcomes such as guest satisfaction and frequency of guest returns. In turn, outcomes like these contributed measurably to the Hotel Paris's strategic goals, including profit margins, market share, and scores on industry satisfaction surveys. Lisa and her team now turn to creating a global HR system that will help to produce the required employee competencies and behaviors. The accompanying HR Scorecard (Figure 17-2) outlines the relationships involved.

On reviewing the data, it was apparent to Lisa and the CFO that the company's global human resource practices were probably inhibiting the Hotel Paris from being the world-class guest services company that it sought to be. For example, high-performing service and hotel firms had formal departure training programs for at least 90% of the employees they sent abroad; the Hotel Paris had no such programs. Similarly, with each city's hotel operating its own local hotel HR information system, there was no easy way for Lisa, the CFO, or the company's CEO to obtain reports on metrics like turnover, absences, or workers' compensation costs across all the different hotels. As the CFO summed it up, "if we can't measure how each hotel is doing in terms of human resource metrics like these, there's really no way to manage these activities, so there's no telling how much lost profits and wasted efforts are dragging down each hotel's performance." Lisa received approval to institute new global human resources programs and practices.

In instituting these new programs and practices, Lisa had several goals in mind. She wanted an integrated human resource information system (HRIS) that allowed her and the company's top managers to monitor and assess, on an ongoing basis, the company's global performance on strategically required employee competencies and behaviors such as attendance, morale, commitment, and service-oriented behavior. To address this need, she received approval to contract with a company that integrated, via the Internet, the separate hotels' HR systems, including human resource and benefits administration, applicant tracking and résumé scanning, and employee morale surveys and performance appraisals.

She took other steps. She contracted with an international HR training company to develop and provide expatriate training for Hotel Paris employees and their families before they leave for their foreign assignments, and to provide continuing short-term support after they arrived. That training company also helped create a series of weeklong "Managers' Seminars." Held once every four months at a different hotel in a different city, these gave selected managers from throughout the Hotel Paris system an opportunity to meet and to learn more about the numerous new HR programs and practices that Lisa and her team had been instituting for the purpose of supporting the company's strategic aims. With the help of their compensation specialist, Lisa and her team also instituted a new incentive program for each of the company's local managers, to focus their attention more fully on the company's service-oriented strategic aims. By the end of the year, the Hotel Paris's performance on metrics such as percent of expatriates receiving predeparture screening, training, and counseling were at or above those of high-performing similar companies, and she and the CFO believed, rightly, that they had their global HR system under control.

practices, wage and salary programs, performance appraisal systems, and safety and health, often using an extensive checklist approach. Audits like these can also identify legal compliance issues the firm needs to address. And they can pinpoint areas that could benefit from today's leading-edge HR management practices—such as those discussed in this book.

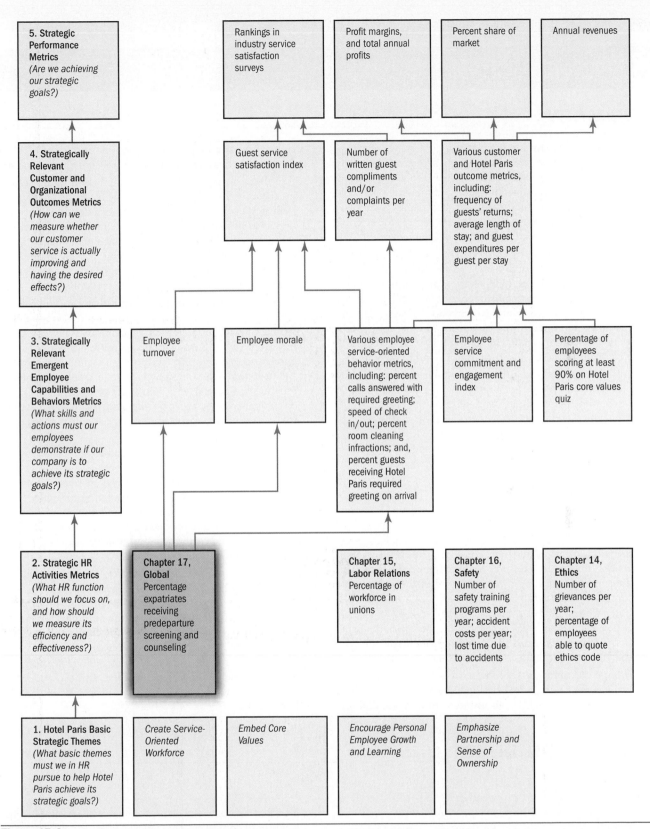

Figure 17-2
HR Scorecard for Hotel Paris International Corporation*

*Note: *(An abbreviated example showing selected HR practices and outcomes aimed at implementing the competitive strategy,"To use superior guest services to differentiate the Hotel Paris properties and thus increase the length of stays and the return rate of guests and thus boost revenues and profitability")*

Review

SUMMARY

1. International business is important to almost every business today, and so firms must increasingly be managed globally. This presents managers with many new challenges, including coordinating production, sales, and financial operations on a worldwide basis. As a result, companies today have pressing international HR needs with respect to selecting, training, paying, and repatriating global employees.

2. Intercountry differences affect a company's HR management processes. Cultural factors suggest differences in values, attitudes, and therefore behaviors and reactions of people from country to country. Economic and labor cost factors help determine local compensation issues. Industrial relations and specifically the relationship between the worker, the union, and the employer influence the nature of a company's specific HR policies from country to country.

3. Countries differ in cultures, legal/political systems, and economies, and so HR practices tend to differ from country to country. For example, "to determine pay" is one of the top reasons for appraising performance in Taiwan, the United States, and Canada but not in Mexico. Similarly, training expenditures for employees range from $241 per employee in Asia to $724 in the United States. In the People's Republic of China, pay incentives play a relatively important role, compared with U.S. pay packages.

4. Research shows that employers engage in three "best practices" to help make their global HR systems acceptable to their local managers around the world. These are: Remember that global systems are more accepted in truly global organizations; investigate pressures to differentiate and determine their legitimacy; and, try to work within the context of a strong corporate culture. To develop effective worldwide HR systems: form global HR networks; remember that it's more important to standardize ends and competencies than specific methods; remember, "you can't communicate enough," and, dedicate adequate resources for the global HR effort.

5. A large percentage of expatriate assignments fail, but the average can be improved through careful selection. There are various sources HR can use to staff domestic and for-

eign subsidiaries. Often managerial positions are filled by locals rather than expatriates, but this is not always the case.

6. Selecting managers for expatriate assignments means screening them for traits that predict success in adapting to dramatically new environments. Such traits include adaptability and flexibility, cultural toughness, self-orientation, job knowledge and motivation, relational skills, extracultural openness, and family situation. Adaptability screening focusing on the family's probable success in handling the foreign assignment can be an especially important step in the selection process.

7. Training for overseas managers typically focuses on cultural differences, on how attitudes influence behavior, and on factual knowledge about the target country. The most common approach to formulating expatriate pay is to equalize purchasing power across countries, a technique known as the balance sheet approach. The employer estimates expenses for income taxes, housing, goods and services, and discretionary costs, and pays supplements to the expatriate in such a way as to maintain the same standard of living he or she would have had at home.

8. The expatriate appraisal process can be complicated by the need to have both local and home-office supervisors provide input into the performance review. Suggestions for improving the process include stipulating difficulty level, weighing the on-site manager's appraisal more heavily, and having the home-site manager get background advice from managers familiar with the location abroad before completing the expatriate's appraisal.

9. Repatriation problems are common but you can minimize them. They include the often well-founded fear that the expatriate is "out of sight, out of mind," and difficulties in reassimilating the expatriate's family back into the home-country culture. Suggestions for avoiding these problems include using repatriation agreements, assigning a sponsor, offering career counseling, keeping the expatriate plugged in to home-office business, and offering reorientation programs to the expatriate and his or her family.

DISCUSSION QUESTIONS

1. You are the president of a small business. What are some of the ways you expect "going international" will affect HR activities in your business?

2. What are some of the specific, uniquely international activities an international HR manager typically engages in?

3. What intercountry differences affect HRM? Give several examples of how each may specifically affect HRM.

4. You are the HR manager of a firm that is about to send its first employees overseas to staff a new subsidiary. Your boss, the president, asks you why such assignments often fail, and what you plan to do to avoid such failures. How do you respond?

5. What special training do overseas candidates need? In what ways is such training similar to and different from traditional diversity training?

6. How does appraising an expatriate's performance differ from appraising that of a home-office manager? How would you avoid some of the unique problems of appraising the expatriate's performance?

7. As an HR manager, what program would you establish to reduce repatriation problems of returning expatriates and their families?

INDIVIDUAL AND GROUP ACTIVITIES

1. Working individually or in groups, write an expatriation and repatriation plan for your professor, whom your school is sending to Bulgaria to teach HR for the next three years.

2. Give three specific examples of multinational corporations in your area. Check on the Internet or with each firm to determine in what countries these firms have operations. Explain the nature of some of their operations, and summarize whatever you can find out about their international employee selection and training HR policies.

3. Choose three traits useful for selecting international assignees, and create a straightforward test to screen candidates for these traits.

4. Use a library or Internet source to determine the relative cost of living in five countries as of this year, and explain the implications of such differences for drafting a pay plan for managers being sent to each country.

5. The HRCI "Test Specifications" appendix at the end of this book (pages 685–689) lists the knowledge someone studying for the HRCI certification exam needs to have in each area of human resource management (such as in Strategic Management, Workforce Planning, and Human Resource Development). In groups of four to five students, do four things: (1) review that appendix now; (2) identify the material in this chapter that relates to the required knowledge the appendix lists; (3) write four multiple choice exam questions on this material that you believe would be suitable for inclusion in the HRCI exam; and (4) if time permits, have someone from your team post your team's questions in front of the class, so the students in other teams can take each others' exam questions.

6. The April 2004 issue of *HR Magazine* contained an article titled "Aftershocks of War," which said that soldiers returning to their jobs from Iraq would likely require HR's assistance in coping with "delayed emotional trauma." The term *delayed emotional trauma* refers to the personality changes such as anger, anxiety, or irritability and associated problems such as tardiness or absenteeism that exposure to the traumatic events of war sometimes triggers in returning veterans. Assume you are the HR manager for the employer of John Smith, who is returning to work next week after one year in Iraq. Based on what you read in this chapter, what steps would you take to help ensure that John's reintegration into your workforce goes as smoothly as possible?

EXPERIENTIAL EXERCISE

A Taxing Problem for Expatriate Employees

Purpose: The purpose of this exercise is to give you practice identifying and analyzing some of the factors that influence expatriates' pay.

Required Understanding: You should be thoroughly familiar with this chapter and with the Web site, www.irs.gov.

How to Set Up the Exercise/Instructions: Divide the class into teams of four or five students. Each team member should read the following: One of the trickiest aspects of calculating expatriates' pay relates to the question of the expatriate's U.S. federal income tax liabilities. Go to the Internal Revenue Service's www.irs.gov. Scroll down to Individuals, and go to Overseas Taxpayers. Your team is the expatriate-employee compensation task force for your company, and your firm is about to send several managers and engineers to Japan, England, and Hong Kong. What information did you find on this site that will help your team formulate expat tax and compensation policies? Based on that, what are the three most important things your firm should keep in mind in formulating a compensation policy for the employees you're about to send to Japan, England, and Hong Kong?

APPLICATION CASE

"Boss, I Think We Have a Problem"

Central Steel Door Corporation has been in business for about 20 years, successfully selling a line of steel industrial-grade doors, as well as the hardware and fittings required for them. Focusing mostly in the United States and Canada, the company had gradually increased its presence from the New York City area, first into New England and then down the Atlantic Coast, then through the Midwest and West, and finally into Canada. The company's basic expansion strategy was always the same: Choose an area, open a distribution center, hire a regional sales manager, then let that regional sales manager help staff the distribution center and hire local sales reps.

Unfortunately, the company's traditional success in finding sales help has not extended to its overseas operations. With the introduction of the new European currency in 2002, Mel Fisher, president of Central Steel Door, decided to expand his company abroad, into Europe. However, the expansion has not gone smoothly at all. He tried for three weeks to find a sales manager by advertising in the *International Herald Tribune*, which is read by businesspeople in Europe and by American expatriates living and working in Europe. Although the ads placed in the *Tribune* also run for about a month in the *Tribune*'s Internet Web site, Mr. Fisher so far has received only five applications. One came from a possibly viable candidate, whereas four came from candidates whom Mr. Fisher refers to as "lost souls"—people who seem to have spent most of their time traveling aimlessly from country to country sipping espresso in sidewalk cafés. When asked what he had done for the last three years, one told Mr. Fisher he'd been on a "walkabout."

Other aspects of his international HR activities have been equally problematic. Fisher alienated two of his U.S. sales managers by sending them to Europe to temporarily run the European operations, but neglecting to work out a compensation package that would cover their relatively high living expenses in Germany and Belgium. One ended up staying the better part of the year, and Mr. Fisher was rudely surprised to be informed by the Belgian government that his sales manager owed thousands of dollars in local taxes. The managers had hired about 10 local people to staff each of the two distribution centers. However, without full-time local European sales managers, the level of sales was disappointing, so Fisher decided to fire about half the distribution center employees. That's when he got an emergency phone call from his temporary sales manager in Germany: "I've just been told that all these employees should have had written employment agreements and that in any case we can't fire anyone without at least one year's notice, and the local authorities here are really up in arms. Boss, I think we have a problem."

Questions

1. Based on this chapter and the case incident, compile a list of 10 international HR mistakes Mr. Fisher has made so far.

2. How would you have gone about hiring a European sales manager? Why?

3. What would you do now if you were Mr. Fisher?

CONTINUING CASE

Carter Cleaning Company Going Abroad

With Jennifer gradually taking the reins of Carter Cleaning Company, Jack decided to take his first long vacation in years and go to Mexico for a month in January 2004. What he found surprised him: While he spent much of the time basking in the sun in Acapulco, he also spent considerable time in Mexico City and was surprised at the dearth of cleaning stores, particularly considering the amount of air pollution in the area. Traveling north he passed through Juarez, Mexico, and was similarly surprised at the relatively few cleaning stores he found there. As he drove back into Texas, and back toward home, he began to think about whether it is advisable to consider expanding his chain of stores into Mexico.

Quite aside from the possible economic benefits, he had liked what he saw in the lifestyle in Mexico and was also attracted by the idea of possibly facing the sort of exciting challenge he faced 20 years ago when he started Carter Cleaning in the United States: "I guess entrepreneurship is in my blood," is the way he put it.

As he drove home to have dinner with Jennifer, he began to formulate the questions he would have to ask before deciding whether or not to expand abroad.

Questions

1. Assuming they began by opening just one or two stores in Mexico, what do you see as the main HR-related challenges he and Jennifer would have to address?

2. How would you go about choosing a manager for a new Mexican store if you were Jack or Jennifer? For instance, would you hire someone locally or send someone from one of your existing stores? Why?

3. The cost of living in Mexico is substantially below that of where Carter is now located: How would you go about developing a pay plan for your new manager if you decided to send an expatriate to Mexico?

4. Present a detailed explanation of the factors you would look for in your candidate for expatriate manager to run the stores in Mexico.

KEY TERMS

codetermination. 658	offshoring, 664	adaptability screening, 668
expatriates (expats), 664	ethnocentric, 666	foreign service premiums, 672
home-country nationals, 664	polycentric, 666	hardship allowances, 672
third-country nationals, 664	geocentric, 666	mobility premiums, 673

ENDNOTES

1. Heinrich Pierer, "Managing a Global Player in the Age of Information," *Management International Review*, October 15, 1999, pp. 9–12.
2. Karen Roberts, Ellen Kossek, and Cynthia Ozeki, "Managing the Global Workforce: Challenges and Strategies," *Academy of Management Executive* 12, no. 4 (1998), pp. 93–106.
3. Ibid., p. 94.
4. Nancy Wong, "Mark Your Calendar! Important Task for International HR," *Workforce*, April 2000, pp. 72–74. See also "Companies Adjust International Assignments in Facing Changing Economy," *Compensation and Benefits Review*, March/April 2003, pp. 10–11.
5. Charlene Solomon, "Today's Global Mobility," *Global Workforce*, July 1998, p. 16.
6. "Fifteen Top Emerging Markets," *Global Workforce*, January 1998, pp. 18–21.
7. David Ralston, Priscilla Elsass, David Gustafson, Fannie Cheung, and Robert Terpstra, "Eastern Values: A Comparison of Managers in the United States, Hong Kong, and the People's Republic of China," *Journal of Applied Psychology* 71, no. 5 (1992), pp. 664–671.
8. Geert Hofstede, "Cultural Dimensions in People Management," in Vladimir Pucik, Noel Tishy, and Carole Barnett (eds.), *Globalizing Management* (New York: John Wiley & Sons, 1992), p. 143.
9. Randall Schuler, Susan Jackson, Ellen Jackofsky, and John Slocum Jr., "Managing Human Resources in Mexico: A Cultural Understanding," *Business Horizons*, May–June 1996, pp. 55–61.
10. Ibid.
11. Valerie Frazee, "Establishing Relations in Germany," *Global Workforce*, April 1997, p. 17.
12. Charlene Solomon, "Destination U.S.A.," *Global Workforce*, April 1997, pp. 19–23.
13. Ibid., p. 21.
14. Annual 2002 figures, www.bls.gov/news.release/ichcc.hr0.htm.
15. "Comparing Employment Practice," *BNA Bulletin to Management*, April 22, 1993, p. 1.
16. "Vacation Policies Around the Globe," *Global Workforce*, October 1996, p. 9.
17. Carolyn Hirschman, "When Operating Abroad, Companies Must Adopt European Style HR Plan," *HR News* 20, no. 3 (March 2001), pp. 1, 6.
18. This is discussed in Eduard Gaugler, "HR Management: An International Comparison," *Personnel*, 1988, p. 28. See also Carlos Castillo, "Collective Labor Rights in Latin America and Mexico," *Relations Industrielles/Industrial Relations* 55, no. 1 (Winter 2000), p. 59.
19. "Inform, Consult, Impose: Workers' Rights in the EU," *Economist*, June 16, 2001, p. 3.
20. Alan Chesters, "Employment Contracts—In Writing or Not?" *Global Workforce*, April 1997, p. 12.
21. Ibid., p. 12.
22. Chesters, "Employment Contracts—In Writing or Not?" p. 13.
23. See, for example, Robert O'Connor, Changes Afoot in EU Pension Regulations," *HR Magazine*, March 2003, pp. 91–95.
24. John Daniels and Lee Radebaugh, *International Business* (Upper Saddle River, NJ: Prentice Hall, 2001), p. 764.
25. Y. Paul Yo et al., "Divergence or Convergence: A Cross National Comparison of Personnel Selection Procedures," *Human Resource Management* 41, no. 1 (Spring 2002), pp. 31–44.
26. John Milliman et al., "An Exploratory Assessment of the Purposes of Performance Appraisals in North and Central America and the Pacific Rim," *Human Resource Management* 41, no. 1 (Spring 2002), pp. 87–102.
27. Ellen Drost et al., "Benchmarking Training and Development Practices: A Multicountry Comparative Analysis," *Human Resource Management* 41, no. 1 (Spring 2002), pp. 67–86.
28. Martin Van Buren and Stephen King, "The 2000 ASTD International Comparisons Report," American Society for Training and Development (2000); this training survey reflects usable responses from 501 U.S. organizations plus over 400 organizations from 47 countries outside the United States.
29. Robert Heneman et al., "Compensation Practices in Small Entrepreneurial and High-Growth Companies in the United States and China," *Compensation and Benefits Review*, July/August 2002, pp. 15–16.
30. Kevin Lowe et al., "International Compensation Practices: A Ten Country Comparative Analysis," *Human Resource Management* 41, no. 1 (Spring 2002), pp. 45–66.
31. Ann Marie Ryan et al., "Designing and Implementing Global Staffing Systems: Part 2—Best Practices," *Human Resource Management* 42, no. 1 (Spring 2003), pp. 85–94.
32. Ibid., p. 86.
33. Ibid., p. 87.
34. Ibid., p. 89.
35. Ibid., p. 90.
36. Ibid., p. 90.
37. Ibid., p. 92.
38. Daniels and Radebaugh, *International Business*, p. 767. See also Castillo, "Collective Labor Rights in Latin America and Mexico," p. 59.
39. Arvind Phatak, *International Dimensions of Management* (Boston: PWS Kent, 1989), p. 106. See also, Charles Hill, *International Business: Competing in the Global Marketplace* (Burr Ridge, IL: Irwin McGraw-Hill, 2001), pp. 564–566.
40. Daniels and Radebaugh, *International Business*, p. 767.
41. Ibid., p. 769; Phatak, *International Dimensions of Management*, p. 106.
42. Phatak, *International Dimensions of Management*, p. 108.
43. Daniels and Radebaugh, *International Business*, p. 769.
44. Based on Pamela Babcock, "America's Newest Export: White Collar Jobs," *HR Magazine*, April 2004, pp. 50–57.
45. Phatak, *International Dimensions of Management*, p. 129.
46. Ibid.
47. Charles Hill, *International Business: Competing in the Global Marketplace*, (Burr Ridge, IL: Irwin, 1994), p. 507.
48. Ibid., pp. 507–510.
49. Ibid., p. 509.
50. Ibid. See also Michael Harvey et al., "An Innovative Global Management Staffing System: A Competency-Based Perspective," *Human Resource Management* 39, no. 4 (Winter 2000), pp. 381–394.
51. Margaret Shaffer and David Harrison, "Expatriates' Psychological Withdrawal from International Assignments: Work, Nonwork, and Family Influences," *Personnel Psychology* 51 (1998), p. 88. See also, Jan Selmer, "Psychological Barriers to Adjustment of Western Business Expatriates in China: Newcomers vs. Long Stayers," *International Journal of Human Resource Management*, June–August 2004, vol. 15, issue 4–5, p. 794 (21).
52. Gary Insch and John Daniels, "Causes and Consequences of Declining Early Departures from Foreign Assignments," *Business Horizons* 46, no. 6 (November–December 2002), pp. 39–48.

53. Paula Caliguri, "The Big Five Personality Characteristics as Predictors of Expatriates' Desire to Terminate the Assignment and Supervisor-Rated Performance," *Personnel Psychology* 53, no. 1 (Spring 2000), pp. 67–88.

54. Jan Selmer, "Expatriation: Corporate Policy, Personal Intentions and International Adjustment," *International Journal of Human Resource Management* 9, no. 6 (December 1998), p. 997–1007.

55. Discussed in Charles Hill, *International Business*, pp. 511–515.

56. Charlene Solomon, "One Assignment, Two Lives," *Personnel Journal*, May 1996, pp. 36–47; Michael Harvey, "Dual-Career Couples During International Relocation: The Trailing Spouse," *International Journal of Human Resource Management* 9, no. 2 (April 1998), pp. 309–330.

57. Michael Schell, quoted in Charlene Marmer Solomon, "Success Abroad Depends on More Than Job Skills," p. 52.

58. Mark Shaffer and David Harrison, "Forgotten Partners of International Assignments: Development and Test of a Model of Spouse Adjustment," *Journal of Applied Psychology* 86, no. 2 (2001), pp. 238–254.

59. Ibid., p. 251.

60. Ibid., p. 250.

61. Ron Garonzik, Joel Brockner, and Phyllis Siegel, "Identifying International Assignees at Risk for Premature Departure: The Interactive Effect of Outcome Favorability and Procedural Fairness," *Journal of Applied Psychology* 85, no. 1 (2000), pp. 13–20. For a discussion of the importance of organizational support in expatriate adjustment, see, for example, Maria Kraimer et al., "Sources of Support and Expatriate Performance: Mediating Role of Expatriate Adjustment," *Personnel Psychology* 54 (2001), pp. 71–99.

62. Carla Joinson, "Cutting Down the Days," *HR Magazine*, April 2000, pp. 90–97; "Employers Shortened Assignments of Workers Abroad," *BNA Bulletin to Management*, January 4, 2001, p. 7.

63. Mason Carpenter et al., "International Assignment Experience at the Top Can Make a Bottom-Line Difference," *Human Resource Management* 30, no. 223 (Summer–Fall 2000), pp. 277–285.

64. Winfred Arthur Jr. and Winston Bennett Jr., "The International Assignee: The Relative Importance of Factors Perceived to Contribute to Success," *Personnel Psychology*, 48 (1995), p. 110; Gretchen Spreitzer, Morgan McCall Jr., and Joan Mahoney, "Early Identification of International Executive Potential," *Journal of Applied Psychology* 82, no. 1 (1997), pp. 62–69.

65. Phatak, *International Dimensions of Management*, p. 119.

66. See, for example, Blocklyn, "Developing the International Executive," p. 45.

67. Blocklyn, "Developing the International Executive," p. 45.

68. Kathryn Tyler, "Don't Fence Her In," *HR Magazine*, 46, no. 3 (March 2001), pp. 69–77.

69. Ibid.

70. Ibid.

71. See Nancy Napier and Sully Taylor, "Experiences of Women Professionals Abroad," *International Journal of Human Resource Management* 13, no. 5 (August 2002), pp. 837–851; Iris Fischlmayr, "Female Self-Perception as a Barrier to International Careers?" *International Journal of Human Resource Management*, 13, no. 5 (August 2002), pp. 773–783; and Wolfgang Mayrhofer and Hugh Scullion, "Female Expatriates in International Business: Evidence from the German Clothing Industry," *International Journal of Human Resource Management* 13, no. 5 (August 2002), pp. 815–836.

72. "International Assignment Policies and Practices," *BNA Bulletin to Management*, May 1, 1997, pp. 140–141, based on a survey by Organization Resources Counselors, Inc., New York City.

73. Hilary Harris and Chris Brewster, "The Coffee Machine System: How International Selection Really Works," *International Journal of Human Resource Management* 10, no. 3 (June 1999), pp. 488–500.

74. Valerie Frazee, "Expats Are Expected to Dive Right In," *Personnel Journal*, December 1996, p. 31.

75. This is based on ibid., p. 30. See also Rita Bennett et al., "Cross-Cultural Training: A Critical Step in Ensuring the Success of National Assignments," *Human Resource Management* 39, nos. 2–3 (Summer–Fall 2000), pp. 239–250, and Jill Elswick, "Worldly Wisdom: Companies Refine Their Approach to Overseas Assignments, Emphasizing Cost-Cutting and Work-Life Support for Expatriates," *Employee Benefit News*, June 15, 2004, pITEM0416600B.

76. Mark Mendenhall and Gunther Stahl, "Expatriate Training and Development: Where Do We Go from Here?" *Human Resource Management* 39, no. 223 (Summer–Fall 2000), pp. 251–265.

77. See, for example, Victor Infante, "Three Ways to Design International Pay: Headquarters, Home Country, Host," *Workforce*, January 2001, pp. 22–24; and Gary Parker and Erwin Janush, "Developing Expatriate Remuneration Packages," *Employee Benefits Journal* 26, no. 2 (June 2001), pp. 3–51.

78. Hewitt Associates, "On Compensation" (May 1989), p. 2.

79. Hill, *International Business*, pp. 519–520; Valerie Frazee, "Is the Balance Sheet Right for Your Expats?" *Global Workforce*, September 1998, pp. 19–26, Stephenie Overman, "Focus on International HR," *HR Magazine*, March 2000, pp. 87–92. See also Sheila Burns, "Flexible International Assignee Compensation Plans," *Compensation and Benefits Review*, May/June 2003, pp. 35–44.

80. Phatak, *International Dimensions of Management*, p. 134. See also, "China to Levy Income Tax on Expatriates," *Asia Africa Intelligence Wire*, August 3, 2004, p. NA. Elec. Coll.: A120140119.

81. Except as noted, this section is based on Martocchio, *Strategic Compensation*, pp. 280–283. See also, Gary Parker, "Establishing Remuneration Practices Across Culturally Diverse Environments," *Compensation and Benefits Review*, Spring 2001, vol. 17, issue 2, p. 23.

82. J. E. Richard, "Global Executive Compensation: A Look at the Future," *Compensation and Benefits Review*, May/June 2000, pp. 35–38.

83. Stan Veliotis, "Offshore Equity Compensation Plans," *Compensation and Benefits Review*, July/August 2000, pp. 39–45.

84. Robert Sauer and Keith Voelker, *Labor Relations: Structure and Process* (New York: Macmillan, 1993), pp. 510–525.

85. Ibid., p. 516. See also Marino Regini, "Human Resource Management and Industrial Relations in European Companies," *International Journal of Human Resource Management* 4, no. 3 (September 1993), pp. 555–568.

86. Quoted from ibid., p. 519.

87. The following is quoted from or adapted from "The Equal Employment Opportunity Responsibilities of Multinational Employers," The U.S. Equal Employment Opportunity Commission: www.EEOC.gov/facts/multi-employers.html, downloaded February 9, 2004.

88. "Terrorism Impact Ability to Import, Export Workers," *BNA Bulletin to Management*, April 3, 2002, p. 111.

89. Ibid.

90. Frank Jossi, "Buying Protection from Terrorism," *HR Magazine*, June 2001, pp. 155–160.

91. Ibid.

92. Ibid.

93. These are based on or quoted from Samuel Greengard, "Mission Possible: Protecting Employees Abroad," *Workforce*, August 1997, pp. 30–32.

94. Ibid., p. 32.

95. Nancy Breuer, "AIDS Threatens Global Business," *Workforce*, February 2000, pp. 52–55.

96. Adapted from Kenneth Laudon and Jane Laudon, *Management Information Systems: New Approaches to Organization and Technology* (Upper Saddle River, NJ: Prentice Hall, 1998), p. G7.

97. Bill Roberts, "Going Global," *HR Magazine*, August 2000, pp. 123–128.

98. Samuel Greengard, "Mission Possible: Protecting Employees Abroad," *Workforce*, August 1997, pp. 30–32.

99. Diane Turner, "NuView Brings Web-Based HRIS to Buildnet," *Workforce*, December 2000, p. 90.

100. Jim Meade, "Web-Based HRIS Meets Multiple Needs," *HR Magazine*, August 2000, pp. 129–133.

101. Carla Joinson, "Save Thousands Per Ex Patriate," *HR Magazine*, July 2002, p. 77.

102. Quoted in Leslie Klaff, "The Right Way to Bring Expats Home," *Workforce*, July 2002, p. 43.

103. Ibid., p. 43.

104. Ibid., p. 43.

APPENDIX FOR CHAPTER 17

HRCI Appendix

This appendix contains the complete test specifications for the Human Resource Certification Institutes certification exams. Note the specific areas of *knowledge* ("knowledge of") listed for each HR functional area.

(Note that HRCI numbers all *knowledge* questions sequentially, with, for instance, the last Strategic Management question numbered 6, and the first Workforce Planning knowledge question numbered 7.)

Appendix A: HRCI Test Specifications

The percentages that follow each functional area heading are the PHR and SPHR percentages, respectively.

1 Strategic Management (12%, 26%)

The processes and activities used to formulate HR objectives, practices, and policies to meet the short- and long-range organizational needs and opportunities, to guide and lead the change process, and to evaluate HR's contributions to organizational effectiveness.

Responsibilities

1. Interpret information related to the organization's operations from internal sources, including financial/accounting, marketing, operations, information technology, and individual employees, in order to participate in strategic planning and policy making.

2. Interpret information related to the general business environment, industry practices and developments, and technological developments from external sources (for example, publications, government documents, media and trade organizations) in order to participate in strategic planning and policy making.

3. Participate as a partner in the organization's strategic planning process.

4. Establish strategic relationships with individuals in the organization, to influence organizational decision making.

5. Establish relationships/alliances with key individuals in the community and in professional capacities to assist in meeting the organization's strategic needs.

6. Evaluate HR's contribution to organizational effectiveness, including assessment, design, implementation and evaluation of activities with respect to strategic and organizational measurement in HR objectives.

7. Provide direction and guidance during changes in organizational processes, operations, planning, intervention, leadership training and culture that balances the expectations and needs of the organization, its employees and other stakeholders (including customers).

8. Develop and shape organizational policy related to the organization's management of its human resources.

9. Cultivate leadership and ethical values in self and others through modeling and teaching.

10. Provide information for the organizational budgeting process, including budget development and review.

11. Monitor legislative environment for proposed changes in law and take appropriate action to support, modify or stop the proposed action (for example, write to a member of Congress, provide expert testimony at a public hearing, lobby legislators).

Knowledge of

1. Lawmaking and administrative regulatory processes.

2. Internal and external environmental scanning techniques.

3. Strategic planning process and implementation.

4. Organizational social responsibility (for example, welfare to work, philanthropy, alliances with community-based organizations).

5. Management functions, including planning, organizing, directing and controlling.

6. Techniques to sustain creativity and innovation.

2 Workforce Planning and Employment (26%, 16%)

The processes of planning, developing, implementing, administering, and performing ongoing evaluation of recruiting, hiring, orientation, and organizational exit to ensure that the workforce will meet the organization's goals and objectives.

Responsibilities

1. Identify staffing requirements to meet the goals and objectives of the organization.

2. Conduct job analyses to write job descriptions and develop job competencies.

3. Identify and document the essential job functions for positions.

4. Establish hiring criteria based on the competencies needed.

5. Assess internal workforce, labor market, and recruitment agencies to determine the availability of qualified applicants.

6. Identify internal and external recruitment methods and implement them within the context of the organization's goals and objectives.

7. Develop strategies to market the organization to potential applicants.

8. Establish selection procedures, including interviewing, testing, and reference and background checking.

9. Implement selection procedures, including interviewing, testing, and reference and background checking.

10. Develop and/or extend employment offers.

11. Perform or administer post-offer employment activities (for example, employment agreements, completion of I-9 verification form, relocation agreements, and medical exams).

12. Facilitate and/or administer the process by which non-U.S. citizens can legally work in the United States.

13. Design, facilitate, and/or conduct the orientation process, including review of performance standards for new hires and transfers.

14. Evaluate selection and employment processes for effectiveness and implement changes if indicated (for example, employee retention).

15. Develop a succession planning process.

16. Develop and implement the organizational exit process, including unemployment insurance claim responses.

17. Develop, implement, manage, and evaluate affirmative action program(s), as may be required.

Knowledge of

7. Federal/state/local employment-related laws (for example, Title VII, ADA, ADEA, Vietnam Veterans, WARN) and regulations (for example, EEOC Uniform Guidelines on Employee Selection Procedures).

8. Immigration law (for example, visas, I-9).

9. Quantitative analyses required to assess past and future staffing (for example, cost-benefit analysis, costs per hire, selection ratios, adverse impact).

10. Recruitment methods and sources.

11. Staffing alternatives (for example, telecommuting, outsourcing).

12. Planning techniques (for example, succession planning, forecasting).

13. Reliability and validity of selection tests/tools/methods.

14. Use an interpretation of selection tests (for example, psychological/personality, cognitive and motor/physical assessments).

15. Interviewing techniques.

16. Relocation practices.

17. Impact of compensation and benefits plans on recruitment and retention.

18. International HR and implications of international workforce for workforce planning and employment.

19. Downsizing and outplacement.

20. Internal workforce planning and employment policies, practices, and procedures.

3 Human Resource Development (15%, 13%)

The processes of ensuring that the skills, knowledge, abilities, and performance of the workforce meet the current and future organizational and individual needs through developing, implementing, and evaluating activities and programs addressing employee training and development, change and performance management, and the unique needs of particular employee groups.

Responsibilities

1. Conduct needs analyses to identify and establish priorities regarding human resource development activities.

2. Develop training programs.

3. Implement training programs.

4. Evaluate training programs.

5. Develop programs to assess employees' potential for growth and development in the organization.

6. Implement programs to assess employees' potential for growth and development in the organization.

7. Evaluate programs to assess employees' potential for growth and development in the organization.

8. Develop change management programs and activities.

9. Implement change management programs and activities.

10. Evaluate change management programs and activities.

11. Develop performance management programs and procedures.

12. Implement performance management programs and procedures.

13. Evaluate performance management programs and procedures.

14. Develop programs to meet the unique needs of particular employees (for example, work/family programs, diversity programs, outplacement programs, repatriation programs and fast-track programs).

15. Implement programs to meet the unique needs of particular employees (for example, work/family programs, diversity programs, outplacement programs, repatriation programs, and fast-track programs).

16. Evaluate programs to meet the unique needs of particular employees (for example, work/family programs, diversity programs, outplacement programs, repatriation programs, and fast-track programs).

Knowledge of

21. Applicable international, federal, state, and local laws and regulations regarding copyrights and patents.

22. Human resource development theories and applications (including career development and leadership development).

23. Organizational development theories and applications.

24. Training methods, programs, and techniques (design, objectives, methods, etc.).

25. Employee involvement strategies.

26. Task/process analysis.

27. Performance appraisal and performance management methods.

28. Applicable international issues (for example, culture, local management approaches/practices, societal norms).

29. Instructional methods and program delivery (content, building modules of program, selection of presentation/delivery mechanism).

30. Techniques to assess HRD program effectiveness (for example, satisfaction, learning, and job performance of program participants, and organizational outcomes such as turnover and productivity).

4 Compensation and Benefits (20%, 16%)

The processes of analyzing, developing, implementing, administering, and performing ongoing evaluation of a total compensation and benefits system for all employee groups consistent with human resource management goals.

Responsibilities

1. Ensure the compliance of compensation and benefits with applicable federal, state and local laws.

2. Analyze, develop, implement and maintain compensation policies and a pay structure consistent with the organization's strategic objectives.

3. Analyze and evaluate pay rates based on internal worth and external market conditions.

4. Develop/select and implement a payroll system.

5. Administer payroll functions.

6. Evaluate compensation policies to ensure that they are positioning the organization internally and externally according to the organization's strategic objectives.

7. Conduct a benefit plan needs assessment and determine/select the plans to be offered, considering the organization's strategic objectives.

8. Implement and administer benefit plans.

9. Evaluate benefits program to ensure that it is positioning the organization internally and externally according to the organization's strategic objectives.

10. Analyze, select, implement, maintain and administer executive compensation, stock purchase, stock options and incentive, and bonus programs.

11. Analyze, develop, select, maintain and implement expatriate and foreign national compensation and benefit programs.

12. Communicate the compensation and benefits plan and policies to the workforce.

Knowledge of

31. Federal, state, and local compensation and benefit laws (for example, FLSA, ERISA, COBRA).

32. Accounting practices related to compensation and benefits (for example, excess group term life, compensatory time).

33. Job evaluation methods.

34. Job pricing and pay structures.

35. Incentive and variable pay methods.

36. Executive compensation.

37. Noncash compensation methods (for example, stock option plans).

38. Benefit needs analysis.

39. Benefit plans (for example, health insurance, life insurance, pension, education, health club).

40. International compensation laws and practices (for example, expatriate compensation, socialized medicine, mandated retirement).

5 Employee and Labor Relations (21%, 24%)

The processes of analyzing, developing, implementing, administering, and performing ongoing evaluation of the workplace relationship between employer and employee (including the collective bargaining process and union relations), in order to maintain effective relationships and working conditions that balance the employer's needs with the employees' rights in support of the organization's strategic objectives.

Responsibilities

1. Ensure compliance with all applicable federal, state, and local laws and regulations.

2. Develop and implement employee relations programs that will create a positive organizational culture.

3. Promote, monitor, and measure the effectiveness of employee relations activities.

4. Assist in establishing work rules and monitor their application and enforcement to ensure fairness and consistency (for union and nonunion environments).

5. Communicate and ensure understanding by employees of laws, regulations, and organizational policies.

6. Resolve employee complaints filed with federal, state, and local agencies involving employment practices.

7. Develop grievance and disciplinary policies and procedures to ensure fairness and consistency.

8. Implement and monitor grievance and disciplinary policies and procedures to ensure fairness and consistency.

9. Respond to union organizing activity.

10. Participate in collective bargaining activities, including contract negotiation and administration.

Knowledge of

41. Applicable federal, state, and local laws affecting employment in union and nonunion environments, such as antidiscrimination laws, sexual harassment, labor relations, and privacy.

42. Techniques for facilitating positive employee relations (for example, small group facilitation, dispute resolution, and labor/management cooperative strategies and programs).

43. Employee involvement strategies (for example, alternate work schedules, work teams).

44. Individual employment rights issues and practices (for example, employment at will, negligent hiring, defamation, employees' rights to bargain collectively).

45. Workplace behavior issues/practices (for example, absenteeism and discipline).

46. Methods for assessment of employee attitudes, opinions, and satisfaction (for example, opinion surveys, attitude surveys, focus panels).

47. Unfair labor practices.

48. The collective bargaining process, strategies, and concepts.

49. Public-sector labor relations issues and practices.

50. Expatriation and repatriation issues and practices.

51. Employee and labor relations for local nationals (i.e., labor relations in other countries).

6 Occupational Health, Safety, and Security (6%, 5%)

The processes of analyzing, developing, implementing, administering, and performing ongoing evaluation of programs, practices, and services to promote the physical and mental well-being of individuals in the workplace, and to protect individuals and the workplace from unsafe acts, unsafe working conditions, and violence.

Responsibilities

1. Ensure compliance with all applicable federal, state, and local workplace health and safety laws and regulations.
2. Determine safety programs needed for the organization.
3. Develop and/or select injury/occupational illness prevention programs.
4. Implement injury/occupational illness prevention programs.
5. Develop and/or select safety training and incentive programs.
6. Implement safety training and incentive programs.
7. Evaluate the effectiveness of safety prevention, training, and incentive programs.
8. Implement workplace injury/occupational illness procedures (for example, workers' compensation, OSHA).
9. Determine health and wellness programs needed for the organization.
10. Develop/select, implement, and evaluate (or make available) health and wellness programs.
11. Develop/select, implement, and evaluate security plans to protect the company from liability.
12. Develop/select, implement, and evaluate security plans to protect employees (for example, injuries resulting from workplace violence).
13. Develop/select, implement, and evaluate incident and emergency response plans (for example, natural disasters, workplace safety threats, evacuation).

Knowledge of

52. Federal, state, and local workplace health and safety laws and regulations (for example, OSHA, Drug-Free Workplace Act, ADA).
53. Workplace injury and occupational illness compensation laws and programs (for example, workers' compensation).
54. Investigation procedures of workplace safety, health, and security enforcement agencies (for example, OSHA).
55. Workplace safety risks.

56. Workplace security risks (for example, theft, corporate espionage, information systems/technology, and vandalism).
57. Potential violent behavior and workplace violence conditions.
58. General health and safety practices (for example, fire evacuation, HAZCOM, ergonomic evaluations).
59. Incident and emergency response plans.
60. Internal investigation and surveillance techniques.
61. Employee assistance programs.
62. Employee wellness programs.
63. Issues related to chemical use and dependency (for example, identification of symptoms, drug testing, discipline).

CORE Knowledge Required by HR Professionals

64. Needs assessment and analysis.
65. Third-party contract management, including development of requests for proposals (RFPs).
66. Communication strategies.
67. Documentation requirements.
68. Adult learning processes.
69. Motivation concepts and applications.
70. Training methods.
71. Leadership concepts and applications.
72. Project management concepts and applications.
73. Diversity concepts and applications.
74. Human relations concepts and applications (for example, interpersonal and organizational behavior).
75. HR ethics and professional standards.
76. Technology and human resource information systems (HRIS) to support HR activities.
77. Qualitative and quantitative methods and tools for analysis, interpretation, and decision-making purposes.
78. Change management.
79. Liability and risk management.
80. Job analysis and job description methods.
81. Employee records management (for example, retention, disposal).
82. The interrelationships among HR activities and programs across functional areas.

Appendix B: Certification Handbook Recertification Guide

Introduction

What Is Certification?

Certification is a voluntary action by a professional group to establish a system to grant recognition to professionals who have met a stated level of training and work experience. Certified individuals are usually issued a certificate attesting that they have met the standards of the credentialing organization and are entitled to make the public aware of their credentialed status, usually through the use of acronyms (i.e., PHR, SPHR, or GPHR) after their names.

Certifications differ from certificate programs because certifications, by definition, include a work experience component. Certificate programs, on the other hand, award certificates once a course of study has been completed and do not require previous work experience.

Why Is Certification Desirable?

Certification sets those with the credential apart—or above—those without it. There are a number of advantages to seeking certification. Certification becomes a public recognition of professional achievement—both within and outside of the profession. For many, achieving certification becomes a personal professional goal—a way to test knowledge and to measure it against one's peers. Others see certification as an aid to career advancement.

Purpose and Use of Certification

PHR and SPHR certifications show that the holder has demonstrated mastery of the HR body of knowledge and, through recertification, has accepted the challenge to stay informed of new developments in the HR field.

The PHR and SPHR exams are completely voluntary. Organizations or individuals incorporating PHR or SPHR certification as a condition of employment or advancement do so of their own volition. Individuals should determine for themselves whether the use of this process, including its eligibility and recertification requirements, when coupled with any other requirements imposed by individuals or organizations, meets their needs and complies with any applicable laws.

The PHR and SPHR designations are a visible reminder to peers and co-workers of the holder's significant professional achievement. PHR and SPHR certified professionals should proudly display their certificates and use the credentials on business correspondence.

Certification Denial and Revocation

Certification may be denied or revoked for any of the following reasons:

- Falsification of work experience or other information on the exam application.
- Misrepresentation of work experience or other information on the exam application.
- Violation of testing procedures.
- Failure to pass the certification exam.
- Failure to meet recertification requirements.

Candidates whose certifications are denied or revoked should contact HRCI for more information about how to appeal the denial or revocation. There is no appeal based on failure to pass the exam or to recertify.

Exam Overview

- 225 multiple choice questions.
- Four hours to complete.
- Administered by computer.
- Administered only in English.

Are You Ready?

- Take the HRCI Online Assessment Exam (www.hrci.org).

There are two levels of certification, the Professional in Human Resources (PHR®) and the Senior Professional in Human Resources (SPHR®). Both exams are generalist (i.e., they assess all the functional areas of the HR field) but differ in terms of focus and the cognitive level of questions. PHR questions tend to be at an operational/technical level. SPHR questions tend to be more at the strategic and/or policy level. HRCI exams are offered only in English.

Test questions on both exams reflect the most recently published test specifications (see Appendix A). The exams are multiple choice and consist of 200 scored questions plus 25 pretest questions randomly distributed throughout the exam (a total of 225 questions). Each question lists four possible answers, only one of which is the correct or "best possible answer." The answer to each question can be derived independently of the answer to any other question. Four hours are allotted to complete the exam. All exams are administered by computer at more than 250 Prometric testing centers. There are no paper-and-pencil exam administrations.

Pretest questions are not counted in scoring. They are, however, essential in building the PHR and SPHR item (or test question) banks and are on the exam to statistically assess their difficulty level and effectiveness at discriminating between candidates who meet the passing standard and those who do not. The information gathered in the pretest process determines whether or not the question will be included on a future exam.

On test day, answer questions that are easy first and mark the more difficult ones to return to later. There is no penalty for guessing, so try to answer all the questions. Unanswered questions are counted as incorrect.

There are survey questions at the end of the exam that candidates are encouraged to answer if time allows. These questions are optional. Responses are confidential. The information collected is used for statistical purposes only.

Exam questions represent the following functional areas in HR. The percentages indicate the extent to which each functional area is emphasized at either exam level.

PHR and SPHR Exam Functional Areas

	PHR	SPHR
Strategic Management	12%	26%
Workforce Planning and Employment	26%	16%
Human Resource Development	15%	13%
Compensation and Benefits	20%	16%
Employee and Labor Relations	21%	24%
Occupational Health, Safety, and Security	6%	5%

Exams reflect the percentages listed above and are reviewed by a panel of certified professionals with subject matter expertise to ensure that the questions are up to date and reflect the published test specifications.

Passing Score

The passing score for both exams (based on a scaled score) is 500. The minimum possible score is 100. The maximum possible score is 700.

For more information about scaled scoring, please see "Understanding the Score Report" and "How the Passing Score Was Set" in the separate HRCI handbook.

HRCI Online Assessment Exam

HRCI offers an online assessment exam comprised of actual exam questions that have appeared on previous exams but were removed from the item bank to develop the assessment exam. Before registering for the exam, consider taking this online assessment exam. The assessment exam exposes candidates to the types of questions that are on the actual exam. For more information about the assessment exam (including fees), visit the HRCI Web site at www.hrci.org.

About Computer-Based Testing (CBT)

Starting in 2004, HRCI will deliver all PHR and SPHR exams by computer at Prometric test centers. Here's what you need to know about this exciting development:

Advantages to Computer-Based Exam Delivery

- Exams will be administered exclusively by computer. Exams will no longer be available in paper-and-pencil format.

- The exams will be administered at more than 250 test centers across the United States, U.S. territories, and Canada. Exams will also be offered internationally wherever a Prometric test center is located. See HRCI's separate Appendix D for more information about taking the exam outside the United States, U.S. territories, or Canada.

- There are two annual testing windows—May 1–June 30, 2004 and November 15, 2004–January 15, 2005.

- Exams will no longer be offered at SHRM conferences.

- Candidates can schedule their exams Monday through Friday and take their exams Monday through Saturday, during the testing windows.

- Candidates will have access to a built-in clock and calculator.

- Individual testing stations will allow for more privacy and test security.

- Immediate (preliminary) pass/fail score results will be provided to candidates before they leave the testing center. Official score reports will be mailed within two to three weeks of testing.

- There are more testing dates.

- There are more test center locations.

■ There will be consistent exam administration and test-taking environments.

■ Candidates are able to mark more difficult questions to return to later.

■ Computer-based testing provides ease of use (no computer experience necessary).

■ A self-paced tutorial shows you how to take the test (including how to mark questions to return to later) to ensure that you are comfortable with the exam administration process.

■ Prometric, the leading provider of computer-based testing, will deliver the exams.

What Will Stay the Same

■ Exam content, number of questions (225), and duration (4 hours).

■ Eligibility requirements.

■ Strict deadline dates.

■ Official score reports will be mailed to candidates.

■ PES will review exam applications, process payments, score the exams, and mail score reports.

For more information about CBT, visit the HRCI homepage at www.hrci.org.

Glossary

action learning A training technique by which management trainees are allowed to work full-time analyzing and solving problems in other departments.

adaptability screening A process that aims to assess the assignee's (and spouse's) probable success in handling a foreign transfer.

adverse impact The overall impact of employer practices that result in significantly higher percentages of members of minorities and other protected groups being rejected for employment, placement, or promotion.

affirmative action Steps that are taken for the purpose of eliminating the present effects of past discrimination.

Age Discrimination in Employment Act of 1967 (ADEA) The act prohibiting arbitrary age discrimination and specifically protecting individuals over 40 years old.

agency shop A form of union security in which employees who do not belong to the union must still pay union dues on the assumption that union efforts benefit all workers.

alternation ranking method Ranking employees from best to worst on a particular trait, choosing highest, then lowest, until all are ranked.

alternative dispute resolution or ADR program Grievance procedure that provides for binding arbitration as the last step.

alternative staffing The use of nontraditional recruitment sources.

Americans with Disabilities Act (ADA) The act requiring employers to make reasonable accommodations for disabled employees; it prohibits discrimination against disabled persons.

annual bonus Plans that are designed to motivate short-term performance of managers and are tied to company profitability.

application form The form that provides information on education, prior work record, and skills.

appraisal interview An interview in which the supervisor and subordinate review the appraisal and make plans to remedy deficiencies and reinforce strengths.

apprenticeship training A structured process by which people become skilled workers through a combination of classroom instruction and on-the-job training.

arbitration The most definitive type of third-party intervention, in which the arbitrator usually has the power to determine and dictate the settlement terms.

at-risk variable pay plans Plans that put some portion of the employee's weekly pay at risk, subject to the firm's meeting its financial goals.

authority The right to make decisions, direct others' work, and give orders.

authorization cards In order to petition for a union election, the union must show that at least 30% of employees may be interested in being unionized. Employees indicate this interest by signing authorization cards.

bargaining unit The group of employees the union will be authorized to represent.

behavior modeling A training technique in which trainees are first shown good management techniques in a film, are asked to play roles in a simulated situation, and are then given feedback and praise by their supervisor.

behavioral interviews A series of job-related questions that focus on how they reacted to actual situations in the past.

behaviorally anchored rating scale (BARS) An appraisal method that aims at combining the benefits of narrative critical incidents and quantified ratings by anchoring a quantified scale with specific narrative examples of good and poor performance.

behavior-based safety Identifying the worker behaviors that contribute to accidents and then training workers to avoid these behaviors.

benchmark job A job that is used to anchor the employer's pay scale and around which other jobs are arranged in order of relative worth.

benefits Indirect financial and nonfinancial payments employees receive for continuing their employment with the company.

bias The tendency to allow individual differences such as age, race, and sex to affect the appraisal ratings employees receive.

bona fide occupational qualification (BFOQ) Requirement that an employee be of a certain religion, sex, or national origin where that is reasonably necessary to the organization's normal operation. Specified by the 1964 Civil Rights Act.

boundaryless organization Organization marked by the widespread use of teams and similar structural mechanisms that reduce and make more permeable the boundaries that typically separate departments.

boycott The combined refusal by employees and other interested parties to buy or use the employer's products.

broadbanding Consolidating salary grades and ranges into just a few wide levels or "bands," each of which contains a relatively wide range of jobs and salary levels.

bumping/layoff procedures Detailed procedures that determine who will be laid off if no work is available; generally allow employees to use their seniority to remain on the job.

burnout The total depletion of physical and mental resources caused by excessive striving to reach an unrealistic work-related goal.

candidate-order error An error of judgment on the part of the interviewer due to interviewing one or more very good or very bad candidates just before the interview in question.

career The occupational positions a person has had over many years.

career anchors Pivots around which a person's career swings; require self-awareness of talents and abilities, motives and needs, and attitudes and values. A concern or value that you will not give up if a [career] choice has to be made.

career cycle The various stages a person's career goes through.

career development The lifelong series of activities that contribute to a person's career exploration, establishment, success, and fulfillment.

career management The process for enabling employees to better understand and develop their career skills and interests, and to use these skills and interests most effectively.

career planning and development The deliberate process through which a person becomes aware of personal career-related attributes and the lifelong series of steps that contribute to his or her career fulfillment.

case study method A development method in which the manager is presented with a written description of an organizational problem to diagnose and solve.

cash balance plans Defined benefit plans under which the employer contributes a percentage of employees' current pay to employees' pension plans every year, and employees earn interest on this amount.

central tendency A tendency to rate all employees the same way, such as rating them all average.

citation Summons informing employers and employees of the regulations and standards that have been violated in the workplace.

Civil Rights Act of 1991 (CRA) It places burden of proof back on employers and permits compensatory and punitive damages.

classes Grouping jobs based on a set of rules for each group or class, such as amount of independent judgment, skill, physical effort, and so forth, required. Classes usually contain similar jobs.

closed shop A form of union security in which the company can hire only union members. This was outlawed in 1947 but still exists in some industries (such as printing).

codetermination Employees have the legal right to a voice in setting company policies.

collective bargaining The process through which representatives of management and the union meet to negotiate a labor agreement.

comparable worth The concept by which women who are usually paid less than men can claim that men in comparable rather than in strictly equal jobs are paid more.

compensable factor A fundamental, compensable element of a job, such as skills, effort, responsibility, and working conditions.

competencies Demonstrable characteristics of a person that enable performance of a job.

competency-based job analysis Describing a job in terms of the measurable, observable, behavioral competencies an employee must exhibit to do a job well.

competency-based pay Where the company pays for the employee's range, depth, and types of skills and knowledge, rather than for the job title he or she holds.

competitive advantage Any factors that allow an organization to differentiate its product or service from those of its competitors to increase market share.

computerized forecast Determination of future staff needs by projecting sales, volume of production, and personnel required to maintain this volume of output, using software packages.

content validity A test that is content valid is one that contains a fair sample of the tasks and skills actually needed for the job in question.

controlled experimentation Formal methods for testing the effectiveness of a training program, preferably with before-and-after tests and a control group.

corporate campaign An organized effort by the union that exerts pressure on the corporation by pressuring the company's other unions, shareholders, directors, customers, creditors, and government agencies, often directly.

criterion validity A type of validity based on showing that scores on the test (predictors) are related to job performance (criterion).

critical incident method Keeping a record of uncommonly good or undesirable examples of an employee's work-related behavior and reviewing it with the employee at predetermined times.

Davis-Bacon Act (1931) A law that sets wage rates for laborers employed by contractors working for the federal government.

decertification Legal process for employees to terminate a union's right to represent them.

decline stage Period where many people face having to accept reduced levels of power and responsibility, and must learn to develop new roles as mentors or confidantes for younger people.

deferred profit-sharing plan A plan in which a certain amount of profits is credited to each employee's account, payable at retirement, termination, or death.

defined benefit pension plan A plan that contains a formula for determining retirement benefits.

defined contribution pension plan A plan in which the employer's contribution to employees' retirement savings funds is specified.

dejobbing Broadening the responsibilities of the company's jobs, and encouraging employees not to limit themselves to what's on their job descriptions.

diary/log Daily listings made by workers of every activity in which they engage along with the time each activity takes.

direct financial payments Pay in the form of wages, salaries, incentives, commissions, and bonuses.

dismissal Involuntary termination of an employee's employment with the firm.

disparate rejection rates A test for adverse impact in which it can be demonstrated that there is a discrepancy between rates of rejection of members of a protected group and of others.

distributive justice The fairness and justice of a decision's result.

downsizing The process of reducing, usually dramatically, the number of people employed by a firm.

early retirement window A type of offering by which employees are encouraged to retire early, the incentive being liberal pension benefits plus perhaps a cash payment.

Economic Growth and Tax Relief Reconciliation Act (2001) (EGTRRA) An act that improves the attractiveness of retirement benefits like 401(k) plans by boosting individual employees' elective deferred limits to $15,000, effective in 2006.

economic strike A strike that results from a failure to agree on the terms of a contract that involve wages, benefits, and other conditions of employment.

Electronic Communications Privacy Act (ECPA) Intended in part to restrict interception and monitoring of oral and wire communications, but with two exceptions: employers who can show a legitimate business reason for doing so, and employers who have employees' consent to do so.

electronic performance monitoring (EPM) Having supervisors electronically monitor the amount of computerized data an employee is processing per day, and thereby his or her performance.

electronic performance support systems (EPSS) Sets of computerized tools and displays that automate training, documentation, and phone support, integrate this automation into applications, and provide support that's faster, cheaper, and more effective than traditional methods.

employee advocacy HR must take responsibility for clearly defining how management should be treating employees, make sure employees have the mechanisms required to contest unfair practices, and represent the interests of employees within the framework of its primary obligation to senior management.

employee assistance program A formal employer program for providing employees with counseling and/or treatment programs for problems such as alcoholism, gambling, or stress.

employee compensation All forms of pay or rewards going to employees and arising from their employment.

employee orientation A procedure for providing new employees with basic background information about the firm.

Employee Retirement Income Security Act (ERISA) Signed into law by President Ford in 1974, the law that provides government protection of pensions for all employees with company pension plans. It also regulates vesting rights (employees who leave before retirement may claim compensation from the pension plan).

employee stock ownership plan (ESOP) A corporation contributes shares of its own stock to a trust in which additional contributions are made annually. The trust distributes the stock to employees on retirement or separation from service. A qualified, tax-deductible stock bonus plan in which employers contribute stock to a trust for eventual use by employees.

employment or personnel planning The process of deciding what positions the firm will have to fill, and how to fill them.

Equal Employment Opportunity Commission (EEOC) The commission, created by Title VII, is empowered to investigate job discrimination complaints and sue on behalf of complainants.

Equal Pay Act (1963) An amendment to the Fair Labor Standards Act designed to require equal pay for women doing the same work as men.

establishment stage Spans roughly ages 24 to 44 and is the heart of most people's work lives.

ethics The principles of conduct governing an individual or a group; specifically, the standards you use to decide what your conduct should be.

ethnocentric The notion that home-country attitudes, management style, knowledge, evaluation criteria, and managers are superior to anything the host country has to offer.

exit interviews Interviews with employees who are leaving the firm, conducted for the purpose of obtaining information about the job or related matters, to give the employer insight about the company.

expatriates (expats) Noncitizens of the countries in which they are working.

expectancy A person's expectation that his or her effort will lead to performance.

expectancy chart A graph showing the relationship between test scores and job performance for a group of people.

exploration stage The period (roughly from ages 15 to 24) during which a person seriously explores various occupational alternatives.

fact finder A neutral party who studies the issues in a dispute and makes a public recommendation for a reasonable settlement.

factor comparison method A widely used method of ranking jobs according to a variety of skill and difficulty factors, then adding up these rankings to arrive at an overall numerical rating for each given job.

Fair Labor Standards Act (1938) This act provides for minimum wages, maximum hours, overtime pay, and child labor protection. The law has been amended many times and covers most employees.

Federal Violence Against Women Act of 1994 Provides that a person who commits a crime of violence motivated by gender shall be liable to the party injured.

flexible benefits plan/cafeteria benefits plan Individualized plans allowed by employers to accommodate employee preferences for benefits.

forced distribution method Similar to grading on a curve; predetermined percentages of ratees are placed in various performance categories.

foreign service premiums Financial payments over and above regular base pay, typically ranging between 10% and 30% of base pay.

401(k) plan A defined contribution plan based on section 401(k) of the Internal Revenue Code.

functional control The authority exerted by an HR manager as coordinator of personnel activities.

functional job analysis A method for classifying jobs similar to the DOL method, but additionally taking into account the extent to which instructions, reasoning, judgment, and mathematical and verbal ability are necessary for performing job tasks.

gainsharing plan An incentive plan that engages employees in a common effort to achieve productivity objectives and share the gains.

geocentric The belief that the firm's whole management staff must be scoured on a global basis, on the assumption that the best manager of a specific position anywhere may be in any of the countries in which the firm operates.

globalization The tendency of firms to extend their sales, ownership, and/or manufacturing to new markets abroad.

golden parachutes Payments companies make in connection with a change in ownership or control of a company.

good faith bargaining Both parties are making every reasonable effort to arrive at agreement; proposals are being matched with counterproposals.

good faith effort strategy Employment strategy aimed at changing practices that have contributed in the past to excluding or underutilizing protected groups.

grade definition Written descriptions of the level of, say, responsibility and knowledge required by jobs in each grade. Similar jobs can then be combined into grades or classes.

grades A job classification system like the class system, although grades often contain dissimilar jobs, such as secretaries, mechanics, and firefighters. Grade descriptions are written based on compensable factors listed in classification systems.

graphic rating scale A scale that lists a number of traits and a range of performance for each. The employee is then rated by identifying the score that best describes his or her level of performance for each trait.

grievance Any factor involving wages, hours, or conditions of employment that is used as a complaint against the employer.

group life insurance Provides lower rates for the employer or employee and includes all employees, including new employees, regardless of health or physical condition.

growth stage The period from birth to age 14 during which a person develops a self-concept by identifying with and interacting with other people.

halo effect In performance appraisal, the problem that occurs when a supervisor's rating of a subordinate on one trait biases the rating of that person on other traits.

hardship allowances Compensate expatriates for exceptionally hard living and working conditions at certain locations.

health maintenance organization (HMO) A prepaid health care system that generally provides routine round-the-clock medical services as well as preventive medicine in a clinic-type arrangement for employees, who pay a nominal fee in addition to the fixed annual fee the employer pays.

home-country nationals Citizens of the country in which the multinational company has its headquarters.

HR Scorecard Measures the HR function's effectiveness and efficiency in producing employee behaviors needed to achieve the company's strategic goals.

human capital The knowledge, education, training, skills, and expertise of a firm's workers.

human resource management (HRM) The policies and practices involved in carrying out the "people" or human resource aspects of a management position, including recruiting, screening, training, rewarding, and appraising.

illegal bargaining items Items in collective bargaining that are forbidden by law; for example, a clause agreeing to hire "union members exclusively" would be illegal in a right-to-work state.

impasse Collective bargaining situation that occurs when the parties are not able to move further toward settlement, usually because one party is demanding more than the other will offer.

implied authority The authority exerted by an HR manager by virtue of others' knowledge that he or she has access to top management (in areas like testing and affirmative action).

indirect financial payments Pay in the form of financial benefits such as insurance.

in-house development center A company-based method for exposing prospective managers to realistic exercises to develop improved management skills.

injunction A court order compelling a party or parties either to resume or to desist from a certain action.

inside games Union efforts to convince employees to impede or to disrupt production—for example, by slowing the work pace.

instrumentality The perceived relationships between successful performance and obtaining the reward.

insubordination Willful disregard or disobedience of the boss's authority or legitimate orders; criticizing the boss in public.

interactional (interpersonal) justice The manner in which managers conduct their interpersonal dealings with employees.

interest inventory A personal development and selection device that compares the person's current interests with those of others now in various occupations so as to determine the preferred occupation for the individual.

job aid Is a set of instructions, diagrams, or similar methods available at the job site to guide the worker.

job analysis The procedure for determining the duties and skill requirements of a job and the kind of person who should be hired for it.

job classification (or grading) method A method for categorizing jobs into groups.

job description A list of a job's duties, responsibilities, reporting relationships, working conditions, and supervisory responsibilities—one product of a job analysis.

job enlargement Assigning workers additional same-level activities, thus increasing the number of activities they perform.

job enrichment Redesigning jobs in a way that increases the opportunities for the worker to experience feelings of responsibility, achievement, growth, and recognition.

job evaluation A systematic comparison done in order to determine the worth of one job relative to another.

job instruction training (JIT) Listing each job's basic tasks, along with key points, in order to provide step-by-step training for employees.

job posting Publicizing an open job to employees (often by literally posting it on bulletin boards) and listing its attributes, like qualifications, supervisor, working schedule, and pay rate.

job rotation A management training technique that involves moving a trainee from department to department to broaden his or her experience and identify strong and weak points to prepare the person for an enhanced role with the company; also, systematically moving workers from one job to another to enhance work team performance.

job sharing Allows two or more people to share a single full-time job.

job specifications A list of a job's "human requirements," that is, the requisite education, skills, personality, and so on—another product of a job analysis.

job-related interview A series of job-related questions that focus on relevant past job-related behaviors.

Landrum-Griffin Act (1959) The law aimed at protecting union members from possible wrongdoing on the part of their unions.

law of individual differences The fact that people differ in personality, abilities, values, and needs.

leveraging Supplementing what you have and doing more with what you have.

line authority The authority exerted by an HR manager by directing the activities of the people in his or her own department and in service areas (like the plant cafeteria).

line manager A manager who is authorized to direct the work of subordinates and is responsible for accomplishing the organization's tasks.

lockout A refusal by the employer to provide opportunities to work.

maintenance stage Period between ages 45 and 65 when many people slide from the stabilization substage into an established position and focus on maintaining that place.

management assessment center A simulation in which management candidates are asked to perform realistic tasks in hypothetical situations and are scored on their performance. It usually also involves testing and the use of management games.

management by objectives (MBO) Involves setting specific measurable goals with each employee and then periodically reviewing the progress made.

management development Any attempt to improve current or future management performance by imparting knowledge, changing attitudes, or increasing skills.

management game A development technique in which teams of managers compete by making computerized decisions regarding realistic but simulated situations.

management process The five basic functions of planning, organizing, staffing, leading, and controlling

mandatory bargaining items Items in collective bargaining that a party must bargain over if they are introduced by the other party—for example, pay.

mass interview A panel interviews several candidates simultaneously.

material safety data sheets (MSDS) Sheets that describe the precautions required by OSHA that employees are to take when dealing with hazardous chemicals, and what to do if problems arise.

mechanical security The utilization of security systems such as locks, intrusion alarms, access control systems, and surveillance systems.

mediation Intervention in which a neutral third party tries to assist the principals in reaching agreement.

mentoring Formal or informal programs in which mid- and senior-level managers help less experienced employees—for instance, by giving them career advice and helping them navigate political pitfalls.

merit pay (merit raise) Any salary increase awarded to an employee based on his or her individual performance.

metrics A set of quantitative performance measures HR managers use to assess their operations.

midcareer crisis substage Period during which people often make major reassessments of their progress relative to original ambitions and goals.

misconduct Deliberate and willful violation of the employer's rules.

mission Spells out who the company is, what it does, and where it's headed.

mixed motive case A discrimination allegation case in which the employer argues that the employment action taken was motivated, not by discrimination, but by some non-discriminatory reason such as ineffective performance.

mobility premiums Typically, lump-sum payments to reward employees for moving from one assignment to another.

national emergency strikes Strikes that might "imperil the national health and safety."

National Labor Relations (or Wagner) Act This law banned certain types of unfair practices and provided for secret-ballot elections and majority rule for determining whether or not a firm's employees want to unionize.

National Labor Relations Board (NLRB) The agency created by the Wagner Act to investigate unfair labor practice charges and to provide for secret-ballot elections and majority rule in determining whether or not a firm's employees want a union.

natural security Taking advantage of the facility's natural or architectural features in order to minimize security problems.

negligent hiring Hiring workers with questionable backgrounds without proper safeguards.

negligent training A situation where an employer fails to train adequately, and the employee subsequently harms a third party.

nonpunitive discipline Discipline without punishment.

nontraditional workers Workers who hold multiple jobs or who are "contingent" or part-time workers, or people working in alternative work arrangements.

Norris-LaGuardia Act (1932) This law marked the beginning of the era of strong encouragement of unions and guaranteed to each employee the right to bargain collectively "free from interference, restraint, or coercion."

occupational illness Any abnormal condition or disorder caused by exposure to environmental factors associated with employment.

Occupational Safety and Health Act The law passed by Congress in 1970 "to assure so far as possible every working man and woman in the nation safe and healthful working conditions and to preserve our human resources."

Occupational Safety and Health Administration (OSHA) The agency created within the Department of Labor to set safety and health standards for almost all workers in the United States.

Office of Federal Contract Compliance Programs (OFCCP) This office is responsible for implementing the executive orders and ensuring compliance of federal contractors.

offshoring Having local employees abroad do jobs that the firm's domestic employees previously did in-house.

On demand recruiting services (ODRS) A service that provides short-term specialized recruiting to support specific projects without the expense of retaining traditional search firms.

on-the-job training Training a person to learn a job while working on it.

open shop Perhaps the least attractive type of union security from the union's point of view, the workers decide whether or not to join the union; and those who join must pay dues.

organization chart A chart that shows the organizationwide distribution of work, with titles of each position and interconnecting lines that show who reports to and communicates to whom.

organizational culture The characteristic values, traditions, and behaviors a company's employees share.

organizational development A special approach to organizational change in which employees themselves formulate and implement the change that's required.

organizational security Using good management to improve security.

outplacement counseling A systematic process by which a terminated person is trained and counseled in the techniques of self-appraisal and securing a new position.

outsourced learning The outsourcing of companies' learning functions to major consulting firms.

outsourcing Letting outside vendors provide services.

paired comparison method Ranking employees by making a chart of all possible pairs of the employees for each trait and indicating which is the better employee of the pair.

panel interview An interview in which a group of interviewers questions the applicant.

pay grade A pay grade is comprised of jobs of approximately equal difficulty.

pay ranges A series of steps or levels within a pay grade, usually based upon years of service.

Pension Benefits Guarantee Corporation (PBGC) Established under ERISA to ensure that pensions meet vesting obligations; also insures pensions should a plan terminate without sufficient funds to meet its vested obligations.

pension plans Plans that provide a fixed sum when employees reach a predetermined retirement age or when they can no longer work due to disability.

performance analysis Verifying that there is a performance deficiency and determining whether that deficiency should be corrected through training or through some other means (such as transferring the employee).

performance appraisal Evaluating an employee's current and/or past performance relative to his or her performance standards.

performance management Managing all elements of the organizational process that affect how well employees perform; the process employers use to make sure employees are working toward organizational goals.

personnel replacement charts Company records showing present performance and promotability of inside candidates for the most important positions.

picketing Having employees carry signs announcing their concerns near the employer's place of business.

piecework A system of pay based on the number of items processed by each individual worker in a unit of time, such as items per hour or items per day.

point method The job evaluation method in which a number of compensable factors are identified and then the degree to which each of these factors is present on the job is determined.

polycentric A conscious belief that only the host-country managers can ever really understand the culture and behavior of the host-country market.

position analysis questionnaire (PAQ) A questionnaire used to collect quantifiable data concerning the duties and responsibilities of various jobs.

position replacement card A card prepared for each position in a company to show possible replacement candidates and their qualifications.

preferred provider organizations (PPOs) Groups of health care providers that contract with employers, insurance companies, or third-party payers to provide medical care services at a reduced fee.

Pregnancy Discrimination Act (PDA) An amendment to Title VII of the Civil Rights Act that prohibits sex discrimination based on "pregnancy, childbirth, or related medical conditions."

preretirement counseling Counseling provided to employees who are about to retire, which covers matters such as benefits advice, second careers, and so on.

procedural justice The fairness of the process.

process chart A work flow chart that shows the flow of inputs to and outputs from a particular job.

profit-sharing plan A plan whereby employees share in the company's profits.

programmed learning A systematic method for teaching job skills involving presenting questions or facts, allowing the person to respond, and giving the learner immediate feedback on the accuracy of his or her answers.

promotions Advancements to positions of increased responsibility.

protected class Persons such as minorities and women protected by equal opportunity laws, including Title VII.

qualifications inventories Manual or computerized records listing employees' education, career and development interests, languages, special skills, and so on, to be used in selecting inside candidates for promotion.

qualified individuals Under ADA, those who can carry out the essential functions of the job.

ranking method The simplest method of job evaluation that involves ranking each job relative to all other jobs, usually based on overall difficulty.

ratio analysis A forecasting technique for determining future staff needs by using ratios between, for example, sales volume and number of employees needed.

reality shock Results of a period that may occur at the initial career entry when the new employee's high job expectations confront the reality of a boring, unchallenging job.

recruiting yield pyramid The historical arithmetic relationships between recruitment leads and invitees, invitees and interviews, interviews and offers made, and offers made and offers accepted.

reengineering The fundamental rethinking and radical redesign of business processes to achieve dramatic improvements in critical, contemporary measures of performance, such as cost, quality, service, and speed.

reliability The consistency of scores obtained by the same person when retested with the identical or equivalent tests.

restricted policy Another test for adverse impact, involving demonstration that an employer's hiring practices exclude a protected group, whether intentionally or not.

retirement The point at which one gives up one's work, usually between the ages of 60 and 65, but increasingly earlier today due to firms' early retirement incentive plans.

reverse discrimination Claim that due to affirmative action quota systems, white males are discriminated against.

right to work A term used to describe state statutory or constitutional provisions banning the requirement of union membership as a condition of employment.

role playing A training technique in which trainees act out parts in a realistic management situation.

salary compression A salary inequity problem, generally caused by inflation, resulting in longer-term employees in a position earning less than workers entering the firm today.

salary survey A survey aimed at determining prevailing wage rates. A good salary survey provides specific wage rates for specific jobs. Formal written questionnaire surveys are the most comprehensive, but telephone surveys and newspaper ads are also sources of information.

savings and thrift plan Plan in which employees contribute a portion of their earnings to a fund; the employer usually matches this contribution in whole or in part.

Scanlon plan An incentive plan developed in 1937 by Joseph Scanlon and designed to encourage cooperation, involvement, and sharing of benefits.

scatter plot A graphical method used to help identify the relationship between two variables.

severance pay A one-time payment some employers provide when terminating an employee.

sexual harassment Harassment on the basis of sex that has the purpose or effect of substantially interfering with a person's work performance or creating an intimidating, hostile, or offensive work environment.

sick leave Provides pay to an employee when he or she is out of work because of illness.

simulated training Training employees on special off-the-job equipment, as in airplane pilot training, so training costs and hazards can be reduced.

situational interview A series of job-related questions that focus on how the candidate would behave in a given situation.

Social Security Federal program that provides three types of benefits: retirement income at the age of 62 and thereafter; survivor's or death benefits payable to the employee's dependents regardless of age at time of death; and disability benefits payable to disabled employees and their dependents. These benefits are payable only if the employee is insured under the Social Security Act.

stabilization substage Firm occupational goals are set and the person does more explicit career planning.

staff manager A manager who assists and advises line managers.

standard hour plan A plan by which a worker is paid a basic hourly rate but is paid an extra percentage of his or her rate for production exceeding the standard per hour or per day. Similar to piecework payment but based on a percent premium.

Standard Occupational Classification (SOC) Classifies all workers into one of 23 major groups of jobs which are subdivided into minor groups of jobs and detailed occupations.

stock option The right to purchase a stated number of shares of a company stock at today's price at some time in the future.

straight piecework An incentive plan in which a person is paid a sum for each item he or she makes or sells, with a strict proportionality between results and rewards.

strategic control The process of assessing progress toward strategic goals and taking corrective action as needed.

strategic human resource management Formulating and executing HR systems—HR policies and activities—that produce the employee competencies and behaviors the company needs to achieve its strategic aims.

strategic management The process of identifying and executing the organization's mission by matching its capabilities with the demands of its environment.

strategic plan A company's plan for how it will match its internal strengths and weaknesses with external opportunities and threats in order to maintain a competitive advantage.

strategy The company's long-term plan for how it will balance its internal strengths and weaknesses with its external opportunities and threats to maintain a competitive advantage.

stress interview An interview in which the applicant is made uncomfortable by a series of often rude questions. This technique helps identify hypersensitive applicants and those with low or high stress tolerance.

strictness/leniency The problem that occurs when a supervisor has a tendency to rate all subordinates either high or low.

strike A withdrawal of labor.

structured or directive interview An interview following a set sequence of questions.

structured sequential interview An interview in which the applicant is interviewed sequentially by several persons; each rates the applicant on a standard form.

succession planning A process through which senior-level openings are planned for and eventually filled.

supplemental pay benefits Benefits for time not worked such as unemployment insurance, vacation and holiday pay, and sick pay.

supplemental unemployment benefits Provide for a "guaranteed annual income" in certain industries where employers must shut down to change machinery or due to reduced work. These benefits are paid by the company and supplement unemployment benefits.

SWOT analysis The use of a SWOT chart to compile and organize the process of identifying company Strengths, Weaknesses, Opportunities, and Threats.

sympathy strike A strike that takes place when one union strikes in support of the strike of another.

Taft-Hartley Act (1947) Also known as the Labor Management Relations Act, this law prohibited union unfair labor practices and enumerated the rights of employees as union members. It also enumerated the rights of employers.

task analysis A detailed study of a job to identify the specific skills required.

team or group incentive plan A plan in which a production standard is set for a specific work group, and its members are paid incentives if the group exceeds the production standard.

telecommuting Where employees work at home, usually with computers, and use phones and the Internet to transmit letters, data, and completed work to the home office.

termination interview The interview in which an employee is informed of the fact that he or she has been dismissed.

test validity The accuracy with which a test, interview, and so on measures what it purports to measure or fulfills the function it was designed to fill.

third-country nationals Citizens of a country other than the parent or the host country.

Title VII of the 1964 Civil Rights Act This act makes it unlawful for employers to discriminate against any individual with respect to hiring, compensation, terms, conditions, or privileges of employment because of race, color, religion, sex, or national origin.

training The process of teaching new employees the basic skills they need to perform their jobs.

transfers Reassignments to similar (or higher) positions in other parts of the firm.

trend analysis Study of a firm's past employment needs over a period of years to predict future needs.

trial substage Period that lasts from about ages 25 to 30 during which the person determines whether or not the chosen field is suitable; if not, changes may be attempted.

U.S. Department of Labor (DOL) job analysis procedure A standardized method by which different jobs can be quantitatively rated, classified, and compared.

unclear standards An appraisal that is too open to interpretation.

unemployment insurance Provides benefits if a person is unable to work through some fault other than his or her own.

unfair labor practice strike A strike aimed at protesting illegal conduct by the employer.

uniform guidelines Guidelines issued by federal agencies charged with ensuring compliance with equal employment federal legislation explaining recommended employer procedures in detail.

union salting A union organizing tactic by which workers who are in fact employed full-time by a union as undercover organizers are hired by unwitting employers.

union shop A form of union security in which the company can hire nonunion people, but they must join the union after a prescribed period of time and pay dues. (If they do not, they can be fired.)

unsafe conditions The mechanical and physical conditions that cause accidents.

unsatisfactory performance Persistent failure to perform assigned duties or to meet prescribed standards on the job.

unstructured or nondirective interview An unstructured conversational-style interview in which the interviewer pursues points of interest as they come up in response to questions.

unstructured sequential interview An interview in which each interviewer forms an independent opinion after asking different questions.

valence The perceived value a person attaches to the reward.

value chain analysis Identifying the primary activities that create value for customers and the related support activities.

variable pay Any plan that ties pay to productivity or profitability, usually as one-time lump payments.

vesting Provision that money placed in a pension fund cannot be forfeited for any reason.

Vietnam Era Veterans' Readjustment Assistance Act of 1974 An act requiring that employers with government contracts take affirmative action to hire disabled veterans.

vision A general statement of its intended direction that evokes emotional feelings in organization members.

Vocational Rehabilitation Act of 1973 The act requiring certain federal contractors to take affirmative action for disabled persons.

voluntary bargaining items Items in collective bargaining over which bargaining is neither illegal nor mandatory—neither party can be compelled against its wishes to negotiate over those items.

wage curve Shows the relationship between the value of the job and the average wage paid for this job.

Walsh-Healey Public Contract Act (1936) A law that requires minimum wage and working conditions for employees working on any government contract amounting to more than $10,000.

wildcat strike An unauthorized strike occurring during the term of a contract.

work samples Actual job tasks used in testing applicants' performance.

work sampling technique A testing method based on measuring performance on actual basic job tasks.

work sharing Refers to a temporary reduction in work hours by a group of employees during economic downturns as a way to prevent layoffs.

workers' compensation Provides income and medical benefits to work-related accident victims or their dependents regardless of fault.

wrongful discharge An employee dismissal that does not comply with the law or does not comply with the contractual arrangement stated or implied by the firm via its employment application forms, employee manuals, or other promises.

Photo Credits

Chapter 1

2   Photodisc #65 Teamwork and Competition
6   Lenore Davis
10 Toyota Motor Manufacturing, Kentucky, Inc.
12 Paul Thompson; Ecoscene/Corbis/Bettmann

Chapter 2

28 Photodisc #52 Global Business and Currency
37 Mugshots/Corbis/Stock Market
41 Marty Katz
60 Tony Freeman/PhotoEdit

Chapter 3

70 RYANSTOCK/Getty Images, Inc.–Taxi
72 Harry Cabluck/AP Wide World Photos
79 Frank OrdoÒez / Syracuse Newspapers/The Image Works
93 AP Wide World Photos

Chapter 4

110 Photodisc-Business and Occupation 2 V43/Getty Images, Inc.
115 Richard Radstone/Telegraph Colour Library/Getty Images, Inc.–Taxi
132 Bruce Ayres/Getty Images Inc.–Stone Allstock
140 Andy Levin/Photo Researchers, Inc.

Chapter 5

150 Photodisc #65 Teamwork and Competition
168 Stuart Isett/Gamma Press USA, Inc.
178 Arnold Zann/Black Star

Chapter 6

192 Photodisc-Business and Occupation 2 V43/Getty Images, Inc.
194 Michael McLaughlin/Julian Richards Agency
208 William Thomas Cain/Bloomberg News/Landov LLC
211 Sylwia Kapuscinski/Detroit Free Press/NEWSCOM
221 Spencer Grant/PhotoEdit

Chapter 7

234 Photodisc-Business and Occupation 2 V43/Getty Images, Inc.
243 Pictor/ImageState/International Stock Photography Ltd.
254 SuperStock, Inc.

Chapter 8

266 Photodisc-Business and Occupation 2 V43/Getty Images, Inc.
271 AGE Fotostock America, Inc.
284 Jim Leynse/Corbis/SABA Press Photos, Inc.
290 Mario Tama/Getty Images, Inc.–Liaison

Chapter 9

308 Photodisc-Business and Occupation 2 V43/Getty Images, Inc.
314 Michael Newman/PhotoEdit
327 Pictor/ImageState/International Stock Photography Ltd.
333 Bob Daemmrich Photography, Inc.

Chapter 10

348 Photodisc #65 Teamwork and Competition
355 Brian Smith
360 Andre Pichette Photography
364 William Mercer McLeod

Chapter 11

388 Mitch Jacobson/AP Wide World Photos
392 Michael Newman/PhotoEdit
401 John Waterman/Getty Images Inc.–Stone Allstock
414 The Tampa Tribune

Chapter 12

436 Photodisc-Business and Occupation 2 V43/Getty Images, Inc.
446 Spartech Corporation
451 Michael S. Yamashita/Corbis/Bettmann
459 Spencer Grant/PhotoEdit

Chapter 13

474 Photodisc #52 Global Business and Currency
480 Stacy Pick/Stock Boston
492 Tova R. Baruch
497 Ann States/Corbis/SABA Press Photos, Inc.

Chapter 14

514 Photodisc-Business and Occupation 2 V43/Getty Images, Inc.
523 Wyatt McSpadden Photography
523 Michael Nagle/Bloomberg News/Landov LLC
537 James King-Holmes/Science Photo Library/Photo Researchers, Inc.

Chapter 15

558 Photodisc #52 Global Business and Currency
561 Culver Pictures, Inc.
582 Michael Newman/PhotoEdit
591 David Burns/AP Wide World Photos

Chapter 16

600 OSHA—Occupational Safety and Health Administration
608 Rollin A. Riggs/New York Times Pictures
619 Richard Pasley/Stock Boston
625 Phil Savoie/Index Stock Imagery, Inc.
640 Spencer Grant/PhotoEdit

Chapter 17

654 Photodisc #65 Teamwork and Competition
658 AUDI AG
665 AP Wide World Photos
670 INSEAD

Name and Organization Index

ABB Business Services, 611
Abosch, Kenan, 470*n*19
Abrahamson, Eric, 307*n*95
Accenture, 237, 291
Acquino, Karl, 653*n*127
ActiveStrategy, 96
Adams, Duncan, 599*n*64
Adams Mark Hotel & Resorts, 280
Adler, Seymour, 232*n*66
Adolf Coors Company, 222
Aerospace Corp., 13
Aetna, 498
African American Network, 63
Agarwala, Tanuja, 27*n*7
Agilent, 661
Airwick Industries, 449
Albert Einstein Healthcare, 86
Albrecht, Karl, 629, 652*n*87
Alderfer, Clay, 470*n*10
Alfred, Winfred, Jr., 305*n*7
Allen, Richard, 470*n*3
Allied Signal, 293
Alliger, George, 148*n*19, 307*n*112
Allmerica Financial Corp, 356
Allred, Brent, 371*n*3
Amazon.com, 540, 568
American Express, 368
American Media, Inc., 271
American Skandia, 446
AmeriCredit, 174–175
Anderson, Cathy, 347*n*49
Anderson, Jack, 425*n*15
Andrews, Tom, 651*n*42
Anfuso, Dawn, 653*n*120
Anheuser-Busch, 21
Antonioni, David, 346*n*3, 347*n*53
Apex Door Company, 304
Apex Environmental, 261
Apollo Travel Services, 282
Appel, Timothy, 27*n*16
Applegate, Jane, 513*n*126&*n*128
Arkin, Anat, 652*n*57
Armagast, Ronald, 435*n*1
Arnold, Edwin, 598*n*26
Arnold, Jeffrey, 74
Arnold, Richard, 471*n*37
Arrowhead Credit Union, 496
Arthur, Winfred, Jr., 231*n*58, 306*n*37
Arthur Andersen, 18, 530
Arzi, Nira, 346*n*8
Ascentis Software Corporation, 504

Ashford, Susan, 305*n*3
Ashworth, Steven, 307*n*105
Assessment Systems Corporation, 212
Atkinson, William, 470*n*28, 652*n*58
AT&T, 677
Attaway, Morris, 557*n*54
Austin, James, 347*n*43
Austin-Hayne Corporation, 326
Avon Products, 290, 292, 293, 294, 576

Babcock, Pamela, 190*n*48, 683*n*44
Bacher, Jeffrey, 473*n*131
Bachler, Christopher, 652*n*88
Bachman, Ronald, 511*n*55
BadReferences.com, 216
Bain, Trevor, 598*n*40
Bain & Company, 289
Baker, Eric, 109*n*23
Bakke, Allen, 62
Baldwin, Timothy, 307*n*111
Baley, Sarah, 471*n*45
Ball, Jeffrey, 597*n*9
Baltes, Boris, 512*n*121
Banham, Russa, 512*n*103
BankAmerica, 364
Banker, Rajiv, 470*n*1
Barclay, Julie, 347*n*46
Barclays Capital, 203
Barker, Tim, 264
Barling, Julian, 651*n*35
Barlow, Wayne, 68*n*46
Barnes, Julian, 101*n*9
Barnes-Farrell, Janet, 346*n*25
Barnes & Noble, 446
Barnett, Carole, 683*n*8
Barr, Jodie, 425*n*23
Barrett, Gerald, 347*n*42, 426*n*58
Barrett, Michael, 108*n*3
Barrick, Murray, 231*n*41&*n*50, 263*n*32
Barron, John, 307*n*111
Barron, Tom, 305*n*24, 306*n*73
Barstow, David, 651*n*7
Bartol, Kathryn, 471*n*71
Baruch, Yehuda, 371*n*15
Barwick, Kenneth, 652*n*57
Bassett, Glenn, 189*n*4, 470*n*30
Bates, Steve, 17, 27*n*5&*n*27, 101*n*22, 231*n*43, 346*n*3&*n*16
Bauer, Talya, 230*n*19
Baumann, Joseph, 470*n*2
Baxter, Gregory, 68*n*25

Baxter Healthcare Corporation, 59
Bayer, Richard, 557*n*73
Baynton, Dannah, 306*n*39&*n*42
Beatty, L. Kate, 510*n*1
Beauchamp, Tom, 556*n*6
Becker, Brian, 84, 87, 92, 101*n*27&*n*34, 597*n*1
Beckett, Helen, 306*n*77
Beehr, Terry, 347*n*59
Beer, Michael, 307*n*95&*n*101
Bell, Cecil, Jr., 296, 307*n*104
Bell, James, 232*n*75
Bellagio Hotel, 194
BellSouth, 213
Benefit Software, Inc., 623
BeneLogic, 495
Bennett, Elizabeth, 598*n*15
Bennett, James, 597*n*6, 684*n*64
Bennett, Rebecca, 231*n*29
Bennett, Rita, 684*n*75
Bennett, Winston, 307*n*112, 668
Bennington, Lynn, 69*n*77
Bennis, Warren, 74, 100*n*3
Bensimon, Helen Frank, 653*n*134
Berardine, Tony, 108*n*7, 109*n*22
Bergal, Gary, 426*n*58&*n*59
Berger, Raymond, 230*n*10
Bergman, Lowell, 651*n*7
Bergman, Mindy D., 67*n*10&*n*13
Bergmann, Thomas, 510*n*1, 511*n*44
Berka, Chris, 232*n*100
Berliner, William, 306*n*30
Bernardin, H. John, 232*n*87, 347*n*42
Bernstein, Susan, 512*n*78
Berta, Dina, 190*n*89, 306*n*53
Betz, Nancy, 230*n*6&*n*15
Bialk, Betty, 511*n*38
Bielema, Michelle, 652*n*47
Bingham, Shereen, 35
Binning, John, 263*n*35
Bisen, Jeffrey, 231*n*56
Bittel, Lester, 557*n*49
Black, Jay Stewart, 305*n*3
Black, Jill, 148*n*28
Blakley, Barry R., 231*n*37
Blanchard, Nick, 283, 305*n*23, 306*n*55&*n*60
Bland, Timothy, 68*n*55, 69*n*90
Blank, Christina, 109*n*17
Blencoe, Allyn, 148*n*8
Blood, Milton, 346*n*19
Bloom, Matt, 425*n*18

703

Blotzer, Michael, 306n63, 651n40, 652n62, 653n99
Blue Cross, 486, 545
Blue Shield, 486
BMC, 497
BMW, 590
Boeing Corp., 591
Bohner, Robert, Jr., 169, 189n44
Bolino, Mark, 347n45
Bolles, Richard, 383, 386n6&n10
Bonpey, Stuart, 69n91
Borgia, Prashant, 307n98
Borofsky, Gerald, 652n47
Boswell, Wendy, 190n58
Bovis Land Lease, 302
Bowers, Molley, 67n11
Bowie, Normal, 556n6
Boyle, Mathew, 512n96
Brada, Paul, 557n79
Brady, W. H., Company, 106
Brett, Jeanne, 470n2
Brett, Joan, 305n25
Bretz, Robert, 425n20
Breuer, Nancy, 684n95
Brewster, Chris, 684n69
Briddle, Daniel, 506
Bridges, Bernisha, 426n47
Bridges, William, 148n26
Bright, Jim, 371n6&n9
British Petroleum, 144, 359
Brockardt, James, 472n82
Brockner, Joel, 684n61
Brookes, Donald, 307n79
Brotherton, Phaedra, 190n83
Brousseau, Kenneth, 371n3
Brown, Deborah Wright, 387n13
Brown, Duncan, 426n53&n60, 427n72
Brown, Jack, 550
Brown, Kenneth, 306n69
Buckley, M. Ronald, 347n43, 556n38
Buhl, William E., 470n21
Bulkeley, William, 262n22&n24, 471n51
Bullard, Peter, 232n90
Burack, Elmer H., 189n2
Burger, Jerry, 263n43
Burger, Warren, 37
Burgnoli, George, 231n54
Burke, Mary, 512n89
Burlingame, Harold, 512n77
Burns, James, Jr., 232n75
Burns, Sheila, 684n79
Burr, Michael, 556n43
Bush, George H. W., 38–39
Bush, George W., 477
Business Advantage, Inc., 291
Business Plan Pro, 77
Busse, Dale, 511n52

Butler, Timothy, 375, 376, 377, 386n5
Butterfield, D. Anthony, 371n36

Cable, Daniel, 306n53
Cabot, Stephen, 598n55
Cadrain, Diane, 232n99, 470n20, 652n79, 653n132
Cahn, Doug, 598n42
Caldwell, David, 263n43
Caligiuri, Paula, 231n44, 683n53
Callender, John, 263n66
Campbell, Andrew, 100n3
Campbell, David, 557n52
Campbell, Donald, 470n15&n29
Campbell, John P., 307n102, 470n15
Campbell Soup Company, 577
Campion, James, 231n56, 252, 264n78&n80
Campion, Michael, 148n10, 252, 262n4, 263n47, 264n68&n71&n78
Camuso, Michael, 557n80
Candrilli, Alfred, 435n1
Cannon-Bowers, Janice A., 305n13
Canon, 141, 413
Capelli, Peter, 231n28
Capital One, 208
Carayon, Pascale, 652n89
Carden, William, 371n1&n4
Carlson, Kevin, 160, 189n19
Carlson, R. E., 263n39&n40, 264n81
Carlson, Tina, 512n82
Carmichael, Katie, 6
Carpenter, Mason, 684n63
Carr, Linda, 307n105
Carrell, Michael, 69n98, 426n29, 586, 596, 598n17&n32&n39&n43&n51, 599n62&n67
Carrier Corporation, 11
Carroll, Darren, 653n110&n135&n137
Carron, Theodore, 148n7
Carter, Jack, 229, 261–262
Carter, Jennifer, 229–230, 261
Carter, Ruth Thaler, 175n, 190
Cascio, Wayne, 115n, 148, 331n, 347
Casey, Judith, 190n63
Cash Creek Casino, 279
Casisom, Jeanie, 471n61
Castagnera, James, 232n75
Castillo, Carlos, 683n18&n38
Catalano, R. E., 307n111
Caterpillar, 583
Caudron, Shari, 27n7, 189n43, 220, 305n8, 471n70, 653n126&n130
Cederblom, Doug, 346n6
Cellar, Douglas, 231n46
Chadd, Charles, 651n21
Chaison, Gary, 599n70
Champy, James, 139, 148n29

Chang, Lei, 426n63
Chanick, Richard, 371n31
Chapman, Mindy, 305n19
Chappell, Lindsey, 138
Charan, Ram, 307n98
Charles Schwab, 293
Chaudhuri, Anita, 263n37
Chayes, Antonio Handler, 69n108
Chesebrough-Ponds USA, 139
Chesters, Alan, 683n20&n22
Cheung, Fannie, 683n7
Chevron, 676
Chiron Corp., 107
Cholewka, Kathleen, 471n62
Christadore, Robert, 511n53
Circuit City, 182
Cisco Systems, 245
Citibank, 106, 446
Citicorp, 656
Citigroup, 549
Citizen's Banking Corporation, 237
Citizens Financial Group, 447
City Garage, 212
Clariant Corporation, 618
Clark, Margaret, 68n31
Clendenning, Donna, 652n71
Click2Learn.com, 284
Clifford, James, 148n1&n2
Coca-Cola, 397, 676
Cocks, David, 450, 471
Cofsky, Kathryn, 426n51
Cohen, Sacha, 68n42
Coil, James, III, 69n97&n109, 557n73&n77
Colgate Palmolive, 668
Collins, Christopher, 189n36
Collins, Judith, 232n89
Collins, Marianne, 148n7
Colvin, Alexander, 101n28
Colvin, Geoffrey, 426n42
CompWatch, 623
Conner, Jeffrey, 557n73
Connerley, Mary, 191n103
Connors, Richard, 69n76
Conseco Inc., 462
Constans, Joseph, 346n20
Constantin, S. W., 263n35
Container Store, 252
Cook, Ellen, 372n41
Cooke, Donna, 232n87
Cooke, William, 598n47
Corinth, William, 652n78
Cornelius, Edwin, III, 148n7&n8
Cox, Taylor, Jr., 69n100
Cox, Walter, Jr., 472n88
Coyle-Shapiro, Jacqueline, 471n79
Crawford, Marnie Swerdlin, 231n37
Crawford, Richard, 27n18

Criterion, Inc., 356
Cropanzano, Russell, 230n18, 556n29&n34
Crowe, Russell, 675
Cruz, Lisa, 297, 419–420
CUC International, 520
Cuerton, Gerald, 598n55
Cullen, Lisa, 652n61
Cullison, Jessica, 512n89
Culotta, Michael, 512n77
Cummings, L. L., 307n102
Cummings, Thomas, 307n95
Cunningham, Edward, 472n128

DaimlerChrysler, 499, 590
Dalessio, Anthony, 263n34
Dana Corp., 411
Danaher, Maria, 371n34
Daniels, Cora, 231n40
Daniels, John, 683n24&n38&n40&n43&n52
Dash, Julekha, 371n20
Davidshofer, Charles, 230n5&n7&n8&n9,
    231n36
Davidson, Oranit, 305n29
Davis, Ronald, 653n106
Dayan, Kobi, 232n59
Deci, Edward, 440–441, 445, 470n12, 471n33
DeCotiis, Thomas, 346n18
DeGroot, Tim, 263n42
Delaney, Jim, 304
DeLaTorre, Philip, 347n36
Dell Computer, 10, 11, 12, 19, 72, 77, 82, 89,
    90, 106, 206, 463
Deloitte & Touche, 363
Delta Airlines, 79, 284–285
Delves, Don, 472n106
Demby, Elayne, 472n104, 512n78
Deming, W. Edwards, 310
DeNisi, Angelo, 148n8, 347n35
Denton, David, 67n4
Designsafe, 616
Dessler, Gary, 88, 89, 90, 473n131
Dewey, Barbara, 426n58
Diamond, Kenneth, 653n111
Dickenson, Terry, 346n19
Dickmeyer, William, 190n73
DiFonzo, Nicholas, 307n98
Digh, Patricia, 69n99
DiLorenzo, Louis, 653n110&n135&n137
Diners Club, 548–549
Dinur, Vossi, 347n49
Dipboye, Robert, 263n36
Discovery Communications, 444
Dixon, Marlene, 262n15
Doherty, Lynn, 189n39
Doherty, Michael, 263n35
Dole Food Co, Inc., 164
Dolmat-Connell, Jack, 395, 425n11

Donkin, Richard, 190n95
Donn, Clifford, 232n96
Donovan, Michelle, 518, 556n12
Doody, Michael, 371n12
Dougherty, Thomas, 263n66
Douglas, Scott, 653n121
Dow Chemical, 356, 661, 662
Dow Jones & Company, 416
Downey, R. G., 347n46
Drake, John, 257, 264n93
Drake, Larry, 67n6
Driver, Michael, 371n3
Drost, Ellen, 683n27
Drucker, Peter, 27n19, 524
Druskat, Vanessa, 347n47
DTX, 454
Dube, Lawrence E., Jr., 232n70
Dunham, Kemba, 557n78
Dunn, Bonnie, 244
Dunnette, M. D., 307n102, 470n9&n15
DuPont, 505, 610
Duracell, Inc., 548

Earhart, Kelli, 512n99
Eastman Kodak., 178–181
Ebbers, Bernard, 520
Eckberg, Steve, 511n24
Eden, Dov, 305n29, 652n92
Einstein Medical, 86, 90
Eisenstat, Russell, 307n95&n101
Electronic Data Systems, 75–76
Ellin, Abby, 190n87
Ellis, Christine, 305n5
Elsass, Priscilla, 683n7
Elswick, Jill, 27n36
Emerson, Sondra, 427n69&n73
Emery, Michael, 306n65&n68
Eneroth, Kristina, 371n3
Enron, 18, 522, 530
Erez, Miriam, 346n8
Erickson, Judith, 652n46
Esen, Euren, 512n89
Esposito, Michael, 68n50, 148n19
Estée Lauder, 290
Estell, Libby, 471n44
Etkind, Steven, 472n84
Evered, James, 148n13&n20
Exchange Bank, 222
Exxon, 676

Falcon, Paul, 557n49
Falconer, Tim, 306n50
Famularo, Joseph, 557n66
Fandray, Dayton, 556n25
Federal Express (FedEx), 80, 204, 529–530,
    535, 562, 567
Fein, Mitchell, 470n26

Feinberg, Mortimer, 336–337
Feinstein, David, 223
Feldacker, Bruce, 67n2&n20
Feldman, Daniel, 190n46&n77
Feliu, Alfred, 653n116&n122&n129&n136
Fellinger, Peter, 346n19
Felsenthal, Edward, 67n9
Feltes, Patricia, 68n22
Fernandez, Maria, 261
Ferris, Gerald, 27n20, 347n43
Fidelity Investments, 368, 492, 493
Fife, Raymond, 426n44
Figlio, David, 425n13
Figura, Susannah, 651n41
Fike Corporation, 222
Fine, Cory, 598n22&n24
Fink, Ross, 68n22
Finnegan, Lisa, 651n25
Fiorina, Carly, 206
First Interstate Bancorp, 82
First Tennessee Bank, 447, 497
First USA Bank, 356–357
First Weigh Manufacturing, 506–507
Fischlmayr, Iris, 684n73
Fisher, Harold E., 307n111
Fisher, Sondra Lotz, 653n103
Fisicaro, Sebastiana, 263n35
Fitz-enz, Jac, 108n12
Fitzgerald, Louise, 35
Fitzgerald, Mark, 598n53
Fleishmann, Scott T., 263n41
Flynn, Gillian, 190n72, 233n113, 511n30,
    512n91, 557n74, 598n28
Fogelman, Danny, 653n112
Fogli, Lawrence, 346n19
Folger, Robert, 556n9
Fontenelle, Gail, 263n36
Foote, David, 371n22
Foote, Kevin, 426n49&n52
Ford, J. Kevin, 307n111
Ford, Robert, 557n88
Ford Motor, 13, 16, 270, 280, 453, 493, 498,
    499, 602, 606, 656, 666
Fossum, John, 598n46&n47&n50&n52
Foster, Ben, 598n30
Foulkes, Fred K., 27n2
Fox, Shaul, 347n49
France, Angela, 557n55&n60
Frank, Andrew, 347n66
Frank, Dwight, 27n20
Frase-Blunt, Martha, 262n13
Frazee, Valerie, 683n11, 684n74&n79
Frazis, Harley, 306n31
Frederickson, James, 426n38
French, Wendell, 307n104
Frey, Jennifer, 370
Friedman, Jeffrey, 392, 425n3

Friedman, Raymond, 69*n*103
Frierson, James G., 68*n*65
Fritz, Norma, 232*n*85
Fry, Richard, 232*n*96
Fuller, Jerry, Jr., 597*n*9
Fusilier, Marceline, 652*n*85

G. Neil Company, 102, 105, 198
Gadiesh, Arit, 75
Galang, M. Carmen, 27*n*20
Gale, Sarah, 190*n*67&*n*76, 231*n*31, 305*n*5
Gamble, John, 472*n*83
Ganger, Ralph E., 306*n*51
Gannett newspapers, 505
Gap, Inc., 364
Garner, Kathleen, 263*n*36
Garonzik, Ron, 684*n*61
Garry, Michael, 109*n*17
Garvey, Charlotte, 305*n*1
Gates, Bill, 155
Gatewood, Robert, 68*n*56, 69*n*73&*n*75
Gaugler, Barbara, 231*n*58
Gay.com, 63
GE Medical, 161, 406–407
General Electric (GE), 16, 161, 170, 206, 319,
    334, 488, 567, 577, 664
General Mills, 413–414
General Motors (GM), 75–76, 78–79, 81,
    159, 282, 453, 499
George, Claude S. G., 26
Gerbman, Russell, 233*n*112, 307*n*88
Gerhart, Barry, 426*n*51&*n*57, 427*n*64&*n*66
German, Mario, 105, 108*n*1
Gerson, Vicki, 108*n*10
Gerstner, Louis, 417–418
Getroncis, 544
Giannantonio, Christina, 27*n*25
Gibbons, Barry, 293
Gibbs, Travis, 230*n*11
Gifford, Robert, 263*n*41
Gilbert, Dan, 470*n*30
Gilbert, James, 75
Gilliland, Stephen, 230*n*16, 264*n*89, 557*n*86
Gilmore, Thomas, 148*n*28
Gilster, Paul, 190*n*74
Gines, Karen, 471*n*50
Gisonny, Richard, 511*n*42
Glater, Jonathan, 471*n*32
GlaxoSmithKline, 411
Glendinning, Peter, 346*n*1, 471*n*67
Glister, Paul, 471*n*47
Gnazzo, Patrick, 517
Goddard, Rogert, 190*n*86
Goldsmith, Howard, 426*n*34,
    472*n*96&*n*99&*n*100&*n*102&*n*111&*n*116
Goldwasser, Donna, 305*n*27

Gombar, Robert, 651*n*12
Gompers, Samuel, 560–561
Goodfellow, Matthew, 573, 598*n*28
Gopher, Daniel, 346*n*8
Gordon, Tim, 652*n*58
Gould, Dennis, 471*n*66
Grady, Teri O., 306*n*49
Grand Casinos, Inc., 107
Granger, Eileen, 306*n*75
Grant, Dennis, 510*n*13&*n*17
Graphic Media, 281
Gratton, Lynda, 101*n*15
Graves, Laura, 262*n*1
Great Western Bank, 244–245
Green, Paul, 264*n*76
Greenberg, Eric Rolfe, 232*n*97
Greenberg, Herbert, 190*n*92
Greene, Barbara, 371*n*8&*n*18
Greengard, Samuel, 101*n*25, 108*n*4&*n*5,
    109*n*14&*n*25, 232*n*68, 556*n*22&*n*26,
    684*n*93
Greenhouse, Stephen, 597*n*3
Greer, Charles, 101*n*14&*n*24&*n*26
Gregures, Gary, 347*n*31
Grensing-Pophal, Lin, 511*n*64
Groe, Gerald, 108*n*8
Gross, Steven, 473*n*131
Grossman, Neil, 511*n*32
Grossman, Robert, 69*n*101, 232*n*63, 651*n*20,
    653*n*109
Grossman, Ronald, 511*n*65
Grote, Dick, 557*n*51
Grover, William, 263*n*35
Gunch, Dawn, 511*n*29
Gundy, Peter, 471*n*65
Gupta, Nina, 473*n*131
Gustafson, David, 683*n*7
Gutherie, James, 472*n*128
Guthime, James, 27*n*19

Ha, Oanh, 470*n*27
Hagmann, Laura, 471*n*71
Hahn, Jeffrey M., 220, 232*n*82
Haines, Victor, 109*n*20
Hakel, Milton, 148*n*8
Hakim, Danny, 101*n*8
Hall, Douglas, 371*n*2
Hall, James, 68*n*55, 598*n*25, 651*n*16
Halloran, Daniel, 372*n*48
Halpert, Jane, 347*n*32
Hamblin, Matt, 511*n*70
Hamel, Gary, 78
Hammer, Michael, 139, 148*n*29
Hammer, Willie, 651*n*26
Hammers, MaryAnn, 109*n*22
Hampson, H. Anthony, 426*n*41
Hane, Edward, 68*n*46

Hannay, Maureen, 512*n*87
Hansen, Fay, 510*n*1
Hansen, Frederick, 470*n*13
Hantula, Donald, 651*n*29
Harbin, Julie, 190*n*48
Harland, Lynn, 347*n*46
Harleysville Group, Inc., 493
Harrington, Ann, 346*n*22, 471*n*38
Harris, Hilary, 684*n*69
Harris, Michael, 470*n*31
Harris, Nicole, 597*n*10
Harris, Paul, 282, 291, 306*n*58, 307*n*91
Harrison, David, 448*n*, 471, 683*n*51, 684*n*58
Hartford Financial Services Group, 637
Hartford Insurance Company, 351
Hartman, Sandra, 534
Hartmen, Sondra, 599*n*60
Hartshorn, Dan, 652*n*49
Harvey, Michael, 683*n*50, 684*n*56
Harvey, Robert J., 148*n*8
Harvey, Tim, 371*n*26
Hastings, Carol, 69*n*102
Hatch, Diane, 68*n*55, 598*n*25, 651*n*16
Hatcher, Chris, 653*n*125
Hatcher, Larry, 472*n*94
Haus, Mick, 232*n*95
Hay Associates, 399
Hay consulting firm, 400
Hayes, Bill, 371*n*14
Hayes, Scott, 231*n*34, 471*n*40
Heath, Chip, 347*n*50
Heavrin, Christina, 426*n*29, 580, 586, 596,
    598*n*17&*n*32&*n*39&*n*43&*n*51,
    599*n*62&*n*67
Heidrick and Struggles, 399
Heilman, Madeline, 69*n*113, 263*n*48
Helms, Marilyn, 470*n*3
Henderson, Andrew, 426*n*38
Henderson, Richard, 148*n*3&*n*5&*n*12,
    425*n*1&*n*10&*n*24, 470*n*24, 471*n*70,
    510*n*19
Hendrickson, Anthony, 108*n*3
Heneman, Herbert, III, 346*n*18
Heneman, Robert, 426*n*48&*n*63, 471*n*74,
    683*n*30
Henn, William, 101*n*24
Henriques, Diana, 556*n*20
Heresy, Robert, 470*n*9
Herskowitz, Elaine, 371*n*35
Herz, Diane, 306*n*31
Herzberg, Frederick, 138, 440
Hester, Kim, 597*n*9
Hewitt Associates, 399, 446
Hewlett-Packard, 206, 288
Hibbing Taconite Steel Plant, 582
Hickman, Julia, 347*n*32
Hicks, Larry, 426*n*50

Hicks, Sabrina, 305*n*2
Higgins, James, 100*n*2
Higgs, A. Catherine, 307*n*105
Hilgard, Ernest R., 470*n*8
Hill, Charles, 683*n*47, 684*n*55&*n*79
Hills, Frederick, 510*n*1, 511*n*44
Hindman, Hugh, 347*n*43
Hirecheck, 217
Hirsch, Barry, 425*n*10
Hirschhorn, Larry, 148*n*28, 307*n*94
Hirschman, Carolyn, 511*n*58&*n*66, 683*n*17
Hispanic Online, 63
Hodgetts, Richard, 424, 425*n*17
Hoffman, James, 652*n*47
Hofmann, David, 651*n*34
Hofrichter, David, 427*n*62
Hofstede, Geert, 657, 683*n*8
Holland, John, 373, 386*n*3
Hollingsworth, Steve, 651*n*14
Holtom, Books, 69*n*103
Hom, David, 512*n*114
Hom, Greg, 651*n*1
Home Depot, 416
Honda, 79, 210–211, 283
Honoree, Andre, 425*n*21
Hoover, Kent, 427*n*89
Hopkins, Shirley, 306*n*46
Hopkins, Willie, 306*n*46, 498*n*, 512*n*99
Horrigan, Michael, 306*n*31
Hotel Paris, 91, 93–97, 142–143, 184–185, 225–226, 241–242, 297–298, 312, 341–342, 366, 367, 419–420, 457–458, 501–502, 550–552, 587–589, 642–643, 678–679
Hough, L. M., 470*n*9
House, Robert J., 307*n*103
Howe, Nancy, 190*n*47
Howie, Robert, 232*n*77
HRdirect, 102
Hudson, Stan, 652*n*58
Huffcutt, Alan, 262*n*4, 263*n*53, 264*n*73
Hughes Electronics, 75–76
Hullin, Charles, 346*n*19
Hunt, Steven, 148*n*23
Hurley, Amy, 27*n*25
Hurst, Robin Rimmer, 264*n*90
Huselid, Mark, 87, 90, 92, 101*n*27&*n*34
Hutcheson, Peggy, 351, 353, 357, 371*n*23
Hymowitz, Carol, 347*n*58

IBM, 11, 83, 107, 291, 417–418, 495, 524, 548, 591, 592, 593, 661, 662
Ilies, Remus, 231*n*49
Immelt, Jeffrey, 275
Incentive Systems Inc., 447
Industrial Health Care, 223
Infante, Victor, 512*n*71, 684*n*77

Insch, Gary, 683*n*52
International Coach Federation, 289
International Paper Corp., 19
International Truck and Engine Corp., 620
Isler, Edward, 557*n*76
Ivanovich, John M., 346*n*17, 470*n*10

J. C. Penney, 524
Jackofsky, Ellen, 683*n*9
Jackson, Brian, 651*n*13
Jackson, Conrad, 652*n*85
Jackson, Susan, 683*n*9
Jacobius, Arlene, 511*n*68
Jacobs, Roger, 651*n*22
Jaffee, Cabot, 231*n*36
Jago, I. Ann, 230*n*37
Janov, Jason, 67*n*14
Janush, Erwin, 684*n*77
Jarrett, M. Quintin, 307*n*110
Jawahar, I. M., 347*n*29
JDS Uniphase, 152–153
JetBlue Airlines, 12, 303–304, 523, 524
John Deere, 83
Johnson, Linda, 652*n*60
Johnson & Johnson, 524, 528
Joinson, Carla, 371*n*5&*n*10, 425*n*14, 684*n*62, 685*n*101
Jones, Casey, 231*n*55, 232*n*60
Jones, Del, 346*n*13
Jones, John, 232*n*84
Jossi, Frank, 69*n*107, 684*n*90
Jourden, Forest, 347*n*50
Judge, Paul, 27*n*10
Judge, Timothy, 231*n*47&*n*52, 262*n*26
Jung, Andrea, 290, 293
Jurgensen, W. G., 426*n*44

Kahanar, Eileen, 510*n*11
Kahn, Randolph, 108*n*3
Kalkstein, Harold Murray, 472*n*85
Kaltenheuser, Skip, 556*n*4
Kaman, Vicki, 425*n*23
Kamel, Hosam, 651*n*38
Kandel, William, 557*n*46
Kanfer, R., 470*n*9&*n*14&*n*15
Kanter, Jeffrey, 472*n*111
Kara, Dan, 189*n*5
Karol Media, 291
Karon, Roy, 306*n*70
Karper, Mark, 232*n*96
Karr, Al, 653*n*106
Karren, Ronald, 262*n*1
Katz, Harry, 598*n*31
Kaul, Pamela, 264*n*87
Kay, Ira, 347*n*60, 472*n*109
Keagy, Jackie, 371*n*19
Kearney, Deborah, 148*n*18

Keaveny, Timothy, 67*n*8, 346*n*17
Kelloway, E. Kevin, 653*n*115
Kemper, Cynthia, 557*n*58
Kennedy, John F., 591
Kernan, Mary, 347*n*42
Kerry, John, 229
Kesselring, Randall, 233*n*108
Kiger, Patrick, 347*n*65, 371*n*25
Kim, Seongsu, 471*n*79
Kim, W. Chan, 557*n*45
Kincaid, William, 651*n*10&*n*45
King, Julia, 471*n*36
King, Stephen, 683*n*28
Kinko's, 204
Kirkpatrick, D., 306*n*72, 307*n*111
Klaff, Leslie, 685*n*102
Klass, Brian, 190*n*77, 427*n*69
Kleiman, Lawrence, 67*n*4
Klein, Howard, 305*n*2
Klein, Robert, 472*n*112
Klineberg, Steven, 69*n*108
Klinefelter, John, 68*n*60
Kmart, 79
Knight Ridder, 564
KnowledgePoint, 326
Knudsen, Liana, 371*n*8&*n*18
Kobata, Mark, 68*n*30
Kochen, Thomas, 69*n*105
Koelling, C. Patrick, 472*n*91
Koen, Clifford, Jr., 599*n*60
Koen, Deb, 371*n*11
Kohl, John, 189*n*35
Kohn, Alfie, 472*n*122, 473*n*129
Komaki, Judi, 652*n*57
Konrad, Alison, 387*n*13
Koonce, Richard, 69*n*98, 371*n*4
Korsgaard, M. Audrey, 556*n* 16
Kossek, Ellen, 683*n*2
Kotter, John, 293, 307*n*95&*n*96&*n*98&*n*100
Kovatch, Kenneth, 470*n*9
Kraft, 671
Kraimer, Maria, 684*n*61
Kravetz, Dennis, 149*n*36
Kravitz, David, 69*n*108
Krell, Eric, 189*n*34, 190*n*64
Kristof, Amy L., 263*n*45&*n*46
Krohe, J., Jr., 525*n*, 556
Krohe, James, Jr., 652*n*87
K*Tec electronics, 463
Kunen, James, 556*n*24
Kurlander, Peter, 472*n*121
Kuzmits, Frank, 109*n*24

Laabs, Jennifer, 190*n*90, 652*n*54, 653*n*114
LaBar, Gregg, 652*n*55
Lachnit, Carroll, 232*n*65, 556*n*8

Lam, Shunyin, 189n6
Lambert, Susan, 512n95
Lampron, France, 108n8
Lance, Charles, 346n27, 347n28
Lane, Irving, 231n36&n57
Langan, Michael, 511n42
Langdale, Don, 263n38
Langdon, Danny, 305n25
Lanza, Bob., 511n60
Larsson, Rikerd, 371n3
Lasek, Marja, 230n1, 232n75
Latham, G., 264n71, 305n9&n26, 306n49,
    307n108, 346n7&n18
Latino Web, 63
Lattanzio, Steve, 511n39
Laudon, Jane, 108n3, 684n96
Laudon, Kenneth, 108n3, 684n96
Lauer, Charles, 190n88
Lavelle, Louis, 426n45, 472n103
Lawler, Edward, III, 290, 307n92, 426n63,
    427n65
Lawrie, John, 189n8
Lazarus, Harold, 472n85
LeBlanc, Manon Mireille, 653n115
LeBlanc, Peter, 426n48&n61
Ledford, Gerald, Jr.,
    426n50&n51&n57&n58&n59&n62&n63
Ledvinka, James, 67n19, 68n56&n65&n66,
    69n73, 230n8
Lee, Barbara, 68n44&n51&n53
Lee, Kai-Fu, 155
Lee, Mushin, 346n3
Lee, Seok-Young, 470n1
Lee, Thomas, 346n8
Lekus, Eric, 512n77
Leon, Mark, 598n20
Leonard, Bill, 14n, 27, 60n, 69, 81n, 101,
    173n, 180n, 190, 222n, 232, 491n, 511,
    536n, 557
Leonard, Declan, 557n55
Letterman, Judith, 513n124
Leung, Alicia, 372n42
Levin, Gregg, 179
Levinson, Edward, 386n4
Levi Strauss & Co., 12, 446
Lewin, Kurt, 292
Lewis, Jason, 306n69
Lewis, Philip, 470n24
Liebowitz, S. Jay, 307n107
Lierman, Bruce, 307n83
Lincoln Electric, 453
Linenberger, Patricia, 67n8
Lipold, Annmarie, 511n41
Lipsig, Ethan, 557n85
Lisko, Richard, 233n108
LKL Associates, Inc., 622
Locke, Edwin, 452

Lockheed Martin, 527, 528
Loess, Kurt H., 346n12
London, Manuel, 347n51
London House, Inc., 221
Longo Toyota, 60, 81
Losey, Michael, 27n2
Lotus Software, 83
Lowe, Kevin, 683n29
Lowry, Phillip, 264n74
Lucas, James M., 100n3
Lundell, Michael, 148n4
Luo, Sonjun, 471n55
Lurie, Mark, 599n65
Luthans, Fred, 425n17
Lyndaker, Marie, 232n96
Lyness, Karen, 372n39

Mabey, Christopher, 347n57
Macalar, Bill, 101n33, 189n1&n3
Macan, Therese, 264n83
MacDonald, J. Randal, 86, 101n31
MacDonald, Scott, 232n96,
    233n101&n102&n103, 512n84
Madigan, John, 351
Mael, Fred, 191n103
Mahoney, Joan, 684n64
Maier, Ayesha, 307n85
Maier, Norman, 288, 307n85
Maiorca, Joseph, 346n19
Making, Peter, 652n57
Mann, Everett, 69n98
Manning, Michael, 652n85
Mansour-Cole, Dana, 557n70
Manus, Bert, 74, 100n3
Mariani, Matthew, 148n13
Marion, Craig, 306n61
Markham, Steven, 472n88
Markoff, John, 189n7
Markowich, M. Michael, 511n24
Marks, Susan, 426n33, 473n133
Marlowe, Cynthia, 263n48
Marra, Janice, 651n38
Marriott, 180, 363, 482, 501, 583
Marshall, Walt, 288
Martin, Christopher, 244n, 262
Martin, David, 347n39, 371n1
Martinez, Michelle, 189n17, 190n54&n59
Martinko, Mark, 653n121
Martocchio, Joseph, 425n1&n27,
    426n46&n54, 427n85, 510n8, 511n64,
    512n108&n113
Maslow, Abraham, 439–440
Masterson, Suzanne, 556n30
Materna, Jessica, 598n57
Matsuoka, Hiroshi, 651n38
Matteson, Michael, 470n10
Matthes, K., 510n18

Matthews, Mike, 306n49
Matusewitch, Eric, 69n79
Mauborgne, Rene, 557n45
Maurer, Richard, 653n141&n145
Mayer, Mary, 232n65
Maynard, Chris, 264
Mayrhofer, Wolfgang, 684n73
McCabe, Darren, 599n73
McCall, Morgan, Jr., 684n64
McCarthy, Michael J., 556n37, 557n59
McCormick, Ernest J., 148n22
McCune, Jenny, 653n124
McCunney, R. J., 223
McDaniel, Ann, 69n118
McDaniel, Kim, 652n59
McDaniel, Michael, 233n109,
    262n1&n2&n6&n9&n30, 263n33
McDonald, James, Jr., 68n34
McDonald's, 281
McDonnell, Sharon, 27n37
McDonnell-Douglas, 47
McGann, Anthony, 346n17
McGovern, T. V., 263n41
McGregor, Douglas M., 470n10
MCI, 18
McIntyre, Nina, 471n52
McKay, Jim, 190n48
McKinsey & Co., 203
McLarney, William, 306n30
McNabb, Robert, 101n29, 426n55, 427n74
McNamara, Paul, 264
McNutt, Robert, 472n95
Meade, Jim, 109n23, 371n24, 512n118, 685n100
Meany, George, 563
Medland, F. F., 347n46
Mehta, Stephanie, 69n97
Meltzer, Mark, 426n34,
    472n96&n99&n100&n102&n111&n116
Melymuka, Kathleen, 372n44
Mendelow, Aubrey, 307n107
Mendelsohn, Susan, 230n19, 231n20
Mendenhall, Mark, 684n76
Men's Wearhouse, 275
Mercedes-Benz, 77, 138
Mercer, William M., Inc., 399
Mercer Human Resource Consulting, 438
Merck, 106
Meredith, Robyn, 190n48
Merrill Lynch, 11, 499, 520, 591
Metiom, Inc., 449
Metro Motors, 446
Meyer, David, 598n40
Meyer, Gary, 346n21
Miceli, Michael, 263n54
Michalak, Donald, 306n35
Michaluk, Dan, 306n69
Microsoft, 155, 168, 393, 620

Middendorf, Catherine, 264*n*83
Middlemist, R. Dennis, 512*n*99
Midvale Steel, 438
Miklas, Donald, 306*n*30
Miklaue, Matthew, 69*n*79
Miles, Raymond, 371*n*3
Milkovich, George, 425*n*18, 511*n*45
Miller, Joseph, 306*n*36
Miller, Marc, 108*n*10
Miller, William H., 148*n*27
Milliman, John, 683*n*26
Mills, Amy, 231*n*56
Mills, Daniel Quinn, 371*n*29
Minehan, Maureen, 425n16, 653*n*104
Ming, Jenny, 364
Mink, Mary, 109*n*16
Minorities Job Bank, 63
Mirabile, Richard, 149*n*35
Mishra, Aneil, 598*n*47
Mitchell, Kristin, 148*n*19
Moberg, David, 598*n*41
Mohr, Erica, 306*n*59
Mohrman, Susan, 307*n*92
Moncarz, Roger, 27*n*12&*n*17
Montebello, Anthony, 307*n*111
Mook, Jonathan, 511*n*43
Moore, Brian, 472*n*87
Moore, Linda, 190*n*94
Moran, John, 68*n*58
Morath, Ray, 191*n*103
Moravec, Milan, 149*n*38
Moretz, Sandy, 651*n*4
Morfopoulos, Richard, 148*n*19
Morgan, Hal, 27*n*22
Morgeson, Frederick, 148*n*10, 262*n*4,
    263*n*46&*n*56, 264*n*68&*n*70&*n*91
Morris, David, 371*n*30
Morris, Sara, 556*n*18
Morrisey, George, 100*n*5
Morrison, Katheryn, 230*n*19, 231*n*20
Morrow, Charlie, 307*n*110
Moskowitz, Rachel, 67*n*6
Motorola, 206, 661
Motowidlo, Stephen, 263*n*42
Muczyk, J. P., 306*n*38
Muhl, Charles, 557*n*65
Murdoch, Rupert, 74
Murphy, Kevin, 230*n*5&*n*7&*n*8&*n*9, 231*n*36,
    232*n*86, 262*n*14, 346*n*30
Murray, Brian, 426*n*51&*n*57, 427*n*64&*n*66
Murray, Kathleen, 512*n*76
Myers, Jeffrey, 651*n*13

Nagao, Denise, 262*n*24
Nakache, Patricia, 512*n*93
Napier, Nancy, 684*n*73
Nash, G. N., 306*n*38

Nash, James, 606, 651*n*6&*n*23, 652*n*52&*n*56
Nasser, Jacques, 16
Nathan, Arte, 194
National Technological University, 283
National Urban League, 63
NCNB, 364
NCR, 21
Neary, D. Bradford, 340, 347*n*67
Neeleman, David, 523, 524
Neiman Marcus, 13
Nelson, Bob, 471*n*41&*n*75
Nelson, Carnot, 263*n*48
Nelson, Emily, 557*n*83
Nelson, James, 472*n*116
Nelson, Katherine, 556*n*11
Neveu, Bob, 232*n*80
Newman, Jerry, 511*n*45
News Corporation, 74
New York Life Insurance, 368
New York Stock Exchange (NYSE), 548
Nextel Communications, 446
Ng, Cheuk Fan, 263*n*41
Nicholson, Gilbert, 231*n*34&*n*54, 232*n*78
Nicholson, Nigel, 472*n*126
Nickel, James, 471*n*73
Niehoff, Brian, 231*n*45
Nighswonger, Todd, 651*n*5&*n*39,
    652*n*75&*n*87, 653*n*95
Nissan Motors, 140, 561, 590
Nohria, Nitin, 307*n*95
Norris, Floyd, 556*n*20
Nortel Networks, 446
Northam, Melissa, 512*n*87
Northrop Grumman Corp., 499
Northrup, Herbert, 598*n*56&*n*58
Northwest Airlines, 578–579
Norwest Corporation, 21
Nowack, Kenneth, 306*n*79, 347*n*56
Nucor Corp., 465–466
Nutt, Paul, 101*n*10
NuView, Inc., 676
Nye, David, 69*n*95

Oakite Company, 449
Obdyke, Louis, 653*n*140
O'Connell, Bill, 471*n*59
O'Connell, Brian, 306*n*76
O'Connell, Joseph, 512*n*83
O'Connor, Robert, 683*n*23
Office Depot, 102
Office Max, 102
O'Leary, Brian, 204
Olson, Craig, 510*n*6
Olson, Howard, 148*n*9
Olson, Madeline Hess, 455, 472
O'Neal, Sondra, 426*n*30, 471*n*73
O'Neill, Ann. M., 233*n*105

Ones, Denize, 347*n*48
Optima Air Filter, 146–147
Oracle Corp., 13
Orlando, Richard, 69*n*104
Osborne, Richard, 556*n*7
Osterman, P., 512*n*94
Ostrosky, Joyce, 556*n*42
Otte, Fred, 351, 353, 357, 371*n*23
Outback Steakhouse, 203–204
Overman, Stephenie, 684*n*79
Overton, Randall, 231*n*33
Owsley, Cynthia, 651*n*38
Ozeki, Cynthia, 683*n*2

Pacific Gas & Electric Company (PG&E),
    286–287
Palmer, David, 252, 264*n*78&*n*80&*n*82
PalmPilot, 620–621
Panepento, Peter, 190*n*48
Pantazis, Cynthia, 306*n*72
Papa John's, 76, 77
Pappas, Michael, 69*n*91
Paquet, Basil, 307*n*111
Parent, Kevin, 426*n*63, 427*n*65
Park Avenue Bank, 284
Parker, Gary, 684*n*77
Parmalat, 18
Parmenter, Eric, 470, 510*n*4&*n*9
Parsons, Charles, 306*n*53
Patterson, Maureen, 231*n*36
Paula, Robert, 231*n*45
Payne, Dinah, 599*n*60
Payne, Richard, 383, 384, 387*n*17
PC Information Technology Services, 506
Peak, Martha, 307*n*87
Pedone, Rose-Robin, 471*n*35
Pell, Arthur, 263*n*65, 264*n*67&*n*69
Pemerl, Dan, 346*n*6
PeopleSoft, 107, 326
PepsiCo, 76, 362, 397, 505
Perrew, Pamela, 557*n*88
Peters, Lawrence, 347*n*35
Petersen, Dan, 651*n*30
Petersen, Donald, 557*n*50
Petit, Andre, 109*n*20
Pfau, Bruce, 347*n*60
Pfeffer, Jeffrey, 425*n*12
Pflug, Warner, 597*n*11
Phatak, Arvind, 683*n*39&*n*41&*n*42&*n*45,
    684*n*65&*n*80
Pickard, Jane, 471*n*73
Pickering, Chris, 27*n*34
Pieperl, Maury, 347*n*62, 371*n*15
Pierce, F. David, 651*n*27
Pierer, Heinrich, 683*n*1
Piktialis, Diane, 27*n*22
Pilla, David, 512*n*104

Pillsbury, 536
Pinto, Michael, 651n3
Piskorski, Thomas, 512n72
Pitney Bowes, 504
Pitt-Catsouphes, Marcie, 190n79
Pittman, Jeffrey, 233n108
Piturro, Marlene, 557n81
Pivec, Mary, 599n73
Pizza Hut, 76
Plachy, Roger, 148n13, 435n1
Ployhart, Robert, 230n15
Poe, Andrea, 471n47, 557n64
Pohley, Katja, 231n58
Poignand, Courtney, 232n100
Porter, Michael, 77, 78, 101n11
Porter, Tom, 189n12
Posthuma, Richard, 262n4, 263n47&n56,
    264n68&n70&n91
Potter, Gordon, 470n1
Pottruck, David, 293
Powell, Gary, 371n36
Prahalad, C. K., 78
Prencipe, Loretta, 598n20
Prewett-Livingston, Amelia J., 263n52
Prezant, Fran, 263n58
Prichard, Robert, 470n15
Pringle, David, 101n7
Procter & Gamble, 76, 397, 548, 656, 661,
    662
Psychological Assessment Resources, 198
Pucik, Vladimir, 683n8
Puncochar, Paul, 652n72
Pursell, Elliot, 264n71&n75

Quinones, Miguel, 230n37, 231n58

Radebaugh, Lee, 683n24&n38&n40&n43
Radio Shack, 493
Ragins, Belle Rose, 371n17
Railton, W. Scott, 651n14
Raimondo, Tony, 229
Ralston, David, 683n7
Raphel, Todd, 307n113
Rasmussen, Keith, Jr., 263n41
Rau, John, 387n15
Raytheon Company, 522
Reasor, Azure, 27n12&n17
Recruitsoft, 177
Reda, James, 426n37
Regini, Marino, 684n84
Reilly, Anne, 470n2
Reilly, Richard, 347n54
Reilly, Robert, 472n82
Reis, Matthew, 306n48
Reitz, Diana, 513n129
Rekus, John, 624, 652n51
Remick, Helen, 427n82

Renn, Robert, 346n10
Rexroad, Max, 556n42
Rice, Charles, 69n97&n109, 557n73&n77
Richard, J. E., 684n82
Richardson, Reed, 580–581, 598n49, 599n63
Richter, Andrew, 427n74
Riggs, Matt, 230n11
Robbins, Howard, 599n73
Roberson, Loriann, 556n16
Roberson, Quinetta, 551
Roberts, Bill, 27n33, 109n21, 189n32,
    557n63, 684n97
Roberts, Della, 653n144
Roberts, Karen, 683n2
Robins, Gary, 262n21
Robinson, Edward, 232n67
Robinson, Karen, 598n14
Robinson, Robert, 68n22
Robinson, Sandra, 231n29
Rockwell, 58
Rodas, Mary, 179
Rodgers, Douglas, 262n19
Rodgers, Johanna, 512n80
Rodriguez, Andrea, 263n58
Rohm & Haas, 622
Romano, Michael, 597n3
Roosevelt, Franklin Delano, 561
Rosato, Donna, 653n133
Rosen, Dean, 68n32
Ross, Timothy, 472n87&n94
Rosset, Allison, 306n59
Rossler, Paul, 472n91
Roth, Philip, 263n53
Roth, William, 148n19
Rotundo, Maria, 67n12
Rowden, Robert, 307n112
Rowe, Patricia, 263n36
Royal Dutch Shell, 666
Rubin, Robert, 264n86
Rupinski, Melvin, 307n110
Ryan, Ann Marie, 230n1&n14&n15, 232n75,
    663, 683n31
Ryan, Nancy, 557n82
Ryan, Richard, 471n33
Rymph, R. Douglas, 556n16
Rynes, Sara, 190n57

Saba Software, 273
Sack, Steven Mitchell, 230n4
Sackett, Paul, 232n88
Sahl, Robert J., 435n1
Salasko, Elizabeth, 189n44
SalesDriver, 449
Salgado, Jesus, 231n46
Salopek, Jennifer, 306n43
Salters, Larry, 387n17
Sanchez, Juan, 347n36

Sand, Robert, 651n15
Sandberg, Jorgen, 148n24
Sandlin, P., 371n21
Sands, S. Scott, 471n64
Santora, Joyce, 306n45
Sapper, Arthur, 651n12
Sarathi, Parth, 264n67
Sarchione, Charles, 207
Saruwatari, Lewis, 263n48
Saturn Corporation, 364
Saudi Petrol Chemical, 622
Sauer, Robert, 684n84
Saulney, Susan, 189n38
Scalia, Antonin, 33
Scanlong, Joseph, 454
Scarpello, Vida, 510n1, 511n44
Schein, Edgar, 375–378, 386n8
Schelberg, Nei, 512n117
Schell, Michael, 684n57
Schepers, Donald, 557n86
Scherer, Lisa, 35
Schmidt, Frank, 148n7, 232n89,
    347n48
Schmidt, Jacqueline, 306n36
Schmidt, Jeffrey, 82, 101n20
Schminke, Marshall, 556n17
Schmit, Mark, 230n14
Schmitt, Neal, 231n32&n56
Schneider, Benjamin, 307n105
Schneider, Sondra, 263n48
Schott, Jennifer, 472n120
Schramm, Jennifer, 189n10
Schroeder, Erica, 306n49
Schroeder, Michael, 27n11
Schroll, Craig, 653n146
Schubert, Margaret, 306n65
Schuler, Randall, 683n9
Schultz, Duane, 262n5, 306n38, 651n37
Schultz, James, 109n20
Schultz, Sydney, 262n5, 306n38, 615n37
Schumacher, Edward, 425n10
Schumann, Paul, 556n2
Schwab, Donald, 346n18
Scott, K. Dow, 472n88
Scott, Lawrence, 652n57
Scott, Miriam, 512n84
Scott, Susanne, 557n70
Scott, W. E., 307n102
Scullion, Hugh, 684n73
Sculnick, Michael W., 69n115
Seabrook, Kathy, 652n66
Seaman, Richard, 471n72
Seattle First National Bank, 498
Segal, Jonathon, 598n35
Seggal, Jonathan, 27n30
Selmer, Jan, 371n7, 372n42, 683n54
Semler, Richard, 472n117

Sesil, James, 472*n*81
Shafer, Richard, 101*n*32
Shaffer, Margaret, 683*n*51
Shaffer, Mark, 684*n*58
Shaller, Elliot H., 68*n*32&*n*34&*n*49
Shand, Dawne, 427*n*70
Shannon, Jones, 101*n*33, 189*n*1&*n*3
Shapiro, Carolyn, 512*n*106
Shapiro, Lawrence, 232*n*77
Shaw, James, 470*n*5
Shaw, Jason, 473*n*131
Shaw, Kathy, 148*n*27
Shay, Robin, 371*n*32
Shein, Esther, 471*n*34
Shell Oil, 661
Sherman, Ellen, 306*n*41
Shippmann, Jeffrey, 149*n*32
Shofer, Charles David, 262*n*14
Short, Larri, 510*n*11
Shotland, Allison, 307*n*112
Siegel, James, 386*n*11
Siegel, Jonathan, 346*n*3
Siegel, Laurence, 231*n*36&*n*57
Siegel, Phyllis, 684*n*61
Siemens, 99–100, 277
Siemens Stromberg-Carlson, 276–277
Silbergeld, Arthur, 512*n*75
Silicon Graphics, 284
Silverhart, Todd, 263*n*34
Silverman, Rachel Emma, 231*n*27
Simmons, Annette, 347*n*38&*n*63
Simmons, Anthony W., 263*n*38
Simon, Steve, 307*n*86
Sims, E. Norman, 189*n*39
Skarlicki, Daniel, 556*n*9
Slack, Kim, 307*n*83
Slater Brothers, 550
Sloane, Arthur, 598*n*13&*n*18&*n*48,
    599*n*61&*n*66
Slocum, John, Jr., 683*n*9
Small, Bruce, 262*n*11&*n*27, 264*n*72
Smith, Adam, 138
Smith, Brian, 347*n*64
Smith, Jack, 148*n*8
Smith, Robert D., 189*n*2
Smith, S. L., 652*n*66
Smith, Sandy, 652*n*57
Smith, Sean, 511*n*46, 651*n*24
Smith, William, 472*n*85
Smither, James, 307*n*90, 347*n*54
Smith-Jentsch, Kimberly A., 305*n*15
Smith & Wesson, 279
Snow, Charles, 371*n*3
Sohn, Rebecca, 386*n*1
Solem, Allen, 307*n*85
Solomon, Charlene, 307*n*83, 652*n*86,
    683*n*5&*n*12, 684*n*56&*n*57

Solomonson, Andrew, 346*n*27, 347*n*28
Son, Byoungho, 346*n*3
Soonhee, Kim, 189*n*28
Sorohan, Erica Gordon, 387*n*18
Sosin, Betty, 471*n*39
Southwest Airlines, 78, 79, 523
Sovereign, Kenneth, 27*n*29, 54, 69*n*80, 159,
    189*n*13, 231*n*21, 305*n*21, 347*n*40, 425*n*7,
    557*n*68, 653*n*107
Spec's Music, 293
Spector, Burt, 307*n*95&*n*101
Spencer, Cassie, 347*n*49
Spencer, James, 231*n*39
Sperling, Richard, 426*n*50
Spreitzer, Gretchen, 598*n*47, 684*n*64
Spychalski, Annette, 231*n*58
Srinivasan, Dhinu, 470*n*1
Stack, George, Jr., 148*n*28
Stahl, Gunther, 684*n*76
Staiman, Jeff, 472*n*105
Stanton, Jeffrey, 346*n*25
Stanton Corporation, 221, 222
Starkman, Paul, 148*n*18
State Capital Credit Union, 107
Steinbrink, John, 471*n*58
Steiner, Dirk, 230*n*16
Sterkel-Powell, Karen, 306*n*46
Stetzer, Adam, 651*n*34
Stevens, C., 189*n*36, 263*n*46
Stevens, Larry, 306*n*69
Stewart, Thomas, 189*n*24
Stiffler, Mark, 471*n*48
Stivarius, Teresa Butler, 232*n*83
Stockham, Sharon, 222
Stoneman, Bill, 262*n*10
Strasse, Tom, 506–507
Strauss, Susan, 262*n*18
Strickland, A. J., III, 101*n*35
Stroh, Linda, 108*n*6&*n*13, 470*n*2
Sudbury, Deborah, 69*n*74, 263*n*60
Sullivan, Michael, 520
Sullivan, Robert, 306*n*30
Sullivan, Sherry, 371*n*1&*n*4
Sundstrom, Eric, 652*n*84
Sun Microsystems, 319, 355, 463, 548
Sunoo, Brenda, 511*n*61, 68*n*32, 189*n*42,
    598*n*55, 652*n*80
SurfControl, 6
Sutcliffe, Virginia, 652*n*63&*n*65
Sutherland, Valerie, 652*n*57
Sutter Health Corporation, 176–177,
    218–219
Sweeney, John, 563
Sweetser, Susan, 190*n*88

Tahbanainen, Maria, 346*n*5
Tahmincioglu, Eve, 653*n*130

Tammaro, Pat, 263*n*59
Tannenbaum, Scott, 307*n*112
Taussig, Reed, 472*n*126
Taylor, Benjamin, 597*n*12
Taylor, Frederick, 138, 442
Taylor, Jason, 597*n*6
Taylor, Paul, 262*n*11&*n*27, 264*n*72
Taylor, Sully, 684*n*73
Tenneco, 620
Tepper, Bennett, 556*n*15
Terpstra, David, 425*n*21
Terris, William, 232*n*84
Test, Alan, 307*n*85
Texas Instruments, 284, 446
Thacker, James, 283, 305*n*23, 306*n*55&*n*60
Thermacore, 454
Thomas, Barry W., 472*n*90
Thomas, Stephen, 425*n*20
Thomas International USA, 213
Thompkins, James, 68*n*60
Thompson, Allison, 189*n*41
Thompson, Arthur, Jr., 101*n*35
Thompson, Cary, 472*n*105
Thompson, Donna, 372*n*39
Thornburg, Linda, 262*n*19
Thornton, George, III, 347*n*49, 371*n*30
Thrutchley, Christopher, 67*n*10
Tichy, Noel, 307*n*98, 683*n*8
Tiffin, Joseph, 148*n*22
Tillett, Scott, 598*n*20
Timberman, Woodrow, 599*n*68
Tinsley, H. E., 263*n*41
Tobin, Nona, 108*n*7, 425*n*27
Tormey, Douglas, 426*n*35
Toscano, Gus, 653*n*109
Toulouse, Chad, 12
Towers Perrin, 476
Toyota, 10, 451, 529, 590
Tracey, William R., 68*n*50
Tramer, Harriet, 513*n*127
Traver, Holly, 307*n*112
TreebaHire™, 245
Trevino, Linda, 556*n*10&*n*11&*n*28&*n*33&
    *n*35&*n*40
Triad International Management, 31
Trilogy Software, Inc., 187–188
Tripathy, Madan Mohan, 652*n*91
Trumbo, D., 262*n*2
Trump, Donald, 25
Truss, Catherine, 101*n*15
TRW, 340–341
Tschirhart, Mary, 598*n*47
TTW, Inc., 339
Tucker, David, 263*n*36
Tucker, Donna, 230*n*10
Tucker, Robert, 149*n*38
Tulgan, Bruce, 472*n*125

Tupperware, 576
Turban, Daniel, 263n66
Turk, Harry, 512n86
Turnasella, Ted, 347n28, 470n7
Turner, Diane, 685n99
Turner, W. Kirk, 67n10
Turner Broadcasting, 536
Tyler, Kathryn, 231n36, 305n17, 306n44, 652n77, 684n70
Tziner, Aharon, 346n20

UCSD Healthcare, 269
Ulrich, Dave, 87, 88, 92, 101n27&n34
Ulrich, L., 262n2
United Airlines, 49
United Auto Workers, 498, 583
U.S. Datatrust, 525
United Steel Workers Union, 454
United Technologies Corp., 517
Upton, David, 101n12, 307n93
U.S. Armed Forces, 282
Useem, Jerry, 512n92

Van Buren, Martin, 683n28
VandeWalle, Don, 305n25
Vanguard, 368, 493
Van Winkle, William, 513n125
Vasilopoulos, Nicholas, 347n54
Vater, John, Jr., 510n10
Velasquez, Manuel, 556n4
Veliotis, Stan, 684n83
Velshi, Ali, 108n11
Vencel, Keith, 177
Verser, Gertrude Casselman, 288
Vest, Michael, 40n, 68
Vettori, F. L., 306n38
Vijayan, Jaikumar, 557n71
Villanova, Peter, 347n43
Vincze, Julian, 100n2
Virick, Meghan, 471n56
VisionPoint Productions, 280
Viswesvaran, Chockalingam, 347n48
Voelker, Keith, 684n84
Volkswagen, 180
Volvo, 77
von der Embse, Thomas, 232n71
Von Hippel, Courtney, 471n74
Vuutari, Vesa, 346n5

Wackenhut Corporation, 221
Wade, Nicholas, 425n19
Wagner, Rick, 80–81
Wagner, William, 230n38
Wah, Louisa, 148n12
Waldroop, James, 375, 376, 377, 386n5

Walker, Garrett, 86, 101n31
Walley, Edwin, 264n85
Wal-Mart, 13, 40–41, 75, 76, 77, 79, 400, 446
Walsh, W. Bruce, 230n6&n12
Walter, Brian, 108n9
Walter, Kate, 556n4
Wanberg, Connie, 293n, 307
Wanderg, Connie, 557n69
Wanek, James, 232n88
Wang Laboratories, 498
Ward, Mathew, 472n111
Wareham, John, 190n53, 387n13
Warner, Daniel, 653n105
Warner, Jack, 347n49
Warner, Jim, 371n19
Warner, Melanie, 100n4
Watkins, Thomas, 598n50
Watson Wyatt Data Services, 399
Way, Philip, 27n24
Weaver, Gary, 556n13&n28&n33&n35& n39&n40
Weaver, Natasha, 305n2
Webb, David, 652n60
Weber, Carline, 426n63, 427n65
WebMD, 74, 75
Weekley, Jeff, 231n55, 232n60, 264n71
Weeks, Bill, 471n63
Wehrenberg, Stephen B., 306n30
Weil, James, 511n57
Wein, Ruth, 69n77
Weinberg, Ronald, 307n111
Weiner, Nan, 427n69
Weinstein, Steve, 557n89
Weintraub, Robert, 306n34
Weitz, Joseph, 263n38
Welch, John (Jack), 314, 346n11
Wellner, Allison, 190n84, 426n44
Wells, Samatha, 232n96
Wells, Susan, 27n28, 189n29, 190n49, 371n38
Wells Fargo, 21, 82
Werner, Jon, 307n86
Westman, Mina, 652n92
Wexley, Kenneth, 305n9&n26, 306n49, 307n108
Wheatley, Marsha, 175
Whitcomb, Chris, 307n82
White, Louis, 307n103
White, Richard, Jr., 232n85
White, William, 426n40&n44
Whitfield, Keith, 101n29, 427n74
Wiener, Richard, 67n7
Wiersma, Uco, 346n18
Wiley, Carolyn, 305n4
Wilk, Steffanie, 231n28
Wilkinson, Margaret, 263n41

Wilkinson, Stephanie, 109n15
William, Sonja, 471n56
Williams, Charles, 347n29
Williamson, Laura Gollub, 262n3&n7&n28, 264n78&n79
Williamson, Mickey, 306n52
Wilson, Cynthia, 237
Wilson, Midge, 347n32
Wilson, Thomas, 470n25
Wimer, Scott, 347n61
Windau, Janaice, 653n109
Wingrove, Clinton, 346n2&n4&n15, 347n30
Wiscombe, Janet, 109n16, 473n132
Witney, Fred, 597n12, 598n13&n19&n48, 599n61&n66
Witt, L. A., 231n51
Wolf, Steven, 347n47
Wonderlic Personnel Test, Inc., 198, 204
Wong, Nancy, 683n4
Wood, Robert E., 472n99
Wood, Russ, 651n41
Woolridridge, Weart, 470n10
Wooten, Kevin, 27n31, 307n103, 556n3
WorldCom, 520, 530
Wright, Al, 427n90
Wright, Thomas, 230n18, 556n29
Wrigley Company, 179
Wuittner, Jeremy, 471n53
Wyatt, Lindsay, 511n66&n69
Wymer, John, III, 69n74, 263n60
Wyse, Rodney, 232n71
Wysong, Marco, 653n98

Xerox Corp., 495

Yager, Edwin, 306n35
Yahoo!, 397
Yandrick, Rudy, 512n100, 556n14
Yates, L. G., 347n46
Yavas, Ugur, 346n12
Yerkes, Leslie, 471n43
Yeung, Sally, 100n3
Yo, Y. Paul, 683n25
Yong, Jane Patterson, 232n75
York, Kenneth, 67n21
Yukl, Gary, 346n7

Zall, Milton, 512n73, 557n53
Zarandona, Joseph, 557n80
Zeigler, James, 651n43
Zimmerman, Eileen, 232n73, 306n71, 471n68, 557n56
Zohar, Dov, 652n46

Subject Index

Absence management, 489
Absenteeism, 584
Accidental death and dismemberment
    coverage, 487
Accidents
    causes of, 611–615
    prevention of, 615–623
Achievement tests, 207–208
Acquired immunodeficiency syndrome
    (AIDS), 40, 632, 676
Action learning, 286–287
Action research, 294, 295
Adaptability screening, 668–669
Adverse action, 219
Adverse impact, 46–48
Advertising, 163–166
    answering, 381–382
    constructing, 164–165
    effectiveness, 165–166
Affirmative action, 31, 32, 60
    equal employment opportunity versus, 60
    steps in, 61–62
Age, as a bona fide occupational qualification,
    48
Age Discrimination in Employment Act
    (1967), 31
    age as bona fide occupational qualification
        and, 48
    alternative dispute resolutions and, 182
    benefits and, 478
    compensation and, 392
    multinational employment and, 674
    promotions and, 360–361
Agency shop, 562
Agreeableness, 207
AIDA (attention, interest, desire, action), 164
Albemarle Paper Company v. Moody, 38
Alcoholism, 625–628
Aligned reward strategy, 395
Alternation ranking method, 317
Alternative dispute resolution, 58, 182
Alternative staffing, 170
American Association of Retired Persons
    (AARP), 179
American Federation of Labor (AFL), 560
American Federation of Labor-Congress of
    Industrial Organizations (AFL-CIO), 563
American Federation of State, County and
    Municipal Employees, 590
American Federation of Teachers, 563, 590
American Postal Workers Union, 585

American Psychological Association, 201
    Ethical Principles of Psychologists and Code
        of Conduct, 201
    Standards for Educational and Psychological
        Testing, 32
American Society for Training and
    Development, 277
American Society of Chartered Life
    Underwriters, 520–521
Americans with Disabilities Act (ADA)
    (1990)
    AIDS and, 40, 632
    benefits and, 479
    compensation and, 392
    compliance of job descriptions, 130
    employee screening and, 217
    employer obligations and, 42–44
    employment interview and, 250
    entrepreneurs and, 53
    health insurance and, 486
    mental impairments and, 41–42
    multinational employers and, 674
    notice forms for, 102
    personality tests and, 207
    physical examinations and, 223
    in practice, 42
    qualified individuals and, 40
    reasonable accommodation and, 40–41
    safety-related screening and, 617
    smoking and, 633
    workers' compensation and, 485
    workplace violence and, 637
Annual bonus, 456, 459–463
Applicant disability, employment interview
    and, 250
Applicant tracking, 176
Application forms
    legal issues and, 181–182
    to predict job performance, 186
    purpose of, 181–182
Application system providers (ASPs), 164,
    219
Appraisal(s)
    avoiding problems with, 329–331
    of expatriate managers, 673
    in practice, 337–338
    soft, 314
    by subordinates, 333
Appraisal interviews, 236, 334–339
    checklist during, 339
    methods of, 336–337

types of, 335–336
Apprenticeship training, 276–277
Aptitude tests, 205
Arbitration, 581
    binding, 581
    interest, 581
    mandatory, 57–58, 182
    nonbinding, 581
    rights, 581
Area wage surveys, 398
Asbestos exposure, 625
Association for Women in Science, 63
At-risk variable pay plans, 456
Attractiveness, effect on interviews, 248–249
Audiovisual-based training, 280
Australia, performance appraisal in, 660
Authority, 6
    implied, 7
    line, 7
Authorization cards, 570
Automated applicant tracking systems and
    applicant screening, 218–219
Automated video-based interview systems,
    245
Automating health care plan administration,
    488
Autonomy, 378

Background information, 219
Background investigations, 213–217
Bakke v. Regents of the University of California,
    62–63
Balance sheet approach, formulating
    expatriate pay in, 671–672
Bargaining, 580–581
    good faith, 578–579
    items in, 578, 579
Bargaining stages, 579
Bargaining unit, 571
Base pay, 410
Basic testing concepts, 195
    reliability, 195
    validity, 195–197
Behavior, 299
    factors shaping ethical, 519–524
    interviewer, 249
    in job analysis, 112
    nonverbal, 247–248
Behavioral interviews, 237
Behaviorally anchored rating scales, 322–324
Behavioral science knowledge, 294

713

Behavior-based safety, 620
Behavior modeling, 289
Benchmark jobs, 398
Benefits, 476–479
    cafeteria approach to, 500, 503–504
    for contingent workers, 491
    executive, 410
    family-friendly, 497–499
    flexible, 500–506
    insurance, 485
    job-related, 498–499
    mental health, 488–489
    for part-time workers, 491
    retirement, 491–495
    supplemental pay, 479
    supplemental unemployment, 485
    survivor's or death, 491
Benefits management systems, 495
Benefits purchasing alliances, 488
*Best International Human Resource
    Management Practices Survey*, 659
Bias, 329
    personal, 331
Big five personality dimensions, 207
Binding arbitration, 581
Biometrics, 537
Bona fide occupational qualification (BFOQ),
    48–49
    age as, 48
    gender as, 49
    national origin as, 49
    religion as, 48–49
Bonuses, 442
    annual, 456, 459–463
Boss's influence on ethical behavior, 520–521
Boundaryless organization, 139
Boycotts, 583
Broadbanding, 415–416
Buckley Amendment (1974), 215
Bumping/layoff procedures, 548
Burden of proof, 38
Bureau of Labor Statistics (BLS), 157, 398
Burk v. California Association of Realtors, 65
Burlington Industries v. Ellerth, 34
Burnout, 630
Business-level/competitive strategy, 76
Business necessity, 49
Business proficiencies, 16
Business-to-consumer (B2C) learning portals,
    285
Business-to-employee (B2E) portals, 285
Bypassing representative, 578

Cafeteria approach, 500, 503–504
California Energy Commission, 74
*California Federal Savings and Loan Association
    v. Guerra*, 32

California Psychological Inventory, 207, 221
Call center, 19
CALPERS (California), 478
Candidate-order error, 247
Candidates, interviewing, 256
Capital, human, 12–13, 17
Career(s)
    defined, 350
    identifying directions in, 374
    making choices in, 372–379
    today, 350–351
Career anchors, 386
    assessing, 378
    identifying, 375–378
Career coaches, 356
Career counselors, 383
Career cycle, 386
Career development, 350, 351–352
    commitment-oriented, 364–366
    innovative corporate, initiatives, 355–358
    roles in, 352–358
Career management, 350
    basics of, 350–352
    career choices in, 372–379
    employee commitment and, 363–366
    enhancing diversity through, 361–363
    job search in, 379–386
Career-oriented appraisals, 355, 365–366
Career planning, 350, 351
    integrating into the employer's human
        resource information system, 358
    workshops for, 356
Career stage, identifying, in career
        management, 372–373
Career success teams, 356
Career tracks, instituting, 363
Carpal tunnel syndrome, 632
Case management, 486
Case study method, 287
Cash balance pension plan, 495
Cash plans, 453
Catastrophic leaves, 482
Centers for Disease Control (CDC), 625
Central tendency, 328
Certification, SHRM, 18, 22
    defined, 690
    denial and revocation, 690
    desirability of, 690
    purpose and use of, 690
Certification Handbook Recertification Guide,
    690–692
Child labor provisions, 391
China, People's Republic of China
    human resource challenges in, 656
    human resource management in, 657
    human resource practices in, 660
    pay incentives in, 661

performance appraisal in, 660
    personnel selection in, 659
Citation, OSHA, 604, 606, 607
Civil Rights Act (1866), 30
Civil Rights Act (1964), 53, 256
    Title VII of the, 30–31, 42, 272, 331, 360,
        390, 590, 637
Civil Rights Act (1991), 33, 38–40, 62, 256
Civil Service Commission, 590
Civil Service Reform Act (1978), 591
Claims-tracking software, 623
Closed shop, 562
Coaching method, 275
Coaching/understudy approach, 286
Codetermination, 658
Cognitive abilities, tests of, 204–205
Collective bargaining, 563, 577–584
    alternatives in, 583–584
    arbitration and, 581
    contract agreement in, 584
    defined, 577–578
    good faith in, 578–579
    hints in, 580–581
    impasses in, 581
    items in, 579
    mediation and, 581
    negotiating team in, 579
    stages in, 579
    strikes and, 582–583
College recruiting, 173–174
Combination plan, 448–449
Commission plan, 448
Commitment-oriented career development,
    364–366
Communications, two-way, 529–530
Communications Workers of America, 592
Company security, 641–642
Comparable worth, 418
Competency-based pay, 412–415
    defined, 412–413
    job analysis, 140–143
    in practice, 413–414
    pros, cons, and results, 414–415
    reasons for using, 413
Compensation
    automating planning process, 421
    for expatriates, 671–673
    job analysis information in, 112–113
    laws on, 390–395
    strategic, 417–418
    union influences on decisions, 394
Compensation factors, 400–401
Compensation surveys, use of Internet for, 399
Competencies, 140, 412
    examples of, 141
    measuring, 359
    promotion and, 358–359

Competency analysis, reasons for using, 140–141

Competency-based appraisals, 317

Competency-based job analysis, 140–143
comparing traditional versus, 141–142

Competitive advantage, 76–77
human resources and, 79–80

Comprehensive Test of Nonverbal Intelligence, 205

Compressed workweeks, 505

Computer-based training (CBT), 281–282, 283, 691–692

Computer-interactive testing, 204

Computerized business planning software, 77

Computerized forecast, 155

Computerized information systems, 156

Computerized interviews, 243–245

Computerized job evaluation, 404–405

Computerized performance appraisal, 326–327

Computerized tools, 616

Computer-related health problems, 630–632

Computers and benefits administration, 504

Concurrent validation, 198

Conscientiousness, 207

Consolidated Omnibus Budget Reconciliation Act (COBRA), 489, 504

Consolidation, 76

Constructive discharge, 540

Content validity, 196–197, 199

Contingency-based recruiters, 171

Contingent workers, 167–170
benefits for, 491

Continuous improvement, 311

Contracts
in collective bargaining, 584
employment, 519, 659
yellow dog, 563

Contrast error, 247

Controlled experimentation, 299

Cooperative line and staff human resource management, 8–9

Coordinative function, 7

Core plus option plans, 504

Corporate campaign, 583

Corporate campus, 356

Corporate-level strategy, 76

Corporate universities, 289

Cost-containment specialists, 487

Cost-inefficient plans, eliminating, 489

Cost leadership, 77

Cost-of-living adjustments, 394, 396

Cost-reduction strategy, 462

Counseling
outplacement, 544
preretirement, 368

Covenant of good faith exception, 538

Covered employment losses, 547

CRA (1991), 52

Crawford Small Parts Dexterity, 205

Creativity, 377–378

Credit unions, 496

Criteria, 196, 197

Criterion validity, 196, 197, 199

Critical incident method, 321–322

Cross-country differences, 660

Cross-cultural sensitivity, 280

Cultural change, 290, 292

Cultural factors, human resource management and, 657

Culture, organizational, 523–524

Cycle, 117

Data security, 641

Data warehouse, 20

Davis-Bacon Act (1931), 390

Debit cards, 503–504

Decertification elections, 576–577

Decline stage in career management, 373, 386

Deductible formula, 459

Defense of Marriage Act (2004), 499

Deferred profit-sharing plans, 453, 493

Defined benefit plans, 492

Defined contribution health care plans, 488

Defined contribution plans, 492, 493

Dejobbing, 137, 139

Demographics, workforce, 13

Depression, employee, 630

Desert Palace Inc. v. Costa, 40

Development practices, global differences and similarities in, 660

Dictionary of Occupational Titles, 129

Differentiation, 77

Dilatory tactics, 578

Direct financial payments, 390

Direct hiring, 168

Directive interviews, 236–237

Disability insurance, 486–490, 487

Disability payments, 491

Disabled, recruiting, 180–181

Disciplinary action, 596

Disciplinary fairness, 516

Disciplinary systems, 527

Discipline
comparing males and females in situations, 534
nonpunitive, 535

Discrimination
defenses against allegations of, 45–52
employment, 361
mandatory arbitration of claims in, 57–58
reverse, 62–63

Discrimination in Employment Act (1967), 53

Discriminatory practice defenses, 50–52

Disease management, 489

Dismissals
grounds for, 538–540
managing, 537–550

Disparate impact, 38–39, 45, 200

Disparate rejection rates, 46–47

Disparate treatment, 39, 45

Distance training, 270, 283–285

Distributive justice, 518

Diversification corporate strategy, 76

Diversity
enhancing, through career management, 361–363
measuring, 61
in workforce, 178–181

Diversity management, 58–60

Diversity training, 280

Domestic partner benefits, 499

Downsizing, 547
adjusting to, 548–550

Drug Free Workplace Act (1988), 224, 628

Drug testing, 223–224

Dual employment, 168–169

Early retirement windows, 494

Ebola virus, 625

Economic Growth and Tax Relief Reconciliation Act (2001), 477, 492

Economic strike, 582

Economic systems, human resource management and, 657–658

Elder care, 498

E-learning, 285

Elections, decertification, 576–577

Electronic Communications Privacy Act (1986), 536, 641

Electronic eavesdropping, 536

Electronic performance monitoring (EPM), 326–327

Electronic performance support systems (EPSS), 282

Emotional stability/neuroticism, 207

Employee(s)
advocacy for, 7
compensation for, 390
dealing with angry, 636–637
defining goals and work efforts of, 312–313
depression of, 630
disciplining, 531
dismissing violent, 636
expatriate, 397
improved screening of, 634–635
privacy of, 535–537, 641–642
retention/dismissal of, 636
rights of, 566
role in career development, 353–355

Employee(s) *(continued)*
  safety of, 602
  safety responsibilities and rights of, 607–610
  testing and selection, 212
Employee Assistance Programs (EAPs), 496
Employee commitment, career management
    and, 363–366
Employee discipline, privacy and, 531–537
Employee handbook, 268
Employee incentive programs, 442–447
Employee leasing, 506–507
Employee orientation, 268–269
Employee participation
  in safety programs, 620
  unions and, 593–594
Employee Polygraph Protection Act (1988),
    220
Employee portal, 20
Employee qualification briefs, 359
Employee recognition programs, 442–447
Employee Reliability Inventory (ERI), 617
Employee Retirement Income Security Act
    (ERISA) (1974), 391–392, 453, 477, 493,
    494
Employee selection, work sampling for,
    208–209
Employee stock ownership plan (ESOP),
    453–454, 493
Employee transportation, 498
Employer Retirement Income Security Act
    (1974), 391
Employers
  rights of, 567
  role of, in career development, 355
  safety responsibilities and rights of, 607–610
  Web sites of, 383
Employer-sponsored dental plans, 486
Employment agencies, 166, 382–383
  private agencies, 166–167
  public and nonprofit agencies, 166
Employment contracts, 519, 659
Employment discrimination, 361
Employment Inventory, 221
Employment laws, need to know, 17–18
Employment planning, 152–157
England, employment contracts in, 659
Enterprise Information Portals (EIPs), 285
Entrepreneurs, human resources for, 134–137,
    172, 291
Equal employment laws, 17
Equal employment opportunity, 30–45
  affirmative action versus, 60
  age discrimination and, 31
  civil rights and, 30–31, 38–40
  court decisions and, 34, 37–38
  disabilities and, 40–44
  employer obligations and, 42–44

equal pay and, 31
executive orders and, 31
Federal agency guidelines and, 32
job analysis information in compliance and,
    113
pregnancy and, 32
role of employee, 36–37
role of manager/employer, 34–35
sexual harassment and, 32–37
state and local laws on, 44
testing and, 200–201
Vietnam veterans and, 32
vocational rehabilitation and, 32
Equal Employment Opportunity Act (1972),
    30, 31
Equal Employment Opportunity Commission
    (EEOC), 31
  conciliation proceedings, 54
  enforcement process, 52
  mandatory arbitration of discrimination
    claims, 57–58
  processing a charge, 52
  responding to employment discrimination
    charges, 54, 56–57
Equal employment opportunity laws, 194,
    200
Equal Pay Act (1963), 31, 53, 391, 400–401
Equity
  external, 396
  impact on pay rates, 396–398
  individual, 397
  internal, 396
  in performance reviews, 516
Equity theory of motivation, 396
Equivalent form estimate, 195
Erratic performance, 44
Essential job functions, 130
Establishment stage in career management,
    372–373, 386
Ethical behavior, factors shaping, at work,
    519–524
Ethical decisions, 517
Ethics
  fair treatment at work and, 516–519
  human resources and, 18, 517, 528
  law and, 517
  meaning of, 517
  policies and codes, 522
  role of human resource management in
    fostering, 524–530
  small business, 530
  training, 526–527
Ethnocentric staffing policy, 666
European Union (EU), 10, 658–659
Evacuation plans, 640–641
Evaluation step in training, 270
"Evil Woman Thesis," 534

Executive(s)
  benefits and perks for, 410
  determining compensation for, 410–411
  development programs for, 286
  incentives for, 456–463
  long-term incentives for overseas, 462
  perquisites for, 500
Executive coaches, 289–290
Executive marketing consultants, 383
Executive Orders 11246 and 11375, 31
Executive recruiters, 171–173, 383
Exit interviews, 236, 544–546
Expatriate assignments, reasons for failure of,
    666–667
Expatriate employees, 397, 664
  compensating, 671–673
  training and maintaining, 669–678
Expatriate managers
  appraising, 673
  selecting, 667–669
Expectancy, 441
Expectancy chart, 199
Exploration stage in career management,
    372–373, 386
External equity, 396
External opportunities and threats, 83
Extraversion, 207

F. A. I. R.: a practical approach to diversity
    and the workplace, 280
Face validity, 201
Fact finder, 581
Fact-finding conference, 56
Factor comparison, 404
Factor comparison job evaluation method,
    427–432
Fair Credit Reporting Act (1970), 215, 217,
    219
Fair Labor Standards Act (1938), 391–392
Fair treatment
  ethics, justice and, 517–519
  role of HR management in fostering,
    524–530
Family and Medical Leave Act (FMLA)
    (1993), 482–484, 632
  benefits and, 479, 504
  compensation and, 392
Family Education Rights and Privacy Act
    (1974), 215
Family-friendly benefits, 497–499
Faragher v. City of Boca Raton, 34
Farm Labor Organizing Committee, 577
FBI Academy, 287
Federal agency guidelines, 32
Federal Labor Relations Act, Title VII of, 591
Federal Personal Responsibility and Welfare
    Reconciliation Act (1996), 180

Federal Privacy Act (1974), 157, 202
Federal Rehabilitation Act (1973), 224
Federal Violence Against Women Act (1994), 33
Federal Wire Act, 641
Feedback, 271
  in performance appraisal, 315
  upward, 333
Fifth Amendment, 30
First impressions, 246–247
Flatter organizations, 139
Flexible benefits programs, 500–506
Flexible schedules, instituting, 363
Flexible spending accounts, 503
Flexible work arrangements, 504, 505–506
Flextime, 504–505
  effectiveness of, 505
Focusers, 77
Food services, 498–499
Forced distribution method, 318–320
Foreign service premiums, 672
Forer Structured Sentence Completion Test, 206
Formal disciplinary appeals processes, 535
Formal promotion policy, 359
Formal structural change, 296
Formal written warning, 337
401(k) retirement programs, 488, 492
Fourteenth Amendment, 30
France, human resource management in, 657–658
Freedom of Information Act (1966), 215
Frustration, 635
Functional control, 7
Functional illiteracy, 279–280
Functional job analysis, 124–125
Functional strategies, 77

Gainsharing plans, 455
  implementing, 455
Gender
  as bona fide occupational qualification, 49
  effect on interviews, 248–249
  issues in testing, 201
Gender-Motivated Violence Act, 633
General aptitude test battery (GATB), 375
General competencies, 141
Generation X women, 418
Geocentric staffing policy, 666
Geographic expansion, 76
Geography, 396
Germany
  employment contracts in, 659
  human resource management in, 657, 658
Gilmer v. Interstate/Johnson Lane Corp., 57
Glass ceiling, 287, 362
  eliminating, 363

Global human resource system, implementation of, 661–663
Globalization, 10–11, 13, 82
Global job analysis, 138
Global organization, staffing, 664–669
Goals
  assigning challenging but doable, 313
  assigning measurable, 313
  assigning specific, 313
  defining for employees, 312–313
Golden parachutes, 462
Golem effect, 275
Good faith bargaining, 578–579
Good faith effort strategy, 62
Grade definition, 403
Grades, 403
Graduate Record Examination, 197
Graphic rating scale method, 315, 317
Graphology, 222
Great Depression, 563
Greece, maximum wages in, 659
Grievances, 584–587
  guidelines for handling, 585–587
  procedure, 585
  sources of, 584–585
Griggs v. Duke Power Company, 37, 50
Gross misconduct, 539–540
Group life insurance plans, 490
Growth stage in career management, 372–373, 386
Guilford-Zimmerman Temperament Survey, 206

Halo effect, 328
Hardship allowances, 672–673
Headhunters, 171
Health
  computer-related problems, 630–632
  workplace hazards in, 623–637
Health care, new trends in controlling costs, 487–488
Health insurance, 486–490
Health Insurance Portability and Accountability Act (HIPAA) (1996), 478, 489–490
Health maintenance organizations (HMOs), 487
Hearing impairment, 41
Heightened security measures, 634
High deductibles, 488
High-performance insight, 540
High-performance work system, 16, 84, 140
Hispanic workers, safety training for, 618
Holidays, 480–481
Home-based salary plan, 397
Home-country nationals, 664
Honesty testing, 220–222

Hong Kong, human resource management in, 657
Hospitalization insurance, 486–490
Hostile environment
  co-workers or nonemployees and, 33–34
  sexual harassment in, 36
  supervisors and, 33
Hotel Employees and Restaurant Employees Union, 583
Hotline, 529
House-Tree-Persona (H-T-P), 206
HRCI test specifications, 685–689
HR eXpress, 21
HRIS (Human Resources Information Systems), 9, 19, 22, 60, 106–108, 217, 678
  Improving Productivity feature, 61, 96, 131, 164, 218, 245, 340, 358, 421, 447, 495, 529, 592, 631, 676
HR Scorecard, 13, 16, 22, 24, 72, 86, 87–97, 98–99, 142–143, 184–185, 225–226, 241–242, 268–269, 297–298, 305, 338, 341–342, 366–367, 419–420, 457–458, 463, 501–502, 550, 552, 587, 589, 642–643, 677–678, 679
Human behaviors in job analysis, 112
Human capital, 12–13, 17
Human process organizational development techniques, 295–296
Human requirements in job analysis, 112
Human resource(s)
  certification in, 18
  challenges for international business, 656–657
  changing role, 10
  competitive advantage and, 79–80
  ethics and, 18
  global differences and similarities in practices, 659–661
  intranets and, 108
  measuring contribution of, 13–16
  strategic challenges, 72–80
  strategic roles of, 80–83
  strategy execution role, 82
  strategy formulation role, 82–83
  technology and, 19–21
Human resource function, auditing, 677–678
Human resource information systems (HRIS), 9, 217
  establishing and computerizing, 101–108
  implementation pitfalls in, 107–108
  Improving Productivity feature, 61, 96, 131, 164, 218, 245, 340, 358, 421, 447, 495, 529, 592, 631, 676
  vendors in, 108
Human resource management, 4–5, 296
  changing environment of, 10–13
  importance to managers, 5

Human resource management *(continued)*
  intercountry differences impact on, 657–659
  line and staff aspects of, 5–7
  responsibilities of line managers, 6–7
  role of, in fostering ethics and fair treatment, 524–530
Human resource manager, 9, 128
  new, 16–21, 468, 670
Human resource portal, 20, 21, 245, 285, 358
Human resource proficiencies, 16
  improving productivity through, 61, 96, 131, 164, 218, 245, 340, 358, 421, 447, 495, 529, 592, 631, 676
Human resource strategy in action, 86–87
Human resource scorecard, 13, 16, 22, 24, 72, 86, 87–97, 98–99, 142–143, 184–185, 225–226, 241–242, 268–269, 297–298, 305, 338, 341–342, 366–367, 419–420, 457–458, 463, 501–502, 550, 552, 587, 589, 642–643, 677–678, 679
Human resource systems
  automating individual tasks, 105
  basic components of manual, 102
  establishing and computerizing, 101–108
  HRIS applications, 107
  HRIS in action, 107
  implementation pitfalls, 107
  implementing global, 661–663
  integration in, 107
  intranets, 108
  online processing, 106
  reporting capability, 107
  system integration, 107
  transaction processing, 106
  vendors, 108
Human resource tasks, automating individual, 105, 176, 245, 421, 488, 495, 590, 676
Hygiene factors, 440

Illegal bargaining items, 563, 579, 633
Illiteracy, functional, 279–280
Immigration law, complying with, post 9/11, 224–225
Impasse, 581
Implied authority, 7
Implied contract exception, 538
Imposing conditions, 578
Impressional management, 247–248
Improved transaction processing, 106
Inadequate concessions, 578
In-basket, 209
Inbound logistics activities, 93
Incentive plans
  implementing effective, 464–465
  reasons for failure, 464
  team/group variable pay, 450–452
  types of, 441

Incentives, 442
  designing and executing effective, 463–466
  for expatriates, 672–673
  long-term, 410, 460–462
  for managers and executives, 456–463
  merit pay as, 443–444
  for professional employees, 445
  programs for, 618–619
  for salespeople, 447–450
  short-term, 410, 456, 459–463
  strategic sales, 450
  supervisor use of, 452
Independence, 378
Independent contractor, 393–394
Indexed options, 460
Indirect payments, 390
Individual differences, law of, 439
Individual equity, 397
Individual factors, influence on ethical behavior, 520
Individual interviews, 243
Individual presentations, 209
Indonesia, personnel selection in, 659
Industrial hygiene, 609, 615
  basic program, 624
Industry wage surveys, 398
Infectious diseases, 625
Informal learning, 277
Information. *See also* Human resource information systems
  background, 219
  computerized, 156
  job analysis, 112–125
  sharing, 549
  withholding, 578
Information technology and incentives, 447
In-house development centers, 289
Injunction, 584
Innovator role, 7
Inside candidates, forecasting the supply of, 155–157
Inside games, 583
Institute for Electrical and Electronic Engineers (IEEE), 166
Institutional barriers, eliminating, 363
Instructional design, in training, 270
Instrumentality, 441
Insubordination, 538, 585
Insurance benefits, 485
Integrated case scenarios, 287
Integrated strategic management, 296
Intellectual capacity, 257
Intellectual factor, probing in interview, 257
Intelligence tests, 205
Intelligent tutoring systems, 281
Intentional discrimination, 39

Interactional justice, 518
Interactive multimedia training, 281–282
Interactive technologies, 281
Intercountry differences, impact on human resource management, 657–659
Interest arbitration, 581
Interest inventories, 207
Interests, measuring, 206–208
Internal candidates, finding, 162
Internal comparison estimate, 195
Internal consistency, 195
Internal equity, 396
Internal sources of candidates, 162–163
Internal strengths and weaknesses, 83
International Association of Firefighters v. City of Cleveland, 62–63
International business, human resource challenges of, 656–657
International labor relations, 673–674
International staffing policy, values and, 665–666
Internet
  recruiting via the, 175–178
  safety improvement solutions and, 631
  training based on, 283–285
  in writing job descriptions, 131
Internships, 174
Interpersonal justice, 518
Interpersonal sensitivity, 549
Interviewees, guidelines for, 264–265
Interviewer behavior, 249
Interviews, 115–116, 209
  administering, 243–245
  appraisal, 236, 334–339
  automated video-based, 245
  behavioral, 237
  closing, 255
  computerized, 243–245
  conducting, 257
  designing and conducting effective, 249, 251–258
  directive, 236–237
  exit, 236, 544–546
  guidelines for, 116
  handling, 385–386
  individual, 243
  job-related, 237
  mass, 243
  nondirective, 236–237
  panel, 243
  personal, 243
  preparing for, 253, 256–257
  pros and cons, 115
  questionnaires in, 116–117
  questions in, 116, 237, 240–241
  reviewing, 255
  selection, 236

serial, 243
situational, 237, 246
specific factors to probe in, 257
stress, 240–241
structured, 236–237, 246, 252–253
structured sequential, 243
structured situational, 249, 251–252
termination, 543–544
types of, 236
unstructured, 236–237, 246
unstructured sequential, 243
usefulness of, 246–249
Intranets, 284
HR and, 108
Involvement system, 454
IQ (intelligence quotient), 205
Italy, maximum wages in, 659

Japan
pay incentives in, 661
personnel selection in, 659
Job(s)
defining, 137
exporting, 11
misunderstanding, 247
Job aids, 282
Job analysis, 112
competency-based, 140–143
global, 138
in a "jobless" world, 137–144
steps in, 113–114
uses of, 112–113
Job analysis information, 112
methods of collection, 114–125
multiple sources of, 125
in performance appraisal, 113
Job classification, 403–404
Job-comparison scale, 430
Job competencies, writing, 142
Job context in job analysis, 112
Job Creation and Worker Assistance Act
(2002), 477
Job descriptions, 112, 114, 273
compliance with ADA, 130
using the Internet for writing, 131
writing, 125–131
Job enlargement, 138
Job enrichment, 84, 138
Job evaluations, 400–405, 412
computerized, 404–405
managerial, 411
point method of, 432–434
preparing for, 401–402
quantitative methods, 427–435
Job identification, 128
Job instruction training, 277–278
Job knowledge questions, 241

Job performance, application forms to predict, 186
Job posting, 162
policy on, 359
Job-related benefits, 498–499
Job-related interview, 237
Job rotation, 138, 275, 286, 355
Job search techniques, 379–383
Job sharing, 505
Job specifications, 112, 114, 273
writing, 132–137
Job stress, 628–629
Job summary, 128
Job title, 128
Johnson v. Transportation Agency, Santa Clara County, 63
Joint venture collaboration, performance appraisals and, 315
Judgments
job specifications based on, 132–133
normative, 517
Justice
distributive, 518
ethics, fair treatment and, 517–519
interactional, 518
interpersonal, 518
organizational, 635
procedural, 518
Just-in-time inventory, 138
Just-in-time manufacturing, 12
Just-in-time workers, 167

Kaufman Adolescent and Adult Intelligence Test, 205
Kenexa CareerTracker, 358
Key employee program, 461
Kidnapping and ransom (K&R) insurance, 675–676
Knights of Labor, 560
Knowledge and experience factor, probing in interview, 257
Know your employment law feature, 22, 50–52, 130, 158, 168–169, 181–182, 202, 215–216, 219, 223–224, 256, 272–273, 331–332, 360–361, 390–394, 442, 477–479, 539–540, 674
Korea
performance appraisal in, 660
personnel selection in, 659

Labor, U.S. Department of
Employment and Training Administration, 277
job analysis procedure, 123–124
Labor laws, 17
Labor Management Relations Act (1947), 564, 566–567

Labor Management Reporting and Disclosure Act (1959), 567
Labor movement, 560–563
AFL-CIO in, 563
history of United States, 560–561
international, 673–674
reasons workers organize, 561–562
today and tomorrow, 590–594
union desires in, 562–563
Labor relations consultants, 569
Land managers, 338–339
Landrum-Griffin Act (1959), 567
Laws. *See also specific*
on compensation, 390–395
equal employment, 17, 194, 200
labor, 17
occupational safety and health, 17
training and, 272
unions and, 563–567
Layoffs, 547–548
alternatives to, 548
Leaderless group discussion, 209
Leadership competencies, 141
Leadership proficiencies, 16, 17
Learning, 299
action, 286–287
informal, 277
motivation, training and, 271–273
programmed, 279
Learning portals, 285
Learning proficiencies, 16, 17
Lechmere, Inc. v. National Labor Relations Board, 576
Lectures, 278–279
Legal and industrial relations factors, 658
Legal constraints on reducing workplace violence, 637
Leveraging, 78
Life insurance, 490–491
Lincoln incentive system, 453
Line and staff aspects of human resource management, 5–7
Line and staff cooperation, 159
Line authority, 7
Line function, 7
Line managers, 6, 9
human resource management responsibilities, 6–7
human resources for, 134–137, 172, 291
Literacy training techniques, 279–280
Local equal employment opportunity laws, 44
Lockout, 583–594
Logrolling, 332
Long-term care, 489–490
Long-term incentives, 410, 460–462
Lump-sum merit raises, 444
Luxembourg, holidays in, 657

Machines, tools, equipment and work aids, in job analysis, 112
Mackay case, 582
Maintenance stage in career management, 373, 386
Make a Picture Story (MAPS), 206
Management assessment centers, 209–210
Management by objectives (MBO), 324–326
Management commitment, safety and, 610–611
Management development, 285–286
Management games, 209
Management malpractice, 53
Management process, 4
Managerial games, 287–288
Managerial job evaluation, 411
Managerial judgment, 155
Managers
    compensating, 410
    competence of, 377
    cooperative line and staff example, 8–9
    development of subordinates, 275
    ethical behavior, 519–524
    expatriate, 667–669, 673
    human resource management jobs, 4–9
    importance of human resource management (HRM) to, 5
    incentives for, 456–463
    line and staff aspects of, 5–7
    new proficiencies, 16
    on-the-job training for, 286–287
Mandatory arbitration, 182
    of discrimination claims, 57–58
Mandatory bargaining items, 579
Marketing and sales activities, 93
Marketing campaign, 292
Mass interview, 243
Material safety data sheet (MSDS), 631
McDonnell-Douglas test, 47
Mechanical Reasoning Test, 205
Mechanical security, 640
Media, 164
Mediation, 581
    voluntary, 57
Mental health benefits, 488–489
Mental Health Parity Act (1996), 477, 488
Mental impairments and the ADA, 41–42
Mentoring, 355
    improving, 363
Mergers, adjusting to, 548–550
Meritor Savings Bank, FSB v. Vinson, 34
Merit pay
    as an incentive, 443–444
    option for, 444
Metrics, 14–15, 87
Mexico
    human resource management in, 657
    performance appraisal in, 660

Midcareer crisis substage, 373, 386
Military campaign, 292
Miniature job training and evaluation approach, 210–211
Minimum wage, 391
Minnesota Clerical Assessment Battery, 212
Minnesota Multiphasic Personality Inventory (MMPI), 204, 206
Minnesota Paper Form Board Test, 205
Minnesota Rate of Manipulation Test, 205
Minorities, recruiting, 63, 179–180
Misconduct, 44, 538
    gross, 539–540
Mission, in strategy, 73–74, 290
Mixed motive, 39–40
Mobility impairments, 41
Mobility premiums, 673
Modeling, 289
Money damages, 39
Monthly Labor Review, 157
Moral standards, 517
Motivation, 257
    psychological needs and intrinsic versus extrinsic, 439–441
    reducing unsafe acts through, 618–619
    training, learning and, 271–273
Motivation factor, probing in interview, 257
Motivator factors, 440
Moving, 292
Multinational corporations (MNCs), 664
MyHRIS, 676

Narrative forms, 322
National Action Council of Minorities in Engineering, 63
National Council on Compensation Insurance (NCCI), 338
National Education Association, 590
National emergency strikes, 567
National Federation for the Blind, 41
National Industry Recovery Act, 561
National Institute for Occupational Safety and Health (NIOSH), 633, 634
National Job Bank, 166
National Labor Relations Act (1935), 564, 566, 569, 571, 582, 590, 593
    independent contractors and, 394
National Labor Relations Board (NLRB), 395, 564, 569, 570, 571, 583–594
National origin as a bona fide occupational qualification (BFOQ), 49
National Recovery Act (1933), 593
Natural security, 639
Needs analysis step in training, 270
Negligent hiring, 194–195
Negligent training, 272
Negotiating team, 579

Network groups, 59
Networking, improving, 363
Neuroticism, 207
Newborn Mother's Protection Act (1996), 477
New Deal, 561
New economy entrepreneurs, unions and, 568
New York Personal Privacy Act (1985), 157
New Workplace feature, 39, 81, 138, 179, 201, 250, 280, 315, 462, 499, 519, 577, 618, 622, 669
9/11 World Trade Center and Pentagon attacks, 270, 637
Nondirective interviews, 236–237, 246
Nonbinding arbitration, 581
Nondeductible formula, 456
Nonpunitive discipline, 535
Nonqualified stock options, 460
Nontraditional workers, 12
Nonverbal behavior, 247–248
Normative judgments, 517
Norris-LaGuardia Act (1932), 563–564
North American Free Trade Agreement (NAFTA), 10, 577

Objective tests, 209
Observation, 117
Obsession, 635
Occupational fraud and abuse, 203
Occupational illness, 603
Occupational orientation, identifying, 373–374
Occupational Outlook Quarterly, 157
Occupational Safety and Health Act (1970), 102, 517, 602, 603–610
Occupational Safety and Health Administration (OSHA), 590, 603–610
    inspections and citations, 604–607
    responsibilities and rights of employers and employees, 607–610
    standards and record keeping, 603–604
Occupational safety and health laws, 17
Occupational Safety and Health Review Commission (OSHRC), 606
Occupational safety in post 9/11 world, 637–642
Occupations, identifying high-potential, 378–379
O'Connor v. Consolidated Coin Caterers Corp., 31
Offer, 393
Office manager, 268
Office of Federal Contract Compliance Programs (OFCCP), 31, 32
Offshoring, 170–171, 664–665
Off-the-job management training and development techniques, 287–290
Off-work safety programs, 622

Old Age and Survivor's Insurance, 491
Older workers, recruiting, 178–179
Older Workers' Benefit Protection Act (1990)
	(OWBPA), 494
Oncale v. Sundowner Offshore Services, 33
On demand recruiting services (ODRS), 173
O*NET, 131, 133, 134, 136
Online award programs, 446–447
Online processing, 106
Online selection software, 488
On-site primary care, 489
On-site visits, 174
On-the-job training, 275–276
On Your Own (When You're) feature, 22, 53,
	77, 134–137, 212–213, 256–257, 291,
	338–339, 354, 452, 506–507, 530, 531,
	568, 575, 610, 612, 660
Openness to experience, 207
Open shop, 562
Operations activities, 93
Opinion surveys, 529
Organizational change
	leading, 293–294
	managing, 290–298
	overcoming resistance to, 292
Organizational culture, 523–524
	influence on ethical behavior, 522–523
Organizational development, 294–298
	human process techniques in, 295–296
	managing, 290–298
Organizational factors, influence on ethical
	behavior, 520
Organizational justice, 635
Organizational renewal, 290–291, 293
Organizational security, 640
Organization charts, 113–114
Organizationwide variable pay plans, 453–456
Orientation, employee, 268–269
Outbound logistics activities, 93
Outplacement counseling, 544
Outside candidates, forecasting the supply of,
	157
Outside seminars, 288
Outside sources of candidates, 163–178
Outsourcing, 20–21, 170–171, 488
Overseas Assignment Inventory, 668
Overtime, 585
Overtime pay, 391
Overtime rates, 442

Paid sick leave, 478
Paired comparison method, 318–320
Panel interview, 243
Paolillo v. Dresser Industries, Inc., 494
Paper-and-pencil honesty tests, 221
Parental leave, 482–484
Participant diary/logs, 117

Part-time workers, 167
	benefits for, 491
*Pattern Makers v. National Labor Relations
	Board*, 566
Pay, performance and, 438–439
Pay cycle, 396
Pay for knowledge, 412
Pay-for-performance plans, 441
Pay grades, 405
Pay incentives, 661
Pay plan, developing workable, 408–409
Pay rates
	determining, 390, 395–398
	equity and its impact on, 396–398
	establishing, 398–407
	fine-tuning, 406–407
Peer appraisals, 332
Pendleton Act (1871), 590
Pension, alternatives to, 494–495
Pension Benefit Guaranty Corporation
	(PBGC), 494
Pension plans, 492–493
Pentagon, 9/11 attacks on, 270, 499, 637
Performance, 14
	pay and, 438–439
Performance achievement plan, 461
Performance analysis, 273–275
Performance appraisal, 338–339, 527
	alternation ranking method in, 317
	behaviorally anchored rating scales in,
		322–324
	comparing performance management and,
		310
	computerized and Web-based, 326–327
	critical incident method in, 321–322
	defined, 310
	global differences and similarities in, 660
	graphic rating scale method in, 316–317
	job analysis information in, 113
	joint venture collaboration and, 315
	legal issues, 331–332
	management by objectives (MBO) in,
		324–326
	narrative forms in, 322
	paired comparison method in, 318–321
	problems and solutions in, 327–331,
		332–334
	realistic, 314
	reasons for, 313
	steps in, 315
	supervisor's role in, 314–315
Performance-based compensation, 390
Performance feedback, 360 degree, 289–290
Performance management, 141, 270, 413
	comparing performance appraisal and, 310
	defined, 310
	reasons for, 310–312

Performance plans, 461–462
Performance standards in job analysis, 112
Permissible bargaining items, 579
Personal bias, 331
Personal characteristics, effect of, on
	interviews, 248–249
Personal contacts, 381
Personal interviews, 243
Personality and interests, measuring, 206–208
Personality factor, 257
	probing in interview, 257
Personal leave, 478
Personal protective equipment, 616
Personal services, 496
Personal supervisory liability, 543
Personnel needs, forecasting, 153–155
Personnel planning, 152–157
Personnel replacement charts, 156
Personnel requirements, using computers to
	forecast, 155
Personnel selection procedures, global
	differences and similarities in, 659
Phantom stock plans, 461
Physical actions, 635
Physical examination, 223
Picketing, 582
Piece rate, 442
Piecework, 390
Piecework plans, 442–443
Placement, reducing unsafe acts through, 617
Plant closing law, 547
Plant rules, 585
Point method, 404
	of job evaluation, 432–434
Point plans, 418
Political campaign, 292
Polycentric-oriented firm, 666
Polygraph, 220–222
Ponticas v. K. M. S. Investments, 194
Portability, 494–495
Position analysis questionnaire, 113–114,
	122–123
Position replacement card, 156
Positive reinforcement programs, 619
Power distance, 657
Predictive validation, 198
Predictors, 196, 197
Preemployment activities, 158
Preemployment information services, 217
Preferred provider organizations (PPOs), 487,
	489
Pregnancy Discrimination Act (1978), 32,
	489
Premium priced options, 460
Preretirement counseling, 368
Pressure to hire, 247
Prima facie case of discrimination, 46

Privacy, 156–157
    employee discipline and, 531–537
    issue of, 202
Private agencies, 166–167
Procedural justice, 518
Process chart, 114
Productivity, improving, 21
Professional, administrative, technical, and
    clerical (PATC) surveys, 398–399
Professional employees
    compensating, 411–412
    incentives for, 445
    union organization of, 591
Professionals in human resources (PHR), 9,
    18, 690
Profit-sharing plans, 453
Programmed learning, 279
Projective tests, 206
Promotions, 358
    establishing guidelines for managing,
        360–361
    horizontal, 359
    making, decisions, 358–359
    vertical, 359
Property loss, security for other sources of,
    641
Proposals and demands, inadequate, 578
Protected class, 37
Psychological needs, intrinsic versus extrinsic
    motivation and, 439–441
Public and nonprofit agencies, 166
Public employees, unions and, 590
Public policy exception, 538
Purdue Peg Board, 205
Purdue Test for Machinists and Machine
    Operators, 208
Puzzle questions, 241

Qualifications inventories, 155
Qualified individual, 40
Quantitative job analysis techniques, 117
Quantitative job evaluation methods, 427–435
Questions
    asking, in interview, 254–255
    job knowledge, 241
    puzzle, 241
    situational, 237, 241
Quid pro quo harassment, 33, 34

Race, effect on interviews, 248–249
Railway Labor Act, 566
Ranking method, 402–403
Rapport, establishing, in interviews, 254
Rating committees, 332–333
Ratio analysis, 154
Reaction, 299
Reactivity, 117

Realistic job previews, 355
Reality shock, 355
Reasonable accommodation, 40–41
Recognition-based awards, 445–446
Recruiting yield pyramid, 161–162
Recruitment
    effective, 157–162
    Internet, 175–178
    job analysis information in, 112
    measuring effectiveness of, 159–161
    new process, 184–185
    organizing function, 159
Reengineering, 139–140
Reeves v. Sanderson Plumbing Products, 529
Reference checks, 213–217
References, giving, 215–216
Referrals, 174–175
Refreezing, 292
Rehiring, 163
Relationship statement, 128
Reliability, 195
Religion as a bona fide occupational
    qualification, 48–49
Repatriation, 676–677
Repetitive trauma injuries, 602
Resistance, overcoming, to change, 292
Responsibilities and duties, 129–130
Restricted policy, 47
Restricted stock plans, 461
Results, 299
Résumé, 383–386
    accomplishments in, 385
    introductory information in, 383
    job objective in, 383, 385
    job scope in, 385
    length of, 385
    making scannable, 385
    personal data in, 385
Retest estimate, 195
Retirement, 366, 368
Retirement benefits, 491–495
Retirement Guidance Planner, 368
Reverse discrimination, 62–63
Reward systems, 527
Rights arbitration, 581
Right to work, 562
Rings of defense approach, 548
Roeder Manipulative Aptitude Test, 205
Role playing, 288, 289
Role reversal, 356
Russia, human resource challenges in, 656

Safety
    behavior-based, 620
    management commitment and, 610–611
    off-work programs for, 622
    reducing unsafe acts by emphasizing, 617

Safety and health audits and inspections,
    620–621
Safety posters, 618
Safety training for Hispanic workers, 618
Salary compression, 396
Salary plan, 448
Salary survey, 398–399
Sales commissions, 390
Salespeople, incentives for, 447–450
Sales quotas, setting, 449–450
Sarbanes-Oxley Act (2002), 18, 442, 529
SARS, 625
Savings and thrift plan, 493
Scanlon plan, 454–455
Scatter plot, 154–155
Scholastic Assessment Test (SAT), 195
Scorecard programs, software systems for
    managing, 96
Scorecard, HR, 13, 16, 22, 24, 72, 86, 87–97,
    98–99, 142–143, 184–185, 225–226,
    241–242, 268–269, 297–298, 305, 338,
    341–342, 366–367, 419–420, 457–458,
    463, 501–502, 550, 552, 587, 589,
    642–643, 677–678, 679
Securities and Exchange Commission, 410
Security, 378
    data, 641
    mechanical, 640
    natural, 639
    organizational, 640
Security audit, 641
Security plan, basic prerequisites for, 638–639
Security program, setting up basic, 639–640
Selection
    employee testing and, 212
    importance of careful, 194–195
    job analysis information in, 112
    reducing unsafe acts through, 617
Selection interview, 236
Self-ratings, 333
Self-service, 19
Seniority, promotion and, 358–359
Seniority-based pay, 396
Senior professional in human resource
    (SPHR) designation, 9, 18, 179, 288, 690
Sensitivity training, 295–296
September 11, 2001, terrorist attacks, 270,
    499, 637
Serial interview, 243
Service activities, 93
Severance pay, 484
Sexual harassment, 32–37, 516
    proving, 33–34
Short-term incentives, 410, 456, 459–463
SHRM certification, 18, 22
Sick building syndrome, 602
Sick leave, 482

Simulated training, 281
Situational interview, 237, 246
Situational questions, 237, 241
Situational tests, 210
16PF, 204
Skill-based pay, 412
Skills
  identifying, 374–375
  transfer of, 271
Slosson Intelligence Test, 205
Small businesses
  ethics for, 530
  free on-site safety and health services for,
    610
  human resources and, 256–258
Small necessities leave laws, 483
SMART, 313
Smoking, workplace, 632–633
Social reinforcement, 289
Social Security, 491
Social Security Act (1935), 392–393
Society for Human Resource Management
    (SHRM), 14, 18, 497
Society of Hispanic Engineers, 63
Soft appraisals, 314
Software systems, for managing scorecard
    programs, 96
Special assignments, 275
Speech impairment, 41
Spurlock v. United Airlines, 49
SRA Test of Mechanical Aptitude, 205
Stabilization substage, 373, 386
Staff functions, 7
Staffing, global organization, 664–669
Staff managers, 6
Standard hour plan, 443
Standard Occupational Classification (SOC),
    129
Standards of performance, 130–131
Stanford-Binet Test, 205
State equal employment opportunity laws, 44
Statistical analysis, job specifications based on,
    134
Stock appreciation rights, 461
Stock options, 453, 460–461
Straight piecework, 443
Strategically relevant human resource system
    policies and activities, 94
Strategically relevant workforce competencies
    and behaviors, 94
Strategically required organizational
    outcomes, 93
Strategic change, 290
Strategic compensation, 417–418
Strategic context of training, 270
Strategic control, 76
Strategic fit, achieving, 77–79

Strategic human resource management
  challenges, 72
  changing environment, 10
  context of thinking, 270
  creating strategy-oriented system, 83–87
  defined, 80
  execution role, 82
  formulation role, 82
  measuring contribution, 13–16
  process, 73–76
  Scorecard, HR feature, 13, 16, 22, 24, 72,
    86, 87–97, 98–99, 142–143, 184–185,
    225–226, 241–242, 268–269, 297–298,
    305, 338, 341–342, 366–367, 419–420,
    457–458, 463, 501–502, 550, 552, 587,
    589, 642–643, 677–678, 679
  Scorecard approach, 87–91
Strategic interventions, 296
Strategic management, 73–76
  integrated, 296
Strategic plan, 72
Strategic planning, types of, 76–77
Strategic sales incentives, 450
Strategy, 13, 72, 75
  translating, into human resource policy and
    practice, 84–86
Strategy execution, 82
Strategy formulation, 72–73, 82–83
Strategy-oriented human resource system,
    creating, 83–87
Stress interview, 240–241
Strictness/leniency, 328–329
Strikes, 582
  national emergency, 567
Stromberg Dexterity Test, 205
Strong-Campbell Inventory, 207
Structural change, 290
Structured interviews, 236–237, 246
Structured sequential interview, 243
Structured situational interview, 237, 249,
    251–252
Subordinates
  appraisal by, 333
  criticizing, 337
  handling defensive, 336–337
Subsidized child care, 498
Substance abuse, 625–628
  screening for, 223
Succession planning, 152, 163, 164, 286
Supervisor
  role in National Labor Relations Board
    (NLRB) election, 574–575
  role of, in performance appraisal, 314–315,
    332
Supplemental pay benefits, 479
Supplemental unemployment benefits, 485
Support activities, 93

Surface bargaining, 578
Survey research, 296
Survivor's or death benefits, 491
SWOT analysis, 74
Sympathy strike, 582

Taft-Hartley Act (1947), 562, 564, 566–567
Taiwan
  pay incentives in, 661
  performance appraisal in, 660
  personnel selection in, 659
Task analysis, 273
  record form for, 273, 274
Tax Reform Act (1986), 494
Team-based organizations, 84
Team building, 296
Team/group variable pay incentive plans,
    450–452
Team incentives
  designing, 450–451
  pros and cons of, 451–452
Technical competencies, 141
Technical/functional competence, 375
Technological advances, 11
Technology, human resources and, 19–21
Technostructural interventions, 296
Telecommuting, 505–506
Teletraining, 283
Temp agencies, 167–170
Terminate at will, 537
Termination interview, 543–544
Terrorism, 270, 499, 637, 675
Test battery, 197–198
Test of Mechanical Comprehensive, 198
Tests/testing
  achievement, 207–208
  basic concepts of, 195–204
  of cognitive abilities, 204–205
  computer-interactive, 204
  equal employment opportunity aspects of,
    200–201
  gender issues in, 201
  honesty, 220–222
  measuring personality and interests,
    206–208
  of motor and physical abilities, 205
  using, at work, 203–204
  validation of, 196, 197–199
  video-based situational, 210
  Web-based, 208
Test takers, individual rights and test security,
    201–202
Thematic Apperception Test, 195–196, 206
Third-country nationals, 664
Thirteenth Amendment, 30
360-degree performance feedback, 289–290,
    334

Time-based pay, 390
Time series design, 299
Time Series Studies, 299
Title VII of the Civil Rights Act of 1964, 30–31, 42, 272, 331, 360, 390, 590, 637
Total performance management process, 338–339
Total quality management (TQM), 310
Toyota Motor Manufacturing of Kentucky, Inc. v. Williams, 42
Trained employees, job specifications for, 132
Training
  apprenticeship, 276–277
  audiovisual-based, 280
  computer-based, 281–282, 283
  defined, 270
  distance learning-based, 270, 283–285
  diversity, 280
  ethics, 526–527
  evaluating, 299–302
  of expatriate employees, 669–678
  five-step, 270–271
  global differences and similarities in, 660
  interactive multimedia, 281–282
  Internet-based, 283–285
  job analysis information in, 113
  job instruction, 277–278
  laws and, 272
  learning, motivation and, 271–273
  literacy techniques, 279–280
  managerial on-the-job, 286–287
  need analysis in, 273
  negligent, 272
  off-the-job management, 287–290
  on-the-job, 275–276
  reducing unsafe acts through, 617–618
  sensitivity, 295–296
  simulated, 281
  strategic context of, 270
  virtual reality, 282
  Web-based, 285–286
  workplace violence, 635
Transaction processing, improved, 106
Transfer of training, 289
Transfers, 358
  handling, 360
Trend analysis, 153
Trial substage, 372, 386
Two-way communications, 529–530

Unassigned duties, job analysis information in discovering, 113
Unclear standards problem, 328
Underemployed, 169
Understudy method, 275
Unemployment insurance, 479–480
Unfair employer labor practice, 564

Unfair labor practices, 566
  committing, 578
Unfair labor practices strikes, 582
Unfreezing, 292
Uniform guidelines, 32
Unilateral changes, making, in conditions, 578
Union(s), 560–561
  desires of, 562–563
  detailed regulation of internal, 567
  employee participation programs and, 593–594
  influences on compensation decisions, 394
  law and, 563–567
  new economy entrepreneurs and, 568
  organizing campaign for, 592–593
  ousting, 576–577
  for professionals, 591
  public employees and, 590
  reasons workers organize into, 561–562
  unfair labor practices of, 566
  for white-collar employees, 591
Union drive and election, 568–577
  campaign, 571
  election, 572–574, 576–577
  hold a hearing, 571
  initial contact, 568–570
  obtaining authorization cards, 570–571
Union salting, 569–570
Union security, 562
Union shop, 562
United Auto Workers (UAW), 561
United Electrical Workers, 577
United Farmworkers, 593
United Kingdom
  holidays in, 657
  human resource management in, 658
U.S. Federal Agencies' Uniform Guidelines on Employee Selection, 113
U.S. v. Paradise, 63
Universities, corporate, 289
University-related programs, 288
Unsafe acts
  causes of, 615
  reducing, 618–619
Unsafe conditions
  as accident cause, 611
  reducing, 615–616
Unsatisfactory performance, 538
Unstructured interviews, 236–237, 246
Unstructured sequential interview, 243
Untrained personnel, job specifications for, 132
Upward feedback, 333

Vacations, 478, 480–481
Valence, 441

Validation
  of test, 197–199
  in training, 270
Validity, 195–197
  criterion for, 197
Value chain analysis, 88–89, 93
Values, 523–524
  international staffing policy and, 665–666
Variable pay, 441
Verbal threats, 635
Vertical integration strategy, 76
Video-based situational testing, 210
Videoconferencing, 284
Video-linked classrooms, 288
Videotaping in workplace, 537
Vietnam Era Veterans' Readjustment Assistance Act (1974), 32
Violence, at work, 633–637
Violence Against Women Act, 633
Virtual reality training, 282
Vision, 74
Vision impairments, 41
Vocational Preference Test (VPT), 373
Vocational Rehabilitation Act (1973), 32, 40
Voluntary bargaining items, 579
Voluntary mediation, 57
Voluntary reduction in pay plan, 548

Wage and Hour Act, 443
Wage curves, 405
Wagner Act, 394. *See also* National Labor Relations Act (1935)
Walk-ins, 174–175
Walsh-Healey Public Contract Act (1936), 390
Washington, County of, v. Gunther, 418
Web-based performance appraisal, 326–327
Web-based testing, 208
Web-based training, 285–286
Web sites, employers, 383
Wechsler Test, 205
Welfare-to-work, 180
Wellness programs, 489
When You're On Your Own feature, 22, 53, 77, 134–137, 212–213, 256–257, 291, 338–339, 354, 452, 506–507, 530, 531, 568, 575, 610, 612, 660
Whistle-blowers, 537
White-collar employees, union organization of, 591
Wide Range Intelligence Test, 205
Wildcat strike, 582
Women
  generation X, 418
  recruiting, 179–180
  sending managers abroad, 669
  in workforce, 361–362

Wonderlic Personnel Test, 212
Wonderlic's Personal Characteristics
    Inventory, 206
Work
    ethics and fair treatment at, 516–519
    factors shaping ethical behavior at, 519–524
    in job analysis, 112
    nature of, 11–13
    using tests at, 203–204
    violence at, 633–637
Work councils, 658
Workday, 393
Work efforts, defining for employees, 312–313
Worker Adjustment and Retraining
    Notification Act (1989), 547

Workers
    boosting diversity in, 59–60
    demographics of, 13
    functions of, 123
    nontraditional, 12
    reasons for organizing into union,
        561–562
    recruiting more diverse, 178–181
    women as, 361–362
Workers' compensation, 485–486
    controlling costs, 485–486, 622–623
Workforce Investment Act (1998), 166
Working conditions, 130–131
Workplace aggression and violence, 527
Workplace health hazards, 623–637

Workplace smoking, 632–633
Workplace violence, legal constraints on
    reducing, 637
Workplace violence training, 635
Work sampling, 160
    for employee selection, 208–209
Works Constitution Act, 658
Work sharing, 505
Work teams, 139
World Trade Center, 9/11 attacks on, 270,
    499, 637
Wrongful discharge suits, avoiding, 540–543
Wygant v. Jackson Board of Education, 62

Yellow dog contracts, 563